William B. Smith

William B. Smith
In the Shadow of a Prophet

Kyle R. Walker

Salt Lake City, 2015
Greg Kofford Books

Copyright © 2015 Kyle R. Walker
Cover design copyright © 2015 Greg Kofford Books, Inc.
Cover design by Loyd Ericson
Cover image, William B. Smith, ca. 1870. Photograph by William B. and Margaret J. Fields, taken at Lyons, Iowa. Courtesy Community of Christ Archives.

Published in the USA.

All rights reserved. No part of this volume may be reproduced in any form without written permission from the publisher, Greg Kofford Books. The views expressed herein are the responsibility of the author and do not necessarily represent the position of Greg Kofford Books.

ISBN 978-1-58958-503-4 (paperback)
ISBN 978-1-58958-504-1 (hardcover)
Also available in ebook.

Greg Kofford Books
P.O. Box 1362
Draper, UT 84020
www.gregkofford.com

2019   18   17   16   .   5   4   3   .   .

Library of Congress Control Number: 2015940492

To my parents, who have always believed in me—
Dennis Lyle Walker, 1943–1987
Sharon Jensen Walker Haworth

Contents

Preface ix

1. Uncle Jesse 1
2. Yankee Childhood 21
3. The Angel and the Plates 41
4. Conversion 63
5. Life in "the Ohio": Missions, Marriage, and Ministry 79
6. In the Shadow of a Prophet 103
7. A Season in Zion, 1836–39 125
8. Newspaper Editor and Illinois Legislator, 1840–43 149
9. President of the Eastern Branches, 1843–45 171
10. Return to Nauvoo 209
11. Time of Reckoning 229
12. Disgruntled Patriarch 257
13. Apostle to Apostate 279
14. "Ho! For Voree": Strangite Apostle and Patriarch 307
15. Church-Building: Quest for Ecclesiastical Station 339
16. Expansion and Collapse 371
17. A Time of Transition 405
18. Civil War Soldier 433
19. The "Brighamites" 459
20. The "Josephites" 495
21. Final Years 531

Appendix A. Wives and Children of William B. Smith 565
Appendix B. "The Elders' Pocket Companion" 583

Bibliography 595
Index 629

Preface

As a member of the founding family of Mormonism, William B. Smith has long been a person of interest in Latter-day Saint history. Six years younger than his prominent elder brother Joseph Smith Jr., the founder of the Mormon religion, Smith was present for his brother's earliest recitations of his revelatory experiences, an early witness to the events connected to the coming forth of the Book of Mormon, and a participant in most of the meetings that laid the groundwork for the establishment for what would eventually become known as the Church of Jesus Christ of Latter-day Saints. Smith held many prominent positions within the movement, as he migrated with the Saints through the states of New York, Ohio, Missouri, and finally to Illinois. He was an active missionary from 1832 through 1845 and had marked success in adding numerous converts to the expanding church.

Smith progressed rapidly through the priesthood hierarchy of the Church, becoming a member of the original Quorum of the Twelve Apostles in 1835. When the Church was headquartered at Nauvoo, Illinois, he was among those trusted by his brother to be initiated into the Quorum of the Anointed (endowed) and be introduced to plural marriage. In the spring of 1844 he also became part of the private Council of Fifty, just prior to the murder of his two older brothers, Joseph and Hyrum. While he resided in Illinois, his was the privilege of representing Hancock County in the state legislature, where he played a key role in defending Nauvoo's controversial charter. Smith successfully published the *Wasp*, a newspaper at Nauvoo, and oversaw the publication of the *Prophet* in New York in 1843-45 during the time he presided over the eastern branches of the Church. These papers were instrumental in defending the Saints' viewpoints at the state and national level. William also succeeded his brother Hyrum as Church patriarch, acting in that calling even before he returned to Nauvoo in May 1845 where the Twelve confirmed this hereditary office. He energetically magnified this calling, bestowing hundreds of blessings of the Saints during the summer of 1845 as patriarch. As the only surviving male member of the Smith family after the summer of 1844, he was looked to by many members of the Church for his views on succession and church policy.

In October 1845, simmering tensions between him and his fellow apostles boiled over, and he was excommunicated in a dramatic break with Brigham Young and the main body of Mormons who eventually settled in Salt Lake City. From that point on, Smith's name all but vanishes from Church history. Saints

William Smith, 1811-1893. Painting by Sutcliffe Maudsley, Nauvoo, Illinois, ca. 1843. Courtesy of John Hajicek.

in the West branded him an apostate, and any mention of his name in LDS Church history decried his rebelliousness and insubordination. For that reason, most of his contributions to the building up of the early Church have been lost to the reader. While there were certainly challenges related to his personality that impacted his leadership and decision making, simply dismissing him from the record fails to account for his vast contributions during the fifteen years between 1830 and 1845.

But William lived an additional forty-eight years, dying at age eighty-two in the obscure town of Osterdock, in northeastern Iowa. The twelve years following his dramatic departure from Nauvoo were equally turbulent as he roared through various factions of the LDS movement. In addition to several unsuccessful attempts at organizing his own church, Smith joined with noted dissidents: James J. Strang, Lyman Wight, Martin Harris, John C. Bennett, George J. Adams, and Isaac Sheen. His interactions with pockets of Saints throughout the Midwest and East are also a valuable resource in understanding the views of those who did not follow Brigham Young's leadership. His voluminous surviving letters not only reveal Smith's attitudes and motives, but also those with whom he interacted.

Finally, in 1878, William linked his experience and aspirations with the Reorganized Church of Jesus Christ of Latter Day Saints (now Community of Christ),[1] under the leadership of his nephew Joseph Smith III. Prior to its organization, William had laid out the blueprint for the formation of his nephew's church. Though the tenets he outlined were eventually adopted by his nephew, RLDS leaders viewed William as a liability. While Joseph III accepted William into his Church on the basis of his original baptism in Joseph's Church, he never appointed William to a prominent position within the movement, even as Church patriarch, and discouraged his attempts to infiltrate the Church's hierarchy. As a result, once again, William's contributions to the formation of the RLDS Church, as well as what he brought to that movement for the better part of fifteen years, have been vastly understated in RLDS histories.

---

1. "Community of Christ" was adopted in 2001, so I reserve it for references to current officers, staff, and departments. During William's lifetime, I refer to the church in which he ended his active ministry and life as the RLDS Church, the Reorganization, or by its full name: The Reorganized Church of Jesus Christ of Latter Day Saints. Joseph's church was initially known as the Church of Christ, then as the Church of Jesus Christ (in Ohio), and simultaneously as the Church of the Latter-day Saints (in Missouri). It was not until 1838 that the name stabilized as the Church of Jesus Christ of Latter-day Saints. Similarly, it took some time for the nomenclature referring to Joseph Smith III's church to assume its final name. The originally informal clustering of those who believed lineal succession was known during the 1850s as the "New Organization." When Joseph III accepted the leadership of these believers, thirty years to the day after the organization of his father's church, it was called the "Church of Jesus Christ of Latter Day Saints." To further differentiate it from the Utah-based church, on February 5, 1873, the name became the "Reorganized Church of Jesus Christ of Latter Day Saints."

With all of William's contributions to Mormonism, it is rather surprising that more has not been written about him. Calvin P. Rudd, a former faculty member from the Salt Lake LDS Institute of Religion, wrote a master's thesis in 1973, but only minimally accessed the vast resources on William owned by the RLDS Church. Nearly everything else written about William is by authors who have focused on his struggle with Church authorities over the scope of his patriarchal authority in 1845. Only one has attempted to highlight his interactions with his nephew Joseph Smith III, and none of the articles have attempted to probe the depths of Smith's complex personality. Consequently, his life has been presented in truncated vignettes. This biography covers his entire life, beginning with William's recollections of and contributions to early Mormon history prior to his 1845 break with Brigham Young and the Twelve and continuing with the events of the final fifty years of his life. From that basis and with due caution about the pitfalls in attempting to "diagnose the dead," in Steven Harper's felicitous phrase, I attempt to sort out the complexities of his enigmatic personality. Despite the abrupt discontinuities, reversals, disappearances, and spectacular public comebacks, this biography bridges those gaps in the life of William B. Smith.

"Why study the process of dissent?" asked Ronald W. Walker in his classic history *Wayward Saints: The Social and Religious Protests of the Godbeites against Brigham Young* (Provo, Utah: Brigham Young University Press, 2009). Answering his own question, Walker clarified that studying dissent assists to flesh out clues related to "personality trait[s]" that help us understand the individual. But, he emphasizes, even more importantly, "the process helps to clarify a historical era. By defining the ideas and policies that divided the apostate from the mainline believer, we find what a former age valued—even to the point of defying old allegiances and old associates. In short, by studying dissent we gain the means to view a society as the participants themselves saw it—and not necessarily as we today assume it to have been" (p. 72). In the case of Willliam B. Smith, we gain additional insights into the dynamics of Mormonism's first family.

My personal interest in William dates back many years, when I first began researching on the Joseph Sr. and Lucy Mack Smith family. Most of what I had heard and read about William prior to my research was adverse and dismissive. Prior research has referred to him derisively, including articles that included in their titles, "Problematic Patriarch," "A Wart on the Ecclesiastical Tree," and the "Persistent 'Pretender.'" I certainly concur with some of these author's perceptions about the challenging nature of William's leadership. By all accounts, William was a complex person who wrestled with insecurities and fits of passion that sometimes overrode his noble desires and family loyalty. But I also began to discover his vast contributions to the upbuilding of Mormonism, including his missionary success, his persuasiveness as a gifted orator, his propensity to accurately portend the future, and his charismatic leadership. I had a desire to highlight all sides of his personality, which I felt was more complex than can be captured in a single article and best evaluated over the course of his life.

I also was drawn to William because of my training as a marriage and family therapist. I became intrigued by his family dynamics, including his birth-order position, the similarity of his temperament with one of his Smith uncles, and his resentment and insecurities related to his prominent older brother's charisma and station. As I immersed myself in the surviving materials, I became captivated by Smith's psyche. Due to my clinical training, I began to pick up on something that previous historians had missed as they attempted to capture Smith's personality—his emotional instability as a critical factor in understanding his personality and behavior. Such an understanding may also help explain why there are conflicting accounts about how William was perceived by those who were acquainted with him—as both rogue and respected citizen; saint and sinner; apostle or an apostate; profligate brother of the Mormon prophet or revered patriarch. For these reasons, William remains for me one of the most fascinating characters in nineteenth-century Mormon history.

As with any book, many have worked behind the scenes to bring it to fruition, and it is a joy to acknowledge my debts to my co-laborers. The many depositories of Mormon history have been invaluable in producing this volume. Foremost among them is the Community of Christ Archives staff in Independence, Missouri. Lachlan Mackay, Barbara Hands Bernauer, Ronald E. Romig, and Rachel Killebrew as well as other librarians have been very helpful as I have researched their vast holdings related to William B. Smith. I also thank those at the LDS Church History Library in Salt Lake City, who have been untiringly helpful. Ronald O. Barney, Michael Landon, and William Slaughter have been particularly helpful in locating materials at the library. David J. Whittaker and Russ Taylor also lent their assistance in researching Smith family sources located at the L. Tom Perry Special Collections at Brigham Young University in Provo, Utah. Several private historians have not only done yeoman's labor in strengthening my book but have been unstintingly generous in joining with me to call this portrait of William B. Smith out of the historical shadows. Erin Jennings Metcalfe and William Shepard have been very generous in sharing numerous sources with me as they have gathered material on William B. Smith through the years. Erin reviewed the entire manuscript and offered helpful feedback, as well as locating and sharing numerous sources with me, including William Smith's pension file, which provided critical documentation for several chapters. She also provided extensive information regarding William's wives and children. Lyndon W. Cook expended considerable effort in transcribing most of Smith's letters, an invaluable resource in helping me to locate the large cache of William's letters in multiple repositories. I also have benefitted from the earlier work of Connell O'Donovan, who has researched extensively on William's interactions with early African-American converts, and made an earlier transcription of William's "Elders' Pocket Companion" (see Appendix B). Jeffrey Smith and Brooks Haderlie, librarians at BYU-Idaho, have been most helpful in assisting with the photographs used in this volume. Alexander L. Baugh and Richard N.

Holzapfel, professors at Brigham Young University, also assisted in locating and sharing photographs from their personal collections. Gracia N. Jones, a representative of the Smith family organization, has also been generous in sharing photographs and other historical items with me throughout the writing of this book; as did Mary Dennis and Estel Neff, Smith family descendants through William's sister Katharine. Michael Marquardt was also generous with his time in helping me to locate sources related to Mormonism's earliest history, as were Richard L. Anderson and Larry C. Porter, retired professors from Brigham Young University. Bruce Blanchard, Reed Stoddard, Dale Sturm, Bill Torngren, and Larry Thurgood were helpful in providing funding for scholarly activities related to the publication. The author would especially would like to acknowledge this volume's editor, Lavina Fielding Anderson. This book was markedly improved due to her very capable editorial expertise and vast knowledge of Mormon history. I wish to also thank Greg Kofford and Loyd Ericson at Kofford Books for their support and encouragement of this project. Their professionalism and competence have made the publication process efficient and enjoyable.

I would also like to acknowledge the following individuals or repositories for their assistance in the publication of this work: Amboy Depot Museum, David and Sue August, Betty Bucholz, Mary Schofield Belden, Beinecke Library at Yale Univesity, Daughters of Utah Pioneers Museum, Elkader Historical Society, Galena/Jo Daviess County Historical Society, John Hajicek, Hancock County Historical Society, Hancock County Courthouse, John C. Hamer, Sharon Jensen Haworth, Robert Intine, Maryellen Harshbarger McVicker, Virgina M. Metzgar, Lee County Courthouse, Rokeby Museum, Lauren Rick, UALR Center for Arkansas History and Culture, Andrew Walker, Drake Walker, Joshua Walker, Kelsie Walker, Kyler Walker, Lucas Walker, Wilson's Creek National Battlefield Museum, and the Wisconsin Historical Society. I would especially like to thank my best friend and spouse, Daylene Walker, for her untiring support over the course of this project.

Chapter 1

Uncle Jesse

Live together in an undivided bond of love ... and if you Join together as one man, you need not want [for] aney thing.
—Asael Smith, 1799

If you say another word about that Book of Mormon, you shall not stay a minute longer in my house, and if I can't get you out any other way, I will hew you down with my broad axe.
—Jesse Smith, 1830

In the fall of 1880, a dramatic scene played out in an obscure village in northeastern Iowa. Two missionaries from the LDS Church in Utah were diligently seeking those interested in the Mormon message. One was twenty-one-year-old Hyrum Jensen from Salina, Utah. The second was twenty-three-year-old B. H. Roberts, trained as a blacksmith and a recent graduate of the University of Deseret, and later a prolific writer and assistant Church historian. Preaching Mormonism as they crisscrossed Clayton County, the elders heard rumors about a surviving brother of the Mormon Prophet Joseph Smith, who apparently resided in the vicinity. Having never met an immediate family member of the founder of the Church he espoused, Roberts resolved to track down William B. Smith. His excitement about such an unexpected opportunity was tempered by uneasiness about what he might expect. Had it been any other member of the Smith family Roberts would likely have suffered no reticence about a visit, but this particular brother gave him pause. Resolute but apprehensive, Roberts recorded in his journal what he had read or heard about the Prophet's younger brother, describing him as "proud, rebellious, pugnacious, and [a] dominant spirit both in his father's house and likewise in the church."[1]

The elders followed the course of the meandering Turkey River, and after much effort and inquiry, they eventually located Smith's residence—a "humble log and frame home in the hills two or three miles west of the town of Elkader." In visiting with local residents en route, Roberts was perplexed by the great admiration they expressed for Smith and his faith. They reported that Smith had successfully defended his brother and Mormonism against a detractor who had earlier come into the town of Elkader and, in doing so, had won the respect of

---

1. Gary James Bergera, *The Autobiography of B. H. Roberts* (Salt Lake City: Signature Books, 1990), 102–4; Truman G. Madsen, *Defender of the Faith: The B. H. Roberts Story* (Salt Lake City: Bookcraft, 1980), 94, 121–22.

the entire community.² What Roberts heard from locals was at variance with his preconceptions about Smith's character.

He was wary as he knocked on the door of Smith's home and was initially taken aback by Smith's sheer physical presence. Though Smith was nearing his seventieth birthday, Roberts reported that he "disclosed a symmetrical physical manhood," standing "erect, full of form, with an aggressive appearance and boldness that would well nigh surpass understanding." After noting his unusual height, Roberts described his "soft, but deep blue eyes, easily converted by the depth of them to almost dark eyes, when animated or stirred with emotion." Smith warmly greeted the missionaries and the three enjoyed a pleasant visit, viewed some relics from the Nauvoo period of the Church's history, and dined together that evening. Smith insisted that they accept his hospitality, and even gave up his own bed, sleeping on the floor, so that the two missionaries would have a comfortable rest before they departed the next morning.³

Instead of the headstrong personality and argumentative approach he had anticipated, Roberts's interaction with Smith was completely the opposite. He recorded in his history that Smith was "tame and submissive," a gracious host, and a man of spontaneous faith, praying without hesitation and even requesting that the LDS elders give a priesthood blessing to his eldest son who was sick with malaria. While Smith did attempt to explicate his idea of succession at one point, Roberts astutely avoided any potential arguments. As they prepared to leave the next morning, Smith startled the Mormons with his supportiveness, voluntarily writing a letter of introduction on their behalf to a friend who lived in a neighboring town. Roberts remembered that Smith requested the man to "receive us as he would himself and see to it than no one insulted us. . . . It was a most feeling and pleading letter in maintenance of his chief proposition to the entertainment of Elder Jensen and me." Long separated from the church the missionaries represented, William Smith was an amiable host despite his persisting religious differences with the Utah-based Church.

If the previous twenty-four hours had not been puzzling enough to Roberts in his attempt to interpret Smith's personality, the scene that transpired as they parted only confused him further. Smith walked the missionaries to the outskirts of town, helping them find the road that led to their destination. As they prepared to depart, Roberts wrote, Smith "extended his hands,"—"long, nervous, powerful hands, taking the hand of each of us," looked into the missionaries' eyes, and "burst into a flood of tears. I had seen men weep before," described Roberts, "but never had I seen any weep like this man. It was a veritable flood of tears accompanied by a clinging, warm clasp of his hand." Smith's overwhelming emotional response surprised the missionaries, and they, in turn, were speechless about why their visit had provoked such a display. "What was it that moved him to such emotions?" Roberts mused in his journal. "Was it the recollection of his own youth when he too under the favor of God had been an

---

2. Bergera, *The Autobiography of B. H. Roberts*, 102–4; Madsen, *Defender of the Faith*, 122.
3. Bergera, *The Autobiography of B. H. Roberts*, 102–4; Madsen, *Defender of the Faith*, 121–22

itinerant missionary going from house to house to present the message of the New Dispensation? The question could not be determined," the missionary finally concluded, "nor all the dramatic experiences of William Smith in the church at Nauvoo, Kirtland, and in New York."[4] Initially prepared for aggression and argumentation, meeting this last Smith brother left the missionaries bewildered, a mystery that their usual categories of "apostates" did not prepare them to penetrate.

Had William's father still been living he likely could have proffered an insightful explanation about his son's enigmatic and fluctuating personality. Such insight had been hard-earned by Joseph Smith Sr., who saw both the strength that stiffened William's resolve as storms of abuse and persecution descended on the despised Mormons, and the pride in his family lineage and sense of "chosenness" that left William vulnerable to adulation and hopes of glory that had gathered around this one surviving son—often less as a glittering robe than as a hampering shroud. Joseph Sr.'s life ended in 1840 in a lengthy illness, episodes of which left him increasingly weak. William, a struggling missionary, barely able to feed his family, yet finding decreasing acceptance among the men who should have been his closest colleagues in the Quorum of the Twelve Apostles, may have felt that he could count on little empathy among his blood kin as well. His father's death in 1840 was followed by that of handsome Don Carlos in 1841, Joseph and Hyrum in June 1844, and Samuel of an unidentified ailment only a month later. His three sisters, though loving and supportive by all accounts, had married men of no great leadership ability—and no such positions were offered them.

As a result, William, who had been isolated partly for his own protection in the East after the rapid deaths of his brothers lamented the loss of a father's steadfast but loving guidance—a father whose own sensitivity to family dynamics had been honed and nurtured during his own upbringing and who keenly saw in William both the strengths of his brother Jesse and also the weaknesses of a proud and capable man whose circumstances did not allow him to flourish as the "master spirit" of his family, religion, and time. As matters stood, William negotiated a lonely disciple's path, one that often left him bewildered and alienated, and taking a proud pose of independence when what he himself and the fledging Church needed was devotion and pastoralism, not a too-ready defensiveness. But during those crucial years of formation, neither Uncle Jesse nor Nephew William found ways to help themselves with their strengths, let alone learn equally important lessons of tender guidance and shared spirituality.

JUST MONTHS after the organization of the Mormon Church, in the latter part of August 1830, Joseph Smith Sr. and his youngest son, fourteen-year-old Don Carlos, traveled from their home in Ontario County some two hundred miles northeast to St. Lawrence County, in upstate New York. Joseph had not seen his parents or siblings in more than eighteen years, and was anxious to renew cordial

---

4. Bergera, *The Autobiography of B. H. Roberts*, 105.

bonds with his family.⁵ Adding to his enthusiasm for the journey was his recent conversion to Mormonism, which he viewed as Christ's New Testament church, restored anew. Its formation had been preceded by the publication of a new book of scripture, the Book of Mormon. His third-born son, namesake Joseph, had only recently been recognized as God's mouthpiece in the newly organized religion, a designation with awesome potential. As a former Universalist, Joseph Sr.'s acceptance of the new faith was a colossal shift away from his former religious ideology.

Almost certainly in the years that had passed since young Joseph had shared with his family that God refused to recognize any existing church as valid, the senior Joseph had contemplated how best to share this staggering message with his family. Not the least difficult was the fact that his family well knew his Universalist beliefs—a firm rejection of Calvinism and general unease with organized religion—so his embrace of a new religion raised questions, perhaps even skepticism and opposition among the relatives who had shared his earlier religious paradigm. Most conspicuous among those skeptical relatives would be his older brother Jesse, who had, during an earlier time, gone through his own religious shift away from Universalism and back to the rigid theologies of Calvinism. Not only would Joseph have to persuade some of his relatives of the necessity of baptism and other religious rites—ceremonies that were at odds with Universalist thought—but at the other end of the spectrum, he would have to contend with his brother's belief in limited election, which was central to Calvinist theology.⁶ But when it came to Jesse, it was more than just the brothers' differing religious philosophies that would make religious dialogue difficult. Headstrong and often belligerent in his views, this eldest son had no hesitation in turning a family disagreement into wrathful expostulation. As a result, family members had learned to be cautious where Jesse was concerned. Often admired and respected among several generations of the Smith family, Jesse's behavior could also, at times, be hostile and aggressive. It would require great skill on Joseph's part to manage

---

5. "Sketch of the Autobiography of George Albert Smith," *Deseret News*, August 11, 1858, 1. Although this autobiography uses the subject's full name, he is more commonly known as "George A.," to avoid confusion with his namesake grandson, George Albert Smith, who was Church president.

6. John W. Welch, ed., "Jesse Smith's 1814 Protest," *BYU Studies* 33, no. 1 (1993): 131–44. Jesse was described as a religious man—"a Covenanter." Richard L. Anderson further described Jesse Smith as "entrenched in Calvinistic theology; in 1836 his brothers were ordered not to talk 'about the Bible at all in his home unless it was upon Limited Election.'" Richard L. Anderson, *Joseph Smith's New England Heritage*, rev. ed. (Salt Lake City: Deseret Book/BYU Press, 2003), 141. I quote from both the 1971 first edition and the 2003 revised edition, specifying the edition in each case. See also John Smith, Journal, August 20, 1836, LDS Church History Library. Anderson further explains that "'limited election' referred to the Calvinistic view that God's predestination defined the saved—thus election to salvation was unconditional and Christ's atonement was limited to that group." Ibid., 278 note 202.

Jesse's erratic personality, deal with his hostile defensiveness, and open his heart to the truths of the new gospel.

Of the nine children of Asael and Mary Duty Smith, it was Joseph who appears to have been closest to Jesse during their youth and early adult years. As the two eldest boys, they were close in age and worked as a team to advance the family farm. But experience had taught even Joseph to be wary of ruffling his eldest brother's temper. Jesse's prickly personality had persisted beyond his youth in spite of his parents' concerted effort to promote a sense of harmony in their home. Their father, Asael, had been especially conscientious in instructing his children to maintain amicable relationships as they matured. In a written charge that he termed a "family address," Asael instructed his adult children to "live together in an undivided bond of love." "You are maney of you," he continued, "and if you Join together as one man, you need not want [for] aney thing. . . I pray, Beseach, and adjure you, by all the relations and Dearness that hath Ever been betwixt us, and by the heart rending pangs of a Dying father, whos[e] Soul hath been ever bound in the bundle of Life with yours, that you know one anoth[e]r [and] visit (as you may) each other [to] comfort, counsel, relieve, Succour, help and admonish one another. . . . And when you have Neither father nor mother Left, be . . . fathers and mothers to each other."[7]

Asael's insistence that his children maintain strong ties was a value that grew out of the deprivation he experienced in his own upbringing. Asael was the youngest child in his family, and his mother died six months after his birth. One year later, Asael's father remarried, leaving him to be primarily raised by his new stepmother. One of Asael's sons later admitted that this second wife, Priscilla, "did not treat him so kindly as some Mothers treat their children," and the pain associated with Asael's childhood was evident in his writings.[8] Asael summarized his feelings about the harshness of his stepmother when he advised his own wife that, if she should remarry after his death, she must always "remember what I have undergon[e] by a Step mother, and Do not estra[n]ge your husband from his own children or kindred."[9] Not only had Asael been mistreated by his stepmother, but as frequently happens in blended families, he felt that the remarriage adversely impacted his relationship with his father. The experience solidified Asael's determination to establish collaborative and supportive relationships in his own home.

As his children reached adulthood, his strong desire for cohesiveness among family members became even more evident. When Joseph Sr. was twenty, Asael

---

7. Asael Smith, "Address to his Family," as quoted in Anderson, *Joseph Smith's New England Heritage* (2003), 166, 173–74.

8. John Smith, Journal, July 20, 1839. See Anderson, *Joseph Smith's New England Heritage* (2003), 253 note 142 for a summary of the genealogical information on Asael's family, primarily contained in *Vital Records of Topsfield, Massachusetts, to the End of the Year 1849* (Topsfield, Mass.: Topsfield Historical Society, 1903).

9. Asael Smith, "Address to his Family," April 10, 1799, photocopy of original in Anderson, *Joseph Smith's New England Heritage* (2003), 166–76.

purchased a tract of land in Vermont, while at the same time leasing his land in Ipswich, Massachusetts. After the Vermont purchase, he planned to send Joseph and twenty-three-year-old Jesse to prepare the land for the family to relocate the next spring. However, those plans were short-lived, as Asael abruptly "changed his mind, as He could not bare to have his boys so far from him as he always loved to have his children close by."[10] Instead, Asael purchased several tracts of land of one hundred acres each; and as historian Richard L. Anderson has observed, "further conveyances hint at partnership with his sons."[11] Even to assure long-term security, Asael could not bring himself to be physically distant from his sons.

Surviving records indicate that Asael and Mary Duty Smith's adult children internalized this need for close bonds by settling near one another. Nine members of the family moved from Vermont to New York between 1806 and 1820. Those who relocated were the parents, Asael and Mary, and seven of the eleven children: Jesse, Joseph, Asahel Jr., Samuel, Silas, John, and Susan. With the exception of Joseph, who moved to Palmyra, New York, all the rest who left Vermont settled near one another in St. Lawrence County, New York. Daughters Priscilla, Mary, and Sarah had all married before the family left Vermont, so they did not follow their parents and siblings to New York. The remaining child, Stephen, had died in 1802, before the family left Vermont.[12]

Asael and Mary Duty Smith had largely succeeded in instilling a sense of unity among their children, but Jesse, for reasons that are not completely clear, was an exception. Prior to the family's removal to New York, Jesse had been involved in some self-promotion at the expense of his father. When Asael turned seventy in 1814, he entrusted his 450-acre farm at Tunbridge, Vermont, to Jesse "with the understanding that he should pay about $600 of debts, which the father was then owing, and distribute to the other children about 100 dollars each. . . . [Asael] reserved to himself a small house and twenty acres of land for his own private residence, putting Jesse in possession of the homestead. Jesse went and settled with the persons to whom his father was owing . . . . He then sued his father for these obligations, and attached his [Asael's] house and twenty acres to secure payment."[13]

Asael's response to such a betrayal was telling. Upon learning of Jesse's deceitful conduct, attorneys advised Asael to countersue "and throw Jesse out of the whole property and leave him to pay the debts." This Asael refused to do, since the idea of a lawsuit in his own family was so repugnant. However, he wept in disappointment at Jesse's double-dealing, pain that was partly assuaged when Silas

---

10. John Smith, Journal, 15–16.

11. Anderson, *Joseph Smith's New England Heritage* (1971), 102.

12. Lamar E. Garrard, "The Asael Smith Family Moves from Vermont to New York, 1806 to 1820," *Regional Studies in Latter-day Saint History: New York*, ed. Larry C. Porter, Milton V. Backman Jr., and Susan Easton Black (Provo, Utah: BYU Department of Church History and Doctrine, 1992), 14–31.

13. Journal History of the Church of Jesus Christ of Latter-day Saints, February 14, 1859, 3, LDS Church History Library.

and John, stung by their father's grief, stepped up to ensure that he was provided for. These two sons were instrumental in relocating their parents to St. Lawrence County, New York, around the year 1814; then each took a five-year turn caring for their parents during their final years.[14]

Family breaches that have lasted for generations have erupted over such behavior. Almost certainly, the other children did not receive the inheritance due to them and would not have condoned Jesse's unfilial greed. The depth of the children's desire to meet their father's goal of unity was a surprising achievement in light of the next development. Jesse recklessly squandered away the Vermont home and property and, a destitute man, eventually followed his family to St. Lawrence County sometime in the 1820s. Instead of shunning their profligate brother or pointing out that his poverty was the just reward for his unfilial behavior, his father and brothers Silas and John "supplied his wants, [and] aided him in procuring a small farm in Stockholm [New York], and assisted in building [him] . . . [a place of] residence."[15] Considering the circumstances, this generosity underscores the Smiths' remarkable ability to be forgiving and supportive of an errant family member. It also reveals the sense of obligation that family members felt toward one another in spite of their differences, something Asael had repeatedly emphasized in the home. While Asael's teachings certainly impacted his family, living with the erratic and temperamental Jesse perhaps did more to improve these qualities in his own children than anything the father had written or taught.[16]

AS THE BUDDING EVENTS of Mormonism began to coalesce in the Joseph Sr. and Lucy Mack Smith family in the late 1820s, the Smiths were eager to share the news with their extended family. Lucy was quick to pen a letter to her brother Solomon, who was closest to her in age.[17] Joseph Sr. similarly desired to share the remarkable events that had occurred during the few previous years with his relatives. He wrote to his father in 1828, informing him that his son Joseph had received several visionary experiences. While Joseph Sr.'s brothers were skeptical,

---

14. Ibid.

15. Ibid.; Anderson, *Joseph Smith's New England Heritage*, 147.

16. Both Joseph Sr. and John Smith were well known for their forbearance in their later ecclesiastical assignments, a quality they developed in their home. As an example, at a time when John was serving on the high council at Kirtland, he was part of a court held on Jared Carter. He was the only individual who came to Carter's defense, urging mercy toward Carter because "he thought that Elder Carter did not express the feelings of his heart so as to be understood & perhaps his heart was not so hard as his words." Minute Book 1, 115-16, 1832-1836 (Kirtland, Ohio), 135, item #7702, LDS Church History Library. Similarly, Joseph Sr. would play the role of mediator in his home on occasion and successfully negotiated peace among family members. (See Chapter 6.)

17. Lucy Smith, Letter to Solomon Mack and wife, January 6, 1831, Waterloo, New York, LDS Church History Library.

his father was immediately intrigued.[18] According to his grandsons, Asael had earlier portended "that something would come forth among his posterity that would revolutionize the world," and that "he always knew that God was going to raise up some branch of his family to be a great benefit to mankind."[19] The letters containing these bold declarations piqued Asael's interest, and he may have wondered if his grandson Joseph would be the fulfillment of his earlier premonitions. Joseph Jr. followed up his father's letter with one of his own, in which, according to cousin George A. Smith, he warned the family that the ungodly risked impending premillennial destruction. "The sword of vengeance of the Almighty hung over this generation," wrote the emerging Mormon Prophet, "and that except they repented and obeyed the gospel and turned from their wicked ways . . . it would fall upon the wicked and sweep them from the earth with the besom of destruction."[20] The apocalyptic warning in his letter caused some of his uncles to reconsider what they had initially dismissed. Joseph Sr.'s younger brother Asahel was most influenced by the letters and appears to have helped pave the way for Asael Sr. to give serious consideration to his grandson's claims.[21]

Joseph Sr.'s eldest surviving son Hyrum also wrote several letters to his grandfather during the years 1828–29, highlighting his support of his brother's claims. Grandfather Asael apparently wrote a letter in return. While none of their correspondence has survived, reference was made to these letters when Jesse wrote to his nephew Hyrum on June 17, 1829. Through correspondence, Hyrum had ascertained his Uncle Jesse's opposition to Mormonism; and in Hyrum's most recent letter to Asael, he referenced Jesse's allegation that Joseph Sr.'s family had been deceived. In doing so, Hyrum provoked Jesse's wrath. After perusing Hyrum's letter to Asael, Jesse fired off an indignant letter to Hyrum attacking the Book of Mormon. Referring to himself in the third person, he angrily stated that "Uncle Jesse did, and still does think the whole pretended discovery . . . a very clear and foolish deception, a very great wickedness, unpardonable, unless you are shielded by your ignorance." He treated the whole story contemptuously and expressed his belief that Joseph Sr.'s entire family had been duped. In the same letter, Hyrum addressed his uncle's skepticism, writing that if his family had been

---

18. "Sketch of the Autobiography of George Albert Smith," 1.

19. The first statement comes from Elias Smith, eldest son of Asahel Smith Jr. Oliver R. Smith, *Journal of Jesse Nathaniel Smith* (Provo, Utah: Jesse N. Smith Family Association, 1970), 336. The second quotation is from "Sketch of the Autobiography of George Albert Smith." George A. Smith, in another account, echoed the phraseology of his cousin Elias when he indicated, "My grandfather, Asahel Smith, heard of the coming forth of the Book of Mormon, and he said it was true, for he knew that something would turn up in his family that would revolutionize the world." George A. Smith, August 2, 1857, *Journal of Discourses*, 26 vols. (London and Liverpool: Latter-Day Saints' Book Depot, 1855–86), 5:102–4.

20. Quoted in "Sketch of the Autobiography of George Albert Smith," 1.

21. Ibid.; Jesse Smith, Letter to Hyrum Smith, June 17, 1829, Joseph Smith Letterbook, 2:59–61, Joseph Smith Papers, LDS Church History Library.

deceived, as Jesse had purported, then God was their deceiver. In response to his nephew's statement, Jesse branded his nephew a "Blasphemous wretch." "How dare you utter such a sentence," Jesse warned, "being hardened in iniquity, you made use of the holy name of Jehovah! for what, why to cover your nefarious designs & impose on the credulity of your Grandfather." Jesse had begun his letter by reflecting on how he had formerly thought of Hyrum as a once-promising nephew. Now that they had come to a religious impasse, Jesse's perception of his nephew had become contemptuous. Jesse had, in essence, disowned Hyrum.[22]

Not content with blasting Hyrum, Jesse continued his letter by criticizing Joseph Sr. and Lucy, whom he accused of having remained emotionally distant since their move to New York. "My complements [sic] to your Father and Mother," Jesse wrote sarcastically to Hyrum, "tell them I wish them to review through [the] years that are past, and say if they have done well in not writing to me these many years, tell them the time has been when they were glad to see me, but I am suspicious that the length of time since we last parted, has in some measure obliterated me from their memory, so that they would not now be pleased to receive a visit from me."[23] Jesse's withering interpretation of his relatives' motives highlights what must have been well-merited insecurity about his place in the family. Clearly, instead of trying to build warmer, closer relationships, his approach was to attack first and blame others for the resulting alienation.

Jesse's letter also failed to consider his responsibility about how his behavior may have contributed to the deterioration of his relationship with his brother and sister-in-law. Besides the financial loss that resulted from Jesse's mismanagement of the family trust, Jesse had contemptuously reprimanded Joseph and Lucy years earlier for attending Methodist Church meetings. While Joseph did not agree with Methodist theology, he was deeply interested in religious issues and had apparently been content, when Lucy asked him to attend with her, to grant that favor. Jesse was so displeased with the young couple and was so persistent in his reproof that Joseph eventually thought it best to stop attending the meetings due to the discord it caused in the extended family. Not satisfied with having thwarted Joseph's attendance, Jesse pressed further, insisting that Joseph should forbid Lucy to attend Methodist meetings as well. His influence was persuasive, as Joseph yielded to the pressure and did as his brother demanded.

Lucy was hurt by Jesse's interference and the influence he had over her husband. While Joseph's father had also expressed dissatisfaction with the young couple's interest in Methodism, Lucy recorded in her history a spiritual dream that pointed to Jesse as being the most outspoken towards them.[24] Shortly after the episode with Jesse and Asael, Lucy was praying that Joseph might become more religiously

---

22. Jesse Smith to Hyrum Smith, June 16, 1829.
23. Ibid.
24. Lucy Mack Smith, *Biographical Sketches of Joseph Smith and his Progenitors for Many Generations* (Liverpool: S. W. Richards, 1853), 54–56.

inclined, which meant his uniting with a formal church organization. The night following her prayer, she received what she interpreted as an inspired dream. In the dream, she viewed a glorious meadow in which stood two trees which were both "very beautiful, well proportioned, and towered with majestic beauty to a great height." The first tree she described in colorful detail in her history, with branches that glistened in the sunlight and swayed with the wind. The tree seemed to be in harmony with the earth and water that surrounded it, and its beauty "increased continually in refulgence and magnitude, until it became exceedingly glorious." In contrast, the second tree lacked the same splendor and light and "stood erect and fixed as a pillar of marble," Lucy recounted, and "no matter how strong the wind blew over it, not a leaf was stirred, not a bough was bent; but obstinately stiff it stood, scorning alike the zephyr's breath, or the power of the mighty storm."[25]

Puzzled by this dream's significance, Lucy was greatly comforted when the interpretation was immediately given to her. The two trees "personated my husband and his oldest brother, Jesse Smith; that the stubborn and unyielding tree was like Jesse; that the other, more pliant and flexible, was like Joseph, my husband." Furthermore, "the breath of heaven, which passed over them, was the pure and undefiled Gospel of the Son of God, which Gospel Jesse would always resist, but which Joseph, when he was more advanced in life, would hear and receive with his whole heart."[26] The dream and its interpretation eased Lucy's uncertainty regarding her husband's salvation, as she felt assured that, at some future point, he would formally unite with an organized church and receive the saving ordinance of baptism. The dream also validated Lucy's view that Jesse's obstinacy and coercion represented the antithesis of Christian fellowship. She never forgot his interference in their relationship; and although there is no evidence that she tried to alienate her husband from his brother, living in Palmyra instead of St. Lawrence County must have put some welcome distance between the two families. Ironically, even though Jesse chastised Hyrum because Joseph and Lucy had not written to him, there is no indication that Jesse had taken the first step by initiating correspondence with them. It is not hard to see that this early experience when Jesse had tried to control their religious lives represented a turning point for Joseph and Lucy toward independence from Jesse's influence.

ALL OF THESE events predated Joseph Sr.'s conversion to Mormonism and the visit he and Don Carlos paid to the family in St. Lawrence County in the summer of 1830. The shape of that visit was influenced by this family history and provides understanding of the family dynamic manifest during their missionary visit. By the 1820s, Joseph was independent enough not to succumb to Jesse's coercive influence; indeed, his newly adopted faith provided the foundation for firm resistance to his intimidating older sibling. Still, reconnecting with Jesse was

---

25. Ibid., 55.
26. Ibid., 55–56.

a bittersweet experience for Joseph. Among all his siblings, Jesse would be the most obdurate with whom to talk about religious issues, let alone rekindle the affinity the brothers had once enjoyed. Nevertheless, Joseph's devotion to his new faith overrode any reservations.

While Joseph and Don Carlos apparently had received no formal call for this particular mission, the father of the Mormon prophet was afire with the desire to kindle the same glowing faith among his relatives. Proselytizing by letter had broached the startling new message, but in-person visits constituted the opportunity to discuss their objections and bear witness to the marvelous experiences connected with the coming forth of the Book of Mormon. Joseph and Don Carlos carried with them copies of the scripture about which Joseph's siblings had only heard.

As they made his way north in the dusty heat of the late summer, their first stop was Potsdam, St. Lawrence County, New York, where they stayed overnight at the home of Joseph's younger brother John and his wife, Clarissa Lyman Smith. The evening's conversation must have included a discussion about the new religion, because they left a copy of the Book of Mormon at the home when they departed the next day. Though initially skeptical, Clarissa and their elder son, George A., were captivated by the book's contents and devoured it through that weekend.[27] Eager to visit with his father and the remainder of his family (most of whom resided nearby in St. Lawrence County) Joseph urged John to transport him and Don Carlos twelve miles to Stockholm, New York, early the next morning. Their next stop was Jesse's home, also in Potsdam, where they learned that their father, Asael, was on his deathbed and hurried on to the home of their brother Silas, with whom Asael and Mary Duty were living. The visitors were much relieved to learn that Asael was recovering from his recent illness but decided that Joseph's surprise visit might have a negative effect on the enfeebled, eighty-six-year-old Asael. Instead, Joseph, John, and Don Carlos returned to Jesse's home for the night.[28]

In spite of his brother's uncertain temperament, Joseph felt responsible to share his message with the whole family, including Jesse. Almost immediately after Joseph, John, and young Don Carlos settled themselves at Jesse's home, they eagerly updated one another on their respective families after so long an absence. During their evening visit, as a matter of course, Joseph brought up the Book of Mormon and spoke of its discovery and translation. Though the rest of the family was anxious to hear what the two missionaries had to say, talk of the "Golden Bible" instantly provoked Jesse's wrath, and the tone of the conversation became abruptly hostile. Jesse threatened Joseph, "If you say another word about that Book of Mormon, you shall not stay a minute longer in my house." He forbade them from bringing copies of the book into his home and denied their preaching "any such damn'd nonsense in his house." Startled by this outburst, his siblings

---

27. "Sketch of the Autobiography of George Albert Smith."
28. Ibid.; Lucy Smith, *Biographical Sketches*, 154.

were even more taken aback by the intensity of his aggression. Jesse warned, "And if I can't get you out any other way, I will hew you down with my broad axe." John, who had had eighteen more years of close interaction with Jesse, commented: "We had always been accustomed to being treated with much harshness by our brother . . . [but] he had never carried it to so great an extent before."[29]

The next morning, after what must have been a broken night's sleep, John took his brother Joseph and Don Carlos again to Silas's home, where Asael and Mary Duty welcomed Joseph and Don Carlos. The meeting was a memorable one, as Asael had feared he would never see Joseph again before his death. Indeed, his health was so fragile that he died that very fall, only months after their visit, so these hours were precious indeed. Additionally, it was Asael and Mary's first meeting with Don Carlos, a handsome, well-spoken teenager. John left a

Clarissa Lyman Smith (1790–1854), married to John Smith, date unknown. Photograph by Savage and Ottinger. Clarissa was baptized in September 1831, just a year after Joseph Sr. and Don Carlos Smith brought copies of the Book of Mormon and preached in the area.

recollection of this glad meeting, which could not have been more different from the previous reunion of Joseph, Don Carlos, and John with the irascible Jesse. "They were overjoyed to see Joseph," John recorded, "for he had been absent from them so long. After the usual salutations, enquiries, and explanations, the subject of the Book of Mormon was introduced. Father [Asael] received it with gladness, that which Joseph communicated; and remarked, that he had always expected something would appear to make known the true gospel."[30] In the remaining months of his life, Asael would read the Book of Mormon nearly through, accept it as scripture, and identify his grandson Joseph as the descendant he had earlier foreseen who "would revolutionize the world" of religious thinking.[31]

However, Asael's belief in the Book of Mormon and his acceptance of his grandson's prophetic calling only provoked Jesse further. Apparently John and Joseph had left Jesse's home early that morning deliberately to avoid another unpleasant scene with their older brother. However, Jesse stormed into Silas's home, shortly after Joseph and Don Carlos had begun to explain the Book of Mormon and other gospel principles to him. When Jesse learned that the conversation was on Mormonism, "his wrath rose as high as it did the night before." According to John Smith's account

---

29. "Sketch of the Autobiography of George Albert Smith"; Lucy Smith, *Biographical Sketches*, 154–55.

30. Lucy Smith, *Biographical Sketches*, 155.

31. George A. Smith, Journal of Discourses, 5:102.

of Joseph's and Don Carlos's experience, Jesse snapped, "My father's mind is weak and I will not have it corrupted with such blasphemous stuff, so just shut up your heads." The effect of this vitriolic reaction on the reunion between Asael and his long-absent son can only be imagined. Joseph attempted to reason with his older brother, but without success until Silas's patience was exhausted. Defying Jesse, Silas replied, "Our brother has come to make us a visit, and I am glad to see him, and am willing he should talk as he pleases in my house." The fuming Jesse replied in such an "insulting manner" and poured out his opinions "so abusively," that Silas asked Jesse to leave the house.[32]

Mary Aikens Smith (1797–1877), married to Silas Smith, ca. 1870. Photograph by Savage and Ottinger. Courtesy LDS Church History Library. Mary was baptized by her nephew Hyrum Smith at Kirtland, Ohio, July 18, 1837. Silas was baptized two years earlier, while still in New York.

With Jesse temporarily out of the way, Joseph and Don Carlos returned to the theme in which Asael (and presumably Mary) manifested such interest. In addition to Asael, Silas and brother Asahel (named for his father) accepted their message, while John remained somewhat skeptical. Perhaps Jesse's persisting opposition was a factor in propelling John to investigate Joseph's claims further. During the weeks that Joseph and Don Carlos remained in the neighborhood visiting their kin, Jesse followed them, attempting to undermine their message. Knowing that John, though unfailingly hospitable to his visiting kin, remained dubious about Mormonism, Jesse went to his home in Potsdam, warning him that their brothers (Joseph, Silas, and Asahel) would soon be at his home. "As true as you live they all believe that cursed Mormon book," cautioned Jesse, "and they are setting a trap for you, to make you believe it." John's independence surfaced against this obvious manipulation, and he pushed back against Jesse's pressure. John caustically thanked Jesse for his concern and reminded Jesse that he considered himself fully capable of sound judgment in religious matters. Jesse conceded that point, but persisted in trying to undermine the missionary effort. "They are as wary as the devil," Jesse insisted, "and I want you to go with me and see our sisters, Susan and Fanny [sister-in-law],[33] and we will bar their minds

---

32. Lucy Smith, *Biographical Sketches*, 155.

33. "Fanny," or Frances, Wilcox was married to Joseph Sr.'s younger brother Samuel. St. Lawrence Co., NY, Surrogate's Court, Probate Records, 1830–1919, vol. 1, 77–78, microfilm 890,065, U.S. and Canada Record Collection, Family History Library, Salt Lake City, Utah. See also, http://josephsmithpapers.org/back/joseph-smith-pedigree-chart, accessed January 14, 2014.

against Joseph's influence." John accepted this invitation, and the two brothers discussed Joseph's missionary influence among the family.[34]

In the meantime, Joseph and Don Carlos were having some success at John's home. John's thirteen-year-old son George had thoroughly studied the Book of Mormon that Joseph and Don Carlos had left with them. One evening while his father was still absent, some religious ministers came to their home to "raise their objections, to find fault with and ridicule the book." Although he was only a boy, George rose to the book's defense. "I commenced to argue in favor of the book, and answered one objection after another, until I came off victoriously and got the compliment of being a very smart boy." Despite this success, George still had doubts about the book's authenticity and systematically wrote out a list of his objections, planning to use these problems in a debate with his Uncle Joseph, which he felt would easily allow him to disprove its authenticity. When Joseph and Don Carlos returned to John and Clarissa's home a few days later, George "undertook to argue with him upon the subject;" but in marked contrast to his debate with the ministers, in just a "half-an hour" Joseph "so successfully removed my objections and enlightened my mind, that I have never ceased to advocate its divine authority."[35]

This new conviction only turned George A. into Jesse's newest target. Though George was a firm believer after his conversation with his Uncle Joseph, when Jesse later attacked him about his conversion, George initially cowered under his influence. Not only were Jesse's sharp tongue and unchecked temper menacing, but his physical stature increased the level of intimidation he could bring to an encounter. Despite this initial desire to escape the confrontation, George A., goaded by his conscience, mustered the psychological strength to stand up in defense of what he felt was true. The resultant debate succeeded in confirming George A.'s belief in the Book of Mormon, but it permanently damaged their relationship. During their debate, Jesse boasted that "Jo dare not talk in my presence" and that even "the devil never shut my mouth." Exasperated by Jesse's intransigence, George blurted out: "Perhaps he [the Devil] opened it, uncle." As soon as the words passed his lips, he realized that contradicting Jesse meant that any possibility of a reasonable discussion had ended. Jesse rebuked George A. so severely that George simply recorded: "I thought I should have lost my identity." When George reported this shattering encounter with Asahel, one of his uncles who shared his newfound faith, Asahel burst out laughing at George's attempt to quell Jesse—apparently amused because he knew firsthand the futility of trying to reason with Jesse and sympathized with the tongue-lashing young George A. had endured. Silas, who also accepted the Mormon message, commented sym-

---

34. "Sketch of the Autobiography of George Albert Smith," 1; Lucy Smith, *Biographical Sketches*, 155.

35. "Sketch of the Autobiography of George Albert Smith," 1; George A. Smith, Journal of Discourses, 5:103.

George A. Smith (1817–1875), ca. 1870. Photograph by Charles R. Savage. Courtesy LDS Church History Library. George was converted to Mormonism through the preaching of his Uncle Joseph Smith Sr., and his first cousin Don Carlos Smith. He was baptized September 10, 1832 at Potsdam, New York.

pathetically on Jesse's excessive reaction to George A.: "If old men begin to talk to boys, they must take boys' play."[36]

Prior to Joseph and Don Carlos's missionary visit, George had always been a particular favorite of his Uncle Jesse, but ever since George A. embraced Mormonism, Jesse "has dispised [sic] me."[37] Given Jesse's prickly response to his parents and siblings, George A. must have taken particular pleasure in his uncle's approbation; and his sudden expulsion from that favored status seems to have been a very painful episode in his life, for he recorded Jesse's rejection in several of his autobiographical writings. It must have been comforting to the teenage George A. that his other uncles listened to—and discounted—Jesse's spite.

Besides his father, Joseph's brothers Asahel and Silas accepted his message. Joseph next turned his attention to his brother John. Asahel and Silas were anxious to let John hear Joseph without interruption, but Jesse remained determined to prevent any such conversation. Apparently the Smith family planned a gathering at sister Susan's home while Joseph and Don Carlos were in the area. The Smith brothers rendezvoused at John's home in Potsdam, where they planned to travel in several wagons to their destination. While at John's house, Jesse "was very careful to hear every word which passed among us, and would not allow one word to be said about the Book of Mormon." Sensing the difficulty, Asahel quietly communicated to his brother, "Now, John, I want you to have some conversation with Joseph, but if you do, you must cheat it out of Jesse. And if you wish, I can work the card for you." John responded with eagerness to speak with Joseph alone. Asahel therefore announced that he would take Jesse in his wagon, which would lead the way, while John drove with Silas. Joseph would accompany the wagons on John's horse. With Joseph on horseback, a conversation could not easily take place. But Asahel's trick was that he would drive far enough ahead of the wagon that they would be out of sight of Silas's wagon, at which point, John and Joseph would return to John's house riding double on John's horse. The plan worked to perfection, and John and Joseph spent a quiet evening alone at John's house.

---

36. George A. Smith, Journal of Discourses, 5:103–4.
37. George A. Smith, Journal and Record Book, 1817–1846, 1–2, LDS Church History Library.

Uninterrupted by Jesse, Joseph was finally able to explain his faith to his brother. John later testified that Joseph "explained to me the principles of 'Mormonism,' the truth of which I have never since denied."[38]

Although John was intially skeptical, his curiosity had been piqued by the letter Joseph Jr. had sent to the family two years earlier in which he described the coming forth of the Book of Mormon and bore his testimony of its divine origin. After reading this letter, John told Clarissa and their children that "Joseph wrote like a prophet."[39] Their visit must have been an unforgettable experience for Joseph Sr., as he had now converted most of his brothers to Mormonism. The brothers caught up with the rest of the family early the next morning and steeled themselves for Jesse's rebuke. The three brothers—Jesse, Silas, and Asahel—censured John "very sharply" for keeping Joseph overnight, but only Jesse's wrath was authentic, since the rest of the brothers had been in on the subterfuge.[40]

John Smith (1781–1854), brother of Joseph Smith Sr., date unknown. Photograph by Edward Martin. Courtesy LDS Church History Library.

The two missionaries eventually succeeded in teaching all the family, while Joseph's siblings carefully kept Jesse out of the way. Joseph's persistence in proselytizing his family bore most satisfying fruit. Except for Jesse, all of his surviving brothers eventually gathered with the Saints in Ohio. In time, seven of the ten living family members either officially united with, or expressed a desire to join the Saints: the parents, Joseph himself, Silas, Asahel, John, and a sister Priscilla.[41] Although Joseph's father died in the fall of 1830, his mother, Mary Duty Smith, traveled to Kirtland in May 1836, expressed a desire to be baptized by her prophet-grandson, and announced her intention to receive her patriarchal blessing

---

38. Lucy Smith, *Biographical Sketches*, 156.

39. John Smith, quoted in "Sketch of the Autobiography of George Albert Smith," 1.

40. Lucy Smith, *Biographical Sketches*, 156.

41. Anderson, *Joseph Smith's New England Heritage*, 142. When John and Joseph Sr. visited their sister Priscilla in 1836, she was much interested in Mormonism. John recorded, "our oldest sister . . . was very much pleased to see us, and received our testimony." In 1858, George A. Smith recorded, "Of my grandfather's family there is but one living—an old lady by the name of Waller, residing in the city of New York. . . . I visited her when I was last back there . . . . She is sanguine in relation to the truth of 'Mormonism,' although she has never embraced it. And, to use the language of her son, she preaches it all the time." "George A. Smith Discourse," both sources cited in Anderson, *Joseph Smith's New England Heritage*, 280 note 204.

from her son Joseph. Her wish was not fulfilled in this life, since the ninety-three-year-old matriarch died less than two weeks after reaching Kirtland.[42]

While the missionary journey of Joseph Sr. and Don Carlos highlighted much of Jesse's abrasive personality, enough historical material has survived to suggest a more nuanced view than simple obstinacy and hostility. George A. Smith indicated that most of the family felt some respect for Jesse, not only because he was the oldest son but also because he had some compensatory qualities. "I had always treated him [Jesse] with the greatest respect," remembered George, "and entertained a very high opinion of him. He was a man of good education . . . [and] naturally elicited from us more or less respect."[43] All of the Smiths, including Jesse, were well versed in Bible study, and their familiarity with the text highlights their uncommon intelligence. Jesse's brother Asahel had "an extraordinary retentive memory, and possessed a great knowledge of the Bible, so much so that he could read it as well without the book as with it." George A. Smith reported that Asahel, after he joined Mormonism, could not lose a debate, due to his knowledge of the scriptures.[44] Similarly, once John began to preach in St. Lawrence County, his neighbors were astounded at his familiarity with the Bible.[45] In common with his siblings, Jesse possessed a strong intellect, and his surviving writings illustrate his familiarity with the biblical text. After evaluating the most detailed of Jesse's surviving writings, John W. Welch described him as possessing the ability to effectively examine the existing doctrinal issues of his day "with a remarkable scriptural facility," quoting from the Bible "extensively, accurately, and readily." Welch further perceived Jesse as being capable of giving "considerable thought to the practical implications of several passages in the Bible" and concluded that he was "articulate and literate."[46]

In addition to his intellectual capabilities, Jesse also appears to have possessed compassion for those who suffered. Following Joseph Jr.'s series of leg surgeries at the tender age of seven, Joseph Sr. and Lucy willingly sent him to recover at Jesse's home in Salem, Massachusetts. This incident would have followed the negative experience of Jesse's attempt to control Joseph and Lucy's attendance at

---

42. This account was not included in Lucy's narrative, but was found in Martha Jane Coray's notebook. Lavina Fielding Anderson, ed., *Lucy's Book: A Critical Edition of Lucy Mack Smith's Family Memoir* (Salt Lake City: Signature Books, 2001), 605–6. See also, Richard Anderson, *Joseph Smith's New England Heritage*, 149–52.

43. George A. Smith, Journal of Discourses, 5:103; George A. Smith, Journal and Record Book, 1817–1846, 1–2, LDS Church History Library, Salt Lake City, Utah.

44. George A. Smith, Journal of Discourses, 5:101.

45. George also indicated that, after his father united with Mormonism "his former Christian friends [were] denouncing him as crazy, saying the improved condition of his health was the result of insanity." Because of this perception, they were subsequently "greatly surprised that a crazy man should know more about the Bible than they all." "Sketch of the Autobiography of George Albert Smith," 1.

46. Welch, "Jesse Smith's 1814 Protest," 134–35.

Methodist meetings, so it shows that they trusted Jesse, regardless of their religious differences, to care for his suffering nephew. Joseph Jr. stayed with his uncle in Salem for an undetermined length of time, and under his care Lucy reported that her son recovered both his strength and health.[47]

Qualities of religiousness, education, and compassion notwithstanding, Jesse's ignoble qualities jeopardized the affectionate unity that Father Asael desired for all his family. While all the Smiths had an independent mindset in common, Jesse took it to a new level. He was so rigid in his views that he lacked empathy for other perspectives and felt so threatened by difference that he often sought to belittle or intimidate others into accepting his interpretations. In summarizing Joseph Sr.'s family of origin, one historian concluded that, while the Smith family were characteristically "religiously committed but open-minded," Jesse was "the notable exception."[48] In time Jesse became an example of irreligiousness among the family, most likely because of his unkindness towards other family members and his stubbornness. Jesse made it difficult for George A. from the point of their debate onward, and George A. described him as exerting "the most cruel tyranny over his [extended] family." Although he was married with ten children, unfortunately, the kinds of family records that would provide examples of his behavior as a husband and father are missing. Obviously, how he behaved in his own home would be the most interesting and enlightening. Any remaining vestiges of respect among his extended family were likely obliterated after the visit of the missionaries.

The experience of Joseph and Don Carlos's mission among their kin in the summer of 1830 illustrates much about the challenging nature of Jesse's obdurate personality. But the episode also highlights the rather remarkable way that his parents and siblings continued to support and tolerate their strong-willed and intimidating brother. Though Joseph, his brothers, and their mother would eventually gather to Ohio in the 1830s, in following Joseph Jr.'s call to gather, it would not be the family's last encounter with Jesse. In spite of the hostility they had experienced in trying to introduce Mormonism to their brother, Joseph and John had still not given up on their brother.

At a high point of missionary activity during the Church's Ohio period, Joseph Sr. and his brother John jointly served a mission to the eastern states in 1836, giving patriarchal blessings to the Saints en route. Upon their return, they stopped to visit their remaining relatives— Jesse, Silas, Priscilla, Mary, and Susan—in Vermont and New York.[49] Time had apparently done nothing to decrease Jesse's animosity. His behavior was markedly cold, and he immediately filed a fabricated lawsuit for an incident that had occurred thirty years earlier against Joseph Sr., confiscating his horse as collateral. Silas paid the fraudulent charge of fifty dollars, enabling Joseph Sr.

---

47. Lucy Smith, *Biographical Sketches*, 65; Lavina Anderson, *Lucy's Book*, 309–10.
48. Richard Anderson, *Joseph Smith's New England Heritage*, 141.
49. Ibid., 280 note 204.

and John to continue their journey. Although the two felt they had been only kind and respectful toward Jesse and had, in turn, only received injustice, they still were concerned about Jesse's welfare. Before leaving the area, the missionaries went into a grove and prayed for their brother.[50] This was their final interaction with Jesse.

Though limited information has survived regarding Jesse, his life appears to have been filled with challenges largely caused by his own behavior. At this final meeting, Joseph and John sensed that Jesse's acerbic personality portended continued estrangement from his family and financial ruin. Their insight into their brother's personality proved accurate. George A. Smith recorded the sad ending to his uncle's life: "Jesse Smith died in 1852 in his 85th year. His numerous family were scattered, and his property wasted away, so that when he died he had no friends able to bury him; and his funeral expenses were defrayed out of the poor fund by the township of Stockholm where he died."[51]

Jesse's behavior and personality appear atypical of Asael and Mary's children who, in every other way, modeled family unity. As historian Lavina Fielding Anderson has summarized, "Jesse's acts of harshness, attempted intimidation, and what seem to be personal malice are puzzling, especially since they apparently run counter to the Smith family tradition of familial affection and devotion."[52] The manner in which the family responded to Jesse's uncharacteristic and difficult personality also reveals much about the family. Limited information makes a full diagnosis difficult, but he appears to have struggled with some sort of emotional instability, which included an impulsive temper, failure to assume responsibility for his misbehavior, entitlement, and a domineering nature.

At the conclusion of their first mission in 1830, as Joseph Sr. and Don Carlos prepared to leave their family and return to Palmyra, Joseph bade his brother goodbye by extending his hand in an affable manner. Jesse apparently shook hands but responded, "Farewell, Jo, for ever," in a brusque tone. Joseph Sr. replied solemnly, "I am afraid, it will be for ever, unless you repent." The sincerity of his declaration combined with the warmth of his handshake was apparently too much even for Jesse's obstinate nature. According to his brother John, he burst into tears and "wept like a child all the while we were riding [for] 4 miles." Jesse never explained the meaning of his tears, and witnesses of the scene were equally puzzled. The tenderness of the scene was at odds with his volatile nature and what the missionaries had witnessed in the weeks they had just spent in New York. Was he prompted by remorse for the way he treated his brother with such harshness after so long an absence? Did he experience the turmoil of recognizing that he had failed to prevent the missionaries' success among his family? Was he

---

50. Following their prayer in behalf of Jesse, Joseph Sr., and John described that the "spirit of the Lord rested upon them," and they prophesied that their brother would "become a pauper, that he should die penniless and that his children should be estranged from him and be scattered." Journal History, February 14, 1859, 1–3.

51. Ibid.

52. Lavina Anderson, *Lucy's Book*, 608.

conflicted by his strained efforts to counteract their message and suppress his own doubts that, just possibly, he was rejecting the truth? Perhaps Jesse did not understand his own emotional response. At Joseph Sr.'s final words, Jesse "melted into tears, . . . made no reply, nor ever mentioned the circumstance afterwards."[53]

AS FAR AS CAN be documented Jesse never met his nephew William B. Smith, but those who knew them well would have recognized the similarities in their personalities. The parting episode involving Jesse and Joseph, which mirrored William's later farewell from LDS missionary B. H. Roberts was one poignant example. Both men experienced interpersonal difficulties, not only because of their religious dogmatism, but also because of the way they attempted to press those views on others. Such behavior was not limited to religion, as both exhibited a sense of entitlement and exploited the kindness of family and neighbors. Endowed with an extraordinary physique, both men would use their physical strength to enforce compliance and intimidate others to get their way. Conversely, both held great influence in their families and in the communities where they resided. Each possessed a keen intellectual capacity, and both were well informed on religious and political issues of their day. The similarities between the two were rather remarkable, and the course of their lives would closely parallel one another.

---

53. Lucy Smith, *Biographical Sketches*, 156.

Chapter 2

Yankee Childhood

> I got into a great many quarrels and contentions with the young men of the neighborhood, But [I] invariably came off victorious.
> —William B. Smith, 1883

Times were hard for the Joseph Smith Sr. and Lucy Mack Smith family at the dawning of a new century. Though the couple's prospects had been promising at the time of their marriage in 1796, several failed business ventures left the growing family destitute. Poverty kept them on the move throughout the New England countryside—no fewer than seven times before they reached Palmyra, New York, in the winter of 1816–17. In spite of economic challenges, Joseph Sr. provided basic necessities for his growing family by teaching school in the winter and farming during the summer months. In reality, he preferred alternative methods of earning a living besides farming (a trait he passed along to his male children), but dire circumstances left him with few alternatives. The year 1810 found them in Royalton, Windsor County, Vermont, where Lucy gave birth to their seventh child, a son they named Ephraim. Adding to the nearly insurmountable burden occasioned by their economic situation, Ephraim died just two weeks after his birth. Infant death was far from a novelty at the time, and their first child had been a stillborn son, but the two short weeks of Ephraim's life must have been an agony of hope, denial, despair, and finally acceptance. It was a time of grief and worry for the Smiths.[1]

The one bright spot during the family's brief stay at Royalton was the birth of their eighth child and fifth surviving son, William, born on March 13, 1811—a year to the day after his deceased brother Ephraim and the same day as his brother Samuel, who was three years older. William was possibly named for a nephew, the adopted son of Lucy's brother Jason, who had lived with the Smiths for a six-month period during the early 1800s.[2] Though he was christened "William,"

---

1. Lucy Mack Smith, *Biographical Sketches of Joseph Smith the Prophet and His Progenitors for Many Generations* (Liverpool: S. W. Richards, 1853), 45–56; Richard L. Anderson, "Alvin Smith," in Kyle R. Walker, ed., *United by Faith: The Joseph Sr. and Lucy Mack Smith Family* (American Fork, Utah: BYU Studies and Covenant Communications, 2006), 86–87.

2. Lucy's brother Jason Mack had adopted a young man named William Smith, whom Lucy describes as a "friendless orphan." Jason left him with Joseph and Lucy's family for six months, probably in 1803, to attend school. Lucy Smith, *Biographical Sketches*, 41, 52; William Smith, *William Smith on Mormonism* (Lamoni, Iowa: Herald Steam Book and Job Office, 1883), 5; hereafter cited as *William Smith on Mormonism*.

in later years he referred to himself as William B. Smith, adopting the initial during the Civil War to differentiate him from many others who shared his name.[3]

Besides his ordinary name, William's birth order position may have also been a factor in his developing personality, as he was sandwiched in the middle of nine surviving children. Growing up at a time when gender roles were firmly prescribed, the age gap between him and his four older brothers (Alvin, Hyrum, Joseph, and Samuel) was large enough that he was not always included in the older children's activities. Instead, he spent more time with Don Carlos, who was five years his junior. Although children's birthdays were not typically observed with elaborate celebrations at that period, it is difficult to know if the natal date, shared with Samuel and an annual reminder of baby Ephraim's death, perhaps contributed to his struggle to establish and maintain a strong sense of identity during his youth.

Soon after William's birth, the family moved east across the Vermont border to Lebanon, New Hampshire, where difficulties continued for the family. In Lebanon, the family was stricken with typhoid fever, an epidemic that spread through the upper Connecticut Valley killing approximately 6,400 people in five months. While older sister Sophronia nearly died and Joseph Jr.'s bout led to osteomyelitis that came close to causing the amputation of his leg, Lucy recounted that two-year-old William also contracted the disease along with the other children. Much of his parents' time and nearly all of their resources for the better part of a year were consumed with nursing their children back to health. These experiences taxed Lucy's strength to its limits and once again exhausted the family's limited financial resources. Joseph Sr. and Lucy had little time for toddler William, especially as Lucy was once again pregnant with Katharine, born on July 28, 1813. It seems likely that William's care was largely left to fifteen-year-old Alvin and, after she had recovered sufficiently, ten-year-old Sophronia, since Hyrum spent hours trying to relieve Joseph Jr.'s pain. Except for Joseph's dramatic operation and Sophronia's near-death, Lucy passes quickly over that dreadful "year of sickness and distress." She summarizes: "Health again returned to our family, and we most assuredly realized the blessing."[4]

---

3. Gary James Bergera, ed., *The Autobiography of B. H. Roberts* (Salt Lake City: Signature Books, 1990), 102. Roberts noted that "the initial ["B"] was [William's] addition to his name which he himself used when in the Union fray to designate him from the many William Smiths that were among the enlisted men." Joseph Smith III appears to have corroborated Robert's account, when he indicated that his uncle was, "later usually called William B. Smith." Richard P. Howard, ed., *The Memoirs of President Joseph Smith III (1832–1914)* (Independence: Herald Publishing House, 1979), 184. Though he didn't elaborate, William also may have been referring to the adoption of the middle initial "B," when he wrote to Joseph III stating, "Joseph you will notice that the letter B in my name <is not> on record in the Revelation apointing the Twelve." William B. Smith, Letter to Joseph Smith III, October 19, 1883, Miscellaneous Letters and Papers, P13, f2311, Community of Christ Library-Archives.

4. Lucy Smith, *Biographical Sketches*, 60–66; Joseph A. Gallup, *Sketches of Epidemic Diseases in the State of Vermont, from Its Settlement to 1815* (Boston: T. B. Wait and Sons,

By 1813 the Smiths had moved back across the New Hampshire border to Vermont. They settled briefly at Norwich where they rented a farm, only to encounter three successive seasons of weather so cold that no crops could be successfully raised. On the basis of glowing reports about plentiful crops of wheat raised in western New York, the family decided on yet another move.[5] William recalled that it was in 1816 when he was "at the age of five," that they moved "into the town of Palmyra, Ontario County, New York."[6]

While William's childhood was filled with economic and health-related challenges, it was also a time when the Smith family experienced a heightened sense of religious zeal. While both parents had a devout religious heritage, in April 1811, just a month after William's birth, Joseph Sr. experienced an increase in his spiritual yearnings. Lucy remembered that her husband's "mind became much excited upon the subject of religion." It is unknown what exactly precipitated this religious awakening, but the timing coincided with his father-in-law Solomon Mack's conversion to the Christian faith, an experience he was eager to share with all he knew. The Smiths were certainly aware of Solomon's transformative experience, as they lived in close proximity to their Mack relatives during William's early childhood. One of William's earliest memories may have been watching his grandfather ride through the Vermont countryside on horseback attempting to peddle his printed autobiography, which recounted his life-changing spiritual experiences and newfound devotion to Jesus Christ.[7]

Ephraim's death and the near-deaths of Sophronia and Joseph Jr. may have also contributed to Joseph Sr.'s increased spirituality. A touching moment in Lucy's autobiography is the description of Joseph Sr. kneeling with her at their

---

1815), 69–70, 75, as quoted in Richard L. Bushman, *Joseph Smith, Rough Stone Rolling* (New York: Alfred A. Knopf, 2005), 20. At a time when Lucy had exhausted herself in caring for Sophronia and Joseph Jr. successively, she related that Hyrum eased her burden by assuming her role. "Hyrum, who was rather remarkable for his tenderness and sympathy, now desired that he might take my place," recounted Lucy, "as he was a good trusty boy, we let him do so. . . . Hyrum sat beside him, almost day and night, for some considerable length of time, holding the affected part of his leg in his hands, and pressing it between them, so that his afflicted brother might be enabled to endure the pain." Lucy Smith, *Biographical Sketches*, 63–64. Later in Palmyra, Katharine spent considerable time in helping to rear her younger sister Lucy, born in 1821, beginning when Katharine was eight. Mary Salisbury Hancock, "The Three Sisters of the Prophet Joseph Smith, Part 1," *Saints' Herald* 101, no. 2 (January 11, 1954): 11.

5. Lucy Smith, *Biographical Sketches*, 66–67.
6. *William Smith on Mormonism*, 5.
7. Solomon Mack had his conversion experience, told as a first-person testimony, printed in pamphlet form. Solomon Mack, *A Narraitve [Narrative] of the Life of Solomon Mack* (Windsor, Vt.: [1811]); "Birthplace and Early Residence of Joseph Smith, Jr.," *Historical Magazine* 8 (November 1870): 315–16, as reproduced in Dan Vogel, ed., *Early Mormon Documents*, 5 vols. (Salt Lake City: Signature Books, 1996), 1:623–26; Richard L. Anderson, *Joseph Smith's New England Heritage*, rev. ed. (Salt Lake City: Deseret Book and BYU Press, 2003), 29.

dying daughter's bedside, their hands clasped together, "pour[ing] out our grief to God, in prayer and supplication, beseeching him to spare our child yet a little longer." The conviction came to both Joseph and Lucy "before we rose to our feet" that Sophronia would live, despite all appearances to the contrary.[8] Joseph had manifested no reluctance to join with Lucy in this exercise of faith; and Lucy also records that he had had the first in a series of seven spiritually significant dreams beginning in the same year William was born and continuing until 1819. Each of the dreams had deep religious meaning to the Smith parents to such an extent that Lucy remembered five of them in sufficient detail to dictate them verbatim twenty-five years later.[9] While William's earliest years were marked by economic and emotional upheaval, it was also a time when spiritual themes were discussed with increasing regularity in the home.

William's parents had, in the early years of their marriage, experienced a high degree of compatibility in their religious views. They jointly shared a theological paradigm that embraced a return to primitive Christianity.[10] Most of Joseph Sr.'s family adhered to the Universalist faith, whose central tenet was that God would ultimately save all of his children—a decided contrast to the uncertainty and doom surrounding Calvinist predestination. Joseph Sr.'s father had also taught him that "outward forms, rites, and ordinances" were unnecessary, as the love of Christ was sufficient to save all humankind.[11] After six years of marriage, however, Lucy's religious views began to shift when she suffered a serious illness that nearly took her life. She described it as "quick consumption," but the symptoms match those of pneumonia—easily fatal in those days before antibiotics. As the family feared the worst, Lucy recounted, "I then looked to the Lord, and begged and pleaded with him to spare my life, in order that I might bring up my children, and be a comfort to my husband." After making "a solemn covenant with God, that, if he would let me live, I would endeavour to serve him according to the best of my abilities," Lucy recovered. True to her word, Lucy sought to fulfill her side of the bargain. She increased her participation in the various religious meetings held in the area where they lived and began a more intensive study of the Bible. "I would hear all that could be said, as well as read much that was written, on the subject of religion," recounted Lucy, "but the Bible I intended should be my guide to life and salvation. This couse I pursued for a number of years. At length I considered it my duty to be baptized, and, finding a minister who was willing to baptize me, and leave me free in regard to joining any religious denomination, I stepped forward and yielded obedience to this ordinance."[12]

---

8. Lucy Smith, *Biographical Sketches*, 60–61.

9. Ibid., 56–74.

10. Lucy Smith, *Biographical Sketches*, 37, 56–57.

11. Asael Smith, "Address to His Family," photographic facsimile reprinted in Anderson, *Joseph Smith's New England Heritage*, 168.

12. Lucy Smith, *Biographical Sketches*, 46–49.

Lucy undoubtedly included her family in her religious quest, as she had done earlier in her marriage when she had pressed her husband to join with her in attending Methodist meetings and as she would do later in Palmyra when she induced the entire family to attend.[13] Lucy ultimately saw it as her responsibility to prevail upon her husband and children to become more religiously inclined. Taking the lead in religious practice within the home was a role she had learned from her mother Lydia and one in which she felt resolute. Lucy's father, Solomon, referred to Lydia as his "instructor" in religious matters, and she was the one who ensured the family engaged in morning and evening prayer.[14] Lucy had observed her mother's example in the home and adopted a similar approach in her own. Lucy's conduct was not unlike that of many mothers in early nineteenth-century America, who were celebrated as "the chief transmitters of religious and moral values."[15] One nineteenth-century historian summarized that while women in the early 1800s well outnumbered men in terms of church membership, they typically "did not conduct their religious lives as disconnected individuals; instead, they drew other members of their families into the congregation." Further,

> While women could not guarantee that their husbands would experience conversion, most could see to it that they faithfully attended on the means of grace. Similarly, while women could not ensure that their children would grow in grace as surely as they grew in stature, they could "train them up in the nurture and admonition of the Lord" and hope that they would enter the covenant as soon as they reached maturity. Popular religious literature told pious women that they could set a powerful example for their household; their "influence" might help bring all the members of their family to God.[16]

In accord with both societal expectations and the teachings and example of her mother, Lucy was the embodiment of a devout wife and mother. She persistently sought to strengthen the religious commitment of her husband and children. At times she met with opposition in her attempt to convert her husband.

---

13. Lavina Fielding Anderson, ed., *Lucy's Book: A Critical Edition of Lucy Mack Smith's Family Memoir* (Salt Lake City: Signature Books, 2001), 291; Lucy Smith, *Biographical Sketches*, 90.

14. Mack, *A Narraitve of the Life of Solomon Mack*, 20. Lydia appears to have dutifully labored to increase Solomon's religious practice throughout their marriage, much as Lucy would do with Joseph Sr. Solomon revealed in his history: "I was distressed to think how I had abused the Sabbath, and had not taken warning from my wife," and that he "had slighted so many warnings from my companion." During the time when he was converted to Christianity, he recalled a particular biblical verse, but indicated, "I was so stupid that I did not know whether these words were in the Bible or not; I asked my wife, and she told me they were, and where they were." Ibid., 21–22.

15. Ruth R. Bloch, "American Feminine Ideals in Transition: The Rise of the Moral Mother, 1785–1815," *Feminist Studies* 4, no. 2 (June 1978): 113, as quoted in Irene M. Bates, "Foreword: Lucy Mack Smith—First Mormon Mother," in Lavina Fielding Anderson, *Lucy's Book*, 3.

16. Nancy Grey Osterud, *Bonds of Community: The Lives of Farm Women in Nineteenth-Century New York* (Ithaca, N.Y.: Cornell University Press, 1991), 262–64.

Though he responded to Lucy's solicitations by attending the occasional church service, Joseph Sr. remained at odds with the organized religions of his day.[17]

Once the family settled in Palmyra and, by their strenuous efforts, had achieved a "comfortable" status, Lucy renewed her quest to find a church that corresponded with her religious views and continued her role of leading out in encouraging the family to attend church services. Joseph Sr.'s earlier reluctance apparently had softened and he did not attempt to prevent Lucy or the children who wished to do so from formally uniting with a denomination, but her husband desisted after attending two or three meetings.[18]

While William doubtless observed the tension in the home over formal religious affiliation, he conversely observed the harmony in his parents' private religiosity. The Smith parents were united in maintaining a spiritual routine in the home. Similar to his description of his mother, William remembered that "my fathers religious habits was strictly Pios and Morral"[19] and that both parents ensured that their children received consistent religious training.[20] In later years, William described his mother as a "pr[a]ying woman" and that the family prayed both morning and evening from his earliest remembrance.[21] "I well remember father used to carry his spectacles in his vest pocked [pocket]," recalled William, "and when us boys saw him feel for his specks, we knew that was a signal to get ready for prayer." If the children were negligent in recognizing their father's motion to his right hand pocket for his eyeglasses, Lucy would chide, "'William,' or whoever was the negligent one, 'get ready for prayer.'"[22] The substance of his parents' petitions often centered on the children, as both Joseph Sr. and Lucy were anxious for them to adopt a religious course throughout their lives. "My parents—father and mother—pourd out their Souls to God the doner of all blessings," wrote William, "to keep and gard their children & keep them from sin and from all evil works."[23]

In addition to family prayer and readings from the Bible, which the parents used as their children's first primer,[24] the Smiths also sang hymns in their family devotionals. William recalled that they sang just after prayer, while the family was still "upon

---

17. Lavina Fielding Anderson, *Lucy's Book*, 291; Lucy Smith, *Biographical Sketches*, 90.
18. Lucy Smith, *Biographical Sketches*, 90.
19. William Smith, "Notes Written on 'Chambers' Life of Joseph Smith,'" ca. 1875, 28, LDS Church History Library.
20. "Sermon by Elder Wm. B. Smith," *Zion's Ensign* (Independence, Mo.) 3 (August 27, 1892): 2.
21. William Smith, "Notes Written on 'Chambers' Life," 29.
22. "Wm. B. Smith's Last Statement," [John W. Peterson to Editor], *Zion's Ensign* 5 (January 13, 1894): 6.
23. William Smith, "Notes Written on 'Chambers' Life," 28–29.
24. John Stafford Interview, 1881, as cited in William H. Kelley, "The Hill Cumorah, and the Book of Mormon," *Saints' Herald* 28, no. 11 (June 1, 1881): 167.

bending knees," a custom adhered to by some Protestants.²⁵ According to William, his father's favorite hymn was penned by John Leland, an American Baptist minister, and William, even in his sixties, could still quote part of it from memory:

> The day is past and gone,
> The evening shades appear;
> O may we all remember well
> The night of death draws near.
>
> We lay our garments by,
> Upon our beds to rest;
> So death will soon disrobe us all
> Of what we here possess
>
> Lord, keep us safe this night,
> Secure from all our fears;
> May angels guard us while we sleep,
> Till morning light appears.
>
> And when we early rise,
> And view th' unwearied sun,
> May we set out to win the prize,
> And after glory run.
>
> And when our days are past,
> And we from time remove,
> O may we in thy bosom rest,
> The bosom of thy love.²⁶

Both parents were steeped in a musical tradition. Music historian Michael Hicks speculates that Lucy may have been a part of the Palmyra Presbyterian choir, since the Mack family both sang and wrote hymns.²⁷ Joseph Sr. apparently had a musical background as well, since William remembered that his father was "a teacher of music by note to a concidera[b]l[e] extent." While the level and type of Joseph's musical education is unknown, at the very least he taught his children to sing. William recalled his father teaching him to raise his youthful voice to the

---

25. William Smith, "Notes Written on 'Chambers' Life," 29; Michael Hicks, *Mormonism and Music: A History* (Urbana: University of Illinois Press, 1989), 4.

26. William Smith, "Notes Written on 'Chambers' Life," 28; *Divine Hymns, or Spiritual Songs, For the Use of Religious Assemblies and Private Christians* (Wilkesbarre, Penn.: Asher & Charles Miner, 1802), 16–17.

27. Hicks, *Mormonism and Music*, 4. Hicks further summarizes the Macks' fondness of music: "Lucy Smith's father, Solomon Mack, was enamored of Isaac Watts's enormously popular *Hymns and Psalms* and tried, rather feebly, to emulate Watts in a set of verses published in his 1811 *Narrative*. Lucy's sisters Lovina and Lovisa, both of whom died young, composed several of their own hymn texts and sang duets on Watts's lyrics. Lucy recalled Lovina chanting Watts with her dying breath. And Lovisa, whose voice was 'high and clear,' sang Watts's 116th Psalm ('My God hath saved my soul from death') later in life with 'angelic harmony.'" Ibid., 15–16 note 17.

tune of "Old Hundredth" (this nickname came from the fact that the tune was "orginally set to the hundredth psalm in the 'old' version of the metrical psalms," more commonly known today by the first line of its text, "Praise God, from Whom All Blessings Flow" but still one of the most renowned of all Christian hymns).[28] Emma Smith later included at least three of the Smith family's oft-sung hymns in the Church's first hymnal, published in 1835.[29]

Although William would have been too young to have seen and understood his parents' united faith exercised on behalf of his dying sister, Sophronia, he would have grown up hearing the story and also understanding its underlying message: that "God had 'power to save to the uttermost all who call on Him'!"[30] Not only did Sophronia recover, which the family understood as a sign of God's divine intervention, but the children certainly absorbed from this experience and many less dramatic occurrences that their parents turned to their faith as a means of coping during difficult circumstances. As William matured, he would have experienced that consistently employed ritual during the family's many hardships. He was shaped, in other words, to seek understanding by employing faith and by his parents' united concern that the children grow strong in their personal faith and united in the family's religious approach to life.[31]

Although we lack anything resembling a complete record of the family's daily activities, it seems likely that the family itself formed the children's essential community. Certainly, from childhood William was drawn deeply into the urgent need to help the family meet their financial obligations. Once the Smiths were situated in Palmyra, Lucy describes a decision-making process that included the children, not just the husband and wife: "We all now sat down, and counselled together relative to the course which was best for us to adopt in our destitute circumstances, and we came to the conclusion to unite our strength in endeavouring to obtain a piece of land."[32] William, who turned six their first spring in Palmyra, would not have been an active discussant, but he was almost certainly present during the family council that Lucy describes.

---

28. Michael Kennedy, Joyce Kennedy, and Tim Rutherford-Johnson, *Oxford Dictionary of Music, 6th ed.* (Oxford, England: Oxford University Press, 2012), 612–13; William Henry Havergal, *A History of the Old Hundredth Psalm Tune: With Specimens* (New York: Mason Brothers, 1854), III–IV.

29. William Smith, "Notes Written on 'Chambers' Life," 29; "Wm. B. Smith's Last Statement"; Emma Smith, comp., *A Collection of Sacred Hymns for the Church of the Latter Day Saints* (Kirtland, Ohio: F. G. Williams & Co., 1835), 55–63, see Hymns #42–43, 48.

30. Lucy Smith, *Biographical Sketches*, 60–61.

31. For a discussion about how death, illness, and financial hardships may have influenced both Joseph Sr. and Lucy's religiosity, see Kyle R. Walker, *The Joseph Sr. and Lucy Mack Smith Family: A Family Process Analysis of a Nineteenth-Century Household* (Provo, Utah: BYU Studies, 2008), 53–62.

32. Ibid., 66, 70.

After two years of effort, the family achieved enough financial stability that they could contract for a hundred-acre farm two miles outside Palmyra.[33] William, writing from memory, later misdated this move to 1821, but correctly recalled: "we moved into Manchester, in the same county . . . where we were engaged in agricultural pursuits, as we had been since my birth."[34] Richard L. Anderson described the financial arrangement: "The Smiths obtained their property on a normal time contract, which arranged that the title would be transferred after a pioneer earned payments by converting the thick forest into productive fields. Terms of purchase were defined in these articles of agreement, a practice commonly called articling."[35] In fact, William remembered the specifics: "This farm had been articled for, to be paid in yearly installments of $100 each."[36] While the price was high compared to similar properties in the region, this farm had all the elements the family would need to succeed.

The early 1820s was a time period marked by strenuous effort for the Smiths, as they united their strength in trying to make a flourishing farm. All who were able joined in clearing and planting the land, constructing a log house and then a frame home, and contributing what they could earn from odd jobs to assist with the annual $100 payment. William remembered that "want of money and the scarcity of provisions . . . [of] necessaty made an imperitive demand upon evrey energy, nerve or member of the family for boath economy and labour which deman[ds] had to be met with the strictest kind of industry."[37] Joseph Jr. similarly recalled: "Being in indigent circumstances [we] were obliged to labour hard for the support of a large Family having nine children and . . . it required the exertions of all that were able to render any assistance for the support of the family."[38] While some of William's brothers hired out for various cash jobs or moved temporarily out of the area to find work, William apparently stayed home where, during the 1820s, he was almost exclusively "engaged as a farmer boy in working on the farm of my father."[39]

---

33. Mormon historians date the Smith family's arrival in Palmyra, New York, to the winter of 1816–17, and estimate their move to their hundred-acre farm as being in January 1819. Karen Lynn Davidson, David J. Whittaker, Mark Ashurst-McGee, and Richard L. Jensen, eds., *Histories, Volume 1: Joseph Smith Histories, 1832–1844*, in THE JOSEPH SMITH PAPERS, general editors Dean C. Jessee, Ronald K. Esplin, and Richard Lyman Bushman (Salt Lake City: Church Historian's Press, 2012), 549. Lucy Mack Smith also indicated: "In 2 years from the time we entered Palmyra . . . we were able to settle ourselves upon our own land [in] a snug comfortable though humble habitation built and neatly furnished by our own industry." Lavina Fielding Anderson, *Lucy's Book*, 321. For a discussion on the timing of this move see, Richard L. Anderson, "Alvin Smith," 88–91.
34. *William Smith on Mormonism*, 5.
35. Richard L. Anderson, "Alvin Smith," 91.
36. *William Smith on Mormonism*, 12.
37. William Smith, "Notes Written on 'Chambers' Life," 28.
38. Davidson, et al., *Histories, Volume 1*, 11.
39. *William Smith on Mormonism*, 12.

"Clearing up a Farm." Sketch by R. E. Robinson in the *American Agriculturist* 39, no. 4 (April 1880).

Clearing the native trees off the land became the initial task of settlers like the Smiths, and the prodigious amount of work required was foremost in William's memory. "The great problem of the early settler was to secure cleared land enough for the growing of crops," described one writer of the process of forest clearing, "in order to get the timber out of the way so the sunlight might reach the ground." Thus, "the forest was the natural enemy," and "the work of clearing involved the heaviest of the heavy physical strains which made up the lot of pioneer activities."[40] Pomeroy Tucker, a resident of Palmyra, described the Smith property as a "nearly wild or unimproved piece of land, mostly covered with standing timber." William's recollection echoed that of Tucker's, describing the acreage as "new" or virgin land, which was "heavely timberd."[41] Experts on this region's horticulture estimate that there were roughly a hundred trees per acre, some of them more than a hundred feet in height, and four or more feet in diameter.[42] "The timber on this land was very heavy," recalled William, and

---

40. Paul W. Brown, "Timber Destruction: The Problem and the Way Out," *America at Work* (St. Louis, Mo.) 6, no. 2 (June 20, 1922), 11.

41. Pomeroy Tucker, *Origin, Rise, and Progress of Mormonism* (New York: D. Appleton and Company, 1867), 12; William Smith, "Notes Written on 'Chambers' Life," 35.

42. Dan Marion, horticulturist and tree pathologist, State College of New York, interviewed by Donald L. Enders, August 10, 1985, and January 24, 1992, Canandaigua, New York, as quoted in Donald L. Enders, "The Joseph Smith, Sr. Family: Farmers of the Genesee," *Joseph Smith, the Prophet, the Man*, ed. Susan Easton Black and Charles D. Tate Jr. (Provo, Utah: BYU Religious Studies Center, 1993), 219. According to Enders, horticulturists continue to estimate that there are approximately 100 trees per acre on

"some of the elms were so large that we had to nigger them off"—a term related to "niggling," which meant dividing the felled trees into large log sections, and then making small fires at the base of the tree where they could be rolled into piles and burned. Because many of the trees on the Smith property "were too large to be cut with a cross-cut saw," as William described, this method of clearing the land saved them considerable chopping.[43]

Mother Smith suggests the extent of the family's labors by recalling that, in their first year on the farm, they constructed a log home and cleared thirty acres.[44] Lucy's statement means, therefore, that the family cut down approximately three thousand trees during their first year using either a cross-cut saw or hand-wielded axes, an effort described by Richard L. Bushman as "herculean achievement." "A skilled woodsman took seven to ten days to clear a single acre," documented Bushman, and a "pioneer working alone could probably clear ten acres the first year, though at the risk of neglecting fences, garden, and the construction of barn and outbuildings."[45] William remembered that the family eventually cleared sixty acres in five years after moving to the farm; and after six or seven years of hard labor, had their farm in good working order. Clearing off the trees "was mostly done in the form of fire" he further recalled, and the resulting ash was typically sold as a cash crop to be made into potash.[46] "Potash, or any of its less refined forms (such as black salts or untreated, raw ashes), became a literal cash staple of the American frontier," described one writer. "Homesteaders, being limited in ways to make money, were provided the financial means by which they could subsist during the first few years of settlement."[47] The standing stumps also had to be burned out, but meanwhile crops—often corn—could be planted in the clearings thus created. William recalled long days "in the field rolling logs or carrying brush"—efforts that "required the utmost exertion [and] endustrey of the family."[48]

---

virgin land in this region of New York, and that there is currently a red oak on the Smith farm that is five feet in diameter. Donald L. Enders, interviewed by Kyle R. Walker, June 7, 2013, Layton, Utah.

43. "The Old Soldier's Testimony. Sermon Preached by Bro. William B. Smith, in the Saints' Chapel, Deloit, Iowa, June 8th, 1884. Reported by C. E. Butterworth," *Saints' Herald* 31 (October 4, 1884): 643–44; Brown, "Timber Destruction," 11.

44. Lucy Smith, *Biographical Sketches*, 70.

45. Richard L. Bushman, *Joseph Smith and the Beginnings of Mormonism* (Urbana: University of Illinois Press, 1984), 48.

46. *William Smith on Mormonism*, 12; William Smith, "Notes Written on 'Chambers' Life," 35.

47. Benjamin C. Pykles, "An Introduction to the Kirtland Flats Ashery," *BYU Studies* 41, no. 1 (2002): 162.

48. *William Smith on Mormonism*, 12; "The Old Soldier's Testimony," 643–44; William Smith, "Notes Written on 'Chambers' Life," 35. William Conklin, an early settler from Erie, Pennsylvania, described what he felt was the most efficient way to clear land, which appears to have mirrored the Smith's approach. "The way I manage is, to go in the first place and cut and pile all the under-brush, then cut up the old logs and cut out the small timber,

"Scenes in a Sugar Bush," published in *Harper's Young People Illustrated Weekly*, May 4, 1880.

It is no wonder that, in later years, William staunchly defended the family's work ethic against accusations of laziness and indolence during this period. Said William, "We cleared sixty acres of the heaviest timber I ever saw. . . . If you will figure up how much work it would take to clear sixty acres of heavy timber land . . . trees you could not conveniently cut down, you can tell whether we were lazy or not." As another example of the family's industry, William claimed that the family tapped approximately twelve to fifteen hundred sugar maples each spring. From these trees, the family typically produced one thousand pounds of sugar per year. Again, he insisted, "to gather sap and make sugar and molasses from that number of trees was no lazy job."[49]

---

say all below one foot through. In this way a man can get over a large piece [of land] in a short time, and it will be but a small job to log it. Then girdle the remainder, and let it stand three or four years, then chop it down in the winter, when the ground is frozen, and all the tops will break up, so all the chopping there is to do, is to cut trees down. When this is done, we put on fires and nigger them off, which is a short job, and easier than chopping. Then the logging and burning is quickly done, as the timber is all dry, light to handle, and good to burn; whereas, if the timber is all cut down green, there is a deal of hard work to chop it, and very heavy work to log it, and slow to burn." Clearing in this way, and by himself, Conklin cleared 35 acres in a matter of six years. Wm. Conklin, "Clearing Land," *Ohio Cultivator* 15, no. 1 (January 1, 1859): 2.

49. J. W. Peterson, "Another Testimony: Statement of William Smith, concerning Joseph, the Prophet," *Deseret Evening News*, January 20, 1894, 11; Lavina Fielding Anderson, *Lucy's Book*, 322.

Corroborating William's reminiscence, historian Donald L. Enders has described the process of sugaring as a "labor-intensive work. . . . Many people could make maple syrup, but it required considerable skill to make sugar and particularly good skill, dexterity, and commitment to make high quality sugar."[50] Neighbors, interviewed much later, vividly recounted this activity. Lorenzo Saunders, William's friend and neighbor in Palmyra, remembered visiting the Smith farm when the family was in the midst of making sugar:

> It was in the Spring I went there to eat sugar. Samuel Lawrence went with me; there was 4 or 5 men making sugar; Their camp was right on the farm; they made several thousands pounds of sugar; You see there was a bounty in the state of New York & they was making a great deal of sugar & they had several boiling places & employed some men. . . . This was in the time of making sugar along in march about the 10th or 15th, & they was in full blast & they used to invite us over to eat sugar. They made sugar every year.[51]

Saunders further recalled that "the Smiths were great sugar makers," and were so successful that one particular year they "took the bounty in the County—of $50.00."[52]

During the early 1820s, in short, the Smiths succeeded in making their one-hundred-acre farm prosper. William took pride in the fact that he had assisted the family as they cleared the land, "and got it under a good fence and cultivation; besides building a good frame house, out-buildings, etc."[53] He also recollected that his father had the secondary occupation of coopering, or barrel-making, and that he taught this skill to at least Hyrum and Joseph Jr., although no evidence has survived indicating that William also learned the trade.[54] Besides building their log and frame homes, the Smiths planted an apple orchard of approximately two hundred trees, which meant that each fall saw the strenuous labor of picking the apples, drying some, storing others in a root cellar, but making most of them into cider which could be transported and sold. They also built a cooper's shop, a barn and pens for their animals, and split-rail fencing running around their fields to protect the growing crops.[55]

Perhaps the clearest evidence of the Smiths' industry in the 1820s was the increase in property value. Shortly after the family moved on the farm, the heavily forested land was valued at $700. Just ten years later, it was valued at $1,300.[56] The $600 increase in property value reflects the rather remarkable productivity that resulted from the Smiths' united labors during this ten-year period. When

---

50. Enders, "The Joseph Smith, Sr. Family," 223.
51. Lorenzo Saunders, interviewed by E. L. Kelley, November 12, 1884, 6–7, E. L. Kelley Papers, "Miscellany," Community of Christ Library-Archives, Independence, in Vogel, *Early Mormon Documents*, 2:151.
52. Lorenzo Saunders, Interviewed by William H. Kelley, September 20, 1884, 4, "Miscellany," Community of Christ Library-Archives, Independence, in Vogel, *Early Mormon Documents*, 2:143–44.
53. *William Smith on Mormonism*, 13.
54. William Smith, "Notes Written on 'Chambers' Life," 35.
55. Enders, "The Joseph Smith, Sr. Family: Farmers of the Genesee," 213, 218–19.
56. Ibid., 219.

Edward Partridge visited and "walked over" the Smith farm in the year 1830 during his investigation of Mormonism, he was struck by the "neatness," "good order and industry which it exhibited." When Lucy recounted to him how the family had sacrificed their prosperous farm for their faith, he concluded that they would not have done so unless the astonishing claims about the Book of Mormon and Joseph Jr.'s prophetic calling were factual. Partridge would have understood and appreciated the colossal effort that had produced this neat and orderly farm; and their willingness to sacrifice it reinforced his own burgeoning faith. He was baptized almost immediately.[57]

William's constant efforts through his teenage years greatly contributed to the prosperity of the farm; but perhaps the unrelenting labor required to make a farm successful prompted him to seek a different profession. William would probably have sought a livelihood elsewhere, even if he had not been drawn into the Mormon ministry from his teen years. Although he bought a farm and spent the closing decades of his life farming, most probably in partnership with his stepson and son (see Chapter 21), he was never content with husbandry alone. Once he reached adulthood, he looked for alternative and entrepreneurial methods of earning a living.

Notwithstanding his time spent working on the farm, William also enjoyed socializing with boys near his own age. He described engaging in the "different amusements of the young men my age in the vicinity." Among other activities, William liked to go hunting and fishing with his younger brother Don Carlos, and two of the neighboring Saunders' boys. Lorenzo Saunders, who was William's age, remembered that he and William often "used to hunt, & fish, & sport, while we was boys together." Lorenzo's brother Benjamin, three years younger than William, also recalled: "We used to coon hunt together . . . with Wm. and [Don] Carlos."[58] William probably spent some of his recreational time fishing in Hathaway Brook which ran through the Smith property and originated near the Hill Cumorah.

Like nearly all rural and frontier men, Joseph Sr. considered a rifle part of his essential equipment and was required to furnish his own firearm for militia mus-

---

57. Lucy Smith, *Biographical Sketches*, 170; Lavina Fielding Anderson, *Lucy's Book*, 504–5. Lucy felt that persecution was the primary reason her family lost their property. She likely recounted the same narrative for Edward Partridge as she had to Oliver Cowdery, at the time of the latter's conversion. When the Smiths were to vacate their frame home and move back to the log home, Lucy warned Oliver of the persecution and sacrifice that would result from his acceptance of Mormonism. She then declared in her history: "I now give up all this for the sake of Christ and salvation, and I pray God to help me to do so, without a murmur or a tear. In the strength of God, I say, that from this time forth, I will not cast one longing look upon anything which I now leave behind me." Lucy Smith, *Biographical Sketches*, 130.

58. *William Smith on Mormonism*, 10; Benjamin Saunders, interviewed by William H. Kelley, ca. September 1884, and Lorenzo Saunders, interviewed by E. L. Kelley, November 12, 1884, both found in "Miscellany," Community of Christ Library-Archives, Independence, both in Vogel, *Early Mormon Documents*, 2:137, 148.

"Boys Fishing in Hathaway Brook on the Joseph Sr. and Lucy Mack Smith farm." Photograph by George Edward Anderson, August 17, 1907. Hathaway Brook originates from the Hill Cumorah and flows north through the Smith farm, and into the Erie Canal at Palmyra. Courtesy LDS Church History Library.

ters, which were standard community functions for New Englanders between ages eighteen [some said sixteen, but most eighteen] and forty-five. Naturally, Joseph Sr. would have hunted to help supply the family with meat, but he also hunted as a form of recreation. During William's youth, he watched his father participate in turkey shoots with their Palmyra neighbors. James Fenimore Cooper described such an event in his 1853 novel *The Pioneers,* where "the ancient amusement of shooting a Christmas turkey [was] one of the few sports that the settlers of a new country seldom or never neglect to observe." Cooper described the bird as typically being "fastened by a string to the stump of a large pine . . . its body was entirely hid by the surrounding snow, nothing being visible but its red swelling head and its long neck." From a distance of approximately one hundred yards, the shooters were typically afforded a single shot in turn, the victor being awarded the turkey as his prize.[59] One of William's friends remembered that Joseph Sr. would genially try to shake his competitors' confidence by "pretending to enchant their guns." He would "blow in the gun and feel around the lock then tell them it was charmed and they could not kill the turky [sic]."[60]

---

59. James Fenimore Cooper, *The Pioneers* (New York: Stringer and Townsend, 1853), 246, 250 as quoted in Andrew F. Smith, *The Turkey: An American Story* (Chicago: University of Illinois Press, 2006), 63.

60. Lorenzo Saunders, interviewed by William H. Kelley, September 17, 1884, 2, E. L. Kelley Papers, Community of Christ Library-Archives, in Vogel, *Early Mormon*

"Turkey Shooting," by Julian Scott, *Harper's Weekly*, January 17, 1874.

The family's love of competition extended to athletics as well. Male adolescents and young men in nineteenth-century America established "a series of informal rankings based on skill," according to one social historian. "They rated each other by weight, height, 'pluck,' spirit, appearance, and all sorts of athletic skills from swimming to stone-throwing to ability at various organized games," which established a type of informal pecking order.[61] The male Smiths were a stalwart band, unusually tall and well-muscled, which would have given them an advantage in such athletic contests. Joseph Jr. was renowned for his love of athletics; and even though his childhood bout with osteomyelitis left him with a slight limp for the rest of his life, he eagerly engaged in matches with adult friends of wrestling, stick-pulling, the standing broad jump, woodchopping, shooting at the mark and a variety of other contests.[62] Joseph himself recounted or recorded his participation and success in athletic contests, demonstrating the important role that such activities continued to play in his life.[63] I have found no record that Joseph Sr. engaged in

---

Documents, 2:127.

61. E. Anthony Rotundo, *American Manhood: Transformations in Masculinity from the Revolution to the Modern Era* (New York: Basic Books, 1983), 41.

62. Alexander L. Baugh, "Joseph Smith's Athletic Nature," in *Joseph Smith: The Prophet, The Man*, ed. Susan Eaton Black and Charles D. Tate Jr. (Provo, Utah: BYU Religious Studies Center, 1993), 137–50; Walker, *The Joseph Sr. and Lucy Mack Smith Family*, 82–88; Rex A. Skidmore, "Joseph Smith: A Leader and Lover of Recreation," *Improvement Era* 43 (December 1940): 716–17, 762–63.

63. Andrew H. Hedges, Alex D. Smith, and Richard Lloyd Anderson, eds., *Journals Volume 2: December 1841–April 1843*, in THE JOSEPH SMITH PAPERS, general editors

wrestling or other athletic contests with his own brothers; but it seems likely that he and his six brothers would have grown up "tussling" and testing their growing strength and skill on each other.[64] George A. Smith, in a life sketch recorded in Joseph Smith Jr.'s history, recorded that "in his [Joseph Sr.'s] young days he was famed as a wrestler, and, Jacob like, he never wrestled with but one man, whom he could not throw."[65] Interestingly, Joseph Sr. also wrestled with his own sons; and as each reached and then surpassed the skill and strength of the older man, it may have been a kind of rite of passage. Hiram Jackway, a Palmyra neighbor of the Smiths, recollected seeing Father Smith and son Joseph wrestle in a nearby hay field. According to Jackway, "Joe threw the old man down, and he cried." When the interviewer asked why Joseph Sr. had become so emotional, Jackway supposed that it was "because Joe was the best man."[66] Although Jackway attributed Joseph Sr.'s weeping to wounded self-esteem—which is possible, given the role physical competence played in defining masculinity in the nineteenth century—another possibility is that Joseph Sr., who was known to be as tender-hearted and loving as his own father, may have been overcome by feelings of joy and pride. His namesake son had come closest to dying during childhood and would face ostracism and hostility as a result of his religious mission. Perhaps this minor evidence of Joseph Jr.'s physical strength and resilience gave Joseph Sr. a moment of reassurance that his beloved son would achieve full manhood. In either case, this vignette is a glimpse of an affectionate and engaged father-son relationship, in contrast to the remote and stern *pater familias* image that is often attributed to the head of a New England household. It also shows the spirited competitiveness that existed among the Smith men. Certainly William likewise participated in such contests of strength with both his father and brothers and, like his brother Joseph, William took pride in his physical prowess.

However, as Joseph's reputation for his "gold Bible" affected the family's standing locally, William's social interactions often turned aggressive. Although

---

Dean C. Jessee, Ronald K. Esplin, and Richard Lyman Bushman (Salt Lake City: Church Historian's Press, 2011), 80, 250, 267, 307, 313.

64. One surviving account documents that Joseph Sr.'s grandsons also participated in and enjoyed wrestling. Samuel H. B. Smith, Samuel's only son, recounted wrestling with his cousin Alvin, Katharine's son, when Samuel stopped by Alvin's home en route to his mission in 1860. "Alvin was very anxious to try his strength with me, being taller and stronger than myself," recorded Samuel, "but I was fortunate enough to throw him every time he tried it." See Samuel H. B. Smith, Autobiography, 1860–1863, 19, photocopy of holograph, in Samuel H. B. Smith Diary Collection, MSS SC 870, L. Tom Perry Special Collections, Harold B. Lee Library, Brigham Young University, Provo, Utah.

65. Joseph Smith, History, 1838–1856, Vol. C–1, created February 24, 1845–July 3, 1845, and November 2, 1838–July 31, 1842, with Addenda September 14, 1840, 20, MS 7513, LDS Church History Library.

66. William H. Kelley, "The Hill Cumorah and the Book of Mormon," *Saints' Herald* 28, no. 11 (June 1, 1881): 166.

some of these exchanges were likely normal play, William had a quick temper and had no hesitation in picking up any gauntlet he perceived as thrown in his direction. "I got into a great many quarrels and contentions with the young men of the neighborhood," William confessed, then boasted, "But [I] invariably came off victorious."[67] The older boys—Alvin, Hyrum, Joseph, and Samuel—were known for their mild dispositions and skill in diffusing a tense situation with a joke or change of subject. More is known about Joseph than the other three, and he, like William, was prompt to resent insults and engage in fisticuffs, although he had no reputation for picking fights or being deliberately quarrelsome. William, however, did not cope well with disagreements, and he seems to have been hyperalert to instances of harassment. No doubt, being associated with the Mormons in Palmyra resulted in many instances where William turned teasing into a fist fight; yet he also seemed drawn to mischief, giving his parents and older siblings concern and occasions for reprimand.[68]

William also confessed that he "enjoyed in common with other boys of my age and circumstances, but limited opportunities for acquiring an education; and being like most youths, more fond of play than study, I made but little use of the opportunities I did have."[69] Still, some of the area's youth, interviewed years later about their Mormon memories, recalled that William occasionally attended school, an indication that the family's economic circumstances had improved.[70] Typically, in that area, school was held during the four- or five-month respite that winter provided from heavy farm labor. Donald L. Enders describes the 1817 record of Palmyra schoolmaster Philander Packard. The Joseph Smith family was in his school district, but regrettably, it lists the attendance of only one child for one day and another for, a half day, during the session that started in September and ran through November 1. Enders comments, "Certainly, the family's poverty was a major factor in limiting educational opportunities." Other Palmyra families sent "up to four children" for "daily attendance." The next most limited attendance is that of a widow's child who attended three full days and two half-days.[71]

---

67. *William Smith on Mormonism*, 13.

68. William indicated in his history that, due to his neglect of spiritual matters, "I received frequent lectures from my mother and my brother Joseph." *William Smith on Mormonism*, 10.

69. Ibid., 6.

70. C[hristopher] M. Stafford, Statement, March 23, 1885, in Arthur B. Deming, *Naked Truths about Mormonism* (Oakland, Calif.), 1, no. 2 (April 1888): 1; William H. Cuyler, Statement, February 27, 1884, as quoted in Clark Braden and E. L. Kelley, *Public Discussion of the Issues between the Reorganized Church of Jesus Christ of Latter Day Saints and the Church of Christ (Disciples) Held in Kirtland, Ohio, Beginning February 12, and Closing March 8, 1884 between E. L. Kelley, of the Reorganized Church of Jesus Christ of Latter Day Saints and Clark Braden, of the Church of Christ* (St. Louis: Clark Braden, 1884), 383.

71. Donald L. Enders, "Treasures and a Trash Heap: An Early Reference to the Joseph Smith Family in Palmyra," *Journal of Mormon History* 40, no. 3 (Summer 2014): 212–13.

As a result, William struggled with spelling and grammar all his life, but he was well-spoken and, according to many Saints' reminiscences, an effective and powerful orator. His scores of surviving letters, preserved in both the Community of Christ Library-Archives and the LDS Church History Library, attest to an expansive vocabulary, familiarity with social issues of his day, and skill as a debater and defender of Mormonism. Like most of his siblings, William probably acquired most of his education as an adult. Still, he received instruction from his parents in the home, which included studying from the Bible.[72] In addition to literacy, these lessons taught ethical and moral principles that had a profound influence on his developing mind. Though he did not fully appreciate his parents' painstaking efforts during his youth—which William described as "wild and inconsiderate"—in later life he remembered with fondness the influence and example of his parents during his formative years.[73]

William would have been too young to recall the brightly prosperous days of his parents' early marriage. By the time he was born, they were deep in poverty and sank still further during his childhood. But from the family's move to Palmyra when William turned six, they slowly struggled upward toward stability, an effort that brought with it increasing respectability in the town's social system. When he was fourteen, however, this decade's worth of progress was reversed under the weight of three interconnected blows: brother Joseph's spiritual experiences beginning in 1820, the death of twenty-five-year-old Alvin in 1823, and the loss of their property in 1825. William, who was twelve when Alvin died, thus spent his teen years struggling with the social ostracism that followed Joseph's talk of angelic visitors and gold plates and their plunge back into poverty two years later. He initially resented the impact of Joseph's visions and visitations on his personal place in the Palmyra community during such a critical developmental period of his life.

---

72. Kelley, "The Hill Cumorah, and the Book of Mormon," 167.
73. *William Smith on Mormonism*, 10; William Smith to D[on] C[arlos] Smith, Plymouth, Illinois, December 1, 1840, in "Communications," *Times and Seasons* 2 (December 15, 1840): 252–53.

Chapter 3

The Angel and the Plates

> The glory of the Lord filled the chamber with a dazzling light, and a glorious angel appeared to him, conversed with him, and told him he was a chosen vessel unto the Lord to make known the true religion.
> —William B. Smith, 1875

> We all had the most implicit confidence in what he said. He was a truthful boy. Father and mother believed him. Why should not the children?
> —William B. Smith, 1891

Just a year before his death, William stood at the pulpit in the Old Stone Church of the Reorganized Church of Jesus Christ of Latter Day Saints in Independence. His brother Joseph had designated this city in the early 1830s as the gathering place for the Saints, where Mormons would establish their Zion prior to Christ's second coming. As a preface, William declared, "There are events and occurrences that take place in human life that fasten themselves upon the memory—that neither time nor old age can obliterate. What a man has seen with his eyes and heard with his ears is an experience that is not easily forgotten. I speak of what I do know and of what my ears have heard and of what my eyes have seen of this Latter Day Work, and of the coming forth of this strange Book of Mormon revelation."[1] As a long-lived member of Mormonism's first family, William would repeatedly be asked to recount his memories of these events for those interested in its history. William's experience, connected to the beginnings of Mormonism during his formative teenage years, would prove to have a profound impact on the remainder of his life.

While the first decade of William's life had been a time of increasing spirituality in the Smith home, the 1820s represented, if it were possible, an era of even greater religious enthusiasm. The Smiths had located themselves in the heart of the "burned-over district" of western New York and were eyewitnesses to the religious enthusiasm that accompanied the Second Great Awakening. The religious fervor so prevalent in the region quickly influenced the Smith home. By the early 1820s, Lucy Mack Smith had succeeded in getting most of the family to attend local church services, as well as the camp meetings—more emotional, intense, and concentrated experiences that did not bypass even villages like Palmyra. William remembered his mother's concern for the family at the time, describing her as a

---

1. "Sermon by Elder Wm. B. Smith. Delivered at the Saints' Church at Independence, Mo.," *Zion's Ensign* (Independence, Mo.) 3, no. 35 (August 27, 1892): 2.

"very pious woman and much interested in the welfare of her children, both here and hereafter." As a result, she used "every means which her parental love could suggest, to get us engaged in seeking for our soul's salvation, or (as the term was) 'in getting religion.'"[2] Joseph Jr. remembered that, as a boy entering his early teens, he attended the preaching services of the various denominations, including revivals and camp meetings, as often as his work permitted.[3] Despite the six years that separated them, William's experience paralleled his brother's. Lucy even succeeded in getting her husband to occasionally attend a church service with the family, though his skeptical views regarding organized religion persisted.[4]

William was only nine when Joseph recounted that he received what is now known as his First Vision. According to Joseph, who left several accounts, including the best-known version now canonized as LDS scripture, he received a joint visitation from God the Father and Jesus Christ who warned him to join no church and that an important work awaited him—later interpreted as translating the Book of Mormon and restoring the New Testament church in its purity. William was an adolescent—aged twelve through nineteen—during the period of the coming forth of the Book of Mormon. His youth during Joseph's earliest vision of the Father and the Son may have been a factor in what he recollected, but William was not the only member of the family who emphasized the events that occurred during the 1823–30 time period in his narrations. The emerging Mormon prophet's recital of a second series of visitations, those of the Angel Moroni with his accompanying message about an ancient record written upon gold plates, was what stood out most clearly in the collective memory of the Smith family.

While William's mother and sister Katharine referenced Joseph Jr.'s First Vision in their recitations, they dedicated significantly more detail to Moroni's initial visits and the subsequent discovery and translation of the Book of Mormon.[5] Likewise, it was the miraculous story of the coming forth of the Book

---

2. William Smith, *William Smith on Mormonism*, 6; hereafter cited as *William Smith on Mormonism*.

3. Karen Lynn Davidson, David J. Whittaker, Mark Ashurst-McGee, and Richard L. Jensen, eds., *Histories: Vol. 1: Joseph Smith Histories, 1832–1844*, Vol. 1 in the Histories series of THE JOSEPH SMITH PAPERS, general editors Dean C. Jessee, Ronald K. Esplin, and Richard Lyman Bushman (Salt Lake City: Church Historian's Press, 2011), 210.

4. Lucy Mack Smith, *Biographical Sketches of Joseph Smith the Prophet and His Progenitors for Many Generations* (Liverpool: S. W. Richards, 1853), 90; Davidson, Whittaker, Ashurst-McGee, and Jensen, *Histories: Vol. 1, 1832–1844*, 208.

5. Lucy Mack Smith, *Biographical Sketches*, 74–78; Kyle R. Walker, "Katharine Smith Salisbury's Recollections of Joseph's Meetings with Moroni," *BYU Studies* 41, no. 3 (2002): 5–17. Interestingly, when William and Mother Smith referenced Joseph's First Vision in their memoirs, both referred the reader to Joseph's published history. *William Smith on Mormonism*, 9; Lucy Mack Smith, *Biographical Sketches*, 74–78. However, Lucy described the visitations of Moroni and the coming forth of the Book of Mormon in meticulous detail in more than fifteen chapters. William and Katharine similarly devoted a significant amount of their recollections to the events during the 1823–30 time period. Lucy may have been prompted to include the First Vision account in her history by her scribe Martha Jane

of Mormon that was the central message of Mormon missionaries whose proselyting efforts began before their church was even organized. One Mormon historian postulated that the reason first-generation Mormons "placed so much emphasis on the idea that the restoration of the gospel began when the angel delivered the Book of Mormon, . . . [was] because that fulfilled biblical prophecy, while the First Vision took a back seat in the literature only because it did not fulfill that prophecy. . . . This event, after all," continued the writer, "was depicted from the beginning as fulfilling the prophecy in Revelation 14:6, where John declared: 'And I saw another angel fly in the midst of heaven, having the everlasting gospel to preach unto them that dwell on the earth.'"[6] The book quickly became the tangible proof of Joseph Smith's prophetic calling, and the instrument utilized by early missionaries to bring about conversion.[7] William's recollections of the

---

Knowlton Coray, as it is not mentioned in the rough draft. A partial notebook by Coray containing what seems to be an outline of important events to include has a notation about the First Vision, but it is "inserted at a slant interlinearly into the list, obviously added as an afterthought." Lavina Fielding Anderson, ed., *Lucy's Book: A Critical Edition of Lucy Mack Smith's Family Memoir* (Salt Lake City: Signature Books, 2001), 141. The list appears on p. 23 of Coray's notebook. Further, in Lucy Mack Smith's October 1845 general conference address at Nauvoo, Lucy begins her narrative by describing Joseph's receiving the plates on September 22, 1827, and recounted that it had been "18 years since I begun to receive this gospel of Glad tidings to all people." "This sequence" writes Anderson, "suggests that she considered the Book of Mormon and not the first vision to mark the beginning of the restoration." LavinaAnderson, *Lucy's Book*, 141.

6. James B. Allen, "Emergence of a Fundamental: The Expanding Role of Joseph Smith's First Vision in Mormon Religious Thought," *Journal of Mormon History* 7 (1980): 52. Terryl L. Givens, *By the Hand of Mormon: The American Scripture that Launched a New World Religion* (New York: Oxford University Press, 2002), 66, similarly points out that Martin Harris's experience with Charles Anthon was viewed by early Mormons as the specific fulfillment of a prophecy contained in Isaiah 29:4–14. "To early converts," explains Givens, "the plates buried in the earth, Harris's experience with the erudite Charles Anthon, and Smith, the untutored farmboy and instrument of God who ushered in the 'fullness of the gospel,' were convincing counterparts of Isaiah's inspired prediction. The Book of Mormon was the element that fulfilled prophecy even as it alerted the world to the imminence of momentous events at last unfolding." See also Richard E. Bennett, "'Read This I Pray Thee': Martin Harris and the Three Wise Men of the East," *Journal of Mormon History* 36, no. 1 (Winter 2010): 178–216.

7. Journals of early Mormon missionaries frequently record using the Book of Mormon as their primary conversion tool. William's brother Samuel, one of the earliest missionaries, set out just months after the Church was organized, in the summer of 1830. In Mendon, New York, he met Phinehas Young who later remembered Samuel's straightforward missionary approach: "There is a book, sir, I wish you to read. . . . It is a revelation from God. . . . If you will read this book with a prayerful heart, and ask God to give you a witness, you will know of the truth of this work." Phinehas thumbed through it and, on the final page, located the testimony of the Three and Eight Witnesses, where it was printed until the 1841 Liverpool edition, when it was moved into the front matter. Phinehas,

genesis of Mormonism focused primarily on the coming forth of the Book of Mormon as well, as he related on one occasion that "it is to be remembered that Joseph Smith was only 17 years of age when he first began his profesional career in the Minestrey," which corresponds to the time Joseph dated his initial visit from Moroni on September 21–22, 1823.[8]

Of course, an additional reason why the Smiths emphasized Moroni's visits and the coming forth of the Book of Mormon as the inauguration of Mormonism may have been that Joseph did not initially share his First Vision experience with his family. It seems odd that Joseph would have been reluctant in 1823 to tell his father about Moroni's visitation, as documented in Lucy Mack Smith's history, if his family had previously accepted his recital of his First Vision in 1820.[9] Furthermore, Joseph's comment to his mother immediately following his First Vision was tellingly vague: "And as I leaned up to the fire piece [place] Mother enquired what the matter was. I replied never mind all is well—I am well enough—off. I then told my mother I have learned for myself that Presbyteriansim is not True."[10] Although neither Joseph or his mother record any further details about this conversation, his reply of "never mind" suggests that Joseph may have avoided further discussion on the subject beyond his comment about Presbyterianism. If he did not tell his family of his First Vision, his attempt to share his visionary experience with a Methodist preacher a few days afterwards, and the preacher's contemptuous response, probably combined to make Joseph even more reticent to discuss his vision. His experience with the preacher also helps to explain why he later feared that his father might also treat his visionary experiences with Moroni with incredulity.[11] Thus, according to William's memo-

---

identifying Samuel as one of the witnesses, questioned him, and Samuel responded by reiterating his faith in the Book of Mormon and its translator: "Yes, ... I know the book to be a revelation from God, translated by the gift and power of the Holy Ghost, and that my brother Joseph Smith, jun., is a Prophet, Seer and Revelator." Phineas [sic] Young, quoted in "History of Brigham Young," *Millennial Star* 25 (June 6, 1863): 360–61.

8. William Smith, "Notes Written on 'Chambers' Life of Joseph Smith,'" ca. 1875, LDS Church History Library; also reproduced in Dan Vogel, ed., *Early Mormon Documents*, 5 vols. (Salt Lake City: Signature Books, 2004), 1:487; Davidson, Whittaker, Ashurst-McGee, and Jensen, *Histories: Vol. 1, 1832–1844*, 220–34.

9. Lucy Mack Smith states that Moroni had previously instructed Joseph to tell his father about the angelic visitation and instructions. When Moroni came to Joseph on the morning of September 22, 1823, he queried Joseph, "Why did you not tell your father that which I commanded you to tell him?" According to Lucy, Joseph replied, 'I was afraid my father would not believe me.'" Lucy Mack Smith, *Biographical Sketches*, 81–82. See also Davidson, Whittaker, Ashurst-McGee, and Jensen, *Histories: Vol. 1, 1832–1844*, 231–32.

10. Joseph Smith, History, 1838–1856, volume A-1 [23 December 1805–30 August 1834], 132, LDS Church History Library, http://josephsmithpapers.org/paperSummary?target=X6D83D120-2EA6-4A7B-AAEE-18CC627FAE1F (accessed April 22, 2014).

11. Davidson, Whittaker, Ashurst-McGee, and Jensen, *Histories: Vol. 1: Joseph Smith 1832–1844*, 214–16; Lucy Mack Smith, *Biographical Sketches*, 81–82.

Camp Meeting at Sing Sing, New York. Engraving from *Harper's Weekly*, August 10, 1859.

ry, the Smiths were introduced to Joseph's sacred mission when he called his family together and told them about his experiences on September 22, 1823, with Moroni.[12] But by the time William's recollections were first recorded (the earliest in 1841), during the Nauvoo period of Church history, William likely would have both heard and read about Joseph's story of the First Vision and would have been familiar with his brother's timeline of events. This may help explain why William blended elements from his own memory with what he either heard or read by the time his accounts were recorded.

None of William's remembrances specifically mention God the Father or Jesus Christ, but he identified rather generally a heavenly messenger—most often an "angel"—as delivering a revelation from heaven. In each account (all but one recorded after age sixty), William mentioned the appearance of a messenger, who subsequently instructed his brother about the ancient Book of Mormon record. At the same time, William highlighted a number of details that parallel his brother's accounts of the First Vision. In William's memory, he combined particulars of Joseph's First Vision, which Joseph reported as occurring in 1820, with the initial visitations of Moroni, happening in September 1823. William's recollections contain elements of both of these visionary experiences, which he had seamlessly merged into one account.

---

12. "William B. Smith: Experience and Testimony," in "Sketches of Conference Sermons, reported by Charles Derry," *Saints' Herald* 30, no. 16 (June 16, 1883): 388; "The Old Soldier's Testimony. Sermon Preached by Bro. William B. Smith, in the Saints' Chapel, Deloit, Iowa, June 8th, 1884. Reported by C. E. Butterworth," *Saints' Herald* 31, no. 40 (October 4, 1884): 643; "Sermon by Elder Wm. B. Smith," *Zion's Ensign* (Independence, Mo.) 3 (August 27, 1892): 2; *William Smith on Mormonism*, 9.

William observed the religious revival that swept through the region where he lived and noted its impact on the family, particularly on his brother Joseph. "At this time of which I am speaking, one of the most extraordinary reformations was being had all over the country," recollected William. "In schoolhouses, [and] in private families the revival meetings were being held and many claimed to be converted to God and professed religion. Methodists, Baptists, Presbyterians and churches of every class or denomination were seemingly engaged in this reformation." He was cognizant of his brother's personal spiritual struggle at the time and, in his reminiscences, always linked Joseph's religious quest with the revivals which were so prevalent in the region. "My brother also, attended these meetings, he was thought to be what was called under concern of mind,[13] such was also the state of the minds of [all] the family."[14] In one account, William's description of the timing of the First Vision generally corresponded with Joseph's, since he dates it at "about four years after my father removed with his family from Vermont to New York [1816]" when Joseph "became concerned on the subject of religion." He also remembered that the whole family was aware that "Joseph's mind was engrossed on religious subjects for some time," and specifically recalled his brother telling him that "there was a lack of wisdom; [and that] he did not know which way to go."[15] William recalled:

> Each sect began to beat up for volunteers, each one saying "We are right," "Come and join us," "Walk with us and we will do you good." . . . Joseph, then about seventeen [fourteen] years of age, had become seriously inclined, though not "brought out," as the phrase was, began to reflect and inquire, which of all these sects was right. . . . Each professed to be the true church. This did not satisfy him, as he was aware that there could be but one way of entering into the Kingdom of Heaven, and that there was but one "straight [sic] and narrow path," etc. All this however was beneficial to him, as it urged him forward, and strengthened him in the determination to know for himself of the certainty and reality of pure and holy religion. He continued in secret to call upon the Lord for a full manifestation of his will, the assurance that he was accepted of him, and that he might have an understanding of the path of obedience.[16]

William related on at least six recorded occasions that the primary reason his brother eventually made up his mind to inquire of God in secret prayer was to ask for direction in deciding which church he should join and that Joseph's seeking

---

13. The phrase "concern of mind" was a common description in early nineteenth-century vernacular for someone who had experienced a religious awakening, become "convicted" of his or her sins, and was actively seeking a religion. "Concern" appears to have been a preliminary step to what might be termed "conviction," or conversion. Some revival preachers specifically directed their sermons toward those who were already under "concern of mind." L. Ives Hoadly, *Preparation to Profess Religion* (Boston: Congregational Board of Publication, 1858), 37–38; Jotham Anderson, *The Recollections of Jotham Anderson, Minister of the Gospel* (Boston: John B. Russell, 1824), 33–41; Asa Mahan, *Autobiography: Intellectual, Moral, and Spiritual* (London: T. Woolmer, 1882), 26.

14. "Sermon by Elder Wm. B. Smith," 2.

15. "William B. Smith: Experience and Testimony," 388.

16. *William Smith on Mormonism*, 7–8.

was in direct response to the great reformation which was going on in the vicinity. It was for these reasons, William remembered, that "at length he determined to call upon the Lord until he should get a manifestation from him," and accordingly he "retired to the woods to ask the Lord for guidance."[17] In only one account did he specify that Joseph was visited by "a glorious angel," whose presence "filled the chamber with a dazzling light."[18] If William was quoted correctly by the newspaper reporter on this occasion, his reference to a "chamber" likely refers to the room where Joseph slept in the Smith home. After Joseph sought seclusion in a nearby grove of trees, William related that his brother, "falling to his knees called for a long time upon the Lord for wisdom and knowledge." William's subsequent recitations correspond with Joseph's several accounts of his First Vision: "While engaged in prayer a light appeared in the heavens, and descended until it rested upon the trees where he was. It appeared like fire. But to his great astonishment, did not burn the trees."[19] In a second account, William similarly recounted that, while his brother prayed, "he saw a pillar of fire descending [and] saw it reach the top of the trees."[20] In a third account, William recalled that "while praying, he [Joseph] saw a bright light, like the brightness of the sun. In that light he saw a personage; and that being pointed him out as the messenger to go forth and declare his truth to the world; for 'They had all gone astray; Every man was going in his own way.'"[21] In a fourth account, he further described Joseph as being so overcome by the light, that he lost consciousness for an undetermined length of time, "but when he came to himself the great light was about him, and he was told by the personage whom he saw descend with the light, not to join any of the churches. That he should be instrumental in the hands of God in establishing

---

17. Ibid., 8. "William B. Smith: Experience and Testimony," 388.
18. William Smith quoted in James Murdock, "The Mormons and Their Prophet," June 19, 1841, *Congregational Observer* (Hartford and New Haven, Conn.) 2 (July 3, 1841): 1; rpt. in James Murdock, "Origin of the Mormons," *Peoria Register and North-Western Gazetteer*, September 3, 1841, n.p., photocopy, M2732.2, LDS Church History Library; also in Vogel, *Early Mormon Documents*, 1:477–80.
19. *William Smith on Mormonism*, 8.
20. "The Old Soldier's Testimony," 643–44.
21. "William B. Smith: Experience and Testimony." Like his brother Joseph, William used "light" and "fire" interchangeably in his various accounts. In his 1835 account, Joseph stated, "I called on the Lord in mighty prayer, a pillar of fire appeared above my head, it presently rested down upon me, and filled me with joy unspeakable, a personage appeared in the midst, of this pillar of flame, which was spread all around, and yet nothing consumed." Dean C. Jessee, Mark Ashurst-McGee, and Richard L. Jensen, eds., *Journals, Vol. 1, 1832–1839*, Vol. 1 of the Journals series of the JOSEPH SMITH PAPERS, general editors Dean C. Jessee, Ronald K. Esplin, and Richard Lyman Bushman (Salt Lake City: Church Historian's Press, 2008), 87–91. In the only account written in his own hand (the 1832 account), Joseph Jr. wrote of seeing a "pillar of light," and had scratched out the word "fire." Davidson, Whittaker, Ashurst-McGee, and Jensen, *Histories: Vol. 1, 1832–1844*, 12, 19.

the true church of Christ."²² Other elements from Joseph's First Vision accounts are also apparent in William's recollections, including his being told that his sins were forgiven him, and that, if he was faithful, he should be shown the "true way."²³

William identified Reverend George Lane, a Methodist minister, as being influential in the Palmyra vicinity and its religious activities at the time of Joseph's visions.²⁴ However, in William's published history and in one additional account, he emphasized Lane's influence in the community after 1820. "In 1822 and 1823," he related, "the people in our neighborhood were very much stirred up with regard to religious matters by the preaching of a Mr. Lane, an Elder of the Methodist Church." In an account related just prior to his death, William provided even more details:

Reverend George Lane (1784–1859). Engraving from *Methodist Magazine*, 9, no. 4 (April 1826).

> A Rev. Mr. Lane of the Methodists preached a sermon on "what church shall I join?" And the burden of his discourse was to ask God, using as a text, "If any lack wisdom let him ask of God who giveth to all men liberally [James 1:5]." And of course when Joseph went home and was looking over the text he was impressed to do just what the preacher had said, and going out in the woods with child-like, simple trusting faith believing that God meant just what he said, he kneeled down and prayed; and the time having come for the reorganizing of his church, God was pleased to show him that he should join none of those churches but if faithful he should be chosen to establish the true church.²⁵

In a second account, William again pointed to Lane's influence on his brother, indicating that Joseph had sought for an answer from God at Lane's instigation. Said William, Joseph's prayer "was in accordance with the instructions given by the Methodist minister, preacher Lane who was one of the principle [sic] leaders of the reformation, that should any after getting what was called religion, have doubted as to what church they should join, that they should go into [sic]

---

22. "The Old Soldier's Testimony," 643.

23. In both the 1832 and 1835 accounts of his First Vision, Joseph Jr. indicated that his sins were forgiven. Davidson, Whittaker, Ashurst-McGee, and Jensen, *Histories: Vol. 1: Joseph Smith Histories, 1832–1844*, 12–13, 116. Similar to what William recounted, Joseph Jr. indicated in an 1840 account that he had received "a promise that the fullness of the gospel should at some future time be made known unto me." Orson Pratt, *A[n] Interesting Account of Several Remarkable Visions, and of the Late Discovery of Ancient American Records* (Edinburgh: Ballantyne and Hughes, 1840), 3–5.

24. "Sermon by Elder Wm. B. Smith," 2.

25. "Wm. B. Smith's Last Statement," 6.

secret prayer and ask God to direct them what to do and what church to join. This is what the brother [Joseph] had done."[26]

While it is possible that the Smiths may have heard Lane preach at some location near Palmyra prior to Joseph's First Vision, which historian Larry C. Porter has described as a viable possibility,[27] William's subsequent description of Lane's preaching appears to have been during 1823–25. When Joseph Smith dictated details of his history to Oliver Cowdery in 1834–35, he also linked Lane to the Palmyra area in the time frame of 1822–23.[28] William would certainly have been familiar with Reverend Lane's sermons in and around Palmyra, but his linking Lane's sermon with the First Vision, including Lane's specific reference to James 1:5, was most likely his own attempt to bring the details into coherence, since Joseph's 1843 account of his First Vision does not assign Lane a role: "I opened the [New] Testament promiscuously on these words, in James, 'Ask of the Lord who giveth to all men liberally and upbraideth not.'"[29] Joseph's description of how he discovered this scripture verse almost at random counters William's statement that Lane's sermon, preached on that very passage as a text, directed taking such a course. William's recollection that Lane preached on joining a church and seeking direction from God still may have been accurate, as a primary purpose of these revivalist preachers was to encourage listeners to seek out a denomination with which to unite. In addition to the possibility that Lane influenced Joseph's prayer which resulted in his First Vision, it is also possible that Lane's preaching may have prompted Joseph to seek to know his standing before God, which resulted in the visitation of Moroni about three years later.

William also remembered that the local Presbyterian minister, Benjamin Stockton, had a marked influence on his entire family, and described Stockton and Lane as preaching in Palmyra on successive nights in a short-lived but initially sincere union designed to bring people to Jesus. The revival William described on this occasion coincides with the period after Joseph reported having

---

26. "Sermon by Elder Wm. B. Smith," 2.

27. Larry C. Porter, "Reverend George Lane—Good 'Gifts,' Much 'Grace,' and Marked 'Usefulness,'" *BYU Studies* 9, no. 3 (Spring 1969): 321–40.

28. Oliver Cowdery initially linked Lane with the First Vision. However, Cowdery later corrected himself, indicating that the events described fit the time period when Joseph Jr. was seventeen. Oliver Cowdery to W.W. Phelps, Letter III, *Latter Day Saints' Messenger and Advocate* 1, no. 3 (December 1834): 42; Oliver Cowdery to W. W. Phelps, Letter IV, *Latter Day Saints' Messenger and Advocate* 1, no. 5 (February 1835): 77–80.

29. Joseph Smith, interviewed by David Nye White, Nauvoo, Illinois, August 21, 1843; in David Nye White, "The Prairies, Nauvoo, Joe Smith, the Temple, the Mormons, &c.," *Pittsburgh Weekly Gazette* 58 (September 15, 1843): 3, photocopy at the LDS Church History Library. Alexander Neibaur also reported that "he [Joseph Smith] wanted to get Religion too[,] wanted to feel & shout like the Rest but could feel nothing, opened the Bible [and] the first Passage that struck him was if any man lack wisdom let him ask of God." Alexander Neibaur, Journal, May 24, 1844, 23–24, LDS Church History Library; also http://josephsmithpapers.org/paperSummary/alexander-neibaur-journal-24-may-1844-extract?p=1.

his First Vision.³⁰ In an account recorded in 1884 when William was seventy-three, he highlighted the broader context of religious enthusiasm in the Palmyra area. "It will be remembered that just before the angel appeared to Joseph," wrote William, "there was an unusual revival in the neighborhood. It spread from town to town, from city to city, from county to county, and from state to state." He further recalled, "My mother attended those meetings, and being much concerned about the spiritual welfare of the family, she persuaded them to attend the meetings."³¹ William often mentioned the Reverend Benjamin Stockton in connection with this revival, whom he correctly identified as the "Presiding Paster [sic] or Shepard" over the Western Presbyterian Church at Palmyra.³² Though Stockton was not officially installed as the minister of the Presbyterian Church until February 1824, he was active in performing ministerial duties in the vicinity of Palmyra for several years prior to that time, beginning in the latter part of 1822.³³ Stockton's services in and near Palmyra overlap with the time period when Joseph reported first being visited by the Angel Moroni.

With undimmed sorrow William would recall Stockton's funeral sermon for William's oldest brother, Alvin, who died in November 1823. Instead of comforting the family, Stockton's harsh denunciation of Alvin as an unbaptized sinner who would not be saved grieved and upset the Smiths. Stockton was obviously using the funeral service as a platform to try and persuade those in attendance, including the Smith family, to join his congregation. William still remembered critical details more than seventy years later: He "preached my brother's funeral sermon and intimated very strongly that he had gone to hell, for Alvin was not a church member, but he was a good boy and my father did not like it." Alvin was beloved by all the family and was described as a kind, hardworking, and dutiful individual. Joseph Sr. was particularly upset with Stockton for making such an insinuation, and he flatly rejected this doctrine that ran counter to his more generous Universalist beliefs. The experience only solidified Joseph Sr.'s belief that all organized religions were corrupt.³⁴

---

30. "Wm. B. Smith's Last Statement," 6.

31. "The Old Soldier's Testimony," 643.

32. William Smith, "Notes Written on 'Chambers' Life of Joseph Smith,'" in Vogel, *Early Mormon Documents*, 1:487.

33. Stockton preached a sermon to the Youth Missionary Society in November of 1822 and performed a wedding on November 26, 1823, just a week after Alvin's death. "Youths' Domestic Missionary Society," *Palmyra Herald* 2 (November 6, 1822): 3; "Married," *Wayne Sentinel* 1 (December 3, 1823): 3; both quoted in H. Michael Marquardt, *The Rise of Mormonism: 1816–1844* (Longwood, Fla.: Xulon Press, 2005), 21–22.

34. "Wm. B. Smith's Last Statement," 6. See also Joseph Smith's description of his brother Alvin, in Andrew H. Hedges, Alex D. Smith, and Richard Lloyd Anderson, eds., *Journals, Vol. 2: December 1841–April 1843*, THE JOSEPH SMITH PAPERS, general editors Dean C. Jessee, Ronald K. Esplin, and Richard Lyman Bushman (Salt Lake City: Church Historian's Press, 2011), 116–17.

Although Lucy probably rejected with equal decisiveness Stockton's prediction about Alvin's ultimate destination, this sermon may have rekindled her desire to unite with a church. Her New Testament study made the necessity of baptism clear, and she had received that rite but without joining a church in 1802 at Randolph, Vermont. She had, at that time, decided "that there was not then upon earth the religion which I sought." In dictating her memoirs almost two decades later, she described the family's flocking to the various meetings of different denominations, attempting to find a measure of consolation to assuage their grief.[35]

Meanwhile, Stockton was undeterred in his efforts to convert the Smith family. During one particular season, probably in the winter of 1824–25, William recollected "a joint revival in the neighborhood between the Baptists, Methodists and Presbyterians and they had succeeded in stirring up quite a feeling." After the completion of the revival, the three churches were all vying for converts.[36] This hectic season may very well have been the same revival that Lucy described in her history, when she recalled that one particular minister (likely Reverend Stockton) "commenced laboring in the neighbourhood, to effect a union of the different churches, in order that all might be agreed, and thus worship God with one heart and one mind."[37] According to William, Stockton was designated "president of the meeting [revival]," probably because he had the only meetinghouse in Palmyra proper. He used his prominent position in the community to his advantage, arguing persuasively that the Smiths should unite with his church. William remembered that Stockton posited "that it was their [the Presbyterians'] meeting and under their care and they had a church there and they [the Smith family] ought to join the Presbyterians." But due to Joseph Sr.'s continuing dislike for Stockton, which had persisted since Alvin's funeral, family members initially declined to take that step. "Our folks hesitated [joining]," remembered William, "as father did not like Rev. Stockton very well."[38]

The evening after Stockton had labored with the Smiths, George Lane persuasively preached in the round-robin revival series.[39] One listener, who attended one of his sermons around this same time period, described the Methodist minister's forcefulness as a preacher. "The exhortations of . . . George Lane, were overwhelming," described the enthusiast. "Sinners quailed under them, and many cried aloud for mercy."[40] William, aware of Lane's reputation, recalled that he was "celebrated throughout the country as a 'great revival preacher,'"[41] and during this revival in

---

35. Anderson, *Lucy's Book*, 357, sentence crossed out in rough draft; Lucy Mack Smith, *Biographical Sketches*, 48.
36. "Wm. B. Smith's Last Statement," 6.
37. Lucy Mack Smith, *Biographical Sketches*, 90.
38. "Wm. B. Smith's Last Statement," 6.
39. Ibid.
40. Life and Times of Rev. George Peck, 108–9, as quoted in Porter, "Reverend George Lane," 332.
41. *William Smith on Mormonism*, 6.

Palmyra, served as "one of the principle [sic] leaders of the reformation."[42] Reverend Lane remembered that, even before he arrived on the scene, "the Lord had already begun a gracious work in Palmyra." He recounted that religious work in the flourishing canal town had "progressed moderately" beginning in the spring of 1824, but by fall "it appeared to break out afresh." Lane may have left his own account of the joint revival held in Palmyra that William had described, when he wrote:

> December 11th and 12th [1824] our quarterly meeting for Ontario circuit was in Ontario. It was attended with showers of blessings, and we have reason to believe that much good was done. Here I found that the work which had for some time been going on in Palmyra, had broken out from the village like a mighty flame, and was spreading in every direction.
>
> When I left the place, [on] December 22nd, there had, in the village and its vicinity, upward of one hundred fifty joined the society, besides a number that had joined other churches, and many that had joined no church.[43]

Notwithstanding Lane's persuasiveness as a preacher, it was Stockton who eventually prevailed with the Smiths. His importunities paid off when the majority of the mature Smiths united with his Presbyterian congregation. Joseph's history notes that his mother Lucy, Hyrum, Sophronia, and Samuel all joined Stockton's congregation.[44] In one account William remembered the same four individuals as joining Stockton's Presbyterian congregation, but in another, he substituted his sister Katharine's name for Sophronia's. His reference to Katharine's formal affiliation was probably a mistake, since his earlier remembrance included Sophronia's name which corresponds with Joseph's recollection, but he may have remembered Katharine's youthful attendance at Stockton's meeting house, which probably mirrored his own.[45]

By the mid-1820s, Benjamin Stockton had been instrumental in establishing what were termed "Sabbath" or Sunday Schools for the youth in the area. *The Wayne*

---

42. "Sermon by Elder Wm. B. Smith," 2.

43. Rev. George Lane, "Revival of Religion on Ontario District," *Methodist Magazine* 8 (1825): 160, as quoted in Porter, "Reverend George Lane," 336.

44. Davidson, Whittaker, Ashurst-McGee, and Jensen, *Histories: Vol. 1*, 208. Historians Milton Backman and James Allen offer corroborating evidence on at least three members of the Smith family joining the Western Presbyterian Church at Palmyra, when they document that the Smiths were visited by Presbyterian church leaders in March 1830 because of inactivity during the previous eighteen months. These three were Lucy, Hyrum, and Samuel. There is no mention of Sophronia, although she was still living in the area. Milton V. Backman Jr. and James B. Allen, "Membership of Certain of Joseph Smith's Family in the Western Presbyterian Church of Palmyra," *BYU Studies* 10, no. 4 (Summer 1970): 482–84.

45. "Sermon by Elder Wm. B. Smith," 2; "Wm. B. Smith's Last Statement," 6. William failed to mention Sophronia's affiliation in this latter account, so he probably mistakenly substituted Katharine's name for Sophronia's. In a third account, William identified only Lucy, Hyrum, and Samuel as joining the Presbyterian Church. *William Smith on Mormonism*, 7. In a fourth account, he left out Samuel and did not identify which sister joined: "My mother and brother Hyrum and a sister were members of the Presbyterian Church." "William B. Smith: Experience and Testimony," 388.

Lucy Mack Smith, 1853. Engraving by Frederick Piercy, *Route From Liverpool to Great Salt Lake Valley* (Liverpool: Franklin D. Richards, 1855).

Sentinel described Stockton's success in raising the necessary funds to establish a library for young people in conjunction with the Sunday School. When it came to the younger generation, Stockton seems somewhat less concerned about their religious affiliation and instead hoped that Palmyra's youth would memorize scripture, learn their spiritual duties, and become familiar with such important scriptural passages as the Lord's Prayer, the Ten Commandments, and Christ's Sermon on the Mount.[46] Lucy ensured that the teenage William accompanied her and the older children to Stockton's meetinghouse on the Sabbath and participate in the Sunday School. "It was in this church presided over by the Rev. Stockton," recalled William, "that I spent much of my boy-hood days, especially the Sabbath in the Sunday Schools of that day."[47] Through his parents' instructions and being involved with the Sunday School, William became deeply familiar with the scriptures and developed a keen interest in Bible-based theology from his youth.

The influence William's mother had on his developing religiosity cannot be overstated, as he frequently described her persistent effort in his history. She enacted a role that was typical of many mothers during the first half of the nineteenth century. Research indicates that in rural New York farming communities like Palmyra, more women than men joined during these revival periods.[48] "Women composed the great majority of members in all churches," noted New York religious historian Whitney Cross, and "dominated revivals and praying circles, pressing husbands, fathers, and sons towards conversion."[49] This pattern held true for the Smiths, as Lucy led out in encouraging family members in church attendance during the mid-1820s, much as she had during the early years of her marriage. William remembered that it was his mother who "prevailed on

---

46. T. Osgood, "Messrs. Editors," *Wayne Sentinel* 2 (December 15, 1824): 2; "Many are inquiring...," *Wayne Sentinel* 2 (December 15, 1824): 2. See also H. Michael Marquardt and Wesley P. Walters, *Inventing Mormonism: Tradition and the Historical Record* (Salt Lake City: Smith Research Associates, 1994), 20, for a discussion of Stockton's religious activities in Palmyra.
47. "Sermon by Elder Wm. B. Smith," 2.
48. Nancy Grey-Osterud, *Bonds of Community: The Lives of Farm Women in Nineteenth-Century New York* (Ithaca, N.Y.: Cornell University Press, 1991), 263.
49. Whitney Cross, *The Burned-Over District: The Social and Intellectual History of Enthusiastic Religion in Western New York, 1800–1850* (Ithaca, N.Y.: Cornell University Press, 1950), 177.

us to attend the meetings, and almost the whole family became interested in the matter, and seekers after truth." She "continued her importunities and exertions to interest us in the importance of seeking for the salvation of our immortal souls, until almost all the family became either converted or seriously inclined."[50] The revivals and camp meetings had greatly impacted the Smith family, and they were split down the middle between those who formally affiliated with a church and those who remained aloof, with Joseph Sr., Joseph Jr., and William falling into the latter category. However, William was only around the age of twelve when his mother and older siblings joined Palmyra's Presbyterian Church, and at that time he and his younger siblings may have been too young to make a decision about formally uniting with the Presbyterians.[51] But evidence suggests that as he matured to adulthood during the decade of the 1820s, he eventually faced that decision. After describing how his mother and siblings joined the Presbyterian Church, William united with his brother Joseph in refraining from joining any church, indicating that "Joseph and myself did not join."[52]

At the same time that the revivals were raging through Palmyra, Joseph Jr. sought to know his standing before God. It had been three years since his First Vision experience; and according to William, Joseph continued to be influenced by local revival preachers and their camp meetings. William was on the cusp of entering his teens when Moroni first visited on September 21–22, 1823, and his personal and spiritual growth appears to have corresponded with Moroni's visits and its aftermath. Lucy ensured that the children continued attending the various denominational meetings that were being held in the area. At the time of Moroni's initial visit to Joseph, William was mature enough to recognize the significance of these events and the influence they had on his family. In all of his recollections regarding the visitation of Moroni, he correctly identified his brother's age as seventeen and the visitation as occurring in 1823. In later life, he recalled the impact of these events on him and his family: "The circumstances that occurred, and the impressions made on my mind at that time, I can remem-

---

50. *William Smith on Mormonism*, 6–7.

51. While the names of baptized children were kept on Presbyterian Church records, as youths matured they were expected to demonstrate activity or face church discipline. While each Presbyterian congregation was apparently free to establish its own bylaws pertaining to membership, a congregation in Owen County, Indiana, operating during this same time period (1820–34) established the age of decision at fourteen. At the organization of its inaugural meeting, the Presbyterian Church at Owen County established: "Further resolved that those who now exceed that age [fourteen] may exercise their own discretion whether they will submit to the authority of the church or not." Kimberly E. Hunter and Christina R. Bunting, "Owen County, Bethany Presbyterian Church Records, 1820–1834," Indiana Historical Society Press, 2014, http://www.indianahistory.org/our-services/books-publications/magazines/online-connections/regional/OwenCoBethanyPresbyRecs.pdf (accessed May 2014).

52. "The Old Soldier's Testimony," 643.

ber better than those which occurred two years ago."⁵³ It was a period filled with excitement and anticipation for the family.

On the day following the Angel Moroni's initial triple overnight visits to the Smith home, William recollected that "my brothers Alvin, Hyrum, Samuel and myself were at work in an adjoining field near the house."⁵⁴ Since it was September, they were doubtless harvesting, a strenuous task. William remembered that Joseph "looked pale and unwell, so that Alvin⁵⁵ told him if he was sick he need not work." William afterward learned that Joseph's weakness was due to "his mind being oppressed by the remembrance of the [previous night's] vision."⁵⁶ Joseph Jr. was so weak from his visionary experiences, related William, that before he reached the house, he "sat down by the fence, when the angel again appeared to him, and told him to call his father's household together and communicate to them the visions he had received, which he had not yet told to any one; and promised him that if he would do so, they would believe it."⁵⁷ William was apparently unaware that the angel instructed Joseph to first tell his father about his revelatory experiences, as both Lucy and Joseph Jr. record.⁵⁸ But William added a significant detail in the sequence of events, indicating that, after Joseph spoke with his father, he then confided Moroni's directive to tell the family about his revelations to his mother. While William and his brothers were still at work in the field, William remem-

---

53. Ibid.
54. "Sermon by Elder Wm. B. Smith," 2. Lucy mentions that her husband Joseph Sr. was also working in the field with his boys. Lucy Mack Smith, *Biographical Sketches*, 81–82.
55. According to Lucy, Joseph Jr.'s pallor caught Joseph Sr.'s attention. "My husband, supposing that he was sick, told him to go to the house, and have his mother doctor him." Lucy Mack Smith, *Biographical Sketches*, 81–82. Joseph Jr. also indicated that it was his father who noticed that he was unwell and "told me to go to the house." Davidson, Whittaker, Ashurst-McGee, and Jensen, *Histories: Vol. 1, 1832–1844*, 117.
56. *William Smith on Mormonism*, 9; Murdock, "The Mormons and Their Prophet," 1.
57. *William Smith on Mormonism*, 9.
58. Lucy remembered that her son Joseph lay down on grass underneath an apple tree in the family's orchard. There Moroni appeared on his fourth visit in less than twenty-four hours and, among other items, repeated from the previous night's counsel, reiterated the need for the boy to tell his father of his visionary experiences. Joseph Jr. expressed apprehension that his father would not believe his account, but Moroni reassuringly said that Joseph Sr. would "believe every word you say to him." Obeying the angel's instructions, Joseph Jr. returned to the field. As Father Smith heard his son's account, the angel's words were literally fulfilled, and he charged his son "not to fail in attending strictly to the instruction which he had received." Lucy Mack Smith, *Biographical Sketches*, 81–82. Joseph left a similar account, recording that "the Angel came to me again and commanded me to go and tell my father what I had seen & heard. I did so. The old man wept and told me that it was a vision from God, and to attend to it." Davidson, Whittaker, Ashurst-McGee, and Jensen, *Histories: Vol. 1, 1832–1844*, 117.

bered that "my mother came to us and said that we were all requested to come into the house, that Joseph had something to tell us."[59]

Once the curious family members had assembled, leaving their chores, Joseph stood up and began to narrate the details of the previous night's experience. William remembered Joseph's exact words: "The glory of the Lord filled the chamber with a dazzling light," and then "a glorious angel appeared to him, conversed with him, and told him he was a chosen vessel unto the Lord to make known the true religion."[60] William further remembered Joseph stating "that the angel had also given him a short account of the inhabitants who formerly resided upon this continent, a full history of whom he said was engraved on some plates which were hidden, and which the angel promised to show him."[61] Besides a history of this people, and more pertinent to his religious quest, Joseph informed the family "that in the record would be found the true gospel, and the true order of Christ's church; for there was no church on earth that would answer the description of the ancient church."[62]

The response of the entire family was revealing. Though astounded by what they heard, they believed his narration largely because they loved and trusted Joseph Jr. "The whole family were melted to tears," William recalled, "and believed all he said. Knowing that he was very young, and had not enjoyed the advantages of a common education; and knowing too, his whole character and disposition, they were convinced that he was totally incapable of arising before his aged parents, his brothers and sisters, and so solemnly giving utterance to anything but the truth."[63] "We all had the most implicit confidence in what he said," William said of his brother on another occasion, "he was a truthful boy. Father and mother believed him, why should not the children? I suppose if he had told crooked stories about other things we might have doubted his word about the plates, but Joseph was a truthful boy.... No sir, we never doubted his word for one minute."[64] Lucy remembered that, in succeeding days, the family would gather in the evenings after the day's work and listen to Joseph Jr.'s description of what he had learned. The Smiths were enthralled. More than twenty years

---

59. "Sermon by Elder Wm. B. Smith," 2.

60. Murdock, "The Mormons and Their Prophet," 1. It is noteworthy that William mentions Moroni's visitation as occurring in his "chamber." In all other accounts, he mentions Joseph's vision as occurring in the woods. This distinction is important, as this was the only time he differentiated between his brother's two earliest revelatory experiences.

61. *William Smith on Mormonism*, 9.

62. "William B. Smith: Experience and Testimony," 388.

63. *William Smith on Mormonism*, 9–10.

64. "Wm. B. Smith's Last Statement," 6. On another occasion, William reiterated his confidence in Joseph's story about obtaining the plates: "All belived it was true, father, mother, brothers and sisters. You can tell what a child is. Parents know whether their children are truthful or not. The proof of the pudding is not in chewing the string, but in eating the pudding. Father knew his child was telling the truth." "The Old Soldier's Testimony," 643.

Reconstructed Smith log home, Palmyra, New York. Photograph by Kyle R. Walker, 2001.

later when Joseph was dead, Lucy recalled nostalgically: "I presume our family presented an aspect as singular as any that ever lived upon the face of the earth—all seated in a circle, father, mother, sons, and daughters, and giving the most profound attention to a boy, eighteen years of age. . . . The sweetest union and happiness pervaded our house."[65] The family immediately rallied around their brother and jointly anticipated his obtaining the record.

William wholeheartedly accepted his older brother's declaration of the miraculous events related to the angel's visits and recalled the family's enthusiasm when Joseph Jr. made his first trip to the Hill Cumorah to obtain the plates. "I well remember the effect produced upon my father's family, when he told them he was to receive the plates; how they looked forward with joy, and waited until the time should come."[66] However, that first attempt ended in disappointment. The same day that he disclosed his revelatory experience to his family, William remembered that Joseph went alone to the designated spot about three miles from their home, "and by digging discovered the plates in a sort of rude stone box."[67] William recorded candidly:

> He did not receive the plates at the time he expected. . . . He had not lived as directed. When he went to get the plates he found them as he was told he should. He took them from the stone box in which they were found, and placed them on the ground behind him, when the thought came into his mind that there might be some hidden

---

65. Lucy Mack Smith, *Biographical Sketches*, 84.
66. "The Old Soldier's Testimony," 643.
67. Murdock, "The Mormons and Their Prophet," 1. Joseph did not mention using a spade or a shovel, but did mention that the "edge [of the stone] all around was covered with earth," and that he had, by unspecified means, "removed the earth off the edge of the stone." He then "obtained a lever which I got fixed under the edge of the stone, and with a little exertion raised it up." Davidson, Whittaker, Ashurst-McGee, and Jensen, *Histories: Vol. 1, 1832–1844*, 232.

treasure hidden with them. While stooping forward to see, he was overpowered, so that he could not look farther. Turning to get the plates, he found they had gone; and on looking around found that they were in the box again; but he could not get them, and he cried out, "Why can't I get the plates as Moroni told me I could?" The angel appeared to him, and told him it was because he had not done as directed. That the plates could not be had for the purpose of making money.[68]

Joseph and the family would have to wait four more years before they received the plates. Like other members of the family, William was saddened that Joseph was initially unsuccessful in retrieving the record and indicated that the family collectively wept in disappointment.[69] It is not clear from William's various accounts what he understood about the annual visits and the four years' delay, but he never expressed any doubt in his older brother's ultimate success. During the four-year interim, he matched his growing, youthful strength against the heavy labors of a newly cleared farm and engaged in various recreational activities with peers near his own age.[70] By the time Joseph, accompanied by his bride, Emma Hale Smith, who joined her prayers for his success with his own faith, received the plates on the night of September 21–22, 1827, William was a robust sixteen-year-old.

Though William insisted that he never saw the plates themselves, he apparently had several occasions to touch them through a covering. "I did not see them [the plates] uncovered," recollected William, "but I handled them and hefted them while wrapped in a tow frock and judged them to have weighed about sixty pounds. I could tell they were plates of some kind and that they were fastened together by rings running through the back."[71] On what appears to be a separate occasion, William lifted the covered plates while they lay on a table, then "thum[b]ed them through the cloth and ascertained that they were thin sheets of some kind of metal."[72] It speaks well for William's integrity that he did not succumb to the temptation to lift the linen frock for a quick glimpse of the plates themselves.

In later life, when William heard accusations that his brother had deceived the neighbors and his family, he reacted defiantly by citing his own experience, asserting that he had "handled them [the plates] and could tell what they were. They were not quite as large as this Bible. [We] could tell whether they were round or square. Could raise the leaves this way (raising a few leaves of the Bible before him). One could easily tell that they were not a stone, hewn out to deceive, or even a block of wood. Being a mixture of gold and copper, they were much

---

68. "The Old Soldier's Testimony," 643.
69. Ibid.
70. *William Smith on Mormonism*, 10.
71. "Wm. B. Smith's Last Statement," 6.
72. William Smith, Interviewed by John W. Peterson and William S. Pender, July 4, 1890, Osterdock, Iowa, typescript with handwritten corrections by John W. Peterson on May 1, 1921, 1, Miscellaneous Letters and Papers, P13, f1490, Community of Christ Library-Archives, Independence, Mo.

The Hill Cumorah, near Palmyra, New York. Stereographic photograph by Underwood and Underwood, 1904. Courtesy Alexander L. Baugh.

heavier than stone, and very much heavier than wood."[73] He estimated the size of the plates to be about "eight to ten inches long, less in width, [and] about the thickness of panes of glass; and together made a pile of about five or six inches high." Apparently recounting what Joseph or others who had actually seen the plates (such as the Three and Eight Witnesses), he indicated that the record was "in a good state of preservation, had the appearance of gold, and bore the inscriptions in strange characters on both sides."[74] He also learned from others, probably Joseph himself, that they believed the characters on the plates had been engraved with some sort of sharp instrument.[75]

William's experience in lifting and feeling the plates through their wrapping was similar to that reported by his sister Katharine or his sister-in-law Emma, both of whom left similar accounts. Apparently it was not uncommon to touch the covered plates or move them from place to place.[76] When Joseph had initially brought the plates to the family home, William remembered that his father was

---

73. "The Old Soldier's Testimony," 644.
74. Murdock, "The Mormons and Their Prophet," 1.
75. "The Old Soldier's Testimony," 644.
76. Katharine's grandson remembered, "[Katharine] told me that while dusting up the room where the Prophet had his study she saw a package on the table containing the gold plates on which was engraved the story of the Book of Mormon. She said she hefted those plates and found them very heavy like gold and also rippled her fingers up the edge of the plates and felt they were separate metal plates and heard the tinkle of sound that they made." "The Prophet's Sister Testifies She Lifted the B of M Plates," 525, typescript copy, LDS Church History Library. Emma Smith related, "The plates often lay on the table without any attempt at concealment, wrapped in a small linen table cloth, which I had given him to fold them in. I once felt of the plates, as they lay on the table, tracing their outline and shape. They seemed to be pliable like thick paper, and would rustle with a metallic sound when the edges were moved by the thumb, as one does sometimes thumb the edges of a book." Joseph Smith III, "Last Testimony of Sister Emma," *Saints' Herald* (October 1, 1879): 289–90.

disappointed that he was unable to view them. "What, Joseph, can we not see them?" he asked his son, to which Joseph Jr. replied, "No. I was disobedient the first time, but intend to be faithful this time; for I was forbidden to show them until they are translated." However, according to William, his brother added rather significantly, "but you can feel them." William said that the family then "handled them," adding these specific details: "Father and my brother Samuel saw them as I did while in the frock. So did Hyrum and others of the family." In later life, several interviewers chided him for not removing the covering to view the plates, one RLDS interviewer remarking that "most people would ha[v]e examined them any way." On this occasion, William "suddenly straiphtened [straightened] up and looked intently at him and said[,] The Lord knew he could trust Joseph and as for the rest of the family we had no desire to transgress the commandment of the Lord."[77]

Once the family became aware of Joseph's charge to bring forth the Book of Mormon, they all became deeply focused on the process. In 1824, when Joseph Jr. once again was not allowed to bring home the plates, Lucy used the pronoun "we"—meaning the family—redoubled their collective efforts to be worthy of obtaining the record. The entire family was involved in obtaining the record and trying to ensure that Joseph could translate it uninterrupted. Various members of the family protected the plates and Joseph himself, one performed scribal duties, others became formal witnesses, and the Smith family was the first to accept his testimony.[78]

William grew impatient in later years in having to defend his faith against accusations that Joseph had borrowed the Book of Mormon text from Solomon Spalding's romance, *Manuscript, Found*, and he repeatedly defended his brother's account of how the Book of Mormon came to fruition. "I am a little too old a man to be telling stories," William responded on one of these occasions at the age of seventy-three, as "there is no money in telling this story. I expect to stand before angels and archangels to be judged for how I have told it." In that context, he would often recount from memory what he knew about the book's translation: "When Joseph received the plates he also received the Urim and Thummim, which he would place in a hat to exclude all light, and with the plates by his side he translated the characters . . . into English. And thus, letter by letter, word by word, sentence by sentence, the whole book was translated."[79] In another instance, he explained why Joseph used a hat, or something similar to exclude the light, in the process of translation. "That they [the Urim and Thummim] were much too large for Joseph and he could only see through one [stone] at a

---

77. William Smith, Interviewed by Peterson and Pender, 1.

78. Lucy Mack Smith, *Biographical Sketches*, 86; Kyle R. Walker, *The Joseph Sr. and Lucy Mack Smith Family: A Family Process Analysis of a Nineteenth-Century Household* (Provo, Utah: BYU Studies, 2008), 22–27; Andrew H. Hedges, "'All My Endeavors to Preserve Them': Protecting the Plates in Palmyra," *Journal of Book of Mormon Studies* 8, no 2 (1999): 16–23.

79. "The Old Soldier's Testimony," 644.

time," he explained, "using sometimes one and sometimes the other. By putting his head in a hat or some dark object it was not necessary to close one eye while looking through the stone with the other."[80]

William also left perhaps the most detailed description of the "Urim and Thummim" and the breastplate to which they could be attached, an indication of his familiarity with these artifacts as well. He either handled or viewed these items, or received a detailed description from his brother. In 1890, he told two RLDS interviewers, John W. Peterson and William S. Pender:

> A silver bow ran over one stone, under the other, arround [sic] over that one and under the first in the shape of a horizontal figure 8 much like a pair of spectacles. . . . The Urim and Thummim was attached to the breastplate by a rod which was fastened at the outer shoulde[r] edge of the breastplate so that when the Urim and thummim was removed from before the eyes it would reach to a pocked [pocket] on the left side of the breastplate where the instrument was kept when not in use by the Seer. I was not informed whether it was detachable from the breastplate or not. From the fact that Joseph often had it with him and sometimes when at work, I am of the opinion that it could be detached. . . . The rod served to hold it before the eyes of the Seer.[81]

After Joseph brought the plates to the Smith home, William recalled that his brother was initially unable to read the characters. "He afterwards made a facsimile of some parts of the inscription," recollected William, "and sent it to professor Anthon of New York city." While failing to mention anything about Martin Harris's role in visiting Anthon, William indicated that the noted professor at Columbia College "pronounced the characters to be ancient Hebrew corrupted, and the language to be degenerate Hebrew with a mixture of Egyptian. He could decipher only one entire word." Later, Joseph discovered that he could translate the record with divine assistance. "After this Joseph Smith was supernaturally assisted to read and to understand the inscription; and he was directed to translate a great part of it. The pages which he was not to translate were found to be sealed together, so that he did not even read them and learn their contents. With an assistant to correct his English, he translated so much of the inscription as now makes the book of Mormon."[82] In an additional account, William related, "He translated them by means of the Urim and Thummim, (which he obtained with the plates), which was placed in a hat to exclude the light, (the plates lying near by covered up), and reading off the translation, which appeared in the stone by the power of God." William then said that, after Joseph kept the record for "a long time in his chamber" and after completing the translation, he eventually

---

80. William Smith, Interviewed by Peterson and Pender, 1.
81. Ibid.
82. Ibid. Martin Harris said that Professor Anthon declared that Book of Mormon characters "were Egyptian, Chaldean, Assyric, &and Arabic, and that they were true characters." Davidson, Whittaker, Ashurst-McGee, and Jensen, *Histories: Vol. 1, 1832–1844*, 240–41.

was "directed by a vision to bury the plates again in the same manner; which he accordingly did."[83]

William later affirmed his belief in his brother's claims: "I believed the testimony of my brother. . . . I always believed he was a servant of God, ever since I heard his statement" of the visitation of the Angel Moroni.[84] With confidence in their son and brother, the Smiths devotedly moved forward in following his directives. Out of the eight surviving children at that point, only William hesitated to devote his full energy to the emerging Church, although he never doubted his brother's revelations. He resented the way the Palmyra community shunned the family after Joseph's visionary experiences were made public, but his experience was tempered by the excitement of what was transpiring through his elder brother. Whether he initially liked it or not, William's fate was forever linked to Mormonism and its golden Bible.

---

83. Murdock, "The Mormons and Their Prophet," 1. In another instance, when William was asked for the plates' location, he responded that they were returned to Moroni. "The Old Soldier's Testimony," 644.

84. "William B. Smith: Experience and Testimony," 388.

Chapter 4

Conversion

> I became awakened to the necessity of embracing the plan of salvation, and of the necessity of publishing a knowledge of Jesus Christ and his gospel among all nations, kindreds, tongues and people. . . . I . . . felt the Spirit of God like a burning fire shut up in my bones.
> —William B. Smith, 1883

While Joseph Smith Jr. was working on translating and publishing the Book of Mormon, William matured to adulthood. By age eighteen, he had developed into an imposing figure of extraordinary strength. One of William's sons remembered that his father "was well built and of powerful physique," in the prime of life, "standing six foot three in his stocking feet."[1] He inherited his tall stature from his father, but in features he more closely resembled the Mack side of the family. He had a prominent nose that was wide at its base and its tip, deeply inset eyes, and thin lips. His cheekbones were high and pronounced, and he had a well-defined, chiseled jaw. One historian described him as "a gaunt, raw-boned, cadaverous-looking youth,"[2] while a niece portrayed William as "tall and elegant in appearance with a clear light olive complexion, wavy brown hair, blue eyes, [and] handsome features."[3] Striking and strong, William attracted attention wherever he went.

Also noteworthy was William's developing personality, which became more discernible during his teens. Some of his earliest memories centered on his parents' religious habits, and his response to these family practices reveals much about William's disposition. Though he came to appreciate their efforts in later life, during his youth he was perturbed by the strictness of their devotion. He was annoyed by the redundancy of his parents' spiritual customs, confessing that he found wearisome their habits of prayer and hymn-singing twice a day. The monotony of singing the same hymns "again and again" irritated the youth, and he felt some resistance against the family's other religious practices, such as Bible reading and

---

1. "Episodes in Genealogical Research: New Light on William Smith," *Deseret News*, July 27, 1935, 8. In later life his height was taken on several occasions, and most commonly he was measured as standing 6'-6'1" tall.

2. Fawn M. Brodie, *No Man Knows My History: The Life of Joseph Smith*, 2d rev. ed. (New York: Alfred A. Knopf, 1971), 163.

3. Mary B. [Smith] Norman (Idaho Falls, Idaho), Letter to Ina [Smith] Coolbrith, March 27, 1908, Miscellaneous Letters and Papers, P13, f951, Community of Christ Library-Archives.

William B. Smith, ca. 1870. Photograph by William B. and Margaret J. Fields, taken at Lyons, Iowa. Courtesy Community of Christ Archives.

church attendance.[4] Despite his mother's continual efforts to get all of the children interested in religion, or perhaps because of it, William recorded that he made no profession of Christianity.[5] When his mother, Hyrum, Sophronia, and Samuel joined the Presbyterian Church in the mid-1820s, William linked himself with his brother Joseph and his father in remaining distant from the various denominations who were vying for converts. Said William, "Joseph and myself did not join," admitting, perhaps partly in jest, "I had not sown all my wild oats."[6] He described himself as spiritually immature and careless regarding the state of his soul. While he joined other family members in attending a variety of religious meetings in the neighborhood, including attending Benjamin Stockton's Sabbath School,[7] he remained unchurched as the saying went, and unconverted.

While his siblings became increasingly interested in seeking salvation, William lagged behind the other children. "I attended the meetings with the rest [of the family]," he recollected, but "did not take so much interest in the matter as the older ones [siblings] did."[8] Yet although he did not realize it at the time, his parents' strict religious training continued to have a profound influence on his development, including the family habits of prayer and hymn singing.[9]

Lucy was also concerned about the family's religious standing in the communities where they resided. Nothing meant more to William's mother than knowing her children were growing up unto the Lord, and her constant efforts ultimately bore fruit. When things started to unravel financially for the Smiths following Alvin's untimely death in November 1823, Lucy clung to her religion and the dignified moral behavior of her children as a means of coping. In a conversation with some of the ladies in Palmyra during this time period, she pointed to her children's character as her greatest accomplishment. "I have never prayed for riches of the world," described Lucy, "but I have always desired that God would enable me to use enough wisdom and forbearance in my family to set good precepts & examples before my children whose lives I always besaught the Lord to spare[,] as also to secure the confidence and affection of my husband[,] that we acting together in the education and instruction of our children that we might in our old age reap the reward of circumspection joined with parental tenderness viz the Pleasure of

---

4. William Smith, "Notes Written on Chambers' Life of Joseph Smith," ca. 1875, 28, LDS Church History Library.

5. William Smith, *William Smith on Mormonism*, 10, 15 (hereafter cited as *William Smith on Mormonism*).

6. "The Old Soldier's Testimony. Sermon Preached by Bro. William B. Smith, in the Saints' Chapel, Deloit, Iowa, June 8th, 1884. Reported by C. E. Butterworth," *Saints' Herald* 31, no. 40 (October 4, 1884): 643–44.

7. "Sermon by Elder Wm. B. Smith. Delivered at the Saints' Church at Independence, Mo.," *Zion's Ensign* 3, no. 35 (August 27, 1892): 2.

8. *William Smith on Mormonism* (Lamoni, Iowa: Herald Steam Book and Job Office, 1883), 6.

9. William Smith, "Notes Written on Chambers' Life."

seeing our children dignify their Fathers name by an upright and honorable course of conduct." "I have been gratified so far," she affirmed to the neighbor ladies about her children's lives, and felt relieved she was not "kept awake with anxiety" about her sons being in "habitual attendance on [at] the Grog Shop & gambling house."[10] Like many mothers, Lucy took great pride in the commendable way her children had matured. The noted exception was William. It wasn't that he was necessarily engaging in irreligious behavior (e.g., patronizing "grog shops"), but more his attitude about spiritual matters. It was the indifference William manifested toward religious matters, so uncharacteristic of the rest of her family, combined with his quick temper, that caused his mother deep concern. In the late 1820s, William recounted that he paid little attention "to religion of any kind," and as a result, "I received frequent lectures from my mother."[11]

Once Joseph Jr. related the circumstances of the angelic visitations of Moroni and his description of the ancient plates, William "fully believed" his brother and became a loyal and interested observer—but not a participant. Though his convictions were apparently sincere, he admitted that his behavior was still "quite wild and inconsiderate." He accepted Joseph's account but his unresponsiveness toward religion generally, including Joseph's, was evident. He responded coolly, for instance, even though Joseph had earlier shared with William the staggering information that he was tasked with the restoration of Christ's New Testament church.[12] William still remained disengaged. He would have turned nine in the spring of 1820, which is the date Joseph assigned to his First Vision, was twelve when Moroni visited Joseph three times in the same night, instructing him about the Book of Mormon, and was sixteen when Joseph retrieved the plates in September 1827. Joseph and his bride, Emma Hale, left Palmyra that fall and were in Harmony, Pennsylvania, and later in Fayette, New York, during the translation of most of the Book of Mormon. It was not until Joseph, Emma, scribe Oliver Cowdery, and new friends from the Whitmer family returned to Palmyra in late June 1829 that William would have had further opportunity to talk with Joseph. Even that visit was brief, since Joseph moved back and forth between Palmyra and Fayette that summer and then moved to Harmony that fall. From then on, Joseph was an exotic and fast-moving visitor. However, William would have been privy to the growing support of family members, including his parents, Hyrum and Samuel, who had all visited Joseph at either Harmony or Fayette during the process of translation, and evidenced their belief in Joseph's appointed mission and revelations.[13]

---

10. Lavina Fielding Anderson, ed., *Lucy's Book: A Critical Edition of Lucy Mack Smith's Family Memoir* (Salt Lake City: Signature Books, 2001), 321–22.

11. *William Smith on Mormonism*, 10.

12. "Wm. B. Smith's Last Statement," *Zion's Ensign* 5, no. 3 (January 13, 1894): 6.

13. Joseph Smith received revelations on behalf of his father and Hyrum in the months of February and May 1829. Michael Hubbard MacKay, Gerrit J. Dirkmaat, Grant Underwood, Robert J. Woodford, and William G. Hartley, eds., *Documents, Volume 1: July 1828—June*

William thus spent his adolescence in what he described as "wild" activities that doubtless included fist-fights with both friends and enemies and, as he grew, was certainly fully prepared to physically challenge anyone who impugned the family honor, including the reputation of his seer-brother. If William's memory was accurate, he was among those present when the Church was organized at Fayette, New York on April 6, 1830, but he was not among those baptized on that day.[14] In 1883 when William was seventy-two, he published a memoir in which he recounted that, at the time the Church was organized, "I fully believed all the circumstances as I have related them, with regard to the visions and revelations which my brother Joseph said he had received and seen, but being young and naturally high-spirited, I did not see the necessity of yielding obedience to the requirements of the gospel."[15] "Yielding obedience," in the terms of the time, meant accepting baptism as a sign of formal denominational membership. One of William's youthful companions, Lorenzo Saunders, even recalled that the teenage William "promised me once that he never would join the Mormons."[16]

William possessed the same independent disposition as many of his relatives, and it would be uncharacteristic of him to let others make a decision regarding his salvation. That step would have to be taken on his own terms and on his own timetable, not unlike some of his Smith uncles, and even some members of his own household, despite their belief in Joseph Jr.'s accounts. Although Lucy was eager for her children to become believers in Jesus Christ and his salvific mission, the question of affiliating with a denomination—perhaps even discussion of a particular denomination's doctrines—may have been a touchy subject, discussed carefully to avoid provoking conflict within the family.[17] Joseph Sr. and Lucy had tried Methodism, Congregationalism, Unitarianism, Presbyterianism, and perhaps the Baptists throughout their married life. They often disagreed about these denominational claims and finally agreed to disagree when Lucy and several of the children affiliated with the local Presbyterian congregation. Perhaps concern about bringing up a sensitive topic also explains why Joseph Jr. was reluctant to

---

1831, THE JOSEPH SMITH PAPERS, general editors Dean C. Jessee, Ronald K. Esplin, and Richard Lyman Bushman (Salt Lake City: Church Historian's Press, 2013), 9–13, 50–55; see pp. 51–52 for Samuel's activities and baptism; see pp. 26–27 for Joseph's movements during this time period. See also Lucy Mack Smith, *Biographical Sketches of Joseph Smith and his Progenitors for Many Generations* (Liverpool: S. W. Richards, 1853), 138–41.

14. *William Smith on Mormonism*, 14. See Note 27 below for further discussion.

15. Ibid., 10, 15.

16. Lorenzo Saunders, interviewed by William H. Kelley, September 17, 1884, 13, notation on reverse side of page, E. L. Kelley Papers, Community of Christ Library-Archives, Independence, Mo., as quoted in Dan Vogel, *Early Mormon Documents*, 5 vols. (Salt Lake City: Signature Books, 1996–2003), 2:134 note 38.

17. Anderson, *Lucy's Book*, 291–92; Kyle R. Walker, *The Joseph Sr. and Lucy Mack Smith Family: A Family Process Analysis of Nineteenth-Century Household* (Provo, Utah: BYU Studies, 2008), 65–68.

tell his father about Moroni's first visitation until the angel reappeared and assured him that Joseph Sr. would "believe every word you say to him."[18]

A parallel example may be Samuel, three years William's senior, who took Oliver Cowdery in the spring of 1829 from Palmyra to Harmony, where Joseph was trying to farm and dictate the Book of Mormon to Emma, who was burdened with her own housekeeping. Even after all the miraculous events related to the coming forth of the Book of Mormon, Samuel was not easily persuaded about the necessity of rebaptism by Joseph Jr. and Oliver Cowdery, even though they presumably testified to him that the authority to baptize had been miraculously conferred upon them by a personal visitation of John the Baptist. They had baptized each other just days earlier and must have been aglow with the experience. Even after Joseph and Oliver "reason[ed] with him out of the Bible . . . [and] showed him that part of the work which we had translated," he still "was not very easily persuaded of these things." "After much enquiry and explanation," recorded Joseph, Samuel resolved to settle the matter through prayer. He accordingly "retired to the woods, in order that by secret and fervent prayer he might obtain of a merciful God, wisdom to enable him to judge for himself: The result was that he obtained revelation for himself sufficient to convince him of the truth of our assertions." Samuel was baptized shortly afterward by Cowdery.[19]

William had a similar disposition as Samuel when it came to accepting authoritative pronouncements by others. It is no surprise that he was thoughtful and cautious when it came to religious matters. His parents had taught them this perspective. But William's indifference set him apart from the rest of the family. Unlike his parents and siblings, he did not apparently experience the burning "need to know" that characterized the rest of the family. During the publication of the Book of Mormon and the Church's organization, other family members were baptized, publicly committing themselves to Joseph and his sacred mission, but eighteen-year-old William was presumably still sowing his "wild oats." In the evening after the Eight Witnesses viewed the Book of Mormon plates in late June 1829 at Manchester, Lucy recorded that a large group participated in a notable meeting in "which we declared those facts that we knew to be true." Besides listening to the experience of the Eight Witnesses, Lucy recorded that her family also participated in the meeting. But the most memorable testimony on that occasion came not from William, but from his younger brother Don Carlos, only thirteen at the time.[20] Similarly, in 1830 it was Don Carlos who accompanied his father on a mission to Joseph Sr.'s relatives and Samuel who launched the first mission focused on distributing the Book of Mormon, while Hyrum preached

---

18. Lucy Mack Smith, *Biographical Sketches*, 81–82.

19. Karen Lynn Davidson, David J. Whittaker, Mark Ashurst-McGee, and Richard L. Jensen, *Histories: Vol. 1: Joseph Smith Histories, 1832–1844*, THE JOSEPH SMITH PAPERS, general editors Dean C. Jessee, Ronald K. Esplin, and Richard Lyman Bushman (Salt Lake City: Church Historian's Press, 2012), 296–98.

20. Lucy Mack Smith, *Biographical Sketches*, 141; *History of the Church*, 4:393.

both at home and at Colesville, New York, before being appointed to preside over the Colesville Branch.[21] No mention is made of William's participation in promulgating the gospel during 1830.

Despite his parents' best efforts to indoctrinate the children and notwithstanding the spiritual home environment of his youth, vital religious questions of salvation and damnation did not resonate for William. Perceiving his apathy, Lucy and Joseph Jr. insisted on engaging him in religious discussions. Initially William may have found this corrective counsel as annoying as his father's leading the family in predictable evenings prayers and hymn singing, but with time he gradually grew more responsive. Indeed, William may have been Joseph's convert. "I was exhorted continually by my parents and brethren," recalled William during his spiritual awakening, but most "especially by Joseph."[22] He does not specify a time period for this intense battle for his soul, but it culminated in the spring of 1830, shortly after the organization of the Church, perhaps when Joseph visited Palmyra in mid-April 1830.[23] To be sure, Joseph would not have overlooked opportunities for sober and intense doctrinal discussions with William on his visits home; and no matter how "wild" William was, he obviously absorbed biblical teachings with enough enthusiasm to pose striking questions and hold his own in family debates. However rough and tumble these discussions between the brothers may have started out, they transitioned into a more serious teacher/learner relationship as Joseph poured out what he was learning through the miraculous Book of Mormon and through the direct ministration of heavenly messengers. The end result, as William recalled, was conversion: "I became awakened to the necessity of embracing the plan of salvation, and of the necessity of publishing a knowledge of Jesus Christ and his gospel among all nations, kindreds, tongues, and people.... I determined to enlist in the glorious cause, and endeavor to bear some humble part in rolling on the great work of the Lord."[24]

---

21. Lucy Mack Smith, *Biographical Sketches*, 151–57; see also Chapter 1 for a further description of Joseph Sr. and Don Carlos's mission. Hyrum was actively proselyting in both the Palmyra vicinity and at Colesville, New York. Some of those whom Hyrum either converted or baptized within the year after the Church was organized include Parley P. Pratt, Ezra Thayre, Emer Harris, and Jared Carter. Jeffrey S. O'Driscoll, *Hyrum Smith: A Life of Integrity* (Salt Lake City: Deseret Book, 2003), 37–43.

22. *William Smith on Mormonism*, 15.

23. Joseph was at Palmyra in mid-April, shortly after the Church was organized, where he received several revelations now recorded in the Doctrine and Covenants. MacKay et al., *Documents, Vol. 1, July 1828—June 1831*, 113–14. It is also possible that William may have traveled to Fayette or Colesville and visited with his brother while Joseph was residing at these locations, although there is no documentary evidence suggesting that William made such a journey until June 9–10, 1830, when he traveled with members of his family to Fayette.

24. *William Smith on Mormonism*, 15.

William indicated that his full conversion did not occur until after the Church was organized,[25] though in a blessing delivered by his father some ten years later Joseph Sr. alluded to William "being faithful in declaring the word, even before the Church was organized."[26] This statement appears to contradict William's own account. Perhaps Joseph Sr. was alluding to William's defense of his brother Joseph's revelatory experiences to Palmyra neighbors even though he was not yet fully devoted to Mormonism himself. Due to his belated conversion in comparison to the rest of the family, the organizational meeting of the Church, held April 6, 1830, at Fayette, New York, just after he had turned nineteen, was less vivid for him than subsequent meetings. As a result, William made contradictory statements later in his life about the location and timing of this historic gathering.[27] His transformation came later that same spring, and he more distinctly remembered events associated with the first conference of the Church, held in Fayette, New York, on June 9, 1830. "After believing I began to repent," wrote William, "and thus the Spirit of

---

25. Ibid., 14.

26. Lucy Mack Smith, *Biographical Sketches*, 267.

27. In his 1883 memoir of his life, William indicated that it was in Hyrum's house, on the Smith farm in Manchester, that the "first conference of the Church of Jesus Christ of Latter Day Saints was held, on the 6th day of April, 1830, at which I was present." *William Smith on Mormonism*, 14. Some historians have utilized this source, along with several others, to argue that the Church was organized at Manchester rather than the traditional site of Fayette. H. Michael Marquardt and Wesley P. Walters, *Inventing Mormonism: Tradition and the Historical Record* (Salt Lake City: Smith Research Associates, 1994), 155 (153–65). But evidence of William's confusion about both the timing and location of the Church's organizational meeting came during his testimony during the Temple Lot Case in 1892. When asked by the defense attorney about "where and when the first conference was held," William sought clarification on the question by asking, "Do you mean the first conference that was held after the organization of the Church?" After the attorney answered "yes sir," William indicated that, "The first conference was held in 1830, on the 6th of April [June 9, 1830], I think. I wouldn't be positive as to whether it was held on the 6th of April, but it was held at Father Whitmer's in Fayette County in the State of New York." Referring to the June 9 conference of the Church, William then added rather significantly, "That is the first conference I have any recollection of." William Smith Testimony, Temple Lot Case Testimonies, 175, U.S. Eighth Circuit Court, 1892, MS 1160, LDS Church History Library. Because he recollected the meeting held on June 9 as the first conference, his 1883 statement that located the organizational meeting at Hyrum Smith's house becomes questionable. Further muddling the picture in William's recollections was his use of the word "conference," which he often used to refer to meetings that occurred after the organizational meeting. William was certainly familiar with the important date of April 6 throughout his service as a Church leader and in several sources had conflated that significant date with the timing of his own conversion. See also MacKay, et al, eds., *Documents—Vol. 1: July 1828–June 1831*, 129, where the editors conclude that the "earliest manuscript and later eyewitness accounts, as well as early financial and legal documents, confirm the correct location [of the Church's organizational meeting] as Fayette Township."

God began to will and to work in me to fit me for the home of my heavenly Father."[28]

Like Martin Harris, who interviewed each member of the Smith family to rule out some sort of deception,[29] William queried each of the Three Witnesses of the Book of Mormon about their experience with the Angel Moroni and their viewing of the metallic plates from which the Book of Mormon was translated. "I have seen the three witnesses, and questioned them closely," recalled William, and felt convinced of the truthfulness of their respective accounts, as each described the same details of their experience. Their testimonies directly impacted William's faith.[30] In later life, he summarized: "The fact also that these tablets [plates] ... were seen by a number of persons, who testify that they not only Saw with their eyes but handled with their hands the said record is Conclusive proof." Even after some of these men disaffiliated from the main body of the Church, William felt that their "standing in society" and reputation as honest men was powerful evidence of the reliability of what they had testified of. "Were I under oath I could not say aught of these men for respectability or for their truthful veracity," proclaimed William, nor has "any one of these person to my knowledge counteracted the testimony ... concerning the real existence of these Mormon tablets."[31] He was not relying on their witness about the existence of plates—he was already certain on that point—but their testimonies about the Angel Moroni and other events related to the establishment of Mormonism verified what he had learned from his brother and other members of the family.

David Whitmer (1805–1888), date unknown. Photograph by R. B. Kice, Richmond, Missouri. Courtesy Community of Christ Archives.

Thus, in the two months between the Church's organizational meeting in April and its first conference in June, William's rigorous searching, doubtless combined with sincere conversations with his parents and Joseph and through humble, personal prayer, caused his spiritual indifference to fall away. He was prepared to make a full commitment to Mormonism. "I felt willing to forsake the world, the flesh, and the devil," recalled William as he prepared to attend the June conference, "and go down into the waters of baptism and take upon me the name of Jesus Christ." He was baptized on June 9, 1830, in the pristine waters of Seneca Lake by David

---

28. "William B. Smith: Experience and Testimony," *Saints' Herald* 30, no. 16 (June 16, 1883): 388.
29. Joel Tiffany, "Mormonism—No. II," *Tiffany's Monthly* 5 (August 1859): 167.
30. "The Old Soldier's Testimony," 644.
31. William Smith, "Notes Written on 'Chambers' Life" 12–15.

Whitmer, at the same time as his two younger siblings, Katharine and Don Carlos. "David Whitmer—don[e] the Baptising in my Case," remembered William, "at the same time with nine others. . . . The Spirit of the Lord was poured out upon us and our hearts made to rejoice in the truth."[32] "I was buried all over in the water," William further recalled of that significant occasion, indicating, "then I was born of the water [and] I felt as if a load fell off my shoulders."[33]

On the second day of that conference, June 10, William was confirmed under the hands of Oliver Cowdery at an evening prayer meeting. The experience included an outpouring of the Spirit, and the events of that evening left an impression that was still burning vividly more than forty years later: "When they laid hands upon me to confirm me," he recounted to an RLDS audience in 1883, "it seemed as though the light of glory rested upon me and on those present, and I received the testimony of the Holy Ghost bearing witness to the truth."[34] Writing in his 1883 autobiography, he detailed some of the spiritual manifestations that others had experienced during the meeting, including Newel Knight's open vision of heaven, in which he heard utterances too sacred to describe and was so overcome with the Spirit that his knees buckled, and he had to be placed on a bed to recover—not once, but twice. William did not witness anything as dramatic as Knight's vision, but he experienced an extraordinary portion of the "Spirit of God like a burning fire shut up in my bones." Afterward, he felt an overwhelming desire to share the gospel message and proclaim to the world the wonderful events connected to Mormonism. As he traveled the thirty miles back to his home in Palmyra, he reported that he had "many solemn thoughts, and serious contemplations . . . concerning the work of the last days, and the great responsibility under which I had just been laid, to live soberly, righteously, and Godly before the world, in order that the Lord might be glorified and honored through me."[35] William had forever linked his fate with Mormonism.

While the excitement of obtaining and translating the record was keen among the Smith family, they may have been unprepared for the skepticism and downright scorn that resulted when they told their miraculous story. By 1829 when the Book

---

32. *William Smith on Mormonism*, 16; William Smith, Osterdock, Iowa., Letter to Edmund Levi Kelley, March 12, 1892, Community of Christ Library-Archives.

33. "William B. Smith: Experience and Testimony," 388. In this account, William says that Oliver Cowdery baptized him. However, as he was preparing to publish his autobiography, *William Smith on Mormonism*, he was able to consult his journal, which had been recently returned to his possession, and wrote a note of clarification to Edmund L. Kelley: "The question on Baptism—I think my answer was that Oliver Cowdery done the Baptising—this is not correct—David Whitmer—done the Baptising in my Case—Oliver don[e] the confirming at father Whitmers Fayette." William Smith to Kelley, March 12, 1892. I have been unable to locate William's personal journal, which apparently has not survived.

34. "William B. Smith: Experience and Testimony," 388.

35. *William Smith on Mormonism*, 15–17. For another account of this same meeting, see Davidson, Whittaker, Ashurst-McGee, and Jensen, *Histories: Vol. 1, 1832–1844*, 386–91.

of Mormon was being published and Joseph was gathering his handful of followers to organize the Church, the Smiths were shunned in the community, residents attempted to organize a boycott to pressure E. B. Grandin against printing the Book of Mormon, and the family's reputation was sullied with charges of laziness, drunkenness, and other irresponsible behavior. William often recounted how his life changed once Joseph Jr. began to make known his prophetic mission. Prior to that time, he felt that the family stood well in the community's esteem. "We never knew we were bad folks until Joseph told his vision," he lamented, as "we were considered respectable till then, but at once people began to circulate falsehoods and stories in a wonderful way."[36] In a second account, William reiterated, "Never did the world talk of disrespect to the family until the story was told of Joseph Smith's mission as a prophet and his angel story told to the world."[37] He was clearly dismayed by this result throughout his life. William's older sister Sophronia suffered so keenly when her friends actively avoided her that she became ill.[38] Joseph Jr. likewise was startled by the level of stigmatization and even hatred that he experienced after making known his visionary experiences.[39]

William also recalled being scoffed at and mistreated by his peers. He actively resented being taunted with such labels as "money-diggers," "angel-believers," "visionary men," and being an accessory to the "gold Bible company." "Owing to the persecution of the religious world in consequence of Joseph's visions, his obtaining the plates and translating them," remembered William of his late teens, "our neighbors conceived an antipathy against us, calling us all manner of names." Both William and Katharine, who was closest to him in age, remembered that their family became a target of religious persecution. Although the community's reaction stopped short of vigilante violence, it went beyond ostracism and name-calling. William said: "Whenever we had meetings at our house they would surround the house, throw stones, sticks and dirt against it, and insult us in all manner of ways."[40] Katharine, who turned seventeen the summer after the Church was organized, remembered that the Book of Mormon had been the focus of their neighbors' unwelcome attentions and, at age eighty-two, recalled that "the mob was around our house nearly every night" after Joseph first obtained the plates.[41]

The hostilities of the Palmyra community apparently did not cease once the Book of Mormon was published. After the Church's organization, Katharine recalled members of the community attending their "prayer meetings." "Some of our neighbors would come to these meetings and ask us mockingly, if we

---

36. "Wm. B. Smith's Last Statement," 6.
37. "Sermon by Elder Wm. B. Smith," 2.
38. Mary Salisbury Hancock, "The Three Sisters of the Prophet Joseph Smith, Part 1," *Saints' Herald* 101, no. 2 (January 11, 1954): 35.
39. Davidson, Whittaker, Ashurst-McGee, and Jensen, *Histories: Vol. 1, 1832–1844*, 13, 216.
40. *William Smith on Mormonism*, 13.
41. Kyle R. Walker, "Katharine Smith Salisbury's Recollections of Joseph's Meetings with Moroni," *BYU Studies* 41, no. 3 (2002): 15–16.

Smith Frame home, Manchester, New York, 2005. Photograph courtesy of Alexander L. Baugh.

expected with our little band to convert the world and make them to believe the golden Bible?"[42] Joseph was fighting off legal harassment and a midnight pursuit in Colesville, then completing his and Emma's move from Harmony to the Whitmer home, so he was infrequently at the Smith home in Palmyra. Joseph Sr. and Lucy were not the kind of people who would quail before taunts or even stones thrown at the house, but the teenagers in the family came of age during a period when fear and genuine risks afflicted their normal daytime activities and, despite their faith in and zeal for Joseph Jr.'s mission, doubtless created a fertile ground for anxiety about their safety—something that remained with William throughout his life. The additional loss of friends and social standing also brought a pain all their own.

In his history William dedicated considerable space to describing the loss of their farm on the border between Palmyra and Manchester (named Farmington until 1822), which was a devastating reversal for the family. After Alvin's death, the Smiths were unable to make the annual 100 dollar payment on their property. They had sunk what little money they had into what William described as the "many improvements we had made" on the farm, which must have included the costs associated with finishing the frame home.[43] As a result, the family failed to make their final payment on their property:

> Father had gone to Pennsylvania to borrow money to pay up, and to liquidate some other claims against us. But while he was gone, the agent with whom we had agreed for the land being removed from office, and a new one coming in who was unacquainted with our circumstances, our neighbors contrived to undermine us by

---

42. Katharine Salisbury (Fountain Green, Ill.), Letter to Dear Sisters, March 10, 1886, *Saints' Herald* 33, no. 17 (May 1, 1886): 260.

43. *William Smith on Mormonism,* 13.

furnishing a man with money, and sending him to the new agent; who, seeing the last payment not settled and the bond thereby forfeited, sold it immediately to this man right from under us. He came with a "writ of ejectment" and turned us all out of doors. Our other creditors then came upon us also, and stripped us of every cent and left us houseless and homeless, and almost friendless, to wander into the wide world and again seek a livelihood.[44]

While the circumstances William described began in 1825, the family was allowed to live in the frame home until 1829, but they knew from that point forward that others would ultimately benefit from all their labors.[45] William summarized his final days on the only property and in the only homes (both log and frame) he had ever known: "Father was gone [to debtor's prison], our farm was gone, [and] our home was gone. The weather was cold, and the hearts as well as the doors of the people seemed closed against us, and our situation was truly deplorable." The Smith parents had experienced financial reversal earlier in their marriage, but this time it was different. The parents had moved into middle age; and starting over at that point was so daunting as to be virtually impossible. Now they would be dependent on their children for their support, a role the children accepted willingly; but the entire family had lost all they had worked for during the previous nine years. William turned to his recently discovered faith for understanding, staunchly declaring: "We thanked the Lord in all our affliction that we were counted worthy to suffer in his cause, and realize[d] that our light affliction here would work for us 'a much more exceeding and eternal weight of glory' in the eternal world."[46]

William had come to adopt his parents' mindset about adversity. Thus, he interpreted the loss of the home and property in Palmyra as persecution and sacrifice, which would be amply rewarded by a God to whom he looked, rejoicing in the blessing of unfaltering faith. Lucy had similarly described in her history how the loss of the farm was due to the fact that the family had turned "their back upon the world and set out in the service of God."[47] Linking their fate to God's purposes gave meaning to the otherwise devastating adversity of losing all they had hoped and worked for. While William adopted a similar worldview, he would not endure the trials during his final years in Palmyra with the same Christian resignation as other members of the family. Being an outcast for his religious convictions did not sit well with him, nor would he tolerate the name-calling and ostracizing he experienced, especially from his peers. He was determined to retaliate when confronted by such injustice.

---

44. Ibid., 13–14.
45. Larry C. Porter, *A Study of the Origins of the Church of Jesus Christ of Latter-day Saints in the States of New York and Pennsylvania* (Provo, Utah: Joseph Fielding Smith Institute for Latter-day Saint History and BYU Studies, 2000), 36–37; slightly updated from his 1971 dissertation by the same title.
46. Ibid., 14.
47. Anderson, *Lucy's Book*, 435–37.

Eastern view of Main Street, Palmyra, New York. Engraving from John W. Barber and Henry Howe, *Historical Collections of the State of New York* (New York: S. Tuttle, 1841).

In this reaction, William's personality mirrored that of his uncle Jesse, and the two men were a match in being impulsive, quick-tempered, and obstinate in their views, although at least at this point William, to his credit, unleashed his temper against the family's enemies rather than, like Jesse, against his own siblings. William's impressive physique backed up his temperament, meaning that he could often get his way. While his physical ability would assist him in becoming a formidable and untiring missionary, traveling to carry the gospel message afar, sometimes his impulsive reactions caused him and his family embarrassment and difficulty. For example, at an early baptismal service conducted by Oliver Cowdery, William noticed a young man, perhaps near his own age, recording the sacred ceremony by writing it down on a board. William interpreted this action as a lack of reverence for the sacred ceremony and attempted to grab the board, surely causing more of a spectacle than the young man's original behavior. When the young man resisted, William reportedly "kicked at him, and clinched [his fists] for a scuffle." David Stafford, a Palmyra resident who witnessed the scene, felt that William's behavior was unbecoming of a recent convert, declaring in his disparaging account, "such was the conduct of these pretended Disciples of the Lord."[48]

William's patriarchal blessing also acknowledges that William did not always react with "meekness" when the family was afflicted by persecution. "Thou hast greatly desired to see thy father's family redeemed from trouble," stated his father in 1834, "and from the power and dominion of those who oppressed them. Verily, this was good desire, but thou hast not altogether desired this thing in meekness,

---

48. Statement of David Stafford, December 5, 1833, Manchester, New York, as quoted in E. D. Howe, *Mormonism Unvailed*, 249–50.

because thou hast not always known the Lord."⁴⁹ In later life, William explained this passage to an editor, who in turn recounted to his readers: "In the days of his youth, bro. William feeling the oppression under which his father[']s family had to pass through, desired anxiously to see them delivered from this oppression, but owing to the inexperience of youth, he would sometimes apply physical force in his and their defence."⁵⁰ Those who spent enough time around William came to know his fiery temper. It was a challenge that would plague him throughout his life.

On other occasions, however, William's physical strength proved providential. In the fall of 1830, Mother Smith and daughters Katharine and Lucy were home alone one evening. Their house was surrounded by what Mother Smith calls "a mob" in search of Hyrum. Not finding him, four men began to search the house for his belongings, which they planned to seize in payment for a debt while others waited outside. Mother Smith recounted:

> Just at this instant, William bounded into the house. "Mother," he cried, "in the name of God, what is this host of men doing here? Are they robbing or murdering? What are they about?" I told him . . . they had taken his father to prison, and had now come after Hyrum, but, not finding him, they were plundering the house. Hereupon William seized a large handspike, sprang up the stairs, and, in one instant, cleared the scoundrels out of the chamber. They scampered down stairs; he flew after them, and, bounding into the very midst of the crowd, he brandished his handspike in every direction, exclaiming, "Away from here, you cut-throats, instantly, or I will be the death of every one of you." [They] seemed to believe what he said, and fled in every direction.⁵¹

In this case, William's wrath, fearlessness, and willingness to threaten violence protected the family. Seventeen-year-old Katharine added the details that the search party arrived in carriages, which denoted a certain level of affluence, and carried dark lanterns, which, like their nighttime arrival, denoted a desire not to be identified. She felt that "if they had found Hyrum it was their intention to have him put to death." Katharine also added that William, in addition to the handspike, armed himself with a "stout club." She corroborated Lucy's account of William's providential arrival and his success in "driving them [the mob] from the house."⁵² William's strength, and accompanying temper, would be both a blessing and a curse to him throughout his long life.

Not long after William drove out these intruders, the Smiths moved from the farm that no longer belonged to them to "the Kingdom," an area near Waterloo,

---

49. William Smith, Patriarchal blessing bestowed by Joseph Smith Sr., December 9, 1834, in H. Michael Marquardt, ed., *Early Patriarchal Blessings of The Church of Jesus Christ of Latter-Day Saints* (Salt Lake City: Smith-Pettit Foundation, 2007), 16.

50. "On the 9ᵗʰ Day of December, 1834 . . . ," *Melchisedek & Aaronic Herald* 1, no. 5 (August 1849): 4.

51. Lucy Mack Smith, *Biographical Sketches*, 163–64.

52. Katharine Salisbury (Fountain Green, Ill.), Letter to Dear Sisters of the "Home Column," May 16, 1886, *Saints' Herald* 33, no. 26 (July 3, 1886): 404–5.

New York.[53] The new locale would provide a temporary respite from the persecution in Palmyra and the whirlwind of activity that had erupted when Joseph first received the plates in the fall of 1827. William had experienced his own spiritual transformation during those years. He had also grown to adulthood during this turbulent and impactful time period. Like others who joined the faith during the early 1830s, he was anxious to know what role he would play in assisting to establish Christ's church, newly restored to the earth.

---

53. Porter, *A Study of the Origins of the Church,*" 104–5.

Chapter 5

Life in "the Ohio": Missions, Marriage, and Ministry

> The little Chagrin river passing through Kirtland will be a witness in the great day of eternity of the many baptisms performed in that stream; in which administration I was . . . a personal participant.
> —William B. Smith, 1883

It was a bittersweet experience for the Smiths to move away from the Palmyra area. It had been their residence for more than thirteen years, but perhaps they had already suffered the major blow when they lost their new home, the blooming farm they had carved out of the virgin forest one tree at a time, along with Alvin's death. All of their children had matured in this location, and daughter Lucy had been born here. But they were taking perhaps their most important possession with them. It was in Palmyra where the family had become united in their faith, where they had finally found peace in their lengthy spiritual quest, and where their son and brother had experienced his miraculous visions.

Also mitigating the pain of leaving was the fact that staying had become painful. Their respected place in their community as hard and honest workers had turned to sneers and jeers, with night invasions of their home, physical attacks on Joseph Jr., and the loss of friends. The last few years in the area had been particularly difficult. Neighbors' animosity had frightened the younger children, and from the Smiths' perspective, outright persecution had seen Joseph Sr. dragged away to debtor's prison.[1] Thus, not only their faith in Joseph Jr.'s mission was pulling them away, but equally strong factors were pushing them out. They were more than ready for a fresh start.

In the fall of 1830, the Smiths settled into the community called "the Kingdom," just a short distance from Fayette and Waterloo nestled into the Finger Lakes region of New York near Seneca Lake. William particularly enjoyed the reprieve from the hostilities he experienced in Palmyra and spoke positively of the family's brief stay—only six months—in the area. William returned to Palmyra at some point that winter, and when asked by his former neighbor Peter Ingersoll how the family was getting along, commented, "We do better there than here; we were

---

1. William B. Smith, *William Smith on Mormonism*, 13–14 (hereafter cited as *William Smith on Mormonism*); Lucy Mack Smith, *Biographical Sketches of Joseph Smith and His Ancestors for Many Generations* (Liverpool: S. W. Richards, 1853), 93–98, 160–65.

too well known here to do much." According to William, the family prospered to a greater degree in their new area of settlement, as their connection to Mormonism had prevented them from obtaining work during their final years in Palmyra.[2] Their new neighbors treated them kindly, provided feed for their animals, and shared their food with the Smiths. Lucy Mack Smith recorded that such acts of generosity "were duly appreciated, for we had experienced the opposite so severely, that the least show of good feeling gave rise to the liveliest sensations of gratitude."[3]

The local residents in and about Waterloo were also more responsive to their religious practices, and some neighbors made a point of calling at the Smith home to join in their evening devotions. Lucy remembered that her home became a place of resort for some twenty people who lived in the vicinity. This group included some of the local youth, who looked up to the tall Smith brothers. Mother Smith recounted, "One evening, soon after we commenced singing, a couple of little boys came in, and one of them, stepping softly up to Samuel, whispered, 'Mr. Smith, won't you pray pretty soon? Our mother said, we must be home by eight o'clock, and we would like to hear you pray before we go.'" The Smiths were touched by the boys' desire and immediately held prayers. The personal attention manifest by the family proved persuasive, as the boys never missed an evening meeting during the rest of the time the Smiths lived in the neighborhood.[4]

While the family enjoyed a season of respite, the Church was expanding into the West. Those in New York were elated to hear of the prosperity that had resulted from the labors of the four missionaries to the Lamanites, who had left New York in October 1830 and were headed on foot to the displaced Indians in the territory across the Mississippi River from Missouri. But the missionaries had marked success in the area of Kirtland, Ohio. They sent back word through a letter written by Oliver Cowdery, and through noted convert Sidney Rigdon and his traveling companion Edward Partridge. These two men traveled east, located Joseph Smith at his parents' home near Waterloo, New York and reported the missionaries' amazing success in and near Kirtland, Ohio.[5] In 1883 at age seventy-two, William remembered the influence of Rigdon's conversion. "Sidney Rigdon was at that time a preacher in the Disciple Church," recalled William, and "was a fluent speaker, and to him these men [the missionaries to the Lamanites] intro-

---

2. Peter Ingersoll, Statement, December 9, 1833, Wayne County, New York, as quoted in E. D. Howe, *Mormonism Unvailed* (Painesville, Ohio: Author, 1834), 236–37.

3. Lucy Mack Smith, *Biographical Sketches*, 167–68.

4. Ibid., 168.

5. Oliver Cowdery, Letter to Our Beloved Brethren (Kirtland, Ohio), November 12, 1830, in Michael Hubbard MacKay, Gerrit J. Dirkmaat, Grant Underwood, Robert J. Woodford, and William G. Hartley, eds., *Documents, Volume 1: July 1828–June 1831*, The Joseph Smith Papers, general editors Dean C. Jessee, Ronald K. Esplin, and Richard Lyman Bushman (Salt Lake City: Church Historian's Press, 2013), 211–14; Mark Lyman Staker, *Hearken, O My People: The Historical Setting of Joseph Smith's Ohio Revelations* (Salt Lake City: Greg Kofford Books, 2009), 93.

Sidney Rigdon, 1793–1876. Engraving from *Contributor*, 8, no. 4 (February 1887).

duced the work and the Book of Mormon." Rigdon then came to New York "and made brother Joseph a visit, being the first time they had ever met." William was particular about this sequence of events, because he was refuting accusations from antagonists that Rigdon had somehow been involved in producing the Book of Mormon.[6]

It is unlikely that William was ordained a deacon during the first year or so after the Church's organization. This early in Mormonism's history, male converts were usually first ordained to the office of teacher—one of the three priesthood offices mentioned in the Book of Mormon.[7] In William's history, he underscored his ordination as teacher and his subsequent ordination as priest but never mentioned being ordained a deacon. Such ordinations were standard procedure for those who preached locally and/or served missions. But William probably labored in "the ministry" even before his ordination as a teacher. Lucy recalls that it was shortly after the Church's organization in April 1830 that "my sons were all ordained to the ministry," even fourteen-year-old Don Carlos.[8] Whether Lucy made a distinction between being ordained, or called, to "the ministry" and being ordained to "the priesthood," let alone to a specific office in the priesthood, is not clear. What *is* clear, however, is that these ordinations endowed participants with a sense of empowerment that enthused them for propounding the restoration message. "I then began to labor a little in the ministry," William recalled, "according to the ability which the Lord had given me. Many Elders were ordained and sent out to preach the gospel. Many were added to the Church." William reflected

---

6. *William Smith on Mormonism*, 17; "William B. Smith: Experience and Testimony," *Saints' Herald* 30, no. 16 (June 16, 1883): 388. The "Spaulding theory," which claims that Joseph Smith produced the Book of Mormon by rewriting an unpublished novel by Solomon Spaulding, with either Rigdon or Oliver Cowdery as a connecting link to Joseph Smith, has produced a voluminous literature, both pro and con.

7. Gregory Prince has written that "the office of deacon did not exist in the Book of Mormon or in the early Restoration. For example, as late as February 1831 a revelation listing the offices in the church identified only elders, priests, and teachers (Book of Commandments, 44:13)." Gregory A. Prince, *Power from On High: The Development of Mormon Priesthood* (Salt Lake City: Signature Books, 1995), 26 note 88, 26, 48. According to historian William G. Hartley, "The earliest mention of ordained deacons is in the *Painesville Telegraph* on October 25, 1831." William G. Hartley, "From Men to Boys: LDS Aaronic Priesthood Offices, 1829–1996," *Journal of Mormon History* 22, no. 1 (Spring 1996), 84–85.

8. Lucy Mack Smith, *Biographical Sketches*, 151.

Grain-Boat on the Erie Canal. Sketch from J. David Williams, ed., *America Illustrated* (Boston, 1883), 88.

on the excitement of the time, when he described how the "work rolled on with unparalleled rapidity."[9]

He was present at the January 2, 1831, conference, where "a revelation[10] was given for the Church to move to the state of Ohio." For William and his family, the revelation called for prompt action, and "therefore, all preparations were made for emigrating to the West."[11] However, some of the Saints apparently did not receive the revelation as the mind of the Lord, and felt, according to John Whitmer, "that Joseph had invented it himself to deceive the people that in the end he might get gain."[12] Perhaps to counter such sentiments or simply to ensure the Saints were spiritually prepared for the migration that spring, William "visited the church calling on every family (as our custom is) . . . [and] prayed with them and did not leave the house untill every member of the family prayed vocally that was over eight years old."[13] It was the first recorded beginning of William's formal Church service, and his ecclesiastical responsibilities would multiply quickly after he arrived in Ohio.

On May 3 or 4, 1831, William left for Ohio with other members of the Fayette Branch of the Church.[14] "Myself, my mother, and some of the family went

---

9. *William Smith on Mormonism*, 18.

10. MacKay, et al., *Documents—Volume 1: July 1828–June 1831*, 229–33; see also 2013 LDS Doctrine and Covenants 38.

11. *William Smith on Mormonism*, 18.

12. John Whitmer, History, 1831–circa 1847, reproduced in Karen Lynn Davidson, Richard L. Jensen and David J. Whittaker, eds., *Histories—Volume 2: Assigned Histories, 1831–1847*, Vol. 2 in the Histories series of the THE JOSEPH SMITH PAPERS, general editors Dean C. Jessee, Ronald K. Esplin, and Richard Lyman Bushman (Salt Lake City: Church Historian's Press, October 2012), 21.

13. Lavina Fielding Anderson, ed., *Lucy's Book: A Critical Edition of Lucy Mack Smith's Family Memoir* (Signature Books: Salt Lake City, 2001), 511.

14. Larry C. Porter, "'Ye Shall Go to the Ohio': Exodus of the New York Saints to Ohio, 1831," in Milton V. Backman Jr. ed., *Regional Studies in Latter-day Saint Church*

on board of a canal-boat to Buffalo," he related, "we then shipped aboard . . . a steam-boat."[15] Mother Smith had attempted to get fifty-four-year-old Solomon Humphrey, a convert brought into the Church by William's brother Don Carlos, or thirty-year-old Hiram Page, one of the eight witnesses to the Book of Mormon, to head the migration. But, Lucy remembered, Page countered with the proposal that "everything should be done just as Mother smith said and [that] I with my sons William and Carlos should have the entire dictation." The company unanimously accepted Page's recommendation, thus reflecting the high regard in which these early converts held the founding family of Mormonism.[16] Accordingly, William, who had turned twenty in March, acted as an assistant to his fifty-six-year-old mother during the migration. Seventeen-year-old Katharine, who was also a part of the company, noted William's role in the journey: "My mother took charge of the company, and with the aid of Bro. Humphr[e]y and my brother William, we accomplished the journey as far as Buffalo" by canal boat.[17]

A detailed record of William's duties and responsibilities has not been preserved, but two examples appear in family reminiscences. The group reached Buffalo in miserable weather—a heavy rainstorm that exacerbated the suffering of the women and children, who were exposed on the boat's flat deck, especially since some of the children were feverish with measles. William accompanied Lucy as the two searched the town for shelter, William holding an umbrella over Lucy, trying to shield her from the drenching rain.

He also saw it as his role to ensure that the migrating Saints avoided worldly behavior. William felt keenly that the traveling Saints should not behave in a way that would sully their reputation as committed Christians. At Buffalo while they were stalled, waiting for a break in the spring ice-jam, some of the exasperated and impatient branch members were arguing with each other, others were "grumbling and murmuring," and, most mortifying, some girls were "flirting, giggling, and laughing" with non-Mormon men aboard ship.[18] William, offended by this misbehavior, quickly came to Lucy's side and whispered, "Mother, do see the confusion yonder; won't you go and put a stop to it!"[19] Lucy promptly did so, not only rebuking their misbehavior but by summoning up their faith and uniting them in a prayer of such fervor that the ice broke up "like bursting thunder," a passage opened up that was barely the width of the ship, and they sailed out onto Lake Erie.[20] "The

---

History: Ohio (Provo, Utah: Brigham Young University Department of Church History and Doctrine, 1990), 15.

15. *William Smith on Mormonism*, 18–19.
16. Anderson, *Lucy's Book*, 512–13.
17. Katharine Salisbury (Fountain Green, Ill.), Letter to Dear Sisters of the "Home Column," May 16, 1886, *Saints' Herald* 33, no. 26 (July 3, 1886): 404–5.
18. Lucy Mack Smith, *Biographical Sketches*, 177, 179; Anderson, *Lucy's Book*, 512–13, 521–23, 528–29.
19. Anderson, *Lucy's Book*, 528.
20. Ibid., 530–36; Lucy Mack Smith, *Biographical Sketches*, 180–81.

ice then closed up behind us," Katharine recalled, "and not another boat passed out for two weeks."[21] Thus, William was a keen observer to his mother's effective leadership skills and faith, which he reinforced by his own observations and alertness. This second incident also demonstrates not only his sense of responsibility for the decorous behavior of the members for whom he was partially responsible but how seriously he took that behavior as a personal standard.

Another important insight comes from this same time period when they were stalled en route. When they encountered another group of Mormons emigrating from Fayette, New York, under the leadership of Thomas Marsh, this future apostle advised her not to mention Mormonism or "we should be mobbed before the next morning." William saw how his mother met this instruction from an experienced elder by promptly exclaiming, "Mob it is, then. . . . We shall attend to prayer before sunset, mob or no mob." The "irritated" Thomas Marsh left, with Lucy's stinging rebuke in his ears: "I should tell the people precisely who I was; 'and . . . if you are ashamed of Christ, you must not expect to be prospered; and I shall wonder if we do not get to Kirtland before you.'"[22] Lucy continued to pray, sing, and share her Mormon faith during their journey to Ohio, an example of boldness in declaring the faith that persisted as an influence on William as an adult.

Katharine also took away memories of that journey's difficulties: "The outlook was anything but pleasant. Children were crying, sisters complaining, wishing they had stayed at home where they could enjoy their comfortable rocking chairs, much as the children of Israel longed for the flesh pots of Egypt. Mother bore all their complainings patiently, and had great charity for and sympathy with them. Her faith was strong in the Lord, for she believed that he had commanded us to go and would carry us safely through."[23]

Unpleasant weather combined with scarce food made for a difficult journey. William noted: "After a long and tedious passage, facing many storms, cold winds and rains, we at length arrived at Fairport [Ohio]."[24] The docking date was likely May 11 or 12, 1831.[25] William and his future brother-in-law, twenty-two-year-old Jenkins Salisbury, then walked the eleven miles to Kirtland to search for Joseph and Emma, who had arrived in early February, Samuel who had reached Ohio later that same month, and Father Smith, who had arrived with Hyrum in March. William related, "We soon discovered their place of residence, and with

---

21. Salisbury to Dear Sisters., Letter to Dear Sisters of the "Home Column," 404–5. Katharine also remembers that the ship paused overnight on the Canadian side of the harbor, making repairs to the waterwheel, before continuing onto the open lake the next day.

22. Lucy Mack Smith, *Biographical Sketches*, 175–76.

23. Salisbury to Dear Sisters of the "Home Column," 404–5; Lucy Mack Smith, *Biographical Sketches*, 180–81.

24. *William Smith on Mormonism*, 19.

25. Porter, "Exodus of the New York Saints," 18.

Life in "the Ohio": Missions, Marriage, and Ministry

View of Lake Erie, 1837. Drawn by Jacques-Gerard Milbert, and engraved by Chavannes, in Jean B. G. Roux de Rochelle, *Etats-Unis d'Amerique* (Paris, 1837).

great joy in our hearts we again conversed with them face to face; while they on their part very gladly received us and bade us welcome."[26]

Kirtland and its environs were home to the Smith family from 1831 to 1838. During the early 1830s, William lived with his parents. Their home became a way-station of sorts for many of the gathering Saints and new converts alike. The Smiths enjoyed watching the work and helping to establish it as Mormonism expanded rapidly in northeastern Ohio. According to William, this new belief "took a general spread through the whole country," and "the gospel spread like wild-fire. Every one was engaged in it."[27]

William became warmly attached to the beautiful, rolling hills of northeastern Ohio, and he returned to this locale on many occasions even after he had moved further west. He assisted his parents in establishing a farm in the area; and, as an unmarried but adult son, his labor was probably critical in the heavy labor of plowing, planting, and harvesting. The precise date of his ordination to the office of teacher in the priesthood is unknown, but he was ordained a priest October 25, 1831.[28] Both his teacher's and priest's licenses have survived, giving

---

26. *William Smith on Mormonism*, 19; Porter, "Exodus of the New York Saints," 5–6, 13–20. Mother Smith recalled that she met her sons Joseph and Samuel shortly after arriving at Fairport, Ohio, apparently near their place of landing. It is possible that William and Jenkins left just prior to this reunion between mother and sons. Lucy Mack Smith, *Biographical Sketches*, 182–83.

27. *William Smith on Mormonism*, 25.

28. William mistakenly dated his ordination to the office of a teacher as October 5, 1830, when in reality it occurred one year later. *William Smith on Mormonism*, 18, 20–21; Lucy Mack Smith, *Biographical Sketches*, 172; Dan Vogel, ed., *Early Mormon Documents*, 5 vols. (Salt Lake City: Signature Books, 1996–2003), 1:487; 1:475, 501.

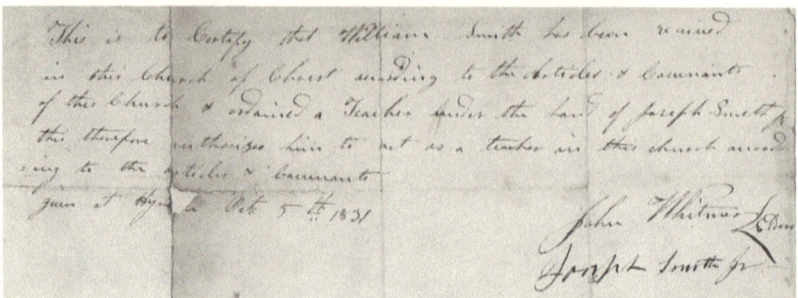

William Smith's Teacher's License, October 4, 1831. Courtesy Community of Christ Archives. It reads, "This is to Certify that William Smith has been received in this Church of Christ according to the Articles & Covenants of this Church & ordained a Teacher under the hand of Joseph Smith jr. this therefore authorizes him to act as a teacher in this church according to the articles & Covenants given at Hyram Oct 5th 1831 John Whitmer Joseph Smith Jr Elders."

a glimpse of how the early Church organized its missionary work and priesthood ordinations. Though his teacher's license was dated October 5, 1831, this date should not be mistaken for his date of ordination, but he had been ordained by at least June 3, 1831. His official license was probably written out later in preparation for his "attending the numerous conferences and visting the branches," as he described in his history, and before traveling abroad as a missionary.[29] Both Lucy and William mention his ordination as a teacher as occurring prior to their migration to Ohio, but in William's history, he mistakenly dated his certificate of ordination one year too early, likely because he did not have the original certificate in his possession in 1883 when he prepared his autobiography.[30]

---

29. Mathew C. Godfrey, Mark Ashurst-McGee, Grant Underwood, Robert J. Woodford, and William G. Hartley, eds., *Documents—Volume 2: July 1831–January 1833*, THE JOSEPH SMITH PAPERS, general editors Dean C. Jessee, Ronald K. Esplin, and Richard Lyman Bushman (Salt Lake City: Church Historian's Press, 2013), 71–74, 72 note 23. These editors note that the "minutes of a conference held circa 3–4 June 1831 in Kirtland, Ohio, lists William Smith as one of the teachers in attendance."

30. If Lucy correctly remembered her timeline, she recalled that "soon after my husband and Joseph left for Kirtland [January–March, 1831], William, being one of the teachers, visited the Church." Lucy Mack Smith, *Biographical Sketches*, 172; *William Smith on Mormonism*, 17–18. When the Community of Christ acquired this document in July 1965, it was through the good offices of Isaac Sheen descendants. "This document... came into the custody of the church early in July through the generosity of Sister Marie Smith of Miami, Oklahoma. According to Sister Smith, these documents were formerly in the possession of Isaac Sheen, first editor of the *Saints' Herald*." "Church Historian Receives Important Document," *Saints' Herald* 112, no. 16 (August 15, 1965): 27. Sheen had taken some of William's possessions from his personal trunk, including this certificate of ordination, when the two of them parted ways in the spring of 1850. (See Chapter 16.)

Life in "the Ohio": Missions, Marriage, and Ministry

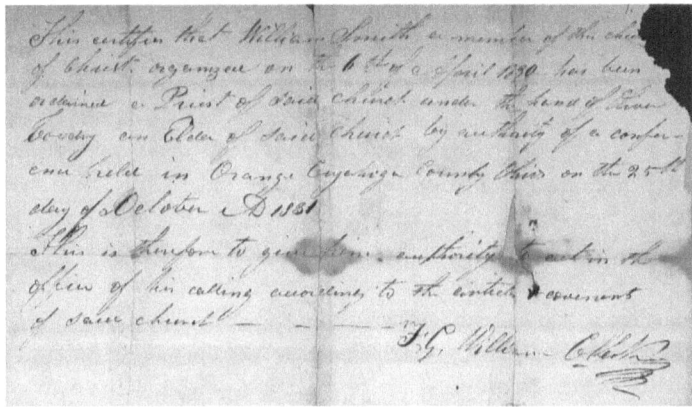

William Smith's Priest's License, October 25, 1831. Courtesy Community of Christ Archives. The license reads, "This certifies that William Smith a member of the church of Christ, organized on the 6th of April 1830 has been ordained a Priest of said church under the hand of Oliver Cowdery an Elder of said church by authority of a conference held in Orange Cuyahoga County Ohio on the 25th day of October AD 1831 This is therefore to give him authority to act in the office of his calling according to the articles & covenants of said church —-FG Williams Clerk"

According to William, after his ordination as a priest, he was "exclusively engaged in the business of my office, attending the numerous conferences and visiting the branches to see that the members were all faithful and that there was no quarreling, or backbiting among the brethren." Thus, at the time when most young men his age would have been acquiring land or establishing themselves in a profession, he was taking a different path. He describes himself as developing a greater determination "to devote my time, talents, and energies in furthering the purposes of God."[31]

William was the last of the Smith brothers to serve a mission—the youngest brother, Don Carlos, had accompanied his father on a mission to relatives in New York in 1830—but between 1832 and the early part of 1833, William served six short missions. The first was in company with his brother Samuel, the two traveling to a neighboring county in Ohio. The next was to New York with his brother Don Carlos, where the two missionaries preached to some of William's former friends, possibly near Waterloo where he had earlier been so warmly received. After several other missions to "different parts of the country" and laboring some in Ohio, William served his longest mission to that point with his brother Hyrum.[32]

In November 1832, the brothers traveled northeast along Lake Erie's shoreline through Ohio and into the northwestern corner of Pennsylvania. They likely fol-

---

31. *William Smith on Mormonism*, 20.
32. Ibid., 21–22.

lowed one of two routes commonly traveled by early Mormon missionaries who sought to promulgate their message in areas east of the newly established Church headquarters. "Missionaries could travel along either the Lake Road, close to Lake Erie, or along the Ridge Road, which was 1 ½ to 2 miles south of the lake," recounted one historian. "The Ridge Road took the elders through the villages of West Springfield, Springfield, Fairview, Swanville, Erie, and North East Township."[33] The Smith brothers likely utilized both of these roads during their missionary travels. As the two missionaries began their proselyting efforts, Hyrum recorded in his journal, "The Lord having opened a way for me to go forth [to preach], therefore I took with me to labor in the gospel, my brother, William, he being ordained to the lesser priesthood."[34] The brothers preached in cities along the way in Ohio until they reached the northwestern edge of Pennsylvania. Eleven years older than William and holding a higher priesthood office, Hyrum took the lead in preaching and baptizing, but the two took turns expounding doctrine. At Thompson, Ohio, Hyrum "spake . . . upon the subject of faith and spake much of the mysteries of the kingdom," while "William spake of the Church—the body of Christ—in the power and demonstration of the spirit, and the congregation was much edified." They baptized and confirmed three individuals.[35] William's focus on the Church as "the body of Christ" shows his sensitivity to the factors that bonded the Saints into a community and the importance of unity, something he had stressed during the Saints' migration from New York to Ohio.

In Pennsylvania, they found several communities who were particularly receptive to their message. During the previous year, two missionary teams had preached in Erie County, Pennsylvania, with some success; Jared Carter and Ebenezer Page were the first to preach in the vicinity on their way to their mission in New York, followed by William's brother Samuel and his companion, Orson Hyde. In February 1832, Samuel and Orson had preached for twelve days at or near Springfield to "large and attentive congregations" where "many were melted down into tears."

---

33. LaMar C. Berrett and Larry C. Porter, *New York and Pennsylvania, Vol. 2*, in Sacred Places: A Comprehensive Guide to Early LDS Historical Sites, LaMar C. Barrett, general series editor (Salt Lake City: Deseret Book, 2000), 313. See also V. Alan Curtis, "Missionary Activities and Church Organizations in Pennsylvania, 1830–1840" (M.A. thesis, Brigham Young University, 1976), 22–25.

34. There is some discrepancy about when they began this mission. Hyrum indicated he began his labors on November 20, 1831, but David Patten wrote that, on November 9, at Springfield, Pennsylvania, "we met with Brothers Hyrum and William Smith. We held a meeting and had a joyful time together, Brother Hyrum baptized six at the close of the meeting; the next day two were baptized." Journal History of the Church of Jesus Christ of Latter-day Saints (chronological scrapbook of typed entries and newspaper clippings, 1830–present), November 9, 1832, 1, LDS Church History Library; hereafter cited as Journal History.

35. Hyrum Smith, Diary, November 23, 1832, p. 1, Box 1, fd. 5, L. Tom Perry Special Collections, Harold B. Lee Library, Brigham Young University, Provo, Utah. See also Jeffrey S. O'Driscoll, *Hyrum Smith: Life of Integrity* (Salt Lake City: Deseret Book, 2003), 70–71.

Five or six individuals were baptized, including one unnamed preacher.[36] Carter and Page, who met up with Smith and Hyde as they were returning from their mission in late April 1832, baptized at least nine during their journeys through Erie County, besides reactivating some of those baptized by Smith and Hyde during their absence. Thus, by the summer of 1832, the gospel had taken root in Erie County, and a small branch was established at Springfield.[37]

By the latter part of November, the Smith brothers were preaching and regulating the affairs of the Springfield Branch. Elders Zebedee Coltrin, John F. Boynton, and William Cahoon met up with the Smith brothers at Springfield, and the five missionaries held a number of preaching meetings in the area. One attendee was fifteen-year-old Benjamin Winchester, the son of local farmer Stephen Winchester and Nancy Case Winchester, who traveled from his home in nearby Lundy's Lane, in Elk Creek Township, to hear the Mormon elders.[38] Though he described himself as "much prejudiced and supposed them [the Mormons] to be among the greatest imposters," out of curiosity he searched until he found the home where the missionaries were to preach. After finding a seat among the interested observers that night, he prepared himself to hear what he described as "these distinguished emissaries of his satanic majesty." He was "somewhat astonished," however, by the service. A simple young man first read a chapter from the New Testament, then preached Christ's gospel as contained in that book, and impressed upon his listeners the necessity of obeying that gospel by accepting baptism and confirmation from an authorized source. Benjamin was enthralled with the elders' preaching and lingered for several days to learn more. At the next meeting, the young elder described "the coming forth of the Book of Mormon, which he said was the record of the remnant of the house of Joseph, who inhabited America." Though Winchester described this doctrine as new and strange, the witness of the Spirit kept him riveted, as he felt pricked in his conscience. "The eyes of the people . . . were opened to understand the scriptures," related Winchester, "which testify of the work of the Lord in these last days, and the manner of its accomplishment. The visions of the prophets were unfolded, and many of their declarations shown to be fulfilling before our eyes. The subject assumed a majesty and glory, which altogether surprised and captivated the audience; and we discovered . . . the stone cut out of . . . the mountain without hands, spoken of by Daniel, which should ultimately fill the whole earth, had already begun to roll. That God had indeed chosen the foolish things of this world to counfound the wise, and the weak things to confound the mighty."

---

36. Orson Hyde, Journal, February 21, 1832, MS 1386, LDS Church History Library.

37. Jared Carter, Journal, January 20, 1832, 48, LDS Church History Library; Steven C. Harper, "The Restoration of Mormonism to Erie County, Pennsylvania," *Mormon Historical Studies* 1, no. 1 (Spring 2000), 7; Cheryl Harmon Bean, "LDS Baptisms in Erie County, Pennsylvania 1831–1833," *Nauvoo Journal* 5, no. 2 (Fall 1993): 60.

38. David J. Whittaker, "East of Nauvoo: Benjamin Winchester and the Early Mormon Church," *Journal of Mormon History* 21, no. 2 (Fall 1995): 32–34.

According to Winchester, the Mormon missionaries continued to preach in adjoining neighborhoods, and their effectiveness created quite a stir throughout the county. The upheaval their preaching created was a confirmatory sign to Winchester, as "the same commotion which the ancient gospel produced, was found still to accompany its promulgation. Some received the truth in the love of it, others used every exertion to withstand it." As for Winchester, his conversion was complete: "After I heard several discourses on the fullness of the gospel, I felt anxious to ally myself to a people who were every where spoken against, and sought the earliest opportunity of doing it."[39] That opportunity came two months later.

The Smith brothers and their companions also influenced another family, Andrews and Elizabeth Tyler. Their son and daughter, Daniel and Almina, both believed from the time that Samuel Smith and Orson Hyde first preached in Springfield in February 1832. However, their father and another brother, William, were vehemently opposed to the Mormons, and threatened to shoot "any 'Mormon' elder who dared to baptize her." Almina remained fixed in her determination to be baptized, even after her father threatened to disown her if she joined the despised sect.

When Hyrum and William Smith arrived on the scene ten months later, Andrews warned them to steer clear of his daughter, who persisted in her desire to unite with the Mormons. "The Elder who baptized her," threatened Tyler, "would do so at his peril." When the Smith brothers met Andrews Tyler, they were unintimidated by the older gentleman. "We shall not baptize your daughter against your wishes," Hyrum calmly reasoned. "If our doctrine be true, and we testify that it is, [and] if you prevent your daughter from embracing it, the sin will be on your head, not on ours or your daughters." This observation caught Tyler off-guard, and his son Daniel recounted that Hyrum's comment "pricked him to the heart. He began to think that possibly the 'Mormons' were right and he was wrong. He therefore decided to counsel his daughter in the matter and then permit her to exercise her free agency [and] would thus relieve himself of any responsibility." After wrestling with how to proceed, he finally decided to allow Almina to make her own decision, which she "had weighed long ago and believed it to be her duty to be baptized." Hyrum recalled that, on December 2, 1832, he and William "held a meeting . . . in the Evening and the Lord was there and Poured out his holy Spirit unto the Convinsing [of] five." Among those present were members of the Tyler family. True to his commitment, Andrews transported Almina by "ox-sled to Lake Erie, a distance of two miles, where, after a hole was cut through three feet of solid ice, she was baptized and confirmed into the Church by Elder Hyrum Smith." Her father watched cautiously from the shore and stayed to witness her confirmation by Hyrum the next morning, before transporting her home. Within

---

39. Benjamin Winchester, *Plain Facts, Shewing the Origin of the Spaulding Story, Concerning the Manuscript Found, and Its Being Transformed into the Book of Mormon; with a Short History of Dr. P. Hulbert, the Author of the Said Story* (Bedford, Mass.: C. B. Merry, 1841), 3–5.

a week of preaching at Springfield, the Smith brothers had baptized sixteen people, greatly strengthening the existing branch. Their influence on the Tyler family was permanent; within a month, Andrews, Elizabeth, and most of their children joined the Church. Daniel, who recounted the details of his family's conversion in his history, was apparently the last to link himself with Mormonism, being baptized on January 16, 1833, at the age of sixteen.[40]

Benjamin Winchester, who heard of the baptisms of some of his associates at Springfield, likely met with the elders again at his home in Elk Creek, as the Smith brothers traveled to this location just a week or so after leaving Springfield. While preaching in the community, in the southwestern part of Erie County, William came in contact with several key individuals who would have an immense impact on his life. Besides befriending Winchester, the Smith brothers met and fellowshipped recent convert Curtis Hodges, age forty-five, and his eldest son Amos, who was about twenty.[41] Curtis probably accompanied Hyrum and William when they returned from their mission to Kirtland later that same month.[42] Both Winchester and members of the Hodges family would play influential roles in William's life during the chaotic Nauvoo period a decade later.

It was also in Elk Creek where the missionaries came in contact with Joshua and Athalia Grant, struggling shingle-makers, and their twelve children.[43] Hyrum recounted in his journal that, on December 10, 1832, the elders "held a meeting in the Evening at Brother grants."[44] William quickly became attached to several of their very capable sons, who were within a few years of his own age, including George D., Jedediah (who would later serve in Brigham Young's First Presidency), and Joshua Jr. Jedediah was the first of the Grant family to embrace the gospel, being baptized by John F. Boynton on March 2, 1833, but the Grants were obvi-

---

40. Daniel Tyler, "Incidents of Experience," in *Scraps of Biography: Tenth Book of the Faith-Promoting Series* (Salt Lake City: Juvenile Instructor Office, 1883), 25–27; Hyrum Smith, Diary, December 2–3, 1832. See also Harper, "The Restoration of Mormonism to Erie County, Pennsylvania," 9–12.

41. Hyrum Smith, Diary, December 10, 1832, recorded that he and William "traveled to Elk Creek to Brother Curtis Hodges." The following day, Hyrum noted that they "held a meeting at Brothers Hodges in the Evening." See also, Bill Shepard, "The Notorious Hodges Brothers: Solving the Mystery of Their Destruction at Nauvoo," *John Whitmer Historical Association Journal* 26 (2006): 281–82.

42. Curtis Hodges was at Kirtland on December 18, 1832, where he arose during an elders' council "and said it was his desire to proclaim the gospel, stating that his situation was such that he could leave home and that his family was so situated that they did not need his assistance & desired to know his duty and what course to take &c as it was his determination to labor in the vineyard." William Smith afterwards preached with Hodges in Erie County, when William returned to the area in February 1833. Minute Book 1, 6, December 18, 1832, item #7702, LDS Church History Library.

43. Gene A. Sessions, *Mormon Thunder: A Documentary History of Jedediah Morgan Grant* (Urbana: University of Illinois Press, 1982), 6.

44. Hyrum Smith, Diary, December 10, 1832.

ously receptive to the Mormon message that the Smith brothers had presented to the family during this mission.[45] Hyrum's notation in his diary about holding a religious meeting at the Grant home during the brothers' mission provides additional evidence of the Grants' support of the traveling elders and their message at this early date. Most later sources indicate rather generally the Mormon elders' influence on the Grants during 1833, but Hyrum's diary indicates that he and William obviously had more influence on the family than they have been given credit for.[46] But it was not just the Grant sons who impressed the twenty-one-year-old missionary, as William was quickly attracted to Grants' daughter Caroline, who would turn nineteen the following month. With dark hair and brown eyes, Caroline was tall, slender, and attractive; but of delicate health. The Grants were responsive to the missionaries and opened their home to the Church ever afterwards. One Jedediah Grant biographer, described how another of the Grant daughters Theda (or "Thedy" as she was nicknamed), who would have turned eleven in 1832, "went up the stairs, which were on the outside of the home, and helped her mother to make ready the bedroom for the Elders, which," remembered Theda, "was then always available whenever any Mormon missionaries visited in the vicinity."[47] Seven-year-old Roxey Ann Grant, whom William would later baptize and marry after Caroline's death, was also present to hear the missionaries' message. The Smith brothers gratefully accepted this dependable hospitality and spent time at the home, as William, fifty years later, remembered that it was during his mission with Hyrum in the fall of 1832 that he first became acquainted with the Grant family.[48]

The Smith brothers baptized seven people in Elk Creek, before returning to Kirtland, where they arrived on Sunday afternoon, December 16, 1832.[49] The *Evening and the Morning Star* reported, "Brothers Hyrum and William Smith have just returned home . . . having baptized twenty-three in Pennsylvania."[50] William's mission with Hyrum demonstrated his commitment to the growing

---

45. Journal History, January 15, 1833, 3. Jedediah Grant's obituary states that John F. Boynton baptized him on March 21, 1833. "Obituary [of Jedediah Grant]," *Deseret News*, December 10, 1856, 5.

46. Theda Grant remembered that her brother "Nelson was a strong Mormon. Amasy [Amasa] Lyman and Orson Hyde baptised Joshua Grant and Thalia H. Grant in 1833 at ———— [blank in original] near Erie, Penn. All of the twelve children were baptised except the oldest, Joseph, and the youngest, Howard." Thedy Grant Reeves, Reminiscence, as told to Joseph Hyrum Grant Jr., November 26, 1904 [sic; should be 1903], Grant Family Records, ca. 1778–1903, Microfilm #1036844, item #10, LDS Family History Library, Salt Lake City.

47. Thedy Grant Reeves, Reminiscence, as told to Joseph Hyrum Grant Jr., November 26, 1904 [sic; should be 1903], Lathrop, Missouri, as quoted in Mary G. Judd, *Jedediah M. Grant: Pioneer, Statesman* (Salt Lake City: Deseret News Press, 1959), 14.

48. *William Smith on Mormonism*, 22.

49. Hyrum Smith, Diary, December 16, 1832.

50. "Extracts of Letters from the Elders Abroad," *Evening and the Morning Star* 1, no. 9 (February 1833): 5–6. Although the Smith brothers baptized twenty-three individuals,

Church. Three days after his return he received the Melchizedek Priesthood and was ordained an elder under the hands of Lyman Johnson.[51]

He remained in Kirtland for a little over a month, where he enjoyed the Christmas holiday with his family, as well as being tutored in spiritual matters by Church leaders. His brother Joseph had spent the summer and fall in Kirtland, working on his revision of the Bible with Sidney Rigdon. During January 1833, Joseph received several significant revelations (LDS D&C 85–88), one foreshadowing the Civil War, and another containing information related to the recently organized School of the Prophets. It was a time of increased understanding and accompanying spiritual gifts. During a conference of high priests and elders (which on this occasion apparently included some of the wives of these early leaders), held on January 22, 1833, Joseph spoke in tongues, followed by Zebedee Coltrin, and then by William, the first, but not the last, time William is recorded as speaking in tongues. "After this the gift [of tongues] was poured out in a miraculous manner until all the Elders obtained the gift together with several members of the Church both male & female. Great and glorious were the divine manifestations of the Holy Spirit. Praises were sang to God & the Lamb besides much speaking & praying, all in tongues." Those present were grateful to be a part of such a marvelous manifestation of the Spirit of God, and the meeting continued late into the night as those present rejoiced that these spiritual gifts had returned from New Testament times to the restored Church of Jesus Christ. The next day, William was present as Joseph washed the feet of those elders who attended the School of the Prophets, following the New Testament pattern where Jesus washed his disciples' feet. Before Joseph washed the feet of his father, he requested a priesthood blessing from under his hands, and William listened as his father prophesied that Joseph would "continue in his Priest[']s office untill Christ come."[52]

By early February, William had returned to Erie County, Pennsylvania, where he and Hyrum had enjoyed such success as a missionary companionship two months earlier. His ordination as an elder and his recent experience connected with the gifts of the Spirit instilled in him the confidence to take the lead as

---

Hyrum named only three in his diary: Daniel Bush, Jonny Mearan, and Alva Gray. Hyrum Smith, Diary, December 6 and December 12, 1832.

51. Minute Book 1, December 19, 1832, 2, LDS Church History Library. William recorded his ordination blessing to the office of Elder in the priesthood as follows: "License, liberty, power and authority are given to William Smith, the bearer of this, to preach the gospel of our Lord and Savior, by the endurance of faith on his name unto the end. Also certifying that he has been received into the Church of Christ; which was organized on the 6thday of April, 1830, according to the articles and covenants of said Church. Furthermore, stating that he has been regularly ordained an Elder in the Church, under the hands of Lyman Johnson, who also is an Elder in the Church. F. G. Williams, Clerk of Conference." Reproduced in *William Smith on Mormonism*, 22–23.

52. Minute Book 1, January 22–23, 1833, 5–6, LDS Church History Library.

a missionary for the first time since his baptism. On February 3, 1833, William was at Springfield, where he met nineteen-year-old Evan Greene (a nephew of Brigham Young) and renewed his acquaintance with the bright and talented John F. Boynton, with whom he and Hyrum had proselyted briefly during their earlier mission. Greene and Boynton, who had begun their mission on January 15, 1833, had been following in the footsteps of the Smith brothers through Erie County, capitalizing on their success. It was this companionship who baptized Benjamin Winchester on January 27, 1833, who had been awaiting such an opportunity since the previous November.[53] It is not clear whether William was present for these baptisms, but he must have rejoiced to see his earlier labors bearing such promising fruit.

In Springfield, William became the recognized leader in the branch and among the missionaries, frequently taking the lead in speaking during the various preaching meetings. One reason for this deference was certainly William's connection to Joseph Jr., which meant that his knowledge of and involvement in Mormonism was deeper than those of the more recent converts. But of at least equal importance were his charismatic presence and noted speaking ability. William also provided leadership by demonstrating the spiritual gifts that he had recently experienced at Kirtland, speaking in tongues at three separate meetings during the week of February 5–13 and thus setting an authorized example for this ecstatic exercise that others could follow with confidence. Greene, who kept almost a daily journal of the missionaries' activities, wrote that on February 6, at a meeting held in the local schoolhouse, William "spake on the subject of the order of God[']s house or the church of Christ and also spake in the gift of tounges." Not everyone present were Mormons, and witnessing William's unusual spiritual expression, "two men arose and began to make some distrubance in the assembly in talking the most abusive maner to Brother Wm and disturbed us considerable." On this occasion William apparently demonstrated unusual restraint, as Greene recorded that "through the grace of God we were able to overcome the devil and they at last left the house in peace and we had a very good meeting."[54]

Combining his missionary efforts with Greene and Boynton, as well as local converts Benjamin Winchester and Amos Hodges, led to noted success. Erie County's proximity to Kirtland meant that converts were continually strengthened by the traveling missionaries who traversed through the region. In a span of six months, from November 1832, when the Smith brothers first arrived in the area, until April 1833, more than 120 individuals were converted in Erie County, Pennsylvania, and several branches of the Church had been organized, including

---

53. Journal History, January 15, 1833, 1–3, LDS Church History Library. This source indicates that the missionary duo also baptized Benjamin's parents, Stephen and Nancy Winchester, on January 27, and baptized two additional family members, Daniel and Paulina Winchester, on February 19, all at Elk Creek.

54. Evan M. Greene, Diary, February 6, 1833, LDS Church History Library.

one at Elk Creek on March 21, 1833.⁵⁵ The success of these early missionaries prompted Joseph Jr. and Sidney Rigdon to visit the area and preach to the Saints in Erie County later in October 1833, as they were traveling as missionaries to Canada. Joseph recounted in his journal on October 6: "Arrived at Springfield [Pennsylvania] on the Sabbath found the Brotheren in meeting Brother Sidney [Rigdon] spake to the people &c—and in the evening held a meeting at Brother Ruds [John Rudd Jr.'s] had a great congregation [that] paid good attention." Joseph also visited the community of Elk Creek two days later.⁵⁶ To this day a small stream in Elk Creek Township is named Mormon Run, an indication of the impact the elders had in the area. According to an early history of Erie County, "Mormon Run received its name because [it was] used as a place of baptism by that sect, who were once numerous in the vicinity."⁵⁷

For William it was not just the excitement of his earlier missionary success that lured him back to the area, but it was also to visit Caroline Grant, whom he had met two months earlier with Hyrum. Nothing in the historical record indicates that William was given a formal missionary assignment to return to the area, but he quickly joined Greene and Boynton, and the three preached together throughout Erie County that February. Evan Greene's journal notes that, on February 10, "Bro Wm spake some concerning the gifts that were bestoed upon the Church of Christ in these last days and gave them the sign of tounges." Over the next few days Smith, Boynton, and Greene all labored together at Girard and then Elk Creek, but their continued success led to noted opposition. At Girard someone cut Boynton's cloak during their evening meeting, and when he discovered it, declared that "the person who did that . . . would die a vagabond or with some malignant disorder." William similary experienced "open opposition" at Girard, after he spoke in the gift of tongues. From Girard the trio moved to Elk Creek, whose Church membership continued to expand, and at which Caroline Grant resided. William preached to a large gathering on February 12, which probably included members of the Grant family; and in contrast to their receipion at Girard, the "considerable large company . . . behaved verry civil." After Boynton preached "about an hour on the order of Gods house . . . Bro. Wm spake a few minutes on the gifts of the gospel of Christ and the manner in which it is preached in these last days." After the meeting,

---

55. Ibid., March 21, 1833; Journal History, January 15, 1833, 3–4; Curtis, "Missionary Activities and Church Organizations in Pennsylvania, 1830–1840," 37.

56. Dean C. Jessee, Mark Ashurst-McGee, and Richard L. Jensen, eds., *Journals— Vol. 1: 1832–1839*, Vol. 1 of the Journals series of THE JOSEPH SMITH PAPERS, general editors Dean C. Jessee, Ronald K. Esplin, and Richard Lyman Bushman (Salt Lake City: Church Historian's Press, 2008), 12–14.

57. In describing Elk Creek river, which crisscrosses Erie County, the *History of Erie County, Pennsylvania* notes that the "East Branch rises in Crawford County, just across the [county] line. It is joined by Frazier's Run at Wellsburg, by Crane Run near Cranesville, by Mormon Run at Thornton's dam, near Albion." *History of Erie County, Pennsylvania*, 2 vols. (Chicago: Warner, Beers & Co., 1884), 1:771.

William left his companions, "and went home with Bro. [Benjamin] Winchester."[58] Although William accepted Benjamin's hospitality in Elk Creek, he also found time to have conversations with nineteen-year-old Caroline Amanda Grant. For both of them, the mutual attraction was strong, and the decision to marry was almost immediate. In his history, William simply noted that it was "in Elk Creek Township, where I became acquainted with a young lady by the name of Caroline Grant, and after a short acquaintance married her on the 14th of February, 1833."[59] Even though Caroline was of age, her parents and siblings found William a suitable marriage partner for Caroline, or almost certainly they could not have so quickly made their decision and carried it out. Traveling missionary William Cahoon and local convert Amos Hodges had apparently witnessed William and Caroline's wedding; when they encountered Greene and Boynton two days later, Greene noted that "they also brought us news of Bro Wm Smith being married." When Greene and Boynton learned of their friend and missionary companion's Valentine's Day wedding, the traveling missionaries had a "time of rejoicing" at the news of this union.[60]

William's influence on the Grant family cannot be underestimated, although surviving details of his interactions are limited because neither he nor they were keeping journals at the time, and later reminiscences by Caroline's sister Theda point to the missionaries who baptized the family. Thus, most historians who have written about the Grant family have missed Smith's influential role in converting the family.[61] The Grants were probably among those whom Greene described in his missionary journal, as being "verry strong in the faith though they had not as yet presented themselves for baptism."[62] Most of the Grant children were baptized within weeks of William's departure after his missionary labors and marriage in Elk Creek, beginning with Jedediah on March 2, 1833, with Boynton performing the ordinance.[63] William probably baptized Caroline around that same time, either at Elk Creek or shortly after they moved into Kirtland.

In addition to the likelihood that he baptized his recent bride, William performed this ordinance for two more siblings, baptizing Theda in the Chagrin River at Kirtland in 1836 and Roxey Ann much later in 1845 in Nauvoo.[64]

---

58. Greene, Diary, February 10–12, 1833.
59. *William Smith on Mormonism*, 22.
60. Greene, Diary, February 16, 1833.
61. Sessions, *Mormon Thunder*, 6–8; Ronald W. Walker, "Qualities That Count: Heber J. Grant as Businessman, Missionary, and Apostle," *BYU Studies*, Special issue, 43, no. 1 (2004), 2–4. Like other Latter-day Saints in Utah, Jedediah M. Grant appears to have minimized William Smith's role and influence in the early Church after the latter was excommunicated in October 1845. That autumn, he and Smith had a falling out, a disagreement that had been intensifying since they had served together in the East during 1843–45.
62. Greene, Diary, February 16, 1833.
63. Journal History, January 15, 1833, 3.
64. Reeves, Reminiscence; William Smith, Letter to Joshua Grant Jr. (Nauvoo, Illinois), August 12, 1845, published in *Nauvoo Neighbor* 3, no. 16 (August 20, 1845): 3.

Life in "the Ohio": Missions, Marriage, and Ministry   97

William had formed a solid bond with his in-laws, even before he married Caroline. George D. Grant named a son born in 1842 William Smith Grant, as a tribute to his influential missionary brother-in-law, and Theda's history is replete with references to William and his influence on the family. Firm in the newfound faith, the Grant family moved to Chagrin, Ohio, some five miles from Kirtland that same year.[65]

William stayed with the Grants in Elk Creek for a honeymoon week after his wedding, then he and Caroline left for Kirtland on February 21. The newlyweds resided for the next few years with Father and Mother Smith, as Hyrum and his wife, Jerusha, and Joseph Jr. and Emma had also begun their married years in the warm generosity of the Smith parents' home. Eleven months after William and Caroline's marriage, on January 7, 1834, they welcomed baby Mary Jane as their first child.[66]

Settling into Kirtland's bustling community, William went to work immediately to improve his family's living situation. He and younger brother Don Carlos both participated in purchasing large tracts of land on the Peter French farm for the temple, in conjunction with their prophet-brother. In addition, William began to chop cordwood for hire.[67] His financial situation improved enough that, by 1835, he began constructing a home just southeast of the Kirtland Temple site, on the corner of Chillicothe and Joseph streets.[68] William recollected that he "engaged in farming, and merchandizing some. My brother Samuel and I cleared about fifteen acres of land, and I commenced a house, as I had means and opportunity, besides assisting all I could in building the Temple."[69]

At the same time, William was progressing spiritually. During the winter following his mission and marriage (1833–34), William once again attended the School of the Prophets held in the upper story of Newel K. Whitney's store, where he enjoyed associating with those interested in furthering their spiritual education. Joseph received many significant revelations during that winter; and the intelligent and articulate William, in marked contrast to his teenage boredom with religion, found great satisfaction in his burgeoning understanding of Church doctrine. He was among those who were present when his brother received the revelation known as the Word of Wisdom (D&C 89), which, among other provisions, discouraged the use of tobacco. According to Zebedee Coltrin's recollections fifty years later, William Smith was among the twenty-one men present, and was almost certainly one of the twenty who threw his pipe and to-

---

65. Grant Davies Atkinson, "A Sketch of the Life of George Davis Grant" (n.p., 1998), 6; Reeves, Reminiscence.

66. "Laid to Rest," *Brookfield Gazette* 12, no. 36 (December 26, 1878): 3.

67. "History of William Smith," *Millennial Star* 27, no. 1 (January 7, 1865), 7–8.

68. *William Smith on Mormonism*, 24–25; Richard N. Holzapfel, T. Jeffery Cottle, and Ted D. Stoddard, eds., *Church History in Black and White: George Edward Anderson's Photographic Mission to Latter-day Saint Historical Sites* (Provo, Utah: BYU Religious Studies Center, 1995), 147, 151.

69. *William Smith on Mormonism*, 24–25.

bacco into the fire to show his support of the revelation immediately after Joseph read it to them.[70]

William would also have grasped the significance of the revelation to construct the Kirtland Temple (D&C 95:8), which announces that a primary purpose of building the Lord's house was "to endow those whom I have chosen with power from on high." He described the Saints' understanding of the endowment at the time as "an additional outpouring of the spiritual gifts and blessings of the church through the means of their industry and sacrifice incurred and undergone on account of its [the temple's] building . . . and [an] outpouring of the spirit that would show that the work was blessed by the Spirit, as a reward for the industry and sacrifice that marked its erection." Upon the temple's completion, according to William's later recollection, the Saints expected "an outpouring of the Spirit"—the same as on the day of Pentecost—"[or] something of that nature that was generally expected and talked of."[71]

Accordingly, William focused much of his energy on that sacred structure. "I used my utmost endeavors to accomplish this work," he recalled, cutting stone in the quarry near the temple, and carrying the stone and mortar that were used in its foundation and walls.[72] Besides the significant physical labors of his strong body, he also collected funds to help finance its construction.[73]

The gifts of the Spirit continued to be manifest during William's ministerial duties at Kirtland, including the gift of healing. One notable experience that stood out to him was the healing of a man who was insane. "A brother by the name of Newcomb moved into Kirtland," recalled William, "and brought with him a brother that was said to be crazy; a person bereft of reason, a raving maniac, and from all appearance possessed of evil spirits." The man was so difficult to control that "he had to be kept in chains, to prevent him from doing harm to anyone." Having tried everything imaginable, his brother finally requested that some of "the Elders of the Church [take] this case in hand." The small group, which included William, "formed a circle around this man of evil spirits, prayed and laid hands upon him, and commanded in the name of Jesus Christ the evil spirits to come out of him; and in less than fifteen minutes afterwards, said crazy man was restored to his reason and released from his chains." William remembered the

---

70. Ibid., 22–23; "October 3, 1883, Statement of Zebedee Coltrin," in Merle H. Graffam, ed., *Salt Lake School of the Prophets Minute Book, 1883* (Palm Desert, Calif.: ULC Press, 1981), 37–38.

71. William Smith Testimony, Temple Lot Case Testimonies, 205–6, U.S. Eighth Circuit Court, 1892, MS 1160, LDS Church History Library. See also, *William Smith on Mormonism*, 22, 25.

72. *Cleveland Herald* report reproduced in "General Conference," *Saints' Herald* 30, no. 16 (April 21, 1883): 242–43.

73. *William Smith on Mormonism*, 22, 25.

Life in "the Ohio": Missions, Marriage, and Ministry   99

Chagrin River—Kirtland Temple in Distance. Photograph ca. 1920, by unknown photographer.

significant impact this "notable miracle" had locally. Word of this miracle spread quickly, creating "much talk and excitement through the country."[74]

According to William's memoir, he participated in "many other notable miracles" at Kirtland, but perhaps the most impressive was the manner in which Mormonism progressed. He watched as the community of Saints took over the city of Kirtland and extended its reach into neighboring communities. He felt that the elders were gladly received among members of all denominations in the area. "To such a degree did this [religious] excitement extend that many of the Methodists and Presbyterians were obliged to give up holding meetings," William recollected, "and vacate their meeting houses in and about Kirtland." The prosperity of the Church "gave a spring to our cause" wrote William, and "filled all hearts with joy and new courage."[75] By the mid 1830s, to his elation, Mormonism was spreading in all directions from Church headquarters, and converts were gathering in great numbers. "The little Chagrin river passing through Kirtland," reflected William, "will be a witness in the great day of eternity of the many baptisms performed in that stream; in which administration I was . . . a personal participant." Among those Smith baptized in the gently meandering river, were his sister-in-law Theda Grant sometime in 1836, and future Utah pioneer and colonizer, twenty-six-year-old Anson Call, on May 21, 1836.[76]

Due to his faithful service as a missionary, his attendance at the School of the Prophets, his participation in Zion's Camp during the summer of 1834, and his labors on the temple, William was also a significant player as the Church's priesthood quorums and hierarchy evolved. Ordained a high priest by Sidney Rigdon

---

74. Ibid., 25–26.
75. Ibid..
76. Ibid., 25–27; Reeves, Reminiscence; Anson Call, Journal, photocopy of holograph in my possession, 7; Thaya Eggleston Gilmore, "Anson Call: Man of Action," *Ensign*, July 2001, 38–43.

on June 21, 1833, he doubtless interpreted this achievement as progress within the ministry that he had chosen as his life's work.[77]

Then, on Saturday, February 14, 1835, William was summoned to a meeting, where he was commended for his participation in Zion's Camp. Under the direction of the First Presidency, the Three Witnesses to the Book of Mormon—Oliver Cowdery, Martin Harris, and David Whitmer—selected twelve men to serve as apostles.[78] William was one of those chosen, but the reminiscences of other participants raise interesting questions about his standing among Church authorities.

According to David Whitmer, he and his brother-in-law Oliver Cowdery had initially selected Phinehas Young, which would have completed the quorum with twelve men, "but Joseph insisted that his brother William Smith should be put in [instead of Phinehas] as it was the only way which he could be saved, otherwise we would not have chosen him."[79] This statement should be considered with caution. When Whitmer made this statement, he had been estranged from the Church for almost fifty years. Was he remembering this episode correctly, or were he and/or Gurley influenced by William's later struggles, which deeply alienated his former colleagues? Was Zenas (or Zenos) Gurley accurately quoting Whitmer, a half century after this conversation had occurred? Furthermore, both Whitmer and Gurley had, like William Smith, been participants in the post-martyrdom turmoil that led to intense conflict among the many Latter-day Saints who chose other expressions of Mormonism besides that led by Brigham Young. William himself amassed a staggering record of affiliation and disaffiliation during this period, and the partings were not always amicable, including his relationship with Gurley.

Two additional sources provide corroboration. Oliver Cowdery, in a letter to Brigham Young in 1848 when he had decided to return to the Church, recollected: "At the time the Twelve were chosen in Kirtland, and I may say before, it had been manifested that Brother Phinehas was entitled to occupy the station as one of the number; but owing to Brother Joseph's urgent request at the time, Brother David and myself yielded to his wish, and consented for William to be selected, contrary to our feelings and judgment, and to our deep mortification ever since."[80]

The second corroborating item is Joseph's growing belief in the prominent role that his family should play in the Church's governing quorums. When William's brother Don Carlos was called to be president of the high priests at Kirtland not

---

77. Minute Book 1, June 21, 1833 (Kirtland, Ohio), 20, LDS Church History Library.

78. Minute Book 1, February 15, 1835 (Kirtland, Ohio), 147–49, LDS Church History Library.

79. Zenos Hovey Gurley, "Questions Asked of David Whitmer at His Home in Richmond, Ray County, Missouri, 1885," MS 4633, LDS Church History Library, also published in Lyndon W. Cook, ed., *David Whitmer Interviews: A Restoration Witness* (Provo, Utah: Grandin Book, 1991), 157.

80. Oliver Cowdery (Elkhorn, Wisc.), Letter to Brigham Young, February 27, 1848, Brigham Young Office Files 1832–1878, General Correspondence, Incoming, 1840–1877, Letters from Church Leaders and Others, 1840–1877, Oliver Cowdery, 1843–1848, LDS Church History Library.

William Smith and Caroline Grant Smith Home, Kirtland, Ohio. Photograph by George Edward Anderson, August 7, 1907. The home was located on the corner of Chillicothe and Joseph Streets. Photograph courtesy LDS Church History Library.

long after William's appointment to the Twelve, there was a similar debate due to his age, as he was still in his teens. Joseph quelled the debate, according to Erastus Snow, who was present, by announcing: "My family have been chosen to preside over the quorums of the priesthood."[81] Through Joseph's intercession, both William and Don Carlos were unanimously sustained in their respective callings.

However, assuming that Joseph did, in fact, make such a statement and that it was transmitted accurately, what he meant by it must remain somewhat conjectural. Perhaps Joseph felt that such an important calling would motivate his younger brother to rise to the significance of the calling, though the Prophet was certainly acquainted with his weaknesses.

The Twelve were subsequently ranked according to age, making William ninth. Though he does not indicate who pronounced his ordination and blessing, he recalled that his ordination took place "under the hands of Oliver Cowdery and Martin Harris"[82] on Sunday morning, February 15, 1835. His blessing was recorded in the Church minutes, and read, at least in part,

> That he may be purified in heart; that he may have communion with God. That he may be equal with his brethren in holding the keys of this ministry That he may be kept and be instrumental in leading Israel forth, that he may be delivered from the hands of those who seek to destroy him: that he may be enabled to bear testimony to the nations, that Jesus lives. That he may stand in the midst of pestilence and destruction, he shall be mighty in the hands of God, in bringing about the restoration of Israel. The nations shall rejoice at the greatness of the gifts which God has

---

81. Erastus Snow quoted in John Henry Smith, *Church, State, and Politics: The Diaries of John Henry Smith*, ed. Jean Bickmore White (Salt Lake City: Signature Books, 1990), 84.
82. *William Smith on Mormonism*, 26.

bestowed upon him, That his tongue shall be loosed, he shall have power to do great things in the name of Jesus. He shall be preserved and remain on the earth until, Christ shall come to take vengeance on the wicked.[83]

This powerful and empowering blessing clearly focused on William's gifts and responsibilities as a missionary, endowing him with talents and motivation. It also communicates the understanding in the Church at that time that the earth teetered on the very brink of Christ's second coming and that the time in which individuals could seek salvation was short indeed.

And in fact, it was only three months later on May 4, 1835, that William, along with other members of the Twelve, departed for a mission to the East. He preached in New York until June 5, then returned to Kirtland with fellow apostles Brigham Young and Orson Hyde to help defend the Prophet Joseph in a court case in Chardon, Ohio, near Kirtland. Following the trial, William returned to the mission field. From an unspecified location, he wrote a letter about his missionary labors that Joseph Smith read to the high council in August 1835. Though the letter has not survived, Joseph indicated that the council approved of William's communication, which "filled our hearts with joy." Joseph, in turn, sent a letter to the Twelve containing items of Church proceedings at Kirtland. A postscript directed to William was appended to the letter which read, "To Elder Wm. Smith: Your house is nearly finished, except plastering, a few days will complete it." William returned from this mission on September 26, moved Caroline and little Mary Jane into their new home, and resumed his duties in the leading councils of the Church.[84]

---

83. Some of the earlier ordinations that day record that Oliver Cowdery acted as voice. Minute Book 1, February 15, 1835 (Kirtland, Ohio), 150–54, LDS Church History Library.

84. Joseph Smith and Kirtland High Council, Letter to Quorum of the Twelve (Kirtland, Ohio), August 4, 1835, in Joseph Smith, "Letter Book" (June 14, 1829–August 4, 1835), 89–90, holograph http://josephsmithpapers.org/paperSummary/letterbook-1#!/paperSummary/letterbook-1&p=105 (accessed March 2, 2015).

Chapter 6

In the Shadow of a Prophet

My brother William said "that I was always determined to carry my points whether right or wrong and therefore he would not stand an equal chance with me."

—Joseph Smith Jr., 1835

By the year 1835, all was prospering in Kirtland, Ohio, headquarters for the blossoming Mormon Church. The Saints excitedly anticipated the completion of the Kirtland Temple, which had required intensive labor and considerable cost to construct since its groundbreaking in June 1833. The ecclesiastical structure of the Church was also largely in place. William's personal growth seems to have corresponded with the prosperity of the Church. He had labored successfully as a missionary, participated in Zion's Camp, and most recently been selected as one in the newly organized Quorum of Twelve Apostles. During the summer after his appointment as an apostle, he served a mission with other members of his quorum both to spread the gospel message and to help regulate the budding eastern branches of the Church.

Mormonism was spreading rapidly throughout the eastern United States and Canada. In mid-July, the twelve were at St. Johnsbury, Vermont, where they held a memorable weekend conference at Levi Snow's barn. The greater Snow family formed a nucleus of devoted members of the Church in the vicinity; and because of the excitement generated by the missionary presence in the area, many were eager to hear more about the Mormon faith. A youth who attended the services that weekend recalled "a big crowd that gathered at the Snow barn. The Mormon Elders sat along the high beams. They let the women folk . . . [have] seats in the bay. The other men and we boys were packed in helter-skelter all around the best we could. It was Sunday but a regular holiday for everybody."[1] Another who attended the Sunday meeting described the apostles sitting on the scaffolding against one wall while a congregation of approximately 1,500 people filled the barn and the yard to overflowing. Though there was no record that William

---

1. Edward T. Fairbanks, *The Town of St. Johnsbury, VT: A Review of One Hundred Twenty-Five Years to the Anniversary Pageant 1912* (St. Johnsbury, Vt.: Cowles Press, 1914), 217–19; Andrew Karl Larson, *Erastus Snow: The Life of a Missionary and Pioneer for the Early Mormon Church* (Salt Lake City: University of Utah Press, 1971), 15–19. Larson notes that the Snow barn was built in the summer of 1832 and that the family lived in it that summer because their home had recently burned down.

Levi Snow's "Mormon Barn," St. Johnsbury, Vermont. Date and photographer unknown. Original in private possession. Courtesy Sharon Jensen Haworth.

preached at the conference, William's impressive height and family connection to the Mormon prophet drew attention. "They looked fresh from the backwoods," described the observer, and the most notable among the group was "the brother of Joe Smith, the chief prophet, who composed one of their number."[2] Many would be baptized in the stream that ran near what came to be known as the Mormon Barn. After the Sunday service on July 19 alone, nine individuals came forward to be baptized.[3] Despite this missionary success, however, there are hints at interpersonal conflicts. Apostle Parley P. Pratt wrote William's Uncle Asahel Smith, on July 21, 1835. "Br Wm Smith is complaining some," wrote Pratt, "though he endured the journey full as well as my self." After the conference in St. Johnsbury concluded, according to Pratt, "The 12 have now gone different ways preaching," and "Wm Smith is yet in the Nabourhood [of St. Johnsbury] a few miles from me[,] if he were here he would write some in this Letter but I can assure you he ever remembers you all."[4] In spite of William's grievances, the four-month mission proved to be a bonding experience for the newly called apostles, who returned to Kirtland that September.

William had moved up quickly in the Church's rapidly coalescing hierarchy and was emerging as a powerful personality within the quorum. At age twenty-four, William was secure in his station in the flourishing church. Since his call

---

2. "Mormonism in New England," *Maine Farmer and Journal of the Useful Arts* 3 (October 9, 1835): 288, as quoted in William Shepard and H. Michael Marquardt, *Lost Apostles: Forgotten Members of Mormonism's Original Quorum of Twelve* (Salt Lake City: Signature Books, 2014), 387.

3. Fairbanks, *The Town of St. Johnsbury, VT,* 218; Jan Shipps and John W. Welch, eds., *The Journals of William E. McLellin, 1831–1836* (Urbana: University of Illinois Press/ Provo, Utah: BYU Studies, 1994), 190.

4. Parley P. Pratt (St. Johnsbury, Vt.), Letter to Asahel Smith, July 21, 1835, MS 7064, LDS Church History Library.

six months earlier, he had not given his fellow Saints any reason to doubt his character. His family, on the other hand, had known something of his disposition of which Church members remained largely unaware. Apprehension about William's inability to handle views that differed from his own and uneasiness about his quick temper had been a concern for the family since his teens. William also acknowledged his inclination to be argumentative with his peers, and several accounts from his youth have survived documenting his heated outbursts. Notwithstanding, such incidents might be considered normal except when examined within the broader context of his life and in light of what he and his family indicated about his personality.[5] Those who knew him best recognized the limitations evident in his character.

Church members who were present during some of the earliest blessing meetings might have picked up on the family's worry for William. When William's prophet-brother Joseph bestowed a blessing upon his head by the laying on of hands on December 18, 1833, he likened his younger brother to a "fi[e]rce lion who divideth not the spoil because of his strength." The comparison suggests William's temper and unmanageability, which must have caused problems in the family as well as problems in the neighborhood. "In the pride of his heart," Joseph continued, "he will neglect the more weighty matters until his soul is bowed down in sorrow and then he shall return and call on th[e] name of his God and shall find forgiveness." The blessing ended on a somewhat positive note, indicating that he would "wax valient" in the Lord's service, "notwithstanding his rebelious heart." For Joseph, William's difficult personality was largely a matter of pride, and he discerned correctly some of the challenges William would continue to experience due to this weakness. He was the only member of the Smith family blessed on the occasion who received any semblance of reproof.[6]

William's father similarly revealed apprehensiveness about certain aspects of his son's personality when, almost exactly a year later on December 9, 1834,

---

5. It was common in early nineteenth-century America for men to manage conflict by using physical force. Historian Robert B. Flanders has summarized, "For people to take the law into their own hands was to be both democratic and faithful to the traditions of the American revolution. . . . It was a regular and ordinary part of the lifestyle." Robert B. Flanders, "Dream and Nightmare: Nauvoo Revisited," in *The Restoration Movement: Essays in Mormon History*, ed. F. Mark Mckiernan, Alma R. Blair, and Paul M. Edwards (Lawrence, Kans.: Coronado Press, 1972), 149. Irene M. Bates has argued that William's behavior was a normal part of the culture of the times. I disagree with her analysis based on William's pattern of behavior that appears to have been above and beyond what was acceptable at the time. Irene M. Bates, "William Smith, 1811–93: Problematic Patriarch," *Dialogue: A Journal of Mormon Thought* 16, no. 2 (Summer 1983): 13–15.

6. Dean C. Jessee, Mark Ashurst-McGee, and Richard L. Jensen, eds., *Journals—Vol. 1832–1839*, THE JOSEPH SMITH PAPERS, general editors Dean C. Jessee, Ronald K. Esplin, and Richard Lyman Bushman (Salt Lake City: Church Historian's Press, 2008), 21–24. Oliver Cowdery also received a warning to forsake several "evils" at the same blessing meeting.

he pronounced William's patriarchal blessing. Among other things, William was told that he had been chastened by the Lord through the many afflictions of his youth so that he would "learn to be obedient to the commandments and faithful to his [the Lord's] precepts." His father was aware of William's pre-conversion struggle, but perhaps of even greater concern to his father was its impact on William's persisting temperament. He continued, "Thou hast greatly desired to see thy father's family redeemed from trouble and from the power and domination of those who oppressed them. . . . But thou hast not altogether desired this thing in meekness, because thou hast not always known the Lord."[7]

His father knew all too well the difficulties William's temperament had created, as his unyielding disposition and lack of spirituality had distressed at least his parents and Joseph Jr. during his adolescence. Yet the family held out hope, that as William's faith and understanding of the gospel increased, he could overcome these challenges. The blessings given by Joseph Jr. and Joseph Sr. were an effort to strengthen William in dealing with these weaknesses. They warned him against the problems that had plagued his youth and shared counsel that would enable him to rise above those challenges. Joseph's insistence that he be called as an apostle doubtless reflected the whole family's desire that this calling would mitigate the imperfections of his personality. If David Whitmer remembered Joseph's instructions to the Three Witnesses correctly (and if Zenas Gurley quoted Whitmer correctly), Joseph saw William's calling as a matter of spiritual life and death, telling Whitmer and Oliver Cowdery that "his brother William Smith should be put in [the Quorum of Twelve Apostles] as it was the only way which he could be saved."[8]

While William's volatile temperament remained a concern to the family, he had managed to keep his aggressiveness largely in check since his call to the prominent position of apostle. It is impossible to predict how he would have fared without this serious ecclesiastical responsibility. Perhaps he would have become as pathologically unpleasant as his uncle Jesse. However, the record of his lapses from appropriate behavior shows that he failed to control these facets of his character, and the pattern raises serious questions about his emotional maturity, even as an adult. In late 1835, just months after his ordination as an apostle, his insubordination and passionate temper erupted publicly, causing great embarrassment to the Church and its prophet. William's lack of empathy and the rigidity of his viewpoints meant he would never do well in a theocracy unless he was in charge—and even that prospect would be fraught by the same set of challenges. Adding to his difficulty was the fact that it was his own brother who was in charge.

---

7. William Smith, Patriarchal Blessing bestowed by Joseph Smith Sr., December 9, 1834, Patriarchal Blessing Book 1, 10–11, LDS Church History Library.

8. Zenos Hovey Gurley, "Questions Asked of David Whitmer at His Home in Richmond, Ray County, Missouri, 1885," MS 4633, LDS Church History Library, also reprinted in Lyndon W. Cook, ed., *David Whitmer Interviews: A Restoration Witness* (Provo, Utah: Grandin Book Company, 1991), 157.

One event was triggered during a high council meeting held at Edmund Bosley's home in Kirtland on October 29, 1835. During the course of the meeting, William brought charges against David Elliott for beating his fifteen-year-old daughter from his first marriage. Joseph Jr., who presided at the meeting, disagreed with William and defended Elliott and his second wife, Mary. After talking with the daughter, Joseph felt that she was trying to create difficulties within the family and was at least partly to blame for bringing the punishment on herself. Although Joseph sternly rebuked Elliott's behavior as inappropriate and as bringing "disgrace upon himself, upon his daughter & upon this Church," the council took no official Church action on Elliott's membership.

William did not accept the council's decision. Later that same evening, when the high council reconvened, he repeated his accusations, this time expanding them to include Mary Elliott, for "also abusing the rest of her children."[9] Lucy Mack Smith was called to give testimony in the case, and Joseph later recorded in his journal the details of what transpired. Because Lucy had not attended the earlier meeting, she began to repeat evidence that had already come out during David Elliott's trial. Joseph apparently tried to abbreviate the proceedings by saying that the evidence had already been heard, but William was irritated and abruptly accused Joseph of "invalidating or doubting Mother's testimony." Joseph took exception to William's objection and, as the presiding authority at the council meeting, "told him he was out of place & asked him to set down." Not one to back down from what he perceived as a confrontation, William stood his ground, refusing either to be silenced or to sit. "I repeated my request," recounted Joseph, but William "bec[a]me enraged," until Joseph "finally ordered him to set down." William's obstinacy was shocking to those in attendance, particularly when he provocatively snapped that "he would not set down . . . unless I [Joseph] knocked him down." "I was agitated in my feeling[s] on . . . account of his stubournness," Joseph recorded, "and was about to leave the house." Dismayed by this open quarrel, Joseph Sr., who was also present, asked Joseph Jr. not to leave and helped allay the hottest feelings until order could be restored. Joseph Jr. said that he "complied" with his father's request, and "the house was brought to order."[10] The high council minutes record, "Sister Elliot confessed her wrong and promised to do so no more consequently the council forgave her. Brother Elliott made his confession and was forgiven, and both he and his wife were restored to fellowship."[11] The two brothers likewise seemed reconciled "after much debate upon the subject," at least from Joseph's perspective. Joseph later indicated that he felt he and William parted that night "with the best of feelings."[12]

---

9. Minute Book 1, (Kirtland, Ohio), October 29, 1835, 126–28, item #7702, LDS Church History Library.

10. Joseph Smith, Journal, October 29, 1835, Jessee, Ashurst-McGee, and Jensen, *Journals, Vol. 1, 1832–1839*, 77–79.

11. Minute Book 1, October 29, 1835, 128.

12. Joseph Smith, Journal, October 29 and 30, 1835, in ibid., 79.

William, however, continued to brood over what he perceived as the high council's unfairness in siding with his brother, both in dismissing the charges against Elliott and in abbreviating Mother Smith's testimony.

It seems likely, however, that the real issue was less about the Elliotts or invalidating Mother Smith's testimony than it was about William's feeling demeaned. Though he certainly disagreed with Joseph's perspective on the case, he felt personally affronted, even insulted, when Joseph abruptly undercut his opinion and the council supported him. The fact that Joseph's voice was naturally more influential among the leading councils of the Church was difficult for William, who was not a naturally submissive or cooperative person, to accept. In this case, he felt that his view was correct and that, therefore, an injustice had been done. Compounding his frustration was the fact that his brother also had more influence within the family. The episode at the high council meeting underscored his resentment toward Joseph's authority. It was an early signal that he would struggle throughout his life with being subordinate to his prophet-brother.

The day after their confrontation, some members of the high council who had been present at the meeting the previous evening reprimanded William, either by letter or more informally in person, for what they felt was his inappropriate conduct. He immediately fired back a hot-tempered letter that, according to Joseph's journal, defended his behavior, denounced the brethren's action as "censur[ing him] unjustly," and argued that his "cause was a just one, and that he had been materially injured." It is evident from William's letter that he not only felt justified in how he behaved at the meeting, but also disagreed with the council's decision and insisted that his colleagues acknowledge his perspective. He felt he was in the right and held dogmatically to his position on the matter. Notwithstanding, he also expressed his hope "to have the matter settled to the understanding of all." A face-to-face meeting seemed like the reasonable next step, and Joseph accordingly wrote to William encouraging him "to call and talk with me, and that I would . . . [talk with] him in the spirit of meekness and give him all the satisfaction I could."[13]

William did not immediately respond and the next day—now two days after the initial episode—Hyrum went to Joseph's home, troubled about the tension in the family. Joseph asked this respected older brother to help them resolve the angry feelings. Coincidentally, while Joseph and Hyrum were conversing, William arrived in response to Joseph's letter of the previous evening. Hyrum had to run some errands but said he would return as soon as possible. William immediately began to rehash the tensions of the meeting. Knowing very well his brother's unpredictable temper and foreseeing the shrewdness that managing the negotiations would require, Joseph asked William to wait until Hyrum returned.[14]

When Hyrum returned, he brought with him Warren Parrish, Joseph's personal secretary. Joseph proposed to William that they allow the two men to help

---

13. Joseph Smith, Journal, October 30, 1831, in ibid., 79–80.
14. Ibid., 80.

resolve their differences that had occurred at the council meeting; "and [that] wherein I had been out of the way I would confess it and ask his forgiv[e]ness, and then he should relate his story and make confession wherein he had done wrong." But almost before Joseph had finished, William flared up at Joseph's implication that he had done anything wrong at the council meeting. William declared that he had not been at fault and then cut to the core of his main grievance with Joseph. According to Joseph's diary, William said "that I [Joseph] was always determined to carry my points whether right or wrong, and therefore he would not stand an equal chance with me." Joseph found his comment offensive because it disregarded his calling as president and prophet of the Church, something he felt that William, of all Saints, should have understood and supported. Still, Joseph did not respond in kind. "[I] did not reply to him in a harsh manner, knowing his inflam[m]atory disposition, but tryed to reason with him and show him the propriety of a complyance with my request"—to have it settled by the two men. After much effort by both Hyrum and Joseph, William finally consented to have a structured discussion regulated by Hyrum and Warren.¹⁵

Joseph began by relating his version of the high council meeting two days earlier, confessed to William where he felt he had done wrong, and asked his forgiveness. William, in turn, gave his side of the story. Joseph was stunned by William's version, since he absolved himself of any wrongdoing whatsoever, "his statements justifying himself throughout in transgressing the order of the council & treating the authority of the Presidency with contempt." Joseph felt that, at the very least, William needed to apologize for disregarding the protocol of a high council meeting and the contemptuous way he had treated the presiding authority. Joseph was firm in his view that both of these formal elements were essential in maintaining order in the Church and its councils. Almost immediately, the two reached an impasse. Hyrum intervened "in the spirit of meekness," trying to help William take responsibility for his errant conduct. William immediately interpreted Hyrum's action as siding with Joseph and accused both of them of inviting him to this face-to-face meeting so they could add "abuse to injury." Once again, he felt, his perspective was being disrespected, while Joseph's view was corroborated. William became increasingly upset while his brothers and Parrish attempted to calm him. "His passion increased," recounted Joseph, and finally, in an impulsive fury, "he arose abruptly and declared that he wanted no more to do with us or the church and said we might take his [preacher's] licence for he would have nothing to do with us." "He became enraged," lamented Joseph. "I joined my brother [Hyrum] in trying to calm his stormy feelings, but to no purpose." William "rushed out the door" despite the efforts of all three men "to prevail on him to stop, but all to no purpose, he went away in a passion."¹⁶

---

15. Ibid.
16. Ibid.

As had been his pattern during adolescence, William never handled conflict mildly. He made good on his threat, ostentatiously sending his preaching license back to his prophet-brother. He then went to their brother Samuel and succeeded in biasing his mind against Joseph. In time, William also persuaded Calvin Stoddard, the husband of their eldest sister, Sophronia, to side with him. Stoddard was all the readier to give William his support since he had recently had his own run-in with the Prophet. The resulting discord in the family caused Joseph deep personal anguish. His family had been his greatest support from the time he was first called to restore the Church, and to see that support eroding troubled him in a way that nothing else could. It further hurt him that William would demean him within the family, as well as attempting to make their disagreement more public than it already was. "I soon learned that he was in the streets exclaiming against, me," wrote Joseph, "which no doubt our enemies rejoice at, and where the matter will end I know not." In his journal it was as if he could not find the words to express the depths of his sorrow, and he wrote mournfully: "The feelings of my heart I cannot express on this occasion."[17]

Joseph loved William and desired to see him take responsibility for his actions. The longer the conflict persisted, the heavier the weight of his sorrow. The distress it caused Joseph was evident to the Saints. Daniel Tyler, one of William's converts from Erie County, Pennsylvania, was aware of his former missionary's struggle and observed the pain it caused Joseph:

> At the time William Smith and others rebelled against the Prophet at Kirtland, I attended a meeting "on the flats" where Joseph presided. . . . I perceived sadness in his countenance and tears trickling down his cheeks. A few moments later a hymn was sung and he opened the meeting by prayer. Instead of facing the audience, however, he turned his back and bowed upon his knees, facing the wall. This, I suppose, was done to hide his sorrow and tears. I had heard men and women pray—especially the former—from the most learned and eloquent. But never until then had I heard a man address his Maker as though He was present listening as a kind father would listen to a dutiful child. Joseph was at that time unlearned, but that prayer, which was to a considerable extent in behalf of those who had accused him of having gone astray and fallen into sin, was that the Lord would forgive them and open their eyes that they might see aright. . . . It was the crowning of all the prayers I ever heard. When Joseph arose and addressed the congregation, he spoke of his many troubles, and said he often wondered why it was that he should have so much trouble in the house of his friends, and he wept as though his heart would break.[18]

The Prophet relied on his faith to help him cope in the days following William's withdrawal from the Church and his distancing himself from the fam-

---

17. Ibid., 79–80; Joseph Smith, Letter to the Editor, June 22, 1835, *Painesville Telegraph* (Kirtland, Ohio), 1, no. 25 (June 26, 1835). See also Joseph Smith, Journal, January 1, 1836, in Jessee, Ashurst-McGee, and Jensen, *Journals, Vol. 1, 1832–1839*, 140, for further evidence of the connection between William Smith and Calvin Stoddard during this period.

18. Daniel Tyler, Reminiscence, in "Recollections of the Prophet Joseph Smith," *Juvenile Instructor* 27, no. 4 (February 15, 1892): 127–28.

ily. Joseph prayed until he "obtained a testimony that Br. William would return to the church and repair the wrong he had done."[19] Joseph found consolation in this reassurance, but he knew that such a course correction would not come easily for William. Joseph felt that the whole conflict was a scheme orchestrated by the Adversary to overthrow his family, and he was fiercely protective of anything that threatened those ties.

When other Church leaders sought to discipline the wayward apostle, Joseph stood faithfully by William throughout their conflict. Just five days after their conflict, on November 3, 1835, William was still on the Prophet's mind when he received a revelation for the Twelve, who were among those who felt that William merited Church discipline. A good portion of the divine communication dealt specifically with William. Since the Smith brothers' blow-up at the high council meeting, some of the apostles had apparently discussed William's standing in their quorum. The revelation instructed: "As for my Servant William let the Eleven humble themselves in prayer and in faith and wait on me in patience and my servant William shall return." Although the indignation and protectiveness of the apostles for Joseph was evident, these instructions cast the matter in a new light. They were to exercise forbearance with their errant colleague and with each other. Tellingly, the revelation went on to rebuke several for committing equal, if not greater, sins than William. The revelation also put a stop to any speculation about his removal from his ecclesiastical office when the pronouncement declared that William would return and that the Lord would yet "make him a polished shaft in my quiver." At the same time, the revelation did not ignore William's mistakes, warning that "if he repent not speedily he shall be brought low and chastened sorely for all his iniquities he has commit[t]ed against me."[20]

William's estrangement from the Church lingered into the winter of 1835–36. Though the Smith brothers were once again interacting, their underlying issues were still unresolved. Joseph was consumed by several major crises that impacted the Church during December, including learning of the Saints' difficulties in Missouri and the personal attacks of Philastus Hurlbut, an apostate. Still, when he learned that William had organized a "debating school," he was initially supportive and found time to attend one of its meetings in William and Caroline's home on December 12.[21] Several Mormon historians have described how the "lyceum movement—part of the larger reform movement of Jacksonian America, with its lectures, dramatic performances, class instruction, and debates—contributed significantly to the education of adult Americans in

---

19. Joseph Smith, Journal, October 31, 1835, in Jessee, Ashurst-McGee, and Jensen, *Journals, Vol. 1, 1832–1839*, 81.

20. Joseph Smith, Journal, November 3, 1835, in ibid., 83.

21. Joseph Smith, Journal, December 12, 1835, in ibid., 120–21. Joseph referred to these meetings held at William's home as the "debating school," and indicated that it was organized without his knowledge. Joseph Smith (Kirtland, Ohio), Letter to William Smith, December 18 or 19, 1835, in ibid., 131–34.

the nineteenth century and provided the cultural context for the schools and debating societies of Kirtland."[22] As one who enjoyed meditating and writing on religious topics throughout his life, William relished the challenge of a thoughtful debate. His debating school, which consisted primarily of young elders near his own age, appears to have been an extension of the School of the Prophets, where the brethren practiced debating religious topics to hone their missionary skills and scriptural knowledge. The Prophet participated on this particular occasion by defending the idea that human happiness was contingent upon God's revealing himself. Their session was then interrupted when Joseph was called out to attend to a sick church member.[23]

Four days later on December 16, Joseph returned to William's home, where the elders picked up debating the same topic. Father Smith and Hyrum were also present. It is not clear how many others were in attendance or who they were, since Brigham Young, Almon Babbit, Jared Carter, William McLellin, and Benjamin F. Johnson are the only other participants identified by name. When the debate concluded, Joseph expressed his reservations about continuing the school. He had, on an earlier occasion publicly expressed similar misgivings about such debates, as he felt there was too "much warmth displayed, to[o] much zeal for mastery, to[o] much of that enthusiasm that characterises a lawyer at the bar, who is determined to defend his cause right or wrong."[24] Just shy of his twenty-eighth birthday, the Prophet had already experienced enough aggravating lawsuits to disdain how the legal system could be manipulated by crafty attorneys, and he resisted the idea that the Saints would employ that same secular approach. He felt that religious topics should be discussed more reverently and that the brethren should show more gentleness and mutual civility in expressing their respective opinions. He had hoped that, with some initial adjustments, the debating school might continue, but the tone he had observed on his first visit had, if anything intensified during the second session. For these reasons, Joseph proposed to those present that the debating school be discontinued, "fearing that it would not result in good."[25]

William, who had organized the school and enjoyed the society, flared up at Joseph's proposal, and perhaps Joseph had been insensitive to his brother's enjoyment of and proprietary feelings about the school he had organized. In any case, he had not taken the basic step of first discussing his proposal with his brother. A heated discussion ensued. William McLellin, an apostle, presumably sided with Joseph but was interrupted by William. The Prophet attempted to intervene, cautioning the two not to have disagreeable feelings for one another due to their rela-

---

22. Ibid., 106 note 155.

23. Joseph Smith, Journal, December 12, 1835, in ibid., 120–21.

24. Joseph Smith, Journal, November 18, 1835, in ibid., 106. About three weeks earlier, he had similarly explained to Apostle John F. Boynton that "it was generally the case, that to[o] much, altercation was indulged in, on both sides and their debates protracted to an unprofitable length." Ibid., October 29, 1835, 77.

25. Joseph Smith, Journal, November 18 and December 16, 1835, in ibid., 106, 124.

tionship as fellow apostles. It is not clear who called for a vote at this critical point; but a majority supported Joseph's proposal regarding "the impropriety of continuing the school." Reacting as he had at the high council meeting two months earlier, William refused to accept the decision. Instead, he brazenly proposed a new topic to be debated at their next meeting, and "assert[ed] that he was in his own house and should insist on continuing the debating school regardless of the consequences."[26] His defiance startled nearly all of those in attendance that night.

After the events of that night, Joseph chose to continue the discussion by letter, apparently hoping that William would be less defensive if he could read and contemplate the argument instead of immediately going on the attack as he often did in face-to-face meetings. Joseph's letter details the point at which the debating school became a battleground: "Br. Hyrum, [then] requested, the privilege, of speaking," recounted Joseph, "[but] you objected, however you said if he would not abuse the school, he might speak, and that you would not allow any man to abuse the school in your house." Whatever Hyrum planned to say was lost in the verbal scuffle that followed, when Joseph, whose "feelings were mortifyed" at William's "inconciderate and stubourn spirit," chastised William for attempting to silence those present and continue the school. William's response became increasingly insolent.[27] For William, it was essentially a replay of the high council meeting. He desired to have an equal voice with Joseph and did not distinguish between their fraternal relationship and Joseph's ecclesiastical position as prophet and president of the Church. The unsettled feelings that had been brewing inside William for several months quickly resurfaced.

Making the issue more complex was the fact that the forbearance that Joseph had manifested toward his brother during the previous two months was waning. That very morning he had been pressed to present a written complaint against William from Orson Hyde to the high council. In the complaint, Hyde expressed frustration that his fellow apostle was receiving substantially more support from the bishop's storehouse than the rest of the twelve.[28] It was not simply their personal difficulty that weighed heavily on Joseph's mind. Rather, William's obduracy and emerging sense of entitlement were becoming ecclesiastical concerns. Although Joseph had allowed a cooling-off period by waiting a few days to write his letter, his exasperation with his younger brother was unmistakable. He confronted him about his insubordination after seeing these elements of his personality surface at

---

26. Joseph Smith, Journal, December 16, 1835, in ibid., 124; Joseph Smith, Letter to William Smith, December 18 or 19, 1835, Joseph Smith, Journal, December 18, 1835, ibid., 131–34.

27. Joseph Smith, Letter to William Smith, December 18 or 19, 1835, ibid., 132; Calvin P. Rudd, "William Smith: Brother of the Prophet Joseph Smith" (M.S. thesis, Brigham Young University, 1973), 44.

28. Orson Hyde, Letter to President [Joseph] Smith, December 15, 1835, in Joseph Smith, Journal, December 17, 1836, in Jessee, Ashurst-McGee, and Jensen, *Journals, Vol. 1, 1832–1839*, 124–28.

the debate meeting, methodically recounting the details of what had transpired in hopes that it would assist his brother in taking responsibility for his faults.

The apparent lone supporter in William's resistance at the meeting that night was Almon Whiting Babbitt, a trained attorney, who also disagreed with the decision to close the school. Babbitt may have also taken offense at Joseph's earlier comments that expressed his antipathy for lawyers. Babbitt later testified, that there "would not have been any difficulty if J. [Joseph, Jr.] Smith had not have got mad." He needled Joseph by claiming that that the only reason he wanted the school closed was because he lost the debate and that he "got mad because he was overpowered in argument." Although Babbitt later confessed that he made these accusations out of anger, they may well reflect William's view of the difficulty. Another witness who was present, Benjamin F. Johnson, probably reflected a more balanced view when he reported that "J. Smith was riled and Wm. Smith was mad."[29]

Father Smith was also present at the conflict. As the heated feelings of his sons escalated, he attempted to intervene by commanding silence. Joseph Jr., whose respect for his father was undeniable, immediately obeyed, but William snapped back that he "would say what he pleased in his own house." Father Smith continued to mediate, attempting to calm their feelings so that there could be an atmosphere in which to amicably settle their differences. Joseph Sr. allowed William to speak his mind but cautioned, "Let the rest hold their tongues." However, Joseph Jr. took exception to William's claim that he was in his own house. There is no question that the house was William and Caroline's residence, but perhaps Joseph felt that William was making an unwarranted claim of entitlement. The Prophet, who had overseen much of the construction of William's home during his absence, felt that the home was just as much his, or rather the Church's, as it was William's. At that moment, Joseph said, "a reflection, rushed through my mind, of the, anxiety, and care I had for you and your family, in doing what I did, in finishing your house and providin[g] flour for your family." Thus, he reacted against William's furious notion that "I should not have the privilege of speaking in my fathers house, or in other words in my fathers family, or in your house." In retrospect, Joseph reflected in his letter to William, "I should have said . . . I helped finish the house"; but what he said was, "I will speak, for I built the house, and it is as much mine as yours." This comment was too much for William's frayed self-control, and he resorted to his fists. As Joseph later recounted the incident—admittedly from his own perspective—"I saw that your indignation was kindled against me, and you made towards me." Joseph admitted that he was not about to either leave or back down at that point: "I was not then to be moved, and I thought to pull off my loose coat, lest it should

---

29. Minute Book 1, December 28, 1835, 130–33. Joseph Smith presented a complaint against Almon Babbitt at the high council meeting on December 28, 1835, about his behavior at the debate meeting and afterward.

tangle me, and you be left to hurt me, but not with the intention of hurting you. But you were too quick for me."[30]

While Joseph was shucking his overcoat, William lunged at him, violently punching him with his fists. Jared Carter and Hyrum Smith both jumped into the melee, only to have William turn on them as well, landing telling blows. When calm was finally restored, Joseph was unable to sit or stand without support. He had to have help—most likely from his father and Hyrum—to reach his own home less than a mile away. He complained about pain in his side, possibly meaning that William had broken, rebroken, or severely bruised some ribs that had been injured during the tar-and-feathering attack in 1832. The next day Joseph reported that he was "at home—quite unwell."[31]

William's animosity toward Joseph went back at least as far as their teens. While the rest of the family universally accepted Joseph's prophetic calling and prominent position in the family, William sometimes resented his older brother and the deference his parents paid him. In later years, William acknowledged that his rather carefree, irreligious youth had elicited frequent lectures from his brother Joseph. Given that he already found the family's religious devotions irritating, William must have experienced his brother's lectures as bossy and preachy.[32] It was also not the first time the brothers had scuffled, and certainly not the first time William had acted disrespectfully toward his older brother. Benjamin F. Johnson recorded another episode that had occurred, apparently at an earlier date during or just after a meeting held in Kirtland, but after the brothers had reached adulthood. "For Insolence to him," Johnson related, "He [Joseph] Soundly Thrashed his Brother William who Boasted himself as Invinsable."[33] Ample evidence exists that both brothers prided themselves on their physical prowess, and Joseph even wrote in his letter to William after their altercation at the debate, "it may be that I cannot boast of being stronger than you."[34] But earlier episodes appear to have been more along the lines of friendly competition, where brothers tested their strength

---

30. Joseph Smith, Letter to William Smith, December 18 or 19, 1835, in Joseph Smith, Journal, December 17, 1836, in Jessee, Ashurst-McGee, and Jensen, *Journals, Vol. 1, 1832–1839*, 132–33.

31. Joseph indicated that William not only "used violence upon my person" during his outburst, but "also upon J.[ared] Carter and some others." He also referred rather vaguely to his "having once fallen into the hands of a mob, and been wounded in my side, and now into the hands of a brother, my side gave way." Joseph Smith, Letter to William Smith, December 18 or 19, 1835, in Jessee, Ashurst-McGee, and Jensen, *Journals, Vol. 1, 1832–1839*, 124. I have found no record describing the 1832 assault that included being "wounded in my side."

32. William Smith, "Notes Written on Chambers' Life of Joseph Smith," ca. 1875, LDS Church History Library, 28; *William Smith on Mormonism*, 10.

33. In Dean R. Zimmerman, ed., *I Knew the Prophets: An Analysis of the Letter of Benjamin F. Johnson to George F. Gibbs, Reporting Doctrinal Views of Joseph Smith and Brigham Young* (Bountiful, Utah: Horizon Publishers, 1976), 20.

34. Joseph Smith, Letter to William Smith, December 18 or 19, 1835, p. 133.

against one another—a recreational activity that the Smith family had engaged in for generations.[35] This episode was different. It had become personal. William had attacked Joseph in an attempt to inflict harm. "But alass!," Joseph wrote William, referring to their conflict, "abuse, anger, malice, hatred, and rage . . . with marks, of violence heaped upon me by a brother."[36] The hurts between the brothers ran deeper than any physical injury William had inflicted upon Joseph.

Though William eventually accepted his brother's prophetic calling, some of his earlier resentments appear to have been rekindled while they were serving together in the leading councils of the church. William felt annoyed that Joseph frequently got his way because of deference to his position as Church president. His brother's prominent role in the family was equally grating. It is evident from Joseph's writings that he strongly felt that he had the prerogative—even the responsibility—to reprove his younger brother for wayward behavior, both because of his ecclesiastical and also because of his birth order in their family.

During the aftermath of their conflict, Joseph asserted his position of having the "duty" to admonish William when he did wrong. In his letter to William, Joseph emphasized that it was "in the spirit of my calling and in view of the authority of the priesthood that has been conferred upon me, [that] it would be my duty to reprove whatever I esteemed to be wrong." He further elaborated that his attempt at reproving William "has been done for the express purpose of endeavouring, to warn exhort, admonish, and rescue you, from falling into difficulties, and sorrows which I foresaw you plunging into, by giving way to that wicked spirit, which you call your passions, which you should curb and break down." Finally, Joseph indicated that it was his "privilege, of reproving a younger brother," and right "to admonish you because of my birthright."[37]

This assertion of authority was difficult for William, as it might be for many younger siblings, and he often protested when Joseph reproved or disagreed with him. In contrast, Hyrum, though older than Joseph and fulfilling ecclesiastical positions that were as weighty, or weightier, than William's, seems to have accepted Joseph's superior position without resentment or resistance. On the contrary, he acknowledged and supported Joseph's demanding position. As one of Joseph's biographers concluded about these two brothers, "William Smith was almost as insecure and unsteady as Hyrum Smith was loyal and unyielding."[38] While that statement probably oversimplifies the two brothers' personalities, Joseph certainly felt that way about his elder brother and provided his own comparison of their differing personalities. When Hyrum visited Joseph two days after the debate meeting debacle, Joseph recorded in his diary: "I could pray in my heart that all my brehtren were like unto my beloved brother Hyrum, who possesses the mild-

---

35. Kyle R. Walker, *The Joseph Sr. and Lucy Mack Smith Family: A Family Process Analysis of a Nineteenth-Century Household* (Provo, Utah: BYU Studies, 2008), 82–83.
36. Joseph Smith, Letter to William Smith, December 18 or 19, 1835, p. 133.
37. Joseph Smith, Letter to William Smith, December 18 or 19, 1835.
38. Truman G. Madsen, *Joseph Smith the Prophet* (Salt Lake City: Bookcraft, 1989), 10.

Hyrum Smith, 1800–1844. Sketch by Frederick Piercy, ca. 1853, based on an earlier drawing by Sutcliffe Maudsley, in *Route from Liverpool to Great Salt Lake Valley* (Liverpool, Franklin D. Richards, 1855).

ness of a lamb and the integrity of a Job, and in short the meekness and humility of Christ, . . . for I never had occasion to rebuke him, nor he me which he declared when he left me to day." While Joseph's tribute to his brother Hyrum is well-known, most have missed the context in which it was recorded. Hyrum and Joseph had just finished discussing their younger brother and his recent misbehavior. Hyrum had been "wounded to the verry soul, with the conduct of William." The adjectives that the grateful Joseph poured out in relation to Hyrum could not have been used to describe William—"mildness," "meekness," "humility," and "integrity." Now, confronted with William's angry response to a well-deserved "rebuke," Joseph could not help finding comfort in Hyrum's assurance that he had never felt it necessary to "rebuke" him.

Joseph must have struggled for a way to heal the relationship with William and to re-establish the brotherly relationship he obviously prized. The difficulty was that their private relationship also had far-reaching and public consequences because of their ecclesiastical relationship.

It was also hard for William to stay in the background while his older brother was continually the focus of attention, both publicly in his civic and church responsibilities, as well as privately in the family. The recipient of his father's name, Joseph Jr. was the fulfillment of both family and scriptural prophecy that all the Smiths unequivocally accepted (2 Ne. 3:15; D&C 1:17, 5:9–10).[39] As Joseph explained to William in the letter he wrote following their scuffle, "I brought salvation to my fathers house, as an instrument in the hands of God, when they

---

39. For Joseph's role in fulfilling a family prophecy, according to two of his grandsons, Joseph's grandfather Asael Smith had earlier portended "that something would come forth among his posterity that would revolutionize the world," and that "he always knew that God was going to raise up some branch of his family to be a great benefit to mankind." The first statement comes from Elias Smith, eldest son of Asahel Smith Jr. Oliver R. Smith, *Journal of Jesse Nathaniel Smith* (Provo, Utah: Jesse N. Smith Family Association, 1970), 336. The second quotation is by George A. Smith, "Sketch of the Autobiography of George Albert Smith." George A. Smith, in another account, echoed the phraseology of his cousin Elias, when he indicated, "My grandfather, Asahel Smith, heard of the coming forth of the Book of Mormon, and he said it was true, for he knew that something would turn up in his family that would revolutionize the world." George A. Smith, August 2, 1857, *Journal of Discourses* 26 vols. (London and Liverpool: LDS Booksellers Depot, 1855–86), 5:102–4.

were in a miserable situation."[40] While William doubtless would have agreed with this statement, he may not have done so graciously. Now in 1835, family members once again were lining up behind Joseph. Hyrum had already defended Joseph at the brothers' meeting after the high council episode. William, still furious, searched for support, turning first to his brother Samuel, who had not been present at the debating school, and then to his brother-in-law Calvin Stoddard, but found only limited sympathy. Father and Mother Smith, concerned about Joseph's injuries as well as the rift in the family, called on him the day after the fracas at the debate meeting. He told them his version of the episode, and they agreed with him that he was not at fault. The next day, Friday, December 18, Hyrum visited Joseph Jr., and the two discussed the altercation. According to Joseph's journal, Hyrum told him that he was "perfectly satisfied, with the course I had taken . . . with him [William], in rebuking, him in his wickedness."[41]

With most of the family siding with Joseph, the cost of holding on to his anger became too great, as it left William feeling ostracized from the Church and also isolated from his family. His strong family ties propelled him toward reconciliation with his brother.[42]

William's father also played a critical role in helping bring about a resolution. He was perhaps better equipped than the rest of the family to deal with William's challenging nature, because of his earlier experience in dealing with his own volatile brother, Jesse, whose temperament resembled William's and had caused the family repeated turmoil. It was Jesse who had threatened to chase Joseph Sr. and Don Carlos out of his house with his broad axe when they had first come to introduce the Book of Mormon to the family in the fall of 1830. It was also Jesse whose siblings often described as punitive and tactless in conversation, heedlessly unleashing a violent temper that alienated him from his relatives. Notwithstanding years of hostility and animosity, Joseph Sr. felt concern about and prayed for his inconstant brother. (See Chapter 1.) All of these experiences seemed to help soften Joseph Sr.'s feelings toward his own obstinate son and give

---

40. Joseph Smith to William Smith, December 18 or 19, 1835, p. 134.

41. Joseph Smith, Journal, December 17 and 18, 1835, in ibid., 128–29.

42. Feelings of inferiority plagued William for the rest of his life. After his prophet-brother's death, he sought an authoritative position like the one Joseph had held. He desired to be patriarch "over the whole church" and hence accountable to no one. He also aspired to leadership positions under various factions of Mormonism, including those led by Brigham Young, James Strang, Joseph Smith III, and Lyman Wight. At least twice he unsuccessfully attempted to establish his own church, with himself as president, an attempt which ultimately failed. In all of these attempts, there is an attitude of inferiority and a sense of entitlement on William's part. He may have felt that, if he could achieve a position of prominence in one of these organizations, he would somehow be validated. Rudd, "William Smith," 124–53; Kyle R. Walker, "William B. Smith," in *United by Faith: The Joseph Sr. and Lucy Mack Smith Family*, ed. Kyle R. Walker (American Fork, Utah: BYU Studies and Covenant Communications, 2005), 274–91.

him a repertoire of useful behaviors in dealing with William. There were times when no one could reach William except his father. Time would reveal that while Joseph Sr. did not trust William in the same way he did his namesake son, he still loved and supported William. The bond between the two was strong, and William remained fiercely loyal to his father throughout his life. His father's love and example helped hold him in their shared faith perhaps more than any other single factor. On several occasions when William faltered in his commitment to the Church, as was the case in 1835, the consoling words and steady example of his father helped him reconcile his differences and refresh his faith.[43]

Two days after their clash, William wrote separate letters to Hyrum and Joseph Jr. confessing his faults and asking for their forgiveness. "Br. Hyrum Smith, called to see me," Joseph recorded in his journal on December 18, "and read a letter that he received from William, in which he asked, his forgivness for the abuse offered to him, at the debate."[44] William's letter to Joseph has survived in its entirety, revealing his emotional instability, conspicuous during this time of conflict, and providing insight into understanding William's psyche. Nowhere in his history were the extremes of his mood more palpable than during the winter of 1835–36. He had gone from complete denial that he had committed any wrongdoing, justifying his behavior and defiantly experiencing no remorse, to the depths of shame and self-loathing. His letter evidences his own bewilderment in how he had reached the point of violently lashing out at those around him. What he personally acknowledged in his letters in the days after the episode provides the most transparent glimpse into his own perception of his temper and personality.

Humbly and self-deprecatingly, William confessed his wrongs to Joseph. "After coming to myself and concidering upon what I have done," William wrote penitently, "I feel as though it was a duty, to make a humble confession to you for what I have done [f]or what took place the other evening." Word of the incident had spread quickly through Kirtland, including among his colleagues of the Twelve. In less than twenty-four hours after his outburst, William reported, "I was called to an account by the 12, yesterday for my conduct . . . and I went over." After citing some of his health concerns, "I told them [the Twelve] that it would be better for them to appoint one in the [Apostolic] office that would be better able to fill it, and by doing this they would throw me into the hands of the church, and leave me where I was before I was chosen." In taking this course, William indicated, "then I would not be in a situation to bring so much disgrace upon the cause, when I [fall] into temptation, and perhaps by this I might obtain salvation." William obviously felt that his apostolic calling surpassed his capacity. He did not trust himself not to repeat such behavior, and he freely confessed that he had explained this position

---

43. Jessee, Ashurst-McGee, and Jensen, *Journals, Vol. 1, 1832–1839*, 140–41; William Smith (Plymouth, Illinois), Letter to D[on]. C[arlos]. Smith, December 1, 1840, printed in *Times and Seasons* 2, no. 4 (December 15, 1840): 252–53.

44. Joseph Smith, Journal, December 18, 1835, in Jessee, Ashurst-McGee, and Jensen, *Journals, Vol. 1, 1832–1829*, 129.

during his meeting with the Twelve in his letter to Joseph. He continued his letter by begging Joseph to release him from the assignment, expressing worry that, if he remained, there might be further repercussions to himself and the Church. Referring to his temperament, William acknowledged, "You know my passions and the danger of falling from so high a station, and thus by withdrawing from the office of the apostleship . . . and remaining a member of the church . . . there is [still] salvation for me." His reference to his "passions," likely referred to his quick temper and obstinacy. He lamented sorrowfully that, if Joseph did not remove him from office, "I am a fraid it will be worse for me, by and by."[45]

In fact, it would be surprising if Joseph had not had second thoughts about his decision to put William in such a prominent calling, especially considering the misgivings of at least David Whitmer and Oliver Cowdery about William's suitability. After all, this rebelliousness had erupted only ten months after his appointment as an apostle and less than two months after a dramatic and public explosion at the high council trial. Certainly those leaders surrounding Joseph questioned the propriety of retaining William in his calling. It was a testament to their faith in Joseph's prophetic calling that they continued to support William despite their reservations. But if Joseph ever entertained any similar feelings, he never made them known. He still put confidence in his brother and faithfully upheld the appropriateness of his calling as an apostle, even though he felt strongly that William had personally wronged him.

William's letter continued on a more personal note, as he remorsefully acknowledged how his outburst had impacted the family and their sibling relationship. "Though I do not know but I have forfeited all right and title to the word brother, in consequence of what I have done," he wrote, ashamed, "for I concider myself; that I am unworthy to be called one." He then penitently sought his older brother's forgiveness:

> Do not think I am your enemy for what I have done, perhaps you may say or ask why I have not remember[ed] the good that you have done to me— When I reflect upon the ingury I have done you I must confess that I do not know what I have been about—I feel sorry for what I have done and humbly ask your forgiveness— I have not confidence as yet to come and see you for I feel ashamed of what I have done, and as I feel now I feel as though all the confessions that I could make verbally or by writing would not be sufficient to atone for the transgression— be this as it may, I am willing to make all the restitution you shall require. . . . I know Brother Joseph you are always willing to forgive. But I sometimes think when I reflect upon the many inguries I have done you I feel as though a confession was not hardly sufficient—but have mercy on me this once, and I will try to do so no more.[46]

The letter is insightful because William appears to have been fully cognizant of his misbehavior, including his stormy temper, and acknowledged actual fear at his inability to control it. Joseph refused to accept William's explanation that

---

45. William Smith (Kirtland, Ohio), Letter to Br. Joseph [Smith], December 18, 1835, in Jessee, Ashurst-McGee, and Jensen, *Journals, Vol. 1, 1832–1839*, 129–30.

46. Ibid.

anger was just part of his personality. That "which you call your passions," Joseph counseled his struggling brother, "you should curb [sic] and break down, and put under your feet, which if you do not you . . . never can be saved, in my view, in the kingdom of God." Those words must have reverberated in William's mind and caused him great consternation. Despite his efforts, William would never overcome the impulsivity of his anger, and by his mid-twenties he had already realized the depth of his struggle. He may have understood something of his personality that Joseph did not and had attempted to warn Joseph about his inability to manage his temper when he asked to be released as an apostle. It was clear that William felt the calling was simply above and beyond his emotional capacity to fulfill.

Joseph, in contrast, felt as though this desire was influenced by Satan. "You desire to remain in the church, but forsake your apostleship," wrote Joseph, "this is a stratigem of the evil one. . . but by maintaining your apostleship," he counseled, "in rising up, and making one tremendous effort, you may overcome your passions, and please God and by forsaking your apostlehip, is not to be willing, to make that sacrafice that God requires at your hand and is to incur his displeasure. . . . When a man falls one step he must regain that step again, or fall another, [and then] he has still more to gain, or eventually all is lost." Perhaps in an effort to lighten the tone of this serious interchange, Joseph penned, "and if at any [future] time you should concider me to be an imposter, for heavens sake leave me in the hands of God, and [do] not think to take vengance on me your self."[47] Joseph sought to counsel his younger brother on where he went astray and how he could prevent such actions from happening in the future, but his greatest desire was to have their conflict permanently resolved. Referring to their conflict, Joseph stated, "[It] cannot be a source of sweet reflection to you nor to me, neither to an honorable father and mother, brothers and sisters." Joseph closed his letter in the language of an invocation: "And now may God have mercy upon my father's house; may God take away enmity from between me and thee; and may all blessings be restored, and the past be forgotten forever. May humble repentance bring us both to thee, O God . . . to enjoy the society of father, mother, Alvin, Hyrum, Sophronia, Samuel, Catherine, Carlos, Lucy . . . is the prayer of your brother."[48]

Even after William's letter of confession, and notwithstanding Joseph's earlier revelation that William would return, Joseph was still troubled about his brother. The spirit in which William's letter was written must have given him increased hope that he and his brother would achieve a reconciliation, but Joseph must also have worried about how William would receive his own letter of response, which did not attempt the disguise the seriousness of the problem. William typically did not receive censure with humility, and Joseph had not shirked from describing in "plainness" where his younger brother had erred as well as laying out the

---

47. Ibid., 134.
48. Ibid.

record from his own perspective of the debate meeting. The day after sending his letter to William, Joseph recorded his apprehensiveness in his journal: "I have had many solemn feelings this day Concerning my Brothe[r] William and have prayed in my heart . . . fervently that the Lord will not cast him off but [that] he may return to the God of Jacob and magnify his apostleship and calling."[49] Though no documentation has survived, William apparently accepted Joseph's letter of correction and reconciliation with unwonted meekness.

As a new year dawned, the two brothers had apparently still not met in person, or if they had, they had at least not discussed their persisting difficulty. Joseph's New Year's resolution was clear—harmony within his family. "My heart is pained within me because of the difficulty that exists in my fathers family," Joseph wrote in his journal on January 1, 1836, and his greatest concern was resolving the division that had resulted from the clash between him and William. "I am determined that nothing on my part shall be lacking to adjust and amicably dispose of and settle all family difficulties," he further recorded.[50] William also seemed ready to reconcile. After having exchanged letters of apology two weeks earlier, the time seemed right for the brothers to meet face to face in a setting that would facilitate settling their differences.

Judging from what he recorded in his journal that morning, Joseph must have orchestrated a meeting of reconciliation for later that same day at his home in Kirtland. Father Smith was present to act as mediator, as well as Martin Harris, a close family friend from Palmyra, in helping them resolve their differences. Joseph Sr.'s role as father, and his relationship to and understanding of William, were critical. In addition, at least Hyrum, Mother Lucy Smith, Emma, and Uncle John Smith were all present to lend their assistance. There is no mention of William's wife Caroline being present, though she probably came as well, considering the meeting's significance. Father Smith led out in organizing the particulars of the gathering, meeting with the men in one room while the women withdrew to a separate room to allow some privacy in the men's discussion. Joseph Sr. began the meeting by offering a fatherly prayer and then "expressed his feelings on the occasion in a verry feeling . . . manner, even with all the sympathy of a father whose feeling[s] were wounded deeply on the account of the difficulty that was existing in the family." Joseph, who left a general account of the meeting in his diary, reported that while his father counseled the brothers, "the spirit of God rested down upon us in mighty power, and our hearts were melted." Whatever their father expressed on the occasion, both Joseph and William were in a mindset to remorsefully discuss their differences and mutually apologize. "Br. William made an humble confession and asked my forgiveness for the abuse he had offered me," related Joseph, "and wherein I had been out of the way I asked his forgiveness, and the spirit of confis-

---

49. Joseph Smith, Journal, December 19, 1835, in Jessee, Ashurst-McGee, and Jensen, *Journals, Vol. 1, 1832–1839*, 135.

50. Joseph Smith, Journal, January 1, 1836, in ibid., 140–41.

sion and forgiveness, was mutual among us all." The two brothers further "covenanted with each other in the Sight of God and the holy angels and the brethren, to strive from henceforward to build each other up in righteousness, in all things and not listen to evil reports concerning eachother, but like brethren, indeed go to eachother [sic], with our grievances in the spirit of meekness, and be reconciled and thereby promote our own happiness and the happiness of the family and in short the happiness and well being of all."

At this point in the family meeting, they called in Mother Smith, Emma, and Joseph's scribe Warren Parrish (who may have arrived late), and the brothers "repeated the covenant to them . . . while gratitude swelled our bosoms, [and] tears flowed from our ey[e]s." Joseph closed the meeting with prayer, and recorded that "it was truly a jubilee and time of rejoiceing."[51]

The resolution appears to have been effective. Joseph Jr. was overjoyed to have his brother return to full-hearted fellowship: "This day has been a day of rejoicing to me, the cloud that has been hanging over us has burst with blessings on our heads."[52] In the next few days following their meeting, William was called to account to the Church and his quorum for his misbehavior. The record suggests that William had been disfellowshipped, either for actions at the high council meeting and afterward when he voluntarily surrendered his preaching license, or for his heated outburst at the debate meeting—perhaps for both. On January 2, Elder Orson Johnson brought charges against William of "unchristian like conduct in speaking disrespectfully of President Joseph Smith Junr. and the revelations & commandments given through him [and] for attempting to inflict personal violence" on him. Six of his colleagues of the Twelve sat in judgment on William that day, and although Joseph was present, he apparently excused himself from presiding. The minutes record that "Elder Wm. Smith then arose and asked permission to speak. He then in the spirit of meekness and humility confessed the charges preferred against him by Elder Orson Johnson and asked forgiveness of the Presidency & council and the whole congregation present." A vote was then called for and "the council and congregation to raise hands if they were satisfied with his confession, which they did with apparent cheerfulness & with united consent."[53] Resolving his differences with his quorum members, William began again to magnify his ecclesiastical assignments.

After more than two months of turmoil, William had finally taken responsibility for his behavior. Regrettably, he had had to hit rock bottom before he finally acknowledged his mistakes, and it is possible to read in the extant records both hopefulness and enduring wariness on the part of those around him. His prophet-brother saw the underlying cause as primarily an issue of pride and had

---

51. Joseph Smith, Journal, January 1, 1836, in ibid.
52. Joseph Smith, Journal, January 3, 1836, in ibid., 141.
53. Minute Book 1, December 29, 1835, and January 2, 1836, 134–35. Members of the Twelve who participated in William's Church trial included Brigham Young, Heber C. Kimball, David W. Patten, Thomas B. Marsh, William E. McLellin, and Parley P. Pratt.

confidence that, if his brother would simply turn to the Lord in faith and humility, he would have the ability to overcome his weakness. While pride may have been a critical element of William's personal struggle, it is not a full explanation. His emotional instability was an integral part of his disposition, much as it appears to have been for his uncle Jesse. At least for a time in the aftermath of this conflict with Joseph Jr., William sensed his fundamental lack of self-control. Psychologically speaking, it seems likely that he had a vision of his own helplessness in the throes of passion that left him aghast. Certainly his letter to Joseph communicates a sense of near-despair that likely explains why he volunteered to withdraw from his apostolic quorum. Perhaps William had proposed the best course for himself when he requested in his letter to Joseph to simply let him remain as an ordinary member of the Church. "Leave me where I was before I was chosen [to the Twelve]," he pled to both his brother and the Twelve. William simply did not possess the emotional stability to lead. Rarely would he manifest this level of insight again. It is a manifestation of Joseph's hopefulness that he fully encouraged and supported his brother continuing in his calling.

For the rest of William's long life, he lapsed into inappropriate responses when a Church leader corrected him or when he encountered opposition either from those in or outside the Church. It was a dangerous combination for someone in such a high-ranking ecclesiastical position. Though Joseph and William would never experience this level of conflict again, William's colleagues in the Church hierarchy would remain wary and distrustful of the Prophet's younger brother.

Chapter 7

A Season in Zion, 1836–39

> Wm Smith one of the twelve saw a vision of the Twelve & Seven in council together in old England & prophecied that a great work would be done by them in the old co[u]ntries & God was already beginning to work in the hearts of the p[e]ople.
> —Joseph Smith Jr., 1836

After reconciling with Joseph and experiencing the emotional relief of feeling at harmony once more with his family, William began the year 1836 by having to account for his actions over the previous two months. On January 2, he made his confession before the Kirtland High Council, which included six members of the Twelve and other leaders who had gathered on that occasion. After making a full and satisfactory confession, the minutes record that "he also covenant[ed] to make confession before the church."[1] That step was certainly necessary considering how public his disagreement was with Joseph. The day after his confession to the high council, on Sunday, January 3, no doubt at the regular preaching service, "Br William Smith made his confession to the Church to their satisfaction, and was cordially received into fellowship again." Perhaps at Joseph's encouragement and to evince a spirit of harmony with his brethren, "br[other] William gave out an appointment to preach in the evening."[2] It was the first time he had delivered a public sermon in more than three months. The group likely met in the Kirtland Temple, which was entering its final phase of construction, and whose main rooms were already being used for Sunday services.[3] At dusk that evening, illuminated by candlelight, William's gift of oration was on full display, and the significance of the moment was not lost on Joseph. He recorded that William "preach[e]d a fine discourse," causing Joseph to summarize the day as one of "rejoicing . . . and I thank my heavenly father for, the union and harmony which now prevails in the Church."[4]

---

1. Minute Book 1, January 2, 1836 (Kirtland, Ohio), 135, item #7702, LDS Church History Library.

2. Joseph Smith, Journal, January 3, 1836, in Dean C. Jessee, Mark Ashurst-McGee, and Richard L. Jensen, eds., *Journals, Vol. 1: 1832–1839*, The Joseph Smith Papers, general editors Dean C. Jessee, Ronald K. Esplin, and Richard Lyman Bushman (Salt Lake City: Church Historian's Press, 2008), 142.

3. Elwin C. Robison, *The First Mormon Temple: Design, Construction, and Historic Context of the Kirtland Temple* (Provo, Utah: Brigham Young University Press, 1997), 79.

4. Joseph Smith, Journal, January 3, 1836, in Jessee, Ashurst-McGee, and Jensen, *Journals, Vol. 1: 1832–1839*, 142.

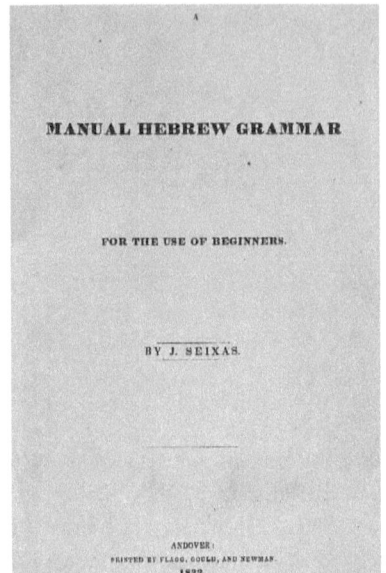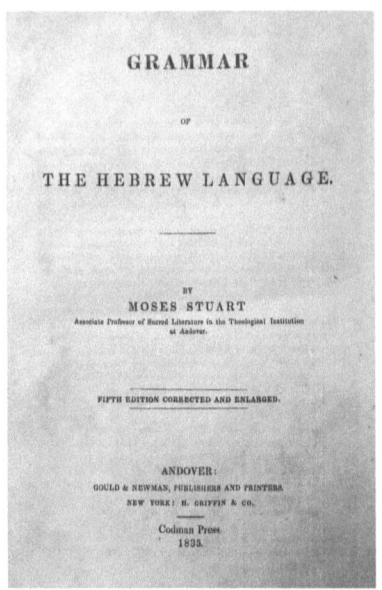

Two Hebrew texts used in the "School of the Prophets." Joshua Seixas's *A Manual of Hebrew Grammar for the Use of Beginners* (Andover, Mass.: Flagg, Gould and Newman, 1833), and Moses Stuart's *A Grammar of the Hebrew Language* (New York: H. Griffin & Co., 1835).

It had been an emotional and embarrassing time period for William, and both he and Joseph were relieved to have the episode behind them. William resumed his duties as one of the Twelve, including participating with his colleagues in the "School of the Prophets"; and by early January, the school's participants, anticipated studying Hebrew. The group had, some months earlier, obtained Hebrew textbooks, which Joseph had begun to study on his own during that winter but then arranged with Hebrew scholar Joshua Seixas, who taught at nearby Oberlin College, to lead the school at Kirtland. Seixas had recently published two editions of his Hebrew grammar text, *A Manual of Hebrew Grammar for the Use of Beginners*. While they waited for Seixas to assume his post, Joseph was elected to teach the class, beginning on January 4, 1836. The Hebrew School began meeting daily except for Sundays and continued that intensive schedule until Seixas began his instruction on January 26.[5] "I attended the school of the prophets this winter and studied Hebrew, under Mr. Sexius [sic] a celebrated teacher of that language," William recalled. He relished the opportunities to improve his education that

---

5. D. Kelly Ogden, "The Kirtland Hebrew School (1835–36)," in Milton V. Backman Jr., ed., *Regional Studies in Latter-day Saint Church History: Ohio* (Provo, Utah: BYU Department of Church History and Doctrine, 1990), 64–71. See also the almost daily entries regarding the Hebrew School in Joseph Smith, Journal, January 4–March 29, 1836, in Jessee, Ashurst-McGee, and Jensen, *Journals, Vol. 1. 1832–1839*, 143–211.

the Church's stay in Ohio offered. He recalled, probably over-optimistically, that "about eight hundred of the members of the Church were his [Seixas's] students during that winter and a large number of them became Hebrew scholars."[6]

However, William's participation in the school was short-lived "owing to some trouble between me and the teacher." William blamed Seixas, claiming that he had "talked against the Church." Reflecting on this episode in later years, his memory is tinged with regret: "I did not attain as great proficiency as I otherwise would have done."[7] But he did not regret the firm stand he had taken. Joseph spent the afternoon of February 26 settling "som[e] misunderstanding between Br. Wm Smith and professor Seixas." William was apparently the only student who had such a conflict, suggesting that his own brashness or oversensitivity may have been contributing factors. While Seixas also had some "misunderstanding" with his students over the sale of Bibles on one occasion, William was apparently the only individual who clashed with him over doctrine. That same month, when Joseph had his own discussion with Seixas and "related to him some of the dealings of God to me—& gave him some of the evidences of the work of the latter days," the Jewish scholar "list[e]ned candidly & did not oppose."[8] Despite the settling of the disagreement, William must have retained a grudge against Seixas, for he refused to continue with his Hebrew studies.

Instead, William focused his energies on the completion of the temple. Toward the end of his life, he reflected on the events connected with the House of the Lord in a sermon he preached there in 1883, at a conference of the RLDS Church. "God told Joseph to build a Temple," William recollected, "but how could he do it without money?" William indicated that the Saints forged ahead anyway, and "they laid the corner stone. Here was a man who would give a day's work. There was a sister who would knit a pair of stockings, and give them to the man who worked on the Temple. They were few and poor."[9] Reflecting on the amount of work it took to build the temple, he personally remembered, "I

---

6. Ogden, "The Kirtland Hebrew School (1835–36)," 77, identifies 115 students who participated in the Hebrew School, commenting, "There were undoubtedly more [who participated], but this number is the best estimate, far below the eight hundred recorded by William Smith."

7. William Smith, *William Smith on Mormonism*, 23; hereafter cited as *William Smith on Mormonism*. Relying on his memory, William mistakenly dated Joshua Seixas's teaching in Kirtland as 1834, but Joseph Smith's contemporary record dates Seixas's arrival in Kirtland on January 26, 1836. Jessee, Ashurst-McGee, and Jensen, *Journals, Vol. 1, 1832–1839*, 173.

8. The dispute between William and Seixas likely occurred on February 26, 1836, when Joseph recorded on that date that he helped settle the misunderstanding between William and Seixas. Thus, William attended the Hebrew School under Seixas's tutelage for exactly one month, from January 26 to February 26, 1836. Joseph Smith, Journal, February 1, February 26, and March 3, 1836, in Jessee, Ashurst-McGee, and Jensen, *Journals, Vol. 1, 1832–1839*, 179, 190–91.

9. "William B. Smith: Experience and Testimony," *Saints' Herald* 30, no. 24 (June 16, 1883): 6.

carried the stone and mortar that put these walls together," and used "my utmost endeavors to accomplish this work, and obtain means for building the temple."[10] The way the temple rose in just a few short years in spite of the poverty of the Church was as remarkable to William as it was to those residents of Geauga County, who witnessed Mormonism blossom before their eyes in the six years since the Saints first arrived.

Later in life William remembered that the Saints had been "promised an endowment of the power of God" in connection with the completion of the temple, as a reward for "their industry and sacrifice incurred and undergone on account of the building of the temple." He further described the endowment as "simply an outpouring of the Spirit, the same as on the day of Pentecost, [or] something similar," and that hope was "something generally expected and talked of."[11] William participated in numerous meetings held during the early months of 1836 preceding the temple's dedication. During that Pentecostal season, beginning in late January 1836, William received several extraordinary spiritual experiences, described in the record as "visions." Beginning on January 22, William participated with other members of his quorum on the top floor of the Kirtland Temple in receiving his washings and anointings, sanctifying prerequisites to being endowed with power from on high in the House of the Lord. A day earlier when Joseph began administering these sacred ceremonies, he had seen in vision his elder brother Alvin (who had not been baptized) and his parents (who were still living) saved in the celestial kingdom. Joseph undoubtedly would have shared such a significant spiritual experience with William when they met the following day, one which would have brought great comfort to the entire family. Although the principle of proxy baptism for the dead had not yet been restored, this vision countered the unsettling funeral sermon preached by Reverend Benjamin Stockton intimating that the unbaptized Alvin had gone to hell.[12] The spiritual outpouring continued that following day, when William joined with other members of the Twelve for their anointings. While encircled together, fellow Apostle Heber C. Kimball re-

---

10. *Cleveland Herald* report reproduced in "General Conference," *Saints' Herald* 30, no. 16 (April 21, 1883): 242; *William Smith on Mormonism*, 22.

11. "William B. Smith: Experience and Testimony," 6; William Smith, Testimony, *The Temple Lot Case* (Lamoni, Iowa: Herald Publishing House and Bindery, 1893), 103.

12. Joseph Smith, Journal, January 21–22, 1836, in Jessee, Ashurst-McGee, and Jensen, *Journals, Vol. 1, 1832–1839*, 168, 171. This news must have been especially comforting to William, who, later in life, was the only family member on record who recounted how his father would not join the Presbyterians as a result of Stockton's funeral sermon. Said William, "He [Joseph Sr.] did not like it [Presbyterianism] because a Rev. Stockton had preached my brother's funeral sermon and intimated very strongly that he had gone to hell, for Alvin was not a church member, but he was a good boy and my father did not like it." "Wm B. Smith's Last Statement," *Zion's Ensign* 5, no. 3 (January 13, 1894): 6.

ported seeing that the apostle "John stood in their midst."[13] It is unknown whether William shared Kimball's vision, but he was least privy to the spiritual occurrences that were frequently part of these sacred gatherings. A week later, when the quorums of Twelve and Seventy met again in the temple to have their anointings sealed, William received his first of several divine manifestations. "Wm Smith one of the Twelve saw the h[e]avens op[e]ned," described a participant, "& the Lords host protecting the Lords anointed." During the same meeting, others, including Joseph Jr. and Zebedee Coltrin, saw Jesus Christ in an open vision.[14]

In a subsequent anointing meeting held on Saturday, February 6, Joseph instructed the Twelve and Seventy to engage in "solemn prayer," and if any "obtain a prophecy or vision to rise & speak that all may be edefied [sic] & rejoice together." During the reverent ceremony that followed, William arose and proclaimed that he "saw a vision of the Twelve & Seven in council together in old England & prophecied that a great work would be done by them in the old co[u]ntries & God was already beginning to work in the hearts of the p[e]ople."[15] While the Twelve had thought of fulfilling Christ's post-resurrection direction to the apostles to take the gospel to the entire world, including the "islands of the seas," William's prophecy was the earliest reference specifically foreshadowing missionary work in the British Isles.

His inspired declaration may even have planted the idea in the mind of his brother, who listened absorbedly to this detailed prophecy and ensured that it was carefully recorded in his history. The following year the Prophet commissioned his first group of missionaries to cross the Atlantic to England. Though William's vision was a remarkably accurate portrayal of what would shortly come to pass, ironically, he would not accompany the other members of the Twelve who later filled that mission.[16]

---

13. Minutes of the School of the Prophets, Provo, Utah, 1868–71, May 18, 1868, 39, MSS 7989, L. Tom Perry Special Collections, Harold B. Lee Library, Brigham Young University, Provo, Utah.

14. Joseph Smith, Journal, January 28, 1836, in Jessee, Ashurst-McGee, and Jensen, *Journals, Vol. 1, 1832–1839*, 174–75, 175 note 343.

15. Joseph Smith, Journal, February 6, 1836, in ibid., 181–82.

16. Ibid.; James B. Allen, Ronald K. Esplin, and David J. Whittaker, *Men with a Mission: The Quorum of the Twelve Apostles in the British Isles* (Salt Lake City: Deseret Book, 1992), 22–28. For the Twelve's commission to preach on "the islands of the seas," see the patriarchal blessings of Orson Hyde, December 29, 1835, and George A. Smith, May 31, 1835, both bestowed by Joseph Smith Sr., reproduced in Michael H. Marquardt, ed., *Early Patriarchal Blessings of the Church of Jesus Christ of Latter-day Saints* (Salt Lake City: Smith-Pettit Foundation, 2007), 30–31, 59. While there are many references regarding the Twelve's commission to take the gospel to all nations, William's prophecy is the earliest reference I can document that specifically mentions missionary work in the British Isles. Two months after William uttered this prophecy, in April 1836, Heber C. Kimball blessed Parley P. Pratt to "go to Upper Canada, even to the city of Toronto, the capital, and there thou shalt find a people prepared for the fulness of the gospel . . . [and] out of this mission, shall the fulness of the gospel spread

Kirtland Temple. Engraving by unknown artist, lithograph published by Henry Howe, *Historical Collections of Ohio* (Cincinnati: Derby, Bradley & Co., 1847).

During the temple's dedication, and during the sacred ceremonies surrounding it, William felt that the Saints were more than rewarded for their sacrifices, and William held vivid memories of what transpired during those months for the rest of his life.[17] On March 27, William participated in the first dedicatory services of the Kirtland Temple. Joseph summarized the feelings of the Saints generally by indicating that the meetings leading up to and including the temple dedication, were "a time of rejoicing long to be remembered!"[18] Three days later, on March 30, William participated in another meeting, held "in the upper story [of the temple]," where he took part in the ordinance of the "washing of feet," similar to Jesus's ministry to his disciples as recorded in the New Testament. All of the quorums of the priesthood met on that historic occasion, and "they [the First Presidency] girded themselves and washed each other's feet in love," remembered William. "There was the washing of the body also and the annointing with oil to represent that the servants had been set apart to the service of God."[19] After the Twelve were washed, they participated in washing the feet of those in the other quorums of the priesthood. Many lingered all day and into the night: "the brethren continued exhorting, prophesying and speaking in tongues until 5 o clock in the morning—the Saviour made his appearance to some, while angels ministered unto others, and it was a penticost and enduement [endowment] indeed, long to be remembered."[20]

---

into England, and cause a great work to be done in that land." Parley P. Pratt [Jr.], ed., *The Autobiography of Parley Parker Pratt, One of the Twelve Apostles of the Church of Jesus Christ of Latter-day Saints, Embracing His Life, Ministry and Travels, with Extracts, in Prose and Verse, from His Miscellaneous Writings* (1874; rpt., Salt Lake City: Deseret Book, 1985 printing), 109–10. See Chapters 8–9 for additional details about why William did not serve with other members of the Twelve on their historic mission to the British Isles.

17. "General Conference," *Saints' Herald* 30, no. 16 (April 21, 1883): 242. William reflected on his earlier experiences associated with the temple's dedication when he returned to Kirtland in April 1883 as a part of the RLDS general conference. (See Chapter 20.)

18. Joseph Smith, Journal, February 6, 1836, in Jessee, Ashurst-McGee, and Jensen, *Journals, Vol. 1, 1832–1839*, 181–82.

19. "William B. Smith: Experience and Testimony," 6.

20. Joseph Smith, Journal, March 30, 1836, in Jessee, Ashurst-McGee, and Jensen, *Journals, Vol. 1, 1832–1839*, 213–16.

The spiritual climax represented by the temple dedication during that eventful year quickly collapsed into worry, crushing poverty, and internal recriminations. The following year, 1837, found the Church-sponsored Kirtland Safety Society Bank plunging toward bankruptcy.[21] Many, including most members of the Smith family, lost money when it eventually collapsed. William apparently did not personally have money to invest, but his parents and several brothers and sisters did.[22] Questions arose among some of Mormonism's unseasoned leaders regarding the scope of Joseph Smith's authority, including some of William's colleagues in the recently established Quorum of Twelve Apostles.

Several historians have highlighted the challenges William's quorum experienced from the time they were called, but more especially during this critical juncture in the Church's history. "Though they [the Twelve] shared important experiences on a mission in the East in 1835 and, after some difficulties, pulled themselves together to receive vital blessings in the Kirtland Temple in 1836, the Quorum seldom functioned unitedly," note James B. Allen, Ronald K. Esplin, and David J. Whittaker, in their careful reconstruction of the apostolic missions in Great Britain. "Relatively young and inexperienced as leaders, some had difficulty reconciling differences between the revealed promise of prominent positions and the reality of their role in Kirtland. Their president, Thomas B. Marsh, an officious leader overly concerned with prerogative, set a tone that made it difficult for the Twelve to grow easily into their new roles."[23] Thus, when challenges subsequently arose associated with the failed banking venture, questions also surfaced about Joseph's competence in temporal matters, and many stumbled in their loyalty. Among the apostles who openly rebelled against Joseph's leadership were John F. Boynton and Lyman Johnson. William, in contrast, remained devoted to his brother throughout this unsettled period of the Church's short history.

Furthermore, during a meeting in the temple in 1837, William's father accused Warren Parrish from the pulpit of mismanaging funds connected with the Kirtland Safety Society Bank. Parrish, who was in the audience, had become a leader of a splinter group in Kirtland. Furious at this public accusation, Parrish tried to drag the Church's patriarch from the stand. William instantly came to his father's rescue. Lucy watched horrified as William spontaneously "sprang from his seat and caught Pa[r]rish in his arms and carried him half way across the house," intending to eject him from the premises. However, in a surprise move, fellow Apostle John F. Boynton turned on William, drew a sword from his cane

---

21. Mark Lyman Staker, *Hearken, O Ye People: The Historical Setting of Joseph Smith's Ohio Revelations* (Salt Lake City: Greg Kofford Books, 2009), 463–548, for a summary of the Kirtland Safety Society banking venture.

22. Marvin S. Hill, C. Keith Rooker, and Larry T. Wimmer, "The Kirtland Economy Revisited: A Market of Critique of Sectarian Economics," *BYU Studies* 17, no. 4 (Summer 1977): 469–70. Joseph Sr., Lucy Mack Smith, Hyrum, Sophronia, Joseph Jr., Samuel, and Katharine are all listed as having invested in the Kirtland Safety Society Bank.

23. Allen, Esplin, and Whittaker, *Men with a Mission*, 22.

and put it to William's chest, warning, "If you advance one step further, I will run you through." Several others surrounded William, and threatened to "handle him severely" if he should touch Parrish again. Significantly outnumbered and confronting such immediate threats, William wisely backed down, limiting his actions to taking his shaken father to safety.[24] This confrontation between two members of the Twelve, who had served closely together in their quorum, and labored as missionaries as far back as 1832, reflected the turmoil of what transpired in Kirtland that season.

William would continue to defend his family as hostilities increased in and around Kirtland. He also occasionally served as Joseph's bodyguard. Once Brigham Young was Church president in Utah, his attitude toward William was derisive, but there were times when he gave William his due in his recollections. During the summer of 1837 when Joseph was returning from Monroe, Michigan, where he had attempted to rescue the Church from its financial difficulties by forming a joint venture with a Michigan bank, Young heard a rumor that some of the disenchanted Saints planned to ambush the Prophet on the road. Brigham and William procured a horse and buggy and drove out to intercept Joseph before he reached Kirtland. They succeeded and, at Joseph's request, William took his place in the stagecoach, while Young whisked Joseph away in the buggy. The stratagem proved successful, and Joseph reached his home safely.[25]

By the end of the year, Kirtland had become hazardous for loyal Saints. Always at the center of persecution, the Smith family experienced more than their share of harassment. In January 1838, Joseph and Sidney Rigdon fled from the city, closely followed by Emma and Phoebe, bringing what household goods they could salvage and their children. Joseph Sr., Lucy, and the rest of the family planned to follow as soon as spring made travel less arduous. This new uprooting would be particularly difficult for William and Caroline, as William owned a beautiful home near the temple and had invested his limited funds in local real estate. Moving would mean leaving everything behind. The extended Smith family had already lost their savings in the collapse of the Kirtland Safety Society Bank.

Caroline had given birth to their second daughter, named Caroline Louisa, in August 1836.[26] Mother Caroline was already experiencing the health problems that would carry her off in 1845, and William must have dreaded the consequences on her health of their departure from Kirtland. Added to the rigors of travel would be caring for baby Caroline, now a toddler, and four-year-old Mary Jane.

---

24. Lavina Fielding Anderson, ed., *Lucy's Book: A Critical Edition of Lucy Mack Smith's Family Memoir* (Salt Lake City: Signature Books, 2001), 597–98; Lucy Mack Smith, *Biographical Sketches of Joseph Smith and His Progenitors for Many Generations* (Liverpool: S. W. Richards, 1853), 211.

25. Elden J. Watson, ed., *Manuscript History of Brigham Young, 1801–1844* (Salt Lake City: Smith Secretarial Service, 1968), 17.

26. Lucy Mack Smith, *Biographical Sketches*, 43.

Joseph Sr., aware of threats against his life, quietly left Kirtland ahead of the rest of the family, traveling southeast some fifty miles to escape his antagonists. He had been targeted for performing marriages without a license, but he was aided in his escape by some of those most outspoken against his son, perhaps a tribute to the veneration in which they still held the aging patriarch. Joseph Sr. eventually reached New Portage, Ohio, which had been home to one of the largest branches of the Church in the early 1830s. Fearing for his safety, the family sent William after his father to ensure that he was safe and had enough to subsist upon. William, who was familiar with the locale, found his father at the home of Edwin D. Woolley in nearby East Rochester, Ohio, in good health, but concerned about his family's security. Woolley was investigating Mormonism and was elated to become acquainted with both the patriarch and an apostle. William reassured his father about his loved ones, and the two discussed plans for the safe departure of their families from the state.[27]

When some of the citizens in the area discovered that William was in town, they invited him to preach. The influence of the Mormons in the area had piqued residents' curiosity, and William expressed his willingness to deliver a Mormon sermon. Some individuals, however, were decidedly opposed to providing a forum for Mormon preaching in their community and threatened to tar and feather William if he made the attempt. One of these, a Mr. Bear, was "a man of unusual size and strength." Not intimidated by these threats, William delivered a persuasive sermon on "The Poor Deluded Mormons." "The singularity of this text excited their curiosity," Mother Smith recalled in her history, "and they stopped in the doorway, saying, wait a little, let us see what he will do with his text; and they waited so long, that they either forgot what they came for, or changed their minds, for they made no further moves towards using their tar and feathers." Mr. Bear, in fact, was so overcome by William's sermon that he "frankly acknowledged his conviction of the truth, and was baptized."[28] Additionally, the influence of Joseph Sr. and William assisted in removing some of Edwin

---

27. Ibid., 216–18; Leonard J. Arrington, *From Quaker to Latter-day Saint: Bishop Edwin D. Woolley* (Salt Lake City: Deseret Book, 1976), 64–65. William had traveled through the area surrounding New Portage several years earlier as part of Zion's Camp. See also Keith W. Perkins and Donald Q. Cannon, *Ohio and Illinois*, Vol. 3 in SACRED PLACES: A COMPREHENSIVE GUIDE TO EARLY LDS HISTORICAL SITES, LaMar C. Berrett, general series editor (Salt Lake City: Deseret Book, 2002), 74–75.

28. Lucy Mack Smith, *Biographical Sketches*, 217–18. Early LDS historians thought this individual was "John Bear," but Bear, a member of the Church who came west, indicated that he was not the individual mentioned in Lucy's account. Possibly another "Mr. Bear" converted during this time or, given the vagaries of nineteenth-century spelling and pronunciation, the name could have been Baer, Berr, Barr, or another variant. See Anderson, *Lucy's Book*, 622 note 248.

Woolley's remaining reservations, and future apostle Erastus Snow performed Woolley's baptism that same winter.[29]

William's skills in oratory had improved during his years in Kirtland due to his many opportunities to preach as a missionary and his association with many of the leading brethren of the Church. His public speaking abilities were further honed by his participation in the short-lived debating school, the School of the Prophets, and the Hebrew school during his stay in Ohio. He continued to polish his speaking style in the ensuing years, as he fulfilled various Church assignments and received instruction from leaders who were better educated than himself. Relatives, Latter-day Saints, and non-Mormons alike described him as a forceful and powerful speaker, and he reportedly enjoyed much success because of his persuasive preaching ability.[30]

Leaving his father temporarily in New Portage, William returned to Kirtland that winter, packed up the family's belongings, and made necessary preparations for the upcoming move. In the summer of 1838, William and Caroline set out for Missouri with all of the Smith family but Joseph and Hyrum, who had gone on ahead.[31] They traveled separately from the larger Kirtland Camp that left two months later.[32] According to Lewis Robbins, who was William's same age and had been baptized a Mormon in 1832, the group was led by William's brother Don Carlos, five years William's junior. Robbins also said that seven families made up their migrating group. In addition to the Robbins family, they included the families of Joseph Sr. and Lucy (which included their daughter Lucy, who turned seventeen that summer), William and Sophronia McCleary, William and Caroline Smith, Jenkins and Katharine Salisbury, Don Carlos and Agnes Smith, and Margaret L. Singley. William and Lewis became fast friends during this trying journey and would later labor together in the East.[33]

They began their journey on May 7, 1838, with seven wagons, fifteen horses, two cows, and seventy-five dollars in cash, but the trip was fraught with challenges, especially financial strictures. Near Terre Haute, Indiana, Don Carlos wrote

---

29. Arrington, *From Quaker to Latter-day Saint*, 64–65.

30. "Episodes in Genealogical Research: New Light on William Smith," *Deseret News*, July 27, 1935, 8; Richard P. Howard, ed., *The Memoirs of President Joseph Smith III (1832–1914)* (Independence: Herald Publishing House, 1979), 185; "Conference Minutes," *Times and Seasons* 2, no. 9 (March 1, 1841): 338.

31. Joseph had left in January, as noted above, and Hyrum said, "I left Kirtland, Ohio, the beginning of March 1838, with a family consisting of ten individuals . . . . I arrived with my family in Far West [Missouri], the latter part of May." Hyrum Smith (Commerce [Nauvoo], Ill.), Letter to the Saints Scattered Abroad, December 1839, *Times and Seasons* 1, no. 2 (December 1839): 21.

32. Lucy Mack Smith, *Biographical Sketches*, 219–21.

33. Lewis Robbins, Autobiographical sketch, circa 1845, 4, MS 18637, LDS Church History Library. William frequently called on Robbins, a friend, to help him with personal and business matters after William left Nauvoo in the fall of 1845.

to his brother Joseph at Far West, reporting that they had already been forced to sell the cows. They also "camped out at night, notwithstanding the rain and cold" because they could not afford to pay for shelter at wayside lodgings. In addition, Agnes was "very feeble [and] Father & Mother are not well." Even though the weather in May should have made for pleasant traveling conditions, Don Carlos wrote that "we have had unaccountable bad roads, had our horses down in the mud, and broke of[f] one wagon tongue . . . and broke down the carriage twice." Despite these difficult circumstances, Don Carlos's faith and optimism remained strong. After summarizing the challenges of the journey, he concluded, "Poverty is a heavy load but we are all obliged to welter under it, . . . [and] may the Lord bless you all and bring us together is my prayer."[34]

William was frequently called on to preach during the migration, but he eventually had to decline such invitations since they were delaying the family's need to complete the journey. Mother Smith was ill most of the way as they encountered torrential rainstorms, and William's sister Katharine was in the late stages of pregnancy. The group was forced to split up, probably after arriving at the Mississippi River, as Mother Smith's illness became acute and Katharine was about to deliver her child. The group split into three for a time.

Lewis, William, and Don Carlos "went into Far West before us" where they met Joseph Jr. and Hyrum "in good health." Katharine stayed in a "negro hut," recuperating from the birth of her son, Alvin, on July 7, 1838, in the care of her older sister Sophronia, and her husband William McCleary. Joseph Sr. and Lucy traveled ahead to Huntsville, Missouri, at a "slow" pace at times "[no] more than 4 miles a day." Lucy was seriously ill, and her recuperation took "some considerable length of time." Katharine, Sophronia, and their families rejoined their parents at Huntsville, then completed the journey together.[35] Robbins said that it took him, the two Smith brothers (and presumably their families), a total of "seven weeks and three days" to complete the migration, dating their arrival in the new settlement of the Saints sometime during the week of June 22–29.[36] It appears that the rest of the family did not arrive until mid-July. William settled

---

34. Don C[arlos] Smith (Nine Miles from Terre Haute, Indiana), Letter to Bro. Joseph [Smith], n.d., in Jessee, Ashurst-McGee, and Jensen, *Journals, Vol. 1, 1832–1839*, 280–81.

35. Lucy Mack Smith, *Biographical Sketches*, 43, 219–21; Anderson, *Lucy's Book*, 626–27, 630.

36. Robbins, Autobiographical Sketch, 4, started for Far West on May 1, 1838, reaching that destination in "seven weeks and three days." However, May 1 appears to have been the date when he started from Kirtland to Norton, Ohio, where he joined the Smith family. Don Carlos Smith, Letter to Joseph Smith, n.d., in Jessee, Ashurst-McGee, and Jensen, *Journals, Vol. 1, 1832–1839*, 280–81, dates their departure from Norton on May 7, making it difficult to determine whether Robbins counted the opening date as their departure from Kirtland or from Norton.

temporarily twenty miles north of Far West, Missouri, in Daviess County, probably near Adam-ondi-Ahman.[37]

It was not the first time William had seen the Saints' promised Zion. Joseph Smith had designated Independence, Missouri, in Jackson County, as the "center place" of the Saints' Zion in 1831 and prophesied that Christ's second coming, which was imminent, would be to the temple the Saints planned to build at that location. William made several trips to the state throughout the 1830s. After the Saints were driven from Jackson County, Missouri, in 1833, Joseph Smith had organized Zion's Camp, a quasi-military expedition to help the exiled Saints regain their lands. William participated in the two-thousand-mile march during the summer of 1834 in a company led by Joseph that included their brother-in-law Jenkins Salisbury. Hyrum led a separate cohort. In later years, William recounted that he had walked to Missouri with "my knapsack on my back" and that he had "slept on the ground" for most of the journey.[38] On the way, he recalled that he frequently acted as "sentinal g[u]ard as a watch over the prophets life." In many instances, he had to stay awake all night on guard duty, an assignment made all the more trying because it occurred during the heat of summer.[39] They reached Missouri only to find that the support they were counting on from the governor would not be forthcoming and that an armed incursion into the state would be most imprudent. At this point, a cholera epidemic broke out in the camp. William was one of those who contracted the dreaded disease. However, an unnamed Mormon sister (who appears to have resided in Missouri) "took him to her house, and nursed him so faithfully [that] he soon recovered" and returned safely to Kirtland.[40] William described the difficulties associated with the trek:

> After staying with the brethren [in Missouri] three or four weeks, and finding that the Governor would not fulfill his promise, and several of our number being taken sick with the cholera and dying . . . we disbanded and made preparations for returning home. I sold a horse which I had bought, and paid my passage back to Kirtland, where I at length arrived in July, after having gone through with a very fatiguing, dangerous and difficult journey, without having accomplished the object for which we undertook the task; except to visit the brethren in Missouri, suffer a great deal of trial and trouble, and come back penniless once more.[41]

As William's description makes plain, he resented the losses he had sustained as a result of the migration. Unlike other members of his quorum who felt that the

---

37. Lucy Mack Smith, *Biographical Sketches*, 221, reports that "Samuel . . . moved to a place called Marrowbone," which was between Far West and Adam-ondi-Ahman in Daviess County and that "William had moved thirty miles in another direction." Perhaps William settled in another area before purchasing land in Daviess County.

38. *William Smith on Mormonism*, 24.

39. William Smith (Osterdock, Iowa), Letter to Bro. [Edmund L.] Kell[e]y, October 15, 1891, Community of Christ Library-Archives.

40. Lucy Mack Smith, *Biographical Sketches*, 201.

41. *William Smith on Mormonism*, 24.

experience taught them essential leadership and cooperative skills, William failed to find any purpose in Zion's Camp and, even in reflecting on the experience later, considered it a "misserable expaditon" [sic] and a disappointment.[42]

He also made two visits to northern Missouri in 1837, before moving there permanently in 1838. Perhaps he was imbued with a desire to be a part of Zion, probably sensing that the Saints' stay in Kirtland was coming to an end. Though little is known about his first visit that year, he was in Far West by early summer and, on June 3, 1837, purchased two tracts of land a mile or so southeast of the center of town. His land lay adjacent to that of Curtis Hodges and his son Amos, two converts from Erie County, Pennsylvania, whom William knew well from his earlier missionary travels through that region.[43] It is significant that William does not appear in any records kept of the councils held in Far West that summer. Subsequent accounts indicate that he was struggling with his faith for a brief time, and those weeks in Missouri seem a likely time for that personal crisis. Though he appears to have stayed true to his brother, he may well have resented the directive to relocate to Missouri and the inevitable prospect loss of his Kirtland property. Thomas B. Marsh and David W. Patten, the two senior members of William's quorum, who had been actively involved in Far West council meetings while present in Far West,[44] wrote to fellow apostle Parley P. Pratt on May 10, appointing a meeting for the Twelve to be held in Kirtland on July 24, 1837.[45] "Thomas lamented that his quorum had not maintained close contact since their 1835 mission," wrote one Marsh biographer, "and that they had not been unified in fulfilling their divine calling as special missionaries. Even more serious to Thomas was the news that some members of his quorum had fallen into apostasy."[46] Marsh certainly would have shared those concerns with William, perhaps sensing William's personal struggle, as well as informing him of the appointed meeting. Marsh hoped to curtail the early signs of disaffection, especially among those of his quorum over which he presided.

William accompanied Marsh and Patten when they left Far West for Kirtland during the month of June. If William's vacillation was not already apparent, he must have disclosed some of his misgivings about the Church during the journey.

---

42. William Smith, Letter to Edmund L. Kell[e]y, October 15, 1891.

43. John Hamer, "Mapping Mormon Settlement in Caldwell County, Missouri," *Mormon Historical Studies* 9, no. 1 (Spring 2008): 25.

44. Minute Book 2 (Far West, Missouri), entries for May 22, 28, June 11, and July 29, 1837, and January 20, February 5–9, 10, 24, March 10, 24, April 13, 1838, ID# 7235, 75–126, LDS Church History Library.

45. Thomas B. Marsh and David W. Patten (Far West, Missouri), Letter to Parley P. Pratt, May 10, 1837, LDS Church History Library, quoted in Lyndon W. Cook, "'I Have Sinned against Heaven, and Am Unworthy of Your Confidence, But I Cannot Live without a Reconciliation': Thomas B. Marsh Returns to the Church," *BYU Studies* 20, no. 4 (Summer 1980), 392–93.

46. Ibid., 392.

Several months later, at a meeting held in Far West the following spring, Patten appraised half of the Twelve "as being men of God, whom he could recommend with cheerful confidence." However, the minutes record, "he spake somewhat doubtful of William Smith from something which he had heard respecting his faith in the work." While he also mentioned five other apostles "as being men whom he could not recommend," William was mentioned first, and Patten singled him out in his remarks that day.[47] Out of Patten's list of apostles he could not recommend as faithful, only William Smith retained his membership during 1837–38.

Shortly after William returned to Kirtland, Julia Priscilla Smith, the daughter of Asahel Smith, and therefore William's first cousin, wrote to her brother Elias: "Wm has got back from Missouri and with him David Patten and T B Marsh. Soon after his r[e]turn he made a confession for past sins and expresses a determination to pursue a different course." Julia may have also pointed to his fluctuating mood as a factor in this brief period of disillusionment, when she added, "He ap[p]ears much engaged and more like Wm than for some time before."[48] Marsh's appointed meeting may have been a factor in restoring William's faith. Historian Lyndon W. Cook summarized that the "difficulties in the Quorum of the Twelve were resolved at the summer meeting in Kirtland, and Marsh's concerns relative to his quroum and their relationship to the First Presidency were satisfactorily addressed in a revelation received by Joseph Smith on 23 July 1837 (D&C 112)."[49]

At a meeting held in Kirtland on September 17, 1837, Joseph Smith and Sidney Rigdon were appointed to go to Missouri and seek out additional locations so "that there may be more stakes of Zion appointed in order that the poor might have a place to gather to."[50] They left Kirtland on September 27, 1837, accompanied by several other Church leaders, including William and Hyrum. "After the city of far west was located by the Whitmers," remembered William of their journey, "Joseph Smith—in company with Sidney Rigdon Hyrum Smith and Vincent Knights [Vinson Knight]—planed an expadition for Missoure over land with team and carri[a]ge—Vin[s]ent Knights being teamster [and] William Smith went along as Special watch gard, Rigden having horse and Buggy riding alone by himself."[51] The group held meetings along the way, and arrived in early November. During this autumn trip, William was actively involved in the business of the Church. Once in northern Missouri, the group officially designated the city of Far West, which John Whitmer and W. W. Phelps had been instrumental in settling in 1836, as the Saints' next gathering place. They conducted

---

47. Minute Book 2, April 7–8, 1838, 116.
48. Julia Priscilla Smith (Kirtland, Ohio), Letter to Elias Smith, August 1837, in Elias Smith Correspondence, 1834–39, MS 70621, LDS Church History Library; terminal punctuation added.
49. Cook, "'I Have Sinned against Heaven,'" 393.
50. Minute Book 1, September 17, 1837, 243, LDS Church History Library.
51. William Smith, Letter to Edmund L. Kell[e]y, October 15, 1891.

other Church business and helped regulate the Saints in Missouri, before leaving for Kirtland on November 10.[52]

According to William's later recollections, after permanently settling in Far West in the summer of 1838, he purchased land in Daviess County, in addition to the two tracts of land he had purchased in 1837 southeast of the temple site in Far West, where he probably intended to build a home. But his plans to construct a home on the beautiful undulating prairie never materialized. By August, William and Caroline were both so ill they were unable to care for their daughters. "We heard that William and his wife, who lived 20 miles away, were very sick," recalled Lucy Mack Smith. "Samuel was at Far West at the time and set out immediately in order to bring them to our house and in a few short days arrived there with them." William's mother was alarmed at their condition, fearing for a time that both might die. Thanks to her careful nursing, they gradually recovered.[53] The Smith parents were living in a large tavern that Joseph Jr. had purchased shortly after he had arrived. William, Caroline, and their daughters lived with Joseph Sr. and Lucy during the remainder of their time in Missouri, and William's unspecified illness was so serious that he was bedfast for more than three months.

As William began to recover under his mother's care, he experienced another vision, which was so precise in describing what afterward transpired that Lucy recorded it in her history. "While William lay sick," recounted his mother, "he had a vision & saw the mob come in [to Far West]—he said he saw them come in thousands & thousands & he said Mother you will be driven & says if I die I want you to take care of my wife [and] I want you to carry my corps[e] wherever you go."[54] Except for William's realistic apprehension that he might not survive his illness, the other elements in this premonition proved accurate. In the fall of 1838, Far West surrendered to the Missouri militia after a short siege.

With all of the Saints, William experienced his share of hardships during the Mormon-Missouri clash in the fall of 1838. At some point during the chaos of the conflict, William discovered that a member of the Missouri militia had appropriated his horse. When he later spotted the soldier riding on his horse, he seized the horse by the bridle and ordered the soldier to dismount. Though the Mormons were outnumbered and the Missourians were plundering Far West, the Missouri militiaman immediately dismounted, leaving the horse in William's powerful hands.[55] Despite recovering one horse, William suffered heavy financial losses in Missouri, a double blow considering that it came on the heels of losing considerable resources in Ohio. He later itemized what he lost to the Missourians, which included a "horse, two horse teams and waggons—one horse and Buggy,

---

52. Minute Book 2, November 6, 7, and 10, 1837, 80–86; Journal History, November 1837, 1.

53. Anderson, *Lucy's Book*, 636–39.

54. Minutes of Address, General Conference, October 8, 1845, uncatalogued holograph, Curtis E. Bolton, LDS Church History Library, quoted in ibid., 639. See also Lucy Mack Smith, *Biographical Sketches*, 225.

55. Lucy Mack Smith, *Biographical Sketches*, 253.

[and] with my family—father and mother, Paid $300, for Claim on 100–60 acres of land in Davi[es]s County, entered 80 acres of land in Cal[d]well Co. paid gold for it, at the land office—dollar and [a] quarter per acres." For the rest of his life William deeply resented leaving Missouri, "without saving a dollar of it under gov Boggs exterminization [sic] order."[56]

Following Joseph and Hyrum's arrest on November 1, 1838, William begged his father to move the family to Illinois. With his health partially restored and his vision already partially fulfilled, he felt impelled to take his family to safety. Although Joseph and Hyrum had been imprisoned with many other Mormon men, "Mr. Smith would not consent to this," recalled William's mother, "for he was in hopes that our sons would be liberated, and peace again be restored." Like so many of the Latter-day Saints, the Church's patriarch could not fathom leaving their promised Zion. "William continued to expostulate with him," Lucy recounted of their exchange, "but to no effect." Joseph Sr. "declared that he would not go away from Far West unless he was called upon to do so by revelation." "Very well," responded William tartly, "I can give you revelation." He recounted his earlier vision, assuring Joseph Sr. that "he himself knew that we would have to leave Far West." But Joseph Sr. was awaiting word from Joseph Jr., not from William. Though he loved William, his experience with his wayward son had not engendered the trust necessary to follow his advice or accept his revelations unquestioningly. However, in an attempt to pacify William, Joseph Sr. encouraged the family to begin making preparations to move so that they would be ready to go if Joseph sent word. Joseph Sr. also sent William to visit Joseph, then being held in Richmond to inquire their course. William was thus relegated to the role of messenger, a role he fulfilled grudgingly. However, he returned with the desired revelation from Joseph Jr. that his family should leave Missouri. Lucy recorded that "this [message] satisfied my husband's mind, and he was willing to remove to Illinois as soon as possible."[57]

Joseph Sr.'s rejection of his revelation stung William. He was upset that his revelation did not have equal weight as that of his brother's. Incensed with his father, he immediately took Caroline and their daughters and left for Illinois, probably in either November or early December 1838. The other apostles were planning to organize and assist the poverty-stricken Saints during the evacuation, most of which occurred in January and February 1839.[58] Despite his immature, though understandable, motivation, William's action probably spared his family the worst of the suffering endured by the Saints who crossed Missouri into Illinois two months later.

---

56. William Smith, Letter to Brother [Edmund L. Kelley], ca. 1893, Suplaiment [sic], Miscellaneous Letters, P19, fd. 49, Community of Christ Library-Archives.

57. Lucy Mack Smith, *Biographical Sketches*, 251–54; Anderson, *Lucy's Book*, 674–75, 679–80.

58. William G. Hartley, "'Almost Too Intolerable a Burthen': The Winter Exodus from Missouri, 1838–39," *Journal of Mormon History* 18, no. 2 (Fall 1992): 16–32.

William established himself in the southeastern corner of Hancock County, in Plymouth, Illinois, some thirty miles south of Nauvoo, where he set up as a tavern-keeper, and sent his team back for his parents and his siblings to use during their migration. Other than this action, William offered little support to the family and none to the body of the Saints. Instead, Don Carlos again stepped forward to lead the family on its journey to Illinois, and Samuel provided housing upon their arrival in Illinois.[59] It was other members of the Twelve who labored tirelessly to ensure that the Saints made it safely out of Missouri.

William's behavior was erratic during the months he left Missouri and tried to find new footing in Illinois. It seems likely that he was experiencing both family and ecclesiastical struggles, which, for him, were always interconnected. His father's distrust of his revelation upset him, which may have impelled him to distance himself from the Church once again. Perhaps the most puzzling feature of William's behavior as he prepared to leave Missouri was launching public tirades against Joseph who, with Hyrum, was imprisoned, facing what would almost certainly be unjust legal proceedings, and certainly in need of emotional support. William's explosiveness naturally upset other members of the Twelve, who saw it as unbecoming behavior for him, both as an apostle and as a member of the Smith family. According to Brigham Young, William "publicly expressed the hope that his brother Joseph would never get out of the hands of his enemies alive."[60] Wilford Woodruff also recorded Brigham Young's memory that William had proclaimed publicly that "Joseph Smith ought to have been hung up by the neck years ago and Dam[n] him he will get it now anyhow." According to Young, Heber C. Kimball had also been present during William's tirade, but his journal does not record anything to this effect.[61] Neither of Young's two recollections was recorded at the time, but it seems likely that time would have heightened—not moderated—Brigham's memory of them, since William was considered an enemy to the Church. Thus, they would have confirmed the public reputation of William that Brigham and other Church leaders held.

Interestingly, these two reports about William's animosity toward Joseph contradict statements he made shortly after reaching Illinois. While it is certainly possible that William was once again expressing long-standing frustrations with his prophet brother and his disagreement with some of his policies, it seems more likely to me that William was acting strategically in expressing these virulent sentiments. Those who were willing to distance themselves from Mormonism and their leaders during this period were usually not targeted by the Missouri militia.

---

59. William Smith, Letter to [Edmund L. Kelley], ca. 1893; Lucy Mack Smith, *Biographical Sketches*, 254–58.

60. Message from the Council of the Twelve, "Hearken, O Ye Latter-Day Saints, and All Ye Inhabitants of the Earth Who Wish to be Saints, to Whom this Writing Shall Come," *Millennial Star* 27 (October 21, 1865): 658.

61. Scott G. Kenney, ed., *Wilford Woodruff's Journal, 1833–1898*, typescript, 9 vols. (Midvale, Utah: Signature Books, 1983–84), February 13, 1859, 5:287.

For example, fellow apostle William McLellin joined the Missouri militia for a time, and Orson Hyde and Thomas B. Marsh signed an affidavit remonstrating against Joseph Smith. Thus, William's outburst was likely an attempt to protect himself, his ailing wife, and his little daughters from having Missouri militia strip them of their goods and even imprison him. Samuel had already made his escape during the opening hours of the siege of Far West, and Don Carlos, who was not an apostle, had been out of the state on a fund-raising mission until December 25, and seems to have eluded the Missourians' wrath.[62] But William's situation was more precarious due to his ecclesiastical position.

Further evidence that his rash statements, assuming that they were remembered and recorded accurately, did not represent his true feelings was a note that he wrote to Hyrum and Joseph in March 1839, three months after they had been incarcerated in Liberty Jail and some five months after William left Missouri. William added a short postscript to his brother Don Carlos's letter. Said William:

> I should have called down to Liberty to have seen you, had it not been for the multiplicity of business that was on my hands & again I thought perhaps that the people might think that the Mormons would rise up to liberate you; consequently too many going to see you might make it worse for you; but we all long to see you, and have you come out of that lonesome place. I hope you will be permitted to come to your families before long, do not worry about them, for they will be taken care of; all we can do will be done, further than this we can only wish, hope, desire, and pray for your deliverance.[63]

Although, in retrospect, it is easy to read this letter as William's excuse for not having given a visit to his incarcerated brothers a high priority, it also contains more positive messages. The letter expressed William's longing to be reunited with his brothers, and his concern about their welfare and that of their families. Though William apparently did little either for the Church or the extended Smith family in the absence of his brothers, the letter contains none of the bitter vindictiveness that the memories of his fellow apostles attribute to him. Considering William's ecclesiastical position, it is also understandable why he would be fearful about the possible repercussions of such a visit. Others were

---

62. Samuel was a target of the Missourians because of his involvement in both the Battle of Crooked River and the election day battle at Gallatin, Missouri. During the latter episode, he had transported a key participant, John Lowe Butler, from the scene. Dean L. Jarman and Kyle R. Walker, "Samuel Harrison Smith," and Roy B. Huff and Kyle R. Walker, "Don Carlos Smith," in *United by Faith: The Joseph Sr. and Lucy Mack Smith Family*, ed. Kyle R. Walker (American Fork, Utah: BYU Studies and Covenant Communications, 2006), 225–27, 371–74; William G. Hartley, *My Best for the Kingdom: History and Autobiography of John Lowe Butler, a Mormon Frontiersman* (Salt Lake City: Aspen Books, 1993), 58–59; Journal History, December 25, 1838, 1.

63. Don Carlos Smith and William Smith (Quincy, Ill.), Letter to Hyrum and Joseph Smith, March 6, 1839, in Joseph Smith Letterbook 2, March 6, 1839, 38–39; handwriting of James Mullholland, LDS Church History Library.

apprehensive about dangers they might experience if they were to visit Liberty Jail, including Andrew Lamoreaux, whom Joseph Sr. sent as a special messenger to Joseph and Hyrum, but who failed to fulfill the assignment.[64]

Whatever the reason for William's outburst at the time he left Missouri, by the time Joseph and Hyrum escaped—or were allowed to escape—reaching Quincy in April 1839, William's fellow apostles considered him out of harmony with the Church. This situation required him to reconcile his statements with his colleagues and account for his conduct.

Just a week or so after arriving in Illinois, Joseph Smith presided at a conference of the Church held at Quincy on May 4, 1839. Part of the business consisted of disciplining those whose behavior in Missouri was seen as disloyal and included testimony about William's conduct in Missouri. If this testimony was the first Joseph had learned about William's outburst before leaving the state, it likely left him surprised and confused, given William's supportive letter in March. Orson Hyde's case also came up at the same conference, and the ensuing discussion may have helped to soften perceptions of William. Both Hyrum Smith and Heber C. Kimball defended Hyde because they had learned of his desire to repent and to return to the Church. Joseph commented, "If my brother Hyrum and Heber C. Kimball will defend Orson Hyde, I will withdraw my motion [against him]."[65] Joseph decided that he wanted to hear personally from both William and Hyde before drawing any conclusions about their standing. In the interim, the conference resolved that "Elders Orson Hyde and William Smith be allowed the privilege of appearing personally before the next general conference of the Church, to give us an account of their conduct; and that in the meantime they be both suspended from exercising the functions of their office."[66]

William likely visited Joseph or Hyrum or both either at Quincy or Commerce (shortly to be renamed Nauvoo) during May, because, by the month's end, Joseph felt reassured about his brother's loyalty. On May 25, Joseph met in council with the Twelve, where "the case of Wm. Smith, the Prophet's brother and one of the Twelve Apostles, came up for investigation and it was decided that Elder Smith, who had been guilty of some willful and irregular conduct while in the state of Missouri, be permitted to retain his standing in the quorum of the Twelve." Wilford Woodruff, who was present as an apostle, recorded in his diary

---

64. Upon learning of Lamoreaux's failure to fulfill this assignment, Bishop Edward Partridge expressed frustration, lamenting that "when another messenger was to be sent, he would go himself, as it was hardly possible to find a man that would do as he was instructed." Lucy Mack Smith, *Biographical Sketches*, 259.

65. *President Heber C. Kimball's Journal*, SEVENTH BOOK OF THE FAITH-PROMOTING SERIES (Salt Lake City: Juvenile Instructor Office, 1882), 77.

66. Church Historian's Office, General Church Minutes, 1839–77, May 4, 1839, CR 100 318, in Richard E. Turley, ed., *Selected Collections from the Archives of the Church of Jesus Christ of Latter-day Saints*, 2 vols., DVD (Provo, Utah: Brigham Young University Press, [December 2002]), Vol. 1, disk 18.

that Church leaders spent the day receiving counsel from Joseph Smith, with the most noteworthy item being that "Brother Wm. Smith was restored to his Quroum."[67] A later account indicated that William was confirmed as a member of the Twelve through Joseph and Hyrum's interposition.[68]

Regardless of any disparaging comments William made about Joseph before leaving Missouri, the two brothers were quickly reconciled after they met in person. In June 1839 Joseph set out to visit Samuel and Don Carlos, who were living in McDonough County, near Macomb, Illinois. En route, he came across William "on the prairie." "Found him in good spirits," Joseph recounted. "Went with him to his house in Plymouth [and] found his family all well [and] staid over night." That evening Joseph and William "had a very satisfactory visit." While Joseph did not indicate whether William accompanied him, he and his party then traveled twenty miles northeast to Macomb where he visited brothers Samuel and Don Carlos.[69]

In early June Joseph requested that the Twelve relocate to Nauvoo, making it more convenient to conduct such business as directing the gathering to the newly established Church headquarters, and regulating the quorums of the priesthood after the Missouri experience.[70] Notwithstanding, William remained at Plymouth for the better part of two years from December 1838 to December 1840. Besides a second visit from Joseph in September 1839, William had only minimal contact with Church leaders at Nauvoo but likely kept apprised of Church business through travelers and through the *Times and Seasons* newspaper.[71] Even after he was received back in fellowship by the general body of the Saints at the October 1839 general conference,[72] William remained distanced from his quorum's activities. Instead, he focused his attention on his prospering hotel-tavern at Plymouth. He was weary of being driven from place to place. For the rest of his life, he felt that requiring the Saints to "gather" at a single location was a mistake—a primary reason that they had been repeatedly persecuted and driven as a people. His remaining at Plymouth was evidence of how seriously he held this view. As the remainder of his quorum departed for missions

---

67. Journal History, May 25, 1839, 1; Kenney, *Wilford Woodruff's Journal*, May 25, 1839, 1:335.

68. "History of William Smith," *Millennial Star* 27, no. 1 (January 7, 1865): 7–8.

69. Joseph Smith, Journal, June 15–17, 1839, in Jessee, Ashurst-McGee, and Jensen, *Journals, Vol. 1, 1832–1839*, 341–42.

70. *President Heber C. Kimball's Journal*, 79; Ronald K. Esplin, *The Emergence of Brigham Young and the Twelve to Mormon Leadership* (Provo, Utah: Joseph Fielding Smith Institute for Latter-day Saint History and BYU Studies, 2006), 151.

71. Joseph Smith, Journal, September 8–14, 1839, in Jessee, Ashurst-McGee, and Jensen, *Journals, Vol. 1, 1832–1839*, 351. Joseph stayed overnight with William and his family on Friday–Saturday, September 13–14, and part of the next day.

72. "Proceedings of the General Conference, held at Commerce, Hancock County, Illinois on Saturday the 5th day of October, 1839," *Times and Seasons* 1, no. 2 (December 1839): 30.

to the British Isles and Jerusalem during the summer and fall of 1839, William remained with his family at Plymouth.

Located near the southeast corner of Hancock County, Illinois, Plymouth had been formally established in January 1836, only three years before William settled there. Round Prairie, several miles to the east in Schuyler County, had been established as a permanent settlement during 1831–32, and the two small communities were closely linked. William had become familiar with the community shortly after its settlement, when he had traveled through the area on journeys to and from Missouri in 1837–38. Local residents remembered that so many of the Mormons who relocated from Ohio to Missouri had passed near their community that they had left a "well-marked and beaten road" that became known as the "Mormon Trail." This general route had, even earlier, long been traveled by various Native American tribes, whose relics were everywhere present at the time Plymouth's first settlers arrived.[73]

When William reached Plymouth in November-December 1838, his first consideration, given his family's impoverished situation, was to establish a firmer financial foundation. William recognized that the budding community afforded an opportunity for substantial growth; a railroad line that was to traverse the state was planned to run directly through the town, and was eventually completed in 1855–56.[74] It is unknown where he obtained work in the community, but he later reported that he initially engaged in some type of merchandising.[75] With the assistance of locals, who were eager to have their struggling, newfound community grow, William and other Saints were able to gain a foothold in the town.

Having been through several financial reversals, William was determined to secure a living for himself, Caroline, and their daughters. Like his father, he was an entrepreneur at heart and was attracted to the prospects of commerce. He felt that he had enough business acumen to be successful and eyed the largest and most promising business in town, a hotel built by Sevier Tadlock. Built on the town square in the same year the town was laid out, the building "answered the triple purpose of dwelling, hotel and store." The first of its kind at Plymouth, the structure was also utilized for most of the town's festivities, including public dances and Independence Day celebrations. When Tadlock hosted such events, he served refreshments, usually charging twenty-five cents a person. Word spread to neighboring communities, including Carthage, and before long, some five or six hundred people would gather for these celebrations.[76] William perceived the hotel's potential; after five months of labor, he seized an opportunity to purchase it.

On April 15, 1839, William borrowed money from local resident Benjamin Whitaker, and the next day he purchased two lots from Sevier and Melinda

---

73. E. H. Young, *A History of Round Prairie and Plymouth, 1831–1875* (Chicago: Geo. J. Titus, Book and Job Printer, 1876), 19–20, 48.
74. Ibid., 105–6.
75. Don Carlos Smith and William Smith to Hyrum and Joseph Smith, March 6, 1839.
76. Young, *A History of Round Prairie and Plymouth*, 41–42, 48.

Mormon Hotel Site, Plymouth, Illinois, ca. 1880. This structure was built on the site of William Smith's "Mormon Hotel" in 1869. An outbuilding, visible at the rear of the home, was likely part of William's original hotel property. Photograph courtesy of Virginia Metzgar.

Tadlock for $750. The hotel stood on one of these two lots (Lot 6, Block 10), situated on the corner of Franklin Street and the town square. The lots included a well, an outhouse, and an extra building where he kept farming tools. Smith described the hotel as a "double log house," which eventually he improved with siding. He then borrowed an additional sum of several hundred dollars to build a stable for the hotel patrons. Property records indicate that, in time, William purchased an adjacent lot, five more lots southeast of the town square, and ten acres—no doubt a farm—just outside of town. He estimated that his investment, including improvements, cost him approximately $2,000 and that the hotel thrived, enabling him to pay off all of his debts, except for a $200 lumber bill, in just under two years. Local residents dubbed his inn the "Mormon Hotel."[77]

William was influential in encouraging his sister Katharine and her husband, William's good comrade, Jenkins Salisbury, to also settle in Plymouth. The Salisburys purchased three lots near the town square, where Jenkins set up his blacksmith shop. In 1842, Samuel moved closer to Plymouth so that he could help manage the hotel. Other Latter-day Saints soon followed, and the influx of Mormons into the small community created quite a stir among the locals. Local historian E. H. Young estimated that nearly half the town of Plymouth in the early 1840s was Mormon—"probably 150 or more in number." Though that number may be exaggerated, in time the Mormon presence in the community had an impact. The missionary efforts of the Mormons in Plymouth during the

---

77. William Smith, Letter to Brother [Edmund L. Kelley], ca. 1893; Young, *A History of Round Prairie and Plymouth*, 64–65.

early 1840s must have found success, as the congregations established before their arrival deteriorated afterward, causing some pastors to relocate. "The Prophet himself came down occasionally and stopped with his friends," continued Young. "He sometimes manifested his love of worldly enjoyments by the spending the night participating in the sports of a merry dancing party at the hotel."[78] One of these visits occurred in the winter of 1842, when Joseph Smith and his entourage were traveling to Springfield for his trial of extradition.[79]

Although William, Samuel, and Katharine seem to have been reasonably well accepted in Plymouth, William's wrath periodically erupted against those who were antagonistic toward the Mormons. In one encounter, William taunted a "gentile" known for "his aversion to the Mormons," stating that "the prophet, Joseph Smith was not arrested yet." "Well, I am sorry for it," the man replied. Infuriated by the comment, William countered that he could "whip [the man] . . . and if he would lay his hand upon him he would do it." The man, certainly aware of Smith's stature, conceded that perhaps William could whip him, but "there is one thing you cannot do—you cannot bully me." He then walked up to William and

> laid his hand upon his shoulder; upon which Smith gave him a stinging blow that nearly upset him. Springing from the counter, Smith followed up his movement, and in the scuffle that ensued, got his head under the gentile's arm, which closed down upon his neck like a vise. His thumb accidentally got into the gentile's mouth, and that was promptly clamped. With a tremendous effort, Smith jerked away with a thumb badly skinned, and sprang out of the door, where he promised to finish the gentile if he would come out. A neighbor passing at the time, stepped between the parties and closed [the] . . . scene.[80]

For good reason, William's neighbors in Plymouth remembered his fiery temper. His interpersonal style impacted his relationships both within and outside the Church. He was not only on the periphery of Zion, but he was also barely hanging on to his fellowship in the Church. While his brethren of the Twelve launched out on their historic mission to England and beyond, William remained settled at Plymouth. The Saints were puzzled at his indifference, and his family and quorum wondered if his commitment to the cause would ever be rekindled.

---

78. Young, *A History of Round Prairie and Plymouth*, 64–65, 87, 91; Herbert S. Salisbury, "Reminiscences of Joseph Smith: As Told by His Sister, Catherine [sic] Smith Salisbury, to Her Grandson, Herbert S. Salisbury," *Saints' Herald* 60, no. 41 (October 8, 1913): 984. Samuel actually ran William's hotel for a time in 1842 before moving to the northernmost part of the prairie near Crooked Creek.

79. Joseph Smith, Journal, December 27, 1842, in *Journals, Vol. 2, December 1841–April 1843*, THE JOSEPH SMITH PAPERS, general editors Dean C. Jessee, Ronald K. Esplin, and Richard Lyman Bushman (Salt Lake City: Church Historian's Press, 2011), 195.

80. Young, *History of Round Prairie and Plymouth*, 70–71.

Chapter 8

Newspaper Editor and Illinois Legislator, 1840–43

> As Democrats we ask for equal justice and equal rights. Give us those rights, and we are content; without them we are deprived of that which was purchased by the blood of our fathers.
> —William Smith, 1842

In September 1840, Joseph Sr.'s health was quickly failing. According to Mother Lucy, his health had never fully recovered from the rigors of the Missouri experience—not only the shock of knowing that Joseph and Hyrum might be executed but then leaving the state during freezing cold, repeated snowstorms, and inadequate food, clothing, and transportation. Now he was dying of what was termed "consumption," a nineteenth-century term for what was most likely tuberculosis.

As he became bedfast, then began coughing up blood, Lucy recognized that the end was near and hurriedly sent for their children. After learning of his father's condition, William immediately made the thirty-mile journey to Nauvoo. In the hours preceding his death, Joseph Sr. desired to leave a father's blessing on each of his children. After recounting some of the miraculous ways William had been blessed in the Lord's service, Joseph Sr. prophesied during William's blessing that he would yet become like a "roaring lion in the forest" in his missionary labors, and be successful in bringing "many sheaves unto Zion."[1]

Joseph Sr.'s final request before he slipped into unconsciousness was that William and Don Carlos sing one of his favorite hymns. Doubtless with great feeling, the brothers sang "Promised Land," written by Baptist minister Samuel Stennett, and made popular during the camp meetings the Smiths often attended during William's youth. It was also likely one of those hymns that the family had repeatedly sung during home devotionals when the boys were children. The stanza that most stood out in William's memory, and most pertinent to the moment, read:

> Where no chilling winds or poisonous breath
> Disturb that peaceful shore,
> Sickness and sorrow, pain and death
> Be felt or feared no more.[2]

---

1. Lucy Mack Smith, *Biographical Sketches of Joseph Smith the Prophet and His Progenitors for Many Generations* (Liverpool: S. W. Richards, 1853), 265–70.

2. John K. Sheen, *Polygamy; or the Veil Uplifted* . . . (York, Neb.: n.p, 1889), 22. Isaac Sheen had apparently kept William Smith's "pocket companion" journal when they split

It was a fitting tribute to their father and his love of hymnody.

While the family jointly mourned the loss of their beloved father, his death was especially poignant for William. From the time he had fled from Missouri, William had been largely preoccupied with his business at Plymouth and, despite his reinstatement into the Church, had done little ecclesiastical work during the past two years. His father's passing changed all of that, instilling in William a greater determination to reform his life and increase his commitment to the faith for which, William believed, his father had given his life.

In a letter he penned to his brother Don Carlos, intended for publication in the *Times and Seasons* newspaper, two months after his father's death, William acknowledged his earlier neglect of his ecclesiastical responsibilities. "I improve the opportunity, that through the medium of the '*Times and Seasons*' the brethren may be informed, respecting the discharge of my duty for some time past," he began. Sensitive to the perceptions of others, he continued, "I am the more disposed to do so as many have thought my course of conduct strange and have had hard feelings respecting me. . . . [I] merely wish to state the circumstances in which I have been placed, which have been a barrier to my preaching the gospel to the extent, which my calling and standing in the church, many would suppose it was my duty to do so." Throughout the letter, he explained the burden of poverty and persecution he had borne: "Ever since I can remember, it has been the lot of my fathers family to suffer great privations and change of circumstances; for when, by our economy and industry we had procured a home, and the comforts of life, as oft has our prospects and comforts vanished and we have been reduced to distress and poverty." But he also manfully accepted responsibility, stating: "I do not wish to exhonerate myself from all blame."

He was pained at the thought that persecution had shortened his father's life and poetically lamented: "The persecution we have suffered . . . has deprived us of the society of one whom we loved; whose voice was more precious than the gold of Opher, the riches of Peru, or ten thousand worlds like this. Oh! May his memory long remain, and his words be written as with a diamond on the tablets of our hearts, and serve as an instructor, a comforter, and rule, to guide us through this unfriendly world." Perhaps reflecting on his lack of support during the family's journey out of Missouri, William expressed his regret that he had not "manifest more filial duty and affection towards a parent whose life and strength had been spent in the cause of truth, and for the salvation of his children."

His letter evidenced a turning point in his life. His father's death plunged him into deep reflection and ultimately reinvigorated his faith. "Believing it to be a duty binding upon me, to 'obey my parents,' and 'bow with reverence to grey

---

with each other in 1850. Sheen passed Smith's journal on to his son John, who included this historical detail in a footnote in his publication on polygamy. (See Appendix B.)

Joseph Smith Sr. Gravestone, Nauvoo, Illinois. Photograph by Kyle R. Walker, 2005.

hairs,'" wrote William, "I feel determined to attend to every duty, and follow the footsteps of our departed sire, come life or death, honor or reproach."[3]

Although he had recently paid off the mortgage on his hotel, William decided to involve other family members in its day-to-day operation, including his brother-in-law, George D. Grant, and his brothers Samuel and Don Carlos, which permitted him to intermittently go to Nauvoo and attend meetings at Church headquarters and to travel as a missionary.[4] He had invested a significant amount of time and money in building up his business. "Purchas[ed] a tavern stand in the town of Plymouth Hancock Co. Illinois 30 miles distant from –Nauvoo," William recalled of his thriving business. "[I] paid $900, for tavern stands—got in debt for it, but [after] the run of [the] business for two years—paid it all up." In addition to the hotel which he had improved by putting siding over the logs, he built "a good stable on the lot for hotell use [and with] the tavern stand . . . were two lots—a good well & out house also an extra building for farming tools."[5] It must have been difficult to leave this thriving business, especially after losing so much of his personal property in Ohio and Missouri. Yet by the following year, on January 1, 1842, William established himself more permanently at Nauvoo, by purchasing lot 1, on block 90, in the names of his daughters, Mary Jane and Caroline Louisa, for $500 from Joseph and Emma Smith. At that price, the lot probably had a standing home, as the deed mentioned not only the transfer of the lot, but also the "premises" and "appurtenences [sic]" to Mary J. and

---

3. William Smith (Plymouth, Ill.), Letter to D[on] C[arlos] Smith, December 1, 1840, in "Communications," *Times and Seasons* 2 (December 15, 1840): 252–53.

4. William paid off his mortgage on August 8, 1840, and sold his prosperous business to Caroline's brother, George D. Grant, for $1,500 on November 10, 1840, who in turn sold the property to Don Carlos Smith the following month, on December 9, 1840. The business appears to have become a family operation, as the property changed hands several times over the next few years, at one point being purchased in the names of William's daughters, Mary Jane and Caroline Louisa. Perhaps he hoped his children would inherit the hotel to help them get their start in life. Book H, Deeds and Mortgages, November 10, 1840, 638–39; Bonds and Mortgages, Book 1, 102; Bonds and Mortgages, Book K, 8; all in Hancock County Courthouse, Carthage, Illinois.

5. William B. Smith, Letter to Brother [Edmund L. Kelley], ca. 1893, Suplaiment [sic], P19, fd. 49, Miscellaneous Letters, Community of Christ Library-Archives.

Caroline L.⁶ William probably moved his family to Nauvoo at that time. Living in the city would also allow him to reconnect with his widowed mother, though little is known of the nature of their relationship during 1842–43. William continued to oversee his hotel business, staying in Plymouth for short periods in the next two years, but after November 1840, he largely left its operation to others.

His father's example of devotion to the Church, coupled with his unswerving love for William, became the catalyst for William's rededicating himself to Mormonism. Two years earlier, William had remained behind when members of his quorum set out for England. Despite intense poverty, personal illness, and sickness that afflicted wives and children, the apostles who fulfilled the mission believed that the Lord would provide for their needs.⁷ In the same letter to the *Times and Seasons*, William explained his decision to remain behind: "My impoverished situation has rendered it necessary for me to use every exertion to support my family." He quoted a scripture—"He who will not provide for his own household is worse than an infidel and hath denied the faith" (1 Tim. 5:8)—and reiterated the persecutions that had been "the lot of my fathers family."⁸

Everything he said about his circumstances at the time of the mission is true, but it still demonstrates that he made a more self-serving decision than those in similar circumstances who actually served their mission. The number and breadth of his reasons, valid though they were, still must have sounded feeble compared to those apostles who had dragged themselves from their sickbeds and made their way to England practically penniless, there to experience a stunning harvest of souls. And in fact, much later in Utah, members of the Twelve, including Brigham Young, would condemn William for not serving in England, stating that he was "better situated to leave his family than any of the members of the quorum who went." This sentiment would be reiterated in subsequent LDS publications when summarizing Smith's life.⁹

---

6. Deed to Caroline Louisa and Mary Jane Smith, January 1, 1842, Hancock County Courthouse, copy of original and transcription available at http://josephsmithpapers.org/paperSummary/deed-to-caroline-louisa-and-mary-jane-smith-1-january-1842 (accessed August 19, 2014).

7. Barely able to stand due to illness, Brigham Young and Heber C. Kimball cheered, "Hurrah, Hurrah, Hurrah, for Israel!" as they left their poverty-stricken wives and sick children. For a discussion on the financial and familial difficulties experienced by those members of the Twelve who fulfilled this mission, see James B. Allen, Ronald K. Esplin, and David J. Whittaker, *Men with a Mission: The Quorum of the Twelve Apostles in the British Isles* (Salt Lake City: Deseret Book, 1992), 67–86.

8. William Smith, to D. C. Smith, December 1, 1840.

9. "History of William Smith," *Millennial Star* 27, no. 1 (January 7, 1865), 7–8; Andrew Jenson, *Latter-Day Saint Biographical Encyclopedia: A Compilation of Biographical Sketches of Prominent Men and Women in the Church of Jesus Christ of Latter-Day Saints*, 4 vols. (Salt Lake City: Andrew Jenson History Company, 1901–30), 1:86–87.

Perhaps even more important than William's poverty was the serious decline in Caroline's already fragile health after being forced from Missouri during November/December 1838. After reading an account in the 1865 *Millennial Star* that noted William's refusal to serve the apostolic mission to England, William defended himself by writing a letter to the *Expositor*, an RLDS periodical published in Oakland, California. "It was well known for years after the saints were driven out of Missouri, that my wife, Caroline Smith, from the exposure she passed through in that inclement season of the year, contracted a disease of which after suffering much she finally died. At the time of the English mission was talked of, my wife was under treatment for dropsy. . . . It would have been absolutely cruel, unjust and anti-Christian to have abandoned a sick wife under such circumstances to undertake a mission to England."[10]

William was not exaggerating Caroline's ultimately fatal illness. Until Samuel, Don Carlos, and George D. Grant moved to Plymouth in the fall of 1840, he could not have left her there without family to provide nursing and without money to pay medical bills. At Caroline's funeral in Nauvoo in May 1845, less than a month after William had brought her back to Nauvoo from a two-year mission in the East, Orson Pratt corroborated William's account. In his sermon, he described Caroline as being "in the line of trouble and the cause of her illness was a fever she took in Missouri and [in] being driven—cold and hunger and fatigue . . . broke down her constitution."[11]

In a parallel circumstance, Parley P. Pratt left England for the United States in July 1840, just three months after his arrival, because he had learned that his wife, Mary Ann, had contracted scarlet fever. Pratt's biographers recount that "he wanted to be with her, to comfort her, and would 'gladly lay down his life' for her and the little ones, but the press of the work meant it would be 'months or years' before he could leave. If Pratt momentarily forgot where his obligations lay, his brethren in the quourm did not. They persuaded him to return to New York, and he set off immediately."[12] William's feelings were probably similar to Pratt's.

William identifies Caroline's illness as "dropsy," a nineteenth-century term for any kind of bodily swelling or edema. These symptoms would cause chronic pain and greatly hamper her mobility, leaving her bedfast at least periodically. Perhaps if she was able to take care of her children and do some cooking, cleaning, and sewing part of the time, she paid for these activities by being required to rest at least part of every day. It seems odd that William was not more explicit

---

10. "William B. Smith," *Expositor* (Oakland, Calif.) 4, no. 8 (August 1888): 3. The *Millennial Star* account included some of Brigham Young's criticisms of William.

11. Church Historian's Office, General Church Minutes, 1839–1877, in Richard E. Turley, ed., *Selected Collections from the Archives of the Church of Jesus Christ of Latter-day Saints*, 2 vols., DVD (Provo, Utah: Brigham Young University Press, [December 2002]), Vol. 1, disk 18, fd. 33.

12. Terryl L. Givens and Matthew J. Grow, *Parley P. Pratt: The Apostle Paul of Mormonism* (New York: Oxford University Press, 2011), 184.

in describing the challenges he faced in caring for Caroline in his 1840 letter to the *Times and Seasons*, but perhaps he included his nursing care along with the family's penury in his citation of 1 Timothy 5:8. If William's version of events was accurate and William's colleagues understood Caroline's condition, it may help to explain why William remained in full fellowship in his quorum while not fulfilling the mission to England. Significantly neither Joseph Smith nor any other apostle reprimanded William about his failure to serve this mission until years later when he had been separated from the Church for two decades.

Perhaps later LDS accounts of the episode and William's explanation reflect different aspects of his disposition during this period. Caroline's illness was a factor in his decision not to serve, and William, as he acknowledged in his *Times and Seasons* letter, was not fully devoted to his calling. Yet it seems inevitable that his absence would have influenced his relationship with his colleagues of the Twelve. He missed out on a great unifying experience that the mission to Great Britain provided for his quorum. James Allen, Ronald Esplin, and David Whittaker, in their history of this mission, summarize the experience: When the "nine apostles—the largest number to meet together since Kirtland—met in council" before bidding farewell to the English Saints in April 1841, they were "unified as they had never been before [;] they no doubt each felt much as Wilford Woodruff felt: 'To meet once more in council after a long separation and having passed through many sore and grievous trials . . . caused our hearts to swell with gratitude to God for his providential care over us.'"[13] While William continued to be sustained as a member of their quorum, the Twelve were also cognizant of his apathy toward his calling, made all the more apparent because this period of apparent indifference came on the heels of his outburst before he left Missouri.

With his father's faith and sacrifice fresh in his mind, William began 1841 with a zeal and energy for the cause that had been previously lacking. For perhaps the first time since he was called to the apostleship, he recognized the significance of his calling and expressed his determination "to magnify my office"—revealingly, by joining his apostolic brethren "on the shores of Europe." He felt that there were prospects on the horizon—perhaps Caroline's health was improving—that would enable him to travel abroad as a missionary. However, his increased zeal and improving family circumstances had come too late. Just two weeks after he expressed his desire to go to England, Joseph Smith wrote to the Twelve requesting them to return to Nauvoo in the spring.[14]

---

13. Woodruff, Journal, April 2, 1841, 2:78, quoted in Allen, Esplin, and Whittaker, *Men with a Mission*, 300.

14. William Smith, Letter to D. C. Smith; Joseph Smith, Letter to the Twelve, December 15, 1840, *Millennial Star* 1 (March 1841): 266; see also Dean C. Jessee, comp. and ed., *Personal Writings of Joseph Smith*, rev. ed. (Salt Lake City: Deseret Book/Provo, Utah: Brigham Young University Press, 2002), 515–22.

William was disappointed that he would not participate in preaching the gospel in England in accordance with his earlier vision in the Kirtland Temple.[15] He did the next best thing by serving several missions closer to home. In this way, he could return frequently when Caroline and the children needed him. Some evidence has survived that indicates that Caroline's condition would, at times, improve, allowing William to travel or for both of them to travel together. One such account comes from Benjamin F. Johnson, an 1831 New York convert, who had relatives in Springfield, Illinois. In the fall of 1839, when he was traveling from Carthage to Springfield, Johnson fell ill and lost consciousness during his journey. "About 4 P.M. I was found unconscious by the roadside," related Johnson, and was found "by the Prophet's brother William and his wife, who were going for wild plums. They took me to their home at Plymouth, and his sister Lucy cared for me tenderly, and grieved much to see me, so very sick."[16] William's sister Lucy, along with other extended family members, undoubtedly helped care for Caroline, both in Plymouth and afterward at Nauvoo during the early 1840s. William and Caroline's going for "wild plums" provides a rare glimpse of a leisurely family outing when they could enjoy each other's company and appreciate normal activities that were not dominated by financial or health worries.

The first of William's short missions occurred the month after his letter to the *Times and Seasons*. On the weekend of January 30–February 1, 1841, he traveled to Walnut Grove, in Knox County, Illinois, where he presided at a three-day conference of the Saints who lived in the region. William likely took Caroline and their two daughters with him on this particular assignment, as Caroline's parents, Joshua and Athalia Grant, had settled at that location and the conference could be combined with a family reunion.[17] Over a hundred members from several branches in the area attended the conference, as well as twenty priesthood officers. It was the first time in more than two years that William had been active in his calling as an apostle. He prayed, conducted Church business, and delivered several sermons, including one in which he spoke of "lively stones" that "are built up a spiritual house, an holy Priesthood, to offer spiritual sacrifices acceptable to God by Jesus Christ" (1 Pet. 2:5). William likely used the biblical passage to encourage those present to both prepare for, and to assist in the construction of a temple. Tellingly, only eleven days earlier, the Prophet had received a revelation commanding the Saints to

---

15. Dean C. Jessee, Mark Ashurst-McGee, and Richard L. Jensen, eds., *Journals, Volume 1: 1832–1839*, THE JOSEPH SMITH PAPERS, general editors Dean C. Jessee, Ronald K. Esplin, and Richard Lyman Bushman (Salt Lake City: Church Historian's Press, 2008), 181–82.

16. Benjamin F. Johnson, *My Life's Review: Autobiography of Benjamin Franklin Johnson* (Provo, Utah: Grandin Book, 1997), 51–52.

17. 1840 U.S. Census, Illinois, Stark County, Roll 70, p. 219. The Grants eventually located at Illinois, Knox County, Walnut Grove. See 1850 U.S. Census, Township 13 N. 3 E., Knox County, Roll M432_113, p. 415A.

construct just such an edifice at Nauvoo.[18] The clerk of the conference reported that "Brother Smith . . . gave great satisfaction to his hearers." As further evidence of his success, he baptized four people on the last day of the conference. The clerk added that the Saints were "highly gratified with the labors of Brother Smith since with us he having deli[v]ered several excellent discourses, and it was moved seconded, and carried unanimously that a vote of thanks be given by this Conference to Brother William Smith for his zealous services at this Conference."[19]

By early 1841, enough time had apparently elapsed that William's verbal outburst in Missouri had been forgotten. Instead, he had aligned himself with Church leadership at Nauvoo and was carrying out his duties with renewed energy. Almost certainly some in the community would have maintained reservations about William, including some members of his quorum, but he had been reinstated through the efforts and influence of his brothers and appeared determined to make good on his commitment. Since the rest of the Twelve were still absent, William's responsibilities increased rapidly during early 1841, drawing him increasingly to the center of Nauvoo life. After proselytizing in Iowa during March with Amasa M. Lyman, William was appointed, during April general conference, to take a mission in the eastern states to collect funds for the construction of the Nauvoo Temple.[20] William immediately left for Pennsylvania, where, by June, he welcomed some of the other apostles as they returned from England. His colleagues of the Twelve were delighted to see the transformation in William's commitment to the cause. Apostle John E. Page wrote to the First Presidency, "I must say in justice to Bro. Wm. Smith that I have been very much pleased with the spirituality of Bro. Smith, and also his zeal with which he has labored in the vineyard of the Lord since I fell into his society in and about Philadelphia. He has been blessed of the Lord to add souls to the kingdom in this region of country. He is truly a destroying storm to sectarianism."[21]

After returning to Nauvoo in November 1841, where he had left Caroline in their new home, William immersed himself in business activities with his brother Joseph, buying and selling land in and around Nauvoo and across the river in

---

18. "Conference Minutes," *Times and Seasons* 2, no. 9 (March 1, 1841): 338; Doctrine and Covenants 124:27–43, 2013 LDS edition; "A Proclamation to the Saints Scattered Abroad," *Times and Seasons* 2, no. 6 (January 15, 1841): 274.

19. "Conference Minutes," 338.

20. "Truth Prevailing," *Times and Seasons* 2, no. 10 (March 15, 1841): 350; Edward Leo Lyman, *Amasa Mason Lyman, Mormon Apostle and Apostate: A Study in Dedication* (Salt Lake City: University of Utah Press, 2009), 54; "Minutes of the General Conference of the Church of Jesus Christ of Latter Day Saints held at the City of Nauvoo . . . ," *Times and Seasons* 2, no. 12 (April 15, 1841): 388.

21. John E. Page (Philadelphia), Letter to the President and Council of the Church of Jesus Christ of Latter-day Saints (Nauvoo), September 1, 1841, in Journal History, September 1, 1841, 5. William also proselytized with his cousin George A. Smith when George first returned to the United States from his mission to England in June 1841. (See Chapter 9.)

Iowa to make farms and home lots available for the flood of converts coming in from England.

William's interaction with William Clayton, a recent convert who had emigrated from England, illustrates his influential role after he had recommitted himself to his calling. Upon his arrival at Nauvoo, Clayton wanted to purchase some property and was referred to Hyrum and William Smith. Hyrum counseled him to settle on the Iowa side of the Mississippi River, counsel that Clayton accepted only reluctantly as he longed to be closer to Church headquarters. However, he eventually purchased a 185-acre farm for three dollars an acre from William on credit in a locale that came to be called Zarahemla, Iowa. He then bought a wagon from William for $60, paying half of it up front. William had invested part of the money from selling property in Plymouth in a Mississippi steamboat, in which he was part owner. He allowed converts like Clayton to work on the steamboat, applying half of his wages to his debts. Such an arrangement benefitted both men. It enabled Clayton to get an immediate start after immigrating to Nauvoo, as well as providing wages that would permit him to pay his debts. William, on the other hand, supported himself and his family from the profits derived from his steamboat enterprise and the interest he earned on the loaned money.

Clayton's experience was typical of hundreds of converts who began arriving from England during the early 1840s. The three Smith brothers—Hyrum, Joseph, and William—oversaw the land business, an industry that thrived given the constant influx of converts.[22] Brothers Samuel and Don Carlos helped run the hotel at Plymouth during this same time period in an effort to support themselves. When traveling to Springfield in December 1842, Joseph indicated that he "arrived at Bro Samu[e]l Smith's [home] in Plymouth," a probable reference to William's Mormon Hotel at which Samuel had been working.[23]

In retrospect, the early 1840s represent the zenith of William's ecclesiastical and civic career. Early in 1842 he reflected on the prosperity and the satisfaction both he and the Saints experienced as they labored together to build the bustling city. Though they had arrived in the state nearly destitute, William mused, "fortune had smiled upon them—Omnipotence interposed in their behalf; homes were providentially provided, prosperity crowned their labors, and an abundance flowed in to alleviate their wants and render them comfortable. . . . The flourishing city of Nauvoo—smiling under the genial sun of happiness and contentment—speaks in language more loud and in strains more eloquent, than any thing that our feeble capacity is competent to introduce."[24] Nauvoo was quickly becoming a river boomtown, and William's voice was becoming an integral part of the community. He was

---

22. George D. Smith, ed., *An Intimate Chronicle: The Journals of William Clayton* (Salt Lake City: Signature Books, 1995), xxii, 80–81; James B. Allen, *No Toil Nor Labor Fear: The Story of William Clayton* (Provo, Utah: BYU Press, 2002), 63–64.

23. Joseph Smith, Journal, December 27, 1842, in Jessee, Ashurst-McGee, and Jensen, *Journals, Volume 1*, 181–82.

24. William Smith, "Introductory," *The Wasp* 1, no. 1 (April 16, 1842): 2.

appointed an assistant chaplain in the Nauvoo Legion in July 1841 and, in May 1842, was appointed to Nauvoo's city council.[25] He enjoyed his prominent role, and his influence expanded quickly as the city prospered.

In the spring of 1842, after moving his family to Nauvoo, William ambitiously sought to establish a newspaper at Nauvoo. The idea had originally been Don Carlos's, who wanted to name it the *Nauvoo Ensign and Zarahemla Standard*. Don Carlos was a seasoned printer, having mastered the trade from his teen years in Kirtland and again at Nauvoo. Prior to his untimely death, probably from pneumonia, on August 7, 1841, Don Carlos saw the need for a newspaper that would report the national and local news, while the *Times and Seasons* would continue to focus almost exclusively on Church business. William picked up where his brother had left off, indicating that Don Carlos had already obtained a good number of subscribers for the proposed paper.[26]

Animosity toward the Saints in the press was also a factor in inaugurating this newspaper. As William indicated in his "Introductory" in the first issue, which appeared on April 16, 1842, "The public press is daily teaming [sic] with slanders, foul calumnies, and base misrepresentations... to turn the tide of popular opinion against us. Shall this state of things be suffered longer to exist without some channel through which we can convey correct information to the world and thereby disabuse the public mind as to the many slanders that are constantly perpatrated [sic] against us?"[27]

The name William chose—*The Wasp*, not only set the paper's tone but also reflected William's personality. Published weekly until April 26, 1843, its burning sting pricked readers throughout western Illinois. "William had definite ideas about the direction his weekly should pursue," wrote historian Jerry C. Jolley of the publication, and "the choice of the name itself indicaties that the *Wasp* would not hesitate to 'sting' those who opposed the editor's views, particularly those distorting Mormonism and advocating hate and persecution against the rising city of the Saints."[28]

If Church leaders needed a voice to counter anti-Mormon sentiment that was increasing in the state, William Smith was an unfortunate choice. Though he

---

25. Andrew H. Hedges, Alex D. Smith, and Richard Lloyd Anderson, eds., *Journals, Vol. 2, December 1841–April 1843*, Vol. 2 of the Journal series of THE JOSEPH SMITH PAPERS, general editors Dean C. Jessee, Ronald K. Esplin, and Richard Lyman Bushman (Salt Lake City: Church Historian's Press, 2011), 511, 521.

26. William Smith, "Introductory"; Roy B. Huff and Kyle R. Walker, "Don Carlos Smith," in *United by Faith: The Joseph Sr. and Lucy Mack Smith Family*, ed. Kyle R. Walker (American Fork, Utah: BYU Studies and Covenant Communications, 2006), 377–80; See also, Kyle R. Walker, "'As Fire Shut Up in My Bones': Ebenezer Robinson, Don Carlos Smith, and the 1840 Edition of the Book of Mormon," *Journal of Mormon History* 36, no. 1 (Winter 2010), 1–40.

27. William Smith, "Introductory," 2.

28. Jerry C. Jolley, "The Sting of the *Wasp*: Early Nauvoo Newspaper—April 1842 to April 1843," *BYU Studies* 22, no. 4 (Fall 1982): 488.

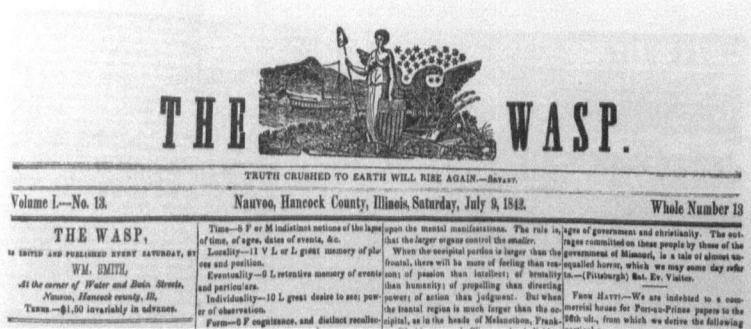

Masthead of the *Wasp* newspaper. Photograph by Kyle R. Walker, 2015.

was well informed regarding political issues that affected the Saints and articulate in expressing his views, his editorial style was too abrasive to win many friends, either for himself or for the Mormons. Although it was an era when "vicious libel was common" among newspaper editors, Smith's editorials were a distraction to the Church's Christian theology.[29] He almost immediately tussled with other newspaper men in the vicinity, most conspicuously with Thomas Sharp, editor of the *Warsaw Signal*. Seven years younger than William, Sharp had been born at Mount Holly, New Jersey, studied law for eighteen months in the late 1830s, was admitted to the Pennsylvania bar in 1840, but moved to Illinois that same year. After practicing law briefly at Quincy, Sharp relocated to Warsaw, another river town just eighteen miles downriver from Nauvoo, also in Hancock County. He purchased the newspaper *Western World* that November, and shortly afterward changed the name to the *Warsaw Signal*, which he edited in 1840–42, and again from 1844 to1846.[30]

Sharp's influence in Hancock County had been on the rise since he had taken over editorship of the *Warsaw Signal* in 1840. On April 6, 1841, when the Saints were celebrating their eleventh anniversary of the organization of the Church, Joseph Smith had invited Sharp to join the festivities. Almost certainly, Joseph meant it partly as a hospitable gesture, but also because he understood Sharp's influential public position as editor of the only non-Mormon newspaper in the county. Sharp accepted the invitation and was the Saints' guest throughout the day. The festivities included laying the cornerstone for the Nauvoo Temple and a ceremonial review of the Nauvoo Legion. In the evening, as an honored

---

29. Ibid., 487.
30. Roger D. Launius, "Anti-Mormonism in Illinois: Thomas C. Sharp's Unfinished History of the Mormon War, 1845," *Journal of Mormon History* 15 (1989): 28; Thomas Gregg, *History of Hancock County Illinois* (Chicago: Charles C. Chapman & Co., 1880), 748–50; Annette P. Hampshire, "Thomas Sharp and Anti-Mormon Sentiment in Illinois 1842–1845," *Journal of the Illinois State Historical Society* 72 (1979): 82.

Sketch of Thomas C. Sharp, 1818–1894. Thomas Gregg, History of Hancock County, Illinois (Chicago: Chas. C. Chapman, 1880), 387.

guest, Sharp dined on roast turkey at the Prophet's home.

However, instead of building feelings of goodwill as intended, the day's events had the opposite effect on Sharp. He was taken aback by the military might of the Nauvoo Legion and reacted with fearful trepidation to Joseph Smith's influence over his followers and the Saints' growing political influence in the county. In May, Sharp summarized his reservations in an editorial: "Whenever they as a people, step beyond the proper sphere of a religious denomination, and become a political body, . . . then this press stands pledged to take a stand against them. [We are] bound to oppose the concentrations of political power in a religious body, or in the hands of a few individuals."[31] In reference to the Nauvoo Legion, Sharp expressed his hope in June that the first step of Illinois's new quartermaster general "will be to remove the arms which have been latterly congregated at Nauvoo, to some place of safe keeping."[32] Sharp continued his opposition to the Mormons in the intervening months, eventually becoming the voice of anti-Mormon sentiment in Illinois.

By the following April, William Smith editorialized bitingly about what he saw as Sharp's abuse of Mormon hospitality:

> It being the native honesty and characteristic of the Latter-Day Saints to be ever co[u]rteous and act with becoming hospitality towards strangers, a generous and polite invitation was given by Gen. Joseph Smith for the stranger [Thomas Sharp] to dine at his table. Accordingly, without many apologies or preliminaries, the work of eating commenced and were all soon satisfied with "roast Turkey" and table dainties. But it appears that this repast did not end the sequel, for notwithstanding the kind treatment, and the courteous manner he was received, after his [Sharp's] return to Warsaw, he commenced a most unwarrantable attack upon us and treated our kindness and mockery and has continued a continual tirade of abuse ever since, and that too without any just cause or provocation whatever.[33]

Tensions between William Smith and Thomas Sharp came to a head simultaneously as the August election began heating up during the summer of 1842. Matters were already simmering. John C. Bennett, a skilled politician who had managed the passage of the Nauvoo City Charter through the state legislature, had fallen spectacularly out of fellowship and disappeared from Nauvoo to hurl

---

31. "The Mormons," *Warsaw Signal* 2, no. 2 (May 19, 1841): 2.
32. "We understand . . . ," *Warsaw Signal* 2, no. 5 (June 9, 1841): 2.
33. William Smith, "The Turkey," *The Wasp* 1, no. 2 (April 23, 1842): 2.

his denunciatory letters from St. Louis. His departure left vacant his seat in the state House of Representatives. Though Bennett recommended Sidney Rigdon or Orson Pratt as his replacement, it was William Smith who was ultimately nominated for the ticket.³⁴ That his name was discussed in the company of Rigdon and Pratt, two of Mormonism's most noted theologians and orators, was not only a commendation of William's speaking ability, but also witnessed the trust he had engendered among his brethren during the previous year. Smith and Sharp feuded throughout the first half of 1842, as Sharp was vehemently opposed to a Mormon representative from Hancock County, most especially because it was the Prophet's brother. William responded with one editorial after another, starting with his sarcastic critique of Sharp's betrayal of the Saints' hospitality and later resorting to personal attacks. "Sharp commented in April 1842 that he had received a copy of the *Wasp* in the mail," recounted one author of their feud, and "'had it been [named] a *Pole Cat* . . . its name would have corresponded perfectly with the character of its content.' William Smith retorted with a glib 'Well done Thom-ASS.'"³⁵ The two frequently resorted to name-calling, and William later sank to belittling Sharp's physical appearance.³⁶ Sharp retaliated in kind. Despite some weeks where William expressed his determination to take the higher ground, probably at the encouragement of some his colleagues, he continued to react to Sharp's attacks. "Some of our friends want our opinion as to the course of certain editors who make it their business to vilify and abuse the character of General Joseph Smith and the Church of Latter Day Saints," wrote William. "We have to say that we shall pay little attention to their contemptible trash and envenomed libels."³⁷ But the sheer amount of ink dedicated to Sharp in *The Wasp*'s newspaper columns evinces William's mindset. He never handled criticism well, even during this most successful season of his life, and Sharp's very personal attacks infuriated him.³⁸

William was elected on the Democratic ticket in August 1842. Ironically, this same ticket brought Thomas Ford to the governor's chair. Sharp's sarcastic editorial on the election results jeered: "How very patriotic must have been the aspirations of Messrs. Davis and Owen,³⁹ when they consented to run on the same ticket with so high-minded—so gentlemanly—so noble a personage, as Bill Smith! He will certainly give dognity [a crude pun that probably responded

---

34. John C. Bennett, "For the Wasp," *The Wasp* 1 (May 28, 1842): 3.

35. Launius, "Anti-Mormonism in Illinois," 29.

36. William Smith, "The Turkey," 2; William Smith, "Just as our paper . . . ," *Wasp* 1, no. 2 (April 23, 1842): 2.

37. William Smith, "Some of our friends. . . ," *Wasp* 1, no. 18 (August 20, 1842): 2.

38. See, for example, William's half-hearted attempt at an apology, in William Smith, "Apology," *Wasp* 1, no. 4 (May 7, 1842): 2; and William Smith, "Sharp, of the Signal . . . ," *Wasp* 1, no. 18 (August 20, 1842): 2.

39. Democratic Senator Jacob Cunningham Davis and Representative Thomas H. Owen.

to William's "Thom-ass"] and weight to our county in the Halls of Legislation! Should not his colleagues feel proud of him?"[40]

For his part, William, rather than being a gracious winner, gloated in *The Wasp* that the margin of victory for some of those on the Democratic ticket had been more than five thousand votes and that Thomas Ford reportedly won by eight to ten thousand votes, no inconsiderable number in a state where some 87,000 residents voted for governor in 1842.[41]

By the time this election had occurred, Church leaders and observers were growing uncomfortable with William's editorial aggressiveness. James Arlington Bennet, a non-Latter day Saint and trusted confidant of Joseph Smith, who ran an educational institution that bore his name at Long Island, New York, expressed misgivings to Joseph about *The Wasp*. In August 1842, he wrote to Joseph, beginning with the complimentary comment that he was disappointed that he was no longer receiving copies of *The Wasp*, and asking Joseph to give "my respects to your brother its Editor." However, Bennet added emphatically, "I dont like the name. Mildness should characterise every thing that comes from Nauvoo and even a name . . . has much influence on one side or the other."[42] The tenor of William's paper had indubitably matched its name from the first issue. Bennet highlighted a development that was becoming all too apparent to Church authorities. By September someone, perhaps Joseph himself, had spoken to William about changing the paper's name, but William resisted. "Some well disposed persons . . . are not pleased with the name 'Wasp,'" wrote William in a September editorial, "preferring a sweeter appellation from the realms of Nauvoo. Well, we have some notion, in time, to change the 'Wasp' to *Honey Bee*. Then the only queery [sic] will be, which has the *sweetest sting?*"[43]

William's election to the legislature seemed like a good opportunity to replace him. William resigned his editorship in December 1842, and the paper was turned over to fellow apostle John Taylor, who, within a few months, renamed it the *Nauvoo Neighbor* and instituted a milder tone to match. Before William left for the legislative session in Springfield, he moved Caroline and their daughters back to Plymouth, if only temporarily, where Samuel and Levira were managing the hotel. William reached the state capital in time to hear Governor Ford's inaugural address on December 8, 1842, and was thunderstruck to hear him assure the people of Illinois that he would attempt to limit chartered cities' rights, referring specifically to Nauvoo as an example of a city that enjoyed too

---

40. "The Election," *Warsaw Signal* 3, no. 5 (August 6, 1842): 2.

41. Ford actually beat Joseph Duncan by approximately 7,000 votes in 1842. "Ford and Moore," *Wasp* 1, no. 17 (August 13, 1842): 3; "The result of the election in Illinois . . . ," *Wasp* 1, no. 18 (August 20, 1842): 2.

42. James Arlington Bennet (Long Island, N.Y.), Letter to Joseph Smith, August 16, 1842, Joseph Smith, Journal, September 7, 1842, in Hedges, Smith, and Anderson, *Journals, Volume 2*, 135–37.

43. William Smith, "Some well disposed persons . . . ," *Wasp* 1, no. 20 (September 3, 1842): 2.

many privileges. "A great deal has been said about certain charters granted to the people of Nauvoo," stated Governor Ford, and "these charters are objectionable on many accounts, but particularly on account of the powers granted. The people of the State have become aroused on the subject, and anxiously desire that those charters should be modified so as to give the inhabitants of Nauvoo no greater privileges than those enjoyed by others of our fellow-citizens."[44] William obviously disagreed and had expected the governor to recognize that he owed his victory in Hancock County largely to its Mormon citizens. Ford's combative remarks set the tone for this politically charged issue throughout the legislative session. Though Nauvoo was not the only city to come under fire for having too-liberal charters, due to Ford's comments and Sharp's opposition in the press, the city became the test case in the state legislature that winter.

Granted in December 1840, principally through the labors of John C. Bennett, Nauvoo's charter afforded the Saints the right to establish a university, a municipal court, and a local militia. The Saints were determined to maintain these legally granted privileges to protect themselves from the injustices they had experienced in Missouri. But William had his work cut out for him in defending the charter from repeal. Led by Thomas Sharp's influential newspaper, other civic leaders were beginning to question the legitimacy of Nauvoo's charter.

Though inexperienced in legislation, William was not inexperienced in oratory. On December 9, 1842, the day following Ford's inaugural address, he took to the House floor and persuasively argued to protect Nauvoo's charter. He focused his defense on the similarity between the charter granted at Nauvoo and those in other prominent cities within the state. Contradicting Ford's claim, William argued that the citizens of Nauvoo have "no greater rights or privileges given them than were already enjoyed by the citizens of Quincy or Springfield; . . . Our condition in that respect is not at all different from Chicago, Alton, and many other chartered cities in this state." He contended that the previous legislature had overwhelmingly approved granting Nauvoo's charter and questioned why things would have changed so significantly in the space of only two years, unless Nauvoo was being singled out due to religious intolerance. In fact, that is exactly what Sharp had argued repeatedly in the *Warsaw Signal*—that the Mormons congregating at Nauvoo held too much political influence in the state. William, for his part, lobbied for a separation of church and state, indicating that a religious discussion should not "at all come under the purview of this legislature." Notwithstanding, Smith also attempted to allay rumors that his church was "strange." "I come right from among them," Smith boldly declared, "and you can all judge whether or not they seem to have the appearance of a strange animal with 7 heads and ten horns."[45]

---

44. *Reports Made to Senate and House of Representatives of the State of Illinois* (Springfield, Ill.: William Waters, 1842), 32.

45. "Speech of Mr. [William] Smith of Hancock County, on the Resolution of Mr. Davis of Bond, to Repeal the Nauvoo Charter, Delivered in the House of Representatives,

William also spent considerable time attempting to counter rumors that the citizens at Nauvoo were hostile toward neighboring communities and the state at large. Sharp's anti-Mormon influence was evident in the issues William was forced to address, including Sharp's allegations that the existence of the Nauvoo Legion was evidence of excessive and potentially dangerous militarism. William told those in the chamber that, while Nauvoo's citizens "have under existing laws drawn a certain portion of the public arms, . . . they have not even that equal portion of arms that they are entitled to by law. . . . It surely cannot be believed that there is any danger of the Mormons breaking out and killing the people," declared William, and he further reassured his colleagues of the House that his constituents had no intention "to molest [even] a hair on the head of a single individual; but, on the contrary, it is their intention in all things to conform to the constitution and laws of the land. . . . Have they not, I would ask, contributed their portion towards replenishing your county and State revenues? Have they ever refused to pay their taxes? Have they not always been both ready and willing to obey both the civil and military laws of this State? Where, then is the necessity that this honorable body should enact a law taking away from them their chartered privileges? Wherein are they [Nauvoo's residents] acting differently from any other citizens?" Reaching the culmination of his speech, Smith asserted, "As Democrats we ask for equal justice and equal rights. Give us those rights, and we are content; without them we are deprived of that which was purchased by the blood of our fathers."[46]

Smith's maiden speech among his colleagues proved persuasive. The House voted 6 to 43 to defeat the charter's repeal, and the Senate similarly voted 22 to 13 to table a similar measure.[47] Thus far Smith had succeeded in fulfilling what he viewed as his central mission in the legislature; but to both his and the Saints' dismay, it was only the beginning of a lengthy debate that persisted throughout the entire winter session and was still lingering ominously as unfinished business when the session closed on March 6, 1843. Keeping tensions simmering was the December 1842 hearing examining Joseph Smith's avoidance of a Missouri extradition attempt. Joseph obeyed an order from Governor Ford and traveled from Nauvoo to Springfield with a party of supporters. He had been in hiding off and on since August to avoid extradition to Missouri because, on May 6, 1842, an unknown assailant, widely believed to be Orrin Porter Rockwell, had shot Missouri's former governor Lilburn W. Boggs in Independence. Although Boggs survived, Rockwell was being blamed for attempted murder and Joseph was seen as an accessory before the act. As Richard Bushman summarized, "To protect the Prophet, Joseph's allies in Nauvoo erected all the legal protections possible, utilizing the Nauvoo municipal courts as the chief bastion. On July 5 [1842], the city council passed an ordinance

---

December 9, 1842," *Wasp* 1, no. 37 (January 14, 1843): 1–2. His description of the many-headed and -horned beast is from Revelation 17:3.

46. "Speech of Mr. Smith of Hancock County," 2.

47. Glen M. Leonard, *Nauvoo: A Place of Peace, a People of Promise* (Provo, Utah: BYU Press/Salt Lake City: Deseret Book, 2002), 307.

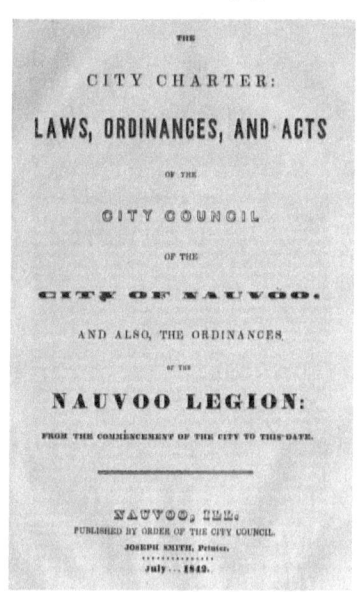

Title Page of city charter, Nauvoo, Illinois. Published by Nauvoo's City Council, July 1842.

empowering the city courts to examine all outside arrest warrants and issue writs of habeas corpus. A warrant for Joseph's extradition would fall under this law, which required the municipal court to review such cases."[48] The manner in which Joseph shielded himself with Nauvoo's municipal court actions prior to his turning himself in was a principal reason Nauvoo's charter had come under scrutiny in the press and during the 1842–43 legislative season. Both Ford and his predecessor, Thomas Carlin, had disregarded the appeals of Joseph and Emma Smith and other Nauvoo civil authorities to ignore Missouri's attempt at extradition and the accusations of recent apostate John C. Bennett. In the end, through the persuasions of Justin Butterfield, the U.S. district attorney for Illinois, Joseph finally presented himself for arrest by Latter-day Saint Wilson Law at Nauvoo, agreeing to have his case tried in Springfield.[49]

On their way to the capital city, Smith and his group lodged at the "Mormon Hotel" at Plymouth. Caroline, likely with the assistance of her two daughters and her sister-in-law Levira Clark Smith (Samuel's spouse), prepared meals for Joseph and his large contingent of at least sixteen. There were not enough beds, even in the hotel, for everyone, and Joseph and Willard Richards slept on buffalo skins on the floor. William had already been separated from his family for the better part of a month, and Caroline and the children must have missed his companionship.

Elizabeth Durfee, married to Jabez Durfee and a good friend of the Smith family, apparently came for the express purpose of providing care and companionship for Caroline so that she could join Joseph's party and meet William in Springfield. Although Willard Richards noted in his journal that Caroline was feeling ill that evening, she and eight-year-old Mary Jane left with Joseph Smith's group the next morning. Six-year-old daughter Caroline remained with Samuel's family at the hotel. It turned out to be a wise decision. The ninety-mile journey from Plymouth to Springfield was arduous, and many of the tavern owners along the way refused to accept the Mormons. The freezing cold was yet another hardship they endured en route. To make matters worse, one of the carriages broke

---

48. Richard Lyman Bushman, *Joseph Smith, Rough Stone Rolling: A Cultural Biography of Mormonism's Founder* (New York: Alfred A. Knopf, 2005), 468–69.

49. Morris A. Thurston, "The Boggs Shooting and Attempted Extradition," *BYU Studies* 48, no. 1 (2009): 13–28; John S. Dinger, "Joseph Smith and the Development of Habeas Corpus in Nauvoo, 1841–44," *Journal of Mormon History* 36, no. 3 (Summer 2010): 135–71.

Old State Capitol, Springfield, Illinois. This building was used as the Illinois State Capitol from 1839 to 1876. Photograph by Kyle R. Walker, 2009.

down just outside of Springfield. The party finally reached its destination on December 30, and Caroline and Mary Jane spent the week with William.[50]

Besides his pending trial, Joseph's mind was also engrossed with the debate surrounding the Nauvoo charter. Just before he left Nauvoo, Joseph had written a lengthy editorial in *The Wasp* defending chartered rights.[51] During their trip to Springfield, Willard Richards recorded that Joseph engaged in some grandiloquent rhetoric, fuming that "to touch the Nauvoo Charter was no better than highway robbery. That since the creation there never had been a repeal of a perpetual charter by God, Angels, or men & that he never would submit to lowering our charter—but they might bring others up to it." Several days later, the Prophet again reiterated, "If a legislature has power to grant a charter for 10 years . . . [it] has no power to revoke it till the expiration thereof."[52] Nauvoo's citizens anxiously awaited the outcome of the legislature that potentially could dramatically alter the affairs of the city.

The Prophet's trial at Springfield was sensationalized in the city and in the press, and members of the House were immediately aware of his presence. On the evening of December 31, while the House was in session, horses drawing a carriage bolted from their owner's control and sped past the capitol. Someone cried out "Joe Smith is running away," which created such a stir among the legislators that they abruptly adjourned to determine the cause of the excitement. The experience

---

50. Hedges, Smith, and Anderson, *Journals, Volume 2*, 195–97, 195 note 39.

51. Joseph Smith, "Remarks on Chartered Rights," *The Wasp* 1, no. 34 (December 24, 1842): 2.

52. Hedges, Smith, and Anderson, *Journals, Volume 2*, 196, 205.

increased curiosity among members of the legislature. The next day, Democratic Speaker of the House Samuel Hackleton called on Joseph Smith and offered him the representatives' hall in the capitol for Sunday preaching. Members of the legislature attended the Latter-day Saint meeting the next day and vigilantly watched the outcome of his trial during the ensuing week. The outcome of Smith's trial would likely influence some of those issues facing the legislature, including attitudes toward Nauvoo's charter. Spectators "of a respectable class" including the likes of Mary Todd Lincoln, other dignitaries, and curious onlookers, also flocked to the capitol to catch a glimpse of the celebrated Mormon prophet.[53]

The Prophet's presence in the city may have regenerated interest in the House of Representatives regarding city charters. Joseph was cleared of all charges on January 5, 1843, but only five days later, Mr. Logan representing Jo Daviess County introduced a bill in the House to amend Nauvoo's charter. Joseph and his associates, likely including Caroline and Mary Jane, had already left the capitol on Saturday, January 7. Wilson Law and Willard Richards composed a fifteen-stanza song after the trial and dubbed it "The Mormon Jubilee," to celebrate Joseph Smith's deliverance. One verse read:

> Our charter'd rights she [Illinois] has maintained
> Through opposition great;
> Long may her charter champions live,
> Still to protect the state.[54]

The party enthusiastically and repeatedly sang this musical tribute on their return journey to Nauvoo, stopping again at Plymouth en route.[55] The experience must have been memorable for Caroline and Mary Jane.

While the Mormons were happily joining in another chorus of "The Mormon Jubilee," Nauvoo's charter was again being debated in the legislature. Once more William took up the defense of the Saints' rights. While reiterating the arguments that he and Representative Thomas Owen had argued the month previous, William attacked what he felt was religious intolerance. He scornfully reported that he had recently overheard a resident of Springfield predict: "10 years shall not roll away, before the people of this State would rise up and expel the Mormons!" He then recounted the atrocities the Saints had experienced in Missouri in an attempt to gain the sympathies of his listeners. "Shall it be said that this State will re-enact the murderous outrages of the State of Missouri? He could, were it not consuming the time of the house, exhibit the crimes and violent proceedings of the Missouri mobs against the defenceless, the weak, and the innocent. He could speak of the

---

53. "The Release of Gen. Joseph Smith," *The Wasp* 1, no. 37 (January 14, 1843): 2; Thurston, "The Boggs Shooting and Attempted Extradition," 29–35.

54. "The Mormon Jubilee," *The Wasp* 1, no. 37 (January 14, 1843): 1.

55. Thurston, "The Boggs Shooting and Attempted Extradition," 47–50. Hedges, Smith, and Anderson, *Journals, Volume 2*, 236–43, describes the jubilant return and visit with Samuel and Katharine and their families at Plymouth.

murder of 17 persons, by a ruthless mob, on their knees, begging for life, and of the sacrifice of a boy whose brains was blown out while imploring for mercy from his savage murderers." William pointed to Joseph's recent acquiescence to state laws by allowing himself to be arrested, going to Springfield, and being acquitted through proper legal channels. It was an example of his constituents' willingness to abide by the laws of the land, William argued, as well as yet another example of the persecution his people continued to experience stemming from the Missouri experience. He concluded by contrasting such lawlessness he witnessed in Missouri with the refinement of "honorable gentleman" of Illinois. He ringingly expressed confidence that members of the House would not act "upon any other principles, than those of honor and constitutional right."[56]

The *Illinois Register*, a Democratic paper published at Springfield, praised William for his persuasive oration: "The bill was defeated through the exertions of Mr. Smith and Mr. Owen, the representatives from Hancock County. Mr. Smith (who we learn is a brother of the prophet) made a powerful speech in defense of his brethren, in the course of which he gave Mr. Davis of Bond county a very severe castigation." The newspaper editor concurred with Smith's argument, "We are opposed to persecution, in all its forms. The Mormons are entitled to the same rights as other citizens but no more. Any attempt to repeal their charters is wrong unless all other [city] charters are repealed also. . . . This idea of depriving the Mormons of rights which other citizens possess, is worse than the edicts of the Spanish inquisition, and will not be tolerated in a free country. Messrs. . . Smith and Owen, are a perfect team in standing up by the rights of their constituents."[57] Even the editor of the Whig-leaning *Sangamo Journal*, normally at odds with the Mormons, conceded that "Mr. Smith, the Prophet's brother, fought ably and manfully against the bill, which was finally laid on the table, on motion of Mr. Logan, by a vote of 60 to 43—tantamount to its defeat."[58]

While William hoped that this second defeat would be the end of efforts to repeal Nauvoo's charter, at the suggestion of an editorial published in the *Illinois Register* on January 20,[59] Senator Davis, a Democrat from Bond County, tried one last approach before the winter session terminated on March 6. Once again, instead of the outright repeal of the charter, Davis proposed amending certain privileges, including exercise of the writ of habeas corpus. Representative Logan

---

56. "House of Representatives," *The Wasp* 1, no. 40 (February 1, 1843): 3.

57. Article from the *[Springfield] Illinois Register*, reproduced in "Nauvoo Charters," *Wasp* 1, no. 40 (February 1, 1843): 2. Concern over the scope of Nauvoo's charter would surface again in 1844, and this time anti-Mormons succeeded in repealing the charter. Leonard, *Nauvoo: A Place of Peace, A People of Promise*, 307–8, 464–68.

58. Article from the *Sangamo Journal*, reproduced in "Nauvoo Charters," *Wasp* 1, no. 40 (February 1, 1843): 2.

59. Article from the *Illinois Register*, reproduced in "Nauvoo Charters," 2.

of Jo Daviess County once again jumped on board, and the bill to amend these privileges eventually passed the House, to William and Owen's dismay.[60]

But the ever-fiery William would not go down without a fight. After the bill passed the House, he arose and proposed to amend the bill's name, a proposal greeted, according to the session clerk, by "profound silence." Smith handed the Speaker of the House a piece of paper on which he had written his proposed title. The Speaker read it and stated: "The amendment is not respectful and not in order." The curious legislators then demanded that the Speaker read the amended title, which he did: "*A bill for an act to humbug the citizens of Nauvoo.*" William's sardonic jest nearly brought down the house, and the clerk reported "profound sensation." The Speaker looked at William for an explanation, and William responded that "he considered the amendment perfectly describing the contents of the bill [and that] he was anxious that things should be called by their right names." He then withdrew his amendment. William must have felt as if divine providence had intervened when, a short time afterward, the Senate preserved the charter intact by a single vote.[61]

On his return to Nauvoo that March, William Smith was hailed as a hero for his success in the legislature. The *Times and Seasons* praised his able leadership: "His talents are known and appreciated, his conduct in the last session of the Legislature proved him to be a man of talent and of genius, a patriot and a statesman, and a man every way qualified to maintain the interests of the people he represented."[62] William's legislative triumph, following on the heels of Joseph's judicial triumph, meant that Nauvoo's citizens faced 1843 with optimism and energy. They did not know that the legislative debate on this particular issue would form a main reason the Saints would be driven from the state some three years later.

---

60. "House of Representatives," *The Wasp* 1, no. 46 (March 15, 1843): 2.
61. Ibid.
62. "For the *Neighbor*," *Times and Seasons* 5, no. 10 (May 15, 1844): 534.

Chapter 9

President of the Eastern Branches, 1843–45

> Had it not been for William Smith, [I] should have been in the Church to this day.
> — Benjamin Winchester, 1845

In his letter to the *Times and Seasons* in December of 1840, William wrote that he stood ready to "visit the churches in different parts of this State [Illinois], and the eastern states" and was ready to "bid adieu for a time, to the land of my nativity, and lift up my voice on the shores of Europe." Caroline's health had improved enough to permit William to travel, and he expressed his desire to "go and assist my brethren [of the Twelve], to prune the vineyard for the last time."[1] While joining his brethren in the British Isles was no longer an option, he instead decided to go east, both to serve as a missionary and to strengthen the branches throughout the eastern states.[2]

The decision to serve as a missionary in the East was critical. Between 1841 and 1845, he spent more time among the eastern Saints than he did in Illinois. For a time, it became a second home to him, as he formed many associations, particularly in New Jersey and Pennsylvania, and made many decisions that permanently influenced the rest of his life. But it also took him away from the main body of the Saints and the First Presidency in Nauvoo. This fact had its pros and cons. A positive effect was that William had opportunities to preside removed from his brother's shadow. A negative effect was that William's leadership experience and ability were limited, and his temperament made it difficult for him to

---

1. William Smith (Plymouth, Ill.), Letter to D[on] C[arlos] Smith, December 1, 1840, in "Communications," *Times and Seasons* 2 (December 15, 1840): 252–53. By "last time," he was paraphrasing a teaching from the Book of Mormon (Jacob 5:62), which communicated the expectation held among early Saints that Christ's second coming was close at hand.

2. As mentioned in Chapter 8, Joseph Smith had written to the Twelve requesting them to return home just weeks after William's letter to Don Carlos was printed in the *Times and Seasons*. Joseph Smith to the Twelve, December 15, 1840, *Millennial Star* 1 (March 1841): 266; see also Dean C. Jessee, comp. and ed., *Personal Writings of Joseph Smith*, rev. ed. (Salt Lake City: Deseret Book and Brigham Young University Press, 2002), 515–22. Most of the Twelve returned to Nauvoo in the summer and fall of 1841. James B. Allen, Ronald K. Esplin, and David J. Whittaker, *Men with a Mission: The Quorum of the Twelve Apostles in the British Isles* (Salt Lake City: Deseret Book, 1992), 304–8.

succeed in that role. When he encountered opposition among resistant Saints or confusion about doctrine and living gospel principles, he was apt to flare up, insisting on deference to his authority, when patience, careful listening, and more consultation with local leaders would have yielded better results and strengthened the unity of the eastern branches.

In April 1841, soon after moving to Nauvoo, he accepted the calling issued by Joseph Smith to serve a mission which had, among other purposes, gathered funds to build the temple. This six-month mission laid the foundation for further service to the area during 1843–45. William responded to the call immediately, leaving within a week after the conference closed. He traveled by steamboat down the Mississippi River to St. Louis. Although he had balked at the mission to England partly because of poverty, funds were not an impediment for this faith-fueled mission. William put his trust in the Lord by traveling without "purse or scrip," as the New Testament and earlier Latter-day Saint revelations stipulated (D&C 24:18, 84:86). In so doing, he was following the model set by his fellow apostles a year earlier when they had embarked on their mission to England. He felt that his faith was immediately rewarded. In a letter to Don Carlos in May, apparently the only one that has survived from this mission, he described: "When I left Nauvoo, I had little or no money, and had it not been for the kindness of a gentleman of the name of Silas Haight . . . I do not know how I should have got along. He being on his way to St. Louis on board the same steamer, and seeing me among the deck passengers, took me into the cabin, and paid my fare to St. Louis." This man was almost certainly Silas Haight, the steamboat's captain. Other sources describe him as both shrewd and profane, but he apparently responded with admiration and sympathy for William's missionary endeavor, not only paying his fare but also making an additional contribution so William could continue his journey. William blessed him and hoped the Lord would "reward him for his kindness, even a hundred fold."[3]

---

3. William Smith (Armstrong County, Pa.), Letter to Elder D[on] C[arlos] Smith, May 8, 1841, *Times and Seasons* 2, no. 16 (June 15, 1841): 444–45. Silas Haight was known as a shrewd businessman who traversed the waterways of the upper Mississippi River for more than thirty years. "Captain Haight was all right as long as everything went right," described one contemporary, "but when things went wrong he would cut loose. He had the steamboat profanity reduced to a science; all of us could swear, but all conceded that Captain Haight was the ranking man on that." Haight would wait for no one at the riverboat landings. On one occasion when his wife was doing some shopping at Burlington, Iowa, Haight impatiently launched his steamboat just as she arrived. As she stood dismayed at the landing, Haight yelled from the boat to go to a particular house until he returned, for he would not be "laying around with a steamboat waiting for women to stock up with needles and thread." Captain E. H. Thomas, "Life on the Mississippi," 1912–13, series of articles published in the *Burlington Saturday Evening Post*, transcription by Georgeann McClure, Iowa History Project, Chapter 37, http://iagenweb.org/history/rivers/burlingtonpost/contents.htm (accessed May 9, 2013).

From St. Louis, William took another steamer south and then east up the Ohio River. Full of missionary enthusiasm, he seized the opportunity to explain Mormon principles to James Murdock, a professor of ancient languages, sacred rhetoric, and ecclesiastical history, who had taught at both the University of Vermont and Andover Theological Seminary. Due to his profession, Murdock had a keen interest in the upstart Mormon religion, with its claim of discovering and translating ancient texts, and William was more than eager to recount important events in Mormonism's first decade. "Curiosity led me to make many inquiries," related Murdock, "all of which he [William] promptly answered, and . . . with great ingenuousness [ingeniousness]." Murdock described William as "thirty years old . . . a sincere believer in the book of Mormon, and an honest, upright man, yet deficient in education." Murdock was captivated by William's firsthand account of many of the events that had impacted the Latter-day Saints and found engaging William's home-spun style of communication, complete with anecdotes and down-country metaphors. Murdock wrote up the interview, had William review it for accuracy, and then sent his account to the *Congregational Observer* in Connecticut, where it was published that summer.[4]

William most likely disembarked near Pittsburgh and gradually made his way east across Pennsylvania, visiting Saints and finding small branches organized in Armstrong, Lancaster, and Chester Counties. From Armstrong County, William wrote to Don Carlos, summarizing his activities for May 8–17. "I have held several meeting, and baptized three," related William. "I find plenty to do; there are calls [for] preaching on every hand." Four days later, he addressed a large congregation that included many Methodists and Presbyterians, in addition to a contingent of Latter-day Saints. Using Hebrews 2:1–4 as his text, he emphasized the "signs and wonders, and with divers miracles, and gifts of the Holy Ghost." William explained that "the above passages of scripture offered me an extensive field of argument, upon the subject of the [restored] gospel." He concluded, "I am happy to say, that the religion of Christ is continuing to gain ground in this vicinity; there is a church of about 40 or 50 members in this place, and [they] are some of the most respectable and intelligent part of the community."[5]

William's ultimate destination was central New Jersey where the Church had already seen marked success. He made this area his headquarters and primarily labored within a sixty-mile radius, with Philadelphia on the west end, and Toms River, New Jersey, to the east. He does not inquire about Caroline, suggesting that he wrote separate letters to her, but no correspondence between them from this mission has survived. He must have made significant portions of this journey on foot, for it taxed even his formidable strength to its limits. He was also suf-

---

4. James Murdock, Letter to *Congregational Observer*, June 19, 1841, in "The Mormons and Their Prophet," *Congregational Observer* 2 (July 3, 1841): 1; see also, Dan Vogel, ed., *Early Mormon Documents*, 5 vols. (Salt Lake City: Signature Books, 1996–2003), 1:477–80. See Chapter 3 for more information on the contents of this interview.

5. William Smith, Letter to Don Carlos Smith, May 8, 1841.

fering from what seems to be a chronic lung infection. In his May letter to Don Carlos, he admitted: "In consequence of my incessant labors, I do not feel very well, my lungs are affected through much speaking; [but] I feel as if I could not forbear . . . and have been influenced to labor beyond my strength."[6]

It was as if William was trying to make up for time lost during the previous two years when he had neglected his apostolic duties. Caring for Caroline had kept him close to home during her bad spells. A contemporary diagnosis of "dropsy" would probably find her suffering either from kidney failure or congestive heart failure, or some other condition that resulted in dangerous retention of water. The home remedies available might have provided short-term relief but not a cure. However, during those brief times when her health improved and spurred on by his newfound commitment, William redoubled his missionary efforts. He seems to have worked continually to the limit of his strength, even though he struggled with respiratory difficulties throughout the summer and early fall.

In Philadelphia William joined fellow apostle John E. Page in late August. Page had been appointed to fulfill a mission to Palestine with Apostle Orson Hyde but remained behind.[7] In a letter to the First Presidency primarily explaining why he had not accompanied Hyde, Page described William's dedication, by way of comparing their conditions: "I believe Bro. Smith is a little apt, like myself, to labor too hard for our own personal good health. I think I have reformed a little for my own good and I think if Bro. Smith would try to do so too, it would militate for his good in the better enjoyment of good health, at least his lungs would hold out better." Page was also pleasantly surprised to observe William's exemplary commitment, commenting that he was "very much pleased with the spirituality of Bro. Smith, and also his zeal with which he has labored in the vineyard of the Lord since I fell into his society in and about Philadelphia. He has been blessed of the Lord to add many souls to the Kingdom in this region of country. He is truly a destroying storm of sectarianism."[8]

While William was acknowledging his limitations and, in essence, reproaching himself for his feebleness, the Saints in the East were impressed with William's effectiveness as a preacher. Although records are not sufficiently complete to provide an analysis of how frequently each apostle spoke, during the

---

6. Ibid.

7. Like William, Page pled poverty and other difficulties that prevented him from fulfilling his mission with the Twelve. When George A. Smith subsequently encountered William Smith and John E. Page in Philadelphia in June 1841, George encouraged Page to leave immediately and catch up with Hyde who was already in Europe. Page never made the journey, though he had collected sufficient funds to do so. Benjamin Winchester (Philadelphia, Pa.), Letter to Joseph Smith, September 18, 1841, Joseph Smith Collection, LDS Church History Library; Allen, Esplin, and Whittaker, *Men with a Mission*, 3–4, 306–7.

8. John E. Page, Letter to the President and Council of the Church of Jesus Christ of Latter day Saints at Nauvoo, September 1, 1841, Philadelphia, in Journal History, September 1, 1841, 2–8.

Nauvoo period William increasingly addressed Church gatherings—even more than many of his apostolic colleagues, providing circumstantial evidence of his persuasive speaking ability. In Armstrong County, Pennsylvania, William felt great power in the Spirit as he preached to some fifty Saints and a number of curious onlookers. While "testifying to the truth of gospel and proclaiming the important message of salvation, the power of the Most High rested upon me," he wrote to Don Carlos in a passage brimming with gratitude. "The spirit of the Lord was manifest, believers rejoiced in the Lord and others who had stood aloof were constrained to acknowledge the truth of the message." William had already baptized three in the region, and more were scheduled to be baptized two days later. Humbly, William thanked God for communicating the message effectively, reporting that his listeners were reportedly astounded at Smith's sermon and said they "had never heard it after this sort."[9]

During the summer, the Twelve began returning from their mission to England. William longed to reconnect with them after the long season of aloofness. He had already joined forces in Philadelphia with John E. Page, the only other apostle who had not gone to the British Isles, and rejoiced when he encountered George A. Smith, William's first cousin, who had been ordained an apostle in 1839. George A. took a circuitous route home after arriving in New York, traveling to New Egypt, New Jersey, where William was staying. During the first week of June, the two cousins preached in the woods and in a schoolhouse in Cream Ridge, New Jersey, on several successive nights.

In less than a week, seven new converts accepted baptism. In teaming up with George A. Smith and John E. Page, William felt a stronger connection to his quorum than he had had for more than two years. William took George A. to Philadelphia, where they reluctantly parted, with George A. continuing his journey to Nauvoo.[10] Still, William must have felt insecure about his place in the quorum. Both George A. Smith and John E. Page were comparatively unfamiliar with his erratic service as an apostle—specifically, his conflict with Joseph Jr. over the debating school which had become public, the fact that he had actually cursed Joseph in the turmoil of the last Mormon months in Missouri, and his refusal of an important missionary assignment. Men like Brigham Young and Heber C. Kimball, with their unwavering loyalty and obedience, were probably growing impatient with what they perceived as excuses, even while they appreciated William's achievements and praised his accomplishments. But George A. also caught a glimpse of some of the challenging aspects of William's personality during their brief labors together that summer. In a private conversation, George A. later remembered that his cousin expressed frustration over the funds he was

---

9. William Smith to Don Carlos Smith, May 8, 1841.

10. "History of George A. Smith," June 4–8, 1841, 39–40, George A. Smith Papers, 1834–75, MS 1322, Box 1, fd. 1, LDS Church History Library. At this point, William had been spectacularly estranged from the Twelve for twenty years, and George A., who was fiercely loyal to Brigham Young, may have had no reason to cast this memory in a more positive light.

The brick schoolhouse in the woods at Cream Ridge, New Jersey, photograph taken in 1905, photographer unknown. Both Joseph Smith and William Smith preached at this location, which was used as an early meeting place for the Saints who resided in Monmouth and Ocean Counties, New Jersey. Courtesy Allentown-Upper Freehold Historic Society.

raising for the temple, recounting that William "considered he was putting means into the hands of Joseph to educate his children, while his [William's] own children were remaining ignorant." George A. defended Joseph: "I think that Joseph has done all he could for his relatives, and I wonder that he has done as much as he has considering the circumstances he had been under."[11] If George A. remembered and reported this exchange accurately, it is another early indication that William felt himself entitled to preferential treatment because of his family connections, even while he was shouldering the same burdens as the other apostles.

Don Carlos died on August 7, 1841. No record has survived of William's feelings, but it must have been a serious blow, especially since Don Carlos was probably the sibling to whom William was closest out of all the family. They had been intimate playmates during childhood and, more recently, had managed their joint business venture with the Mormon Hotel at Plymouth. He had also missed the healing that would have come as tributes poured in from the community and the Saints joined in mourning during the funeral. It seems likely that William appears to have sublimated his sorrow by throwing himself even more fervently into his mission. He returned

---

11. "History of William Smith," *Millennial Star* 27, no. 1 (January 7, 1865): 8. This source dates the conversation as occurring in 1843, but the account referred to and George A.'s recollection of attending "a woods meeting" with William in New Jersey better fits the summer of 1841. "History of George A. Smith," June 5–7, 1841, 39.

to Nauvoo in November 1841, bringing with him the triumph of a very successful mission. First, he had baptized twenty-five converts and witnessed the baptisms of many more performed by Erastus Snow, Benjamin Winchester, and other traveling missionaries with whom he had labored. The eastern branches had been materially strengthened by his efforts. He had set a high standard for himself in terms of strenuous and unremitting work, with the result that he had demonstrated his commitment to the Church and to his apostolic calling.

After his return to Nauvoo, his ardor about the work remained high. He enthusiastically reported on the prosperity of the eastern branches: "Calls for preaching are very numerous and the field for labor is very extensive." He felt that "twenty five or thirty elders could be busily engaged."[12] The branches in the East were blossoming by the early 1840s, and William could confidently share his optimism that the success of the Church in the area would continue.

He was eager to return to the East as soon as possible, but events kept him in Nauvoo that winter. Caroline was experiencing another difficult episode in her illness.[13] In addition to Don Carlos's death, Father Smith had died less than a year earlier, and Lucy, along with other family members, would have also needed William's support. Another impediment to returning to the mission field was William's increasing responsibilities in Nauvoo during the next year and a half. Five months after his return, in April 1842, William launched his weekly newspaper, the *Wasp*, a project that absorbed much of his time. In August, he was elected a Democratic representative from Hancock County to the Illinois House of Representatives, which meant that he was in Springfield full time between December 1842 and March 1843. (See Chapter 8.) By then, the renamed newspaper had been shifted to John Taylor, freeing William to return to the East.

Although William had engaged in land transactions with Joseph and Hyrum during the early part of 1841, his six-month absence had resulted in de facto separation from the business. During the spring of 1842, he still sought to purchase and sell land, only to encounter what seemed like reluctance from Joseph to include him in business affairs, possibly because Joseph found William overly willing to engage in speculative real estate deals. Soon after he had left for his eastern mission, William wrote to Joseph in August 1841 asking his brother to deed him two lots at Nauvoo, including one that was "on the hill near the Temple." "I want to sell [one]," he confided, "in order to b[u]y me a small farm near Plymouth."[14] This motive suggests speculation, a difficult business to manage from a distance. Apparently Joseph took no action on this request, but in the spring of 1843, after he had finished his work in the Illinois legislature, William again asked Joseph for the deed to the lot near the temple. According to a later account by Brigham Young, Joseph

---

12. "Elder William Smith . . . ," *Times and Seasons* 3, no. 2 (November 15, 1841): 599.
13. Ibid.
14. William Smith (Chester County, Pa.), Letter to Joseph Smith, August 5, 1841, LDS Church History Library.

"told him he would do so [transfer the lot] with great pleasure, if he would build a house and live upon it; but he would not give him a lot to sell." William assured Joseph that he planned to build his home there, so Joseph transferred the property to him. Then, "a few hours afterwards," William broke his agreement with Joseph and tried to sell the lot for $500 to James Ivins, a convert and friend from William's eastern mission. Joseph directed the city clerk to void the transfer to William. Just as William had tried to make the sale without talking over his changed plans with Joseph, so Joseph apparently acted with equal abruptness. Thus, when William learned that Joseph had nullified the transaction, he predictably became "so offended that he threatened Joseph." Once again, the two brothers demonstrated short-fuse reactions that plunged them into an adversarial confrontation. Although the details of the confrontation are limited, Joseph apparently followed up with a second, more thoughtful approach that avoided an open breach.[15] But the bottom line was that William did not get title to the property.

Instead of the lot near the temple, William said that in May 1843 he purchased a sandy lot near the river for $300 and contracted with Reuben Hedlock to construct a home for him and his family. To his surprise, however, only weeks later, Hedlock was called as a missionary to England. He was not successful in that assignment. After more than two years in England, the First Presidency sent Parley P. Pratt, John Taylor, and Orson Hyde to England to straighten out the mission's confused financial and administrative affairs. When they discovered that Hedlock had misappropriated to his own use the funds that the Saints had been saving with great sacrifice so that they could migrate, the apostles excommunicated Hedlock in October 1846. According to William, who wrote this account in third person, "the sequel to the story is, in the fact that Hadlock [sic] never returned from his mission to England, and William Smith found himself minus of money, house and lot."[16]

Brigham Young's 1865 account incorrectly dated this disagreement over the deed to the lot as occurring in May 1844, an account which was repeated in later LDS publications. Young conjectured that Joseph was getting rid of William

---

15. Brigham Young published an account of the brothers' conflict over the lot in 1865 as "History of William Smith," *Millennial Star* 27, no. 1 (January 7, 1865): 7–8, and Andrew Jenson republished Young's account in his own "William Smith," *Historical Record* 3, no. 5 (March 1886): 44–45, and again in *Latter-day Saint Biographical Encyclopedia: A Compilation of Biographical Sketches of Prominent Men and Women in the Church of Jesus Christ of Latter-day Saints,* 4 vols. (Salt Lake City: Andrew Jenson History Company, 1901–30), 1:86–87.

16. "William B. Smith," *The Expositor* (Oakland, Calif.) 4, no. 8 (August 1888): 3. When William read Andrew Jenson's 1886 republication of Young's account, he felt that Jenson reported the conflict over the lot inaccurately. According to William, Jenson was mistakenly describing the lot near the Mississippi River, where William had contracted with Hedlock to build his house. Andrew Jenson, "William Smith," *Historical Record* 3, no. 5 (March 1886): 44–45; In his *Expositor* account, William does not mention the deed and its cancellation for the lot near the temple.

when he assigned him to take a second mission to the East, describing it as the last time Joseph and William met before Joseph's death. Young thus implied that the two brothers parted with hostile feelings. However, these events actually occurred in the spring of 1843, not 1844. Young, who was probably assisted by George A. Smith in compiling the account, remembered that William was "accompanied by his family" when he left on this mission, corresponding to the events of 1843. William briefly returned to Nauvoo in the spring of 1844, but Caroline and their daughters remained in the East.[17] Thus, the Young/Smith account, by collapsing the May 1843 disagreement over the deed with William's brief return to Nauvoo in April-May 1844, erases several significant events in William's life during that brief time period: His endowment and induction into the Quorum of the Anointed, his attendance at important meetings with Joseph and other members of the Twelve during those critical months, and his enthusiastic "electioneering" in Joseph's campaign for the U.S. presidency. The skimpy evidence available also suggests that the two brothers successfully worked through their differences over the property in the spring of 1843, not, as Young stated, that the conflict was so volatile that Joseph "deemed it prudent to keep out of the way, until William left on a steamboat for the East."[18] Additional evidence of the harmonious relationship between the two brothers is that, on May 10, 1843, Joseph himself drove William and his family in Joseph's carriage to the upper landing as "they were intending to start on their missions, but no steamboat came." (The only consequence was that William and his family had to wait a day or two, but they definitely departed as soon as possible, since William's name does not appear in the minutes of any meetings in the days following.) William was naturally upset with Young, and Andrew Jenson's later reprint's of Young's versions, that cast him and Joseph as adversaries. Referring to the conflict, William protested in his 1888 *Expositor* correction, "I did not suppose it would become Church history."[19]

By at least the spring of 1843, William was introduced to plural marriage, further evidence that he remained in Joseph's trusted inner circle. Although the details of this introduction and his reaction have not survived, both Joseph Smith and Brigham Young likely played a role. Before William left for the East on May 10, 1843, Brigham Young sealed him and Mary Ann Covington Sheffield, a recent convert from England. Covington had been married to James Sheffield in England but had left her alcoholic husband a few months prior to sailing for

---

17. "History of William Smith," 7–8; Verifying that Caroline and her daughters remained in the East when William traveled to Nauvoo in April-May, 1844, is Caroline's letter to William, written from Philadelphia on May 5, 1844. Caroline Grant Smith (Philadelphia, Pa.), Letter to Jedediah M. Grant, May 5, 1844, LDS Church History Library.

18. "History of William Smith," 7–8; Jenson, *Latter-day Saint Biographical Encyclopedia*, 1:86–87. William was still alive when Jenson wrote his biographical sketch in about 1886, and responded to what he felt were its inaccuracies. "William B. Smith," *The Expositor* (Oakland, Calif.) 4, no. 8 (August 1888): 3.

19. "William B. Smith," *The Expositor* (Oakland, Calif.) 4, no. 8 (August 1888): 3.

America in a company led by Orson Hyde. The company had reached St. Louis so late in the season that they had been forced to winter there for four months until the ice melted.[20] They reached Nauvoo in April 1843.

William initially met Mary Ann that month at Montrose, Iowa, at the home of William's uncle Asahel Smith, just after her company completed their journey to Nauvoo. Thus, the two could not have known each other longer than a month when this marriage occurred. Mary temporarily lived in Orson Hyde's home, where Joseph Smith introduced her to the principle of plural marriage. "I went to live at Orson Hyde's and soon after that time Joseph Smith wished to have an interview with me," recalled Covington decades later in being interviewed for the Temple Lot Case. "He had the interview with me, and then asked me if I had ever heard of a mans having more wives than one, and I said I had not. He then told me that he had received a revelation from God that a man could have more wives than one." A short time afterward, Joseph came to her again, informing her that "his brother William wished to marry me as a wife in plural marriage if I felt willing to consent to it." Within a few weeks of arriving at Nauvoo, Mary Ann moved in with Agnes Coolbrith Smith, the widow of William's brother Don Carlos. Agnes had been sealed as a plural wife of Joseph Smith on January 6, 1842. According to Mary Ann's later recollection, her own sealing occurred at Agnes's home, the two-story printing office on the northeast corner of Water and Bain Streets. She identified Brigham Young as the officiator but did not remember the presence of any witnesses. It is not clear whether Caroline was also instructed in "the principle" and gave her consent to the marriage. In any case, Caroline and William left only few weeks later. Though their time together was brief, Mary Ann reported that William "treated me very well."[21]

Mary Ann Covington Sheffield Smith Stratton West, 1815–1908. Courtesy Daughters of Utah Pioneers.

It is possible that William had not been instructed as thoroughly as other members of the Twelve by his brother and other leaders prior to his leaving

---

20. Myrtle Stevens Hyde, *Orson Hyde: The Olive Branch of Israel* (Salt Lake City: Agreka Books, 2000), 148–49.

21. Mary Ann [Covington Sheffield] West, Testimony, in United States testimony 1892, Court of Appeals (Eighth Circuit), 495–96, MS 1160, LDS Church History Library. Although for convenience, I usually cite the published version, in this case and a handful of others, the original transcript provides crucial details. For Agnes Coolbrith Smith's sealing to Joseph Smith, see, Todd Compton, *In Sacred Loneliness: The Plural Wives of Joseph Smith* (Salt Lake City: Signature Books, 1996), 153–54.

Nauvoo, as he later seemed to believe that he could exercise the sealing power—a right strictly reserved to a small handful of Joseph's confidants and only in Nauvoo. William's absence from Nauvoo for the following year also meant that William missed the extensive instruction that the Prophet provided to the Twelve, sometimes on a daily basis in the spring of 1844.[22] This situation and William's enthusiasm for the new doctrine may help explain why he later seemed to feel that he could endow others with sealing power and to instruct them regarding plural marriage. Over the next two years, William introduced plural marriage to key leaders in the East, and word inevitably circulated throughout the eastern branches that William both approved of and was involved in polygamy.

But another reason may have simply been William's willingness to breach conventional morals, especially given Caroline's gradually worsening illness. A year earlier in May 1842, two women implicated William as part of the group John C. Bennett and Chauncey L. Higbee had led into adultery and "spiritual wifery." The first, twenty-seven-year-old Sarah Miller, testified before Nauvoo's High Council on May 24, 1842, that Higbee had visited her that same month, made "seducing insinuations," and told her it was not a crime for a single woman to be sexually intimate if they kept the affair secret. When Higbee visited her a second time, "William Smith came with him & told me that the doctrine which Chancy Higby had taught me was true."[23] Whether William knew all of the details of Higbee's earlier argument is unclear from the fragmented minutes.

The second woman, also investigated by the high council, was Catherine Fuller Warren. Significantly, the holograph high council minutes show that some sections of Warren's testimony referring to William were crossed out, perhaps to protect William, or perhaps because this portion of Warren's testimony was unsubstantiated during the high council's investigation. A third woman, Melinda Lewis, who must have been a near neighbor to Warren, gave the high council the names of other men who made presumably illicit visits to Warren but specifically testified "[I] have never seen Wm Smith there [at Warren's home]." A fourth woman, Matilda Nyman, testified that William attempted to seduce her but "I refused because I had come to the determination to break off such conduct." (Nyman had earlier suc-

---

22. Ronald K. Esplin, "Joseph, Brigham and the Twelve: A Succession of Continuity," *BYU Studies* 21, no. 3 (Summer 1981): 302–7, 319–20; Alexander L. Baugh and Richard Neitzel Holzapfel, "'I Roll the Burthen and Responsibility of Leading This Church Off from My Shoulders on to Yours': The 1844/1845 Declaration of the Quorum of the Twelve Regarding Apostolic Succession," *BYU Studies* 49, no. 3 (2000): 5–19.

23. John S. Dinger, ed., *The Nauvoo City and High Council Minutes* (Salt Lake City: Signature Books, 2011), 415–16 note 40. Dinger notes that the words added in italics from the minutes he quotes "come from the original [minutes], a photocopy of which exists in the Valeen Tippets Avery Papers at Utah State University." Sarah Miller's quotation about William was in italics and was apparently thus eliminated from some surviving transcriptions.

cumbed to the blandishments of Chauncey Higbee, a lapse she deeply regretted.)[24] While William's connection with these women is somewhat unclear and there are conflicting accounts as to William's participation with Bennett and Higbee, he was sufficiently implicated that the high council felt it necessary to convene a court for William, probably during that same summer of 1842.

In a late reminiscence, Lorenzo Snow recounted some details of the circumstances surrounding William's trial in a council meeting of the Twelve in Salt Lake City. According to Apostle Abraham H. Cannon's remarkably detailed diary, Snow said:

> William Smith, one of the first quorum of apostles in the age had been guilty of adultery and many other sins. The Prophet Joseph instructed Brigham (then the President of the Twelve) to prefer a charge against the sinner, which was done. Before the time set for the trial, however, Emma Smith talked with Joseph and said the charge preferred against William was done with a view to injuring the Smith family. After the trial had began Joseph entered the room and was given a seat. The testimony of witnesses concerning the culprit's sins was then continued. After a short time Joseph arose filled with wrath and said, "Bro. Brigham, I will not listen to this abuse of my family a minute longer. I will wade in blood up to my knees before I will do it." A rupture between the two greatest men on earth seemed imminent. But Brigham Young was equal to the danger, and he instantly said "Bro. Joseph, I withdraw the charge." Thus the angry passions were instantly stilled.[25]

I have not been able to find any evidence to corroborate the detail that members of the high council were attempting to "injure" the Smith family. Perhaps due to her influential position as the newly appointed president of the Relief Society, Emma had learned something from sisters in her organization that had led her to make that claim. Either way, her timely intervention may have

---

24. Testimonies of Sarah Miller, Catherine Fuller (Warren), Matilda Nyman, and Melinda Lewis, Testimonies in Nauvoo High Council cases, 1842 May, MS 24557, LDS Church History Library. Dinger's transcription of the *The Nauvoo City and High Council Minutes*, 416–18, which quotes Warren's testimony, contains no reference to William. See ibid., 415–16 note 40 for the portion mentioning William that was deleted from the transcript.

25. Dennis B. Horne, ed., *An Apostle's Record: The Journals of Abraham H. Cannon* (Clearfield, Utah: Gnolaum Books, 2004), April 9, 1890, 144. Horne notes that "the parallels between this story and the following related by former BYU professor Truman G. Madsen are striking: 'This is a story still carried in the family lore of Brigham Young's descendants but, so far as I know, never recorded. It says that in a meeting the Prophet rebuked Brigham Young from his head to his feet for something he had done, or something he was supposed to have done but hadn't—the detail is unclear. And it may well have been that the Prophet was deliberately putting Brigham Young to a test. When he had finished the rebuke, everyone in the room waited for the response. Brigham Young rose to his feet . . . . In a voice everyone could tell was sincere, he said simply, "Joseph, what do you want me to do?" And the story says that the Prophet burst into tears, came down from the stand, threw his arms around Brigham, and said, in effect, "Brother Brigham, you passed."'" Truman G. Madsen, *Joseph Smith, the Prophet* (Salt Lake City: Bookcraft, 1989), 87–88, quoted in ibid., 144–45 note 13.

helped sway the outcome in William's favor, and although Joseph demonstrated a pattern of defending his brother William throughout his tenure in the Twelve, perhaps both he and Emma were responding to the lack of evidence of actual adultery on William's part. According to Sarah Miller's testimony, William had corroborated Higbee's teaching but had not committed adultery with Miller. While he may have made a direct approach to Nyman, she describes herself as rebuffing his attempt at seduction.[26] Whatever the extent of William's connection to Bennett and Higbee that spring, during July and September 1842, he vigorously condemned their actions in *The Wasp*.[27] Furthermore, Bennett and Higby were excommunicated, but William was not formally disciplined.

BY APRIL 1843, as part of the seasonal missionary assignments, most of the Twelve went east to preach and collect funds for the temple and Nauvoo House. Joseph assigned William to return to the eastern branches "with his sick wife."[28] Caroline's condition had not improved over the winter, and William hoped that a change of scene and access to better medical care would help her. In a pamphlet published in 1844 before returning to Nauvoo, William defended himself against what he considered to be "slanders." In this pamphlet, William justified his travels by recounting his hope of finding "some superior medical skill, that might restore my family to health again, if not to their former youthful bloom."[29] Although it was only Caroline who seemed to be "sick and helpless," William did not want to be separated more than necessary from his daughters Mary Jane, who had turned nine in January 1843 and Caroline Louisa who was a few weeks shy of her seventh birthday.

On the same day that blossoms first appeared on apple trees in Nauvoo, a sure indicator of warmer weather for travel, teams of missionaries prepared to head east, including most of the Twelve. As mentioned above, on May 10, William, Caroline, and their two daughters prepared to embark on a Mississippi River steamboat. Accompanying the group was Caroline's brother Jedediah M. Grant, who would help care for his sister and work as William's missionary companion. Joseph recorded in his journal: "Took my brother William, [and] Elders

---

26. At least two historians, citing Catherine Fuller Warren's May 25 testimony, conclude that William had committed adultery: D. Michael Quinn, *The Mormon Hierarchy: Origins of Power* (Salt Lake City: Signature Books, 1994), 634; Robert D. Hutchins, "Joseph Smith III: Moderate Mormon" (M.A. thesis, Brigham Young University, 1977), 33 note 104.

27. "Bennettiana," *The Wasp* 1, no. 15 (July 23, 1842): 2; "Bennett," *The Wasp* 1, no. 16 (July 30, 1842): 2; "Dr. Bennett, the late Mormon general . . . ," *The Wasp* 1, no. 21 (September 10, 1842): 2.

28. Joseph Smith, Journal, April 19, 1843, Hedges, Smith, and Anderson, *Journals, Volume 2*, 363–69.

29. William B. Smith, *Defence of Elder William Smith, Against the Slanders of Abraham Burtis and Others* (Philadelphia: Brown, Bicking & Guilbert, 1844), 12. He also pointed out the seriousness with which he took his ecclesiastical responsibilities of preaching, baptizing, and strengthening the young branches of the Church.

J. M. Grant, E[benezer] Robinson and Horace K. Whitney in my carriage to the Upper Steam Boat landing and back. They were intending to start on their mission, but no steamboat came."[30] The group probably departed the next day and was followed by most of the Twelve, who were dispatched in the following two months. The Twelve traveled in small groups, some holding meetings along the way in Cincinnati, Pittsburgh, Philadelphia, and New York.[31] William missed most of these gatherings due to his pressing need to get Caroline and the children settled in New Jersey. He was the only apostle whose family was traveling with him. Except for the brief return to Nauvoo in April-May 1844 already mentioned, William would remain in the East until April 1845.

By summer William and his family had settled themselves in Hornerstown, New Jersey, a city in the same region where William had lived two years earlier. In September he relocated to Philadelphia, at "No. 418 North Tenth Street . . . above Callo[w]hill Street."[32] Initially, he spent much of his time nursing Caroline and laboring in the branch established at Philadelphia. When eight of the Twelve held a conference in Boston on September 9–11, 1843, William "did not Enjoy the Pleasure of the Company of the twelve while they were . . . hear [sic] as much as I wanted to on account of . . . my wife being Sick," he explained in an October letter to Joseph, but still felt that their labors had "don[e] a vast deal of good." William remained optimistic that Caroline would recover. She was under the care of "a doctor in these parts celebrated for the cure of dropsy" who was "working wonders upon her. The proespect of her being released of her Loathsom diseas will Keep us till spring before returning to Nauvoo."[33] At that point, he was envisioning a mission of about a year before returning to Nauvoo. In fact, it would extend more than twice as long.

After William established his family and Caroline's health was stabilized, his efforts turned to the status of the eastern branches. William's colleagues of the Twelve left for Nauvoo in October.[34] Though William was not specifically assigned to preside over all the eastern branches, he was the highest-ranking Church authority in the area. The Philadelphia members viewed him as "an eyewitness to many of the

---

30. Journal History, May 10, 1843, 1.

31. Hedges, Smith, and Anderson, *Journals, Volume 2*, 369 note 946. Heber C. Kimball left Nauvoo for his eastern mission on June 10. Stanley B. Kimball, ed., *On the Potter's Wheel: The Diaries of Heber C. Kimball* (Salt Lake City: Signature Books and Smith Research Associates, 1987), 51. Wilford Woodruff, George A. Smith, and Brigham Young left Nauvoo on July 7. Elden J. Watson, ed., *Manuscript History of Brigham Young 1801–1844* (Salt Lake City: Smith Secretarial Service, 1968), 134.

32. Walter W. Smith, "History of the Philadelphia Branch," *Journal of History* (Lamoni, Iowa) 12, no. 1 (January 1919): 117–18.

33. William Smith (Philadelphia, Pa.), Letter to Joseph Smith, October 28, 1843, LDS Church History Library.

34. Watson, *Manuscript History of Brigham Young*, 152; Scott G. Kenney, ed., *Wilford Woodruff's Journal, 1833–1898*, typescript, 9 vols. (Midvale, Utah: Signature Books, 1983–85), 2:318.

stirring scenes incident to the establishment and progress of the Church of Jesus Christ in these last days," as "an able defender of the truth," and as a preacher who, during 1843, "added strength to the church in Philadelphia by his testimony."[35] Regrettably, with time, William's labors among the Saints in the East would be riddled with conflict. While William's charismatic personality and oratorical gifts initially drew people to him, his leadership ability did not have Joseph's staying power. Whereas those who knew Joseph best seemed to increase in love for and loyalty to him, William did not share leadership well and lacked Joseph's gift for intimacy. His personality was frequently prickly, and his officious style of leadership frequently upset both his colleagues and those over whom he presided. Although a dynamic leader, he had no gift for submission as a subordinate, and he stubbornly resisted opposition to his views and policies. He became most rancorous when his decisions were challenged in public by those he supervised.

William must certainly have hoped for a renewal of the warmth and support he had experienced during his 1841 mission, but branch members, who had endured dozens of sermons urging them to support massive and faraway projects like the Nauvoo Temple and Nauvoo House, were more restrained in opening their pocketbooks. Furthermore, John C. Bennett's disquieting disclosures in his *The History of the Saints; or, an Exposé of Joe Smith and Mormonism*, published in the fall of 1842,[36] had created uneasiness about visitors from Church headquarters. Bennett's sensational lectures in New York and Massachusetts, even preceding his book, had also alarmed many members.[37] Even though they well understood apostasy and the probability of self-justifying accusations, some felt a new defensiveness about being Mormon. Particularly alarming were Bennett's disclosures about polygamy. Thomas S. Terry, an eighteen-year-old Pennsylvania convert of less than a year, heard a Mormon elder, Joseph H. Newton, preach in favor of plural marriage in Philadelphia even before William's arrival. Newton had baptized him at Philadelphia on March 12, 1842, with the result that he could not deny the information, even though, when he heard Newton preach "the Doctrine of the Plurality of wives" in the "Spring of 1843," he recognized Newton's injudiciousness. Newton had, he wrote, "betrayed the confidence which Elder Brigham Young had place[d] in him, [and] it upset the whole Branch except

---

35. Walter W. Smith, "History of Philadelphia Branch," 118.

36. Ibid. Bennett had been excommunicated in May 1842 at Nauvoo and had retaliated by publishing a series of exposé letters in the *Sangamo Journal*, which included at least partially accurate reports that leaders at Nauvoo were practicing polygamy. He compiled his letters into John C. Bennett, *The History of the Saints; or, an Exposé of Joe Smith and Mormonism* (Boston: Leland & Whiting, 1842). For more information on Bennett and his activities in Nauvoo and afterward, see Brian C. Hales, *Joseph Smith's Polygamy, Volume 1: History* (Salt Lake City: Greg Kofford Books, 2013), 523–45.

37. Andrew F. Smith, *The Saintly Scoundrel: The Life and Times of John C. Bennett* (Urbana: University of Illinois Press, 1997), 114–28.

two."[38] Terry respected Newton, but broke with him when Newton disaffiliated from the Church in 1844 and became a prominent member of Sidney Rigdon's post-Nauvoo movement in Pittsburgh in late 1844. Newton's information provided some credibility to Bennett's accusations and caused great upheaval among the members. William found himself in a quandary, having to defend the Church against accusations of plural marriage, while at the same time accepting and engaging in the practice. Basically, he followed his colleague's example at Nauvoo of issuing public denials and shifting the accusation from "plural marriage" to "spiritual wifery" which he could, in good conscience, deny.

Many of the eastern branches had been established since the late 1830s and had been functioning fairly autonomously during the last half-decade. William's arrival and his assumption of authority in gradually overseeing all the eastern branches, combined with his forceful personality and demanding leadership style conflicted with the working relationships established by many of the presiding elders (equivalent of branch presidents) in the region. Joseph Smith had earlier perceived some potential conflict as authorities from Nauvoo traveled among the eastern branches; and, on January 13, 1840, about a month after he had visited with President Martin Van Buren at the nation's capital, the Prophet instructed the Philadelphia Branch "that traveling elders should be especially cautious of encroaching on the ground of stationed and presiding elders, and rather direct their efforts to breaking up and occupying new ground."[39] Such instructions naturally provided reasons for local leaders to resist measures from visiting authorities that they found troublesome, and William would have done well to adopt this approach during his tenure in the East. Unfortunately, his personality directed him toward a more authoritarian style. Just two years after Joseph's counsel to the Philadelphia Branch and just months before William settled in the area—and not even accounting for the disruption caused by Newton's preaching on polygamy—the branch had already experienced "some misunderstanding among the officers about their rights and duties, [and] some conflict between traveling elders and the presiding authorities [which had] engendered strife."[40] The current uneasiness of the Saints in the East, combined with

---

38. Thomas S. Terry, Autobiographical sketch, 1857, 6–7, Val A. Browning Library, Dixie State University, St. George, Utah. Terry's autobiography is catalogued as a "journal," but this material was written retrospectively and defends his decision to remain attached to the Twelve. See also Stephen J. Fleming, "Discord in the City of Brotherly Love: The Story of Early Mormonism in Philadelphia," *Mormon Historical Studies* 5, no. 1 (Spring 2004): 15; Jenson, *Biographical Encyclopedia*, 3:261; Maurine Carr Ward, "Philadelphia Pennsylvania Branch Membership: 1840–1854," *Mormon Historical Studies* 6, no. 1 (Spring 2005): 84; Thomas J. Gregory, "Sidney Rigdon: Post Nauvoo," *BYU Studies* 21, no. 1 (Winter 1981): 55–56.

39. Walter W. Smith, "The History of the Philadelphia, Pennsylvania, Branch," *Journal of History* (Lamoni, Iowa) 11, no. 3 (July 1918): 366; also cited in Stephen J. Fleming, "Discord in the City of Brotherly Love: The Story of Early Mormonism in Philadelphia," *Mormon Historical Studies* 5, no. 1 (Spring 2004): 6.

40. Walter Smith, "History of Philadelphia Branch," (January 1919), 112–13.

William's abrasive personal style, meant that a clash was inevitable. Rather surprisingly, however, once established in the East, the thirty-two-year-old William formed an alliance with two other powerful personalities who were influential in the Church—George J. Adams, who was William's age, and twenty-four-year-old Samuel Brannan. Adams had a bombastic personality, enjoyed preaching, and thrived on public conflict. His effectiveness as a missionary and familiarity with the Bible were equal to those of any preacher in the country. He had been baptized in Philadelphia in 1841 and, since that time, had resided primarily in the eastern branches. According to Clarence Day, who documented Adams's 1866 ill-advised colonization venture to the Holy Land, Adams, was "of medium size, black curly hair, sharp dark eyes, intelligent forehead, Roman nose, lips that shut up like a clamshell." His personality was characterized by "great firmness if not absolute obstinacy."[41]

George J. Adams, 1811–1880. Photograph taken ca. 1866 by an unknown photographer. Photograph from *New England Magazine* 36, no. 2 (April 1907).

Not the least of Adams's qualities was his background as an actor, and he recited Shakespeare with much the same relish that he quoted scripture. He had earlier been instrumental in bringing the theater to Nauvoo, as he and his brother-in-law, Thomas Lyne, performed a series of plays in the Masonic Hall to the delight of the Saints. A good part of his success as a debater, in which he nearly always emerged victorious, was due to his skill as an actor. One editorial described Adams as "proverbial for his burning eloquence and withering sarcasm" and characterized his oratorical skill as "like the mountain torrent quenching the flames of iniquity."[42] Adams had an

---

41. Clarence Day, *The Journey to Jaffa* (n.d., n.p.) 30, quoted in Vickie Cleverley Speek, *God Has Made Us a Kingdom: James Strang and the Midwest Mormons* (Salt Lake City: Signature Books, 2006), 38.

42. Peter Amann, "Prophet in Zion: The Saga of George J. Adams," *New England Quarterly* 37, no. 4 (December 1964): 477–500; "The Star in the East," *Zion's Reveille* (Voree, Wisc.) 1, no. 12 (December 1846): 1; John S. Lindsay, *The Mormons and the Theater; or, The History of Theatricals in Utah; with Reminiscences and Comments, Humorous and Critical* (Salt Lake City: Century Printing, 1905), 3–7. In time he would prove to be a rogue and an alcoholic, who exploited many of his followers through his religious pretenses. Adams later used his acting skills in creating a coronation ceremony that literally crowned James Strang as king of Beaver Island. Speek, *God Has Made Us a Kingdom,"* 119–22. By the late 1850s, Adams established himself as a prophet of his Church of the Messiah; in 1866, he led members of

uncanny ability to win over an audience, honed during his many exploits as an actor. Edmund C. Briggs, who later served as an apostle in the RLDS Church, described Adams as "the eloquent elder," who "was one of the most intellectual and fascinating ministers of the gospel I ever heard. It was a grand feast to the soul to hear him preach Christ and repeat the Lord's prayer. He was an elocutionist of the richest type in word painting I had ever heard in the pulpit."[43] Heber C. Kimball once contrasted his own simple, straightforward style of speaking to Adams's elaborate but fragile style. Adams was a "polished stone" while Heber and Brigham Young were "rough Stones out of the mountain."[44] Kimball's condemnation likely pointed to an aspect of Adams's personality that would ultimately lead to difficulty—his egotism and unwillingness to be governed by Church authorities. Adams's larger-than-life personality was a character trait that he and William held in common. They could easily have turned into competitors; but ironically, they became cooperative partners in spreading Mormonism's message along the eastern seaboard.

While Samuel Brannan was less eccentric than Adams, history would reveal him to be an aspiring and conflicted character. An energetic and enthusiastic convert, he threw himself into the work. Because he had skills in journalism, he largely oversaw the publication of a Church-sponsored newspaper, the *Prophet*, which issued its first number on May 18, 1844, and its last on December 15, 1845 (by then

---

his church across the Atlantic Ocean to Palestine in an attempt to establish Zion. Adams lost control over his Jaffa Colony due to his alcoholism and eventually returned to the United States. A number of his followers also returned to the states, where a good number joined the Reorganized Church of Jesus Christ of Latter Day Saints. Reed M. Holmes, *Dreamers of Zion: Joseph Smith and George J. Adams, Conviction, Leadership, and Israel's Renewal* (Portland, Ore.: Sussex Academic Press, 2003), 81, 92–160. When a recommendation was made to receive Adams into the RLDS Church in 1878, Joseph Smith III consulted with counselor in the First Presidency W. W. Blair who answered, "I can only say, I would have nothing to do with G. J. Adams for the present. His accession to the church would be a source of weakness and scandal to the church, and a hindrance to the work generally. His career in respect to the church when connected with J. J. Strang, was and is regarded as very corrupt—wilfully and intentionally corrupt. And his career in respect to the Jaffa Colony was very bad indeed. For us to pick up and place in the ministry such *proven* bad men, is, to my mind, to defile the church. . . . He needs remodeling and reconstructing from foundation to capstone." W. W. Blair, Letter to Joseph Smith III, December 9, 1878, quoted in Holmes, *Dreamers of Zion*, 156.

43. Edmund C. Briggs, *Early History of the Reorganization: Autobiographical Sketches and Incidents in the Life of the Author* (Independence: Price Publishing Company, 1998), 89.

44. Referring to himself and Brigham Young, Kimball related, "we are not Polished stones like . . . Elder Adams . . . . But we are rough Stones out of the mountain, & when we roll through the forest & nock the bark of[f] from the trees it does not hurt us even if we should get a Cornor nocked of[f] occasionally. For the more they roll about & knock the cornors of[f] the better we are. But if we were pollished & smooth when we get the cornors knocked of[f] it would deface us. This is the case with Joseph Smith. He never professed to be a dressed smooth polished stone, but was rough out of the mountain & has been rolling among the rocks & trees & [it] has not hurt him at all." Heber C. Kimball quoted in Scott G. Kenney, ed., *Wilford Woodruff's Journal, 1833–1898*, September 9, 1843, 2:297.

Samuel Brannan, 1819–1889. Engraving from Oscar T. Shuck, ed., *Representative and Leading Men of the Pacific* (San Francisco: Bacon and Company, 1870).

renamed the *New York Messenger*), under his management. In between he filled its columns with news from Nauvoo, a plethora of letters from leaders—especially from William and Adams, and even dabbled in politics during the 1844 national election. After the deaths of Joseph and Hyrum Smith, when it became inevitable that the Saints must leave Nauvoo, Brannan organized an epic migration west for 230 convert Saints on the ship *Brooklyn*. At one point, just prior to their departure, he ambitiously petitioned Brigham Young to install him as one of the Twelve, in order to supervise affairs once he arrived in California. The group departed on February 4, 1846, ironically on the same day that Brigham Young sent the first wagons across the Mississippi River from Nauvoo. The *Brooklyn* sailed around Cape Horn, stopping in Honolulu, before landing at present-day San Francisco just before the California gold rush. Brannan promptly set out toward the East, intercepting Brigham Young at the Green River and encouraging him to continue to the fertile fields of California. Young squelched that proposal in no uncertain terms, having decided instead on the harsher but more isolated Great Basin as the Saints' new Zion.

Brannan periodically waffled in his commitment to the Church and eventually left Mormonism permanently. He made a fortune by supplying miners during the gold rush but squandered it through alcoholism and womanizing. He did not have enough money to pay for his own funeral when he died in 1889. He is remembered as both a hero and a scoundrel.[45]

Again, he and William could have turned into bitter competitors but instead seemed to appreciate and enjoy each other's ambitious personalities and admire their influence. By early fall 1843, the Twelve who were serving missions in the

---

45. Will Bagley, *Scoundrel's Tale: The Samuel Brannan Papers* (Logan: Utah State University Press, 1999), 15–17, 118, 131–34, 208–14. Bagley labels Brannan a scoundrel "based on his involvement in the vigilante movement, the dishonesty that surrounded his many filibustering schemes, and the scandalous conduct of his personal life rather than on his actions as a businessman or religious leader." "It is hard to tell the rags-to-riches-to-rags story of Brannan's life," continues Bagley, "with his forays into alcoholism, gambling, political corruption, and adultery—without turning the story into an object lesson, but Brannan himself expressed no remorse for any of his actions." Other contemporaries of Brannan, described his "energy, abilities, force of character and courage" as "very great," and that he had "more conspicuously shown [such traits] in the face of those obstacles and dangers that would have hampered and filled with dread less bold and talented men" (15–17).

East returned to Nauvoo, leaving William as the only apostle in the East, and hence its presiding authority. In his association with these two men, William quickly found the recognition and status he craved. Adams and Brannan revered the youthful and charismatic apostle, and Smith reciprocated that support by promoting the two men among the eastern Saints. Within months of Smith's arrival in the east, Smith, Adams, and Brannan were acting as an unofficial presidency over all of the eastern branches of Mormonism, demonstrating unusual unity on all Church matters. Smith admired Adams, whose oratorical gifts were second to none and, in an attempt to increase his standing, deemed him the "thirteenth apostle."[46] Under Brannan's editorship, the *Prophet* became the outlet for the trio's authoritative voice among the eastern branches.

Smith relished the opportunity to preside. He was most content when he was in charge, and being removed from Church headquarters at Nauvoo meant there would be no one looking over his shoulder on the decisions he made. It seems likely that the autonomy he enjoyed in presiding over the eastern branches was a reason for remaining in the East much longer than he initially anticipated, coupled with the realistic fear that another Illinois mob might rise up to slay the last surviving Smith brother. (Samuel had died of an undiagnosed illness in July 1844.) But part of the motivation may well have been William's personal empire-building, encouraged by Adams and Brannan's similar ambitions.

Between October 1843 and December 1844, William Smith launched an ambitious effort to bring the scattered eastern branches under his leadership and, even more dangerously, began to implement practices of his own volition, independent of authorities at Nauvoo. For example, he taught both Adams and Brannan the concept of plural marriage and bestowed the sealing power on them. William likely knew he was overstepping his bounds by instituting such practices outside Nauvoo, but after the deaths of his brothers Prophet and Patriarch, he perceived that both offices, especially that of patriarch, devolved upon him; as an apostle, he held as much authority as any member of his quorum. In any case, he seemed determined to move ahead with the practice. He kept in his possession detailed scriptural arguments defending the practice, as well as a marriage ceremony apparently based on the one used for his sealing to Mary Ann Covington.[47]

---

46. According to William, it was his brother Joseph who had designated Adams the "thirteenth apostle." William Smith (Peterborough, N.H.), Letter to Brigham Young, October 16, 1844, Brigham Young Office Files 1832–1878, Letters from Church Leaders and Others, 1840–1877, William Smith, 1844–1857, LDS Church History Library.

47. William had these items written up probably in November 1844, in what he termed "The Elders' Pocket Companion." He likely used the arguments contained therein to introduce George J. Adams, Samuel Brannan, and others to accept the practice of polygamy. His "Pocket Companion" was given to Isaac Sheen, along with other personal items, by William's second wife, Roxey Ann Grant, around 1850. Sheen's son John, reproduced portions of William's "Pocket Companion" in his book, John K. Sheen, *Polygamy, or The Veil Lifted* (York, Neb.: n.p., 1889). See Appendix B.

The Saints in the East, particularly those who served in leadership positions, responded more reluctantly to William's leadership than he liked, especially as they got to know him better and after he intensified his authoritarian demands in an effort to gain their compliance. Fellow apostles would later question how impetuously he would remove from office those who disagreed with him.

For example, within a few months of reaching New Jersey, during the summer and early fall of 1843, William clashed with Abraham Burtis, presiding elder of the New Egypt Branch who had been baptized in 1837 and helped organize the first branches in the state at New Egypt and Toms River. Smith and Burtis had met two years earlier when Smith had preached in the area as a missionary, but their relationship had apparently been cordial at that point. When Smith returned, however, the two men apparently sparred over plural marriage, which Burtis rightly suspected had been embraced by Nauvoo Church leaders and which William denied. Burtis also took exception to Smith's assertion of authority in the area, not an unreasonable position since William did not have specific authorization from the First Presidency to provide leadership in the eastern branches. As Smith became aware that Burtis objected to his leadership, he publicly censured Burtis at a Church meeting held on December 2, 1843, at Cream Ridge, New Jersey, that included members from all branches in the region. William recounted the history of their conflict to those in attendance at the conference, indicating that Burtis, upon learning of the death of a young man in the area, said "what a pity it was not Bill Smith" and then asserted that he "would do all he could against me, and then leave the Church." William put his self-defense in a pamphlet in which he labeled Burtis's behavior toward him as "unchristian like" and "slander[ous]." William also complained that Burtis's opposition was "not against me alone, but against all the authorities," perhaps a veiled reference to plural marriage. Smith further took umbrage at Burtis's wife, Sarah, whom William described as "behaving very disorderly" at a Church meeting where William had presided, where she apparently laughed at him, "treating me with mocks and frowns." William felt that even with all that had transpired, he would still "freely forgive them, when they repent, although they have tried to do me a serious injury." He worried that Burtis's disaffection, "if he persisted in it . . . would ruin him [Burtis], break up the Church there [New Egypt] or make a division in it."[48]

In time their clash had become dangerously personal, as Burtis apparently sought to discourage Caroline's attending physician from continuing his care. "I think the labour of Mr. Burtis," William alleged in a letter to Jedediah Grant, "to try to influence him [the doctor] to abandon his effort to cure my wife, has been quite unsuccessful." Caroline was beyond help and would soon die, but both William and Jedediah felt that Burtis was meddling in a private family matter and reacted wrathfully. "Concerning the vain and unholy attempt of Mr. Burtis, to persuade Dr.

---

48. Wm. Smith, Letter to Mr. [Abraham] Burtis (New Egypt, N.J.), September 16, 1843, as quoted in William Smith, *Defence of Elder William Smith, Against the Slanders of Abraham Burtis and Others*, 11–13.

Newell to give up your wife to the ravages of death," wrote Jedediah to William in late November, "exhibits the inherent meanness of Mr. B. so conspicuously, that the eyes of the blind will be opened, to see the courrption of a fallen, depraved, unmerciful being... entirely desititute of those inherent qualities, which renders a man a blessing to society."[49] The conflict spilled over to other members of the New Egypt Branch. While most supported Smith, several sympathized with Burtis. As their differences became increasingly public, Smith wrote Burtis, inviting him to a face-to-face meeting where he hoped they could resolve their differences. According to Smith, "Burtis remained inexorable, savage, and impenitent, threatening me with the law." When William visited Burtis at his home, he said Burtis "leaned back in his chair, against the wall, his eyes red with anger, and sparkling with rage." William expressed his fear to Burtis that he would not only lose his Church membership, but would "cross his name out of the Church of Christ. He [Burtis] replied 'go ahead, go ahead, I defy your authority,'" and according to William, repeatedly said "you are a liar."[50]

As early as October 1843, William had written to Burtis, "suspending him from acting in the office of an Elder," and summoned a council of elders from the local New Jersey branches to assist in restoring order. William convened an earlier Church council that met to discuss Burtis's case on October 18, at New Egypt. Probably because William was the person in conflict with Burtis, he appointed Jedediah M. Grant to preside. Burtis was invited to attend in his defense, but before even responding to the accusations, "became offended and withdrew from the conference, refusing to offer any rebutting testimony." According to the minutes, Jedediah then "offered a motion that his license be demanded, and he be suspended until he makes satisfaction." However, William, who obviously felt that Burtis's actions warranted more severe punishment, "offered an ammendment, that he be cut off from the Church, which was carried, [with] only two dissenting [votes]."[51] Sarah Burtis was probably cut off at the same time, but Abraham's case became more public due to his position as branch president. Smith, who never dealt well with criticism, had obviously prevailed in this contest of competing authority but still did not feel that Burtis had been adequately punished, given the upheaval in the New Egypt Branch. Smith convened a meeting on December 3 for the general Church membership in the entire area to recount what had transpired in the Burtis episode. To ensure that those Saints in the area understood who was at fault, he published his small pamphlet telling his side of the story, which included testimonies from members of the New Egypt Branch

---

49. William Smith (Hornerstown, N.J.), Letter to Jedediah M. Grant, November 26, 1843, and Jedediah M. Grant (Philadelphia, Pa.), Letter to William Smith, November 28, 1843, both quoted in William Smith, *Defence of Elder William Smith*, 12–16.

50. William Smith, *Defence of Elder William Smith*, 17, 20–21.

51. William Smith, Letter to Jedediah M. Grant, November 26, 1843; and Jedediah M. Grant, Letter to William Smith, November 28, 1843. See also Peter Crawley, *A Descriptive Bibliography of the Mormon Church, Volume One, 1830–1847* (Provo, Utah: BYU Religious Studies Center, 1997), 235.

condemning Burtis, and reporting the proceedings of both councils. Naturally, he defended his behavior and the decision of the elders' council to sever Burtis from the Church. From a less emotionally charged perspective, it is clear that William was letting his insecurities speak.

In addition to getting his version on the record, William probably saw the pamphlet as a way of forewarning the Saints in other branches that they could expect a similar fate if they failed to support William's superior authority. After reproving those in the New Egypt Branch, some of whom Smith felt were "putting at defiance the authorities of the Church [and] trampling upon all rule and Church government," he ended on a more conciliatory note. In a rare moment of introspection, Smith wrote, "That I have foibles, (and perhaps many) I shall not attempt to deny. I do not esteem myself above the rest of mankind." At the final (all-member) meeting, he offered to leave the area if the Saints did not want him there and asked those present to stand if they wished him to spend the winter in their midst. Reeling from the loss of their branch president and threatened by the loss of their membership in the Church, all those present stood in support of the intimidating apostle.

William was much gratified by this show of support and hoped the decision of the council, along with the publication and distribution of the proceedings, would "soon pass into oblivion, and there sleep forever," marking an end to resistance to his leadership in the area, but the trouble was just beginning.[52] The difficulties he experienced at New Egypt had been of such a disruptive magnitude it may have prompted him to relocate his family to Philadelphia in September. But the show of support for William's leadership manifest at the conference, helped William feel comfortable enough that he returned to the area in the fall of 1844, settling at Bordentown, New Jersey, about ten miles west from New Egypt.[53] In the meantime, William stayed actively involved in overseeing the New Jersey branches.

Benjamin Winchester was another leader who had been very influential as a missionary in the East and with whom Smith would eventually clash. Winchester had baptized Abraham Burtis in 1837 during an early mission through that part of New Jersey and had done much to build up the branches in the eastern states. Local history records that "in 1837, Elder Benjamin Winchester preached the first Mormon sermon in Ocean County, in a school house in New Egypt. . . . He made some fifty converts, who were baptized; among them was Abraham Burtis, who became a preacher."[54] Up to this point in their history, Smith and Winchester had enjoyed an amiable relationship. The two had known each other more than ten years. In 1832–33, William had been one of the missionaries working in the Erie, Pennsylvania, area when Winchester joined the Church.[55] Winchester had

---

52. William Smith, *Defence of Elder William Smith*, 18–24.

53. Walter Smith, "History of Philadelphia Branch," 117–18.

54. Edwin Salter, *History of Monmouth and Ocean Counties* (Bayonne, N.J.: F. Gardner & Son, 1890), 252.

55. Winchester specifically mentions Evan Greene and John Boynton as the elders who converted him in February 1833, but William Smith was actively proselyting with

great success as a missionary in the East, and his education was evident in several publications he wrote in defense of Mormonism. William had sent a note to *The Wasp* in April 1843, complimenting Winchester's recently published *Synopsis of the Holy Scriptures and Concordance*: "I have just perused a book, written by Elder B. Winchester, on the priesthood, and I have no hesitation in saying that it is a good work, and would recommend it to the traveling elders, as a worthy and valuable pocket companion."[56]

That support apparently continued at least until the time of the Smith-Burtis episode. When the two leaders collided in the fall of 1843, Winchester, a friend to both men, was drawn into the conflict and unsuccessfully acted as intermediary in an attempt to help them reconcile their differences. During the first meeting of New Jersey leaders, when Smith called for the vote whether to excommunicate Burtis, Winchester was one of two members who opposed the motion, which naturally angered William.[57] In a letter to his brother Joseph in October 1843, just two weeks after the meeting, William grumbled that Burtis had become a "particular favorite of Winchester."[58] Their differences apparently persisted in the months following Burtis's trial, and by the fall of 1844, Smith and Winchester were increasingly at odds.

Title Page of Benjamin Winchester's *Synopsis of the Holy Scriptures and Concordance* (Philadelphia, 1842).

Winchester's reputation had been deteriorating in the early 1840s, as he disputed with other presiding leaders at Nauvoo. In 1841, Joseph Smith recorded that he had personally given Winchester a "severe reproof" on the occasion for his "folly and vanity," and in 1842 the Quorum of the Twelve had suspended Winchester for "disobedience to the First Presidency." In 1843 Winchester was again reproved before the leading councils at Nauvoo, who also divested him

---

Greene and Boynton during this same month in this area of Elk Creek, Pennsylvania. Benjamin Winchester, *The Origin of the Spaulding Story, Concerning the Manuscript Found* (Philadelphia: Brown, Bicking & Guilbert, 1840), 2–5; Evan M. Greene, Journal, 1833 January–1835 April, 7–9, LDS Church History Library.

56. William Smith, Letter to the Editor, *The Wasp*, 1, no. 51 (April 19, 1843): 3. For more information on Winchester's *Synopsis of the Holy Scriptures*, see Crawley, *Descriptive Bibliography*, 1:199–201.

57. William Smith, *Defence of Elder William Smith*, 18–21.

58. William Smith, Letter to Joseph Smith, October 28, 1843.

of his preaching license due to his rebelliousness. One witness at the council recorded that "Winchester was entirely used up by Bro. Joseph and Bro. Young before the council of the Twelve and his license [was] taken from him. It was his last kick until he reformed. I never heard a man get such a scoring since the Lord made me as Winchester got at that time."[59] He then returned to Philadelphia, obviously disgruntled and upset. Thus, when William Smith called the first meeting over Burtis's behavior, Winchester may well have felt inclined to withhold support from yet another apostle.

In early September 1844, their differences had advanced to an extent that Smith felt it necessary to rebuke Winchester from the stand during a Church conference in Philadelphia. Winchester, who was present at the meeting, arose following Smith's comments and stated that "the quorum [of the Twelve] had slandered him, had taken his license [and] that he had spent four hundred dollars in going and returning from Nauvoo and other places, to answer to charges proffered against him, and the Twelve had never explained the reason why he was suspended." This, he explained, was the primary reason why he no longer sustained the authorities of the Church. Smith described this defense as a "ridiculous" outburst and, in early September 1844, gave public notice that Winchester was excommunicated.[60] Winchester quickly went on the offensive against Smith and, according to Jedediah Grant, "was traveling from house to house in Philadelphia, stirring up conversations about polygamy, while refusing to preach because he did not want to bring any female to her ruin, as he claimed other missionaries had."[61] During the winter of 1844–45, Winchester made no effort to conceal his contempt for the apostle. He later declared, "Had it not been for William Smith, [I] should have been in the Church to this day."[62]

As he had handled the conflict with Abraham Burtis, William immediately sought to curtail Winchester's influence among the Saints by publishing several dis-

---

59. Journal History, October 31, 1841, January 1 and 12, 1842, 1; David J. Whittaker, "East of Nauvoo: Benjamin Winchester and the Early Mormon Church," *Journal of Mormon History* 21, no. 2 (Fall 1995): 51–52, 59–60; George J. Adams (Springfield, Ill.), Letter to Peter Hess, July 7, 1843, MS 730, LDS Church History Library, also quoted in Whittaker, "East of Nauvoo," 59.

60. "Minutes of a Conference in Philadelphia," *Prophet* 1, no. 17 (September 14, 1844): 1; William Smith, "Official Notice," *Prophet* 1, no. 17 (September 14, 1844): 2. I have found no evidence or date of an actual Church court that ruled on Winchester's membership.

61. Quoting in Whittaker, "East of Nauvoo," 67, summarizing the contents of Jedediah M. Grant (Philadelphia, Pa.), Letter to Brigham Young, September 4, 1844, LDS Church History Library, also in Journal History, September 4, 1844, 5–6.

62. Samuel Brannan published an editorial denouncing William after he left the Church in the fall of 1845 in which he includes this quotation. Brannan had probably heard the statement from George B. Wallace, who had reported having a conversation with Benjamin Winchester in Pittsburgh two weeks earlier. Samuel Brannan, "Beware of Strong Delusion, Lest Ye believe a Lie and Be Damned," *New-York Messenger* 2, no. 20 (November 15, 1845): 157; also reproduced in *Times and Seasons* 6, no. 18 (December 1, 1845): 1045.

paraging editorials in the *Prophet*. At this point, Joseph and Hyrum had been slain three months earlier and the turmoil was still rocking the Church. In one editorial in September, Smith made it clear that Winchester was prohibited from preaching in the name of the Church and referred to his behavior by quoting Revelations 21:8: "All liars shall have their part in the lake which burneth with fire."[63] After Winchester aligned himself with Sidney Rigdon's movement in Pennsylvania that same fall, William felt he needed to undermine Winchester's standing further, especially among the branches where Winchester was having some success. He published another derogatory letter on November 23, 1845, in the *Prophet*, which implied, among other things, that Winchester was a thief and an accessory to the murder of his brothers, Joseph and Hyrum while at Nauvoo. "We are told that the partaker [of spoils] is as bad as the thief," wrote William in the conclusion of his published letter, "and that no murderer hath eternal life abiding in him [1 John 3:15]. Benny, remember that the blood of the Prophets is still crying for vengeance." He quoted Shakespeare on the power of guilt: "'Suspicion still haunts the guilty mind. The thief doth fear each bush and officer,'" He then demanded, "How is it with you Benny? Reflect on thy own black deeds, O thou child of hell! Repent before thou die, and art called to judgment with thy sins upon thy head!"[64] David Whittaker, in an important article about Winchester's Mormon career, admitted that William Smith's letter "must rank as one of the most libelous in the early Church."[65] It seems unlikely that William really believed that Winchester was linked to individuals involved in his brothers' assassination. Rather, in trying to diminish Winchester's reputation, William linked him with those who harbored the same spirit as those who had murdered his brothers. Either way, in accusing him of breaking the law and being an accessory to his brothers' murder, William had crossed a legal line, and Winchester immediately filed suit for slander against Smith (the editor), Brannan (the publisher), and Jedediah Grant (the distributor) of the *Prophet*. William's unfounded accusations entangled him in an expensive and lengthy lawsuit. While Adams and Grant attempted to countersue Winchester for

---

63. Smith, "Official Notice," 2; "Meeting of the Mormons Last Evening," *Prophet* 1, no. 26 (November 16, 1844): 2.

64. In William's rebuke of Winchester, he quoted Shakespeare's *King Henry VI*. William Smith (Bordentown, N.J.), Letter to Brother [Samuel] Brannan, November 1, 1844, in *Prophet* 1, no. 27 (November 23, 1844): 2. In a subsequent letter published in the *Prophet*, William wrote, Winchester "is now an excommunicate, and as such published to the world. And I have no hesitation in saying that I believe him to be one of the most consummate falsifiers that ever disgraced humanity; and the public are notified that this imposter and apostate has no authority from the Church of Latter day Saints to preach or to administer any of the ordinances belonging to the Gospel." William Smith (New York City), Letter to Elder [Samuel] Brannan, *Prophet* 1, no. 30 (December 14, 1844): 3.

65. Whittaker, "East of Nauvoo," 70.

slander, ultimately it was William who remained mired in the difficult predicament through the winter of 1844–45.[66]

In September Smith wrote to Brigham Young, explaining "that necessity requires the immediate attention of the Quorum in the case of Benj. Winchester," and, in a follow-up letter written in December, solicited statements from Nauvoo that would verify what he had written about Winchester, and requested they be put "into the form of affidavits." William avoided dealing with the fact that he had implicated Winchester in the murder of his brothers and instead wanted "to show onley that (B. Winchester was more or less engaged in the Law infraction at Nauvoo)."[67] But no such evidence was forthcoming, and William was forced to retract his earlier accusations. In a letter to Samuel Brannan intended for publication in the *Prophet*, Smith clarified that it was not his intent "to charge B. Winchester with being accessory to the murder of my Brother—but engaged more or less, I believe, in the Law infraction." It was less than a complete retraction and was definitely not an apology, though he continued: "A small mistake sometimes makes trouble, and it is not my intention to charge any person wrongfully."[68]

Though William succumbed to the serious pressure to publicly soften his former allegation, privately he held doggedly to his position, lamenting the possibility of going to prison because he was "telling the truth about Winchester." Smith's polarized thinking made it difficult for him to engage in introspection or take responsibility for his misconduct in situations where he was in error. Because he perceived Winchester as possessing an "apostate spirit," he easily disregarded evidence to the contrary, remaining stubbornly hostile to his former colleague. "Where this thing may terminate in I cant Say," he wrote to Brigham Young or Heber C. Kimball in March 1845, referring to the lawsuit. "The whigs & Rigdenits [Rigdonites] have c[ol]lected together & conspired aghainst me & no doubt will send me to the Ju[d]g[e] or prison."[69]

---

66. Ibid., 70–71; William Smith (Bordentown, N.J.), Letter to Elder S[amuel] Brannan, December 17, 1844; "Arrest," *Prophet* 1, no. 31 (December 21, 1844): 2. Wilford Woodruff, who traveled through the eastern branches in October-December 1844 (see below), was undeniably troubled by William's behavior and reported to Brigham Young: "Wm [Smith] wrote a piece accusing Winchester of having a hand in murdering his brothers, & he [Winchester] has got out warrants for him, one about to taken [Samuel] Brannan for printing it & have taken Elder Grant for selling the papers." Wilford Woodruff (Philadelphia, Pa.), Letter to Pres. Brigham Young, December 3, 1844, Brigham Young Office Files 1832–1878, Letters from Church Leaders and Others, 1840–1877, Wilford Woodruff, 1844, LDS Church History Library.

67. William Smith (New York City), Letter to Brigham Young, September 9, 1844; and William Smith (Bordentown, N.J.), Letter to Brigham Young, December 26, 1844, both in Brigham Young Office Files 1832–1878, Letters from Church Leaders and Others, 1840–1877, William Smith, 1844–1857, LDS Church History Library.

68. Smith to Brannan, December 17, 1844.

69. William Smith (Philadelphia, Pa.), Letter to Brigham Young or Heber C. Kimball, March 1845, Brigham Young Office Files 1832–1878, Letters from Church Leaders and

William's continuing apprehension was not completely misplaced. In March 1845, as he passed through Philadelphia, he was arrested and taken before Mayor John Swift, for libel. William recounted being "taken before the mare [Mayor] of the city & put under 3 thousand dollar bond to appear to the may term of co[u]rt[.] I gave bonds to the amount of 2000 the mare [Mayor] reducing the bail 1000." Thanks to the Saints' generosity, they provided security for the $2,000 bond assuring William's appearance at the May term of court.[70]

By the winter of 1844–45, the eastern branches were deteriorating under the leadership of Smith, Adams, and Brannan. Smith's brash style had upset a number of presiding elders, at least some of whom found his punitive attribute toward Burtis unjustified. The three men, acting together, had replaced many of those who opposed them, leading to further discontent and apprehension. In some branches, members were divided in their support of the authorities from Nauvoo, and some had left the Church altogether. Smith continued to spar with other leaders during his tenure in the East, including George T. Leach, presiding elder at New York City, John Hardy, president of the Boston Branch, the largest in the East, and prominent New Jersey convert John Horner, who had been baptized in 1840 by Erastus Snow.[71]

Plural marriage was the tinder that ignited the controversies, and William's leadership in the East came under closer scrutiny in October of 1844, when fellow apostle Wilford Woodruff made a two-month tour of the eastern branches before departing to preside over the Church in England. While visiting the Westfield, New Jersey, branch, Woodruff wrote to Brigham Young in October that he had received a spiritual prompting to ask a Church member what he thought about "marriage for eternity." Woodruff admitted that he found the impulse strange under the circumstances, as it was the furthest thing from his mind, but he obeyed the prompting and posed the question to Elder Quartus S. Sparks, who served as

---

Others, 1840–1877, William Smith, 1844–1857, LDS Church History Library.

70. Whittaker, "East of Nauvoo," 71–72; "William Smith," *Peoria Democratic Press* 4, no. 11 (April 23, 1845): 2; Samuel Brannan (New York), Letter to Brigham Young and Heber C. Kimball, July 22, 1845, Brigham Young Office Files 1832–1878, General Letters, 1840–1877, Be-Br, 1845, LDS Church History Library.

71. Wilford Woodruff (Boston, Mass.), Letter to President [Brigham] Young, October 9 and 14, 1844, Brigham Young Office Files 1832–1878, Letters from Church Leaders and Others, 1840–1877, Wilford Woodruff, 1844, LDS Church History Library; John Hardy, *Startling Developments of Crim. Con.! Or Two Mormon Apostles Exposed in Practising the Spiritual Wife System* (Boston: Conway and Company, 1844); John M. Horner, "Adventures of a Pioneer," *Improvement Era* 7, no. 7 (May 1904), 512–13. Horner and Smith's difficulty probably occurred during the winter of 1843–44. On May 10, 1844, the *Times and Seasons* printed a notice: "We are authorized to state that the difficulty heretofore existing between Elder William Smith, one of the 'Twelve,' and Elder John Horner, has been settled. Elder Horner has therefore had his license restored to him again, and is satisfied that opposition to the constituted authorities is bad policy." Both Horner and Smith were in Nauvoo at the time the notice was published. "Notice," *Times and Seasons* 5, no. 10 (May 15, 1844): 535.

branch president at Hartford, Connecticut, and who was serving as a missionary in the area.[72] Sparks informed Woodruff that a particular sister had been "sealed to her husband" by Samuel Brannan, thus making them spouses for eternity. Curiosity piqued, Woodruff continued his inquiries and eventually determined that leaders were sealing couples in eternal union. He also heard rumors, which he apparently was able to confirm, that plural marriage was also being taught and practiced.[73] In the early fall of 1844, either Adams or Brannan had likely sealed William Smith to Sarah Ann Libby and Hannah Maria Libby, biological sisters who had joined the Church at Lowell, Massachusetts, on May 15, 1844, and had been members of the branch since that date. Historian T. Edgar Lyon summarized that Woodruff "reported William B. Smith was in Boston [Lowell?] . . . living with two young female members of the church, blood sisters, whom he claimed were his plural wives properly sealed to him by priesthood authority." Sarah Ann was twenty-six and Hannah sixteen at the time of their marriages to William, and both worked in the textile mill industry which was such an integral part of Lowell's economy.[74] Again, it is not known whether William consulted Caroline about this step, or if he did, what her reaction was. Adams and Brannan also received plural wives with very little oversight, but the details are sketchy and evidence scant. At the very least, as their Church trials would reveal the following spring, they had engaged in both teaching and practicing polygamy in the East in 1844–45, and rumors continued to circulate throughout the eastern branches that Smith and his colleagues secretly supported the practice.[75]

After William had engineered Winchester's excommunication in September 1844, Winchester immediately affiliated with Sidney Rigdon's Church of Jesus

---

72. Quartus Strong Sparks joined the Church in 1838, had been installed as president of the branch at Hartford, Connecticut, on January 4, 1845. "Hartford Conference," *Prophet* 1, no. 38 (February 8, 1845): 2–3.

73. Woodruff to Young, October 9 and 14, 1844.

74. T. Edgar Lyon, "Nauvoo and the Council of the Twelve," in *The Restoration Movement: Essays in Mormon History*, rev. ed., ed. F. Mark McKiernan, Alma R. Blair, and Paul M. Edwards (Independence, Mo.: Herald House, 1992) 198 note 37; Martha Mayo and Connell O'Donovan, "Members and Missionaries of the Lowell, Mass. Branch of The Church of Jesus Christ of Latter-Day Saints, 1835–1860," unpublished web document, http://people.ucsc.edu/~odonovan/lowell_members.html#hannah_lib, accessed September 12, 2014. I have been unable to locate the reference Lyon cites documenting that William was living at Lowell with these two "blood sisters" whom he identified as his plural wives. However, later references include verification that Sarah Ann and Hannah Libby were sealed to William at some point between June 1844–August 1845. Joseph F. Smith (Salt Lake City), Letter to William Smith, July 12, 1884, MS 1325, Box 31, fd. 3, pp. 58–67, LDS Church History Library; Joseph Fielding Smith, *Blood Atonement and the Origin of Plural Marriage* (Salt Lake City: Deseret News, 1905), 49.

75. Dinger, *Nauvoo City and High Council Minutes*, 548–50, 549 note 18; Willard Richards, Diary, May 24, 1845, Willard Richards Papers, 1821–54, Vol. 11, May 4–23, 1845, MS 1490, Box 1, LDS Church History Library.

Christ of Latter Day Saints, headquartered in Pittsburgh. Smith, Adams, and Brannan challenged the Rigdonites both in public and in the press throughout the winter of 1844–45. William Smith felt that these various dissidents were conspiring against him, using plural marriage as their primary weapon of attack. "Benny [Winchester] with all the Rigdonites are desperate aghainst me," Smith wrote to leaders at Nauvoo, "for I have be[e]n the principle means of saving the Eastern Churches from Rigdonism hence the set determination to ruin me & get me out of the way or into prison." He further noted: "Bennys hobby in public aghainst the 12" was utilizing the "mutch fuss swirling about [the] spiritual wife practice." He expected more support from Nauvoo in defending himself against Winchester and the Rigdonites, but the Quorum of Twelve Apostles holding fast at Nauvoo were consumed by their own challenges, including repelling dissident claims to leadership, finishing the temple, and negotiating a reasonable departure date with increasingly hostile neighbors.[76] With attacks against Smith and his colleagues about plural marriage, combined with Winchester's slander lawsuit against Smith, many of the branches were on the verge of collapse.

Hannah Maria Libby (Smith Smith), 1828–1906. Photograph taken ca. 1862–1873, by Edward Martin, George A. Smith photograph collection. Courtesy LDS Church History Library.

Woodruff, for one, was shocked at what he had discovered, for it was his understanding that such priesthood ceremonies were under strict control of authorities at Nauvoo and that Brannan absolutely was not authorized to perform sealings. He hypothesized that Smith had played a role in sanctioning Brannan's actions and quickly went on to Boston, where Smith, Adams, and Brannan had scheduled a Church meeting in early October.[77]

Woodruff's unannounced arrival during the meeting apparently caught Smith by surprise. While they continued conducting Church business, Woodruff took his seat on the stand next to Smith. Rather than acknowledging and welcoming his fellow apostle, Smith, Adams, and Brannan all seemed "somewhat emberressed [sic] at my presence," Woodruff reported. He leaned close to Smith and quietly queried: "How [is it that] Br. Brannan came to be marrying people for eternity[?]." Smith admitted that he had "appointed him to do it." "His Administrations are not legal," protested Woodruff. Smith contradicted: "Yes they are[.] Any Elder can do it that has power to marry at all." Woodruff disagreed. The sealing power "is

---

76. William Smith to Young or Kimball, March [no day], 1845.
77. Woodruff to Young, October 9 and 14, 1844.

Wilford Woodruff, 1807–1898. Photograph taken ca. 1850, by Marsena Cannon. Courtesy LDS Church History Library.

a right exclusively belonging to the quorum of the Twelve or the president of the quorum." Woodruff obviously felt that the sealing power was vested only in the president of the Church—even though at this time there technically was no Church president (the First Presidency would not be reorganized until December 1847), but Brigham Young was fulfilling that function as president of the Quorum of the Twelve. Even the Twelve, as Woodruff saw the situation, needed Young's authorization to seal. Smith countered, "That has reference to exclusive privileges [i.e., plural marriages] and not reference [to] sealing a man to his wife for eternity, for any Elder can do that." Woodruff was stunned at Smith's interpretation of the sealing power and his understanding of his rights. Woodruff recorded, "I will confess some feelings came across me that made me squirm all over."[78] By now, the disagreement between the two apostles had certainly disrupted the meeting, and Woodruff dropped the subject, merely passing on a detailed report to Young before leaving the United States in December.

This conversation, however, foreshadowed the objections the Twelve would have with William Smith in succeeding months. While Woodruff's greatest concern was the unauthorized use of the sealing power, he found other actions unsettling. During the Boston meeting, John Hardy, who had been the Boston Branch's president since February 1843, resigned from his position and was quickly replaced by Joseph T. Ball, an African American convert specifically selected by Smith, Adams, and Brannan. Woodruff disagreed with this abrupt change as he felt the trio of leaders were "running all over all rights of presiding Elders, on the Claim that Wm Smith was one of the Twelve." He felt that Hardy was a good man and competent leader but that Smith, Adams, and Brannan were "leagued together in all things" and that anyone who "opposed them in their deeds, they would trample them down until presiding Elders were loosing [sic] their posts and some ready to come out in battle array openly against the Church."[79]

Woodruff was also concerned about the mission finances. Speaking of Smith and Adams, Woodruff wrote, "I have some reason to believe they have spent hundreds of dollars of Temple money for their own use."[80] That suspicion was strengthened when Woodruff attended a meeting with Smith at Peterborough,

---

78. Ibid.
79. Ibid.
80. Woodruff to Young, October 9 and 14, 1844.

New Hampshire, when "the Saints brought forward their tithings for the Temple all of which Elder Wm Smith took to the amount of $150 for the Temple and $25 or $30 dollars for his own use."[81] Woodruff understood that three leaders had collected donations from the Saints saying they were for the Nauvoo Temple but instead were being used to support the *Prophet* and for such personal use as defending Smith in his lawsuit with Winchester. William's manner of collecting money may have also disturbed Woodruff. Preaching in New Bedford, Massachusetts, during the same season Woodruff was in the area, a reporter from the *New York American* recorded that William concluded his sermon with these emphatic words: "Brethren, I will say here, for the credit of the audience, that at our last meeting I collected some two dollars, while at the same time the expenses of the hall were six dollars. Now, I wish in all soberness to assure, my dear friends, of one solemn truth, and that is, that rather than pay all expenses, preach for nothing, and find myself into the bargain, *I will see the whole generation damned first!*"[82] After spending October and November among the eastern Saints, Woodruff summarized these concerns in a letter on December 3 to Brigham Young, concluding with a plea that if he wished to "save the eastern churches to delegate some one of the Twelve from Nauvoo that will act [in concert] with you to come and take charge of them for awhile." Further, he warned Young about the need to "keep an eye upon Bro. William and Adams" by insisting that both men come to Nauvoo.[83]

William either failed to understand that being introduced to plural marriage did not give him authority to oversee, teach, or perform such unions, or he had simply assumed that prerogative. By late October 1844, Brigham Young received the first of Woodruff's lengthy communications, "relative to the injudicious course pursued by Elders William Smith, Geo J. Adams and Samuel Brannan."[84] When the Twelve realized what William was doing, they were stunned. On December 3, Woodruff had sent another report, which further expressed his concerns: "By careful observation I can see things cropping out that is leading to Apostacy and acting against our interest. God knows I don't want to injure Bro. Smith, nor Bro. Adams. For the sake of the Smith family, I want William Smith [to stay in the church], if possible, but I know that you ought to be apprised of things as they are."

He further questioned Smith's support of the Twelve: "William and Adams at times talk much about sustaining the Twelve, but I Think it is for effect more than any thing else. Wm. Smith told Elder [Jedediah] Grant that the Twelve had not sustained him, nor had he risen through their influence, but on his own. Neither should he feel himself bound hereafter to defend the character of the Twelve, or be accountable to that quorum, but he was led by visions and

---

81. Kenney, *Wilford Woodruff's Journal*, October 18, 1844, 2:475.
82. "Coming to the Point," *New York American*, October 10, 1844: 2.
83. Woodruff to Young, December 3, 1844.
84. Journal History, October 22, 1844, 1.

revelations for himself." Grant passed these remarks on to Woodruff, explaining, in mitigation of his brother-in-law's comments, that William "was somewhat excited when he made these remarks." Still, it was not an attitude that would have set well with the Twelve at Nauvoo.

Even more unnerving was the fact that Jedediah Grant voluntarily added a postscript to Woodruff's letter, stating: "The statements of Bro. Woodruff I verily believe are just and true, and some of them I know are true to the letter. My views agree with him in all things."[85] Grant had grown increasingly uncomfortable with how the branches were being managed under his brother-in-law's heavy hand.

Woodruff continued his journey to England where he also found plenty of mismanagement to absorb his energies. When his reports reached Brigham Young and the other members of the Twelve, William Clayton summarized their reaction on December 19, 1844: "Read 2 letters from Elder Woodruff to President Young concerning Wm Smith and G. J. Adams showing that they are in opposition to the Twelve and have collected money in the east for the Temple and have used it. There are warrants out for them in N York and Boston and all seems confusion and sorrow wherever they go."[86]

Already wary of Smith's inconstant behavior throughout his tenure as an apostle, Young acted without delay upon receiving Woodruff's letter. In the December 1, 1844, issue of the *Times and Seasons* (the issue was late enough that Woodruff's letter, written December 3, reached Nauvoo before it went to press), the Church announced that Parley P. Pratt had "been appointed by the council of the Twelve to go to the city of New York, to take charge of the press in that city . . . and to take the presidency of all the eastern churches."[87] Smith was, in essence, being replaced. John Taylor, editor of the newspaper, had attempted to frame Pratt's appointment as judiciously as possible, by inserting a rather lengthy notice next to the announcement. "We have just received a communication from Elder William Smith," described Taylor, "[who] would have been here some time ago had it not been for the sickness of his wife; he went to the east for the purpose of recruiting her health, which, we are sorry to be informed, is fast failing. He has been laboring for some time among the eastern churches, and purposes returning here as soon as circumstances will permit."[88]

Smith had not been consulted about the decision to replace him and was startled when that issue of the *Times and Seasons* reached him, especially as he was not in-

---

85. Woodruff to Young, December 3, 1844.
86. George D. Smith, ed., *An Intimate Chronicle: The Journals of William Clayton*, 152. The "warrants" were related to Winchester's lawsuits against Smith, Adams, and Grant.
87. "Elder Parley P. Pratt . . . ," *Times and Seasons* 5, no. 22 (December 1, 1844): 727.
88. In his notice, Taylor also commended William Smith for his missionary service, offered condolences for the deaths of his three brothers the previous year, expressed sympathy for Caroline's lingering illness, and assured him that "his old friends the Twelve have not forgotten him." John Taylor, "We have just received . . . ," *Times and Seasons* 5, no. 22 (December 1, 1844): 727.

tending to return to Nauvoo until spring. He fired off a seething letter to Heber C. Kimball on December 21, 1844. He recounted his labors to establish, support, and distribute the *Prophet* throughout the East, as well as his tireless efforts to combat "Rigdonism," and had "called on the churches to stand by the 12." But most upsetting to him was feeling that he had been replaced by Pratt and undermined by Woodruff, who, he correctly surmised, had sent negative reports about him to leaders at Nauvoo. Wrote William, "if PP Pratt [has] come hear [sic] to find fault with me & to userp more power than I have got we shall have a drawn game." William flared up at the notion that Pratt was also appointed "to take the presidency of all the eastern churches." The wording ignored his own authority, because "it do[e]s not even honor me in my office as one of the 12[.] I must say this step has surprised me mutch. . . . I acknowledge no man as my superior in the quorum but one [Brigham Young], & him in his place as one of the 12 & prophet," William continued, "the rest as my equal in power at home abroad in the land & on the sea." After pointedly referring by name to Woodruff and Pratt, William emphasized, "I want the 12 to understand that I am one of that Number."[89] Yet surely William Smith must have known that Pratt could not have replaced him unless Brigham Young had sanctioned the appointment.

The events that transpired during the winter of 1844–45 taxed William's already limited patience to its fragile limits. With Pratt's appointment as leader in the East, William began to question whether he held equal status with other members of the Twelve. After all, Woodruff's assessment of the eastern branches had been accepted unreservedly and without any sort of attempt at consulting with him. And since William was not only an apostle, like Woodruff and Pratt, he was also heir to the Church patriarch's office. After mentioning the deaths of his brothers Joseph and Hyrum, William underscored, "Remember to[o] that I am one of the Smith family & all are not." He interpreted his fellow apostles as being equal, or slightly inferior to him in authority, so they were overstepping their ecclesiastical authority.[90] If Pratt was called to replace him, then was he not viewed as the more capable leader?

Pratt responded promptly to his new assignment, traveling through Bordentown, New Jersey, where William and his family were living, on December 24, 1845, and probably arriving in New York City a day or two afterward.[91] Almost immediately after his arrival, on January 1, 1845, Pratt announced his appointment in the *Prophet*: "I, Parley P. Pratt, being duly appointed by the first presidency of the whole Church to the special presidency of the Church of the Eastern States . . ." In the ensuing weeks he forged ahead in setting the branches in order, which included criticizing the leadership of William Smith and his colleagues. He also published an editorial in the *Prophet* on January 1, which, among other things, cautioned the

---

89. William Smith to Kimball, December 21, 1844.

90. William Smith (Bordentown, N.J.), Letter to Heber C. Kimball, December 21, 1844, Brigham Young Office Files, 1832–78, Box 42, fd. 13, LDS Church History Library.

91. William Smith (Bordentown, N.J.), Letter to Brigham Young, December 26, 1844, Brigham Young Office Files, 1832–78, Box 42, fd. 13, LDS Church History Library.

Saints against supporting causes that were not sanctioned by the Twelve. "In this way," Pratt continued, "thousands of dollars are drawn from the saints and from the elders, while the temple cause is neglected." He pointedly opined that "vast sums" of money had been expended "by men who have but little experience in publishing, and perhaps pay double for the paper and printing."[92]

Parley P. Pratt had also heard accounts of Adams claiming he was an "Apostle," similar to what Woodruff indicated in his letters to Young, and a claim William had personally promoted during his tenure in the East. Pratt immediately published a notice in the *Prophet* countering that sentiment in no uncertain terms.[93] William could not have misread these statements as a critique of his own leadership. After reading these, and other similar-themed editorials, which continued into the ensuing months, William wrote in frustration, "I notice . . . [in] the times & seasons [the brethren] has But vary Lidle conffidence in my hard Labour to Save the Eastern Churches & keep up the prophet [newspaper]."[94] William believed his reputation was being damaged. In addition to this injury, he felt undermined and unappreciated for his lengthy service among the eastern Saints.

Writing on behalf of the Twelve on January 9, 1845, Heber C. Kimball carefully replied to Smith's hasty and imprudent letter written on December 21. After having "read it carefully myself several times," Kimball wrote, "it has also been repeatedly read to the brethren of the Twelve." Church leaders perceptibly knew they needed to handle William delicately, especially after receiving his impassioned letter. In defense of Pratt's appointment, Kimball referred to an earlier letter written by William to Brigham Young, dated October 16, 1844, in which he indicated: "I should have come to Nauvoo this fall But the sickness of my family prevents [it]." Based on that letter and a report they had received from George J. Adams, Kimball wrote, "We expected you to come as quick as possible [to Nauvoo]," and understood "that you had retired from travelling and was with your family in Jersey and there probably would remain untill you returned to Nauvoo." As to William's insinuation that Parley might be viewed as holding superior authority over William, Kimball explained, "when you and he are together you are one." He praised Smith for "standing up against error, and defending the churches against Rigdonism and s[c]hisms"; on that front, Kimball noted, "We have not doubted your integrity." Then, Kimball moved to the key phrase in the letter by passing on the Twelve's request: "Now brother William it is my wish, and the wishes of the Twelve that you would come to Nauvoo, as soon as the health of your family will possibly permit." He reminded him that the patriarchal

---

92. Parley P. Pratt, "Regulations. For the Publishing Department of the Latter-day Saints in the East," *Prophet* 1, no. 33 (January 4, 1845): 2; reprinted in the *Times and Seasons* 6 (January 15, 1845): 778.

93. Parley P. Pratt, "Elder G. J. Adams," *Prophet* 1, no. 33 (January 4, 1845): 2. For the full document, see Chapter 11.

94. William Smith to Young or Kimball, March [no day], 1845.

office awaited him, "which is your legal right," and that "Nauvoo will necessarily be your home henceforth . . . for your usefulness is needed here."⁹⁵

Though Kimball's letter pacified Smith for a time and assured his support of Pratt in his new position, it ignored most of the concerns leaders had about William's service in the East. Church authorities likely thought it best to deal with Smith in person. After receiving Kimball's letter, William wrote a letter to the *Prophet* in late January that must have reassured Pratt. William announced that he was "much rejoiced" at Pratt's arrival and that he would "continue to labor in conjunction with Elder Pratt, in the eastern churches until spring. It is well known however, by the saints that I contemplate leaving for the west soon, and I feel highly pleased to leave the presidency of the eastern churches in such competent hands, and I hope the saints will do all in their power to sustain them."⁹⁶ Though his feeling of being undermined was calmed for the time, most of the concerns Smith expressed in his December 1844 letter to Kimball would resurface after he returned to Nauvoo.

Winchester's lawsuit with William had dragged on since November 1844, with his arrest for libel in Philadelphia in March 1845, which placed him under the necessity of arranging for a $2,000 bond that he would need to settle with his former colleague. The need to leave the East for Nauvoo apparently motivated him to settle the suit, to which Winchester agreed if Smith and Brannan would pay him $600 in damages—$300 to pay for books published by Winchester⁹⁷ and the other $300 for libel. Brannan secured $300, and another former editor of the *Prophet*, George T. Leach, secured the other $300, and paid off Winchester in April 1845.⁹⁸ William also undoubtedly agreed to issue a more formal retraction of his

---

95. Heber C. Kimball (Nauvoo, Ill.), Letter to William Smith, January 9, 1845, LDS Church History Library.

96. William Smith, Letter to Dear Brother [Brannan], ca. January, 1845, *Prophet* 1, no. 36 (January 25, 1845): 3, also reprinted as "Letter from Eld. Wm. Smith," *Times and Seasons* 6 (February 15, 1845): 814.

97. When Pratt took over leadership in the East at the beginning of the year, he counseled Saints: "Let the books, tracts, periodicals, pamphlets, &c of Mr. B. Winchester and others no longer be patronized by the Saints." Pratt, "Regulations," 2. However, at least for a time, Winchester's publications were still being sold in England, and he probably demanded his money either for the sale or publication costs associated with printing, or for both. Samuel Brannan (New York City), Letter to Brigham Young and Council, July 22, 1845, Brigham Young Collection, LDS Church History Library.

98. William mentioned the settlement with Winchester at a meeting with the Twelve held on May 5, 1845, the day after he returned to Nauvoo. Willard Richards, Diary, May 5, 1845, Willard Richards Papers, 1821–1854, MS 1490, LDS Church History Library. Brannan wrote in July to Brigham Young that "in order to get Br. Wm Smith exhonerated from 2000 dollar bonds when he was arrested in Philadelphia by B. Winchester—that he might go to the west with his family, I gave Winchester my note for three hundred dollars that Brother [Reuben] Hadlock was owing him in England for books, payable in four months from the last of March, which I shall have to pay the last day of this month." Brannan to Young and Kimball, July 22, 1845; See also Samuel Brannan, Letter

accusations against Winchester in the *Prophet* as part of the suit's resolution. "As much speculation has been had in regard to an article published in the Prophet, some time back, in reference to Mr. Benjamin Winchester," wrote William, "I wish to correct the public mind on this subject. . . . As far as the charge of his being accessory to the death of my Brothers is concerned, it was far from my intention of imputing it to him, and that was not the meaning of the 'Law infraction.' The language was harsh, but I trust this article will amply correct it."[99]

Caroline was well enough to travel but still seriously ill when the family departed for Nauvoo on April 19, 1845. Pratt, along with many other leaders and lay members in the East, must have bade him farewell with relief. Although Pratt himself was well known for a pugnacious approach to dissent, he knew that a more conciliatory approach in leadership and especially patience would be necessary to restore order in the troubled branches. "We . . . taught the Church to beware of all impure and wicked doctrines and practices," Pratt summarized in his autobiography, "and not to receive any Elder or minister who sought to seduce them by any false teachings. With these exercises and the continual labors of Elders [Ezra T.] Benson, [Pelatiah] Brown, [Jedediah] Grant and many others, with myself, we succeeded in setting in order the church and reestablishing pure gospel principles."[100] Jedediah Grant, whose personality and actions had drawn Woodruff's approval,[101] became a stabilizing influence in the Philadelphia Branch. In June, a month after the Smith family departed for Nauvoo, Samuel Brannan recognized the need for a less combative approach. "There is more flies caught with molasses than vinegar," Brannan wrote placatingly to Brigham Young.[102] William was no longer one of the sources of conflict in the eastern branches, but his stormy leadership left many unanswered questions about his conduct in the East. His relocation in Nauvoo would bring up not only these questions but a prickly series of new issues.

---

to Brigham Young, August 29, 1845, Brigham Young Office Files 1832–1878, General Letters, 1840–1877, Be-Br, 1845, LDS Church History Library; Whittaker, "East of Nauvoo," 72. Whittaker summarizes the resolution of Winchester's lawsuit against William Smith as follows: "Because the lower courts were nonreporting courts, records are not extant either of the case or verdict. Presumably it was settled by summer 1845, possibly because Smith had backed down publicly from his original stand and possibly [because] Samuel Brannan had settled a $300 bill he owed Winchester for books sold to Reuben Hedlock in England." Whittaker, "East of Nauvoo," 72 note 125.

99. William Smith, Letter to the Editor of the Prophet, *Prophet* 1, no. 46 (April 5, 1845): 3.
100. Parley P. Pratt [Jr.], ed., *Autobiography of Parley P. Pratt* (Salt Lake City: Deseret Book, 1985), 300.
101. Woodruff to Young, December 3, 1844.
102. Samuel Brannan, Letter to Brigham Young, June 2, 1845, quoted in Bagley, *A Scoundrel's Tale*, 70.

Chapter 10

Return to Nauvoo

> She was a fond mother, an affectionate wife, a devoted friend, and the strong ties of affection which existed between us can never be broken, nor can time or eternity ever efface from my heart the virtue and graces of my Caroline.
>
> —William Smith, 1845

Despite his lengthy service and numerous connections throughout the eastern branches—or perhaps because of it—William longed to return to Nauvoo. His tenure as president of the eastern branches had been a tumultuous two years. As early as November 1844 while Wilford Woodruff was visiting the branches and accumulating much information that did not reflect well on William, William mused nostalgically: "Nauvoo contains almost all that is near to me." Its soil had been sanctified by the graves of his father and four brothers. He yearned to see "my poor old mother, almost worn out with years and trouble," and, perhaps pointedly, reminded Phelps that he, Mother Lucy, "and three sisters . . . are all of that family, who were the founders of Mormonism and the church of Christ in these last days."[1]

William had been to Nauvoo only once since his departure with Caroline and their daughters in May 1843. Only weeks before Joseph and Hyrum's assassinations, he had led a group of forty or fifty converts to Nauvoo, arriving on April 22, 1844, and followed two days later by twenty-eight-year-old Jedediah Grant, who shepherded another group of about twenty. William spent the evening of the 22nd with Joseph, reporting on the status of the eastern branches.[2] William remained in Nauvoo for less than a month, departing on May 10, 1844, just as events were coalescing that would lead to the deaths of Joseph and Hyrum a month later.

In her only known surviving letter, Caroline wrote to Jedediah on May 5, 1844. She had diligently fulfilled her promise to write William every two weeks during his absence, and although disappointed not to receive any letters from either

---

1. William Smith (Bordentown, N.J.), Letter to W. W. Phelps, November 10, 1844, in *Prophet* 1, no. 27 (November 23, 1844): 3.

2. Joseph's diary notes that a heavy thunderstorm the day before had raised the water level so significantly that it stopped all of the mills in Nauvoo, perhaps because the canals that fed the water-powered mills were ruined by the high water. Scott H. Faulring, ed., *An American Prophet's Record: The Diaries and Journals of Joseph Smith* (Salt Lake City: Signature Books, 1987), 472; Journal History, April 22, 1844, 1, and April 24, 1844, 1; "More Mormons," *Nauvoo Neighbor* 1, no. 52 (April 24, 1844): 2.

Jedediah or William that week, she remained in good spirits. "This morning all nature wears a Smile and how can I ware a frown (in the middle of the beauties and Splendurs of a May day morning)." Her chronic illness was an ever-present concern: "The distroyer has drawn a cloud over my sky a frown on my brow and a veil over my once happy face but yet I look forward to a day not far distant when the dist[r]oyer Shall leave [me] . . . clear of his poysonous influence and then I can injoy life with a knowledge of the injoyment for most assuredly I understand the bitter an[d] then why not appreciate the sweet."[3]

Jedediah M. Grant, 1816–56. Engraving by Frederick Piercy, 1853, in *Route from Liverpool to Great Salt Lake Valley* (Liverpool, 1855). Jedediah was Caroline's younger brother, who served as a missionary with William during his eastern mission (1843–45), and later served in the LDS First Presidency (1854–56) with Brigham Young in Utah.

Caroline expressed affection for William, instructing Jedediah to "tell Wm I wold like to see him an hour or two mightly well about this time." William "must keep up his spirits and do the best he can and not give himself trouble about my sufring for . . . want of means for I have been vary well provided for so far." The Philadelphia Saints had generously provided for her needs during William's absence. This letter suggests that the two enjoyed a close relationship and that Caroline especially appreciated the devoted care he had provided during her prolonged illness. Ten-year-old Mary Jane and seven-year-old daughter Caroline "are talking about theye [their] father evry day and asking me when he will come." They asked their uncle to "give their love to father." Caroline Louisa had tenderly saved a piece of everything she had collected since her father left to share with him upon his return.[4]

The *Nauvoo Neighbor* announced warmly: "We are happy to say that our well beloved brother *William Smith*, has returned once more to our goodly city, in first rate health and spirits." Perhaps referring to his success in defending Nauvoo's controversial charter in the 1842–43 legislative session, the editorial described Smith as "the same old champion of the rights of man," and "the same unguided advocate for the extension of '*Mormonism Unveiled*' power, dominion, grace and glory."[5] Probably because of that legislative service, William and Sidney Rigdon both addressed a large congregation of Saints about Joseph Smith's presidential platform on April 27. Two days earlier William had been inducted into

---

3. Caroline Grant Smith (Philadelphia, Pa.), Letter to Jedediah M. Grant, May 5, 1844, Grant Family Papers, 1844–1893, MS 3370, LDS Church History Library.
4. Ibid.
5. "More Mormons," *Nauvoo Neighbor* 1, no. 52 (April 24, 1844): 2.

the Church's political unit, the Council of Fifty, which had been organized in March.[6] William also served on a committee that helped draft resolutions to be adopted after a political state convention meeting held in the city.[7]

On Sunday, May 12, William listened to Joseph preach from the "Stand" near the unfinished Nauvoo Temple on the topic of the resurrection and vicarious work for the dead. It was the last sermon he heard his prophet-brother preach. That same day, he was initiated into the privileged Quorum of the Anointed and received his endowment along with Almon W. Babbitt. After the sacred ceremony, William joined in prayer with the other men, imploring "deliverance from our enemies and exaltation to such officers as will enable the Servants of God to execute Righteousness in the Earth."[8]

Nine days later, on May 21, William boarded the steamboat *Osprey* with Heber C. Kimball, Brigham Young, and a host of other elders. He had seen Joseph, Hyrum, and Samuel Smith for the last time in this life. Most of the departing elders were making a double mission—to preach the gospel and to campaign for Joseph as a presidential candidate.[9] Just prior to William's departure, he published a notice in the May 15 issue of the *Nauvoo Neighbor:* "Elder William Smith (late representative) wishes to say to the friends and voters of Hancock county, that in consequence of the sickness of his family, now in the hands of a doctor in the city of Philadelphia, he relinquishes the idea of offering himself as a candidate for a seat in the next Legislature of Illinois." William recommended Hyrum as a "suitable and capable person" to take his place.[10] Although William made Caroline's health his top priority, he must have been pleased that others had considered him likewise "suitable and capable" to represent Hancock County with its dominantly Mormon population in the state legislature.

In the month following his return to Philadelphia, William cared for Caroline and, with other members of the Twelve, campaigned for Joseph. Although he limited his travel outside Philadelphia, he wrote a letter to George T. Leach, who was then editing the *Prophet* at New York, encouraging him to "hand out the banner for Gen. Joseph Smith, and let the world know that we are not afraid to advocate his claims to the Presidential Chair." William also traveled part of the way toward

---

6. Quinn notes that the Council of Fifty was revealed to Joseph Smith on April 7, 1842, but its organization was not established until March 10, 1844. D. Michael Quinn, "The Council of Fifty and Its Members, 1844–1945," *BYU Studies* 20, no. 2 (Winter 1980): 164–65, 196.

7. Journal History, May 17, 1844, 1; Faulring, *An American Prophet's Record*, 474–75.

8. Faulring, *An American Prophet's Record*, 478.

9. Journal History, May 21, 1844, 1; Heber C. Kimball wrote on May 21, 1844: "I left Nauvoo in company with about 50 or sixty of the Elders of Isreal." During his journey east, Kimball noted in several journal entries that he was traveling and boarding with William Smith. Stanley B. Kimball, ed., *On the Potter's Wheel: The Diaries of Heber C. Kimball* (Salt Lake City: Signature Books and Smith Research Associates, 1987), 60–63.

10. "To the Friends and Voters of Hancock County," *Nauvoo Neighbor* 2, no. 3 (May 15, 1844): 2.

Washington, D.C., with Heber C. Kimball and Lyman Wight, who intended to give politicians what William termed "Davy Crockett and Mormon Politics."[11] Kimball fell ill during his return from Washington, D.C., but made it as far as Philadelphia where he praised the "good care taken of me" at William's home on June 13, 1844.[12] Caroline was largely bedfast, by this point, but apparently could instruct the branch sisters and perhaps also her daughters in caring for the ailing apostle.

William was in Boston on June 29, where he met with seven of the Twelve for a conference in the morning and preached a public sermon that evening. Joseph and Hyrum had been murdered in Carthage two days before, but the news had not yet reached the Twelve. On Tuesday morning, July 9, 1844, at Salem, Massachusetts, William and Heber C. Kimball were together when they found the newspapers "full of News of the death of our Prophet." Kimball's first reaction was denial.

Title Page of *General Smith's Views of the Powers and Policy of the Government of the United States* (Nauvoo, Illinois, 1844).

He was unwilling to "to believe it, fore it was to[o] much to bare."[13] Experience had taught both men to be skeptical of what they read about Mormonism in the press. Heber does not describe William's reaction, but it was probably similar—a combination of dread and hope. Within days, the initial report was confirmed; Hyrum and Joseph had been murdered at Carthage, Illinois, on June 27.

By August 1844 William learned that his brother Samuel had also succumbed to what was termed "bilious" fever, leaving William as the only surviving male member of the Smith family.[14] Family friends at Nauvoo wrote to William, informing him of his brothers' deaths, how Lucy was bearing the shock, and expressing

---

11. William Smith (Philadelphia), Letter to Respected Br. [George T.] Leach, June 3, 1844, *Prophet* 1, no. 6 (June 22, 1844): 2. The *Prophet* had begun publication on May 18, 1844, with Leach as its first editor. He was followed by William Smith, from June 29 to July 13, 1844, and then by Samuel Brannan from July 20, 1844 to May 24, 1845.

12. Stanley Kimball, *On the Potter's Wheel*, 68–74.

13. Ibid., 73–74.

14. Samuel contracted an undiagnosed illness or suffered an internal injury during the same time that his brothers were murdered at Carthage and he endured a high-speed chase on horseback in attempting to come to their rescue. He died approximately one month after his brothers, on July 30, 1844. Dean L. Jarman and Kyle R. Walker, "Samuel Harrison Smith," in *United by Faith: The Joseph Sr. and Lucy Mack Smith Family*, ed. Kyle R. Walker (American Fork, Utah: BYU Studies and Covenant Communications, 2006), 230–35.

their sympathies.[15] "My farther [father] & Brothers are gone," William lamented in a letter to Brigham Young on August 24, "& I am But a youth & alone & who will be my friend hear on Earth."[16] The shock was all the greater because his older brothers had provided some of the direction and reassurance of his father, since his death in 1840, which had also profoundly impacted William. To lose three older brothers all at once, and on the heels of losing both his father and Don Carlos in 1841, was disorienting. He was thirty-three, but the fact that he called himself "a youth" is telling evidence of the loneliness and vulnerability he felt after that fateful summer of 1844. The direct murders of Joseph and Hyrum and the violence-related death of Samuel made William apprehensive about returning to Nauvoo with the rest of the Twelve. His caution was confirmed in a letter from Willard Richards, which, William said, warned him "not to return to the scene of the recent sad events in the west, as it might continue the excitement, and endanger not only my own life, but the lives of hundreds, perhaps thousands, of the saints."[17]

Even if Smith wanted to return to Nauvoo immediately, Caroline's health was too precarious. William wrote to Brigham Young in late August 1844: "It is vary uncertain when I can get to Nauvoo. I should of started before this but feared my wife would not live to get their. She has had the water drawn off once since you left and must be tapped again in a few days so you can see how fast She is hast[e]ning to the grave."[18] For these reasons, William would be delayed nearly a full year before returning to Nauvoo. Obviously, this "heroic" medical procedure, though temporarily successful, brought only brief relief to the suffering Caroline.

It would doubtless have provided comfort had William been with the Saints in Nauvoo where he could experience the brotherhood of his quorum members, but instead he coped emotionally by immersing himself in responsibilities for the branches over which he presided, defending himself against accusations of impropriety, and wrangling with the ongoing lawsuit filed by Benjamin Winchester. (See Chapter 9.)

A sense of deep sadness and trepidation lay just under the surface of his busyness, and he would occasionally give vent to his emotions. Letters from this period, some published in the *Prophet*, are tellingly personal, almost as though he turned to pen and paper when sorrow overcame him. "My helth is vary poor. My afflictions have worn me down," he wrote Brigham Young not long after the tragedy at Carthage. "I am left alone (as a mear Sipher) no doubt.... I hope you will not for-

---

15. Hugh Herringshaw (Nauvoo, Ill.), Letter to William Smith, August 28, 1844, in *Prophet* 1, no. 19 (September 21, 1844): 2; Jonathan C. Wright (Nauvoo, Ill.), Letter to William Smith, August 28, 1844, *Prophet* 1, no. 31 (December 21, 1844): 2–3.

16. William Smith (Bordentown, N.J.), Letter to Brigham Young, August 24, 1844, Brigham Young Office Files 1832–1878, Letters from Church Leaders and Others, 1840–1877, William Smith, 1844–1857, LDS Church History Library.

17. William Smith, "A Proclamation," *Warsaw Signal* 11 (October 29, 1845): 1. The letter William refers to may be the one quoted in Journal History, June 30, 1844, 3–4. If not, the original Richards letter may no longer be extant.

18. William Smith to Young, August 24, 1844. Terminal punctuation added.

get me." Referring to the two apostles to whom he felt closest, William instructed Young to "tell Brother Cimball I never wanted to see him so bad in my life. Tell Brother White [Lyman Wight]," who was the eldest apostle at age forty-eight, and fifteen years William's senior, "that I shall look to him for protection [now] that my farther and Brothers are gone."[19] He lamented his emotional confusion: "Like the ship broken upon the wave so my helth and constitution through privations troubles & afflictions has become recked & will be inposible to right again."[20]

The traumatic image of his brothers' murder as recounted in the eastern newspapers haunted him. He obviously felt a need to process his loss more deeply but was geographically separated from those who were most likely to understand his feelings: "I must say," he wrote to newspaper editor and family friend W. W. Phelps, "I wish I could think more of Nauvoo than I do, yet it is not Nauvoo! . . . . When I reflect that there lie the sliver [sic] locks of an aged and martyred father, martyred by a Missouri persecution, in the grave, numbered with the dead; and four brothers." Unable to attend the viewing and funeral, he envisioned Joseph and Hyrum "with mangled bodies, and garments red with crimson gore. Oh! The fatal steel and barbarous murder! Their blood is still unavenged, and the cruel murderers are longing [sic] about seeking for more; what have others to expect?"[21] Communications from Nauvoo produced feelings of foreboding, which in time, deepened toward paranoia. At times, William's despondency led to feelings of depression and listlessness, and he wrote almost longingly about following his father and brothers to the grave. "Oh my god Nauvoo looks like a desolation to me," he wrote heartrendingly. "Where is Hyram where is Joseph where is Samuel & where will my poor old mother be soon. I have no desire to live only to do the will of god."[22] He was haunted by the probability that "I too may soon be called to seal my testimony with my blood."[23] At times he seemed surprised that out of all the male members of his family, he was the one who remained. He sought comfort in asserting that four out of five had died as a result of their faith, and, hence, had a crown laid up for them above. Still, his grief was pronounced. "If we look into the families of those who have been taken away by the hands of wicked men and apostates," he recounted to his friend Samuel Brannan, "we will hear the widows moan, and orphans cry, whilst floods of tears bedew their cheeks. But, Oh! Let me turn away from this awful scene—close mine eyes—and not attempt to tell the sad tale."[24]

---

19. Ibid.

20. William Smith (Peterborough, N.H.), Letter to Brigham Young, October 16, 1844, Brigham Young Office Files, LDS Church History Library.

21. William Smith (Bordentown, N.J.), Letter to W. W. Phelps, November 10, 1844, *Prophet* 1, no. 27 (November 23, 1844): 3.

22. William Smith to Brigham Young, October 16, 1844; terminal punctuation added.

23. William Smith to W. W. Phelps, November 10, 1844.

24. William Smith (Bordentown, N.J.), Letter to Samuel Brannan, November 1, 1844, *Prophet* 1, no. 26 (November 16, 1844): 3.

Lithograph of Joseph and Hyrum Smith, by Moses Marlin, date unknown. After their deaths, many Latter-day Saint artists memorialized the Smith brothers in numerous paired renderings.

Five months after the murders, William lamented to Brannan: "The health of my family is still very bad, and no prospects for the better," he wrote in November 1844. "Persecution has almost robbed me of every jewel I possessed—my wife is now fast declining, and soon must (unless God interposes) be numbered with the silent dead."[25] In fact, Caroline's health steadily declined during the winter. By December she was "vary sick & cannot set up in bead [bed] mutch less travel."[26]

Lucy Mack Smith, who was dealing with her own overwhelming grief, wrote to William on January 23, 1845. Although she had wept on receiving a letter from her only surviving son, she encouraged Caroline not to lose heart: "My Dear daughter Caroline do not imagine your Mother forgets you. . . . My prayers and supplications are poured out by night and by day for you and I do hope that God will in mercy Spare you to come back to Nauvoo that we may behold your face again in the flesh." Well aware of how lingering illness could diminish the will to live, she urged Caroline to "trust in God my Dear child and try to live so that we may meet again." She also passed on messages from the three Smith daughters: Caroline's sisters-in-law "pray for you and they wish me to give their love to you and say that they remember you always in their prayers." She reminded William to "kiss them [his daughters] for me and tell them Grand Mother longs to see them."[27]

Although Lucy was experiencing her own pronounced grief with her recent losses, "it would have been some satisfaction to me, if I had expected his [William's] immediate return," recorded Lucy in her history, "but his wife was lying at the point of death, which compelled him to remain where he was. His case was, if it were possible, worse than mine, for he had to bear all his grief alone in a land of strangers, confined to the side of his dying wife, and absent from those who felt the deepest interest in his welfare; whilst I was surrounded with friends, being in the midst of the Church; my daughters, too, were with me, and from

---

25. William Smith to Brannan, November 1, 1844.
26. William Smith (Bordentown, N.J.), Letter to Heber C. Kimball, December 21, 1844, Brigham Young Office Files 1832–1878, Letters from Church Leaders and Others, 1840–1877, William Smith, 1844–1857, LDS Church History Library.
27. Lucy Mack Smith (Nauvoo, Ill.), Letter to William Smith, January 23, 1845, LDS Church History Library.

their society I derived great comfort."[28] In the hiatus from violence in the months immediately following the murders of Joseph and Hyrum, William began planning his return to Nauvoo if Caroline's health permitted.

In December 1844, Caroline's younger sister, Roxey Ann, traveled from the Grant family home in Walnut Grove, Illinois, to Philadelphia to help nurse her sister. William described her as a "faithful sister and devoted friend." She stayed with the Smiths for next six months, tenderly watching over Caroline.[29] Her care allowed William to intermittently travel throughout the eastern branches to conduct Church business. It was a time of vacillating emotions for the household. William and Caroline frequently expressed their expectation and hopefulness for her full recovery, only to be disappointed a few weeks later when her edema would return, causing painful swelling in her abdomen. In June 1844, en route to his proselytizing-campaigning mission, Heber C. Kimball had stayed with the Smiths in Philadelphia and had described what was apparently a procedure new to him in attempting to remove the fluid in her abdomen: She was "tapped" and had "two gallons taken from hur," weighing an estimated twenty pounds. He also indicated that Caroline mustered the strength to come out of her bedroom to see him. Caroline received enough relief from this procedure that she accompanied William and Kimball to New Brunswick, New Jersey, and then Boston, Massachusetts, where seven of the Twelve had gathered. On July 3 Kimball reported that he had spent the afternoon with "Wm. Smith and wife, [and] had a good time," which included attending the "comedietta" *Husbands, Wives, and Lovers* at the Boston Museum that evening.[30] But by late August, William despondently reported to Brigham Young that she had already "had the water drawn off once since you left and must be tapped again in a few days."[31]

Besides the well-established Church branches that initially drew the Smiths to the vicinity in 1843, they had also hoped to put Caroline in the care of a renowned physician, William Augustus Newell, who practiced in Bordentown. Newell had graduated from the University of Pennsylvania's medical school in 1839 and was living in New Jersey's Pine Barrens while William Smith was undertaking his first mission there in 1841. Newell, who later served as governor of New Jersey and as a U.S. congressman, continued his medical practice.

---

28. Lavina Fielding Anderson, ed., *Lucy's Book: A Critical Edition of Lucy Mack Smith's Family Memoir* (Salt Lake City: Signature Books, 2001), 751.

29. In a letter to Brigham Young in December 1844, William wrote that he had "just received your line by the hands of Sister Roxey Ann." William Smith (Bordentown, N.J.), Letter to Brigham Young, December 26, 1844, Brigham Young Office Files 1832–1878, Letters from Church Leaders and Others, 1840–1877, William Smith, 1844–1857, LDS Church History Library. See alsoWilliam Smith (City of Joseph [Nauvoo, Ill.]), Letter to Joshua Grant Jr., August 12, 1845, *Nauvoo Neighbor* 3, no. 16 (August 20, 1845): 3.

30. Heber C. Kimball, Diary, July 13, 21, 27, and July 3, 1844, in Stanley B. Kimball, *On the Potter's Wheel*, 68–72.

31. William Smith to Brigham Young, August 24, 1844.

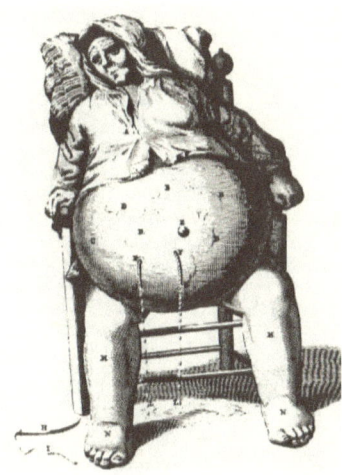

Woman being "tapped" for dropsy. Sketch from Frederik Dekkers's *Exercitationes Practicae circa Medendi Methodum* (Leyden, 1695).

Among his distinguished patients were John Quincy Adams and Tad Lincoln, Abraham's son, whose life he would be credited with saving in the 1860s. When William's family lived in Pennsylvania and New Jersey in 1843–45, Newell lived at least part of the time at Imlaystown, New Jersey, less than five miles from where William and Caroline were staying in Hornerstown, New Jersey, in the summer of 1843.[32] Newell made repeated house calls over the course of their two-year stay, both in New Jersey, and afterward in Pennsylvania. Both William and Jedediah Grant spoke highly of Newell in their letters, describing his "boundless popularity" in the region. His acquaintance confirmed "him to be not only a skillful practi[ti]oner, but a high-minded philanthropist, above the persuasions of men governed by prejudice or passion."[33] They must have entertained high hopes that Newell would be able to cure Caroline's "dropsy," but it was not to be.

Not long after the family had arrived in the East, William had written to Joseph at Nauvoo in late October 1843, explaining that Newell was "celebrated for the cure of dropsy" and was "working wonders upon her [Caroline]." William hopefully anticipated Caroline's relief from "her Loathsome diseas."[34] A month later William wrote to Caroline's brother, Jedediah M. Grant, that the "health of my family is about as usual, no change has taken place of late, either for the better or worse, if any at all, we think it is in our favor." He tried to find optimism in the fact that "Dr. Newell . . . appears quite as cheerful as ever."[35]

"Tapping," although it succeeded in draining off excess fluid, was painful since it required a sufficient accumulation to generate severe pressure on the organs and muscles. It likely involved inserting a hooked needle through the skin in multiple locations (most probably the abdomen), with the fluid then draining

---

32. Lloyd R. Applegate, *A Life of Service: William Augustus Newell* (Tom's River, N.J.: Ocean County Historical Society, 1994), 1–8; Frant V. Sperduto, "William A. Newell, Class of 1836," *Journal of the Rutgers University Libraries* 29, no. 3 (1966): 74–75.

33. Jedediah M. Grant (Philadelphia, Pa.), Letter to William Smith, November 28, 1843, in William Smith, *Defence of Elder William Smith against the Slander of Abraham Burtis, and Others* (Philadelphia: Brown, Bicking & Guilbert, 1844), 15–16.

34. William Smith (Philadelphia, Pa.), Letter to Joseph Smith, October 28, 1843, Joseph Smith Collection, LDS Church History Library.

35. William Smith (Hornerstown, N.J.), Letter to Jedediah M. Grant, November 26, 1843, in *Defence of Elder William Smith*, 13–14.

from that area. Naturally, the risk of infection from this procedure was quite high. Although medical diagnoses of nineteenth-century ailments are far from reliable, Caroline's repeated bouts of edema suggest either kidney failure or congestive heart failure, neither of which could be cured by removing the retained fluid, even though it would provide some relief of symptoms. Furthermore, the repeated "tappings" in themselves took a toll on Caroline's health. While Newell's medical treatment had likely prolonged Caroline's life, by the spring of 1845, both William and Caroline sensed the inevitability of her demise. Caroline's greatest desire was to see her family and fellow Saints one last time and "lay her body among those of her brethren and sisters at Nauvoo." William himself had never stopped yearning to find himself again in Nauvoo. Thus, they made plans to go, even knowing that the journey itself might prove fatal to Caroline.[36]

Engraving of William Augustus Newell, 1817–1901. From the *Allentown Messenger*, date and engraver unknown. Courtesy of the Allentown-Upper Freehold Historical Society.

The long New Jersey winter finally gave way to spring, and they left Philadelphia on April 19, 1845, accompanied by Roxey Ann and their two daughters. It was a bittersweet experience for the family to leave the Saints, especially the women who had selflessly cared for Caroline. William probably had more mixed feelings, including relief at distancing himself from Parley P. Pratt, his personal conflicts with local leaders, and Winchester's lawsuit. The Smiths' desire to return to Nauvoo was filled with both anticipation and apprehensiveness. They longed to see their families and view Nauvoo's progress, but William must also have been anxious to determine his standing in his quorum.

They probably traveled as much as possible by riverboat as offering the least stressful form of travel to Caroline. They reached Nauvoo on Sunday, May 4, 1845, "after a journey of two weeks and one day," wrote William. In a notice he published on May 10 in the *Nauvoo Neighbor*, he mingled pathos and happiness: "It was with much difficulty I could keep my wife alive to reach this point; but thank God, we have met with our friends once more, who are alive; and rejoice to see Nauvoo, the holy Zion of our God."[37] The *Nauvoo Neighbor* also published a welcoming notice: "Among the Saints who arrived in this city, on Sunday last, were *Elder Wm Smith* and family. Mrs. Smith is very feeble, and the elder[']s

---

36. William Smith to Joshua Grant, August 12, 1845.

37. William Smith (Nauvoo, Ill.), to Dear Brethren, May 10, 1845, *Nauvoo Neighbor* 3, no. 2 (May 14, 1845): 2–3.

health has been somewhat impaired by a few days illness. He will soon be sound again in this abode of peace, animation, and industry."[38]

Emma Smith graciously welcomed William, Caroline, the two little girls, and Roxey Ann into the Homestead[39] into which she and Joseph had moved when they first reached the town site in April 1839. Although Emma was caring for her own five children, including David Hyrum, who had been born in November 1844 after Joseph's death, she treated them "kindly and affectionately" and took personal pains to see that Caroline "received every attention that the strongest love and affection could dictate."[40] After mustering all of her strength to make the journey, Caroline must have lapsed with relief into Emma's capable hands. She apparently had developed a great affinity for her sister-in-law, once commenting that "the Lord never made a better woman than Sister Emma."[41] William stayed sometimes at Emma's admittedly crowded home and sometimes across the street at the Mansion House, where he roomed with James Monroe, a young schoolteacher, who accepted William's daughters as pupils along with the other Smith children. When William began giving patriarchal blessings (see Chapter 12), Monroe acted as his scribe, and his detailed diary provides important insights into William's psyche during that turbulent summer of 1845.

Smith was awestruck with how the city had expanded in the year since his last visit. He described the population as between fifteen and twenty thousand—almost certainly an overestimate—but was particularly impressed by the magnificent limestone temple, which dominated the city's landscape. "Yesterday I took a look through the temple," William wrote in his May 10 article for the *Nauvoo Neighbor*. "This is truly an imposing and a stupendous work; it has progressed beyond all expectation;—one would hardly imagine, so far from Nauvoo, considering the time and the means, and the greatness of the work, that as much would have been done as has been. . . . From two to three hundred laborers are at work upon the walls, the stone, the timber and the inside work. The yard, a wall about the Temple is designed to save it from the common, and is quite like your eastern church yards. It will enclose six acres, —and to conclude, Nauvoo still looks beautiful." He expressed admiration and appreciation to the Saints who had labored so faithfully and contributed so much of their limited means for its construction. "It is my prayer to Almighty God," he concluded, "that peace and true fidelity will continue in the camp of the Saints, until we can do the work the Lord has called us to do."[42]

---

38. "Among the Saints . . . ," *Nauvoo Neighbor* 1, no. 147 (May 7, 1845): 2; Stanley Kimball, *On The Potter's Wheel*, 108.

39. By this date, Emma had leased the Mansion House, which stood on the opposite corner of Water and Main Streets, to William Marks.

40. William Smith to Joshua Grant, August 12, 1845; Linda King Newell and Valeen Tippetts Avery, *Mormon Enigma: Emma Hale Smith*, 2d. ed. (Urbana: University of Illinois Press, 1994), 210, 349 note 4.

41. Caroline Grant Smith, quoted in William Smith to Joseph Smith, October 28, 1843.

42. William Smith to Dear Brethren, May 10, 1845.

Nauvoo, ca. 1846. Photograph by Charles W. Carter of earlier daguerreotype attributed to Lucian Foster. Courtesy LDS Church History Library.

Even though Caroline's life was ebbing away, William willingly picked up the ecclesiastical assignments expected of the Twelve, including preaching services. The Saints were anxious to hear from the Prophet's only surviving brother, and an estimated ten thousand eagerly gathered to hear him on a windy Sabbath in mid-May, just a week after his arrival, at the "Stand" near the temple. "It is with humbling [humility] I rise to address this large assembly of people," he began, "with grief mingled with joy." He had arrived in Nauvoo struggling with "chills and fever," and apologized that his "lungs" were incapable of producing the volume needed for such a large assembly, but pressed on: "I am happy once more at meeting my brethren and friends in this city," he began. "[Although] I have been deprived of the enjoyment of your society, I have had you in remembrance—it is needless for me to enter into those cries that have sorrowed your hearts—which has thrown such a gloom over the Church and the world. I presume there is none that have felt the stroke so much as myself. I fell [sic] down alone. The only one left of the family that have born[e] the burden of the day." His pleasure in "the kind faces of friends" was tempered by sorrow that he could not "hail the kind voices of my Fr. [father] and brothers but alas they are gone." Smith spoke of the Church's foundation laid by his brother Joseph, and the temple that he had inaugurated, which was now nearing completion. "Though they may kill our prophets," William declared confidently, "the Church will roll on triumphant." He concluded by encouraging unity among the Saints, and asking those assembled to remember him in their prayers. Following several other speakers, Smith was also afforded the signal honor of dismissing the congregation by prayer.[43]

---

43. Church Historian's Office, Journal, 1844–79, May 11, 1845, CR 100 1, Box 1, fd. 33, LDS Church History Library.

Hearing the Prophet's brother speak rekindled feelings of gratitude for the contributions of the founding family of Mormonism. It was approaching the one-year anniversary of the Carthage tragedy, and the absence of their beloved leader was ever-present in the Saints' thoughts. Zina Diantha Huntington Jacobs recorded in her diary that "it brought Peculiar feelings to hear the last one of the family that are living of the Males speak to the saints."[44] A report in the *Nauvoo Neighbor* described "an uncommon large audience listened to a discourse from *Elder W. Smith* on Sunday forenoon. And who could hear without reflecting that he was the *last* man of five brothers who had carried this kingdom in their arms *when it was a child?*"[45] George A. Smith and Brigham Young were cordial and complimentary when they spoke following William's Sunday sermon. Young even encouraged the members to meet William's pressing financial needs. James Monroe, listening attentively during the meeting, recorded that, following Smith's sermon, Young "spoke in a commendatory manner of William Smith, but I thought rather coolly."[46] There were still many lingering questions regarding Smith's presidency over the eastern branches of the Church.

Meanwhile, Caroline, though she survived the arduous journey home, was steadily weakening. As her condition deteriorated, one visitor reported she had been "tapped" on at least twenty separate occasions, which certainly included the procedures performed in New Jersey and Philadelphia. Caretakers estimated that more than fifty-three gallons of fluid had been drained from her body during these procedures. Zina Jacobs lamented sympathetically, "The extent of her suffering no one knoweth."[47] William summoned Caroline's parents from their residence in Walnut Grove, Illinois, and they arrived around May 20, just a few days before their daughter passed away. "During the last period of her illness she suffered much pain and distress," recounted William in a letter to Caroline's brother Joshua, giving the sad news of her death. "Doctors could do her no good. Almost everything was tried to relieve her, but of no avail." It was some consolation that "her wishes" to die among the Saints and be buried there "were gratified." In her final moments, Caroline mustered her strength and "bore a strong and faithful testimony to the truth." Her suffering finally came to an end in the evening of May 22, 1845.[48]

---

44. Maureen Ursenbach Beecher, ed., "'All Things Move in Order in the City': The Nauvoo Diary of Zina Diantha Huntington Jacobs," *BYU Studies* 19, no. 3 (Spring 1979): 310.

45. "Meeting," *Nauvoo Neighbor* 3, no. 2 (May 14, 1845): 2; emphasis in original.

46. Church Historian's Office, Journal, May 11, 1845; James M. Monroe, Journal, May 11, 1845, LDS Church History Library.

47. Beecher, "'All Things Move in Order in the City,'" 311.

48. William Smith to Joshua Grant, August 12, 1845. Nauvoo cemetery records indicate that Caroline died from "dropsey of the abdomen." Fred E. Woods, "The Cemetery Record of William D. Huntington, Nauvoo Sexton," *Mormon Historical Studies* 3, no. 1 (Spring 2002): 152; Lyndon W. Cook, comp., *Nauvoo Deaths and Marriages, 1839–1845* (Provo, Utah: Grandin Book, 1994), 70.

As was the custom of the day, William's friend and scribe James Monroe "sat up with the body" through the night. The next morning the house "was in an uproar," preparing for the ten o'clock funeral. Monroe noted somewhat censoriously that little was done "to see whether the family had any way to come to the stand or to help any about fixing, and the relations seemed to manifest no interest in honoring her remains."[49] Perhaps they were simply delayed since, just before the service began, a procession of carriages traveled from Emma Smith's home to the "Stand" east of the temple. Monroe "rode up in the wagon with the corpse as one of the [pall] bearers." Brigham Young, Heber C. Kimball, and perhaps other members of the Twelve did not attend the funeral because of concerns about their safety; the trial of Joseph and Hyrum's accused murderers was then taking place at Carthage. Brigham Young wrote to Parley P. Pratt on May 26: "Brother Wm. Smith's wife died last thursday evening and was put in the tomb of Joseph on Saturday at 10 AM. He held a meeting at the stand but we could not be with him on account of exposing ourselves to arrest by the enemy."[50]

Four members of the Twelve attended: John E. Page, Amasa M. Lyman, George A. Smith, and Orson Pratt, the latter delivering the eulogy and funeral sermon. Caroline's casket was placed in the center of the congregation, and the Smiths and Grants who attended were seated next to it. Despite Monroe's comment about deficiencies in the family's care, William and his two daughters were surrounded by relatives who shared his grief: his mother Lucy, Caroline's mother Athalia Grant, Emma Smith, Mary Fielding Smith, and, although not mentioned, assuredly his three sisters and their families. Pratt opened his discourse on the fall and resurrection, taking as his text 1 Corinthians 15:43: "It is sown in dishonor; it is raised in glory: it is sown in weakness; it is raised in power." It was a fitting verse of scripture for the occasion, especially in light of the suffering Caroline had endured. One listener described Pratt's remarks as "excellent," while another indicated it was "uninteresting but very good notwithstanding."[51] In the second part of Pratt's sermon, he recounted the history of Caroline's illness, dating it to the hardships she had endured in being driven from Missouri. "Our beloved sister, whose remains are now before us, has fallen asleep with the assurance of a glorious resurrection, and she will come up," he promised, "being numbered with those who have washed their robes and made them white in the blood of the lamb, having passed through great tribulations. She has a right to this honor." Pratt also movingly sought to comfort William and the "two orphan children left to mourn the loss of their beloved mother." With pathos, he ob-

---

49. Monroe, Journal, May 22–24, 1845, 69–70.

50. Brigham Young (Nauvoo, Ill.), Letter to Bro. [Parley P.] Pratt, May 26, 1845, Brigham Young Office Files 1832–1878, Letterbooks, 1844–1877, Copybook, August 27, Fred E. Woods, "The Cemetery Record of William D. Huntington, Nauvoo Sexton," *Mormon Historical Studies* 3, no. 1 (Spring 2002): 152; LDS Church History Library.

51. Beecher, "All Things Move in Order in the City," 311; Monroe, Journal, May 24, 1845, 70.

Caroline Amanda Grant Smith, 1814–45. Painting by Sutcliffe Maudsley, Nauvoo, Illinois, ca. 1843. Courtesy of John Hajicek.

served, "They most bitterly weep over her departed remains. A father's care will but inadequately supply the loss of a mother's tenderness, and they will, doubtless see many times, when they will most keenly feel their loss; but, time, the grand panacea for all earthly wounds, will, gradually, heal their grief and they will live in hopes of again meeting her in heaven, and there with renewed pleasure receive her parental care." William requested that the congregation sing "Old 100th" (also known as "Praise God from Whom All Blessings Flow") for the closing song, a hymn he had sung repeatedly as a youth growing up in his Palmyra home.[52] If Brigham Young was accurate in appraising the danger to the apostles, William jeopardized his own safety by attending the funeral service, but the support of the Nauvoo community certainly provided him a measure of comfort.

About three months later, William wrote to his twenty-six-year-old brother-in-law, Joshua Grant, who had been absent on a mission in North Carolina at the time of the funeral, describing Caroline's final days:

> When she had thus finished her course and enjoyed the last desires of her heart, her spirit bade adieu to this world of suffering, pain and trouble, and like the weary traveller, when at last he reaches home, she can now realize and appreciate the sweets of rest. Go tell the man who was brought up in affluence and ease, who never travelled the rugged paths of this life, and whose life was never wasted with pain and disease, that there is haven of rest beyond the grave, a paradisical home where pain and disease are never known, and it affords him no joy, no consolation; but tell the sick, the pained, the afflicted—who have been borne down under a load of afflictions all their life long, that there is such a haven of rest, where sickness and death never enter, and how consoling is the news—how heavenly the prospect, and how ecstatic the bliss, which such promise affords them.[53]

After the funeral services, those in the congregation filed past the casket. It was then deposited in the Tomb of Joseph near the temple. But within a few days, some of the temple workmen complained of the unpleasant odor caused by the summer heat, and William transported the body to the graveyard several miles outside the city while he prepared a more permanent place in Emma's garden. By fall, Caroline had been reinterred in the Smith family cemetery which was part of Emma Smith's homestead property, buried near William's four brothers and his father. He purchased a number of stones to mark the grave, and built a fence around the site to mark her final resting place.[54]

---

52. Church Historian's Office, General Church Minutes, 1839–1877, May 24, 1845, CR 100 318, LDS Church History Library, reproduced in *Selected Collections*; "Funeral of Mrs. Caroline Smith," *Times and Seasons* 6 (June 1, 1845): 918–20; "Obituary," *Nauvoo Neighbor* 3, no. 4 (May 28, 1845): 3; William Smith, "Notes Written on 'Chambers' Life," 29.

53. William Smith to Joshua Grant, August 12, 1845.

54. Ibid.; William Smith (Augusta, Iowa Territory), Letter to Pres. B[righam] Young or Lewis Robbins, September 28, 1845, Brigham Young Office Files 1832–1878, Letters from Church Leaders and Others, 1840–1877, William Smith, 1844–1857, LDS Church History Library.

Smith Family Cemetery, Nauvoo, Illinois. Joseph Smith Sr., Lucy Mack Smith, Hyrum, Joseph, Samuel and Don Carlos Smith, along with Caroline Amanda Grant Smith, are all buried in this cemetery. Photograph by Kyle R. Walker, 2010.

Roxey Ann Grant had stayed on during Caroline's final illness to nurse and care for her but then insisted on returning to her aging parents in Walnut Grove, Illinois. Before she left Nauvoo, however, she requested baptism, an ordinance she had hesitated to perform until she heard Caroline's final testimony. In William's letter to Joshua, he described baptizing her in the Mississippi River and confirming her a member of the Church.[55]

William summarized his feelings for Caroline in this same letter: "She was a fond mother, an affectionate wife, a devoted friend, and the strong ties of affection which existed between us can never be broken, nor can time or eternity ever efface from my heart the virtue and graces of my Caroline. When I look on my little girls, her offspring, my emotions are better imagined than described; and I long for the time when I shall again enjoy the sweets of her society, and rejoice in her presence. But she has gone, and we can only mingle our tears together for her loss."[56]

Shortly after Caroline's death, William moved his daughters into the home formerly occupied by William Marks on Water Street, not far from Emma's Homestead. Marks's home was available because Marks had, by business arrangement, rented the Mansion House from Emma. William arranged for his mother and three sisters (he does not mention his sisters' husbands), to also take up

---

55. William Smith to Joshua Grant, August 12, 1845.
56. Ibid.

residence and, he hoped, tend to homemaking: "My little girls were running wild, and my clothes needed some attention." However, his sisters had young children of their own, and his mother, who turned seventy that year, was ill for much of the summer. To provide his girls with more structure and education, William had enrolled them in James Monroe's school on May 5, the day after they reached Nauvoo. They did well, considering the turmoil and unsettled circumstances, although at times Caroline Louisa required some extra discipline. William later described himself as "more fond of play than study" during his youth, and Caroline Louisa may have had the same tendency.[57] On at least one occasion, she had to stay after school because she had not done her homework. In another instance, she left school without permission, ignoring Monroe's attempt to call her back. As a result, he refused to "receive her back again, as she had gone off without liberty and would not come back when I called her." Monroe reported on another occasion, "I had considerable trouble with Caroline and I do not know what will be the end of it. She says she won't and shouldn't get her lesson. And I tell her that she shall not come to school until she does. I think she has learned it, but has not recited it yet."[58]

Monroe was in a difficult position. Schoolteachers in the nineteenth century were seen as important authority figures who could enforce their rules by severe corporal punishment, although girls, especially young ones, were seldom flogged as frequently as boys. The twenty-three-year-old Monroe had been a schoolteacher in Nauvoo for three years and had taught high school in Utica, New York, for several years previous to his gathering with the Saints.[59] He was thus trying to maintain a difficult balance between his friendship for William, his sympathy for the motherless Caroline, and his role as a schoolteacher who could be relied on to keep order in his classroom. As these examples show, he had not yet found the right note with Caroline. Tellingly, he also records that he had kept fourteen-year-old Julia Murdock Smith, Joseph and Emma's adopted daughter, after school several times, once with Caroline, and that she also once left the classroom without permission. Monroe overheard Julia complaining about him, stating that Monroe "had no more heart than a hog." When he confronted her for her lack of respect, she "went to crying," then apologized, and demonstrated a willingness to complete her lessons.[60] Though Julia was much older, she, much like Caroline, had lost a beloved parent, and her surviving parent was burdened with many other obligations.

For William, straitened finances added to the complexities of his grief and attempts to understand where he fit in the rapidly changing social and ecclesiasti-

---

57. William Smith, *William Smith on Mormonism* (Lamoni, Iowa: Herald Steam Book and Job Office), 6.

58. Monroe, Journal, May 19 and 22, 1845, 68–70.

59. Edward Hogan, "The Curious Case of James Madison Monroe," *Sunstone* no. 172 (August 2013), 32.

60. Monroe, Journal, May 22, 1845, 69–70.

cal structure. He hoped to trade or sell some of his property in Plymouth for land in Nauvoo and advertised: "Notice to Emigrants. Brethren wishing to purchase land, houses, or city lots, will do well to call on me, at Mrs. Emma Smith's or the Mansion. . . . ALSO—I have some landed property with houses and out offices on, in the interior of this county, which I will sell or exchange for property in this city."[61] The real estate market had cooled considerably since William had last lived in the city, and given the increasingly clear realization that the Saints were facing another migration west, buying property was not an attractive option. Apparently William found no takers to his offer so he looked instead to his ecclesiastical office to earn his livelihood.

It had certainly been a time of confusion and upheaval for William since he and his family had returned to Nauvoo three weeks earlier. He had lost his companion of twelve years, felt misgivings about his standing in his quorum, and experienced apprehension about being a Smith in post-martyrdom Nauvoo. While he was relieved that Caroline's sufferings had finally come to an end, his were only beginning. He had hoped that Nauvoo would afford him the peace that his eastern mission had not, but he was about to experience the most tumultuous era of his entire life.

---

61. William Smith, "Notice to Emigrants," *Nauvoo Neighbor* 3, no. 3 (May 21, 1845): 3.

Chapter 11

Time of Reckoning

> There is more danger from William than from any other source, and I fear his course will bring us much trouble.
> —William Clayton, May 1845

The weeks following William's return from his eastern mission on May 4, 1845, were filled with a whirlwind of activities and emotions. His relocating to Nauvoo afflicted him with a bout of "chills and fever," which he pushed past so that he could care for Caroline until her death less than three weeks later on May 22.[1] There was little time to grieve her loss. His daughters, ages eleven and nine by the end of that summer, were dealing with their own sorrow. By moving into the William Marks home on Water Street, he had at least some assistance from his sisters, but he probably expected more help with childcare and housekeeping from his mother and sisters than they were able to provide. His plural wife, Mary Ann Covington, lived next door in the former *Times and Seasons* printing office.[2] She had no children of her own to care for, but existing records do not clarify her relationship with William. It was certainly not the situation taken for granted among plural wives in Utah that one would take over caring for the children of a deceased sister-wife.

William knew that rumors were circulating through Nauvoo critiquing his leadership among the eastern LDS branches. Instead of building a record of devotion, humility, and hard work which would become its own defense, he immediately sent a lengthy letter to the *Nauvoo Neighbor* which defended his reputation against "spiritual wifery" and, not incidentally, attacked the Boston Branch president, John Hardy, whom William had summarily dismissed in October 1844. Hardy had retaliated by publishing a pamphlet publicly accusing William, Adams, and Brannan of "spiritual wifery."[3] "In my own defence, so far as the charge of spiritual wifery is concerned," stated William, "I know of no such doctrine in the church of Christ nor have I any alliance with such a system. . . . The marriage contract should be kept sacred and holy, and the introduction of any law or

---

1. James M. Monroe, Journal, May 4, 1845, 56; September 1841–June 1842, and April–May 1845, MS 7061, LDS Church History Library.

2. Mary Ann [Covington Sheffield] West, Testimony, in United States testimony 1892, Court of Appeals (Eighth Circuit), 499–500, MS 1160, LDS Church History Library.

3. John Hardy, *Startling Developments of Crim. Con.! Or Two Mormon Apostles Exposed, in Practising the Spiritual Wife System in Boston* (Boston: Conway and Company, 1844).

government that would throw off the sacred obligations of this contract, as laid down by Jesus Christ in his holy gospel, would open a gate to a flood of licentiousness that would destroy the morals of any people." He concluded that "man should love his wife and cleave unto her, and they twain should be one flesh."[4]

Joseph had used the same method by differentiating between "celestial marriage" and "spiritual wifery"—not commenting on the first but denouncing the second and thereby leaving both members and nonmembers who were not privy to this coded language to conclude that Mormons accepted only monogamy. Whatever the technical accuracy of this argument, its intent was to conceal the practice—a dilemma faced by all of the members of the Twelve and others who were engaged in plural marriage. William included with his letter to the *Nauvoo Neighbor* a signed statement from sixteen Boston members vouching for his character.[5]

Subtitle page of John Hardy's *Startling Developments of Crim. Con.! Or Two Mormon Apostles Exposed, in Practising the Spiritual Wife System in Boston* (Boston, 1844).

Such a position at least had the merit of following the policy then espoused by the Church leaders in Nauvoo, but they must have been uncomfortable with its appearance in the Church-sponsored newspaper. John Taylor was then the editor, and it seems strange that he would have allowed its publication. Even denials were acknowledgments of the ongoing controversy. William almost certainly was not aware that Wilford Woodruff had warned Brigham Young in his three letters written in October–December 1844 that William's impetuous action against Hardy and others had generated harsh feelings, making some former leaders "ready to come out in battle array openly against the Church." He warned Young specifically about Hardy, whom he described as "about to wield the pen against the Church." Woodruff had earlier recommended that instead of being "so very tenacious" in punishing these eastern leaders, "I would rather they would

---

4. William Smith (Nauvoo, Ill.), Letter to Dear Brethren, May 10, 1845, *Nauvoo Neighbor* 3, no. 2 (May 14, 1845): 2–3.

5. Ibid.

let things rest a little here."[6] When William's conflicts continued after his return to Nauvoo, leaders in the city likely felt the validity of Woodruff's recommendation. They were weary of William's combative approach and given his record for the past ten years, almost certainly viewed William as the instigator of his feuds.

If those challenges were not enough concerns, William was also apprehensive about his physical safety. Hostility toward Mormons had not abated, and even though there was little support for vigilante assassination per se, the specific deaths of Joseph and Hyrum were not viewed as completely unjustified. On May 30, not quite a month after William's return to Hancock County, the five men accused of murdering Joseph and Hyrum were all acquitted by a jury in Carthage—not a development that would have reassured him.[7] It is impossible to say whether the verdict would have been different if Brigham Young had encouraged the Saints to participate in the legal process, but he was unwilling—not without reason—to risk his own life or that of others by being witnesses.

In spite of these emotional challenges, William willingly accepted assignments to preach to the Saints, which helped him reconnect with the expanding body of Church members at Nauvoo. The immense harvest of converts from Great Britain during the previous two years meant that many had never personally met this younger brother of the Prophet. The *Nauvoo Neighbor*, which had enthusiastically announced William's return and sympathetically reported on his health problems, anticipated that he would "soon be sound again" thanks to the "peace" that prevailed in Nauvoo.[8] However, beneath this placid surface, an undercurrent of tension ran between William Smith and the rest of the Twelve—issues that remained unresolved. (See Chapter 9.)

One of the major issues was William's standing with the Twelve. He felt displaced and diminished by Parley Pratt's assignment as "Presiding Elder of the Church of Jesus Christ of Latter day Saints in the Eastern Branches."[9] As the surviving male Smith, William obviously expected to inherit Hyrum's position as Church patriarch. Less certain were Hyrum's additional positions as assistant president and as a counselor in the First Presidency—but there is no question that William coveted that increased status, nor is there any question that Brigham Young viewed such aspirations as a challenge to his own authority.

---

6. Wilford Woodruff (Boston, Mass.), Letter to Brigham Young, October 9 and 14, Brigham Young Office Files 1832–1878, Letters from Church Leaders and Others, 1840–1877, Wilford Woodruff, 1844, LDS Church History Library.

7. Those accused of murdering Hyrum and Joseph Smith were acquitted on May 30, 1845. Dallin H. Oaks and Marvin S. Hill, *Carthage Conspiracy: The Trial of the Accused Assassins of Joseph Smith* (Urbana: University of Illinois Press, 1975), 184–86.

8. "Among the Saints . . . ," *Nauvoo Neighbor* 3, no. 1 (May 7, 1845): 2. Notice of William's return to Nauvoo was also reprinted under the title of "From the *Nauvoo Neighbor*," *Prophet* 1, no. 52 (May 24, 1845): 3.

9. Parley P. Pratt and Samuel Brannan, "What Is 'Mormonism?'" *Prophet* 1, no. 47 (April 12, 1845): 4.

Furthermore, William's often fragile self-esteem made him overreact to slights, whether intended or not.

No doubt increasing William's apprehension was the Nauvoo High Council brusque handling of William's ecclesiastical colleague, George J. Adams. In mid-March 1845, Brigham Young had summoned Adams to come to Nauvoo to account for his behavior under William's supervision. He had already been disfellowshipped once on February 10, 1843, for "adultery." According to non-Mormon Charlotte Haven, he had returned from his mission "with . . . a wife and child, although he had left a wife and family here when he went away." Adams confessed his guilt and, seven months later, was restored to full fellowship on September 7, 1843.[10] This new court, attended by six apostles, six high councilors, and one member of the presiding bishopric, convened on March 15, 1845. Brigham Young led out by announcing that he had "objections to brother Adams' conduct, and to the course he has taken." Then he cited specifics: "When brother Adams came home last fall, I asked him if he had any money for the temple; he said no, [that] he had handed everything to Wm Smith. Since then Wm Smith has wrote and said he sent some money and some cloth by brother Adams for the temple; we have not got it." Adams announced defensively that he was willing to meet with "any committee this council might appoint, and settle the whole account with them," but the minutes record no additional explanation about the donations. Young also reported that Adams was allegedly claiming that "the Church owes him something from six hundred to one thousand dollars in money" and asked for an explanation. The sketchy minutes do not provide details, but Adams did, in fact, explain "how the church owed him money." The council was disconcerted by his response. Young demanded that Adams "'bring the names of those who donated money,' saying [that] other agents had collected 'hundreds of dollars' without any trouble meeting their [personal] expenses, while Adams 'lost $200 coming [to Nauvoo], but [Young] dont believe it.'" Young also pointed out an apparent discrepancy in his report, stating that Adams "told us in the fall it was $150 now it is $200."

Young next asked Adams to explain a report that he was claiming "some great authority over every body else, and also that he was appointed Joseph Smith's Spokesman."[11] This report stemmed from Wilford Woodruff's specific charge: "I

---

10. Joseph Smith, Journal, February 10, 1843, in Andrew H. Hedges, Alex D. Smith, and Richard Lloyd Anderson, eds., *Journals, Volume 2: December 1841–April 1843*, THE JOSEPH SMITH PAPERS (Salt Lake City: Church Historian's Press, 2011), 259, see esp. 259 note 383; John S. Dinger, ed., *The Nauvoo City and High Council Minutes* (Salt Lake City: Signature Books, 2011), 470–71; Charlotte Haven (Nauvoo, Ill.), Letter to My Dear Friends at home, September 8, 1843, in William Mulder and A. Russell Mortensen, *Among the Mormons* (New York: Alfred A. Knopf, 1958), 126–27. Haven had linked Adams's behavior with rumors she had heard at Nauvoo regarding polygamy.

11. Dinger, *The Nauvoo City and High Council Minutes*, 547–49, and 549 note 17, where Dinger quotes D. Michael Quinn's transcription of these minutes, in D. Michael Quinn Papers, Beinecke Rare Book and Manuscript Library, Yale University, New Haven, Connecticut.

also beg of you not to send Elder Adams into the eastern churches, or anywhere else, until he can learn that there is authority in the Church unto whom he is amenable. For I believe him to be reckless and do not believe he regards any authority in this Church where he is out of the presence of the Twelve. He is such a great Apostle to the Gentiles and [thinks] he is head and shoulders above all others." Furthermore, Woodruff reported that William Smith had promoted Adams as "the great apostle to the Gentiles as Paul, even the 13th apostle (which claim was held up to me)."[12] Reinforcing these reckless and unorthodox claims (assuming that they had been reported correctly) was a notice Parley P. Pratt had published on January 4, 1845, in the *Prophet*, two months before Adams's court: "Whereas various inquiries are daily saluting my ears in relation to Elder Adams, who is represented by some as claiming to be an Apostle, holding equal authority with the Twelve and even keys above them, and independent of them, such as [to] administer sealing blessing[s], &c. Now, without pretending to lay any of these things to his charge or expressing any judgment whether he pretends to these claims or not, and without any design to censure him, I take this opportunity to say, once [and] for all, that he holds no such authority."[13]

Apparently no record has survived of Adams's response to this very public reproof, but Brigham Young demanded a reply at this March trial. According to the high council minutes, Adams "denied having said that he was appointed Joseph's spokesman."[14]

The third and final accusation charged Adams with unauthorized plural marriage sealings. Young stated that he knew "through personal revelation that Adams and William Smith had both married 'scores' of women back east." Young's exaggeration makes it sound as though he had grown irritated with Adams by this stage of his hearing. In another sweeping generalization, Young claimed that he was "all the time receiving letters from the East giving account of your prostituting young women and ruining the churches." The sketchy minutes record only that "Adams plead guilty and begged for mercy." Then in a classic blame-shifting move, he admitted that he had "promise[d] [William] not to tell" authorities at Nauvoo.[15]

Nearly everyone attending the court spoke. "Many hard things were proven against him," recorded one participant; Adams, who had apparently gone into the proceedings confident that he could bluff his way through, ultimately confessed his mistakes, "and agree[d] to be one with the Twelve and do right here after." As the council neared its conclusion, "Prest. Young . . . said he wanted Brother Adams to sit down and write that he had done wrong, that he asks forgiveness,

---

12. Woodruff to Young, October 9 and 14, 1844; Wilford Woodruff (Philadelphia, Pa.), Letter to Brigham Young, December 3, 1844, Brigham Young Office Files 1832–1878, Letters from Church Leaders and Others, 1840–1877, Wilford Woodruff, 1844, LDS Church History Library.

13. P. P. Pratt, "Elder G. J. Adams," *Prophet* 1, no. 33 (January 4, 1845): 2.

14. Dinger, *The Nauvoo City and High Council Minutes*, 549.

15. Ibid., 549 note 18.

and is willing henceforth to listen to council, and do right without incriminating any one else; also that the proper authorities of this Church are here, and that he is with the Twelve and will be with them to bear off this Kingdom. I want brother Adams to write this freely and confess his iniquities." He sweetened this punishment by promising, "a mans confession will never do him hurt unless he turns round and does wrong again." Adams additionally promised to turn over donations that he had, in fact, collected for the temple fund and further pledged to provide from his records or from memory "the names of those who donated money" and have a settlement. Adams's trial ended on a conciliatory note, with each member of the council "expressing a strong desire for brother Adams' salvation," but he did not follow through on any of these three commitments.[16]

It seems fairly certain that Adams had already spent the Saints' contributions. Thus, making a list of donors and donations would only confirm his dishonesty. A written confession could be published, thus strongly eroding his already shaky reputation. Nor did his willingness to "receive council" bear any fruit. The Church never received the Saints' contributions, and apparently by April 10, Adams had fled from the city, never to return. As a result, the April 15 issue of the *Times and Seasons* carried the news of his trial and excommunication.[17] By the time William and Caroline returned to Nauvoo on May 4, Adams was living in Augusta, Iowa Territory, on the western side of the Mississippi River. Ambitiously, he attempted to organize a schismatic offshoot led by Joseph Smith III (then age twelve), even though neither young Joseph nor Emma gave him any encouragement. By early fall, Adams also dangled the patriarchal office in this new church before William while promoting himself as a spokesman for the martyred Joseph Smith in his new organization. He thus flatly contradicted his own protestations during his trial that he had ever made that claim.[18]

Perhaps the public nature of Adams's trial was a factor in his decision to remain permanently disaffected. The high council published a stern rebuke in the *Times and Seasons*, accompanying the notice of his excommunication: "His conduct has been such as to disgrace him in the eyes of justice and virtue," this notice read. "Under the sacred garb of religion, he has been practising the most disgraceful and diabolical conduct." They concluded by putting leaders in the East on notice: "Let this be a warning to other elders, if there are any guilty of like conduct."[19]

---

16. Ibid., 549–50, 549 note 17; George D. Smith, ed., *An Intimate Chronicle: The Journals of William Clayton* (Salt Lake City: Signature Books, 1995), 160, 166.

17. Brigham Young, "Notice to the Churches Abroad," *Times and Seasons* 6 (April 15, 1845): 878. The notice began, "This may certify that Elder George J. Adams has been disfellowshipped and cut off from the church of Jesus Christ of Latter-day Saints."

18. George D. Smith, *An Intimate Chronicle*, 166; George J. Adams (Burlington, Iowa Territory), Letter to A. R. Tewkesberry, June 14, 1845, MS 697, LDS Church History Library.

19. "Notice to the Churches Abroad," 878.

Although Adams's testimony was obviously unreliable, he tried to shift much of the blame to both William Smith and to Samuel Brannan, the two other leaders who presided over the eastern branches during 1843–45. Shortly after Adams's trial, Brigham Young summoned Brannan to Nauvoo to investigate the circumstances which had come to light during Adams's court. By that time, Brannan had shifted his allegiance from William to Pratt and was editing the *Prophet* with him. Based primarily on Adams's testimony, the Nauvoo High Council had excommunicated Brannan *in absentia* on April 10, 1845, the same date they had formally disciplined Adams. Brannan learned of the decision in a letter from Brigham Young to Parley P. Pratt written on the same day as the decision: "We have this day excommunicated George J. Adams, and Samuel Brannan, for abominations that are not necessary to mention now. They will be published in our next paper. This is, therefore, to notify you beforehand of the fact, that you may have the advantage in negotiating any necessary business." He continued: "There are other Elders in the East, that have reason to beware, for we are resolved that if men will not be wise and virtuous, they shall not have our confidence or fellowship."[20] Brannan must have been chagrined by the irony of preparing to reprint the high council's notice from the *Times and Seasons* in the very newspaper he helped to publish.[21]

However, unlike his former colleague, Brannan was genuinely penitent and immediately wrote a letter that was published in the same issue of the *Prophet* as the notice of his excommunication. In it, he humbly expressed his willingness to "yield obedience" to the Twelve and submit to whatever punishment they saw fit, praying that "in the future, my mind and heart may not be guided otherwise." He continued, "The blow is truly a severe one, but I feel to bear it patiently, and even more if required. If I have deviated from the path of rectitude—violated the commandments of God, or been the means of bringing reproach upon his cause, I look upon myself as being bound to make restitution for the same." His contrition after learning of this punishment was a factor in the positive outcome of his case. On May 11, he left New York City to meet with the authorities at Nauvoo, arriving about three weeks after William Smith.[22]

Both William and Parley P. Pratt sent Brigham Young encouraging reports that aided in Brannan's restoration of membership. Pratt wrote to Young on May 7—probably soon after he received Young's April 10 letter. He assured Young that Brannan had "labored faithfully and diligently, since I came here last winter, and has set a good example . . . and has at all times possessed a Spirit of willingness

---

20. Brigham Young (Nauvoo, Ill.), Letter to Parley P. Pratt, April 10, 1845, Brigham Young Office Files 1832–1878, General Correspondence, Outgoing, 1843–1876, 1845 January-May, LDS Church History Library.

21. Brigham Young, "Notice to the Churches Abroad," *Prophet* 1, no. 51 (May 10, 1845): 2.

22. Samuel Brannan, Letter to Brethren and Friends, *Prophet* 1, no. 51 (May 10, 1845): 2.

to hearken to counsel."²³ The same could not be said of Adams, Pratt admitted. Adams was initially disinclined to take responsibility for his behavior, had been previously disfellowshipped, and ultimately rebelled against the Twelve after learning of the high council's decision. "I hope the church will not restore him [Adams] again to confidence and fellowship, without good reason," Pratt wrote sternly in the *Prophet*, "as he has already been a great injury to the cause, and a stumbling block to thousands."²⁴ Pratt felt that Brannan, on the other hand, should not bear full responsibility for some of his mistakes. "I hope that your honorable body will strike at the root of the evils which may have entangled him" he wrote, "for I consider him at worst, as only one of the branches. That is I consider that he may have been led, or influenced by Others, on whom justice ought to rest with greater weight and severity."²⁵ Pratt's reference to "Others" certainly pointed to Smith—the presiding authority in the East.

William Smith also passionately defended Brannan immediately after he returned to Nauvoo, although his motives were undoubtedly self-serving. In his first meeting with the Twelve on May 5, just a day after he arrived with his wife and daughters, William expressed his desire that Brannan be restored to fellowship because he felt that Brannan was "innocent of the charge brought against him."²⁶ This, along with Pratt's report about Brannan, influenced the Twelve positively, but before they made a final decision, they still wanted to hear from both Brannan and Smith about what had transpired in the East. Brannan arrived in Nauvoo on May 23 after a twelve-day journey, and immediately sought out William. Caroline had died only the day before, and William was dealing simultaneously with her loss and with making funeral arrangements. Both men called that same day on other members of William's quorum, including Brigham Young. Although the details of their exchange have not survived, William's manner during these brief visits concerned Church leaders, although their only immediate action was to schedule a hearing on Brannan's case for the following afternoon. That same evening, however, the Twelve held a meeting at which Smith was not present. According to William Clayton, "the improper course of Wm. Smith was the subject of conversation." This discussion lasted late into the evening, and chief among their conclusions was William's aspiration to "rule the Church and monopolize the whole to himself."²⁷ William

---

23. P. P. Pratt (New York), Letter to Brigham Young, May 7, 1845, Brigham Young Office Files 1832–1878, Letters from Church Leaders and Others, 1840–1877, Parley P. Pratt, 1845, LDS Church History Library.

24. Parley P. Pratt, "We publish the above . . . ," *Prophet* 1, no. 51 (May 10, 1845): 2.

25. Pratt to Young, May 7, 1845. See also Pratt, "We publish the above . . . ", for a similar description of Pratt's view on Brannan's standing in the Church.

26. George A. Smith, "My Journal," *Instructor* 83 (September 1948): 418; Willard Richards, Diary, May 5, 1845, MS 1490, Box 1, LDS Church History Library.

27. William Clayton dutifully recorded in his journal the disposition of William Smith, as well as Church leaders' feelings about William at the time. George D. Smith, *An Intimate Chronicle*, 166. See also Journal History of the Church of Jesus Christ of

must have been physically exhausted and in emotional turmoil; perhaps he had made stronger statements than he actually intended, but perhaps, understanding these factors, the rest of the Twelve were willing to confirm the patriarchal office on him, despite their misgivings.

The next day, May 24, 1845, was a very memorable date in the life of William Smith. In the morning, he paid his last respects to Caroline at her funeral and burial. Just a few hours later, at three in the afternoon, the Council of the Twelve convened at John Taylor's home to hear Samuel Brannan's case. The twenty-six-year-old Brannan[28] faced his Church trial with continued penitence, allowing William to lead out in the explanations. The council included eight members of the Quorum of the Twelve, besides William. While surviving details of the hearing are fragmented, the principal accusation against Brannan was an allegedly improper relationship with Sarah Wallace, a Latter-day Saint woman at Lowell, Massachusetts, who had died two months earlier on March 15 of consumption.[29] William Smith, Samuel Brannan, and Sarah's brother, George B. Wallace, all gave testimony. Sarah, the "principal accuser," had not left a letter or any other document of accusation, but according to her brother, who was also a Mormon, Brannan had seduced Sarah under religious pretenses and shortly afterward had had William perform their sealing. Whether Smith was aware of their alleged sexual transgression at the time of the marriage is not clear from the minutes, but William simply recounted that Brannan asked him if he had any objection to his marrying Sarah. Sarah "manifested [a] strong attachment for Brannan," and so "I married them [and] did not consider he . . . was under under any obligation to any one else," William testified. "Married them by all the authority [I] possessd for time & Eternity, and had a right &c to do [so] as an apostle of J. Christ." Apparently, at some point after their wedding, Brannan recounted that he "walked with Sis Wallace in public &c. [and] She had discovered that the time would come when men would have more wives than one." Indeed, Brannan himself may have informed her that he had been married civilly to Eliza Ann Corwin, though the specific date of their marriage[30] is unknown. However, the

---

Latter-day Saints (chronological scrapbook of typed entries and newspaper clippings, 1830–present), May 23, 1845, 1, LDS Church History Library.

28. Brannan was born on March 2, 1819, at Saco, Maine. Will Bagley indicates that Brannan's family first affiliated with the Church in 1832, and moved to Geauga County, Ohio the following year. Will Bagley, *A Scoundrel's Tale: The Samuel Brannan Papers* (Logan: Utah State University Press, 1999), 23–24.

29. Sarah Wallace died on March 15, 1845. J. W. Crosby, "Obituary," *The Prophet* 1, no. 47 (April 12, 1845): 3.

30. According to Bagley, *Scoundrel's Tale*, 49, 67, 97 note 59, Brannan and Sarah Wallace were married "only months after Brannan's legal marriage to Ann Eliza Corwin." However, Bagley does not document the date of either marriage and probably relied on circumstantial evidence from Brannan's trial on May 24, 1845. Samuel and Eliza had their first child on October 17, 1845, so they were almost certainly married by January

secrecy surrounding his and Sarah's union, evident in the details recorded at this Church court,[31] reveals that this was a plural marriage. William continued that Sarah next heard "Father [Freeman] Nickerson preach . . . that if anyone should get hold of his skirts or any else, on the spiritual wife system, they would to go to hell. & she believed it. Sis Wallace wrote Brannan upbraiding him with the humbug & charging me with assisting Brannan." Nickerson was the presiding elder at the branch in nearby New Bedford, Massachusetts, and his sermon, according to her brother George, "worried her to think she must be Brannans [wife]." According to both William and George, Sarah was upset with Brannan and also with William Smith, whom she reprimanded privately for teaching plural marriage. She felt that she had been misled into accepting a union that the Nauvoo leaders would not have recognized as valid. That sentiment was strengthened once Parley P. Pratt arrived in the East. George testified that "Pratt told her the sealing was not according to the Law of God," and that "unless he [Brannan] repented he could not be crowned in the celestial kingdom."[32]

Pratt, along with William's fellow apostles who were present at the hearing, had two objections to the union. First, William Smith did not have authority to perform sealings, including plural marriages, without direct authorization from Brigham Young at that time. Second, a marriage "for eternity" reinforced the rumors of plural marriage that were circulating through the eastern branches. Though this was certainly a plural marriage, William Smith testified to the council that, at the time he performed the wedding, he understood it to be Brannan's first marriage—in effect, placing blame squarely on Brannan's shoulders. William proclaimed his innocence by saying that "P. P. Pratt must have supposed that Brannan was married to two [women], at once."[33]

Smith's account of events, as they can be reconstructed from the minutes, show him carefully sidestepping any responsibility on his part for teaching or authorizing plural marriages outside of Nauvoo, though the evidence is overwhelming that he had and that Brigham Young and other leaders knew it.[34] Smith's failure to take

---

1845—but it seems evem more likely that they had been married during the previous six months. I have also been unable to identify a marriage date.

31. At one point during the investigation, Brannan testified that he "would correspond with her [Sarah]" while he was away, "but [I] did not write for fear some one would get the letter," and realize it was a plural marriage. Willard Richards, Minutes of Trial of Samuel Brannan, May 24, 1845, Church Historian's Office, General Church Minutes, 1839–77, CR 100 318, Box 1, fd. 34.

32. Willard Richards, Minutes of Council, May 24, 1845, Church Historian's Office, General Church Minutes, 1839–77, CR 100 318, Box 1, fd. 34.

33. Willard Richards, Minutes of Council, May 24, 1845, Church Historian's Office, General Church Minutes, 1839–77, CR 100 318, Box 1, fd. 34.

34. Besides the testimony given during Brannan's trial, the earlier confession of George J. Adams, combined with what he had learned from Wilford Woodruff's earlier letters, must have left little doubt in Young's mind that William was authorizing plural marriages

responsibility for this errant conduct left Adams and Brannan abandoned when, it seems more likely, they were following his lead, though perhaps over-enthusiastically. By October 1845, after hearing of William's excommunication, Brannan wrote a strong letter to Brigham Young denouncing William. He had obviously felt duped by his former leader. "Unless he repents, and that sincerely too," Brannan wrote, "I never shall do the work I have done for him over again." It sounds as if he felt that William had abandoned him during his trial by manipulating the testimony to present himself in the best light possible. Brannan seems to be expressing resentment at having the brunt of the responsibility thrust on him when he protested, "I am no traitor, neither will I be crucified for a traitor."[35]

Since Sarah, the "principal accuser," had died and because Brannan's excommunication *in absentia* had already inflicted severe "suffering" on him, the high council reinstated his membership. He had made a good impression because, as Young put it, he had "borne his chastisement like a Saint." In fact, on May 10, Brigham Young had written to Pratt asking him to rebaptize Brannan privately, based on consultation by letter with Pratt and in person with William Smith. However, Brannan had already left for Nauvoo before Pratt received Young's letter.[36] Brannan's continued penitence during his trial on May 24 resulted in a unanimous vote to restore him to full fellowship, but William's testimony caused the council increasing concern. Both Adams and Brannan had cast William in a dubious light, putting him at the center of what Wilford Woodruff had earlier described in his letters to Young as the "vortex of recklessness"[37] that had created turmoil among the eastern Saints. Of particular anxiety were William's irresponsible and unauthorized use of the sealing power and his loose version of plural marriage. Even if William did not know that Brannan's union with Sarah had been a plural marriage, Church leaders at Nauvoo were still upset that Smith was using the sealing power and bestowing it on others without authorization.

William was the only member of the Twelve who had been audacious enough to use the sealing power and authorize plural marriages outside of the trusted circle at Nauvoo.[38] In addition to performing the admittedly confused

---

during his mission to the East. Dinger, *Nauvoo City and High Council Minutes*, 548–50; Woodruff to Young, October 9 and 14, 1844; Woodruff to Young, December 3, 1844.

35. Samuel Brannan (New York), Letter to Brigham Young, October 9, 1845, Brigham Young Office Files 1832–1878, General Correspondence, Incoming, 1840–1877, General Letters, 1840–1877, Be-Br, 1845, LDS Church History Library.

36. Brigham Young (Nauvoo, Ill.), Letter to P. P. Pratt, May 10, 1845, Brigham Young Office Files 1832–1878, General Correspondence, Outgoing, 1843–1876, 1845 January-May, LDS Church History Library.

37. Woodruff to Young, December 3, 1844.

38. However, in November-December 1847, Brigham Young reprimanded Parley P. Pratt and John Taylor because they had "committed an insult on the Holy Priesthood" by entering into plural marriages that he had not authorized. Young had, earlier that summer, instructed the apostles that "no man has a right to Attend to the ordinance of

marriage between Brannan and Sarah Wallace, he had taken advantage of his presiding position to be sealed to two sisters: Sarah Ann Libby and Hannah Maria Libby. And if the remonstrations of the disgruntled Boston Branch president, John Hardy, are accurate, William had also been engaged to a "Miss Annis" of the New Bedford Branch. These marriages would have been performed by Adams, Brannan, or Joseph T. Ball. Ball was an African American member whom Smith installed to replace John Hardy as president of the Boston Branch. William had personally instructed at least Adams and Brannan and probably Ball about plural marriages and had bestowed upon them the sealing power.[39]

Further evidence that Smith was performing plural marriages comes from his "pocket companion," a short journal that he kept in the fall of 1844, containing lengthy scriptural arguments defending the practice of plural marriage, as well as a written ceremony for performing such unions.[40] (See Appendix B.) Many of his conflicts with presiding elders in the eastern branches erupted over plural marriage and how he dealt with leaders who opposed polygamy, which was, after all, the public position then being taken by the Church.

Though William appears to have been intentionally vague with his colleagues about the extent he had used the sealing power, he obviously believed that he held the right to exercise such authority. He must have known that Young and his fellow apostles would oppose his perspective, which was why he had sworn Adams to secrecy about the practice. The day before Brannan's trial—the very day of Caroline's death—William had visited Newel and Elizabeth Ann Whitney in their home where he had expressed resentment toward Brigham Young and Heber C. Kimball because, as Elizabeth Ann reported, he felt the two men "had taken rights from him."[41]

---

sealing except the President of the Church or those who are directed by him so to do." Pratt's biographers explain that "Pratt and Taylor, however, interpreted 'or those who are directed by him to do so' to give them latitude." Their interpretation of the sealing power at this point appears very similar to William's understanding. Terryl L. Givens and Matthew J. Grow, *Parley P. Pratt: The Apostle Paul of Mormonism* (New York: Oxford University Press, 2011), 259, 270–71.

39. Joseph F. Smith, *Blood Atonement and the Origin of Plural Marriage* (Salt Lake City: Deseret News Press, 1905), 49; John Hardy, *History of the Trials of Elder John Hardy before the Church of the Latter-day Saints in Boston, for Slander, in Saying that G. J. Adams, S. Brannan, and Wm. Smith were Licentious Characters* (Boston: Conway and Company, 1844). Martha Mayo and Connell O'Donovan's research on members of the Lowell Branch tenattively identifies Annis's first name as Sarah. Martha Mayo and Connell O'Donovan, "Members & Missionaries of the Lowell, Mass. Branch of the Church of Jesus Christ of Latter-Day Saints, 1835–1860," http://people.ucsc.edu/~odonovan/lowell_members.html#annis (accessed September 9, 2014).

40. William Smith, Pocket Companion, ca. fall 1844, reproduced in John K. Sheen, *Polygamy, or The Veil Lifted* (York, Neb.: n.pub., 1889). See Appendix B.

41. Heber C. Kimball had learned this information from the Whitneys and recorded it in his diary. Stanley B. Kimball, ed., *On the Potter's Wheel: The Diaries of Heber C. Kimball* (Urbana: University of Illinois Press, 1987), 114–15.

This same view surfaced during Brannan's hearing, when it became clear that William felt that employing the sealing power was among his privileges. As he had argued to Woodruff the previous winter,[42] Smith claimed that right because of his apostolic authority—authority that other members of the Twelve were also exercising. During Brannan's trial, William had stated with apparent emphasis that he had sealed Brannan and Wallace "with all the authority [I] possessed" and underscored that he "had a right . . . to do [so] as an apostle." According to the minutes, William "felt interested in [discussing] the subject" of his authority, "& wished the council if they chose to say whether or not he had a right so to do.—whether he [had] a right to mar[r]y Brannan & do what he had done. Or whether [he] was to be rode on a rail, & put down, or not." William's argumentative tone and lengthy speech on the subject, apparently went on for "quite a time."[43] Although not present during Brannan's trial, William Clayton succinctly summarized Smith's position in his journal that week: "Wm says he has sealed some women to men and he considers he is not accountable to Brigham nor the Twelve nor any one else."[44] According to the minutes from Brannan's hearing, Young agreed that William had a right to perform marriages—actually, any Mormon elder did—but "did not couple any other of Wm[']s acts, in this decision."[45] In other words, while William could perform marriages, Young could not tolerate his use of the sealing power without explicit authorization. Young was clarifying his role to William Smith as president of the Quorum of the Twelve, emphasizing that he stood in Joseph's place in holding the keys of the sealing power. Though William Smith certainly recognized Young as the presiding authority in the Church as indicated in his earlier letters, his absence for the entire preceding year may have limited his understanding about use of the sealing power after Joseph's death. Certainly, he disagreed with Brigham's restrictive explication. Young followed the precedent regarding sealings set by Joseph Smith prior to his death, where Joseph had closely overseen all sealings by either performing them himself or giving his personal authorization.[46]

The differences between Smith and the Twelve remained at an impasse during Brannan's hearing. Following the decision to reinstate Brannan, the discussion on use of the sealing power was shelved, only to resurface a few months later. Church authorities were obviously uncomfortable with William's deportment and views related to the sealing power during Brannan's trial but decided to take a conciliatory stance toward this last surviving brother of the Prophet, hoping to draw him into greater harmony with the quorum. Perhaps Caroline's funeral only a few hours

---

42. Woodruff to Young, October 9 and 14, 1844.
43. Richards, Minutes of Council, May 24, 1845; Bagley, *A Scoundrel's Tale*, 67–68.
44. George D. Smith, *An Intimate Chronicle*, 166.
45. Richards, Minutes of Council, May 24, 1845; Bagley, *A Scoundrel's Tale*, 67–68.
46. Brian Hales, *Joseph Smith's Polygamy, Volume 1: History* (Salt Lake City: Greg Kofford Books, 2013), 120 note 47, 604–5, 607.

earlier suggested that William's emotional and spiritual resilience were at a low ebb, making the time inopportune for a hard-hitting and prolonged discussion.

Instead, they took up the topic of the patriarchal office, which was clear-cut by comparison. William could assume that he inherited the office upon the deaths of his brothers but asked about formal ordination. After all, Young had assured him by letter that the office was his if he desired it, although he hinted that William could have designated one of his paternal uncles as the patriarch.[47] William had no desire to yield this office previously held by his father and older brother Hyrum. So on the same day as Caroline's funeral and Brannan's trial, William "asked the views of the council about his patriarchal office" and received renewed assurances from Brigham Young that "it was his right" to receive the office of Church patriarch.[48] At that juncture, the mood in the room changed markedly. Willard Richards recorded in his diary that "there was a warm interchange of good feeling[s] between Wm Smith and the Quorum."[49] George A. Smith recorded that the "brethren present expressed their feelings towards Elder Wm. Smith." Their congeniality touched William's sympathy, and he reciprocated by "lifting both hands to heaven expressing the same."[50] The apostles then encircled William with "all of the Twelve present laying their hands on him except W. Richards who wrote the blessing," while Brigham Young ordained William as Church patriarch and pronounced a blessing upon him.[51]

A limited transcript of the ordination written by Williard Richards has survived. This summary records that Young said "we lay our hands up[on] you of the tw[elve] to set you apart & ord[ain] you a patriarch to the whole [church]," and blessed Smith to "preside over all other patriarchs." He promised that William would be given the "right power [and] glory pertaining to that office—praying our heave[n]ly father to pour out [the] H[oly] S[pirit] [to] fill your whole system." He further blessed Smith with the "revelatory" capacity to declare the "lineage [and] determine the parentage" of the Saints and to identify the "calling gifts & blessing[s] god has in store" for them. Significantly, Young also blessed William that he would manifest "love [and] t[r]anquility to [the] Twelve," that they would become "more & more united," something William had been inwardly wrestling with in the hectic month since his return. Longtime Smith family friend Lewis Robbins was also present to witness the historic occasion, but left no record of his impressions that day. The evening ended on a positive and spiritual note.[52]

---

47. Brigham Young (Nauvoo, Ill.), Letter to William Smith, September 28, 1844, *Prophet* 1, no. 25 (November 9, 1844): 2.

48. Richards, Minutes of Council, May 24, 1845.

49. Richards, Diary, May 24, 1845.

50. "Memoirs of George A. Smith," May 24, 1845, 300.

51. Richards, Diary, May 24, 1845; Richards, Minutes of Council, May 24, 1845, 301.

52. Patriarchal Blessing bestowed by B[righam] Young on William Smith, May 24, 1845. Brigham Young Office Files 1832–1878, President's Office Files, 1843–1877,

While it might seem odd that fellow members of the Twelve conferred the patriarchal office on William given their concerns about his current attitude, they probably assumed that doing so did not create a significant risk—in fact, that withholding it would confuse members, few of whom were aware of William's alleged misbehavior in the eastern branches. After all, the patriarchal office provided only restricted authority "over all other patriarchs." Members of the Twelve were also probably not aware at that point of the extent which William had used the sealing power and had been teaching plural marriage. Smith also began giving patriarchal blessings before his ordination, while still in the East, which probably was less of a surprise considering the hereditary nature of the office.[53] William apparently took his office seriously enough to immediately begin giving blessings. Notwithstanding, Young appears to have desired that he be officially recognized in that capacity, specifically instructing William by letter in September 1844 that, if he desired the office of presiding patriarch he should "come to Nauvoo as soon as possible, and receive your ordination of Patriarch by the proper authorities, so that you may officiate in giving the Saints their patriarchal blessings."[54] While it is unknown whether Smith continued bestowing patriarchal blessings after receiving Young's directive, the other apostles may have still been uncomfortable with William's assumption that he was entitled to the office. But during the meetings held on May 24, 1845, William appeared willing to hearken to Young's counsel. He was also the last surviving adult man in the Joseph Smith Sr. family. He held a special place in the Saints' affections due to his family connection, and his quorum colleagues appear to have been willing to tolerate some of his eccentricities, or even outright mistakes, because of those ties. As Wilford Woodruff had written to Young in December 1844, "for the sake of the Smith family," if it was at all possible, "I want William Smith [to remain in the church]."[55] Undoubtedly Woodruff's statement not only reflected the view of his fellow quorum members but also that of the membership at large. William Smith knew this and had used it to his advantage repeatedly throughout his tenure as an apostle, and more especially after the deaths of his brothers.

Recommends, Certificates, and Ordination Records, 1843–1871, Blessing of William Smith, 1845 May 24, LDS Church History Library.

53. Benjamin Winchester in a sermon in November 1844 stated: "I have loved brother William Smith! and I love him still. I received a patriarchal blessing under his hands! and I believe it was given by the spirit of God! and I am determined to try and have it all fulfilled." Benjamin Winchester, quoted in "Meeting of the Mormons Last Evening," *Prophet* 1, no. 26 (November 16, 1844): 2. According to D. Michael Quinn, "Smith gave this blessing before mid-September when the two men condemned each other as apostates." Quinn, *The Mormon Hierarchy: Origins of Power* (Salt Lake City: Signature Books, 1994), 214, 426 note 152.

54. Brigham Young to William Smith, September 28, 1844.

55. Woodruff to Young, December 3, 1844.

Offering him the office and validating it through ordination may have also been a goodwill gesture toward the entire Smith family, with whom all Mormons deeply sympathized. While Smith's colleagues may have hoped that this gesture would satisfy William's ambition, as it turned out, nothing they did seemed to placate Smith for long. He immediately used the ordination to increase his standing in the Church's hierarchy. It was a difficult predicament for Church leaders who revered the Smiths, yet had to try and manage the most difficult and inconstant personality in the family. Had it been any other Smith brother who had survived, this situation likely would not have developed. William's ordination as patriarch created a quandary that kept leaders reeling throughout the summer and would be a decision they would almost immediately regret, although they could not have anticipated what later became visible as William's ulterior motives in obtaining the office.

Parley P. Pratt, 1807–1857. Daguerreotype photograph by unknown photographer, ca. 1850–1857. Courtesy LDS Church History Library.

The exchange of good feelings between Smith and the council following his ordination did not last. Young likely left the meeting confused by Smith's convoluted explanation of the sealing he had performed on Brannan's behalf. Even more disconcerting was Smith's assertion that he did not need to account to Young or the Twelve for his behavior. William apparently dodged disclosing the extent to which he had used the sealing power in the East, including bestowing it on Brannan, Adams, and possibly others. As early as December 1844, Woodruff had learned from Caroline's brother that William, who was in a temper, did not "feel himself bound hereafter to defend the character of the Twelve, or be accountable to that quorum, but he was led by visions and revelations for himself."[56] If he was still maintaining this position in May 1845 in Nauvoo, a clash was inevitable.

In the meantime, disconcerting reports about William continued to arrive from the East, especially from Parley P. Pratt. In October 1845, soon after he had been excommunicated, William published his own defensive version of events in the *Warsaw Signal*: "News was arriving from the east, by letters and various other ways, to the Council, and others, containing eulogiums on the boasted righ-

---

56. Ibid.

teousness of Parley P. Pratt, and condemning the acts of his predecessors."[57] In an attempt to bring the eastern branches into harmony with Church practice and policies, Pratt began to openly criticize misbehavior by Smith, Adams, and Brannan, using the *Prophet* to spread the word as far as possible. As Pratt familiarized himself with the status of the eastern branches, he grew increasingly troubled by reports about Smith's behavior, including more specific details of his sealings. During the same week as Brannan's trial, Pratt wrote a pointed editorial explaining that uniting couples and families for eternity was of such a sacred nature that it could take place only in the not-yet-completed house of God, and most especially with the express authorization of he who held the keys of that power (Brigham Young), which could not occur in the outlying branches of the Church. Said Pratt:

> How frequently a man and his wife, or a young couple about to be married, present themselves to me, with a request to be sealed to each other; that is, married for eternity. Do I ever grant their request? No; for the best of all reasons.—I have no authority so to do under present circumstances; and, were I to do it, it would only be deceiving them; as such a sealing would not stand, or be recognized in the resurrection; unless performed according to the strict law of God, and of the keys of the sealing powers, and in connection with the ordinances of endowment which belongs to God's sanctuary [temple], and no where else.[58]

In another reference to the trio of leaders—Smith, Adams, and Brannan—and the plural marriages they had considered their privilege, Pratt referred to the sealing power as allowing for "no confusion, unlawful connection, or unvirtuous liberties."[59] Although he did not name Smith, Adams, and Brannan, it was obvious whom he meant and that he vigorously condemned them for claiming such privileges when they had presided in the area. This editorial, printed on May 24, reached Nauvoo that same week, just days after William had argued with other members of the Twelve over who controlled the keys of authorizing the use of the sealing power.

Perhaps the doctrinal divergence between Smith and the Twelve might have been resolved had Pratt's editorial not reignited William Smith's ire. Although few details have survived about their relationship during Joseph Smith's lifetime, the personalities of the two apostles did not seem likely to mesh well. Pratt's biographers Terryl Givens and Matthew Grow describe him as an individual who spoke impetuously and with an "unflinching bluntness" that regularly proved "divisive" with those whom he interacted. In contrast was Heber C. Kimball. "Brigham Young once commented on the 'want of tact' in some elders 'to know how to win the people,'" report Givens and Grow. Young "used Pratt's friend Heber Kimball, a phenomenally successful missionary, as an example of a softer,

---

57. William Smith, "A Proclamation," *Warsaw Signal* 11, no. 32 (October 29, 1845): 1.

58. Parley P. Pratt, "This Number Closes the First Volume of the 'Prophet,'" *Prophet* 1, no. 52 (May 24, 1845): 2.

59. Ibid.

gentler approach. 'Come, my friend, sit down; do not be in a hurry,' he would say to strangers. Then he would 'preach the Gospel in a plain, familiar manner, and make his hearers believe everything he said.... 'Come along now'; and he would lead them into the waters of baptism.' Pratt, on the other hand, was a missionary without subtlety."[60] During Joseph Smith's lifetime, Pratt, an ardent missionary, remained at the center of Church activity, laboring as one of the movement's brightest theologians and most prolific writers.

William Smith was much less devout than Pratt in his religious practice and more tolerant of those who may have been considered outside mainstream Mormonism. His friendships with Brannan and Adams, and the Hodges family (see Chapter 12), were an example of how he was frequently drawn to those on the fringes of the movement, as was the case in his friendships. "William is a very sociable, and would be called the world over a jolly dog," noted one non-Mormon observer of Smith's personality. "I could not help thinking him out of place among the ascetic looking, long headed fellows, his coadjutors of the Twelve."[61] Among William's colleagues in the Twelve, he seems to have been most drawn to Heber C. Kimball, as Kimball's affable manner most closely paralleled his own personality. Of course, the exception to Smith's easygoing ways came when he was confronted or criticized. His sensitive ego meant that he frequently overreacted when challenged. Consequently, Smith responded defensively to Pratt's harsh accusations when they appeared in the *Prophet*. He was especially belligerent during this time when he felt uneasy about his status among the Saints. Although William never received correction meekly, Pratt's indirect but widely distributed reproof sent Smith into a rage.

The editorial also gave William additional reason to believe that his authority as an apostle was being undermined, something he had certainly supposed during the previous six months. Ever sensitive to injustice, he was incapable of remaining passive and felt impelled to do something to counter Pratt's very public sentiments. He decided to use the power of the press, as editing *The Wasp* and the *Prophet* had helped him promote his agenda throughout his tenure as a Church leader. He immediately wrote a short announcement about Brannan's reinstatement and sent it to John Taylor to be published in the *Nauvoo Neighbor*: "The Saints will notice by the restoration of Elder Brannan that no wrong has been done by him or his former councilor [George Adams] . . . as is insinuated by P. P. Pratt in the last No. of the Prophet," Smith penned. He then included a

---

60. Terryl L. Givens and Matthew J. Grow, *Parley P. Pratt: The Apostle Paul of Mormonism* (New York: Oxford University Press, 2011), 76, 79; Brigham Young, April 6, 1857, *Journal of Discourses*, 26 vols. (London and Liverpool: LDS Booksellers Depot, 1855–86), 4:305.

61. [J. A. Harris], "A correspondent from the Albany Atlas writing from Nauvoo . . . gives the following description of a call made upon the family of Joe Smith," *Cleveland Herald* 11, no. 70 (September 13, 1845): 1. E. D. Howe had helped launch the *Cleveland Herald*, so the paper had long had an interest in Mormonism.

statement which revealed his most primary motivation for writing—retaliation against Pratt: "And I really hope for the future that there will be no more of this low, back handed impeachment Among brethren of the same faith and especially from those who are no better than they should be."[62]

For obvious reasons, Taylor would not print Smith's vitriolic announcement. Not only did Smith's statement ignore the mistakes that both Adams and Brannan had committed in the East, but Taylor—and the other apostles as well—would obviously judge inappropriate William's open attack on Pratt. When Smith learned that Taylor would not publish it, he grew increasingly rancorous. He wrote to Taylor again, insisting that he had a right to defend himself against the "suspicion thrown upon me by Elder PP Pratt." He warned Taylor, "I clame as my right to speak in the neighbor in defence of my own wrights & if I am not allowed this priviledge [by] the Brethren [and they] will not do it for me I shall take sutch steps as conscience may dictate to preserve my influence & my friends abroad."[63] Smith's threat was vague, but his anger was undisguised. He clearly intended to protect his erratic reputation at all costs. When Taylor ignored this letter as well, Smith grew even more furious. To schoolteacher James Monroe, who was acting as William's scribe for patriarchal blessings, he exploded that the *Nauvoo Neighbor* was a "little stinking paper, just fit for Jack——t."[64]

In the days following his ordination as Church patriarch, Smith ruminated on how he might restore his damaged reputation. However, instead of stepping back from the emotional brink to analyze and correct the messages he was receiving, he continued to nurse his anger. He felt his voice was being restricted and his character sullied in the eyes of the Saints. He learned that he was being excluded from some of the meetings that included the Church's highest ranking officials. He later recounted how he felt that the Church "proceedings . . . were kept entirely hidden from me" during the summer of 1845. "The disposition of the Temple funds, counselling with regard to the affairs of the church, I . . . had nothing to do with."[65] Insecure about his status, Smith resolved on a tactic that he hoped would restore his reputation and expand on his Church position. Though he had occasionally entertained thoughts about aspiring to a more prominent position within the movement following his brothers' deaths, it was not until his return to Nauvoo that he began to maneuver for such a position among the main body of Saints. His feeling that his authority was being undermined brought his ambition to the surface.

In October of 1844, when Woodruff had visited the eastern branches of the church, the first topic that William Smith brought up was, according to

---

62. William Smith, "The Saints Will Notice . . . ," unpublished announcement, ca. May 1845, Brigham Young Office Files 1832–78, Box 42, fd. 13, LDS Church History Library.

63. Wm. Smith, Letter to Elder Tailor [sic], Editor of the *Neighbor*, ca. May/June 1845, Box 42, fd. 13, Brigham Young Office Files 1832–78, LDS Church History Library.

64. James M. Monroe, Journal, May 29, 1845, 72, MS 7061, LDS Church History Library.

65. William Smith, "Proclamation," 1.

Woodruff, "the office of Patriarch and said it was his right, should contend for it, through death and the grave, etc."⁶⁶ If Woodruff is reporting the tone of this conversation accurately, William did not mention the office mildly but extremely pugnaciously. Two months earlier in late August, he had demanded in a letter to Brigham Young: "Will the Bretherin remember me & my clames in the Smith family[?]"⁶⁷ Once in Nauvoo, William perceived his influence in the Church diminishing, and he responded by seeming fixated about acquiring the patriarchal office. He wanted to secure his place in the Church's hierarchy, even though Young had already assured Smith that the office of patriarch was his if he should desire it.⁶⁸ Almost immediately after being ordained presiding patriarch, Smith began to expand the position to increase his standing among the Saints.

In the week following his ordination as patriarch, William sent a letter to the *Times and Seasons* announcing that he was ready to bestow patriarchal blessings on the Saints. He underscored his unique position as the only surviving son of Joseph Sr., his calling as an apostle, and his recent ordination as the patriarch. Adjacent to William's letter was a lengthy article written by an assistant editor, W. W. Phelps, regarding the office of patriarch. Whether Smith had any influence on Phelps's editorial is unknown, but it seems likely, since it enunciated his own evolving view of his authority. "William is the last of the family," began Phelps, "and truly inherits the blood and spirit of his father's house, as well as the priesthood and patriarchal office from his father and brother, legally, and by hereditary descent." Phelps thus emphasized William's inheritance of the office "by lineage," suggesting that this element was more important than his ordination. Although this letter appeared in the May 15 issue, William actually wrote it and Phelps published it after his ordination on May 24, as this issue of the *Times and Seasons* had been delayed by at least ten days, and probably into mid-June. Other members of the Twelve were likely surprised at William's letter because, at the time of his ordination, there had been a "warm interchange of good feeling[s]" between William and the Twelve.⁶⁹

---

66. Woodruff to Young, October 9 and 14, 1844.

67. William Smith (Bordentown, N.J.), Letter to Brigham Young, August 24, 1844, Brigham Young Office Files 1832–1878, Letters from Church Leaders and Others, 1840–1877, William Smith, 1844–1857, LDS Church History Library.

68. "As it regards the Patriarch of the whole Church," Brigham Young had written William Smith in September 1844, "there has not been any appointed yet in the place of brother Hyrum, and I do not calculate to do any thing but what is strictly according to the mind and will of God; the right rests upon your head, there is no doubt, and all will remain as it is until we have further communications from you; but if you feel disposed, you can bestow it upon Uncle John or As[ah]el; and if not disposed to do so, but feel to have it yourself, we wish you to come to Nauvoo as soon as possible, and receive your ordination of Patriarch by the proper authorities, so that you may officiate in giving the Saints their patriarchal blessings." Brigham Young (Nauvoo), Letter to William Smith, September 28, 1844, *Prophet* 1, no. 25 (November 9, 1844): 2.

69. Richards, Diary, May 24, 1845.

William Wines Phelps, 1792–1872. Photograph by Edward Martin, 1862–1873. Courtesy LDS Church History Library.

It was probably Phelps who also inserted an earlier note in the December 1, 1844, issue of the *Times and Seasons*, which further muddled the extent of William's authority by asserting that, once ordained patriarch, "he will stand in the same relationship to the Twelve, as his brother Hyrum did to the First Presidency, after he was ordained patriarch."[70] Hyrum had inherited the office of patriarch and had also been ordained to it, but he had separately been ordained as assistant president of the Church. The implication was that William would likewise receive both offices. Thus his authority would be greater than that of the Twelve, and he would, logically, become Church president.

William Smith's May letter in the *Times and Seasons* also included a defense of his behavior in the East and his views on succession—which had begun to shift as a result of his resentful feelings. "As to my presidency over the eastern churches," asserted William, "I am confident that my precept and example have been unexceptionable in the eyes of all good Saints." He also counseled the Saints: "Support and uphold the proper authorities of the church—when I say authorities, I mean the whole, and not a part; the *Twelve*, and not one, two, six, eight, ten, or eleven, but the whole *Twelve*;—follow me as I follow Christ."[71] The purpose of his letter was twofold. First, William was clearly attempting to restore his reputation by asserting that his behavior in the East had been proper. Second, he was attempting to rally the Saints to support him as possessing equal authority with other members of the Twelve. He referred to himself as "the last of the [Smith] family" and then asked, "Shall I be sustained by this community?"—a reference to both his ecclesiastical authority and his need for financial support.[72]

This letter was an important turning point, as it was the first time William had publicly acknowledged disagreements with other members of the Twelve. Its emphasis on lineal priesthood also concerned leaders since it essentially ignored Brigham Young's authoritative role as president of the Twelve. Both articles created confusion among the Saints about the extent of Smith's authority in the Church. Young and the rest of the Twelve immediately felt the need to correct those implica-

---

70. "We have just received . . . ," *Times and Seasons* 5, no. 22 (December 1, 1844): 727.
71. William Smith, "Patriarchal," *Times and Seasons* 6 (May 15, 1845): 904.
72. Ibid., 904.

tions. Most assuredly with input from other members of the Twelve, John Taylor was appointed to respond to the editorials written by both Phelps and Smith.

In the days following William's ordination, and because of what had been outlined in the *Times and Seasons*, the authority of the patriarchal office became a point of debate. In referring to the scope of William's authority as patriarch, Phelps began his editorial by writing that William held "the office of Patriarch over the whole church." Taylor focused on this phrase as dramatically overstating William's authority—especially given Phelps's emphasis on lineal priesthood and William's aggressive claims to the sealing power that he had expressed during Brannan's trial. George J. Adams was already promoting Joseph III as the lineal successor to Joseph Smith, in organizing a faction of Mormonism across the Mississippi River in Iowa, and authorities at Nauvoo had learned that William was sympathetic to his views.[73] Additionally, as questions and confusion about Joseph Smith's successor continued, they included speculation that a Smith would likely be appointed as the presiding authority in Nauvoo. Prior to Samuel's death on July 30, 1844, there were rumors that this younger brother of Joseph and Hyrum would emerge as the new prophet of Mormonism. "The Mormon mantle has fallen upon Sam Smith," wrote one editor in an eastern newspaper, "who has been, or is to be inducted into office with all due solemnity, and take upon himself the entire government of the 'Latter Day Saints' as prophet and patriarch chief."[74] After Samuel's death, the speculation and discussion shifted to the probability that William would assume the prophetic role. William's former antagonist, Thomas C. Sharp, conjectured in his *Warsaw Signal*, "that it is rumored that Bill Smith is making trouble for the Twelve, in Nauvoo, and will either compel them, quietly, to surrender their power and submit to him, or else he will throw himself in open rebellion."[75]

The Twelve felt they needed to suppress William's ambition, as they certainly understood his motives. The June 1 issue of the *Times and Seasons*, which was printed on or about June 25, 1845, contained John Taylor's lengthy editorial clarifying the authority of the patriarchal office. "Since the publication of the last *Times and Seasons*," began Taylor, "we have frequently been interrogated about the meaning of some remarks made by Eld. Wm. Smith in an article headed patriarchal, and also concerning some expressions in the editorial [written by

---

73. William Clayton recorded in his journal on May 23, 1845, that "W[illiam] Smith is coming out in opposition to the Twelve and in favor of Adams. The latter has organized a church at Augusta, Iowa Territory with young Joseph Smith for President, Wm Smith for Patriarch, Jared Carter for President of the stake and himself for spokesman to Joseph." George D. Smith, *An Intimate Chronicle*, 166.

74. [Horace Greeley and Thomas McElrath], "The New Monarch of Mormondom," *New York Weekly Tribune*, 3, no. 152 (August 10, 1844): 2.

75. Thomas C. Sharp, "Trouble in the Holy City," *Warsaw Signal* 2, no. 15 (June 11, 1845): 2; "New Order of Things at Nauvoo," *Sangamo Journal* (Springfield, Ill.) 14, no. 40 (June 26, 1845): 2.

Phelps] connected therewith; and as the nature of the office of Patriarch, does not seem to be fully understood, we thought a little explanation on this point might not be amiss."[76] This conversational, almost casual, introduction does not make the equally important point that the Twelve wanted this editorial to counteract views William had expressed in a form that William would certainly understand, even if the general Church membership did not, after his return to Nauvoo. As Brigham Young had with the claims of Sidney Rigdon and James J. Strang, he was taking swift, though in this case indirect, action to rein in the aspiring brother of the Prophet.

Taylor also rebuked Phelps and downplayed his authority to pontificate on the subject by referring to him as a "junior editor" and dismissing his editorial as having been written "rather hastily." Taylor then got to the core of his topic: "We have been asked, 'Does not patriarch *over* the *whole* Church place Brother William Smith at the head of the whole church? Ans[wer]. No. Brother William is not patriarch *over* the *whole* church; but patriarch to the church." Taylor further clarified the role of a patriarch in relation to the Twelve, indicating that the office was bestowed on William by the Twelve. "Can a stream run higher than its fountain?" asked Taylor. "We think that every one will see that Br. William Smith's patriarchal office will not exalt him higher in regard to priesthood than he was before, as one of the Twelve; but will rather change the nature of his office."[77]

The most surprising portion of Taylor's editorial related to Smith's calling as an apostle. "In all probability if Br. William magnifies his calling [as Patriarch] he will not be able henceforth to attend to the duties of an apostle; but officiate in the same capacity in regard to blessing as his brother Hyrum did. Not as [a] president of the church; but as patriarch to it." Thus, while he acknowledged Hyrum's role as a member of the First Presidency for a time, Taylor indicated that when Hyrum "was ordained patriarch he gave it up"—and by "it," Taylor here means as a counselor in the First Presidency, and another was ordained in his stead (Wm. Law)." This statement, not unexpectedly, was genuinely confusing, as Hyrum actually received a more expansive role—being appointed a prophet, seer, and revelator in an office that was later deemed "assistant" or "associate president" of the Church, on January 19, 1841, when William Law replaced him as a counselor in the First Presidency.[78] Even Brigham Young postulated that, had Hyrum survived, he would have been Church president by virtue of his office as associate president.[79]

---

76. [John Taylor], "Patriarchal," *Times and Seasons* 6 (June 1, 1845): 920. John Taylor mentioned drafting this editorial in his journal on June 23, 1845, where he also recorded the contents of the subsequently published editorial. Dean C. Jessee, ed., *John Taylor Nauvoo Journal* (Provo, Utah: Grandin Book, 1996), 63–66.

77. Ibid., 920–21.

78. Ibid., 922; Hedges, Smith, and Anderson, *Journals, Volume 2*, 492; Jeffrey S. O'Driscoll, *Hyrum Smith: A Life of Integrity* (Salt Lake City: Deseret Book, 2003), 232–34.

79. "October Conference Minutes," *Times and Seasons* 5, no. 19 (October 15, 1844), 683–84.

In spite of the confusion this statement created, Taylor's main point was unmistakable; William was never ordained to any office in the First Presidency or as an assistant president. Thus, his claims to authority rested on either his office as Church patriarch or as an apostle. In either case, to put it bluntly, Young, as senior apostle, outranked him. After a fairly lengthy clarification on the office of patriarch, Taylor succinctly concluded, "President Brigham Young is the president and head, and presides over all patriarchs, presidents and councils of the church."[80]

In his final paragraph, Taylor also included a warning to William. He could maintain his position as patriarch and as one of the Twelve if he would "maintain his dignity" in those offices and be acquiescent to "President Brigham Young," who was head over all the Church.[81] The message was clear. Taylor's editorial not only clarified the role of the presiding patriarch in the Church but also reproved William for his overreaching and admonished him to mend his ways if he wanted to maintain either or both positions.

The inner circle of leaders in Nauvoo undoubtedly saw this rebuke as harsh, especially given William's probable physical fatigue from Caroline's final days of life and the emotional turmoil that accompanied her death and funeral. Still, William had actually brought it on himself by publishing his letter to the *Times and Seasons*. Rather than expressing contrition and loyalty, he had justified his behavior in the East and angled for a higher station in the Church hierarchy. At this time of external danger from hostile non-Mormons and turmoil within as different men competed for Church leadership, William had crossed a line with his public claims. Silence from the other Church leaders could have meant either that they saw his claims as valid or, at least, that they were uncertain. Either interpretation was not tolerable. William's public claims demanded a public response.

While Smith *may* not have been responsible for the views promoted in Phelps's editorial, the other General Authorities knew that Smith held many of those same opinions. He had expressed such viewpoints during Brannan's trial only days earlier, and they had learned from Newel Whitney and Elizabeth Ann Whitney that William was fuming because he felt he should have more authority than he was being allowed.[82] Even if the other apostles had had reports from no one except Wilford Woodruff and Parley P. Pratt, those reports would have still been alarming, but now they had been reinforced by George J. Adams's and Samuel Brannan's confessions during their respective trials that had unquestionably implicated William. And even if Adams and Brannan had been trying to shift more responsibility from their shoulders to William's, William's statements in his own defense had created more alarm, not reassurance. In fact, as May ended, Nauvoo leaders had a clearer sense about the scope of William's ambition.

---

80. Taylor, "Patriarchal," 922.
81. Ibid., 922.
82. Stanley Kimball, *On the Potter's Wheel*, 114–15.

William Clayton recorded in his journal the perspective of Young and other leaders toward William during May's critical last week. Undoubtedly, that perspective had been included in Taylor's editorial. At a meeting on May 23, where leaders discussed Smith's case, they concluded that William was indeed aspiring to be the president of the Church. A week later, while leaders prayed over many pressing matters, Clayton detailed that they "especially" pled "that the Lord would over-rule the movements of Wm. Smith who is endeavoring to ride the Twelve down."[83] Revealingly, Smith was absent from both of these meetings, and unquestionably it was because of what they perceived as his recalcitrant disposition.

A reasonable question is why the other General Authorities did not ask William to help clarify the role of the presiding patriarch during the tense week of May 23–30. As one of the Twelve, he was a part of the Church's governing body, and no one challenged the validity of his calling and ordination as Church patriarch. The answer lay in William's reckless attitude and behavior. Almost certainly, if Taylor had consulted Smith about the forthcoming editorial, it would have led to another clash. Ever since William had been called as an apostle in Kirtland, his history demonstrated that, once he made up his mind, there was no reasoning with him. During Brannan's trial, he had obstinately insisted on arguing about his right to use the sealing power. As a result, the Twelve chose to sidestep Smith. They were responding in kind to his own preemptive step in going to the *Times and Seasons* after John Taylor refused to publish either of William's announcements. Both decisions only escalated their differences. Communication between the two parties was at a stalemate, doubtless exacerbated by personal distrust between Brigham and William that could only temporarily be papered over.

When Smith read Taylor's "clarification," he was predictably incensed. In his self-justifying letter to the *Warsaw Signal* in October, he described: "I published a short notice on the subject of the office of patriarch, [and] it was soon scanned and criticised, . . . without even my knowledge or consent." He felt that Taylor's explanation reduced the office to being "equal only to any common father over his family . . . robbing me of my lawful rights in the Smith family, rights by lineage, etc." William also jeered that Taylor had "done a brave thing when he published his false notions and misstatements with regard to my patriarchal office, at a time when he knew I had not the power of defence."[84]

James Monroe, to whom William spilled out his outraged feelings, recorded: "William is wonderfully angry because they would not print a piece of his in the Neighbor in reply to an insinuation of P. P. Pratt in the New York Prophet." Monroe further summarized the widening chasm between the two parties by recording William's complaint "that B. Young is not a whit beyond himself or any other of the Twelve. That he is merely President by courtesy. That he has no higher keys and that the whole Twelve are presidents over the Church and not B.

---

83. George D. Smith, *An Intimate Chronicle*, 166–67.
84. William Smith, "A Proclamation," 1.

Young and that he does not stand in Joseph's shoes." Monroe speculated: "His words seem to posture a rupture between him and the Twelve, but I hardly know how it will come out. Most probably to his disadvantage, as the authority of the Twelve is too firmly rooted to be broken up very easily."[85]

Irene M. Bates and E. Gary Smith, co-authors of a group biography of the patriarchs who have held this office, highlighted the confusion surrounding the Church patriarch's authority as a primary factor in William's conflict with other members of the Twelve that began in May of 1845.[86] However, considering the context of the previous six months, it seems clear that William was simply using his ordination as a tool to increase his standing and influence in the Church, which he felt had been eroded steadily ever since Parley P. Pratt had arrived

William Clayton, 1814–1879. Engraving by unknown artist, date unknown. Engraving in author's possession. Clayton frequently recorded William's viewpoints and temperament in his journal during the summer of 1845.

in the East. He felt singled out among the Twelve for having privileges enjoyed by his brethren diminished and stripped from him. What William failed to recognize was that his behavior and perceptions were escalating the problem. He had refused to acknowledge his wrongdoing by his unauthorized use of the sealing power, exacerbated by his defiant, public self-defense when he arrived in Nauvoo. His refusal to subordinate himself to Brigham Young and the collective voice of the Twelve was at the core of his difficulty. Had he acquiesced to the Twelve, there would have been no debate over the authority of the patriarchal office. The more zealously William defended himself, championed lineal rights, and defied the Twelve, the more strongly the Twelve felt they needed to restrict his influence in Nauvoo. The more he felt undermined, the more he defied the Twelve. It was a vicious cycle to which William was blind and from which, as a consequence, he could not extricate himself. At earlier points in his history, Joseph or Hyrum or both had been successful in calming William's temper, and had let brotherly love and concern mitigate consequences that William probably well deserved. And

---

85. Monroe, Journal, May 29, 1845, 72.

86. Irene M. Bates and E. Gary Smith, *Lost Legacy: The Mormon Office of Presiding Patriarch* (Urbana: University of Illinois Press, 1996), 79–95. Also see these authors' earlier publications about William Smith and his role as patriarch: Irene M. Bates, "William Smith, 1811–93: Problematic Patriarch," *Dialogue: A Journal of Mormon Thought* 16, no. 2 (Summer 1983): 11–23; E. Gary Smith, "The Patriarchal Crisis of 1845," *Dialogue: A Journal of Mormon Thought* 16, no. 2 (Summer 1983): 24–35.

he, in turn, had responded to their affection and concern with an outpouring of warmth and love that had mended the relationship.

But William no longer had a brother, or even a friend close enough to play a brother's role, in helping him deal with his grief, his anger, and his wounded pride. As a result, he had spilled his intemperate views into the public record, insulted his colleagues in the quorum, and challenged Brigham Young directly. It was a foregone conclusion that he would continue to clash with the Twelve. William Clayton recorded in his diary the view that was becoming all too apparent to Church officials: "There is more danger from William than from any other source, and I fear his course will bring us much trouble."[87] Clayton's perceptions would prove remarkably accurate.

---

87. George D. Smith, *An Intimate Chronicle*, 166.

Chapter 12

Disgruntled Patriarch

> If the brethren did not want me or my councils . . . I would leave them. Let . . . the Twelve say so—Let the Bishops say so—Let the police say so, and I am gone. But mark it, . . . where I go, there also the Smith family [will] go, and with them also goes the Priesthood.
> —William Smith, June 25, 1845

After the Church courts of Adams and Brannan, William Smith was increasingly viewed with suspicion. The descriptions of his activities in the East—combined with his erratic loyalty, assertions of authority, and mixture of cooperation and insubordination after returning to Nauvoo—had not endeared him to other members of the Twelve. Brigham Young, having successfully squelched attempts from Sidney Rigdon for Church leadership, sympathizers with the Law brothers, and the even more serious contest posed by James J. Strang, was alert to challenges from other directions.

Little is known about Brigham's personal relations with William in Kirtland, but William's quick withdrawal from Missouri when Brigham was mobilizing all possible resources to evacuate the Saints must have looked like a lack of commitment. Furthermore, David W. Patten, president of the Twelve before his death at the battle of Crooked River, had expressed doubts about William, and William had, in fact, cursed Joseph, probably in a moment of flaring temper that he later regretted. William was called up for possible discipline in May 1839 at Quincy in proceedings where others, such as Orson Hyde, were also reprimanded. (See Chapter 7.) Although William was confirmed in his membership, he distanced himself from the Twelve, moved to Plymouth, Illinois, where he ran a hotel, and declined a call for all the apostles to serve missions. Many of them were in ill health themselves, and this undertaking, particularly the Great Britain mission, came at enormous sacrifice to their impoverished and ill families. All of these events must have positioned William as someone not completely dependable on Brigham's scale of judgment.

For William's part, while he doubtless respected and admired Brigham's leadership abilities, he had a hard time submitting himself wholly to another's decisions—even when that person was his own brother whom he accepted as a prophet. The deaths of his father in 1840 and Don Carlos in 1841 were a serious emotional blow to William's sense of familial stability, and the loss of his three remaining brothers within a matter of weeks in 1844, coupled with Caroline's steady decline that made her death inevitable, must have increased his insecurity.

Worse, Brigham's closeness to Joseph may have set up an unconscious feeling of having been supplanted in that valued relationship—a feeling that became explicit when Brigham Young replaced him with Parley P. Pratt as president of the eastern branches. John Taylor's editorial publicly limiting William's claims of authority as patriarch was also an implied rebuke that chafed William's sensitive feelings. The Twelve doubtless saw their efforts as attempts to communicate the importance of acting in unity with them, but for William, they constituted punishment and suppression, even oppression.

Ten years later in 1855 when William briefly tried to realign himself with Mormonism, he wrote to Brigham Young, expressing the negative feelings he associated with this time period. He compared himself to an "Irishman"—a common ethnic slur of the time that linked the Irish with barbarism and lack of civilized behavior, very nearly in the same category of exclusion as African Americans, Native Americans, and (later) the Chinese. In fact, asserted William, he felt "a peg or two lower than an Irishman" when compared to other members of the Twelve and the privileges they enjoyed.[1] William's diminished status was also apparent to Church members. Omar Olney, a lay member of the Church, who later supported William Smith's church at Covington, Kentucky, said that he had "ever felt sympathy for William Smith, since I heard some of the twelveites say in Nauvoo, 'that he was too tall and if he would come back to Nauvoo, they would make him shorter by a head.'"[2]

Humiliatingly, Sidney Rigdon, who by now had organized an offshoot of Mormonism in Pittsburgh, Pennsylvania, called the Church of Jesus Christ of Latter Day Saints, had announced William's pending appointment as patriarch in his newspaper, and said he had "been taken from the quorum of the twelve to fill that office." Reflecting their faction's perception of William's diminished role, Rigdon concluded his article by the jeering query: "Come down a peg, eh?"[3]

On May 29, 1845, schoolteacher James Monroe, who had almost immediately become William's secretary and his confidant, 'talked with Aunt Emma some about the course of William Smith," recording the details in his diary. Though Monroe much admired William, "I told [her] that his character has not stood

---

1. William Smith (Springfield, Ill.), Letter to Brigham Young, May 7, 1855, Brigham Young Office Files 1832–1878, Letters from Church Leaders and Others, 1840–1877, William Smith, 1844–1857, LDS Church History Library.

2. "Shorter by a Head," *Melchisedek and Aaronic Herald* 1, no. 8 (February 1850): 4. Little is known about Omar Olney. Despite his fairly unusual name, I have been unable to determine whether he was related to noted dissident Oliver Olney, who had been excommunicated in 1842 and had written several pamphlets remonstrating against the Twelve at Nauvoo. Omar was living at Hunts Hollow, New York, affiliated with William Smith's Church of Jesus Christ of Latter Day Saints in 1849–50, and acted as an agent for Smith's newspaper. "List of Agents for this Paper," *Melchisedek and Aaronic Herald* 1, no. 5 (August 1849): 2.

3. [Sidney Rigdon] "As We Thought," *Messenger and Advocate* 1, no. 5 (January 1, 1845): 73.

very high . . . and that we should be quite cautious about believing that a man had met with a sudden change as it was rather difficult for a man to change his nature." At this point, Monroe would have known William for about a month, yet he was already wary of trusting the errant apostle based on what he had heard and observed of his uneven temperament. Emma apparently disagreed. She freely acknowledged her brother-in-law's volatile history and temperament but pointed out that changing one's "course of conduct . . . had been done" and that, if a man wanted to do so, "he should be encouraged." She was still mourning the deaths of Joseph and Hyrum a year earlier and had quick sympathy for William, who was dealing with Caroline's death—though expected—only seven days earlier. Smith's challenges were more complex than Emma realized, and as the summer wore on, Emma, Church leaders, and the members would be exposed to William's inability to regain his emotional stability. Monroe remained cautious. Two days before his conversation with Emma, he had heard "something from William Smith which makes me think he intends to take a stand somewhat in opposition to the Twelve. . . . I shall stand aloof and find out, if I can [determine] which of them is right and if neither of them is right I shall do the best I can." He was obviously at a crossroads of his faith.

Emma's defense of William may have been motivated by their shared ideology. When Monroe asked for her views of William's current religious philosophy, which certainly included upholding the Smith family, Emma responded that "he seemed to talk well on the subject" and "seemed to have correct principles."[4] Although she stopped short of expressing unqualified support, she would certainly have found William's position preferable to Brigham Young's. She had only reluctantly and briefly supported plural marriage and, in the months following Joseph's death, saw Brigham Young as strongly supporting and encouraging the temple, plural marriage, and adoption sealings as among the most important of Joseph's works. Before the Saints left Nauvoo, he authorized a growing number of new plural marriages and had positioned the endowment as so crucial a part of the gospel, that in the ten-week period that ended only on the eve of the evacuation of Nauvoo, some 5,600 Saints were endowed in the barely finished temple.[5]

For her part, Emma identified more closely with men like William Marks, Nauvoo's stake president, who strenuously opposed polygamy. He doubtless brought her great comfort by sharing with her a conversation he had with Joseph "about three weeks" before his assassination. According to Marks, the Prophet confessed that he had "'been deceived'" in generating the practice of plural marriage and that it must be stopped or "'it will prove our destruction and overthrow.'" He authorized Marks to try those practicing polygamy in the Nauvoo

---

4. James M. Monroe, Journal, May 29, 1845, MS 7061, LDS Church History Library.
5. George D. Smith, "Nauvoo Roots of Mormon Polygamy, 1841–46: A Preliminary Demographic Report," *Dialogue: A Journal of Mormon Thought* 34, nos. 1–2 (Spring/Summer 2001): 150–56; James B. Allen and Glen M. Leonard, *The Story of the Latter-day Saints* (Salt Lake City: Deseret Book, 1976), 169–70.

High Council and "'cut them off, if they will not repent and cease the practice.'" For his part, Joseph would "'go into the stand, and preach against it with all my might.'"⁶

Nothing came of this proposal since it coincided with the publication of the *Expositor* and the eruption of violence that Joseph Smith could not control. Still, assuming the accuracy of this report, Emma would have felt even more resistant to Brigham Young and other leaders who promoted plural marriage. Perhaps she was unaware that William Smith was one of those who supported the practice. But in August, he took a step that put his support on the public record—to Brigham Young's consternation (see Chapter 13)—and Emma distanced herself from her brother-in-law ever afterward.

Emma Hale Smith and David Hyrum Smith, ca. 1845, by an unknown photographer. Courtesy Community of Christ Archives.

In the intervening weeks, however, the two found common ground in their expectations about property held in Joseph Smith's name. Emma had already clashed with the Twelve over Joseph Smith's estate, and it would continue to be a hotly contested point between her and Church leaders. William was also interested in obtaining property held in his brother's name. Within twenty-four hours of returning to Nauvoo, William had advertised that he was ready to sell property, and it may have been that he and Emma desired to jointly sell properties held in Joseph's name. Monroe recorded that William "intends to go on publishing books to which they [the Twelve] claim the right, and spoke as if he thought they intended to apply the money from tithing to such purpose in order to reap the benefit of it."⁷ Either way, Smith felt entitled to at least a portion of the profits derived from the sale of Church publications because of his family connection. Within days after leaving Nauvoo in October, he expressed his resentment: "Brigham Young, John Taylor, and Willard Richards with the appointed Bishops have assumed the publishing of the Church Documents, the Book of Covenants, and also Joseph's private history, as their own property entirely regardless of the rights of the Smith family."⁸ Other members of the Smith family, including Emma, had similar proprietary feelings, and it was an issue that Church leaders and the Smiths never fully resolved.

---

6. Marks put his recollection of this conversation into print eight years later. William Marks, "Epistle," *Zion's Harbinger and Baneemy's Organ* 7, no. 3 (July 1853): 53, quoted in Mark A. Scherer, *The Journey of a People: The Era of Restoration, 1820 to 1844* (Independence, Mo.: Community of Christ Seminary Press, 2013), 408.

7. Monroe, Journal, May 27, 1845.

8. William Smith, "A Proclamation," *Warsaw Signal* 2, no. 32 (October 29, 1845): 1.

Leaders were dumbfounded when William complained in a public sermon on June 15 "that he and his connection[s] had been neglected." Heber C. Kimball irritably recorded in his diary that the Smiths "had all they wanted, when they asked for it."[9] Kimball's daughter, Helen, recalled that, no matter what the Twelve did to gratify William, he "was always dissatisfied."[10] She may have observed that behavior personally or heard her father's complaint, as he recorded on May 30, 1845: "Wm Smith not sattisfid other wise the Twelve are one."[11] This greed and sense of entitlement would mar William's relations with his colleagues until his excommunication in October.

But this public whining was overshadowed by a more spectacular flare-up during June that involved the Curtis Hodges family. Two of Curtis's sons, William and Stephen, were convicted of murder in Iowa that same summer. While members of the Hodges family had joined the Church at an early date, by 1843 Curtis had been excommunicated, and some of his sons were involved in a loosely organized gang of thieves. As historian Bill Shepard recounts, William and Stephen murdered a Mennonite minister and the minister's son-in-law in Lee County, Iowa Territory, during a botched robbery. They were convicted and sentenced to execution by hanging. During their trial, a third brother, Amos, was jailed in Nauvoo, charged with a robbery in that city. A fourth brother, Ervine, threatened to kill Brigham Young if he did not secure the release of his brothers. Ervine also threatened Nauvoo policeman Elbridge Tufts for testifying against his brothers at their trial. That same night, Ervine was attacked and stabbed numerous times with a bowie knife near Brigham Young's home. His wounds were not immediately fatal, and puzzlingly, although he was conscious for a short time before he died, he refused to name his assailant.[12]

William Smith's relationship with the Hodges family went back some thirteen years, as he and Hyrum had fellowshipped and proselyted members of the family during a mission to Erie County, Pennsylvania, in 1832.[13] William was

---

9. Heber C. Kimball, Journal, June 21, 1845, in Stanley B. Kimball, ed., *On the Potter's Wheel: The Diaries of Heber C. Kimball* (Salt Lake City: Signature Books and Smith Research Associates, 1987), 123. See also Kyle R. Walker, "Looking After the First Family of Mormonism: LDS Church Leaders' Support of the Smiths after the Murders of Joseph and Hyrum," *John Whitmer Historical Association Journal* 32, no. 1 (Spring/Summer 2012): 17–32.

10. Jeni Broberg Holzapfel and Richard Neitzel Holzapfel, eds., *A Woman's View: Helen Mar Whitney's Reminiscences of Early Church History* (Provo, Utah: BYU Religious Studies Center, 1997), 261.

11. Heber C. Kimball, Journal, May 30, 1845, in Stanley Kimball, *On the Potter's Wheel*, 118.

12. Bill Shepard, "The Notorious Hodges Brothers: Solving the Mystery of Their Destruction at Nauvoo," *John Whitmer Historical Association Journal* 26 (2006): 260–86.

13. According to Hyrum's diary, he and William "traveled to Elk Creek to Brother Curtis Hodges." The following day, they "held a meeting in at Brothers Hodges in the Evening." Hyrum Smith, Diary, December 10, 1832, Box 1, fd. 5, L. Tom Perry Special Collections, Lee Library, Brigham Young University, Provo, Utah. Parents Curtis and Lucy Hodges had been baptized in Kirtland on November 6, 1832, just a few weeks before Hyrum and William began their mission to Erie County. Shepard, "The Notorious Hodges Brothers," 281–82.

initially upset that Nauvoo was plagued by proximity to a "gang of thieves and murder[er]s [who] had their headquarters in this place and they must be rooted out";[14] but when he learned their identity, he came to their defense, warned William and Stephen before their capture to flee, and provided bail for Amos. William suspected that Ervine had been murdered by the Nauvoo police.[15] "Wm. Smith has given bail for another brother of the Hodges who was in custody for robbing," recorded William Clayton, and "is railing against the movements of the Twelve and says he has authority here to do as he has a mind to and the people shall know it. It appears he is determined to cause us trouble."[16] The rest of the Twelve firmly insisted that the Hodges brothers must answer to the law for their actions.

Tufts was outraged when he learned that William had not only put up Amos's bail but was urging him to flee the city. Worse, Smith brazenly ordered Tufts to let him go free. According to William's account, Tufts retorted that "he did not care a damn for what I said and further insulted me [by saying] that he had his council from others and should follow it." William's temper flared, and he burst out that he "would not bear it"—especially because Tufts downplayed William's ecclesiastical authority, an issue that lay at the core of William's insecurities. Grabbing Tufts by the shirt collar, he began to punch him repeatedly, easily fending off Tufts's attempts to defend himself with his cane. According to Clayton, Smith beat Tufts "shamefully" for what authorities felt was a "matter of small consequence."[17] To William, however, it meant everything. Tufts had insulted his personal honor and denigrated his ecclesiastical authority.

The consequence, after William's temper had cooled, was fear for his personal safety. Although the state legislature had repealed the Nauvoo city charter early that January, the municipal police, under the direction of the Twelve, kept order in the city and guarded Church authorities. By attacking Tufts, Smith had lost that protection. While he had previously felt uneasy about his safety where other Illinois citizens were concerned, now he felt unsafe in the city itself. On June 25, Smith appealed to Brigham Young: "Tuft[s] is surrounded by groups of men threatening me & I am not safe." He accused the police of spreading rumors that it was "no more harm to rais[e] a cane over an apostles head & beat him for a crime" than it was to physically subdue other malefactors. "Something must be done" for his protection, William demanded. "I will not risk my life in the hands of such men, they must either give me satisfaction or quit the police." Young should "regulate this matter," so it would be "clipped in the bud. I will not be watched and guarded by such men, and something is necessary, an action on the

---

14. Monroe, Journal, May 13, 1845.

15. Shepard, "The Notorious Hodges Brothers," 269.

16. George D. Smith, ed., *An Intimate Chronicle: The Journals of William Clayton* (Salt Lake City: Signature Books, 1991), 169.

17. Ibid., 169; William Smith (Nauvoo, Ill.), Letter to Pres. B[righam] Young, June 25, 1845, in Dean C. Jessee, ed., *John Taylor Nauvoo Journal* (Provo, Utah: Grandin Book, 1996), 69–70.

Masonic Hall, Nauvoo, Illinois. Photograph taken ca. 1930, by Curt Teich & Co., Chicago, Illinois.

subject immediately for my protection [or] I will . . . die."[18] John Taylor, noting the fracas in his journal on June 25, summarized, "Our mind was the Policeman was doing his duty, and Bro. Wm. Smith was in the wrong; and his life was not in jeopardy."[19]

Still, Brigham was willing to try and calm William's fears, even though he doubtless perceived the problem as less danger to William than injury to his oversensitive feelings. On June 25, the same day William wrote Young, the apostles called a meeting in the Masonic Hall with William and police officers. What began as negotiation between Smith and the Nauvoo police quickly blazed up into a contest of power between William and Brigham during the three-hour meeting.[20] For Smith, the key issue was less about his relationship to the police than about his status among the Church authorities. There are at least six different sources for this meeting: William's own account, published in late October after his excommunication, John Taylor's detailed Nauvoo diary entry written the same date, and brief summaries in the diaries of George A. Smith, Willard Richards, Heber C. Kimball, and Hosea Stout, chief of Nauvoo's police.

According to William's version, the meeting was an exercise in attempting to intimidate him. As he entered the third-story meeting room, he found "some fifty or sixty police-men all armed with their Bowie-knives, pistols, and hickory clubs." The "door [was] guarded, and the man whom I had supposed a particu-

---

18. William Smith to Brigham Young, June 25, 1845.

19. Jessee, *John Taylor Nauvoo Journal*, 70.

20. Willard Richards recorded that the meeting started at 6:00 P.M., and Hosea Stout reported that the same meeting was "dismissed about dark." Willard Richards, Diary, June 25, 1845; Juanita Brooks, ed., *On the Mormon Frontier: The Diary of Hosea Stout, Volume 1, 1844–1848*, 1:49.

lar friend of mine"—possibly Tufts—"was chuckling with sparkling eyes to think he had me in his power." The accounts by Stout, Taylor, George A. Smith, Richards, and Kimball record no threatening elements. In fact, even William's account appears somewhat contradictory, as he describes Young greeting him with a friendly handshake and a "smiling countenance." Still, his version of the story stresses the element of threat and danger: "Various circumstances induced me to believe myself hedged in, and I looked at the door and at the window, but with a very faint hope of escape; it was death to jump from the window, and the armed police prevented escape from the door." He continued, "It was now quite dark, and wagons and carriages were all in readiness, so that with the greatest of ease I could have been sent on a long mission to preach the Gospel."[21]

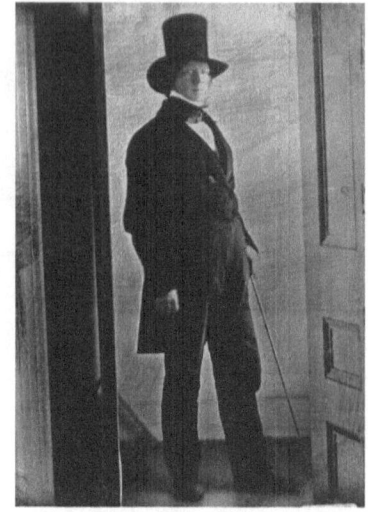

Brigham Young, 1801–1877. Daguerreotype by unknown photographer, ca. 1845. Courtesy LDS Church History Library.

According to William, Brigham Young first asked him to explain his "grievances." William responded defiantly, "I answered the call . . . and in fervent tones both long and loud, spoke of my grievances. . . . I told them I considered my right to teach the church altogether unimpeachable; as was also my right to counsel the police, and to assist in controlling the public sentiment." George A. Smith described William's remarks as "a very long and pathetic speech against Bro. Tufts and [his] family."[22] William then stressed his main point: "If the brethren did not want me or my councils . . . I would leave them. Let . . . the Twelve say so—Let the Bishops say so—Let the police say so, and I am gone." In his final declaration, he invoked what he considered to be his most telling threat: "But mark it, . . . where I go, there also the Smith family [will] go, and with them also goes the Priesthood."[23]

Those present listened with apparent patience to William's hour-long diatribe, but this final statement exposed William's sense of superiority because of his lineal connection. Brigham Young spoke next, rebuking William roundly for telling the police to let the Hodges escape. The officers, he insisted, were "fulfilling the law, having men in their custody, who I believe to be murderers, and who had threatened my life." Young then focused on Smith's threat to leave the Church, taking the priesthood with him: "When the Twelve act as counsel,

---

21. William Smith, "Proclamation," 1.
22. George A. Smith, "Memoirs of George A. Smith," June 25, 1845, in George A. Smith Papers, 1834–1875, MS 1322, Box 1, fd. 1, LDS Church History Library, 306.
23. William Smith, "Proclamation," 1.

they act unitedly, and not separately," announced Young firmly, "and I am their mouthpiece." Next, Young challenged William's sense of privilege and entitlement, the first time he had done so directly since William's return. Significantly, he addressed the whole group, not William personally. It was a rhetorical strategy that sidestepped the appearance of a debate between the two men and instead positioned Brigham as a leader addressing a congregation about a problem which happened to be William's beliefs:

> We could live in peace here before William Smith came; and since he came there has been the devil to pay; he has been throwing out hints all the time, that the presidency belonged to him, producing discord. I have reason to believe, and before we get through with this matter, think I can prove, that he told General Deming that I was the instigator of that murder (of Ervine Hodges). I will not stand such things, nor will I be nosed about by Wm. Smith; but while he remains one of the counsel like my-self and the rest of the brethren, he shall be subject to that counsel; and I will have an investigation into these matters; and I will not sustain William Smith in any principle of unrighteousness; neither shall any of these Police be put out of their office on his account for they are good men, and have done their duty.[24]

As for William's claim that the priesthood was his personal possession, due to his family connection, Young spelled out the doctrine of priesthood transmittal explicitly. William reported him as saying: "We received the priesthood from God through Joseph Smith and not through William, and . . . he had no authority or power to curse the Twelve Apostles who received the priesthood from Joseph." Young also declared, "I will let William Smith know that he has no right to counsel this church. . . . [And] furthermore, that where the Smith family goes the Church will not go, nor the priesthood either!"[25]

John Taylor recorded that Smith "seemed to be humbled under the influence of what Brother Brigham had said; he having spoken with great power." William then retracted most of what he had said, responding that "he did not mean that he would take the priesthood away with him; but that he would take his family away; and that he had not said, that he had a right to the presidency;—but that he always said that Brother Brigham was the head of the church; and that he did not wish any of the Police to be dismissed, he only wished to know if he would be safe."[26] Tufts was present, but it seems unlikely that he and the other Nauvoo policemen present felt that William's revised statement was an adequate apology for beating Tufts and demanding his dismissal. Notwithstanding, as the meeting dragged on for another hour, and after some additional remarks from Young, the council "agreed to compare his [William's] statement with Bro. Tufts and

---

24. Taylor, Journal, June 25, 1845, in Jessee, *John Taylor Nauvoo Journal*, 72; terminal punctuation added.
25. William Smith, "Proclamation," 1.
26. Taylor, Journal, June 25, 1845, in Jessee, *John Taylor Nauvoo Journal*, 73.

be satisfied, For we could then settle the whole matter in a few minutes."[27] This strategy apparently worked, and Young "called upon the Police to know if they would stand by Brother William, and support him. They all answered 'yes.' He then called upon Brother William to know if he would support the Police. He answered 'yes.'"[28]

The meeting thus ended with this fragile treaty of peace and mutual esteem covering the serious rifts of hostility and suspicion. Brigham Young probably felt that another major crisis had been averted, but it seems unlikely that he interpreted the solution as permanent. Whatever William's immediate feelings, as he mulled over the details of the meeting, he felt his good will slipping away. Once again, he decided that he had been insulted and humiliated. He fumed to his mother and his sisters, telling a version that probably closely followed his "Proclamation" account, stressing the conspiracy to diminish his authority and compel him to submit to the Twelve. The Smith family had long seen their world—not without good reason—as one in which they were persecuted for righteousness's sake, and they rallied to provide emotional support that must have soothed William's abraded ego and smoothed over the fact that he had definitely been relegated to the place that Brigham and the Twelve designed for him. The one statement Smith had not retracted had to do with taking his family and fleeing the city, and from that time forward, he began to consider leaving Nauvoo and branching out on his own.[29]

William had become skillful at playing the role of victim, and he convinced his family that he was in danger from Church authorities and their supporters. Sisters Katharine and Lucy, both tall women, were afraid to go out of the house alone lest they be mistaken for William.[30] William's paranoia influenced his remaining family members and certainly intensified their mistrust of Young and other leaders despite the care and support being lavished upon them.

Another definite effect of William's narrative of victimhood was to arouse the fears of his mother, then age seventy, that the life of her only surviving son was in danger. In a late recollection, William's niece, Mary Bailey Smith Norman, remembered that she spent the evening with Grandmother Lucy at the Marks home, recalling when William left and returned after this lengthy meeting. "Uncle William brought his two little motherless girls, Mary Jane and Caroline to his mother to take care of them." William dressed for the meeting in "a large circular cloak . . . and a broad brim[m]ed slouch hat, drawn well down over his face, so as to conceal as much as possible his features as he suspected that

---

27. George A. Smith, "Memoirs of George A. Smith," June 25, 1845, 306, in George A. Smith Papers, 1834–1875, MS 1322, Box 1, fd. 1, Special Collections, Marriott Library, University of Utah.

28. Taylor, Journal, June 25, 1845, in Jessee, *John Taylor Nauvoo Journal*, 73.

29. William Smith, "Proclamation," 1.

30. Mary B. (Smith) Norman (Idaho Falls, Idaho), Letter to Ina (Smith) Coolbrith, April 24, 1908, P13, f 955, Community of Christ Library-Archives.

he might be assassinated before he reached the hall." According to her account, William did not return until "sometime after midnight," and, the next day, "told grandmother [Lucy] about his experience the night before," freely expressing apprehensions about his safety and a belief that if he left the city "they [presumably the police] would follow him and murder him."³¹ Lucy took this highly colored account seriously. Her anxiety took the form of a significant dream sequence that very night of June 26–27 and she reported the details on June 27—coincidentally the anniversary of Joseph and Hyrum's murders—to a small group that included William, her three daughters and their husbands, Leonora Taylor (John Taylor's wife), and William's cousin Elias Smith. She "saw William in a room full of armed men and he having no weapons. They would have crushed him down, if it had not been for the power of God." The dream closely paralleled William's version of the meeting.

William had also shared with his mother his view that his voice was being diminished in the governing councils of the Church, an element that also figured in another sequence of Lucy's dream. An unidentified divine "messenger" assured Lucy that her family "were the first founders, fathers, and heads of this Church, raised up in these last days." He continued:

> Thy son William he shall have power over the Churches, he is father in Israel over the patriarchs and the whole of the Church, he is the last of the lineage that is raised up in these last days. He is patriarch to regulate the affairs of the Church. He is President over all the Church, they cannot take his apostleship away from him. The Presidency of the Church belongs to William, he being the last of the heads of the Church, according to the lineage, he having inherited it from the family from before the foundation of the world.³²

If William had personally dictated the contents of her dream—especially the triple repetition that the presidency of the Church was his by lineal right—it could not have reflected his views more precisely.

The contents of this dream, which Lucy and the family considered revelatory, came under immediate scrutiny and had promptly been written down, possibly at William's instigation. John Taylor recorded that, when he came home that evening, Leonora "showed me a copy of a vision that Mother Lucy Smith had, stating that her son William was head over the Church."³³ Surviving accounts suggest that it was William who ensured that his mother's vision was recorded. Since, according to William Clayton's diary entry on June 30, Lucy had her own copy of the revelation, it seems that at least two and perhaps more copies had been made. According to Clayton, Mother Smith's "new revelation" had at some

---

31. Mary B. (Smith) Norman (Idaho Falls, Idaho), Letters to Ina (Smith) Coolbrith, March 27, 1908, and April 24, 1908.

32. Taylor, Journal, June 27, 1845, in Jessee, *John Taylor Nauvoo Journal*, 73–75. Taylor recorded a list of sixteen people who "were present at the time this vision was related" by Lucy. He was not among them, but apparently heard the account immediately from his wife.

33. Taylor, Journal, June 27, 1845, in Jessee, *John Taylor Nauvoo Journal*, 73.

point been "corrected and altered by William Smith so as to suit his wishes by representing him as the legal successor of Joseph in the presidency."³⁴ Brigham Young sent George A. Smith and his father, John, to visit Lucy two days later, on June 29. At that point, expressing apprehensions of her own, Lucy told George A. that she did not want her vision read publicly because it "was not written down correctly and that it was only for her own children and not for the Priesthood or church."³⁵ This retreat was apparently welcome news, and, on June 30, seven members of the Twelve, including Brigham, visited Lucy and read aloud what George A. Smith termed a "revised copy of her vision." In response, Lucy herself reiterated that "she thought that we had not a correct copy of her vision," an implication that William may indeed have doctored the wording. Despite Lucy's comment, John Taylor stated in his diary that "we know that it is . . . a correct copy."³⁶ But in making this statement, Taylor was certainly relying on his wife's copy of the vision, which may have also been reworked by William, even though Leonora had been present when Lucy related her vision. Perhaps Taylor was indicating that the essence of the dream had been correctly recorded.

Brigham Young immediately sent John and George A. to invite him to the meeting with Mother Smith on June 30, but William flatly refused. According to George A., "He spoke very hard against Bro. Brigham and said he had the right, by birth to lead the church and that all he wanted was his rights and he would have them at all events." George added that William exhibited a bitter spirit and threatened that "he had friends" who would apparently support him in his views. "My father also failed to change his [William's] mind," George recorded.³⁷

The situation teetered on the edge of another explosion. On June 30 a majority of the Twelve and other leaders called on Lucy and her family. Young had apparently reached the limit of his patience with William's claims and forthrightly told Mother Smith that William "was aiming at power, and authority, and priesthood that did not belong to him" and that Church leaders "would not allow him to tread upon his [Young's] neck or any other man's." He further clarified his perception of Smith's calling as patriarch, which followed the general outline of John Taylor's editorial in the *Times and Seasons* less than two weeks earlier. If William desired to be president of the entire Church, Young continued, the Church "should have their choice," but, he scoffed, neither "the Church . . . [nor] would the Twelve consent to it; for if it had been put to them, I do not suppose twenty would have voted for him out the many thousands there are in the Church."³⁸

Lucy responded by rephrasing and retracting. She thought that "William did not want it [the presidency]," and explained that "she did not profess to be a revelator only for herself and family, [and] that she wanted peace, union, and

---

34. George D. Smith, *An Intimate Chronicle*, 169–70.
35. George A. Smith, "History of George A. Smith," 84–85.
36. John Taylor, Journal, June 30, 1845, Jessee, *John Taylor Nauvoo Journal*, 77.
37. George A. Smith, "Memoirs of George A. Smith," June 28, 1845, 308.
38. Taylor, Journal, June 30, 1845, in Jessee, *John Taylor Nauvoo Journal*, 77.

harmony" with the authorities.[39] If William had indeed doctored her letter, Lucy seemed as confused as everyone else about William's eccentric behavior, but she insisted on her motherly support. John Taylor recorded in his journal that "we prayed with Mother Smith before we left her; and she and the family manifested good feelings. I am sorry the old lady should be troubled, she is a good woman and has past [sic] through much trouble for the cause of truth, and has the respect and confidence of the whole Church."[40] Lucy's daughters and sons-in-law only played a minimal role in the discussion but presumably were also relieved that this crisis ended amicably.

But William, who had stubbornly stayed away, remained a question mark. William responded, not by appraising his own behavior as a contribution to the conflict, but as a conspiracy against him and his family. He refused to attend meetings of the Twelve for the next week or so. His distance and obstinacy were disconcerting to Church leaders who warily awaited his next move.

Thus, surprisingly, the month of July turned out in retrospect to be a period of peace, after the turmoil and grief of May and the explosive confrontation among William, the Twelve, and the Nauvoo police in June. William seemed to pull himself together, step back from the ongoing conflict with his associates, and immerse himself in his work as patriarch. In July, William concentrated on his patriarchal calling, apparently finding peace and joy as he opened himself to the Spirit.

Shortly after his ordination confirming his inherited appointment, he placed an advertisement in the *Nauvoo Neighbor*, publicizing his appointment as presiding patriarch, and announcing, "I am now ready to receive the calls of the Saints, and confer upon them their patriarchal blessings as they may desire."[41] Christine Elyse Blythe summarized that "in 1840, the going rate for a patriarchal blessing was one dollar. If this payment remained the same, according to those blessings documented from June 1845 to October 1845 . . . William would have made around three hundred dollars in a six-month period." By comparison, Blythe continues, "In 1840 a laborer received $12 a week in Illinois, but this wage included room and board and much more strenuous labor—especially when considering William would have given most blessings either in his own home or that of the receipient, meaning his overhead or travel expenses were virtually nonexistent."[42] But it probably was not as lucrative as Blythe described. Smith would later complain that many Saints did not have cash on hand to pay him, and to his credit, Smith bestowed the blessings anyway.[43] After reading Smith's advertisement, Thomas Sharp, editor of the anti-Mormon *Warsaw Signal* with

---

39. Ibid.
40. Jessee, *John Taylor Nauvoo Journal*, 79.
41. William Smith, "Notice," *Nauvoo Neighbor* 3, no. 6 (June 11, 1845): 3.
42. Christine Elyse Blythe, "William Smith's Patriarchal Blessings and Contested Authority in the Post-Martyrdom Church," *Journal of Mormon History* 39, no. 3 (Summer 2013): 76–77.
43. William Smith (City of Joseph [Nauvoo], Ill.), Letter to Jesse C. Little, August 20, 1845.

whom William had jousted in *The Wasp*, chided Smith for receiving remuneration for his blessings. Sharp particularly questioned Smith's motives given the narrative of persecution that formed the preface to William's announcement: "After having been for so long a time buffeted upon the waves of affliction; after having sacrificed all of this world's goods, by mobs at different times, and after having suffered so much sorrow and afflictions from the loss of friends and relatives . . . . I hope my brethren and sisters will remember their old and tried friend, (William Smith.)." Sharp noted Smith's business acumen, writing that "Bill Smith has been appointed Patriarch, and he shows himself in the start, a business man; for he advertises in the Neighbor, that he is ready to confer Patriarchal Blessings and in the usual style prays for the patronage of the saints." Sharp reprinted Smith's advertisement in his paper, and added the parody: "Common blessings 50 cents—Extraordinary blessings $1.00—Children half price—Women gratis."[44]

William's achievement as presiding patriarch was prodigious. In a three-month period, from June to early September, he pronounced more than three hundred blessings on behalf of the Saints. According to the existing records, of the approximately three hundred blessings he pronounced on individual Saints, 144—almost 50 percent—were given in July.[45]

In his numerous blessings, Smith included the lineage of the recipient, a practice established by Joseph Jr. and carried on by Joseph Sr. and Hyrum, which linked modern-day Saints with the biblical house of Israel. In bestowing these blessings, he frequently prophesied, a gift that he had occasionally exercised in Ohio and Missouri, but for which no documentation exists during his presiding over the eastern branches.[46] Smith included much of what he described as the "unfolding" or "future destiny" of the recipient throughout his blessings. One of his more notable blessings was upon Abigail Abbott, in which he prophesied that some member of her posterity would "be led on to avenge the blood of the Prophets and Patriarchs," and "lead a mighty people from the wilderness" in conjunction with a man named "Nishcosh." As evinced in this blessing, Smith effortlessly blended biblical and Book of Mormon references, declaring that Abigail's descendant would be "named after the name of his father . . . who was

---

44. Thomas Sharp, "Mormon Gull-Traps," *Warsaw Signal* 2, no. 16 (June 18, 1845): 1.
45. Marquardt, *Early Patriarchal Blessings*, 279–372.
46. Smith uttered several notable prophecies during the 1830s. (See Chapter 7.) In 1835, at a Church conference, he had an open vision of the Twelve's future mission to England. Dean C. Jessee, Mark Ashurst-McGee, and Richard L. Jensen, eds., *Journals, Volume 1: 1832–1839*, Vol. 1 of the Journals series of THE JOSEPH SMITH PAPERS, general editors Dean C. Jessee, Ronald K. Esplin, and Richard Lyman Bushman (Salt Lake City: Church Historian's Press, 2008), 181–82. He also described the Missourians' siege of Far West in remarkable detail some three months before it occurred. Lucy Mack Smith, *Biographical Sketches of Joseph Smith and His Progenitors for Many Generations* (Liverpool: S. W. Richards, 1853), 219–25.

a descendant from the tribe of Judah," while Nishcosh "shall be a descendant of Nimrod," a mighty hunter among the Jaredites.[47]

In Chester Potter's blessing, bestowed on the one-year anniversary of the deaths of Joseph and Hyrum Smith, William declared that Potter would, "even in heaven . . . be called to administer as a ministering spirit to those who are the heirs of Salvation."[48] This pronouncement linked Potter's future mission with the three disciples of Jesus mentioned in the Book of Mormon, and John the Beloved in the New Testament, who were never to taste of death, but to remain on the earth to "minister for those who shall be heirs of salvation who dwell on the earth." The twenty-three-year-old Potter must have been elated to be linked to these revered apostles.[49] Although these pronouncements about the future may seem extraordinary to modern readers, they were fully consistent with the spirit of William's father, Joseph Sr., who did not restrain his desire to pour out an abundance of promises.[50]

However, William Smith was unique among his predecessors, as well as in the tradition established among his successors, in providing proxy patriarchal blessings for at least two women.[51] At this point, the Saints were familiar with and enthusiastic about the ritual of baptism performed by proxy for deceased relatives, and, to a more limited extent, the sealing of a deceased spouse to the surviving spouse.[52] It was natural for some Saints to seek a patriarchal blessing for a deceased loved one, and Smith initially complied with their request. Some weeks after bestowing two proxy blessings, he wrote to Brigham Young. Although his letter to Young has not survived, Young's response on August 10 makes it clear that William asked whether the practice was advisable—an unusual step for

---

47. References are to 2 Nephi 3:15, Ether 2:1–4, and Genesis 10:8–9. Marquardt, *Early Patriarchal Blessings*, 244–45.

48. Marquardt, *Early Patriarchal Blessings*, 254. See also D&C 132:16–17, 2013 LDS edition.

49. Ibid., 254. See LDS D&C 7:6, and 3 Nephi 28, 2013 LDS edition.

50. See, for example, Joseph Sr.'s blessing bestowed upon Lorenzo Snow on December 15, 1836, wherein he prophesied that Snow should "have power to translate thyself from one plannet to annother—power to go to the moon if thou shalt desire it. Power to preach to the spirits in prison—power like Enoch to translate thyself to heaven,—thou shalt have power to rend the vail of heaven and see Jesus standing on the right hand of his Father." Marquardt, *Early Patriarchal Blessings*, 94–95.

51. William Smith, blessing bestowed on Delilah Maxwell in behalf of Mary Maxwell, June 30, 1845, and blessing bestowed on Mary Ann Peterson in behalf of Ann B. Peterson, July 16, 1845, both in Marquardt, *Early Patriarchal Blessings*, 259, 328.

52. For example, Hyrum Smith's deceased first wife, Jerusha Barden, was sealed to him on May 29, 1843, with his second wife, Mary Fielding, acting as Jerusha's proxy. Another example was Newel Knight, who was sealed to his deceased first wife, Sally Coburn, on January 19, 1846, with his second wife, Lydia Goldthwaite, acting as Sally's proxy. Lyndon W. Cook, *Nauvoo Marriages and Proxy Sealings 1843–1846* (Provo, Utah: Grandin Book, 2004), 3, 90.

William, who was fully inclined to make his own decisions without seeking permission or confirmation. In his response, Brigham Young informed William that it was contrary "to the order of the church to confer Patriarchal Blessings on the dead by proxy, until baptism &c has been attended to for them by proxy, which must be done in the Lord's House, therefore, any thing of the kind done at this time would be of no effect."[53] While Young's response left open the possibility of proxy blessings, he seemingly discouraged the practice, and there is no record of other proxy blessings after this date.

At times Smith appears to have used his blessings to shore up his own ecclesiastical authority in the minds of the Saints. In a blessing given to Nathan Packer on June 19, Smith stated, "This blessing is confer[r]ed upon thy head by one who holds the authority of the Patriarchal office at this time over the whole church of God."[54] The blessing was bestowed just a week before Taylor's editorial "Patriarchal" appeared in the *Times and Seasons* emphasizing that William was not patriarch "*over* the whole church; but patriarch *to* the church"; obviously the debate over the scope of his authority preceded the editorial's publication.[55] "Still, the expression '*over*' the Church appears five times in the blessings William gave in June," according to Blythe, "and the phrase 'prophet and patriarch' appears six times, showing that William took seriously the claim that the offices of prophet and patriarch were connected—even one and the same."[56] The emphasized phrase became a contested point with John Taylor and other Church leaders, and claiming jurisdiction in the course of pronouncing his blessings may have been William's subtle way of retaliating against what he felt were limitations being imposed on him by other General Authorities. In another blessing, William indicated that the blessing was bestowed "by the highest authority in the Church of God on the earth."[57] At times his pronouncements may have confused the Saints about the extent of his authority, as Smith conferred one particular blessing "by the sealing authority."[58]

---

53. Brigham Young, Letter to Brother Wm Smith Patriarch, August 10, 1845, Brigham Young Office Files 1832–1878, Letters from Church Leaders and Others, 1840–1877, William Smith, 1844–1857, LDS Church History Library.

54. Marquardt, *Early Patriarchal Blessings*, 233.

55. William was upset after reading Taylor's editorial published in the June 1, 1845, issue of the *Times and Seasons*. Despite the date, this issue was apparently not published and distributed until at least June 26. William read Taylor's editorial on June 26, 1845. William Smith (Nauvoo, Ill.), Letter to Brigham Young and the Council of the Twelve, June 30, 1845, reproduced in George D. Smith, *An Intimate Chronicle*, 170.

56. Blythe, "William Smith's Patriarchal Blessings," 76.

57. Blessing bestowed on William A. Beebe, by William Smith, June 21, 1845, in Marquardt, *Early Patriarchal Blessings*, 239–40; also in D. Michael Quinn, *The Mormon Hierarchy: Origins of Power* (Salt Lake City: Signature Books, 199), 216.

58. Blessing bestowed on Anna Landers, by William Smith, June 23, 1845, in Marquardt, *Early Patriarchal Blessings*, 241.

Although an analysis of the language of William's blessings provides glimpses of underlying turmoil and William's personal struggle to maintain a station equal to that of the other apostles, it seems likely that the majority of Saints who received one of his blessings felt strengthened by it. Even those who personally disliked William still viewed their patriarchal blessing as heaven-inspired. Such was the case with Benjamin Winchester, who had earlier denounced Smith in strong terms and had even sued him for slander during his tenure in the East. (See Chapter 9.) Yet even after William had excommunicated him, Winchester reflected positively on his blessing: "I have loved brother William Smith! . . . . I received a patriarchal blessing under his hands! and I believe it was given by the spirit of God! and I am determined to try and have it all fulfilled."[59] There were stretches during that summer when Smith was blessing as many as ten individuals per day. Those who acted as scribes in recording his blessings included English convert John O. Angus, Scottish convert and clerk Robert Campbell, James Monroe, and most frequently his brother-in-law Arthur Millikin.[60]

Most of these blessings were given at Nauvoo, but during the last week in July 1845, William traveled to the Union Branch in Pike County, Illinois. There on July 29 alone, William bestowed blessings on sixteen local members.[61] Evidently, William felt safe enough to leave the county at this point, although he remained intermittently obsessed about his safety during the rest of the summer and fall.

After a relatively peaceful July, the next stage in the conflict emerged in early August. William wrote to Brigham Young on August 9. The letter that has not survived, but Young referred to it in his reply the next day, quoting William several times. William was apparently unhappy that many of the Saints were too poor to pay for their patriarchal blessings and complained that his colleague-apostles were not encouraging Saints to receive their blessings from him. He apparently attributed this reluctance to "fear of offending the Twelve or Uncle John [Smith]." Joseph Smith Jr. had ordained John on January 10, 1844[62] as a local patriarch. At that point, Hyrum was the Church patriarch, the office that William held over the "whole church." Brigham wrote reassuringly, "If the people you bless do not pay you, you [can] depend on the trustees for support, [and] it is right they should bring you Trustee orders . . . so that [you] can get their pay of those who get their blessings." Thus, despite William's tendency to exploit the

---

59. Benjamin Winchester, quoted in "Meeting of the Mormons Last Evening," *Prophet* 1, no. 26 (November 16, 1844): 2.

60. William Smith Patriarchal Blessing Book; Monroe, Journal, May 28–29, 1845, 72.

61. For information on the Union Branch, see Joseph Wood (Perry, Pike County, Ill.), Letter to Bro's. Smith and Robinson, March 26, 1840, in *Times and Seasons* 1, no. 6 (April 1840): 7–8; Marquardt, *Early Patriarchal Blessings,* 354–71.

62. Joseph Smith, Journal, January 10, 1845, in Scott H. Faulring, ed., *An American Prophet's Record: The Diaries and Journals of Joseph Smith* (Salt Lake City: Signature Books, 1987), 439; Irene M. Bates, "Uncle John Smith, 1781–1854: Patriarchal Bridge," *Dialogue: A Journal of Mormon Thought* 20 (Fall 1987): 83.

Saints' generosity, Brigham and those closest to him were still willing to treat William with extraordinary consideration and meet his financial needs at a time when funding for completing the temple was at a crisis stage. Young expressed confusion at Smith's supposition that the apostles had been sending Saints to Uncle John Smith for their blessings: "We know not what it [your accusation] is made out of. The Twelve have never thrown a straw in your way, but done every thing they could for you and will continue to do so." In fact, "we are also unquestionably informed that Uncle John has not blessed any, or very few for some time, on account of his health and when they have called on him he has told them to go to Willia[m] and get their blessing."[63]

On August 12, William reported in the one letter he apparently wrote that summer to Caroline's brother Joshua, Jr. that he was kept continually busy by "the many calls of the brethren to receive their patriarchal blessings" but repeated his frustration that he did not always receive his pay.[64] A week later, Smith complained to Jesse Little that he was finding it difficult to support himself "in the exercise of my [patriarchal] office," because, as he recounted, "the people are so poor."[65] Church leaders, still anxious to keep this erratic apostle as a supporter, intervened with assurances.[66]

Although William's August 9 letter to Brigham Young focuses on William's perception of his patriarchal calling—which no one was challenging or denigrating—it reveals William's unpleasant sense of privilege which, not surprisingly, reignited his colleagues' mistrust. Rather than the attitude of humility and service that had been typical of Samuel and Hyrum, William flaunted his sense of entitlement. As early as December 1835, only ten months after being called as an apostle, William's fellow apostle Orson Hyde protested to Joseph that "Elder Wm Smith could go to the Store[house] and get whatever he pleased . . . until his account has amounted to seven Hundred Dollars." In contrast, "while we were abroad this last season, we strain[e]d every nerve to obtain a little something for our familys and regularly divided the monies equally . . . not knowing that William had such a fountain at home from whence he drew his support." Hyde petitioned Joseph to rectify the disparity. Acting in simple fairness, Joseph arranged for storehouse credit to be extended equitably to all members of the Quorum of the Twelve.[67]

---

63. Brigham Young (City of Joseph [Nauvoo], Ill.), Letter to Brother Wm Smith Patriarch, August 10, 1845, Brigham Young Office Files 1832–1878, General Correspondence, Outgoing, 1843–1876, 1845 June-August, LDS Church History Library.

64. William Smith (Nauvoo, Ill.), Letter to Joshua Grant Jr., August 12, 1845, in *Nauvoo Neighbor* 3, no. 16 (August 20, 1845): 3.

65. William Smith to Jesse C. Little, August 20, 1845.

66. Young to Brother Wm Smith Patriarch, August 10, 1845.

67. Hyde underscored the point he was making by telling what he called the parable of the twelve sons: "Pardon me if I speak in parables or parody. A certain good shepherd had twelve sons and he sent them out one day to go and gather his flock which were scattered upon the mountains and in the vallies afar off they were all obedient to their fathers

William, however, did not learn the obvious lesson that, among the Twelve, he was one of equals. He continued to regard high-level financial support as his prerogative. His appropriation of temple donations from the eastern Saints for his personal use had upset Wilford Woodruff and Parley P. Pratt, who viewed William as taking arrogant liberties with consecrated funds. Once Pratt assumed leadership in the East, he ensured that all funds donated for the temple were carefully recorded and that the donors were given receipts.[68] Other members of the Twelve also received financial assistance due to their full-time labors in the ministry, but none interpreted "the labourer is worthy of his hire" (Luke 10:7) to the extent that William did. He had become adept at living off the charity of the Saints. To solicit donations, Smith typically assured a sympathetic response by highlighting his family connection, history of persecution, and extensive Church service. His approach proved persuasive. John Hardy, the presiding elder of the Boston branch whom Smith had cut off and replaced, angrily recounted in his 1844 exposé how Smith and George J. Adams had utilized "old and oft repeated stories . . . when begging for money—viz. how much they had suffered and the persecution they had undergone, and how much they had suffered by false brethren!" According to Hardy, Smith's repeated use of such fund-raising tactics made many Saints uncomfortable.[69] This aspect of entitlement had escalated during William's eastern mission, now became increasingly apparent to Saints at Nauvoo that summer, and continued to manifest itself when he affiliated with other factions of Mormonism later in life.

At some point during the summer of 1845, Smith went to the extreme of demanding a regular portion of the Saints' tithing in addition to arguing that he should personally profit from the sale of Church publications. According to Orson Hyde, "William Smith . . . claimed that it was his right to have one-

---

mandate, and at Evening they returned with the flock, and one son received wool enough to make him warm and comfortable and also rec[eive]d of the flesh and milk of the flock, the other eleven received not so much as one kid to make merry with their friends." Orson Hyde, Letter to Joseph Smith, December 15, 1835, quoted in Jessee, Ashurst-McGee, and Jensen, *Journals, Volume 1*, 124–28, 128 note 216.

68. A month after Pratt arrived, William wrote in the *Prophet*: "All the Saints that gave money into my hand at Peterborough, Lowell, New Bedforb [sic] New York and other places for the Temple, shall have their names recorded in the Book of the Law of the Lord, as soon as I can get to Nauvoo in the Spring. . . . The Saints will understand that a book is now open at the Prophet office by Elder P. P. Pratt, so that all eastern churches under his presidency can forward their tithing and have their names recorded. This you will see Brethren is a new arrangement authorized by the authorities at Nauvoo." William Smith, "Notice," *Prophet* 1, no. 37 (February 1, 1845): 2. In July, Pratt wrote an editorial stating: "Elders that collect money from the saints, and promise to go to Nauvoo and work it out on the temple, cannot be ignorant of the fact, that they are doing wrong, and had better repent." [Parley P. Pratt], "Notice," *New-York Messenger* 2, no. 1 (July 5, 1845): 6.

69. John Hardy, *Startling Developments of Crim. Con.! Or Two Mormon Apostles Exposed, in Practising the Spiritual Wife System in Boston* (Boston: Conway and Company, 1844), 5.

twelfth part of the tithing set off to him, to be appropriated to his own individual use, or in any way that he thought proper. This was not allowed any one of the Twelve; and he was the only one that ever asked or expected such a thing."[70] Church leaders were already supporting William and his family. Brigham Young announced in conference the month after William's excommunication that "we furnished him a span of horses, and a carriage and a house, and Brother [Heber C.] Kimball became responsible for [paying] the rent of it."[71] Church leaders had earlier rented the Jonathan Browning home for Mother Smith and her daughter Lucy's family in September 1844, and had hired a young woman to wait on Lucy in ensuring that her needs were met.[72] After William's return from the East, he, his mother, sisters Katharine and Lucy, and their families all moved to the commodious William Marks home on Water Street, which the Church was renting for them.[73] This very material support, reinforced by the money William made from giving patriarchal blessings, meant that the Church was indeed supporting the entire Smith family with the exception of Sophronia, whose husband, a wagon maker, provided ample income for his family.[74]

When the Twelve denied William's demands for further temporal support, he became even pricklier about his status. Other members of the Twelve who had worked closely with him through the years knew all too well his difficulties with authority and his sense of entitlement. On at least six separate occasions, four prior to the death of his prophet-brother, his behavior was aberrant enough that his standing in the Church had been called into question by his associates. Each time he had managed to retain his standing, but typically because Joseph and Hyrum

---

70. [Orson Hyde], "Cause for Which William Smith Was Excluded from the Church!," *Frontier Guardian* 2, no. 1 (February 6, 1850): 2.

71. "Conference Minutes," *Times and Seasons* 6, no. 16 (November 1, 1845): 1014.

72. Editors of the RLDS edition of Lucy Mack Smith's history included this lengthy footnote: "At the time of the tragedy at Carthage, Grandmother Smith was living with Joseph, and continued living with Emma until in September following, when she removed with her son-in-law, Arthur Millikin, and her daughter Lucy, into a house known as the Ponson [Peter Poncin] house, hired for them by the church, which also hired a girl to wait upon her and help generally." Lucy Smith, *Biographical Sketches of Joseph Smith the Prophet and His Progenitors for Many Generations* (Lamoni, Iowa: Reorganized Church of Jesus Christ of Latter Day Saints, 1912), 95 note 1. Though Nauvoo residents later identified this home as the "Ponson House," trustees did not sell the home to Peter Poncin until 1847, several years after Lucy had lived in the home. At the time Lucy and members of her family lived in the home, it still belonged to Jonathan Browning. Dale L. Berge, "The Jonathan Browning Site: An Example of Archaeology for Restoration in Nauvoo, Illinois," *BYU Studies* 19 (Winter 1979): 209–10.

73. William Smith, "Notice," *Nauvoo Neighbor* 3, no. 6 (June 11, 1845): 3; Mary B. (Smith) Norman to Ina (Smith) Coolbrith, April 24, 1908.

74. "Biographical Sketch of John Lyman Smith," *Millennial Star* 56, no. 34 (August 20, 1894): 542; Kyle R. Walker, "Looking After the First Family of Mormonism: LDS Church Leaders' Support of the Smiths after the Murders of Joseph and Hyrum," *John Whitmer Historical Association Journal* 32, no. 1 (Spring/Summer 2012): 17–32.

had interceded for him.[75] Despite these personality challenges, Joseph had often included his younger brother at the highest level of the decision-making process in the Church, but in his absence and with the stress of continued challenges over succession, William was more vulnerable. Although Joseph clearly loved William, he had not placed full confidence in him, knowing that William's prickly personality could lead to petulance, lashing out at and even withdrawing from the family and his ecclesiastical colleagues.

After Joseph's death, Church leaders acknowledged William's lengthy Church service, and—more especially—the importance of showing support for the Twelve from this last surviving Smith son. Thus, they continued to manifest greater clemency toward the wavering apostle than his behavior probably merited. Adams had been severed from the Church, both *in absentia* and in person, and Brannan had been excommunicated *in absentia* but had manifested a contrition that had resulted in the restoration of his membership. (See Chapter 11.) Clearly, William was the guiding spirit behind the transgressions of Adams and Brannan, but his colleagues merely issued a mild reprimand for his similar, if not greater, transgressions. This partiality may have been due to Smith's sidestepping a direct confession of everything he had taught during his eastern mission and entangling the court in a discussion of sealing authority rather than plural marriage per se until they dropped the subject.

Still, the leaders had been apprised of at least some of his indiscretions. At George J. Adams's trial, Brigham Young revealed part of his willingness to put up with Smith, when he sourly and accurately indicated: "There is but one principle that can save William. He has a brother who is a prophet in the church." Young counseled those present at Adams's trial that "we dont want you to say a word against Wm because [he] is bound to be saved. Joseph [Smith] got a promise of it." Joseph's spiritual witness that his brother would eventually receive salvation had infused his own approach to dealing with his errant sibling, and Young initially adopted a similar approach. Foremost in Young's mind may have been the Prophet's teaching regarding wayward children: "When a seal is put upon the father and mother, it secures their posterity, so that they cannot be lost, but will be saved by virtue of the covenant of their father and mother."[76] That teaching also likely comforted Mother Lucy, who struggled between love for this surviving son, confusion at his erratic behavior, and steadfast family loyalty with its implications for William's leadership. Comprehending her son's complex personality was certainly made more difficult given the absence of her husband and two sons who often mitigated William's volatility; still, she desired that he rise to the position in the movement that would reflect the great contributions and sacrifice of her family.

---

75. "History of William Smith," *Millennial Star* 27, no. 1 (January 7, 1865): 7; "Conference Minutes," *Times and Seasons* 6, no. 16 (November 1, 1845): 1008, 1019; Kyle R. Walker, "William B. Smith," 246–307.

76. Joseph Smith, quoted in Larry E. Dahl and Donald Q. Cannon, eds., *Encyclopedia of Joseph Smith's Teachings* (Salt Lake City: Deseret Book, 1997), 493.

However, an unfortunate consequence of the leaders' persistent forbearance enabled William to continue his erratic behavior and defiance unchecked. They were almost certainly hesitant about confronting him directly because William's typical response to chastisement, as Joseph and Hyrum had painfully learned in 1835, was an explosion that resulted in personal hostilities and scandal on the entire Church. Young now had the additional burden of placating William to maintain the support of the Smith family at a time when he could not count on Emma's compliance.

In his demanding letter to Brigham Young written on August 9, William boldly asked that the Church purchase the William Marks home for him (which the trustees were already renting on the Smith family's behalf), and, according to Young, "present[ed] for payment . . . [several] bills" amounting to "$74.25" in cash. After stating definitively that the "Trustees have not one dollar on hand" to pay his debts, Young replied diplomatically that if the Church purchased the Marks home, "they will purchase it for the church for you to live in." In other words, the title would be in the Church's name, but William and the other Smiths might continue to live in the home rent free. Brigham also reminded William that the payment for patriarchal blessings "surely give[s] you a better chance of living than any other one of the quorum," and—with a note of genuine asperity—that he had "already received more assistance from the church funds than all the rest of the Twelve put together."[77]

Unlike his oldest brother, Alvin, William apparently had never made a sustained financial contribution to the family's well-being. Even now, when he was the family's "sole remaining support," as Lucy had termed him in her January 1845 letter while he was still in the East, he did not seem to feel that it required him to earn a living and support his mother and sisters.[78] As Lucy Mack Smith's historian summarized: While "William was in a sorry financial plight himself, it is also true that there is no record of his contributing in any way to Lucy's support. Rather, his public expressions of pity and concern for his 'poor old mother' can be read, without any great stretch of the imagination, as designed to raise funds and bolster his claims to authority within the church. . . . William's future public statements also tended to be along these same lines: making use of Lucy's age and poverty to rouse pity and open pocketbooks."[79] Both Church leadership and lay members began to recognize Smith's modus operandi, and as a result, the Saints' veneration for him declined. By summer's end, William's loyal family would be among the few who still esteemed the faltering apostle.

---

77. Young to Wm Smith, August 10, 1845.

78. Lucy Mack Smith (Nauvoo, Ill.) to William Smith, January 23, 1845, LDS Church History Library.

79. Lavina Fielding Anderson, *Lucy's Book: A Critical Edition of Lucy Mack Smith's Family Memoir* (Salt Lake City: Signature Books, 2001), 784.

Chapter 13

Apostle to Apostate

> While I write to you, my brethren, the feeling that I have been wronged and abused, is struggling for the mastery.
> —William Smith, October 1845

William lay low for nearly two weeks after he had met with Church leaders and the police at the Masonic Hall, although he did write to Brigham Young the week following the meeting seeking reconciliation. Smith's attempts at renegotiating interpersonal conflicts on paper had sometimes proven to be an effective strategy—as, for example, after his fist-fight with Joseph in 1835 in Kirtland. In person, William frequently began with good intentions but often flared into hostile and combative encounters. Writing his thoughts had, at least on occasion, required him to think through his message more calmly and smooth out some of his spiky self-justifications. It is a boon to the historian that, during the summer of 1845, he again turned to his pen in an effort to solve his conflicts with the Twelve.

On June 30, William wrote a lengthy and important missive addressed to Young and the Twelve, taking up first John Taylor's "clarification" in the *Times and Seasons* about the patriarchal office. Smith questioned: "Why was not the article shown to me as it was an article touching my office and standing in the church, [yet] nothing was said to me on the subject[?]. This with other like circumstances since my return from the east, and for my hard labor there, have received no favor nothing but hints of abuse, whilst other men can be applauded to the skies, and that too for the fruits of other mens labors. I am sick and tired of such partiality. Only give me my just dues, that in truth, justice and honor demands, and all is well."[1]

This passage begins with a reasonable question but, in only three sentences, has deteriorated into self-pity, showing that William positioned himself as a victim. He once again referred to the wording of John Taylor's *Times and Seasons* editorial statement, asserting that his ordination blessing, pronounced by Young himself had set him apart as "patriarch over the whole church." He asked Young

---

1. Both William Clayton and John Taylor recorded William Smith's letter in their respective journals, the versions varying slightly from one another. The variations are inconsequential. See William Smith (Nauvoo, Ill.), Letter to Brigham Young and Council of the Twelve, June 30, 1845, in George D. Smith, ed., *An Intimate Chronicle: The Journals of William Clayton* (Salt Lake City: Signature Books, 1995), 170–71; also copied in Dean C. Jessee, ed., *John Taylor Nauvoo Journal* (Provo, Utah: Grandin Book, 1996), 77–78.

to correct the misunderstanding in the *Times and Seasons* and give him the right to "visit all branches of the church and intrude on no mans rights, and further, to attend to all of the ordinances of God, no man being my head." If Young complied, Smith would "reconcile all difficulties and Elder Young can stand as the president of the church . . . by my most hearty wish and consent."

But William's sweeping demand would have made William independent—not answering for his actions to Young or to the other apostles. Young would naturally reject this condition on sight. Even if William agreed to recognize Young's office, he was setting up an untenable situation. In case of disagreement (which was almost inevitable), the members of the Church would have two authoritative voices giving directions. Then, to strengthen his position, William ended the letter by citing his Smith lineage, already a very touchy subject: "I want all men to understand that my fathers family are of the royal blood and promised seed and no man or set of men can take their crown or place in time or in eternity."[2] William concluded his letter with what sounded more like an ultimatum than conciliation, by stating that "the above is my proposition and will settle all difficulties at once and these are my avid sentiments and no equivocation."[3] The right to utilize the sealing power was a key issue because it related to Church governance. It remained at the core of William's conflict with the Twelve and had been a point of explicit disagreement ever since he had reached Nauvoo in May. William's argument that he should hold a more prominent place in the Church's hierarchy, including the right to use the sealing power without oversight, was his foremost concern.

It was also, of course, Brigham Young's foremost concern. Despite the calmer tenor of this letter to Young, Smith was showing no inclination to recognize Young's authority as president of the Twelve or even the authority of the Twelve as a whole. In point of fact, the Twelve were less concerned about the exact wording of William's ordination than his interpretation of "over the whole church." William's references to lineal authority and his view that he could officiate in any ordinance without oversight were a demand that they simply could not meet. While the tone of the letter generally evinced a spirit of conciliation, Church leaders and Smith continued to differ in their views on the scope of his authority. In his letter of response, written the same day he received William's, Young reiterated his view that there were "some ordinances in the church that cannot be administered by any person out of this place at present, but must be done here"—by which he meant both eternal and plural sealings. "As to your having the right to administer

---

2. George D. Smith, *An Intimate Chronicle*, 170–71; Jessee, *John Taylor Nauvoo Journal*, 77–78. Willard Richards, who recorded William's blessing of ordination, added: "Wm Smith was ordained Patriarch *to* [not "over"] the whole church of Jesus Christ of Latter Day Saints and to preside over the patriarchs." Willard Richards, Diary, May 24, 1845, emphasis mine; Willard Richards Papers, MS 1490, LDS Church History Library.

3. Quoted. in George D. Smith, *An Intimate Chronicle*, 170–71; see also Jessee, *John Taylor Nauvoo Journal*, 77–78.

all ordinances, in the world and no one standing at your head, we could not sanction, because the president of the church stands at the head of all the officers in the Church." Though there was technically no president of the Church at this point, Young was obviously recognized and acting as the de facto president. With input from the Twelve and the assistance of his clerk William Clayton, Young, maintaining a calm but unambiguous tone, judiciously delineated his perspective on the authority of the presiding patriarch: "As to your right to officiate in the office of Patriarch, we say you have the right to officiate in all the world, wherever your lot may be cast, and no one to dictate or control you excepting the Twelve, which body of men must preside over the whole Church in all the world." Young urged William to deal with him directly rather than making his differences a public matter and expressed his hope that "there will be no [hard] feelings" from the exchange. Continuing the accommodating tone of his letter, Young concluded: "If this [letter] does not meet with your feelings Brother William [write] me again, or come and see me, and we will make all things right for we surely want peace and the salvation of the people."[4] Apparently William neither wrote to Young nor visited him; if he did, this encounter has not survived in the documentary record, and it seems likely that an in-person visit would have produced enough fireworks to have also produced a record. As a result, it seems likely that William was temporarily mollified by Young's combination of recognizing his authority, even while setting limits on what the patriarchal office involved.

The dialogue paused there, even though the tensions would erupt later. William continued exercising his calling and bestowed at least twenty-seven blessings between June 25 and July 3—the two weeks following his momentous and ominous clash with fellow leaders at the Masonic Hall and three days after the two men's exchange of letters on June 30.[5] However, Young's private perception of William since his return from the East spilled out in a letter to Wilford Woodruff that same week, on June 27, 1845, not only the anniversary of Joseph and Hyrum's murders but also the the day after Mother Smith's three-part dream affirming William's supremacy because of his lineage. "The course of E[lde]r Wm Smith since his return to Nauvoo has not been such as we could have wished," Young wrote regretfully. "He seems to think he ought to be president of the church, & since he was ordained a Patriarch to the whole church he has endeavored to get up an influence among the Saints to persuade them that the office of Patriarch necessarily makes him president. We think to the contrary knowing

---

4. Brigham Young (Nauvoo, Ill.), Letter to William Smith, June 30, 1845, Brigham Young Office Files 1832–1878, General Correspondence, Outgoing, 1843–1876, 1845 June-August, LDS Church History Library. William Clayton took Young's dictated response and summarized its contents in his journal. George D. Smith, *An Intimate Chronicle*, 171. John Taylor also copied the letter in his journal; it varies only slightly from the original. Jessee, *John Taylor Nauvoo Journal*, 79.

5. H. Michael Marquardt, comp., *Early Patriarchal Blessings of the Church of Jesus Christ of Latter-day Saints* (Salt Lake City: Smith-Pettit Foundation, 2007), 248–86.

better, & there are but very few that will listen to him for a moment. He seems determined to cause us trouble, but our prayers continually ascend up to our heavenly father to over-rule William & save him if possible." Writing of himself in the third person, Young penned confidently: "However we know that God is with his Servant Brigham and will sustain him in his place, & we have no fears that the Saints will do likewise, should it come to a trial [vote]."[6]

It was not until Sunday, July 6, two weeks after the meeting with the Twelve and six days after the exchange of letters that William made his next public appearance by attending a preaching service at the stand near the temple. Enough time had apparently elapsed since his confrontation with Young that he felt comfortable meeting with other leaders during Sunday worship services. In a gesture obviously meant to communicate harmony and reconciliation, Young invited Smith to be the opening speaker. Nothing was evident in either man's remarks that day that hinted at persisting differences. Smith preached a persuasive sermon on the importance of premillennial temple work. Young immediately followed this address by encouraging the Saints to receive their patriarchal blessings from William—even specifying that he would be available for these blessings on Monday, Wednesdays, and Fridays "in his own dwelling house—formerly occupied by Wm. Marks."[7]

Church leaders continued to manifest rather remarkable patience as William jockeyed for additional recognition and a more prominent role in the Church's hierarchy. (See Chapter 12.) In mid-June, William had complained from the pulpit that not enough was being done to recognize his family.[8] Responding to this dissatisfaction (as well as to soothe Lucy and perhaps Emma as well), after almost three weeks of conflict in various forms, the Twelve hit on the idea of holding a dinner for the entire Smith family and their in-laws, assigning Bishops Newel K. Whitney and George Miller as hosts. This dinner was designed to honor the Smiths for the significant role they had played in the restoration movement and acknowledging the losses and persecution they had experienced as a result. They were especially solicitous of William, encouraging him to invite any and all of his friends to the celebration. "Near [to] all the conexions of Brother Wm. either by birth or marriage were present, besides a number of Wm[']s particular

---

6. Brigham Young (Nauvoo, Ill.), Letter to Wilford Woodruff, June 27, 1845, Brigham Young Office Files 1832–1878, General Correspondence, Outgoing, 1843–1876, 1845 June-August, LDS Church History Library.

7. Willard Richards, Church Historian's Office, General Church Minutes, July 6, 1845, CR 100 318, LDS Church History Library, in Richard E. Turley, ed., *Selected Collections from the Archives of the Church of Jesus Christ of Latter-day Saints,* 2 vols., DVD (Provo, Utah: Brigham Young University Press, [December 2002]), 1:18.

8. William voiced his complaint during a Sunday worship service on June 15, 1845. Stanley B. Kimball, *On the Potter's Wheel: The Diaries of Heber C. Kimball* (Urbana: University of Illinois Press, 1987), 123.

Nauvoo Mansion House, completed in 1843. Photograph taken ca. 1880s, by an unknown photographer.

friends," recorded William Clayton, who also attended.[9] The dinner took place at the Mansion House on July 9, and details of the occasion were recorded by Lyman O. Littlefield and published in the Church-sponsored newspaper: "To day our city has been enlivened by a public dinner given in honor of the Smith family.... And from what a listening ear can gather from the chat of some in attendance, the feast was a sumptuous and luxurious one, and every thing came off with decorum, affording a high degree of pleasure to the guests." The Twelve went so far as to provide carriages to transport all members of the extended Smith family to and from the dinner. Littlefield recorded the universal sentiment that, "as carriages were employed in taking to and fro the widows and children of that venerable family, clad in mourning, my reflections were quickened with the thought, that in a period of about two years, four brothers have fallen, and left behind them wives and children to lament their loss.... What company could be more worthy to surround the festive board than this, who, perhaps felt a momentary alleviation from their heavy sorrow, by mingling in the hilarity of the occasion."[10] In a significant symbolic act, Brigham Young, Heber C. Kimball, and other members of the Twelve served the food to about fifty members of the Smith family who participated in the occasion. The six-hour long celebration lasted from 2:00 p.m. until dusk, and included entertainment by a band.[11]

Perhaps commenting disapprovingly on William's participation, Daniel H. Wells more than twenty years later recalled that "the evening was spent cheer-

---

9. George D. Smith, *An Intimate Chronicle*, 173.

10. Lyman O. Littlefield, "Still Later from Nauvoo," *New-York Messenger* 2, no. 5 (August 2, 1845): 6.

11. "Dinner to the Smith Family," *New-York Messenger* 2, no. 6 (August 9, 1845): 4.

fully." William was unqualifiedly in disfavor with Church leaders in Utah by the time Wells recalled the event, prompting him to add that "the spirit of Wm. and his associates was very different from the spirit of the Twelve." Wells described William as "anxious to dance off some of his superstition and sectarianism. It chanced that they had a very poor fiddle, and the strings kept breaking. This Elder [William], thinking, I suppose, to tickle our ears, who were not in the Church [Wells had not yet been baptized], proposed that we should lay hands on the fiddle." William's mockery repelled Wells, who adjudged William as a "miserable hypocrite."[12] In almost identical language, Clayton recorded in his contemporary diary that, while "the evening was spent cheerfully . . . the spirit of Wm. and his associates was very different from the spirit of the Twelve."[13]

Notwithstanding, the dinner had the effect for which the Twelve had hoped, and both William and his mother affectionately and appreciatively addressed the audience. Though Lucy's remarks were not recorded, William proposed a toast of "pure water" to President Young and the bishops: "May their kindness be rewarded, may their power be increased, their purses never fail, their good will continue, [and] their desires be accomplished. . . . In the name and in behalf of all my relatives," Smith concluded, "I present my thanks to the President and Bishops for the kind manifestation of their good feelings towards the remnants of that family." Those present then drank while "standing," and while being showered "with great applause."[14]

This rather extravagant expression of goodwill by Church leaders at the dinner temporarily assuaged William's discontentment, and as already discussed (Chapter 12), during the month of July, he appears to have set his differences aside, concentrated on his patriarchal duties, and acted in harmony with the rest of the Twelve. The respite was only temporary, however, since it still did not give Smith what he really desired—a more prominent voice in the leading councils of the Church. Throughout the summer of 1845, William vacillated between submitting to the will of the Twelve and going defiantly off in his own direction. He had never learned the art of graceful submission to authority—or even subordinating his own desires to achieve a larger goal that depended on cooperation. This trait constantly resurfaced during the summer of 1845, beginning with his entrance to Nauvoo carrying a fairly large chip on his shoulder from being replaced by Parley P. Pratt in the eastern branches.

Nothing in his personal life provided a needed element of serenity either. He had left Nauvoo for his eastern mission in May 1843, as a freshly converted polygamist. Two years later, he returned with a dying wife, and less than a month after Caroline's death, Brigham Young officiated at William's marriage to Mary Jane Rollins on June 22, which was technically a monogamous second

---

12. Daniel H. Wells, August 18, 1867, *Journal of Discourses*, 12:137–38.
13. George D. Smith, *An Intimate Chronicle*, 173.
14. "Dinner to the Smith Family," 4.

marriage.¹⁵ His first plural wife, Mary Ann Covington, to whom he had been married for some two years, lived next door to William in the former printing office on the corner of Water and Bain Streets, and he maintained his secret relationship with her during his brief visit to Nauvoo in April-May 1844 and after his return from his eastern mission. Mary Jane Rollins thus became, for all practical purposes, his second civilly recognized wife. She was the eldest daughter of Enoch Perham Rollins and Sophia Philbrook Rollins, born December 25, 1829, at Bangor, Maine. Her family had only recently migrated to Nauvoo, in August 1844, after having converted to Mormonism in 1841.¹⁶ This family was not, apparently, related to the better known family of Mary Elizabeth Rollins Lightner, who became one of Joseph's plural wives in 1842. "I have broken through sectarian tradition, and in the course of about a month taken another wife," recounted Smith somewhat defiantly in explaining this hasty marriage in an August letter to Caroline's brother Joshua Grant. He acknowledged, "Some have found fault with me for marrying so soon."¹⁷

The American and British "respectable" tradition at this period was for the bereaved spouse to observe about a year of mourning before contracting another marriage, though widowers in William's age group (ages thirty to thirty-four) remarried more quickly than any other age group, especially when the widower had children under the age of twelve, which was the case with William.¹⁸ Joseph Smith had, in fact, buttressed this tradition in July 1838: "We do disapprove of the custom which has gained in the world, and has been practiced among us, to our great mortification, in marrying in five or six weeks, or even in two or three months, after the death of their companion. We believe that due respect ought to be had, to the memory of the dead, and the feelings of both friends and children."¹⁹ This counsel was apparently part of Joseph's larger program of assuring that the Mormons were seen as observing the decent conventions of society. However, five months later he earnestly counseled his brother, Hyrum,

---

15. Maureen Ursenbach Beecher, ed., "'All Things Move in Order in the City': The Nauvoo Diary of Zina Diantha Huntington Jacobs," 313; Stanley Kimball, *On the Potter's Wheel*, 123.

16. "Died. Enoch Perham Rollins," *Deseret News*, December 19, 1877, 11.

17. William Smith (Nauvoo, Ill.), Letter to Joshua Grant Jr., August 12, 1845, in *Nauvoo Neighbor* 3, no. 16 (August 20, 1845): 3.

18. Demographer Albert E. McCormick, in his analysis of nineteenth-century remarriage trends, found that widowers in William's age range (ages thirty to thirty-four), remarried more quickly than any other age group, a pattern he attributes to the need to care for motherless children: "There was direct relationship between the number of children a widower had and the rapidity with which he remarried. Simply stated, the more children a widower had, the more quickly he acquired a second spouse. This was particularly true for widowers with children under the age of twelve." Albert E. McCormick Jr., *Historical Demography through Genealogies: Explorations into Pre-1900 American Population Issues* (Bloomington, Ind.: iUniverse, 2011), 35–36. William and Caroline's two daughters were both under age twelve when he married Mary Jane Rollins.

19. Joseph Smith, "In obedience to our promise . . . ," *Elders' Journal* 1, no. 3 (July 1838): 43.

to reestablish a stable home as soon as possible after the death of his first wife, Jerusha Barden, on October 13, 1837, and apparently even suggested British convert Mary Fielding as an appropriate candidate. Hyrum, who had five children ranging in age from three months to ten years, married again on December 24, 1837. Hyrum carefully explained, "It was not because I had less love or regard for Jerusha, that I married so soon, but it was for the sake of my children."[20]

William was in a somewhat similar situation and apparently drew criticism as a result. "Some have turned against me," William wrote snappishly to Brigham Young just three days after his marriage, "becaus[e] I had the audacity to get married."[21] Clearly, he expected Brigham, who had performed the sealing, to defend him against this criticism. About six weeks after this marriage, William explained to Joshua Grant that he had "hired a woman to take charge of my household affairs"—apparently an unsuccessful arrangement that had brought "censure and jealousy of some good brethren and sisters." Of greater concern, he explained, "my little girls were running wild, and my clothes needed some attention," but he assured his brother-in-law "that neither short nor long steps [would] . . . cause her [Caroline's] bright image to fade from my mind, or erase her worth and good qualities from my memory."[22]

The timing of his marriage was only a part of what made fellow Saints uncomfortable. Mary Jane Rollins was fifteen at the time of the wedding, which made her only four years older than Mary Jane Smith, the elder daughter of William and Caroline. Upon learning of Smith's marriage, Thomas Sharp gleefully wrote, "Patriarch Bill Smith, brother of the Prophet, whose wife died four weeks since, was again married on last Sunday . . . having been a widower about 18 days [actually twenty-eight]. His bride is about 16 [sic] years of age and he is 35 [actually thirty-four]. Bill will do very well for a father in the church but his wife won't do for mother."[23] This age discrepancy and the marriage of girls in their younger or mid-teens was not scandalous, but perhaps all three factors may have tested the limits of societal norms, especially when coupled with rumors about William's misbehavior in the East.

Others questioned, in politer terms, the appropriateness of Mary Jane Rollins as an apostle's wife. Helen Mar Kimball, who turned seventeen in 1845 and was thus near Mary Jane's age, described her as a "very pretty young girl." The "character she bore was not of the best," but "she was good enough for him." (Helen Mar made this disparaging statement in 1883 when William was universally regarded with opprobrium in Utah.) Helen Mar added that William had "married the girl for spite, [and] at all events they were not happy, and it was only a

---

20. Hyrum Smith, quoted in Pearson H. Corbett, *Hyrum Smith Patriarch* (Salt Lake City: Deseret Book, 1976), 164; Jeffrey S. O' Driscoll, *Hyrum Smith: A Life of Integrity* (Salt Lake City: Deseret Book), 163. Neither source identifies to whom or when he made this explanation.

21. William Smith to Brigham Young, June 25, 1845.

22. William Smith to Grant, August 12, 1845.

23. "Patriarch Bill Smith," *Warsaw Signal* 2, no. 18 (July 2, 1845): 2.

short time before they separated."²⁴ She does not explain her statement about William's motives nor whom he would have spited by the marriage. Furthermore, Mary Jane was either unaware of his existing plural marriage to Mary Ann Covington or, at the very least, could not adapt to such an arrangement.

William was sealed to a second plural wife, Priscilla Mogridge, in either July or August. The complications were obvious, and Mary Jane left William just two months after they had wed on June 22. The gossipy *Warsaw Signal* reported that William "got into difficulty with his wife on account of his being intimate with an English girl that lives with his family, and it is reported that his wife has left him."²⁵

Priscilla Mogridge Smith Lowry Williams Staines, 1823–1899. Daguerreotype photograph taken ca. 1850s, by an unknown photographer. Courtesy LDS Church History Library.

Mary Jane's leaving also coincided with William's ill-advised public announcement of plural marriage on August 17, 1845 (discussed below). Two weeks later on August 31, Willard Richards, Brigham Young, Heber C. Kimball, George A. Smith, and John Taylor visited William and heard him "tell about his wife who had left him."²⁶ All five apostles were themselves polygamists so they presumably sought to console William. The end of this marriage certainly impacted Smith's two young daughters, who must have spent the summer in turmoil given their mother's death, their father's rapid remarriage, his continuing conflict with the other apostles, Mary Jane's unhappy departure, and moving to at least two different houses in just three months.

If Sharp's account can be trusted, William's polygamous marriages negatively impacted his already fragile marriage to Mary Jane Rollins. Priscilla Mogridge, like William's first plural wife Mary Ann Covington, was an English convert. Born on March 11, 1823, at Widbrook, Wiltshire, England, she was the seventh of nine children born to John Mogridge and Mary Crook Mogridge.²⁷ According to Mogridge's personal history, she was converted at age nineteen and baptized in an

---

24. Jeni Broberg Holzapfel and Richard Neitzel Holzapfel, eds., *A Woman's View: Helen Mar Whitney's Reminiscences of Early Church History* (Provo, Utah: BYU Religious Studies Center, 1997), 261.

25. "From Nauvoo," *Warsaw Signal* 2, no. 27 (September 3, 1845): 2. The "English girl" could have been either Mary Ann Covington or Priscilla Mogridge.

26. Willard Richards, Journal, August 31, 1845, Box 1, Volume 11, Willard Richards Papers, 1821–1854, MS 1490, LDS Church History Library.

27. Edward W. Tullidge, *The Women of Mormondom* (New York: Tullidge and Crandall, 1877), 285; Connell O'Donovan, "The Orphan Child: Priscilla Mogridge Smith Lowry Williams Staines (1823–1899)," *John Whitmer Historical Association Journal* 32, no. 1

ice-covered river apparently during the winter of 1842–43. "We looked upon the gathering as necessary to our salvation," wrote Priscilla. During the intervening year after her baptism and confirmation, she was "filled with an irresistible desire to join the saints who were gathering to America."[28] She left all of her family and sailed from Liverpool on December 27, 1843, to New Orleans aboard the *Fanny* with about 210 other Mormon converts, reaching Nauvoo on board the *Maid of Iowa* April 13, 1844.[29] William's brief final visit to Nauvoo occurred in April-May 1844 before the deaths of his brothers, and it is possible that he made her acquaintance before returning to Caroline in the East on May 21.[30] Their next opportunity to meet was in the summer of 1845 when William pronounced her patriarchal blessing on July 11.[31] The marriage probably occurred during the relatively conflict-free month between July 9 and August 10. Priscilla testified forty-eight years later in Utah: "I was taught that principle [of plural marriage] by William Smith in 1845" and married him shortly afterward. "He told me that his brother had received a revelation to that effect," recalled Mogridge, "and he taught it to me, and practiced it." She could not definitively remember the officiator's name—possibly "Lee" or "Lane"—and could not recollect ever being introduced publicly as William's wife—which fit the pattern of secrecy then governing polygamy.[32]

Although dates are not available for all of William's plural unions in Nauvoo, it was likely during this same relatively peaceful month that Brigham Young authorized William's sealing to at least five more wives: Mary Jones, Henriette Rice, Lucinda Curtis, and Mary Jane Rollins's sister Ann Sophia Rollins. As discussed in Chapter 11, he had already married sisters Sarah Ann Libby and Hannah Maria Libby, most certainly while he was still in the East in the fall of 1844. Because of the issue of authority, Brigham Young obviously considered these marriages invalid, so he would almost certainly have intended to reperform these sealings once the Libby sisters migrated to Nauvoo.

Meanwhile, William's first plural wife, Mary Ann Covington, to whom he had been sealed in May 1843, had waited patiently for William's return to

---

(Spring/Summer 2012): 80–81, notes that several of Priscilla's siblings joined the Church but that only Priscilla migrated to America.

28. Tullidge, *The Women of Mormondom*, 286, 288.

29. Fred E. Woods, *Gathering to Nauvoo* (American Fork, Utah: Covenant Communications, 2002), 167–68; Joseph Smith, Journal, April 13, 1844, in Scott H. Faulring, ed., *An American Prophet's Record: The Diaries and Journals of Joseph Smith* (Salt Lake City: Signature Books, 1987), 471.

30. William had led a group of forty to fifty eastern Mormons to Nauvoo in April 1844. (See Chapter 10.) He subsequently left Nauvoo on May 21, 1844, headed east with Heber C. Kimball and a large contingent of traveling missionaries who were also engaged in Joseph's presidential campaign. Stanley Kimball, *On the Potter's Wheel*, 60.

31. Marquardt, *Early Patriarchal Blessings*, 312–13.

32. Priscilla M. Staines, Testimony, Temple Lot Case Testimonies, 528–29, U.S. Eighth Circuit Court, 1892, MS 1160, LDS Church History Library.

Mary Elizabeth Jones Smith Hall, 1828–1901, date and photographer unknown. Courtesy Daughters of Utah Pioneers

Nauvoo in May 1845 when they apparently renewed their relationship. Covington lived with Agnes Coolbrith Smith, Don Carlos's monogamous widow and Joseph's plural widow, at the former printing office on Water Street, now a residence. It was next door to the Marks home where William was living with his mother, two of his three sisters, and their families.[33] If his legal wife, Mary Jane Rollins, is included in the number, William had nine wives by August 1845—which possibly contributed to the emotional turmoil that was sweeping through his life. Only his sealing to Mary Ann Covington and the two Libby sisters lasted longer than three months, and all of his plural marriages ended when William was dropped from the Quorum of the Twelve and excommunicated in October 1845. None of these women had children with him. None of them accompanied him out of the Church and out of Nauvoo. (See Appendix A for information on William's wives and their respective children.)

Whether William was pushing for more sealings or whether Brigham Young had encouraged him is not known. Young had officiated in at least three of William's plural sealings, two during July-August. Perhaps in allowing—or even encouraging—more sealings, Young hoped that William's dissatisfaction with his station would be placated. This, combined with the dinner sponsored by the Twelve and hosted by the bishops to honor the Smith family, certainly were efforts to maintain William's loyalty. These plural unions also evidenced his alignment with Church leaders during this one-month period.

Additionally, rumors were swirling throughout Hancock County that William would soon marry his brother's widow, the prominent matriarch Emma Hale Smith. The *Warsaw Signal* published what others had only speculated: "It is gossiped about, that Smith will, in a decent time marry Emma, widow of his brother, the Prophet. . . . If this union is effected we shall look for a complete revolution in the Holy City during the course of the summer."[34] While these rumors were only minimally credible, typical of Thomas Sharp's *Warsaw Signal*, if William had considered the possibility of marrying Emma, there is no indication in any existing documentation that either of them had harbored anything remotely like a romantic interest in each other. Thus, if William had considered

---

33. Mary Ann West, Testimony, Temple Lot Case Testimonies, 499–500, U.S. Eighth Circuit Court, 1892, MS 1160, LDS Church History Library.

34. "Trouble in the Holy City," *Warsaw Signal* 2, no. 15 (June 11, 1845): 2.

the possibilities of such a marriage, he may have seen it as strengthening his claim to leadership. For Emma's part, while she had compassionately nursed Caroline through her final illness, she does not seem to have relied on William for protection, advice, consolation, or anything closer than a possible conjunction of business interests in Joseph's estate holdings.

On the other hand, William had lived intermittently at Emma's home while Emma was nursing Caroline. Perhaps this time spent under Emma's roof provided grist for the ill-founded rumors about their relationship. But it is also possible that William may have influenced Emma's thinking more than Emma's biographers have given him credit for. After he left Nauvoo in the fall of 1845, a letter from William to Emma referred to their earlier efforts "to reform the Church." William was frustrated that Emma had not signed the letter supporting William's claims, while Jenkins and Katharine Salisbury and Arthur and Lucy Millikin had been supportive—although William may have assumed more support than actually existed. "Brother Salisbury has just returned to St. Louis without obtaining your name," wrote William regretfully. "Judge my surprise Emma when you now refuse to help me . . . after the many times I have talked with you on this subject and asked what I Should do to save my fathers familey." William definitely saw each episode squarely from how it influenced him, so it is likely that he saw one or two conversations as "many" and also assumed that Emma agreed with him as long as she did not verbally disagree. But Emma left no independent record, so we are left to speculate about the extent and content of these "many" conversations. According to William, Emma's "answer" about reforming the Church "was for me [William] to proclaim against the Spiritual wife doctrine [and] the usurpation of the 12."[35] Like other surviving Smiths, Emma was sympathetic to the idea of lineal rights. Additionally, William and Emma both shared the perception that they were entitled to Joseph's estate, including the publication of scripture. For example, Emma refused to surrender Joseph's Bible containing his textual revisions to the Twelve. She and William viewed such items as Joseph's personal property and felt that any profits received from its publication should go to the family.[36]

Extant records of the summer of 1845 provides glimpses of William associating with Emma. In early August, William took Emma and several other women on a carriage ride through the city. As they traveled down Hyde Street and crossed in front of Erastus Snow's duplex home, Snow's two wives, Artimisia Beaman and Minerva White, stuck their heads out the window and, according to a late memory that William shared with nephew Joseph III in 1883, "yelled out, at the

---

35. William Smith (St. Louis, Mo.), Letter to Sister Emma [Smith], [November] 21, 1845, LDS Church History Library.

36. William Smith, "A Proclamation," *Warsaw Signal* 2, no. 32 (October 29, 1845): 1; Linda King Newell and Valeen Tippetts Avery, *Mormon Enigma: Emma Hale Smith* (Urbana: University of Illinois Press, 1994), 203–9.

top of their voices 'There goes Bill Smith with his spiritual wives.'"[37] William further stated that the women in the carriage with him also overheard Snow's wives rehearsing, "there he goes dont you see him that's just what I thought about Bro William; I always thought he loved the Women."[38] The comment most assuredly upset Emma, a decided opponent of the practice, and William, of course, took exception to the remark, but some of the other women in his carriage very well may have been among his recently married plural wives. While Snow's wives were commenting on William's character, he defended, not himself, but rather the practice of plural marriage and later mentioned the incident in a sermon. Without referring to Snow's wives by name, he prayed that God would "curse . . . [and] damn such hypocrites," who were themselves "up to here (putting his hand to the top of his head)," in spiritual wifery. However, William refused to see that the comment was less about the practice than it was about his reputation.

As another clue about William's reputation, Frances ("Fanny") Corwin, who had lived in New York when William presided over the eastern branches, had rebuffed his attempts to teach her about the practice and, once while she was still in New York, "requested him to refrain from coming to her house, as his conduct was not accordance with her ideas of propriety."[39] According to Helen Mar Whitney's 1883 recollections of events in June 1845, she happened to be at the home of one of Joseph Smith's plural wives when William stopped by and, despite Helen Mar's presence, reportedly gave her a "long and eloquently worded" proposal of marriage, "telling her not only [of] his devotion to her, but of a wonderful vision, or revelation that he had received, concerning her and himself, picturing out her future state in glorious colors. . . . His poor suffering wife had passed away previous to this and he thought it a flattering inducement to offer a young lady the privilege of standing first." According to Helen, she thought it beneath her to "even deign a reply, but cast his letter to the flames." When William showed up at their door some days afterward, Helen Mar was again present and heard him ask for "that letter." "When she coolly informed him that it had been destroyed," described Whitney, "his countenance, which had already became a shade or two darker with pent up wrath, (which he did not try to conceal) grew darker still and the look he gave her as he turned to leave resembled anything but that of a Saint."[40] Jedediah Grant, William's brother-in-law and confidential colleague during his eastern mission, revealingly contrasted the way William had

---

37. William B. Smith, Letter to Joseph Smith III, [October 19, 1883], Miscellaneous Letters and Papers, P13, f2311, Community of Christ Library-Archives.

38. "A Synopsis of the First Chap. of the Gospel of St. William," August 17, 1845, Nauvoo, Illinois, reported by George D. Watt, LDS Church History Library.

39. Frances Corwin, quoted by Caroline Barnes Crosby, in Edward Leo Lyman, Susan Ward Payne, and S. George Ellsworth, eds., *No Place to Call Home: The 1807–1857 Life Writings of Caroline Barnes Crosby, Chronicler of Outlying Mormon Communities* (Logan: Utah State University Press, 2005), 361.

40. Holzapfel and Holzapfel, *A Woman's View*, 260–61.

tried to teach plural marriage with Joseph's typical approach. Joseph's version "would elevate them [women], make them virtuous and happy, while that of his profligate brother would make them wretched and miserable, would debauch and degrade them."[41]

The brief period of harmony between William and the Twelve in July and early August was starting to teeter out of its precarious balance by August 9, when William again picked up his pen—and his argument—over the authority to seal. His letter has not apparently survived, but Young answered it the next day on August 10, quoting and paraphrasing the main points William made. From Brigham's answer, we can deduce that William again reiterated his belief that he held the right to officiate in every ordinance in the Church. To bolster his argument, he described being present for "Joseph's teachings up stairs in the [red] brick store" which the Twelve had attended in April-May 1844, and at which, he claimed, Joseph had bestowed on him—along with the rest of the Twelve—"power to build up the kingdom of God."[42]

William also produced a second document that recaps, in greater detail, the arguments he laid out for Brigham. This second document was published in the highly skeptical *Warsaw Signal* by his old enemy, Thomas Sharp, who had obviously decided that embarrassing Brigham and the other apostles was more satisfying than annoying the comparatively powerless William once again. Introducing William's "Proclamation," Sharp wrote, "he [William] is doubtless, actuated, in this expose, by selfish and interested motives, and were it not for the fact that he has been virtually stripped of power in Nauvoo . . . [it] would never have appeared before the public. . . . Notwithstanding we can give Smith but little credit for his motives," Sharp concluded, "we yet believe his statements."[43] As a result, it seems plausible that the *Signal* reproduced William's "Proclamation" accurately.

In it, William announced: "I was present with Joseph at the last council that was held previous to the Twelve and others going on their electioneering campaign. It was at this time that I receive[d] my initiation into the highest priesthood lodge, was washed and anointed, and clad with the sacerdotal robe of pure white, and ordained to be priest and king, and invested with all the power than any man on earth ever did possess."[44] This is an obvious description of William's reception into the Quorum of the Anointed, which took place on

---

41. "Discourse. By President J. M. Grant," *Deseret News,* April 2, 1856, 4.

42. Brigham Young (City of Joseph [Nauvoo], Ill.), Letter to William Smith, August 10, 1845, Brigham Young Office Files 1832–1878, General Correspondence, Outgoing, 1843–1876, 1845 June-August, LDS Church History Library.

43. Thomas Sharp, "Proclamation of Bill Smith," *Warsaw Signal* 2, no. 32 (October 29, 1845): 2. This is Sharp's editorial note, which headed William's "Proclamation" in the same issue.

44. William wrote this "Proclamation" after he left Nauvoo in September, and Sharp published it in in the *Warsaw Signal* 2, no. 32 (October 29, 1845): 1, 4. I believe that it accurately describes William's mindset and understanding of his authority after his return to Nauvoo.

May 12, 1844.[45] "In consequence of these endowments and ordination received from under the hands of Joseph," reasoned William, "I hold as much power and as many keys to seal and bind on earth, as can possibly belong to Brigham Young; [because] this power was conferred equally on all the Twelve."[46]

In Young's reply on August 10, he acknowledged the importance of what had transpired at those significant meetings. "You refer to 'Joseph's teachings up stairs in the brick store that the Twelve have power to build up the kingdom of God,'" wrote Brigham, "which the Twelve well recollect." But he further clarified that he and the Twelve "also recollect that Joseph said that the sealing power is always vested in one man." In fact, according to the revelation on celestial marriage that Hyrum read to the Nauvoo High Council on August 12, 1843[47] (now canonized as LDS Doctrine and Covenants 132:7): "I have appointed unto my servant Joseph to hold this [sealing] power in the last days, and there is never but one on the earth at a time on whom this power and the keys of this priesthood are conferred." Brigham continued quoting Joseph: "There never was, nor never would be but one man on the earth at a time to hold the keys of the sealing power in the church, [and] . . . all sealings must be performed by the man holding the keys, or by his dictation, and that man is the president of the church." Young meticulously spelled out his role as the presiding authority in the Church to ensure there would be no misunderstanding. If William still held to the view that Hyrum possessed the same authority equal to Joseph's, Young illustrated his view with an example that differentiated between the two men's respective authority. "Hyrum held the patriarchal office legitimately, [and] So do you. Hyrum was counseller, [and] so are you. But the sealing power was not in Hyrum legitimately neither did he act on the sealing principle only as he was dictated [to] by Joseph." Perhaps Hyrum was similarly confused about the extent of his authority. Young recounted that "this was proven" in one particular case, when Hyrum "did undertake to seal without counsel, & Joseph told him if he did not stop it he would go to hell and all those he sealed with him."[48]

---

45. Faulring, *An American Prophet's Record*, 478; Andrew F. Ehat, "'They Might Have Known He Was Not a Fallen Prophet'—The Nauvoo Journal of Joseph Fielding," *BYU Studies* 19, no. 2 (Winter 1979): 148–49.

46. William Smith, "A Proclamation," 1.

47. Brian C. Hales, *Joseph Smith's Polygamy, Volume 2: History* (Salt Lake City: Greg Kofford Books, 2013), 139–44.

48. Young to William Smith, August 10, 1845. The sealing Young referred to occurred on June 23, 1843, when Hyrum sealed Parley P. Pratt and his monogamous second wife, Mary Ann Frost Stearns, without Joseph's authorization. When Joseph learned of the sealing, he cancelled the ceremony and later performed the sealing himself. See Brian C. Hales, *Joseph Smith's Polygamy, Volume 1, History* (Salt Lake City: Greg Kofford Books, 2013), 619–21. See also Andrew F. Ehat, "Joseph Smith's Introduction of Temple Ordinances and the Mormon Succession Question" (M.A. thesis, Brigham Young University, 1982), 66–71.

While William may have missed what has been termed the "last charge" meeting held sometime between March 24 and 26, 1844, in which Joseph Smith gave the Twelve additional priesthood keys along with a charge to "'bear off the Kingdom' to all the world," William had returned to Nauvoo a few weeks later and apparently received similar instructions from his brother. But he had missed much of the evolution of these responsibilities which had come when the Twelve met together almost daily during the spring of 1844, as he was in Nauvoo for only one month. In addition, Parley P. Pratt described that, during the same pivotal "last charge" meeting, "Joseph conferred 'the keys of the sealing power' on Brigham Young as president of the Twelve. The Prophet taught them that it was the 'last key,' the 'most sacred of all,' and that it pertained 'exclusively to the first presidency.'"[49]

William's absence from Nauvoo during this critical training period under Joseph's tutelage may help to explain his confusion regarding the sealing power. Though Smith acknowledged Young's authority as president of the Twelve, he failed to recognize that Young's position gave him the ultimate power in administering sealing privileges or delegating that authority (usually case by case) to others. William persistently resisted Young's responsibility, especially because it positioned him in a role inferior to Young's. He expected to have a dominant voice during this time of transition in the Church, and once again, his misapprehension led to a cascade of unwise decisions.

On Sunday, August 17, several days after being mocked by Snow's wives during the carriage ride, and perhaps speaking directly to these women, Smith retaliated by preaching a sermon, the likes of which had never been heard publicly at Nauvoo. For some reason, perhaps due to hostilities which were increasing that month, John Taylor was the only other apostle present. Smith titled his remarks "A Synopsis of the First Chap[ter] of the Gospel by St. William."[50] Perhaps he meant it jocosely, but it came across as irreverent, even arrogant. In his discourse, he proclaimed that, as the sermons of the ancient apostles had been canonized, so should his, and that he would preach freely on his views. The sermon had a decidedly aggressive tone. He knew that he was stepping across the line that mandated secrecy where plural marriage was concerned, but William had frequently taken his own course, and his audacity in preaching a polygamous sermon was no exception. "I have concluded for my part, that while I live, in Nauvoo, & practice Mormon religion, the best course, I could take, would be an independent course," he stated at the outset of his sermon, "that course which will be the most congenial, and the most suitable to my own circumstances and

---

49. "Proclamation of Parley P. Pratt," January 1, 1845, *Millennial Star* 5 (March 1845): 151, as quoted in Ronald K. Esplin, "Joseph, Brigham and the Twelve: A Succession of Continuity," *BYU Studies* 21, no. 3 (Summer 1981): 319–20. Esplin here discusses Joseph's "last charge" to the Twelve.

50. "A Synopsis of the First Chap. of the Gospel of St. William." My search of journals and early documents for this period provides no clue about the unexplained absence of the other apostles, even though many of them were unquestionably in Nauvoo.

feelings, and leave the rest of the matter with the People, and with my God, not trying to please anybody, only myself." William set the background for what he was to reveal by summarizing the histories of Jacob, David and Solomon from the Old Testament who were justified before the Lord in marrying more wives than one, until David transgressed by arranging for Uriah's death so he could marry Bathsheba and until Solomon transgressed in worshipping false gods with some of his foreign wives.

At the pinnacle of his sermon, Smith declared, "If a Sister gives me her hand upon the Spiritual Wife system, to share with me the fate & destinies of time, and eternity, I will not be ashamed of her before the public. What I do in the secret chamber I would do in the broad daylight. . . . I will not be ashamed, to be seen with you in the street." William derisively referred to the incident passing the Snow home several days earlier: "I rode in my Waggon with some of the sisters," he recounted, adding contemptuously, "and if I did wrong I will get some of the Sisters to Baptize me." He then stated somewhat cuttingly, "Now dont get scared brethren, and leave the congregation before I get through, it is such an awful doctrine I know and I am just the man to get into the business, and get out of it too, for I am not the author of God's works, nor am I to blame, for what he has revealed." His conclusion was a brash declaration that what he had spoken was "the Gospel according to St. William in the Name of Jesus Christ Amen."[51]

Those present were stunned by what they had heard. Many of the sisters present "threw up their white handkerchiefs" to cover their faces in disgust, and a good portion of the congregation walked away while Smith was still speaking.[52] John Taylor remembered that it was not only "the principles advanced by him" that caused many to leave, but it was also "the manner in which they were stated." Taylor regretted that he was the only other apostle present and felt "exceedingly pained" at his "unpleasant" task of correcting "one of the Twelve[,] my brother in the Quorum, and the brother of Joseph."[53] It was a task made even more difficult because Taylor already had a prickly history with William Smith and knew he would not take public correction calmly. Taylor waited edgily on the stand for Smith to conclude his remarks and immediately responded. While he acknowledged that Smith's teachings had biblical precedence, Taylor, who by this point had seven wives, stated flatly that he personally would have "nothing to do with the Gospel according to St. William." He recorded in his journal that he "arose and without appearing to advert to him, wishing to leave him out of the question as much as possible . . . told the people I must preach from William's text." Taylor clarified that while the prophets of the Old Testament were justified in taking more than one wife, he challenged William's implication; "Can we draw inference from

---

51. Ibid.

52. William B. Smith, Letter to Joseph Smith III, [October 19, 1883]; George D. Smith, *An Intimate Chronicle*, 178. See also William Smith, "Elders' Pocket Companion," in Appendix B.

53. Jessee, *John Taylor Nauvoo Journal*, 97.

that, that every man in this Congregation, shall take him many wives[?]" By phrasing his objection as a rhetorical question, Taylor was able to sidestep the conclusion William had drawn from the same evidence. Furthermore, as Taylor reflected in his journal, he disagreed with the "crude manner" in which William made his argument, since it would lead to "corruption, adultery and every other wicked thing both in men and women [by] . . . letting loose the reins of government" over the practice. At the same time, he was careful to state that he did not "find fault" with William "if he has a mind to ride [with], three or four Ladies, in his carriage."[54]

John Taylor, 1808–1887. Engraving by Frederick Piercy, 1853, in *Route From Liverpool to Great Salt Lake Valley* (Liverpool, 1855).

As Taylor attempted the unhappy task of countering William's argument while simultaneously not repudiating polygamy, William interrupted him in mid-sentence: "I wish to say that if Bro. Taylor, intends to take up my subject in this manner, I wish to have the privilege to answer him as he proceeds for I do not intend to be put down, and brow beaten every time I speak on this stand." Hoping to ease the tension, Taylor replied, "It is not my intention to put Bro. William down, or cast any reflections upon Bro William's sermon, but I am here today to speak & offer a word of caution." According to Taylor, William interrupted him twice more during his remarks, forewarning that he would "rise" in rebuttal "as often as he thought proper" and that Taylor "had no business to qualify his remarks and that in so doing I was implicating him and teaching principles that were incorrect." After several back-and-forth exchanges, Taylor placatingly said: "I was Bro. William's friend and I knew that if he only heard me through, he would aquiesce in the principles I advanced." After Taylor spoke while the "Spirit of God . . . rested upon me in power," William "then arose and made an apology, for what he had said," reassuring Taylor that "he [William] had always been my friend and was my friend still." Taylor quoted William as concluding the exchange with the announcement: "Bro. William and Bro. Taylor are [both] right, I expressed it different, and meant no harm by what I have said." Thus, this potentially explosive episode was patched up, at least in public. In his private reflections, Taylor expressed his gratitude that he had been present to counter Smith's eccentric discourse.[55] While Taylor astutely avoided

---

54. Jessee, *John Taylor Nauvoo Journal*, 98–99; "A Synopsis of the First Chap. of the Gospel of St. William."

55. Jessee, *John Taylor Nauvoo Journal*, 98.

debating Smith on such a sensitive topic, the experience naturally intensified the distrust the Twelve felt toward him.

Those who stayed to hear the meeting's conclusion were uncomfortable with both William's teachings and his quarrelsome demeanor toward Taylor. Hosea Stout indicated that, as Taylor began speaking, "William showed considerable feelings."[56] According to Zina Diantha Huntington Jacobs, one of Joseph's plural wives, after "Wm Smith Spoke to the People . . . . Elder Ta[y]lor made an appropriate reply," because, as she categorically stated, "it was needed."[57] In a late reminiscence, as evidence of the lasting impact of William's sermon, Cyrus Wheelock recalled the occasion when William "undertook to prove that it [polygamy] was right . . . and he preached so many strange things there to the people that Elder John Taylor got up and corrected him." Wheelock further remembered that "William Smith is the only man I ever heard preach it [polygamy] publicly in Nauvoo."[58] William Clayton, who had carefully tracked shifts in William's disposition since his return, penned in his journal on August 17: "His course today will evidently hurt him in the estimation of the saints more than any thing he has done before."[59]

Word spread quickly about the disastrous sermon. At a meeting of the Twelve later that same day—which William did not attend—his discourse on "Spritual wifeism" was the topic of discussion, and William's cousin George A. Smith prayed "that the course—Wm Smith had pursued might fall on his own head."[60] The *Warsaw Signal*, probably relying on second-hand information, summarized: "Bill, from the stand, avowed that the Spiritual Wife System was taught in Nauvoo secretly—that he taught and practiced it, and he was not in favor of making any secret of the matter. . . . This bold declaration created quite a sensation amongst the Saints and Bill is in hot water in consequence of it."[61]

Although there was no open break with the Twelve, it is possible to reconstruct in retrospect the developments that led to William's decision to leave Nauvoo, a decision he had certainly made by the end of August or by early September. As early as August 20, he announced plans to visit the eastern branches, bestowing patriarchal blessings as he traveled. He went so far as to seek the sanction of the Twelve and, probably with some relief, they agreed. They prepared a notice of his pending departure on August 24 to be printed in the *Times and Seasons*.[62]

---

56. Juanita Brooks, ed., *On the Mormon Frontier: The Diary of Hosea Stout*, 2 vols. (Salt Lake City: University of Utah Press, 1964), 1:57–58.

57. Beecher, "All Things Move in Order in the City," 318.

58. Cyrus H. Wheelock, Testimony, 542, 1892, U.S. Eighth Circuit Court, MS 1160, LDS Church History Library.

59. George D. Smith, *An Intimate Chronicle*, 178.

60. George A. Smith quoted in Willard Richards, Diary, August 17, 1845.

61. "From Nauvoo," *Warsaw Signal* 2, no. 24 (September 3, 1845): 2.

62. William Smith (Nauvoo, Ill.), Letter to Jesse C. Little, August 20, 1845, typescript by Ireta Andersen, November 16, 1932, Utah State Historical Society; George D. Smith,

Inopportunely for William, Parley P. Pratt arrived two days later on August 26, and the eight months he had presided alone in the East had obviously brought new disclosures of misbehavior on the part of William Smith, George J. Adams (who had decidedly disaffiliated), and Samuel Brannan, who was exerting himself to show loyalty to the Twelve and especially to Pratt. When Parley heard that William was planning to return to the eastern branches, he reacted with consternation. "On Sunday last the Council decided to let Wm. Smith go East by the authority of the church, to give Patriarchal blessings," recorded William Clayton in his diary on August 27, "but on the representation of Brother Parley today of Wms course and feelings of the people in the East towards him it was decided that he had better not go." Pratt strenuously recommended that William remain at Nauvoo where the other apostles could monitor his behavior and attitude.[63]

The apostles unanimously agreed with Pratt's recommendation, cancelled William's patriarchal journey, told John Taylor, editor of the *Times and Seasons*, not to insert the notice regarding Smith's mission,[64] and assigned Willard Richards to write William informing him of the council's decision. Richards did so on August 27, ten days after William's ill-advised "First Epistle." "I am instructed by a council of the Twelve & Bishops," the letter began, "to say to you that the council has taken into consideration the piece which had been written for publication in the paper related to your eastern mission this fall, and decided that it is not wisdom to publish it." Richards explained to William that the reason was that "most of the brethren in the eastern branches are now making every exertion to remove to Nauvoo, [and] it will be wisdom for you to remain here, & give them their patriarchal blessings on their arrival."[65] William was astute enough to recognize Pratt's influence on this abrupt turnabout by his colleagues of the Twelve, who only days earlier had been supportive of William's proposal.

Cancelling his mission was the final straw for William, and he began seriously planning to leave Nauvoo with or without the consent of the Twelve. As an exacerbating factor, apparently he did not feel fully confident that the Nauvoo police had his safety as their preeminent goal, and the Hodges murders—as both killers and as victims—must have left him even more uneasy. Thus, around September 12, his brother-in-law Jenkins Salisbury, and Hiram Stratton, a Zion's Camp veteran, came to him urgently with a report that Church leaders and the Nauvoo police had plans to dispose of Smith. "I did not leave that place [Nauvoo] too soon," William recounted a month afterward, "for the very day of my departure it was whispered to me that a secret plot was already concocted for taking away my life."[66] Salisbury and Stratton had likely based their report on hearsay, as neither man held a position in one of the

---

An Intimate Chronicle, 178.

63. George D. Smith, *An Intimate Chronicle*, 179.

64. Ibid.

65. Willard Richards, Letter to Elder Wm Smith, Patriarch, Nauvoo, Illinois, August 27, 1845, in Willard Richards Papers, MS 1490, Box 3, fd. 5, LDS Church History Library.

66. William Smith, "A Proclamation," 1.

leading councils or the police force, but Smith at once believed their report and feared for his life. In 1855, when William was briefly exploring the option of rejoining the LDS Church, he wrote a sympathy-seeking letter to Brigham Young: "The day I left Hyram Stratten and J Salsbury called to see me on a special Mission as they said to inform me that your council and Police had decided to distroy my life the following night." William admitted that their "account of things in a tone of earnest zeal threw me into a dreadful state of excitement." This report, combined with the other stresses and threats, had "almost deranged my senses."[67] He hurriedly packed a few belongings, including several patriarchal blessing books, took his two daughters, and slipped out of Nauvoo that same night, escorted by Salisbury and Stratton. Although he does not give the date of his escape, it was between September 11 and 14, 1845—most probably the night of September 12–13.[68] It is not clear why he thought that his two young daughters would be safer with him, living a fugitive's life, than in the care of their grandmother and aunts and, at least theoretically, under the protection of the Nauvoo police. Killing white women and children was considered outrageous during this time period, and the murders of an eleven-year-old and a nine-year-old would have been viewed as monstrous.

Although he had little time to plan, he initially made his way to his Uncle John Smith's home. Although John and Clarissa briefly sheltered him, they were disturbed by his behavior and surprised by his conviction that his life was in danger at Nauvoo. John immediately reported to Brigham Young that William had angrily declared that he would go east that fall and that, "by God . . . this

---

67. William Smith (Springfield, Ill.), Letter to Brigham Young, May 7, 1855, Brigham Young Office Files 1832–1878, Letters from Church Leaders and Others, 1840–1877, William Smith, 1844–1857, LDS Church History Library. Hiram Stratton was disfellowshipped several months later, on January 18, 1846, "for unchristianlike conduct." "Notice," *Times and Seasons* 6, no. 21 (January 15, 1846): 1096.

68. I derive this span of dates from three other sources. First, Calvin Rudd dates William's departure from Nauvoo as occurring on September 12, 1845, citing an undated letter housed at the RLDS Auditorium at the time he wrote his thesis (1973). Calvin P. Rudd, "William Smith: Brother of the Prophet Joseph Smith" (M.A. thesis, Brigham Young University, 1973), 124. I conducted a thorough search of all of William Smith's letters at the Community of Christ Library-Archives and was unable to verify this date. I found a possible candidate for Rudd's letter, but in it, William Smith states only that he left Nauvoo in "September 1845." William B. Smith, Letter to Joseph Smith III, October 19, 1883. Second, Smith pronounced his final recorded patriarchal blessing upon Andrew S. Gibbons at Nauvoo on September 11, 1845. Marquardt, *Early Patriarchal Blessings*, 430. Third, three days later on September 14, a constable came to Nauvoo from Carthage with writs for arresting William and several other apostles. However, Rudd, "William Smith," 124, states that "the constable later indicated that William Smith was excused from the writ and was not expected to be seen," most logically because he had already left the city. I therefore conclude that William left Nauvoo between September 11 and 14, 1845.

people should know before spring who their leader was."⁶⁹ William then crossed the Mississippi River and went north to Augusta, Iowa, where George J. Adams was residing. Notwithstanding his defiant pronouncement, Smith would have reason to pause before making his final break with the Twelve.

Church leaders were surprised when they learned that William had left Nauvoo. Apostle Orson Hyde, who later learned first hand of William's fears for his safety, assured his fellow apostle that "there is no one here that wishes to harm the hair of your head."⁷⁰ Helen Mar Whitney quoted Proverbs 28:1 to express her confusion at William's action: "'The wicked flee when no man pursueth,' which words applied to William Smith."⁷¹ Almost certainly, they misunderstood the intensity of William's anxiety about his safety, or what it meant to be a Smith in post-martyrdom Nauvoo. Two of his brothers had been assassinated and a third had died almost immediately afterward of undiagnosed afflictions brought on by his efforts to ride to his brothers' rescue. Willard Richards had, in fact, counseled William to stay out of Nauvoo for almost a year because the Saints were unsure whether an attack would be made on this last surviving Smith son.⁷² He had attempted to defend the Hodges brothers—friends who were, in fact, guilty of murder—only to have a third Hodges brother murdered within a few rods of Brigham Young's house. His conflict with Elbridge Tufts of the Nauvoo police was also a contributing factor. In short, William felt that his life was in jeopardy, and when he heard the second-hand reports from two of his closest friends that his fears were real, he felt that flight was his only option. In his hurry to flee the city, Smith had not even paused long enough to tell his mother good-bye, an indication of his apprehension. Another measure is his insistence on taking eleven-year-old Mary Jane, who was so seriously ill that, on August 31, Willard Richards had noted it in his diary.⁷³ On September 28, some two weeks after he fled Nauvoo, William said that "one of my lidle girls" (meaning Mary Jane) was "violently sick with the Billious & intermitting fevor & is now lying at the point of death."⁷⁴ Thus, her illness had lasted a month. William's hurried night journey

---

69. Brigham Young, Journal, September 16, 1845, 61, Brigham Young Office Files, 1832–78, CR 1234 1, LDS Church History Library.

70. Orson Hyde (Nauvoo, Ill.), Letter to William Smith, October 28, 1845, in *Warsaw Signal* 2, no. 36 (November 26, 1845): 1.

71. Holzapfel and Holzapfel, *A Woman's View*, 160.

72. Richards to Brigham Young, June 30, 1844; William Smith, "A Proclamation," 1.

73. Richards wrote that "at dark went to Wm Smiths to see his sick child. Found Young Kimball Geo A Taylor & Geo Grant [there]." Willard Richards, Diary, August 31, 1845, Willard Richards Papers, MS 490.

74. William Smith (Augusta, Iowa Territory), Letter to Pres. B[righam] Young or Mr. Lewis Robbins, September 28, 1845, Brigham Young Office Files 1832–1878, Letters from Church Leaders and Others, 1840–1877, William Smith, 1844–1857, LDS Church History Library.

from Nauvoo and then through several cities in Iowa Territory could not have helped her condition.

Smith's indecisiveness after leaving Nauvoo is evidence of the impetuosity of his decision. The first word the Twelve received after the simple fact of his flight was Uncle John Smith's report on September 16, 1845, of William's flamboyant defiance and outrageous claim to leadership.[75] At that point, William was traveling north along the Iowa side of the Mississippi River. He stopped briefly at Fort Madison, then spent several weeks at Augusta, Iowa, and "then fled to a place . . . on the Skunk River, where I had a cousin," whose name he could not recall.[76] At the end of September, he wrote Brigham Young a mild and conciliatory letter from Augusta, describing plans to "make a visit to my friends & attend a blessing meeting" (apparently bestowing patriarchal blessings to the Saints in Iowa). "I am afraid that my sick child will keep me from Nauvoo one or two weeks yet," he explained to Young, "so be patient with me. . . . I will get there as soon as I can." His personal safety and Mary Jane's health were his foremost concerns, "but," wrote William, "I would like to attend the [October] Conference if the health of my girl will permit & the mob[s] do not prevent me." He requested that Church leaders reassure his mother that he was safe and reiterated his desire to return to Nauvoo as soon as his "lidle girls" health improved. Thus, despite his door-slamming exit, William was still ambiguous about which path he was going to follow and was obviously fishing for information from Brigham Young. In the letter to Young, he included a note to Lewis Robbins, a friend from his Ohio days, requesting that he "get a team & hall the grave stones I have bought for my wife to the grave in Emmas garden." Further communicating indecisiveness, he also requested Robbins to get him "a lot of wood for winter . . . for I may be detained some time from home."[77]

A decade later in his 1855 letter to Brigham Young, William acknowledged the possibility that Jenkins Salisbury and Hiram Stratton may have overstated the danger when he fled Nauvoo. "As to the falshood of them witnisess," Smith wrote, "if they did lie to me I was not to blame but the affect was all the same to me as it produced the excitement and . . . the fears as a matter of coarse [and I responded] as any man would have done under the same Sirconstances." He said the warning from his friends "coupled with the awful feeling that had rested upon me for the twelve months previous on the account of the murder of Joseph & Hyrum in Carthage Jail" contributed to his mindset at the time he left.[78]

William's apprehension continued during September, and he remained convinced that people in both Iowa and Illinois wanted him dead. At times his behavior bordered on paranoia. Furthermore, hostilities were escalating in Hancock

---

75. Brigham Young, Journal, September 16, 1845, 61.
76. William Smith Testimony, Temple Lot Case Testimonies, 185–86, U.S. Eighth Circuit Court, 1892, MS 1160, LDS Church History Library.
77. William Smith, Letter to Young or Robbins, September 28, 1845.
78. William Smith, Letter to Young, May 7, 1855.

County in September 1845, with vigilante groups of non-Mormons attacking outlying settlements, burning barns and haystacks, and knocking down houses.[79] It was a precarious time for the Saints, and more especially for their leaders. Just days after Smith fled Nauvoo, authorities arrived from Carthage on September 15 with arrest warrants for many of the Twelve, including William Smith.[80] When William heard about these writs, he described his anxieties in his September 28 letter to Brigham Young: "Hyrum & Joseph were killed by falling into the hands of the governor to answer to the writs, & should the mob rage to that extent now in Hancock I would advise that the Brethren keep clear of writs & out of the hands of the governor." He also outlined his own tentative plans: "Should danger increase upon me hear [sic]," wrote William, "I shall take measures for my safety in some more distant parts."[81]

He continued this lengthy letter by claiming that a mob at Fort Madison had come together to kill him but he managed to escape through "the prairie full [of] men." At Augusta, he felt that the locals were "raising a mob to come after me at this place" and claimed, "I have received several messages warning me to flee for my life." He does not describe how he learned about the first two mobs (although he obviously believed they existed) nor who the messengers were. "The mob has sworn to kill me & extinguish the whole Smith blood family," he wrote.[82] It is true that Mormon opponents had earlier threatened that, not only should the Latter-day Saints be driven from the state, but also that there should not be a Smith left in the state.[83] William was alert to such threats and, given the turmoil of the times, obviously lacked the resources to appraise how real the danger was, but his letter documents genuine fear.

William also included an important item in his letter to Young, indicating that "[George J.] Adamsit[e]s are scarce & I do not hear from him." Although William denied association with Adams in Augusta, Church leaders in Nauvoo were obviously hesitant about accepting this assurance. On May 23, 1845, William Clayton recorded the Twelve's view that Adams had "organized a church at Augusta, Iowa Territory with young Joseph Smith for President, W[illia]m Smith for Patriarch, Jared Carter for President of the stake and himself for spokesman to Joseph." In truth, if William linked his ambitions with those of Adams, he would certainly have a more prominent role than the one he experienced at Nauvoo. Clayton had noted in May that "W[illiam] Smith is coming out in opposition to the Twelve and in favor of Adams,"[84] but he made no mention of Smith's support of Adams in the intervening months. Despite William's claim in his September 28 letter that

---

79. Glen M. Leonard, *Nauvoo: A Place of Peace, A People of Promise* (Salt Lake City: Deseret Book/Provo, Utah: Brigham Young University Press, 2002), 587–621.

80. Journal History, September 15, 1845, 1.

81. William Smith, Letter to Young or Robbins, September 28, 1845.

82. Ibid.

83. Richards to Young, June 30, 1844; William Smith, "A Proclamation," 1.

84. George D. Smith, *An Intimate Chronicle*, 166.

he was not affiliated with Adams, George A. Smith had learned on September 26 in a letter from James Brown, a Latter day Saint at Augusta who was loyal to Brigham Young, that William was "safely quartered in G[eorge] J. Adams house in Augusta."[85] "William Smith is in Augusta," Brown had written to Young, and "what his business is I have to guess[.] He has stopped with a decenter [dissenter] that is living in G. J. Adams House." Brown also contradicted William's claim that he was giving patriarchal blessings to Iowa Saints: "He hasent visited any of the Brethren that I can learn." Furthermore, Jared Carter and a member of the Gibbs family, whom Brown had earlier identified as devoted followers of Adams, "has bin [been] round among the people to raise means to build William Smith a house in Augusta."[86] Though William did not stay long enough for those plans to materialize, the conflicting statements indicate that he was at a crossroads and likely did not fully comprehend the magnitude of his pending decision. Ultimately, as he acknowledged in his "Proclamation," "the feeling that I have been wronged and abused, is struggling for the mastery."[87] He allowed that feeling to prevail and stayed away from Nauvoo.

William Smith's decision to break away from the main body of the Saints was the hinge upon which the rest of his life turned. Yet he could not accept being part of the Mormon community when he felt that it would require him to accept diminished status and authority. While leaders at Nauvoo knew that Smith was unhappy with events related to his station, they did not foresee how far he would go in seeking retaliation. His family seemed as confused at his precipitous departure as everyone else. Samuel W. Richards later recalled a conversation with Lucy Mack Smith at Nauvoo that same fall in which she referred "to the course of another son [William], which had not been so much in harmony with her wishes, but had caused her much anxiety and sorrow, because of his waywardness. Calling him by name" remembered Richards, she then declared with unconscious irony: "'He has endeared himself to me by the trouble he has made me.'"[88]

During the sustaining of Church officers at the October general conference held on October 6, William's name was presented as one of the Twelve. Parley P. Pratt promptly objected, indicating that he could not "conscientiously, uphold and sustain Brother William as one of the Twelve Apostles" because he had "proof positive that he is an aspiring man; that he aspires to uproot and undermine the legal Presidency of the Church that he may occupy the place himself." Pratt con-

---

85. George A. Smith, "History of George A. Smith," September 26, 1845, 113, George A. Smith Papers, MS 1322, Box 1, fd. 1, LDS Church History Library.

86. James Brown (Augusta, Iowa Territory), Letters to Brigham Young, September 24, 1845, and June 13, 1845, both in Brigham Young Office Files 1832–78, General Correspondence, Incoming, 1840–1877, General Letters, 1840–77, Be-Br, 1845, LDS Church History Library.

87. William Smith, "A Proclamation," 1.

88. Lucy Mack Smith, quoted by Samuel W. Richards, "The Duty of Marriage," *Contributor* 13, no. 4 (February 1892): 167.

tinued, "In the second place, while Brother William was in the east, to my certain knowledge, his doctrine and conduct have not had a savory influence; but have produced death and destruction wherever he went. This also I am well prepared to prove. I have been waiting in all long suffering for an alteration in Brother William's course but up to the present time I have been disappointed. For these two reasons I would plead for one, that we no longer sustain him in his office till a proper investigation can be had, and he make satisfaction."[89]

Other leaders were cognizant of William's defiant public statements, his erratic behavior during the preceding summer, his over-enthusiastic embrace of polygamy, and his current association with the flagrant apostate George J. Adams. Pratt's objection was immediately seconded, and the conference body unanimously withdrew fellowship from Smith as one of the Twelve and as Church Patriarch. Notwithstanding the decision of the conference, Church leaders assumed that Smith would return shortly and that the issues between them would be resolved. Two days later on October 8 when Brigham Young was preaching to the conference, he commented that William "has run away in a time of trouble; but I suppose will come back when it is peace."[90] Young misjudged Smith, as he would soon learn.

It is not clear when or how William learned that the conference had rejected him as apostle and patriarch in what amounted to a withdrawal of fellowship. But at that point, it likely was not a factor in his decision to write an antagonistic pamphlet. Rather, the conference's approval of Pratt's motion only confirmed the path he had already chosen, adding vitality to his course. With the assistance of George J. Adams, Smith produced a lengthy sixteen-page pamphlet titled "A Proclamation," denouncing the Twelve. He then traveled 180 miles up the Mississippi River to the bustling lead-mining city of Galena, Illinois. Here he printed 500 copies on one of the town's printing presses at a cost of $40 and sent copies "to all [the] newspaper editors that I could think of," including the *St. Louis Republican* and the *Warsaw Signal*.[91]

The bitterness that had been building since Pratt had replaced him in the East, along with the turmoil of his station that had occurred during the summer of 1845, came spewing out in Smith's publication. Smith included in his pamphlet his version of being supplanted as president over the eastern branches, the murder of Ervine Hodges (in which he implicated the Nauvoo police and Brigham Young), threatening elements connected with the June 25 meeting at the Masonic Hall, the tussle over the scope of his patriarchal authority, and what he considered the scorn with which Church leaders had treated his mother's revelation on the anniversary of the martyrdoms. While he spoke disparagingly

---

89. Parley P. Pratt, quoted in "Conference Minutes," *Times and Seasons* 6, no. 16 (November 1, 1845): 1008.

90. Brigham Young, quoted in ibid., 1014.

91. William Smith Testimony, Temple Lot Case Testimonies, 186, U.S. Eighth Circuit Court, 1892, MS 1160, LDS Church History Library.

William Smith's "Proclamation," as published on the entire front page of Thomas C. Sharp's *Warsaw Signal*, October 29, 1845.

about several of his apostolic colleagues, including Parley P. Pratt, John Taylor, and Willard Richards, he reserved his most venomous attack for Brigham Young. "I will state unequivocally at the outset," William began his pamphlet, "that it is my firm and sincere conviction, that, since the murder of my two brothers, usurpation and anarchy . . . have crept into the church. . . . Under the reign of one whom I may call a Pontius Pilate, under the reign I say of this B. Young, no greater tyranny ever existed since the days of Nero." At variance with his earlier views, Smith declared that Young held no superior position over any other member of the Twelve. "What, my brethren, I would ask you, are the claims of Brigham Young to the keys above the rest of the Twelve?" Smith queried. "They are keys which Joseph never conferred on Brigham Young, nor was power ever given to him to lead the church in his place as his successor." Rather disingenuously, Smith included an exposé of polygamy, disclosing that "Brigham Young, H. C. Kimball, and Willard Richards" all had "several houses filled up with women who have been secretly married to [them]." He also outlined his shifting view of succession, promoting the "rights of the Smith family," including mentioning for the first time publicly the right of "little Joseph [Smith III], the son of Joseph Smith [as] . . . the lawful heir to the office, being the oldest son of the deceased prophet." He concluded his pamphlet by threatening an independent course: "The Twelve did not ordain me one of their number, nor decree my lineage in the Smith family, and I shall never suffer myself to be controlled by Brigham Young or any of his coadjutors."[92]

When copies of his tract reached Nauvoo on October 15, Church leaders were stunned at William's accusations and disclosures. They felt that William was not only guilty of "abusing" both "President B. Young," but also the entire "12 and the church."[93] Authorities at Nauvoo were further appalled that Smith sent

---

92. William Smith, "A Proclamation," 1, 4.

93. Thomas Bullock, Journal, October 15, 1845, in Greg R. Knight, ed., *Thomas Bullock Nauvoo Journal* (Orem, Utah: Grandin Book, 1994), 19; Juanita Brooks, *On the Mormon*

a number of these pamphlets to Thomas Sharp, unquestionably the fomenter of anti-Mormonism and proposal of the assassinations, and William's former nemesis. Sharp exuberantly gave the entire front page of his *Warsaw Signal* to Smith's contemptuous pamphlet. Sharp, though pleasantly surprised to find an anti-Mormon ally in Smith, remained skeptical of his motives.[94] Orson Hyde wrote William a letter of reaction on October 28 that Sharp, with equal glee, also published. In addition to expressing surprise at the contents of William's pamphlet, Hyde lamented: "And to cap the climax, that you should send a bundle of these pamphlets to Tom Sharp, as if thereby to win the sympathy of the very man whom you have the best reason to believe was the ready instigator of the murder of your brothers. . . . *Wm. that was a cruel thrust.*"[95]

On October 19, extracts from William's "Proclamation" were read to the Twelve, the high council, and a gathering of Saints. The pamphlet was so scornful toward the Twelve that Church leaders felt they must call for an immediate vote on his standing. The gathering unanimously voted to cut William off from the Church, and reportedly not one hand was raised in a contrary vote.[96] In 1850, Hyde, in his own newspaper, the *Frontier Guardian*, summarized the grounds for Smith's excommunication: "[For] a wish to appropriate the public funds of the church to his own private use—for publishing false and slanderous statements concerning the church: and for a general looseness and recklessness of character which ill comported with the dignity of his high calling."[97]

William's abandonment of Nauvoo marked the end of a turbulent summer for Smith. He had clashed with his brethren of the Twelve on a variety of issues, including the scope of his authority as the presiding patriarch, control of the Nauvoo police, the handling of the Hodges brothers' crimes, and his audacious and coarse public sermon on plural marriage. In a matter of four months, he had managed to alienate the confidence of almost all of the Saints at Nauvoo. Yet his familial connection meant that he still possessed great influence among many of the Saints who were scattered throughout the branches of the Church in remote regions in the East and Midwest. These were the individuals Smith would seek out in the ensuing decade.

Frontier: The Diary of Hosea Stout, 1844–1861, 2 vols. (Salt Lake City: University of Utah Press, 1964), 1:85.

94. "Proclamation of Bill Smith," 2.

95. Hyde to William Smith, October 28, 1845, in *Warsaw Signal* 2, no. 36 (November 26, 1845): 1; italics in original.

96. Orson Hyde, "William Smith," *Frontier Guardian*, 2, no. 1 (February 6, 1850): 2; Orson Hyde (Nauvoo, Ill.), Letter to Samuel Brannan, October 20, 1845, in *New-York Messenger* 2, no. 19 (November 8, 1845): 8.

97. Hyde, "William Smith," 2.

Chapter 14

"Ho! For Voree":
Strangite Apostle and Patriarch

> I go in for honors now days as well as rights.
> —William B. Smith, 1846

With the flamboyant George J. Adams in tow, William successfully published his pamphlet, titled "A Proclamation" at Galena, Illinois, in early October 1845. While it was being printed, Smith formed part of the audience before whom Adams performed in a theatrical play in the city. Writing on October 8 to David Rogers, a Latter-day Saint whom William and Adams had known in the East, and who was still in New York, Smith recounted, "I am happy to tell you this evening while I am penning this short note that our old friend Adams has a splendid performance in this city entitled Lady of Lyons.[1] He played to a full house last evening [and] he thinks of continuing one month." Adams's dynamic performances attracted "crowded congregations," an interesting slip of the mind for William, who was accustomed to religious gatherings rather than dramatic ones.[2]

Rogers turned his letter over to Orson Pratt, the presiding authority in the East during the time of Smith's excommunication, who made a copy which he sent to Church authorities at Nauvoo, thus keeping them apprised of William's movements. Because Smith referred to his "Proclamation" and forewarned Rogers that there would be a "gathering . . . of old friends" in the East, Church leaders inserted a notice in both the *New-York Messenger* and *Times and Seasons* warning the eastern Saints against Smith's intentions. Apostle Orson Pratt further cautioned Saints in the region: "If after all the instruction you have received, you suffer yourselves to be influenced and led away by apostates, such as Rigdon, Adams,

---

1. Terminal punctuation added. The play *Lady of Lyons* was a five-act romantic melodrama written in 1838 by Edward Bulwer Lytton. It formed the basis for the opera *Leonora* [1845] by William Henry Fry, which was "the first publicly performed opera with continuous music by a native American composer." Edward Bulwer Lytton, *The Lady of Lyons; or, Love and Pride*; Donald Jay Grout and Hermine Weigel Williams, *A Short History of Opera*, 4th ed. (New York: Columbia University Press, 2003), 570.

2. William Smith (Galena, Ill.), Letter to Brother [David] Roggers [sic], October 8, 1845, copied by Orson Pratt and sent to Brigham Young, Brigham Young Office Files, Letters from Church Leaders and Others, 1840–1877, William Smith, 1844–1857, LDS Church History Library.

Galena, Illinois, ca. 1852. Photographer unknown. Courtesy Galena & U.S. Grant Museum, Galena, Illinois.

William Smith, and others who have been legally cut off from the church—your sins shall be upon your own heads."[3]

Adams's earnings as an actor likely provided the $40 with which Smith published and distributed 500 copies of his pamphlet to newspapers throughout the state and beyond, as well as paying his own passage downriver to St. Louis.[4] Smith indicated in his letter to Rogers that his pamphlet would be ready for distribution by October 10, and he undoubtedly left within days of its mailing.[5]

Smith boarded a steamboat at Galena, where he traveled south on the Mississippi River, probably disembarking near Rock Island, Illinois. From there he traveled forty overland miles to Walnut Grove (Altona), Illinois, where he left his daughters in the care of their Grant grandparents, Joshua and Athalia, and their aunt Roxey Ann. A week earlier, in a letter he had written to his friend Lewis Robbins on October 5, William had expressed his intention "to take my children to

---

3. The warning was published by editor Samuel Brannan as "Beware of Strong Delusion, Lest Ye Believe a Lie and Be Damned," *New-York Messenger* 2, no. 20 (November 15, 1845): 5; rpt. under the same heading in *Times and Seasons* 6, no. 18 (December 1, 1845): 6–7. The quotation is from "Farewell Message of Orson Pratt," November 8, 1845 (New York City), Letter to *New-York Messenger* 2, no. 20 (November 15, 1845): 1.

4. William Smith, Testimony, Temple Lot Case Testimonies, 185–86, U.S. Eighth Circuit Court, 1892, MS 1160, LDS Church History Library.

5. William Smith, Letter to [David] Roggers [sic], October 8, 1845.

father Grants."⁶ After a brief stop at the Grants, who probably had not yet learned of William's disaffection, he headed southwest, traveling through Galesburg, Illinois, back toward the Mississippi River. At some point on the river he caught the steamboat *Di Vernon* in order to continue his trip south, paying $3.00 for passage to St. Louis. He was joined en route by several other Saints after the steamer stopped near Nauvoo. They included George B. Wallace, whom Smith had met in the Eastern States Mission and who had testified at Samuel Brannan's trial in Nauvoo. In his journal on the weekend of October 18–19, Wallace recorded details of a conversation with his former colleague as they traveled downriver toward St. Louis. During this trip, which usually took about a day and a half, William "revealed to me his plans of operation," recorded Wallace. Those plans included his intention to stop in St. Louis and "to hold a conference, then [he was] going east."⁷

While the *Di Vernon* had been docked near Nauvoo, William communicated his intentions to Jenkins Salisbury, perhaps through a messenger. Salisbury had successfully urged Smith's surreptitious departure from the city September 12 because his life was at risk in Nauvoo. Now Salisbury also professed apprehensions about his own safety. He fled from Nauvoo for St. Louis within a month of receiving William's communication, leaving his wife, Katharine, and children behind him. For the next few months, he became Smith's most ardent supporter in the extended Smith family.⁸

Smith's self-justifying "Proclamation" in the *Warsaw Signal* had cost him his Church membership and, once published, took on a life of its own. Samuel Brannan, who had been a core member of Smith's leadership trio in the East during 1843–45, dismissed the "Proclamation" as "actuated by purely selfish motives alone, for his own personal emolument; and aggrandizement, at the sacrifice of the lives of his best friends, and the defamation of the character of the whole church; . . . [E]ven if true,"

---

6. William Smith, Letter to Lewis Robbins, October 5, 1845, handwritten copy in Brigham Young Office Files, 1832–78, Letter from Church Leaders and Others, 1840–1877, William Smith, 1844–1857, LDS Church History Library.

7. George Benjamin Wallace, Journals, October 18–19, and 23, 1845, MS 22868, LDS Church History Library; E. W. Gould, *Fifty Years on the Mississippi; or, Gould's History of River Navigation*, 513, identifies this steamboat as the first *Di Vernon*, which made its maiden voyage in the fall of 1842. A second *Di Vernon* or *Die Vernon* steamboat was built in 1850.

8. Salisbury was in St. Louis by at least November 12, 1845, and probably earlier. William Smith (St. Louis, Mo.), Letter to Orson Hyde, November 12, 1845, in *Warsaw Signal* 2, no. 36 (November 26, 1845): 2. See also William Small (St. Louis, Mo.), Letter to Benjamin Winchester, November 24, 1845, in *Messenger and Advocate of the Church of Christ* 2, no. 2 (December 1845): 7–8; and Katharine Salisbury (Fountain Green, Ill.), Letter to Dear Friend, February 26, 1889, P19, f 46, typescript copy in the Community of Christ Archives, Independence, Mo. In early April 1846, Jenkins Salisbury wrote a letter to Thomas Sharp, editor of the *Warsaw Signal*, denouncing the Twelve and justifying his efforts to flee Nauvoo to save his own life the previous year. His letter to Thomas Sharp, published in the *Warsaw Signal* 3, no. 2 (April 8, 1846): 2, claimed: "A Brighamite of high standing with his master, being influenced towards me by feeling of personal friendship, warned me not to stay in this county [Hancock] through the summer on peril of my life."

concluded Brannan, it was "unchristianlike," because it brought "persecution and affliction upon the innocent."[9] Certainly Brannan was in harmony with Nauvoo leaders, who vehemently denounced Smith's exposé. Orson Hyde, writing to Brannan on October 20, 1845, reported a consensus among Church authorities that Smith's pamphlet "contained the most wicked and malicious falsehoods of apostacy that has ever gone out of the Church."[10] These misrepresentations, enhanced by his status as an apostle and as the only surviving brother of his prophet-brother, intrigued Saints who lived in outlying branches of the Church who were interested in Smith's perspective on succession and gave weight to his views.

Smith landed at St. Louis on Sunday evening, October 19, 1845, and he was joined by Adams and Salisbury in mid-November.[11] In an attempt to garner support, the three men began to energetically publicize their disclosures against the Twelve. Due to its location and commercial prominence, St. Louis became a way-station for many Latter-day Saints both before and after Joseph Smith's death. St. Louis "played two important roles in Mormon history," summarized one historian, "as a city of refuge and as an emigrant center. As a large and tolerant city, it gave protection to Mormons in the 1830s when they fled persecution in western Missouri and to the refugees from Illinois mobs in the mid-1840s."[12] Hundreds of Mormons traveled to the booming port city to earn enough money to make their way west, while others, who were disaffected from the main body led by Brigham Young, hoped to start over in St. Louis. As a result, as one St. Louis Saint described, the city had become "the first [place] where apostates vomit their venom and explode their spleen."[13] Smith had been preceded in his course by such notable dissidents as Sidney Rigdon, who penned a lengthy letter outlining his differences with leaders at Nauvoo, while laying over at St. Louis on his way to Pennsylvania in September 1844, and John C. Bennett, who compiled his *The History of the Saints* at St. Louis, preached against leaders at Nauvoo at some of the same venues that Smith would occupy.[14] William, who had passed

---

9. Samuel Brannan, quoted in "New York Conference," *Times and Seasons* 6, no. 17 (November 15, 1845): 13–14.

10. Orson Hyde (Nauvoo, Ill.), Letter to Samuel Brannan, October 20, 1845, in *New York Messenger* 2, no. 19 (November 8, 1845): 8.

11. Wallace, Journal, October 19, 1845. William Small indicated that Adams and Smith first preached together in St. Louis on November 16, 1845, though William had been preaching in the city prior to that date. William Small, Letter to Benjamin Winchester, November 24, 1845.

12. Stanley B. Kimball, "The Saints and St. Louis, 1831–1857: An Oasis of Tolerance and Security," *BYU Studies* 13, no. 4 (Summer 1973): 490.

13. James Kay (St. Louis, Mo.), Letter to Dear Brother Ward, February 10, 1846, in *Millennial Star* 7, no. 9 (May 1, 1846): 135–37, quoted in Kimball, "The Saints and St. Louis," 491.

14. In January 1843 Bennett preached in the Lyceum Hall, admission fee: twelve and a half cents per person. Smith preached in the same building in November 1845 and charged the same amount as Bennett. Rigdon had stopped in the city in September 1844, long enough to publish a lengthy letter outlining his opposition to the Twelve, which several St. Louis newspapers printed. Kimball, "The Saints and St. Louis," 496–97, 501.

St. Louis, Missouri, 1853. Engraving by Frederick Piercy, *Route From Liverpool to Great Salt Lake Valley* (Liverpool: Franklin D. Richards, 1855).

through the city often, knew about its importance to various groups of Latter-day Saints. Smarting from his rejection in 1845, he became increasingly bitter toward those who he felt were responsible for repeated injustices and followed up his virulent pamphlet with an extensive preaching campaign against leaders at Nauvoo.

William Small, a follower of Sidney Rigdon, documented that "William lectured four nights at the Mechanic's Institute, to tolerable large audiences," during the week of November 9–15, just prior to Adams's arrival in the city. Then on Sunday, November 16, Small recounted that "Adams and William lectured three times . . . to overflowing congregations."[15] Smith and Adams launched a series of lectures with the admission price of twenty-five cents. Their combined efforts almost immediately attracted coverage in a local newspaper that headlined its report, "Grand Flare-up in the Mormon Church in St. Louis."[16] James Kay, a Latter-day Saint still loyal to the Twelve, attended these lectures and summarized: William "contends the church is disorganized, having no head, that the twelve are not, nor ever were, ordained to be head of the church, that Joseph's priesthood was to be conferred on his posterity to all future generations, and that young Joseph [III] is the only legal successor to the presidency of this church."[17] It was not the first time William had presented himself as an advocate for his nephew's

---

15. William Small, Letter to Benjamin Winchester, November 24, 1845.

16. "Grand Flare-up in the Mormon Church in St. Louis," *People's Organ,* November 21, 1845, quoted in Kimball, "The Saints and St. Louis," 503; "Trouble in the Mormon Camp," *Warsaw Signal* 2, no. 36 (November 26, 1845): 2.

17. James Kay (St. Louis, Mo.), Letter to Brother Ward, November 22, 1845, *Millennial Star* 7, no. 9 (May 1, 1846): 134–35.

lineal right to lead the Church, but his preaching in St. Louis was the first time he had done so in public and had linked Joseph III to his plan.[18] As usual, he did so without the approval or consent of either young Joseph or Emma.

William had begun promoting the concept of lineal rights in his "Proclamation" published in October 1845, and specifically mentioned Joseph Smith III. William declared that "I have faith in the doctrine of legal descent, lineage & blood," and certainly included himself when he remonstrated against leaders at Nauvoo for "depriving his [Joseph Smith's] lineal successors of the right to teach and direct the church and correct evils."[19] The first time that the documentary record shows William expressing his view that Joseph III would become Church president was on August 20, 1845. Writing to Jesse C. Little from Nauvoo, William expressed his belief that "little Joseph" would be "his fathers successor although some people would fain make us believe that the Twelve are to be the perpetual heads of this church to the exclusion of the Smith family."[20] The lineal argument was persuasive for three reasons: (1) It clarified confusion by sweeping aside legalistic claims, arguments, and reports of events that took place secretly, especially the rapid evolution of leadership developments during the previous year; (2) It spoke to the Saints' longing to recapture some of the charismatic father's "glow" through his son; and (3) While Americans had politically renounced a monarchy, it still appealed to many of them, especially with the waves of British converts who arrived with every ship.

St. Louis newspapers, however, viewed William's stories and views with a jaundiced eye. One reporter wrote, "with regard to the lecturer, Smith, now in town, there is one common sense fact which strikes us, and that is, that could he find an audience in Nauvoo, he would not now be seeking one in St. Louis."[21] Another article poked fun at William's old-fashioned speaking style: "that peculiarly effective sing-song and nasal character which distinguished the primitive reformers." The writer extracted a portion of William's sermon delivered on Tuesday, October 28, 1845, in the hall of the Mechanics' Institute: "Ses I to Brigham Young, ses I, 'How is it a-going to be about the young Joseph, who should, in right, be the head of the church, as his father and family have stood the brunt [of] the storm?' Ses he, ses Brigham Young, 'If we go to preachin' young Joseph now, these enemies on our borders will shoot the young prophet as they did his father;' and so they set the head of the church aside, and ever since it ain't bin gittin' along at all!"[22]

---

18. William Smith, "A Proclamation," *Warsaw Signal* 2, no. 32 (October 29, 1845): 1, 4.
19. Ibid., 1.
20. William Smith, Letter to Jesse C. Little, August 20, 1845 (Nauvoo, Ill.), typescript by Ireta Anderson, November 16, 1936, Utah State Historical Society.
21. "The Mormons—Oregon," *Weekly Reveille* (St. Louis, Mo.) 2, no. 17 (November 3, 1845): 1.
22. "Mormonism—The Young Joseph!" *Weekly Reveille* (St. Louis, Mo) 2, no. 17 (November 3, 1845): 1; reproduced in "Mormon Oratory," *True American* (Lexington, Ky.) 1, no. 19 (November 25, 1845): 1.

James Kay was surprised that Smith successfully influenced LDS branch president James Riley to support his claims, as Riley had, previous to Smith's arrival, outspokenly announced that he would "fellowship no man unless he publicly protested to obey and uphold the twelve as the rightful authorities of the church."[23] Riley apparently went to Nauvoo to investigate some of William Smith's claims, which certainly included William's disclosures regarding the practice of polygamy at Nauvoo. His short visit must have brought shocking disclosures, for Riley returned to St. Louis "a bitter enemy to the Church."[24] Within weeks of Smith, Adams, and Salisbury's arrival, the LDS branch at St. Louis was teetering on the verge of collapse. According to Kay, "Two high priests were disfellowshipped, one seventy, and a number of other officers from this branch I suppose will join the Smith party."[25]

Despite the effectiveness of Smith and Adams's preaching, the two men were not completely unified in their views. Adams apparently still held some negative feelings toward Joseph Smith for disfellowshipping him in 1843 when it was discovered that he had been guilty of adultery.[26] In one of his St. Louis sermons,

---

23. Kay to Ward, February 10, 1846.

24. This account comes from Thomas Wrigley, who remained loyal to Brigham Young and the Twelve while residing at St. Louis during the time William Smith preached in the city and afterward. Kate B. Carter, *The Mormons in St. Louis* (Salt Lake City: Daughters of Utah Pioneers, 1962), 97.

25. Kay to Ward, February 10, 1846. According to Stanley B. Kimball: "The *People's Organ* of November reported that on Wednesday 19 November, at the regular meeting in the Mechanics Institute someone publicly 'denied the spiritual right of the Twelve to the patriarchal government and accused the Twelve of robbery, assassination, and adultery.' The chairman tried to stop the proceedings, but was prevented from doing so by many shouts of 'Sit down, let him speak, privilege, go on . . . etc.' According to the reporter, one of the denunciators was a 'Brother Riley.'" Quoted in Kimball, "The Saints and St. Louis," 503–4.

26. Non-Mormon Charlotte Haven reported in 1843 that Adams "returned from a two years' mission in England, bringing with him a wife and a child, although he had left a wife and family here when he went away." Charlotte Haven (Nauvoo, Ill.), Letter to My dear friends at home, September 8, 1843, in William Mulder and A. Russell Mortensen, eds., *Among the Mormons* (New York: Alfred A. Knopf, 1958), 126–27. In a letter Adams had written to Joseph Smith in February 1843, he halfheartedly acknowledged his wrongdoing: "Whatever I have done, you know, and you also know I have sincerely repented months ago." He then implored the Prophet, "Now, my dear Brother, if you can save me without a public trial, I trust I will never forget it while memory lasts." Notwithstanding his plea, Joseph mandated that "Elder Geo. J. Adams be silenc[e]d & called to Nauvoo with his family." Adams confessed to adultery in May and was restored to fellowship, but his reputation came under closer scrutiny from that point up to and including his excommunication in the spring of 1845. (See Chapter 11.) George J. Adams (Boston, Mass.), Letter to Joseph Smith, February 23, 1843, in Journal History, February 23, 1843, 1–2; John S. Dinger, ed., *The Nauvoo City and High Council Minutes* (Salt Lake City: Signature Books, 2011), 470–71. Joseph Smith, Journal, February 10, 1843, in Andrew H. Hedges, Alex D. Smith, and Richard Lloyd Anderson, eds., ournals, Volume 2: December 1841–April 1843, THE JOSEPH SMITH PAPERS, general Editors Dean C.

Adams stated that he "would not spoil a good story for relation's sake." Glancing at William sitting behind him on the stand, Adams baldly stated that Joseph, just before leaving for Carthage, confessed to Adams that if he "had hearkened to the councils of my God and kept his commandments, I should not have been in the situation I am in now; if I had laid aside my drums, and fifes, and guns, swords, and pistols, and attended to my calling, this people should have been a glorious people." Whether his story was true, embellished for effect, or made up out of the whole cloth, Adams clearly implied that Joseph was a fallen prophet, seduced by his own fantasies of power. Adams's rhetoric resembled the "fallen prophet" claims that Rigdonite adherents were then promoting in the city.[27]

Although William did not denounce or correct Adams, he could not condone such a view, instead consistently asserting that Joseph was not a fallen prophet. For his part, Adams was also reluctant to formally organize according to Smith's design. Notwithstanding these differences, the two men found common ground in denouncing the Twelve. "We have had W. Smith and G. J. Adams lecturing and showing the corruptions and iniquities of the people at Nauvoo," reported William Small in an account that was later published in Sidney Rigdon's newspaper. "They have caused much excitement, and many of the twelveites have separated themselves, and now begin to open their eyes." As an example of their success, he reported on a meeting held on Thursday November 20, "in the Lyceum Hall, to a respectable audience of about five hundred." While their preaching caused great excitement and some disruption among all branches of Mormonism in the city, relatively few ended up actually embracing Smith's views. At one point in his lecture, Smith asked those opposed to the Twelve to stand, "when some twenty arose."[28] This bare handful (assuming that a significant number were not willing to take a public stand) likely included at least some Rigdon supporters, who would have opposed the Twelve, but who were not necessarily in favor of Smith.

In accordance with his earlier threat to Church authorities at Nauvoo, William also attempted to rally his mother and remaining siblings with his repeated declaration that the Twelve had undermined "Smith family rights."[29] Jenkins Salisbury traveled back and forth between St. Louis and Nauvoo, becoming Smith's messenger in communicating his views to the extended Smith family. At some point, Salisbury likely brought William's daughters with him to the city, since they were

---

Jessee, Ronald K. Esplin, and Richard Lyman Bushman (Salt Lake City: Church Historian's Press, 2011), 259, see especially 259 note 383.

27. In fact, this account of Adams's lecture was reported by Rigdonite follower William Small, in Letter to Benjamin Winchester, in *Messenger and Advocate of the Church of Christ*, November 24, 1845, 407–8.

28. Ibid.

29. William Smith, "Proclamation," 1; William Smith, Letter to Lewis Robbins, October 5, 1845.

"Ho! For Voree": Strangite Apostle and Patriarch   315

Wilkins Jenkins Salisbury, 1809–1853. Daguerreotype photograph taken ca. 1850, photographer unknown. Courtesy Mary Dennis. Photograph of original by Kyle R. Walker.

with William in late November when he left St. Louis for Cincinnati.[30] Salisbury also informed William that Emma Smith's support had waned. Almost certainly, her sympathies had dissolved when William preached his sermon on polygamy at Nauvoo in August, but William had apparently been too consumed with his ongoing conflict with Church leaders to notice. William hastily wrote to his sister-in-law on November 21: "Judge my serprise Emma when you now refuse to help me reform the Church after the many times I have talked with you on this Subject and asked what I Should do to save my fathers family . . . and the answer was to Come out and proclame against the Spiritual wife doctrin[e] [and] the usurpation of the 12."[31] William also defended himself, albeit quite awkwardly, against a report that William's brother-in-law, Jedediah M. Grant, had picked up in St. Louis and taken to Nauvoo. This embarrassing report was that William was living with Elizabeth Weston, an unmarried woman, at St. Louis. In nineteenth-century terms, the fact alone of sharing living quarters would have been evidence of immoral behavior. Jedediah certainly thought so. William protested that, a month earlier when he reached St. Louis, he had moved in with William Weston, an acquaintance from his years in Plymouth, Illinois. However, within a week or so of his arrival, Weston and his family left St. Louis for New Orleans, leaving behind Weston's sister, Elizabeth. William assured Emma that the family was Catholic, that "the young girl [is] a perfect stranger to me," and that "no woman affairs Shall—entangle me or hinder my work."[32] William's explanation probably meant little to Emma, as she had already decided to distance herself and her sons from William's aspirations.

Hoping to expand his influence, William left his small band of followers at St. Louis under the leadership of Jenkins Salisbury, and by the latter part of November, he, his daughters, and Adams were traveling east to Cincinnati, Ohio.[33] William

---

30. In a letter written on January 27, 1846, to Lewis Robbins, William said, "I have my little girles with me." William Smith (Cincinnati, Ohio), Letter to Lewis Robbins, January 29, 1846, Brigham Young Collection, 1832–78, General Correspondence, Incoming, 1840–77, LDS Church History Library.

31. William Smith (St. Louis, Mo.), Letter to Emma Smith, [November] 21, 1845, LDS Church History Library.

32. Ibid.; see also the discussion in Irene M. Bates and E. Gary Smith, *Lost Legacy: The Mormon Office of Presiding Patriarch* (Urbana: University of Illinois Press, 1996), 93–94.

33. Small to Winchester, November 24, 1845, 407–8.

recounted, "I followed several months lecturing and giving expositions of the different principles of our faith at different places," which included the two river-port cities. He indicated that he targeted these cities because they were locations where he had previously "been successful in making converts to the faith."[34] In their advertisement for preaching, the two men occasionally sought to heighten interest by disclosing details about the practice of "spiritual wifery" at Nauvoo in lectures at which "ladies will not be admitted."[35] Accordingly, word about these lectures spread quickly through the city.

William's new proselytizing followed the pattern he had already established. In 1835 during his conflict with his brother Joseph in Kirtland, he had quickly tried to polarize the Smith family and others who would listen to his version of the quarrel. In 1845 after his break from the Twelve, he detailed his opposition in his lengthy "Proclamation," sending copies "to all these newspaper editors that I could think of" and traveling to St. Louis and Cincinnati, two major Mormon outposts, to find sympathizers.[36] While publishing his opposition gave his views widespread dissemination, it also gave time for Church authorities to deflect his influence among the eastern branches. Due to his inflated self-importance, Smith rashly confided his intentions to some of his former associates. Writing to a former colleague in October 1845, Smith mentioned his intention to visit Saints in the east who had better "lay low for the Black ducks[37] for in the fall of the year ther[e] is a dreadful coming or gathering of old friends."[38] Smith assumed his former colleagues would join his effort, but most remained loyal to Brigham Young and ended up reporting the contents of William's letters to Brigham Young and other Church authorities.[39]

In an article published in the *Times and Seasons*, leaders responded to William's threats: "We would respectfully give notice to those reverend gentlemen, that while we 'are looking out for black ducks,' they had better look for Yankee girls, for they might find their match." Referencing Smith and Adams's loose version of plural marriage during their mission among the eastern branches, the article continued, "Wounded virtue has not been healed, and might require a balm. We would say there are letters and documents in the hands of elders in the east, of Wm. Smith's writing, that should cause a reign of silence, at least for the space of a half an

---

34. William Smith, Testimony, Temple Lot Case Testimonies, 185–86, U.S. Eighth Circuit Court, 1892, MS 1160, LDS Church History Library.

35. "Trouble in the Mormon Camp," 2; *Cincinnati Daily Commercial*, quoted in Andrew F. Smith, *The Saintly Scoundrel: The Life and Times of Dr. John Cook Bennett* (Urbana: University of Illinois Press, 1997), 146.

36. William Smith, Testimony, 185–86.

37. This was likely a hunting reference. Ducks migrated in the fall and hunters would "lay low for black ducks" in order to have a better shot at their target.

38. William Smith, Letter to Roggers [sic], October 8, 1845.

39. "Beware of Strong Delusion," 1045–46.

hour."⁴⁰ It was a direct warning that undermined William's course by pointing out his hypocrisy in preaching against "spiritual wifery." It was also Brigham Young's most explicit warning that William was in no position to denounce polygamy.

Samuel Brannan, who continued to edit the Church's newspaper in New York, also weighed in on William's threat. Brannan had a particular dislike for Smith because he felt that Smith had duped him, leading to his being briefly excommunicated. In a letter to Brigham Young on October 9, Brannan predicted that, "if he wishes to keep himself from trouble, shame, and disgrace, that if he has any feeling for the character of his family, and his martyred brethren, that he stay where he is, or go where he is not known. For we, the church in New York, have no desire to see him, unless he repent speedily." Highlighting William's willingness to live off the Saints' charity, he added that, if William "comes into this country . . . he will have to go to work on the dock rolling molas[s]es or else starve."⁴¹

Another leader in the East who had earlier associated with Smith was William I. Appleby, president of the Recklesstown Branch in New Jersey. In September, a few weeks before Smith's excommunication, Appleby recorded, "I dreamed Joseph the Martyred Prophet came to me" with what he described as an inspired warning. "He sat down in a chair fronting me, near by, with a writing in his hand; he commenced instructing and counselling me, with tears rolling down his cheeks, [warned me] never to find fault, no[r] lift my hand against the Servants of God." A month later, Appleby received a packet of William's pamphlets, which he interpreted as the fulfillment of Joseph's warning to remain loyal to the Twelve. He warned his branch against Smith and succeeded in blocking William from drawing away members of his branch and assuring their commitment to the Twelve.⁴²

Although William probably planned to go to New York, he made it only as far east as Cincinnati where he met up with the disreputable John C. Bennett, who had been lecturing about the health benefits of the tomato, medicine, and surgery at the Botanico-Medical College in the city. Rumors had earlier linked William with Bennett during Bennett's amorous adventures in Nauvoo in 1842. After Joseph Smith's death, Bennett expressed interest in uniting with some branch of Mormonism but did not initially support William's leadership. While Bennett claimed to hold William in high regard, he rejected William's proposal

---

40. Ibid., 1046–47. He was probably alluding to Revelations 8:1: "And when he had opened the seventh seal, there was silence in heaven about the space of half an hour."

41. Samuel Brannan (New York), Letter to Brigham Young, October 9, 1845, LDS Church History Library; "New York Conference," *Times and Seasons* 6, no. 17 (November 15, 1845): 13–14. Brigham Young Office Files 1832–1878, General Correspondence, Incoming, 1840–1877, General Letters, 1840–1877, Be-Br, 1845, Church History Library.

42. William I. Appleby, Autobiography and Journal, September 19 and October 30, 1845, 148–49, MS 1401, fd. 1, LDS Church History Library; Stephen J. Fleming, "'Sweeping Everything before It': Early Mormonism in the Pine Barrens of New Jersey," *BYU Studies* 40, no. 1 (2001): 89.

to form part of his First Presidency.⁴³ Lacking full support from either Adams or Bennett, William moved ahead with an organization attempt by holding a meeting of a small number of followers on January 6, 1846. Those who linked themselves with Smith's church included William Jarman, James Riley (the former branch president at St. Louis), Jared Carter, and a J. Lewis.

Adams's name was noticeably absent from the minutes, since he had returned to St. Louis to pursue his acting career. Their most pressing difference may have been over William's insistence on defending his prophet-brother's character. William ensured that one of the first resolutions adopted at his organizational meeting had to do with the full acceptance of his brothers: "That, whereas, we, the Church of Jesus Christ of Latter Day Saints, believe that Joseph and Hyram Smith our martyred brothers, lived and died accepted of the Lord." He rejected Sidney Rigdon and George J. Adams's arguments that Joseph had fallen from his lofty calling, either by introducing polygamy or because of his political ambition. Still, Adams's influence showed itself in the organizational meeting, which advocated most of the items that Adams had outlined at Augusta, Iowa, the previous spring. One resolution recognized "Joseph Smith [III], the son of Joseph Smith . . . [as] successor to his father, holding the keys of this dispensation, with power and authority from his father, according to Book of D & C." In addition, those present received William "as the Patriarch, Guardian, and Councillor of the Church, holding the same office and authority as his brother Hyrum." Despite Emma's stony silence, the conference attempted to solicit her support by receiving her "in the Church with all the authority conferred upon her by her husband, and also, as a Councillor in the Church." William published the conference minutes in a one-page handbill formatted like a newspaper and announcing a second conference to be held in St. Louis on April 6, 1846. Here, he hoped to unify the Saints in the two locales and gather additional Saints to support his movement.⁴⁴

The April 6 meeting never took place. Although William had barely laid the groundwork for a church organization, he became distracted by the emergence of James J. Strang, who was having success in gathering up those Mormons who did not support Brigham Young's leadership. Two years younger than William, Strang had been baptized by Joseph Smith at Nauvoo in February 1844. He had been familiar with Mormonism prior to his baptism, as his wife's aunt, Lydia Perce Smith, and her husband, Moses Smith, (no relation to the Joseph Smith family) had joined the Church before 1837 and settled in Burlington, Wisconsin.

---

43. John C. Bennett (Cincinnati, Ohio), Letter to Dear Friend [James Strang], March 28, 1846, Beinecke Library, Yale University, New Haven, Connecticut. Bennett's biographer noted that Bennett wrote to Sidney Rigdon, Dr. Robert Foster, and George Adams during the period after Joseph Smith's death. Many factions of Mormonism were also interested in having Bennett join their movement. Andrew Smith, *The Saintly Scoundrel*, 144–47.

44. *Minutes of a Conference, Held by the Church of Jesus Christ of Latter Day Saints* (Cincinnati, Ohio: William Smith, 1846): 1, photocopy of original in my possession; Kay to Ward, February 10, 1846.

James J. Strang, 1813–1856. Photograph taken ca. 1850, photographer unknown. Courtesy William Shepard, original in collection of John Hajicek.

James and Mary Strang followed in 1843. After his baptism, Strang was commissioned by Hyrum Smith and Sidney Rigdon to explore possible gathering places for the Saints in Wisconsin Territory. Strang claimed that Joseph Smith had written a letter appointing him to be his successor on June 18, 1844, just nine days before the assassinations. Strang was a charismatic leader and bolstered his claims by describing his ordination by angels and discovering and translating plates buried in a hill near his home in Voree, Wisconsin.[45]

William Smith learned of Strang's assertions through the proselyting efforts of Samuel Searls, one of the earliest Strangite missionaries from Eaton County, Michigan, who had arrived in Cincinnati not long after Smith, and preached in the city on February 20, 1846. Many who were disaffected from the Church authorities at Nauvoo found Strang's message attractive. Among them was George J. Adams, who was back in Cincinnati by March, and John C. Bennett. Bennett wrote an editorial for the *Cincinnati Daily Commercial* entitled "Ho! For Voree," reporting that, after Searls arrived in the city, "both branches of the Mormons here, the Rigdonites and Twelveites, disbanded, and all but three [individuals] acknowledged the power and glory of the new Prophet [Strang]." William Smith, who failed to take any additional steps in the direction of further organization, also considered linking his aspirations with the emerging leader. Bennett further recounted, "We presume that William Smith, who has been lecturing here, will join the new Prophet, and Voree will become a second Nauvoo."[46] And in fact, Strang provided a church structure where Smith, Adams, and Bennett eventually—though temporarily—found common ground.

Both Bennett and Adams wrote to Strang that spring and petitioned him to accept their support but also strongly suggested that he should give them prominent positions in his movement. Adams requested that Strang install him as an apostle, while Bennett asked that he be restored to his place in the First Presidency. All three men, Smith, Adams and Bennett, spoke highly of each other in their correspondence with Strang. For example, Bennett wrote glowingly that "William Smith, I do hope and trust, will go up and take his place, for he is

---

45. Vickie Cleverley Speek, *"God Has Made Us a Kingdom": James Strang and the Midwest Mormons* (Salt Lake City: Signature Books, 2006), 15–22; Andrew Smith, *The Saintly Scoundrel*, 146–47.

46. John C. Bennett, "Ho! For Voree," *Voree Herald* 1, no. 3 (March 1846): 2; Andrew Smith, *The Saintly Scoundrel*, 147.

a noble soul. I respect William very highly. He is one of God's noblemen, and my heart's desire and prayer to God is that he may be with us, and one of us. I have written him fully on the subject." In a second letter a few days later, Bennett again expressed support of Strang and encouraged him to write directly to William or send a messenger to proselyte him. Bennett encouraged Strang to offer Smith the patriarchal office and to come to Voree with "his mother, with the mummies and papyrus—[and] the bodies of Joseph and Hyrum." He predicted: "All these things would have an astonishing effect in congregating the people at Voree." Bennett concluded: "Make a desperate effort now, for it is highly important." While the eccentric Bennett went overboard in sketching the disinterment of the Smith brothers' remains, Strang responded attentively to Bennett's other suggestions.[47]

John Cook Bennett, 1804–1867. Engraving from his book *The History of the Saints; or an Expose of Joe Smith and Mormonism* (Boston: Leland & Whiting, 1842).

In addition to Strang's success, William was also preoccupied with the evacuation of Nauvoo by most of the Twelve's followers in February 1846. He had earlier had his eye on Church properties at Nauvoo, publicly scolding Church authorities for attempting to sell the Nauvoo Temple to the Catholic Church,

---

47. For example, Strang, on Bennett's suggestion, changed the name of his paper from the *Voree Herald* to *Zion's Reveille*. Bennett also praised Adams: "Brother Adams is doing up the work most gloriously for you in Cincinnati. He comes down like a blighting tempest upon the factions of the Twelveites and Rigdonites." Similarly, Adams wrote to Strang that "I had much conversation with the Dr [Bennett] and find him a Gentleman in every sense [and] is a varry Strong friend of yours as also the prosperity of Voree and the Church." Adams continued. "I sincerely hope he will take his place in the Church altho he has many varry many inducements to remain in the world. His place is in the Church the Same to the Prophet that Joshua was to Moses, that Joab was to David. I [k]now he will have opisition among his friends but I hope he will come up and take his place like a man of God. . . . No man has ever been appointed in his place in these stations his council and influence and name would under present circumstances be a tower of strength [as] he has great influence over many of the followers of Rigdon, as well as William Smith." John C. Bennett wrote four letters from Cincinnati, Ohio during this period: Letter to James J. Strang, March 24, 1846, Community of Christ Library-Archives; Letter to Dear Friend [James Strang], March 28, 1846; Letter to Dear Brother [James Strang], April 2, 1846; Letter to Dear Brother [James] Strang, March 27, 1846. The latter three holographic letters are part of the James J. Strang Collection, Beinecke Library, Yale University (hereafter cited as Strang Collection).

which William labeled the "mother of harlots."⁴⁸ With most of the Saints now absent from the city, Smith seized upon the opportunity to gather up both property and the remaining Saints to his cause. Jenkins Salisbury, in a letter to Thomas Sharp designed for publication, noted that "Wm. Smith, brother of the late Mormon Prophet, informs me, that he has returned here for the purpose of gathering his family together, with all such of the Mormons as are willing to be guided by his counsel and remove *immediately* out of the state. . . . He furthermore intends by right of his Patriarchal office over that portion of the Mormons which are or can be recognized as the church formerly organized by his brother, to adopt such measures, according to law, as well secure to the real church all *real estate* and other property which rightly belongs to the church."⁴⁹ Just weeks after Brigham Young began leading the vanguard company of pioneer Saints to the West, William moved toward the abandoned city.

The *Warsaw Signal* reported in early March 1846: "The Patriarch Bill Smith passed up the river on Saturday morning last [March 7th]. He was in fine spirits, and seemed to think, now the Twelve are gone, that he can shine at Nauvoo. He says he is in favor of the Saints leaving the City and scattering over the country, but not of emigrating or settling in one body at one spot. He did not seem hostile to Strang," the editor significantly added, and "it may therefore be that he will yet become the Patriarch of Strang's Church."⁵⁰ Thomas Sharp's predictions were remarkably accurate.

After an absence of nearly six months, William reached Nauvoo on Sunday, March 8, 1846. He immediately put the Saints who had remained behind on notice that he had returned and would be a force to be reckoned with. According to Thomas Bullock, William landed at Nauvoo about 2:00 P.M. "with a parcel of drunken rowdies who commenced firing guns in the air and creating a disturbance and alarm." One of these "rowdies" was undoubtedly Jenkins Salisbury, whose son, Solomon Salisbury, recalled that his father had returned from St. Louis in March 1846. As William sauntered through town, he discovered W. W. Phelps's wife, Sally, who was working in her garden. William and W. W. had been good friends prior to William's break from the Twelve. He approached her

---

48. William Smith (St. Louis, Mo.), Letter to Samuel Brannan, November 14, 1845, LDS Church History Library. Also, in the meeting of organization held at Cincinnati, Ohio, the group resolved "that whereas, the present leaders at Nauvoo design to sell or rent the Temple and Church property at Nauvoo, to the Catholics, or others . . . [we] forbid any and all persons, from buying or renting either the Temple, or any Church property at Nauvoo as it will be contested by the original Church, and it is the property of the Saints, not the Twelve; who have no control over it in the absence of the First Presidency." William Smith, *Minutes of a Conference, Held by the Church of Jesus Christ of Latter Day Saints* (Cincinnati, Ohio: William Smith, 1846), 1.

49. W. J[enkins] Salisbury (Nauvoo, Ill.), Letter to Mr. [Thomas] Sharp, *Warsaw Signal* 3, no. 2 (April 8, 1846): 2; emphasis in original.

50. "The PATRIARCH Bill Smith," *Warsaw Signal* 2, no. 50 (March 11, 1846): 1.

cordially, extended his hand, and greeted her: "How do you do Sister Phelps?" Smith's reputation obviously preceded him, as Sally responded curtly, "Don't Sister Phelps me!" Bullock was quick to note that the Saints who were still in Nauvoo initially paid little attention to Smith and his shenanigans.[51] Orson Hyde corroborated Bullock's account, noting in a letter to Brigham Young that "brother William Smith arrived here Sunday afternoon, but none bade him welcome except his own friends or relatives."[52]

Nauvoo was a hotbed of activity during the spring of 1846. The Saints had hoped that their departure from the county would decrease hostilities, but conflict with local residents persisted. In September, these hostilities culminated in the remaining Saints, many of them poor and ill, being driven from the city after an unequal armed combat called "the Battle of Nauvoo." The harassed and uncertain Saints, relying on Brigham Young's promise that no one would be left behind, regarded non-Mormons and dissidents with deep distrust, and William Smith's family ties no longer qualified him as one of the Saints. Referring to the turmoil in the city after Young's departure in February, W. W. Phelps wrote from Nauvoo in late March: "Every thing has free toleration now [with] no restraint." In an attempt to protect the faithful from outside influences, Phelps reported an increase of "whistling, whining, whittling, and I do not know but wh——g!"[53]

William Smith also became the target of those making efforts to safeguard the Saints who were waiting to depart for the West. One newspaper report indicated that Orrin Porter Rockwell and Jack Redden had been sent from Young's camp to Nauvoo as informal police officers and speculated that William Smith's return to the city was the primary reason these two rough-and-ready frontiersmen had arrived: "they [the pioneer camp], therefore, determined to halt . . . and also sent back their bullies, Rockwell and Redding [Redden] to frighten certain obnoxious persons out of Nauvoo."[54]

William again moved into the Marks home with his children, where his mother, sisters, and their children were still living. The same day William arrived in the city, Luke Johnson, one of the Twelve who had been disaffected from the Church since December 1837, sought reinstatement from the Saints left in Nauvoo. "Bro. Luke Johson came on to the stand after my preaching," recounted Orson Hyde in a letter he wrote to Brigham Young several days afterward, "con-

---

51. Greg Knight, ed., *Thomas Bullock Nauvoo Journal* (Provo, Utah: Grandin Press, 1994), 61–62; Solomon J. Salisbury, "Old Nauvoo Days Recalled," *Autumn Leaves* 37 (April 1924): 153.

52. Orson Hyde (Nauvoo, Ill.), Letter to Brigham Young, March 10, 1846, Brigham Young Office Files 1832–1878, Letters from Church Leaders and Others, 1840–1877, Orson Hyde, 1846, LDS Church History Library.

53. W. W. Phelps (Nauvoo, Ill.), Letter to Prest. Brigham Young, Willard Richards, and Camp of Israel, March 23, 1846, Willard Richards Papers, 1821–1854, MS 1490, Box 4, Folder 1, February 12, 1846–October 26, 1846, LDS Church History Library.

54. "Movements of the Mormons," *Warsaw Signal* 2, no. 52 (March 25, 1846): 2.

William Marks Home, Nauvoo, Illinois. Most of the Smith family, including William and his daughters, lived in this commodious home in 1845–46. Photograph, ca. 1930, photographer unknown.

fessed his sins—[and] obtained the heart[y] approbation of some eight thousand." After the meeting, many of the congregation followed Hyde to the end of Main Street, near the unfinished Nauvoo House, to witness his rebaptism. William was apparently an interested but distant observer. "When the people retired from the water," making their way back up Main Street, Hyde said that "William stood in the door of the mansion [House] and saw the hundreds of people pass by, but not one turned aside to greet him." Hyde further noted that William "keeps hid up mostly," but the following day (March 9) he preached "to about 30 rowdies from the South door of the mansion [House]. He stood within the fence and his auditors in the street. A respectable looking gentleman rode up and asked what was going on," recounted Hyde with derision, when "one of his auditors replied, 'We have got a damned fool of a jackass here with his ears drawn up, and he is trying to bray.'" Hyde also predicted something that he surely hoped for: "I will prophesy that he leaves this place soon."[55]

Less than two weeks after his arrival, William launched a vigorous agenda. For days, he "bucked rails" to construct a stand and enough seats in the yard near the Marks house to accommodate "a great congregation." He then announced his intention to preach on Sunday, March 22. However, that morning, he found that vandals

---

55. Hyde to Brigham Young, March 10, 1846. See also William Shepard and H. Michael Marquardt, *Lost Apostles: Forgotten Members of Mormonism's Original Quorum of Twelve* (Salt Lake City: Signature Books, 2014), 283–84.

had smeared all of his benches and his stand with outhouse sewage.⁵⁶ This tasteless tactic had apparently been used on other occasions to urge outsiders to leave the area. "Most of the apostates [followers of Brigham Young] had gone," remembered William, "and those left in charge of the place under the command of Orson Hyde were very hostile. They indecently bedowled [sic] the seats of my meeting ground & committed various offences." William was further incensed as he felt that these same individuals "killed my dog and threw him into my mother's well."⁵⁷

While acknowledging that Hyde was not personally responsible for such acts, William felt he bore some responsibility because "such things as these were suffered to go on unrestrained by their leaders."⁵⁸ Phelps acknowledged in a letter to Brigham Young that "some of the boys . . . anointed his [William's] stand and seats—which made them 'smell strong' of the latter end; this with rain kept Saint William indoors when he poured out wrath on the Twelve."⁵⁹ Both the stench and the weather may have prevented Smith from preaching that day, but his persistent determination to publicize his message did not diminish. A local paper reported that the "Patriarch Bill Smith is, we learn, flourishing in Nauvoo. At first they prohibited him from speaking, but finally he obtained a hearing and has since been going it to his own satisfaction."⁶⁰

Smith's return to Nauvoo set him on a different course for the next year of his life. Within days of his arrival, Smith met with Strang adherent Hiram Stratton and fellow apostle John E. Page at Page's house.⁶¹ Page was already supporting Strang by the time William arrived at Nauvoo, having been disfellowshipped by Brigham Young on February 9 because he had publicly declared his support of the emerging leader. Strang would appoint him an apostle the following month, at a conference held in Voree, Wisconsin, on April 6–7.⁶² William was searching for a place among the Saints, as well as an avenue to retaliate against the Twelve, and he found it in the Strangites. According to William, it was when he met with Page in Nauvoo that he had "for the first time been apprised of an appointment

---

56. Isaac Paden (Knoxville, Ill.), Letter to James J. Strang, May 17, 1846, Strang Collection; Mary B. (Smith) Norman (Idaho Falls, Idaho), Letter to Ina (Smith) Coolbrith, April 24, 1908, p13, f 955, Community of Christ Library-Archives.

57. William Smith, Epistle, ca. 1850, 5, William Smith Papers, 1850, MS 3697, LDS Church History Library.

58. Ibid.

59. Phelps to Young, Richards, and Camp of Israel, March 23, 1846.

60. "Patriarch Bill Smith," *Warsaw Signal* 2, no. 51 (March 18, 1846): 2.

61. Knight, *Thomas Bullock Nauvoo Journal*, 61–62.

62. John E. Page (Nauvoo, Ill.), Letter to James J. Strang, February 1, 1846, Document 10, Strang Collection; Elden J. Watson, ed., *Manuscript History of Brigham Young, 1846–1847* (Salt Lake City: Elden J. Watson, 1978), 31; "Conference at Voree," in John Hajicek, ed., *Chronicles of Voree, (1844–1849)* (Burlington, Wisc.: J. J. Hajicek, 1922), April 6–7, 1846, 62–67. For more information on John E. Page's history, including his support of James Strang, see William Shepard, "Shadows on the Sun Dial: John E. Page and the Strangites," *Dialogue: A Journal of Mormon Thought* 41, no. 1 (Spring 2008): 34–66.

made by Joseph Smith to James J. Strang." After learning further details from Page, he said, "I took pains to gather all the evidence that could be adduced to see if there was any foundation at all for the claims of Mr. Strang." He met with Emma Smith, who remembered that Joseph had received a letter from Strang before his death and had intended to respond. According to William, Emma also informed William that Joseph III remembered a woman coming into their home at Far West, Missouri, and stating that the Church would ultimately go to Voree. (Joseph III was only six at the time of this alleged prophecy).[63] William listened to Page's preaching and the glowing descriptions of Strang's success in Wisconsin.

By mid-March, he decided to merge his objectives with Strang and, like Adams and Bennett, immediately began to maneuver for a high rank in Strang's movement. On March 17, only nine days after reaching Nauvoo, William wrote his first letter to Strang: "I have Perused with beccoming intrest your serial letters sent to my Mother and Sister Emma; also some of your Papers Voree Herald &c with your attendant remarks on the order of the church, which clearly evinced the true spirit of old Mormonism." In this and subsequent letters, William presented himself as a victim of the Twelve's machinations, describing in detail how he had been wronged and attempting to ascertain whether Strang would validate his claims as patriarch and apostle.[64] He continued his correspondence with Strang throughout that spring, expressing his confidence that Strang had been designated as Joseph's successor. It is difficult to decipher whether Smith was truly convinced of Strang's calling as Joseph's successor or whether he saw Strang's rising movement as an opportunity to meet his personal ambitions and receive the recognition that his excommunication had stripped away with his offices. William's almost immediate and dramatic shift away from the idea of lineal succession, something Strang opposed but which William had vigorously advocated since leaving Nauvoo, supports the latter interpretation.[65] Either way, Smith had linked his fate to Strang's budding movement by the spring of 1846.

William's subsequent correspondence with the faction's leader reveals how the two men's aspirations coalesced between March 1846 and May 1847, allowing William to gain important leadership positions in Strang's expanding organization. By May 1846, William was publicly acknowledging his allegiance to Strang at a time when Strang's followers were having some success at Nauvoo.

---

63. Emma Smith, quoted in William Smith (Nauvoo, Ill.), Letter to James Jesse Strang, March 1, 1846 [date incorrect], *Voree Herald* 1, no. 7 (July 1846): 31.

64. William Smith (Nauvoo, Ill.), Letter to Brother [James] Strang, March 17, 1846, Strang Collection; William Smith (Nauvoo, Ill.), Letter to Dear Brother Strang, April 12, 1846, *Voree Herald* 1, no. 6 (June 1846): 3–4.

65. While Strang conceded that the patriarchal office "goes by lineage," as well as the Aaronic order of priesthood, "the office of prophet, of lawgiver to God's people and shepherd of the whole flock of God does not." James J. Strang (Voree, Wisc.), Letter to Dear Brother [Orange L. Wight], September 13, 1848, *Gospel Herald* 3, no. 27 (September 21, 1848): 4–6.

Edward Thompson, writing to Hugh Herringshaw in late May 1846, described the scene at Nauvoo that spring as Twelveites, Rigdonites, and Strangites vied for converts in the absence of most of the Twelve. After Orson Hyde had completed his sermon during one preaching service, Jacob Syfritt,[66] a Rigdon adherent, took to the stand as soon as Hyde sat down. Syfritt announced "that a conference of the C of J C of LDS was then in session near the old stand & requested all the honest in heart to attend." Some attendees had not heard what Syfritt had said, so he "repeated it again to the utmost of his voice." "When I go to Nauvoo I generally go to the Strang meetings," wrote Thompson, as "they have quiet [quite] a congregation & have great liberty & power in preaching." Thompson was obviously supporting Strang's claims at the time, as he included one of Strang's pamphlets in his letter, indicating that "he claims to be the man that was <u>appointed</u> by Joseph not ordained," an emphasis that differed from Sidney Rigdon's claim to successorship through his ordination as a member of the First Presidency. According to Thompson, "Wm Smith his mother Emma & family" supported Strang at the time, along with "Prest. [William] Marks [and] J.E. Page."[67] Orson Hyde, writing from Nauvoo in late March to Brigham Young who was on the trail west, indicated that "the Lord has given me just power enough to hang on in the storm and keep my head above water." He further complained, "It is no very desirable job to stay where hell boils over every breeze that blows," but expressed his willingness to "still, do as you say."[68] Hyde was relieved when he finally was able to depart from the abandoned city that fall.

Smith had much to gain by coupling his aspirations with Strang's. He continued his correspondence through the spring, and met with Strang in person by the summer and fall of 1846. In late December, he spelled out his requirements to Strang in exchange for his support. William wanted Strang to publicly acknowledge that he had been wronged by other members of the Twelve while he had resided at Nauvoo, give him a place in Strang's Council of the Twelve Apostles, and sustain him as the "presiding patriarch *over* the Church." This phrase, "over the Church," was critical to William, as it had generated John Taylor's public rebuke in print a year earlier. William also petitioned Strang to formally declare

---

66. Jacob Syfritt had been a part of the Philadelphia Branch when William Smith was presiding over the eastern branches of the Church in 1843–45. Syfritt had also served as a counselor to Benjamin Winchester. He was residing in Philadelphia in 1849 and appears to have aligned himself with William Smith's movement in 1849–50. "Jacob Syfret" (*sic*) appears as an agent for William Smith and Isaac Sheen's newspaper. "List of Agents for This Paper," *Melchisedek and Aaronic Herald* 1, no. 5 (August 1849): 2.

67. Edward Thompson (Keokuk, Iowa), Letter to Hugh Herringshaw, May 26, 1846, MS 22665, LDS Church History Library. I have not been able to identify either Thompson or his correspondent.

68. Orson Hyde (Nauvoo, Ill.), Letter to Dear Brethren, March 27, 1846, Brigham Young Office Files 1832–1878, Letters from Church Leaders and Others, 1840–1877, Orson Hyde, 1846, LDS Church History Library.

that Smith was indeed the presiding or chief patriarch, which also entitled him to be a member of the First Presidency—much like the position his brother Hyrum had held before his death. Wrote William bluntly, "I go in for honors now days as well as rights. If [I am] a councilor . . . [in] the Presadency why not say so? If [I am] one of the three presidents why not say so? or if [I am] a Presadent protem in the place of litle Joseph [Joseph Smith III] etc. . . . why [not] name it? I know of no nameless offices in the Church. If any think me a Signfant [insignificant] they will find themselves mistaken."[69] William hungered for public recognition of these positions. Not only would it satisfy his personal ambition, but he felt that a public declaration in Strang's expanding newspaper would fully clear his name and restore his reputation among the Saints still in the Midwest and in the East. It was what he had desired of leaders at Nauvoo the previous summer but had been denied.

Strang also had much to gain by extending the hand of fellowship to the younger brother of the Prophet. In one of his earliest letters to Strang in March, William had coupled his support of Strang's movement with that of the entire Smith family. He included the names of his mother, sisters, and their spouses on two letters, implying that his family unitedly supported Strang.[70] William's younger sister Katharine later issued an affidavit: "I now in truth declare that I never signed my name to such [a] certificate of document; neither did I give my consent for anyone to sign it. I never knew anything about Strang or his work, nor heard of him for several years after I left Nauvoo. I do not believe that my mother, Lucy Smith, or my sisters, Lucy Millikin and Sophronia McClerrie [McCleary], signed any such certificate. . . . So I say the whole thing was a forgery. Whoever the perpetrator was, his acts will surely be revealed sometime, as justice will prevail."[71] And in fact, Jenkins and Katharine were actually absent from Nauvoo when Smith included their names.[72] Obviously, William exploited his family to make himself a more appealing candidate in Strang's movement. He may have assumed that his family would unquestioningly follow his direction, and it is true that they had provided sympathetic support during the summer

---

69. William Smith (Knoxville, Ill.), Letter to James Jesse Strang, December 25, 1846, Strang Collection; terminal punctuation added.

70. William Smith (Nauvoo, Ill.), Letter to James J. Strang, March 1 [sic], 1846, *Voree Herald* 1, no. 7 (July 1846): 3; "Opinions of the Smith Family," *Voree Herald* 1, no. 6 (June 1846): 1.

71. Katharine Salisbury (Fountain Green, Ill.), Letter to Editors of *Saints' Herald* 46, no. 78 (March 26, 1899): 261..

72. The Salisburys were absent from Nauvoo from March 1846 through the fall of 1847. They also were not among Smith family members who lived at Knoxville, Illinois, during the winter of 1846–47. Salisbury, "Old Nauvoo Days Recalled," 153–54; Kyle R. Walker, "Katharine Smith Salisbury," in Kyle R. Walker, ed., *United by Faith: The Joseph Sr. and Lucy Mack Smith Family* (American Fork, Utah: BYU Studies and Covenant Communications, 2006), 324–27.

Stone House built in the 1840s, where James J. Strang's newspaper, the *Voree Herald*, was printed. Photograph courtesy of John Hajicek.

of 1845 when he had been in Nauvoo. His device worked, for Strang remained unaware of Smith's manipulation and longed to have the support of the entire Smith family, which would strengthen his claim as Joseph Smith's successor.

What began then, in March 1846, would be a merger of convenience for the two men. Strang would add credibility to his own cause by recruiting the surviving Smiths and the Egyptian mummies—both of which William promised. For Smith, Strang would give him what he most desired: a restoration to his former calling as an apostle, as well as a more prominent position in being "chief patriarch" and holding a position akin to Hyrum's as assistant president. Both men were motivated to unite their talents in Strang's budding organization.

In early June, William took his two daughters to their grandparents' home in Walnut Grove, Illinois, where they remained for the entire summer, while William traveled to Voree where he finally met with Strang in person.[73] On June 11, 1846, Strang and Aaron Smith, Moses Smith's brother and Strang's counselor, ordained William "to the office of Patriarch and f[a]ther unto the whole Church according to his right by revalation [sic] and blessing. Also to be an Apostle and Special witness of the name of Christ in the world . . . holding his former place in the Quorum of the Twelve." The minutes indicate that William then participated in other ordinations, including ordaining John C. Bennett to the office of high

---

73. William did not return for his daughters until fall when he "found one of my children very sick." William Smith, Epistle, ca. 1850, 5.

priest.[74] William remained in Voree for most of the summer, where, according to his own report, "I preached in Voree & baptized a large number of Saints."[75] On July 28, he published an announcement in Strang's newspaper, *Zion's Reveille*: "Inheriting, as I do, the office of patriarch by lineal descent from my progenitors, and having been ordained thereunto, by the first presidency, and being thereby fully invested with the patriarchal authority, I deem it necessary to at this time to address you a few lines." He assured readers that, "as to the claims of Brother James J. Strang, I entertain no doubt whatever, as to his appointment by my brother Joseph, and his confirmation by angelic administration . . . [and by revelation] unto me." He encouraged the Saints to join him and Strang at Voree—the great "gathering place appointed of God." He signed the letter emphatically, "Patriarch of the whole church."[76]

William demonstrated his loyalty to the emerging prophet when he traveled with James J. Strang to Kirtland, Ohio, in early August 1846. Strang held a conference on August 7–10 at the former Mormon headquarters to officially organize his own church. William was an active participant. He recollected that he "preached 3 times in the temple and baptized nine."[77] During the Kirtland conference, Smith was once again acknowledged as the "chief patriarch," presiding over "the whole church." Furthermore, Strang ensured that his followers understood that as patriarch, Smith "held a seat in the councils of the first presidency, as coadjutor . . . by virtue of his patriarchate." Strang had thus extended to William that which he most desired—a position in the Twelve, the office of presiding Patriarch *over* the entire church, and the public announcement of his positions in Strang's newspaper.[78] William's friend and collaborator George J. Adams followed Smith into Strang's church and also moved quickly up his hierarchy of leadership, being appointed a member of the First Presidency.[79]

Satisfied for the time being, in September 1846 William returned to Illinois. "On the way I called at Voree, Wisconsin where I preached one sermon," he recounted. "I [then] returned to Knoxville and Walnut Grove Ill., where I had left my children."[80] By November 1846, he and his daughters had settled at Knoxville, Illinois, in his own residence, where he planned to spend the winter near his mother, his sisters Sophronia and Lucy, and their families. They had come to Knoxville to avoid the Battle of Nauvoo in September, and were living in tight

---

74. Hajicek, *The Chronicles of Voree*, 82–84.
75. William Smith, Epistle, ca. 1850, 5.
76. William Smith (Voree, Wisc.), "Letter to the Church of Jesus Christ of Latter Day Saints, July 28, 1846," in *Zion's Reveille* 1, no. 12 (December 1846): 3.
77. William Smith, Epistle, ca. 1850, 5.
78. "The First Presidency," *Zion's Reveille* 1, no. 12 (December, 1846): 3; "Patriarchs," *Zion's Reveille* 2, no. 1 (January 14, 1847): 3. These issues of the *Zion's Reveille* reveal how Strang responded to each of Smith's requests by publishing those items in his paper.
79. "The First Presidency," *Zion's Reveille* 1, no. 12 (December 1846): 1.
80. William Smith, Epistle, ca. 1850, 5.

quarters with Isaac Paden, a Church leader who had only recently shifted his loyalty from Brigham Young to James Strang, and who was presiding over a branch of approximately thirty-six Strangites organized in the city.[81] About a month after their arrival, William recounted, "on hearing that my folks was—at Knoxville I hastened to give them council what to do. I found my Mother 2 sisters and their families—at the house of Brother Padens all—stowed into a room about 15 by 12 feet with only a small grate fire Place to Cook by." Describing these circumstances in a letter written to Strang on December 7, William indicated "in this Condition—they have been living for 4 weeks waiting for help and teams from Voree."[82] The Smiths presumably attended this loosely organized Strangite branch during the winter of 1846–47, which, combined with William's declarations that all his family supported Strang, became the foundation for rumors that Lucy Smith and all her children were Strangites. Surviving accounts are contradictory about the level of support William's mother and sisters actually gave Strang. According to a correpondent for the *Friends' Weekly Intelligencer* of Philadelphia, "I have now in my possession, a letter from William Smith, another from his mother, and a third, signed by her two married daughters and their husbands, acknowledging their full belief in Strang's appointment by Joseph, to be the president of the church. . . . These documents were presented to us by Lucy Smith, the mother of the deceased prophet." The *Racine Advocate*, however, countered: "It is said that Lucy Smith, the mother in Israel of the Mormons, and the rest of the Jo. Smith family, insist, that they do not believe that Strang of Voree, was ever appointed a prophet by Jo. Smith, so that Strang had better act under some other more improbable authority."[83] If the Smith women had considered the possibility of affiliating with the Strangites, they ultimately decided against it. In the spring of 1847, they returned to Nauvoo and only William made the trip to Voree that season.

William corresponded frequently with Strang throughout the winter of 1846–47;[84] but after associating with Strang for only a few months, Smith's

---

81. Isaac Paden (Knoxville, Ill.), Letter to Brigham Young, January 26, 1846, Brigham Young Office Files 1832–78, General Correspondence, Incoming, 1840–77, General Letters, 1840–1877, M-P, 1846, LDS Church History Library; Isaac Paden (Knoxville, Ill.), Letter to James J. Strang, May 17, 1846, Strang Collection. The Knoxville Branch of Strang's church appears to have been one of the largest at the time outside of headquarters at Voree. At the October 1846 conference held in Voree, a J. Savage reported that the Knoxville Branch had thirty-six members. Hajicek, *Chronicles of Voree*, 108.

82. William Smith (Knoxville, Ill.), Letter to James J. Strang, December 7, 1846, Strang Collection.

83. "Correspondence of Friends' Weekly Intelligencer," *Friends' Weekly Intelligencer* (Philadelphia) 3, no. 29 (October 17, 1846): 226; "Can't Get the Papers," *Racine Advocate* (Wisconsin Territory) 4, no. 43 (September 16, 1846): 1. The letters referred to in the *Intelligencer* presumably have not survived—if they had once existed.

84. William Smith, Note to James J. Strang, ca. November 1846, Strang Collection; William Smith, Letter to James J. Strang, December 2, 1846; William Smith, Letter to James J. Strang, December 7, 1846; William Smith, Letter to James J. Strang, December

reputation among the Strangites was already failing. Rumors were circulating at Voree that Smith had been intimate with a female member of Strang's church to whom he was not married, or at least so it appeared on the surface. Despite his pronouncements to the contrary, Smith continued to espouse polygamy after his excommunication in 1845, an action that he had begun as early as 1843 at Nauvoo and for which he had been punished for preaching about in August 1845. Although his prolific burst of plural marriages in 1845 did not, as far as we know, result in any kind of permanent relationship or the births of any children, Smith continued to secretly teach and advocate for the practice during his association with Strang and afterward. William had most likely been sealed to Evanade Archer[85] by fellow Strangite Benjamin Ellsworth, while he lived at Ellsworth's residence in Voree during the summer of 1846. Ellsworth had been closely linked to both Smith and John C. Bennett during his affiliation with Strang. This union was problematic not only because of the secrecy surrounding their sealing, but also because William was still legally married to Mary Jane Rollins, although she had left him in August 1845. Publicly he seemed to be a widower or divorcé. Knowing he had not obtained a divorce from Rollins, William had Evanade sealed to him in a private ceremony that apparently only he, Ellsworth, and possibly Bennett knew about. Benjamin's wife Sarah, who was apparently unaware that her husband or William Smith supported polygamy, discovered their relationship—which appeared to outsiders like adultery—and was probably the source of rumors about the relationship which emerged at Voree and beyond. Benjamin would afterward be excommunicated for his involvement in the episode and for teaching "corrupt doctrines in regard to marriage and social intercourse." At a church court in August 1847, after serving as president of the Seventies Quorum and then being nominated to be an apostle in Strang's church, Benjamin Ellsworth was abruptly excommunicated for "teaching and practicing the spiritual wife system."[86]

19, 1846; William Smith (Knoxville, Ill.), Letter to James J. Strang, December 25, 1846, Strang Collection; William Smith to James J. Strang (Knoxville, Ill.), Letter to James J. Strang, February 10, 1847, in "Letter from the Patriarch," *Zion's Reveille* 2, no. 7 (February 25, 1847): 3–4.

85. Evanade Archer was born about 1827 in Green County, Indiana, to John W. Archer and Mary Saunders Archer. The Archers joined the Church in Indiana around 1835 and moved to Clay County, Missouri, that same year. They gathered with the Saints at Nauvoo and, after the death of Joseph Smith, followed James J. Strang to Voree. Clark V. Johnson, *Mormon Redress Petitions: Documents of the 1833–1838 Missouri Conflict* (Provo, Utah: BYU Religious Studies Center, 1992), 127, 599. Evanade and William had no children, and she apparently stayed in Voree while William went off, first to Kirtland with Strang, then to Knoxville for the winter of 1846–47. They may have resumed a marital relationship during his brief return to Voree before settling in Knoxville for the winter, and during his brief visit in April 1847. (See below and also Appendix A for information on Evanade Archer.)

86. Hajicek, *Chronicles of Voree*, 151. Sarah Ellsworth, Testimony before James J. Strang, April 23, 1847, John C. Gaylord accuser vs. William Smith accused, Complaint

In the meantime, both John C. Bennett and George J. Adams were trying to fend off similar accusations during their brief glory days as highly placed leaders in Strang's church. As early as October 1846, Bennett was accused of "teaching False Doctrine, (such as) Polygamy, and Concubinage." Aaron Smith, Strang's first counselor, excommunicated Bennett while Strang was still in the East laboring as a missionary. Once Strang returned, he reversed the action, reinstating Bennett. But the accusations could not be adequately answered or ignored and ultimately led to a major division in Strang's church. They ultimately resulted with Bennett's excommunication for "various immortalities," which became official in October 1847.[87]

In early 1847, while presiding over the Strangite branch in Boston, Adams's persuasive talents failed to convince members of his own branch, who disfellowshipped him "for immoral conduct [and]. . . for teaching that fornication and adultery is justifiable under certain circumstances." Strangite follower and Church leader at Boston, John Hardy, who split with the leader in the winter of 1846–47, expanded his unease beyond the admittedly flamboyant Adams by warning in a splinter group's newspaper, "If you wish to support the Eastern churches, shun Wm. Smith as you would deadly poison." Hardy's earlier interactions with Smith in the year 1844, when William excommunicated Hardy, certainly influenced his negative perception of the Church leader. William was then in Illinois, but his reputation since uniting with Strang had already reached the eastern seaboard. Hardy further argued that, "when Strang came East, if he had not been connected with such men as Wm. Smith, John C. Bennett, and G. J. Adams, he would have got ten [converts] to where he got one."[88] Strang had taken a colossal risk by rewarding the support of these admittedly effective and charismatic individuals with their high positions, but whose questionable character resulted in matters quickly spiraling out of control.

As reports about Adams and Smith filtered back to Strang in Voree in the fall of 1846, the Church leader faced a dilemma. John C. Bennett had already injured Strang's church by engaging in what some Strangite dissenters described as "damnable heresys and doctrines that the devil J. C. Bennett W. M. Smith and others have introduced or tried to." Strang biographer Vickie Cleverley Speek summarized that these "writers said they were concerned for the safety and reputation of the women of Voree and that they could not, in good conscience, refer

---

for Adultery, Document 181, Strang Collection.

87. Andrew F. Smith, *The Saintly Scoundrel*, 154–65; Hajicek, *Chronicles of Voree*, 151; Speek, *God Has Made Us a Kingdom*, 48–49.

88. John Hardy, quoted in "By express . . . ," *The New Era and Herald of Zion's Watchmen* (Elkhorn, Wisc.) 1, no. 2 (February 1847): 3. In another letter to Strang from Boston, Alden Hale, a Strangite member, revealed his opinion that "if G. J. Adams has set in flame all places where he has been as he has Boston . . . it would take but few such fires to nearly obliterate Mormonism from the world." Alden Hale (Lowell, Mass.), Letter to James Strang, January 1, 1849, General Correspondence, fd. 361, Strang Collection.

potential immigrants to Voree while the 'devil' Bennett was there." These dissenters certainly referred to the same kinds of activities for which Bennett had been excommunicated for in Nauvoo.[89] Strang did not want to risk reducing his membership further. Now, two more of his most prominent leaders were the explosive center of rumors about polygamy; and although Bennett's version differed substantially from what Joseph Smith taught at Nauvoo, it was a doctrine that had caused many of Strang's adherents to reject leadership from the Twelve. Nor did the stories diminish with time. They actually intensified as the months passed, until, by the summer of 1847, Strang was forced to take action.

There is some evidence that Strang had drawn back from the kind of searching interviews that may have exposed Smith and Adams's earlier support of polygamy. In August 1846 when William was laboring as a Strangite missionary in Kirtland, he had written Strang a confidential postscript in one of his letters to Strang that hinted at polygamy. He warned Strang about the Saints in Philadelphia where Smith had personally presided in 1843–45: "I forgot to mention to you that the Phila[delphia] Saints are mostly spiritual wife believers[,] especially some of the most prominent female leaders." He did not name names or provide details, but it seems too significant a topic for him to have "forgot[ten] to mention" it, presumably in a personal conversation about polygamy. Strang had publicly taken a hard line against polygamy, but the conversation with William had apparently taken place on two levels: ostensible agreement that it was a corrupt principle but underlain with the intriguing possibilities of secret-keeping, and the possibility that it may actually have had divine approval. What Strang actually knew is not clear; he did not keep anything like a detailed confidential diary or, like Joseph Smith, had an intimate disciple like the compulsive recordkeeper William Clayton to whom he spoke freely. Strang had certainly heard rumors and reports from many sources about Smith, Bennett, and Adams and their marital expansiveness, so despite public denials from all three, it seems a stretch to think he did not have some knowledge of their checkered careers of, at best, plural sealings, and at worst, outright promiscuity. Strang's denunciations of polygamy as "heretical" and an "abomination"[90] reassured those who found the conflicted and confusing reports of Nauvoo polygamy a reason to turn away from the Twelve, but it was a thin crust over a potential volcano.

No documents have survived of what William and Strang had discussed where polygamy was concerned—including the eight plural wives William had left behind him when he fled from Nauvoo in September; but perhaps the par-

---

89. For example, four men from Kirtland wrote: "We shall not at this time undertake to innumerate the many damnable heresys and doctrines that the devil J. C. Bennett W.M. Smith and others have introduced or tried to, but thanks be to God there is Eyes Eares and Some understanding in and among the Saints." Jacob Bump, Leonard Rich, Amos Babcock, and S. B. Stoddard, Letter, October 16, [1846], Community of Christ Library-Archives, quoted in Speek, *God Has Made Us a Kingdom*, 49.

90. James J. Strang, "Official," *Zion's Reveille* 2, no. 21 (August 12, 1847): 4.

allel situation with George J. Adams provides a model. Before Adams joined with Strang in July 1846 on the basis of his former baptism, and while Adams was still corresponding with Strang about, not only membership, but the high position he could expect as a reward for doing so, he attempted to dispel rumors about his sexual reputation. Referring to other factions of Mormonism, Adams told Strang "they have reported that I was fond of women [but] it is a base lie." Strang freely forgave Adams but warned: "As for these complaints that you say are made against you I have only to say now that if you are guilty, you must do so no more."[91] If William Smith had made a similar confession to Strang and, like Adams, committed to shun the practice, he did not keep that commitment, nor could he, in a small community like Voree, keep knowledge of it from Strang.

By December William learned that negative reports about him had reached Strang at Voree about his behavior while he had lived in Voree the previous summer. On December 2, 1846, William wrote to Strang, assuring him that he had "renounced the spiritual wife doctrin and I wish you to think of me as you see and hear me by my own acts and words and not as others may say. Even J C Benit has a wrong Conception of me in woman afairs," William emphasized, perhaps trying to distance himself from the troubled leader. "I want it Expressly understood that I have not taught the spiritual wife doctrin to no soul living man nor woman." Again presenting himself as a victim, Smith lamented that he "must be abused as never man was abused by the Voree saints" and thus be "rob[b]ed of all [my] friends.... for no man has suffered more than I have in the late revolutions of the church." Smith then appealed to his greatest advantage—one that had proved decisive in Strang's willingness to incorporate Smith into his evolving ecclesiastical organization. William reminded Strang that he was "the main spoke in the Smith family" and half-threatened that "it would be poor incouragement to my old Mother and Sisters [if] the first day of my arrival in Voree [they] would find me in Church trouble." As he had done earlier, he asked Strang to publish William's standing in the Strangite newspaper and add a description (by which he obviously hoped for praise) of his role in Kirtland when Strang officially reorganized his church. The *Voree Herald* had reported the conference but rather suprisingly failed to mention William's contributions or even his presence.[92] Several weeks later, apparently dissatisfied with Strang's silence, Smith rolled out another heavy gun of persuasion, reminding Strang that he had "the [Egyptian] mummies & [church patriarchal blessing] records . . . and [they] will be of great benefit to the Church [if] we Can get them to Voree."[93]

---

91. George J. Adams (Cincinnati, Ohio), Letter to James J. Strang, March 27, 1846, Strang Collection; James J. Strang, Letter to George Adams, May 5, 1846, fd. 60, Strang Collection, quoted in Speek, *God Has Made Us a Kingdom*, 39–40.

92. William Smith (Knoxville, Ill.), Letter to James Jesse Strang, December 2, 1846, Strang Collection; "Kirtland," *Voree Herald* 1, no. 9 (September 1846): 1.

93. William Smith (Knoxville, Ill.), Letter to James Jesse Strang, December 19, 1846, Strang Collection. As discussed later, the mummies were technically in Lucy's possession,

Strang met William's demands with wholehearted, public endorsement as William wished, thus ignoring, at least temporarily, the issue of polygamy. In addition to the distance between Knoxville and Voree, the rumors at Voree most certainly put an end to his polygamous relationship with Evanade. Strang gambled that he could keep William satisfied and compliant, at least for the time being. The December issue of the *Zion's Reveille,* printed after Strang received William's letters written on December 2, 7, and 19, contained Strang's endorsement of all three items on Smith's list: (1) his honorable standing in the Church, (2) his participation in Kirtland Conference, and (3) acknowledgment of his offices. It continued with condolences for Mary Jane Rollins's death (mentioned in William's December 2, corrected in his December 7 missive), and, as a fifth item, the fact that William had been prevented from attending the October conference by illness. Strang acknowledged William, indeed, "held a seat in the councils of the *first presidency*" (the other counselor was George J. Adams), as the "Chief Patriarch . . . *of the whole church,*" and had offered dedicated ministry in Kirtland in the summer of 1846.[94] Although not acknowledging that William had been sealed to Evanade Archer, which Strang may have not yet confirmed, he went so far as to publish that William's "Brighamite wife" (Mary Jane Rollins) had died, thus leaving William unquestionably free to remarry.[95] This odd position, though clarifying William's right to remarry, contradicted the fact that William had explained twice that Mary Jane was not dead—first in a letter on December 7 and again on December 19. He repeatedly asked Strang to use his legal training to assist him "to get a Bill [of divorce]" from Mary Jane, petitioning, "will you be my friend and assist me in this thing?"[96] Both letters appear to have reached Strang before the December issue of the *Zion's Reveille* went to press, meaning that Strang may have intentionally published this false report of Mary Jane's death to help protect Smith's deteriorating reputation.

Strang's public support continued through the April 1847 conference of the Church in Voree, which William attended. The conference sustained him as

---

but William obviously assumed that he had a right to them and did, in fact, take possession of them in 1848 for a time.

94. "The First Presidency," *Zion's Reveille* 1, no. 12 (December 1846): 1; "William Smith," *Zion's Reveille* 1, no. 12 (December 1846): 3; emphasis in original.

95. "William Smith," *Zion's Reveille* 1, no. 12 (December 1846): 3.

96. In this same issue of the *Zion's Reveille,* Strang acknowledges the receipt of William's December 19 letter to John C. Bennett. "William Smith . . . ," *Zion's Reveille* 1, no. 12 (December 1846): 3. It seems likely that Strang would have also received William's letter written to him on the same date, and two earlier letters from William written that same month. In this letter William states, "The (Confidential) report concerning my (2nd) wife being dead is contradicted my only safe way is to get a Bill [of divorce] this I shall try my best to accomplish next Spring." William Smith to Strang, December 19, 1846; emphasis in original. See also William Smith to Strang, December 2, 1846, and William Smith to Strang, December 7, 1846.

"Patriarch to the church," and he was appointed to go on a mission to England with John E. Page.[97] However, barely two weeks later, on April 23, Sarah Ellsworth testified before Strang that she knew personally that William had roomed with Evenade Archer at the Ellsworth home during William's visit to Voree in the summer of 1846. Sarah had been instrumental in sending Evenade away, assuming their relationship was adulterous.[98] Sarah's testimony left no doubt in Strang's mind that Smith was guilty of either adultery or polygamy. And needless to say, he also had incontrovertible evidence that Smith had lied in how he represented himself.

After the conference, William returned to Knoxville, Illinois, where he continued his missionary efforts for Strang during the remainder of April. But in Voree, Strang now faced a dilemma. As a religious leader requiring impeccable moral behavior from his followers, he could not allow his apostle-patriarch-counselor to flout requirements for sexual rectitude. But excommunicating Smith for either polygamy or adultery risked losing Smith family support, the physical presence of Lucy and her three daughters, and the almost-mystical presence of the Egyptian mummies that provided yet another link to the Joseph Smith-like persona that had proved so persuasive in converting many of his adherents.

Ultimately, Strang decided on a compromise in the weeks after the April conference and in the wake of Sarah Ellsworth's testimony. He would drop Smith as an apostle and probably as a counselor in the First Presidency (though that was not specifically mentioned) but retain him as the patriarch, since, as Strang reasoned, William's lineal right to the office was unquestionable. Though no details have survived regarding the discussion between Strang and Smith about how they came to this decision, it appears that William had agreed to the arrangement before Strang published the announcement in the July issue of the *Zion's Reveille*.[99] Whether with William's consent or not, Strang provided the face-saving explanation that "at the request of Elder Wm. Smith and the sanction of the Conference, he (Smith) was discontinued as a member of the traveling High Council or Twelve Apostles." The next line read, "Elder Wm. Smith was sustained by the sanction of the Conference in the office of Patriarch to the church, as his legal right by lineage." Using the word "request," implied that William was overwhelmed by his dual roles and wished to concentrate on being patriarch. The truth would have been far more disconcerting to Strang's followers.

Although Smith's sentiments regarding Strang's compromise have not survived, he initially agreed to it, perhaps believing that once the issue had blown over he would be reinstated as an apostle. But by the time the newspaper came out in July, the impulsive William had already decided to sever his connection with Strang. Perhaps he had received word about Sarah Ellsworth's testimony

---

97. "The Minutes of the Annual Conference of the Church of Jesus Christ of Latter Day Saints, Held at Voree April the 6th, 1847," *Zion's Reveille* 2, no. 16 (July 8, 1847): 3–4.

98. Sarah Ellsworth, Testimony before James J. Strang, 1–2.

99. "The Minutes of the Annual Conference of the Church of Jesus Christ of Latter Day Saints, Held at Voree April the 6th, 1847," 67–68.

given at Voree. He put himself in the best light: "When I arrived in Knoxville [Illinois] in May 1847," recollected William, "I made a declaration against Strang[s] impositions."[100] The statement, of course, ignored how his own misconduct contributed to his losing his apostolic office and his falling out of favor with Strang. By early June he had made overtures of reconciliation with Brigham Young, then en route to the West with the vanguard company of the Saints, by writing to Orson Hyde. When Hyde failed to open the door to restoring William to his former callings, Smith returned to the effort he had launched in St. Louis and Cincinnati in the winter of 1845–1846 of organizing his own church and positioning himself as its president and prophet until Joseph III came of age.[101] After passing the summer brooding about possible avenues to power, William began publicizing his message in August 1847.

Strang's compromise had unraveled within a matter of weeks, though Smith's remonstrance against Strang probably had not reached the would-be prophet until late summer, and Strang felt he had no other option but to deal with William's indiscretions publicly. The August issue of *Zion's Reveille* announced: "It becomes our painful duty to give public notice that William Smith, the Patriarch, has been sometime since suspended, pending a trial of [for] gross immorality." On October 6, 1847, the conference excommunicated Smith for "adultery," meaning his polygamous union with Evenade Archer.[102] (See Chapter 15 for William's frenetic activities between June and October.) Smith retaliated by claiming that Strang had used deception in conferring his impressive "endowment," using a mixture of phosphorous and oil to create a glowing effect that he claimed to be the "illumination" of the Holy Ghost. He also denounced Strang as an imposter who manufactured and buried the plates, then "found" them by claimed revelation to cast himself as a prophet and translator in the Joseph Smith mode.[103] Even before Strang's conference officially excommunicated William, the two men had denounced one another.

Ironically, Strang himself began the surreptitious practice of polygamy just a year or so after excommunicating William Smith, John C. Bennett, Benjamin Ellsworth, and others who had accepted the practice. He definitely reserved the privilege for himself, leaving his wife Mary in Voree while he traveled on mis-

---

100. William Smith, Epistle, ca. 1850, 6.

101. William Smith (St. Louis, Mo.), Letter to Orson Hyde, June 22, 1847, Brigham Young Office Files 1832–78, Letters from Church Leaders and Others, 1840–1877, William Smith, 1844–1857, LDS Church History Library. See also Walker, *United by Faith*, 282–83.

102. "It becomes our painful duty . . . ," *Zion's Reveille* 2, no. 23 (August 26, 1847): 3. By October it was official, as the paper reported that "William Smith, Patriarch, [has been] excommunicated for adultery. . . . And the whole congregation lifted their hands against him." "Conference of the Church of Jesus Christ of Latter Day Saints, at Voree," *Gospel Herald* 2, no. 30 (October 14, 1847): 2.

103. "Conference of the Church of Jesus Christ of Latter Day Saints, at Voree," 2; William Smith (Ottawa, Ill.), Letter to the Editor, September 16, 1847, *Ottawa Free Trader*, rpt., as "A Late Mormon Miracle," *Gospel Herald* 2, no. 40 (December 23, 1847): 2–3.

sionary and preaching journeys with his youthful masculine-appearing secretary, "Charley Douglass," who was actually Elvira Field. Surprisingly, George J. Adams survived this purge of polygamists, probably because he spent most of his time in the East, far removed from Voree and close scrutiny. Even more ironically, when Adams came to St. James, Michigan, on Beaver Island, in July 1849, Adams performed Strang's sealing to Elvira, probably using the ceremony William had taught him. A year later, also on Beaver Island, Adams led out in ordaining Strang as "King of Beaver Island." His flair for the dramatic took visible form in a grand ceremony staged on July 8, 1850. Utilizing background scenery and stage props, Adams crowned Strang "king of heaven and earth," placing a literal crown covered with gold tinsel and studded stars on his head, while Strang held a scepter in his hand. Adams stayed on as one of Strang's closest associates until he fell out of favor later that fall.[104]

At this point, William refused to give up polygamy, a lack of personal discipline and restraint that would cost him dear in every organization he created or affiliated with. Strang would experience similar turmoil as his polygamous unions became increasingly publicized, eventually contributing to his murder. Perhaps Strang and Smith had more in common than either man realized. Theirs was a brief, but important union. Smith's extensive ecclesiastical experience no doubt influenced Strang's thinking, and Strang's missionary success in gathering scattered Saints to his cause informed Smith in his own sporadic efforts to get his own organization off the ground. While the two men pursued different paths after their separation, during their brief association in 1846–47, the two powerful personalities merged their aspirations in the obscure gathering place of Voree, Territory of Wisconsin.

---

104. Speek, *God Has Made Us a Kingdom*, 67–68, 120–28.

Chapter 15

Church-Building: Quest for Ecclesiastical Station

> I appoint unto you a stake of Zion in this land, even in the land of Palestine, wherein thou dwellest, to be a place of gathering . . . for your temporal salvation.
> —Revelation to William Smith, 1847

Lee County, Illinois, factored into the Mormon story at an early date, and the area's citizens were well aware of the Mormon presence in the state by the late 1830s. Not only had Mormonism been sensationalized in the press and throughout the state generally, but in time, as the Mormon missionaries began to proselyte throughout the state, dozens of citizens in Lee and its adjoining counties converted to the faith. Additionally, Emma Hale Smith's older sister Elizabeth, age thirty-six when she and her husband, Benjamin Wasson, had moved from New York to Illinois, had been some of the area's earliest settlers. They built a home in Palestine Grove, in the heart of Lee County, in December 1837.[1]

At the encouragement of both Emma and Elizabeth, other members of the Hale family soon followed their lead. Emma penned a note to her forty-six-year-old elder brother David in 1841, in which she encouraged him and his family to move westward. "I feel quite anxious that all of my Father's family should come and settle in this country," she wrote, "as I think it is far better than any other place east of here." Emma also revealed her yearning to have her family unite with Mormonism: "I should also like to have you all investigate our doctrines and all become good Mormons." It had been a lonely venture when she had gone against her father's wishes and married Mormonism's founder, and she had experienced little, if any, interaction with her family as she repeatedly made new homes during the Saints'

---

1. The Wasson family had moved from Harpersville, New York, to Farmington, Illinois, in late August 1836. According to Elizabeth's daughter Clara, by that winter Benjamin had bought land in Palestine Grove and almost immediately began construction of a log house. They moved into the completed home in December 1837. The Wassons became prominent members of the community in which they resided, near present-day Amboy, Illinois. Clara Wasson became a noted schoolteacher, and the family built an early schoolhouse on their property that was used as both a school and a social hall that was known as the "Wasson Schoolhouse." Inez A. Kennedy, *Recollections of the Pioneers of Lee County* (Dixon, Ill.: Inez A. Kennedy, 1893), 57–59, 94–95; *History of Lee County* (Chicago, H. H. Hill and Co., 1882), 337.

frequent moves through Ohio, Missouri, and finally Illinois. She was elated at the prospect of having her sister and family nearby after nearly ten years of separation. However, her earlier experiences in Harmony, Pennsylvania, where she had met and married Joseph Smith, tempered her approach when speaking of her religion with her family. She added cautiously in her letter, "but there is no compulsion as to the subject of our religion, you can live here if you are not Mormons."[2]

Primarily because the Wasson family had settled in the area and spurred on by Emma's encouragement, four more of Emma's siblings migrated from New York and Pennsylvania to northern Illinois during the 1840s: sisters' Trial (or Tryal), and brothers Jesse, David, and Alva. In addition, Emma's Uncle Nathaniel Lewis, who had strongly opposed Joseph Smith when he and Emma lived in Harmony, Pennsylvania, moved to the area with his wife, Sarah, sons Hiel, Joseph, and Levi, and daughter Sophia. Several neighbors of the Hales also relocated to Lee County, including Asa Searles, who had attended school with Joseph Smith while he lived in Pennsylvania. Searles, who recollected wrestling with the future prophet during their early manhood, described Joseph as a "large, strong fellow [who] could handle any of the boys."[3] Though none of her siblings accepted Mormonism, Emma's nephew, Lorenzo Wasson, joined the Church in 1842, to the delight of both Emma and Joseph, and Lorenzo's younger brother Harmon soon followed.[4] Benjamin and Elizabeth Wasson's daughter Clara must have also experienced a

Elizabeth Hale Wasson, 1800–1874. Sketch by J. Manz, in Inez A. Kennedy, *Recollections of the Pioneers of Lee County* (Dixon, Ill.: Inez A. Kennedy, 1893).

---

2. Lorenzo D. Wasson, Emma Hale Smith, and Joseph Smith (Nauvoo, Ill.), Letter to David Hale, February 20, 1841, MS 7395, LDS Church History Library.

3. Asa Searles, quoted in Kennedy, *Recollections of the Pioneers of Lee County*, 61; *History of Lee County*, 308, 354–55, 386, 397, 400–401. For information on the Lewis family and their opposition to Joseph Smith and Mormonism, see Dan Vogel, ed., *Early Mormon Documents*, 5 vols. (Salt Lake City: Signature Books, 1996–2003), 4:293–321.

4. After a meeting held on March 20, 1842, Joseph Smith went to the Mississippi River "to attend to the ordinance of baptism," not far from his home. "The bank of the Mississippi was lined with a multitude of people, and President Joseph Smith went into the river and baptized eighty persons for the remission of sins, and what added joy to the scene was, that the first person baptized was M[r]. L. D. Wasson, a nephew of Mrs. Emma Smith—the first of her kindred that has embraced the fullness of the Gospel." Joseph Smith Jr., *History of the Church of Jesus Christ of Latter-day Saints*, ed. B. H. Roberts, 2nd rev. ed., 7 vols. (Salt Lake City: Deseret Book, 1971), 1:86 (hereafter cited as *History of the LDS Church*); see also Richard P. Howard, ed., *The Memoirs of President Joseph Smith III (1832–1914)* (Independence: Herald Publishing House, 1979), 36.

warm relationship with her aunt and uncle, as she asked Joseph Smith to perform her wedding to William Backenstos at the Mansion House in Nauvoo on October 4, 1843.[5]

In June 1843, Joseph and Emma Smith decided to take a much-needed vacation to visit the Wassons at Palestine Grove.[6] Although Joseph traveled often in the region and even as far as Washington, D.C., soon after settling in Nauvoo, Emma seldom left Nauvoo except for a rare shopping trip to St. Louis to furnish the Nauvoo House in 1843. Thus, it was unusual for Joseph and Emma to take a trip together, let alone one that included their children, so this family visit must have been warmly anticipated. It was after they reached Palestine Grove, while the Smiths were staying with Elizabeth and Benjamin, that Joseph was arrested at pistol point by Joseph H. Reynolds, a sheriff from Jackson County, Missouri, and Harmon T. Wilson, a constable from Carthage, Illinois. Their purpose was to extradite him to Missouri. The arrest did not go as smoothly as Smith's captors hoped, for local residents protested both the legality and the manner in which Wilson and Reynolds conducted the arrest. Citizens in nearby Pawpaw were also upset when Joseph's captors prevented him from preaching in their community and finally threatened Wilson and Reynolds with legal action. The outnumbered law officers finally conceded, allowing the Prophet to deliver a discourse that lasted an hour and a half.[7]

Alva Hale, 1795–1881. Sketch by unknown artist, in *History of Lee County* (Chicago: H. H. Hill, 1881).

Other residents, including members of Emma's family, came to Joseph Smith's defense and helped deter his captors from transporting him across the Mississippi River into Missouri. These individuals were also instrumental in securing legal aid for the Prophet, which materially aided in his eventual release. Joseph Wood, who acted as a member of Joseph Smith's counsel during his arrest and who was also a Latter-day Saint living near Pawpaw, Illinois, would later play a prominent

---

5. Scott H. Faulring, ed., *An American Prophet's Record: The Diaries and Journals of Joseph Smith* (Salt Lake City: Signature Books, 1987), 417.

6. "Missouri vs. Joseph Smith," *Times and Seasons* 4, no. 16 (July 1, 1843): 242; Thomas Gregg, *The Prophet of Palmyra* (Chicago: Charles H. Chapman & Co., 1880), 209–11. Both of these sources identify Palestine Grove, Illinois, as the location of the Benjamin Wasson home where Joseph Smith was arrested. The Wassons lived near Palestine Grove, which later came to be known as Amboy, Illinois, one mile north of where William Smith located in 1847. Kennedy, *Recollections of the Pioneers of Lee County*, 58.

7. Kennedy, *Recollections of the Pioneers of Lee County*, 101–3.

role in William Smith's organization.⁸ During his arrest, Joseph Smith preached eloquently in the county, leaving a favorable impression among his listeners. After he was secure in Nauvoo, the Saints sent their heartfelt thanks to the residents of Lee County. At a public meeting in Nauvoo, the Saints "Resolved unanimously" that the "citizens of Dixon, Pawpaw Grove, and Lee County generally, in this state, receive the warmest thanks of this meeting for the firm patriotism, bold and decided stand taken against lawless outrage and the spirit of mobocracy, as manifested in the arrest or capture of General Joseph Smith, while on a visit to his friends in that district of [the] country. . . . They have shown themselves republicans, patriots, and worthy citizens of this state."⁹

Clara Wasson Backenstos, 1823–1905. Sketch by J. Manz, in Inez A. Kennedy, *Recollections of the Pioneers of Lee County* (Dixon, Ill.: Inez A. Kennedy, 1893).

Joseph Smith's sensational arrest and his preaching in Lee County opened the way for missionary success in the area. While visiting Emma's relatives and before his arrest, the Prophet had preached at the home of John Hook and in a log schoolhouse—probably the "Wasson schoolhouse" where his twenty-year-old niece Clara taught school. Both the home and the schoolhouse were located in the vicinity of Palestine Grove.¹⁰ Lee County historians indicate that Joseph Smith preached in the vicinity more than once; however, his only visit to the area that can be documented was in the summer of 1843. Ephraim Ingalls, an early resident of the county who later worked as a surgeon in Chicago, remembered that Joseph Smith attended a Sunday service conducted by the Reverend Joseph Gardner, in which Gardner, prompted by "curiosity," invited Smith to give the closing prayer. Following the meeting's conclusion and "after the audience was dismissed," remembered Ingalls, "Smith said to Gardner in an apologetic way, 'I was never gifted in prayer.'"¹¹ During the June 1843 visit that he and Emma made

---

8. It was Joseph Smith III who tentatively identified Joseph Wood as being an attorney who assisted his father during this time period. Joseph III, who was present with the family during his father's arrest, said: "I am of the opinion this same Wood afterward became associated with Uncle William B. Smith, but of this I am not certain. If so, his first name was Joseph." Joseph III also indicated that both Lorenzo and Benjamin Wasson helped to secure legal aid for Joseph Smith. Howard, *The Memoirs of President Joseph Smith III*, 36.

9. "A Public Meeting in Relation to the Late Arrest of General Joseph Smith," *Nauvoo Neighbor* 1, no. 12 (July 19, 1843): 3.

10. *History of Lee County*, 308.

11. Kennedy, *Recollections of the Pioneers of Lee County*, 390–92; see also Anthony J. Becker, *The Biography of a Country Town: U.S.A.* (Amboy, Ill.: Spencer-Walker Press, 1954), 119.

Joseph Smith, sketch by Frank Taylor, based on an earlier sketch by Benjamin West during Joseph Smith's habeas corpus hearing in Springfield, Illinois, in January 1843. From *Harper's Weekly* 27, no. 1372 (April 7, 1883).

to the area, another resident recollected that Joseph Smith debated "a Methodist preacher named Headly, regarding the authenticity of the 'Book of Mormon.'"[12] Still others remembered that both Hyrum Smith and Sidney Rigdon preached in or near Palestine Grove, but this occasion was separate from Joseph and Emma's June 1843 visit.[13]

The Hook family was most impressed not only with Mormonism's prophet, but also with his doctrine. In the months following Joseph Smith's visit, thirty-four-year-old LDS missionary William Anderson began preaching in the area. Anderson lived just across the southern border of Lee County in Bureau County and had been converted by a group of LDS missionaries who preached at his home in July 1841. He was baptized the following month, then traveled to Nauvoo for the October general conference where he was ordained to the priesthood and received his patriarchal blessing from Hyrum Smith. Anderson may have already known the Hook family—both families had moved from Maine to Illinois in the late 1830s—but there is no documentation of an earlier relationship.

Aaron Hook Sr. and Rhoda Gibson Hook, with their sons William and John, left Maine on August 26, 1839, in two horse-drawn wagons, arriving two months later, on October 28. Aaron Jr. had established his home in Lamoille, Bureau County, Illinois, two years earlier. If he did not already know William Anderson, he certainly became acquainted with him rapidly, since they were near neighbors. After staying with Aaron Jr. for several months, the entire Hook family, including Aaron Jr., settled a few miles to the north at Palestine Grove in February 1840. William Anderson, who had been preaching in Chicago and other parts of northern Illinois in the spring of 1843, had reached Lee County by that fall. Like Joseph Smith before him, he also accepted the John Hook family's invitation to preach there and found the extended family eager to hear his message. John, his brother Aaron, their families, and their mother, Rhoda, all became Latter-day Saints by the fall of 1843 as a result of Anderson's preaching. Anderson likely baptized the Hooks in the Green River, which flowed within a stone's throw of

---

12. *History of Lee County*, 309.
13. Kennedy, *Recollections of the Pioneers of Lee County*, 96; Becker, *The Biography of a Country Town*, 119.

Green River, near Palestine Grove (later Amboy), Illinois. Photograph taken by Chase, ca. 1908.

their property. Afterward he held regular preaching services in the Hook home.[14] Mormonism thus gained a firm foothold in Palestine Grove, a relationship that would figure largely in William's future religious activities. (See Chapters 16–17.)

When William Smith initially fled from Nauvoo in mid-September 1845, he went to Iowa and sought refuge with George J. Adams, his colleague from the East, who had made his disaffection public. Adams had been making efforts to establish a church of his own, an important tenet of which was that Joseph III was his father's rightful successor. Adams had announced this position as early as May 1845 and offered William Smith the patriarchal office within his church.[15] Adams's teachings coincided with William's view that the Smith family should play a more prominent role in the Church's hierarchy. During the ensuing winter, William seems to have

---

14. *History of Lee County*, 284, 308–10, 406–7; Pearl Wilcox, *Regathering the Scattered Saints in Wisconsin and Illinois* (Independence: Pearl Wilcox, 1984), 74; Andrew Jenson, *Latter-day Saint Biographical Encyclopedia: A Compilation of Biographical Sketches of Prominent Men and Women in the Church of Jesus Christ of Latter-Day Saints* (Salt Lake City: Andrew Jenson History Co., 1901–36), 2:585–86. Aaron and Matilda Hook's names appear on the Nauvoo Scroll Petition, under the date of November 28, 1843, at Nauvoo. Clark V. Johnson, ed., *Mormon Redress Petitions: Documents of the 1833–1838 Missouri Conflict* (Provo, Utah: BYU Religious Studies Center, 1992), 591–92. In the 1850 census for Amboy, William's children Rhoda, Rosanna, and Aaron, along with their grandmother Rhoda, are all living in the John Hook household. Grandmother Rhoda is referred to as the "widow Hook" in later sources. 1850 U.S. Census, Illinois, Lee County, Amboy Township, Roll M432_116, 117A, image 88.

15. George D. Smith, ed., *An Intimate Chronicle: The Journals of William Clayton* (Salt Lake City: Signature Books, 1991), 166.

believed that he and Joseph III should both fulfill important roles—positions that were waiting for them due to the Saints' desire for a Smith leader. Smith's subsequent experience reinforced his belief that the idea of lineal succession resonated with Saints who remained in the Midwest while those led by the Twelve were plodding across Iowa in the early spring of 1846. Adams and Smith had proselytized for a time at St. Louis and Cincinnati, gaining a handful of adherents, but then switched their allegiance to James J. Strang in the spring of 1846. For Smith, the association with Strang lasted for approximately one year.

After his break with Strang, in June 1847 Smith wrote two letters to Orson Hyde, who headed the Church in Kanesville, Iowa, where he helped organize western migration. William was trying to ascertain whether he might be restored to his former ecclesiastical positions as apostle and patriarch, but he also asked Orson Hyde for funds to move to Utah.[16] Probably still smarting from the way William had behaved when he returned to Nauvoo in March 1846, Hyde responded firmly, making no promises on either point and making it clear that William's sincerity had yet to be proved.[17] (See Chapter 19.) Upset with Hyde's lack of enthusiasm for his reinstatement, William reconsidered the possibilities of establishing a church that would rival those led by Brigham Young and James Strang, despite his notable failure to do so up to that point. This time, Smith contemplated a church in which he would play an increasingly prominent role. He immediately sought to identify individuals who would sympathize with his feelings and support his leadership.

Due to his extensive missionary efforts, Smith was well aware of which outlying Mormon branches were the strongest. In early 1841, he had proselyted in northern Illinois and presided over a church conference held in Walnut Grove Township in Knox County. The conference included a number of different branches from surrounding counties. According to the minutes, members who

---

16. William Smith (St. Louis, Mo.), Letter to Dear Bro. [Orson] Hyde, June 2, 1847, Brigham Young Office Files 1832–1878, General Correspondence, Incoming, 1840–1877, Letters from Church Leaders and Others, 1840–1877, Orson Hyde, 1847–1848, LDS Church History Library; William Smith (St. Louis, Mo.), Letter to Orson Hyde, June 22, 1847, Brigham Young Office Files 1832–1878, Letters from Church Leaders and Others, 1840–1877, William Smith, 1844–1857, LDS Church History Library.

17. Orson Hyde (Council Bluffs, Iowa), Letter to William Smith, June 22, 1847, Brigham Young Office Files 1832–1877, Letters from Church Leaders and Others, Orson Hyde, 1847–1848, LDS Church History Library. William summarized how he interpreted Hyde's letter in an 1847 publication: "Cease your whining about your martyred brothers; cease your whining about your poor old mother, cease your preaching, and go to work at some business, and get money, and join the camp in the west. Go to the camp, if you have to go on foot without money." William Smith and Aaron Hook, *William Smith, Patriarch & Prophet of the Most High God. Latter Days Saints, Beware of Imposition!* (N.p., ca. 1847), 1, M293,1, LDS Church History Library; hereafter cited as Smith and Hook, *William Smith, Patriarch & Prophet*. See Chapter 19 "The Brighamites," for a further discussion on William's relationship with Young's followers after the deaths of Joseph and Hyrum.

Thomas, 1786–1879, and Hannah Tourtillott, 1797–1878, ca. 1870. Photograph courtesy of Maryellen Harshbarger McVicker, photographer unknown.

attended felt that William "gave great satisfaction to his hearers, [being] highly gratified with the labors of Brother Smith," which left them with a favorable impression of the thirty-year-old apostle.[18] In addition to living in Knoxville, Illinois, during the winter of 1846–47, his more recent association with Strang had introduced him to clusters of Saints in northern Illinois and southern Wisconsin who had not gone west under Brigham Young's leadership. When he renewed his efforts to organize a church in August 1847, William targeted Lee County as a particularly promising area.

At least part of the reason William was drawn to Lee County was his earlier association with Aaron Hook Jr., who had lived in Palestine Grove since 1840.[19] Like Smith, Hook had also joined James Strang's church for a brief period after Joseph Smith's death, and it was during that period when he and William forged their friendship. William had stayed with Hook at Palestine Grove in the fall of 1846. Another of his hosts was sixty-year-old Thomas Tourtillott, who lived in the very southwest corner of Lee County, in Hanno (later Sublette) Township. Tourtillott had migrated from Bangor, Maine, to Illinois in 1839, most likely with the Hook family, and had also affiliated with Strang.[20]

---

18. "Minutes of a Conference held at Walnut Grove, Knox [C]o. Ill. January 30th, 1841," *Times and Seasons* 2, no. 9 (March 1, 1841): 12.

19. Kennedy, *Recollections of the Pioneers of Lee County*, 86.

20. The son of a Revolutionary War veteran, Captain Abraham Tourtellotte, and his wife, Leah Mansell Tourtellotte, Thomas was born April 23, 1786, at Orono, Maine. In 1826, he married Hannah, born April 8, 1797, at Howland, Maine. Duane A. Tourtillott, "Book of Remembrance," 1978, Tourtillott Family Papers, Wisconsin State Archives, University of Wisconsin at Green Bay; Anthony J. Becker and Lillian A. Rapp,

During the fall of 1846, William borrowed Tourtillott's horse and rode a hundred miles to Walnut Grove Township near Altona, in Knox County, Illinois, to visit his daughters, who were living there with their grandparents, Joshua and Athalia Grant, and their aunt Roxey Ann. When William returned the horse some weeks later, the Tourtillotts "treated me with great hospitality and kindness" while he recovered from a five-week bout of "chills and fever." In April 1847, William traveled with Thomas Tourtillott and Aaron Hook to Strang's general conference, then again visited his daughters at Walnut Grove Township.[21]

William remained in Walnut Grove Township during April-May 1847 with the Grants. In May, William's divorce from Mary Jane Rollins was finalized in Knox County, and he acted promptly. Only days later, on May 19, he married twenty-two-year-old Roxey Ann Grant, Caroline's younger sister.[22] James J. Strang and William's friend Hiram Stratton (also a Strangite), had been instrumental in providing the necessary legal documentation to complete the divorce.[23] Roxey Ann had periodically taken care of William and Caroline's young daughters, providing stability and a growing attachment, while Caroline's deteriorating health intermittently confined her to her bed. In November 1844, Roxey Ann had traveled from her parents' home in Knox County to the East Coast to help care for Caroline during her downward-spiraling illness, then had accompanied William and her dying sister to Nauvoo in May 1845. There she helped Emma nurse Caroline and, after Caroline's funeral, accepted baptism from William in the Mississippi River. He had tried to persuade her to stay on and help care for his daughters, but she insisted on returning to Knox County where her parents, both in their sixties, needed care.[24] Roxey Ann had returned to Nauvoo at least once, as she received her washing and anointing and endowment in the Nauvoo Temple on February 2, 1846.[25] During 1846–47 after William had taken his daughters and left the city by night with only a few hours' notice, it seems likely that Roxey Ann had taken the major responsibility for the girls while William

---

Sublette, Illinois: Our Bit of U.S.A: Sublette Centennial (Mendota, Ill.: Sublette Centennial Committee, 1954), 11, 76. John Hook was also born at Orono, Maine, on October 16, 1814. *History of Lee County*, 406.

21. William Smith, Epistle, ca. 1850, 5, William Smith Papers, MS 3697, LDS Church History Library.

22. William and Roxey Ann were married by probate justice R. T. Hannaman, who served in that position from 1837 to 1839, and again from 1843 to 1849. William Smith and Roxey Ann Grant Marriage License, Marriage Index Book 1, 84, Knox County Courthouse, Galesburg, Illinois.

23. William Smith vs. Mary Jane Smith, May and June Terms, 1847, Circuit Court Records, Knox County Courthouse, Galesburg, Illinois. Included in the file is Hiram Stratton's sworn statement regarding Mary Jane Rollins Smith's disreputable character while at Nauvoo, notarized by James J. Strang. The divorce was final on May 12, 1847.

24. William Smith (Nauvoo, Ill.), Letter to Joshua Grant Jr., August 12, 1845, *Nauvoo Neighbor* 3, no. 16 (August 20, 1845): 3.

25. Nauvoo Temple Endowment Register, 263, Land and Records Office, Nauvoo, Illinois.

was affiliating with Strang. The marriage was a logical choice, as Roxey Ann had never married, obviously had developed a close bond with her two nieces, and, as far as is known, had no inkling of William's multiple plural marriages during the later summer and early fall of 1845.

In August 1847, William publicly declared that he had broken with Strang. Aaron Hook and Thomas Tourtillott apparently followed his lead. After attending the April 1847 Strangite conference in Voree, Hook and Tourtillott returned to their homes in Lee County, where Hook opened his home to dispersed Saints in the area and hosted regular church meetings. Though the group he gathered around him was small, Hook "sometimes preached, and was an influential man among those of his faith."[26] William described the thirty-year-old Hook as a "vigorous man," with a "strong intellect, and athletic powers."[27]

These regular preaching services began in the fall of 1847, and William Smith returned to their community, enthused with the revived vision of launching his own denomination. Roxey Ann and William's two daughters probably stayed behind in Knox County during his early missionary efforts that fall. Recounting his general movements during this time period, William announced in an 1850 "Epistle" that he went "to Palestine Grove with an intention of obtaining possession of a place for a temporary gathering or resting place for the church, where I organized a stake of Zion according to the commandments of God, and continued laboring and baptising in this place, and the region round about from the fall of 1847 to the fall of 1848."[28] Not only was William warmly received by those who shared his Mormon heritage, but the locals also treated him respectfully because of their earlier experience with Joseph Smith at the time of his arrest in 1843.

Besides the Hooks and Tourtillotts, William likely knew at least some of the local families who had some affiliation with Mormonism but who had not felt motivated to move, either to Nauvoo, or to any other "gathering" place. Smith quickly decided that this region was ideal for mobilizing these scattered Saints into a supportive group. Among those who lived in the region and who had become Mormons during Joseph Smith's lifetime, were Lorenzo and Harmon Wasson (sons of Emma's sister, Elizabeth), Edwin and Permelia Cadwell, Alva and Sabrina Smith (no relation to William), Susannah Williams, Stephen and Erepta Richardson,[29] Experience Stone, and other members of the extended

---

26. *History of Lee County*, 310.

27. William Smith, Letter to the Saints Scattered Abroad, *Melchisedek and Aaronic Herald* (Covington, Ky.) 1, no. 8 (September, 1849): 1.

28. William Smith, Epistle, ca. 1850, 6.

29. Stephen and Erepta Wilder Richardson joined the Church at Charleston, Virginia, being baptized by Lyman Johnson and confirmed by Orson Pratt. Stephen was ordained a priest at Nauvoo on April 6, 1843, and the couple received their endowments in the Nauvoo Temple on January 9, 1846. They joined William Smith's church at Palestine Grove sometime during 1847–50. Wilcox, *Regathering the Scattered Saints in Wisconsin and Illinois*, 84–85; William Smith (et. al.) (Shelburn [Palestine Grove], Ill.), Letter to

Stephen Richardson (1799–1888) and Erepta Wilder Richardson (1802–1889), ca. 1880. Photograph courtesy of Maryellen Harshbarger McVicker, photographer unknown.

Hook family.[30] William naturally knew some of Emma's relatives, even if their contacts were infrequent. He knew, or knew about, others who had moved in from New York and Pennsylvania—northeasterners who held the same values and ideology as himself. "The people are friendly," he would later comment, further confirming his conviction that Palestine Grove was a promising location for this second effort to organize his own church.[31]

Smith had been involved in community building from his early twenties in Kirtland, followed by additional experiences in Far West and especially Nauvoo. His leadership skills in presiding over the scattered eastern branches also stood him in good stead as he planned his own church. Palestine Grove offered all of the ingredients for his own version of Zion. The "rocky ford" of the Green River (formerly called Inlet Creek or Rock River) had been a natural ford, since, at that location, the river bottom was solid rock. For centuries Native Americans had crossed at this point on the trail from Council Bluffs to Chicago. By the time the Hooks settled in the area, the native peoples were still wintering near the crossing, a tradition that had persisted for generations. Rhoda Hook, John and Aaron's wid-

---

the Honorable Senators & Representatives of the United States in Congress Assembled, January 29, 1850, Brigham Young Office Files 1832–1878, Utah Delegate Files, 1849–1872, John M. Bernhisel to Brigham Young, 1849–1866, 1849–1850 March-May, LDS Church History Library.

30. Wilcox, *Regathering the Scattered Saints in Wisconsin and Illinois*, 84–85, 89.

31. Smith and Hook, *William Smith, Patriarch and Prophet*, 1.

John Hook Home and Tavern. Date and photographer unknown. Courtesy Community of Christ Archives.

owed mother, traded with the friendly Indians who camped near her home.[32] The river crossing became a natural stopping place for the early white settlers as well, and by the 1840s, a number of businesses had been established near this location.

Though the community had existed since the mid-1830s, it was not until 1844 that a small town was platted on the west side of the crossing and designated by the name of Rocky Ford. In November 1847, only three months after Smith arrived on the scene, a new plat was created and the town, renamed Shelburn, was expanded to include sites on both sides of the river. "Palestine Grove," referring to the extensive timberland in the southernmost part of the county, predated both of these town names and originally referred to a much larger geographical area, not a specific town site. Later, after the area was more settled, it referred to the much smaller and more specific location of Rhoda Hook's property, just a quarter mile northwest of the ford. William Smith used all three of these city names—Rocky Ford, Shelburn, and Palestine Grove—interchangeably in his correspondence to describe the same location.[33]

Besides a saw mill, a distillery, and two stores being established in the community, a flouring mill termed a "corn cracker" was built in 1844 just a few miles south of the crossing on the river, the first of its kind in the county. The town also had a schoolhouse, which doubled as a meeting house for community worship

---

32. Kennedy, *Recollections of the Pioneers of Lee County*, 91–92.

33. Writing to his followers in 1847, Smith said that "Palestine Grove, or Rocky Ford, now known as the town of *Shelburn*, is situated on a public state road, leading from Peru (the head of navigation on the Illinois River) to Dixon, Rock River, and Galena." Smith and Hook, *William Smith, Patriarch and Prophet*, 1. The more specific location of Palestine Grove was platted in 1854 at the request of Rhoda Hook and marks the location where William Smith established his following.

Crossing of the Green River at Rocky Ford (Palestine Grove or Shelburn). Sketch by J. Manz, in Inez A. Kennedy, *Recollections of the Pioneers of Lee County* (Dixon, Ill.: Inez A. Kennedy, 1893).

services, separate from those held in the Hook home.[34] The Hooks' home and property was near the crossing, and in time, they expanded their home so they could offer facilities to feed and shelter travelers. Though their inn had no sign, early travelers who crisscrossed through the area were well aware of its location. By 1842, the mail carrier used the "Hook Tavern" as a primary station on his route, staying at the location on Monday nights as he went north and Friday nights on his return trip. This Hook home also became the central gathering place where the area's scattered settlers came together for "concerts, lectures, puppet shows," and other forms of entertainment, such as politicking and preaching.[35]

A road maintained by the state, termed by locals the "Peru and Galena state road" because it ran between the two cities, ran right through the settlement, and when a stage line was established, it also followed this route. Perhaps the most significant element in community-envisioned growth was that the Central Railroad, then under construction in the state, was popularly planned to run parallel to the Peru and Galena road, passing right through the town of Shelburn. (It was finished in 1854, but ended up being constructed a mile or so to the north.) Smith was perceptive enough to recognize the town's potential, and the fact that the Hooks' home and tavern were at the center of the town's activity made this locale even more appealing. Rhoda Hook also owned forty acres of property in the town, and Smith saw the prospect for growth and gathering on her property as ideal.[36]

---

34. *History of Lee County*, 281; Kennedy, *Recollections of the Pioneers of Lee County*, 60, 92–95; Smith and Hook, *William Smith, Patriarch and Prophet*, 1.

35. Wilcox, *Regathering the Scattered Saints*, 72–73; Kennedy, *Recollections of the Pioneers of Lee County*, 91.

36. A copy of Rhoda E. Hook's purchase of forty acres of section 21 in Amboy Township, signed by President James Polk on September 1, 1845, is reproduced in

Smith's experience as a leader and his effectiveness as a preacher were immediately evident after his arrival, and Mormon influence in the area immediately expanded. Smith found a sympathetic ear in Aaron Hook. Both men energetically denounced other branches of Mormonism and strongly desired to reestablish the Church as it had existed during Joseph's day. Though William attempted to pick up where he had left off before being distracted by Strangite possibilities, he had certainly lost a number of initial converts by switching his allegiance to Strang. A former supporter who remained with Strang was George J. Adams, who continued to play a prominent role in Strang's movement, instructing Strang regarding polygamy, and also crowning Strang "King of heaven and earth" using his own theatrical props to supply a crown, scepter, and robes.[37]

Another who remained with Strang was Stephen Kettle, who also lived nearby at La Moille, across the county line in Bureau County. Apparently Smith and Kettle could not get along after Smith denounced Strang, perhaps because the two were vying for converts in the region. At one point, in late August 1848, their differences spilled over into violence. According to Kettle, who would later file charges against him for assault and battery, William "did make an assault and with his hands and feet did . . . beat[,] bruise and injure [me]." While William was initially found guilty of assault and battery by a judge in Bureau County and fined twenty-five dollars, he appealed the decision in Lee County, and the case was dropped.[38]

Notwithstanding the erosion of these more notable personalities, Smith forged ahead, trying to regenerate interest in his budding movement. A major task for Smith and Hook during the fall of 1847 was articulating clear beliefs that would provide their church with a distinctive identity. On August 28, William announced a revelation that, among other things, instructed: "I appoint unto you a stake of Zion in this land, even in the land of Palestine, wherein thou dwellest, to be a place of gathering . . . for your temporal salvation." The revelation continued, "In this stake . . . my people shall build unto me an house that shall be for the cleansing of the sanctuary, and for the saving of the sons of Jacob." The "cleansing" probably was an announcement that a goal was returning the church to its original purity, making it distinctive from other factions of Mormonism

---

Becker, *The Biography of a Country Town*, 96. The *History of Lee County* notes that, "until the fall of 1844, when the first land sales were held at Dixon, the inhabitants of Amboy Township [where the Hook property was located], were squatters." Rhoda formalized her land transaction less than a year later. *History of Lee County*, 284–85.

37. Vickie Cleverley Speek, *"God Has Made Us a Kingdom": James Strang and the Midwest Mormons* (Salt Lake City: Signature Books, 2006), 92, 119–22.

38. General no. 111, Circuit Court, Lee County, Illinois, vs. William Smith, Criminal Action, term 1849, record B, p. 42, Illinois State Archives, Illinois Regional Archives Depository, Regional History Center, Founders Memorial Library Room 400, Northern Illinois University, DeKalb, IL. Special thanks to Erin Jennings Metcalfe for locating and sharing this source. For more information about Stephen Kettle's association with Strang, see John J. Hajicek, ed., *Chronicles of Voree, 1844–1849* (Burlington, Wisc.: J.J. Hajicek, 1992), 80.

that were also vying for converts. It then built up to the crucial point: "And now I command my servant William Smith and my servant Aaron Hook, whom I have appointed to be thy counsellor, to begin from this hour to proclaim the glad tidings of salvation, even the redemption of Zion, and to set in order all things pertaining to my Church." William published this revelation in a one-page broadside that also included his denunciation of nine of the Twelve Apostles[39] and James J. Strang. A third item on this broadside was his editorial, written for the occasion, pointing out the incongruity of claiming that "the Prophet was a transgressor when he fell, . . . and [yet] there is a crown and sceptre awaiting him. . . . We leave the Saints to judge of the consistency of the premises upon which the usurper Strang claims his appointment to the leadership of the Church." Smith continued pointedly, "The Saints will know how to appreciate the labors and claims of any man who would thus charge the Prophet Joseph, after all the good he has done in 17 years of hard labor and toil to bring the fulness of the gospel to the nations of the earth, saying nothing of the many times he was mobbed, tarred and feathered, and left on the ground for dead, and at last, without means of defence, murdered outright in Carthage." William emphatically declared that his brother Joseph had died a "martyr, and not a transgressor," as Strang claimed. He and Hook also emphasized the importance of gathering to the area, as well as the necessity of engaging in missionary work.[40]

While Smith had been lured into cooperation with both Adams and Strang by the promise of prominent positions, this time there would be no question about who was in charge. In this, and subsequent revelations, Smith denominated himself "First President, Prophet, Seer, Revelator, Translator, and Patriarch over the whole church of Jesus Christ of Latter Day Saints."[41] The proliferation of titles helped buttress William's sense of security about heading this newly reorganized church. He reverted to the explanation he had argued for in vain in Nauvoo—that because of his ordination as patriarch he was entitled to the multiple positions Hyrum held as Assistant President of the Church and Patriarch over the Church.

"I have appointed thee, my servant William Smith, to take the place of my servant Hiram Smith, thy brother," read a second revelation William dictated in late 1847, "as Patriarch unto the whole Church, and to preside over my people, saith your God, and no power shall remove thee therefrom; and thou shalt be the Prophet Seer Revelator, and Translator unto my church during the minority of him who I have appointed from the loins of Joseph thy brother." Despite this clear reference to Joseph III's right to leadership, succeeding events revealed that William had little, if any, intention of turning the presiding role over to his nephew. In fact, this second revelation in 1847 included the caveat: If Joseph III "does that which

---

39. The three who were not cut off were Lyman Wight, John E. Page, and William himself.
40. Smith and Hook, *William Smith, Patriarch and Prophet*, 1.
41. Joseph Wood, *Epistle of the Twelve* (Milwaukee, Wisc.: Sentinel and Gazette Steam Press Print, 1851), 3.

is wicked and corrupt before me, and hardens his heart and stiffens his neck with pride and rebellious sc[h]ism, then thou my servant William, shalt continue to exercise all the authority with which I have this day invested thee, and thou shalt not only be the successor of Hiram, thy brother, but of Joseph, thy brother also, in all things." This second revelation continued: "For thou art the 'President of the High-Priesthood of the Church' . . . inherited by lineal descent,—therefore I say unto my servant William Smith, arise and set all things in order . . . for unto my servant William have I given to act in the place of the legal heir of Joseph whom I have appointed to receive commandments for my church, if he continue faithful."[42]

This pronouncement was the culmination of what William had desired for three years, and he was exhilarated to see it coming to fruition. The August 28 revelation had assigned Aaron Hook the position of Smith's first counselor, and they called their regrouped organization the "Palestine Grove Branch" or the "Palestine Stake of Zion" of the Church of Jesus Christ of Latter Day Saints.[43]

William and Aaron Hook did not view their church as a new organization but rather as a reestablishment of Joseph's original church, correcting the "apostasy" into which the Twelve, by usurping authority at Nauvoo, had led it. On January 10, 1848, William's small group of followers met at the home of Thomas Tourtillott in Lee County, where they appointed six men to write a proclamation announcing to the scattered Saints that a prophet had been appointed and denouncing all other factions of Mormonism. The six leaders, which included Smith, Aaron Hook and Tourtillott—and reminiscent of how William's brother Joseph had inaugurated Mormonism—crafted their document in the intervening months and published it on March 24, 1848. A major focus was vindicating William's character and authority. Referring to other factions of Mormonism, the proclamation read that "the works of all those will be brought to nought, who have, by treachery and deceit, sought to destroy the Smith family, the lawful Priesthood of the Church, and more particularly William Smith, one of the subjects of this epistle, to whom we wish now to call your attention as the only remaining brother of the martyred Prophet, as a man approved of by God." Also noteworthy during these early months of organization was Smith's continued support of vicarious work for the dead, where he mentioned that "all the baptisms for the dead performed before the death of my servant Joseph are acceptable unto me, and from this time let my servant William appoint a stake in every state, and let this ordinance, all washings, anointings, endowments, and other ordinances, be performed by those whom he shall hereafter appoint in those stakes." William's description appears, at least at the time, to closely resemble the temple ordinances practiced at Nauvoo.[44]

---

42. William Smith, *A Revelation Given to William Smith, in 1847, On the Apostacy of the Church and the Pruning of the Vineyard of the Lord* (N.p., 1848), 1–2, M293.1, LDS Church History Library.

43. Smith and Hook, *William Smith, Patriarch and Prophet*, 1.

44. The other three men who were appointed to help write the proclamation were Alva Smith, John Landers, and Nathaniel Berry. "To the Scattered Saints," *Zion's Standard:*

Church-Building: Quest for Ecclesiastical Station

Thomas and Hannah Tourtillott Home, near Sublette, Illinois. Ca. 1920, photographer unknown. Courtesy Maryellen Harshbarger McVicker.

It was clear from Smith's initial revelation and by labeling Palestine Grove a "branch," that Smith and Hook envisioned their organization quickly expanding throughout the country and eventually filling the world. Their little branch would ultimately become the center of the kingdom of God. Smith hoped that, once established, the scattered branches of his blossoming church would accept him as the successor to his brother, and adhere to his revelations. Despite these great aspirations, however, growth was initially meager. In the fall of 1847, when Brigham Young returned from Utah to Winter Quarters and learned of Smith's attempt to organize, he derisively commented, "Wm. Smith has set up shop for himself, has one member to his Church & he is his [own] 1st counselor."[45] In reality, Smith and Hook had, in the first four or five months, expanded their church to approximately twenty to thirty followers and, Young's jibe to the contrary, William did have a first counselor in Hook.[46]

The Hook property, located just northwest of the crossing of the Green River, became the center of activity for William's budding church. Aaron Hook apparent-

---

A Voice from the Smith Family (Princeton, Ill.: P. Lynch, March 24, 1848), 1; see also William Smith, *A Revelation Given to William Smith, in 1847*, 2.

45. Brigham Young and Willard Richards (Winter Quarters, Neb.), Letter to Orson Spencer, November 25, 1847, Brigham Young Office Files 1832–1878, General Correspondence, Outgoing, 1843–1876, 1847 October-December, LDS Church History Library.

46. William Smith said that he had thirty followers, and LDS missionary George W. Bratton said he had twenty to thirty. Testimony of William B. Smith, Temple Lot Case Testimonies, 170, United States Testimony 1892, U.S. Eighth Circuit Court, MS 1160, LDS Church History Library; Geo[rge] W. Bratton (Ottawa, Ill.), Letter to Brigham Young, February 26, 1848, Brigham Young Office Files 1832–1878, General Correspondence, Incoming, 1840–1877, A-C, 1848, LDS Church History Library.

ly also built a home on his mother's forty acres and eventually "fitted up his house with a hall which was used for their [church] services."[47] In accordance with his first revelation, William established himself more permanently in the Palestine Grove area, and began construction on a home on Rhoda Hook's property. "In Palestine grove I built a house costing me Some $300, on the Ladies Hook land," William recalled some forty years later.[48] However, he willingly accepted help—and even urged contributions and labors—from his followers. Writing from Palestine Grove in 1851, one follower noted: "President William Smith has a bad cold, $20.00 has been raised on the credit of the Lodge to finish purchasing materials for finishing the house."[49] In the meantime, William lived with Aaron Hook and called Aaron's older brother, John, as stake president over Palestine Grove Branch.[50] Smith's group eventually managed to lay out a town that they named Palestine Grove a quarter of a mile northwest of the river crossing. Local residents recall "talk of building a temple" on a prominent hill in their newly established community.[51]

Smith's extensive church-building experience provided a clear template of how to launch his new organization and increase its membership. As Joseph's early church had done in each gathering location, William sought to establish a newspaper that would disseminate information regarding his beliefs and expand his church. He petitioned funds from his supporters to purchase a printing press with which to publish "useful knowledge and the preservation of faith."[52] When the necessary means were not forthcoming, he resorted to job-printing by papers in more populous areas in northern Illinois, including the *Ottawa Free Trader* and the *Princeton Herald*. At Ottawa, Smith published several lengthy publications, one of which included his entire August 1847 revelation. In March 1848, Smith managed to publish a single issue of *Zion's Standard: A Voice from the Smith Family*, which he may have hoped would become his church's official newspaper. P. Lynch, editor of the *Princeton [Illinois] Herald*, in nearby Bureau County, produced this rare exemplar, whose contents reflected William's persisting perception that he and his family had repeatedly been treated unjustly.[53]

Ironically, he no doubt felt that his own family were among his persecutors. He no longer had any documented support from his remaining siblings,

---

47. *History of Lee County*, 310.

48. William Smith, Letter to Brother [Edmund Levi Kelley], ca. 1893, Suplaiment [sic], P19, fd. 49, Miscellaneous Letters, Community of Christ Archives.

49. Joseph Wood (Palestine, Ill.), Letter to Jason W. Briggs, September 30, 1851, Miscellaneous Letters and Papers, P13, f80, Community of Christ Archives.

50. When the 1850 U.S. census was enumerated, William was living with Aaron Hook in Amboy, Lee County, Illinois; see also "An Extract of Conference Minutes," *Melchisedek and Aaronic Herald* 1, no. 6 (September 1849): 4.

51. *History of Lee County*, 310.

52. Smith and Hook, *William Smith, Patriarch and Prophet*, 1.

53. William Smith, *Zion's Standard: A Voice from the Smith Family* (Princeton, Ill.: P. Lynch, March 24, 1848); Smith and Hook, *William Smith, Patriarch and Prophet*, 1.

Lewis Crum Bidamon, 1806–1891. Photograph by D. W. McClure, date unknown. Courtesy Community of Christ Archives.

Emma, Mother Smith, or even his briefly enthusiastic brother-in-law, Jenkins Salisbury. William visited relatives some time between December 1847–January 1848 at Nauvoo shortly after establishing his church at Palestine Grove, hoping to enlist their support and the influence of their names. His exuberance received a decided splash of cold water when he called on Emma and her new husband, Lewis Bidamon, whom she had married in December 1847, soon after William had received his second revelation. Although Bidamon and Emma were, as always, cordial to family members, neither one took his claims seriously. Bidamon, who was a lapsed Congregationalist and at the time of their interaction a self-proclaimed deist, treated the whole conversation with contempt, laughing and making fun of religion generally. In a letter in 1893 to RLDS presiding bishop Edmund L. Kelley, Smith recounted indignantly, "While I set at his table [Bidamon] he asked me what [I] thought of the mistakes of Moses," in an apparent attempt to belittle his faith. As the conversation continued, William unable to make a dent in Bidamon's religious paradigm, described: "I became disgusted with him," due to his apparent skepticism. Though he did not record Emma's reaction, she apparently made no effort to extend her hospitality to William personally to welcome his religious view. Although details are scanty, learning two years earlier that he was still supporting plural marriage created a permanent rift in their relationship. Emma was certainly perceptive enough—and had seen examples from others besides William—to recognize that William would have seized any opportunity to exploit the name and influence of Joseph III, then barely fifteen. Furthermore, the situation in the Midwest was still unstable, and she was not anxious to promote any activities that would intensify the already existing tensions and conflict.

William next tried to enlist Lewis and Emma to look after William's property at Plymouth, Illinois, perhaps hoping to reap some income from rental. When they refused, William became further upset.[54] This negative visit created a rift that

---

54. William B. Smith, Letter to Brother [Edmund L. Kelley], ca. 1893. Joseph Smith III similarly recollected "how scornfully he [Lewis] had treated the Bible, and how, in my case, he had scoffed at and sought to throw distrust and discredit upon that Word which I had received as guidance in my religious life and was striving so hard to obey." Joseph III further recounted that, just a year before Lewis's death, he felt that his stepfather had softened toward religion. Joseph III challenged him to receive the ordinance of baptism.

persisted for decades. In fact, the next positive documented interaction was in 1878, the year he linked himself to the Reorganized Church and just months before Emma's death. Perhaps they had mended differences earlier, but the relationship appears to have been strained at least until the early 1860s.[55] Interestingly, William also avoided proselyting Emma's relatives living near Palestine Grove, some of whom communicated with Emma during the time William was building up his church in the area. Writing in May 1848 to his Aunt Emma, Harmon Wasson wrote that "neither Wm Smith [or] any of his crue [crew] have ever attempted to convert any of this neighborhood[, they] probably think we are not smart enough to appreciate their motives[.] at all events they let us alone which probably is wisdom in them." Wasson also expressed his contempt for those who were supporting William, writing that "the Hook[']s tribe are the Lowest of the low & they are Bill[']s main support."[56]

At this point, William's sister Sophronia had been widowed, and she and her only surviving daughter Maria moved to the eastern edge of Hancock County, in Fountain Green, Illinois. By the year 1850, they were living in the same household with Sophronia's sister Lucy and her husband, Arthur Millikin, and their four children, where Arthur was working making saddles. Lucy Mack Smith, who was living at Nauvoo in the late 1840s, was also living with daughters Sophronia and Lucy by the year 1850. Katharine, her husband Jenkins Salisbury, with their four children ranging in age from fourteen to six months, were living nearby in Webster (formerly Ramus and Macedonia), Illinois, where he worked as a blacksmith, but they certainly were not prospering financially.[57] During the same visit, William ran into additional conflict with his relatives. He had earlier assisted

---

"He looked me squarely in the face," Joseph III recorded of Lewis's reply, "and then with tears trickling over his whitened cheeks said, solemnly and faintly, 'Joseph, it is too late!' 'Too late, Major?' 'Yes, my boy; it is too late.' . . . . Kneeling with others at his bedside, I offered up a most earnest prayer for him and for the peace of his soul. . . . As if in the nature of a direct answer to my plea, the wasted man with bowed head and feeble hands hanging low, in the humility of conscious guilt scarce daring to look up, murmured low, pleadingly and with earnest fervor, 'Lord, be merciful to me, a sinner!'" Mary Audentia Smith Anderson, ed., *Joseph Smith III and the Restoration* (Independence, Mo.: Herald House, 1952), 466–69.

55. William B. Smith (Hannibal, Mo.), Letter to Joseph Smith III, January 25, 1879, in *Saints' Herald* 26, no. 4 (February 15, 1879): 62. William called on Lewis in 1886 and "took tea with him and wife. The Major [Lewis] showed me over the ground where some of our relatives were laid away for their final resting place."

56. Harmon Wasson (Binghamton, Ill.), Letter to Emma [Smith] Bidamon, May 14, 1848, Wilford C. Wood Collection, MS f413, LDS Church History Library.

57. 1850 U.S. Census, Illinois, Hancock County, September 17, 1850, Roll M432_109, 296B, image 60; Gracia N. Jones, "Sophronia Smith Stoddard McCleary," and Kyle R. Walker, "Katharine Smith Salisbury," both in Kyle R. Walker, ed., *United by Faith: The Joseph Sr. and Lucy Mack Smith Family* (American Fork, Utah: BYU Studies and Covenant Communications, 2006), 182–89, 326–32.

Mother Lucy in brokering a deal with Church trustees, which resulted in deeding Mother Smith the Joseph B. Noble home at Nauvoo. (See Chapter 19.) The trustees, Almon W. Babbitt and Joseph Heywood, made the transfer reluctantly, fearing, not without cause, that William would somehow get possession of the property. Although William certainly had a tendency to regard family property as his own, his mother and sisters were upset at this imputation of William's motives. Mother Lucy wrote an indignant letter that scorchingly denounced them for infringing on her motherly feelings, and implying that they wanted her to promise to turn William out of her house before they would make the transfer.[58]

In fact, as time revealed, William did have designs on the property. Just a year after the trustees deeded the home to Mother Smith on April 11, 1846, Lucy then deeded the home to her daughter Lucy and son-in-law Arthur Millikin on March 24, 1847, while they were still in Knox County.[59] Nine months later when William visited Nauvoo, in the winter of 1847–48 and discovered that the transaction had taken place, he was incensed. He felt entitled to the property, likely because he had acted as his mother's advisor in obtaining the home. Church trustee Almon Babbitt wrote Brigham Young on January 31, 1848, that William "has got at loger heads with A[rthur] Milliken and Lucy, because Mother Smith made a deed of the property that the Trustees deeded to her to Milliken[;] hence, you see that the Smith family are divided up."[60] Perhaps trying to pacify William, Mother Lucy allowed him to take the Egyptian mummies she had received from her son Joseph in Kirtland and which she had carefully watched over for many years, showing them to visitors for a small fee that was significant as a means of support. William desired to profit from the mummies as early as April 1847, and attempted to sell them outright to Brigham Young and the Church on the trail west that same month, using Reuben Miller as an intermediary. Nothing came of his offer of $1,600, and it is unclear if Lucy endorsed William's attempt to sell

---

58. Lucy Smith (Nauvoo, Ill.), Letter to Messrs. Babbitt, Heywood, and Hulmer [sic], March 22, 1846, *Voree Herald* 1, no. 8 (August 1846): 3.

59. Lucy Mack Smith apparently transferred the property for $1,000 to her daughter, Lucy, and her husband, Arthur Millikin. They possibly rented the home by the late 1840s but were living in Fountain Green, Illinois, by 1850. They, in turn, sold the property for a mere $200 on March 9, 1852. The preceding transactions had been recorded in Hancock County Deeds, Book P, 435–36, entry #8477 (June 5, 1846); and then Book S, 188–89, entry #10437 (June 1, 1847). The $200 transaction was recorded in Book 33, entry #4530 (March 9, 1852), according to Susan Easton Black, Harvey B. Black, and Brandon Plewe, *Property Transactions in Nauvoo, Hancock County, Illinois, and Surrounding Communities (1839–1859)*, 7 vols. (Wilmington, Del.: World Vital Records, Inc., 2006), 2878, 3785 (volumes paginated continuously).

60. Almon W. Babbitt (Nauvoo, Ill.), Letter to Brigham Young, January 31, 1848, Brigham Young Office Files 1832–1878, General Correspondence, Incoming, 1840–1877, A-C, 1848, LDS Church History Library.

the mummies at that time.⁶¹ During another trip to Nauvoo during the ensuing winter, William apparently persuaded Lucy to loan him the mummies as a source of income; but as Babbitt noted, "William Smith has got the Mummies from Mother Smith and refuses to give them up."⁶² It is unclear what Babbitt meant by "give them up," but it probably meant that Smith refused to return them to Mother Smith so that she could continue to earn a small subsistence by exhibiting them to visitors who passed through Nauvoo.

If William had arrived in Nauvoo confident in his conviction that "the Smith family [must] gather themselves together" and "give heed to the counsel of my servant William," as his second revelation mandated, it was evident that the Smiths themselves did not consider themselves bound by this revelatory instruction.⁶³ The only documented support from his family after this period was that two brothers-in-law, Jenkins Salisbury and Arthur Millikin, briefly acted as agents for the *Melchisedek and Aaronic Herald* in August 1849.⁶⁴ This paper was printed at Covington, Kentucky, with the support of Isaac Sheen. Salisbury occasionally corresponded with Smith during this period, but his letters seem limited to information about Nauvoo and Mother Smith's health.⁶⁵ None of the Smiths relocated to Palestine Grove, and no relatives attended his conferences or held positions in his church. Though William occasionally visited his family in and around Nauvoo, he remained more or less estranged from them during the decades of the 1850s and 1860s, uncharacteristic of usual relations within the family. His three sisters stayed in close contact with each other and their mother throughout the remainder of their lives.⁶⁶

How William explained this skepticism to himself is not clear, but his typical pattern would have been to perceive himself as a martyr, suffering ill treatment because of his high calling. William returned to Palestine Grove determined to

---

61. Reuben Miller (Burlington, Iowa Territory), to Bro [Brigham] Young, April 21, 1847, Brigham Young Office Files 1832–1878, General Correspondence, Incoming, 1840–1877, General Letters, 1840–1877, M-P, 1847, LDS Church History Library.

62. Almon W. Babbitt to Brigham Young, January 31, 1848.

63. William Smith, *A Revelation Given to William Smith in 1847*, 3.

64. "List of Agents for This Paper," *Melchisedek and Aaronic Herald* 1, no. 5 (August 1849): 2.

65. "Mother Smith, mother of the martyred prophets . . . ," *Melchisedek and Aaronic Herald* 1, no. 5 (August 1849): 4. Salisbury had written to William that "Mother Smith . . . has been sick, nigh unto death, and although she has recovered, it is not expected that she will live long." William also attached the name of Jenkins Salisbury to his petition to Congress in 1850, but there is no evidence that Salisbury was present at Palestine Grove. William likely attached Salisbury's name *in absentia* to bolster support for his petition. William Smith, Letter to the Honorable Senators & Representatives of the United States in Congress Assembled, January 29, 1850.

66. Kyle R. Walker, "The Joseph Sr. and Lucy Mack Smith Family: A Family Process Analysis of a Nineteenth-Century Household" (Ph.D. diss., Brigham Young University, 2001); published under the same title as part of the BYU Studies/Joseph Fielding Smith Institute for Latter-day Saint History, 2008), 21–43. All quotations are from this 2008 edition.

move ahead without his family, although he seems to have exaggerated claims of their support when he felt that such claims would bolster his own leadership authority. In the meantime he continued to take advantage of local newspapers who continued an interest in Mormonism's exoticism as a well-tested means of selling papers. His description of the flourishing church and glowing descriptions of Palestine Grove encouraged gathering, inquiries about the church, and lengthy doctrinal treatises. Smith described Palestine Grove as unexcelled in Illinois. "The land is fertile, and locations can be had cheap, and the people are friendly," wrote Smith. "No part of Illinois that I have ever visited, excels this point for timber convenient to prairie, and for facilities of almost every kind, mills, &c., and water power to carry any amount of machinery. There is at present a grist mill within three miles of this place, called a valuable, first-rate flouring mill, that runs the year round. There is a saw mill in this place, and a still [distillery] in full operation, which could be easily converted into a cloth-dressing machine, carding machine, or a flouring mill. . . . Corn, wheat, and all kinds of grain are raised here, and in growing time the fields look green and luxuriant with grain, well rewarding the laborer's toil."[67] According to Smith, Palestine Grove was a flourishing paradise. Although it is unlikely that he would have dwelled on any disadvantages, Palestine Grove was, in fact, blossoming during the late 1840s and early 1850s. Local history corroborates Smith's observations, by identifying Palestine Grove and Binghamton (several miles northeast), as the two most promising villages in the region.[68] William's experience in selling real estate and gathering the Saints to Nauvoo made him an effective promoter in his attempt to gather the scattered Saints to the area.

In 1848 Smith and Hook began to expand their missionary efforts beyond Lee County. In February, Smith lectured at Ottawa, La Salle County, Illinois, preaching in the courthouse on February 16 and 23. George Bratton, a Latter-day Saint loyal to Brigham Young, attended these lectures, and described Smith's tone as filled with "bitterness," while Smith himself appeared to be a "very unhappy man and looks, as I told him[,] like a broken down politician." Smith charged 20 cents per person for these lectures, but as a fund-raising attempt, they were a complete failure. Bratton saw Smith as quite "humbled" after his lack of success in Ottawa and hoped that William might return to the main body of the Church. Bratton encouraged Young to send Jedediah or George Grant to try and reinvigorate William's faith in the body of the Church under the Apostles.[69] For his part, William was so distressed and humiliated that he returned to Palestine Grove, determined never to return to Ottawa. He was, however, not ready to consider reaffiliating with Brigham Young, and Bratton had underestimated Smith's resolve.

---

67. Smith and Hook, *Patriarch and Prophet of the Most High God*, 1.
68. *History of Lee County*, 281–85, 310–14.
69. Bratton to Brigham Young, February 26, 1848.

Because William was enjoying only nominal success in his attempt to organize the scattered Saints in northern Illinois that first year, he cast about for ways to expand his influence beyond the state. His publications did not have the readership that Smith and Hook desired. In October 1848, nine months after the Ottawa fiasco, Smith and Hook launched an ambitious missionary effort that targeted scattered branches in Ohio, and states along the eastern seaboard, where Smith had spent considerable time as a missionary. Roxey Ann remained behind with William's two teenage daughters at Walnut Grove, Illinois, living with or near her parents, who certainly assisted in raising their granddaughters. His marriage to Roxey Ann and her proximity to her parents meant that she led out in providing a mostly stable home for Mary Jane and Caroline, though William's only intermittent involvement in his daughter's lives during the late 1840s and early 1850s would most assuredly have had a negative influence on their development. While he demonstrated love and concern for his two maturing daughters, he was often preoccupied with his own ambitions for much of their upbringing, relying heavily on others for their day-to-day care. This was again the case beginning in October 1848 and continuing through November 1849, when William was absent from home, traveling as a missionary in an attempt to expand his fledgling church.

By November 1848, Smith and Hook had reached Cincinnati, Ohio, where they found a significant number of Saints who were searching for direction. Smith had influenced some in this area of Ohio when he had preached there three years earlier, shortly after he broke with leaders at Nauvoo. Smith and Hook likely reestablished contact with some of these former adherents once they arrived in the vicinity. They also met an influential leader named Isaac Sheen, who had been trying to organize and keep together a group of scattered Saints in the vicinity. Sheen probably had provided the impetus for William to come to the city, as Sheen's son John remembered that his father wrote to William prior to his arrival, wherein he had advocated for "the lineal priesthood doctrine." Sheen had been baptized in Philadelphia by Erastus Snow in 1840, had considered going west with Brigham Young's group in 1846, but instead had gone south to Missouri. When he had enough money to purchase a printing press, he moved in 1847 to Covington, Kentucky, just across the river from Cincinnati, where he began publishing his religious views in December. Sheen and Smith found common ground around the concept of lineal succession, and shortly after the two missionaries arrived, Sheen decided to link his group with Smith's church. Isaac's son John remembered the group's inaugural meeting, which probably took place in mid-October 1848: "I have a distinct memory of the hall and gathering and it was there resolved that it was 'young Joseph's right by lineage,' [to lead the church] etc., and that William should stand in his stead until Joseph should come of age."[70]

---

70. John Kirk Sheen, "Isaac Sheen First Editor of the 'Herald,'" *Saints' Herald* 57, no. 4 (January 26, 1910): 94–95; "A Trio," *Gospel Herald* (Voree, Wisc.) 2, no. 39 (December 16, 1847): 184.

Isaac Sheen, 1810–1874. Photograph taken ca. 1866, by R. Thompson, Sandwitch [sic], Illinois. Courtesy Community of Christ Archives.

Smith and Sheen's united efforts would complement each other in a way that neither of them could do separately. William's experience as a missionary and administrator was invaluable, while Sheen's writing and editorial skills were equally essential in publicizing the church's message. Accordingly, William continued proselytizing, while Sheen edited and published the church's newspaper. The first issue appeared in February 1849 and was named the *Aaronic Herald*. By the second issue, which appeared in March, they had expanded the title to the *Melchisedic and Aaronic Herald*, (spelling "Melchizedek" at least three different ways in this, and subsequent issues). Although they hoped to have the newspaper published monthly, issues appeared intermittently, with the final issue rolling off the press in April 1850. While the lack of funds prevented the paper from being published more regularly, it proved successful in spreading the message of William's Church of Jesus Christ of Latter Day Saints.

Within weeks of their arrival, Smith, Hook, and Sheen succeeded in establishing a branch of their church at Covington. By August 1849, Sheen wrote a glowing report about the church's prosperity near Cincinnati and Covington: "The work of the Lord is progressing even far beyond our most sanguine expectations. A very flourishing branch of the church has been raised up in this place since our prophet Wm. Smith has been amongst us. Numbers have been baptised and more are expecting to be, and others are investigating the matter."[71] Establishing a branch in the area was not without its challenges. A Latter-day Saint branch devoted to Brigham Young was also functioning in the area, and the two factions often collided with one another in their struggle for adherents. William suspected that Brigham Young had instructed branch members to form a committee to investigate Smith and Sheen's movements and keep him informed.[72] On one occasion, Smith debated a "Brighamite" named J. W. Pugh on William's lineal claim to be Joseph's successor. Much of Smith's rhetoric centered on the "lasciviousness" of the LDS leaders, an obvious reference to the practice of polygamy. Since William himself had participated in Nauvoo polygamy, he had firsthand and detailed knowledge of what had transpired at Church headquarters. Such understanding made him a persuasive

---

71. Isaac Sheen, "Advice to the Saints," *Melchisedek and Aaronic Herald* (Covington, Ky.) 1, no. 5 (August 1849): 3.

72. "A Singular Committee," *Melchisedek and Aaronic Herald* (Covington, Ky.) 1, no. 3 (May 1, 1845): 3.

debater with the "Brighamites," even though he naturally concealed his own role in the practice. Had his hearers known of Smith's own participation and acceptance of polygamy he would have certainly lost all credibility. The *Melchisedek and Aaronic Herald* celebrated what they felt was Smith's victory at the debate, recounting that "the loud acclamations of the assembled hundreds in favor of him might be heard for squares around—mingled with the hisses of a few Brighamite serpents." After the meeting, as Smith returned home, he "was greeted with plaudits, 'Hurra[h] for Wm. Smith—I'm for Wm. Smith.'"[73]

Smith relished any opportunity to attack Brigham Young and his former colleagues of the Twelve, particularly in retaliation for any of the slights and offenses William felt he had suffered because of them. Once the *Melchisedek and Aaronic Herald* was up and running, he and Sheen ensured that a good portion of nearly every issue was dedicated to denouncing Young and those who had gone west under his leadership.

William and Aaron Hook's next step, now that the Church of Jesus Christ of Latter Day Saints in Covington was under the able leadership of Isaac Sheen, was to go east to labor among the branches where William had devoted much effort during his earlier missions. According to his account in 1850, William summarized that he and Hook visited "Philadelphia, New Jersey, New York, Hartford, Windsor, Ellington, & Mansfield in Conn., baptizing, organizing and setting in order the churches."[74]

By the latter part of November 1848, Smith and Hook were at Philadelphia, where they experienced much more success than in any of the other branches they visited. William's presence in the city generated significant interest, especially after he advertised: "The only surviving brother of the Prophet Joseph Smith, would preach at the hall, northeast corner of Seventh and Callowhill Streets." A local historian recounted how "Elder Smith's presence attracted considerable attention among the Saints, as also among the nonmembers. Many were curious to see the brother of the dead Prophet, many of the Saints remembering him from their acquaintance while he lived in Philadelphia. He visited the Saints and began regular services at the hall . . . teaching lineal priesthood as applied to the presidency of the church." William's timing was fortunate, as Sidney Rigdon's church had all but collapsed the previous year, and William was able to draw a number of these Saints to his church. After his inaugural speech on November 25, 1848, his branch gained a modest number of consistent adherents, including Jacob Syfritt, who was afterward appointed a bishop, as well as Theodore H. Dennis, Adam Long, William Small, and Joseph Lightcap, among others. Both Syfritt and Small had been a part of Rigdon's church.[75] Before the end of

---

73. "Good News," *Melchisedek and Aaronic Herald* (Covington, Ky.) 1, no. 7 (October 1849): 4.

74. William Smith, Epistle, ca. 1850, 6.

75. Walter Wayne Smith, "Philadelphia Branch," *Journal of History* (Lamoni, Iowa) 13, no. 4 (October 1920): 521–24. William Small was, at one point, an apostle in Rigdon's

Philadelphia, Pennsylvania, ca. 1850. Engraving produced by Thomas Kelly, London, England, 1856.

November, William also published and distributed a short pamphlet containing his second revelation received in 1847, along with a lengthy announcement regarding his prophetic appointment entitled "To the Scattered Saints," and a short message directed specifically to Latter Day Saints in Philadelphia. The publication reiterated the tenets of his Church of Jesus Christ of Latter Day Saints and additionally instructed Saints to avoid gathering with Brigham Young, who he portended were going "to perish in a desert land." Rather, "God says stay at home," stressed William, as "you can get salvation in this land without going to the valley of the Great Salt Lake, Brigham Young's hiding place." The publication also highlighted: "the Saints will understand that it will be their privilege if they desire, to be baptised for their dead, and attend to all the ordinances of God's House, in the respective Branches of the Church where they reside."[76]

During the ensuing month, William used Philadelphia as a home base from which to proselyte across Pennsylvania's border into New Jersey. During the first week of December, Smith and Hook were in Cream Ridge and Hornerstown, New Jersey, where several branches of the Church had remained intact since the late 1830s. Smith had labored as a missionary in this area for seven months in 1841, and resided with his family in the region for nearly two years, from May 1843–April 1845, during his presidency over the eastern states. Many Saints still in the vicinity remembered him well. The two preached on the "ridge" near Hornerstown with some success, and learning of their presence, an LDS member loyal to the Twelve, Stephen Curtis, immediately informed William Appleby, presiding elder of the LDS Church in the area. Some of the Saints in that area of New Jersey were apparently unaware of William's disaffiliation and excommunication in 1845

---

church. Richard S. Van Wagoner, *Sidney Rigdon: A Portrait of Religious Excess* (Salt Lake City: Signature Books, 1994), 388–93, 385 note 43.

76. William Smith, *A Revelation Given to William Smith*, 8.

and accepted his message based on their belief that he was still representing the Church led by Brigham Young. "Mr. Smith not informing them [of] but what he was," recorded Appleby, misrepresented himself as "one of the Twelve, and in Good standing in the Church, until he had received their names to 'uphold the Smith family.'" Taking advantage of the Saints' lack of information about his history, William successfully convinced "some seven or eight members of the Church residing at Hornerstown" that he was "to be the Guardian of little Joseph Smith [III], and President and Ruler of the Church." One of these converts was John Huggins, who, after his conversion to William's church, was ordained an elder and assigned to prepare a place for him to preach the Sunday following their arrival.[77]

However, Appleby immediately traveled to Hornerstown to rectify the situation. Appleby was anything but ill informed about William's history. He had been well aware of Smith's tempestuous leadership and heretical teachings when he had presided over the eastern branches several years earlier. Even more specifically, he had documentary evidence of William's apostasy from the Church at Nauvoo, as William had sent a bundle of his "Proclamation" pamphlets to the Saints in that area of New Jersey in 1845. When these pamphlets arrived, Appleby recorded in his journal, "Elder Wm Smith, [who] had been expelled from the Church, . . . published a Pamphlet against the 'twelve' composed of all manner of absurdity's almost, and sent a package to where I resided. But his Pamphlet took no affect on me, although there was quite a time with some of the disaffected members of the Church after Joseph's death, in regard to who should stand as President of the Church. Some were for Sidney Rigdon, some for William Smith (very few) and others for J. J. Strang." He felt that he had been forewarned by Joseph Smith himself in a dream just days before William's pamphlets arrived in his neighborhood in the fall of 1845 and was thus prepared to take prompt action to prevent their distribution.

Once Appleby learned that Huggins had located a preaching venue for William, he prepared to debate the former apostle. According to Appleby, however, once William learned that Appleby was planning to show up and challenge him, William sent Hook in his place. It seems likely that William foresaw a collapse of credibility, if he and Appleby were to debate face to face, since Appleby was well informed about William's heresies, including his practice of plural marriage during 1843–45. Smith and Hook differentiated their Church of Jesus Christ of Latter Day Saints from Brigham Young's by stressing the concept of lineal succession, but also repudiated the "Brighamites" for practicing plural marriage. Thus, Appleby could, from his own knowledge, have greatly embarrassed William on the basis of his inconsistency. It no doubt seemed prudent to William to avoid a possibly mortifying confrontation with his former colleague.

---

77. William Appleby, Autobiography and Journal, December 2, 1848, 246–47, MS 1401, fd. 1, LDS Church History Library; Stephen J. Fleming, "'Sweeping Everything before It': Early Mormonism in the Pine Barrens of New Jersey," *BYU Studies* 40, no. 1 (2001): 88–91.

Appleby carefully took notes during Hook's sermon held at the "bricks on the Ridge" (probably the Cream Ridge Schoolhouse) so that he might counter his and Smith's claims the following day. The next day he apparently convinced John Huggins of his error in accepting Smith's leadership. Appleby confirmed Huggins's repentance for being duped by rebaptizing him a member of the Church. On Monday evening, according to appointment, Appleby took the stand in the same location on the ridge to respond to Hook and Smith. Appleby recounted that "an overflowing congregation" gathered that evening, and "listened with breathless attention for some two hours." "I replied to Mr. Hook (he being present) [and] investigated Mr. Smiths claims," recounted Appleby, "the result was [that] all the Members led astray was restored back to the Church again. All being satisfied that his claims were groundless." Not only did those present agree with their branch president's reasoning, but they unitedly felt that William had "endeavored to deceive them." The upshot of the evening was William's loss of credibility and Appleby's success as he called on his members, "with uplifted hands [to covenant] . . . to do their duty and uphold the lawful authorities of the Church."[78]

Hook must have left the meeting dejected. Shortly after Appleby had rectified the situation, Smith and Hook abandoned the area and continued their missionary labors elsewhere. However, in retaliation for undermining his missionary efforts, William later pronounced a curse upon Appleby, prophesying he should, "die with the plague," and that his "bones shall consume away in the tomb of the flesh." Sheen highlighted Smith's prophecy in the June 1849 issue of their paper because he and William felt that it had been fulfilled. Wrote Sheen, "we can only say now, for want of space, that Appleby is dead. He died with the cholera on his way to Council Bluffs" en route to Salt Lake City. The fact that Appleby had purportedly died while gathering with Brigham Young and the Saints in the West warned other Mormons who might follow the same course. In actuality, Appleby safely migrated to Utah where he lived another twenty years, dying May 20, 1870. Smith and Sheen were forced to recant the mistake in the August issue of their paper, adding somewhat lamely that, in reference "to the prophecy of Pres. Wm. Smith concerning Mr. Appleby, surely God has plenty of time to fulfill all his judgments, and the messenger of death is still on the alert."[79]

William and Hook left Philadelphia in January 1849 to continue their labors northward. Jacob Syfritt presided over the branch after their departure, which continued successfully for the better part of two years. This Philadelphia branch would be William's most prosperous unit outside Palestine Grove and Covington.[80]

---

78. Appleby, Autobiography and Journal, December 2, 1848, 246–47.

79. "Mr. Appleby," *Melchisedek and Aaronic Herald* (Covington, Ky.), 1, no. 4 (June 1849): 3; "Wm. I. Appleby, if the truth is told by the Frontier Guardian, is still alive . . . ," *Melchisedek and Aaronic Herald* (Covington, Ky.) 1, no. 5 (August 1849): 4.

80. Walter Wayne Smith, "Philadelphia Branch," *Journal of History* (Lamoni, Iowa) 13, no. 4 (October 1920): 521–24; "Information Wanted," *Melchisedek and Aaronic Herald* 1, no. 5 (August 1849): 4. Appleby indicated that, after William Smith preached in

Front page of the *Melchisedek and Aaronic Herald*, volume 1, no. 9 (April 1850).

Smith and Hook enjoyed modest success as they continued to travel through the various eastern branches, assigning those they converted to join their missionary effort. By March Aaron Hook was proselyting in Boston, before going to visit relatives in his native land near Bangor, Maine, while converts Selah Lane and Samuel Capin proselyted along with William in Connecticut.[81] According to a "proclamation" William wrote on March 19, 1849, and published in his newspaper, these elders were to "plant stakes, ordain Elders, organise churches, and to gather the scattered remnants of Israel."[82] Once the *Melchisedek and Aaronic Herald* was launched in February 1849, the newspaper frequently highlighted the success of these missionaries. Before the year was out, a branch of the church was established at Hartford, Connecticut, and converts united with Smith's church in New York, Massachusetts, New Jersey, Ohio, and Pennsylvania. In addition, elders laboring closer to church headquarters at Palestine Grove, made converts in Illinois, Iowa, and Wisconsin.[83]

Selah Lane, an early convert to Mormonism under Joseph Smith's leadership with whom William had been acquainted in Kirtland in the 1830s, was one of William's converts as he labored in the East. Daniel Tredwell, a close associate of Lane, was confused about how someone as bright as Lane "could have had the effrontery to insult common sense in advocating Mormonism." It was likely Lane's "refinement and learning" that also impressed Smith, and these traits helped make Lane a persuasive missionary after he teamed up with William and his new church.[84]

Hornerstown, New Jersey, in early December 1848, he returned to Philadelphia. William Ivins Appleby, Autobiography and Journal, December 2, 1847, 246–47.

81. "Information Wanted," *Melchisedek & Aaronic Herald* (Covington, Ky.) 1, no. 5 (August 1849): 4; "Progress Additional," *Melchisedeck and Aaronic Herald* (Covington, Ky.) 1, no. 3 (May 1, 1849): 2.

82. "A Proclamation to the Saints . . . ," *Melchisedek and Aaronic Herald* (Covington, Ky.) 1, no. 5 (August 1849): 1.

83. "Progress Additional," *Melchisedeck and Aaronic Herald* 1, no. 3 (May 1, 1849): 2; "List of Agents for this Paper," *Melchisedek and Aaronic Herald* (Covington, Ky.) 1, no. 5 (August 1849): 2.

84. Daniel M. Tredwell, *Personal Reminiscences of Men and Things on Long Island, Part 1* (Brooklyn, N.Y.: Charles Andrew Ditmas, 1912), 242.

Lane quickly gained prominence in William's church. A revelation that William received in March 1849 called Lane into the First Presidency as the other counselor with Aaron Hook and assigned him and Hook to select twelve men to serve as apostles. However, by the summer's end, he had separated himself from William's church for unknown reasons. Smith knew that he needed someone of great loyalty to serve as his counselor and turned to Isaac Sheen to replace Lane. Sheen's commitment to William Smith and his church had been unwavering since Smith had arrived in Covington the previous year, and he wholeheartedly accepted the tenets as outlined by Smith and Hook at Palestine Grove. Once Smith completed his intense eight-month mission, at a special conference of the church in June 1849 at Covington, Sheen was called as a counselor in the First Presidency.[85]

William resided at Covington for the summer and fall of 1849,[86] while he simultaneously maintained the Palestine Grove Branch in Illinois and his position as church president. Through missionary efforts and the medium of Sheen's impressive efforts in bringing out the *Melchisedek & Aaronic Herald* regularly and containing important ecclesiastical and theological information, William's Church of Jesus Christ of Latter Day Saints enjoyed modest success in 1849. In addition to the special conference in June 1849 in Covington, another was scheduled for October that same year. Smith had expended considerable effort in building up the Covington Branch and in spreading his message throughout the eastern states. The branch at Covington was a marked success; and through Sheen's instrumentality, newspaper readership was increasing.

Their combined efforts were blossoming to such an extent that Smith determined to relocate church headquarters to Covington. That fall William expressed his intention to travel to Walnut Grove, pack his belongings, and bring Roxey Ann and his daughters back to Covington. He had been gone the better part of the year, devoting his time to missionary efforts and presiding over his church at Covington. Sheen summarized Smith's efforts: "Pres. Wm. Smith has been laboring among us about three months, and his labors have been greatly blessed, whilst his life and conversation among us has been in strict accordance with his profession as the Prophet of the Most High. We have had the pleasure also of perusing letters from the saints in the Eastern States, and we find that in all parts of the country the saints coincide with us in bearing testimony to the excellency of his character."[87] Sheen was becoming Smith's most ardent supporter. But his glowing assessment of William's character was about to be challenged so forcefully that he would soon vehemently denounce him as an imposter.

---

85. "Special Conference," *Melchisedek and Aaronic Herald* (Covington, Ky.) 1, no. 4 (June 1849): 4.

86. "A Certificate," *Melchisedek and Aaronic Herald* (Covington, Ky.) 1, no. 6 (September 1849): 4.

87. Isaac Sheen, "The Work of the Lord," *Melchisedek & Aaronic Herald* (Covington, Ky.) 1, no. 6 (September 1849): 2.

Chapter 16

Expansion and Collapse

> They threw off the mask, in a council called the Priests' Lodge, and confessed to the belief and practice of polygamy in the name of the Lord. . . . This created in some minds a terrible conflict between faith and infidelity.
>
> —Jason W. Briggs, 1875

When William returned to Palestine Grove in January 1850, his budding church was prospering. Though they were small, branches had been established in Hartford, Connecticut, and Philadelphia, Pennsylvania, while the majority of his followers resided in his strongholds of Palestine Grove, Illinois, and Covington, Kentucky. William, along with his small team of missionaries, had ardently labored to build up his church in the East from October 1848 until June 1849, when William returned to Covington. During this eight-month mission, as he gathered adherents to his cause, most were immediately assigned to assist him and the others in their missionary labors. Their combined efforts helped gather converts in a smattering of cities along the eastern seaboard, primarily in New Jersey, Pennsylvania, New York, Connecticut, and Massachusetts.[1]

With the publication of the *Mechisedec and Aaronic Herald* newspaper and the flourishing of his church in the Covington/Cincinnati region, Smith envisioned permanently relocating with his family to that area. The September 1849 issue of the *Mechisedec and Aaronic Herald* paper announced: "Bro. William is going to leave us for a few weeks, and is going to visit his family, and bring them here." Roxcy Ann, who was living at Walnut Grove (Altona), Illinois, was doubtless surprised by William's decision to move the family to Covington instead of settling in Palestine Grove, where construction had begun on their home. His hasty plan did not materialize as quickly as he had hoped. Roxey Ann had not seen her husband for nearly a year and must have been disappointed that he had to return to Covington for his

---

1. Samuel T. Capin and Selah Lane were two converts to William's church. By the spring of 1849, they were engaged in missionary work, proselytizing in Connecticut. "Progress Additional," *Melchisedec and Aaronic Herald* 1, no. 3 (May 1, 1849): 2; Walter Wayne Smith, "Philadelphia Branch," *Journal of History* (Lamoni, Iowa) 13, no. 4 (October 1920): 521–24. The August issue of the *Melchisedek and Aaronic Herald* contained a list of agents for the newspaper, which may well contain the names of those whom the missionaries had converted during their mission. "List of Agents for This Paper," *Melchisedeck and Aaronic Herald* 1, no. 5 (August 1849): 2. As already noted (Chapter 15), the spelling of "Melchisedec," the use of "&/ and," and the title of the paper itself varied considerably from issue to issue.

church's conference after staying in Illinois for only two weeks. Apparently those two weeks were not sufficient for William to make arrangements to uproot his family, so William returned to Covington alone where he presided over his church's conference during the first week of October and continued his church-building efforts.[2]

After the October conference, Smith and Sheen busied themselves in preparing material for the paper and, in the ensuing months, drafted two letters to oppose the Mormons' efforts to achieve statehood for their huge territory of "Deseret" in the West. Brigham Young and other Mormon leaders had drafted a petition for statehood in Salt Lake City in the summer of 1849 and appointed Isaac Sheen's brother-in-law, Almon W. Babbitt, and John M. Bernhisel to take it to Washington, D.C. William Smith personally disliked Babbitt because, as one of the trustees appointed by the Twelve to dispose of property in Nauvoo after Joseph and Hyrum's deaths, he had, William felt, cheated the Smith family. William and Sheen sent the first letter, dated December 31, 1849, to the U.S. House of Representatives, in care of Kentucky Senator Joseph R. Underwood; while the second, written just one day later on January 1, 1850, went directly to U.S. President Zachary Taylor. In these letters Smith and Sheen lambasted "Salt Lake Mormonism" as diametrically in opposition to the pure principles of virtue, liberty, and equality." They claimed that

> the rulers of the Salt Lake Church are bitter and inveterate enemies of our government. They entertain treasonable designs against the liberties of American freeborn sons and daughters of freedom. They have elected Brigham Young (who is the president of their church) to be the Governor of the proposed State of Deseret. Their intention is to unite church and state and whilst the political power of the Roman pontiff is passing away, the American tyrant is endeavoring to establish a new order of political popery in the recesses of the mountains of America.[3]

While the two letters essentially made the same points, the letter to Zachary Taylor was shorter and focused on their opposition to the possible appointment of Brigham Young as a territorial governor: "If a territorial government is established in that land," wrote Smith and Sheen, "we hope that [a] Governor will be appointed who is not a Salt Lake Mormon, and that all the office holders in that territory may be men who are opposed to Salt Lake Mormonism." After he returned to Illinois in January 1850, William and his followers at Palestine Grove sent two similarly worded petitions—one general letter to Congress, and one to Illinois State Representative John Wentworth—and William attached the names of fifty-six followers at Palestine.[4] Both Senator Underwood and John

---

2. "The Work of the Lord," *Melchisedek & Aaronic Herald* 1, no. 6 (September 1849): 2.

3. William Smith and Isaac Sheen (Covington, Ky.), Letter to the House of Representatives of the United States of America, December 31, 1849, House Miscellaneous Documents, 31st Congress, 1st Session, Document No. 43; William Smith and Isaac Sheen (Covington, Ky.), Letter to President Zachary Taylor, January 1, 1850, National Archives.

4. William Smith (et. al.) (Shelburn [Palestine Grove], Ill.), Letter to the Honorable Senators & Representative of the United States in Congress Assembled, January 29, 1850; William Smith (Shelburn [Palestine Grove], Ill.), Letter to the Hon. John Wentworth, January 25, 1850;

Wentworth summarized the contents of his petition in Congress. John M. Bernhisel described that William Smith's petitions "created quite a sensation in both wings of the Capitol and were ugly things to face." Reflecting on the impact of their letters, Smith and Sheen felt elated with the "effect it has produced," and proudly claimed that "our principles have been promulgated in the Senate of the United States and by telegraphic dispatches in nearly all the daily papers in the Union."[5] Despite the impact of William's petitions, it wasn't the primary reason Deseret was ultimately denied statehood. Historian Eugene Campbell declared that "the church's application for statehood was doomed to defeat," regardless of Smith and Sheen's petition. According to Campbell, this was due to Deseret's large geographical size (nearly one sixth of the size of the United States) and its limited population (far short of the 60,000 people required by the Northwest Ordinance for statehood). Instead, "Utah became part of the Compromise of 1850, which admitted California into the Union as a free state and created Utah and New Mexico as territories." Countering Smith and Sheen's appeal, Brigham Young would be appointed territorial governor in 1851.[6]

William returned to Illinois in January to spend time with his family and church followers at Palestine Grove. Roxey Ann happily welcomed her husband's return that winter and his help in rearing their growing family. In addition to William's two teenage daughters by Caroline, the couple's first child had been born on September 21, 1848, at Palestine Grove and named Thalia after Roxey Ann's mother. William had been present for Thalia's birth but had left on a lengthy mission when she was only about a month old. When he finally saw her again in 1850, Thalia was already fifteen months old.[7] William's relentless efforts at building up his church had often left Roxey Ann alone to deal with these responsibilities during the three years of their marriage. Unlike his whirlwind dash in September 1849, William seemingly consulted Roxey Ann about permanently moving to Covington, and Roxey Ann apparently agreed. Though details are limited, she and the children either accompanied William when he left in March 1850 or came on their own a few weeks afterward. In a letter that William wrote to Sheen on April 29, 1850, he made several references to Roxey Ann being in Covington.[8]

---

and John M. Bernhisel (Washington, D.C.), Letter to Brigham Young, March 21 1850, all in Brigham Young Office Files 1832–1878, Utah Delegate Files, 1849–1872, John M. Bernhisel to Brigham Young, 1849–1866, 1849–1850 March–May, LDS Church History Library.

5. "Memorial to Congress," *Melchisedek & Aaronic Herald* 1, no. 8 (February 1850): 4. John M. Bernhisel summarized the effect of these petitions in a letter he wrote to Brigham Young in March 1850. Bernhisel to Young, March 21 1850.

6. Eugene E. Campbell, *Establishing Zion: The Mormon Church in the American West, 1847–1869* (Salt Lake City: Signature Books, 1988), 205–6.

7. "Records of Early Church Families," *Utah Genealogical Magazine* 26, no. 19 (July 1935): 105.

8. William Smith (Shelburn, Ill.) to Brother [Isaac] Sheen, April 29, 1850, in *Daily Nonpareil* (Cincinnati, Ohio) 3, no. 185 (May 20, 1850), 2; reprinted in *Frontier Guardian* 2, no. 2 (June 26, 1850): 3.

Cincinnati, Ohio, 1848. Daguerreotype photograph taken by Charles Fontayne and William S. Porter, from the Kentucky side of the Ohio River. From the Collection of the Public Library of Cincinnati and Hamilton County.

After staying in Illinois for only a month, William was anxious to get back to Kentucky in February 1850 but could not travel on the ice-blocked Illinois River.[9] He finally reached Covington on March 20.[10] The months away from his bustling duties at Covington had given him time to consider how best to expand his church, and he was reconsidering the merits of Covington or Texas as headquarters. During the same time that Smith and Sheen were organizing in 1848–50, William learned more about Lyman Wight's own branch of Mormonism, which he had established along the Pedernales River, near Fredericksburg, Texas. Wight, who turned fifty-four in May 1850, had been an apostle with William and also a member of the Council of Fifty at the time of Joseph Smith's death. Joseph had assigned him to explore the Texas area to determine whether it would be an appropriate gathering place if the Saints were forced out of Nauvoo. After Joseph Smith's death, Wight remained committed to this plan, defying Brigham Young's orders to abandon the mission. He also refused to follow the Saints once they migrated west. After a lengthy investigation, including personal inquiries by several missionaries whom Brigham Young sent to Texas, John Smith announced at Fort Douglas in December 1848, in Young's presence, that Wight was "cut off from the Church."[11] By 1848, William was certainly aware that Wight had rejected the Twelve's authority and had pursued, with some success, an inde-

---

9. "President Wm. Smith . . . ," *Melchisedek & Aaronic Herald* 1, no. 8 (February, 1850): 4.

10. "A Revelation, Given March 20, 1850, in Covington, Kentucky . . . ," *Melchisedek & Aaronic Herald* 1, no. 9 (April 1850): 1.

11. Melvin C. Johnson, *Polygamy on the Pedernales: Lyman Wight's Mormon Villages in Antebellum Texas, 1845–1858* (Logan: Utah State University Press, 2006), 29–57, 118–22.

pendent course by establishing his colony in Texas. Anxious to expand his own organization, William wrote to Wight in the spring or early summer of 1848, attempting to ascertain Wight's perspective on the succession question in general and how William, specifically, might fit into the picture.[12]

William's letter has not survived, but Wight's response, written on August 28, 1848, refers to a number of items William discussed. It took months for this letter to reach William who was traveling energetically throughout the East. Wight's letter had originally been sent to Nauvoo, then forwarded to Palestine Grove, then to Walnut Grove, Illinois (where Roxey Ann's parents resided), and finally to Philadelphia, where it eventually found its way into William's hands in the spring of 1849.[13] It turned out to be well worth the wait, and Smith could not have been more elated with Wight's perspective. While he had always held the Smith family in high regard, Wight had enjoyed a close personal relationship with Mormonism's founder Joseph Smith. His esteem for the family was evident in his letter to William, and William's teachings regarding a lineal successor resonated with Wight. "Brother William," wrote Wight, "we hold you . . . as being the Patriarch of the whole church, and the blessing of prophet and seer to rest upon his [Joseph Smith's] oldest son if he will receive it, if not, we shall look unto you until the Lord shall make some one of his posterity willing to receive it."[14]

Not surprisingly, William had freely shared with Wight his negative perceptions about how Brigham Young and the trustees at Nauvoo had treated him and his "aged mother" after the deaths of his brothers. To William's satisfaction, Wight, by now no friend of Brigham's, responded with indignation. William had so often rehearsed and embellished the events during the summer of 1845 and afterward that he had become adept at soliciting the sympathies of those who had been away from Nauvoo when these events occurred. Predictably William made no mention of the Joseph B. Noble home that the Church trustees transferred to Mother Smith at William's request. (See Chapter 19.) Instead, William highlighted the conflict preceding the transfer in an attempt to rouse Wight's sympathies, much as he had done with James Strang two years earlier. William's version of events accomplished his purpose. In his letter of response to William, Wight expressed his ire that Mother Smith should be "proscribed in her living" and that "if she sees fit to come to Texas she can have all she wishes for her support on earth, and a home for her children; and if she wishes her bones to be carried to Nauvoo, I pledge myself it shall be done. If she wishes to remain there, our support will not be withheld from her."[15]

---

12. Smith and Sheen published it as Lyman Wight (Zodiac Mills, Tex.), Letter to Brother William Smith, August 22, 1848, *Melchisedic and Aaronic Herald* 1, no. 2 (March 1849): 1.

13. William Smith (Ellington, Conn.), Letter to Dear brother Lyman Wight, April 21, 1849, *Melchisedek and Aaronic Herald* 1, no. 4 (June 1849): 1.

14. Wight to Smith, August 22, 1848.

15. Ibid.

Sympathizing with Lucy's deplorable state as portrayed by William, Wight wrote her a separate letter, assuring the aged matriarch of his compassion for her plight: "Alas! Shall I say in the space of a few years, is it possible that you was deprived of sons the most noble of all the earth, and left with one son and three daughters to mourn the loss of five of the most affectionate sons that were ever born of a woman[?]" His entire community voted that she "should stand as John said Mary stood when he was on the isle of Patmos. She had a crown of gold upon her head and twelve stars in that crown. And that you are the mother of the Angel of the seventh and last dispensation of God on earth." Wight unreservedly accepted William's depiction of the Church trustees, probably because they reinforced his own conflicts with Brigham Young and the other Twelve at Nauvoo in the preceding years. He denounced Brigham Young and Orson Hyde for their treatment of the Smith family and expressed an equally strong commitment to provide a comfortable living for Mother Smith, wherever she chose to live. In a postscript from Lyman to his son Orange, whom he had sent to Illinois, he urged: "[Never] cease to labor with the Smith family as long as there is one remaining upon the face of the earth." He further asked Orange to "tell William I respect him as a friend and a brother in Christ Jesus our Lord, [and] that according to his address [letter] his mind is perfectly right."[16]

Lyman, 1796–1858, and Harriet Wight. Photograph ca. 1850s, photographer unknown. Courtesy Community of Christ Archives.

As outlined in his letter, Wight's view concerning succession and the preeminence of the Smith family paralleled William's. William also relished Wight's fervent support; he craved public recognition that thus validated his own perspective of his ecclesiastical standing. Enthusiastically, he published these letters—and subsequent letters from Wight—in his and Sheen's newspaper. "Your letters dear brother Wight breathe a kind spirit not only to one member of the family but to the whole family," wrote William in reply. "You may be assured you have friends among us." Smith immediately began planning how he and Wight might join forces: "I should like to see you much, brother Wight," wrote William, "to talk with you further upon these matters, to council together concerning the order of arrangements for the furtherance of the cause, the redemption of Zion, &c.

---

16. Postscript to Orange Wight in Lyman Wight (Zodiac Mills, Tex.), Letter to Mother [Lucy Mack] Smith, August 21, 1848, *Melchisedeck and Aaronic Herald* 1, no. 3 (May 1, 1849): 4.

&c."¹⁷ The two leaders continued corresponding throughout the year, as Smith wrestled to know how best to merge their organizations.

Linking William's organization with Wight's would more than double the size of his church, as Wight, in his letter to Mother Smith, claimed that their original group of 150 had expanded to 240 by August 1848.¹⁸ Wight was also excited about the prospect of merging with Smith and, upon learning of William's Church of Jesus Christ of Latter Day Saints, sent several representatives including his son Orange to visit the branch at Palestine Grove long before he even received a response from William. It was heady evidence of Wight's enthusiasm for William's movement. Orange visited Nauvoo in the summer of 1848 where he called on Lucy Mack Smith, and encountered William, who was also in town, probably visiting his mother before departing on his lengthy eastern proselyting mission. From Nauvoo, William brought Orange to his home at Palestine Grove. In a letter to Lyman, William related, "Bro. Orange was at my place in Palestine, Ill., some time in August or the first of September last [1848]." He found Orange "in good spirits [while] he stayed at my house and in the neighbourhood some five or six days." William felt comfortable enough with Orange's message of support from his father in regards to linking their objectives that he even sent one unidentified "family" to accompany Orange on his return trip to gather with the Wightites in Texas.¹⁹ The informal visit was a success, and Orange assuredly reported favorably to Lyman Wight about Smith and his church. Due to this visit, combined with teachings contained in Smith's subsequent letters, Lyman and his followers fully supported William's Church of Jesus Christ of Latter Day Saints. In November 1849, they sustained Smith "as Prophet, Seer, revelator and translator," with a qualifier—"untill some one of the posterity of Joseph Smith his deceased brother shall come forward and take [his] [p]lace."²⁰ Smith reciprocated such support by validating Wight's mission to Texas and by appointing Wight a member of his First Presidency in September 1849.²¹

---

17. William Smith (Ellington, Conn.), Letter to Lyman Wight, April 21, 1849, *Melchisedek and Aaronic Herald* 1, no. 4 (June 1849): 1–2.

18. Wight to Mother Smith, August 21, 1848. Wight may have exaggerated his colony's population to win William's support. Melvin C. Johnson, in his history of Wight's colony, *Polygamy on the Pedernales*, 4, estimates that "the colony's population never reached more than 175 at any given time."

19. William Smith to Wight, April 21, 1849. Orange visited other scattered Mormons in Illinois during his mission, and he and his father may have also had thoughts of merging their church organization with James J. Strang's. However, this plan, if actually contemplated, never materialized. Orange L. Wight (Mount Sterling, Ill.), Letter to James J. Strang, August 22, 1848, *Gospel Herald* 3, no. 27 (September 21, 1848): 4.

20. Lyman Wight [Zodiac, Tex.], Letter to William Smith, November 4, 1849, *Melchisedek & Aaronic Herald* 1, no. 8 (February 1850): 1; Heman C. Smith, "Lyman Wight on Succession," typescript transcript of a document written in the hand of Heman C. Smith, Community of Christ Library-Archives, quoted in Johnson, *Polygamy on the Pedernales*, 126.

21. William Smith to Wight, April 21, 1849; William Smith (Covington, Ky.), Letter to the Saints Scattered Abroad, Greeting, September 30, 1849, *Melchisedek & Aaronic*

William also immediately consulted with Isaac Sheen on how best to unite their organization with Lyman Wight. Obviously William had been deliberating about merging with Wight during the past year, after receiving his former apostolic colleague's letter and meeting with Orange Wight. Wight had no intention of leaving his thriving community at Zodiac, Texas,[22] so Smith and Sheen considered moving their own headquarters to Wight's community. Wight championed his settlement as the best gathering place, claiming, with considerable exaggeration, that it could sustain "ten thousand families . . . in a luxurious manner and have enough left over to buy a county in Missouri." He further highlighted Zodiac's prosperity by detailing such possessions as "not less than 1,000 head of cattle" and enough mills to support large numbers of people. "This will probably be one of the best seasons for emigration that has been known since Texas has been settling," urged Wight, "as crops of all kinds transcend the anticipations of our eldest farmers. . . . The fat valleys of Texas are large, and in beauty surpasses all understanding." He described the climate as one of the "most congenial places for old age and infirmity."[23]

William was convinced. By the summer of 1849, he and Sheen were seriously contemplating taking their disciples at Covington, Palestine Grove, and elsewhere to Texas and communicated those intentions to Wight. Wight responded enthusiastically, suggesting that Sheen "pack up press type and paper" so that Sheen could "re-publish all the revelations God has seen fit to give through the mouth of Br. Joseph."[24] Wight's proposal to reprint Joseph's revelations bothered William—not because William had doctrinal differences with Joseph's revelations but rather because Wight did not mention publishing William's revelations along with Joseph's. In the April 1850 issue of the *Melchisedek and Aaronic Herald*, William inserted the following statement in an article that enthused about the possibilities of a move to Texas: "The revelations which God hath given to him [William] are of equal validity to those which were given through Joseph. They agree with them in style and doctrine."[25] This clarification was important to William—an attempt to ensure that he was perceived as being on an equal plane with his influential older brother.

Once Smith returned to Covington in March 1850, three weeks before he convened his April conference, Smith received a revelation commanding his followers

---

Herald 1, no. 6 (September 1849): 1, and continued in 1, no. 7 (October 1849): 1.

22. Writing to William on July 26, 1849, Wight explained: "The reason, Br. William, of my being so firm in my decision to have you come to this place is from the solemnity of my mission given by Br. Joseph, not yet performed, and the thirteen million souls in Mexico who have not yet heard the gospel, and the noble hearted inhabitants of Texas, who have open arms to receive thousands on thousands of poor emigrants." Lyman Wight (Zodiac, Tex.), Letter to Brother William Smith, July 26, 1849, *Mechisedek & Aaronic Herald* 1, no. 6 (September 1849): 2–3.

23. Wight to William Smith, July 26, 1849.

24. Ibid.

25. "Texas," *Melchisedek and Aaronic Herald* 1, no. 9 (April 1850): 2.

William B. Smith, ca. 1870. Photograph by H. P. Brown. Courtesy Community of Christ Archives.

to "get ye up from this land, and go ye out [from] among the gentiles who have decreed thy destruction"—even though there appears to be no evidence of hostility or persecution. He hinted that the migration would take place in two phases: "in summer" (that is, immediately) "and in winter" (a few months later). The revelation continued: "Therefore let my servant William Smith and my servant Isaac Sheen . . . gather together all their means, with their families and with the poor . . . and depart immediately from this land, to the land that I have appointed for the gathering of my people, in the land of Texas, to the place of my servant Lyman Wight." The significant revelation was announced at the church's conference three weeks later, and published in its entirety in the April issue of the *Melchisedek & Aaronic Herald*.[26] William had already sent at least one family from Palestine Grove to Zodiac Mills, Texas.[27] He followed up immediately with plans to move as many of his followers as possible to the newly appointed gathering place.

However, Smith's aspirations frequently raced ahead of practicality. It was an ambitious financial undertaking that William and his followers were unprepared to meet. William had frequently discouraged those Saints who were still in the East and Midwest from following "B. Young to a salt land thousands of miles off in the wilderness," since that journey had inflicted untold "suffering . . . upon [his] followers."[28] Perhaps William failed to realize that Wight's settlement, according to Wight's proposed route (discussed below), was more than 1,400 miles to the southwest, whether traveling from either Covington or Palestine Grove, and even farther for his followers on the East Coast. The proposed migration was one hundred miles longer than Young's pioneer overland journey of 1846–47 from Nauvoo to the Salt Lake Valley. William likely felt that his proposed migration would not entail the same hardships as Young's because they could travel on the Ohio and Mississippi Rivers for at least a thousand miles. Still, that mode of transportation would require great expense and effort. Smith expected financial assistance from Wight, especially to underwrite his own family's expenses.[29] Wight responded to that request by assuring William, "I shall send you from four to five hundred dollars" after their spring planting was completed, but there seems to be no evidence that Wight sent such funds.

Wight also needed time to prepare for this major influx. Once he began reading William's statements about relocating to Texas, both as published in issues of the *Melchisedek & Aaronic Herald* and in William's personal communica-

---

26. "A Revelation, given March 20, 1850, in Covington, Kentucky, to William Smith . . . ," *Melchisedek & Aaronic Herald* 1, no. 9 (April 1850): 1.

27. William Smith to Wight, April 21, 1849.

28. William Smith, Epistle, ca. 1850, William Smith Papers, MS 3697, LDS Church History Library.

29. At a conference at Covington in early April 1850, one of the resolutions instructed "the branch of the Church under the superintendence of Bro. Lyman Wight, to send money for the removal of the Smith family to that place." "The Greatest Annual Conference," *Melchisedek and Aaronic Herald* 1, no. 9 (April 1850): 2–3.

tions, Wight expressed his own reservations. Wight counseled him to wait until his followers could pay their debt incurred to repair a broken dam, and plant spring crops. In November 1849, Wight reported that his colonists were two months behind in paying a $500 debt to repair the dam, which would limit the funds they could send to underwrite the migration.[30] Wight had initially been enthralled at the prospect of William's relocating his Church of Jesus Christ of Latter Day Saints to Texas. Especially dazzling was William's promise that the whole "Smith family [was] moving to Texas." In July 1849 Wight's enthusiasm spilled out in a letter to William spelling out the best route for migration: "Should you with all the Smith family and friends conclude to move this fall, my advice to you would be to commit yourselves, [to gathering] teams and wagons and all that you have to the broad waves of the Mississippi, with an almighty prayer to God that you might all arrive safe at Shreveport in Louisiana, on Red River. And give us timely notice to meet you there, which is a distance of about four hundred and fifty miles, and we will be there with from one to ten wagons as the case may require, and with from one to five hundred dollars as you think you will stand in need of." He also committed to sending some of his strongest men to assist them once they arrived in New Orleans or, if they decided to travel across the Gulf of Mexico, to Port Lavaca.[31] But time apparently tempered Wight's enthusiasm as he realized that such a significant inundation of Saints would certainly tax his small colony's limited resources.

William forged ahead with plans anyway, largely following Wight's advice on the route and hoping to expand his numbers along the way by intercepting some of Brigham Young's followers who were migrating from Europe, by way of New Orleans. "We would say to the saints in England, Scotland, Ireland, Wales and the adjacent islands that emigration may be carried on to this land[,] the promised land of Joseph, without going further west than the Cordilleras mountains with but little more expense and trouble than it would require to land at the northern sea ports. [Port] Lavacca [sic] or Galveston is the landing place in Texas. From there," instructed William in an an 1850 "Epistle," "proceed by land to Zodiac Mills near Fredericksburgh in Texas."[32] The *Mechisedek and Aaronic Herald* further announced as part of its report on the April 1850 conference: "Pres. Smith expects to emigrate to Texas with a company in the fall. In this re-

---

30. William expressed his intent of relocating at least some of his followers to Texas as early as April 21, 1849, while he was still serving as a missionary in the East. See William Smith (Ellington, Conn.), Letter to Lyman Wight, April 21, 1849, *Mechisedek and Aaronic Herald* 1, no. 4 (June 1849): 1–2. For Wight's response, see Lyman Wight [Zodiac Mills, Tex.], Letter to William Smith, November 4, 1849, *Melchisedek and Aaronic Herald* 1, no. 8 (February, 1850): 1. By February 1850, William wrote that it was "expected that after the [April] conference a company of Saints will emigrate from this place [Covington] to Texas." "The Annual Conference," *Melchisedek & Aaronic Herald* 1, no. 8 (February 1850): 4.

31. Wight to William Smith, July 26, 1849.

32. William Smith, Epistle, ca. 1850, 8.

Wightite Mill, near Marble Falls, Burnet County, Texas. Photograph ca. 1910, photographer unknown. In 1851 Lyman Wight moved his colony fifty miles northeast of Fredericksburg, Texas, to this community near Marble Falls.

gion [Covington] and also in the Eastern and Western States there are many that are preparing for the gathering at that time." Smith and Sheen even announced a special conference to be held in Texas on the anniversary of Joseph Smith's birth, December 23, 1850.[33] But beyond announcing the proposed itinerary, William had apparently given little thought to the practical complications of paying for steamers to transport his followers to New Orleans, chartering a ship to cross the Gulf of Mexico to Galveston, and then buying enough wagons to transport the group the final three hundred miles overland journey to Zodiac Mills. While William often inspired his followers with his exuberant visions for church, community, and temple building, very few of his inspirations were realized, as he lacked the forethought and pragmatism to bring them to fruition, nor did he have Joseph's ability to hold the loyalty of capable lieutenants to whom he could delegate the necessary tasks.

In the meantime, Smith shuffled the First Presidency to give Wight a more conspicuous post in his church. Sheen remained in the First Presidency, and William's long-time colleague Aaron Hook graciously agreed to step down as counselor in the First Presidency to allow Wight the loftier position. Hook instead became a counselor *to* the presidency, and Alva Smith, a convert from Illinois who had temporarily held that position, was reassigned as one of the Twelve Apostles.[34] As a result of their correspondence, William also became

---

33. "The Greatest Annual Conference," 2–3.

34. Toward the end of the conference, Sheen apparently encouraged Hook to again accept his position in the First Presidency. The minutes record: "We return our thanks

imbued with many of Wight's teachings, including his emphasis on communal living and his millennial fervor for returning to Jackson County, Missouri, to build the long-prophesied temple to prepare for Christ's second coming.[35] At one point, as a result of their communications, Smith proposed organizing the poor in Cincinnati and Covington into a United Order, to ensure that those who were too poor to migrate might have enough to subsist on until they could join those who had gone ahead to Texas. "It is our intention," proclaimed Smith in a letter to the Saints in November 1849, to establish a "United Order of a Stake of Zion in the State of Ohio [which] shall be for the benefit of the poor who are unable to get to Texas. . . . It is thought expedient by the first presidency of the church that the scattered Saints who are deprived of the priviledge [sic] of assembling together to receive instruction, and who are unable to get to Texas, should, in the present emergency, move into this stake of Zion."[36] It was the way William and his colleagues had of dealing with the poor who could not afford the 1,400-mile journey to Texas. However, despite considerable discussion about establishing this communal order, that organization never materialized. Smith began proclaiming Wight's colony as a "branch" of his own Church of Jesus Christ of Latter Day Saints. He also anticipated that his followers would participate in the endowments of the Zodiac temple Wight had constructed on two and a half acres and which his followers had begun using in 1849.[37]

Meanwhile, in preparation for their merger, Lyman sent four representatives from his colony in Texas to the Church of Jesus Christ of Latter Day Saints at Covington to help prepare for the move and participate in several church conferences. They included Otis Hobart, Stephen Z. Curtis, Joseph D. Goodale, and Silas Caldwell, but Hobart, one of Wight's most prominent members, fell ill in Covington in December 1849, with an unidentified "painful bodily affliction" and died several weeks later at age fifty, on January 17, 1850.[38] Only Sheen was present when he died, as William had returned to Palestine Grove. Smith then had the challenging task of appropriately memorializing Hobart during the April 1850 conference. William's March 20 revelation contained this tribute: "Now I say concerning my servant Otis Hobart whom I have taken unto myself, whose works I have accepted, and is justified before me, behold he is with me, and his spirit mingleth in the councils of the martyred prophets." The minutes record that, although Hobart had passed away three months earlier, he was to be "[re]

---

to brother Isaac Sheen for expressing his willingness to recede from his office in the Presidency of the Church, in order that brother Aaron Hook might hold that office." "The Greatest Annual Conference," 3–4.

35. William Smith, Epistle, ca. 1850, 6–7.

36. William Smith, Letter to the Saints Scattered Abroad, September 30, 1849.

37. "Texas," *Melchisedek & Aaronic Herald* 1, no. 9 (April 1850): 2; "Prophet's Department," *Melchisedek & Aaronic Herald* 1, no. 7 (October 1849): 1; Johnson, *Polygamy on the Pedernales*, 125–28, 137–43.

38. "Death," *Melchisedek & Aaronic Herald* 1, no. 8 (February 1850): 4.

interred with his robes on him,"³⁹ a reference to the sacred garments he had previously received as part of Wight's endowment ceremony in his temple at Zodiac Mills. Smith ensured that other members of Wight's colony were recognized and participated actively in the conference; seven of Wight's branch being appointed apostles, including Goodale and Curtis, who were present for the conference.⁴⁰

Curtis, Goodale, and Caldwell must have felt satisfied with this memorial service and with the conference in general, since William not only validated Wight's Texas mission, but also made the first official announcement that his Church of Jesus Christ of Latter Day Saints would gather at Zodiac Mills beginning immediately. In addition, Goodale and Curtis were called to serve missions in Michigan and Pennsylvania respectively.⁴¹

At some point between Hobart's arrival in December 1849 and his death in January 1850, he confided enough information to Isaac Sheen that the editor became convinced that Wight's members were practicing polygamy at Zodiac Mills. Hobart's daughter, Mary Ann, had married Lyman Wight as a plural wife five or six years earlier. But whether it was this family fact or other information, Sheen found Hobart's admission during his final illness persuasive and began to suspect that William knew Wight's members were practicing polygamy. Forty years later, Isaac Sheen's son, John, wrote in an exposé including the information: "Through the visit an[d] death of Otis Hobart it was learned that the 'devil' [i.e., polygamy] was in Texas and that William was not above suspicion."⁴² Sheen must have immediately questioned William about Hobart's disclosure when Smith returned in March, and William's denial (or possibly his attempt to explain it) did not persuade Sheen. The editor's perplexity was understandable. From the very first number of their paper, Smith had denounced polygamy in the strongest terms, referring to the "spiritual wife doctrine" practiced among the "Brighamites" as the most compelling evidence of their delusion.⁴³ Smith and Sheen had, less than four months earlier, sent their counter-petitions to Congress and the U.S. president, opposing statehood for Deseret because the Mormons were practicing

---

39. "A Revelation Given March 20, 1850, in Covington, Kentucky, to William Smith . . . ," *Melchisedek & Aaronic Herald* 1, no. 9 (April 1850): 1; "The Greatest Annual Conference," 4.

40. The Twelve Apostles appointed at William's April 1850 conference included: "In Texas, William P. Eldrige, Andrew Balentine, Spencer Smith, Joseph D. Goodale, Stephen Curtis, Orange L. Wight, Irvin Carter; in the Northern States [Palestine Grove and Covington], George Baily, Nathaniel T. James, Henry Nisonger, Edwin Cadwell and Alva Smith." "The Greatest Annual Conference," 3. Reinterring a body was not uncommon in the nineteenth century, but dressing the corpse seems unlikely. They may, however, have laid the robes in the coffin over the body.

41. "The Greatest Annual Conference," 2–4; Johnson, *Polygamy on the Pedernales*, 127–28. Caldwell apparently did not receive an assignment.

42. John K. Sheen, *Polygamy: or, The Veil Lifted* (York, Neb.: n.pub., 1889), 14; Johnson, *Polygamy on the Pedernales*, 80, 127.

43. "The Man of Sin," *Aaronic Herald* (Covington, Ky.) 1, no. 1 (February 1, 1849): 2.

polygamy. Rhetorically, they demanded why Congress would consider admitting Deseret into the Union while its people were attempting to "legalise adultery, fornication, incest, and all manner of wickedness."[44] Although William's denials were temporarily successful, Sheen became increasingly distrustful and determined to discover if Smith indeed supported the practice.

Following the April 1850 church conference, Smith immediately left Roxey Ann and the children at Covington while he returned to Palestine Grove, probably to begin preparing his followers in that region to relocate to Texas. According to John Sheen, within days, Isaac "laid a plan to entrap William" by sending him a letter inquiring about the doctrine of plural marriage. As a result, Isaac "succeeded in getting a polygamous letter [of response] from William."[45] William eagerly took the bait, hoping that Sheen would also become an advocate of polygamy. In his reply to Sheen, he apparently distinguished between a marriage performed and recognized by God and "cemented by the sealing power" and a marriage performed by man, which would not endure beyond the grave nor be recognized by God in mortality. Smith viewed "gentile" marriages, performed without priesthood authorization, in the same category as baptisms performed outside the faith. He repeated the arguments that had been developed in Nauvoo that "the ancient patriarchs had more wives than one," and that "this was allowed by the law of God, or it would not have been so, . . . for priesthood purposes in propagating a multitude of those to whom the promises were given."[46] Beyond any doubt, Sheen now knew that Smith believed in the practice of plural marriage. He apparently wrote William a response in mid-April that has not survived but which denounced Smith's teachings in no uncertain terms.[47]

After receiving Sheen's letter condemning polygamy, William immediately recognized his blunder and quickly backpedaled. On April 29, he wrote Sheen from Palestine Grove (Shelburn), explaining that he had written "when I was quite sick, and I wish you to correct the errors, if any, and do it for my good and not for my injury." But he also sensed the extent of Sheen's disapproval and foresaw negative consequences in Covington. "Do not let the devil triumph over us now," he pled with Sheen. "We have done a good work, and a very small matter would destroy it all. Brother Sheen, I claim protection at your hand; if I have done wrong in any respect I am willing to make restitution to the last farthing. I claim a right of trial according to the law of God face to face; if I have committed

---

44. Sheen and Smith to the House of Representatives, December 31, 1849.

45. Sheen, *Polygamy*, 14.

46. "Extract from Wm. Smith's Fornication Letter," *Daily Cincinnati Commercial* 12, no. 299 (May 22, 1850): 4. Evidence suggests that Smith may have tried to teach these principles to Sheen's wife, Drusilla, as Orson Hyde later revealed that Sheen was upset because Smith had "invaded his domestic circle." [Orson Hyde], "Bill Smith," *Frontier Guardian* 2, no. 11 (June 26, 1850): 3.

47. Isaac Sheen, "Wm. Smith—The Imposter," *Daily Nonpareil* (Cincinnati, Ohio) 3, no. 185 (May 20, 1850): 2.

an offence show me my error in a Christian spirit—not in the spirit of a savage. I can do no more than to offer my life and body as a sacrifice." He asserted that he was "determined by the grace of God to set my face against all sin" and begged Sheen to say nothing on the subject until they could meet in person. "I shall come to see you," William concluded in his letter, "I must have a talk with you."[48]

But he was relying, rather unrealistically, on his personal charisma to persuade Sheen to again become a supporter. In truth, William had no intention of changing his views regarding plural marriage. By this point, they were too engrained in his thinking. His attempt to explain away and even to recant his statements were a last-ditch effort to retain his followers at Covington. He must have been relieved that Sheen appeared temporarily willing to accept William's sincere apology "and his determination to forsake it [polygamy]," but Sheen's forbearance was temporary. He was only waiting for a face-to-face interview before he made a final decision. William immediately caught a steamer and headed for Covington, apparently assuring himself that he could persuade Sheen to remain silent. There was more at stake for William than simply retaining his followers. Although the quality of his marriage to Roxey Ann is not well documented, he was apparently apprehensive about her reaction to the accusation that he advocated polygamy, even though he apparently did not have any additional wives at the time. At some point during 1849–50, she had flatly refused to go with him to Texas in the projected fall 1850 move. "My wife says that she will not go to Texas," William wrote Sheen in his quasi-apology, quasi-explanation on April 29, "for fear of the spiritual [wife] doctrine. I have told her better, but all to no avail."[49] Perhaps William did not know the extent that Wight's followers were engaging in the practice, but at the very least he knew that Wight had been introduced to those teachings at Nauvoo. Roxey Ann correctly surmised the Wight's followers were practicing plural marriage in Texas and may have had her own suspicions about William's support of the practice. In his letter to Sheen, William begged him not to reveal his damaging admissions to Roxey Ann. "My letters," wrote William, "do not open them, but keep them safe for me. I do not wish that my wife should have perusal of all my letters. She is easy excited; keep then these things sacred until I come. I hope that none of our difficulty will be named to her, that all may remain in quiet."[50]

Even before William reached Covington, however, it was clear that Sheen could not be convinced. On the basis of William's letters admitting polygamy, Sheen repudiated the letters to Congress and the U.S. president, rejecting in the strongest terms Smith's deceit in simultaneously denouncing the very practice among the "Brighamites" that he personally espoused. On May 4, Sheen wrote to

---

48. William Smith (Shelburn, Ill.), Letter to Isaac Sheen, April 29, 1850, *Daily Nonpareil* (Cincinnati, Ohio) 3, no. 185 (May 20, 1850): 2.
49. Ibid.
50. Ibid.

Kentucky's representative in Congress, Richard H. Stanton, condemning Smith's "accusations against the Deseret Mormons" as "the ebullitions of a malicious heart, and have been made by him to divert attention from his own outrageous villainy and licentiousness." John M. Bernhisel, who was sent by leaders in Salt Lake City to spearhead efforts for Deseret's statehood, ensured that Stanton was made aware of Sheen's recantation.[51]

William had reached Covington by mid-May, and his private meeting with Sheen took place on May 18, 1850. Sheen had enough evidence in his possession to establish William's deception. He was also astute enough to discount William's excuse of "illness." William's thorough scriptural reasoning had not been written while William was incoherent. Now William was caught in a difficult dilemma. If he acknowledged his support of the practice, he ran the risk of losing Sheen, his press, members of the local branches, and possibly Roxey Ann as well. On the other hand, he could not deny that he had, at some point, supported the practice since he had already disclosed as much in his April 29 letter. During their conversation, William quickly determined that his previous strategy of pleading delirium and promising repentance would not retain Sheen's loyalty. Instead, he changed tactics and boldly tried to convince Sheen that God approved of and authorized the practice. Sheen remained incredulous. William's vacillation demolished his credibility, and Sheen was disgusted by William's duplicity. "He has professed the greatest hostility to the plurality wife doctrine," Sheen recounted in a letter to the editor of the *Daily Cincinnati Commercial* only four days later "but on the 18th ult. [May] he told me that he had a right to raise up posterity from other men's wives. He said it would be an honor conferred upon them and their husbands, to allow him that privilege, and that they would thereby be exalted to a high degree of glory in eternity. He said that the Salt Lake Mormons had no authority to do such things, but that the authority belonged to him."[52] Indeed, William had apparently even tried to sidestep Isaac and convince Sheen's wife Drusilla of that teaching at some point during his stay in Covington.[53] But neither of them was convinced. When William finished his argument, according to Sheen, "I told him instantly that I would have no more connection with him, and that such damnable iniquity, I never had, and never would participate in."[54] Sheen was shattered by William's betrayal and disillusioned by his disclosures. In his letter to the *Commercial*, which appeared on

---

51. Isaac Sheen (Covington, Ky.), Letter to Hon. R[ichard] H. Stanton, May 4, 1850, reproduced in *Frontier Guardian* 2, no. 11 (June 26, 1850): 3. See also John M. Bernhisel, May 15, 1850, Letter to the Editors of the *Union*, and R[ichard] H. Stanton, May 14, 1850, Letter to House of Representatives, both reproduced in *Frontier Guardian* 2, no. 11 (June 26, 1850): 3.

52. "Wm. Smith—Fornication—Adultery," *Daily Cincinnati Commercial* 12 (May 22, 1850): 4.

53. Orson Hyde later wrote, that "*Br. William* has invaded his [Sheen's] domestic circle, and the fangs of the monster pierced the fountain of his most sensitive feelings." Orson Hyde, "Bill Smith," *Frontier Guardian* 2, no. 11 (June 26, 1850): 3.

54. "Wm. Smith—Fornication—Adultery," 4.

May 22, he denounced Smith as an imposter, also branding him a "hypocritical libertine." Sheen proclaimed that he was no longer connected with any branch of Mormonism or any other religion.[55]

When Roxey Ann and the children had moved to Covington, they brought with them a "leather trunk" containing some of William's most valuable records—a journal, two patriarchal blessing books, and one of the two fair copies of Lucy Mack Smith's history.[56] (The other had gone to Salt Lake City with the Church Historian's records.) Roxey Ann's arrival coincided with Smith's two letters, the first attempting to enlist Sheen's belief in polygamy, and the second backtracking but also attempting to deny his admission. The timing could not have been worse for William.

Although William had begged Sheen not to mention these letters to Roxey Ann, Sheen did not consider himself bound by the request. Roxey Ann's reaction was exactly what William had feared. Taking William's young daughter, Caroline Louisa (Mary Jane stayed with William) and her own toddler Thalia, Roxey Ann returned to her parents in Walnut Grove, Illinois. She took some of William's belongings and either sold the leather trunk to Sheen or left it and its remaining contents for Sheen to dispose of as he wished. Sheen initially denied selling the contents of William's trunk, writing in May 1850 that he had "witnesses to prove that Smith's statement concerning the Church Records are totally false; his wife [Roxey Ann], who has left him, in consequence of his licentiousness has either taken them with her, or has disposed of them."[57] However, John Sheen later wrote that Roxey Ann "gave into father's hands a lot of [William's] papers and books" and that "he felt justified in keeping them." Brigham Young's history records that Sheen apparently gave a volume of patriarchal blessings to Almon W. Babbitt (Sheen's brother-in-law), who unsuccessfully tried to sell them to LDS leaders in Salt Lake City on Sheen's behalf in 1854. Young's history documents that William had taken one patriarchal blessing book, including blessings by his father and Hyrum, without permission when he fled from Nauvoo in the fall of 1845. The meandering course of this important volume was documented by LDS leaders in the year 1859: "In 1850 Wm. Smith, then residing with Isaac Sheen, Covington, Kentucky, in consequence of a serious misunderstanding which arose between him and Sheen, . . . resulted in Williams' [sic] leaving Covington in too great a hurry to take the record [patriarchal blessing book] with him. Sheen retained it and subsequently placed it in charge of A. W. Babbitt . . . with instructions to sell it to the Church for $3,000, if he could, but not to take less than $500.00." After Babbitt's death in 1856, George A. Smith obtained the blessing book from Benjamin F. Johnson, one of the administrators of Babbitt's estate.[58]

---

55. Ibid.

56. Stanley B. Kimball, "New Light on Old Egyptiana: Mormon Mummies, 1848–71," *Dialogue: A Journal of Mormon Thought* 16, no. 4 (Winter 1983): 87 note 30.

57. "Wm. Smith—Fornication—Adultery."

58. "History of Joseph Smith, Senior, Patriarchal Record," Journal History of the Church of Jesus Christ of Latter-day Saints, February 11, 1859, 1–2, LDS Church History Library.

John Sheen claimed that "William's journal was given to him [William] when he came to Plano, Ill., in 1878 to be regenerated, or whitewashed by the Reorganization." Isaac Sheen, who was a member of the Reorganization, must have retained the journal in his possession until his death in 1874, and then gave it to Joseph III, who, in turn, presented it to William. Sheen continued, "'Mother Smith's History' (in manuscript) was GIVEN by Uncle Almon [Babbitt] to Orson Pratt, who had it published."[59]

Babbitt, who met Roxey Ann during this period when she discovered her husband's disloyalty, supported her decision to leave William.[60] William's older daughter, sixteen-year-old Mary Jane, stayed with William, but Roxey Ann, who was pregnant with her second child by William, had moved to her parents' home in Walnut Grove by November 1850, bringing with her two-year-old Thalia, and her niece and step daughter, Caroline Louisa.[61] Not long after Roxey Ann left him, William filed for a divorce, which was, at least in part, an attempt to recover his records. After a lengthy legal battle, the divorce became final in April 1853, awarded by the Knox County, Illinois Circuit Court. (See Chapter 17.)[62] Roxey Ann and William's second child, Hyrum Wallace, was born August 17, 1850.[63]

Smith turned his back on those who rejected his leadership, never to return to Covington. He lost a very talented member in Sheen, as well as his very valuable newspaper and press, but the damage was more far-reaching in the area of Covington than William had anticipated.[64] In an attempt to hold members who were thinking of deserting his branch, Smith immediately wrote to the editor of the *Daily Cincinnati Commercial*, who published portions in a summary two days after his fateful conversation with Sheen and two days before Sheen's own denunciation appeared. In it, William claimed that "Isaac Sheen has been cut off from the 'Church of Jesus Christ of Latter Day Saints,' . . . by President WM. SMITH, the brother of Joseph, the only . . . true representative of God on Earth!" The editor further summarized William's letter, "The 'Prophet of God' alleges that Sheen, who lives in Covington, has taken advantage of his former high position in the true church, and joined with Babbitt, a

---

59. Sheen, *Polygamy*, 15; emphasis Sheen's. (See Appendix B.)

60. William Smith (Turkey River, Iowa), Letter to Brigham Young, July 13, 1856, LDS Church History Library: "I notice also that you have the Scoundrel of a Babbit about you—Sur[e]ly you must love rotten mutton or you would not have that cut throat of a lickskillet in your rankes[.]"

61. U.S. Census, 1850, Illinois, Lee County, Amboy Township, September 12, 1850, Roll: M432_116, 117B, image 89, and Illinois, Knox County, Township 13 N. 3 E., November 8, 1850, Roll: M432_113, 415A, image 416.

62. Final Decree, Bill of Divorce, Roxey Ann Smith vs. William Smith, April 26, 1853, Knox County Circuit Court, April Term, Knox County Courthouse, Galesburg, Illinois.

63. "Records of Early Church Families," 105.

64. After the establishment of the RLDS Church in 1860, Isaac Sheen devoted his talents as an editor and newspaper publisher to that cause, publishing *The True Latter Day Saints' Herald* from 1860 to 1865.

'Salt Lake Mormon,' taking with him Wm. Smith's records of the true church . . . as kept by the 'Prophet of God.' . . . . There appears to be no doubt, however, in the true Prophet's mind," wrote the editor caustically, "that truth will prevail in spite of Satan, Babbitt, Sheen, Salt Lake Mormons, or any other combination or representatives of Satan. Ahem! So we go."[65] The only "alliance" linking Sheen with Salt Lake Mormons was his brother-in-law Almon Babbitt, to whom Sheen had given Smith's patriarchal blessing book. Sheen's response, published in the *Daily Cincinnati Commercial* two days later, explained, "I did not wait for him [William] to cut me off, and he [now] has no Church in Covington to cut any one off." As for William's accusation that Sheen was affiliating with "Salt Lake Mormons," Sheen wrote "I have no connection with their church, and never intend to have." More damning was Sheen's reference to "a letter" which he had in his "possession . . . written by Wm. Smith, in which he advocates the plurality of wife doctrine. I have another letter written by him on the 29th ult., in which he asks my forgiveness for his participation in such iniquity, and his determination to forsake it. Recent events show that his pretended repentance was base hypocrisy." Sheen attached a portion of William's polygamous letter to his own, which the *Daily Cincinnati Commercial* published in the same issue. If members of the branch were on the fence regarding whom to follow, the contents of the letter permanently turned them away from Smith. Following Sheen's public denunciation of Smith, all but one of the members of his branch in the Covington region left him.[66]

Following his break-up with Sheen, Smith retreated to Palestine Grove, Illinois, and his still-loyal group of followers there. He obviously felt hurt that Roxey Ann had returned to her parents and had left him, although it is difficult to reconstruct his thinking. He blamed Sheen and Babbitt for her decision to leave him and, like his over-optimistic approach to Sheen, probably felt that if he had been there when she discovered his letters he could have persuaded her to stay with him. Admittedly, letters in his trunk had been written from women members to William in what Roxey Ann later described as "very endearing language." Still, he might have legitimately argued that he had not taken any new wives after his marriage to her. These letters, one from a sister living in St. Louis requesting he send her promised monies—(probably Mary Ann Covington, who lived in the city in 1846), and several sent to William from sisters in the East (probably the Libby sisters in Lowell, possibly written in the summer of 1845 after William returned to Nauvoo), were from plural wives whose unions had ended shortly after he left Nauvoo in the fall of 1845.[67] But Smith had often overestimated his influence, and Roxey Ann probably would have left him anyway because of his deceit regarding his continued support of the practice. Some six years later, William was still agitated about what had occurred during that eventful spring of 1850 in Kentucky. In a letter written to Brigham Young in the mid-1850s,

---

65. "A Prophet Robbed and Deserted—Excommunication of Elder Sheen," *Daily Cincinnati Commercial* 12 (May 20, 1850): 1.

66. "Wm. Smith—Fornication—Adultery."; "Extract From Wm. Smith's Fornication Letter."

67. Kimball, "New Light on Old Egyptiana," 87 note 30.

Smith fumed, "I notice also that you have that Scoundrel of a [Almon] Babbit[t] about you.... [H]e is the man that Paid Isaac Sheen one thousand dollars for my trunk of Books and advised my wife to seperate [sic] from me."[68]

The break with Sheen dissolved the proposed move to Texas and the memorial conference of December 23. But Smith remained determined to build up his Church of Jesus Christ of Latter Day Saints with himself as leader. After all, he still had the full support of his branch at Palestine Grove in Lee County, whose members remained largely unaware of his sentiments regarding polygamy. He also felt he had the continued backing of Wight and his followers, whom he continued to sustain in leadership positions in his organization. During 1850–51, however, Smith focused his efforts closer to his home in Lee County, Illinois, traveling extensively through northern Illinois and southern Wisconsin. He primarily targeted clusters of Saints who had formerly affiliated with James J. Strang's organization and who had been left leaderless after Strang's removal to Beaver Island, Michigan, and the exposure of his practice of plural marriage. Smith found groups of Saints in northern Illinois, whom he and his followers continued to proselyte. Many had been searching for something to strengthen and regenerate their faith, and they found it in William Smith's theology of lineal succession.

Among them was twenty-three-year-old William Wallace ("W.W.") Blair, born in Holly, New York, in 1828, and whose family had been some of the earliest settlers in the region of Palestine Grove, in Lee County. Although still relatively young, Blair was described as an individual who "loved truth and admired consistency in doctrine." The Blairs lived less than a mile east of the Hook property. William certainly knew Blair as a near neighbor during his comings and goings at Palestine Grove, but it was not until 1851 that the two men formed a more intimate relationship. Blair, who had joined the Church prior to Joseph Smith's death in 1844, was among those drawn to William's message. He was described as being "quite skeptical on religious questions" following the death of Joseph Smith. "Unsatisfied with what he heard," according to one colleague, "[and] disappointed in what he saw, he lost faith in professing Christians, and in Christian professors. But when he heard 'the eleventh hour message' delivered by William Smith, a brother of the Palmyra seer, he accepted it in good faith, and adhered to it thenceforth to the end. It was to him the Good Shepherd's voice."[69]

Blair also left his own account of his conversion to William Smith's movement: "Residing near Amboy, Lee County, Illinois, I became interested in the doctrine of Christ taught by a body of Latter Day Saints, less than twenty in number, located in that vicinity, and on the eighth day of October, [1851,] after thorough conviction of the truth of that doctrine, I was baptized by Elder

---

68. William Smith (Turkey River, Iowa), Letter to Brigham Young, July 13, 1856, Brigham Young Office Files, 1832–1878, Letters from Church Leaders and Others, 1840–1877, William Smith, 1844–1857, LDS Church History Library.

69. Mark H. Forscutt, "Statement of Obituary," in Frederick B. Blair, comp., *The Memoirs of President W. W. Blair* (Lamoni, Iowa: Herald Publishing House, 1908), 202–3.

William B. Smith, brother of Joseph the Seer, and confirmed by him and others, and after four days, in answer to silent, fervent prayer, was as literally baptized with the Holy Spirit as I had previously been of water." His wife and mother also united with Smith's organization. "For weeks and months afterward" Blair continued, "my highest anticipations in respect to the peace and love and spiritual blessings of the gospel were more than realized."[70] William also found a warm reception at Waukesha and Beloit, Wisconsin, and converted a number of influential Saints to his organization who became effective leaders, including the prominent Briggs family at Beloit. Jason W. Briggs, just two years younger than Blair at age twenty-five, had joined the Mormons in 1841, and united with William's church in the winter of 1850. William subsequently ordained him to be the presiding elder over the Beloit Branch.

William Wallace Blair, 1828–1896. Date and photographer unknown. Courtesy Community of Christ Archives.

Smith was impressed with the energetic Briggs, and he quickly moved up in the hierarchy in Smith's Church of Jesus Christ of Latter Day Saints. Within a few months of his baptism, William called Briggs as an apostle. Briggs recollected that, during the next year, seven or eight branches of the church were established in Wisconsin, the largest of them at Beloit and Waukesha. He estimated that, at its peak, those who affiliated with Smith's church in Wisconsin numbered several hundred.[71] In a history published in 1875, Briggs reconstructed the reasons that Smith's teachings resonated with so many Saints in this area:

> William Smith; who, in the spring of 1850, called a Conference, at Covington, Kentucky; from which time he visited many of the branches and scattered Saints, teaching "lineal Priesthood" as applying to the Presidency of the Church; and thus disposing of all pretenders already arisen, or to rise out of the posterity of the original President of the Church. This principle, though pretty clearly shown in the books, had been almost entirely overlooked, or forgotten by the Saints; but when their attention was thus called to it, many at once received it as the solution of the question of "Presidency." Wm. Smith taught also, in connection with this [teaching], that it was his right, as the only surviving brother of the former President, and uncle (and natural guardian) of the seed of Joseph, to stand, during the interim, as President, pro tem.

---

70. Frederick Blair, *The Memoirs of President W. W. Blair*, 5.

71. Pearl Wilcox, *Regathering of the Scattered Saints in Wisconsin and Illinois* (Independence, Mo.: Pearl G. Wilcox, 1984), 29–31; Jason W. Briggs (Beloit, Wisc.), Letter to Joseph Smith III, November 20, 1853, MS 4632, LDS Church History Library.

And in this there seemed a general acquiescence on the part of the Saints among whom he labored; and he was so acknowledged, and began to organize. Many branches, and nearly all the Saints in Northern Illinois and Southern Wisconsin were identified with this movement, and among them was enjoyed a large measure of spiritual gifts.[72]

Though it is unclear if Jason's brother Edmund formally united with Smith's organization, a third brother, Silas, affiliated with their brother Jason's branch at Beloit and accepted Smith's teachings regarding lineal descent of the priesthood. Edmund remembered Smith's visits to Beloit and Waukesha, where he was "preaching and teaching the doctrine of lineal priesthood." He was "the first man that ever taught that [doctrine] there," recalled Edmund. "William Smith was gathering up these old members of the church [through] preaching lineal priesthood."[73] Edmund was especially impressed with another convert who also had leanings toward Smith's movement, Zenas H. Gurley, who was in the Yellowstone Branch in Wisconsin.[74] Many of those who converted during this time were assigned key positions in Smith's organization.

Leadership in Smith's church was in a constant state of flux. It had started with Smith as president and Aaron Hook as his sole counselor. William later temporarily added Selah Lane as a counselor to his First Presidency, who, after he left William's church, was replaced by Isaac Sheen. Once Lyman Wight linked his church-building efforts with William, Hook graciously agreed to step down as counselor in the First Presidency to allow Wight the loftier position. Hook was subsequently appointed as a counselor *to* the First Presidency, until Sheen broke with Smith, then Hook was reinstated in the First Presidency, and William's church continued to sustain Wight as a member of the same presiding council in absentia. In the spring of 1851, William's church produced its first publication since the breakup with Sheen, a twenty-seven-page pamphlet, *Epistle of the Twelve*, published in Milwaukee, Wisconsin.[75] The pamphlet laid out scriptural arguments for lineal priesthood, citing biblical and Book of Mormon passages to provide a framework for cataloguing William's succession claims. It also provided a list of the leaders of his church, including the names of his Twelve Apostles. Two lived in Palestine Grove, two in Strang's former headquarters of Voree, Wisconsin, and the remaining eight with Wight's group in Texas.[76] Obviously, Smith desired

---

72. Jason W. Briggs, "History of the Reorganization of the Church of Jesus Christ of Latter Day Saints, Chapter 1," *The Messenger* (Salt Lake City) 2, no. 1 (November 1875): 1.

73. E. C. Briggs, Testimony, *The Temple Lot Case* (Lamoni, Iowa: Herald Publishing House and Bindery, 1893), 207.

74. Edmund C. Briggs, *Early History of the Reorganization: Autobiographical Sketches and Incidents in the Life of the Author* (Independence, Mo.: Price Publishing Company, 1998), 31–34. This autobiography was originally published serially in the *Saints' Herald*.

75. Joseph Wood, *Epistle of the Twelve* (Milwaukee, Wisc.: Sentinel and Gazette Steam Press Print, 1851).

76. The apostles were listed as: "William P. Eldridge, Irvin Carter, Andrew Balentine, George Bailey, Spencer Smith, Edwin Cadwell, Joseph D. Goodale, Alva Smith, Stephen

to remain on good terms with Wight, but his intention to relocate his church to Texas had cooled by the year 1851. In the publication, Smith expressed his hope that "brother Lyman Wight will be present" for an important conference to be held on April 6, 1851, and instead of reiterating his former intention to relocate their church to Texas, the *Epistle* detailed that "the First President [William] and Spokesman [Joseph Wood] intend visiting President Lyman Wight and the Saints with him, at the Cordilleras [Texas], as soon as they are permitted to do so." Smith also included several of Wight's letters, written to William and his mother Lucy, in the publication.[77]

The new star in William's organization was Joseph Wood, who had acted as one of Joseph Smith's attorneys in 1843 when a Missouri sheriff and Carthage constable arrested the Prophet in Lee County and tried to hustle him into Missouri, only to be thwarted by a combination of legal efforts and a large turnout of Nauvoo's men. Wood had joined the Church in its first years, serving a mission to Michigan in 1832–33 with Apostle David W. Patten and Jared Carter as two of his companions.[78] Wood had apparently experienced his own challenges with marital fidelity, being excommunicated in 1834 for adultery but being reinstated at some unknown date.[79] Wood was given an exalted new position imme-

---

Curtis, Jason W. Briggs, Orange L. Wight, Ira J. Patten" (capitalization standardized). Interestingly, although Joseph Wood was "President of the Quorum of Twelve," he was not a member of the Twelve per se. The pamphlet noted that "Brother Ira J. Patten, the last name on the list, is a brother of the Apostle David W. Patten, who suffered martyrdom for the cause of Christ during the persecution in Missouri." The pamphlet specified that the "members of this Quorum are all equal; but when they are in Council, and the Spokesmen [Joseph Wood], who is their legitimate President, is absent, the oldest man present (in courtesy to age,) presides. The oldest man may also, (in the absence of the Spokesmen) convene said Quorum for business." Ibid., 2.

77. Wood, *Epistle of the Twelve*, 22–23.

78. Richard P. Howard, ed., *Memoirs of President Joseph Smith III* (Independence: Herald Publishing House, 1979), 36; Lycurgus A. Wilson, *Life of David W. Patten: The First Apostolic Martyr* (Salt Lake City: Deseret News, 1904), 6; Jared Carter, Journal, entries for December 13, 1832–January 20, 1833, MS 1441, LDS Church History Library. According to Carter, when he arrived in Michigan on December 13, 1832, he found that Joseph Wood had "lost his armer [sic], because of the many temptations of the evil one and the great persicution from the wicked. He being young & [illegible] he has seased to lead the little flock of God as he had ought to have done."

79. At least one author claims that Wood was cut off from the Church for practicing "some form of polygamy," but the evidence available suggests it was more likely adultery. Phillip R. Legg, *Oliver Cowdery: The Elusive Second Elder of the Restoration* (Independence, Mo.: Herald Publishing House, 1989), 80. See also Brian C. Hales, *Joseph Smith's Polygamy, Volume 1: History* (Salt Lake City: Greg Kofford Books, 2013), 169. Joseph Smith (Kirtland Mills, Ohio), Letter to J. G. Fosdick, February 3, 1834, LDS Church History Library, states that Wood was "cut off from the Church" on that date for, among other items, "indulging in . . . [a] lustful spirit." Letter also available at http://josephsmithpapers.org/paperSummary/letter-to-j-g-fosdick-3-february-1834, accessed

diately beneath William's own. The *Epistle* announced: "JOSEPH WOOD [is] God's spokesman for, and Counsellor to the said WILLIAM SMITH, President of the Quorum of the Twelve Apostles and the whole ministry; also, a Prophet, Seer, Revelator, and Translator; holding the keys of ministry of this latter day dispensation, equally and jointly with the said WILLIAM SMITH." Wood lived fifteen miles east of Palestine Grove in Paw Paw, Illinois, where he had practiced as a lawyer "for many years"; he moved to Palestine Grove in early 1851, where he and Smith were inseparable for the next two years.[80]

Joseph Smith III, who claimed to have access to much of the history of his uncle's organization during this time, summarized this period only generally, saying that William's loosely organized church "flourished for a time" and that he was able to gather in "quite a number of members."[81] William's Church of Jesus Christ of Latter Day Saints peaked during 1850–51, thriving as the scattered Midwest Saints found hope in William's central tenet that ecclesiastical leadership should remain centered in the Smith family. The branch at Palestine Grove expanded to more than sixty persons and was strengthened by Smith's earlier missionary efforts in the eastern United States, as some of his adherents gathered to Lee County. He also had the support of nearly all of the clusters of Saints in northern Illinois and southern Wisconsin, bringing total numbers to around three hundred, even with the collapse of the Covington Branch. If Wight's colony is included as part of his organization, then at its height, Smith's followers numbered somewhere between four and five hundred.[82] After the collapse of William's branch at Covington, Palestine Grove once again became the focal point of William's church-building. In the 1851 *Epistle of the Twelve,* Smith and Wood again encouraged gathering to the locale: "There is a stake or place of gathering at Palestine Grove, rocky ford of the inlet, near Shelburn, Lee County, Illinois. This is a beautiful, healthy situation; the gentiles are very friendly; [and] the brethren own considerable land at the stake."[83] Smith's followers laid the granite cornerstone on the most prominent hill near the town for the projected temple in the early 1850s, but the project fizzled, probably due to a lack of funds.[84]

December 12, 2014. However, evidence of his return to fellowship is documented when he built up several branches of the Church in Illinois in the 1840s. Joseph Wood (Perry, Ill.), Letter to Bro's. [Ebenezer] Robinson and [Don Carlos] Smith, March 26, 1840, *Times and Seasons* 1, no. 6 (April 1840): 87–88.

80. Wood, *Epistle of the Twelve,* 3, 21–22; *History of Lee County* (Chicago: H. H. Hill and Company, 1881), 88.

81. Howard, *The Memoirs of President Joseph Smith [III],* 184.

82. *History of Lee County,* 310.

83. Wood, *Epistle of the Twelve,* 21.

84. *History of Lee County,* 310; Inez A. Kennedy, *Recollections of the Pioneers of Lee County* (Dixon, Ill.: Inez A. Kennedy, 1893), 392. In 2010, I examined portions of the surviving granite foundation stone at the Amboy Illinois Central Depot Museum, Amboy, Illinois.

Temple Hill, Palestine Grove, Illinois. Photograph 2010 by Kyle R. Walker.

Smith's organization prospered in the area until the fall of 1851. Apparently he still had not learned that his Illinois members would, like those in Covington, react with repugnance to his belief in polygamy. Even though it seems that Sheen's denunciations had not reached the members in Illinois, William failed to capitalize on this advantage and began secretly introducing polygamy to some of his most trusted leaders at Palestine Grove. He established what he termed the "Priests Lodge" for men, and a "Priestess Lodge" for women. It is not clear how he explained Roxey Ann's absence, although his apparent commitment to remaining in the area would have naturally raised questions about their lack of a stable home and about her role in this new order. He obviously patterned this select group after the Quorum of the Anointed that Joseph had established for those endowed at Nauvoo and also initiated them into polygamy, although there is only one record documenting how William explained his theology and that he had performed plural sealings. In a letter written about a woman identified only as "Sister C____," who lived in Waukesha, William reprimanded her for apparently expressing second thoughts about being sealed to Joseph Wood. "Sister C___ belongs to Brother W[ood], and her salvation turns upon the view which he may take of her course of conduct towards him," wrote William. "If she turns a somerset [sic] and refuses to be reconciled to him she is lost—worlds without end." William also included a brief revelation in his July 18, 1851, letter about this unnamed sister, which among other things, provided the only known details regarding his enigmatic Priests Lodge: "Concerning those females who have received the priesthood by being sealed to my servants William Smith and Joseph W[oo]d," read the revelation, "and have been washed and anointed and ordained under their hands having been received into the priestess lodge—having taken the covenant thereof; if they, or either of them, shall fall, or altogether turn therefrom, she or they shall be excluded therefrom and from my church also." The Priests Lodge included at least Smith, Aaron Hook, and Joseph Wood, while the Priestess Lodge included some women of the Hook family, including Aaron and John's niece Rosa Hook, and several other unidentified women who resided in Palestine Grove, and at least two female members of the Waukesha Branch in Wisconsin.[85] However, most of his followers remained unaware of Smith's secret lodge.

William's leadership came into question beginning with the 1851 publication of his and Wood's *Epistle of the Twelve*. Joseph Wood had been instrumental in its publication, and possibly its most inflammatory teaching was that William no longer claimed to be holding the president's office in guardianship for Joseph Smith III. Absent from its contents was any mention of Joseph Smith's son as legal heir to the office. In fact, there was no mention of him at all. This was a marked change from William's 1847–50 rhetoric about holding the office pro tem for his young nephew. Even though he had gradually begun making bolder claims for his own rights as Church president, in this pamphlet, Wood, obviously representing William's position, contended that William had inherited the right to preside over the entire church. "Our brother William Smith [as] the only surviving son of the good old Patriarch, and of course the only surviving brother of Hyrum and Joseph Smith," argued Joseph Wood, is "consequently the *only* living heir to the Patriarchy and the First Presidency over the church." He reiterated the same concept four different times in the publication. Perhaps even more remarkable was that William expanded his claim that he had been ordained his brother's successor. He had, previous to this time, claimed that his apostolic ordination gave him the right to preside over the Church, holding the church together until his nephew came of age, but now he and Wood claimed a previously undocumented special blessing or ordination that gave him authority superior to that held by his colleagues of the Twelve: "Previous to President William Smith's leaving Nauvoo, on his mission to the East, for the last time during the earthly existence of his brothers, President Joseph Smith ordained him a Prophet, Seer, Revelator, and Translator, and then informed him that he had all the necessary ordinations to lead the church, [in his time,] then leaped, smote his feet together, and observed that it was done."[86]

Furthermore, William followed up this claim in his correspondence with the leaders of his outlying branches, claiming that the sons of Hyrum and Joseph would now be dependent on William and his posterity for any designated leadership positions. Responding to a letter of inquiry from David Powell, a member of William's church at Waukesha, William explained: "As to questions in regard to my right of standing as Joseph's successor, I reply, In my first step in acting as the representative of Joseph's son [Joseph Smith III], the matter was not made plain to

---

85. William Smith (Palestine, Ill.), Letter to Sister C_____, July 18, 1851, in *Dixon Telegraph* 2, no. 51 (April 30, 1853): 4. The newspaper article used the blanks in a conventional attempt to mask those involved in the "Lodge," especially the women.

86. "President William Smith was ordained by his brother Joseph Smith," in Wood, *Epistle of the Twelve*, 3–7, 18; brackets in original, capitalization standardized.

me then as it now is. The increase of light began small at first, and so increased by degrees until the full right of my authority was made known by revelation." In this letter to Powell, written on Christmas Day 1851, William went on to explain that as the only surviving son of Joseph Smith Sr., and because "[I] was ordained before Joseph's death, Prophet, Seer, Revelator and Translator . . . . it is in this manner my inheritance is preserved unto [me and] my children, and thus answering the revelation I have received of late on this subject." Speaking of himself in the third person, he noted, "Should William have no son, he would have power to ordain one of Joseph's sons, provided one of them came forward and claimed rights. But should William have a son or sons, the right of Patriarchy, not by expediency, but by law, rests in his family."[87] At this point, his only son, Hyrum Wallace, was sixteen months old and in the custody of his mother who was divorcing William.

As a result of this publication and this letter to Powell, which underscored William's bolder claims, some of his followers, especially some of his key leaders, began to feel uneasy about William's ambition. Former apostolic colleague John E. Page had already noticed a shift in William's ever-evolving conception of his right to the presidency: "It is well known that, after Joseph Smith's death, Wm. Smith set himself up as the 'guardian' of the church, till Joseph, the prophet's son should become of lawful age to take his place as the President of the Church," described Page in a Strangite newspaper. "W[illia]m," Page queried sarcastically, "why did you not take the President's office at the first? O[h], I suppose you *forgot* that you was ordained to that office by Joseph." Page, who was supporting Strang at the time, perceptively asked, "Why [then] did you adhere to James J. Strang as the President of the church [and] as Joseph's successor[?] . . . Why, if you know that now [your ordination by Joseph] you [also] knew it from the first. O[h], you '*forgot it.*' Oh! what a set of forgetful prophets!" Page cuttingly concluded, "I wonder who the old prince of tophet will send next to say that they were ordained by Joseph Smith to be his successor and they '*forgot it.*'"[88] Jason W. Briggs, one of William's apostles and branch president at Beloit, also expressed discomfort about William's changing perception of his role as president prior to the conference held on October 6, 1851,[89] and his 1875 memory of that

---

87. Wm. Smith, *President*, Letter to Brother [David] Powell, Palestine Stake of Zion, Illinois, December 25, 1851, *Messenger* (Salt Lake City) 2, no. 2 (December 1875): 1–2; emphasis on "President" in original.

88. John E. Page, "Forgetful Prophets," *Gospel Herald* 2, no. 38 (December 9, 1847): 8. "Tophet" is mentioned in Isaiah 30:33 and 2 Kings 23:10, and Page was probably referring to "Tophet" as the "prince of hell" or the devil.

89. Joseph Wood (Palestine, Ill.), Letter to Jason W. Briggs, September 30, 1851, P13, f80, Community of Christ Library-Archives. In Wood's letter to Briggs, which was sent prior to the October 6 meeting in which the disclosures were made, Wood copied a revelation to William Smith that included instructions to Jason Briggs: "And, now, Behold, I say concerning my servant, Jason W. Briggs, hast thou not murmured in thine heart against me? Now this is the thing that I have against thee, thou hast not trusted to

conference identified it as another point at which William's aspiration outran his achievements. Once again—and again fatally—William overestimated his influence among his followers, not only in his grandiose decision to claim the presidency but also in introducing polygamy. According to Briggs, up until this conference, William had, both publicly and privately, "uniformly condemned all the excesses known to exist among the different factions [of Mormonism], and especially polygamy." But it became apparent during the course of the conference that Smith, Hook, and Wood "not only believed in the principle of a plurality of wives, but were really in the practice of it stealthily, and under the strongest vows of secrecy." Briggs recounted with revulsion how, at a meeting well attended by branch leaders, "they threw off the mask, in a council called the Priests' Lodge, and confessed to the belief and practice of polygamy in the name of the Lord." Besides a handful of followers who had covertly been initiated as members of William's secret lodge, the remainder of those present at the conference were thunderstruck by his disclosures. Briggs said that the revelation "created in some [of our] minds a terrible conflict between faith and infidelity."[90]

The word spread rapidly among William's disciples. William may have thought that his unqualified claims to be the Church's only legitimate president would provide enough momentum to override resistance to polygamy, but instead, just the opposite occurred. His claims about polygamy eroded his claims to presidential authority. The disillusioned Briggs returned to Beloit, "perplexed with this intermingling of truth and falsehood, of right and wrong; light and darkness." During weeks of struggle, he "sought unto God for its solution, in fervent and continued prayer," and his torment was resolved by receiving a personal revelation denouncing Smith and Wood. Briggs energetically distributed his revelation among all the branches of Smith's church, especially those in southern Wisconsin, and succeeded in drawing away most of William's followers over the next several months.

Many who had followed Smith and Hook from the very first now wavered in their support. William feebly attempted to minimize the damage, using the same means that had failed with Sheen, namely backpedaling about what he had actually said at the October 6 meeting. Counting on his charisma, he declared himself preeminent in receiving revelation and exclusively authorized to cut off dissidents. He held conferences at Palestine Grove on November 24 and again on December 3. He also wrote to branch leaders in southern Wisconsin, informing them that Briggs was no longer a member in good standing. Briggs countered, as

---

my word, nor given heed to the counsel of my Spirit; nor was it justifiable in thee, to give way to a fearful Spirit while listening to the bickerings of enemies; and also to the lying slanders of secret conspirators against my servants, William Smith and Joseph Wood. It was for this cause that darkness came over thy mind; and a cloud, and condemnation resteth upon thee until thy heart shall be entirely cleansed from sin and unbelief."

90. Jason W. Briggs, "History of the Reorganization of the Church of Jesus Christ of Latter Day Saints, Chapter 1," 1.

Sheen had done, by quoting William's own words and explaining that the continued references to the "Celestial Law" in his letters "is a pretended revelation to him, authorizing polygamy, apportioning the number of wives according to grade of office in the Church, from half a dozen to several hundred. It repudiated gentile marriages," added Briggs, indicating that he had "seen it [the revelation], and of course kn[e]w what it contained." Though most of Briggs's efforts to combat Smith centered on polygamy, Briggs also disagreed with William's efforts to expand his governing role within the Church of Jesus Christ of Latter Day Saints.[91]

Jason W. Briggs, 1821–1899. Date and photographer unknown. Courtesy Community of Christ Archives.

Briggs's tireless efforts and the already existing abhorrence most members felt about polygamy undermined support for William in Wisconsin. In his home branch of Beloit where William had more than thirty followers, Briggs convened two separate meetings on November 24, 1851. At the morning meeting, he read aloud his revelation denouncing Smith and Wood and their teachings. "But as Esau despised his birthright," read one portion of Briggs's revelation, "so has William Smith despised my law, and forfeited that which pertained to him as an Apostle and High Priest in my Church. And his spokesman, Joseph Wood, shall fall with him," continued the revelation, "for they are rejected of me. They shall be degraded in their lives, and shall die without regard . . . for they have wholly forsaken my law, and given themselves to all manner of uncleanness, and prostituted my law and the keys and power entrusted to them, to the lusts of the flesh, and have run greedily in the way of adultery." The evening meeting "soon took the character of an investigation," recounted Briggs, "and many facts, relative to the erroneous teachings of Wm. Smith and Wood were brought out. Ample opportunity for any to defend them was given, which was attempted by one or two, after which . . . a motion was made and duly seconded to withdraw the hand of fellowship from them. The vote was almost unanimous in the affirmative; with only two voting against it."[92]

Briggs quickly sent letters and representatives to three other branches in Wisconsin, articulating his objections to William's aspirations to the presidency and his promotion of polygamy. Briggs contacted the "Nephi Branch, in

---

91. Ibid., 1; Jason W. Briggs, "History of the Reorganization of the Church of Jesus Christ of Latter Day Saints, Chapter II," *Messenger* 2, no. 2 (December 1875): 1–2; Wm. Smith to Brother Powell, December 25, 1851.

92. Briggs, "History of the Reorganization, Chapter 1," 1; Briggs, "History of the Reorganization, Chapter II," 1.

Expansion and Collapse

Places associated with William Smith's church-building efforts. Courtesy John C. Hamer.

Walworth County, one at Voree, and one in Waukesha County, Wisconsin." By February 1852, Briggs was visiting these branches in person and persuading the presiding officers and members to sign a formal statement repudiating William's leadership. He also sent this statement of repudiation to a branch of Mormons at Yellowstone, in Lafayette County, led by Zenas H. Gurley.[93]

Once again, events had overtaken William's ability to cope. As he struggled to manage the catastrophe in Palestine Grove, he neglected his outlying branches. His only surviving branch in the East after the rupture with Isaac Sheen was at Philadelphia. The branch had functioned fairly autonomously for more than two years, first being established during William's eastern mission in the winter of 1848–49. But by 1851 some of his more prominent followers had left the area. William's bishop, Jacob Syfritt, had become disaffected during the fall of 1849 and joined a faction of Mormonism led by George M. Hinkle. By the latter part of 1850, Syfritt's congregation was expanding, while William's gradually declined. By 1851, the same year William's branches in the Midwest began renouncing his leadership, the Philadelphia Branch also disbanded.[94] Smith had neither the time, or following, to maintain the branch.

William's relationship with Lyman Wight in Texas also began to wane, probably as an inevitable result of the lack of momentum stemming from the summer of 1850. The distance between the two settlements made both communication and consolidation of their respective organizations difficult, if not impossible. Wight also became aware of William's aspirations to retain leadership of the Church indefinitely. William sent Wight a copy of his and Wood's pamphlet, in which he had included two of Wight's letters. He urged Wight to attend his conference in April 1851, but Wight was not enthusiastic about Wood's repeated emphasis that William Smith was "the only living heir to the Patriarchy and First Presidency over the church," and particularly suspected the new claim that Joseph had ordained William to be his successor.[95] Wight was also practicing polygamy and probably would not have taken exception to William's stance (although it is not clear if he knew about it), but he was adamant that Joseph III or another son of the late Prophet should become Church president. Wight quickly pinpointed William's aspirations, questioned his motives, and found it unlikely that William would relinquish the office once Joseph III came of age. It was an unreconcilable difference. Wight recorded in his journal on December 26, 1851, "William Smith proffered to receive me as I was, provided I would receive him as president of the Church and Joseph Wood as God's spokesman. For an absolute refusal I was disfellowshiped."[96]

---

93. Briggs, "History of the Reorganization, Chapter II," 1–2.

94. Walter W. Smith, "History of the Philadelphia Branch," *Journal of History* (Lamoni, Iowa) 12, no. 1 (January 1919): 521–25.

95. Wood, *Epistle of the Twelve*, 5, 24.

96. Lyman Wight, Journal, quoted in Joseph Smith III and Heman C. Smith, eds., *The History of the Reorganized Church of Jesus Christ of Latter Day Saints*, 4 vols. (Independence, Mo.: Herald Publishing House, 1952 printing), 3:34.

"Morman" Cemetery located on "Morman" Road, Palestine Grove, Illinois. Photograph 2010 by Kyle R. Walker.

But although William had demolished his own best chances to create and lead a viable church, his influence was far from ended. His numerous followers in the region picked up the scattered pieces and, imbued with William's convictions about lineal succession, formed what shortly afterward became the Reorganized Church of Jesus Christ of Latter Day Saints.

William remained in Palestine Grove for two more years, becoming entangled in several lengthy lawsuits stemming from his practice of polygamy. But the town of Palestine Grove disappeared almost as quickly as his religious movement. The Illinois Central Railroad, finished in the area in 1854, changed its course to run a mile or so north through the newly established community of Amboy. As a result, the post office at Shelburn (Palestine Grove) closed, and businesses all but died out within a few years. The flour mill burned to the ground on two different occasions, leaving the community without its central business.[97] Today, nothing of significance remains of this once-bustling community. The hill where the proposed temple was to be built is overgrown with brush and trees and littered with farm implements. The once-busy road from Peru to Galena, Illinois, that passed through the heart of Palestine Grove is no longer in use. The quietly meandering Green River intersects a few scattered farm homes, which are set between two cemeteries. One is the old "Morman" cemetery, located on the very rural "Morman" road, where even the majority of gravestones have been removed by descendants to prevent vandalism. The misspelled road and cemetery are all that remain of William's once-thriving headquarters.

---

97. Anthony J. Becker, *The Biography of a Country Town: U.S.A.* (Amboy, Ill.: Spencer-Walker Press, 1954), 88–107.

Chapter 17

A Time of Transition

> There was teachings and practices by him [William] which no man of God ever taught & practiced without cursings. This and that put together placed this branch of the church in this place between hope & fear and as the presiding Elder I was in deep trouble [day and] night Such as [I] never [had] experienced & was driven to cry unto the [Lord] continually for weeks
> —Jason W. Briggs, 1853

William's attempt at organizing his own church during the five years spanning 1847 to 1852 had been a remarkable accomplishment. He had successfully unified many of the scattered Saints from Covington to Connecticut, and from the Pedernales River in Texas to Palestine Grove in Illinois, focusing their attention on the concept of lineal succession. He had established a thriving community on the Hook property in Lee County, Illinois, where his followers could gather. He had acquired a press, published a newspaper, and even commenced work on a temple. In just a few short years, William had succeeded in assembling a cadre of leaders who were proficient at explicating and carrying out his directives. His church-building efforts had generally followed the template established by his prophet-brother Joseph, whose religious movement had met with unprecedented success in the fourteen years between its establishment in 1830 and his death in 1844. As one of its Twelve Apostles and as a family member, William had learned firsthand about community- and church-building.

This time period also reflected the first time where William was recognized as head of a religious movement. He had gradually developed that role, moving from the poignant status of being the last surviving brother of the charismatic Prophet Joseph, to being the family spokesman for his brother's values, to positioning himself as the guardian for the boy Joseph III, to speaking with authority as the leader in his own right. Now, at the peak of his influence, his voice was the mind and will of God to his followers. It was a station he had coveted but had only gradually come to articulate after the murders of his brothers. Possibly he had silently desired the status of Joseph and Hyrum even before their deaths. He had always struggled against being a subordinate and had limited tolerance for views that differed from his own, as evidenced in his clashes with Joseph, his challenges with branch leaders during his eastern mission, and in his epic wrestle with Brigham Young and the Twelve over the extent of his authority after he returned to Nauvoo in 1845. Now, preeminent in his small but thriving church community, he should have been satisfied, but he was not.

William's chronic feelings of entitlement and insecurity made it difficult, if not impossible, for him to ever experience any prolonged period of contentment. The precarious combination of these core elements in William's personality repeatedly undercut his success. These characteristics dominated the troubled and conflicted period in 1844–45, when he perceived leaders at Nauvoo as undermining his authority, even as they confirmed his patriarchal status, encouraged Church members to support him, and authorized his marriage to at least five plural wives. Brigham Young's power in the climactic showdown during the summer and fall of 1845 had William fleeing the city—he claimed in fear for his life but definitely in recognition of his diminished status. His tenuous self-concept never recovered. William's repeated efforts to cut off his former colleagues of the Twelve and ally himself with men like George Adams, James Strang, and Lyman Wight, whom he perceived as sources of friendly authority, repeatedly failed. Even his success in his own organization evinced his preoccupation with retrieving his lost power and being recognized as the charismatic and powerful religious spokesman for God that his brother had been. He became fixated on the perceived injustices of that time period for the remainder of his life.

But influential though the events of 1844–45 were on William's future years, his response to those threats to his identity was not an isolated episode, and his insecurities had not begun after the deaths of his brothers Hyrum and Joseph. They were amply evident much earlier in his life, even during childhood. Any event that threatened his fragile identity brought these inherent qualities to the surface. After William reached adulthood, the way these core feelings were manifest became predictable: to contest and dismiss all competitors to his authority, to expand upon his ecclesiastical station through receiving and publishing his revelations, and to increase his status by adding polygamous unions.

When necessary, he was quick to use his superior physical strength to enforce his views and intimidate others. One Latter-day Saint acquainted with William at Nauvoo, described him as a "boastful, bullying individual."[1] Indeed, many Mormons were afraid of William. Freeman Nickerson was fearful of testifying against Smith during John Hardy's church trial during William's eastern mission, because he felt "that Smith would kill him when he got home, [as] he had such [a] horrible temper."[2] Helen Mar Whitney described William as "certainly an odd one in that family—was very genteel, good looking and capable of appearing in the most refined modern society." But as an example of his irregular behavior, she recalled that, when he came from the East in May 1845, "the next day after his

---

1. George Morris, *Autobiography* (Provo, Utah: Brigham Young University Library, 1953), 31.

2. John Hardy, *Startling Developments of Crim. Con.! Or Two Mormon Apostles exposed, in Practising the Spiritual Wife System in Boston* (Boston: Conway and Company, 1844), 9.

arrival at Nauvoo, instead of coming to the meeting, which was held by the roadside east of the temple, he rode flauntingly by in a fine carriage dressed in deep mourning [attire] with no one but himself and driver. He could have taken any other road as well, but it looked as though he did it just for the purpose of creating a sensation."[3] Such tactics eventually aggravated William's followers, and once his ambition and entitlement became transparent, they lost respect for and confidence in his leadership. Few understood William's underlying insecurities that drove his behavior, and neither William nor his followers would have perceived him as unconfident. His impressive physique with his accompanying bellicosity, combined with his convincing gift at oration, veiled his underlying self-doubts.

His family connection to Mormonism's founder meant that his followers and co-workers tolerated his behavior longer than they otherwise would have. William felt that menial labor was beneath his high station and, as a result, rarely attempted to earn a living by a trade or even a profession, although he was quite successful as an innkeeper. Ephraim Ingalls, a physician near Palestine Grove, was summoned to set an arm that William broke when he

> cut some poles from the tops of fallen trees. Going home he fell from the load and broke his arm. I was sent for, but as I was ten miles away it was some time before I reached him and the placing of it in proper dressings gave him considerable pain. During this he suspended his groans long enough to say: "I was never blessed when I engaged in manual labor. I think I have another work to perform." That he should think a special providence was punishing him for bringing home a load of wood to keep his family from freezing, caused me to smile, notwithstanding my sympathy for him in his suffering.[4]

William was no Hyrum, whose steadfast loyalty and unqualified support of Joseph gave him enormous influence and honored positions within the Church, even though such supportiveness required him to step back when Joseph was taken with glamorous newcomers like John C. Bennett. Nor was William another Joseph. It is irresistible, though ultimately inconclusive, to compare William's personality traits to those of his more successful brother. Both men had a restless streak that, even when they were technically settled in one community, made repeated trips elsewhere, not to mention changing their places of residence often. The brothers were more interested in earning their livelihood through business ventures than farming, similar to their father. Both Joseph and William attracted and impressed acquaintances readily but William frequently alienated and shrugged off even his earliest friends. Both men were handsome and charismatic. Although information about the internal workings of William's marriage to Caroline is scanty, what documentation is available shows mutual affection and support, just as Joseph's most ardent expressions of love and

---

[3]. Jeni Broberg Holzapfel and Richard Neitzel Holzapfel, eds., *A Woman's View: Helen Mar Whitney's Reminiscences of Early Church History* (Provo, Utah: BYU Religious Studies Center, 1997), 260.

[4]. Ephraim Ingalls, quoted in Inez A. Kennedy, *Recollections of the Pioneers of Lee County* (Dixon, Ill.: Inez A. Kennedy, 1893), 390–97.

appreciation were reserved for his legal wife, Emma, even while he married dozens of women as plural wives in Nauvoo. William's first documented step outside the bounds of conventional matrimony was his plural marriage to Mary Ann Covington in Nauvoo in 1843, although both Parley P. Pratt and Wilford Woodruff believed that he was engaged in either plural or improper relations with women in the eastern branches during 1844–45. No doubt the combination of Caroline's lingering illness, the principle of plural marriage, and William's sense of entitlement combined with his need for admiration and attention to make him less than strictly moral around impressionable women. Both men believed that God had called them to the work of church-building; but Joseph produced both the new scripture of the Book of Mormon, in addition to an outpouring of revelations, and also a system of ordination and organization that assured the continuation and expansion of his church while William did neither.

William Smith, 1811–1893. Photograph taken ca. 1880, by unknown photographer. Courtesy of Mary Dennis.

To the believer, such parallels are inconsequential. The simple answer is that Joseph was a true prophet and William was not. To the psychologist, arriving at a simple, clear-cut answer is impossible given the lack of data. But Joseph died in a hail of bullets, while William died of old age at eighty-two in 1893, having spent his last three decades on the margins of his nephew's church after the collapse of his own movement. The visible parallels may be less important than invisible qualities that, with the passage of time, have become increasingly blurred. Undeniably, however, some flaws in William's personality help explain why, just at the height of his success in organizing his Church of Jesus Christ of Latter Day Saints as a faction of Mormonism rivaling Strangism, he let it all slip through his fingers, alienating and rescattering his followers.

As he perceived his church organization crumbling all around him, William floundered, trying to retain his followers. He immediately announced a revelation denouncing his main detractor, Jason W. Briggs, and sent his spiritual decree to his branches in Wisconsin and Illinois. But Briggs had received his own revelation that countered Smith's and crushed his former leader's influence by publicizing William's support of polygamy. Briggs's ambitious, doctrine-centered missionary efforts through southern Wisconsin proved more persuasive than William's denunciations and denials.[5] It was not simply William's acceptance of polygamy that caused such dissonance among his adherents, but his leadership style. Lyman

---

5. Jason W. Briggs, "History of the Reorganization of the Church of Jesus Christ of Latter Day Saints, Chapter 1," *Messenger* 2, no. 1 (November 1875): 1; Jason W. Briggs,

Wight and his Mormon colony in Texas had views on plural marriage that harmonized with Smith's, but Wight grew irritated with his colleague's personal aspirations, as William's self-promotion progressively overshadowed his teachings. Once William's followers detected his ambition and motives, they chilled toward him. Pinpointing Smith's personal qualities, Edmund Briggs recollected, "Everybody that knew William Smith, and worked with him, rejected him."[6] Edmund's brother Jason later stated that, by the summer of 1852, "the Saints in Northern Illinois and Southern Wisconsin had almost entirely renounced the leadership of Wm. Smith and Joseph Wood, causing an utter dissolution of their organization."[7] Though he possessed the charisma that initially drew others to him, unlike his prophet-brother he was unable to retain their support for any significant length of time. Greater intimacy simply resulted in quicker disillusionment across the board.

Such disillusionment during this stage of his life also affected members of his own family. At the same time his Church of Jesus Christ of Latter Day Saints was collapsing, his marriage was also unraveling. Roxey Ann left him in May 1850, after she discovered he was advocating plural marriage among his followers at Covington. Most of Roxey's family had gone west with Brigham Young, but her parents remained in Illinois; and if William had any vestiges of credibility left with them, he lost it by the way he callously treated their daughter and ignored their two children following the separation. William initiated divorce proceedings in Lee County six months after they had separated, in November 1850.[8] Part of his motivation may have been his desire to regroup, mobilize his shattered resources, and remarry, but his primary purpose appears to have been financial. Smith was incensed that Roxey Ann had kept his leather trunk, eventually allowing Isaac Sheen to keep and disperse some of its contents in the early 1850s. In his application for divorce, William accused Roxey Ann of disposing of his personal property, a trunk that he described as containing "a large quantity of books, & the records, journals and proceedings of The Church of Jesus Christ of Latter day Saints," which he inflated as valued "to at least the sum of five thousand dollars."[9]

"History of the Church of Jesus Christ of Latter Day Saints, Chapter II," *Messenger* 2, no. 2 (December 1875): 1–2.

6. "Testimony of E. C. Briggs," in *Temple Lot Case* (Lamoni, Iowa: Herald Publishing House and Bindery, 1893), 207.

7. Jason W. Briggs, "History of the Reorganization of the Church of Jesus Christ of Latter Day Saints, Chap[ter]. IV," *Messenger* 2, no. 4 (February 1876): 3.

8. *William Smith vs. Roxey Ann [Grant] Smith*, Bill of Divorcement, filed November 20, 1850, Lee County Circuit Court, Illinois, April Term; photocopy in my possession. I sincerely thank both Erin Jennings Metcalfe and Bill Shepard for generously sharing their collected research regarding William's legal cases in Knox and Lee Counties, Illinois.

9. *William Smith and Roxey Ann Smith*, Defendant's [Roxey Ann's] answer, filed May 11, 1852, Knox County Circuit Court, April Term 1852, as quoted in Stanley B. Kimball, "New Light on Old Egyptiana," *Dialogue: A Journal of Mormon Thought* 16, no. 4 (Winter 1983): 87 note 30.

Upon learning that William had initiated divorce proceedings and was seeking compensation for his allegedly stolen books, Roxey Ann retaliated by filing a lawsuit of her own in neighboring Knox County (where she was living with her parents), charging William with abandonment, accepting and practicing plural marriage without her knowledge and consent, and failing to support her and their two children. William was unwise in seeking compensation from Roxey Ann as part of the divorce; for in her own suit against him, she presented evidence that eventually led the state to charge William with bigamy. In May 1852, Roxey Ann issued a statement of defense, declaring that she had in her possession "a letter from a female in St. Louis requesting the said complainant [sic] to send her money he had promised, and two or three letters from females in the East . . . written in a very endearing language." Apparently William had kept up a correspondence with several of his wives who were residing in the East (probably the Libby sisters in Lowell, possibly written in the summer of 1845 after William returned to Nauvoo) and Mary Ann Covington (who lived in St. Louis in 1846). These letters had been in William's trunk; and along with William's April 1850 letter to Isaac Sheen defending polygamy, they had prompted Roxey Ann to leave William in the first place. She also denied William's depiction of the value of the items in his trunk, describing it as an "an old leather trunk," containing "a few old books such as an 'old blessing book' used by the father [Joseph Smith Sr.] of the said complainant, an old dictionary, some old Hymn books, a memorandum book kept by the said complainant of some of his public acts, and a few old weekly newspapers."[10]

Their legal wrangling dragged on for several years, its slow progress probably caused by the two divorce cases in two different counties, before finally coming to trial in the spring of 1853 in Lee County. In a prepared statement issued in Knox County on April 25, 1853, R. L. Hannaman, Roxey Ann's attorney, declared that "on or about the 4th day of March AD 1850, the said William Smith wickedly disregarding the solemnity of his marriage vows, and the sanctity and contract of matrimony, and the marriage state hath wickedly and willfully deserted and absented himself from the bed and board of your oratrix [plaintiff] without any reasonable cause for the space of more than two years." The statement further asserted that Roxey Ann had "been put to great inconvenience to support herself and two infant children," and her attorney requested William to "answer charges of neglect." Roxey Ann's attorney included a sworn statement from Amos Ward, possibly one of William's former adherents, who lived near Roxey Ann and her parents in Knox County. Ward corroborated Roxey Ann's statement, testifying that, to his knowledge "the said Defendant [William] has not . . . furnished his said wife or children with any means of support since he abandoned them." Hannaman further asked, on Roxey Ann's behalf, that the Knox County Court

---

10. *William Smith and Roxey Ann Smith*, Defendant's [Roxey Ann] answer; William Smith (Shelburn, Ill.), Letter to Brother [Isaac] Sheen, April 29, 1850, *Daily Nonpareil* (Cincinnati, Oh.) 3, no. 185 (May 20, 1850): 2.

Roxey Ann Grant Smith, 1825–1900. Date and photographer unknown. Courtesy of Dianna Smith.

dissolve their marriage, issue a decree granting her sole "custody of the said children," and ordering William to pay the court costs. Though William had instigated the legal action that ultimately led to the trial that took place in Lee County back in 1850, these prepared statements in Knox County likely reflect the substance of Roxey Ann's defense during the trial.[11]

The reality was that William was broke, which probably was part of his motivation to try and obtain compensation for the items in his trunk—although trying to extract money from his estranged wife seems more like an act of revenge than one of calculated financial profit. Most of what he had obtained had been provided for him by his followers, who had attended to his every need, including providing him with property and financially underwriting the construction of his home at Palestine Grove.[12] As his followers abruptly deserted the movement, William lost not only their spiritual backing, but also their financial support. He could not even afford legal counsel for Roxey Ann's countersuit, but eventually he persuaded his former church "spokesman" Joseph Wood and Wood's law associate Edward Southwick, who practiced at Dixon, Illinois, to act for him. These two were part of a team of attorneys who had defended William's brother Joseph in the summer of 1843 in Lee County.[13]

---

11. R. L. Hannaman, Letter to Honorable Hezekiah M. Weed, re: *Roxey Ann Smith vs. William Smith*, Bill of Divorce, filed April 25, 1853, April Term, Knox County Circuit Court, Knox County Courthouse, Knoxville, Illinois; photocopy in my possession.

12. Joseph Wood (Palestine Stake of Zion, [Ill.]), Letter to Jason W. Briggs, September 30, 1851, Community of Christ Library-Archives, notes that "President William Smith has a bad cold, $20.00 has been raised on the credit of the Lodge to finish purchasing materials for finishing his house, to be paid at April Conference." In 1892, William recollected, "In Palestine grove I built a house costing me Some $300, on the Ladies Hook land." William Smith (Osterdock, Iowa), Letter to Edmund Levi Kelley, October 3, 1892, P19, fd. 49, Community of Christ Library-Archives.

13. In 1856, both Joseph Wood and Edward Southwick are listed as lawyers practicing at Dixon, Illinois. John Livingston, *Livingston's Law Register: Containing a Complete List of Lawyers in the United States* (New York: Livingston, 1856), 113. At the April 1853 trial, William's attorneys are identified as "Southwick and Jos. Wood his solicitors." *William Smith vs. Roxey Ann Smith*, Bill for Divorce, April Term 1853, Lee County Circuit Court, Chancery Book A, 11, 21, Chancery Book B, 246, Lee County Courthouse, Dixon, Illinois. Joseph Smith III identified these same two individuals as defending his father when he was arrested in Lee County, Illinois. Richard P. Howard, ed., *The Memoirs of Joseph Smith III, (1832–1914)* (Independence, Mo.: Herald Publishing House, 1979), 36.

In addition to accusing her of stealing his trunk, Smith attempted to undermine Roxey Ann's character by accusing her, ironically, of practicing "spiritual wifery."[14] When Isaac Sheen learned of William and Roxey Ann's divorce case, he apparently sent a letter in defense of Roxey Ann's reputation, as he felt she had been a victim of Smith's treachery.[15] It probably did not bode well for Smith that Joseph Lewis, Emma Hale Smith's first cousin, and one of Joseph Smith's early antagonists, sat on the jury in Roxey Ann's suit against William. After a lengthy legal process that had dragged on for some two-and-a-half years, the twelve-man jury issued a verdict in favor of Roxey Ann at the April 1853 term. The judge ordered Smith to "take nothing by his said bill of complaint; and that he pay the costs of this cause."[16] Back in Knox County where Roxey Ann had filed her own divorce suit, the court shortly afterward granted Roxey Ann her divorce based on her charge of desertion, requiring William to pay all court costs and attorney's fees.[17] William fumed, not only about losing his trunk of documents, but also in being held liable for the fees stemming from divorce proceedings he himself had instigated.

During the divorce proceedings, it became readily apparent that William had been practicing polygamy. In addition to the women's letters that Roxey Ann had found in William's trunk, she and her attorney also obtained a letter William wrote to a discontented female member of his enigmatic Priests' Lodge, who lived in Prairieville (Waukesha), Wisconsin. Perhaps Jason W. Briggs had played a role in obtaining the letter and sending it to Hannaman, as he had proselytized against William in this particular branch the previous year (1852), persuading the entire Waukesha Branch to support his views. "As to sister C__'s case, on which you ask my council," William had written from his headquarters in Palestine Grove, "Brother W[oo]d is appointed of the Lord to hold the keys of this dispensation with me, [and] it is not my province to interfere with any of his wives." The letter went on to discuss "those females" who had been "sealed to my servants William Smith and Joseph W[oo]d." The document was read during Smith's divorce proceedings, and certainly was a key piece of evidence in Roxey

---

14. "Mormonism in This County," *Dixon Telegraph* 2, no. 48 (April 9, 1853): 2.

15. "Mormonism Again," *Dixon Telegraph* 2, no. 52 (May 7, 1853): 2, reports: "A gentleman writes us from Cincinnati, an article in defence of Mrs. Smith, William Smith's wife; and insists we publish it, as an act of justice to her. We suggest to our correspondent, that by our statement of what Smith alleged [polygamy] against her in his application for a divorce, we by no means asserted its truth; and that the result of her application in Knox County for the same purpose, if favorable to her, will be a very complete vindication of her character." The editor apparently never published Sheen's letter, writing that "as this [the outcome of the pending divorce] will probably be soon determined, it will perhaps be better that we should await that decision."

16. *William Smith vs. Roxey Ann Smith*, Bill for Divorce, April Term 1853, Lee County Circuit Court, Chancery Book A, 21, Lee County Courthouse, Dixon, Illinois.

17. Final Decree, Bill of Divorce, *Roxey Ann Smith vs. William Smith*, April 26, 1853, Knox County Circuit Court, April Term, Knox County Courthouse, Galesburg, Illinois.

Palestine Grove (also known as Shelburn and Rocky Ford), Illinois. Photograph 2010, by Kyle R. Walker.

Ann's defense.[18] Not only did the letter undermine William's credibility, but it was equally embarrassing to William's attorney Joseph Wood, who was present in the courtroom when the letter was read. Once the state identified Smith and Wood as polygamists, the state attorney filed charges of bigamy against Smith, while Wood distanced himself from his former church colleague ever afterward.

Adding to William's mounting legal difficulties in Palestine Grove was his secret marriage to John and Aaron Hook's niece, fifteen-year-old Rosanna ("Rosa") Hook, which probably took place in the early part of in 1852. Rosa's mother, Mercy, had died before 1843; and after Mercy's death, her father, William L. Hook, returned to his native state of Maine, where he remarried and remained for more than seven years.[19] During their father's absence, Rosa, her twin sister Rhoda, and their brother Aaron were left in the care of their grandmother Rhoda Hook at Palestine Grove, where they joined William's church along with

---

18. William Smith (Palestine, Ill.), Letter to Sister [name replaced by line in publication], July 18, 1851, in *Dixon Telegraph* 2, no. 51 (April 30, 1853): 2; "The foregoing communication . . . ," *Dixon Telegraph* 2, no. 51 (April 30, 1853): 2.

19. I have been unable to locate a death record for Mercy Hook, but William Hook had married Abigail Wallingford in Howland, Maine, by 1844. William and Abigail were still in Howland in August 1850. By 1855, they had relocated to Lodi, Wisconsin. Stephen Clay Balliet, *The Balliet, Balliett, Balliette, Balyeat, Bolyard, and Allied Families* (Lehigh County, Penn.: Thos. J. Moran's Sons, 1968), 647; 1850 U.S. Census, Maine, Penobscot County, Howland, Roll M432_266; 284B, image 145; Wisconsin State Census, 1855, Columbia County, Lodi; 1860 U.S. Census, Wisconsin, Columbia County, Lodi, Film #1032686, Line 48, image 00389. Special thanks to Erin Jennings Metcalfe for her research in identifying William L. Hook's movements during the 1840s and 1850s.

other members of the family. When Joseph Farwell, a near neighbor of William and the Hooks, learned that William and Rosa were living together, he brought charges of adultery in the county court against William on October 14, 1852. Farwell was aware that William was still legally married to Roxey Ann, since the divorce, filed in 1850, would not conclude for another six months. Possibly Rosa disclosed the details of her union to William to sixty-year-old Joseph Farwell, as Farwell testified that he not only believed they were living together as a couple but was also "informed" that it was so. In a village as small as Palestine Grove with its two hundred inhabitants, it would have been difficult to keep such an union secret, and Farwell could also have been "informed" of their secret (and illegal) marriage from other neighbors. William's church activities came under greater scrutiny by 1852 during the scandalous divorce, especially after William had disclosed his support of polygamy to some of his most prominent followers just one year earlier.

William's unorthodox religious views and interpersonal difficulties fueled neighborhood gossip. Rumors regarding William's support of polygamy not only reached his non-Mormon neighbors, but also the handful of followers still in the vicinity, including W. W. Blair and Edwin Cadwell, who must not have been present during the shocking October 6, 1851, meeting where William announced the principle of polygamy. By the fall of 1852, W. W. Blair recorded that "trials of a very distracting character came to me through the doings and teachings of leading officers in the little branch, and with a determination not to fellowship nor walk in communion with minsters or members of that kind, at the closing of a morning service in the branch on a Sunday, Elder Edwin Cadwell and myself stated the leading features of our grievances, and the stumbling-blocks we had encountered, and there and then publicly, quietly withdrew. In this we were soon followed, in a quiet manner, by a few others."[20] The rumors surrounding William's polygamous union to Rosa Hook was the final straw for the dwindling members of William's Church of Jesus Christ of Latter Day Saints at Palestine Grove.

Not long after Rosa was polygamously sealed to Smith in the spring of 1852, she apparently fell in love with a young man nearer her own age who was living with the Hooks in the summer of 1852, meaning that her marriage to William was essentially over in a matter of three or four months. She also complained that Smith had coerced her into marrying him. According to the *Dixon Telegraph*, Rosa had been "induced to believe that it was necessary for her salvation that she should become his spiritual wife."[21] Feeling that she had been manipulated into the marriage,

---

20. Frederick B. Blair, comp., *The Memoirs of President W. W. Blair* (Lamoni, Iowa: Herald Publishing House, 1908), 5–6.

21. "Mormonism in This County." A later report probably based on hearsay, suggests that William was polygamously married to both Rosa and her twin sister Rhoda. The adverse editorial contained in St. Louis's *Missouri Republican* stated, while living at Palestine Grove "the rascal [William Smith] there became acquainted with a family in which were two girls, twin sisters, of comparatively tender age. There he committed a

Rosa apparently swore an affidavit before justice of the peace Frederick Dutcher at around the same time as Joseph Farwell's testimony (October 1852), although her account has not survived. According to her uncle Aaron Hook, shortly after her sealing to Smith, Rosa subsequently "seceded" from William's "faith" and moved out of Illinois to Newark, Wisconsin, not far from Beloit, probably in the winter of 1852–53.[22] When she and Farwell went to the authorities with their accusations against Smith, Rosa was presumably pregnant. As the Palestine Grove community became aware that Rosa was expecting, rumor suggested that William was the father. The state, even before charging William with bigamy based on the outcome of his divorce proceedings in April 1853, brought charges in October 1852 of adultery, bastardy (or paternity) in April 1853, and rape (for which he was indicted in September 1853), based on the testimony of Rosa and Farwell.[23]

However, other members of Hook family defended William against these charges. After Rosa relocated to Wisconsin, her uncle Aaron Hook solicited testimony from her in an attempt to clear William's name. Aaron Hook and Jotham T. Barrett reported in their letter to the editor that "from the statements that are now made by the girl [Rosa], which we have from *reliable sources*, we learn the facts that the real author of her troubles is a young man that was in the employ of the family, with whom she resided all last summer." The "troubles" Hook and Barrett referred to was assuredly Rosa's pregnancy, meaning that the father of her child was the unnamed young man living in the Hook household, not William. Rosa's initial accusations against Smith may have been an attempt to end the unwanted secret marriage and exonerate herself and her young lover from blame for her pregnancy. The child apparently died shortly after birth, as no surviving record exists of her giving birth to a child in 1852–53. According to Aaron Hook and Jotham Barrett, Rosa had apparently been pressured by her young lover to "swear against Mr. Smith through the influence of bribery, flattery, promises, &c," to cover the embarrassment of this misbehavior. After relocating to Wisconsin, on March 29, 1853, Rosa recanted her initial accusations, stating: "I sincerely and honestly clear William Smith from all the charges made in my affidavit." More damaging to Rosa's character was that the remainder of the Hook

---

double crime of seducing one of the sisters, and perpetrating a rape upon the other, and fled to this city." "Important Arrest," *Missouri Republican* 32, no. 101 (April 28, 1854): 2.

22. Aaron Hook and Jotham T. Barrett made a statement in April 1853 that Rosa had not been "a member of Mr. Smith's Church, having for a long time since seceded from the faith." Aaron Hook and Jotham T. Barrett (Shelburn, Ill.), Letter to the Editors, April 19, 1853, in "Slander Refuted," *Dixon Telegraph* 2, no. 51 (April 20, 1853): 2.

23. *The People of the State of Illinois vs. William Smith*, Bond, In Charge of Adultery, Lee County Circuit Clerk, Dixon, Illinois, October 15, 1852; *The People of the State of Illinois vs. William Smith*, Bastardy, Lee County Circuit Clerk, April 7, 1853, Criminal Record, Book B, 348, Dixon, Illinois; *The People of the State of Illinois vs. William Smith*, Indictment for Rape, Lee County Circuit Clerk, September 21, 1853, Criminal Record, Book B, 400, Dixon, Illinois.

family, including Rosa's grandmother and uncles, all sided with Smith. Aaron Hook ensured that Rosa's sworn statement of repudiation was published in the *Dixon Telegraph* along with Hook and Barrett's letter of April 19, 1853.[24]

While more details about William and Rosa's brief union may never be fully known, Rosa's initial testimony had caused pandemonium among county residents, resulting in the state's filing the triple charges of adultery, bastardy, and rape against Smith during the same time that his divorce was drawing to a conclusion. While Rosa's second affidavit, subsequently published in the *Dixon Telegraph*, may have helped clear the charges of rape and bastardy, it did not necessarily exonerate William of bigamy. The evidence presented during the divorce case confirmed that Smith was both teaching and practicing plural marriage, which assuredly provided credibility to Farwell's accusations. His indiscreet handwritten letters, penned during the time his church was flourishing in the area, found their way to the press and were subsequently published in local newspapers.[25] Being the brother of the celebrated Mormon prophet sensationalized his case throughout the state and meant that William's stay in Lee County made a lasting impression on the shocked but titillated residents.[26]

William's interactions with his two daughters by Caroline cannot be clearly documented, but apparently they stayed in or near Palestine Grove during the le-

---

24. Hook and Barrett (Shelburn, Ill.), Letter to Mr. Editor, April 19, 1853, and Rosa A. Hook (Newark, Wisc.), Statement, March 29, 1853, both cited in "Slander Refuted," *Dixon Telegraph* 2, no. 51 (April 30, 1853): 2. Erin Jennings Metcalfe has conjectured that Rosa may have given birth to Lorenzo Osborne during this time period (1852–53), and that he may have been William and Rosa's child; but the 1860 U.S. Census for Wisconsin—the earliest source mentioning him by name—lists Lorenzo as being born in Wisconsin in 1854 to Rosanna and her husband, Samuel J. Osborne, whom she had married that same year. The 1870 U.S. Census for Wisconsin gives the same year of birth but lists Lorenzo's birth place as Illinois. Later accounts vary about the year of his birth. Without further documentation or DNA testing, and based on the account from Aaron Hook and Jotham Barrett published in the *Dixon Telegraph*, I have concluded that Lorenzo was not William's child and that the baby born to Rosa and her unnamed lover likely died before her marriage to Samuel Osborne. Erin Jennings Metcalfe, "Rosanna and Rhoda Hook," ca. 2011, unpublished manuscript, in author's possession, 2; 1860 U.S. Census, Wisconsin, Columbia, Lodi, Roll M653_1401, 387, image 396; 1870 U.S. Census, Wisconsin, Dane County, Madison, Roll M593_1708, 331B, image 667.

25. William Smith, Letter to Sister [name replaced by line], 2.

26. The 1881 *History of Lee County* refers to William's teachings in the area as "heresy." "Lee county has been visited by religious heresy and fanaticism under the banner of Mormonism. After the murder of the great Mormon high priest, Joe Smith, his brother, William Smith, with a small band of followers, took up their residence in Lee county, about twelve miles south of Dixon, where they kept up their organization and meetings for some time." The history then records the jury's decision in favor of Roxey Ann in William's divorce case including a portion of William's polygamous letter, quoted in this chapter. *History of Lee County* (Chicago: H. H. Hill, 1881), 88.

Caroline ("Carrie") Scott, 1862–1883. Photograph ca. 1880, by unknown photographer. Daughter of Andrew and Mary Jane Smith Scott, and granddaughter of William Smith and Caroline Grant Smith. Courtesy of Gracia Jones.

gal turmoil of the early 1850s. It is not clear what interactions Roxey Ann had with her nieces/stepdaughters during this time, especially after she took her two young children and returned to her parents' home in Knox County, Illinois. Mary Jane at age seventeen married a Scottish immigrant, twenty-two-year-old Andrew Scott, on October 24, 1852, in Lee County. Andrew farmed for a living in Brooklyn Township in Lee County after the two wed. Two decades later in the 1870s, he, Mary Jane, and their four children, moved to Brookfield in Linn County, Missouri, where Andrew became a bank president, suggesting comfortable family circumstances. Mary Jane affiliated with the Baptist Church but unfortunately developed symptoms of her mother's condition at age forty-three and, despite the best efforts of her attending physician, succumbed to "dropsy of the heart" just two weeks before her forty-fifth birthday.[27]

Caroline and William's second daughter, Caroline Louisa, lived for a time in Walnut Grove with Roxey Ann after her father split with Isaac Sheen in 1850. During the early 1850s, when William seemed on track to build his thriving Church of Jesus Christ of Latter Day Saints, she lived with William; and apparently he maintained enough of a home despite his frequent travels that it was a workable arrangement. Just a year after Mary Jane's marriage, seventeen-year-old Caroline wed twenty-one-year-old James S. Quince in Lee County on December 8, 1853.[28] Quince worked for many years as a railroad engineer at Amboy, Illinois, just a mile or so north of Palestine Grove. During the Civil War, James enlisted and served as a corporal in Company I of the 89th Illinois Regiment. For unknown reasons, the family, which by then included five children, moved to Fort Worth, Texas. In an eerie replay of Mary Jane's fate, Caroline

---

27. Mary Jane Smith, marriage to Andrew Scott, October 24, 1852, First Marriage Register, 1839–73, Marriage Records of Lee County, Illinois, Book A, 46, Lee County Courthouse (old), Dixon, Illinois; "Laid to Rest," *Brookfield [Missouri] Gazette* 12, no. 36 (December 26, 1878): 3; 1880 U.S. Census, Missouri, Linn County, Brookfield, Roll 700, film 1254700, 426A; Harry D. Galley, *Joseph Smith Senior's Children* (Rock Island, Ill.: Harry D. Galley, 2000), 31–32.

28. Caroline Smith and James S. Quince, First Marriage Register, 1839–73, December 8, 1853, Marriage Records of Lee County, Illinois, Book A, 57, Lee County Courthouse (old), Dixon, Illinois. Both daughters married at age seventeen.

died on January 9, 1878, the same year as Mary Jane's death, at age forty-one.[29] What contact William maintained with these two daughters is not known, given the absence of any reports of visits or the survival of any letters. William was at Brookfield, Missouri, just a month after Mary Jane's death, probably to offer his condolences to his son-in-law and grandchildren, but he was apparently not present at her death and makes no mention of any business but proselytizing in his sole letter written while at Brookfield.[30] His surviving letters are voluminous but rarely mention Caroline Louisa, Mary Jane, or their children.

By the spring of 1853, William had lost his lawsuits. He was broke and, except for the Hook family and perhaps Jotham Barrett, had lost all of his followers in the Palestine Grove area. With his legal troubles mounting and his reputation in question, Smith fled from Lee County in the spring of 1854 leaving several of his legal trials still pending. He may have felt that the widespread publicity meant there no way he could get a fair trial in Lee County, and his impoverishment meant that he could not afford legal representation. He traveled down the Illinois River toward St. Louis.

Historian Stanley B. Kimball, who attempted to reconstruct the movements of Joseph Smith's Egyptian mummies and papyri after his death (they were in Mother Lucy's possession immediately after the martyrdom in 1844), speculated that William may have sold or rented the mummies or papyri during the first third of the 1850s to provide a sort of living. He had obtained the mummies from his mother during a visit to Nauvoo in the year 1847. Perhaps Lucy loaned William the mummies because he was so upset with her for transferring her home, deeded to her by Nauvoo's Trustees, to her daughter Lucy and her husband Arthur Millikin. (See Chapter 19.) "William was seldom gainfully employed," summarized Kimball, "was often in financial straits, and owned very little." "William may have sold or leased the antiquities to one of the many circuses playing along the Illinois River. The local press included 134 references to twenty-eight different circuses playing this area of Illinois during 1848–56, some featuring 'Museums of Wonder.'"

Kimball believed that A. Combs, who eventually consummated a sale of the mummies with Emma Smith Bidamon just ten days after Lucy Mack Smith's death in 1856, was likely the individual with whom William brokered a deal. Kimball conjectured that "William rented, leased, or sold all or part of the antiquities under circumstances that precluded concluding the transaction until

---

29. Frank E. Stevens, *History of Lee County Illinois* (Chicago: S. J. Clarke Publishing, 1914), 1:121–22; 1870 U.S. Census, Illinois, Lee County, Amboy, Roll M593_246, 216A; Galley, *Joseph Smith Senior's Children*, 32–34.

30. William Smith (Brookfield, Mo.), Letter to Richard Randall, February 13, 1879. William made no mention of his family in his letter to Randall, confining his remarks to describing his missionary labors for the RLDS Church.

A Facsimile from the Book of Abraham, no. 3. As published in the *Times and Seasons* newspaper at Nauvoo, 3, no. 14 (May 16, 1842).

the death of his mother to whom the mummies and papyri legally belonged."[31] Kimball's argument is bolstered by a later account from Joseph Smith III: "We learned that while living near Galesburg [Knox County, Illinois], William undertook a lecturing tour, and secured the mummies and case of records, as the papyrus was called, as an exhibit and aid to making his lectures more attractive and lucrative." Apparently, at a later and unspecified time, according to Joseph III, "Uncle William became stranded somewhere along the Illinois River, and sold the mummies and the records with the understanding that he might repurchase them. This he never did."[32] Acquiring such profits may help explain how William was able to pay his passage down the Illinois River, obtain housing in St. Louis, and eventually pay for legal representation in his ongoing battle with the disillusioned but determined Roxey Ann.

Once in St. Louis, Smith went to work in the thriving river city and, according to one newspaper report, had hopes of escaping west to Salt Lake City. Even assuming that Brigham's Saints would have welcomed him—far from a sure prospect— he would not have had time to set this plan in motion. Though William knew he was a wanted man, he probably didn't realize that L. McCuen, sheriff of

---

31. Kimball, "New Light on Old Egyptiana," 87–89. H. Donl Peterson also believed that William likely sold the mummies and/or papyri to A. Combs. H. Donl Peterson, *The Story of the Book of Abraham: Mummies, Manuscripts, and Mormonism* (Salt Lake City: Deseret Book, 1995), 257–58.

32. Joseph Smith III (Lamoni, Iowa), Letter to Bro. Heman C. Smith, October 24, 1898, in *Saints' Herald* 46, no. 2 (January 11, 1899): 18.

Lee County, had been tracking him ever since he discovered that Smith had left the county without paying the legal costs for which he was liable, making him technically in contempt of court. McCuen eventually followed him to St. Louis, teamed up with several local officers, and went to Smith's dwelling on Market Street, between Seventh and Eighth Streets, in the heart of the city. He captured Smith late at night, on April 25, 1854, took him across the Mississippi River, and shortly thereafter returned him to Lee County to await trial.

The *Dixon Telegraph* recounted this thrilling chase and Smith's capture: "Bill Smith, the Mormon Prophet and brother of Joe Smith, the renowned founder of the Mormon Church . . . is now closely confined in the jail at this place. He being indicted, gave bail for his appearance at the last Circuit Court, but, having got some presentiment—and we think it would hardly require any supernatural power to give it to him—that the case rather favored the side of the people, he vacated these parts. But owing to some disarrangement in the Mormon under ground railroad, or the adroitness of the person in pursuit, he was brought to a halt at St. Louis, and marched back to Dixon." The reporter described Smith as a "large and powerfully built man, with good manners, and about forty-two years of age."[33]

Recognizing his desperate circumstances, William once again appealed to former colleague Joseph Wood for legal assistance. But like nearly all of his former adherents, Wood had decisively distanced himself from Smith by 1854. The *Dixon Telegraph* reported, "[William's] friend Joseph [Wood] has lately resumed the practice of the law; and to him Bill wrote 'for God's sake' to come over and help him. Joe replied that he had quit practicing law 'for God's sake;' but that if Bill would send him fifty dollars, he would try his case for him; but that if he did not send the money, he 'would appear against him, and could send him to the Penitentiary, like a d——n [demon?].'" The paper subsequently reported that William was unable to raise money to pay Wood's fee and forfeited his bail, leaving him locked in jail awaiting trial.[34] In early May, William spent several tense weeks in jail, while at the same time repeatedly attempting to get some Hook family members to come to his aid. After three weeks in the common jail, several of his friends, including Aaron Hook and Hook's mother Rhoda, finally and with apparent reluctance, supplied his bail of $1,000 and may have also helped him secure legal aid. William meekly returned to his home on the Hook property while awaiting his trial.[35]

In characteristic fashion, William, in an account written decades later, said that he "disfellowshipped" Joseph Wood, ironically enough "for his belief in Polygamy."

---

33. "Mormonism in This County," *Dixon [Illinois] Telegraph* 2, no. 48 (April 9, 1853); "Important Arrest," *Missouri Republican* 32, no. 101 (April 28, 1854): 2; "Bill Smith, the Mormon Prophet," *Dixon Telegraph* 3, no. 52 (May 4, 1854): 2.

34. "More Trouble in the Church," *Dixon Telegraph* 3, no. 44 (March 9, 1854): 2.

35. Bond posted by Rhoda E. Hook, Aaron Hook, and Elnathan Gibbs, in *The People of the State of Illinois vs. William Smith*, Indictment for Rape, Bond or Recongnizance, Lee County Circuit Clerk, May 15, 1854, Dixon, Illinois.

William recounted that Wood "afterwards put out for Salt Lake amoung a people of his own kind."³⁶ Smith once again secured Edward Southwick, the Dixon attorney, as his legal counsel, with assistant Shepard G. Patrick replacing Joseph Wood. Wood steered clear of William, an obvious attempt to avoid prosecution for his own involvement in polygamy, which had been made public in the divorce proceedings. William's lawyers successfully filed for a continuance of his case and later petitioned the court for a change of venue.³⁷ With his name and reputation constantly being held up and mocked in the press, Smith and his attorneys obviously felt that Lee County could hardly provide a dispassionate jury. While the court obligingly changed the venue to La Salle County, the state's attorney for Lee County (identified only by his surname, Miller) eventually decided Smith's case was no longer worth pursuing. The sheriff had been repeatedly frustrated in his attempt to locate witnesses, and most, like Rosa Hook, had reportedly left the state. Rosa herself, who by now had presumably lost her child, was living in Wisconsin, first in Newark, then in Lodi, and thus avoided participation in the trial she helped instigate without a cumbersome extradition procedure. Even if she had been persuaded or ordered to return to Lee County, her swearing an affidavit recanting her accusations against William severely weakened the case, and the lack of witnesses made it difficult to prove that Smith, still enmeshed in the divorce proceedings, was actually guilty of bigamy since he could have argued that he had assumed a quick decision on his divorce suit and remarried based on that assumption. As a result, Miller dropped the bigamy charges in March 23, 1853, followed by the bastardy and rape charges after an initial hearing on May 15, 1854, four months later in September 1854. Miller concluded to "prosecute this case no farther," and Smith was subsequently discharged.³⁸

Although he had been cleared of all charges brought by the state, Smith's reputation was severely damaged. He left the county in August 1854, dejected and under a cloud of suspicion. He was such a conspicuous citizen that local histories documented Smith's stay in the area, his relationship to Mormonism's founder,

---

36. William Smith (Osterdock, Iowa), Letter to Edmund Levi Kelley, October 15, 1891, Community of Christ Archives. I have found no evidence that Joseph Wood ever moved to Salt Lake City. It may have been William's way of dismissing Wood, who had rejected him.

37. Bastardy change of venue to La Salle County, in *People of the State of Illinois vs. William Smith*, Bastardy, Lee County Circuit Clerk, September 21, 1853, Criminal Record, Book B, 398, and Chancery Record, Book B, 399, Dixon, Illinois.

38. *The People of the State of Illinois vs. William Smith*, trial March 23, 1853, Lee County Circuit Court, Dixon, Illinois, Illinois Regional Archives Depository, Northern Illinois University, Regional History Center, DeKalb, Illinois; *The People of the State of Illinois vs. William Smith*, Trial for Bastardy, Criminal Record, April 7, 1853, Book B, 348, September 21, 1853, Book B, 398, and Chancery Record, Book B, 399, Lee County Circuit Clerk, Dixon, Illinois; *The People of the State of Illinois vs. William Smith*, Indictment for Rape, May 15, 1854, September 18, 1854, Criminal Record, Book B, 459–60, 466, Lee County Circuit Clerk, Dixon, Illinois.

and his "heretical" teachings about polygamy.³⁹ Jason W. Briggs, who had broken with Smith's church in the fall of 1851, continued to follow Smith's movements. He was puzzled about how Smith had escaped legal punishment for his actions in Lee County but felt certain that he had "not escaped the Lords."⁴⁰

In August 1854, William, then living seventy miles south in South Hampton, Peoria County, Illinois (apparently new territory for him), wrote to Brigham Young, exploring the possibilities of reinstatement into the Utah-based Church of Jesus Christ of Latter-day Saints. Exactly what Brigham knew about the initial success and plummeting fortunes of William's Church of Jesus Christ of Latter Day Saints, followed by the decidedly unsavory legal complications of the divorce, countersuit, and indictments brought by the state against William is not known; but Brigham did not answer this letter. William followed up with two more letters, one in May 1855, and the third in July 1856 two months after Mother Lucy's death. Polygamy had been publicly announced in Utah in August 1852, making moot William's excursions into that form of marriage; but Brigham apparently ignored all three letters. William's letters evinced only a half-hearted attempt at recognizing his mistakes, and he continued to demand restoration to his former Church positions, a demand Young was unwilling to meet. (See Chapter 19.)⁴¹

Hyrum Wallace Smith, 1850–1935. Pictured here with his second wife, Rosalia ("Rosa") Damitz. Date and photographer unknown. Photograph courtesy of Dianna Smith.

William apparently made no attempt to establish contact with his two children by Roxey Ann, who had been granted sole custody. Possibly, he never even saw his son Hyrum Wallace, as Roxey Ann left William in the spring of 1850 while she was pregnant with him. Hyrum Wallace was born August 17, 1850, at Altona, Knox County, Illinois, joining daughter Thalia, who had been

---

39. *History of Lee County*, 88; Stevens, *History of Lee County Illinois*, 275–76.

40. J[ason] W. Briggs (Beloit, Wisc.), Letter to Joseph Smith III, November 20, 1853; *History of Lee County*, 88.

41. William wrote three letters to Brigham Young during 1854–56. (See Chapter 18.) Young did not respond to any of these letters. William Smith (South Hampton, Ill.), Letter to Brigham Young, August 8, 1854; William Smith (Springfield, Ill.), Letter to Brigham Young, May 7, 1855; William Smith (Turkey River, Iowa), Letter to Brigham Young, July 13, 1856, all in Brigham Young Office Files, 1832–78, Letters from Church Leaders and Others, 1840–1877, William Smith, 1844–1857, LDS Church History Library.

Thalia Grant Smith, 1848–1924, with her first cousin Heber J. Grant, ca. 1923, photographer unknown. Used by permission of Gracia Jones.

born September 21, 1848, in Lee County, Illinois. Roxey Ann's parents provided a home for them in Walnut Grove Township, Knox County, Illinois, from the time she left William in 1850 until 1868 when she took the children and moved to Lathrop, Missouri, for unknown reasons. Ironically enough, she thus spent the rest of her life just twenty miles from Far West and Liberty, dying in 1900 at age seventy-five. As an adult, H. Wallace married and moved to California, while Thalia remained single, teaching school in rural Lathrop, Missouri.

In 1923, when she was seventy-five, Thalia began a regular correspondence with Heber J. Grant, William's nephew and her first cousin, which represented the culmination of a relationship which had begun thirty years earlier. (Heber's father was the brother of Thalia's mother.) Grant sent Thalia a copy of the Book of Mormon and other religious tracts produced by the LDS Church in Salt Lake City. In 1923, Grant was elated to learn that Thalia had become converted to the LDS faith, largely because of Grant's influence. Thalia had written to Grant, "I had always wanted to know about the Latter-day Saints and in the Mormon Bible [Book of Mormon]. I have you [Grant] to thank for your patience and perseverance in sending me these things to open my eyes to the truth, as I had always been taught that Mormonism was a delusion, that Joseph Smith was a 'Dreamer' and nothing more." Grant baptized Thalia the following year, at Independence, Missouri, on April 26, 1924. Thalia's description of what she knew about Mormonism and Joseph Smith reveals that Roxey Ann had distanced herself and her children from Mormonism after ending her marriage to William.

Grant and Thalia also corresponded with Thalia's brother H. Wallace about his Mormon roots, sharing information on doctrinal issues and their joy at Thalia's conversion, but such attempts at converting him were evidently unsuccessful. Grant had visited both Roxey Ann and Thalia while they were living in Lathrop, Missouri, prior to Roxey Ann's death in 1900, and reported that "from the first time that I met her [Thalia's] mother, the widow of William Smith and my father's sister, I was very favorably impressed with mother and daughter as very splendid people."[42]

---

42. Heber J. Grant (Salt Lake City), Letter to "My dear Cousin Thalia [Smith]," September 5, 1923, 136–37; October 15, 1923, 229–31; November 6, 1923, 266–67; Heber J. Grant, Letter to "My dear cousin Wallace [Smith]," November 6, 1923, 265; Heber J. Grant, Letter to Miss Mariana Shreve, December 3, 1923, 355–57; Heber J. Grant, Letter to S. O. Bennion, February 12, 1924, 666. These four letters are in Heber J. Grant Letters, MS

As for William, he eventually made his way farther south to Springfield, Illinois, where he eagerly proselytized the small pockets of Mormons in the area, some of whom he converted to his views. However, there was no organizational structure into which they could fit; and LDS traveling elder Thomas Colburn vigorously followed William, detaching these few scattered followers from William's usual message on the importance of lineal succession, given the more complete and promising Mormon gospel that the thriving movement in Salt Lake City could offer. Colburn reported that Smith had "long been laboring with might and main to poison the minds of all as far as his influence extends, against the authorities of the church of Christ in Utah.... He [Smith] had endeavored to give a public lecture against polygamy, at the hall in Springfield," but it was poorly attended. William's image in the press, including his trial for bigamy the previous year, prompted caution. Thus, Colburn continued to find additional Mormons in and around Springfield who had, briefly followed William Smith, but had found more than ample reason to doubt William's staying power.[43]

Smith eventually retreated to northeastern Iowa where he again revived his dream of establishing a healthy Mormon branch to compete with the Utah Mormons and returned to Kirtland, Ohio, as a prospective gathering place. William still owned property in the area and may have also hoped to create some financial stability after the turmoil and impoverishment of the first half of the 1850s. In the fall of 1855, he found a smattering of Mormons still in the area, lacking leadership and an organization. Stephen Post, who had followed James J. Strang for a time and kept a detailed journal, was among those who visited Kirtland during this same time. He resided across the border in Centerville, Pennsylvania, where he labored as a blacksmith. According to Post, Kirtland was a "land barren of faith" and the local Mormons "as people without a shepard."[44] It was the kind of situation where Smith could mobilize his impressive physical presence, eloquence in speech, and charisma to attract followers.

At Kirtland, William reconnected with a figure from his past, seventy-two-year-old Martin Harris, one of the three witnesses of the Book of Mormon, whom William had known since his boyhood in Palmyra, New York. Harris had remained in the Kirtland vicinity for most of his life, even after the main body

---

1234, Box 21, fd. 2, LDS Church History Library. Grant quotes Thalia in his letter to Shreve; I was allowed to see Grant's outgoing, but not his incoming, correspondence. After learning of Thalia's conversion, Grant wrote, "I rejoice beyond my power to tell you that you have arrived at the point where you believe in the Book of Mormon [as] an inspired work. Surely, if the Book of Mormon is an inspired work, Joseph Smith was indeed a prophet of the living God, and the Gospel of the Lord Jesus Christ as proclaimed by Joseph Smith and his successors—Brigham Young and others—is in very deed the plan of life and salvation." Heber J. Grant, Letter to "My dear Cousin Thalia [Smith]," August 21, 1923, 96–97.

43. Thomas Colburn, Letter to the Editor, May 31, 1855, in *St. Louis Luminary* 1, no. 28 (June 2, 1855): 3.

44. Stephen Post, Journal, April 11, 1856.

Martin Harris, 1783–1875. Photograph by Charles W. Carter of an earlier photo by Savage & Ottinger, ca. 1870. Courtesy LDS Church History Library.

of Saints had moved on to Missouri in 1838, and then established Nauvoo in Illinois in the early 1840s. After the Twelve left most of the Mormons westward, Martin had become the self-appointed caretaker of the Kirtland Temple. Smith found the magnificent temple he helped construct in a dilapidated condition. "The town [of Kirtland] had a sorry look, and the condition of the Temple was pitiful," described one observer. "Its walls inside and out, also its trimmings and decorations, were badly defaced."[45] Another recounted that where "the pulpits of the Temple used to be richly cushioned and trimmed with red velvet and silk tassels," such luxuries were now absent, along "with the gilt and curtains! The walls, once spotlessly white, are profusely profaned with the autographs of visitors. Counts, congressmen, and circus-riders—poets, privates, pedlars and pudding-heads—lads, lassies, ladies and one lord have scrawled their names and the day and year . . . on the once immaculate walls."[46]

William and Martin had both supported James J. Strang after Joseph Smith's death; but like William, Martin's affiliation lasted less than a year.[47] The two had crossed paths when William accompanied Strang to Kirtland in August 1846. During the Strangite conference held August 7–10, William was acknowledged as Patriarch over the Church and a member of the First Presidency, while Harris was appointed to Strang's high council.[48] When the two men renewed their acquaintance nearly a decade later in 1855, Smith importuned Harris to assist him in reorganizing the Church in the area. With the support of Chilion Daniels, Smith and Harris notified Mormons in the greater Kirtland area of a conference to be held on October 6, 1855. Just prior to the conference, both Smith and Harris participated in a spiritualist episode conducted by a "prophetess" called Miss Sexton, who channeled a revelation from both Old and New Testament prophets authorizing them to begin organizing.

Stephen Post, whom the two men summoned to serve as secretary for the conference, recorded that "Br Martin Harris had published a proclamation pur-

---

45. Blair, *Memoirs of President W. W. Blair*, 35–36.
46. "Mormon Times in Kirtland," *Cleveland Daily Plain Dealer* 15, no. 114 (May 17, 1859): 3.
47. Though Harris's affiliation with Strang was brief, his commitment was strong enough that he served a six-week mission to England in 1846. H. Michael Marquardt, "Martin Harris: The Kirtland Years, 1831–1870," *Dialogue: A Journal of Mormon Thought* 35, no. 3 (Fall 2002): 19–25.
48. "Kirtland," *Voree Herald* 1, no. 9 (September 1846): 1–2; "William Smith," *Zion's Reveille* 1, no. 12 (December 1846): 2–3.

Tiered priesthood pulpits, Kirtland Temple. Stereographic photograph by J. B. King, 1906. Copy in author's possession.

porting to be given by Moses, Elias, Elijah & John through a Miss Sexton a Spirit medium of Cleveland. Wm Smith got a revelation given through the same medium, [and] read to me the purport of which was that We Moses Elias Elijah & John again come unto you &c & go on to give directions to different elders about reorganizing the church and appointing them to select a place for the gathering of the saints." To protect the identities of those tasked with the reorganization, Smith assigned pseudonyms to those key leaders, much as Joseph had done to participants in Zion's Camp and in Missouri.[49]

Several Mormons came to the conference from nearby Erie, Pennsylvania, including Simeon Atwood and a Sister Soule, as well as a handful of Saints from the more immediate area of Kirtland. One of those present was Hiram Stratton, an individual who had also earlier supported James J. Strang, and who had been influential in persuading Smith to support Strang some ten years earlier at Nauvoo. Harris acted as president during the weekend conference, while Smith and Daniels took turns preaching. Reminiscent of Kirtland's heyday, Smith and Harris took their places in the temple's tiered priesthood seats on the east end of the building and stood at the ornately carved and painted pulpits as they explicated their tenets and preached. Perhaps due to lack of numbers, they adopted twelve resolutions, rather than formally organizing during the gathering, though the resolutions make their intent to do so clear. Included in their ideology was a declaration of their "full confidence in the raising up and calling of Joseph Smith

---

49. Stephen Post, Journal, October 5, 1855.

Jr. as translator, seer, & prophet," their belief in the veracity of the Bible, Book of Mormon, Doctrine and Covenants as containing the "fulness of the gospel," and their rejection of the "doctrines of the plurality of wives." Those present seemed unaware of Smith's involvement in polygamy just a few years earlier in his own failed organization. The group set a date for another conference to be held on April 6, 1856, hoping to garner more support in the ensuing months. Before the conference adjourned, Harris ensured that he read his revelation received through Miss Sexton to those present.[50]

It does not appear that the proposed April conference ever took place. Harris's wife had decided to migrate to Utah in the year 1856 without her husband, and William had returned to the Midwest, settling in northeastern Iowa.[51] Still, Harris and Smith were anticipating taking organizational steps by 1857. Harris continued to preach during the intervening time period and succeeded in winning at least one adherent. The *Painesville Telegraph* reported that, on April 24, 1857, Harris "baptized a happy convert in the river, near the Geauga Mills."[52] Smith had also returned to the area, residing just across the state line in Warren, Pennsylvania. He preached in Warren and Erie Counties in an attempt to gather followers;[53] and near October 25, 1857, Smith and Harris formally organized their church. (Stephen Post noted in his journal on that date that William Smith "is now trying to organize as President in Kirtland.") In anticipation of formally organizing, William had, a month earlier, written to Post in an attempt to get him to serve as a printer. William obviously envisioned producing a newspaper, as he had done in his earlier organization, and the exigency was evident in the

---

50. "Resolutions Passed at a Conference of Elders," in ibid., October 6–7, 1855; Greg R. Knight, *Thomas Bullock Nauvoo Journal* (Orem, Utah: Grandin Book, 1884), 62. A few years after Smith and Harris's organization collapsed, in the summer of 1860, W. W. Blair and James Blakeslee visited the Kirtland Temple and met with some of these same individuals. Blair recounted, "On Sunday, the nineteenth of August [1860], . . . brother Blakeslee and I attended a meeting in the Temple where Simeon Atwood, of Erie, Pennsylvania, and Leonard Rich, of Kirtland, were the speakers. By their request Elder Blakeslee and myself took seats in the stand with them and Martin Harris." Blair, *Memoirs of President W. W. Blair*, 36.

51. Marquardt, "Martin Harris," 34–35; William Smith, Letter to Brigham Young, July 13, 1856. Martin's first wife, Lucy Harris, presumably had died in 1836, and he had married Caroline Young a few months later, on November 1, 1836. Martin and Caroline had six surviving children (one additional daughter died as a child), whom Caroline took with her to Utah in 1859. Marquardt, "Martin Harris," 10, 34; Dennis A. Wright, "Caroline Young Harris: The Kirtland Wife of Martin Harris," in *Regional Studies in Latter-day Saint Church History: Ohio and Upper Canada*, edited by Guy L. Dorius, Craig K. Manscill, and Craig James Ostler (Provo, Utah: BYU Religious Studies Center, 2006), 111–23.

52. "Elder Martin Harris . . . ," *Painesville Telegraph* 35 (April 30, 1857): 3, quoted in Marquardt, "Martin Harris," 34–35.

53. William Smith to the Editor, May 19, 1857, (Warren, Penn.), in *New-York Daily Tribune* 17, no. 5025 (May 28, 1857): 5.

fact that William sent his request in what Post described as a "revelation" appointing him to the position.⁵⁴ However, since they had last met in Kirtland in the fall of 1855, Post had transferred his loyalty to Sidney Rigdon's diminishing movement. Rigdon had received a revelation on March 17, 1856, calling Post "to a great work assisting my servant Sidney Rigdon in preparing the way before me, and Elijah which should come." According to Rigdon's biographer, "Rigdon and Post, two yoked visionaries, while seeing each other face-to-face only once, would correspond with each other for [the next] twenty years."⁵⁵

Neither William, Martin, nor any other member left a record of the date or details about the organizational meeting. They presumably adopted the same designation William had used for his organization at Palestine Grove: the Church of Jesus Christ of Latter Day Saints. However, surviving details about their organization are limited, probably because it was short-lived. It is also possible that they met infrequently—that after their initial efforts to organize in October, William returned to his home across the border in Pennsylvania, and only periodically gathered at Kirtland for designated meetings. Not until May 1858 is there another mention of their organization at Kirtland, when Jeter Clinton, a traveling missionary from Salt Lake City, reported that Smith and Harris were again together in the city, where they had "organized a church of their own," meaning that their organization had survived in one form or another for at least seven months.⁵⁶ There was also a notable difference since their initial gathering on October 6, 1855, as William managed to assume primacy of leadership. Enoch Beebe, who was bound for Utah with a group of missionaries returning from England, recounted to leaders in Provo, Utah, on June 22, 1858, that he had stopped in Kirtland on his way and that "Martin Harris had reorganized the Church in [that] place with 6 members." He added rather significantly that the group had "appointed Wm. Smith their Leader Prophet Seer & Revelator."⁵⁷

While William Smith and Martin Harris struggled to garner support, their organization began to unravel almost immediately; and within months of their initial organization—by June 1858, "Harris kicked Smith out of the place & damned him to Hell."⁵⁸ While it is unknown what exactly transpired, the sole surviving account reveals that Harris's negative reaction and stinging rejection stemmed from Smith's overweening ambition. The local paper pointed to the challenges associated

---

54. Post, Journal, October 25, 1857.

55. Sidney Rigdon, Letter to Stephen Post, March 17, 1856, quoted in Richard S. Van Wagoner, *Sidney Rigdon: A Portrait of Religious Excess* (Salt Lake City: Signature Books, 1994), 402–4.

56. Journal History, May 18, 1858, 3.

57. Scott G. Kenney, ed., *Wilford Woodruff's Journal, 1833–1898*, 9 vols. (Midvale, Utah: Signature Books, 1983–85), June 22, 1858, 5:199.

58. Ibid. Woodruff heard this report from "Enoch Beese" [Beebe?], who had stopped in Kirtland with other traveling missionaries. See also Post, Journal, October 25, 1857; Max J. Evans, "The Stephen Post Collection," *BYU Studies* 14, no. 1 (Autumn 1973): 100–103; Marquardt, "Martin Harris," 34–35.

with Smith's personality, recounting that "William Smith, a brother of the Prophet Joe, came from Pennsylvania to Kirtland and another attempt was made to galvanize the 'dead body' of Mormonism there." However, "Smith put on so many airs there was no living with him," the editor summarized, "and he was requested to go away." Smith and Harris's organization dissolved immediately. Harris remained at his post as self-appointed caretaker of the Kirtland Temple, and Smith retreated back across the state line to Erie County, Pennsylvania.[59]

While Smith never completely relinquished his personal ambition to lead a branch of Mormonism, by the late 1850s his prospects of ever establishing a viable church organization had passed. However, his personal life acquired a new and long-overdue stability, and he brought a bride to Pennsylvania. During his stay in Ohio and Pennsylvania, he had become acquainted with Eliza Elsie Sanborn, the thirty-year-old daughter of Enoch Sanborn and Lois Elliot Sanborn, originally from Cattaraugus, New York.[60] Enoch and Lois had joined the Mormons during the 1830s and moved to Kirtland, Ohio, in the spring of 1836. Possibly nine-year-old Eliza joined the Church after reaching Kirtland, though her older brother Alden, who would have turned eighteen in 1836, stated that while "my father was a Mormon," he himself apparently had not joined, though he "attended meetings both in Nauvoo and . . . in Kirtland." The family moved with the Saints, following Joseph Smith to Missouri, then to Illinois; and at one point, Eliza resided "just across the street from him [Joseph] in Nauvoo." After Eliza's parents died in Illinois, she and her two siblings returned to Ohio in the fall of 1840 to be closer to their extended family.[61] Eliza married James Brain on November 18, 1845, in Cuyahoga County, Ohio, and the couple had four children. However, in June 1857, Eliza petitioned successfully for a divorce for James's "willful absence" and reverted to her birth name.[62] Eliza may have supported William's recent attempt at organizing the short-lived Church of Jesus

---

59. "Mormon Times in Kirtland," 3; Marquardt, "Martin Harris," 35.

60. "Obituary. Mrs. Eliza E. Smith," *Elkader Weekly Register* 12, no. 18 (March 14, 1889): 1. Eliza was born on April 16, 1827.

61. Alden Enoch Sanborn, Testimony, quoted in *Public Discussions of the Issues between the Reorganized Church of Jesus Christ of Latter Day Saints and the Church of Christ [Disciples] Held in Kirtland, Ohio Beginning February 12, and Closing March 8, 1884 between E. L. Kelley, of the Reorganized Church of Jesus Christ of Latter Day Saints and Clark Braden, of the Church of Christ* (St. Louis: Clark Braden, 1884), 393–94; Erin Jennings Metcalfe, "Eliza Elsie Sanborn," 1–2, 2010, unpublished manuscript in my possession.

62. James Brain and Eliza Sanborn applied for a marriage license in Cuyahoga County, Ohio, on November 17, 1845. Ohio, County Marriages, 1790–1950, microfilm 872467, item 1, image number 371, LDS Family History Library. Their four children were Byron Bradford (born October 21, 1846), Mary Lois (1848), Ward (1851), and Clara (January 17, 1851). Ward and Clara may have been twins. Mary and Ward were living with William and Eliza in Erie, Pennsylvania, in 1860, while Byron lived with his father in Kirtland. 1860 U.S. Census, Pennsylvania, Erie County, Venango, Roll M653_1108, 1061, image 454; 1860 U.S. Census, Ohio, Lake County, Willoughby, Roll M653_996,

Christ of Latter Day Saints at Kirtland, and William certainly knew the Sanborn family during the Kirtland-Nauvoo period. He likely became reacquainted with Eliza when he first returned to Kirtland in October 1855. About five months after Eliza's divorce, and during the same time William and Harris were building up their church, the pair married on November 12, 1857, at Kirtland, Ohio.[63]

William and his new bride moved across the state line into Venango Township, Erie County, Pennsylvania, approximately eighty miles from Kirtland. William seemed to have found new stability and acted the part of a father in caring for Eliza's children, who then ranged in age from eleven to six. In time, most of them developed a fondness for William and considered him their father. In marrying Eliza Sanborn, Smith's life had come full circle. It had been in Erie County, Pennsylvania, while serving the Mormon Church as a twenty-one-year-old missionary that he had met and married Caroline Grant nearly a quarter of a century earlier. His marriage to Caroline had been his most successful relationship, and he must have hoped that his marriage to Eliza would mark the end of the tumultuous twelve years since Caroline's death. The couple resided in Erie County for their first three years of marriage. On July 24, 1858, their first child was born—named William Enoch for his father and Eliza's father. To distinguish him from his father, he was nicknamed Willie.[64]

Despite their long ties to Mormonism, William and Eliza chose to distance themselves from the faith during their earliest years of marriage. Not long after his failed attempt to organize with Martin Harris, William withdrew from all factions of Mormonism. The *Cleveland Daily Plain Dealer* reported in May 1859 that William, after his failed partnership with Martin Harris, "renounced Mormonism, and is now scouring the rural districts of Pennsylvania with a one-horse panorama of Palestine."[65]

During 1858–60, William led a stable life in Erie County but did not altogether abandon evangelizing. For a time, he entertained the notion of using his well-honed oratorical skills to earn his livelihood. Wearied of being unrecognized among varying factions of Mormonism, he decided to link his fate with the Baptists. Smith preached on behalf of that sect throughout southern Pennsylvania, but the

---

297, image 133. For information on Clara, see Ohio Deaths, 1908–1953, Microfilm 1991300, image number 1849, LDS Family History Library.

63. Daughters of the American Revolution, New Connecticut Chapter (Painesville, Ohio), "Probate Court Marriage Records, Lake County Ohio, 1840–1865," typescript, 102, Morley Library, Painesville, Ohio. The entry reads: "Smith, Wm., m., Eliza E. Sanburne, November 12, 1857."

64. "Records of Early Church Families," *Utah Genealogical Magazine* 26, no. 19 (1935): 105; 1870 U.S. Census, Iowa, Clayton County, Boardman Township, Roll M593_383, 152A, image 31.

65. "Mormon Times in Kirtland," 3. See also Jeter Clinton's account, in Journal History, May 18, 1858, 1. In an letter to the *New York Tribune* in May 1857, William announced: "Permit me to say that I am not a Mormon." However, in this account he was probably indicating that he was not affiliating with Brigham Young's followers in Salt Lake City.

reality was that he could never truly divorce himself from his roots. His declaration that he was no longer a Mormon was more of a rejection of existing factions than a renunciation of his faith. His firm conviction regarding the restoration of Christ's New Testament church found its way back into his sermons, and the Baptist vestrymen in Pennsylvania tried him for heresy, probably in 1859–60.[66]

His brief affiliation with the Baptists apparently preceded his also brief venture into exhibiting what the *Cleveland Plain Dealer* had called a "one horse panorama of Palestine." Mormon historian Dale Broadhurst commented that Smith's display was likely "a small scale imitation of John Banvard's Holy Land panorama, featured in his New York City museum during the 1850s. The *New York Tribune* of December 27, 1852, advertised that 'Banvard's Panorama of Palestine' was currently 'on exhibition' in that city; while the *New York Evening Telegram* of Jan[uary] 10, 1889, remembered the Banvard diorama as having been a 'famous' local attraction. Mobile versions of these mural paintings were commonplace during the mid-19th century."[67] Although William had parted with the mummies at an earlier but undetermined date, he may have retained, if only temporarily, portions of the papyri, which he had obtained from his mother and which he may have included in his traveling display.

William was apparently unsuccessful in these modes of earning a living and he reluctantly resigned himself to farming and carpentry, neither of which he enjoyed, to provide for his family.[68] Land was cheaper in the West, so after three years in Erie County, the family moved seven hundred miles to rural Elkader in Clayton County, Iowa, in 1860.[69] William had briefly resided near this locale during 1856 without attracting attention. At least two of Eliza's children by her previous marriage joined the family in Iowa. Thus, at age fifty-one, Smith was starting over in an area where no one knew his name, or his relationship to Mormonism's founder.

---

66. Howard, *The Memoirs of President Joseph Smith III*, 184; William B. Smith, Testimony, January 29–30, 1892, Temple Lot Case,

67. Kevin J. Avery, "Movies for Manifest Destiny: The Moving Panorama in Phenomenon in America," online article http://www.tfaoi.com/aa/3aa/3aa66.htm, published 1999 (accessed February 20, 2015). See also "Mormon Times in Kirtland," 3, notes and commentary by Dale Broadhurst, note 3, http.//www.sidneyrigdon.com/dbroadhu/OH/miscoh09.htm (accessed February 14, 2012).

68. 1860 U.S. Census, Pennsylvania, Erie County, Venango, Roll M653_1108, 1061, image 454. While visiting his first cousin Joseph Smith III in Nauvoo in the year 1860, Joseph F. Smith recounted in a letter to his wife Levira, "Joseph [III] received a letter from Uncle William from which we learned he [William] had sowed his wild oats etc. and that he was farming now for a living!" Joseph F. Smith (Colchester, Ill.), Letter to Levira A. Smith, June 28, 1860, Joseph F. Smith Papers 1854–1918, Correspondence between Joseph and his wife Levira 1859–1867, MS 1325, LDS Church History Library.

69. "Obituary. Mrs. Eliza E. Smith," 1.

Chapter 18

Civil War Soldier

> Amid the clash of arms, the fatigue of march and the swamps and sloughs of the burning south [William] devoted three years of his life to the land that gave him birth, and from these fields of strife he returned again to his home, crippled with aches from which he never recovered.
> —Samuel Murdock, 1893[1]

By the early 1860s, Smith found himself scrambling to try and make ends meet for his growing family. Not only was he supporting his wife, Eliza, and their son Willie, but William assisted in caring for at least two of Eliza's children from her previous marriage—Mary and Ward Brain, ages twelve and nine. Eliza's two other children, fourteen-year-old Byron and eight-year-old Clara, remained with their father for a time after their mother's remarriage, but Byron later moved to Iowa to be near Eliza after she and William relocated to Elkader in Clayton County in 1860. William and Eliza helped Eliza's eldest son Byron get his start once he eventually married, allowing the newlyweds to live in their home while Byron labored as a farmer on William's property.[2]

When William married thirty-year-old Eliza Sanborn in 1857, he was, for all intents and purposes, starting all over again at age forty-six. Mary Jane and Caroline, his daughters by his first marriage, had married and were raising families of their own. The turmoil of the previous fourteen years had taken its toll on William's emotional health, and his marriage to Eliza marked a turning point in his life. William sought a simpler life by moving far away from areas where Mormonism had flourished, as well as judiciously avoiding places where he had experienced legal difficulties. He kept a low profile in the ensuing decade, occasionally revealing his biblical fluency by preaching a more general form of Christianity but concealing his Mormon roots. Writing to nephew Joseph III in

---

1. Samuel Murdock, "The Rev. William B. Smith," *Elkader Weekly Register*, November 23, 1893, 5.

2. Mary and Ward were living with William and Eliza in June 1860, while Byron was living with his father, James Brain. Byron enlisted in the Union Army in 1863 and, after the war, was living right next to William and Eliza in Elkader, Iowa, in 1870. Ward presumably died sometime during the 1860s. Mary died at fifteen on January 11, 1865. William was serving in the army at the time of Mary's death. She is buried next to her mother in the East Lake Cemetery in Elkader, Iowa. U.S. Census, 1860, Pennsylvania, Erie County, Venango, and Ohio, Lake County, Willoughby; U.S. Federal Census, 1870, Iowa, Clayton County, Boardman Township.

the late 1860s, William recounted that, accompanying his move to Elkader, he "concluded to remain silent on the subject [of Mormonism], still preaching occasionally, notwithstanding." He was stepping away from the "calumny so common in these Mormon affairs." He declared that he did not "care anything about these matters now," adding significantly, "nor do I let these matters fret my spirit."[3]

Obscuring their ties to Mormonism was common among most of Smith's relatives who remained in the Midwest at one point or another, with the noted exception of William's mother Lucy. His sister Katharine, for example, remained in Hancock County after the deaths of her brothers and had tried to conceal her connection to the founder of Mormonism. Being known as a Smith resulted in hardships for her and her children. "I received the most ill treatment," Katharine's eldest son Solomon recalled of his youth growing up in Hancock County, "there I was called a Mormon, boycotted, abused, slandered. I received no invitations to parties of any kind. There were no young folks that . . . would invite me to their parties or have anything to do with me. I was an outcast." William's two remaining sisters, Sophronia and Lucy, who also remained in Illinois, quite soon moved across the Hancock County line into McDonough County, to avoid the ostracism that Katharine and her family experienced.[4] Like his sister-in-law Emma Hale Smith Bidamon, William had reached the point of desiring a reprieve from the unrest that had been his lot since he had first united with Mormonism. Following his marriage to Eliza, he left behind his polygamous exploits, along with his aspiration of establishing himself at the head of a religious movement. In their obscure new home in Elkader, William and Eliza could hope for anonymity and making an adequate living in Iowa's fertile rolling hills.

However, his plans to become a farmer did not last long, possibly because he disdained manual labor. With the outbreak of the Civil War in late 1861, Smith was caught up in the national epic. As a youth in Palmyra, New York, William had seen the social tensions engendered by slavery both in New York and throughout the country at large. Cultural anthropologist Mark L. Staker has documented the influence of racial tensions on the Smith family during their fourteen-year stay in New York. While Joseph was pursuing the translation of the Book of Mormon during the late 1820s, New York was already implementing emancipation laws. Although

---

3. William B. Smith (Elkader, Iowa), Letter to Dear Nephew [Joseph Smith III], October 16, 1868, in *True Latter Day Saints' Herald* 1, no. 15 (January 1, 1869): 22–23.

4. Solomon J. Salisbury, "Old Nauvoo Days Recalled," *Autumn Leaves* 37 (April 1924): 155. See also Kyle R. Walker, *United by Faith: The Joseph Sr. and Lucy Mack Smith Family* (American Fork, Utah: Covenant Communications/BYU Studies, 2006), 322–31. Katharine's granddaughter, Mary Salisbury Hancock, wrote: "My Grandmother & Grandfather with their family having moved into the very midst of this mob infested [Hancock] County was forced to keep quiet if they were to save their lives. . . . Those who remained at and near Nauvoo," also recalled Mary "with the mobs & violence around about the Saints kept very quiet." Mary Salisbury Hancock, Autobiography, ca. 1963, 6; original in possession of Mary Dennis; photocopy of holograph in my possession courtesy of Mary Dennis.

the state had more slaves than Missouri in 1817, by the time Mormons immigrated to Ohio in 1831, the practice was virtually nonexistent in New York. Staker notes that New York not only had the highest concentration of blacks in the country during the 1820s, a situation in which the Smiths would have become keenly aware of their plight; but in their first neighborhood in Palmyra, "free blacks and runaways congregated in noticeable numbers. . . . Because the region had an open, sparsely populated border with Canada, it was attractive to slaves seeking freedom; but the sympathetic attitude of the local population also helped to make the area a magnet for runaways. The town of Ontario just north of Palmyra bordered Lake Ontario and Ontario, Canada, to the north. Palmyra operated at least four stations on the Underground Railroad where slaves moved north to the border."[5]

In addition, abolitionist thought infiltrated religious ideology which swept through western New York, including sermons at camp meetings in which the Smiths participated. Methodists in New York were so outspoken against slavery that they refused to license "preachers, exhorters, or traveling preachers who were slave-owners."[6] While Presbyterians were typically less sympathetic to the anti-slavery movement than Methodists, Staker discovered that Presbyterians in Palmyra were an exception. "The Reverend George R. H. Shumway of Palmyra's Western Presbyterian Church was a 'conductor' on the Underground Railroad and regularly hid runaways in his church buildings, continuing a tradition apparently established by his predecessors before the Smith family arrived in Palmyra."[7] This was the same church with which William's mother and siblings affiliated in the mid-1820s and where William regularly attended Sunday school during his youth. Slavery and abolitionist thought were hotly contested issues everywhere during William's youth. Such sentiments continued once the Smith family moved to northeastern Ohio, where many escaping slaves also passed through the area on their way to Canada by crossing Lake Erie.[8] William was thus indoctrinated with the anti-slavery sentiment that permeated these regions during his maturing years.

During the Civil War, William's views harmonized with those on the Union side of the conflict. In addition to being raised in Vermont and New York, he had spent considerable time in the northeastern United States as an adult. During his earlier missionary journeys, he had resided in New Jersey, Philadelphia, Boston, and New York City. As a newspaper editor in the antebellum North, he was keenly aware of reports and editorials about abolitionist activities that saturated the press in major cities along the eastern seaboard. With other early members of the Latter-day Saint movement, Smith's earlier experience in Missouri solidified his ideological differences from the beliefs of Southerns. As a collective body, the

---

5. Mark Lyman Staker, *Hearken, O Ye People: The Historical Setting for Joseph Smith's Ohio Revelations* (Salt Lake City: Greg Kofford Books, 2009), 120.

6. Quoted in ibid., 121.

7. Ibid., 122.

8. According to Staker, "Geauga County was the last stop on the Underground Railroad just before runaways crossed over Lake Erie into Canada" (29–30).

Engraving of author recording narratives of former slaves housed at Philadelphia. Engraving by unknown artist, ca. 1817, In Jesse Torrey, *A Portraiture of Domestic Slavery, In the United States* (Philadelphia, Jesse Torrey, 1817).

Saints were decidedly opposed to slavery; and such views, combined with cultural differences of a predominantly northeastern Church membership, quickly drew suspicion and violence from their Missouri neighbors during 1831–39.[9]

But even among those of William's faith and his cultural region of western New York, William may have been an exception, as Staker notes that "feelings about slavery and those about race were two entirely different issues. Those who opposed slavery were not necessarily liberal on racial issues; and . . . even some white abolitionists argued that blacks did not have a soul or were not literally God's children."[10] William differed from those who held such views. Rather, he felt acute compassion for the plight of African Americans throughout his life. Although he did not see his primary ministry as lying among blacks, there is reason to believe that he extended more religious privileges for this particular group than any other early

---

9. During the Mormon-Missouri conflict in 1836, the citizens of Clay County, Missouri, drafted a number of resolutions, including, "These are the reasons why these people [Mormons] have become objects of the deepest hatred and detestation to many of our citizens. They are eastern men, whose manners, habits, customs, and even dialect are essentially different from our own. They are non-slaveholders and opposed to slavery; which, in the peculiar period, when abolition has reared its deformed and haggard visage in our land, is well calculated to excite deep and abiding prejudices in any community." "Public Meeting," *Messenger and Advocate* 2, no. 11 (August 1836): 2.

10. Staker, "Hearken, O My People," 139 note 7, cites as an example: "Englishman Basil Hall, *Travels in North America*, 2 vols. (Edinburgh: William Blackwood, 1833) 1:29–30, 140–41, [who] traveled in 1827 from New York City to Rochester, passing Palmyra en route. He noted that some Americans in western New York believed blacks did not have a soul and that many whites refused to show them even the most basic civility."

Mormon leader. As the first of four points of evidence, during his eastern mission, prior to November 1844, he ordained a black convert in Lowell, Massachusetts, Q. Walker Lewis, to the office of elder in the Church's Melchizedek Priesthood. Lewis, who worked as a barber in Lowell, was well known as a radical abolitionist; both he and his extended family actively participated in the Underground Railroad.[11] Lewis and Smith labored together for more than a year after Lewis was ordained an Elder, while Smith presided over the eastern branches. The Church had not yet established a policy on priesthood for black men, but there is no evidence that he ever considered rescinding his ordination of Lewis. In 1847, two years after Smith left the area, William I. Appleby, then presiding elder in the region, recorded with surprise: "In the [Lowell] Branch there is a coloured Brother," documented Appleby, "an Elder ordained by Elder Wm Smith while he was a member of the Church, contrary though to the order of the Church or the Law of the Priesthood, [(] as the Descendants of Ham are not entitled to that privilege) by the name of Walker Lewis. He appears to be a much humble man, and an example for his more whiter brethren to follow."[12] While Appleby appears to have been skeptical that blacks should be extended such privileges, Smith apparently—at least in this case—did not base eligibility for priesthood on race.

The second example was a black convert named Joseph T. Ball, who was baptized before September 1833, and who afterward attended Mormonism's Boston Branch.[13] Members of Ball's family were prominent participants in the Massachusetts Abolition Society in the 1830s, and in 1833 two of his sisters helped form the Boston Female Anti-Slavery Society, serving as officers during the years 1835–38.[14]

During the fall of 1844 when William was presiding over the eastern branches, he ordained Ball a High Priest and then called him as president of the Boston Branch,

---

11. Connell O'Donovan, "The Mormon Priesthood Ban and Elder Q. Walker Lewis: 'An Example for His More Whiter Brethren to Follow,'" *John Whitmer Historical Association Journal* 26 (2006): 66–71.

12. William I. Appleby, Autobiography and Journal, 1848–56, May 19, 1847, 171–72, MS 1401, fd. 1, LDS Church History Library.

13. Connell O'Donovan, "Joseph T. Ball, 1804–1861: Mormonism's First African American High Priest," unpublished manuscript, 2011, 6; copy in my possession courtesy of O'Donovan. O'Donovan cites a letter written from Joseph Smith to Vienna Jaques, dated September 4, 1833, that mentions "Brother Ball" arriving in Kirtland "from Boston." Joseph Smith (Kirtland, Ohio), Vienna Jaques, September 4, 1833, in Gerrit J. Dirkmaat, Brent M. Rogers, Grant Underwood, Robert J. Woodford, and William G. Hartley, eds., *Documents, Volume 3: February 1833–March 1834*, in THE JOSEPH SMITH PAPERS (Salt Lake City: Church Historian's Press, 2014), 288–96. They establish "Jaques" as her preferred spelling of their surname.

14. Frances E. Willard and Mary A. Livermore, eds., *A Woman of the Century: Fourteen Hundred-Seventy Biographical Sketches Accompanied by Portraits of Leading American Women in All Walks of Life* (Buffalo, N.Y.: Charles Wells Moulton, 1893), 50; Debra Gold Hansen, *Strained Sisterhood: Gender and Class in the Boston Female Anti-Slavery Society* (Amherst: University of Massachusetts Press, 1993), 79, 95–96, 110–12; *Special Report of the Bristol and Clifton Ladies' Anti-Slavery Society* (London: John Snow, 1852), 6.

Preamble to the Constitution of the Boston Female Anti-Slavery Society.

Believing slavery to be a direct violation of the laws of God, and productive of a vast amount of misery and crime; and convinced that its abolition can only be effected by an acknowledgement of the justice and necessity of *immediate emancipation*,—we hereby agree to form ourselves into a Society **TO AID AND ASSIST IN THIS RIGHTEOUS CAUSE AS FAR AS LIES WITHIN OUR POWER.**

From the constitution of the Boston Female Anti-Slavery Society, ca. 1836. *Annual Report of the Boston Female Anti-Slavery Society* (Boston: Isaac Knapp, 1837).

---

the largest outside of Nauvoo. Ball was the earliest known African American to be appointed to this prominent position, where he served from October 22, 1844 to March 1, 1845. Wilford Woodruff included Ball's name in his letter to Brigham Young written October 9, 1844, as being leagued together with Smith, George J. Adams, and Samuel Brannan in what he felt was the mismanagement of the eastern branches, and in being involved in Smith's loosely governed form of polygamy. During that same month (October 1844) when other leaders resigned their offices due to their disdain for Smith's leadership, including Boston Branch President John Hardy, Ball remained loyal to Smith. Woodruff recorded, "Elder Wm Smith & myself attended a church meeting together there [in Lowell, Massachusetts and] all the mail [sic] members resigned their offices in that branch of the Church except one coloured brother who was an elder." Ball was then ordained both a High Priest and appointed branch president by Smith. Perhaps because he had supplanted Hardy, Hardy also mentioned Ball being closely aligned with Smith and Adams in a publication he produced outlining his reasons for leaving the Church. These sources verify William's trust in Ball as a leader, as the two labored harmoniously while William presided in the area.[15] Joseph Ball followed Smith to Nauvoo in the summer of 1845, and felt sufficiently close to Smith that he came to him to receive his patriarchal blessing on July 14, 1845, during which blessing William expressed his "respect and esteem" for Ball. In Ball's patriarchal blessing, William stated, "the powers and blessings of the holy Priesthood are upon thine head after the order of Melchisedec [sic] [having] even [been] ordained a High Priest by the Spirit of

---

15. Wilford Woodruff (Boston, Mass.), Letter to Brigham Young, October 9, 1844; and Wilford Woodruff (Scarborough, Maine), Letter to Brigham Young, November 16, 1844, both in Brigham Young, Office files, 1832–1878, General Correspondence, Incoming, 1840–1877, Letters from Church Leaders and Others, 1840–1877, Wilford Woodruff, 1844, LDS Church History Library; John Hardy, *Startling Developments of Crim. Con.! Or Two Mormon Apostles Exposed, in Practising the Spiritual Wife System in Boston* (Boston: Conway and Company, 1844), 3–4.

Revelation from under my hands which is again confirmed by the same authority and sealed on earth & Ratified in heaven, and no power under the heaven shall take it from thee, for upon thine head has been ordained this authority & power from before the foundation of the world." William's blessing that Ball was preordained to receive the priesthood "before the foundation of the world" is an interesting reference that counters later interpretations about blacks and the priesthood, even though Ball himself disappears from the documentary record after a brief affiliation with Strang—possibly under William's influence—in the late 1840s.[16]

As a third example, Smith's sympathies toward African Americans were further strengthened during his association with Isaac Sheen during 1847–50. Before Sheen and Smith organized their Church of Jesus Christ of Latter Day Saints, Sheen was a zealous abolitionist. A convert from Quakerism, Sheen believed that "all men," including those of color, "were created free and equal." Sheen had personally participated in the Underground Railroad, risking his own safety to transport slaves northward to freedom.[17] The home of Stephen and Erepta Richardson, two of William's loyal followers living near Palestine Grove, was also utilized as a stop on the Underground Railroad during this same time period. Descendants remember that "the living room floor in the house lifted up and there was a place for slaves to hide under the floor. Then the floor was put back in place and covered with a rug. They [the runaway slaves] were never caught."[18]

During their three-year merger, it seems likely that Smith and Sheen welcomed African Americans Elijah Ables and his wife, Mary Ann Adams Ables, to their meeting place in Covington, Kentucky, just across the Ohio River from where the Ableses lived in Cincinnati. Elijah Ables was among the most prominent African Americans in Mormon history, having been ordained to the Melchizedek Priesthood in 1836 by Joseph Smith. Later that same year, he was installed as a member of the Quorum of Seventy at Kirtland.[19] Since one of Smith's apostles at that time, Henry Nisonger, lived with the Ables family, both Russell Stevenson, Ables's biographer, and Connell O'Donovan have speculated that the Ables family may have affili-

---

16. Patriarchal Blessing of Joseph T. Ball, July 15, 1845, in H. Michael Marquardt, ed., *Early Patriarchal Blessings of the Church of Jesus Christ of Latter-day Saints* (Salt Lake City: Smith-Pettit Foundation, 2007), 320; O'Donovan, "Boston Mormons—Joseph T. Ball," 89–90. Charles Greenwood to James J. Strang, July 1, 1849, Item #351, Box 2, Folder 41, James Jesse Strang Collection, Beinecke Library, Yale University, New Haven, Conn., quoted in O'Donovan, "Boston Mormons—Joseph T. Ball," 45–46.

17. John Kirk Sheen, "Isaac Sheen First Editor of the 'Herald,'" *Saints' Herald* 57, no. 4 (January 26, 1910): 94–95; Connell O'Donovan, "William Smith, Isaac Sheen and the Melchisedek & Aaronic Herald," http://www.connellodonovan.com/herald.html (accessed March 6, 2015).

18. E-mail communication from Maryellen Harshbarger McVicker to Kyle R. Walker, April 9, 2015.

19. Russell W. Stevenson, *For the Cause of Righteousness: A Global History of Blacks and Mormonism, 1830–2013* (Salt Lake City: Greg Kofford Books, 2014), 10, 210.

ated with Smith and Sheen's organization, though evidence suggests that Elijah Ables remained loyal to Brigham Young while living at Cincinnati. Stevenson summarizes: "Ables had personal contact with virtually all of William Smith's followers in Cincinnati," and several of his former missionary companions, including Zenas Gurley and James Blakeslee, transferred their loyalty to William Smith's Church of Jesus Christ of Latter Day Saints during this period. When Smith and Isaac Sheen parted ways in May 1850, William lived with Elijah and Mary Ann for a time. Whether Ables attended Smith's church or not, Smith appears to have at least maintained an amiable relationship with Ables during his stay in Cincinnati, providing further evidence that he did not exclude co-religionists on the basis of race.[20]

Elijah Ables, 1808–1884. Date and photographer unknown. Courtesy LDS Church History Library.

In an 1868 letter to the *Clayton County Journal* in defense of Mormonism, William wrote that "the Republican party abolished Slavery in the United States, and it established the principle of human liberty and equal rights for all time to come." He further referred to slavery as one of the "twin relics of barbarism," echoing the Republican platform of the previous decade and, toward the end of his life, in 1892 when he was eighty-one, William movingly urged RLDS Church members not to exclude blacks from any privileges in the RLDS Church, a movement which he then embraced.[21] In the 1890s there was an on-going discussion regarding RLDS Church members' feelings about extending Mormon priesthood authority to African Americans. Some twentieth-century RLDS historians and most members felt that the race issue was resolved in 1865 when Joseph Smith III received a revelation during a conference where "the question was raised in regard

---

20. Russell W. Stevenson, "A Negro Preacher": The Worlds of Elijah Ables," *Journal of Mormon History* 39, no. 2 (Spring 2013): 216–21; Isaac Sheen, "A Prophetic Family Arrangement," *Covington Daily Union*, June 5, 1850, 2; O'Donovan, "William Smith, Isaac Sheen, and the Melchisedek and Aaronic Herald." Despite William's willingness to extend priesthood privileges to blacks, Stevenson noted that William's "debt to Ables's hospitality did not prevent him from making a coarse racial pun on Brigham Young's name. He claimed that Joseph 'placed his hands upon Brig Ham [two words] Young's head and pronounced these words: You are the lineage of Cain through the loins of Ham.'" "B. Young's Lineage," *Melchizedek and Aaronic Herald* 1, no. 8 (February 1850): 4, as quoted in Stevenson, "A Negro Preacher," 219–20.

21. William Smith, "Mormonism," quoted in "Clayton Co. Journal," *True Latter Day Saints' Herald* 1, no. 15 (January 1, 1869): 23; "Extracts from Letters," *Saints' Herald* 39, no. 40 (October 1, 1892): 631.

to the ordination of Africans to offices in the priesthood." During the ensuing discussion, W. W. Blair, who was present, remembered that lay member Joseph Robinson "spoke in tongues," which Joseph III interpreted, revealing that "'prejudice of race, color, and caste would soon be done away among the Saints,' and that 'every nation and people' would 'soon have gospel ministers of their own.'"[22] This revelation was canonized as Section 116 in the RLDS edition of the Doctrine and Covenants. Yet historian William D. Russell has documented that racial tensions continued to plague the Church as late as the 1960s. Though the 1865 revelation was "permissive on the ordination of blacks," recounted Russell, even the revelation itself "has been criticized by RLDS liberals for its apparent suggestion of a segregated ministry and for its note of caution, warning against haste in ordaining Negro men." Furthermore, by the 1890s, Joseph Smith III had retreated from his position of "liberality during the 1860s and 1870s" and advocated "separating the races in church and establishing separate branches where practicable so that black priesthood could minister to their own race."[23] Informed about deliberations that were taking place in the RLDS Church regarding the integration of blacks in congregations and priesthood offices, William was at the forefront in expressing his view on human rights during these years of indeterminacy, which ran counter to the more conservative direction taken by Joseph III and other leaders during that decade. Smith wrote to the *Saints' Herald* in 1892: "The Constitution of these United States makes no distinction in the human family; all men are born free and equal." Smith quoted the Apostle Paul that "God has made of one blood all nations." "If such are the facts founded upon a just *law*," continued Smith, "by what authority have we the right to say that a colored man has no right to be ordained to all the powers of the priesthood, necessary for the building up the church of Christ in any part of the world, among any race of people, whether black or white." Smith had done just that earlier in his ecclesiastical career when he served as a traveling missionary overseeing the eastern branches, when he ordained Q. Walker Lewis an elder, ordained

---

22. William D. Russell, "A Priestly Role for a Prophetic Church: The RLDS Church and Black Americans," 39; Frederick B. Blair, comp., *The Memoirs of W. W. Blair* (Lamoni, Iowa: Herald Publishing House, 1908), 113.

23. Russell further noted that "despite the 1865 revelation . . . very few blacks were ordained to the priesthood. It was not until 1889 that a black man was ordained to the Melchisedec priesthood." Perhaps the ordination of Emanuel Eaton that year had been the impetus that prompted further discussion on the issue of race relations. Russell further cites Joseph III's 1893 statement on race relations that underscored his evolving view on the integration of blacks in the RLDS Church: "Church privileges and equal access to God's mercy do not necessarily destroy the social distinctions which wisdom and peculiarities of condition impose and make distinctive. Any attempt to urge the unrestrained intercourse of all classes, races, and conditions will stir up strife and contention far more dangerous to the welfare and unity of the church, than the principle contended for will justify." This statement appeared just six months after William's views on human rights were published in the *Saints' Herald*. Russell, "A Priestly Role for a Prophetic Church," 39–41, 45–46.

Joseph T. Ball a High Priest and appointed him to preside over the Boston Branch, and fellowshipped Elijah Ables in Cincinnati. "To preach a full gospel is no half way work in this latter day dispensation; hence, as I understand it," emphasized Smith, "the colored race has a right to the priesthood in all its powers of administration subject to the ruling authority of Christ's church."[24] It was a position RLDS leaders did not adopt at the time. Though William expressed these sentiments just a year before his death in 1893, they provide a window into an inclusive attitude toward blacks that was evident throughout his adult life.

Thus, there was no question about which side Smith supported when the Civil War engulfed the nation. While Smith left no documentary evidence of which I am aware about his motives in enlisting, it probably was two-fold. The first may have been his grim financial status. Although he was attempting to farm, he was never very successful or satisfied at that trade and had lost all of his property and savings after his movement collapsed in the early 1850s. One report indicated that by the 1860s, Smith "was so poor that he could not provide a morsel of food for his wife."[25] Just before the move, William had tried preaching for the Baptists, laboring as a carpenter, and working as a traveling showman. On December 23, 1863, just two months before Smith enlisted, the federal government called for 300,000 volunteers between ages eighteen and forty-five. To make the offer more appealing, the government offered an enlistment bonus of seventy-five dollars for a one-year enlistment, a hundred dollars for a two-year enlistment, and three hundred dollars for a three-year enlistment. Furthermore, at the time of Smith's enlistment, the government promised volunteers regular pay at $13 per month.[26] It was an attractive offer.

Don Carlos Salisbury, 1841–1919. Photograph ca. 1861, photographer unknown. William's nephew who served in the Civil War, 1861–64. Courtesy of Mary Dennis.

---

24. "Extracts from Letters," *Saints' Herald* 39, no. 40 (October 1, 1892): 631.

25. Fred C. Collier, ed., *The Office Journal of President Brigham Young: Book D, 1858–1863*, March 17, 1860 (Hanna, Utah: Collier's Publishing, 2006), 58.

26. William C. Moffat, Jr., "Soldier's Pay"; Mark M. Boatner III, "Pay," in *The Civil War Dictionary*, rev. ed. (New York: Vintage Books, 1988), 624–25: "Union privates were paid $13 per month until after the final raise of 20 June '64, when they got $16." However, Boatner notes that, while soldiers were supposed to be paid every two months, they were fortunate if they got their pay every four months during their time of service.

Don Carlos Salisbury led the charge of his Union unit at Utica, Livingston County, Missouri, driving out the Confederates and capturing their flag, which was afterward displayed in a Springfield Museum. Courtesy of the Illinois State Military Museum in Springfield, Illinois. Department of Military Affairs, Springfield, Illinois.

A second motivation was patriotic loyalty. Don Carlos Salisbury, the twenty-year-old son of William's sister Katharine, enlisted in May 1861 out of a sense of duty. He served for almost three years, in Missouri, Tennessee, and Alabama. During his training at Quincy, Illinois, Salisbury indicated that his company were in "good spirits for they think we may have a little fun with Missouri."[27] A month later, his unit, the 16th Illinois Volunteer Infantry, fought at Utica, Livingston County, Missouri. During the fracas Salisbury led the charge that drove out the Confederates and captured their flag. He was promoted to the rank of corporal for his bravery, and the captured flag hung in a Springfield museum for many years after the war. Salisbury always felt that the fierce fighting in northwest Missouri was part of God's retribution on the state for having driven out the Saints, a sentiment he shared with the extended Smith family.[28] William, who had been driven from the state and experienced firsthand the injustices of the Saints in the state, certainly would have concurred with his nephew's sentiments.

Writing in 1862 to his brother Alvin, Salisbury expressed how much he longed to see his family. However, his sense of duty outweighed his desire to return home and gave him grit to endure the hardships associated with war. "When I think of

---

27. Don Carlos Salisbury (Quincy, Ill.), Letter to Mother, Brothers, and Sister, May 8, 1861, L. Tom Perry Special Collections, Brigham Young University, Provo, Utah.

28. Herbert S. Salisbury, "The Western Adventures of Don Carlos Salisbury," July 18, 1945, 1, unpublished manuscript, typescript in my possession.

you I think of my country," wrote the young soldier, "and the thought strikes me that I would not enjoy myself at home until peace is restored to this once happy country." He linked his military service with his commitment to God: "I have set my heart on something higher than worldly affairs," he wrote ardently, praising the faith that allowed him to find happiness "under all misfortunes." Like thousands of others enmeshed in this ambiguous and bloody war, he found in his faith strength to face even death: "There is one happy thought that bears them [Christians] up and that is if they don't meet again in this world they will meet in heaven." His only note of sorrow was his wish "that all my relations were Christians."[29] Writing to his cousin Maria, he asked her to assure her mother, Salisbury's Aunt Sophronia, that he was "a second Lamoni to her."[30] Since Lamoni was a convert-king in the Book of Mormon, it seems most likely that, in a mental slip, he confused Lamoni with "Moroni," the name of two separate righteous leaders in the Book of Mormon. The allusion suggests that Joseph and Lucy's daughters passed on their faith in Mormonism to their children, even though, during the 1860s, neither William nor his sisters were affiliated with any branch of Mormonism.

William may have also been motivated to volunteer by the example of additional family members, including his son-in-law James S. Quince, who had married Caroline Louisa, and his stepson, Byron Brain, Eliza's son by her first husband. Both of these younger relatives enlisted before William took that step. Quince, who had enlisted in the Union Army in August 1862 for a three-year term, was eventually promoted to the rank of sergeant in June 1864, and to first sergeant six months later.[31] Byron, who was eighteen years old, enlisted in the Iowa Cavalry for three years in June 1863.[32] Although we know nothing of their motivations, it seems probable that war would have seemed more glamorous to

---

29. Don Carlos Salisbury (Tuscumbia, Ala.), Letter to Dear Brother Alvin [Salisbury], August 28, 1862, L. Tom Perry Special Collections, Harold B. Lee Library, Brigham Young University, Provo, Utah (hereafter Perry Special Collections).

30. D.[on] C.[arlos] Salisbury (Tuscumbia, Ala.), Letter to Mariah Woolley, August 28, 1862, photograph of holograph in my possession, courtesy of Mary Dennis. Salisbury was raised by his Aunt Sophronia, who was better off economically that his own mother Katharine. Sophronia provided Don Carlos with a quality education, sending him to both common and cadet schools. Walker, "Katharine Smith Salisbury," in *United by Faith*, 329.

31. James S. Quince enlisted on August 12, 1862, at Brooklyn, Illinois, and was mustered in on August 25 in Chicago. He was mustered out at Nashville, Tennessee on June 10, 1865. "James S. Quince," Illinois Civil War Detail Report, Illinois Civil War Muster and Descriptive Rolls Database, Illinois State Archives, http://www.ilsos.gov/isaveterans/civilMusterSearch.do?key=205673 (accessed November 5, 2013).

32. Byron B. Brain enlisted on June 28, 1863, and was mustered in on July 10 as part of the 7th Regiment of the Iowa Cavalry. He was not mustered out until June 22, 1866. "Iowa in the Civil War," transcribed by Sharon D. Franklin, http://iagenweb.org/civilwar/regiment/cavalry/07th/coH.html (accessed March 10, 2015); Iowa Civil War Union Units 1st through 9th, https://familysearch.org/learn/wiki/en/Iowa_Civil_War_Union_Units_1st_through_9th (accessed March 11, 2015).

a young man than to a middle-aged one. In fact, although the war began with the popular view that the conflict would be swift and decisive, by February 1864 when William actually enlisted, the reality of the long-drawn-out combat with its enormous casualties, deadly illnesses, and strategic fumbling would have made it difficult to keep a romantic image alive. William's enlistment came after the epic Battle of Gettysburg where more than 50,000 soldiers had died, memorialized movingly in Abraham Lincoln's famous Gettysburg Address. Eight of the ten bloodiest Civil War battles had already been fought. The tide of the war had certainly turned in the North's favor, but 1864 would be a critical year as the Union Army moved deeper into the South and secured key cities in the West.

Thus, although William has not left a personal record of his motivations, it seems doubtful that he was inspired by dreams of glory and instead made his decision in the face of the statistical reality that he could be killed, injured, or impaired by the lack of reliable supplies, harsh weather, or poor medical care if he fell ill. Like his nephew Don Carlos Salisbury, William saw preserving the Union as a holy cause. Indeed, only three generations away from the fervor of the Revolutionary War, these Americans saw a logical overlapping between religious faith and patriotism. In a commemorative speech about William ten days after his death, a friend from Elkader made the connection explicit. William, he said, "had an abiding faith in the high and holy destiny of his country and her men and when the terrible civil war broke out he left his little family where rest and peace and comfort had their abode, hastened to the front, [and] joined the Union army."[33] In fact, William did not "hasten" nor did he go to "the front," but he was willing to put his life on the line. He enlisted at Rock Island, Illinois, late in the war, and while the closest combat zones were in Missouri and Kentucky, most of the major battles in these states had already been fought by 1864. But Union and Confederate units were still skirmishing on the western front, and William's Civil War service would primarily be in maintaining some key strongholds in the state of Arkansas.

As soon as the spring thaw opened the Mississippi River for travel on February 19, 1864, he left Elkader. Most likely, he traveled to nearby Guttenberg, twenty-one miles to the southeast of Elkader, where he boarded a steamer and headed downriver, sharing the majestic waterway with a huge slabs of ice. "The ice came floating down the river in sheets acres large," described one witness of this extraordinary display during the same month Smith traveled. "The unevenness of the river banks caused the ice to pile up on dry land in heaps as large as a good sized house. It was truly magnificent to behold—it displayed the power and grandeur of God's works."[34] After traveling downriver about two hundred miles, William probably reached Rock Island, Illinois, that same day, where the Mississippi turns sharply

---

33. Murdock, "The Rev. William B. Smith," 5.
34. Lafayette Rogan, Diary, 1864, Illinois State Historical Library, Springfield, quoted in Benton McAdams, *Rebels at Rock Island: The Story of a Civil War Prison* (DeKalb: Northern Illinois University Press, 2000), 78–79. Rogan is also the source of dating the spring break-up on February 19, 1864.

Prison at Rock Island, Illinois. Lithograph produced in 1864 by C. Vogt and H. Lambach at Davenport, Iowa.

west for some thirty miles from its general southward direction. This point, about a hundred miles north of Nauvoo, is marked by the dramatic Rock Island, which lies between Moline and Rock Island, Illinois, and Davenport, Iowa, its limestone cliffs jutting abruptly twenty feet above the river, a heavy growth of forest running along its ridge. During the summer of 1863, the federal government constructed a prison surrounded by a twelve-foot-high fence on the island to house the growing number of Confederate prisoners. It was originally designed to house ten thousand; and in December 1863, it had received its first prisoners—some five thousand—but the number had swelled to nearly eight thousand by February 1864 when Smith arrived. An estimated twelve thousand Confederates were imprisoned at Rock Island during its eighteen months of operation, beginning in December 1863 and ending July 1865. Nearly a fourth of the Confederates were suffering from pneumonia and an outbreak of smallpox, their sufferings exacerbated by limited rations and very little medical care. During the first four months of operation, nearly one thousand prisoners died at Rock Island Prison, and nearly two thousand by the end of its operation.[35] While William stayed in Rock Island for several days, he witnessed firsthand the cruel realities of war.

At Rock Island, on February 21, 1864, Smith enlisted as part of the 126th Illinois U.S. Volunteer Infantry, initially organized September 4, 1862, and now replenishing its former strength with volunteers. William was approaching his fifty-third birthday, which technically made him ineligible to enlist. According to his nephew Joseph Smith III, he "misstated his age, making him appear some

---

35. McAdams, *Rebels at Rock Island*, xi–xii, 3, 61; Boatner, "Rock Island Prison," in *The Civil War Dictionary*, 705.

ten years younger than he really was."³⁶ Army recruiters, desperate for volunteers, were known to turn a blind eye to very youthful eighteen-year-olds. Nearly a million under age eighteen—more than 100,000 of them age fifteen and under—have been documented. In parallel fashion, a disproportionate number of forty-four-year-olds stepped up to the recruiter's table.³⁷ William's visage and complexion may have been comparatively unlined; but in March 1860, Brigham Young had described him as having hair that was "white as a sheet."³⁸ Doubtless a bottle of dye solved this problem, at least until he was firmly enlisted. His enlistment record describes him as six feet tall, dark-haired, with blue eyes and a light complexion, and lists his profession as "minister."³⁹

William enlisted for three years, entitling him to a bonus of between one hundred and three hundred dollars, to be paid at his time of discharge based on the length of service he completed. He also would have received the upfront bonus of seventy-five dollars promised to volunteers who enlisted between December 1863 and April 1864.⁴⁰ At the time of his enlistment, he gave his name as "William B. Smith." There are no earlier records in which he uses this initial, supporting his comment in 1883 when he was seventy-two to Joseph III that he [Joseph III] "will notice that the letter B in my name is not in [the] record in the Revelation apointing the Twelve."⁴¹ After his visit with William in the year 1880, B. H. Roberts, apparently listening to William recount this information firsthand, recorded afterward that "the initial ["B"] was [William's] addition to his name which he himself used when in the Union fray to designate him from the

---

36. Howard, *The Memoirs of President Joseph Smith III*, 91.

37. American Civil War Research Database, Enlistment Age Distribution, All Years Union Army, www.civilwardata.com/ca_demo2.html (accessed November 19, 2013).

38. Brigham Young, quoted in Collier, *The Office Journal of President Brigham Young*, 858. Given how common the name "William Smith" was, family historians were confused for years about whether William had, in fact, served in the Civil War or whether his records had been misfiled with those of another William Smith. Calvin P. Rudd, in researching his master's thesis on William, discovered a letter, written by William's son, Edson Don Carlos Smith, who would have turned two in 1864. Edson was familiar with his father's service in the war but wanted to document his father's company and length of service. In 1938, Edson "corresponded with a resident of Dixon, Illinois," whose research found that "a William B. Smith" from Clayton County, age forty-four, "joined Company G of the 126th Illinois Infantry in February 1864." Clyde E. Buckingham (Dixon, Ill.), Letter to Edson D. C. Smith, December 22, 1938, LDS Church History Library; quoted in Calvin P. Rudd, "William B. Smith: Brother of the Prophet Joseph Smith" (M.A. thesis, Brigham Young University, 1974), 154.

39. "William B. Smith, Company G, 126 IL US INF.," Illinois Civil War Muster and Descriptive Rolls, Illinois State Archives, http://www.ilsos.gov/isaveterans/civilMusterSearch.do?key=237510 (accessed March 11, 2015).

40. Moffat, "Soldier's Pay"; Boatner, "Pay," *Civil War Dictionary*, 624.

41. William B. Smith, Letter to Joseph Smith III, October 19, 1883, Miscellaneous Letters and Papers, P13, f2311, Community of Christ Archives.

William B. Smith, 1811–1893. This is the earliest known photograph of William, taken ca. 1862, photographer unknown, about the time he enlisted in the Civil War. Photograph of original by Kyle R. Walker, 2005. Courtesy of Mary Dennis.

many William Smiths that were among the enlisted men."[42] Roberts's memory of William's reasoning for adopting the middle initial "B" was accurate, as there was a "William F. Smith" who enlisted the same month as William, and who also was part of Company G of the 126th Illinois Infantry.[43] William continued to use this initial for the rest of his life.

From the recruiting station, it seems likely that William traveled by railroad with other volunteers 150 miles to Springfield, Illinois, on the same day as his enlistment (February 21, 1864), where he was officially mustered into the army. At each stop, the citizens hailed the volunteers as patriotic heroes. One Civil War historian recounted that, as the soldiers traveled to their destination, "their course was often a triumphal procession, with crowds gathered along the way to shower the volunteers with praise. Company commanders were required to make speeches in every small town through which they passed as the units halted to be honored with picnics and banquets."[44] Smith doubtless appreciated being part of a cause that was so significant and must have savored the praise he received as part of the group from Illinois citizens, who had, only a few years earlier, run him out of the state.

His volunteer unit was in Springfield from February 21 to around March 19. While stationed in the city, Smith would have been issued a standard uniform, with either a blue or gray jacket, "trousers cut in the same style as U.S. regulation jackets, two flannel shirts, two pairs of socks and a stout pair of shoes." He would have also been issued a broad-brimmed black hat and a Springfield rifle musket.[45] But even so brief a stay must have brought bittersweet memories. He had served as a state legislator for four months in 1842–43 and had lived there in brief snatches during the 1850s. The city represented the pinnacle of Smith's ecclesiastical and political career during the early 1840s. It would be intriguing to know if he reconnected with some of his political or religious acquaintances who still lived in the area.

Smith's stay in Springfield lasted about three weeks. On March 21, 1864, he arrived in Arkansas where he joined the 126th Illinois Infantry.[46] According to the examining surgeons' report in William Smith's pension file, Smith had expected to

---

42. B. H. Roberts, *The Autobiography of B. H. Roberts*, 102. Lavina Fielding Anderson, *Lucy's Book: A Critical Edition of Lucy Mack Smith's Family Memoir*, 874, identifies William as having a middle name: "Bunnell." This name is an error, and William never used more than the initial "B."

43. J. N. Reece, *Report of the Adjutant General of the State of Illinois, Volume VI, Containing Reports for the Years 1861–66* (Springfield, Ill.: Journal Company Printers and Binders, 1900), 485.

44. Carl Moneyhon, "1861: 'The Die Is Cast,'" *Rugged and Sublime: The Civil War in Arkansas*, edited by Mark K. Christ (Fayetteville: University of Arkansas Press, 1994), 11.

45. Robin Smith and Ron Field, *Uniforms of the Civil War* (London: Lyons Press, 2001), 121–22.

46. Report of the Adjutant General, June 29, 1866, Washington D.C., in William B. Smith, Complete Pension File, invalid pension filed August 26, 1865, Certificate no.

be appointed a chaplain at the time of enlistment due to his extensive experience as a minister.[47] Chaplains were typically appointed by field officers and company commanders, however, and his lack of formal religious affiliation may have prevented him from receiving the post. In July 1862, Congress decreed: "No person shall be appointed a chaplain in the U.S. army who is not a regularly ordained minister of some religious denomination, and who does not present testimonials of his present good standing as such minister with recommendation for his appointment as army Chaplain from some authorized ecclesiastical body, or not less than five accredited ministers belonging to said denomination."[48] At the time, Smith was not affiliated with any denomination and certainly would not have been able to provide testimonials from five "accredited ministers." If he requested to be a chaplain, he almost certainly would have been denied on these grounds.

Joseph III reported in about 1911, eighteen years after William's death, that when Lieutenant Colonel Horatio L. Birdsall learned of Smith's religious training, "he was offered the chaplaincy of his regiment, but declined the post, preferring to keep his place in the ranks."[49] Joseph III's information certainly came from William himself, and perhaps it represented William's more palatable explanation of why he ended up as an ordinary foot soldier. If he was prompted primarily by monetary reasons, then service as a chaplain would have been more lucrative and less risky. (A chaplain would have been paid $100 per month.) Still, William may have relished the role to engage in combat. Some thirty years earlier, Smith had been among those who expressed disappointment that Zion's Camp did not involve a pitched battle with hostile Missourians.[50] Perhaps, even as a middle-aged man, his blood was stirred by the genuine risks of bloody conflict. As a chaplain, he would have had to remain at a distance. It seems compatible with his hot temper that he would have thrilled to the experience of armed strife.

William reached Company G, of the 126th Volunteer Illinois Infantry on March 21, along with the reinforcements of eight new volunteers. Under the command of Captain Gabriel Armstrong, they were part of General Frederick Steele's Arkansas campaign to clear Confederate troops from the state and to maintain strongholds in Arkansas from Little Rock to its state line with Tennessee,

---

79175, Box 48086, 128, National Archives, Washington D.C. Special thanks to Erin B. Jennings Metcalfe for acquiring and sharing William's entire pension file.

47. Asa Hearr and M. Staples (examining surgeons), Report, June 27, 1882, in William Smith Pension File, 123.

48. Quoted in Edward McPherson, *The Political History of the United States of America, during the Great Rebellion, from November 6, 1860, to July 4, 1864* (Washington D.C.: Philip & Solomons/D. Appleton & Co., 1864), 279–80.

49. Howard, *The Memoirs of President Joseph Smith III*, 91.

50. Writing in *William Smith on Mormonism*, 24, he stated: "After having gone through with a very fatiguing, dangerous and difficult journey, without having accomplished the object for which we undertook the task; except to . . . suffer a great deal of trial and trouble, and come back penniless once more."

formed by the Mississippi River. He joined a group of seasoned soldiers, who had fought in several key battles in Tennessee and Mississippi for more than a year. Most notably, the 126th Illinois Infantry had participated in the successful siege at Vicksburg, Mississippi, during the summer of 1863. Shortly after the Confederates surrendered Vicksburg on July 4, 1863, the 126th Illinois Infantry was transported by railroad to Helena, Arkansas. Under the command of Colonel Frederick Steele, who had gained prominence during the battle at Vicksburg, the unit had then participated in several skirmishes in Arkansas.[51] Both sides of the conflict recognized the importance of controlling the Arkansas River Valley as its routes for transporting troops and supplies throughout the South were critical. Civil War historian Mark Christ summarized that 1863 saw a

> change in Union strategy in the central Trans-Mississippi. Following the signal Confederate defeats at Pea Ridge and Prairie Grove in northwest Arkansas . . . and amid the ongoing siege of Vicksburg, Mississippi, Federal strategy turned toward control of the verdant Arkansas River Valley. The region was the key to control of Arkansas and Indian Territory, splitting both down the middle, and provided not only an opportunity to bisect the Trans-Mississippi Confederacy but also to close Arkansas as an avenue for Confederate invasion of Missouri. The capture of Little Rock, the state capital, would also further President Lincoln's political goal of reestablishing loyal state governments throughout the [S]outh.[52]

Before the summer of 1863 had ended, federal troops were preparing to capture Little Rock, the state's capital and a major Confederate stronghold since the outbreak of the war. On August 10, Steele marched his troops quickly despite blistering temperatures from Helena to Little Rock. Illness swept through the ranks. Many died from the "debilitating malarial diseases of the region's miasmic swamps," while dehydration exacted its own toll and exacerbated other conditions. Despite these disadvantages, after several minor battles Steele's troops successfully expelled the Confederates from the city on September 10.[53]

In March 1864, Smith arrived at De Valls Bluff, Arkansas, fifty miles east of Little Rock, where Union forces were attempting to maintain control of the White River. In January 1863, the federal army had slowly advanced up the White River, battering its small riverside towns of St. Charles, Clarendon, and De Valls Bluff into submission. Mary Patrick of St. Charles bitterly lamented that the Yankees had left "our pretty town in ashes—Our Church and Sunday-school library burntd—our graveyard despoiled."[54] The Memphis and Little Rock Railroad was still in full operation through the area, and the higher elevation of De Valls Bluff above the White River would, the officers hoped, promote

---

51. "History of the One Hundred and Twenty-Sixth Infantry," *Report of the Adjutant General of the State of Illinois*, 491; Mark Christ, *Civil War Arkansas, 1863: The Battle for a State*, (Norman: University of Oklahoma Press, 2010), 5.

52. Christ, *Civil War Arkansas*, 5.

53. Ibid., 145–96; quotations on 156–57.

54. Mrs. Mary S. Patrick, Diary, January 1863, as quoted in ibid., 91.

improved health among the soldiers. Colonel Steele had used De Valls Bluff as his base of operations before seizing Little Rock, and it remained a hub for activities in the valley during 1864–65.[55]

De Valls Bluff must have figured prominently in Smith's memory during the tour of duty of the new volunteers, who spent from March 21–July 20, 1864, at that location. The capture of Little Rock in early September 1863 had increased federal momentum throughout Arkansas, but the Confederate Army, commanded in that region by General Jo Shelby, was determined to regain control of the Arkansas River Valley. "I will enlist you in the Confederate army; or I will drive you into the Federal ranks," Shelby declared to the valley's residents. "You shall not remain idle spectators of a dream enacted before your eyes." If nothing else, he hoped to disrupt Union traffic in and around Little Rock and De Valls Bluff. For a few months, the balance of power wavered between the two armies, and some Union commanders drew their forces back to the safety of Little Rock and De Valls Bluff. However, by June 1864 the Confederate forces retreated to the north in a state of disarray, greatly hampering their effectiveness. By summer's end, morale was low among Confederate soldiers and civilians, and even the determined Shelby could not overcome the disorganization he found among his troops. The Confederate forces in Arkansas had passed the peak of their threat in the state.[56]

However, Union forces had to confront a new enemy—repeated waves of illness, malaria, and dysentery. During July 1864, for example, about one-fifth of the 5,556 enlisted soldiers at nearby Helena, Arkansas were listed as sick, earning the Union soliders' nickname "Hell-in Arkansas."[57] Summer heat dried up the mud that turned roads into quagmires, but the hot weather brought disease including dysentery, anopheles mosquitos swarming out of the swamps to spread malaria, while haphazard enforcement of hygienic regulations in the camp provided ideal conditions for typhoid epidemics. The swamp water was contaminated and stagnant.[58] One soldier, writing in his journal described "a stench that can be smelt in those marshes which is very offensive." They were forced to drink the swamp water "after takeing a stick and pushing of[f] the thick green scum."[59] Hundreds of Union soldiers wounded in the Arkansas River Valley were transported to De Valls Bluff, in hopes that the higher elevation would leave some of the problems behind. They still lacked proper medical care, and another soldier described how the sick detachment that had been left behind at Clarendon after

---

55. Ibid., 160–61.
56. Daniel E. Sutherland, "1864: 'A Strange, Wild Time,'" in Christ, *Rugged and Sublime*, 124–27.
57. Jeannie M. Whayne, Thomas A. Deblack, George Sabo III, and Morris S. Arnold, *Arkansas: A Narrative History* (Fayetteville: University of Arkansas Press, 2002), 188. See also (no author), "Hell-in Arkansas," http://civilwarhelena.com/history/hell-in-arkansas/ (accessed March 3, 2015).
58. Christ, *Civil War Arkansas*, 106.
59. Franklin Spillman Denny, Diary, quoted in Christ, *Civil War Arkansas*, 150.

Landing on the White River at De Valls Bluff, Arkansas. Photograph taken ca. 1863, photographer unknown. In the collection of Wilson's Creek National Battlefield. Image courtesy of the National Park Service.

taking the town "had come up on the boats & they had to lie on the bank of the River. Very many of them are very weak & exhausted & dispirited. There were very many sick belonging to all the different Reg[imen]ts. And for some reason no preparation was made for them, and all is hurry and bustle yet they are left to do the very best they can for themselves, or go untended."[60] In spite of the numerous sick at De Valls Bluff, Arkansas Civil War historian Mark Christ felt that "Steele made a good choice selecting De Valls Bluff as a base of operations, for the fast-moving White River kept a clear channel scoured for most of the year, giving the town regular access to steamers and gunboats."[61]

At this point, in May 1864, William Smith entered the documentary record for the first time since his arrival in Arkansas on March 21. He fell ill with "dysentery, chills and fever." Although youth was no protection from illness, his advanced age probably meant reduced vitality. According to William, in a document he prepared seeking an invalid's pension after the war, these symptoms also triggered what was likely a hereditary condition of neuralgia, the symptoms of which are often exacerbated by stress. At age sixty-four when he applied for a disability pension, he described: "About the month of May 1864 while on duty as a Soldier I was attacked with rheumatism in my back and hips. Also about that same time I became afflicted with neuralg[i]a in my face and head which became very severe in its character [and] invariably my right Eye and Ear completely destroying the Sight of my right Eye and materially injuring the hearing of my right ear."[62] He

---

60. James B. Lockney, Journal, quoted in Christ, *Civil War Arkansas*, 160.
61. Christ, *Civil War Arkansas*, 161.
62. William B. Smith (Elkader, Iowa), Letter to United States Pension Office, July 19, 1875, William B. Smith Pension File, 41–42.

was under the care of the overworked company surgeon Dr. Vernon R. Bridges during May and June. "Some days he [Smith] would be able to do duty," remembered fellow soldier William H. Ziegler, who was providing a statement in support of William's disability pension, and other days "he would be under the surgeons care." Ziegler's recollection documents that Smith's condition fluctuated; and it is possible, though not certain, that he participated in Arkansas skirmishes at Clarendon on June 26–28, 1864, and Pine Bluff on July 1. His condition worsened after that time, and he was granted a thirty-day furlough beginning July 20.[63]

Vernon R. Bridges, Williams attending physician. Photograph ca. 1864, photographer unknown. Original in private possession.

Smith apparently returned to Elkader, Iowa, where, as he wrote in his disability application, family members made "applications of oils and lineaments[,] plasters & eye water."[64] While muster rolls report him as being at "home" on this furlough, he may have also been treated part of that time in one of the many hospitals set up in river towns along the northern Mississippi, where they were safe from Confederate raids. During the year 1863 alone, for example, 7,396 sick and wounded soldiers had been transported to hospitals near Keokuk, Iowa. In July 1864, the same month Smith began his furlough, the steamer *Kate Kearney* delivered more than a hundred invalid soldiers to Keokuk, a pattern that continued throughout the remainder of the year. While an unknown percentage of these soldiers failed to recover, many returned to the battlefield, as was the case in April 1864, when more than one hundred soldiers recovered sufficiently to return to war. Steamboats like the *Kate Kearney*, the *Diligent*, the *Schuyler*, the *Sunnyside*, and the *Gladiator* were pressed into service to transport soldiers up and down the river over the course of the war.[65] Smith's recuperation was not quick, and his furlough was extended to approximately three months. He returned to De Valls Bluff by steamer in late October or early November.[66]

---

63. Statement of William H. Ziegler, September 3, 1893; Report of Adjutant General, June 29, 1866; both in William B. Smith Pension File, 98, 128.

64. William B. Smith (Elkader, Iowa), Letter to United States Pension Office, May 2, 1882, William B. Smith Pension File, 59.

65. William J. Petersen, *Steamboating on the Upper Mississippi: The Water Way to Iowa* (Iowa City: State Historical Society of Iowa, 1937), 180–89. Petersen records that, in July 1864, the *Kate Kearney* arrived in Keokuk "with over a hundred invalid soldiers. Throughout the year [1864] steamboats brought wounded soldiers to Keokuk and the ports above. They departed with fresh troops for below" (188).

66. Report of Adjutant General, June 29, 1866, William B. Smith Pension File, 128.

57th U.S. Colored Infantry band at Little Rock, Arkansas, ca. 1865. Courtesy UALR Center for Arkansas History and Culture.

Throughout the winter of 1864–65, Smith and his unit were assigned to defend posts along the White River in eastern Arkansas. He saw action at De Valls Bluff in December and again at the mouth of the White River the following February, as small bands of Confederate guerrillas attacked Union strongholds in the area. During the first half of 1865, William's unit was strengthened by several newly formed African American units, comprised primarily of ex-slaves from Arkansas and Mississippi. These "colored units," commanded by white officers, greatly assisted Union forces in holding southwestern Arkansas during 1865.[67] In the final months before the war's end in April 1865, the federal army was in firm control of the state. General William T. Sherman reached Savannah, Georgia, on December 21, 1864; and less than four months later, on April 9, Confederate General Robert E. Lee surrendered his army to Ulysses S. Grant at Appomattox Court House in Virginia. In the summer of 1865, William Smith and his unit were transferred to Pine Bluff, a city on the Arkansas River, forty-four miles south of Little Rock. The 126th Illinois Infantry helped keep order in the city and assure uninterrupted riverboat traffic in this area of southwestern Arkansas after

---

67. Moneyhon, "1865," 147–49: "In addition to Arkansas's white Unionists, the Federal forces were bolstered by black regiments raised within the state. Approximately three thousand men of the 11th, 57th, 83d, 54th, 79th, 112th, and 113th U.S. Colored Infantry were stationed at Little Rock and Pine Bluff, and another two thousand black troops were assigned to the fortifications at Helena. Filled with ex-slaves from the plantations of Arkansas and Mississippi, these regiments were commanded by Northern white officers. The black soldiers often were used as laborers—they loaded and unloaded steamships and railroad cars, drove teams, or constructed fortifications—but they were prepared for combat. That spring [1865], black infantry units often accompanied Federal raids through the southwestern part of the state and performed well."

the war. Smith was mustered out by Lieutenant Charles S. Hussey, who had been a leader over the 60th U.S. Colored Troops Infantry, at Pine Bluff on July 12, 1865. William had served his country for nearly a year and a half.[68]

According to Joseph III, William returned from the war "without a scratch," meaning that he was not physically injured in battle.[69] While true, that statement does not acknowledge the permanent damage to his health from illness. Samuel Murdock, Smith's neighbor in Clayton County during the next three decades, gave a more detailed description: "Amid the clash of arms, the fatigue of march and the swamps and sloughs of the burning south," he wrote in a memorial statement a few days after William's death, "[William] devoted three years of his life to the land that gave him birth, and from these fields of strife he returned again to his home, crippled with aches from which he never recovered."[70] Less than a month after returning Elkader, Smith submitted a petition for an invalid's pension as a veteran, describing the symptoms listed above.[71]

Seventeen years after the war's end, in an update to his petition, Smith reported to his examining doctor that his "rheumatism[,] loss of sight and deafness have gradually increased until at the present time he has so little use of his right arm that he is unable to perform manual labor, has lost the sight of his right eye so that is of little or no use to him whatever, and his deafness somewhat increased."[72] These symptoms, particularly the diminished sight and hearing on his right side, could have resulted from the loud explosions of rifle fire, since he would have been holding his weapon against his right shoulder, but it is more likely that these physical symptoms were exacerbated by the stress of warfare. Although any diagnosis at this historical distance is difficult, Smith appears to have been experiencing symptoms that most closely resemble trigeminal neuralgia (named for the trigeminal nerve) which causes such severe and unremitting pain, especially in the face, that it has been nicknamed the "suicide disease." According to his own account, recollections of family members, and evaluating physicians, he frequently complained of aches on the right side of his face and body.[73] Joseph

---

68. "William B. Smith, Company G, 126 IL US INF," Illinois Civil War Muster and Descriptive Rolls, Illinois State Archives, http://www.ilsos.gov/isaveterans/civilMusterSearch.do?key=237510 (accessed March 11, 2015); Nathaniel B. Baker, "Sixtieth United States Infantry: History of the Regiment," in *Report of the Brig.-Gen. Nathaniel B. Baker, Adjutant General and Act'g Q. M. G. and Act'g as P. M. G., to Hon. William M. Stone, Governor of the State of Iowa* (Des Moines, Iowa: F. W. Palmer, 1867), 620–22.

69. Howard, *Memoirs of President Joseph Smith*, 91, 185

70. Murdock, "The Rev. William B. Smith," 5.

71. Declaration for Invalid Pension, August 8, 1865, William Smith Pension File, 46.

72. Statement of A. B. Hanna, March 30, 1882, William Smith Pension File, 91–92.

73. William B. Smith, Letter to U.S. Pension Office, July 19, 1875; Statement of A. B. Hanna, March 30, 1882; William E. Smith (Dundee, Minn.), Letter to U.S. Pension Office, ca. October 1889, 77–79, in William B. Smith Pension File; and Edson D. C. Smith, (Dundee, Minn.) to U.S. Pension Office, June 6, 1892, 80, in William B. Smith Pension File.

III also struggled with facial neuralgia off and on from age of fifty-seven until his death in 1914. Intriguingly, and perhaps further substantiating that this was a hereditary condition, both William and Joseph III began to experience these symptoms in their fifties—the onset in both instances during periods of stress.[74]

Smith had also likely contracted a parasite in the Arkansas swamps, from which he suffered for the rest of his life with chronic diarrhea, internal and external hemorrhoids, and piles. It is possible that he also endured symptoms that closely resemble celiac disease. Numerous reports included in his disability petitions indicated that Smith could deal only with a limited and carefully prepared diet and that the "food often passed undigested." Family members and physicians refer to his struggle with "chronic diarrhea," "internal piles or hemorrhoids," and "abdominal pains" after eating.[75] The combination of trigeminal neuralgia and celiac disease, both of them painful and debilitating, made it difficult for him to function, and he spent much of the remainder of his life with only a restricted ability to perform manual labor. Both of his children by Eliza recall him as permanently disabled and in need of constant assistance in his later years.[76]

Notwithstanding his continuing health challenges, Smith was proud of his service to his country. "I served in the army in the War of Rebellion nearly two years until the war closed," he declared in an 1892 deposition, "until I was no longer needed in the service of the government and was discharged."[77] In the ensuing years, he made great efforts to attend the annual reunion of Civil War soldiers in northeastern Iowa. A fellow soldier, William Ziegler, paid him perhaps the best tribute, when he was asked to verify Smith's Civil War disabilities: "William B. Smith was a good soldier and an honorable man and what statement he may make concerning his disabilities wherever and when contracted can be relied upon as [a] man of truth."[78]

---

74. Joseph Smith III first reported his symptoms of neuralgia during a demanding mission to Utah and the West Coast. Joseph Smith III, Letter to J[ohn W.] Peterson, November 8, 1893, and Joseph Smith III (Lamoni, Iowa), Letter to William B. Smith, October 26, 1893, P13, f439, both in Community of Christ Library-Archives; Howard, *The Memoirs of President Joseph Smith III*, 160. Roger D. Launius conjectures that "the likelihood of Joseph Smith, Jr., having the same affliction [neuralgia] is considerable," but that "since he died a relatively young man, it never appeared sufficiently for diagnosis." He cites an account of a "painful toothache" during Joseph's incarceration in Liberty Jail as a possible episode of neuralgia. Roger D. Launius, *Joseph Smith III Pragmatic Prophet* (Urbana: University of Illinois Press, 1988), 230–31, 244 note 43.

75. Edson D. C. Smith, to U.S. Pension Office, June 6, 1892; Statement of A. B. Hanna, July 27, 1867, William Smith Pension File, 133; Statement of H. Hamilton, October 17, 1879, William Smith Pension File, 143; Statement of A. B. Hanna, March 30, 1882.

76. William E. Smith, Letter to U.S. Pension Office, ca. October 1889; Edson D. C. Smith, to U.S. Pension Office, June 6, 1892.

77. Testimony of William B. Smith, Temple Lot Case Testimonies, 211.

78. Murdock, "The Rev. William B. Smith"; Statement of William H. Ziegler, July 20, 1889, in William B. Smith Pension File, 100.

Chapter 19

The "Brighamites"

I hope Brother Brigham will forgiv[e] me for I have said many harsh things concerning him yet I know him to be a man of God[.] He shall never complain of me hereafter for I have decreed that my tongue shall no more speak evil of the ruler of my people him whom god has honer[e]d.
—William B. Smith, 1847

The deaths of Joseph and Hyrum Smith in June 1844, followed within a month by the death from an undiagnosed illness of a third brother, Samuel H. Smith, left thirty-three-year-old Apostle William B. Smith as the only surviving son of Joseph Smith Sr. and Lucy Mack Smith. He was serving a mission in the East and stayed there, following the advice of those who feared that his life might be in danger if he rushed back to Nauvoo with the other apostles who were scattered throughout the East on similar missions to promote Joseph Smith's candidacy for the U.S. presidency. Thus, William was not in Nauvoo during Sidney Rigdon's attempt to position himself as the Church's "guardian" based on his position in Joseph Smith's First Presidency, nor was he present as Brigham Young, president of the Quorum of the Twelve, arrived at the last minute and thwarted Rigdon's attempt.

In short, in the immediate follow-up of Joseph and Hyrum's murders William was united with and a staunch supporter of the Quorum of the Twelve Apostles, of which he was a member. But within a matter of months, this unity frayed, intensifying to the point of an open breach within a year. The first signs of trouble emerged with startling promptness after William's return from his eastern mission. Members of the Twelve at Nauvoo became increasingly concerned about William's leadership in the East. Brigham Young learned from Apostle Wilford Woodruff, who traveled through the eastern branches during the months of October-December 1844, that William had authorized plural marriages, bestowed the sealing power on several of his colleagues, and diverted the eastern Saints' temple donations to his own ends.[1] Young acted almost immediately after receiving Woodruff's report, sending

---

1. Wilford Woodruff (Boston), Letter to Brigham Young, October 9, 1844; Wilford Woodruff (Boston), Letter to Brigham Young, October 14, 1844; Wilford Woodruff (Philadelphia), Letter to Brigham Young, December 3, 1844; all in Brigham Young Office Files 1832–1878, Letters from Church Leaders and Others, 1840–1877, William Smith, 1844–1857, LDS Church History Library; John S. Dinger, ed., *The Nauvoo High City and High Council Minutes* (Salt Lake City: Signature Books, 2011), 548–50, 549 note 17–18.

Parley P. Pratt to assume leadership over the eastern branches in December 1844.[2] Pratt's appointment sent William into a simmering rage, but a letter from Heber C. Kimball temporarily pacified William. Kimball assured him that leaders at Nauvoo were expecting him to return to Nauvoo immediately—one reason that had factored into their appointment of Pratt—and that until he left for Nauvoo, the two apostles should "act as one."[3] But the experience made William uneasy about his ecclesiastical station ever afterward.

Yet William Smith's catalogue of difficulties with Church authorities had not begun during his eastern mission, becoming particularly evident after his call as one of the apostles in 1835. After his appointment to the Twelve, William's Church membership had been called into question on at least six separate occasions, stemming from his struggle with insubordination, a sense of entitlement resulting from his position as a member of the Smith family and his apostleship, and his expectation of being supported from Church funds.[4] Within months after William was called an apostle, Orson Hyde had written a formal complaint to Joseph Smith about the injudicious way William was drawing on the bishop's storehouse for money and supplies. After highlighting the disparity between William and the rest of the quorum, Orson Hyde suggested that Joseph should either "take the baskets off from our noses or put one to Williams nose or if this cannot be done, reconcile the parable of the twelve sons with the superior privileges [sic] that William has." Hyde elaborated his allusion to the parable of the twelve sons, which appears in the Doctrine and Covenants (LDS 38:26–27), in his letter to Joseph: "Pardon me if I speak in parables or parody. A certain good shepherd had twelve sons and he sent them out one day to go and gather his flock when were scattered upon the mountains and in the vallies afar off they were all obedient to their fathers mandate, and at Evening they returned with the flock, and one son received wool enough to make him warm and comfortable and also rec[eive]d of the flesh and milk of the flock, the other eleven received not so much as one kid to make merry with their friends."[5] Hyde's report that William

---

2. Church leaders at Nauvoo published an editorial that read, "Elder Parley P. Pratt has been appointed by the council of the Twelve to go to the city of New York, to take charge of the press in that city . . . and to take the presidency of all the eastern churches." "Elder Parley P. Pratt . . .," *Times and Seasons* 5, no. 22 (December 1, 1844): 727.

3. Heber C. Kimball (Nauvoo, Ill.), Letter to William Smith, January 9, 1845, LDS Church History Library.

4. "History of William Smith," *Millennial Star* 27, no. 1 (January 7, 1865): 7; "Conference Minutes," *Times and Seasons* 6, no. 16 (November 1, 1845): 1, 12; Kyle R. Walker, "William B. Smith," in Kyle R. Walker, ed., *United by Faith: The Joseph Sr. and Lucy Mack Smith Family* (American Fork, Utah: Covenant Communications and BYU Studies, 2006), 246–307.

5. Orson Hyde, Letter to Joseph Smith, December 15, 1835, as quoted in Dean C. Jessee, Mark Ashurst-McGee, and Richard L. Jensen, eds., *Journals, Vol. 1: 1832–1839*, THE JOSEPH SMITH PAPERS, general editors Dean C. Jessee, Ronald K. Esplin, and Richard Lyman Bushman (Salt Lake City: Church Historian's Press, 2008), 124–28. Joseph

was receiving special privileges as early as December 1835 exposed a core attribute of William's personality, and it was a perception that most members of the Twelve came to share about William during his decade-long tenure as an apostle.

Though observable throughout his adult life, William Smith's sense of entitlement became most noticeable after his return to Nauvoo in May 1845. Brigham Young had initially been sympathetic to William's plight, expressing personal support as well as encouraging the Saints to "rem[em]ber bro Wm. Smith . . . . [and] be kind to him [and] dont be afraid of [sharing] your substance and the S[avior] will bless you."[6] Additionally, Young indicated that, after William returned to Nauvoo, "we furnished him a span of horses, and a carriage and a house, and Brother [Heber C.] Kimball became responsible for the rent of it."[7] William was living rent-free in the home formerly occupied by William Marks, and, like his father and brother Hyrum, continued the privilege of charging for his patriarchal blessings, by which means he earned his livelihood.[8] Even though the Church was completely supporting William and public statements about him were positive, even laudatory, his dissatisfaction persisted and even intensified throughout that summer. His discontentment was in part due to his completely accurate perception that the Twelve drew the line at expanding his priesthood "privileges" to the point of allowing him to claim a major role in the succession, a view which, to William's mind, involved an expectation of increased temporal support. William was obviously pressing the limits of the Twelve's forbearance, but he never seemed satisfied and continued to expect even more from the Church and its leaders.

While William jockeyed for a more prominent role in the Church's hierarchy throughout the summer of 1845, Church authorities responded with rather remarkable patience. The summer was tempestuous. The Church was still in shock and mourning for the loss of Joseph and Hyrum, external enemies were pressing more threateningly on the outlying Mormon villages, and the already impoverished community was being urged to make superhuman efforts to complete the Nauvoo Temple. William, rather than providing support and employing his impressive tal-

---

responded by ensuring that storehouse resources were extended equitably to members of the Quorum of the Twelve. Ibid., 128 note 216.

6. Young made this statement at a Church gathering in Nauvoo on May 11, 1845. Church Historian's Office, General Church Minutes, 1839–77, May 11, 1845, 15, CR 100 318, Box 1, fd. 33, in Richard E. Turley, ed., *Selected Collections from the Archives of the Church of Jesus Christ of Latter-day Saints*, 2 vols., DVD (Provo, Utah: Brigham Young University Press, [December 2002]), 1:18.

7. "Conference Minutes," *Times & Seasons* 6, no. 16 (November 1, 1845): 1014.

8. Brigham Young (City of Joseph [Nauvoo], Ill.), Letter to Brother Wm. Smith, August 10, 1845, Brigham Young Office Files 1832–1878, General Correspondence, Outgoing, 1845 June-August, LDS Church History Library. Christine Elise Blythe summarized that "in 1840, the going rate for a patriarchal blessing was one dollar." Christine Elyse Blythe, "William Smith's Patriarchal Blessings and Contested Authority in the Post-Martyrdom Church," 76–77.

ents to meet these challenges, had become one of the problems, demanding favors and being only temporarily satisfied with each new concession. The Twelve, especially Brigham himself and John Taylor, expended considerable effort in clarifying the extent of William's patriarchal authority, intervened to resolve a physical fistfight he had with the Nauvoo policeman Elbridge Tufts, muted his efforts on behalf of the Hodges brothers who had been convicted of theft and murder, and negotiated solutions to William's financial and family demands. (See Chapters 12–13.) William's misconduct was discussed at least six times that summer by the Twelve in meetings which William did not attend. This record provides evidence of increasing uneasiness with his conduct and what they saw, with justification, as underlying disloyalty.[9] As early as mid-June, when William had been back in the city less than two months, he complained publicly that not enough was being done to honor his family.[10] Church leaders went to great lengths to try and resolve his dissatisfaction, which included hosting a grand dinner party honoring the Smith family and all their relations. Although the dinner showered William, Mother Lucy, his sisters, their husbands, and members of the extended family with praise and attention, it only temporarily assuaged William's feelings.[11] The Twelve cannot be blamed for feeling that William's chronic discontentment was a bottomless well.

In late July or early August, Brigham Young was having a carriage constructed for his own family and had apparently promised Mother Smith a ride in the finished carriage. Lucy had often enjoyed taking carriage rides with Joseph before his death, and it was kind gesture by Young. However, William responded by launching a rumor that Joseph had actually been constructing the carriage for their mother before his death. Under his prodding, he encouraged Lucy to ask for the carriage, the horse, and its harness as a gift. Young was obviously surprised at Lucy's approach and correctly surmised that William's avarice lay at its roots, but her goodwill as the matriarch of the family and his personal affection for Lucy prevented him from turning it into an open quarrel. He immediately wrote Lucy on August 2, informing her that, when the carriage was complete she should not only have it but "all that I have is at your command to make you happy [in] the little time you have to live with us." He also promised to call on her as soon as

---

9. See, for example, George D. Smith, ed., *An Intimate Chronicle: The Journals of William Clayton*, (Salt Lake City: Signature Books, 1991), 166, 170–76; Dean C. Jessee, ed., *John Taylor Nauvoo Journal* (Provo, Utah: Grandin Book, 1996), 63–79, 90–99; Stanley B. Kimball, *On the Potter's Wheel: The Diaries of Heber C. Kimball* (Salt Lake City: Signature Books, 1987), 109, 114–15, 118, 124.

10. Heber C. Kimball recorded in his journal: "Wm. Smith said last Sabath [June 15, 1845] on the stand, that he and his connection had been neglected and so forth. This was fols [false] as they had all they wanted, when they asked for it. This gives me sorrow." Stanley Kimball, *On the Potter's Wheel*, 123.

11. George Smith, *An Intimate Chronicle*, 173; Lyman O. Littlefield, "Still Later from Nauvoo," *New-York Messenger* 2, no. 5 (August 2, 1845): 38; "Dinner to the Smith Family," *New-York Messenger* 2, no. 6 (August 9, 1845): 44.

it was convenient, and concluded, "May the Lord Bles[s] you and comfort your h[e]art—I am your son and fr[i]end as ever."[12] In fact, he gave the carriage to Mother Smith so that the elderly woman could travel around the city in comfort, but he was also obviously motivated by a desire to avoid rancor with the family. William Clayton summarized in his journal, "Out of respect for Mother Smith the brethren would rather indulge the whole family than to have hurt feelings."[13]

This generous gift did not placate William. Only a couple of weeks later in mid-August, William wrote to Brigham Young asking for seventy-five dollars to help him pay some personal debts. Young, keenly aware of the need to spend every available penny on the temple's construction, informed him bluntly that the Church did not have such sums available and pointed out that William had "already received more assistance from the church funds than all of the rest of the Twelve put together."[14] This was not an argument that William would have considered satisfactory, and his need—which the rest of the Twelve would have considered simple greed—was becoming increasingly difficult for leaders to ignore.

A wiser man would have recognized that he was exhausting the Twelve's patience and taken pains to establish more collegial relationships; but in fact, William felt entitled to Church properties to such an extent that, at one point in the summer of 1845, Orson Hyde recalled in 1850 that William "claimed that it was his right to have one-twelfth part of the tithing set off to him, to be appropriated to his own individual use, or in any way he thought proper." Even though Hyde was probably not the most accurate source—due to his exasperation with William by this point—it was a significant complaint. According to Orson Hyde, "he was the only one [of the Twelve] that ever asked or expected such a thing."[15] A year earlier (four years after William's excommunication), Hyde referred to this same theme and hotly expressed his exasperation. He flatly accused: "He [William] would confess many things that he was not guilty of; but the church required him to confess fully the things that he was guilty of. He never wished the priesthood for any other purpose than to use it as a key to sensuality, avarice

---

12. Scott G. Kenney, ed., *Wilford Woodruff's Journal, 1833–1898*, typescript, 9 vols. (Midvale, Utah: Signature Books, 1983–85), February 13, 1859, 5:287–88; Brigham Young, Letter to Lucy Smith, August 2, 1845, Brigham Young Office Files 1832–1878, General Correspondence, Outgoing, 1843–1876, 1845 June-August, LDS Church History Library; also cited in Dean C. Jessee, "The Writings of Brigham Young," *Western Historical Quarterly* 4, no. 3 (July 1973): 285–86.

13. George Smith, *An Intimate Chronicle*, 176.

14. Young to Wm Smith, August 10, 1845. See Chapter 13 for a further description of the dinner. For a further discussion on LDS Church leaders' efforts to care for the Smiths after the summer of 1844, see Kyle R. Walker, "Looking After the First Family of Mormonism: LDS Church Leaders' Support of the Smiths after the Murders of Joseph and Hyrum," *John Whitmer Historical Association Journal* 32, no. 1 (Spring/Summer 2012): 17–46.

15. Orson Hyde, "Cause for Which William Smith Was Excluded from the Church!" *Frontier Guardian*, 2, no. 1 (February 6, 1850): 2.

and ease."¹⁶ Though this accusation was doubtless inflamed by Hyde's personal irritation with William, he had put his finger on a point in Smith's personality that grated on the Twelve. As the hot and turbulent summer of 1845 drew toward a close, Church leaders' patience with William had worn thin even while William's unmet expectations caused him to experience increased frustration.

After his excommunication, departure from Nauvoo, and increasingly irresponsible trajectory through other Mormon groups, some members of the Twelve were openly relieved that they no longer had to accommodate William's shenanigans, demands, and excuses. At a meeting of the Twelve in Salt Lake City in December 1852, when William was making his final, futile effort to establish his own church, his cousin, Apostle George A. Smith, "rejoiced to see the union of the quorum & their disposition to do right. We dont have to feel that one of the quorum like Lyman Wight is drawing off one way & John E. Page another & A Wm Smith Commiting iniquity & we have to sustain him against our feelings."¹⁷ William's tenure as an apostle had been a long and difficult journey, but it was decidedly over.

Many former friends and relatives in the LDS movement had seen events in the explosive autumn of 1845 as presenting them with a choice between loyalty to family and loyalty to the Twelve. Most permanently severed relationships with William, particularly after he denounced the Twelve in the pamphlet that Thomas Sharp had been only too willing to print for him. Despite William's lengthy absences from the body of the Twelve and the prickly relationships he generated when they were in closer proximity, their shared apostleship had provided a meaningful bond. But after October 1845, William never again saw any member of his quorum, with the exception of Orson Hyde—and those encounters could hardly be called a reconciliation. When he left Nauvoo, he left eight plural wives behind him. One of them, thirty-year-old Mary Ann Covington, who swore an affidavit in the Temple Lot case in early 1892, probably spoke for the other wives as well in saying that she considered her marriage at an end because "Smith had gone off and left the church." In answer to a follow-up question, she added that she also considered that his action cancelled "the eternity part of it." William had never contacted her after he left Nauvoo, and "I don't think Smith will ever come where I am [in eternity] to claim me."¹⁸ She clearly felt that William had abandoned her while also abandoning their shared Mormon faith.

Smith relatives who were loyal to Brigham Young's leadership after the death of Joseph Smith also felt that they needed to choose between family and faith. William's Uncle John Smith, along with John's son George A., rejected William's attempt to persuade them to support him as Joseph's successor in late June 1845.

---

16. Orson Hyde, "We Have Just Read a Letter . . . ," *Frontier Guardian* 1, no. 1 (February 7, 1849): 2.

17. Quoted in Kenney, *Wilford Woodruff's Journal*, December 22, 1852, 4:157.

18. Testimony of Mary Ann [Covington Sheffield] West, Testimony, Temple Lot Case, in United States testimony 1892, Court of Appeals (Eighth Circuit), 501–02, MS 1160, LDS Church History Library.

George A. Smith, 1817-1875. Photograph taken ca. 1870, photographer unknown. Courtesy Mary Dennis.

John and George appealed to family feeling in attempting to sway William toward loyalty to the Twelve, and Uncle John "reasoned with him and endeavored to show him the falsity of his position," but with little effect. George remembered that William "evinced a very bitter spirit and declared himself President of the Church and said he would have his rights."[19] A year later, when he briefly returned to Nauvoo in March-May 1846, the excommunicated William approached his widowed aunt Mary Aikens Smith (widow of William's uncle Silas Smith), and her two sons, Silas, age fifteen, and Jesse, age eleven. They were preparing to go West with the body of the Saints when William appeared at their home, trying "to start a church for himself," according to Jesse's recollection. "He came to our house and asked us to join his church; this, we however, declined to do."[20] George A. was both angry and mortified by William's behavior, explaining in an 1857 sermon that William had attempted to trade on Joseph's name to increase his standing among scattered Mormons. "I considered it was the worst thing a man could do to endeavour to build himself up on the merits of others," expostulated George A. "For cousin William to go and endeavour to pull down the work of his brother, I felt that he has disgraced the family and the name." He felt so embarrassed by how William had shamed the family that, when he traveled through the eastern states in 1856–57 laboring for Deseret's statehood, he concealed the family connection.[21] In the same sermon in Salt Lake City's Bowery, George A. went further: "The husbandman found a rattlesnake cold and frozen, and he took it, and he put it in his bosom, and kept it there till it was warm; and then the snake coiled about the husbandman and destroyed his life."[22] William felt that he had been neglected and abused by the Twelve; but for their part, the Twelve, returned the feeling in full measure. Even William's relatives in the West detested him for his malevolent attacks and hostilities that went on for a good part of his life.

However, William was not through with Mormonism nor, for that matter, was Mormonism through with William. Although Hyde considered William a

---

19. Journal History of the Church of Jesus Christ of Latter-day Saints (chronological scrapbook of typed entries and newspaper clippings, 1830–present), June 28, 1845, 1, LDS Church History Library.

20. Oliver R. Smith, ed., *Six Decades in the West: The Journal of Jesse Nathaniel Smith* (Provo, Utah: Jesse N. Smith Family Assn., 1970), 9.

21. George A. Smith, August 2, 1857, *Journal of Discourses*, 26 vols. (London and Liverpool: LDS Booksellers Depot, 1855–86), 5:102.

22. Ibid.

reprobate by 1849–50, he had earlier been the first to reach out to William, writing a direct, but compassionate letter to his former colleague the same month as his excommunication (October 1845), inviting him to return to the city of the Saints.[23] Hyde may have been sympathetic because he had experienced his own period of estrangement from the Mormon faith during the Mormon-Missouri conflict in 1838, a turbulent period of conflicting loyalties complicated by a serious illness that he said affected his judgement. This separation lasted only a few months; and by February 1839 he had acknowledged his error, mistakes, sought forgiveness from Joseph Smith, and eventually returned to full fellowship. Almost immediately after his reinstatement in the Church, Hyde had also successfully intervened to assist W. W. Phelps, another wavering Church member during the Missouri crisis, in his return to Mormonism.[24]

Alluding to his own poignant episode with apostasy, Hyde hoped to draw William back into the Church fold.[25] "I want to be your friend," he wrote compassionately from Nauvoo to William, who was then in St. Louis. "I beseech you in the name of God to come speedily back to Nauvoo. You shall not be harmed.—Your mother's heart is grieved and broken. You are her son, she feels for you, and all the church feel for you. . . . All would be glad to forgive you, if you will only come within the reach of our forgiveness, in your person, and in your spirit. You may think that you have no friends in Nauvoo, but, William, I know that your best, and only real friends are here." Obviously familiar with Smith's fears as outlined in his pamphlet, Hyde also attempted to calm William's anxiety regarding his safety should he return, reassuring him that "there is no one here that wishes to harm the hair of your head."[26]

Rather than responding to this friendly outreach, William was in no mood for reconciliation, and Hyde's letter infuriated him. He had never done well in owning his part in a conflict and often boiled over at any hint of wrongdoing on his part. Hyde candidly referred to William's misconduct when he presided over the Eastern branches of the Church: "I know what you [have] done in the east and presisely what your influence is there." He also sought to give William a spiritual sign, by "which you may know yourself that God is not pleased with your course," predicting, "Not one of your plans or schemes will succeed according to your expectation." (He was, as it turned out, completely prescient.) But overall, Hyde's tone was one

---

23. Orson Hyde (Nauvoo, Ill.), Letter to William Smith, October 28, 1845, as quoted in *Messenger and Advocate of the Church of Christ* 2, no. 2 (December 1845): 413–14.

24. William W. Phelps (Dayton, Ohio), Letter to Brother Joseph [Smith], June 29, 1840; and Orson Hyde and John E. Page, Letter to Presidents Joseph Smith, Hyrum Smith, Sidney Rigdon, n.d., n.p., both quoted in *History of the Church*, 4:141–43; Myrtle Stevens Hyde, *Orson Hyde: The Olive Branch of Israel* (Salt Lake City: Aspen Books, 2000), 97–109.

25. Hyde referenced his own apostasy in his correspondence with William in 1847. William alluded to Hyde's statement in a letter to Lyman Wight, while laboring as a missionary in Connecticut, April 21, 1849, published in *Melchisedek and Aaronic Herald* 1, no. 4 (June 1849): 1–2.

26. Orson Hyde to William Smith, October 28, 1845.

of conciliation, and he concluded warmly: "With feelings of great anxiety, for your welfare, both here and hereafter. I am your friend and well wisher."[27]

Although Hyde meant well, William's temper flared, and he wrote a lengthy reply in November that reiterated his grievances with leaders at Nauvoo and alienated him further. Once again, he complained that the Twelve were restricting his Church privileges. "You are well advised of the fact, that I have been wronged & robbed by my pretended friends," William wrote uncompromisingly, "among whom I rank your saintly self." Furthermore, as the sole surviving male Smith, he felt he should have a more prominent role in the governing councils of the Church, and he concluded by repeating the accusations that his life was in danger in Nauvoo, thanks to the Twelve, including Hyde. He wrote sarcastically, "Sir, were you aware of the injuries and wrongs which your so very kind hearted brethren have committed, and their secret plottings to rob you of every thing calculated to sweeten life or render existence desirable, no atonement could heal the wounds inflicted upon your feelings." William announced that he had every right to function "independent" of the Twelve. "I am fixed in my course," he continued, "and firm as the Rock of Gibralter."

As for Hyde's warning that his organizational plans would come to naught, Smith countered bitterly: "As regards the course I am taking, make yourself as contented as possible . . . as to my success for I think my chances are quite as encouraging as yours possibly can be in the event of your departure to the wild and cheerless far-west." He outlined for Hyde his plan to creating his rival church: "My life and exertions will be . . . to perpetuate the names of my father's family, and with honor to my noble martyred brothers Joseph and Hyrum wipe away the disgrace, the stain, the evils that, since their deaths have crept into the church." He believed that the Smiths—namely himself—must play a more prominent leadership role. He referred to distancing Joseph and Hyrum's names from the "stain" of polygamy, thus restoring the Church to its original purity.[28] Though this approach should have created a moral conundrum for William, who had unequivocally accepted the practice (and would do so on during at least two later flirtations with other Mormon movements), he knew that this course would be his best chance of gathering adherents to his cause and assumed, with some justification, that the Twelve (or his former plural wives) would guard his secret because polygamy was still not a topic for public discussion. It was as if he issued a counter-threat to Hyde, even though they both knew of William's duplicity. He signed the letter defiantly, "Patriarch of the Church."[29] He also made the letter public by sending it to the *Warsaw Signal,* and their letters were subsequently published in Sidney Rigdon's Philadelphia paper, the *Messenger and Advocate of the Church of Jesus Christ.*

---

27. Ibid.
28. William Smith, Letter to Orson Hyde, November 12, 1845 (St. Louis), in *Messenger and Advocate of the Church of Christ* (Pittsburgh) 2, no. 2 (December 1845): 414–16.
29. Ibid.

Although William rejected this overture, Hyde remained the foremost apostle with whom Smith had interaction in the ensuing decade. As the highest-ranking Church official still in Nauvoo after Brigham Young headed out across Iowa in February 1846, Orson Hyde thwarted Smith's influence in Nauvoo when William paid the city a recruiting trip in March 1846. Again, during 1848–52, Hyde was local Church president, migration coordinator at Council Bluffs and Kanesville, Iowa, and editor of the influential *Frontier Guardian*. Thus, Hyde was on the shifting front lines in the identity wars between the Strangites, the "New Organization" gradually coalescing around the hope that Joseph III would step up and fill his dead father's shoes, and the followers of Alpheus Cutler of the Council of Fifty, not to mention the waves of Mormon converts flooding upriver toward the jumping-off point in Nebraska for the next decade.[30] There were no face-to-face meetings, although they were in Nauvoo together in the spring of 1846, but Smith continued to correspond periodically with Hyde during his post-Mormon years.

Orson Hyde, 1805–1878. Photograph by Marsena Cannon, ca. 1855. Courtesy LDS Church History Library.

The first time Smith returned to Nauvoo after he broke from Brigham Young's leadership, was on March 8, 1846, about a month after the main body of Saints had left for the West.[31] At that point, he became aware of a promise Brigham Young had made to his mother to care for her during her final years. Lucy's son Joseph had apparently promised her a home when he was still alive, and, according to Lucy, "since his [Joseph's] death the promises were renewed all last Summer and Winter [1845]." In fact, Lucy further stated that before he left Nauvoo in February 1846, "the last thing that Brigham said to me was, I should have a home and be provided for, in all my wants."[32] Indeed, Brigham had been attentive to Mother Smith's needs. One year earlier, on July 24, 1845, trustees at Nauvoo paid one hundred dollars for a lot that they gifted to Lucy.[33] About a week later, on August 2, Brigham

---

30. Hyde, *Orson Hyde: The Olive Branch of Israel*, 225–84.

31. Greg R. Knight, ed., *Thomas Bullock's Nauvoo Journal* (Orem, Utah: Grandin Book, 1994), 60-61.

32. Lucy Smith (Nauvoo, Ill.), Letter to Messrs Babbitt, Heywood and Hulmer [Fulmer], March 22, 1846, in *Voree Herald* 1, no. 8 (August 1846): 3.

33. Hancock County Deeds, Book O, 99, entry #7383; Book P, 435–36, entry #8477; Book S, 188–89, entry #10437, in Susan Easton Black, Harvey B. Black, and Brandon Plewe,

Nauvoo Trustees. Almon W. Babbitt, 1812–1856, on the left. Engraving by unknown artist. Joseph L. Heywood, 1815–1910, in the middle. Courtesy LDS Church History Library. John S. Fullmer, 1807–1883, from Frank Eshom, *Pioneers and Prominent Men of Utah* (Salt Lake City: Utah Pioneers Book Publishing Company, 1913).

Young and Heber C. Kimball had purchased several blocks of property in the heart of Nauvoo from Emma Smith for $550, at least one of which they intended to transfer to Lucy and her daughters. These purchases not only assisted Emma in providing for her family but would also ensure that Lucy and her daughters would be looked after. William Clayton recorded that the authorities "then went to Mother Smiths and took her into the Carriage to show her the Blocks and give her her choice which of the two she would have to be deeded to herself and her daughters." After Lucy chose her lot, Clayton recorded that "she [Lucy] wants a house building of the same pattern as Brother [Heber C.] Kimballs," one of the finest structures in all of Nauvoo.[34] However, with the hurried migration, leaders knew they would be unable to construct such a home and, instead, discussed alternatives with Lucy to ensure that her needs would be met for the remainder of her life. According to Orson Hyde, the presiding authority left at Nauvoo in the spring of 1846, "we offered to pay Mother Smith two hundred Dollars yearly, and furnish her a house to live in rent free, and pay the amount monthly or quarterly."[35] In March 1846, Lucy pressed the Church-appointed trustees, Almon Babbitt, Joseph Heywood, and John Fullmer, who worked in conjunction with Orson Hyde to complete the details of the transaction.

Lucy felt satisfied with this arrangement that would provide her with a comfortable home, while the proposed monthly allowance would provide for her needs during her final years. To the trustees' surprise, however, once William

---

eds., *Property Transactions in Nauvoo, Hancock County, Illinois and Surrounding Communities (1839–1859)*, 7 vols. (Wilmington, Del.: World Vital Records, 2006), 6: 3784–85.

34. George Smith, *An Intimate Chronicle*, 176.

35. Orson Hyde, Letter to Dear Brethren (Nauvoo, Ill.), March 27, 1846, Brigham Young Office Files 1832–1878, General Correspondence, Incoming, 1840–1877, Letters from Church Leaders and Others, 1840-1877, Orson Hyde, 1846, LDS Church History Library.

arrived in Nauvoo, he intervened between the trustees and his mother, advising Lucy to refuse the offer. Instead, according to Orson Hyde, William encouraged his mother to make as "large a grab" as possible, which meant obtaining legal title to an existing home in Nauvoo as opposed to the yearly salary and rent-free home. He was afraid that, once the majority of Mormons left for the West, she would not see the promised monies. Orson Hyde felt that William's motives were self-serving and that he wanted the property himself after his mother's death. Subsequent developments reveal that this was, in fact, his motive.[36]

The three trustees, especially Babbitt, were uncomfortable negotiating with William, and were hesitant to make the transfer. After all, the trustees, which unofficially included Orson Hyde, were well aware of Smith's record of making seemingly endless demands for Church funds. To add to their discomfort, William was also now openly supporting James J. Strang's movement.[37]

Babbitt and Heywood met with Mother Smith on March 10, 1846, only two days after William's return, and, according to William, informed her "that unless we [meaning him, Lucy, and presumably her daughters] acknowledge the Twelve as the heads of the church, Mother Smith could have no inheritance at Nauvoo."[38] However, it soon became apparent that the trustees' were less concerned with Lucy than with William. After a few weeks, trustees wrote to Lucy, bluntly informing her that they would not transfer the home while she allowed "William to stay about her house." They were concerned about Smith's motives and his influence on the Saints remaining in Nauvoo now that he was supporting Strang; but from the Smith family's perspective, the request was insensitive and impractical.[39] Isaac Paden, a Latter-day Saint residing at Knoxville, Illinois, who supported Strang, protested:

> I wrote to Bro. Babbit that my astonishment had been aroused to a greater height than it ever had before that such an unreasonable hard hearted request cant be asked at the hands of Mother Smith a woman of her age an old lady placed under such circumstances connected with the Church as she and now be drove to the necessity (after wading through seas of trouble) to drive from her imbrace and Shut her door against her only living son on earth it was asking too much[.] I then plead in behalf of the Church in behalf of Mother Smith in behalf of humanity and Gods sake to withdraw the inhu-

---

36. Orson Hyde, "Mother Smith," *Frontier Guardian* 1, no. 21 (November 14, 1849): 2; Orson Hyde to Dear Brethren, March 27, 1846. When William visited Nauvoo in 1848 and discovered that his mother had transferred title to the Joseph B. Noble home to his sister, Lucy, William was irate over the transaction. Almon W. Babbitt (Nauvoo, Ill.), Letter to President Brigham Young, January 31, 1848, Brigham Young Office Files 1832–1878, General Letters, 1840-1877, A-C, 1848, LDS Church History Library.

37. William Smith (Nauvoo), Letter to James Jesse Strang, March 17, 1846, James Jesse Strang Papers, 1829–70, WA MSS-186–189, Beinecke Rare Book and Manuscript Library, Yale University, New Haven, Conn.

38. William Smith (Nauvoo), Letter to Brother [James] Strang, March 11, 1846, in *Voree Herald* 1, no. 4 (April 1846): 7.

39. Isaac Paden (Knoxville, Ill.), Letter to James M. Adams, April 4, 1846, James Jesse Strang Collection, Beinecke Rare Book and Manuscript Library, Yale University, New Haven, Conn.

man Request and pay her yearly a reasonable sum together with a comfortable house and let the old ladys Children eat drink and sleep under her Roof as she wished.[40]

The request was unreasonable on its face, despite William's history, which certainly urged caution. Surely an elderly widow would desire her only remaining son to be at her house as often as possible, as Paden argued. This was not the first time that Almon Babbitt, in particular, had offended members of the Smith family. He had been particularly injudicious in his consultations with Emma Smith after her husband's death.[41] At the same time, it is understandable why the trustees were hesitant to negotiate with William.

Mother Smith responded indignantly in repudiating the trustees' condition: "You would have me forsake my children in order that you may give me a living, but let it not be said that in the Church of Jesus Christ of Latter Day Saints, a mother has to forfe[i]t . . . the cords of affection that bind her to her children, or she shall not have a subsistence." She reminded them of Brigham Young's promise of a home before he had left for the West, revealing her sentiment that "I think if he were here he would not do as you have done."[42] Lucy's statement revealed her positive feelings toward Young and other leaders who had left for the West and blamed the trustees for the situation while William, for his part, blamed Young.

After learning of the stand-off between the trustees and Lucy, Hyde wrote to Brigham Young seeking counsel: "We offered to pay Mother Smith two hundred Dollars yearly, and furnish her a house to live in rent free, and pay the amount monthly or quarterly," related Hyde, "but 'Bill' [William] puts the old lady up to refuse that offer. He wants a good property deeded to her, that at her death he may have it. We are not disposed to do it, unless you counsel us to do so. We have told the old lady that we are willing to support her handsomely."[43]

While the particulars of Young's response have not survived, he appears to have directed them to either give her title to a home at Nauvoo or the yearly salary, leaving the decision to be worked out between Mother Smith and the trustees. He may have also steered them away from negotiating with William. Immediately after receiving Young's directive, the trustees recognized their error in how they had handled the situation and began discussing these options with Mother Smith. However, this time around they sidestepped William and instead involved Lucy's son-in-law Arthur Millikin in the negotiations. Millikin proposed that he would be willing to care for his mother-in-law for the remainder of her life if there was some "inducement" at Nauvoo that could be "secured to him." The two parties agreed that, if trustees purchased the Joseph B. Noble

---

40. Paden to Adams, April 4, 1846.
41. Richard P. Howard, ed., *The Memoirs of President Joseph Smith III (1832–1914)* (Independence: Herald Publishing House, 1979), 38.
42. Lucy Smith (Nauvoo, Ill.), Letter to Messrs Babbitt, Heywood and [F]ulmer, 3.
43. Orson Hyde (Nauvoo, Ill.), Letter to Dear Brethren, March 27, 1846, Brigham Young, Office Files 1832–1878, General Correspondence, Incoming, 1840–1877, Letters from Church Leaders and Others, 1832–1877, Orson Hyde, 1846, LDS Church History Library.

Arthur, 1817–1882, and Lucy Smith Millikin, 1821–1882. Both photographs by Charles R. Savage, date unknown. Courtesy LDS Church History Library.

home for Lucy, she would, in time, transfer the title to the Millikins. It was, in essence, the exact same thing that William had desired, but Church authorities at Nauvoo obviously trusted Millikin, husband of daughter Lucy, over William. Millikin agreed that, if he would ultimately receive title to the home, he and his wife would ensure that Mother Smith was provided for until her death. Both sides felt satisfied with the arrangement, and trustees purchased the home from Noble, and transferred the property to Lucy on April 11, 1846. George A. Smith, who was on the trail west, recorded two days later, "The trustees gave mother Smith a deed of conveyance of a house and lot, in the city of Nauvoo, built and occupied by Joseph B. Noble, valued at twelve hundred dollars, which she took possession of."[44] Though William was aware that the property was being deeded to his mother, neither the trustees nor Mother Smith informed William that Arthur and Lucy Millikin would ultimately receive title to the property. William undoubtedly felt he deserved credit for the transaction as they two parties ultimately agreed on his original proposal.[45]

As part of the transaction, to suppress William Smith's persisting complaints against the Twelve, trustees at Nauvoo published a document asserting that they had treated the Smith family equitably. The broadside, *To the public*, began: "The

---

44. Minutes of a Conference held at Nauvoo, April 8, 1846, Leonard J. Arrington Papers, 43–54, Box 12, fd. 2, Merrill-Cazier Library, Utah State University, Logan, Utah; Church Historian's Office, History of the Church 1839–circa 1882, CR 100 102, 17, *Selected Collections*, DVD #2, also cited in Journal History, April 13, 1846, 1; Hancock County Deeds, Book P, 435–36, June 5, 1846, entry #8477, in Black, Black, and Brandon Plewe, *Property Transactions in Nauvoo*, 2878.

45. Babbitt to Young, January 31, 1848.

Joseph B. Noble/Lucy Mack Smith Home, Nauvoo, Illinois. Photograph by Kyle R. Walker, 2005.

following document . . . will show how much honesty, sincerity, or good faith, there is in Wm. Smith's pretended claims to any portion of the Church property. In the first place, he had no claim: But, to avoid any difficulty or contention, the Trustees agreed to give to his mother the property."[46] The document was signed by William, his sister Lucy, and her husband, Arthur Millikin, but not by either of the other two sisters or their husbands, and not by Lucy Mack Smith or Emma. The trustees felt that this approach was necessary to deflect claims that William would almost certainly make soon that the Church was once again neglecting the Smith family. It read:

> This is to certify, that we, the members of the Smith family, in consideration of Mother Smith have received from the Church of Jesus Christ of Latter-day Saints, a deed of conveyance of a house and lot in the city of Nauvoo, Hancock county; built and occupied by Joseph B. Noble, valued, in ordinary times, at the sum of twelve hundred dollars. We hereby in consideration of the above named and mentioned donation, and deed of conveyance, declare ourselves perfectly satisfied with the dealings of said church with Mother Smith; and freely acknowledge that the said church is hereby released from all moral and legal obligation to us or either of us. In testimony whereof, we have hereunto set our hands, this thirteenth day of April, in the year of our Lord one thousand eight hundred and forty six, at Nauvoo, Hancock county, Illinois. Wm. Smith, Arthur Millikin, Lucy Millikin.[47]

---

46. Peter Crawley, *A Descriptive Bibliography of the Mormon Church* (Provo, Utah: BYU Religious Studies Center, 1997), 354–55.

47. Ibid. The aging Lucy did not sign it, presumably because Arthur, daughter Lucy, and William were acting on her behalf.

Despite this precaution, William continued for years, in each organization with which he affiliated, to assert that the Twelve had robbed the Smith family of their rights to monies but always neglecting to mention that Church leaders had transferred the Noble home to his family.[48] To counter William's persisting accusations, a scornful Orson Hyde wrote an indignant article in the *Frontier Guardian* explaining the background, spelling out that title to the Noble home had been transferred to Lucy, and certifying that William, Arthur, and Lucy, as representatives of the family, had released "the Church from any further obligation for Mother Smith's support. . . . These are the facts of the case," challenged Hyde, "and if William does not remember the whole circumstances, we will refresh his memory."[49]

To The Public. Broadside printed by Nauvoo Trustees, 1846. Courtesy LDS Church History Library.

During the same month of March 1846 while William was battling the trustees over the property issue, he openly proselytized for Strang at Nauvoo. On March 17 he had written to Strang indicating his support, and within two months he would be appointed an apostle and patriarch in Strang's church. (See Chapter 14.) According to Orson Hyde, William "put up his advertisements" inviting all the Saints remaining in the city to attend a meeting to be held Sunday, March 22, where he would "preach in his mothers yard" in the large grove near the William Marks home where he was staying. For the appointed Sunday, he and his brother-in-law Jenkins Salisbury constructed a number of makeshift log benches in the grove while William prepared to preach from a makeshift stand. According to his niece, Mary Bailey Smith, the daughter of his dead brother Samuel, then also living in the home, William had already preached several times that month and was beginning to have some influence among the Saints who heard him. In a gossipy letter Mary wrote some sixty years later to her cousin Ina Coolbrith, daughter of Don Carlos Smith, then living in California, she recounted, "I was delighted with prospects of seeing many people together," and more especially because "William was going to preach too; how grand that did seem." It was a

---

48. William ensured that the slight was published in James J. Strang's newspaper later that summer. Lucy Smith, Letter to Messrs Babbitt, Heywood, and Hulmer [Fulmer], March 22, 1846, in *Voree Herald* 1, no. 8 (August 1846): 3. By the late 1840s, William was again recounting how his family had been neglected by Young and his colleagues as he corresponded with Lyman Wight in Texas. Lyman Wight (Zodiac Mills, Texas), Letter to William Smith, August 22, 1848, in *Melchisedic and Aaronic Herald* 1, no. 2 (March 1849): 1.

49. Hyde, "Mother Smith," 2.

child's reaction, and Mary was, in fact, only a week shy of her ninth birthday at the time. She anticipated the entertainment that the preaching would be and described how she "wandered through the grove, watched the men at work," in expectation of "the pleasure we would have on the following Sunday." However, to her dismay and disgust, when the family awoke on the appointed day, someone had smeared the benches with outhouse sewage, effectively cancelling the preaching. Probably rehearsing William's tales of victimhood, Mary remembered that "after this he [William] made no more attempts at public speaking."[50] In actuality, William preached with some success that spring in Nauvoo, his talents as a preacher coming to the fore.[51]

According to the Smith family tradition as Mary explained it, William blamed Brigham Young for the act, although he was leading the migration some fifty-five miles from Nauvoo at the time. William apparently retaliated by having an envelope containing a bullet delivered to Orson Hyde while he was preaching at the stand in Nauvoo on April 8, 1846. William denied the accusation; but if he in fact had delivered the threat (or approved the action), it rekindled his anxieties about his own safety, whether real or imagined. Four days after the incident he wrote melodramatically to James Strang, "I am cautioned, my life is threatened, and some have said that I will be a murdered man in one weeks time."[52]

Accusations reached a climax when Young and Smith accused each other of being involved in the murder of Ervine Hodges, which had occurred a year earlier during the summer of 1845. Though there is no direct evidence that either man played a role in Hodges's murder, it reveals how rumor and innuendo influenced both men's views of one another, tainting the relationship between the Twelve organizing the exodus west and the Smith family.[53] As late as 1857, William took the extreme step of accusing Young of poisoning Samuel Smith. Samuel had died

---

50. Mary B. [Smith] Norman, Letter to Ina [Smith] Coolbrith (Idaho Falls, Idaho), April 24, 1908, P13, f 955, Community of Christ Library-Archives. Isaac Paden also described this incident, recounting that he was aware of the "anointing of William Smiths stand & seats which he had fixed in his Mothers door yard[.] I spoke my mind in full to those who approbated the act in this wise they that did the act should be looked upon as below the Brute creation and those who approbated such acts were as bruitbeasts and no better than them that did the acts." Paden to Adams, April 4, 1846.

51. Just ten days after William arrived in Nauvoo, the *Warsaw Signal* reported, "Patriarch Bill Smith is, we learn, flourishing in Nauvoo. At first they prohibited him from speaking, but finally he obtained a hearing and has since been going it to his own satisfaction." "Patriarch Bill Smith," *Warsaw Signal* 2, no. 51 (March 18, 1846): 2.

52. Wm. Smith (Nauvoo, Ill.), Letter to Dear brother Strang, April 12, 1846, in *Voree Herald* 1, no. 6 (June 1846): 3.

53. Juanita Brooks, ed., *On the Mormon Frontier: The Diary of Hosea Stout, 1844–1861*, 2 vols. (Salt Lake City: University of Utah Press, 1964), 1:147; William Smith, "A Proclamation," *Warsaw Signal* 2, no. 32 (October 29, 1845): 1; Bill Shepard, "The Notorious Hodges Brothers: Solving the Mystery of Their Destruction at Nauvoo," *John Whitmer Historical Association Journal* 26 (2006): 260–86.

on July 30, 1844, at Nauvoo, just a month after Hyrum and Joseph were killed at Carthage, Illinois; but all contemporary accounts report symptoms of a fever, and possibly internal injuries, suffered after being chased between Carthage and Nauvoo on horseback on the day of his brothers' murder. William knew very well that Young was in the East with other members of the Twelve, including William himself, at the time Samuel died in Nauvoo. But such rumors circulated for years, marring the relationship between the Twelve and the Smiths in the Midwest. It was part of the larger narrative that the Twelve had robbed the Smiths of their rightful inheritance.[54] It is no surprise that Mormons in the West saw William as a rogue and a reprobate, creating a lasting impasse between Mormons who followed Brigham Young and the Smith family who remained in the Midwest.

When Smith linked his aspirations with Strang in 1846–47, Brigham Young and the Twelve were concerned about William's influence on the Smith relatives who remained in Nauvoo—basically all of Joseph Sr. and Lucy's children and grandchildren except for Hyrum's children by both Jerusha and Mary, and two of Samuel's four surviving children. Young and the Twelve seem to have been caught off guard by Strang's success in attracting the Mormons who remained behind and took steps to counter his influence. In this game of religious politics, endorsement by members of the Smith family was a powerful counter; but William's tendency to make unsubstantiated statements leaves the real feelings of Lucy and her daughters largely a matter of conjecture. Still, William boldly claimed that the whole Smith family was supporting Strang, and William published letters to that effect in Strang's newspaper.[55]

Possibly because of the disturbing effect of these rumors, in January 1847, Young recorded: "I dreamed of seeing Joseph the prophet last night and conversing with him, that Mother Smith was present and very deeply engaged reading a pamphlet, when Joseph with a great deal of dignity turned his head towards his mother partly looking over his shoulder, said, 'Have you got the word of God

---

54. Dean L. Jarman and Kyle R. Walker, "Samuel Harrison Smith," in Walker, *United by Faith*, 230–35; William Smith (Warren, Penn.), Letter to the editor, *New York Tribune* 17, no. 5025 (May 28, 1857): 5. For an example of how William's hearsay accounts were perpetuated among descendants of the Smith family, see Mary B[ailey Smith] Norman, Letter to Ina [Smith] Coolbrith, March 27, 1908, P13, f 951, Community of Christ Library-Archives.

55. William Smith, "Opinions of the Smith Family," *Voree Herald* 1, no. 6 (June 1846): 1. While this source indicated that Mother Smith, the Salisburys, and the Millikins all supported Strang, Katharine Salisbury later denied ever having signed any statement in support of Strang, making the documents William had printed in Strang's newspaper suspect. Her repudiation suggests that William apparently felt that he had the support of the remaining Smith family without having to consult them. Katharine Salisbury, Letter to Elder George Lambert, February 10, 1899, and Josephine Salisbury to Bro. George [Lambert], [February 10, 1899], P21, f92, Community of Christ Library-Archives. Katharine Salisbury, Letter to Elder George Lambert, February 10, 1899, and Josephine Salisbury to Bro. George [Lambert], [February 10, 1899], P21, f92, Community of Christ Library-Archives.

there?' Mother Smith replied, 'There is truth here.' Joseph replied, 'That may be, but I think you will be sick of that pretty soon.'"[56] Later that same month, Young heard that William and Mother Smith, along with William's daughters, were living together at Knoxville, Illinois. In a general letter to the Saints from Young and the other apostles, Young recorded, "At the last report she [Lucy] was a Strangite, but we think she will not be [for] long." He then reflected amiably, "It would rejoice our hearts if Mother Smith was with us so that we could minister to her necessities."[57]

Young hoped to persuade the Smiths to espouse the cause of the Twelve and thus help unify the Church. He also knew that Lucy's support would have influenced the rest of the family. On April 4, 1847, as Young prepared to lead the vanguard company out of Winter Quarters toward the Rocky Mountains, he took the time to write again to Mother Smith: "Beloved Mother in Israel," he began, "our thoughts, our feelings, our desires & our prayers to our Heavenly Father in the name of Jesus are often drawn out in your behalf. . . . We felt that we could not take our leave without addressing a line to Mother Smith, to let her know that her children in the Gospel have not forgotten her. . . . If our dear Mother Smith should at any time wish to come where the Saints are located & she will make it manifest to us, there is no Sacrifice we will count too great to bring her forward & we ever have been, now are and shall continue to be, ready to divide with her the last loaf."[58] But this warmth and kindness did not extend to William. He had burned too many bridges.

William's short-lived relationship with Strang ended in the spring of 1847, and he married Roxey Ann Grant, Caroline's younger sister on May 19, 1847.[59] (See Chapter 15.) Just prior to his marriage he made a rather remarkable—though brief—turnabout in his attitude toward Brigham Young and the Church. It is unknown what influence Roxey Ann may have had William's attitude, but the marriage coincided with an attempt at reconciliation. It is also possible that the relationship simply made it obvious that William's life had been a succession of disasters since 1845 and that he needed sources of stability—marital, familial, and financial. William first spoke with Reuben Miller in late March or early April 1847, while Miller was living at Burlington, Iowa Territory; and Miller afterward asserted in a letter he wrote to Brigham Young that he had "touched the main Spring of his [William's] heart." Like William, Miller had also supported

---

56. William S. Harwell, *Manuscript History of Brigham Young* (Salt Lake City: Collier's Publishing, 1997), 11.

57. The Twelve Apostles (Winter Quarters, Neb.), Letter to the Saints, January 27, 1847, in Harwell, *Manuscript History of Brigham Young*, 25.

58. Brigham Young for the Council of the Twelve (Winter Quarters, Neb.), Letter to Lucy Mack Smith, April 4, 1847, Brigham Young, Office Files 1832–1878, General Correspondence, Outgoing, 1843–1876, 1847 March-May, LDS Church History Library.

59. William Smith and Roxey Ann Grant Marriage License, Marriage Index Book 1, 84, Knox County Courthouse, Galesburg. Probate justice R. L. Hannaman, who served in that position in 1837–39, and again in 1843–49, performed the ceremony.

Strang at Voree, Wisconsin, during 1846 and, due to his disloyalty, certainly had lost some credibility with Church authorities on the trail west. In his letter, Miller claimed to have had a "confidential" conversation with William, and indicated his belief that William was willing to "climb any reasonable mountain, And give a just, frank, and Candid acknowledgment of his errors, to the people among whom he wishes a restoration and who he has injured." But it was also clear from Miller's account that William's return was contingent on his being restored to his former offices. Miller queried Young, "Taken [sic] all things into consideration, Can William return to his fomer position, and standing, in the church of God[?]"[60]

Reuben Miller, 1811–1882. Engraving by unknown artist. Courtesy LDS Church History Library.

Church leaders did not reply to Miller's letter for more than five months; and when they did, they censured Miller for thinking that a case as complex and serious as William's could be handled in such a cavalier fashion. Willard Richards, representing Church leaders' views in his letter of response, wrote, "How could you expect that any council instititued for the salvation of Israel would act upon [one] such testimony alone, in deciding such an important matter?"[61] By the time Miller finally received Richards's letter, William was already launching his own Church of Jesus Christ of Latter Days Saints.

Although William had rejected Hyde's earlier invitation to return to Nauvoo in the fall of 1845 and had disgusted Hyde by his efforts to further exploit the Church, it was to Hyde that William reached out two months after his conversation with Miller, on June 2, 1847. In a rather astonishing reversal, William wrote to Hyde, confessing his errors since 1845 and requesting reinstatement. With apparent sincerity and humility, he wrote:

> For the last two or three months, my mind has been seriously pondering over the scenes that have passed since we last met in council to deliberate on the affairs of the kingdom of God, and the many causes that have led to our separation. . . . I am made sensible, that I have done wrong on my part in leaving the church as I did, and

---

60. Reuben Miller (Burlington, Iowa Territory), to Bro [Brigham] Young, April 21, 1847, Brigham Young, Office Files 1832–1878, General Correspondence, Incoming, 1840–1877, General Letters, 1840-1877, M-P, 1847, LDS Church History Library. Reuben Miller rejoined the LDS Church on October 19, 1846, eventually migrated to Salt Lake City, where he afterward served as bishop of the Mill Creek Ward for more than thirty years.

61. Willard Richards (Platte River, 110 miles west of Fort Laramie), Letter to Reuben Miller, September 17, 1847, Willard Richards Papers, 1821–1854, MS 1490, Box 3, fd. 7, available on *Selected Collections from the Archives of the Church of Jesus Christ of Latter-day Saints.*

in carrying this warfare so far, and contrary to . . . my known duty and the dictates of my conscience. But, I must still be permitted to add, that it is not without a cause that I have felt justified in the course I had taken although to me now it is a source of much regret. . . . [T]hen perhaps again I was wrong; and therefore, done wrong, since two wrongs cannot make a right, to me it will ever be a source of regret, while I reflect upon the evil that is done, and the blessings I have lost. Now, I pray for a termination of this unhappy warfare, unhappy because I feel unhappy. . . . Tell the brethren that I am sorry, heartily sorry, and want them to forgive me in what I have done, and that I am willing to do right, and stray no longer from the fold of the good shepherd, but return to them. Will you forgive me[?] It is my desire and determination to go with them, as soon as I can get means, to fit myself for the journey. . . . As soon as circumstances will permit I am ready to attend to the requisitions of the Gospel and ordinances necessary for restoration, or, as counsel shall direct.[62]

Apparently he did not receive an answer as quickly as he wished, for three weeks later, he wrote again to Hyde reiterating his desire to gather with the Saints in the West. William added, "I hope Brother Brigham will forgiv[e] me for I have said many harsh things concerning him yet I know him to be a man of God. He shall never complain of me hereafter for I have decreed that my tongue shall no more speak evil of the ruler of my people him whom god has honer[e]d." He concluded remorsefully, "I say to all—I know that I have sinned against heaven and in the light of my brethrin and am no longer worthy to be called . . . brother but I trust in the god of Joseph and my brethrin to help me in this time of tro[u]ble."[63]

These insightful letters reveal William's recognition of his earlier mistakes and his error in not acknowledging Brigham Young's leadership. The two letters to Hyde were the most penitent he would ever write to LDS leaders and contained the most detailed recognition of his misconduct. The letters also reveal William's turmoil in acknowledging his earlier mistakes, his despondency in being separated from the Church he helped build up, and his sorrow in being estranged from his former friends and colleagues. But sandwiched between the expressions of remorse and contrition in both letters were pleas for money, an all-too-familiar refrain that must have undercut Hyde's appraisal of William's sincerity. "I would be glad to join the camp as soon as convenient," wrote William, "but I need not tell you, that we are all very destitute at present of the means sufficient for our removal to the mountains."[64] "Pleas[e] send me a written dockument [sic] that will give the Saints [in St. Louis] a right to assist me in making preparation for the [Journey] west," he reiterated in his second letter, "that I may be to work

---

62. William Smith (St. Louis, Mo.), Letter to Dear Bro. [Orson] Hyde, June 2, 1847, Brigham Young, Office Files 1832–1878, General Correspondence, Incoming, 1840–1877, Letters from Church Leaders and Others, 1840–1877, Orson Hyde, 1847–1848, LDS Church History Library.

63. William Smith (St. Louis, Mo.), Letter to Orson Hyde, June 22, 1847, Brigham Young, Office Files 1832–1878, General Correspondence, Incoming, 1840–1877, Letters from Church Leaders and Others, 1840-1877, William Smith, 1844–1857, LDS Church History Library.

64. William Smith to Hyde, June 2, 1847.

and have some means of living life."⁶⁵ As he had done in negotiating an advantageous position with Strang, William also included his mother in the bargain. While he acknowledged to Hyde that he had not yet "apprised" Mother Smith of "my present intention of going west," he added rather significantly, "but [she] will most probably go with me."⁶⁶

Already mistrustful of William's motives, Church leaders reacted strongly against his request for financial support, and Hyde put responsibility for their conflict squarely on William's shoulders. After assuring William that he "was glad to receive your letter" and "I am not your enemy," Hyde got directly to the point: "You seem to think that there have been wrongs on both sides and now wish this unhappy warfare to cease[.] But I cannot admit, neither will the Council of the 12 admit that their has been any wrong on their part or on the part of the Church in their conduct towards you[,] Neither the Shadow of Wrong," Hyde emphasized. He continued his defense of the manner in which the Church handled William's erratic behavior: "We have done our Duty towards you [and] our Garments are clean," adding, "If there is any warfare with you Your own conscience is your antagonist." Hyde further referred to William's efforts to block the sale of Church properties when he had returned to Nauvoo in 1846, indicating that his "opposition . . . hedged up our way that we could not sell property to any advantage." Hyde briskly told William to earn his own way and not expect to be supported out of Church funds. "I can recommend to you no better way to get help of a pecuniary nature then the course I took when in a condition similar to your own," wrote Hyde, meaning his estrangement during the Missouri crisis. "I Bought me a Good ax and went to chopping cord wood and put up my 2 cords per day, thus I sustained myself and family and obtained means to Gather with the Saints. And I also took some money," Hyde explained, "and Goods of the hard Earnings of my own hands as a sin offering to the authorities of the Church when I met [with] them." Hyde encouraged his fellow apostle to adopt a similar approach, explaining that "a course of this kind will prove to the church that Conscience and principle and not want have induced your return to the church."⁶⁷

Hyde also wrote to St. Louis branch president Nathaniel Felt at the same time he sent his letter to William. (Felt had queried Hyde about whether he should provide financial assistance to William.) Hyde astutely counseled Felt to wait until William went "to work with his own hand, and earn[ed] $50 or $100. Then," explained Hyde, "I could have some confidence that he was sincere in his desires to return to the Church. . . . Just so soon as he will go to work and lay up $100 by his own industry and perseverance I will give him $100 more[.]

---

65. William Smith to Hyde, June 22, 1847.
66. Ibid.,
67. Orson Hyde (Council Bluffs), Letter to William Smith, June 22, 1847, Brigham Young, Office Files 1832–1878, General Correspondence, Incoming, 1832–1877, Letters from Church Leaders and Others, 1840–1877, Orson Hyde, 1847–1848, LDS Church History Library.

But he must now help himself Before I can help him or recommend the Saints and Church abroad to do it."⁶⁸ In other words, Hyde would not send money nor would he authorize agents in St. Louis to let Smith ask the Saints to pay his way to Council Bluffs without his first earning a portion of his support. Hyde was testing William's sincerity and the depth of his remorse for his past history of financially exploiting leaders and lay members alike.

But Hyde's direct approach did not sit well with William, who never handled confrontation mildly. Although he was dramatic enough to have worked himself up to acknowledge himself in the wrong—and may, in fact, have genuinely felt repentant—it did not last. He felt insulted that Hyde had, in essence, ignored his confession and required proof of his reformation by earning his own way. William did not respond directly to Hyde, but the letter was a turning point, and both men referred to it in the ensuing years as demarcating their impasse. Three months after receiving Hyde's answer, in September 1847, William published his own interpretation of Hyde's admittedly blunt advice, apparently not realizing that most readers would probably agree with Hyde, not with him: "William, cease your whining about your martyred brothers; cease your whining about your poor old mother; cease your preaching, and go to work at some business, and get money, and join the camp in the west. Go to the camp, if you have to go on foot without money."⁶⁹ William was still fuming about what Hyde had unsympathetically written in 1847 of William needing "to go to work like an honest man and support himself by his own industry . . . cease to be idle and learn to tell the truth and to be a virtuous man."⁷⁰

Rapidly, William returned to his earlier aggressive stance and predictably retaliated. His obvious expectation of financial support and restoration to his Church offices confirmed Hyde's suspicions. He complained to the more sympathetic Lyman Wight that Hyde had "advised his brethren [at St. Louis] to shut up the bowels of compassion and charity against me, and post me to the

---

68. N[athaniel] H. Felt (St. Louis, Mo.), Letter to Orson Hyde, June 1, 1847; and Orson Hyde (Council Bluffs, Iowa), Letter to Nathaniel Felt, June 29, 1847, both in Brigham Young, Office Files 1832–1878, General Correspondence, Incoming, 1832–1877, Letters from Church Leaders and Others, 1840–1877, Orson Hyde, 1847–1848, LDS Church History Library. In his letter to Hyde, Felt wrote that "Wm Smith is now in this place [St. Louis], and has called on me and seems desirous of coming back into the Church and expresses himself willing to do all in his power to make amends for all the wrong he has done. He assured us he had been very unhappy and had done many things that were wrong when he knew they were wrong." As evidence of his sincerity, Felt recounted that William was willing to make his confession public, to the extent that he would "send circulars around to different parts of the country." William had also asked Felt for financial help in emigrating, and Felt asked Hyde if he thought it was proper "for me to baptize [William], when called upon for that purpose."

69. William Smith, *William Smith, Patriarch & Prophet of the Most High God. Latter Day Saints Beware of Imposition!* (Ottawa, Ill.: William Smith, September 1847).

70. Hyde, "Mother Smith," November 14, 1849, 2.

wilderness on foot and alone without money . . . and take to malling [mauling] rails or chopping wood."[71] Smith felt that such menial work was beneath his high station and announced: "I have therefore chosen to follow my calling instead of apostatizing and going to 'chopping wood,' . . . having a more noble work to accomplish."[72] While Smith's motive seems to have been his desire for financial support, Hyde's conditions, expressed in a tone of exasperation and combined with William's angry response, make it difficult to determine Smith's true motive. Was he merely seeking financial support and hence posing as the prodigal son; or was he sincere in his request and then offended by Hyde's stipulations?

In Hyde's *Frontier Guardian* article of November 14, 1849, in which he defended the Church leaders against accusations of neglecting the Smith family, Hyde summarized what was doubtless the perspective of his fellow apostles on William's request for reinstatement. Scornfully, he wrote that William "has made some two or three applications to us since we have been at the [Council] Bluffs to come back to the Church; . . . but the idea of labor with his own hands for [his] support, which was every where interwoven [as] a condition of his return, was so opposed to every feeling of his nature, that he cries 'Sour grapes—wicked Brighamites—apostates—oppressors of the Smith family—usurpers of power,' &c." The fact of the matter was that Church leaders did not trust William. Hyde had been in a position to observe William's erratic trajectory through several Mormon groups during 1845–47 and was justly exasperated about William's continued claims that the Church neglected Mother Smith and the family. Hyde had firsthand knowledge of the transaction of deeding Mother Smith the Noble home. He had William's signature and that of the Millikins on a document acknowledging that the trustees had acted fairly toward the family and did not hesitate to put these facts in print. Hyde phrased William's complaint sarcastically: "[Now,] when Mother Smith wants a support, then the Brighamites are oppressors if they will not support her. Shame on a man, in the prime of life, that will whine because somebody else will not support his mother!"[73]

Yet William did not seem to have learned much from this lesson. On at least five occasions during 1847–60, counting the letters to Brigham Young and Hyde, when William hit rock bottom, he turned to LDS leaders, seeking recognition and financial support. It seems to have surprised and offended him each time to be greeted with measured conditions and even suspicion. Those who knew William best, including Brigham Young and Orson Hyde, did not hasten to embrace his announcements of repentance, consistently setting up another emotional explosion from William over what he perceived as rejection and leading to a new round of tirades against the Church. It was a pattern that had no possibility of producing fruitful results.

---

71. William Smith to Lyman Wight, April 21, 1849.
72. Ibid.
73. Orson Hyde, "Mother Smith," 2,

During his attempts to organize his own Church of Jesus Christ of Latter Day Saints in 1847–53, William expended great efforts to denounce the Church in the West, often dedicating a significant segment of Isaac Sheen's *Melchisedek* [sic] *and Aaronic Herald,* to that end. He made no effort to restrain his disdain for Brigham Young's followers as he sparred in 1849–50 with Hyde in their respective newspapers. When the state of Deseret was making its first petitions for statehood, Smith and Sheen penned several lengthy letters to Congress, attempting to discredit Church leaders in the West. Reiterating accusations from his 1845 "Proclamation," Smith charged Salt Lake Mormons with treason, counterfeiting, and murder. These letters were read during the committee hearings on Deseret's petition and may have influenced the negative decision. (See Chapter 16.)[74] After Sheen discovered William's support of polygamy, Sheen followed up with an apologetic letter, concluding, "I find that his [Smith's] accusations against the Deseret Mormons are the ebullitions of a malicious heart, and have been made by him to divert attention from his own outrageous villainy and licentiousness. I have been credibly informed that to the memorial which William Smith sent from Illinois he attached the names of persons who never authorized him to do so."[75] Hyde printed Sheen's letter but took the occasion to rebuke him, reminding Sheen that he had "recognized this scoundrel [William] as your brother," and as "President Smith," "when he was lying against the church and slandering it."[76]

Once his own organization unraveled in the early 1850s, William again turned to the LDS Church for validation. However, by the time William petitioned Young for reinstatement in the mid-1850s, he had lost all credibility. Leaders in the West questioned Smith's sincerity and distrusted his motives. Each year, from 1854 to

---

74. William Smith, "A Proclamation," 1, 4; William Smith and Isaac Sheen (Covington, Ky.), Letter to the House of Representatives of the United States of America, December 31, 1849, House Miscellaneous Documents, 31st Congress, 1st Session, Document No. 43; William Smith and Isaac Sheen (Covington, Ky.), Letter to President Zachary Taylor, January 1, 1850, National Archives; and William Smith et. al., (Shelburn [Palestine Grove], Ill.), Letter to the Honorable Senators & Representative of the United States in Congress Assembled, January 29, 1850; William Smith, (Shelburn [Palestine Grove], Ill.), Letter to the Hon. John Wentworth, January 25, 1850; and John M. Bernhisel (Washington, D.C.), Letter to Brigham Young, March 21 1850, all in Brigham Young, Office Files 1832–1878, Utah Delegate Files, 1849–1872, John M. Bernhisel to Brigham Young, 1849–1866, 1849–1850 March-May, LDS Church History Library. Historian Eugene Campbell indicated that "the church's application for statehood was doomed to defeat," regardless of Smith and Sheen's petition. According to Campbell, this was due to Deseret's large geographical size (nearly one sixth the size of the United States) and its limited population (far short of the 60,000 people required by the Northwest Ordinance for statehood). Eugene E. Campbell, *Establishing Zion: The Mormon Church in the American West, 1847–1869* (Salt Lake City: Signature Books, 1988), 205.

75. Isaac Sheen (Covington, Ky.), Letter to Hon. R. H. Stanton, May 4, 1850, in *Frontier Guardian* 2, no. 11 (June 26, 1850): 3.

76. Orson Hyde, "Bill Smith," *Frontier Guardian* 2, no. 11 (June 26, 1850): 3.

1856, William wrote to Brigham Young attempting to resolve their former rift, though the letters did not communicate the same level of contrition as his 1847 letters to Hyde. Writing from Peoria County, Illinois, on August 8, 1854, William addressed his letter to the "Honorable Brigham Young, President of the Church & Council." "It is not my porpos in writing these few linnes to provoke controverse nor to envite reproche," began William, "as I have alrady experianced quite enough of such things in the . . . events and changes of the last ten years." While William once again acknowledged Young as president of the Church in the letter, most of what he wrote rehashed his view that he should be recognized as an apostle and as the patriarch to the Church. In reference to these callings but also revealing something of his personality, William declared: "One thing is certain[,] I shall never submit willingly to suffer the disgrace of a wrong. . . . Nor am I willing to relinquish claims that Justly belongs to me in the Church and the kingdom of God. Such a sacrifice would be dearer to me than life itself." Still, he hoped that a resolution might be realized. "As you may well supose," recounted William of their conflict, "the warfair has progressed [and] accusation has been the principle material of the war. True or false—causes—real or imaginary—have had to do with the matter on boath sid[e]s of the question [and] the affects also have been the same wheather for better or worse[,] for good or for evil. Such then has been the state of affairs growing out of a misunderstanding as well also as a misaprehension of this small affair which at the first could have all been settled by a word from the proper source and saved all this world of confusion." He besought Young "to look into this matter and see if a reconciliation or a settlement of our long standing difficulty can be had upon honorable principles in regard to all parties concerned." William signed his letter "Apostle and Patriarch of the Church of Jesus Christ of Latter day Saints," which would not have set well with Young, since William was petitioning Young for reinstatement to these offices.[77]

Brigham Young, 1801–1877). Daguerreotype by Marsena Cannon, ca. 1850. Courtesy LDS Church History Library.

There is no indication that Young responded to William's letter, as he probably did not have any particular reason to do so. Neither man had changed his views in any substantial way in the intervening decade; and William's virulent

---

77. William Smith (South Hampton, Ill.), Letter to Brigham Young, August 8, 1854, Brigham Young, Office Files 1832–1878, General Correspondence, Incoming, 1840–1877, Letters from Church Leaders and Others, 1840–1877, William Smith, 1844–1857, LDS Church History Library.

public attacks in 1850 only widened the chasm between them. William wrote to Young again eight months later, on May 7, 1855, his tone even more hostile, reiterating his view that he had been "robbed of my Apostleship [when] I accepted of the Patriarchal office." Probably because he was being restricted in his influence during the summer of 1845, including being excluded from important decision-making meetings, Smith felt that he had been curtailed as an apostle—"an office that I legitimately held from under the hands of Joseph." William demanded, as conditions of his coming to Utah, that the Twelve recognize these offices and also make the public aware of his unfair treatment. "Brother Brigham I want you to deel honorable with me and Just say to the Saints and [to] the world—that as to this office of the Apostle Ship I have a just claim and when this is done No man in all the Mormon rankes would be more willing to do you and the Church of god honorable justice than myself." In this letter, William returned to the fall of 1845 when he had fled from Nauvoo after his friends Hiram Stratton and Jenkins Salisbury told him that his life was in danger. William acknowledged for the first time that Stratton and Salisbury might have deceived him about the danger but claimed that the "fears" and "excitement" this warning produced "almost deranged my senses."[78] While William was unquestionably apprehensive about his safety during those final weeks in Nauvoo, attributing his apostasy to a frenzied emotional state was simply insufficient. It may have explained his flight but not his earlier behavior among the eastern branches and certainly not the zigzag course his life had taken since the fall of 1845. Brigham Young, like Orson Hyde, undoubtedly saw this half-hearted attempt at taking responsibility for his apostasy as an unsatisfactory confession.

In February 1849, about a year and a half after William and Orson had exchanged their unsatisfactory correspondence, Hyde had again used his newspaper to expose William's activities and his own dim view of them. He had pointed out ironically: "As bad as he [William] represents the church to be, he has written two or three letters to us, confessing a part of his sins, and desiring to get back into this '*wicked and abominable church*:' but the church would not receive his confession, and consequently would not receive him. He would confess many things that he was not guilty of," summarized Hyde, "but the church required him to confess fully the things that he was guilty of."[79]

In his 1855 letter to Young, and after receiving no response, William again strongly hinted that he needed cash: "On account of my impoverished Sircomstances I shall defer my visit to the [Salt Lake] vall[e]y until next spring." Such references to his poverty certainly would have been a bitter reminder of how

---

78. William Smith (Springfield, Ill.), Letter to Brigham Young, May 7, 1855, Brigham Young, Office Files 1832–1878, General Correspondence, Incoming, 1840–1877, Letters from Church Leaders and Others, 1840–1877, William Smith, 1844–1857, LDS Church History Library.

79. Orson Hyde, "We Have Just Read . . . ," *Frontier Guardian*, 1, no. 1 (February 7, 1849): 2; emphasis Hyde's.

William had used his Church and family connections to benefit financially for most of his adult life. Nor did William sweeten this demand by concluding with his well-worn list of grievances: "I have rights Brother Brigham, and I want them and it is in regard to my Apostleship[.] Now deal just[ly] with me upon this matter and I am your man and true hearted friend and Brother until death."[80] Such stipulations, presented in a demanding tone, did nothing to foster his reconciliation with leaders in Salt Lake City. Whatever benefit the Twelve may have seen by having William publicly enlisted in their cause had dwindled and disappeared.

Lacking the personal insight to realize how Young and other leaders perceived him, William felt ignored and unwanted when Young again did not respond. In his third and final letter to Young, written a year later on July 13, 1856. Smith wrote, this time plaintively: "Brigham I thought once to get up a correspondance with you but this I see you refuse to do for reasons best known to yourself. I have now given up all hopes of ever seeing you or that Salt Lake Cuntry." William reported to Young about hearing a rumor that his brother-in-law George D. Grant had said, "William Smith would not live one hour were he to come to Salt Lake." It could have been an exaggeration or a downright fabrication; but assuming that it was accurate, William interpreted it as a threat from Church leaders. It could just as easily have been the Grant brothers' anger at William's unauthorized polygamy—which amounted to adultery in their eyes—while he was married to Caroline and his neglect and refusal to provide a stable home for their second sister, Roxey Ann, during their marriage. But death threats fit William's perception of Church leaders in the West, who had wrested his Church offices from him and usurped governance of the Mormon kingdom away from the Smith family. William concluded his letter to Young on a fiery note: "If god Almighty do[e]s not judge a hoast of you for your damnable deeds and send you to hell, then there is no use for a devle, you and your gang about you hav[e] treated me <u>real</u> mean."[81] It was the last line he ever wrote directly to Brigham Young.

At this point, William went to Warren, Pennsylvania, crossing over the state line to Kirtland, Ohio, in a brief, but unsuccessful, attempt to form an organization with Martin Harris. William had married Eliza Sanborn in 1857 after he and Martin Harris parted ways, by 1858, he had engaged in several fruitless professional pursuits. However, in April 1860, the "New Organization" that had been coalescing around Zenas Gurley and Jason W. Briggs had its hopes fulfilled when Joseph III and his mother attended the conference and Joseph, responding to spiritual confirmation, accepted leadership in the group that became the Reorganized Church of Jesus Christ of Latter Day Saints (now Community of Christ). For reasons that have not been preserved, in May, William set aside his differences with

---

80. William Smith to Young, May 7, 1855.

81. William Smith (Turkey River, Iowa), Letter to Brigham Young, July 13, 1856, Brigham Young, Office Files 1832–1878, General Correspondence, Incoming, 1840–1877, Letters from Church Leaders and Others, 1840–1877, William Smith, 1844–1857, LDS Church History Library.

Mormonism long enough to be rebaptized as a member of the LDS Church by an Elder J. J. Butler, an LDS missionary laboring in Erie, Pennsylvania. On May 14, future LDS Apostle Albert Carrington came in to Brigham Young's office in Salt Lake City, "and read a letter from Wm. Smith bro. of the Prophet in which he desired to come . . . to the valley and be restored to his former associations, he stated he had been rebaptised." In the same mail was "another letter . . . from J. J. Butler stating he had baptized Wm Smith, and that his course had been to sustain the authorities of this Church."[82] It appears that Butler acted on his own volition in rebaptizing Smith, as there is no record that the leaders in Salt Lake City expected this development, nor does Butler mention whether William's wife, Eliza, or any of her children old enough for baptism had accepted that ordinance. Once again, at least part of William's motivation may have been financial. Brigham Young's office journal contains a report in mid-March 1860 from an unidentified informant that William "was so poor that he could not provide a morsel of food for his family."[83] Given William's history, it seems reasonable that he was hoping for financial assistance in moving him and his family to Utah. Such assistance was not, however, forthcoming; and his rebaptism evidenced his persisting, albeit vacillating, desire to be reunited with his former brethren.

Predictably, it did not last long and he turned hopefully toward his nephew, Joseph III. The first of his many letters to this new Church leader rehearsed his frustrations toward Young for his neglect and exploitation of the Smith family. "I wrote to him [Brigham] to remunerate me for some of the losses I had sustained [during] the break-up of the Church," wrote William only two months after being rebaptized a Mormon, "and you can see how willing the man is to get influence from the Smith family." Joseph III had no reason to like or trust Brigham Young, and the two were now in direct competition over which church was the true successor of Joseph Smith Jr.'s movement, but Joseph III was also prudent enough to see that William was both a liability and an advantage. The RLDS Church was poor. Joseph III supported his growing family as editor of the Church's magazine, the *True Latter Day Saints' Herald*, and thus did not attempt to subsidize William nor offer him office as either an apostle and/or patriarch. Nor did he invite William to join him at Church headquarters, first, Plano, Illinois, and later Lamoni, Iowa, and still later, Independence, Missouri. Instead Joseph kept William at a judicious distance over the remaining years of William's life. He expressed sympathy and emotional support, however, and was quick to publish a portion of William's letter complaining about the LDS Church.[84]

---

82. Brigham Young, Office Journal, May 14, 1860, CR 1234 1, Box 72, fd.5, LDS Church History Library; Paul M. Edwards, "William B. Smith: The Persistent Pretender," *Dialogue: A Journal of Mormon Thought* 18 (Summer 1985): 131–32.

83. Brigham Young, Office Journal, March 17, 1860.

84. "Wm. Smith's Contradiction of a Utah Rumor," *True Latter Day Saints' Herald* 7, no. 1 (July 1860): 172. The rumor alluded to is not known, but the article said that Wm.

Whatever plans William may have made to relocate to Salt Lake City dissolved under his continued poverty and the indifference he perceived from leaders in Salt Lake City. In 1857, in summarizing the history of the Smith family while speaking to the Saints at Salt Lake City in a Sunday sermon, George A. Smith recapitulated the feelings of the Saints in the West toward William when he lamented: "The Saints could have carried William upon their shoulders; they could have carried him in their arms, and have done anything for him, if he would have laid aside his follies and wickedness, and would have done right." Acknowledging their shared family connection, George A. concluded: "For a man to have good blood in his veins, and then to go and disgrace that blood, is perhaps [a] double responsibility."[85]

In the latter part of 1860, William and Eliza moved to Elkader, Iowa, where William tried his hand again at farming and, in February 1864, enlisted for a brief term of service as a Union soldier. During these years, William kept a low profile about his ties to Mormonism.

Though William was most often hostile in public statements about "Brighamites," his periodic in-person interactions with LDS missionaries were surprisingly positive. One of the earliest of these was in 1848, when Smith was beginning to organize his church at Palestine Grove and encountered thirty-five-year-old George W. Bratton when he was preaching in Ottawa, Illinois. Bratton, just one year William's junior, had grown up in Erie, Pennsylvania, and was living in the county when William and Hyrum Smith had been missionaries in the area in 1832–33.[86] The unexpected meeting of the two men in Ottawa in 1848 apparently led to several conversations that must have been congenial enough to convince Bratton that Smith would come back into the fold with the right approach. Bratton wrote to Brigham Young, "Now let me intercede for him [Smith], if it is yet posible— Let Br. Jed[ediah] or George Grant Come into Palestine grove, where he Resides with 20 or 30 fol[lowers], Com[e] Authorized with terms for Wm.[,] but go to him first [and] be particular in persuading his wife [Roxey Ann,] then preach to his followers in mildness and Wm and all is Caught." Bratton did not feel authorized to carry out such a course of action and reported that he had been "Counciled to let him Alone" by some Church leader in the region, perhaps Erastus Snow in St. Louis or Orson Hyde at Council Bluffs. Still, he felt this approach would prove effective and suggested the Grant brothers for this mission. Bratton warmly concluded, in his letter to Young, to give Smith "all

---

included a slip of paper—perhaps some story about William from a Utah source—that William described as "Brigham is making use of my influence against you."

85. George A. Smith, August 2, 1857, *Journal of Discourses*, 5:102.

86. Bratton did not join the Church until January 21, 1846, but had lived in Nauvoo since 1841, laboring as a woodworker on the interior of the Nauvoo Temple. Chaundelle Hill Brough, comp., "History of George Washington Bratton," July 2004, https://familysearch.org/photos/stories/1703275/history-of-george-washington-bratton (accessed December 30, 2013).

the clemency you can."[87] Brigham Young had other pressing priorities in 1848; and by 1849–50, after William's clashes with Orson Hyde, he probably seemed a less likely candidate to be wooed back into the fold.

Thomas Colburn, a fifty-four-year-old LDS missionary from Utah, was given the assignment in 1855 to "hunt up the lost sheep" in the northern and eastern states, "and endeavor to gather them into the fold." When he and his missionary companion W. W. Rust, stopped at Springfield, Illinois, to visit a member of the Church, they were surprised to meet William Smith living with a Latter-day Saint named Jonathan Palmer and even more surprised by his friendly welcome. As Colburn related in a letter published in the Mormon newspaper in St. Louis, Smith "grasped me by the hand, [and] said it done him good to take an old Mormon by the hand." Colburn asked what he was doing in Springfield, and Smith replied that "he was preaching the first principles of the Gospel," but when Colburn pressed him further, inquiring if he preached the gathering and acknowledged the authorities in Utah, "his reply was rather evasive, said he and the authorities had had some misunderstanding, the same as Peter and Paul, that he had [recently] written to President Young, saying he was willing to abide his decision." As the missionaries prepared to leave, Colburn said Smith "wished me to give him the hand of fellowship." Colburn replied that "under existing circumstances I could not, and advised him, if he was honest hearted, as he appeared to be, he had better repair immediately to the vallies of the mountains and report himself, and abide the decision of the First Presidency."[88]

About four weeks later when Colburn was returning to Utah, he again stopped in Springfield and had a long visit with Smith about his religious views. This encounter was less cordial, and Smith was initially "displeased to see a brace of Salt Lake Mormons. . . . He had been laboring with might and main to poison the minds of all as far as his influence extends against the authorities of the church of Christ in Utah." Predictably, Smith launched into his narrative of persecution, claiming that the Brighamites had "shamefully treated, persecuted and abused' [him] . . . through misrepresentation, and a lack of knowledge concerning him." Colburn's reaction was a combination of compassion and straightforward counsel, with the result that William finally "said he was willing to submit his case to, and abide the decision of Pres. Brigham Young, provided he could retain his Apostleship, if so he was willing to be a Brighamite and be numbered as one of the Salt Lake Mormons."[89] Colburn must have influenced William to consider reconciliation with authorities in Salt Lake City, because after their initial visit

---

87. Geo[rge] W. Bratton (Ottawa, Ill.), Letter to Brigham Young, February 26, 1848, Brigham Young, Office Files 1832–1878, General Correspondence, Incoming, 1840–1877, General Letters, 1840–1877, A-C, 1848, LDS Church History Library.

88. Thomas Colburn, Letter on May 2, 1855, to Elder [Erastus] Snow, Editor, in *St. Louis Luminary* 1, no. 24 (May 5, 1855): 2.

89. Thomas Colburn, Letter to the editor, May 31, 1855, *St. Louis Luminary* 1, no. 28 (June 2, 1855): 3.

William composed a letter to Brigham Young on May 7, 1855, and Colburn personally carried Smith's handwritten letter with him to Salt Lake City to deliver to Young—the second letter William wrote to Brigham Young in the mid-1850s.[90] As with William's first letter, Young did not answer.

Besides his baptism in 1860 by J. J. Butler, this 1855 encounter was almost William's last meeting with an LDS missionary. In the fall of 1880 when William was sixty-nine, twenty-three-year-old British convert B. H. Roberts, a future member of the First Council of the Seventy, and his twenty-one-year-old missionary companion Hyrum Jensen, visited William in Elkader, Iowa. (See Chapter 1.) Eliza Sanborn Smith, mistaking them for RLDS missionaries, first greeted the missionaries warmly. When she learned her mistake, the "atmosphere became frigid, especially on the part of Mrs. Smith. She was vehement in her expression of her opposition to us in very uncomplimentary, not to say insulting, attacks upon our people in Utah." Eliza had apparently accepted William's tales of mistreatment by LDS Church leaders unquestioningly. Only after Roberts assured Eliza that they had not come with the "vain hope to convert him [William] to Mormonism, ... but merely wanted to see him as a brother of the prophet and make some inquiries of him," did she finally relent and invite them into the home. William also intervened with his wife, "express[ing] a desire for such a visit."[91]

Although the missionaries expected William to react with animosity similar to Eliza's, his reception of the two itinerant elders turned out to be the complete opposite. He treated them as brothers of the same faith and was astonishingly affable and compassionate. He invited them to eat with him and Eliza and then to stay the night. "After the table was cleared," recorded Roberts of the memorable evening, "William Smith with us sat about the table in an interesting and animated conversation. William Smith disclosed some photographs and manuscript papers, which were of great interest to us. At that time we were not very well informed as to the Nauvoo period history of the church, and William had his own way in the explanations that he gave of his difficulties in Nauvoo. Never before had we seen copies of the *Times and Seasons*, several of which William had." The elders were engrossed by William's accounts of these early events of Church history and were equally impressed by his physical stature and features, which made a lasting impression on Roberts. Roberts noted in his journal, that William "expressed at this table conversation complete faith in the divine calling of his brother and the ultimate triumph of the work he had introduced in the world."[92]

Later that night William directed them to a bed in an upstairs room. The next morning "we were awakened . . . by the rising of William Smith from an opposite corner of the room where he had slept upon a palate [sic] improvised from some

---

90. William Smith to Young, May 7, 1855.

91. Gary James Bergera, ed., *The Autobiography of B. H. Roberts* (Salt Lake City: Signature Books, 1990), 103.

92. Ibid., 104.

B. H. Roberts, 1857–1933. Photograph taken ca. 1880, photographer unknown. Carte de visite in author's possession.

miscellaneous clothes. He had surrendered his own bed to us, and I felt like severely reproaching myself for having taken the man's bed." After feeding the missionaries breakfast, William walked them into town, and, since Eliza had evidently not thawed as far as welcoming them, wrote a letter of introduction to a neighbor, a well-to-do farmer named Robinson," urging him to provide the missionaries with hospitality while they were in the area. According to Roberts, "It was a most feeling and pleading letter in maintenance of his chief proposition to the entertainment of Elder Jensen and me." As he led the missionaries to the outskirts of town and said goodbye, William gave each of them a "clinging warm clasp of his hand."[93] The young elders were bemused by these acts of exceptional kindness, especially when nearly everything they knew about him was that he had been determinedly hostile toward their denomination. Perhaps time had softened his understanding of their differences.

After Smith's separation from the Church at Nauvoo at a period when loyalty was most desired and needed, leaders of the LDS Church never trusted William again after he rebuffed Orson Hyde's invitation in 1845. They never offered him what he most earnestly desired—the restoration of his former ordinations as an apostle and as patriarch to the Church—nor would they meet his expectation of financial support. Although he made a few gestures toward reconciliation, he remained outwardly hostile toward Brigham Young and the Church in Utah, seizing moments of public interest to issue sensational statements about their hostility to the U.S. government, their "invention" of polygamy, and, above all and repeatedly, their robbing the Smith family of its rightful inheritance.[94] Church leaders in the Salt Lake Valley denounced him and rejected his claims in the 1850s when his accusations became part of the general national opprobrium the Mormons faced during the Utah Expedition.[95] Young's denunciation of William was most vehemently expressed after Orson Pratt had, with Lucy's permission, published her family memoir in 1853, focused on the sufferings and sacrifices of the Smith family in establishing the Church of Jesus Christ of Latter-day Saints. In 1865, Brigham ordered the destruction of her book, calling it a "tissue of lies" and apparently

---

93. Ibid., 104–5.

94. William Smith, "Proclamation," 1, 4; "Bill Smith," *Daily Commercial Register* (Sandusky, Ohio) 4, no. 304 (May 23, 1855): 2; William Smith (Warren, Penn.), Letter to the *New York Tribune* 17, no. 5025 (May 28, 1857), 5.

95. Brigham Young, June 7, 1857, *Journal of Discourses*, 4:345; George A. Smith, August 2, 1857, *Journal of Discourses*, 5:102.

taking particular umbrage at its relatively few but positive references to William.[96] Yet during at least three encounters with LDS missionaries, William responded cordially in face-to-face interactions. He eventually looked to the RLDS Church for validation which, though not fully satisfying, was still less prickly as his expectations and his physical energies slowly waned during old age. (See Chapter 20.)

Two of William's children later joined the LDS Church. Thalia, William's daughter by Roxey Ann, remained with her mother in the Midwest, living in Lathrop, Missouri. After a lengthy correspondence with her first cousin and LDS Church President Heber J. Grant, she was baptized by Grant on April 26, 1924, and died seven months later at age seventy-six.[97]

William's youngest son by Eliza, Edson Don Carlos Smith, was also baptized a member of the Church of Jesus Christ of Latter-day Saints on February 13, 1931, in Tacoma, Washington. At the age of thirty, he had been baptized a member of the RLDS Church and had accepted Joseph III's firm position that plural marriage had been invented by Brigham Young and the Twelve, even serving as an RLDS branch president in Wisconsin. But after confronting the evidence that his uncles—and his own father—had been polygamists in Nauvoo, presented to him by an RLDS member of the Seventy, T. W. Chatburn, Edson became "skeptical." Chatburn told Edson that "the revelation on plural mar-

---

96. Lavina Fielding Anderson, ed., *Lucy's Book: A Critical Edition of Lucy Mack Smith's Family Memoir* (Salt Lake City: Signature Books, 2001), 100–113. At a meeting with Brigham Young in February 1859, Wilford Woodruff recorded that Young expressed his desire that LDS historians should "revise" and "correct" Lucy's book. Young indicated on that occasion, one of his foremost objections to the publication was "that book makes out William Smith according to Mother Smith's statement to be full of the Holy Ghost & the power of God." According to Wilford Woodruff, who recorded Young's sentiments on the occasion, "Young said Wm. Smith is the most wicked man I ever saw in my life," citing William's outburst in Missouri toward his brother Joseph, and the role he had played in the construction of Young's carriage in Nauvoo as examples. Kenney, *Wilford Woodruff's Journal*, 5:287–88.

97. After learning of Thalia's conversion, Grant wrote, "I rejoice beyond my power to tell you that you have arrived at the point where you believe in the Book of Mormon [as] an inspired work. Surely, if the Book of Mormon is an inspired work, Joseph Smith was indeed a prophet of the living God, and the Gospel of the Lord Jesus Christ as proclaimed by Joseph Smith and his successors—Brigham Young and others—is in very deed the plan of life and salvation." Heber J. Grant, Letter to My dear Cousin Thalia [Smith], August 21, 1923 (Salt Lake City), in Heber J. Grant Letters, MS 1234, Box 21, fd. 2, 96–97, LDS Church History Library. On April 26, 1924, Heber J. Grant baptized and confirmed Thalia a member of the LDS Church in Independence, Missouri. Record of Members Collection, Missouri, Central States Mission, 1904–, 552–53, Reel 4269, CR 375 8, LDS Church History Library; Heber J. Grant, *The Diaries of Heber J. Grant, 1880–1945 Abridged* (Salt Lake City: Privately Published, 2010), 327. Thalia died on November 27, 1924; and despite his busy schedule, Grant traveled to Independence to attend her funeral. *Ninety-Fifth Annual Conference of the Church of Jesus Christ of Latter day Saints, April 4, 5 and 6, 1925* (Salt Lake City: Church of Jesus Christ of Latter-day Saints, 1925), 6.

Edson Don Carlos Smith, 1862–1939, with his third wife, Hannah Christine Hansen, 1863–1940. The couple, pictured here dressed in white, worked in the Salt Lake Temple in Salt Lake City, Utah. Photograph taken ca. 1930s, photographer unknown. Courtesy of Gracia Jones.

riage was first received by Joseph the Prophet and that he practiced polygamy, also Hyrum and my father [William]." Edson was at first unconvinced, as he indicated that "my father [William] taught me differently," but after Chatburn indicated that this is "well known by the present leaders of the [RLDS] church," Edson ended up leaving the faith. His baptism into the LDS Church was the culmination of some thirty years of searching, and he indicated that he experienced a miraculous healing of his knee at the time of his baptism. In an attempt to make sense of his father's life, Edson affirmed: "Now as to my father, I have this to say, he was a good, kind father and I loved him very much and still do. But he surely made a mistake when he abandoned his calling as an apostle of the first Quorum of the Twelve and his patriarchal office as the patriarch of the Church and refused the leadership of Brigham Young."

Shortly thereafter, Edson made sure that he performed vicarious temple ordinances for his father. In recounting his father's story for an LDS audience, he queried: "Why ponder over [the] . . . mistake[s] of my father? I have seen to it that he has been reinstated into the true Church and the true work of God and have received from him from the spirit world that he is satisfied and pleased with his reinstatement. This represents the temple work I have done for him now. Let God be true regardless of the mistakes of men."[98]

---

98. "Baptism Heals: Nephew of Prophet Joseph Smith Relates Experience," *Deseret News*, January 9, 1932, 6; "Episodes in Genealogical Research: New Light on William Smith," *Deseret News*, July 27, 1935, 7.

Chapter 20

The "Josephites"

> We had the benefit of [William's] experience, testimony, and wisdom, and were pleased to have what prestige his name and former associations brought to us.
>
> —Joseph Smith III

William, who had turned thirty-three three months before his brothers' murders in June 1844, had positioned himself solidly with his colleagues of the Twelve. In a letter to Brigham Young on August 24, 1844, William affirmed his belief that, with Joseph's death,

> the 12 come next . . . as presiding officers & govern the Church in all things temporaly & Spiritualy recieving revalation from Joseph as the ancient Apostles did from Christ through the president of the Corum [Quorum] for the instruction & government of the Church. This will constitute a proper head & keep confusion & disorder out the Church. the President bein[g] supported by the prayr & united faith of the rest of the 12. . . . This duty than involves [devolves] upon you Brother Young as head & revelator to receive revelations from Joseph for the government of the Church."[1]

However, William was not only an apostle but, given Hyrum's death, was soon appointed Church patriarch, a hereditary position which Hyrum had assumed upon Joseph Sr.'s death, due both to his father's bestowal of the office and by revelation to Joseph. (Hyrum was also assistant Church president, a little-understood office that would create confusion later as William and Brigham tangled over jurisdictional issues.) In the same letter to Young, William asked that leaders at Nauvoo "remember me & my clames in the Smith family,"—a reference to his desire that he be formally appointed as the presiding patriarch. William acknowledged in his letter to Young that the office of Church patriarch was to be governed by the Twelve, and he carefully explained his understanding of the calling. The patriarch was a "father to the whole Church." He continued: "A Patriarch can be a prophet & revelator, not to the Church as government but to the church as his children in Patriarchal blessings upon their heads in prophecing teaching & fartherly care &c."[2] Young wrote to Smith the following month, indicating that he was "happy to inform you that your mind is precisely the same

---

1. William Smith, (Bordentown, N.J.) Letter to Brigham Young, August 24, 1844, LDS Church History Library. In quotations from holograph documents, I have added terminal punctuation and initial capitals for clarification.
2. Ibid.

as my brethren the Twelve," and that "the right [of the Patriarchal office] rests upon your head."[3]

Yet as early as May 1845, William was at least entertaining the notion that Joseph Smith III might succeed his father as Prophet and President.[4] He also sought to expand the authority of the presiding patriarch beyond what he had outlined in his earlier letter to Young. By the end of that same summer, after months of sparring with his colleagues of the Twelve over the scope of his own authority, William began to promote lineal succession in his communications. Intriguingly, even at this early date, he vacillated between promoting his own right to preside over the Church and the right of his nephew, young Joseph.[5]

How had William's views on succession shifted so dramatically in the course of one year? The answer lay in William's perception that he was steadily being distanced from his apostolic office and being relegated to the lesser role as presiding patriarch, which had little governing authority and which was supervised by the Twelve. These perceptions prevented him from seeing how his own misconduct had led the Twelve to restrict his influence after he returned to Nauvoo. William came to perceive it as a conspiracy hatched by the Twelve to curtail his influence in the Church and to appropriate Joseph Smith's accumulated wealth to their own emolument. His fragile self-image and inability to acknowledge his mistakes prevented him from considering an alternative view. These characteristics, combined with his personal ambition, led him on a different course—that of promoting Smith family rights. His subsequent history reveals that, while William had been imbued with a sense of specialness about being a Smith, his belief that he or his nephew should lead the Church surfaced only after he perceived the diminishing of his own role in the Church. Almost at once, he became an opportunist, desperately searching for an exalted station among any faction of Mormonism that would support his own self-importance. He was clearly retaliating against

---

3. Brigham Young (Nauvoo, Ill.), Letter to Beloved Br. William [Smith], September 28, 1844, LDS Church History Library.

4. On May 23, 1845, William Clayton recorded in his journal that "William Smith is coming out in opposition to the Twelve and in favor of [George J.] Adams. The latter has organized a church at Augusta, Iowa Territory with young Joseph Smith for President, Wm Smith for Patriarch." George D. Smith, ed., *An Intimate Chronicle: The Journals of William Clayton* (Salt Lake City: Signature Books, 1991), 166.

5. Journal History, June 28, 1845, 1. On August 20, 1845, William wrote to Jesse C. Little, his former eastern colleague: "Emma is well and also little Joseph his fathers successor although some people would fain make us believe that the Twelve are to be the perpetual heads of this church to the exclusion of the Smith family, but every one who has read the book of Doctrine and Covenants must be aware that Priesthood authority is hereditary and descends from Father to son and therefore Josephs oldest son will take his place when he arrives at the age of maturity." William Smith (Nauvoo, Ill.), Letter to Jesse C. Little, August 20, 1845, typescript by Ireta Anderson, Utah State Historical Society, Salt Lake City.

the Twelve as his enemies by wresting power from them and heightening his own reputation, which was waning among the Saints at Nauvoo.

After fleeing from Nauvoo in mid-September 1845, William first affiliated with George J. Adams, who had earlier advocated Smith family rights, and William subsequently promoted his twelve-year-old nephew's future leadership while attempting to gather adherents in St. Louis and Cincinnati in 1845–46.[6] William used his nephew's name to help strengthen his own right to power, though he did so without young Joseph's participation or consent. Those in the Twelve saw William as using Joseph III's family position to strengthen his own position. Evidence that William was indeed pumping up his own authority by using his nephew's name came when William linked his ambition with James J. Strang during 1846–47. (See Chapter 14.) During that time he completely shelved the idea of his own or his nephew's right to the presidency in favor of Strang, as long as Strang elevated William to a prominent office within his movement.

Once William broke with Strang in May 1847 and revived his efforts at church-building, he also revived the idea of lineal succession. In August 1847 he launched his own "Church of Jesus Christ of Latter Day Saints" and, without the permission of Emma Hale Smith or Joseph III, began to vociferously promote his nephew's right to succeed his father as prophet and president. (See Chapter 15.) He established his headquarters in the heart of Lee County, Illinois, where a handful of disillusioned Mormons were farming at Palestine Grove (also known as Rocky Ford and later Shelburn). Exuberant over even this limited success, in time William modified the idea of lineal succession so that it focused on his own right to preside. Many of his followers became uneasy at this evidence of his personal ignoble ambition—discomfort that William failed to mitigate— and they eventually broke with his church organization.

By the fall of 1853 William's Church of Jesus Christ of Latter Day Saints had disintegrated. Although its six-year duration showed moments of success and provided excitement and adulation for William, it also resulted in bitter alienation and scorn heaped upon him by those who felt betrayed by him. William did not try to reorganize his church in the area. Since his brothers' murders in 1844, William had arguably affiliated with more factions of Mormonism than any other single individual. He had linked his aspirations with the Mormonism movements established by his brother, by Brigham Young's leadership after Joseph Smith's death, by George J. Adams in Iowa, by James J. Strang in Wisconsin, by Lyman Wight in Texas, by Isaac Sheen in Kentucky, and by Martin Harris in Ohio. In addition, William had associated with a host of noted dissidents, including Benjamin Winchester, William Marks, John C. Bennett, William McLellin, Reuben Miller, John E. Page,

---

6. George D. Smith, *An Intimate Chronicle*, 166; James Kay to Brother Ward (St. Louis, Mo.), November 22, 1845, *Millennial Star* 7, no. 9 (May 1, 1846): 134–35; "Mormonism— The Young Joseph!," *Weekly Reveille* (St. Louis, Mo.) 2, no. 17 (November 3, 1845): 1; "Mormon Oratory," *True American* (Lexington, Ky.) 1, no. 19 (November 25, 1845): 1. (See chaps. 11–12.)

Jared Carter, Jason W. Briggs, and Zenas H. Gurley, to name a few. He had additionally formed his own promising offshoot of Mormonism but had undercut its expansion by his own ambition and support of polygamy.

William's travels and Church experience were widespread. In all of his associations, he craved the recognition that he felt his family name merited, and he tried to play a governing role, experimenting with ways of occupying a role of major influence—if not openly seeking supreme leadership—in every organization with which he affiliated. In 1857, as his last attempt at church organizing fell to pieces, William married Eliza Elsie Sanborn at Kirtland, Ohio. Little is known about the quality of the marriage or the meshing of their personalities; but at least the timing was significant. Whether she influenced him directly to give up his insatiable ambition, this marriage represented something of a turning point, a mellowing of his religious ambition, and the abandonment of his fascination with his polygamy. The couple moved the remote area of Clayton County, Iowa, settling in the city of Elkader in 1860, far from any branch of Mormonism.[7] During the decade of the 1860s, he apparently withdrew from this cycle of religious attachment followed by disaffiliation, tried to earn a living in a variety of mostly unsuccessful ways, and joined the Union Army during the last months of the Civil War.

During the 1850s, young Joseph III came to manhood, and the repeated efforts of Zenas Gurley and his son Samuel, brothers Jason and Edmund Briggs, and W. W. Blair influenced Joseph to give serious consideration for more than seven years to their advancing organization. Although Emma and her second husband, Lewis Bidamon, were earnest Christians in belief and behavior, Emma had been deliberately silent on the Mormon-related experiences of Missouri and Nauvoo—the only periods when her children would have been old enough to have some memories of their own. And she definitely had not encouraged Joseph III to see himself as heir apparent to the ultimately fatal combination of forces that had brought Joseph's church a skyrocketing number of converts but also his death. When the hopeful Saints of the "New Organization" called a conference at Amboy for April 6, 1860, praying fervently for God to make known His will to young Joseph, Joseph's mature reflection and his own intense and humble spiritual seeking confirmed his call to continue his father's work. Loyally, Emma accompanied him to the conference. As she had given him complete space and time for his reflections, now she gave him her support. He was twenty-seven, and William, at this point, was forty-nine. In what became known as the Reorganized

---

7. Daughters of the American Revolution, New Connecticut Chapter (Painesville, Ohio), "Probate Court Marriage Records, Lake County, Ohio, 1840–1865," typescript at the Morley Library, Painesville, Ohio, 102. The entry reads: "Smith, Wm., m., Eliza E. Sanburne, November 12, 1857." William and Eliza were living in Venango Township, Erie County, Pennsylvania, in June 1860, according to the federal census. They moved to Elkader, Iowa, in the latter half of 1860. U.S. Federal Census, Pennsylvania, Erie County, Venango, Roll M653_1108, 1061, image 454; "Obituary. Mrs. Eliza E. Smith of Elkader," *Elkader Weekly Register* 12, no. 18 (March 14, 1889): 1.

The "Josephites" 499

Joseph Smith III, 1832–1914. Daguerreotype photograph, ca. 1850s. Courtesy LDS Church History Library.

Church of Jesus Christ of Latter Day Saints, William would finally find a religious home, though not the exalted position he craved, and was reasonably contented during the last fifteen years of his life.

Attending the conference were core members of William's organization who had continued to hold services in and around William's former headquarters through the decade of the 1850s. This group included members of the Hook family, W. W. Blair, Jason and Edmund Briggs, Alvah Smith (no relation to William), Isaac Sheen (who traveled from his home in Cincinnati), Israel Rogers, James Blakeslee, Samuel Powers, John Gaylord, William Marks, Jacob Doan, and Jotham Barrett.[8] Joseph III had arrived from Nauvoo the evening before the conference convened and was hosted by Experience Stone, a Mormon who had been a faithful follower in William's church and whose deceased relatives were buried in William's "Morman" cemetery nearby.[9] Among those who participated in ordaining Joseph III were several of William's former adherents: Zenas Gurley, Samuel Powers, and W. W. Blair.[10] In establishing a press, Joseph III and his associates turned to William's former editor, Isaac Sheen. William's fingerprints were ubiquitous on the foundations of the RLDS Church.

---

8. W. W. Blair (East Paw Paw, Ill.), Letter to Edwin Cadwell, Aaron Hook, and Jotham Barrett, March 7, 1856, P13, f111; Conference Minutes of a Meeting Held in Amboy, Illinois, June 10, 1859, P13, fd. 111 both in Community of Christ Library-Archives, Independence.

9. Richard P. Howard, ed., *Memoirs of President Joseph Smith III, (1832–1914)* (Independence: Herald Publishing House, 1979), 73, 81; Anthony J. Becker, *The Biography of a Country Town: USA* (Amboy, Ill.: Spencer-Walker Press, 1954), 118–20. The misspelled "Morman Cemetery," is located on the misspelled "Morman Road," about a mile south of present-day Amboy.

10. Joseph Smith III and Heman C. Smith, eds., *The History of the Reorganized Church of Jesus Christ of Latter Day Saints, 1805–1890*, 4 vols. (Independence: Herald House, 1896), 3:251 (hereafter *History of the Reorganized Church*, by volume and page); Howard, *The Memoirs of President Joseph Smith III*, 184. Samuel Powers and his wife, Maria, lived in Beloit, Wisconsin, and were baptized by Zenas H. Gurley Sr. in 1852. However, Samuel had earlier been "convinced in his heart the Latter Day Saints message was from Heaven, but he rebelled against obeying it." Either William Smith or his followers at Beloit had played an influential role in Powers's ultimate conversion, as the Beloit Branch unitedly supported William's Church of Jesus Christ of Latter Day Saints during the two years before Powers's baptism. Pearl Wilcox, *Regathering the Scattered Saints in Wisconsin and Illinois* (Independence, Mo.: Pearl Wilcox, 1984), 37–38.

Gravestones of the Stone and Doan families, located in William's "Morman" Cemetery, Palestine Grove, Illlinois. Photographs at the Amboy Depot Museum, Amboy, Illinois.

Although William's own church disintegrated by 1853, he had learned that two ideas appealed strongly to the scattered Saints who had looked to him for leadership: the idea of lineal succession, and restoring the Church to its original "purity" by publicly opposing polygamy. Some of his most prominent adherents pointed to Smith's role in introducing them to this first idea of succession. "William Smith was gathering up these old members of the church," recalled Edmund Briggs, Jason's younger brother. Edmund had become an RLDS apostle and was presiding bishop in 1892. According to those recollections, Smith had appealed to the former Mormons in Beloit, Wisconsin, by "preaching and teaching the doctrine of lineal priesthood," and was "the first man that ever taught that [lineal succession] there."[11] After William's church collapsed in the early 1850s, Jason W. Briggs and Zenas Gurley, two of his alienated disciples, almost immediately picked up the banner. William may have been a fallen prophet, but the idea of lineal succession rang true to them.

Briggs's revelation, a founding document of the Reorganization,[12] appropriately credits William as "represent[ing] the rightful heir to the presidency" dur-

---

11. E. C. Briggs, Testimony, *Abstract of Pleading and Evidence in the Circuit Court of the United States, Western Division at Kansas City—The Reorganized Church of Jesus Christ of Latter day Saints vs. The Church of Christ at Independence* (Lamoni, Iowa: Herald Publishing House and Bindery, 1893): 207 (hereafter *Temple Lot Case*).

12. Jason W. Briggs's revelation was reproduced in its entirety in the official history of the Reorganized Church and sanctioned by Joseph Smith III. *History of the Reorganized*

Zenas H. Gurley, 1801–1871. Date and photographer unknown. Courtesy Community of Christ Archives.

ing those intervening years. Consequently, then, Smith's organization should receive more credit in RLDS history than it has. Admittedly, a check on giving William that credit presents the dilemma of expressing too much enthusiasm for the organization of a fallen prophet who had not only advocated polygamy in Palestine Grove and Covington, but also at Nauvoo, during his eastern mission in 1843–45, afterward at Nauvoo, and then again when he associated with James J. Strang at Voree. Later RLDS histories, like LDS histories, found William Smith's morals and ambitions distasteful—with the result that they minimized his influence, except for passing references. For example, Richard P. Howard, RLDS Church historian, stated that Smith's Church "represented yet another small and isolated move toward reorganizing the church."[13] The most recent history of the Community of Christ continues that theme, noting quite cursorily that the "[Jason W.] Briggs group stayed with [William] Smith for less than a year when they discovered that, like Strang, he also embraced polygamy."[14] Other histories emphasized how various members "briefly" affiliated with Smith's group. Some, like Apostle Edmund Briggs, sought to completely eliminate William's role in the evolution of the RLDS Church, even denying that Jason ever affiliated with William's church, although the record clearly shows that Jason had served as an ardent apostle from 1850 to 1851.[15] The truth was that William Smith had more influence than Reorganization historians have been comfortable attributing to him, as dozens of Joseph III's earliest followers could credit William for reinvigorating their faith in Mormonism.

Most of William's followers continued in the faith of what he had taught them even after they considered him a fallen prophet and denied his leadership. When they petitioned Joseph III to assume the position of prophet-president, they were speaking for a tenet that William had promoted recurrently for nearly eight years after the murders of his brothers. Those who had affiliated with William's church and who then embraced the Reorganization, read like a who's who in early RLDS Church history: the three Briggs brothers (Jason W., Edmund, and Silas), Zenas H. Gurley, James Blakeslee, W. W. and Winthrop

---

Church, of Jesus Christ of Latter Day Saints, 1805–1890, 3:200–204.

13. Richard P. Howard, *The Church through the Years, Vol. 1* (Independence: Herald Publishing House, 1992), 331.

14. Mark A. Scherer, *The Journey of a People: The Era of Reorganization, 1844 to 1946* (Independence: Community of Christ Seminary Press, 2013), 80–81.

15. Edmund C. Briggs, Testimony, *The Temple Lot Case*, 207.

Blair, Israel Rogers, Isaac Sheen, Jotham Barrett, Edwin Cadwell, Jacob Doan, Experience Stone, her sons Stephen and Lardner, and a host of others.[16] While it was William Smith who united these future influential leaders around the idea of lineal succession, it was Joseph III who, blessed with the patience and prudence that William lacked, reaped the ultimate harvest. It was William who had successfully instilled in many of these founding members of the Reorganization the conviction that the presidency should pass from father to son—a doctrine that became a cornerstone of the Reorganization. RLDS historian Alma R. Blair wrote that, while those who eventually joined the Reorganization "were united in their stance against polygamy and in their belief in the authority of their new prophet," it was "the idea of lineal succession [that] proved most fruitful in combining them and the structure which had emerged."[17] The RLDS Church adopted what William had most strongly promulgated in his teachings, including his public renunciation of polygamy.

William had successfully gathered a strong group of Mormons scattered throughout Illinois and Wisconsin at and around Palestine Grove in Lee County, Illinois. It served as his headquarters from 1847 to 1853. In 1854 the community was renamed Amboy, centered slightly apart from Palestine Grove so that it could establish its business center close to the railroad, which arrived in November 1854.[18] The irony was that William himself would not be present to participate in these foundational RLDS events.

In fact, William had made another foray into Mormonism, being rebaptized LDS in the spring of 1860 (exact date not known), about the same time as the official organization of the RLDS Church. Though details are skimpy, a Mormon elder named J. J. Butler performed the ordinance, obviously without the approval of the First Presidency in Utah. No contemporary account of the conversations, conditions, or immediate results of this rite have been preserved.[19] William's financial situation likely prevented him from immediately moving west, and he also had well-founded doubts that Brigham Young and the Twelve would restore him to his prominent ecclesiastical offices. They had, in fact, already appointed

---

16. Ibid., 146; Howard, *Memoirs of Joseph Smith III*, 184. Jason Briggs and W. W. Blair were both designated apostles in William Smith's church.

17. Alma R. Blair, "The Reorganized Church of Jesus Christ of Latter Day Saints: Moderate Mormons," in *The Restoration Movement: Essays in Mormon History*, edited by F. Mark McKiernan, Alma R. Blair, and Paul M. Edwards (Independence: Herald Publishing House, 1992), 211.

18. Becker, *The Biography of a Country Town*, 107–14.

19. Brigham Young Office Journal, May 14, 1860, CR 1234 1, Box 72, fd. 5, LDS Church History Library, reads: "A. Carrington came in and read a letter from Wm. Smith, bro. of the Prophet, in which he desired to come to the valley and be restored to his former associations. He stated he had been rebaptised. Another letter was also read from a J. J. Butler stating he had baptized Wm. Smith, and that his [William's] course had been to sustain the authorities of this Church."

Joseph Sr.'s brother John, then John's namesake son, as presiding patriarch.[20] Would they undo this action or make another kind of adjustment to welcome someone as volatile as William? Furthermore, William had earlier (1847) made such an appointment a condition for returning to the LDS Church and immigrating to Utah, and it is probably fair to say that Brigham Young was unwilling to accommodate such demands.[21]

Thus, only months—perhaps only weeks—later, William learned that Joseph III had accepted the presidency over a movement that promised to become a full-fledged church. One can only imagine William's thoughts as he contemplated the horns of this particular dilemma. For an individual who currently felt unrecognized and unappreciated for his service, he must have felt rejected, even insulted, to be excluded from these landmark events. He had ample reason to know that Briggs and Gurley viewed him with suspicion and would not have welcomed his participation, but he probably assumed that his nephew would, at some point, extend a formal invitation to him—including a position in his organization. Joseph III, however, made no such move and never explained, in any account that has survived, the motives for his reticence. He was well aware of William's flamboyant, self-serving, and morally questionable history and was exercising considerable caution where his unstable uncle was concerned.

For his part, William doubtless leaped to the conclusion that his former followers who were now affiliating with the Reorganized Church had delivered disparaging reports to young Joseph. His inflated sense of self-importance did not allow him to admit that even a strictly factual report about his activities since 1845 would have been troubling to Joseph III and to the sincere and humble Church members now gathering around the new prophet. William's prickly sensitivities slipped out in letters he wrote almost a decade later, persistently shadowing his fifteen-year affiliation with the Reorganization.[22]

In July 1860, the newly baptized William, who had obviously received no messages of welcome from Utah, decided to take the first step toward the new organization. He wrote to Joseph III, shrewdly positioning himself as a supporter: "I shall sustain your present position as the lawful head and leader of the Mormon Church." He also complained in the letter that Brigham Young had taken "spoils" from Nauvoo, including William's own "property." William claimed, "I wrote to him to remunerate me for some of the losses I had sustained in the break-up of the Church, and you can see how willing the man is to get influence from the

---

20. Irene M. Bates and E. Gary Smith, *Lost Legacy: The Mormon Office of Presiding Patriarch* (Urbana: University of Illinois Press, 1996), 104–50.

21. William Smith (St. Louis, Mo.), Letter to Orson Hyde, June 22, 1847, Brigham Young Office Files 1832–1878, Letters from Church Leaders and Others, 1840–1877, William Smith, 1844–1857, LDS Church History Library.

22. See, for example, William B. Smith (Elkader, Iowa), Letter to Dear Nephew [Joseph Smith III], October 16, 1868, in *True Latter Day Saints' Herald* 1, no. 15 (January 1, 1869): 22–23.

Smith family." William was probably referring to Young's completely ignoring his half-hearted petitions for reinstatement during 1854–56. Despite his LDS baptism, William must have deduced, by this point, that Brigham Young was not going to restore him to the Twelve or to the patriarchy, so he openly angled for a position in Joseph III's movement. He appealed to his nephew's sympathy by recounting some of their common grievances against Brigham Young and the Saints in the West but made exaggerated claims that he had received "many invitations to join them [Salt Lake Mormons], from delegates sent from Salt Lake." This claim was an obvious ploy to heighten Joseph's interest in soliciting William's participation in the RLDS Church. William then assured the newly installed president: "I am your friend . . . and be assured, Joseph, that I have no feelings against you or any of those who have joined in with you."[23]

The other challenge William faced if he were to join the RLDS Church was overcoming the opposition from his former followers who had been repelled by his disclosures about polygamy and his personal ambition. He obliquely addressed this issue in his letter when he mentioned that he held no animosity toward those who had joined with the Reorganization.[24] William was clearly anxious to determine what feelings RLDS leaders held toward him, and he made it clear that he was available for membership and, obviously, high office. If Joseph III responded, his letter has not survived, but he had William's letter published immediately—almost certainly because of William's complaints about Brigham Young and to show that this last remaining Smith brother was his supporter. The fact of publication, with or without Joseph III's comments, evinced at least tacit support. One wonders how Isaac Sheen, newly appointed editor of the *True Latter Day Saints' Herald*, felt about publishing William's letter, given the acrimonious end of their relationship ten years earlier.

A short time after William wrote Joseph III this first letter, he confronted his nephew over what William must have considered slander and enmity, but which Joseph III doubtless considered full justification for treating his uncle warily. In Joseph III's memoirs, dictated in 1911–14 when he was in his early eighties, he recounted in general terms that, in 1856, he received "documentary evidence" from Edmund C. Briggs and Samuel H. Gurley about William's Church of Jesus Christ of Latter Day Saints at Palestine Grove. Almost certainly, Briggs and Gurley would have included William's shattering revelation in October 1851 supporting polygamy. The congregation had rejected William's leadership, though not Mormonism per se; and Briggs and Gurley had used this painful episode to petition Joseph III to assume presidency of the Church. Joseph did not describe the contents in detail in his memoir (and flatly rejected this effort at persuasion), but he described the "documentary evidence" as involving William's

---

23. "Wm. Smith's Contradiction of Utah Rumor," *True Latter Day Saints' Herald* 1, no. 7 (July 1860): 172.

24. Ibid.

"several religious movements," primarily "his career at Binghamton [Palestine Grove] and in Lee County, and his work in connection with one Joseph Wood, Aaron Hook, and others."[25] Edmund's brother Jason had documented much of William's morally dubious activities, which had led to the dissolution of Smith's church and had followed Smith's movement for several years afterward.

Joseph III later referred to the collection in an interview with Salt Lake Mormon David Seeley: "William Smith, father's brother, attempted organization, and to build up and gather a church together; once at Covington, KY., and afterward at Binghampton or Palestine Grove, Illinois; both failed, and both suffered persecution from which, Wm Smith fled and stayed away until it blew over; part of which persecution, was for things of a similar nature to those for which your people now suffer [i.e., polygamy]; and of which I do not care to inform you, though I hold the evidence to prove them."[26] In short, Joseph III undoubtedly had evidence in his custody that William had practiced polygamy.

How William learned that his nephew had these materials is not known, but it triggered the confrontation, their first known face-to-face meeting since 1848 when Joseph III was in his mid-teens. According to Joseph III, William "came to Nauvoo and demanded their surrender." William certainly wanted to distance himself from his history of polygamy and his legal difficulties connected to his Church organization in Lee County. But Joseph III refused to relinquish the documents, as he felt that they were "placed in my hands without reservation, or obligation on my part to make any specific use of it." William was furious and, as a result, Joseph wrote, William "remained aloof from me until several years after I identified myself with the Reorganization."[27] Whether this quarrel occurred before or after Joseph published William's July 1860 letter complaining about Brigham Young and angling for a position in Joseph's church is not clear. However, it does explain why William retreated from all branches of Mormonism for several years and why Joseph III was content with distance.

Then, typically, time smoothed out William's ruffled feelings. By the latter part of 1868, while William was living in Elkader, Iowa, and Joseph was living at Plano, Illinois, "relations of a more or less friendly character were then established between us; he visited me from time to time, and so far as I was concerned no significance or ulterior motive on his part was attributed to these visits." During some of these exchanges, the fifty-seven-year-old uncle and his thirty-six-year-old nephew discussed their differing ideas of what should be included in the newly established Reorganization.[28] In a letter William penned to his nephew on October 16, 1868, he indicated that "sometime I will tell you where I think

---

25. Howard, *Memoirs of President Joseph Smith III*, 184.

26. Joseph Smith III (San Bernardino, Calif.), Interviewed by David Seeley (Utah Mormon), January 1889, Miscellany Collection, P19, fd. 47, Community of Christ Library-Archives.

27. Howard, *Memoirs of Joseph Smith III*, 184.

28. Ibid.

your plan of church building in this New Organization is at fault."²⁹ Certainly one of these differences had to do with William's perspective on the office of patriarch, and his continuing hope to be appointed an apostle. Judging from future correspondence, other Church items that may have been a part of their discussions included vicarious work for the dead, the temple endowment, and opposition to polygamy, which both men recognized as a foundation stone of the Reorganization. Joseph III described their differences thus: "In our interviews he frankly stated his objection to certain movements of the Reorganized Church, and I as frankly maintained their necessity and integrity."³⁰

In reality, William was too late to have much of a voice in what offices or practices might be included in the Reorganization. Most of these issues had been decided by the early 1860s. Though he had often got his way in his various ventures in other factions of Mormonism, William met his match in his nephew. While the two relatives had divergent personalities in many ways, both men shared the quality of holding firmly to their viewpoints. Joseph III was not about to be coerced into accepting William's views regarding Church offices or practices; and having obtained William's papers from Briggs and Gurley, he knew what William had been trying to accomplish in his own affiliations and short-lived organization. He remained wary of his Uncle William and his ambition.³¹

While feelings between the two men gradually improved on the personal plane, William continued to remain distant from the Reorganization. His occasional letters expressed interest in what was transpiring in the emerging church, but he had no other ties with any branch of Mormonism when he settled in Elkader. His LDS baptism changed nothing in his relations with the Utah church. In October 1868, William explained to Joseph III: "According to my philosophy on the true plan of salvation to save all men, I am not in sympathy (very strongly) with any of the present organized bands of Mormons, your own not excepted. Still out of respect to yourself, and that of your father's family, I would not impede your progress." His prickly pride was still wounded by the fact that many of his former followers now formed the nucleus of the Reorganized Church's leadership. He felt that these men had rejected him and did not appreciate his earlier labors. William also revealed these feelings in a sharply worded complaint in the same letter: "You may also judge that I seek not the society of those who have so meanly misrepresented my acts, and doings, while I was honestly and sincerely laboring to save the church from the monstrous imposition of Brighamism." Then, he protested, but without much conviction: "Lest some of your adherents . . . think that I am swinging for a place (seat) in the New Organization, I would inform them that I am satisfied perfectly with my present position; and should

---

29. William Smith to Dear Nephew, October 16, 1868.

30. Howard, *Memoirs of Joseph Smith III*, 184.

31. Paul M. Edwards highlights many of William's interactions with Joseph III in his "William B. Smith: The Persistent 'Pretender,'" *Dialogue: A Journal of Mormon Thought* 18, no. 2 (Summer 1985): 128–39.

I hereafter seek a change in . . . connection with any religious class of professors, I think that I could suit myself much better than to unite with any class of L. D. Saints or Mormons that I have any knowledge of at present."[32] Joseph III's answer, if he responded, has not survived, but he certainly knew better than to take this lofty lament at face value.

Despite these denials, William deeply yearned to be recognized and elevated to a prominent position in the RLDS Church, just as he had consistently sought a similar goal in every church with which he had affiliated since his excommunication in Nauvoo in 1845. In November 1872 he declared, "I most cordially endorse the Reorganization" and affirmed his belief that Joseph III was the "legal" president of the Church, even though William himself was still formally unaffiliated.[33] It is not known whether any visitors or correspondents suggested that he become a member of the New Organization, but his own letters continue to protest his religious independence.

In spite of his distance from any particular branch of Mormonism, William's persisting faith in its doctrine compelled him to undertake what he described as a "mission" in Delaware County, Iowa, in 1873, during which he preached at least fourteen different sermons on Mormonism. "These meetings were well attended," described William in a letter to Joseph III, "while much prejudice was removed from the minds of the people; and . . . I could soon make many additions to the faith in these parts." This missionary success was William's effort to persuade Joseph III to give him a prominent role in the developing church. "At present I have not invited any to baptism," William continued, "for the reason that I choose not to do so, until there is a more perfect understanding and fellowship with the Reorganized Church on this matter." Though he expressed support of his nephew's church in several letters during the early 1870s, he made it clear that his full support was contingent on being granted an important office. Toward the end of this letter, William probed, "Joseph, you can do as you think best, if I can be of any use or benefit to the Church, you can place my name before the Church for admission."[34]

Like the feelers he had extended toward Brigham Young two decades earlier, William was offering a quid pro quo: his full support of the Reorganization with whatever influence his Smith name and family connection could bring

---

32. William Smith to Dear Nephew, October 16, 1868.

33. William B. Smith (Elkader, Iowa), Letter to Respected Nephew [Joseph Smith III], November 11, 1872, in *True Latter Day Saints' Herald* 19, no. 23 (December 1, 1872): 723, averred: "I do most cordially endorse the Reorganization; and further state now, as I always have done from the time of the great apostasy in 1844 and 1845, that the legal presidency of the Church of Jesus Christ of Latter Day Saints, belongs of right, to the oldest son of the martyred prophet, Joseph Smith, who was the first prophet of the church, and the [one] called of God."

34. Wm. B. Smith (Elkader, Iowa), Letter to Joseph [Smith III], December 12, 1873, *True Latter Day Saints' Herald* 21, no. 1 (January 1, 1874): 19–20.

in exchange for reinstatement in his coveted priesthood offices. Joseph III had no trouble deciphering the proposed bargain. William had already signed "Patriarch," to one of his letters to Joseph, evincing his belief that he still held the office.[35] Although Joseph was manifestly unwilling to take William's advice on organization and doctrinal aspects of the Reorganization, William urged Joseph to visit him in Elkader and preach. "There are many here who would be glad to hear you speak," wrote William, "and [I] would procure the Church in Elkader for you to speak in." He concluded his invitation by warmly encouraging Joseph III to "think me your friend" and again repeated his urgent invitation to "come, come and see us."[36] Joseph III reciprocated William's warmth by publishing his letters in the Church's newspaper, thus keeping his name periodically before the members, but he otherwise remained cautious. He never traveled to Elkader and, as nearly as can be reconstructed from the correspondence, he never wrote first and sometimes did not respond at all, except to have William's letters published.

Either there is a gap in the correspondence or William allowed five more years to pass before he again wrote to his nephew in January 1878. This time, he spelled out his expectations should he unite with the Reorganization. Though William's letter has not survived, Joseph III's answer on January 12, 1878, identifies two of William's "propositions." He apparently appealed to be restored to the office of presiding patriarch, including an expanded role as part of the First Presidency, much like Hyrum at the time of his death. William also wanted to be recognized as an apostle, with all of the original authority he had held in his brother's church. Joseph's answer quickly deflated William's aspirations. According to Joseph, the Quorum of the Twelve had been dissolved by Brigham Young's exodus to Utah. While this "did not destroy individual baptism, nor necessarily individual priesthood," explained Joseph III, "the character of that priesthood, and the particular office in it, must in all cases be determined upon the consideration and examination of each individual case." As for William's "proposition" to become part of the governing council of the RLDS Church, Joseph III observed, perhaps wryly, that he (Joseph III) "already had the compliment [of] . . . having been appointed by revelation." "Besides this," cautioned Joseph III, "you are now well advanced in years, [and] the time for you to have attempted an organized resistance to the Reorganization if ever contemplated by you, is past. . . . The prestige of my fathers name now belongs to me, and it is now assured to me."[37]

While Joseph III was blunt enough to make it clear that William had very little to contribute to the Church organization and that no office would be bestowed upon him, he was perceptive enough to recognize William's desire to unite with the Reorganization. After sternly spelling out that William's conditions for member-

---

35. William Smith to Respected Nephew, November 11, 1872; Edwards, "William B. Smith," 132.

36. William Smith to Dear Nephew, October 16, 1868.

37. Joseph Smith III, Letter to William B. Smith, January 12, 1878, in Joseph Smith III Letterbook 1, 275–79, Community of Christ Library-Archives.

ship would not be met, he then warmly opened the door to William on his status as a member: "I stand ready to welcome you into the church with both hands," wrote Joseph III, "and I am also willing to endorse any legitimate act done by you, that clear proff [proof], or the spirit testifies to be correct." The RLDS president further described how formally linking William's name with the Reorganization would vindicate his "honor and integrity . . . with a recognition of your office as an High Priest, the highest grade known to the Melchisedek Priesthood, and carrying with it the right to officiate in every ministerial office in the church." He urged, "Now is your golden opportunity to throw the power of your mind, and the influence of your name into the scale in favor of the work, for which your honorable place is rapidly being made." He then, intriguingly dangled dazzling possibilities before his uncle: "I am ready to recognize you publicly in this office [High Priest], at once; leaving the question of apostleship, and patriarchate to be settled subsequently, as the necessity of the case may demand, wisdom direct, or the spirit command."[38]

This cordial invitation—stressing the influence of William's name and family connection and the "golden opportunity" which would give him an "honorable place"—though not the titles William coveted—certainly appealed to William, who had felt undermined and rejected by all factions of Mormonism for many years. Joseph III adeptly checked William's office-seeking, which had been an unsavory aspect of his religious activities for more then thirty years, but simultaneously promised him an honored place, though its dimensions were not specified, if he formally affiliated. William almost certainly interpreted the offer of an "honorable place" as the first step in on-going negotiations which, he must have flattered himself, he could win.

Joseph III recognized the strength and credibility that the Reorganization would receive if all remaining members of his father's immediate family united with the Reorganization. Five years earlier, Joseph III had made personal visits to William's sister Katharine, then a sixty-year-old widow living in Fountain Green, Illinois. He invited her to formally unite with the RLDS Church, an invitation she accepted; and he personally officiated in baptizing and confirming her.[39] RLDS members came to view her as a living link between the church Joseph Smith had established and the Reorganization; and in her later years, she would occasionally be asked to share her recollections of early Mormon history, once at a session of the annual RLDS Church conference.[40]

William's two remaining sisters, Sophronia (who died in 1876) and Lucy (who died in 1882), were received into the RLDS Church in April 1873 on

---

38. Ibid.

39. "The Record of the Pilot Grove [Illinois] Branch of the Church of Jesus Christ of L.D.S.," entry for June 17, 1873, 25, Community of Christ Library-Archives. The entry in the minutes reads: "Cathcrinc Salisbury Born at Wind[s]or Co Vermont Rebaptised at Colchester McDonough Co. Illinois June 17th 1873 By Joseph Smith Confirmed same Day. Same place by Joseph Smith."

40. Kyle R. Walker, "Katharine Smith Salisbury's Recollections of Joseph's Meetings with Moroni," *BYU Studies* 41, no. 3 (2002): 4–17.

Joseph Smith III home in Plano, Illinois. Photograph by Kyle R. Walker, 2009.

their original baptisms, but they were living in Colchester, McDonough County, Illinois, and only minimally participated in the Reorganization, since there were no RLDS branches in their locale.[41] But William's case was unique among the remaining Smiths, because William's sisters did not have any desire for station nor, in fact, was there much of a formal role for RLDS women in terms of leadership. In addition, Joseph III had firsthand knowledge of William's troubling history. From the beginning of their relationship, Joseph III was perceptive enough to know he must handle William's reinstatement prudently, particularly as William's ambition for prominence and important office resurfaced.

A few months later, Joseph III invited William to attend an RLDS conference during the first week in April 1878, in Plano, Illinois, which he had made Church headquarters in 1865. William not only accepted the invitation but arrived early with the goal of having significant conversations about the offices he could expect if he were to unite with the Reorganization. Joseph III hosted William in his own home in Plano and showed no reluctance to discuss William's wishes in a prolonged conversation that lasted several days. William pressed his proposals, but Joseph continued to tactfully check William's ambition and deflect his request for station. Recalling this episode in his memoirs, Joseph III described their maneuvers: "He demanded to be received into the church upon his former membership, to be allowed to retain his standing as an apostle, and that his several attempts at church

---

41. *History of the Reorganized Church*, 4:3–4. See also Gracia N. Jones, "Sophronia Smith Stoddard McCleary," and Nathan H. Williams, "Lucy Smith Millikin," both in Kyle R. Walker, ed., *United by Faith: The Joseph Sr. and Lucy Mack Smith Family* (American Fork, Utah: Covenant Communications/Provo, Utah: BYU Studies, 2006), 193, 421–23.

Stone Church in Plano. This early RLDS meetinghouse was dedicated in November 1868. The original pews and pulpit are still in use by the local Community of Christ congregation. Photograph by Kyle R. Walker, 2009.

rebuilding should be recognized by us." Joseph III clearly foresaw the disruption that would follow from placing William in a position of authority, due to William's combative personality and competing aspirations. He countered by pointing out the much more active, democratic role that the conference played in RLDS affairs. Joseph III explained: "While we might be willing to receive him [William] into fellowship on his original baptism, his priesthood standing among us would have to be determined by the conference." He also felt that it would be a serious mistake to sanction William's earlier church-building efforts, since so many of them, including William's own church, had crashed on the rock of polygamy. As a result, Joseph cautiously stipulated that "whatever work he [William] had done in church building was to be frankly and openly examined, its recognition and acceptance, wholly or in part, to depend upon its nature, quality, and value to or effect upon the church itself, as might be determined after such examination and analysis."[42]

This wariness and the involvement from the beginning of others—many of whom had witnessed William's chaotic behavior during the 1840s and 1850s—was not the response William desired, even though he must have anticipated it based on their earlier communications. He may have hoped that his share of Smith charisma could charm his nephew during their face-to-face meetings and override Joseph III's objections. But in a rare moment of realistic evaluation, he must have understood that being formally reunited with a faction of Mormonism, no matter what restrictions it came with, would bring him some of the recognition he had lacked for more than twenty-five years.

---

42. Howard, *Memoirs of President Joseph Smith III*, 184–85.

Another kindly act by Joseph III may have softened William's feelings toward his nephew. Though Joseph III never returned the Briggs and Gurley papers related to William's Palestine Grove church, he returned William's personal journal, which Isaac Sheen had been holding.[43] The journal had been taken from William's trunk when he and Sheen had parted ways in the spring of 1850, and William was relieved to finally have this record of the earliest incidents of his life, which he used in composing his 1883 autobiographical account, *William Smith on Mormonism*.[44]

The two Smiths, though cordial, remained at an impasse as the conference commenced in the stone church in Plano, on April 5, 1878. Joseph III continued to stand firm on his former offer: membership recognized upon William's previous baptism, and confirmation of his office as a high priest, but nothing more alluring. "Thus we stood upon these differences when conference convened," recollected Joseph III, "and for the first few days of the session. He seemed determined that I should pledge myself to an unqualified reception and acceptance of him and of his work, while I was equally firm in my position not to recognize, endorse, or approve any such work until a full knowledge of the facts concerning it, frankly presented and thoroughly canvassed, should warrant us in doing so." In taking this position, Joseph had the full support of other officers in the Reorganization. Consequently, three days into the conference William reluctantly gave in. According to Joseph III, "he authorized me to present to the assembly his request to be received upon his original baptism."[45] Joseph III turned the final decision about William's reception into the RLDS Church over to a committee of three men, none of whom had been damaged directly by William's earlier chaotic behavior, although all of them were in a position to have knowledge of it: Elijah Banta, William H. Kelley, and George A. Blakeslee. The committee duly considered William's case and recommended that he be received as a member on his original baptism which had been performed in Fayette, New York, on June 9, 1830.

Joseph III apparently reserved to himself the decision of which priesthood office should accompany William's reception. On April 8, 1878, William was received as

---

43. Isaac Sheen's son John recollected: "William's Journal was given to him [William] when he came to Plano, Ill., in 1878." John K. Sheen, *Polygamy; or, The Veil Lifted* (York, Neb.: N.pub., 1889), 15.

44. William's holograph journal has not been located, but evidence that he used it is that he had earlier said Oliver Cowdery baptized him at Fayette, New York, on June 9, 1830. "William B. Smith. Experience and Testimony," *Saints' Herald* 30, no. 24 (June 16, 1883): 388. However, after reading his journal, he correctly identified David Whitmer as having performed the ordinance. William Smith (Osterdock, Iowa), Letter to Edmund Levi Kelley, March 12, 1892, Community of Christ Library-Archives. Even after he had published his history, in which he correctly identified David Whitmer as his baptizer, he had mistakenly mentioned Cowdery as the individual who had baptized him in an earlier letter to Edmund Kelley written in 1892, afterward correcting the mistake.

45. Howard, *Memoirs of President Joseph Smith III*, 184–85. See discussion above for the correct identification of David Whitmer as having baptized William.

Emma Hale Smith Bidamon, ca. 1870. William visited Emma at Nauvoo in January 1879, just months before her death on April 30. Photo courtesy of Mary Dennis.

an official member of the Reorganized Church and, in accord with Joseph III's earlier offer, allowed to "occupy... the office of High Priest."[46] After eighteen years of being unaffiliated with any movement of Mormonism, William was gratified, rejoicing in a degree of the recognition that he had so ardently desired for decades. "We had the benefit of his experience, testimony, and wisdom," Joseph III summarized of his uncle's acceptance of the Reorganization, "and were pleased to have what prestige his name and former connections brought to us."[47] After nearly two decades of posturing, William was electrified to have a visible place in the RLDS Church, and threw his whole effort in support of the movement.

Within a year of his linking himself with his nephew's church, and notwithstanding he was nearing his sixty-eighth birthday, William began a lengthy six-month mission to Iowa and Missouri as a demonstration of his newfound commitment. Though he had preached both Christian and Mormon sermons near his home in Elkader, he had not actively proselyted as a missionary for any particular church organization in more than twenty years. A gifted preacher, William relished meeting with Saints, holding curious audiences spellbound, and receiving the deference of RLDS members who enjoyed this connection to Mormonism's founder.

Smith began his mission on New Year's Day 1879,[48] preaching first at Montrose, Iowa. While preaching in the city, he made the effort to cross the Mississippi River and visit Emma Hale Smith Bidamon and her husband, Lewis, at Nauvoo, just four months before Emma's death.[49] Thirty years earlier, William had asked Emma

---

46. The committee reported: "We, your committee appointed to consider the propriety of receiving William B. Smith into the church on his original baptism, respectfully report and recommend that said William B. Smith be so received as a member; and upon the rule long since obtained and acted upon by the Reorganization, namely, that 'it is a matter of conscience' upon the part of the individual as to his being rebaptized when once it is shown that he has received a legal baptism, we report that satisfactory evidence shows that said William B. Smith was baptized by Oliver Cowdery, in the early days of the church." Howard, *Memoirs of President Joseph Smith III*, 184–85.

47. Ibid., 185.

48. Wm. B. Smith (Keokuk, Iowa) Letter to Dear Nephew [Joseph Smith III], May 28, 1879, *Saints' Herald* 26, no. 13 (July 1, 1879): 206.

49. William Smith (Hannibal, Mo.), Letter to Joseph [Smith III], Dear Nephew, January 25, 1879, *Saints' Herald* 26, no. 4 (February 15, 1879): 62.

and Lewis to look after his property in Plymouth, Illinois; not only had they refused, but Lewis had scoffed at his religious efforts and William had stormed out of Nauvoo.[50] William did not record the details of this 1879 visit, but apparently they had let bygones slip away. Seven years later in 1886, William recounted another cordial visit with Lewis and his second wife, Nancy Abercrombie.[51]

From Nauvoo, William continued his labors at the RLDS branch across the Mississippi River at Montrose. His effectiveness as a missionary was evidenced when several who listened to him preach desired baptism but decided to wait until the spring thaw broke up the ice still clogging the Mississippi River. Smith reported to Joseph III: "Waiting for a change in the climate, for a week's time, or two weeks, would not materially damage a brother or sister's faith in case they were honest and true-hearted believers in the work; and if they were not, it is just as well that such saints should back out before obeying the gospel, as for them to back out after they have joined themselves to the body of Christ."[52]

William continued south to Keokuk, where the RLDS Saints had established a larger congregation and had "a very neat and comely house for public worship." Word of his coming had preceded him, as RLDS Apostle John H. Lake ensured that William's preaching appointments were advertised in the local paper. William preached every evening for a week and recorded that his hearers manifested "more than becoming interest." He felt that his visit not only strengthened the Saints in the area but helped instill in others a desire to know more about the RLDS faith.[53]

William was at Hannibal, Missouri, on January 25, where he stayed with a John Taylor, president of the RLDS branch, while he preached. He then headed directly west, visiting Saints near Bevier, Brookfield, and Hamilton, then reached Kingston in March, in the heart of Caldwell County, Missouri. A letter has survived from William to Richard Randall, who was caring for a brother who had gone insane. William knew something of the burden of caring for an incapacitated

---

50. William Smith (Osterdock, Iowa), Letter to Edmund Levi Kelley, October 3, 1892, Community of Christ Library-Archives: "I visited Nauvoo in [18]47 [or] 48—tried to get Bidamon to look after [my property] but know he was to[o] Infidel to do anything laughed and mad[e] fun of religion—while I set at his table and asked me what [I] thought of the mistakes of Moses, I became disgusted with him—so never called on him—again—untill here in very late–years."

51. Of his 1886 visit to Nauvoo, William commented: "On Monday, July 5th, called on Major Bidamon, in Nauvoo, Illinois, and took tea with him and [second] wife [Nancy Abercrombie]. The Major showed me over the grounds where some of our relatives were laid away for their final resting place. Nauvoo is now a city of vineyards, with many houses still empty. The sad reminiscences that crowded my memory did not create in me a very strong desire to remain long in the city." William Smith (La Crosse, Ill.), Letter to Joseph Smith III, July 17, 1886, *Saints' Herald* 33, no. 30 (July 31, 1886): 469–70.

52. Smith to Dear Nephew, January 25, 1879.

53. Ibid.

loved one from the lengthy terminal illness of his first wife, Caroline Grant. With the empathy born of experience, Smith wrote tenderly to Randall, "This must be a sevear trial for you and I sympathise with you in this your trouble it cirtingly must place a great burden upon your mind and I pray my father in heaven that he will give you strength to endure this—and give you patience—while you labour to discharge your duty towards a kindred relative so near to household life."[54]

Traveling through Missouri called up memories of earlier incidents in Mormonism's troubled history in that state. William had first traversed the state in 1834 as part of Zion's Camp, then twice in 1837, once when he accompanied Joseph and Hyrum as the Saints were beginning to settle in northern Missouri. By the summer of 1838, the entire Smith clan had settled in northern Missouri, only to be driven from the state during the winter of 1838–39. At the time, William had accepted his brother's revelations appointing the land of Missouri as the location of the Saints' Zion, where they would build the New Jerusalem as prophesied by John the Revelator (Rev. 3:12, 21:2). Like many early Mormons who clung to Joseph Smith's revelations, William anticipated that his brother's prophecies about Missouri would be realized during his lifetime. It had been a matter of discussion in William's correspondence with Lyman Wight in 1848–51. Wight was also passionate to see the holy city established. When William arrived in Caldwell County in the spring of 1879 and preached to the Saints at Kingston, just a few miles from Far West, it rekindled his desire to see the Saints return to their promised Zion. He wrote excitedly to Joseph Smith III in March 1879: "Tell the Saints through the *Herald*, if admissible, that Zion in Missouri is *redeemed*; and that the feelings and spirit of the people in this Far West district, as almost universally expressed, are 'Come in, come in, ye Mormon Saints, and possess the goodly land.'"[55] William was obviously taking this hospitable attitude rather optimistically and urged Joseph III, "All around the old city of Far West land and farms are for sale, and at reasonable figures; and such is the civilized condition of the country, that Saints can purchase land and live on it without molestation." Enthusiastically he described Far West's "beauty for landscape and richness of soil. This is a great farming country, stock of every kind, and fruit and honey. For the last forty years the timber has grown in great abundance, splendid groves nearing the city, mark the spots where forty years ago, there was nothing but bare prairie; once patches of hazle brakes, but now beautiful groves of timber, large enough for rails or other uses have grown up for fire or farming purposes."[56]

With fiery enthusiasm, he appointed a meeting to be held on March 30, 1879, at the Far West temple site. There, standing on one of the temple

---

54. William Smith (Brookfield, Mo.), Letter to Richard Randall, February 13, 1879, Richard Randall Papers, 1878–1914, MS 5764, LDS Church History Library.

55. Wm B. Smith (Kingston, Mo.), Letter to the Editor, ca. March 1879, *Saints' Herald* 26, no. 8 (April 15, 1879): 125.

56. Ibid.

Temple Site at Far West, Missouri. Photograph by George Edward Anderson, taken May 16, 1907. Courtesy LDS Church History Library.

cornerstones,[57] William preached to a large crowd of Saints and interested country people. Filled with millennial fervor and a keen sense of the injustices he had experienced decades earlier, William recounted the history of the Saints at Far West. The enthralled audience listened to his firsthand, though certainly enhanced, recollections of his participation in the ceremony of laying the temple cornerstones on July 4, 1838, "at a time when the blood of the Saints was made to drench this Missouri soil." He concluded: "A more civilized spirit has taken possession of the masses of the people of the state of Missouri," and we then "invite our brothers in the East and elsewhere, to emigrate to this land and secure their inheritances in Zion, by purchase."[58] It was a nostalgic experience for Smith who had once owned property in the area, and it would be the highlight of his mission. The Church's response did not match Smith's enthusiasm, and Joseph Smith III almost certainly had marked reservations against allowing William to encourage and direct immigration and settlement.

Gomer Griffiths, a convert of less than two years who was later appointed an RLDS apostle, accompanied William in his travels through northern Missouri, and remembered with fondness being tutored by the seasoned missionary. "I was with him when he visited [the] Far West Temple Lot, and preached on the corner-stone of the Temple," recalled Griffiths. "He took for his subject, 'What is a Temple;' and delivered one of the finest and ablest discourses on that topic it has ever been my lot

---

57. Wm. B. Smith, Letter to the Editor, ca. March 1879.

58. William's sermon at Far West was later published in the official *History of the RLDS Church*, 4:253–54.

Gomer Griffiths, 1856–1922. Photograph taken ca. 1888, by unknown photographer. Copy from postcard in my possession.

to listen to." Griffiths further appreciated the "encouragement and assistance" he received from the older missionary, as the two labored throughout the state that season.[59]

Whether William was cognizant of it, while he preached in Kingston and Far West he was less than twenty miles from his divorced wife Roxey Ann, who had not remarried, and was now living in Lathrop. Living with her were her two children by William, Thalia and H. Wallace, who were now thirty and twenty-eight respectively. It seems probable that word would have reached Roxey Ann and the children that William was preaching fairly nearby, but apparently they made no effort to contact him, and he may not have been aware of their presence. In contrast, when William preached in Brookfield, Missouri, two months earlier, he apparently visited the family of his daughter, Mary Jane, who had died in late December 1878, at age forty-four like her mother, leaving her husband, Andrew Scott, and their four children ranging in age from twenty-five to ten. Smith was apparently a welcome visitor as he comforted the grieving family. Mary Jane's death must have brought painful memories of Caroline's lingering death after several years of suffering. Her obituary noted somberly: "Medical skill and remedies were as naught to her, beyond temporary alleviation of her suffering,"[60] which had certainly been the case with her mother. Caroline Louisa, William and Caroline's second daughter, had died just months earlier in Texas.[61] After this point, however, the documentary record does not show that William had continuing contact with his grandchildren.

Smith might have extended his mission, but Eliza wrote in May, summoning him home "with pressing calls for my attention to affairs there."[62] He made

---

59. "Autobiography of Gomer T. Griffiths," in *History of the Reorganized Church of Jesus Christ of Latter Day Saints*, 4:719.

60. William had two daughters by his first wife Caroline, and the eldest, Mary Jane, lived with her husband and children at Brookfield, Missouri, during the decade of the 1870s. Mary Jane had died of "dropsy of the heart" (edema) just a month earlier, on December 21, 1878. Her husband, Andrew, was president of a bank in the city. The couple had four children: Alice, Mary ("Nettie"), Caroline ("Carrie"), and Frank. "Laid to Rest," *Brookfield Gazette* 12, no. 36 (December 26, 1878): 3; Harry D. Galley, *Joseph Smith Senior's Children* (Rock Island, Ill.: Author, 2000), 31–34.

61. Galley, *Joseph Smith Senior's Children*, 34–35. See also, Appendix A.

62. William B. Smith (Hannibal, Mo.), Letter to Brethren of the Herald, May 26, 1879, *Saints' Herald* 26, no. 12 (June 15, 1879): 189.

a circuitous route home, delivering several sermons in St. Louis and preaching in some of the same cities along the Mississippi River, not reaching Elkader until mid-June 1879. He obviously found the mission experience rewarding, and wrote Joseph III of his intention to serve another mission "as soon as I get affairs in a proper condition at home."[63] In the years that followed, Smith served numerous short missions throughout Iowa and adjoining states—typically lasting a month or a few weeks, but occasionally going as far afield as Illinois, Minnesota, and even Ohio and Michigan.

Joseph III, who must have had some misgivings about William as a missionary, was pleased and relieved by William's success and generously praised him. Wherever he went, Joseph wrote in February 1879, he heard Saints say, "God Bless Bro. William," and "He has done us good." The relieved Church president reported with approbation: "Your testimony is carrying weight with it, and the fact of your preaching the gospel, in its primitive charter, tells like golden measures for the church."[64]

Through his missionary service, William solidified his place within the movement, yet his labors were not entirely free of controversy. Members in at least one locale complained that he collected funds and encouraged gifts for himself and his family. He had long engaged in this practice during his earlier missionary travels when the Mormon elders depended on members and other hospitable people for food and lodging. William did not see such personal fund-raising as incompatible with his calling and appointment as a missionary. RLDS members were quick to feed and house traveling missionaries and occasionally contributed cash to assist with traveling expenses, but they were far from wealthy. William's approach was apparently unorthodox for RLDS itinerant preachers, who "were required to be self-sustaining and simultaneously provide for their own families."[65]

William made no attempt to conceal his receipt of money and other gifts in his letters to the *Saints' Herald* and to Joseph III. "I could not close this epistle with a justified conscience without comment or compliment to the kind Saints of Keokuk," William wrote in one letter to Joseph III, "for they responded cheerfully in assisting me on my journey."[66] In another letter to the *Saints' Herald*, William noted the "kindness shown me at Renick, Randolph county, Missouri." He praised "the generous and thoughtful kindness of the sisters in that branch of the Church who remembered my wife and family with several good presents that will make their hearts glad."[67] He obviously expected such support from members during his travels but, learning that there had been complaints, apologized to Joseph III, citing poverty as his justification: "As I had been from home on a mission, in northwest

---

63. Wm. B. Smith to Dear Nephew, May 28, 1879.

64. Joseph Smith III, Letter to William B. Smith, February 20, 1879, Joseph Smith III Letterbooks, Book 2, P6, 115–16, Community of Christ Library-Archives.

65. Ronald E. Romig, "Alexander H. Smith: Remembering a Son of Joseph and Emma Smith," *Journal of Mormon History* 37, no. 2 (Spring 2011): 34.

66. William Smith to Dear Nephew, January 25, 1879

67. William B. Smith to Brethren of the *Herald*, May 26, 1879.

Missouri, some five months, and the time drew nigh for my return home; and as I had exhausted nearly the last dollar in expenses coming down from Far West I did not think it improper to speak of this subject before the Saints, asking them to assist me in my expenses to my home. If this is my offending," William humbly offered, "I will say to the Saints . . . that if I ever come that way again, that I will try to do better next time, and say nothing about money."[68] His apology apparently rectified the situation, as the documentary record shows no further complaints from the Church members about William's expectations.

Despite his missionary success, William obviously desired reinstatement as Church patriarch, an office Joseph III was clearly unwilling to grant him. Within months, William began suspecting that his former followers were weakening his influence with his nephew. He wrote to Joseph on the topic apparently in early February, while he was only a few weeks into his mission. This letter has not survived; but Joseph's answer, written on February 20, 1879, communicates William's sensitive self-concept and his near reflex of blaming others when matters did not go his way. Joseph III responded: "So far as the patriarchy of the church is concerned there will probably be but one opinion concerning where it goes, when the question is brought up before the church—I believe that opinion to be in your favor." Still, Joseph III downplayed both its necessity and authority, putting William off with the mild assurance that it would, "at a propitious time . . . be presented and disposed of."[69]

But without absolutely foreclosing the option, Joseph III also took no action to appoint William to that office. William blamed the enmity of Zenas Gurley and Jason Briggs, even though he had no direct evidence that they had been poisoning Joseph III's well where he was concerned, and Joseph reassured William: "You do Jason W. Briggs and Zenos H. Gurley Sr. a[n] injustice wherever you think to say either of these brethren ever attempted, in any wise[, to] lessen your influence with me, or to belittle your work at any time to me." Joseph responded to what was obviously at least a second letter with some exasperation in May 1879. "I have tried several time[s] to make you comprehend this. Such language as you use in your last letter respecting him [Briggs], are quite inconsistent [with] anything ever said by him to me of you."[70] William had apparently attacked Briggs and Gurley, but Joseph had rejected this effort to alienate Joseph from the two stalwarts and bluntly counseled William to share his opinions about past events in a manner "so as to not bring about personal conflict. . . . It is calling names and charging bad motives that hurt people."[71]

---

68. William B. Smith (Elkader, Iowa), Letter to Joseph [Smith III], Dear Nephew, April 4, 1880, *Saints' Herald* 27, no. 10 (May 15, 1880): 158–59.

69. Joseph Smith III to William B. Smith, February 20, 1879.

70. Joseph Smith III, Letter to William Smith, May 6, 1879, Joseph Smith III Letterbooks, Book 2, P6, 163–65, Community of Christ Library-Archives.

71. Joseph Smith III, Letter to William Smith, July 12, 1879, Joseph Smith III Letterbooks, Letterbook 2, P6, 257–58, Community of Christ Library-Archives.

William's ability to tactfully resolve conflict had never been well-honed, and his impetuousness and insecurities were just as palpable in his writings to his nephew as they had been in his interpersonal interactions. After calming William's misgivings about his reputation, Joseph III, whose social skills were much better developed, often complimented his uncle on the positive impact he was having on the Church and assured him of his personal friendship. This approach typically pacified William, if only temporarily. For example, in that same May letter, Joseph concluded with compliments and blessings: "You are a tower of strength to the church, so long waiting for something humble to lean upon stronger than themselves; and that your declining years may shine like the sun in resplendent glory . . . is the prayer of your nephew, 'Little Joseph.'"[72]

However, some RLDS leaders indeed had concerns about William's aspiration for the patriarchal office, especially when he began to publish his arguments in the *Saints' Herald* that such an appointment was necessary. Joseph III, as editor, seems to have been remarkably willing to let William make his case public; but those who had been involved with William during the late 1840s and 1850s could not have expected William's reputation to escape unscathed from all that had transpired during the collapse of his own Church. "William accepted his work as a missionary with vigor," described historian Paul M. Edwards of William's ambition, "but nothing about his demeanor suggested that he was giving up his desire to be recognized as the patriarch." Rather, he brought up the need for appointment to that office "wherever he went," although, as far as is known, he never took the step of delivering patriarchal blessings to the members. Clearly, he felt the need for authorization and formal recognition of his position. "There was concern among Church leaders about William's determination to affirm the office itself," continued Edwards. In March 1881, Jason Briggs wrote contemptuously to fellow apostle and bishop William Kelly: "What do you think of the pipe laying to spring a patriarch upon us? And what a specimen." Further, Briggs called the office a "wart on the ecclesiastical tree, unknown in the Bible, or Book of Mormon," while venting his wish to completely eliminate the office.[73] Whatever discussions there may have been between the Church president and his colleagues about the office of patriarch, Joseph III chose to look forward and not backward.

William was especially sensitive to references to himself and his church organization (and dissolution), when his former followers began publishing vignettes about the early history of the RLDS Church. He took particular exception to the writings of Zenas H. Gurley and W. W. Blair, probably because they neglected his own efforts.[74] This restraint doubtless had Joseph's approval since he knew that, if William's past was brought into the open, it could lead to conflict for the

---

72. Ibid. For an additional example, see Joseph Smith III to William B. Smith, February 20, 1879.

73. Briggs, quoted in Edwards, "William B. Smith," 134.

74. Which specific works roused his ire is not clear, possibly editorials or letters in the *Saints' Herald*.

Joseph Smith III, 1832–1914. Photograph taken at Council Bluffs, Iowa, ca. 1905, by Riley. Photo courtesy of Mary Dennis.

Reorganization. Writing to William, Joseph III assured William that he had spoken with Blair about a particular historical publication and that Blair "takes out allusions to you where he can do so with propriety, in order not to annoy you; and we have talked the matter over." But he also warned William, "Your acts in the past will . . . hardly be called into question, unless it be because of your own indiscretion in urging it on."[75]

Joseph III further cautioned William about his interactions both with members and nonmembers over disagreements. When William told Joseph III in a letter that has not survived that he contemplated visiting David Whitmer, Joseph responded on May 6, counseling William against a combative approach. "I believe that David Whitmer may be met, much better by fair argument than denunciation." He further counseled his uncle, "Let me entreat [you] to deal gently with erring ones."[76] Joseph III was perceptive regarding William's personality; and if William had adopted his nephew's prudent counsel and moderate approach, it would have greatly improved his relationships.

Joseph III's tactic in dealing with William was to encourage him to let "bygones to be bygones" and to leave behind "the past, the erroneous past." In a letter on May 15, 1879, he counseled: "True, many things of the past were good and right . . . but [even] the sifting out of these good things causes so much irritating dust and ashes of bad thing[s] to rise, that I think it better to let the sifting alone when it can be done safely."[77] Although he did not specifically allude to polygamy, it was clearly on his mind; and he often cautioned William about what he *should* remember. This was most evident when William was writing *William Smith on Mormonism* (1883). Joseph III wrote bluntly to William:

> I have long been engaged in removing from Father's memory and from the early church, the stigma and blame thrown upon them because of Polygamy; and have at last lived to see the cloud rapidly lifting. And I would not consent to see further blame attached, by a blunder now. Therefore, uncle, bear in mind our standing today before the world, as defenders of Mormonism free from Polygamy, and go ahead with your personal recollections of Joseph and Hyrum. . . . And if you are the wise

---

75. Joseph Smith III to William Smith, July 12, 1879.
76. Joseph Smith III to William Smith, May 6, 1879. I have been unable to locate any evidence that William ever met with Whitmer during his mission to Missouri.
77. Joseph Smith III, Letter to William Smith, May 15, 1879, Joseph Smith III Letterbooks, Letterbook 2, P6, 203A–204, Community of Christ Library-Archives.

man I think you to be, you will fail [to] remember anything contrary to the lofty standard of character at which we esteem these good men. You can do the cause great good; you can injure it by injudicious sayings.[78]

William got the message, and "fail[ed] to remember" anything in his 1883 publication that would reflect poorly on the image of Joseph Smith Jr. and RLDS Church.[79]

William and his sister Katharine both proved to be loyal assets to the Reorganization in their final years. Joseph III and other RLDS leaders requested sworn statements on at least one occasion from both that would distance their Church from polygamy and the Nauvoo endowment—items of controversial doctrinal divergence from the Mormon Church headquartered in Salt Lake City. For example, in 1883, Joseph III specifically and pointedly asked: "Was the so called Revelation on Plural marriage the Polygamic Revelation ever presented to the twelve before or since [Joseph Smith's] death to your knowledge if so state the date and time when such Revelation was presented and by whom[?]" William responded in a sworn statement, "No mention was made to me of any Plural marriage Revelation by any one nor did I ever see the said Revelation not until within the last 2 years some one having sent it to me by mail."[80] On one occasion, just after giving his nephew a statement denying polygamy, William assured Joseph III, "What I have stated I am willing to qualify under oath & could say much more if needed."[81]

Thus, William acted as a ready witness and made numerous denials of polygamy during his fifteen-year association with the RLDS Church, either at his nephew's request or at his own volition. He was, however, misrepresenting the facts. Joseph Jr. dictated the revelation that is now LDS Doctrine and Covenants 132 on July 12, 1843, and Hyrum Smith read it to the Nauvoo High Council on August 12, exactly a month later.[82] William had been sealed to his first plural wife, an English convert named Mary Ann Covington, by Brigham Young in April 1843.[83] The ensuing summer William was in the East. However, in April and May 1844, William had led a group of forty or fifty Saints to Nauvoo, arriving on April 22 aboard the steamboat *Charlotte*. During his brief stay in Nauvoo, he was inducted into the Council of Fifty. On Sunday, May 12, he was endowed, initiated into the

---

78. Joseph Smith III, Letter to William Smith, March 11, 1882, Community of Christ Library-Archives.

79. William Smith, *William Smith on Mormonism* (Lamoni, Iowa: Herald Steam Book and Job Office, 1883).

80. William Smith sworn statement, October 22, 1883, Clayton County, Iowa, before T. G. Price, Notary Public; published as, "The 'Endowment': Statement of William B. Smith, The Only Surviving Brother of the Seer," *Saints' Advocate* (Plano, Ill.) 2, no. 6 (December 1879): 65.

81. William B. Smith, Letter to Joseph Smith III, October 19, 1883, Miscellaneous Letters and Papers, P13, f2311, Community of Christ Library-Archives.

82. See discussion in Brian C. Hales, *Joseph Smith and Polygamy*, 3 vols. (Salt Lake City: Greg Kofford Books, 2013), 2:139–61.

83. Mary Ann [Covington Sheffield] West, Testimony, in United States testimony 1892, Court of Appeals (Eighth Circuit), 496–97, MS 1160, LDS Church History Library.

Quorum of the Anointed, and joined in the group prayer "for deliverance from our enemies and exaltation to such officers as will enable the Servants of God to execute Righteousness in the Earth."[84] On May 21, William left Nauvoo in company with Heber C. Kimball, Brigham Young, and other missionaries who were campaigning for Joseph as a candidate for the U.S. presidency. When he returned in 1845, almost a year after the murders of Joseph and Hyrum, he married Mary Jane Rollins (monogamously) a month after Caroline's death but had been sealed polygamously to Mary Jones, Priscilla Mogridge, Henriette Rice, Lucinda Curtis, Ann Rollins, and Sarah and Hannah Libby, none of whom stayed with him or apparently considered themselves his wives by the time he married Roxey Ann Grant.[85]

Katharine also firmly denied polygamy: "I was at his [Joseph Smith's] house many times, and I conversed with him about many subjects, but I never heard him at any time mention such a thing as the plural-wife system or order. And I heard nothing of such a doctrine existing until a year after his death. At that time, on coming to Nauvoo, I was informed that Brigham Young and others were practicing that system."[86] It seems likely that she genuinely did not know about plural marriage or about the Nauvoo endowment. During the first half of the 1840s, she and her family of numerous children lived in Plymouth, Illinois, some forty miles from Nauvoo. Joseph Smith visited her at least once,[87] but she could seldom come to Nauvoo. Thus, she could truthfully state that she had no knowledge of the temple rites performed in Nauvoo because she never received them and apparently was unaware of Joseph and Hyrum's participation in polygamy. William knew about both because he had been present and a participant. Despite his certain knowledge, he was still willing to give testimony to the contrary if it meant undermining Mormonism in the West. This attitude, which at least technically amounts to perjury, was, he felt, justified, both as retaliation against Brigham Young and the Twelve for rejecting him and as a worthy means of building up his nephew's church.

When leaders of the LDS Church in the West learned of William's statements they were surprised. After William's nephew Joseph F. Smith, then an apostle, read one of William's statements denying polygamy, he wrote to his uncle in 1884 asking him to "reconcile some things you have said with your career in

---

84. Scott H. Faulring, ed., *An American Prophet's Record: The Diaries and Journals of Joseph Smith* (Salt Lake City: Signature Books, 1987), 478; Jedediah S. Rogers, ed., *The Council of Fifty: A Documentary History* (Salt Lake City: Signature Books, 2014), xl, 49.

85. Lavina Fielding Anderson, *Lucy's Book: A Critical Edition of Lucy Mack Smith's Family Memoir* (Salt Lake City: Signature Books, 2001), 875; George D. Smith, *Nauvoo Polygamy: . . . "but we called it celestial marriage"* (Salt Lake City: Signature Books, 2008), 623–24.

86. "Aunt Katharine Salisbury's Testimony," *Saints' Herald* 40, no. 18 (May 6, 1893): 275; also published in *History of the RLDS Church*, 5:207.

87. This visit took place on January 9, 1843, when Joseph Smith and his entourage were returning from his trial at Springfield, Illinois. Andrew H. Hedges, Alex D. Smith, Richard Lloyd Anderson, eds., *Journals, Volume 2: December 1841—April 1843*, THE JOSEPH SMITH PAPERS (Salt Lake City: Church Historian's Press, 2011), 242–43.

Katharine Smith Salisbury, 1813–1900, with RLDS Church leaders, taken at Burlington, Iowa, 1896. Both Katharine and William were viewed as living links between Joseph Jr.'s original church and the RLDS Church and often shared their recollections. Seated, second from left, is Alexander Hale Smith, Joseph and Emma's son, with Katharine on his left. Photo courtesy of Mary Dennis.

Nauvoo, and your connection with Sarah and Hannah Libby, Priscilla Morgridge & others?" He reminded William that "some of these women are [still] living and can speak for themselves."[88] William did not respond.

In the final decade of his life, William continued to serve a number of brief missions for the RLDS Church and presided at various worship meetings and conferences in northeastern Iowa. When his health allowed, Smith enjoyed traveling to the annual April conferences of the RLDS Church. He also participated in other notable Church events, such as the dedication of a chapel at Montrose, Iowa, on September 2, 1883.[89] After thirty-two years of marriage, Eliza passed away in 1889, and William married Rosa Goyette La Ture Surprise, an RLDS Church member who attended the Clinton, Iowa Branch, in December of that same year. The couple moved approximately fifteen miles southeast, settling in Osterdock, Iowa, where William and Eliza's youngest daughter Loie May lived. (See Chapter 21.) In his final years he was instrumental in organizing a branch of the RLDS Church in Osterdock. At its organizational meeting, William was unanimously chosen as branch president. In addition to presiding at meetings,

---

88. Joseph F. Smith (Salt Lake City), Letter to William Smith, July 12, 1884, MS 1325, Box 31, fd. 3, pp. 58–67, LDS Church History Library. Joseph F. Smith was responding to a letter that William had written on June 25, 1884, that apparently has not survived. The women Joseph F. names had been sealed to William as plural wives between September 1844 and August 1845.

89. Howard, *Memoirs of President Joseph Smith III*, 206; *History of the RLDS Church*, 4:433.

The "Josephites"

Illustration by Frank Taylor of RLDS members gathering at the Kirtland Temple for a session of general conference. *Harper's Weekly* 27, no. 1372 (April 7, 1883).

he occasionally preached in a local church or in his own home to a small group of RLDS followers, which included members of his growing posterity.[90]

The pinnacle of William's experience with the RLDS Church came in 1883, when the Church planned its annual April conference to be held in Kirtland rather than the usual location of Lamoni, Iowa, where Joseph III had established the Church's headquarters in 1881. Having assisted in the construction of the Kirtland Temple, William was delighted to be involved in such a significant reunion. Like his missionary travels through Missouri in 1879, his presence at the conference triggered reflections on this earlier period of his turbulent life. It was gratifying to have attention showered upon him because of his connection to Joseph Smith and to the temple dedication almost fifty years earlier. Joseph III recalled kindly that William's "tall form was conspicuous and added dignity to the assembly." William fully enjoyed the honor of sitting in the tiered priesthood pulpits that rose prominently on each end of the spacious assembly room.[91]

William was further recognized during the week-long conference. He offered the opening prayer at one session, preached several sermons, and was appointed to preside at another session.[92] Reorganite Saints also requested that William re-

---

90. Osterdock Branch Minutebook, Book 1 (small), entry for June 11, 1893; see also Osterdock Branch Minutebook, Book 2 (large), entry for August 19, 1893, both in Community of Christ Library-Archives.

91. Howard, *Memoirs of President Joseph Smith III*, 184–85, 207.

92. "General Conference," *Saints' Herald* 30, no. 16 (April 21, 1883): 242–43. See also Kevin Bryant, "'Attracting No Little Attention': The RLDS Return to Kirtland, 1883

CERTIFICATE OF APPOINTMENT AND LETTER OF RECOMMENDATION.

Lamoni, Iowa, *May 12th* 188*3*.

Elder *William B. Smith:*

This is to Certify to you and to all whom it may concern, that at the Session of the General Conference of the Reorganized Church of Jesus Christ of Latter Day Saints, held at *Kirtland, Ohio, April 6th to 15th,* 188*3*, you were *appointed as a minister* in ~~charge of~~ the Mission that is comprised in the following named Countries, States, Territories, or portions thereof, to-wit: *Iowa & Illinois*

to preach therein the Gospel of Jesus Christ, and to administer in the ordinances thereof, agreeably to the laws and regulations of said Church, and according to the authority conferred upon you at your Ordination and by your Appointment to ~~to~~ said field of labor, as certified in this Letter.

And, furthermore, the Church having confidence in you, does, through us, commend you to the hospitality and care of the Saints where you may labor, and to their ministrations and aid, as well as to that of all others who love truth and righteousness, according as any may be able and willing to thus minister to you. And we also commend you to the Officers, Managers, and Agents of Railway lines and other modes of public conveyance, for such courtesies, permits, or lessened rates of fare as they may be able, consistently with their rules, regulations, or powers, to grant to Ministers of the Gospel.

Trusting that you will, by wise and upright conduct and conversation, merit the trust and confidence of all these, as well as of the Church, we affix the Seal of said Church to this document, and subscribe ourselves your brethren and fellow laborers in the Lord.

Joseph Smith
President of the Church.

Henry A. Stebbins
Secretary of the Church.

William B. Smith Certificate of Appointment, dated May 12, 1883, and signed by Joseph Smith III. Courtesy Community of Christ Archives.

late his reminiscences of early Mormon events, including the coming forth of the Book of Mormon. He was happy to comply, and Saints and newspaper reporters listened eagerly to William's firsthand recollections of Mormonism's earliest events. It was a captivating portrayal of a cherished Mormon narrative. After recounting his brother's quest for truth and the impact of his revelatory experiences on his family, William reaffirmed his belief in his brother's prophetic mission—something he had done repeatedly. His remarks were published in their entirety in the *Saints' Herald*.[93]

A reporter from the *Cleveland Herald* asked about William's involvement in the construction of the temple fifty years earlier. William described carrying "the stone and mortar that put these walls together." When the reporter asked how he liked the conference, William enthusiastically quipped: "Just as well as it is possible for anyone to do. I shouldn't want to enjoy it any better for fear I might evaporate." He concluded the interview by describing what "a great pleasure" it was for him "to again enter the blessed old building." The reporter described Smith as "a tall, spare gentleman, seventy-two years of age, and is apparently as deeply in love with the Church and cause as was his brother."[94]

The conference experience was intensely satisfying to William. He was gratified by the attention he received during the proceedings and by the eagerness with which those present listened to his account of building up Mormonism, his personal sacrifices, and the expression of his faith. The Saints admired him as a tangible link between their organization and the earliest days of the Church. Before leaving Kirtland, Joseph Smith III asked William if he were enjoying himself. William straightened up and, with a twinkle in his eye, replied, "Enjoying myself? Why, I couldn't possibly enjoy myself more unless I were *bigger*—and even that is a little doubtful!"[95]

William's response revealed his contentment, but such moments of satisfaction were fleeting. He had primarily held himself aloof during the eighteen years between the RLDS Church's organization in 1860 and his formal acceptance of membership and priesthood in 1878. Although he proved himself an energetic missionary and basked in the attention he received, the other titles he coveted eluded him.

William's insatiable desire for higher office was evident in the letters he wrote toward the end of his life, evincing his continuing insecurities. At one point in March or April of 1882 when he was turning seventy-one, William argued in a letter to the *Saints' Herald* that the Church's hierarchy was incomplete without a patriarch: "If the keys of revelation given to Joseph Smith are to be held by a successor, why are not the keys of the patriachate given to Hyram [sic] Smith to be

---

General Conference," *John Whitmer Historical Association Journal* 29 (2009): 59–60, 71.

93. "William B. Smith. Experience and Testimony," *Saints' Herald* 30, no. 24 (June 16, 1883): 388.

94. "General Conference," 242, reproducing *Cleveland Herald* report.

95. Howard, *Memoirs of President Joseph Smith III*, 185, 207.

held by him, or a successor in office, also upon the same principle?"⁹⁶ The *Saints' Herald*, still being edited by Joseph III, published this public and pointed hint that he should be appointed to that office. However, Joseph continued to delay, never completely ruling out the possibility and thereby keeping William hoping for an eventually positive decision. Just a year before William's death, he made the same argument to RLDS Apostle William H. Kelley. "My nephew is lame on Some of these points," he confided to Kelley, whom he hoped to make his advocate. "The Church under him not yet perfect in its organization."⁹⁷

Alexander Hale Smith, 1838–1909). Son of Joseph and Emma Hale Smith, who was appointed patriarch of the RLDS Church and a member of the First Presidency in 1897, the two positions that William coveted. Photograph by J. Handers & Son, Chicago, Illinois, ca. 1885. Courtesy of Estel Neff.

Joseph's caution was not harsh or punitive, and the two appear to have enjoyed an amicable relationship, both on paper and in person. Joseph simply had an organizational astuteness and managerial ability that William himself lacked. He obviously agreed that organizational completeness required a patriarch—just that it could not be William. After William's death in 1893, Joseph waited a respectable five years, then appointed his brother Alexander Hale Smith to two positions which were sustained by conference action: as a counselor in the First Presidency (1897–1902) and also as the RLDS Church's first Patriarch/Evangelist.⁹⁸

Joseph had judiciously outwaited William. A "yes" would have brought an unstable person into the inner organizational circle that was dealing with other problems. A flat "no" would have outraged William and probably sent him on a rampage of retaliation, protest, and complaints to anyone who would listen, creating a dangerous source of divisiveness and possibly triggering revelations about matters he had agreed to "forget." If William had still been alive when Joseph III appointed Alexander, he would have felt equally injured. His contributions were undeniable—but so were his weaknesses.

Joseph's delicate balance managed to accomplish something that Joseph Smith Jr., Brigham Young, and James J. Strang had not. He wisely checked his uncle's aspirations but often published his letters, a favor that William relished.

---

96. William B. Smith, Letter to the *Saints' Herald*, ca. March/April 1882, *Saints' Herald* 29, no. 8 (April 15, 1882): 119–20.

97. William Smith (Osterdock, Iowa), Letter to William H. Kelley, October 7, 1892, Community of Christ Library-Archives.

98. Alexander H. Smith Letter Book, 1897–1901, MS 17756, LDS Church History Library; Ronald E. Romig, ed., *Alexander: Joseph and Emma Smith's Far West Son* (Independence: John Whitmer Books, 2010), 110–11.

In his private correspondence, Joseph III also showered his uncle with praise, admiration, and affection. Joseph's success in handling his unpredictable uncle was a remarkable achievement, as he provided his aspiring relative just enough of a role to retain his loyalty, while never granting him any real governing authority in the Church. It probably also helped that William never resided near the headquarters of the RLDS Church, limiting his in-person interactions to the occasional conference. As a result, William served faithfully in the Reorganization during the final fifteen years of his life.

On the other hand, Joseph III unquestionably employed William to meet his own ends. He solicited statements from him that supported the historical narrative Joseph was creating about the Restoration, while keeping him at arm's length from what William really wanted. After William's death, Joseph III and future RLDS historians minimized his role and influence on their organization. William's obituary as published in the *Saints' Herald* was noticeably short, abbreviated his many contributions during Joseph Jr.'s lifetime, minimized his role in keeping alive the concept of lineal succession, and downplayed his multiple missions during his last fifteen years.[99] Even the obituary of William's wife, Eliza, published in the *Saints' Herald* four years earlier, took up more column inches than William's.[100] Ironically, it was the LDS Church, from which William had long been estranged, that published a lengthier obituary.[101]

In his testimony during the Temple Lot Case, William asserted that while "I was living in Lee County, Illinois he had a following that "numbered up some where between thirty and fourty [sic] member[s]." He recounted that he became identified with the Reorganized Church about sixteen years earlier. As for the following he had—"Well . . . I turned them all over as far as I was concerned into the hands of my Nephew."[102] It was easier for him to believe that narrative than the truth—which was that they had rejected his leadership. There is little evidence that he ever understood that he, himself, had scuttled his own organization through his overweening pride and overconfident assumption that his charisma would overcome all doctrinal objections. Perhaps that was an admission he could not make, even silently. Still, William had in truth performed an indispensable role in keeping alive the concept of lineal succession, and the Reorganized Church ultimately provided him with a theology and structure where he had a place—one that still brought him a measure of attention and respect.

---

99. "Died. Smith," *Saints' Herald* 40, no. 49 (December 9, 1893): 787.

100. "SMITH—Mrs. Eliza E., wife of W. B. Smith," *Saints' Herald* 36, no. 13 (March 30, 1889): 207.

101. "William B. Smith," *Deseret Evening News* 27, no. 24 (December 19, 1893): 4.

102. William B. Smith, Testimony, in United States testimony 1892, Court of Appeals (Eighth Circuit), 170–71, MS 1160, LDS Church History Library.

Chapter 21

Final Years

> For nearly a third of a century this good man lived in and about Elkader known and respected by all. . . . His whole life has been one of rectitude and honor.
> —Samuel Murdock, 1893

When thirty-six-year-old attorney John T. Stoneman took the pulpit at the Universalist Church in Elkader, Iowa, on Wednesday, January 29, 1868, he was in for a surprise. The future Iowa state senator had apparently lectured disparagingly on "Joe Smith, the Mormon Prophet" on previous occasions throughout the Midwest, and had no reason to suppose that his stop in this rural northeastern Iowa town would prove to be any different. "He traced the history of Joe Smith and Mormonism from its earliest invention," described a local reporter, and "he backed his statement[s] with historical facts and incidents, and made happy comparisons between the Mormon and Mohometan bibles. The leading ideas of the Mormons, and of Joe Smith, especially, his habits and inclinations, were all presented by Mr. Stoneman in the liveliest and most attractive manner. His delivery was unexceptional, and his lecture throughout displayed a perfect knowledge of the subject he was discoursing upon." But sitting among his numerous and attentive listeners was a "common farmer," who, at the completion of the lecture, arose from the audience and announced: "This lecturer had grossly misrepresented his [Joseph Smith's] claims, his conduct, and the effect of his life's work—and most of all his character." This ordinary looking farmer "startled the audience" and Stoneman when he then announced himself as none other than William B. Smith—brother of the celebrated Mormon prophet about whom Stoneman had been discoursing.

William and Eliza had moved to the country town of Elkader in 1860, eight years earlier, with at least three of Eliza's four children by her first marriage, along with William and Eliza's son William Enoch Smith. After eight years, he was no stranger to the local residents. He may even have known the unnamed reporter on the Stoneman lecture, but it is also true that William had made no effort to announce his Mormon connections earlier—and what name could be more common than "William Smith"? He asserted from the floor that both Mormonism and his brother Joseph had been greatly misrepresented and offered to set the record straight, "if he could obtain the use of the hall, to set forth the truth in relation to his brother, the Mormon prophet," with his knowledge of firsthand information.

The Round Church, Elkader, Iowa. This church was built in 1857 by the Congregationalists, and later sold to the Universalists. It was torn down in 1909. Photograph taken ca. 1900, photographer unknown. Courtesy of Betty Buchholz and the Elkader Historical Society.

"At the close of the latter's [Stoneman's] lecture," and after learning his identity, "some of the audience called upon Mr. Smith for some remarks." The intrigued audience encouraged Smith to take the podium and immediately respond in detail to Stoneman's lecture, but William, apparently "not expecting this" and feeling "unprepared" to make a thoughtful reply, "declined to speak until the following evening." In the intervening time, excitement grew among Elkader's inhabitants. Local residents were so enthusiastic to hear what he had to say, that "the hall [Universalist Church] was instantly pledged, and one of the merchants of the town also proposed that money be raised for the purchase of a new suit of clothes for William Smith in which to appear before the public, ... [which] was immediately supplied" once he confirmed that he would fill the appointment.[1]

The ensuing evening found the Universalist Church filled to overflowing with high expectations. The *Clayton County Journal*, published weekly at Elkader, recounted how "everybody was on tip-toe" to hear Smith's response. The reporter set the scene with gusto: "It was hardly expected that a common farmer, such as Mr. Smith appeared to be, could say many 'smart things,' or be in any way

---

1. "Mormonism. Lecture by Mr. Stoneman—Reply of a Brother of Joe Smith," *Clayton County Journal* 16, no. 38 (February 6, 1868): 2; Gary James Bergera, ed., *The Autobiography of B. H. Roberts* (Salt Lake City: Signature Books, 1990), 106–7.

eloquent, but the fact that he was a brother of the Mormon prophet and himself once prominently connected with the Mormons led the curious and the seekers after truth to the church." Elkader's citizens were not disappointed. "To the amazement of the community," the fifty-six-year-old Smith "delivered a very logical and effective reply to the lecture." The local reporter recounted that "he not only spoke very readily, but, being entirely conversant with the subject, having made it a life of study, he elicited many facts and presented them in the most striking language." Indeed, William's skill is not surprising. He had spent the better part of his life since his teen years defending his Mormon faith. He had forgotten none of his skills as an articulate and persuasive debater, but "he also displayed a native wit and sarcasm that many times brought down the house with thunders of applause." For entertainment-starved townspeople enduring an Iowa winter, this lecture and its rebuttal were first-rate fare. William himself must have been pleased by the reporter's conclusion that the residents of Elkader "readily believed that Mormonism wasn't half as bad [as] . . . many suppose[d]," and that Joseph Smith "had just as good a right to be a prophet as any man mentioned in the Bible."[2] The *Clayton County Journal* does not chronicle the response of the New York educated lawyer, or if he was present the following evening during Smith's reply; but if he was, he must have left town chagrined at being defeated by a local farmer of far less formal education.

Further evidence of William's success in this public encounter is that the editor of the *Clayton County Journal* invited William to write a series of columns explaining Mormonism in even greater detail than allowed for during his evening of rebuttal. "Doubtless every one of our readers would gladly hear [more] about Mormonism from so eminent a source," concluded the reporter of the episode.[3] Although he was nearing his sixtieth birthday and had not actively proselyted for nearly a decade, William's intellect and oratory talent had apparently not diminished. He followed up his lecture with at least two articles about Mormonism, being careful to delineate between his belief in "primitive Mormonism," and Brigham Young's version in Utah, which embraced polygamy.[4]

---

2. "Mormonism. Lecture by Mr. Stoneman—Reply of a Brother of Joe Smith"; Bergera, *Autobiography of B. H. Roberts*, 107.

3. "Mormonism. Lecture by Mr. Stoneman—Reply of a Brother of Joe Smith."

4. William fulfilled the editor's request and wrote at least two columns about Mormonism for the *Clayton County Journal*. He sent excerpts from the articles to Joseph Smith III, who had them reprinted: "Extracts from the *Clayton Co. Journal*," in *True Latter Day Saints' Herald* 15, no. 1 (January 1, 1869): 23–25. "The iron horse is rapidly approaching the capitol of polygamy," wrote William in one article for the paper, "and thousands will turn their eyes towards Utah, but the devilish system of social servitude, incorporated by Brigham Young and his hypocritical, blood-stained Elders and Apostles will prevent them from making that territory their home. Tens of thousands of soldiers will rally at the first call to wipe out these law-breakers and adulterers, and it needs the voice of Congress, and the command of the President to teach them that there is 'a God in Israel.'"

At the time William delivered his defense of Mormonism at Elkader's Universalist Church, he had been acquainted with the area for eight years. William had briefly teamed up with Martin Harris at Kirtland, Ohio, in the fall of 1855, but this experiment was short-lived.[5] Furthermore, William had then been at loose ends, maritally speaking. He had married Roxey Ann Grant in May 1847, but the marriage had been much interrupted by William's constant travels, efforts at church-building, and especially when his support of polygamy became known. Roxey Ann separated from William in the spring of 1850 (the two divorced in 1853), then resided with her parents in Walnut Grove, Illinois, taking H. Wallace and Thalia, their two children. His two daughters by Caroline, for whom Roxey Ann had provided a mother's care, had married in their late teens and established homes of their own. After William's association with Martin Harris failed to produce a core of believers, William disappears from the documentary record for several months. However, by July 1856, he was living at Turkey River in northeastern Iowa, located on the Mississippi River and thirty miles southeast of Elkader.[6]

How William spent the summer and fall of 1856 has not been documented; but in the spring of 1857, William returned to Kirtland with renewed enthusiasm for building up a church in the area. In addition to preaching locally, he crossed the state line into Pennsylvania where he preached in Erie and Warren Counties.[7] This second effort was ultimately no more successful than the first, but during the time he was organizing with Harris in October 1857 William remained in the area, in part because of an attraction to the recently divorced thirty-year-old Eliza Elsie Sanborn Brain. The two wed at Kirtland on November 12, 1857.[8] William, who was sixteen years Eliza's senior, apparently had benefited from the turmoil that had marred his earlier marriages and, from all that can be learned, willingly assumed fatherly responsibility for Eliza's four children by her previous marriage, ranging in age from eleven to six. Almost immediately, they added a son, William ("Willie") Enoch Smith, born on July 24, 1858.[9] After struggling for three years to earn a

---

5. Stephen Post, Journals, 1835–1879, October 5, 1855, MS 1304, LDS Church History Library.

6. William Smith (Turkey River, Iowa), Letter to Brigham Young, July 13, 1856, Brigham Young Office files 1832–1878, Letter from Church Leaders and Others, 1840–1877, William Smith, 1844–1857, LDS Church History Library. From this locale, he wrote his third and last letter to Brigham Young, a combination of wheedling for a restoration of his position as apostle and patriarch and angry denunciation of how "mean" Brigham's treatment had been. There is no record that Brigham responded to any of these letters.

7. William Smith (Warren, Penn.), Letter to the Editor, May 19, 1857, *New-York Daily Tribune* 17, no. 5025 (May 28, 1857): 5.

8. Daughters of the American Revolution, New Connecticut Chapter (Painesville, Ohio), "Probate Court Marriage Records, Lake County Ohio, 1840–1865," typescript, 102, Morley Library, Painesville, Ohio. The entry reads: "Smith, Wm., m., Eliza E. Sanburne, November 12, 1857."

9. "Records of Early Church Families," *Utah Genealogical Magazine* 26, no. 19 (1935): 105; 1870 U.S. Census, Iowa, Clayton County, Boardman Township, 27.

Final Years 535

Elkader, Iowa. Photograph taken ca. 1852, photographer unknown. Courtesy Betty Buchholz and the Elkader Historical Society.

living by preaching for the Baptist Church and by various sales-related ventures in Pennsylvania, William and Eliza relocated their family seven hundred miles to the west, in Elkader, Iowa, in the latter part of 1860.[10]

Why they chose Elkader remains a minor mystery. There is no indication that William had ever passed near Clayton County, Iowa before 1856. Apparently the closest he had come had been Galena, Illinois, eighty miles away. The explanation may be, not that he was drawn to the area, but rather than he was attempting to avoid other regions where he was no longer welcome. He would undoubtedly have sought to distance himself from Illinois, which had enmeshed him in legal difficulties in Lee and Knox Counties that had only recently been settled. Initially welcoming Saints in southern Wisconsin had also rejected his leadership and his Church organization, and so he probably avoided that region as well.

The town of Elkader is located in the heart of Clayton County, just fifteen miles west of the Mississippi River. The town was founded twenty years before

---

10. Two of Eliza's children, Mary and Ward Brain, were living with William and Eliza when the 1860 U.S. Census was enumerated, and one more, Byron, also by her previous marriage, was living with William and Eliza in Elkader when the 1870 U.S. Census was enumerated. Erin Jennings Metcalfe documents Mary Lois Brain's death in Elkader on January 11, 1865. "Records of Early Church Families," *Utah Genealogical Magazine* 26, no. 19 (1935): 105; 1860 U.S. Census, Pennsylvania, Erie County, Venango, Roll M653_1108, 1061, image 454; 1870 U.S. Census, Boardman, Clayton County, Iowa, 27; Erin B. Jennings Metcalfe, "Eliza Elsie Sanborn," ca. 2010, unpublished manuscript in my possession, 3. See Eliza's obituary for documentation about the family's relocation to Elkader in 1860. "Obituary. Mrs. Eliza E. Smith of Elkader," *Elkader Weekly Register* 12, no. 18 (March 14, 1889): 1. See Chapter 17 for additional details on William's marriage to Eliza Elsie Sanborn and for information on her previous marriage and affiliation with Mormonism.

Turkey River, as it flows through Elkader, Iowa. Photograph taken ca. 1925, photographer unknown. Copy in author's possession.

William set foot in the area, its first explorers being miners hoping to find lead similar to the rich deposits of Galena, Illinois, and Dubuque, Iowa. Elkader was established as the county seat in 1860, the same year the Smiths arrived. The Turkey River bisects both the county and the town, picking up enough speed to power a grist mill. In addition to a handful of small businesses, the town also boasted a two-story brick schoolhouse, three church houses (Methodist, Catholic, and Universalist), and a weekly newspaper.[11] Thus, William could easily see Elkader as a good place to raise his young family, buy affordable property, and farm for a living. On September 6, 1862, he and Eliza welcomed a second son named for William's deceased younger brother, Edson Don Carlos. The family was complete when daughter Loie May was born on May 8, 1866.[12]

William and Eliza probably rented a home for a few years, since land records show that they purchased two forty-acre tracts in 1865 after William's brief adventure with the Union Army. They paid $100 for the first tract on October 7. Located about five miles north of town and bordering the west bank of the Turkey River, it would have been suitable for farming. They paid $300 for the second forty-acre tract on November 18, but the two properties were not contiguous. This acreage lay two miles northwest of downtown Elkader. Here, near a little creek that quietly meandered into the Turkey River, William and Eliza

---

11. A. T. Andreas, *Illustrated and Historical Atlas of the State of Iowa* (Chicago: Lake Side Press, 1875), 435–36.

12. "Records of Early Church Families," 105; "Episodes in Genealogical Research: New Light on William Smith," *Deseret News*, July 27, 1935, 7–8; Harry D. Galley, *Joseph Smith Senior's Children* (Rock Island, Ill.: Harry D. Galley, 2000), 46–47.

William and Eliza Smith's Home, Elkader, Iowa. Date and photographer unknown. Courtesy Gracia Jones.

constructed a two-story wood-plank structure, described by B. H. Roberts as a "humble log and frame home in the hills two or three miles west of the town of Elkader."[13] Six years later, they purchased a tract of forty acres that shared a property line with their home place. They paid $400 for it, but generously transferred it to their twenty-seven-year-old son Willie for only five dollars in 1885, to help him get a start in life when he and his wife, Anna Jane Harris Smith, were expecting their second child.[14]

Given William's social/religious turmoil and his psychological volatility, he could not be called an encouraging marriage prospect in 1857; but Eliza's personality seems to have tempered William's unpredictable nature. The marriage and the move marked a turning point in William's turbulent life. Descriptions of her personality mention that she was both loving and firm, "quiet in her manners," and possessing a "retiring disposition." These traits, assumed to be suitable for a nineteenth-century lady, did not mean she was meek and malleable. Beneath her reserve was a clear mind and steadfast determination in matters of importance. When she filed for divorce from her first husband, James Brain, in 1857, she was only one of five women petitioning for a divorce; and she insisted on reverting

---

13. Bergera, *Autobiography of B. H. Roberts*, 103.

14. William B. Smith purchased the first property for $100 from Louis and Frances Davis on October 7, 1865. The second tract of land, where the Smiths constructed their home, was purchased on November 18, 1865, in Eliza's name for $300 from Henry Carter. The additional forty acres was also purchased from Carter, on April 8, 1871. Land and Record Book Z, 584; Land and Record Book B-2, 48; Land and Record Book 38, 37; Quit Claim Deed Record, number 55, all at the Clayton County Courthouse, Elkader, Iowa.

to her birth name of Sanborn.¹⁵ A second example is the portrait left by LDS missionary B. H. Roberts and his companion, Hyrum Jensen, who visited the Smiths in 1880. Roberts described William as respectful and cordial—expressing a desire to "pleasantly entertain us"; but the encounter with Eliza was neither. Apparently she had absorbed and resented William's view of himself as being maltreated by the Utah-based church and was "vehement in her expression of her opposition to us in very uncomplimentary, not to say insulting, attacks upon our people in Utah." Roberts summarized the marriage as a near-caricature of the henpecked husband: "Mrs. Smith . . . dominated the household, and William, once the proud, rebellious, pugnacious, and dominant spirit both in his father's house and likewise in the church was now tame and submissive enough to his arrogant and dominating wife."¹⁶

Eliza Elsie Sanborn Brain Smith, 1827–1889. Photograph by Hale, ca. 1875, Elkader, Iowa. Courtesy Gracia Jones.

The missionaries' depiction of Eliza's personality was in striking contrast to that of her neighbors, who felt that "she was accommodating to all, and was always ready to extend a helping hand to a neighbor or friend in distress."¹⁷ It is easy to see that Eliza felt protective of William and stood ready to deflect any proposition with which the Mormon missionaries might try to lure him into any involvement that would have disrupted their hard but peaceful life. In any event, although she willingly provided supper, breakfast, and a night's shelter, she did not encourage a longer stay and probably foresaw that the memories aroused by their visit would bring both nostalgia and sorrow to William. The fact that she could behave with both exemplary neighborliness and protective defiance obviously made for a successful marriage for their thirty-two years together, and no record that I have been able to find shows William embroiled in the kinds of interpersonal conflicts and religious ambitions that had kept his earlier years distressed and turbulent.

In describing William's encounter with John T. Stoneman, the *Clayton County Journal* described William as "follow[ing] the occupation of a farmer in the vicinity of Elkader, and upon Sundays occasionally preaching," although it does not specify whether he affiliated with one of the three denominations in

---

15. "List of Letters Remaining in the Cleveland Post Office, August 4th, 1857, Ladies' List," *Plain Dealer*, August 4, 1857, 3; "Petition for Divorce," notice in unidentified newspaper, ca. July 16, 1857; both cited in Metcalfe, "Eliza Elsie Sanborn," 2.

16. Bergera, *Autobiography of B. H. Roberts*, 103.

17. "Obituary. Mrs. Eliza E. Smith of Elkader," 1.

Final Years 539

Judge Samuel Murdock, 1817–1897 (center). From Realto E. Price, *History of Clayton County, Iowa* (Chicago: Robert O. Law Co., 1916).

town.[18] Farming was obviously a fallback position. Those who knew him best knew that his ambitions had always been centered in religious activities—and, furthermore—that he had never liked farming. When his Mormon nephew Joseph F. Smith learned of William's plans, he exclaimed in a letter to his wife Levira: "Joseph [III] received a letter from Uncle William from which we learned he [William] had sowed his wild oats etc. and that he was farming now for a living!"[19] It is true that William was only moderately successful as a farmer and remained constantly vigilant for alternative occupations.

At some point during his years in Elkader, he worked at the law office of Samuel Murdock, one of six attorneys who practiced in the town. Murdock had been the first attorney to establish a practice in Clayton County, later served as a judge, and was one of the best-respected citizens in the region. Murdock's effectiveness as an attorney brought him distinguished status. William's experience as Hancock County's representative in the Illinois state legislature in 1842–43 no doubt honed his understanding of both political and legal issues. When Murdock became aware of William's political experience, he invited him to do occasional work clerking in his law office. Such experience was highly valued in frontier America, and William had been offered a similar position in the Nauvoo law office of George Edmunds in the spring of 1846. Edmunds, who shared an office with Almon W. Babbitt in Nauvoo, offered to tutor Smith in the legal trade if he would "drop all his Gospel." William, caught up in the throes of the succession crisis and experiencing his own ambitions, declined the offer.[20] William had also experienced his own share of legal challenges, a hard but thorough mentorship in understanding the law. The legal profession also seemed to be a promising avenue given William's keen mind, skill as a debater, ability to think on his feet, and his thoughtfulness in scrutinizing difficult topics. Additionally, Murdock and Smith shared a common interest in Native American history, which for Smith was expressed most powerfully in the Book of Mormon. Murdock was an avid explorer of Native American mounds, from which he collected artifacts and which he estimated to number some 100,000 in

---

18. "Mormonism. Lecture by Mr. Stoneman—Reply of a Brother of Joe Smith."

19. Joseph F. Smith (Colchester, Ill.), Letter to Levira A. Smith, June 28, 1860, Joseph F. Smith Papers 1854–1918, Correspondence between Joseph and his wife Levira 1859–1867, MS 1325, LDS Church History Library.

20. Greg R. Knight, ed., *Thomas Bullock Nauvoo Journal* (Orem, Utah: Grandin Book, 1994), 64.

Clayton County alone. William likely worked only part-time or on a project basis for Murdock, as existing records do not suggest that he earned a consistent wage or spent regular days at Murdock's office. It does seem clear, however, that the two men developed an affable relationship.[21]

Smith's foremost passion remained laboring as a minister of the gospel, which had become an integral part of his identity. When he identified himself by profession, he most often called himself "Minister," or "Latter Day Saint Minister," and his near neighbors referred to him as the "Reverend William B. Smith."[22] After a carefully negotiated union with the RLDS Church, he attended an RLDS general conference in 1883 at which he begged leaders for a missionary appointment. Though RLDS missionaries were expected to be self-sustaining during their labors, due to his connection to Mormonism's founder, he was often the recipient of monetary gifts during his travels. (See Chapter 20.) He announced that it was his desire to be appointed as a missionary but revealingly added that he wished "to be relieved from the monotony of a life confined on a farm where necessity of hard labor like a canker worm is constantly destroying my ministerial . . . and spiritual life; and that my . . . temporal life may be prolonged."[23] Certainly his health was a factor in his avoidance of farm labor, but his dislike of the unremitting physical labor was probably a more important factor. Although Iowa land was rich and the expanding population meant that, despite bad years, there was a consistent market for agricultural project, William disliked farming and does not seem to have been particularly successful. His letters contain complaints about losing money on his crops. If he could find a buyer, he would sell his farm. "Times are very hard with me just now," he wrote to Joseph III in spring of 1880, "my farming resources have been so much cut off, for the few years passed by the chinch bug and drought, that I have realized no surplus of means; only what necessity demands for the immediate support of my family. I have tried to sell out, that I might locate in some more favorable spot of earth, but there is no sale for property here, and I must wait the Lord's time."[24] Three years later, William described a major flood, his account laced with humor:

---

21. *Portrait and Biographical Record of Dubuque, Jones and Clayton Counties, Iowa* (Chicago: Chapman Publishing, 1894), 502–4; *The History of Iowa County, Iowa, Containing A History of the County, Its Cities, Towns, &c.* (Des Moines: Union Historical Company, 1881), 64.

22. See 1850 U.S. Census, Illinois, Lee County, Amboy Township, Roll: M432_116, 117B, Image 89; 1880 U.S. Census, Iowa, Clayton County, Boardman Township, Roll: 333, 278D, Image 0199; Statement of L. E. Wagner, October 28, 1887, 31, in William B. Smith Pension File; Samuel Murdock, "The Rev. William B. Smith," *Elkader Weekly Register* 16, no. 49 (November 23, 1893): 16.

23. "Elder Wm. B. Smith, of the High Priests Quorum, Present, Reports," *Saints' Herald* 30, no. 17 (April 28, 1883): 269.

24. W[ilia]m. B. Smith (Elkader, Iowa), Letter to Joseph [Smith III], March 21, 1880, *Saints' Herald* 27, no. 8 (April 15, 1880): 122.

The clouds opened a general avalanche and poured down big rivers of waters, and following down a little spring brook that passes near my house, it spread itself out almost as majestic as the great father of waters; and in passing my house it took along with it a light two horse wagon that I had for family use. . . . This outpouring of such a body of water all at once, tore up some of my wire fence, taking posts out of the ground, "asking no questions for conscience's sake," and some [of the] rail fence I suppose will soon find a lodgement in the Gulf of Mexico.[25]

Several times William described inclement weather that destroyed his crops, his detailed complaints no doubt hoping to bring sympathy—and more material expressions of concern—regarding his difficult economic plight. "My garden [is] all spoiled under watter for near two weeks," he wrote to RLDS presiding bishop Edmund L. Kelley in 1892, "Potato, beens, peas unions [sic] and sweet corn all gone up and [it is] still raining at this writing. . . . My kitchen was flooded with whatter & all boats had to be used all about the place."[26]

Notwithstanding his dislike of farming, no doubt Eliza's steadiness and more resolute personality evened out William's volatile reactions to adversity and prevented him from making impulsive decisions. Beginning in the 1870s, he rented his three small farms of forty-acres each to neighbors, which provided some additional income.[27] Certainly as Willie and Edson became teenagers, they helped keep the family afloat. Though very little has survived documenting Eliza's activities during their thirty-two-year marriage, Eliza probably assisted by leading out in home chores, raising their three children, and in caring for their animals. She also nursed William during his episodes of illness. Edson remembered his father as a "hard working man," who, through persevering effort, eventually succeeded in paying off their farm.[28] Notwithstanding, the Smiths remained at the lower end of the socio-economic ladder, particularly as William moved into the final decade of his life.

His failing health had been a continual challenge from the time of his service in the Civil War. After he returned from the war in the summer of 1865, he immediately petitioned the U.S. government for an invalid's pension. Although not injured in battle, his right ear and right eye were affected; and he suffered from digestive distress that he may have contracted through a parasite in the Arkansas swamp. His attending physician since coming to Elkader, A. B. Hanna, reported seeing Smith in the fall of 1865 and indicated that he was battling with "Rheumatism, deafness, and partial loss of sight of right eye." "I found him quite hard of hearing," continued Hanna in his notes, "the sight of right eye so much impaired that he could not see objects distinctly and the right arm was somewhat impaired from the effects of

---

25. William Smith (Elkader, Iowa), Letter to Joseph Smith III, July 23, 1883, *Saints' Herald* 30, no. 32 (August 11, 1883): 507–8.

26. William Smith (Osterdock, Iowa), Letter to E[dmund] L. Kelley, July 2, 1892, P19, fd. 49, Community of Christ Library-Archives.

27. Statement of L. E. Wagner, October 28, 1887, 31, William B. Smith Pension File.

28. "Episodes in Genealogical Research: New Light on William Smith," 8.

William B. Smith, 1811–1893. Photograph by Clark, taken January 1891, at Hannibal, Missouri. Courtesy Community of Christ Archives.

rheumatism." Hanna saw Smith again in the year 1867, and "found him growing worse as to such complaint[s] . . . until at the present time he has so little use of his right arm that he is unable to perform manual labor, has lost the sight of his right eye so that it is of little or no use to him whatever, and his deafness somewhat increased." Smith was experiencing symptoms of neuralgia on the right side of his face and body, a hereditary condition present in the Smith line, sometimes exacerbated by stress.[29] Joseph Smith III's biographer Roger D. Launius described the excruciating pain associated with his struggle with neuralgia, indicating that after his intial bout which first appeared in his mid-forties during a demanding mission to Utah, "the ailment flared up periodically ever after. Known as the 'suicide sickness' during the nineteenth century because the terrible pain presumably drove the sufferer to suicide, the largely hereditary disease was caused by a nerve growing directly into the skull without the usual tissue shielding it from contact with the bone. It was particularly painful whenever the weather changed dramatically, and sometimes when it did not" summarized Launius of the condition, "making it difficult for the sufferer to talk, eat, or even move his head." William, whose condition appears to have mirrored his nephew's, was forced to suffer through these intermittent bouts of neuralgia, as nothing could be done to treat the condition in the late 1800s.[30] In William's case, his symptoms first emerged while he was in the army. Hanna, who provided medical care for the family prior to William's military service, made a statement that William had not complained of any of these symptoms prior to his enlistment.[31] William apparently never fully recovered his hearing, sight, or full use of his arm, all on the right side of his body. His initial pension of six dollars a month was granted July 12, 1865.[32]

Besides neuralgia, William struggled with symptoms that a modern diagnostician may have identified as celiac disease. From William's complaints, doctors frequently reported a host of digestive ailments, including chronic diarrhea, stomach pain, and piles. At one point doctors also discovered that he had developed a fairly

---

29. Joseph Smith III also struggled with neuralgia throughout his life. See, for example, Joseph Smith III, Letter to J[ohn W.] Peterson, November 8, 1893, Community of Christ Library-Archives; Joseph Smith III (Lamoni, Iowa), Letter to William B. Smith, October 26, 1893, P13, f439, Community of Christ Library-Archives; Richard P. Howard, ed., *The Memoirs of President Joseph Smith III*, 1832–1914 (Independence, Mo.: Herald Publishing House, 1979), 160.

30. Launius also conjectures that "the likelihood of Joseph Smith, Jr., having the same affliction is considerable," but that "since he died a relatively young man, it never appeared sufficiently for diagnosis." He cites an account of a "painful toothache" during Joseph's incarceration in Liberty Jail as a possible episode of neuralgia. Roger D. Launius, *Joseph Smith III Pragmatic Prophet* (Urbana: University of Illinois Press, 1988), 230–31, 244 note 43.

31. Statements of A. B. Hanna, July 27, 1867, March 30, 1882, 91–92, 133, in William B. Smith Pension File.

32. U.S. Pension Office, Letter to Edson D. C. Smith, March 14, 1916, copy of typewritten letter, 21, in William B. Smith Pension File.

serious umbilical hernia, and was forced to wear a "truss," a nineteenth-century contraption worn around the waist to apply constant pressure on the protrusion. Respiratory illnesses, evident earlier in life, also continued to plague him in later years. Sons Willie and Edson both reported that William's physical condition intermittently impacted his ability to engage in manual labor. According to Willie, William was periodically so ill that he "had to be lifted on and off of his bed" by family members and could move about his home only with difficulty.[33] Yet at least some of these physical symptoms occasionally subsided during in the 1870s and 1880s, helping to explain why he was able to undertake several missions, at least one of them lasting for six months after he was accepted in the RLDS Church on his original baptism. However, these stretches of vigorous health were punctuated by other periods when his symptoms returned and he again experienced ill health.

His Civil War pension provided a steady but inadequate income in providing for his family. On at least ten occasions, he had local doctors evaluate his worsening symptoms, hoping to increase the amount of his pension. His pension was increased from $6 to $8 in 1867, to $12 in October 1879, and finally to $14 in December 1887, where it remained until his death six years later.[34] However, not all of the doctors he visited concurred with William's assessment of his symptoms, and some even questioned the veracity of his complaints. A trio of doctors who examined William in 1882 at Dubuque, Iowa, noted in their report that William said he was unable to perform any manual labor but occasionally preached gospel sermons. While preaching a sermon probably required only minimal physical effort, especially by comparison with farm work, it still involved traveling, walking, and standing for a protracted period of time while speaking. These doctors' report did not present the picture of a failing invalid; rather, they summarized that his "physical condition [is] good for a man of his years" and actually recommended decreasing the amount of Smith's pension. An intriguing, and perhaps relevant note in their report is that William was a "Bro. of Jo [the] Mormon Prophet," which suggests both that William's conversation went beyond strictly medical matters and also that the trio of doctors may have let their skepticism about Mormonism influence their evaluation of William's health problems. Still, another doctor who evaluated Smith that same year submitted a similarly cautious evaluation to the U.S. Pension Office: "I think the old man [Smith] has got about all that he is entitled to. I can't make any thing out of the multiplicity of complaints alleged."[35]

---

33. William E. Smith (Dundee, Minn.), Letter to U.S. Pension Office, ca. October 1889, 77–79, in William B. Smith Pension File; and Edson D. C. Smith, (Dundee, Minn.) to U.S. Pension Office, June 6, 1892, 80, in William B. Smith Pension File.

34. U.S. Pension Office, Letter to Edson D. C. Smith, March 14, 1916, 21, William B. Smith Pension File.

35. Asa Kearr, M. Staples, and C. M. Balderseage, Examining Surgeon's Certificate, June 21, 1882, 123, William B. Smith Pension File; K. F. Rerdy, Examining Surgeon's Certificate, April 5, 1882, 125, William B. Smith Pension File. Even A. B. Hanna,

Final Years

William and Eliza Smith's property, 1970. Photograph by Mary Schofield Belden.

Perhaps William's nearest neighbor, L. E. Wagner, gave the most accurate portrayal of William's activities during his declining years as part of a statement submitted to the Pension Office in 1887 when William would have been seventy-six. Wagner agreed that William sometimes

> had to be cared for by his neighbors and friends, and lived by hired help[.] He is the owner of a Small farm which Joins my land, and for many years Since his return from the Service of the United States as a Soldier, he has rented his farm consisting of only 40 acres to his neighbors for use and cultivation, not being able to work the land himself on account of his General disability. I also state that I have not seen him engaged or Attempt any manual labor for these many years, excepting only some light work about his house, such as bringing in wood and watter, or milking a cow by sitting on a chair.[36]

William had never led an affluent life, although the early 1840s, while living at Plymouth and Nauvoo, and perhaps his years presiding over the LDS branches in the East, had been the most financially comfortable. But during his seventies, his final years were marked by poverty. He struggled to earn enough by renting out his small farms, by keeping a cow and a garden, possibly a pig each season, almost certainly chickens, and by preaching a sermon when he could, for which

---

the Smith's family doctor at Elkader, occasionally challenged the accuracy of William's complaints. In an evaluation he completed in 1874 he noted that there was not a "particle of increased disability in the case and he [William] is in possession of a good state of health." Hannah concluded, "His case is fifty percent better than it was at the last biennial examination . . . therefore I find no increase of disability, consequently no increase of pension can be recommended." A. B. Hanna, Examining Surgeon's Certificate, March 18, 1874, 137, William B. Smith Pension File.

36. Statement of L. E. Wagner, 31.

he probably received a portion of the weekly collection. Certainly, he relied anxiously on his monthly pension.

But William also turned to the RLDS Church in hopes of receiving a pension or at least a periodic allowance. Community of Christ Archives contain about three dozen letters in which the focus gradually shifted from reporting family news and expressing bright hopes for the Reorganization to imploring material assistance. He had tried a similar approach with his begging letters to Brigham Young and other LDS leaders during the late 1840s and 1850s—only to receive absolutely no encouragement—but RLDS leaders, despite the constant scramble for funds, were occasionally able to send him small amounts.

Edmund Levi Kelley, 1844–1930. Date and photographer unknown. Courtesy Community of Christ Archives.

The first of these letters where William made a direct pitch for funds was written in October 1880 [37] when he was sixty-nine years old and continued until within a few months of his death. While he occasionally appealed to Joseph Smith III for support, he typically petitioned Edmund L. Kelley, who, after 1890 was the Presiding Bishop, and supervised the distribution of Church funds, and in whom William found a sympathetic ear. These letters are not easy reading, since William's unattractive sense of entitlement once again becomes evident. William dusted off many of the same tactics he had employed earlier: references to his extensive missionary service, being victimized and mistreated by the Twelve in Nauvoo, and his lineage as part of Mormonism's founding family.

Writing to Bishop Kelley in 1891, William rhetorically demanded: "Who is it that stands next to the oldest claim in the Church for either moral worth or for the amount of labour done—in planting the standard of this latterday work[?]— and in planting this standard in the world, who is it may we not also ask that has been the greatest sufferers—during the trials—that the Church has had to pass through since the date of its organizatino [sic] in 1830?"[38] With such grandiose rhetoric, William apparently hoped to persuade Kelley that he merited a reward; but Kelley, who was not born until 1844, did not have memories of the Ohio-Missouri-Nauvoo glory days that William was obviously counting on; and Joseph III's appraisal of William to Kelley, affectionate though it might have been, would not have encouraged liberality toward his manipulative uncle. William often sent

---

37. W[ilia]m. B. Smith (Elkader, Iowa), Letter to Respected Nephew [Joseph Smith III], October 24, 1880, *Saints' Herald* 27, no. 23 (December 1, 1880): 369.

38. William Smith (Osterdock, Iowa), Letter to Edmund Levi Kelley, October 15, 1891, P19, fd. 48, Community of Christ Library-Archives; terminal punctuation added.

lengthy descriptions of what he described as a "short brief of my labors in the Church," hoping to persuade Kelley of his worthiness of financial support. A repeated—and no doubt wearisome—theme was his claim that the Church owed him for his lifetime of labors. "Now brother [Kelley] the question arises = Am I to loose [lose] all the honor or glory of all this labour done for the 50 years that are passed? And what I now ask for Brother is that the Bishope place a certain sum per <u>month</u> for my support."[39] Kelley apparently did not respond. In other letters, William implored Kelley to send funds so he could, for example, finish his kitchen, buy a stove, or purchase wood to heat his house—sketching the prospect of entertaining in comfort whatever RLDS dignitaries passed through Elkader. He also depicted himself as unable to serve a mission due to his shabby attire.[40] In one such letter he queried Kelley, "[You] don't want Gentiles to know Jo Smith's Brother is too poor to owne a good ministerial coat[?]"[41] Some of the numerous letters William sent to Kelley were written on brown paper sacks, a vivid indication of the poverty in which he and Eliza were living. In one letter in June 1892 when he was eighty-one, he described their suffering during the previous winter when he had been forced to dismantle the fence around his yard and burn the lumber to heat the house.[42]

While Kelley's letters of response did not survive, and copies were not retained at RLDS Church headquarters, William's continued correspondence documents Kelley's responsiveness to his needs. Though Kelley deflected William's request for a regular, monthly allowance, he frequently sent William small sums of money, typically ranging from $5 to $25.[43] It is unknown whether Kelley acted on his own, or in consultation with Joseph III; but these periodic gifts, combined with William's pension and the rent from his farm, were William's only sources of income during his final years, which passed in a pathetic chronicle of increasing poverty and ill health.

In retrospect, it seems likely to me that William's violent middle years—between 1845 and 1865—had taken a toll on William's emotional health. The psychological stress of grandiose schemes followed by destructive disappointment

---

39. William Smith (Osterdock, Iowa), Letter to Edmund Levi Kelley, ca. October-November, 1891, P19, fd. 48, Community of Christ Library-Archives.

40. William B. Smith (Osterdock, Iowa), Letters to Edmund Levi Kelley, September 6, September 15, October 19, and November 12, 1891, and June 1, 1892, all letters in P19, fds. 48 and 49, Community of Christ Library-Archives.

41. William B. Smith, Letter to Edmund Levi Kelley (Independence, Mo.), August 26, 1892, P19, fd. 49, Community of Christ Library-Archives; terminal punctuation added.

42. William B. Smith to Edmund Levi Kelley, June 1, 1892.

43. William B. Smith, (Elkader, Iowa), Letter to George A. Blakeslee, February 20, 1885; William B. Smith (Osterdock, Iowa), Letters to Edmund Levi Kelley, October 15 and October 19, 1891, and March 30, and June 1, 1892; William B. Smith, Letter to Edmund Levi Kelley, June 1, 1892; all letters in P19, fds. 48 and 49, Community of Christ Library-Archives.

and initially warm friendships that chilled into mistrust and dislike certainly contributed to his poor physical health. Although he had been able to distract himself with the next church-building project or position himself as a martyr to enemies both in and out of the Church, the ceaseless round of activity came to a stop after his last church-building effort fizzled. He had to face the record of his many shattered relationships and the fact that his reputation had been materially damaged among many of his former friends and family.

Tellingly, some doctors noted items related to William's emotional health when they evaluated his pension requests or just provided medical care for the family. A. B. Hanna, William's family physician for many years, noted during one visit that William was experiencing what he termed "dyspeptic feelings," which, in nineteenth-century vernacular could have referred to either William's persistent digestive problems or his gloomy and irritable mood. Both seem likely; but Hanna recounted on a subsequent visit that William's "mind is dull and torpid," and he had "no life or energy of spirits."[44] While insufficient information has survived to make a reliable diagnosis, these brief entries by a medical professional suggest evidence of an ongoing struggle to deal with what we would probably call depression today. Such negative feelings would be both a cause and an effect that influenced William's significant physical distress.

Time and distance from the turmoil of his past probably helped improve his emotional health. His removal to northeastern Iowa provided a literal reprieve from the stressors he had experienced when he was raging through the Midwest, dazzled by his own ambitions but lacking the self-discipline either to make a stable home for his family or to settle into a religious life that would bring greater peace. In one of his earliest letters to his nephew Joseph Smith III, written in October 1868, William recounted, "Since my sojourn in this part of the country, I had concluded to remain silent on the subject [of Mormonism], still preaching occasionally, notwithstanding."[45] An eighteen-year hiatus from affiliating with any particular faction of Mormonism probably helped improve his emotional stability if only by reducing the frequency of bristling encounters with former friends and co-believers who, he felt, were undermining and ignoring him. As William moved into his fifties, a new marriage, and a chance to become a more thoughtful and consistent father, he achieved a simpler life. The quiet little community of Elkader on the banks of Iowa's Turkey River was willing to accept him on his own terms—not as a scandalous Mormon, not as the brother of a murdered prophet and patriarch. He had no need to fear attacks by anti-Mormons. Like his sisters and their children, anonymity afforded a welcome period of peace. Both in his own marriage and in Joseph III's firm instructions to forget Nauvoo polygamy, William's self-indulgent

---

44. Statements of A. B. Hanna, July 27, 1867, September 4, 1873, 133, 135, in William B. Smith Pension File.

45. William Smith (Elkader, Iowa), Letter to Dear Nephew [Joseph Smith III], October 16, 1868, *Saints' Herald* 8, no. 1 (January 1, 1869): 22–23.

delusions about his own form of plural marriage were gone. His ambitions to preside over a thriving church receded into the background, although they revived with sufficient energy that he besieged his nephew for recognition and position for a time—but Joseph III simply outwaited him. Besides more than year's service to his country in the Civil War and his occasional missionary travels, Smith spent the remainder of his life in Clayton County.

In that peaceful setting, William found the respect and acceptance that he had lacked up to that point in his life. His teachings and example greatly impressed the local citizens in the area where he resided during his final thirty years of his life. After his ties to Mormonism became known, and before uniting with the Reorganized Church, he became a defender of Mormonism throughout the region where he resided. In 1875 he traveled to Buckland, Alamakee County, Iowa, and, according to William, "succeeded in removing much of the prejudice of the people against the faith of the true Latter Day Saints."[46] His preaching was influential enough, according to B. H. Roberts, that when he and his companion Hyrum Jensen from Salt Lake City visited the area during the 1880s, he recorded: "I can bear witness of William's return to a defense of truth in Elkader, where I met up with the evidence of such a return. At a drug store in Elkader where Elder Jensen and I called to inquire specifically as to the location of William Smith's home, the hotel proprietor or manager, when he learned the nature of our mission, stated that all through their country, people had become convinced through William Smith that his brother Joseph had as much right to be a prophet in these days as Ezekiel or Amos or any of the old prophets had in ancient times."[47] Smith succeeded in establishing a respectable reputation in Elkader. As his ties to the Reorganization became better known, the old-timers nicknamed him "Mormon Smith," a title he came to embrace.[48] In one of his letters to Bishop Kelley, William commented on Elkader's citizens: "These Egyptians are not all Egyptian nor are they Israilitis [Israelites] by either faith Blood or by example [, but] still seam very willing for Mormon Smith to take charge of their Sunday School." In fact, the various denominations in the area not only trusted William to teach and preach but also assigned him to fill out their "Reports of Sunday Schools" to send to the Iowa State Sunday School Association.[49]

By the 1880s William had made his peace with his nephew's church and was firmly entrenched in the RLDS movement, an affiliation he kept for the rest of his life. He preached regularly in his region of Iowa and occasionally went into neighboring states. Writing to Joseph III in 1880, he reported that he had delivered more than forty-five sermons and received "invitations from all parts of the country,

---

46. W[ilia]m B. Smith, Letter to Joseph [Smith III], ca. December 1878, *Saints' Herald* 26, no. 1 (January 1, 1879): 1–2.

47. Bergera, *Autobiography of B. H. Roberts*, 106.

48. Al Ehrhardt (Elkader, Iowa), Letter to LDS Church, August 8, 1973.

49. William B. Smith (Osterdock, Iowa), Letter to Edmund Levi Kelley, June 1, 1892, P19, fd. 49, Community of Christ Library-Archives.

saying 'come over and help us.'"⁵⁰ Though RLDS Church leaders only appointed him a "minister," William was recognized throughout northeastern Iowa as a leader, overseeing the handful of RLDS branches in the region. Just a few years before his death, William established a small branch of the RLDS Church at Osterdock, Iowa, some twenty miles southeast from Elkader. This branch elected him as the group's presiding elder. William's son Edson recalled that his father was "a forceful preacher of righteousness, and my heart was made to burn within me whenever I heard a discourse delivered by him."⁵¹ Joseph Smith III concurred, stating that his Uncle William "spoke well in church services, preached with old time fervor and *éclat*, and bore a strong and fervent testimony to the truth of the latter day message, which was well received wherever he labored."⁵²

In 1883 William published a short autobiography, *William Smith on Mormonism*, which focused primarily on the earliest events of the Restoration. Its subtitle was, significantly, "A True Account of the Origin of the Book of Mormon." In 1845, William's mother, Lucy, explained in the only letter she wrote him that has survived: "People are often enquiring of me the particulars of Joseph's getting the plates seeing the angels at first and many other things." These repeated calls from curious visitors, including members, were, in fact, one of her reasons for dictating her own autobiography: "I have told over many things pertaining to these matters to different persons to gratify their curiosity[,] indeed [I] have almost destroyed my lungs giving these recitals to those who felt anxious to hear them [and] have now concluded to write down every particular as far as as [is] possible."⁵³ William, who outlived his mother by forty years, was also called upon to deliver his recollections of these early events, and he recognized the growing interest among both Mormons and others to learn his views on those experiences. His desire to publish his reminiscences was twofold. First, he could point to his pamphlet when individuals asked about the founding of Mormonism, including the coming forth of the Book of Mormon. He also hoped to make a profit by selling his forty-one-page pamphlet, much as his mother had in publishing her own memoir.

William promoted his autobiography in his personal correspondence and also in the RLDS *Saints' Herald*: "I hope that all Latter Day Saints will not be slow in forwarding their small tribute in exchange for the book entitled William Smith on the Origin of this Latter Day Work. It is a pamphlet of forty-one pages, nicely printed, and covered with blue and yellow paper, containing an account of the angel's visits to Joseph Smith, and the marvelous finding of the golden plates;

---

50. W[illia]m B. Smith (Elkader, Iowa), Letter to Joseph [Smith III], March 21, 1880, *Saints' Herald* 27, no. 8 (April 15, 1880): 122.

51. Edson D. C. Smith, quoted in "Episodes in Genealogical Research: New Light on William Smith," *Deseret News*, July 27, 1935, 8.

52. Richard P. Howard, ed., *The Memoirs of President Joseph Smith III (1832–1914)* (Independence, Mo.: Herald Publishing House, 1979), 185.

53. Lucy [Mack] Smith (Nauvoo, Ill.), Letter to William Smith, January 23, 1845, LDS Church History Library.

Final Years

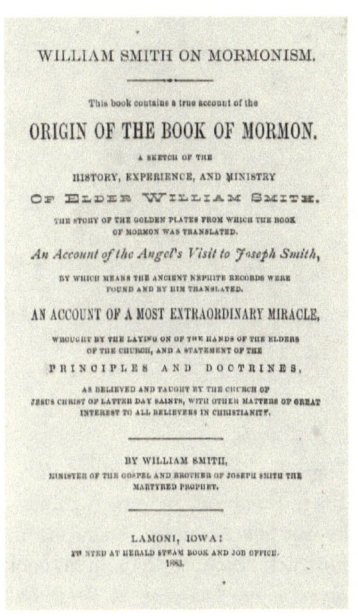

Title page of *William Smith on Mormonism* (Lamoni, IA: Herald Steam Book and Job Office, 1883). Copy in author's possession.

also an engraving of Mother Lucy Smith, the mother of this prophet and seer of the last days; also an engraving of the author of this work." He asserted that "this work, small though it is, should be in the hands of all who believe in the divine mission of Joseph Smith." He set the price at twenty-five cents per copy, or five for a dollar.[54]

His publication was a success, as the first printing was sold out by the summer of 1885, and William asked RLDS leaders to sponsor the printing of a thousand copies of an expanded second edition, which would include an addendum about his perspective on what led to the deaths of his brothers Hyrum and Joseph. Joseph III apparently did not share William's enthusiasm for inserting the additional—perhaps controversial—information in the RLDS publication of his history, since it would almost certainly have resurrected reports and rumors of plural marriage. Apparently they reached a compromise. The RLDS Church appears to have published additional copies of the pamphlet in 1885, but it was unchanged from the original printing,[55] including the conclusion that conveyed a more hospitable spirit of Christian fellowship: "There is no period, or condition in human life with those that are the followers of Christ, that the enjoyment in the spiritual life is greater than when the heart and soul reach far out for the salvation of all mankind, for such is the spirit of the gospel that Christ came to establish on earth. There is a beauty and an excellence in the thought that carries the mind to the far off distant land of India's Coral strand, where the messengers of peace preach the gospel to unregenerate man, telling him of a Christ and a crucified Savior, who

---

54. William Smith (Elkader, Iowa), Letter to Joseph Smith III, March 2, 1884, *Saints' Herald* 31, no. 12 (March 22, 1884): 181; William B. Smith, Letter to the Editor, April 6, 1885, *Expositor* (Oakland, Calif.) 1, no. 5 (May 1885).

55. William B. Smith (Elkader, Iowa), Letter to William W. Blair, July 24, 1885, *Saints' Herald* 32, no. 32 (August 8, 1885): 514. The two editions of his pamphlet *William Smith on Mormonism* may have only been distinguishable by the color of the cover, the first printed with gray-blue wrappers, and the second in salmon-colored wrappers. There is an example of the pamphlet in salmon-colored wrappers at L. Tom Perry Special Collections, Harold B. Lee Library, Brigham Young University, Provo, Utah. I own a copy of the pamphlet in a gray-blue wrapper. If there was a second printing in 1885, the date of publication remained the same (1883).

died to save a world from ruin and sin. The gospel is a message of Peace unto all nations, kindred[s], tongues and people."⁵⁶

William remained an ever-ready defender of Mormonism, representing his brother or family's character whenever they came under attack. In 1874, William and Robert Chambers published an anthology, *Chambers's Miscellany*, that contained a lengthy chapter entitled "History of the Mormons."⁵⁷ It contained a number of derogatory statements about William's family and his brother Joseph. When a copy reached William, he reacted defensively, poring over the volume for many days, perhaps months, to produce a thoughtful rebuttal. His reply eventually contained some thirty-five pages of handwritten notes, which William hoped his neighbor Charles Knecht would edit and publish for him before his death—a request that was never fulfilled.⁵⁸

Engraving of Joseph Smith, 1805–1844, based on an earlier painting by Sutcliffe Maudsley. Engraving by Frederick Piercy, ca. 1853, in his book *Route From Liverpool to Great Salt Lake Valley* (Liverpool: Franklin D. Richards, 1855).

In *William Smith on Mormonism*, William boldly proclaimed as his personal testimony that his brother Joseph was a modern prophet and that supernatural circumstances had accompanied the coming forth of the Book of Mormon. "Enough has been said in the personal experience of my early history to show not only the sincerity of my faith in the latter day work; but also the fact of my unshaken confidence in my brother Joseph Smith as a true Prophet of God," he penned toward the end of his publication. "And that the statements given in the preceding lines concerning the strange vision[s] shown to Joseph Smith, are true; and the translation of the record as found by the brother as stated, is also true, and in no other way did Joseph Smith compile, or compose the Book of Mormon only as stated by the gift and power of God."⁵⁹

It was similar to the personal witness that he had written to his good friend W. W. Phelps in 1844, shortly after the murder of Joseph and Hyrum:

---

56. William Smith, *William Smith on Mormonism* (Lamoni, Iowa: Herald Steam Book and Job Office, 1883), 39.

57. William Chambers and Robert Chambers, *Chambers's Miscellany of Instructive & Entertaining Tracts*, 3 vols., rev. ed. (London: W. and R. Chambers, 1874), 3:426–57.

58. William Smith, "Notes Written on 'Chambers' Life of Joseph Smith,'" ca. 1875, 28, MS 2807, LDS Church History Library, also reprinted in Dan Vogel, ed., *Early Mormon Documents*, 5 vols. (Salt Lake City: Signature Books, 1996–2003), 1:481–89.

59. William Smith, *William Smith on Mormonism*, 28.

But it is said in Mormonism there is a charm,—a mystery that the world cannot explain; I admit it; it has a charm more inviting than all the magicians' and sooth sayers' of Egypt and a mystery that sectarians cannot unravel;—Why? Because they have not the spirit of Christ, which is the spirit of prophecy. Mormonism has inferiors, but no superiors; it acknowledges no twin-sister but heaven; no superior but God; no king but Jesus; with unparalleled rapidity it has rolled on, "out-vied the muttering crowd," and accumulated its thousands, who are now rejoicing in the fullness of the gospel revealed and brought to light by the prophet Joseph. If it should be asked, then, is Mormonism true, a thousand intelligent voices reverberate yes! yes! yes![60]

Toward the end of his life, William took comfort in his belief "that I have never turned my back upon the testimony of him whom God called to lay the foundation of this latter day work."[61] It was consolation for his many failed attempts to find a replacement faith after he rejected, and was rejected by, his colleagues in the Quorum of the Twelve.

William also ensured that he perpetuated his witness of Mormonism's origin within his own family, which may have been an additional purpose for his publishing *William Smith on Mormonism*. His son Edson recalled that William would often declare his testimony of Joseph's prophetic calling to Edson's mother, Eliza: "Mother, Joseph was a prophet—a true prophet of God," his son recollected him saying. He bore his testimony of Joseph to his wife Eliza so often that she was eventually convinced of the truth of Mormonism and he subsequently baptized her into the RLDS faith.[62] Edson remembered that, in conversations with the children, William "ever spoke in endearing terms of his brother Joseph and held him to be a prophet of the God to the end of his days." Edson was fond of listening to his father recount the particulars of the earliest events of the Restoration, especially the coming forth of the Book of Mormon and the visitation of Moroni. "I used to have my father repeat the stories to me of how the Prophet found the plates and of the Angel's visits to him," recalled Edson. "He gave me the details a number of times, his story being practically the same as is recorded in the Church history books."[63] According to Edson, William's children never forgot the stories their father told them.

During his years in Elkader, William became a securely accepted member of the community—"respected in the community" was how Edson put it; and the citizens had no hesitation in "frequently call[ing] upon [him] to speak in

---

60. William Smith (Bordentown, N.J.), Letter to Dear Brother W. W. Phelps, November 10, 1844, *Prophet* 1, no. 27 (November 23, 1844): 3.

61. William Smith (Elkader, Iowa), Letter to Joseph Smith III, April 18, 1884, *Saints' Herald* 31, no. 19 (May 10, 1884): 290.

62. Edson D. C. Smith, quoted in "Episodes in Genealogical Research," 8; Susan Easton Black, comp., *Early Members of the Reorganized Church of Jesus Christ of Latter-day Saints*, 5 vols. (Provo, Utah: BYU Religious Studies Center, 1993), 5:690.

63. Edson D. C. Smith, quoted in "Episodes in Genealogical Research," 8.

public meetings and when they wanted a man to be chaplain."⁶⁴ Attorney Samuel Murdock corroborated the family remembrance: "For nearly a third of a century this good man lived in and about Elkader known and respected by all, and it was here that we would often see him at the reunion of the soldiers, the reunion of the old settlers, sitting on both grand and petit juries, then at the bed of sickness, now in the pulpit, and then opening assemblies with prayer and dismissing them again with a benediction, or perhaps hastening to the house of mourning to whisper consolation to weeping friends."⁶⁵ Murdock similarly praised him on another occasion, relating how William had "preached to us, lectured to us, pronounced funeral services over our dead, sat upon our juries, mingled in our conversations, [and] acted as chaplain on our national holidays." Just months before William's death, Murdock himself defended Mormonism due to his affinity for his close friend and neighbor after an antagonistic article toward Mormonism appeared in the *Dubuque Times*. "He has raised up in this county a bright and honorable family, all of whom are doing well," stated Murdock, "and none of whom has ever caused him to blush."⁶⁶

Edson Don Carlos Smith, 1862–1939. Date and photographer unknown. Courtesy of Buddy Youngreen.

During the final decade of his life, William also paid frequent visits to his only surviving sister, Katharine Smith Salisbury, who still resided in Hancock County, Illinois. She outlived William, who died in 1893, by seven years, within months of the dawning of the twentieth century. Katharine's children and grandchildren recalled fondly that William "frequently came to Hancock County and visited in the . . . Salisbury home in Fountain Green [Illinois] Township. Here he and [K]atharine talked long hours day after day reliving the early years of Latter Day Saintism." The two were united in their support of the Reorganization toward the end of their lives, and descendants remembered that "now in their old age they clung to each other like a couple of children." Eliza and William's own children apparently did not accompany him on these visits, which required paying for river passage on a steamer, probably from Guttenberg to Keokuk, Iowa. During these excursions into Illinois, William would usually preach in the Eagle or Hickory Grove schoolhouses, both of which were just a few miles

---

64. Ibid.

65. Murdock, "The Rev. William B. Smith," 5.

66. Samuel Murdock, quoted in "A Timely Defense," *Saints Herald* 40, no. 19 (May 13, 1893): 294.

Katharine Smith Salisbury, 1813–1900. Photograph ca. 1885, by unknown photographer. Courtesy of Estel Neff.

from his sister's home, on the eastern edge of Hancock County. While he reportedly never converted anyone, the people came out in droves to hear the brother of the celebrated Mormon prophet, enthralled by this living witness of their county's history from a period that most had only heard or read about. On one visit in January 1879, Smith brought with him Gomer Griffiths, a young RLDS missionary. They took turns preaching each evening for a week to overflow crowds at a local schoolhouse, where William tutored the younger missionary. A member of the RLDS faith for only two years and quite uncertain of his preaching ability, Griffiths remembered that he "received much encouragement and assistance from him [William]" during the time they preached together. "I am thankful I had the privilege of traveling with 'Uncle' William," Griffiths reminisced appreciatively, "and my testimony is that he was a noble and faithful man, one of the kindest and best of friends." Griffiths later served as an apostle in the RLDS Church.[67]

William apparently healed past wounds with other members of his family as well, including with his youngest sister, Lucy Smith Millikin, who died in 1882. In 1848 Smith had been angry when their mother deeded the Joseph B. Noble home (a gift to her from the Church) to Lucy and her husband, Arthur Millikin. During that same time, he was also offended when Emma Smith Bidamon, Joseph's widow, and her second husband, Lewis Bidamon, refused to look after his property in Plymouth, Illinois. During those years, these acts formed part of the panoply of hurts, rejections, and rebuffs that he felt he was receiving from everyone. But along with his ambitions to preside over his own church, he gave up these grudges and frequently made an effort to stay in touch with all of the extended Smith family still in the Midwest. Documentation is too skimpy to determine when or how often he visited them, whether Eliza encouraged these visits, whether she and the children accompanied him, or whether the relatives were equally welcome at Elkader. Lucy, Arthur, and their children lived in Colchester, Illinois, and the two siblings appar

---

67. Warren L. Van Dine, "Catharine Smith Salisbury," typescript, 1972, 29, Community of Christ Library-Archives; Joseph Smith III and Heman C. Smith, eds., *The History of the Reorganized Church of Jesus Christ of Latter Day Saints, 1805–1890*, 4 vols. (Independence: Herald House, 1896), *The History of the Reorganized Church of Jesus Christ of Latter Day Saints, 1873–1890* (Independence, Mo.: Herald House, 1952), 4:719. Also see Joseph Smith III's account of preaching in these two schoolhouses when visiting William's sisters near the Hancock and McDonough County line, in Joseph Smith, "Hail the New Year," *True Latter Day Saints' Herald* 20, no. 1 (January 1, 1873): 17–18.

Eagle Schoolhouse, Fountain Green, Illinois. Photograph by Kyle R. Walker, 2010.

ently enjoyed an amiable relationship before her death. Similarly, William stopped to see Emma when his missionary travels brought him through Illinois and even visited Lewis and his second wife after Emma's death.[68]

Old age brought a much-welcome mellowing to William. He more readily forgave offenses and also apparently had overcome his impetuous temper. His son Edson, who became aware of his father's history of interpersonal conflicts only late in life, characterized William's final thirty years as peaceful: "My father was a very spiritual man; he did not use profane language . . . [and] he never had any disturbances with anyone," said Edson, in a statement that stands in sharp contrast to William's turbulent earlier life.[69]

Interestingly, Smith's mellowing appears to correspond with several prophecies about his life, including a line from a blessing, bestowed by his brother Joseph that read, "in the pride of his heart he will neglect the more weighty matters until his soul is bowed down in sorrow."[70] Perhaps this line from his blessing is what his brother Joseph was referring to when, according to several apostles, who recalled the statement in 1857, he stated that William "would become a good man

---

68. William B. Smith (Hannibal, Mo.), Letter to Joseph Smith III, January 25, 1879, *Saints' Herald* 26, no. 4 (February 15, 1879): 62; William Smith (Galien, Mich.), Letter to William H. Kelley, June 5, 1883, Community of Christ Library-Archives; William Smith (La Crosse, Ill.), Letter to Joseph Smith III, July 17, 1886, *Saints' Herald* 33, no. 30 (July 31, 1886): 469–70.

69. Edson D. C. Smith, qtd in "Episodes in Genealogical Research," 7.

70. H. Michael Marquardt, comp., *Early Patriarchal Blessings of the Church of Jesus Christ of Latter-day Saints* (Salt Lake City: Smith-Pettit Foundation, 2007), 6.

William "Willie" Enoch Smith, 1858–1929, and family. Willie is seated and wearing a hat. Date and photographer unknown. Courtesy LDS Church History Library.

when He became an old man."[71] It is unknown who among the group brought up Joseph's alleged statement, but several present recalled Joseph saying something to that effect, generating a discussion about what Joseph meant. Brigham Young, who does not appear to have personally recalled the statement, added a prediction of his own: "Whether Joseph said it or not I will say in the name of the Lord that if Wm. Smith lives untill He is 65 or 70 years old He will become a good humble man. He will do the best he can. He will have to answer for his sins," declared Young, adding that "when a man give[s] way to the power of the Devil he finds it hard to recover himself again." Young asked Wilford Woodruff, a meticulous journal keeper, to record his prophecy and directed him to "put it into the Church History."[72]

The decade of the 1880s saw William's three children by Eliza marry and move away. Willie, at age twenty-three, married Anna Jane Harris on September 11, 1881, in Clayton County. They had two daughters while still living in Elkader, before Willie relocated his family to Dundee, Nobles County, Minnesota, sometime during 1887–88, where he labored as a farmer. Willie sold the forty acres

---

71. Brigham Young, quoted in Scott G. Kenney, ed., *Wilford Woodruff's Journal, 1833–1898* (Midvale, Utah: Signature Books, 1983–85), June 14, 1857, 5:58. The First Presidency and apostles who were gathered on this occasion included Brigham Young, Heber C. Kimball, Daniel H. Wells, Wilford Woodruff, George A. Smith, Charles C. Rich, and Amasa Lyman.

72. Ibid.

deeded to him by his father before moving to Minnesota, which probably helped him purchase farmland in Dundee.[73]

Edson married Marion C. Nichols just two years after his older brother married, on September 20, 1884, also in Clayton County, at age twenty-two. Edson and his family left Elkader with Willie's family, also living in Dundee for about ten years, before moving to Chippewa Falls, Wisconsin, some 180 miles north of Elkader. Edson also labored as a farmer.[74] William and Eliza's youngest child, Loie May, married Perry Jackson Bolsinger on March 11, 1886, at Elkader, and the couple settled in Clayton County near Osterdock, Iowa, just twenty miles southeast of Elkader. Loie May taught school in the area, while Perry farmed for a living.[75]

Loie May Bolsinger, 1866–1925. Date and photographer unknown. Courtesy of Buddy Youngreen.

Not long after the children had married and moved away, in February 1889, William's wife Eliza began experiencing what doctors diagnosed as paresis or paralysis, which typically included the loss of muscle function caused by damage to the nervous system. She may have had a stroke, for she died just four weeks after her symptoms first began, on March 7, 1889. Her obituary described her as an individual who "was always ready to extend a helping hand to a neighbor or friend in distress, and many can testify to her noble character of soul and mind."[76] This service certainly extended to her husband, as she had consistently and com-

---

73. William E. Smith, Letter to U.S. Pension Office, ca. October 1889; 1900 U.S. Census, Minnesota, Nobles County, Graham Lakes, Roll 778, 3A; Harry D. Galley, *Joseph Smith Senior's Children* (Rock Island, Ill.: Harry D. Galley, 2000), 41–42. By 1910, Willie and Anna had moved their family farther west, settling near Mitchell, Davison County, South Dakota, where Willie continued to farm for a living. 1910 U.S. Census, South Dakota, Sanborn County, Logan, Roll T624_1486, 15B.

74. Sometime after 1910, Edson and Marion relocated to Kootenai, Idaho, where Marion passed away on May 1, 1920, and Edson afterward moved to Olympia, Washington. While living in Washington, Edson met with LDS missionaries and was baptized into the LDS Church headquartered at Salt Lake City at a meeting held in Tacoma, Washington, in 1931. (See Chapter 19). Edson D. C. Smith, quoted in "Episodes in Genealogical Research," 7–8; Edson D. C. Smith to U.S. Pension Office, June 6, 1892; 1910 U.S. Census, Wisconsin, Chippewa County, Chippewa Ward 1, Roll T624_1703, 1A; 1920 U.S. Census, Idaho, Kootenai County, Kootenai, Roll T625_291, 27B; Galley, *Joseph Smith Senior's Children*, 42–46.

75. Galley, *Joseph Smith Senior's Children*, 46–49; 1900 U.S. Census, Iowa, Clayton County, Mallory, Roll 425, 4A.

76. "Obituary. Mrs. Eliza E. Smith, of Elkader," 1.

passionately nursed him through his numerous illnesses. The epitaph on Eliza's gravestone in Elkader's city cemetery reads:

> She has gone to rest sweetly sleeping
> A light from our household has gone
> A voice we loved is stilled
> A Place is Vacant in our hearts
> That never can be filled
> She was a faithful wife and a good mother[77]

After the funeral, William traveled with Willie and Edson to their homes in Dundee, where he spent several months before returning to Elkader. After Eliza's death, William apparently desired to be closer to his children, and he sold his property and home in Elkader and moved twenty miles southeast to Osterdock, Iowa. He purchased a lot and small home in Osterdock, not far from where his twenty-four-year-old daughter, Loie May, and her husband were living.[78]

About eight months after Eliza's death, Smith married Rosanna ("Rosa") Goyette La Ture Surprise, a twice-widowed Frenchwoman who lived less than a hundred miles southeast in Clinton, Clinton County, Iowa, on December 21, 1889.[79] Rosa had been born at Montreal, Quebec, Canada, on May 16, 1830, and was nineteen years younger than Smith. She was fifty-nine, and he was seventy-eight. She had been baptized a member of the RLDS faith in 1880 and attended the RLDS Clinton Branch. William likely came to know her through their shared faith, as he frequently traveled and preached at the RLDS branches organized in northeastern Iowa. Rosa had first married Joseph La Ture in 1847 near Montreal, Quebec, Canada, and had two children before Joseph died at Lockport, New York, five years later. She then married Samuel Surprise at Lockport around 1854, where they lived for five years, before moving to Iowa in about 1859, residing at Dubuque and then Bellevue. She had six children with Samuel, before he left the family to find work, and according to Rosa, then "lost his mind and

Eliza Elsie Sanborn Brain Smith gravestone, Elkader or East Side Cemetery, Elkader, Iowa. Photograph by Mary Schofield Belden, 1970.

---

77. Transcription quoted in Metcalfe, "Eliza Elsie Sanborn," 3–4.
78. Documentation of the property is in William B. Smith's U.S. Pension file, indicating that Rosanna rented the property and home for four dollars a month after William's death in 1893. Statement of J. H. Hill, Clayton County Recorder, April 22, 1899, Part II, 82, William B. Smith Pension File.
79. Marriage License #12066, Book 1, 219, Clinton County Courthouse, Clinton, Iowa.

died in an [insane] asylum in Cook Co. Ill[inois]," on January 27, 1879. Rosa owned no property at the time of her marriage to William, and all of her children were raised and had moved out. She was described as a "kind and gentle woman." Though William died only a little more than three years later, Rosa was described as "untiring in her efforts to soothe his declining years," and "to watch over his tottering footsteps."[80] Not long after their marriage, the two moved into William's home in Osterdock.

William's three decades in Elkader had been a time of withdrawal and solitude, which had given him time to reflect upon his earlier life. The process brought him to at least a partial recognition that he himself had caused many of his earlier conflicts and that it also limited his effectiveness as a leader. Just a year before his death, he confessed to Joseph III, speaking of himself in third person, "Your Uncle William's make up is of that nature that it might do for him to stand in the lead [at the head] of a large body of people," William confided, most especially if there were limitations placed on "the exercise of equal rights among human beings."[81] Though this partial acknowledgement was embedded in a declaration about his independent nature, which he viewed as a positive attribute, later in life William acknowledged that his domineering personality had limited his success as a leader and contributed to his inability to retain his followers. "Experience will teach you what men can say in time to come, and how they will revile that which we have thought was for the best at the time," he wrote to his nephew somewhat regretfully. Continuing his letter in this pensive mood, he confided to Joseph III, "Your father's course in life was not faultless; neither can, or will it be said of you, Joseph [III], fifty years hence, that all was right in every particular. Nor do I expect such an approval to fall on all the acts of my former life."[82]

Notwithstanding William's repeated bouts of poor health and his straitened economic circumstances, those who met with him during his last years were frequently impressed by his physique. LDS missionary B. H. Roberts, visiting in the fall of 1880 in Elkader, noted, "He was an unusually tall man and, though emaciated, disclosed a symmetrical physical manhood." Roberts, who was then twenty-three, five feet nine inches tall and 190 pounds, estimated the physically superior William to weigh 215–30 pounds in the prime of his life, and was impressed that despite his age—William was then sixty-nine—"stood erect, [and] full of form."[83] Joseph Smith III, who failed to inherit the Smith men's height of at least six feet

---

80. Statement of Rosanna Smith, June 21, 1902, 29, Part 1, Widow's Pension, William B. Smith Pension File; John R. Neely (Chicago, Ill.), Letter to N. A. Lowry, April 21, 1903, 52, Part 1, Widow's Pension, William B. Smith Pension File; "Obituary. Mrs. Eliza E. Smith, of Elkader," 1; Murdock, "Rev. William B. Smith," 5.

81. "Extracts from Letters," *Saints' Herald* 39, no. 40 (October 1, 1892): 631.

82. William B. Smith (Elkader, Iowa), Letter to Dear Nephew [Joseph Smith III], October 16, 1868, *True Latter Day Saints' Herald* 15, no. 1 (January 1, 1869): 22–23.

83. Bergera, *Autobiography of B.H. Roberts*, 104–5; Truman G. Madsen, *B. H. Roberts Defender of the Faith* (Salt Lake City: Deseret Book, 1980), 184.

(he was only five feet eight inches tall), similarly remembered that, even in his final years, William "still walked erect, and carried himself with a distinctly military air and step."[84] His extraordinary strength helped carry him through the progressive and recurrent illnesses from which he suffered during his final thirty years of life.

Psychologically, William also demonstrated resiliency and complexity that left even so astute an observer as B. H. Roberts confused. Because Roberts was aware of William's determined public stand against polygamy and his support of the Reorganized Church, he must have approached Elkader with his missionary companion, Hyrum Jensen, with a certain amount of trepidation. Thus, the warm welcome he received from the former apostle and patriarch confused him. Although Eliza did not stint in expressing her negative opinions about Mormonism, William was a gracious host, feeding the two missionaries supper and breakfast and, although they did not know it until the next day, giving them his own bed while he slept on the floor. (See Chapter 1.) The next day, William wrote a letter to a possible contact in Elkader, urging this friend "to receive us as he would himself and to see to it that no one insulted us." He walked with them to the outskirts of town and, in saying farewell, "burst into a flood of tears accompanied by a clinging warm clasp of his hand." Three times, Roberts looked back as they continued on their way, and each time, William was also looking at them, giving them "a farewell wave of the hand."[85]

Roberts, an ardent missionary, must have asked himself if this last Smith brother could be reclaimed for the LDS Church with return visits and repeated efforts—although he and his companion were unable to change their plans at that point. But he brooded over the encounter, confounded by the contrast between William's public persona and his private actions. "What was it that moved him to such emotions?" Roberts asked himself. "Was it the recollection of his own youth when he too under the favor of God had been an itinerant missionary going from house to house to present the great message of the New dispensation?" Roberts finally concluded, that "the question could not be determined, nor all the dramatic experiences of William Smith in the church at Nauvoo, Kirtland, and in New York."[86] The fact remains, however, that the memories of longtime LDS General Authorities who had weathered William's combative and aggressive assaults on Mormonism contrasted sharply with Roberts's personal experience, and his own history did not try to follow William's career after he affiliated with Joseph III's Reorganization.

William's final years also manifest emotional resilience. Despite his grief over Eliza's death, he adjusted to the new marriage and the new town and, even into his eighties, continued to preach Mormonism in northeastern Iowa. Edson remembered

---

84. Howard, *Memoirs of President Joseph Smith III*, 185. See Launius, *Joseph Smith III: Pragmatic Prophet*, 5, for the physical description of Joseph III.

85. Bergera, *Autobiography of B. H. Roberts*, 105.

86. Ibid.

that his father was always "studying on religious subjects and writing down his thoughts and experiences." According to Edson, William went on a self-called RLDS mission each summer during his last years, in itself a measure of at least some periods of vigorous health.[87] However, while on a preaching tour in Minnesota in the summer of 1893, probably while visiting his sons and their families, he contracted influenza. He returned to Osterdock where Rosa nursed him during this final illness. He died on November 13, 1893, at age eighty-two. His funeral services were held "in his little church at Osterdock"—apparently the modest church meetinghouse where the local branch met, and where he had sermonized since coming to Osterdock three years earlier. He was buried in the Bethel Cemetery, adjacent to the little chapel.[88]

William B. Smith, 1811–1893, ca. 1893. Photographer unknown. Courtesy Gracia Jones.

The local paper carried his obituary, written by his former employer Samuel Murdock of Elkader. Murdock praised William as a "good and virtuous man," with an impeccable reputation since moving to their community thirty years earlier, a final tribute that marked a striking contrast to William's turbulent years in Ohio and Illinois. "For nearly a third of a century this good man lived in and about Elkader," wrote the venerable judge, "and was known and respected by all." He also described William's children as having the "highest respectability" in the community. "His whole life has been one of rectitude and honor, devoted to his God, his fellow men, and the land that give him birth, and let no one now cast reproach upon it." At an earlier date, an editorial in the paper had similarly described Smith as a man who was "candid, honest, and upright—a citizen of whom rumor speaks no evil."[89] W. H. Kephart, an RLDS minister, who lived in a neighboring county, was present and "conducted the last sad rites" at the Bethel Cemetery.[90] RLDS leaders responded to his death with surprising neglect, probably relieved to have his knowledge of and participation in plural marriage pass into obscurity.

William's life was truly an American story in its pitches and plunges, its ambitions and combats. His life had been inconstant and eventful, with his conflict-

---

87. Edson D. C. Smith, qtd in "Episodes in Genealogical Research," 8.

88. Ibid.; "Died.—Smith," *Saints' Herald* 40, no. 49 (December 9, 1893): 787; Murdock, "Rev. William B. Smith," 5. William's wife Rosa identified the cause of his death as "La grippe," a French term for the influenza. Statement of Rosanna B. Smith, 29, William B. Smith Pension File.

89. Murdock, "Rev. William B. Smith," 16; "Extracts from the *Clayton Co. Journal*," in *True Latter Day Saints' Herald* 15, no. 1 (January 1, 1869): 23–25.

90. "Died.—Smith," 787.

Bethel Church, Osterdock, Iowa. William preached in this building as president of the RLDS Branch established in the area. William's gravestone is in the foreground. Photograph by Kyle R. Walker, 2010.

ing loyalties, and a marital history that included five civil and nine plural wives. He fathered seven children but seems to have lost touch with his two daughters by Caroline, both of whom had moved out of state, and was estranged from his two children by Roxey Ann. His ambitions frequently outran his ability to discipline and channel his undeniable talents. Among his contributions before the murders of Joseph and Hyrum were his service as a representative to the Illinois legislature, as editor of one newspaper in Illinois and one in New York, and his able and persuasive preaching that brought hundreds into the faith.

One constant was his pride in his heritage and the triumph of a movement that had begun in his own home, even while he reshaped his personal history to fit at least five expressions of the Mormonism launched by his brother Joseph. He obviously had manifested some of the charisma that drew devoted disciples to his brother, but those very qualities of compassion, affection, and enthusiasm frequently ended in injured feelings, agonizing rejection, desire for retaliation, and launching a new scheme before he could properly prepare for its success. The cycle of disappointing others, which led to their rejection of him, was all too often a prelude to his own violent rejection of them, so that he left behind him a trail of damaged and mistrustful former friends, allies, wives, and children.

William's unstable emotions certainly contributed to his erratic behavior. He was impulsive and angry, remembered by many for his passionate temper. There were also periods of despondency and self-loathing. Nevertheless, after his frantic activities to find or make a new spiritual home during the later 1840s and 1850s, he succeeded in reining in his ambitions, settling into a community that accepted

William B. Smith's original (left) and replacement (right) headstones. Note also the Grand Army of the Republic (G.A.R.) marker, indicating that William was part of a fraternal organization for veterans of the Union Army. Photograph of original by Al Ehrhardt, ca. 1970. Photograph of replacement headstone by Kyle R. Walker, 2010.

him on his own terms, and becoming a stable husband and kindly father and stepfather despite wrestling with poverty.

Had William's father still been living, he may have warned William against the path taken by his own volatile brother Jesse and persuaded him to build on the strength that might have stiffened William's resolve during storms of persecution to temper his pride in his family lineage and also to accept discipleship humbly. As it was, William's sense of "chosenness" resulted less in a glittering robe than a hampering shroud. William's loneliness must have been intense. He was often bewildered and alienated but fell back on a proud pose of independence when what he and the fledgling church needed was devotion and pastoralism.

In his pamphlet *William Smith on Mormonism*, he closed his life story with a song entitled "Gospel Missionary Hymn" by Daniel March (1816–1909), a minister and hymnwriter from Massachusetts. William included one of the final stanzas, a verse that had poignant application to his own life experience:

> If you cannot be the watchman,
> Standing high on Zion's wall
> Pointing out the path to heaven,
> Offering life and peace to all;—
> With your prayers and with your bounties,
> You can do what heaven demands;
> You can be like faithful Aaron,
> Holding up the prophet's hands.[91]

In the end, it was a role he finally, and reluctantly, accepted and, in doing so, made his greatest contributions to the Smith family church headed by his nephew, Joseph III.

---

91. William Smith, *William Smith on Mormonism*, 41.

Appendix A

Wives and Children of William B. Smith

Civil Wives and Children

1. Caroline Amanda Grant Smith

Caroline Amanda Grant was born January 22, 1814, at Windsor, Broome County, New York. She was the second daughter, and the sixth of twelve children born to Joshua Grant and Athalia Howard Grant.[1] She first met William when he was serving as a missionary during the winter of 1832–33 in Erie County, Pennsylvania. The two wed on February 14, 1833, near or at the Grant home in Elk Creek Township, Erie County, Pennsylvania.[2] They were married for twelve years, before Caroline died of "dropsy of the heart" on May 22, 1845, at Nauvoo, Hancock County, Illinois.[3] She was initially buried in the "tomb of Joseph" near the Nauvoo Temple, reinterred in the Nauvoo Cemetery, and finally moved by William to her final resting place in the Smith Family Cemetery in Nauvoo.[4]

a. Mary Jane Smith Scott. Mary Jane Smith was born January 7, 1834, at Kirtland, Geauga County, Ohio.[5] At age seventeen Mary Jane married a Scottish immigrant, twenty-two-year-old Andrew Scott, on October 24, 1852, at Rocky

---

1. Thedy Grant Reeves, Reminiscence, as told to Joseph Hyrum Grant Jr., November 26, 1904 [sic; should be 1903], 1, Grant Family Records, ca. 1778–1903, Microfilm #1036844, item #10, LDS Family History Library, Salt Lake City.

2. Evan M. Greene, Diary, February 16, 1833, LDS Church History Library.

3. William Smith (City of Joseph [Nauvoo, Ill.]), Letter to Joshua Grant Jr., August 12, 1845, *Nauvoo Neighbor* 3, no. 16 (August 20, 1845): 3. Nauvoo cemetery records indicate that Caroline died from "dropsey of the abdomen." Fred E. Woods, "The Cemetery Record of William D. Huntington, Nauvoo Sexton," *Mormon Historical Studies* 3, no. 1 (Spring 2002): 152; Lyndon W. Cook, comp., *Nauvoo Deaths and Marriages, 1839–1845* (Provo, Utah: Grandin Book, 1994), 70.

4. William Smith, Letter to Joshua Grant, August 12, 1845; William Smith (Augusta, Iowa Territory), Letter to Pres. B[righam] Young or Lewis Robbins, September 28, 1845, Brigham Young, Office Files, 1832–1878, Letters from Church Leaders and Others, 1840–1877, William Smith, 1844–1857, LDS Church History Library.

5. "Laid To Rest," *Brookfield Gazette* 12, no. 36 (December 26, 1878): 3. Lucy Mack Smith, in *Biographical Sketches of Joseph Smith the Prophet and his Progenitors for Many Generations* (Liverpool: S. W. Richards, 1853), 43, lists Mary Jane's birth as January 1835, but that date appears to have been a mistake in light of later sources.

Ford (Shelburn or Palestine Grove), Lee County, Illinois.[6] Andrew farmed for a living in Brooklyn Township in Lee County after the two wed. Two decades later in the 1870s, he, Mary Jane, and their four children, moved to Brookfield in Linn County, Missouri, where Andrew became a bank president. Mary Jane affiliated with the Baptist Church in Brookfield, but unfortunately developed symptoms of her mother's condition at age forty-three, and succumbed to "dropsy of the heart" just two weeks before her forty-fifth birthday. She died at Brookfield, Linn County, Missouri, on December 21, 1878.[7]

b. Caroline Louisa Smith Quince. Caroline Louisa Smith was born in August 1836, at Kirtland, Geauga County, Ohio.[8] Just a year after her older sister Mary Jane's marriage, seventeen-year-old Caroline wed twenty-one-year-old James S. Quince in Rocky Ford (Shelburn or Palestine Grove) Lee County, Illinois, on December 8, 1853.[9] Quince worked for many years as a railroad engineer at Amboy, Illinois, just a mile or so north of Palestine Grove. During the Civil War, James enlisted and served as a corporal in Company I of the 89th Illinois Regiment. For unknown reasons, the family, which by then included five children, moved to Fort Worth, Texas, in the 1870s. Caroline died on January 9, 1878, the same year as her sister Mary Jane's death, at age forty-one.[10]

2. Mary Jane Rollins Smith Williamson Taylor

Mary Jane Rollins was the eldest daughter of Enoch Perham Rollins and Sophia Philbrook Rollins, born December 25, 1829, at Bangor, Maine.[11] She migrated with her family to Nauvoo in August 1844, after having been baptized into the LDS Church on February 8, 1841.[12] William married Rollins at Nauvoo on June 22, 1845, with Brigham Young performing the ceremony.[13] Just two months

---

6. Mary Jane Smith, marriage to Andrew Scott, October 24, 1852, First Marriage Register, 1839–73, Marriage Records of Lee County, Illinois, Book A, 46, Lee County Courthouse (old), Dixon, Illinois.

7. "Laid to Rest," 3; 1880 U.S. Census, Missouri, Linn County, Brookfield, Roll 700, film 1254700, 426A; Harry D. Galley, *Joseph Smith Senior's Children* (Rock Island, Ill.: Harry D. Galley, 2000), 31–32.

8. Lucy Mack Smith, *Biographical Sketches*, 43.

9. Caroline Smith and James S. Quince, First Marriage Register, 1839–73, December 8, 1853, Marriage Records of Lee County, Illinois, Book A, 57, Lee County Courthouse (old), Dixon, Illinois.

10. Frank E. Stevens, *History of Lee County Illinois* (Chicago: S. J. Clarke Publishing, 1914), 1:121–22; 1870 U.S. Census, Illinois, Lee County, Amboy, Roll M593_246, 216A; Galley, *Joseph Smith Senior's Children*, 32–34.

11. Ann S. Elmer Wilson, "Enoch Perham Rollins," unpublished manuscript, n.d., 1, copy in author's possession.

12. "Died. Enoch Perham Rollins," *Deseret News*, December 19, 1877, 11.

13. "Married," *Nauvoo Neighbor* 3, no. 9 (July 2, 1845): 3; Maureen Ursenbach Beecher, ed., "'All Things Move in Order in the City': The Nauvoo Diary of Zina Diantha

Appendix A: Wives and Children of William B. Smith 567

Caroline Louisa Smith Quince, 1836–1878, headstone, Fort Worth, Texas. Photograph courtesy of Erin Jennings Metcalfe.

later, in late August, Mary Jane left William, apparently over her unwillingness to accept plural marriage.[14] The two divorced on May 12, 1847.[15] Although her family migrated to Utah, Mary Jane never did. She later married Francis R. Williamson at St. Louis, Missouri, in 1847.[16] After Williamson's death, she married William N. Taylor 1860, also in St. Louis.[17] Mary Jane died of pneumonia on March 18, 1879, at St. Louis.[18]

3. Roxey (or Roxie) Ann Grant Smith

Roxey Ann Grant was born March 16, 1825, at Naples, Ontario County, New York.[19] She was a younger sister to William's first wife, Caroline Amanda Grant. Roxey Ann helped care for Caroline during a five-month period, from December 1844–April 1845, while the family was living in Philadelphia during William's presidency over the eastern branches and afterward at Nauvoo in May 1845. (See Chapter 10.) William baptized Roxey Ann at Nauvoo during the same month as Caroline's death, in May 1845.[20] William and Roxey Ann were married two years later, in Knox County, Illinois, on May 19, 1847.[21] The couple separated in May 1850 after Roxey Ann

---

Huntington Jacobs," *BYU Studies* 19, no. 3 (Spring 1979): 313; Stanley B. Kimball, *On the Potter's Wheel: The Diaries of Heber C. Kimball* (Salt Lake City: Signature Books, 1987), 123.

14. Thomas Sharp, "From Nauvoo," *Warsaw Signal* 2, no. 24 (September 3, 1845): 2; Willard Richards, Journal, August 31, 1845, Box 1, Volume 11, Willard Richards Papers, 1821–54, MS 1490, LDS Church History Library.

15. William Smith vs. Mary Jane Smith, May and June Terms, 1847, Circuit Court Records, Knox County Courthouse, Galesburg, Illinois.

16. Marriage Record of Francis R. Williamson and Miss Mary J. Rawlings, October 29, 1847. *Missouri, Marriage Records, 1805–2002.* Online database. (Provo, Utah: Ancestry.com Operations, 2007), 76.

17. Marriage Record of W. N. Taylor and Mary Jane Williamson, October 29, 1860, by F. A. Morris, *Missouri, Marriage Records, 1805–2002.* Online database. (Provo, Utah: Ancestry.com Operations, 2007), 126.

18. "Died—Taylor," *Globe-Democrat* (St. Louis, Missouri), March 19, 1879, 5.

19. Reeves, Reminiscence, 1.

20. William Smith (City of Joseph [Nauvoo, Ill.]), Letter to Joshua Grant Jr., August 12, 1845, *Nauvoo Neighbor* 3, no. 16 (August 20, 1845): 3.

21. William and Roxey Ann were married by probate justice R. L. Hannaman, who served in that position from 1837 to 1839, and again from 1843 to 1849. William Smith and Roxey Ann Grant Marriage License, Marriage Index Book 1, 84, Knox County Courthouse, Galesburg, Illinois.

discovered that William supported polygamy. (See Chapter 16.) After a lengthy legal battle, their divorce became final on April 26, 1853.²² Roxey Ann retained custody of their two children (Thalia and Hyrum Wallace) after the divorce. She did not marry again. She and their two children lived in Walnut Grove Township (Altona), Illinois, near Roxey Ann's parents, for more than a decade after the divorce. By 1870, she and the children relocated to Lathrop, Clinton County, Missouri, where Roxey Ann died on March 30, 1900.²³

Thalia Grant Smith, 1848–1924. Photograph taken ca. 1923 by unknown photographer. Courtesy of Gracia Jones.

a. **Thalia Grant Smith.** Thalia Grant Smith was born September 21, 1848, at Altona (Walnut Grove Township), Knox County, Illinois, the eldest child of William and Roxey Ann Grant Smith.²⁴ After her parents' divorce in 1853, Thalia stayed with her mother and her grandparents in Knox County and, after more than decade, relocated to Lathrop, Clinton County, Missouri, "about the year 1870." She worked as a schoolteacher in Lathrop for many years. She was a member of the local Christian Church, and was "one of the charter members of the Women's Missionary Society of this congregation."²⁵ After a lengthy correspondence with her first cousin and LDS Church President Heber J. Grant, she was baptized by Grant on April 26, 1924, in Independence, Missouri, where she died seven months later at age seventy-six.²⁶ Heber J.

---

22. Final Decree, Bill of Divorce, Roxey Ann Smith vs. William Smith, April 26, 1853, Knox County Circuit Court, April Term, Knox County Courthouse, Galesburg, Illinois.

23. Reeves, Reminiscence, 2; Galley, *Joseph Smith Senior's Children*, 20–21.

24. "Death of Miss Thalia Smith," *Lathrop Optimist* 16, no. 2 (December 4, 1924): 1; Galley, *Joseph Smith Senior's Children*, 37–38.

25. "Death of Miss Thalia Smith," 1.

26. After learning of Thalia's conversion, Grant wrote, "I rejoice beyond my power to tell you that you have arrived at the point where you believe in the Book of Mormon [as] an inspired work. Surely, if the Book of Mormon is an inspired work, Joseph Smith was indeed a prophet of the living God, and the Gospel of the Lord Jesus Christ as proclaimed by Joseph Smith and his successors—Brigham Young and others—is in very deed the plan of life and salvation." Heber J. Grant (Salt Lake City), Letter to My dear Cousin Thalia [Smith], August 21, 1923, in Heber J. Grant Letters, MS 1234, Box 21, fd. 2, 96–97, LDS Church History Library. On April 26, 1924, Heber J. Grant baptized and confirmed Thalia a member of the LDS Church in Independence, Missouri. Record of Members Collection, Missouri, Central States Mission, 1904–, 552–53, Reel 4269, CR 375 8, LDS Church History Library; Heber J. Grant, *The Diaries of Heber J. Grant, 1880–1945 Abridged* (Salt

Grant also attended and spoke at her funeral service after her death on November 27, 1924.²⁷

b. Hyrum Wallace Smith. Hyrum Wallace Smith was born August 17, 1850, at Altona (Walnut Grove Township), Knox County, Illinois. He was the second child and only son of William Smith and Roxey Ann Grant Smith.²⁸ His parents separated while Roxey Ann was pregnant with him, and there is no evidence that Hyrum Wallace ever knew or interacted with his father. He moved to Lathrop, Clinton County, Missouri, with his mother and sister Thalia around 1870.²⁹ Hyrum Wallace married Margaret ("Maggie") Waller on January 20, 1881. Maggie died less than a year later, apparently due to complications during childbirth, on January 11, 1882. Hyrum Wallace then married Rosalia ("Rosa") Catherine Damitz on January 2, 1887. Hyrum Wallace and Rosa moved to Inglewood, California, after Roxey Ann's death, and Hyrum Wallace died in Inglewood on January 27, 1935.³⁰ Heber J. Grant, Hyrum Wallace's first cousin and president of the LDS Church, attended and spoke at his funeral held on January 30, 1935.³¹

4. Eliza Elsie Sanborn Brain Smith

Eliza Elsie Sanborn was born on April 16, 1827, at Cattaraugus, New York, the daughter of Enoch Sanborn and Lois Elliot Sanborn.³² Enoch and Lois had joined the Mormons during the 1830s and moved to Kirtland, Ohio, in the spring of 1836. The family moved with the Saints, following Joseph Smith to Missouri, then to Illinois; and at one point, Eliza resided "just across the street from him [Joseph] in Nauvoo." After Eliza's parents died in Illinois, she and her two siblings returned to Ohio in the fall of 1840 to be closer to their extended family.³³ Eliza married James Brain on November 18, 1845, in Cuyahoga County, Ohio, and

---

Lake City: Privately Published, 2010), 327. Thalia died on November 27, 1924, and despite his busy schedule, Grant traveled to Independence to attend her funeral services. *Ninety-Fifth Annual Conference of the Church of Jesus Christ of Latter day Saints, April 4, 5 and 6, 1925* (Salt Lake City: Church of Jesus Christ of Latter-day Saints, 1925), 6.

27. "Death of Miss Thalia Smith," 1.
28. "Records of Early Church Families," *Utah Genealogical Magazine* 26, no. 19 (July 1935): 105; Galley, *Joseph Smith Senior's Children*, 39.
29. "Death of Miss Thalia Smith," 1.
30. Galley, *Joseph Smith Senior's Children*, 39–41.
31. Grant, *The Diaries of Heber J. Grant*, 404.
32. "Obituary. Mrs. Eliza E. Smith," *Elkader Weekly Register* 12, no. 18 (March 14, 1889): 1.
33. Alden Enoch Sanborn, Testimony, quoted in *Public Discussions of the Issues between the Reorganized Church of Jesus Christ of Latter Day Saints and the Church of Christ [Disciples] Held in Kirtland, Ohio Beginning February 12, and Closing March 8, 1884 between E. L. Kelley, of the Reorganized Church of Jesus Christ of Latter Day Saints and Clark Braden, of the Church of Christ*, 393–94; Erin Jennings Metcalfe, "Eliza Elsie Sanborn," 2010, 1–2; unpublished manuscript in my possession.

the couple had four children. However, in June 1857, Eliza petitioned successfully for a divorce on the grounds of James's "willful absence" and reverted to her birth name.[34] During William's stay in Ohio and Pennsylvania during 1855–57, he had become reacquainted with Eliza, when she was about thirty years old. Eliza likely supported William's attempt at organizing the short-lived Church of Jesus Christ of Latter Day Saints at Kirtland, and William certainly knew the Sanborn family during the Kirtland-Nauvoo period. About five months after Eliza's divorce and during the same time that William and Martin Harris were building up their church, the pair married on November 12, 1857, at Kirtland, Ohio.[35] The couple had three children (William Enoch, Edson Don Carlos, and Loie May) during their thirty-two-year marriage. Eliza died at Elkader, Iowa, on May 7, 1889.[36]

a. William Enoch Smith. William ("Willie") Enoch Smith was the first child born to William B. Smith and Eliza Elsie Sanborn Smith, born on July 24, 1858, at Erie, Erie County, Pennsylvania.[37] He moved with his parents to Elkader, Clayton County, Iowa in 1860.[38] He was married to Anna Jane Harris by T. E. Fleming on September 11, 1881, in Clayton County, Iowa, at twenty-three.[39] They had two daughters while still living in Elkader, before Willie relocated his family to Dundee, Nobles County, Minnesota, where he labored as a farmer. Sometime during 1887–1888, Willie sold forty acres deeded to him by his father before moving to Minnesota and probably used

---

34. James Brain and Eliza Sanborn applied for a marriage license in Cuyahoga County, Ohio, on November 17, 1845. Ohio, County Marriages, 1790–1950, microfilm 872467, item 1, image number 371, LDS Family History Library. Their four children were Byron Bradford (born October 21, 1846), Mary Lois (1848), Ward (1851), and Clara (January 17, 1851). Ward and Clara may have been twins. Mary and Ward were living with William and Eliza in Erie, Pennsylvania, in 1860, while Byron lived with his father in Kirtland. 1860 U.S. Census, Pennsylvania, Erie County, Venango, Roll M653_1108, 1061, image 454; 1860 U.S. Census, Ohio, Lake County, Willoughby, Roll M653_996, 297, image 133. For information on Clara, see Ohio Deaths, 1908–1953, Microfilm 1991300, image number 1849, LDS Family History Library.

35. Daughters of the American Revolution, New Connecticut Chapter (Painesville, Ohio), "Probate Court Marriage Records, Lake County Ohio, 1840–1865," typescript, 102, Morley Library, Painesville, Ohio. The entry reads: "Smith, Wm., m., Eliza E. Sanburne, November 12, 1857."

36. "OBITUARY. Mrs. Eliza E. Smith, of Elkader," 1.

37. "Records of Early Church Families," 105.

38. "OBITUARY. Mrs. Eliza E. Smith, of Elkader," 1.

39. Galley, *Joseph Smith Senior's Children*, 42.

Appendix A: Wives and Children of William B. Smith   571

Edson Don Carlos Smith, 1862–1939 (left), with unidentified son and grandson. Photographer unknown. Courtesy LDS Church History Library.

the money to buy farmland in Dundee.⁴⁰ He died on February 13, 1930, at Mitchell, Davison County, South Dakota.⁴¹

b. Edson Don Carlos Smith. Edson Don Carlos Smith was the second son of William B. Smith and Eliza Elsie Sanborn Smith, born at Elkader, Clayton County, Iowa on September 6, 1862.⁴² Edson married Marion C. Nichols two years after his brother's marriage, on September 20, 1884, also in Clayton County, at twenty-two. Edson and his family left Elkader with his brother Willie, also relocating to Dundee, Minnesota, for about ten years, before moving to Chippewa Falls, Wisconsin, some 180 miles north of Elkader. Like Willie, Edson also farmed.⁴³ Edson Don Carlos Smith was baptized a member of the Church of Jesus Christ of Latter-day Saints on February 13, 1931, in Tacoma, Washington. At thirty, he had been baptized a member of the RLDS Church and served as an RLDS branch president in Wisconsin. But after confronting the evidence that his uncles—and his own father—had been polygamists in Nauvoo, presented to him by an RLDS member of the Seventy, T. W. Chatburn, Edson became "skeptical" and left the faith. His baptism into the LDS Church was the culmination of some thirty years of searching. Shortly thereafter, Edson made sure that he performed vicarious temple ordinances

---

40. William E. Smith to U.S. Pension Office, ca. October 1889; 1900 U.S. Census, Graham Lakes, Nobles, Minnesota, Roll 778, 3A; Galley, *Joseph Smith Senior's Children*, 41–42. By 1910, Willie and Anna had moved their family farther west, settling near Mitchell, Davison County, South Dakota, where Willie continued to farm for a living. 1910 U.S. Census, Logan, Sanborn, South Dakota, Roll T624_1486, 15B.

41. Galley, *Joseph Smith Senior's Children*, 41.

42. Edson Don Carlos Smith, State of Utah Death Certificate, February 14, 1939, copy of original in my possession; "Records of Early Church Families," 105.

43. Sometime after 1910, Edson and Marion relocated to Kootenai, Idaho, where Marion passed away on May 1, 1920. Edson then moved to Olympia, Washington. In Washington, Edson met with LDS missionaries and was baptized in 1931 into the LDS Church at Tacoma, Washington. (See Chapter 19). Edson D. C. Smith, quoted in "Episodes in Genealogical Research: New Light on William Smith," 7–8; Edson D. C. Smith to U.S. Pension Office, June 6, 1892; 1910 U.S. Census, Chippewa Ward 1, Chippewa County, Wisconsin, Roll T624_1703, 1A; 1920 U.S. Census, Kootenai, Kootenai County, Idaho, Roll T625_291, 27B; Galley, *Joseph Smith Senior's Children*, 42–46.

for his father. (See Chapter 19.)[44] Edson married Lethe Newton on December 3, 1921, at Coeur d'Alene, Kootenai County, Idaho. After Lethe's death, He married Hannah Christine Hansen on April 18, 1932, at Salt Lake City. Toward the end of his life, Edson worked as a watchman at the LDS Church Administration Building, and as a Salt Lake Temple groundskeeper. He died in Salt Lake City on February 13, 1939.[45]

c. Loie May Smith Bolsinger. Loie May Smith was the only daughter and third child of William B. Smith and Eliza Elsie Sanborn Smith, born on May 8, 1866 at Elkader, Clayton County, Iowa.[46] She married Perry Jackson Bolsinger at Elkader, Iowa, on March 11, 1886. The couple moved to Osterdock, Clayton County, Iowa.[47] Loie May taught school and Perry farmed.[48] After the death of Loie May's mother, Eliza, William moved to Osterdock to be near Loie May and her family. Loie May died at her home in Osterdock, Iowa, on May 10, 1925.[49]

5. Rosanna Goyette La Ture Surprise Smith

About eight months after Eliza's death, William married Rosanna ("Rosa") Goyette La Ture Surprise, a widowed Frenchwoman who lived less than a hundred miles southeast in Clinton, Clinton County, Iowa, on December 21, 1889.[50] Rosa had been born at Montreal, Quebec, Canada, on May 16, 1830, and was nineteen years younger than Smith.[51] She had been baptized a member of the RLDS Church in 1880 and attended the RLDS branch in Clinton, Iowa. William likely came to know her through their shared faith, as he frequently traveled and preached at the RLDS branches organized in northeastern Iowa. Rosa had first married Joseph La Ture in 1847 near Montreal, Quebec, Canada, and had two children before Joseph died at Lockport, New York, five years later. She then married Samuel Surprise at Lockport around 1854, where they lived for five years, before moving to Iowa in about 1859, residing at Dubuque and then Bellevue. She had six children with Samuel, before he left the family to find work. According to Rosa, he then "lost his mind and died in an [insane] asylum in Cook Co. Ill[inois]," on January 27, 1879. Rosa owned no property at the time of her marriage to William, and all of her children were raised and had

---

44. "Baptism Heals: Nephew of Prophet Joseph Smith Relates Experience," *Deseret News*, January 9, 1932, 6; "Episodes in Genealogical Research: New Light on William Smith," *Deseret News*, July 27, 1935, 7.
45. Edson Don Carlos Smith, State of Utah Death Certificate, February 14, 1939.
46. Mae Bolsinger, Standard Certificate of death #22–923, Clayton County, Mallory Township, Osterdock City, in Galley, *Joseph Smith Senior's Children*, 46.
47. Galley, *Joseph Smith Senior's Children*, 46.
48. Ibid., 46–49; 1900 U.S. Census, Mallory, Clayton County, Iowa, Roll 425, 4A.
49. Galley, *Joseph Smith Senior's Children*, 46.
50. Marriage License #12066, Book 1, 219, Clinton County Courthouse, Clinton, Iowa.
51. Galley, *Joseph Smith Senior's Children*, 22.

moved out. Not long after their marriage, the two moved to Osterdock, Iowa. Though William died only a little more than three years later, Rosa was described as "untiring in her efforts to soothe his declining years," and "to watch over his tottering footsteps."[52] Rosa died April 6, 1923, at Clinton, Iowa.[53]

Plural Wives

1. Mary Ann Covington Sheffield Smith Stratton West

Mary Ann Covington was born in Hedfordshire, England, to Berril and Elizabeth Hodges Covington, on March 31, 1815. Mary Ann reported that she joined the LDS Church in 1841 at Bedford, England, being baptized by either James or William Lavender. She had married James Sheffield in England in 1836, but had left her alcoholic husband a few months prior to sailing for America in a company led by Orson Hyde.[54] The company had reached St. Louis so late in the season that they had been forced to winter there for four months until the ice melted.[55] They reached Nauvoo in April 1843. William initially met Mary Ann that month at Montrose, Iowa, at the home of William's uncle Asahel Smith, just after her company completed their journey to Nauvoo. Mary temporarily lived in Orson Hyde's home, where Joseph Smith introduced her to the principle of plural marriage. "I went to live at Orson Hyde's and soon after that time Joseph Smith wished to have an interview with me," recalled Covington decades later in being interviewed for the Temple Lot Case. "He had the interview with me, and then asked me if I had ever heard of a mans having more wives than one, and I said I had not. He then told me that he had received a revelation from God that a man could have more wives than one." A short time afterward, Joseph came to her again, informing her that "his brother William wished to marry me as a wife in plural marriage if I felt willing to consent to it." Within a few weeks of arriving at Nauvoo, Mary Ann moved in with Agnes Smith, the widow of William's brother Don Carlos and a plural wife of Joseph. According to Mary Ann's recollection, her own sealing occurred at Agnes Smith's home, the two-story printing office on the northeast corner

---

52. Statement of Rosanna Smith, June 21, 1902, 29, Part 1, Widow's Pension, William B. Smith Pension File; John R. Neely (Chicago, Ill.), Letter to N. A. Lowry, April 21, 1903, 52, Part 1, Widow's Pension, William B. Smith Pension File; "OBITUARY. Mrs. Eliza E. Smith, of Elkader," 1; Murdock, "Rev. William B. Smith," 5.

53. "Funerals—Mrs. Rosanna Smith," *Clinton Herald*, (April 7, 1923): 6; "Drop Report—Pensioner, Rosanna Smith," April 25, 1923, Part 2, 91, in William B. Smith Pension File.

54. Mary Ann [Covington Sheffield] West, Testimony, in United States testimony 1892, Court of Appeals Eighth Circuit, 497–98, MS 1160, LDS Church History Library; Ruby Brown Clayson, "Biography of Mary Ann Covington Stratton West," unpublished typescript paper, ca. 1958, 1, MSS 2817, L. Tom Perry Special Collections, Brigham Young University, Provo, Utah.

55. Myrtle Stevens Hyde, *Orson Hyde: The Olive Branch of Israel* (Salt Lake City: Agreka Books, 2000), 148–49.

of Water and Bain Streets. She identified Brigham Young as the officiator but did not remember the presence of any witnesses. Though their time together was brief, Mary Ann reported that William "treated me very well."[56] The two separated when William left the Church in September 1845. In her Temple Lot testimony, Mary Ann probably spoke for all of William's plural wives at Nauvoo, when she said she considered that William had "divorced himself from me . . . . when he went away [to the] east." She said she married Joseph A. Stratton in December 1846; and after Stratton died on October 30, 1850, she married Chauncey W. West in 1851 in Salt Lake City.[57] She died in Ogden, Utah, on October 5, 1908.[58]

2. Sarah Ann Libby Smith Smith

Sarah Ann Libby was born on May 7, 1818, at Ossipee, New Hampshire, to Nathaniel Libby and Tirzah Lord Libby. Her father died on July 18, 1840. Sarah, her younger sister Hannah, and their mother moved to Lowell, Massachusetts. At Lowell, Sarah worked as a carder in the textile mills and as a pastry cook.[59] Sarah Ann was baptized at Lowell on May 18, 1844, and was sealed to William Smith in the fall of 1844, when William presided over the eastern branches of the Church.[60] Sarah and William's marriage was dissolved when William left Nauvoo in September 1845. Sarah and her sister Hannah migrated from Lowell to Nauvoo, Illinois, in September-October, 1845, arriving on October 20.[61] Shortly afterward, on November 20, 1845, Sarah was sealed to George A. Smith, William's first cousin.[62] The sealing was re-

---

56. Mary Ann [Covington Sheffield] West, Testimony, in United States testimony 1892, Court of Appeals Eighth Circuit, 495–96, MS 1160, LDS Church History Library.

57. Ibid., 498–99.

58. "Respected Pioneer Dies at Ogden," *Evening Telegram* (Salt Lake City) 7, no. 20177 (October 5, 1908): 11.

59. Connell O'Donovan, "Members and Missionaries of the Lowell, Mass. Branch of The Church of Jesus Christ of Latter-Day Saints, 1835–1860," unpublished web document, http://www.connellodonovan.com/sarah_libby.html (accessed April 12, 2015).

60. T. Edgar Lyon, "Nauvoo and the Council of the Twelve," in *The Restoration Movement: Essays in Mormon History*, rev. ed., edited by F. Mark McKiernan, Alma R. Blair, and Paul M. Edwards (Independence, Mo.: Herald House, 1992), 198 note 37. I have been unable to locate the reference Lyon cites documenting that William was living at Lowell with these two "blood sisters" whom he identified as his plural wives. However, later references add credibility to what Lyon recounted, including verification that Sarah Ann and Hannah Libby were sealed to William at some point between June 1844–August 1845. Joseph F. Smith (Salt Lake City), Letter to William Smith, July 12, 1884, MS 1325, Box 31, fd. 3, pp. 58–67, LDS Church History Library; Joseph Fielding Smith, *Blood Atonement and the Origin of Plural Marriage* (Salt Lake City: Deseret News, 1905), 49.

61. Hannah M. Smith Autobiographical Letter (Provo, Utah), to Charles Warren Smith, or his heirs, or Sarah M. Colton, or her heirs, or Grace Libby Smith, or her heirs, March 5, 1881, placed in a Relief Society box of the Provo Fourth Ward, 1, typescript copy in my possession.

62. Merlo J. Pusey, *Builders of the Kingdom: George A. Smith, John Henry Smith George Albert Smith* (Provo, Utah: Brigham Young University Press, 1981), 60.

peated in the Nauvoo Temple on January 26, 1846.[63] She gave birth to John Henry Smith on September 18, 1848. He later became a member of the Quorum of the Twelve Apostles and a member of the First Presidency in Salt Lake City. Sarah was also the grandmother of George Albert Smith, who later became president of the LDS Church. Sarah migrated to Utah but struggled with poor health and died at Salt Lake City on June 12, 1851.[64]

3. Hannah Maria Libby Smith Smith

Hannah Maria Libby Smith Smith, 1828–1906. Hannah (seated front row, center) is pictured here as part of the Provo Third Ward Relief Society Presidency. Photograph by James Fennemore. Courtesy LDS Church History Library.

Hannah Maria Libby was the third daughter of Nathaniel Libby and Thirza Lord Libby, born at Ossipee, New Hampshire, on June 29, 1828.[65] She worked in the fabric mills at Lowell, Massachusetts, with her mother and her older sister Sarah Ann, who was also a plural wife of William Smith.[66] She was baptized with Sarah at Lowell on May 18, 1844, and was sealed to William during the fall of 1844.[67] The two separated once William left the Church in September 1845. She migrated with her sister Sarah Ann to Nauvoo, arriving on October 20, 1845.[68] She was subsequently sealed to William's cousin, George A. Smith, on November 20, 1845, with the sealing being repeated in the Nauvoo Temple on January 26, 1846.[69] In addition to rearing her five children (only three of whom survived childhood), Hannah helped raise her nephew John Henry Smith, after Hannah's sister Sarah died in 1851. Hannah died at Provo, Utah on September 21, 1906.[70]

---

63. Lyndon W. Cook, *Nauvoo Marriages and Proxy Sealings 1843–1846* (Provo, Utah: Grandin Book, 2004), 149.

64. Pusey, *Builders of the Kingdom*, 84.

65. Hannah M. Smith Autobiographical Letter, 1; State of Utah—Death Certificate, Hannah Maria Smith, September 21, 1906, copy in author's possession.

66. O'Donovan, "Members and Missionaries of the Lowell, Mass. Branch."

67. Lyon, "Nauvoo and the Council of the Twelve," 198 note 37; Joseph F. Smith to William Smith, July 12, 1884; Joseph Fielding Smith, *Blood Atonement and the Origin of Plural Marriage*, 49.

68. Hannah M. Smith, Autobiographical Letter, 1.

69. Pusey, *Builders of the Kingdom*, 60; Cook, *Nauvoo Marriages and Proxy Sealings 1843–1846*, 149.

70. State of Utah—Death Certificate, Hannah Maria Smith, September 21, 1906, copy in author's possession.

4. Priscilla Mogridge Smith Lowry Williams Staines

Priscilla Mogridge, like William's first plural wife Mary Ann Covington, was an English convert. Born on March 11, 1823, at Widbrook, Wiltshire, England, she was the seventh of nine children born to John Mogridge and Mary Crook Mogridge.[71] According to Priscilla's personal history, she was converted at age nineteen and baptized during the winter of 1842–43. "We looked upon the gathering as necessary to our salvation," wrote Priscilla. During the intervening year after her baptism and confirmation, she was "filled with an irresistible desire to join the saints who were gathering to America."[72] She left all of her family and sailed from Liverpool to New Orleans on December 27, 1843, aboard the *Fanny* with about 210 other Mormon converts, reaching Nauvoo on April 13, 1844.[73] William's brief final visit to Nauvoo occurred in April-May 1844 before the deaths of his brothers, and it is possible that he made her acquaintance during that time period.[74] Their next opportunity to meet was in the summer of 1845 when William pronounced her patriarchal blessing on July 11.[75] The marriage probably occurred during the relatively conflict-free month between July 9 and August 10. Priscilla testified forty-eight years later in Utah: "I was taught that principle [of plural marriage] by William Smith in 1845" and married him shortly afterward. "He told me that his brother had received a revelation to that effect, and

Priscilla Mogridge Smith Lowry Williams Staines, 1823–1899. Photograph taken after her marriage to William C. Staines, ca. 1880, photographer unknown. Courtesy Daughters of Utah Pioneers.

---

71. Edward W. Tullidge, *The Women of Mormondom* (New York: Tullidge and Crandall, 1877), 285; Connell O'Donovan, "The Orphan Child: Priscilla Mogridge Smith Lowry Williams Staines (1823–1899)," *John Whitmer Historical Association Journal* 32, no. 1 (Spring/Summer 2012):-80–81, notes that several of Priscilla's siblings joined the Church but that only Priscilla migrated to America.

72. Tullidge, *The Women of Mormondom*, 286, 288.

73. Fred E. Woods, *Gathering to Nauvoo* (American Fork, Utah: Covenant Communications, 2002), 167–68; Joseph Smith, Journal, April 13, 1844, in Scott H. Faulring, ed., *An American Prophet's Record: The Diaries and Journals of Joseph Smith* (Salt Lake City: Signature Books, 1987), 471.

74. William had led a group of forty to fifty eastern Mormons to Nauvoo in April 1844. (See Chapter 10.) He subsequently left Nauvoo on May 21, 1844, headed east with Heber C. Kimball and a large contingent of traveling missionaries who were also engaged in Joseph's presidential campaign . Kimball, *On the Potter's Wheel*, 60.

75. Marquardt, *Early Patriarchal Blessings*, 312–13.

he taught it to me, and practiced it." She could not definitively remember the officiator's name—possibly "Lee" or "Lane"—and could not recollect ever being introduced publicly as William's wife—which fit the pattern of secrecy then governing polygamy.[76] The couple separated when William fled Nauvoo in mid-September 1845. She then married Samuel R. Lowry in 1846 at St. Louis, Missouri, but the two had separated by the early 1850s. Priscilla then married Thomas S. Williams in 1854 in Salt Lake City. After his death, she married William Carter Staines in 1865. Priscilla died on January 4, 1899, at Salt Lake City.[77]

5. Mary Jones Smith Hall

Mary Elizabeth Jones was the second child born to William Jones and Elizabeth Hughes Jones on March 17, 1828, at New York City. She was baptized in 1841 at Nauvoo,[78] where she married William Smith in late summer 1845. Mary Ann Covington, the first of William's plural wives, remembered that she was present during this sealing ceremony and that Brigham Young performed the sealing at the home of Agnes Coolbrith Smith. Covington was particular about the sequence of William's sealing to Mary Jones, indicating that it took place after his civil marriage to Mary Jane Rollins (June 22, 1845), and after his sealing to Priscilla Mogridge. She also recollected that Mary Jones continued to reside with her parents after she and William were sealed.[79] As with William's other plural wives, the couple separated after William left Nauvoo in September 1845. Mary married Job Pitcher Hall at Winter Quarters, Nebraska on February 26, 1848, and the Jones family followed Brigham Young to the West.[80]

6. Henriette Rice Smith

Henriette Rice was the daughter of Ira Rice and Sarah Ann Harrington Rice, born at Ypsilanti, Washtenaw, Michigan, about 1831. The family joined the LDS Church in Michigan in 1840, and had relocated to Nauvoo by 1842.[81] Henriette was sealed to William by Brigham Young in Nauvoo on August 8, 1845.[82]

---

76. Priscilla M. Staines, Testimony, Temple Lot Case Testimonies, 528–529, U.S. Eighth Circuit Court, 1892, MS 1160, LDS Church History Library.

77. O'Donovan, "The Orphan Child: Priscilla Mogridge Smith Lowry Williams Staines," 86–87, 102–03, 107, 112–13.

78. Mary Roe Porter, *History of Job Pitcher Hall* (n.p., James Varley Roe and Mary Roe Porter, 1960), 8–9, 19.

79. Mary Ann (Covington) West Testimony, Temple Lot Case Testimonies, 496, 509–511, U.S. Eighth Circuit Court, 1892, MS 1160, LDS Church History Library.

80. Porter, *History of Job Pitcher Hall*, 23.

81. Eva A. Rice and Loretta C. Rice, *Footprints of Ira Rice* (Logan: Utah State University, 1973), 8, 10. Ira received his patriarchal blessing from William Smith August 4, 1845. Ibid., 10.

82. Under the date of August 8, 1845, Brigham Young recorded in his journal, "In the evening went to Wm Smiths and sealed [him] to Miss Rice." Brigham Young Office Files 1832–1878, Brigham Young Journals, 1832–1846, LDS Church History Library.

Henriette also separated from William once he left the Church in September 1845. She died the following year while the Saints were migrating from Nauvoo.[83]

7. Lucinda ("Lucy") Ellen Curtis Smith Merdock Douglas Flanders

Lucinda Ellen Curtis was born on March 24, 1829, at Hanover, Chautauqua County, New York, to Thomas Curtis and Persis (Percy) Baldwin Curtis.[84] Her parents joined the Church in 1835 in New York, and shortly afterward gathered with the Saints at Kirtland, Ohio. Lucinda recalled being baptized at age eight in 1837 at Kirtland, Ohio.[85] Lucinda's father died when they were migrating with the Saints to Missouri, and her mother afterward married Edward Johnson. Lucinda and William were probably married at Nauvoo during July-August, 1845.[86] The two were separated when William abandoned Nauvoo in September 1845. A family record documents that, when William fled Nauvoo, leaving her behind, it "was a terrible experience for Lucy."[87] Afterward, she was sealed to John Hatfield as a plural wife. The two apparently separated a short time later, and Lucinda then married Charles Merdock at St. Joseph, Missouri, on April 5, 1850. After Merdock's death on January 6, 1853,[88] she married Daniel

Lucinda Ellen Curtis Smith Merdock Douglas Flanders, 1829–1915. Photographer and date unknown. Courtesy Community of Christ Archives.

---

83. Writing to William Smith in November 1846, James L. Blanchard indicated that he had visited "the old man," apparently a reference to Henriette's father, Ira Rice. Blanchard then wrote, "however he is no friend of yours[.] His daughter she that was called your wife is dead[.] I suppose you have heard of this before." James L. Blanchard (Oquawka, Ill.), Letter to William Smith, November 6, 1846, Beinecke Library, Yale University, New Haven, Connecticut.

84. Missouri Death Certificate, Lucinda E. Flanders, File # 8046, March 21, 1915, copy in my possession; John Slayton, Jr., comp., *Descendants of James Rising (1617–1688)*, published web document, 1999, unpaginated, entry for Thomas Curtis, available at http://www.genealogy.com/forum/surnames/topics/rising/19/ (accessed April 20, 2015).

85. Pearl Wilcox, *Saints of the Reorganization in Missouri* (Independence, Mo.: Pearl Wilcox, 1974), 75–76; Slayton, *Descendants of James Rising*.

86. Nelson Winch Green, *Fifteen Years among the Mormons: Being the Narrative of Mrs. Mary Ettie V. Smith* (New York: H. Dayton, 1859), 121–22, 124.

87. Slayton, *Descendants of James Rising*.

88. Charles Merdock marriage to Lucinda (Lucy) E. Curtis, April 5, 1850, Saint Joseph, Buchanan County, Missouri, Pedigree Resource File, CD # 135, Church of Jesus Christ of Latter-day Saints. Black and Black, Annotated Record of Baptisms for the Dead, 3: 1612.

Douglas, then Jasper Delaney Flanders on March 25, 1860.[89] She and Jasper then united with the Reorganized Church of Jesus Christ of Latter Day Saints, their family forming the nucleus of the Delano RLDS Branch, in Dekalb County, Missouri.[90] Lucinda died at Stewartsville, Missouri, on March 21, 1915.[91]

8. Ann Sophia Rollins Smith Beckstead Roberts

Ann Sophia Rollins was the second child born to Enoch Perham Rollins and Sophia Philbrick Rollins, born at Bangor, Maine, on March 5, 1831.[92] She moved with her family to Nauvoo in August 1844, after having been baptized with her family into the LDS Church on February 8, 1841.[93] She was a younger sister to Mary Jane Rollins, who was civilly married to William on June 22, 1845.[94] Ann received her patriarchal blessing from William on July 8, 1845, and the two were probably sealed that same month.[95] They separated when William left Nauvoo in September 1845. She later married Sidney M. Beckstead on June 11, 1850,[96] and, after his death in 1864, married Edward K. Roberts April 19, 1869.[97] She died at Annabella, Utah, on May 13, 1885.[98]

9. Evenade Archer

Evanade Archer was born about 1827 in Green County, Indiana, to John W. Archer and Mary Saunders Archer.[99] The Archers joined the Church in Indiana around the year 1835, relocating to Clay County, Missouri, that same year. They gathered with the Saints at Nauvoo and, after the death of Joseph Smith, followed

---

89. When she married Jasper D. Flanders in 1860, she was listed as "Lucinda E. Douglass." Marriage of Jasper Flanders to Lucinda E. Douglass, March 25, 1860, by William W. Riggs, JP. Missouri State & County Records on Microform, Dekalb County, Missouri Marriage Book "B" (1845–1867), 12, 24, Woodruff roll 16, film cabinet 91.

90. Wilcox, *Saints of the Reorganization in Missouri*, 75.

91. Missouri Death Certificate, Lucinda E. Flanders, File # 8046, March 21, 1915, copy in my possession.

92. Wilson, "Enoch Perham Rollins," 2.

93. "Died. Enoch Perham Rollins," 11.

94. "Married," *Nauvoo Neighbor* 3, no. 9 (July 2, 1845): 3.

95. "Patriarchal blessing of Ann S. Rollins," Nauvoo, Illinois, July 8, 1845, in H. Michael Marquardt, comp., *Early Patriarchal Blessings of The Church of Jesus Christ of Latter-Day Saints* (Salt Lake City; Smith-Pettit Foundation, 2007), 303; Green, *Fifteen Years among the Mormons*, 121–22, 124.

96. Wilson, "Enoch Perham Rollins," 4.

97. Frank Esshom, *Pioneers and Prominent Men of Utah* (Salt Lake City: Utah Pioneers Book Publishing, 1913), 1135.

98. "Deaths. Sarah A. B. Elmer," *Salt Lake Tribune*, September 16, 1944, 18. This is also the date on Ann's headstone.

99. Archer Association Family Group Records, call #RTMIS00004, 5–6, LDS Family History Library, Salt Lake City.

James J. Strang to Voree, Wisconsin.[100] William and Evanade were presumably sealed by Benjamin Ellsworth at Voree, Wisconsin, in the summer of 1846. (See Chapter 14.) Evanade and William had no children, and apparently Evanade stayed behind in Voree while William went off, first to Kirtland with Strang, then to Knoxville for the winter of 1846–47. They may have resumed a marital relationship during his brief return to Voree September 1846 before William settled in Knoxville County, Illinois, for the winter and during his brief visit in April 1847. The two apparently separated after William broke from Strang in 1847. Evanade's family migrated to Davis County, Iowa, in the 1850s, and I have been unable to locate her death date.[101]

10. Rosanna ("Rosa") Hook Smith Osborne Blake

Rosanna Hook was born in 1837 at Howland, Maine, to William and Mercy Hook. Aaron Hook Sr. and Rhoda Gibson Hook, with their sons William and John, left Maine for Illinois, arriving on October 28, 1839. Aaron Jr. had established his home in Lamoille, Bureau County, Illinois, two years earlier. After staying with Aaron Jr. for several months, the entire Hook family, including Aaron Jr., settled a few miles to the north at Palestine Grove in February 1840.[102] Rosanna's mother, Mercy, died before 1843; and after Mercy's death, her father, William L. Hook, returned to his native state of Maine, where he remarried and remained for more than seven years.[103] During their father's absence, Rosanna, her twin sister Rhoda, and their brother Aaron were left in the care of their grandmother Rhoda Hook at Palestine Grove, where they joined William's church along with other members of the family. William Anderson, a near neighbor to Aaron Jr.,

---

100. Clark V. Johnson, *Mormon Redress Petitions: Documents of the 1833–1838 Missouri Conflict* (Provo, Utah: BYU Religious Studies Center, 1992), 127, 599. John W. Archer is listed as a high priest in Strang's church, in the November 1846 issues of the *Zion's Reveille*. "The Pseudo-Mormon Clique," *Zion's Reveille* 1, no. 11 (November 1846): 1. The Archer family entered into a communal order established by Strang in 1848. By 1849, John had withdrawn from the order, and sought legal recourse in recovering items that he had consecrated. Documents in the Case of John W. Archer vs. James J. Strang and John Cole, MSS 408, L. Tom Perry Special Collections, Harold B. Lee Library, Brigham Young University.

101. 1860 U.S. Census, Union, Davis County, Iowa, Roll: M653_317, 795, image 283.

102. *History of Lee County*, 284, 308–10, 406–7; Pearl Wilcox, *Regathering the Scattered Saints in Wisconsin and Illinois* (Independence, Mo.: Pearl Wilcox, 1984), 74.

103. I have been unable to locate a death record for Mercy Hook, but William Hook had married Abigail Wallingford in Howland, Maine, by 1844. William and Abigail were still in Howland in August 1850. By 1855, they had relocated to Lodi, Wisconsin. Stephen Clay Balliet, *The Balliet, Balliett, Balliette, Balyeat, Bolyard, and Allied Families* (Lehigh County, Penn.: Thos. J. Moran's Sons, 1968), 647; 1850 U.S. Census, Maine, Penobscot County, Howland, Roll M432_266; 284B, image 145; Wisconsin State Census, 1855, Columbia County, Lodi; 1860 U.S. Census, Wisconsin, Columbia County, Lodi, Film #1032686, Line 48, image 00389. Special thanks to Erin Jennings Metcalfe for her research in identifying William L. Hook's movements during the 1840s and 1850s.

who had been preaching in Chicago and other parts of northern Illinois in the spring of 1843, began preaching in Lee County by that fall. Anderson preached at the home of John Hook and found the extended family eager to hear his message. John, his brother Aaron, their families, and their mother, Rhoda, all became Latter-day Saints by the fall of 1843 as a result of Anderson's preaching. Anderson likely baptized the Hooks in the Green River, which ran near John Hook's home. Afterward he held regular preaching services in the Hook home.[104] During the time William was building up his Church of Jesus Christ of Latter Days Saints at Palestine Grove, William married fifteen-year-old Rosanna Hook, the niece of his counselor Aaron Hook, likely in the early part of in 1852. The two had separated by the summer of 1852 when Rosanna fell in love with a young man nearer her own age. Although she brought accusations against William that led to the state charging William with criminal conduct, Rosanna later recanted her accusations, and William was eventually cleared. (See Chapter 17.) Rosanna had moved to Wisconsin by 1853, where she married Samuel J. Osborne in 1854.[105] She married William J. Blake in 1866, divorced him, then married him again in 1868.[106] She died at Madison, Wisconsin, on October 13, 1893.[107]

---

104. *History of Lee County*, 284, 308–10, 406–7; Andrew Jenson, *Latter-day Saint Biographical Encyclopedia: A Compilation of Biographical Sketches of Prominent Men and Women in the Church of Jesus Christ of Latter-day Saints* (Salt Lake City: Andrew Jenson History Co., 1901–36), 2:585–86. Aaron and Matilda Hook's names appear on the Nauvoo Scroll Petition, under the date of November 28, 1843, at Nauvoo. Clark V. Johnson, ed., *Mormon Redress Petitions: Documents of the 1833–1838 Missouri Conflict* (Provo, Utah: BYU Religious Studies Center, 1992), 591–92. In the 1850 census for Amboy, William's children Rhoda, Rosanna, and Aaron, along with their grandmother Rhoda, were all living in the John Hook household. Grandmother Rhoda is referred to as the "widow Hook" in later sources. 1850 U.S. Census, Illinois, Lee County, Amboy Township, Roll M432_116, 117A, image 88.

105. 1860 U.S. Census, Lodi, Columbia County, Wisconsin, Roll: M653_1401, 387, image 396.

106. "Wisconsin Marriages, 1836–1930," index, William J. Blake and Rosannah Osborn, July 8, 1866, Lodi, Columbia, Wisconsin, FamilySearch, https://familysearch.org/pal:/MM9.1.1/XRLS-N31, accessed April 9, 2015; "Wisconsin Marriages, 1836–1930," index, William J. Blake and Rosanna Osborne, November, 28, 1868, Madison, Dane, Wisconsin, FamilySearch, https://familysearch.org/pal:/MM9.11/XRLX-S3V, accessed April 9, 2015.

107. "Anna Blake," October 13, 1893, Madison, Dane County, Wisconsin, in Wisconsin Pre-1907 Vital Records Collection, Volume 1, 0431, Wisconsin Historical Society, Madison, Wisconsin.

Appendix B

"The Elders' Pocket Companion" By William Smith

As contained in John K. Sheen, *Polygamy; or, The Veil Lifted* (York, Neb.: n. p., 1889).

THE
ELDERS' POCKET COMPANION.[1]
Being

A Series of Brief Treaties on Babtism for the dead. Spiritual Wife doctrine applied to the Millenium, and Plurality Wife Doctrine as practiced by the Ancient Prophets and Patriarchs &c.

Also,

The Power and authority of the Priesthood with the duties of Elders, Priests, Teachers and Deacons, Members &c.– Mode of Baptism, Manner of Administering the Sacrament – Settling difficulties, &c. &c. with a brief sketch of the faith, and rise of the Church of Latter Day Saints.

Together

with a Short Biography of Joseph Smith Sr and his family—Martyrdom of Joseph & Hiram Smith, the Prophet and Patriarch of the Church &c—The whole designed to assist the Elders, Members &c.

By W. SMITH, One of the twelve. "A wise man seeketh after knowledge and findeth it"– But a fool despiseth it. – Mormon Scripture.

"Behold the former things are come to pass and new things do I declare. Before they spring forth I tell you of them.["]["""] Isa. xlii:9.

Dear Brethren Greeting
As I am informed that Elder Grant[2] is about to publish a Pamphlet touching the claims of Elder Rigdon [*See Note below*—*J. K. S.*][3] and the twelve to the Presidency of the Church of Christ.[4] And as it is expected, Great will be the mystery of ungodliness exposed by the Rigdonites on various plans and schemes devised by their own imagination. And as I profess to know some things, that the world does not; I shall endeavor to reason upon some that will I trust, be a benefit to all that is seeking after truth and knowledge. Jesus said unto his disciples, "Unto you is given to know the mysteries of the kingdom." But to them that were without he spoke in Parables[5], and so do we.[6] I hold it a maxim, that I have as good a right to know the mysteries of the third heavens, as Paul, and if Paul saw and heard, things, ["]unlawful for men to utter," so have I. And Because men of meaner spirits do not, seek after, or aspire for the glory of the stars, Is that a reason, others should not seek to know the power and fullness, of their salvation in the celestial world? No man shall contract or chain my belief; the soul is free to act, like the bird uncaged,--mantled with charity, which is the bond of perfectness, and peace, "believeth all things, and endureth all things."[7] Free to roam where it pleases, in the midst of the Boundless fields of knowledge; until like

Paul, it can comprehend, the height, and depth, of the eternal world; comprehend all mysteries, and upon this principle I stand Gods free man, Christ said "fear not them that can kill the body," but fear him that can (not will) destroy both soul and body in hell"[8] Thus I am not bound by human creeds, or the fear of man And to satisfy the inquiring mind I think it proper to address the saints, on some other points of doctrine, (altogether different from the one Elder Grant, has taken in hand, as no doubt, but he will do justice to the subject.) And this I do for the benefit of the church, that they may be saved, and conducted through the storm that is now gathering around them, and be protected from the ravening wolves, who are seeking to destroy the flock I -----[9] proper for me to state that since the great Mormon exposures By J. C. Bennett the ----- ----- ----- [spiritual] wife system, has become so notorious in all the churches, and also in the world abroad, as a matter of public rumor, that situated as I have been, among different people, for the last two years,[10] involved upon me has been the arduous task, of answering to the thousand and one questions asked concerning the subject above alluded to. And no doubt <u>hundreds</u> of persons may be brought to testify, that I have (from what will appear in the sequeal) taught them plurality wife doctrine. This would not have been the case however had things been otherwise, with these men. Just at this present time A struggle is being made to divide the Church, destroy the twelve and make Elder Rigdon the <u>Prophet and Head</u> of the same. A right that belongs to the twelve who acc[o]rding to the Law of God legally hold that office; Hence to displace these men, it becomes needful to destroy their character, influence &c. by falsehoods slander, or anything else, that will accomplish the object of those engaged in it

Therefore it is to be expected that doctrine will be most grossly misrepresented, and especially where it suits them to accomplish their base and wicked purposes in carrying out their plan. It could not be otherwise expected; in relation to many instances where questions of a singular character have been asked, if some things should be said to gratify, the most curious and inquisitive. Solomon said ["]answer a fool according to his folly, lest he be wise in his own conceit."[11] These kind have got the desire of their heart and will perish in their own corruption. But so far from teaching what has been represented it is entirely in the reverse. And since some few of these men (Rigdonites) who appear the most conspicuous, and have taken it upon them to betray the most unlimited confidence according to their own statements <u>if provided what they say is true</u>. It will be seen in the course of my remarks what I have taught and said, both publicly and privately. And as my belief in doctrine is founded upon the Bible, and revelation, the word of God Then let <u>Judas's</u> betray and grumble, on, the LORD knows them that are his, and will prove the Just, he will never forsake them. And to this day, ----- ----- -----, I can say he has never forsaken me, neither has he forsaken the twelve that has been called and chosen But our enemies God will judge.

When Jesus left the earth 1800 years ago the government fell upon the twelve, Peter, James and John presiding &c Joseph our Prophet is gone, and God has given the twelve the keys of this last ministry, and their power still remains to bind on earth, and seal in heaven. In the language of the Poet

"Ye chosen twelve, to you are given,
The keys of this last ministry–
To every nation under heaven
From land to land from sea to sea."[12]

To seal matrimonial contracts, remission of sins by Baptism, and to Baptise the living for the dead, &c Christ gave this power to his disciples in former times and it remained with them and God has given this power to the twelve in these last times, and none can take it away. Then let ["]the heathen rage and the people imagine vain things."¹³ The scriptures must be fulfilled. See Rev. vii. 2 to 4. The servants of God must be sealed; and who is to do this work, the ministers God sends, and these must have <u>Priesthood Power</u>. These too, are to "come up through great tribulation" (16v).¹⁴ This the Prophet Joseph the twelve and others have done. We are also told in the sixth Chap of Rev. 10, 11 v. that these will be persecuted unto death &c. Jer. xvi. 16. Speaks of Fishers and hunters being sent to gather Israel &c. Christ said he would send his angels, to gather his elect from the four corners of the earth." <u>Angels</u> are sometimes servants; and servants angels, in scripture in many places, and these will have power to do the work of these last days, of the fulness of times <u>to seal, Bind, gather, save</u> on earth and heaven for time and also for eternity. Although some have already sealed their testimony with their blood, others would rob them of their glory, Despoil the Church of its Power, &c– ----- the true servants of God, of their Priesthood, Oh! shame on such men, that would be guilty of such foul treachery, consummate ignorance and folly. Daniel said this kingdom the God of heaven should set up, "should break in pieces all other kingdoms and stand forever. And not be given to others ----- -----[."]¹⁵

With these remarks I shall content myself to proceed, and give my opinion on the following subjects, under their respective heads, which are three peculiar doctrines in the Bible

First. The Doctrine of Baptism for the <u>Dead</u>.

2. The Spiritual Wife system (so-<u>called</u>)

3. Is the plurality of wives, a, <u>doctrine</u> as practiced by the ancient <u>Prophets and Patriarchs</u>. First. Baptism for the Dead **Omitted.**¹⁶

NOTE.—All italics are mine [Sheen's]. Words underscored are so marked in copy. References to Celestial Revelation are Mine.¹⁷

[*Page 10*] Second. THE SPIRITUAL WIFE SYSTEM: SO CALLED.

This doctrine is different from the one under the head of "plurality of wife doctrine." Yet it is plural, but *not confined* to the probationary state, but to the resurrected. "In that day says Isa iv. 1. Seven women shall take hold of one man, and say we will eat our own bread, and wear our own apparel, only let us be called by thy name, to take away our reproach." It is evident this refers to the Millennium from what follows in the five following verses, otherwise it is a circumstance connected, with the preparatory work of the coming of Christ. We shall take the liberty however of applying it to the Millennium, as the above passage most unquestionably sits forth the order–the glory and beauty of that day, when the earth shall bloom again as in the Garden of Eden redeemed from sin, and Zion shall be called holy, and all that remain in her and in Jerusalem &c. At this time all the wicked will be destroyed, and the saints will be few, and further in the Millennium the mortal saints who remain in the flesh, at the time of Christ's coming, will multiply and replenish the earth. See Isa. lxv. 20 to 25. And those born during the Millennium are the ones Satan is going forth to tempt and deceive after the Millennium. See Rev. xx. 7, 8. It will be then no doubt as it was in the days of old, a reproach for women not to generate, and bare children but it will be done without the pang, and sting of sin attendant now, Isa. lxv, 23. This I give as my opinion, based upon the scriptures referred to.

There is another point connected with the subject I wish to notice, ie. all marriages solemnized in the ancient church was sealed by the Priesthood for time and eternity. [*C. Rev.*, *par. 2.*]¹⁸ Hence marriages out of the Church is not considered legal. "Be ye not unequally yoked with unbelievers."¹⁹ Marriage is a sacred ordinance, and was always solemnized in the church by a man holding the Priesthood, And not as the custom is among the Gentiles, for time only, and not for eternity by Priesthood authority, but by Gentile Law, which makes this kind of marriage legal only so far as the laws of man are concerned, in the sight of men and not of God. [*C. Rev., par. 2.*]²⁰

It is evident that to seal contracts for time and also for eternity [*C. Rev., par. 2.*]²¹ it would require the same power and authority that it would to baptise. This was the extent and power given to the ancient disciples, to bind on earth and seal in heaven. This to[o] was the key to solve the mystery of the question propounded by the Saducees, "Whose wife shall she be in the resurrection, for all had her to wife."²² The first that had her in time, had her also in eternity is sealed, for the first contract held good. The rest had her only in time. In eternity there is no marrying, [*C. Rev., par. 4.*]²³ for the marriage covenant takes place here in time under the law of the Holy Priesthood ["I am the Lord thy God, and will give unto thee the law of my Holy Priesthood.—*C. Rev., par. 11.*]²⁴ and must remain when sealed by that authority, for time and eternity.

But the question might be asked can a man be sealed to more than one woman? I answer they can, for if a man has several wives, and they are all dead, but one, he can be sealed up [to] them all, by the one living standing up for the dead, and thus acting by proxy, he can claim them all in the resurrection. As in case of Baptizing the living for the dead. And Here I would ask where would be the Justice of depriving the men of the first, second or third wife, he had been married to them all here for time, and also for eternity, by the Priesthood, and if not in time sealed as before mentioned, for the privilege is greater as I think I have clearly shown. The man loved them all had children by them all, and one was as near and dear to him as the other. And again, we shall not lose the power of recognition in the eternal world; this will constitute our happiness in part. But cut <u>one, two or three</u> off from our presence where is the fullness of their glory – they would be lonely stars. Paul said "man was the head of woman as Christ is head of the Church." Therefore man is not without the woman in the lord neither the woman without the man in the Lord.²⁵ [*See Note below*]²⁶

Hence they are as the Angels, "not marrying nor given in marriage in the resurrection." [*C. Rev., par. 4.*]²⁷ Therefore this takes place before, and are as the Angels of God to enjoy each others society, wives, children, husband, &c to live and love all, (not one) and this makes us happy. For in the language of the Poet.

"Love is the golden chain that binds
  The happy minds above"
And he's an heir of heaven who finds
  His bosom swell with love"²⁸

This will exalt us to a Kingdom of power and glory, [*C. Rev., par. 6.*]²⁹ for Christ has promised, to those—["]who are faithful over a few things shall be made ruler over many things"³⁰ Thus I have given a brief sketch of the doctrine that has *so long racked and distracted the Brains of Mormon Apostates*' And I have given it as my own sentiments and upon my own responsibility; [* *"placed under restrictions."–Hyrum Smith*]³¹ and I do not wish the Church, or those of my brethren the "twelve" to be charged, or made responsible for them for I am indebted to no one for the most of the points I have noticed above, But for the fact that I have been grossly misrepresented, induced me to give this *explanation* and in this manner, I *have always* represented and *taught it*. And while

I hold even the ashes and tomb of a martyred Prophet, and Brother sacred, or venerate the Patriarch of the Church of Christ, slain for the cause of God, and esteem Joseph Smith as the head of this last dispensation, while I have any regard for truth, or of *reverence for the REVELATION* of God and the scriptures of divine truth—I shall contend for the above faith, and sentiments, in the manner I have taught and explained them; and applied them to time and place. In these no doubt I shall be misrepresented. I must expect that all manner of evil will be spoken agains[t] me, "falsely for Christ sake" "For so persecuted they the Prophets that were before me"[32]

In conclusion on this subject I would say to husbands and wives, [to] "be spiritual minded is life eternal"[33] Husbands respect and love your wives, wives love your husbands, a[d]hereing to the Good advice given by the Apostle Peter 1 Epis. iii. Let this be done and all will be well: we shall have peace at home, peace abroad—peace In the church—peace among our neighbors—peace in our families—peace in our councils, and firesides. And we shall have Spiritual Fathers, Spiritual Mothers, Spiritual Brothers, Spiritual Sisters, Spiritual husbands, and Spiritual wives. And thus I shall end by inserting a form for sealing under the Priesthood for time and eternity, for the gratification of the reader.

The man standing on the right of the lady; with their right hands Joined. The one holding the Priesthood and authority of officiating, and sealing in the ordinance standing before them, Says, "You and both you (calling them by name) mutually agree to be each others companion, husband and wife; for time and all eternity, covenanting to observe all legal duties, and obligations, enjoined upon you in this marriage contract, according to the law of God. To stand by each other, nourish & cherish, each other in sickness and in health, in prosperity, and in adversity, To forsake all others, and cleave unto each other, according to the Power of this covenant Bond, (including all*[34] lawful exceptions) This you covenant to do? (And when the parties shall answer in the affirmative) Then the man of God shall say: "I seal you up unto Eternal life *against all sins*, except the sin against the Holy Ghost, *which is the shedding of innocent blood*,[35] *which sin I do not* say shall be forgiven in this world or in the world to come) To come forth in the resurrection of the Just, conferring upon you the resurrection power; That no power shall separate you, from each others society in eternity, exalted at God's right hand To thrones, kingdoms, Powers and dominion, with the *blessings* of Abraham, Isaac and Jacob—and all the Holy Apostles, and prophets. And in consideration of the above covenant, and by the authority of the *Holy Priesthood*, I confer upon you all the *blessings* in common with this holy order, in time, and also eternity. And in the name of Jesus Christ and by the authority of this holy order Priesthood annointing in the Laws of God, I pronounce you husband and wife. Even so Amen.

*If either dies reserving the privilege of marrying again here in time &c. It is proper here to state, that no one has authority to act in this holy order, except he holds the Melchezedeck Priesthood, and has received his annointing and endowment to act in this high, holy and sacred calling. {Here insert the marriage vow Times and Seasons, May 1, 1844}[36]

We now come to the subject under the third Head, viz. PLURALITY WIFE DOCTRINE as practised by the Ancient Prophets and Patriarchs'

As a great deal has been said in this our day, about pure religion, virtue and holiness, and obedience to the commands of God, Let us enquire what it is? I believe virtue and pure undefiled religion, consists in obeying every commandment of God and hearkening to his holy laws with the strictest obedience rather than to the precepts, or proscriptive views of men. When men and women do this, they are a virtuous and holy people and if all people would only hearken to the law and commandments of God, there would be no need of any [of] the Laws of men, and such it will be when Christ comes, See L [--] xiv. 11.³⁷ We are commanded to place God, always first in our thoughts, to adore and admire him, above all and his law as supreme, and not man, Hence to obey God and not man in whatever he shall command, is our impearative [sic] duty, and the work of righteousness virtue and true holiness will be the result, without which no man can see the Lord.

Hence the consideration of which we are bound first to God and his law, Secondly to obey all his commandments, thirdly, man to be subject to them, and thereby becoming prepared for the Kingdom of immortal Glory, and ["]Joint heirs with Jesus Christ"³⁸ which constitutes, all the principles of pure religion. As we are about to introduce the reader to a singular subject and we hope that he will lay aside all prejudice., and impar[t]ially investigate the same and consider the words of God p[a]ramount to men's and of all earthly consideration.

But in regard to the righteousness or correctness of the Doctrine practised by the ancient Prophets &c. I shall leave the impartial reader to judge for himself (I shall not) but leave you and the Bible to contest it. But as I before observed, I give my own individual opinion, (and not for an example for the Church of Christ in this our day) That there must have been a law or *Justification* [*C. Rev. par, 1.*]³⁹ appears evident, Do not understand me, to say what God will do, or what he will not do, He does as he pleases, and works after the council of his own will. Upon this subject I will give a few quotations from the scriptures, concerning the usages and practices of some of the Ancients Prophets and Patriarchs.

Having given my opinion on this subject to many already, and misrepresentations grown out of it, which is the only apology I offer for the appearance of this article. And that the grounds on which my opinion is founded might be made manifest.

First. Abraham who was the Father of many nations and a righteous man, yet we find him believing in, and practicing this doctrine, and [it] does it appear to me (as before observed) *there must have been a law of Justification* under which those ancient Prophets and Patriarchs acted, if not so they were all transgressors, and the whole tribes of Israel, were brought forth in adultery, Jesus himself (according to the flesh) sprang from the seed of David, the house of Judah, yet Jesus was of the lawful seed.

We find it recorded in Gen. xvi Chap. that Abraham had two wives, viz Sarah and Hagar. It appears that Sarah had no children, and desired Abraham to take Hagar to wife, so she (Sarah) might obtain ----- [children?] by her, so Abraham took Hagar, Sarah's handmaid to wife. and from her was born Ishmael, – again we find that Abraham had also his concubines. See Gen. xxv, 6. "But unto the sons of the concubines which Abraham had, Abraham gave gifts and sent them away from Isaac his son" &c. Yet we find that Abraham was beloved of the Lord, and received the *promise* that in him, and his seed should all the families of the Earth be blessed. And that the Lord would ["]bless them, that b[l]essed him (Abraham) and curse them that cursed him." See G[e]n. 1 to xii, 1 to 3. Also we find that when Abraham returned from the s[l]aughter of the Kings, Melchisedeck, Priest of the Most High God met him, blessed him, and administered bread and wine unto him. Gen. xiv. 18, 20. Again Kings should come from him, and the whole land of Canaan, given to him by the Lord, for an [']everlasting possession,' Gen. xvii 1 to 10, also v. 22 where it is recorded that "God left off talking with him and went up from Abraham"

Secondly, Jacob, [etc. etc.]⁴⁰

"Surely there must [have] been a law of Justification, or a special commandment, or else they must have been illegitimate children."

Thirdly, cites Gideon.
Fourthly, cites David.
Christ sprang from Judah, etc.
Fifthly, cites Solomon.⁴¹

"What bad men these must have been, if all is true that men say in these days about Prophets. For my part I cannot see why it is that there should be such a great difference among Prophets, all are called by the same God and inspired by the same spirit, and governed by the same law. For no one will doubt I presume, but that the gospel was preached to Adam, Noah, Abraham, Moses &c.

Hence the strange singularity of the above doctrine Is such I shall not attempt to explain but leave it for more skillful hands. perhaps some of those officious, knowing ones, that talk so much about Spiritual Wives &c can give us, some light on the subject as they are great on these tactics. To solve these to me inexplicable problems, requires more genius than I profess to be master of. But so far from proving myself an Egotist, a Bigot or Infidel to say these were wicked Prophets, and abominable characters; would be to dispise the scriptures and charge God foolishly, for he says he "gave unto David his master's wives unto his own bosom—2 Sam xii, 8 and for me to find fault and rail against the word of the God of Heaven would be folly in the extreme, trampling under my feet holy things, and doing dispite to the spirit of his grace. I would say to those who do, in the words of the inspired writer "Come not thou into my sanctuary." No doubt David sinned in the case of Uriah the Hittite, and in taking to him wives of the nations (perhaps) that God had commanded, the children of Israel, they should not mingle with, as in the case of Solomon – See 1 Kings xi. 1 to 3. In the *Book of Jacob IN THE BOOK OF MORMON* it is written, that "David and Solomon truly had many wives and concubines, which thing was abominable before the Lord." "Wherefore my brethren, (says Jacob) hear me and hearken to the word of the Lord: for there shall not any man among you have save it be one wife; and concubines, he shall have none: For I, the Lord God delighteth in the chastity of women. And whoredoms are an abomination before me; thus saith the Lord of Hosts" &c "FOR IF I WILL, *saith the Lord of Hosts raise up seed unto me*. I WILL COMMAND MY PEOPLE; *otherwise, they shall hearken unto these things*.'"⁴²

Thus we see the grounds in my estimation in which the ancient Prophets were Justified, that is, when God wanted "to raise up seed unto himself, he would command his people" otherwise it was an abomination in his sight. But says one, that is recorded in the Book of Mormon What of it, God knows. Angels, and men knows that the Book of Mormon, is true, and it is of more value to the Saints, being translated by the gift and power of God than the garbled translation of the uninspired linguistics of King James. Although we hold the Bible as sacred, and perhaps more so, than any other denomination.

When I commenced this subject I informed my reader that I was not going to lay down a precedent, for any one; and in this I do not wish to be misunderstood. I have only observed that in my opinion there must have been a law of Justification, under the dispensation of the ancient prophets, and I have given the reason and grounds upon which I base that opinion. And as such I freely and fairly give it to all people, "sink or swim"—live or die—and if I am wrong, it is subject to be contradicted, by those who may please to differ with my opinion. If they can do it on Bible or scripture grounds, I have no objection. I am not to blame, for what is written in the Bible, I did not make it, or translate it. And further we are commanded "to search the scriptures, for in them ye think that ye have eternal life," and they are they "which testify for me."[43] And furthermore, "whatsoever was written aforetime, was written for our pro[f]it and learning."[44]

"The man of God may be perfect thoroughly furnished by every good work,"[45] God has not spoken, falsely, but truth eternal truth is his law, and commandments, And he is still the God of Abraham, of Isaac—and of Jacob, The God of all the Holy Prophets, and Apostles— And Christ said he ["]did not come to do away with the Law and the Prophets but to fulfill them."[46] so let it be – Amen.

As we have now got through with the foregoing peculiar subjects, I shall here insert for the benefit of all a brief synopsis of the Faith (etc.)[47]

---

1. William Smith's "Elders' Pocket Companion" apparently has not survived, nor has his personal journal. When William and Isaac Sheen parted ways in the spring of 1850, Sheen, in Covington, Kentucky, kept a number of William's documents in William's "leather trunk." While William's journal was eventually returned to him when he united with the RLDS Church in 1878, Isaac's son John retained William's "Elders' Pocket Companion." (See Chapter 16.) John K. Sheen included much of what was contained in the "Elders' Pocket Companion" in his publication *Polygamy; or, The Veil Lifted* (York, Neb.: n.p., 1889), which Sheen said originally contained "35 pages of fools-cap paper (2d page blank)" (p. 15). I wish to acknowledge Connell O' Donovan and Erin Jennings Metcalfe for their previous transcription of William's "Elders' Pocket Companion," available at http://www.connellodonovan.com/pocket_companion.pdf, accessed April 5, 2015. I have used an original copy of John K. Sheen's *Polygamy; or, The Veil Lifted*.

2. Jedediah M. Grant, 1816–58. Grant served with William when William presided over the eastern branches of the Church during 1843–45. William was married to Grant's sister, Caroline Amanda Grant, at the time.

3. This bracketed note was in the original, and read as follows: "NOTE.—The *Prophet* of Dec. 28, *1844* says: 'We have just received a small pamphlet from Elder Grant of Philadelphia, and for sale at this office at 15 cents per copy, bearing the title 'Grant's Rigdon.'"

4. Jedediah M. Grant, *A Collection of Facts, Relative to the Course Taken by Elder Sidney Rigdon, in the States of Ohio, Missouri, Illinois and Pennsylvania* (Philadelphia: Brown, Bicking & Guilbert, 1844). Peter Crawley observed, of Grant's pamphlet, that he "obviously composed *A Collection of Facts* in response to the disaffections in the Philadelphia branch. The *Prophet* of December 28, 1844, noted that it had just received copies and had them for sale at the office for 15 cents each. The following week it reported that Rigdon had brought suit against Grant over the tract." Peter Crawley, *A Descriptive Bibliography of the Mormon Church, Volume One* (Provo, Utah: BYU Religious Studies Center, 1997), 284; "We have just received a small publication from Elder Grant . . . ," *Prophet* 1, no. 32 (December 28, 1844): 2.

5. William is quoting Matthew 13:11–13.

6. According to Sheen, all underlining was in Smith's original handwriting.

7. See 1 Corinthians 13:7.

8. See Matthew 10:28.

9. Probably the original was illegible, and Sheen replaced such words and passages with dashes.

10. William left for his eastern mission around May 10, 1843. Besides a brief return trip to Nauvoo for one month in April-May 1844, he resided in the East for nearly two

Appendix B: "The Elders' Pocket Companion" By William Smith

years. (See Chapter 9.) Journal History, May 10, 1843, 1; Joseph Smith, Journal, April 19, 1843, in Hedges, Smith, and Anderson, *Journals, Volume 2,* 363–69.

11. See Proverbs 26:5.

12. This is Parley P. Pratt, *The Millennium, and other Poems: To Which Is Annexed, A Treatise on the Regeneration and Eternal Duration of Matter* (New York: W. Molineaux, 1840), 57.

13. See Acts 4:25.

14. He is actually referring to Revelations 7:14.

15. See Daniel 2:44.

16. Sheen eliminated William Smith's outline on baptisms for the dead, likely because he was most interested in William's teachings regarding plural marriage

17. John K. Sheen wrote this note in the original pamphlet.

18. Bracket inserted by Sheen. "C. Rev." refers to Celestial Revelation—referring to LDS Doctrine and Covenants 132 (2013 ed.). Sheen is specifically referring to Doctrine and Covenants 132:7.

19. See 2 Corinthians 6:14.

20. Brackets inserted by Sheen. He refers to Doctrine and Covenants 132:7.

21. Ibid.

22. See Matthew 22:28.

23. Brackets inserted by Sheen. See Doctrine and Covenants 132:15–16.

24. Brackets and quotation inserted by Sheen. See Doctrine and Covenants 132:28.

25. See 1 Corinthians 11:3, 11.

26. Sheen wrote on page 18 of his publication: "Note.—The reader will remember that 'The Elders' Pocket Companion,' by W. Smith, one of the Twelve, contains internal evidence of having been written in *1844.* And [on] April 6, 1845, Brigham Young quoted these two texts more fully (See Times & Seasons July 1, 1845) and exclaimed: 'Now brethren, these are Paul's sayings, not Joseph Smith's spiritual wife system sayings.' Joseph the younger [Joseph Smith III] has sought to make capital against Brigham on account of this speech and has placed an unfair construction upon it; for it is plain that what was meant was: You say Joseph Smith taught a spiritual wife doctrine, now I tell you Paul teaches this in the texts quoted, now this is Paul's doctrine. The he adds: This is Joseph Smith's doctrine of spiritual wives; or Paul and Joseph teach the same doctrine. At any rate this speech of Brigham's was made in *1845,* some months after William Smith's 'Elders' Pocket Companion' was written and he is answering charges made against him dating back to the winter of 1843–1844. See pages 7 and 8 of this pamphlet." See also, "SPEECH Delivered by President B. Young, in the City of Joseph, April 6th, 1845," *Times and Seasons* 6, no. 12 (July 1, 1845): 953–57.

27. See Doctrine and Covenants 132:15–16.

28. This hymn, "The Grace of Christian Love," was written by Joseph Swain. William misquotes it slightly, substituting "minds" for Swain's "souls," and "swell" for Swain's "glow." J[oseph] Swain, *Walworth Hymns* (London: J. Mathews, 1792), 32; Samuel Willoughby Duffield, *English Hymns: Their Authors and History* (New York and London: Funk & Wagnalls, 1888), 234–35.

29. See Doctrine and Covenants 132:19.

30. See Matthew 25:21.

31. Bracketed insertion by Sheen. Sheen appears to be quoting a statement Hyrum Smith made in response to an inquiry by Brother Richard Hewitt, after hearing someone teach in his community, China Creek, Hancock County, that after one obtained "a certain priesthood" he could "have as many wives as he pleases, and that [that] doctrine is taught

here [in Nauvoo]." Hyrum responded that the "mysteries of God are not given to all men; and unto those to whom they are given they are placed under restrictions to impart only such as God will command them; and the residue is to be kept in a faithful breast, otherwise he will be brought under condemnation." Hyrum Smith (Nauvoo, Ill.), Letter to the brethren of the Church of Jesus Christ of Latter day Saints, living on China Creek, in Hancock County, March 15, 1844, in *Times and Seasons* 5, no. 6 (March 15, 1844): 474.

32. See Matthew 5:11–12.

33. See 2 Nephi 9:39 and Romans 8:6.

34. Sheen inserted these words in an asterisked note: [* "and shall inherit thrones, kingdoms, principalities, and powers." Etc. –*C. Rev. Par. 6.* J. K. S.]. See Doctrine and Covenants 132:19.

35. Sheen inserted the following: "[See Celestial Revelation; paragraph 6; also as follows: "The blasphemy against the Holy Ghost, which shall not be forgiven in the world, nor out of the world, is in that ye commit murder, wherein ye shed innocent blood, and assent unto my death, after ye have received my new and everlasting covenant saith the Lord God; and he that abideth not this law, can in *nowise* enter into my glory, but shall be *damned*, saith the Lord."—*C. Rev. par. 10* J. K. S.]." See Doctrine and Covenants 132:27.

36. Brackets and notation by Sheen. William Smith's "Elder's Pocket Companion" contained the complete marriage vow. See "The Marriage Vow," *Times and Seasons* 5, no. 9 (May 1, 1844): 527.

37. Sheen apparently found this section illegible. Perhaps William was alluding to Acts 5:29, or Romans 13:1.

38. See Romans 8:17.

39. Bracketed insertion by Sheen. See Doctrine and Covenants 132:1.

40. Brackets inserted by Sheen. Sheen then noted, "It is hardly necessary to print any more of the ----- contained in the third treaties [treatise] of William Smith's, suffice it to say the whole of the treaties [sic] is an argument for A Law of Justification, and in order to save time and space I will simply give a synopsis of the balance and extract the important parts."

41. The previous four lines may be Sheen's insertion, summarizing that William had cited examples from the lives of Gideon, David, and Solomon in defense of plural marriage.

42. Sheen inserted the following footnote: "'MENE, MENE, TEKEL, UPHARSIN!' Shades of 'Nephi-Moroni!' Great Julius Caesar, and shades of the martyred Prophet and Patriarch!—the Royal Blood of Ephraim accuseth the golden tablets, even the Book of Mormon. The English of the Book of Mormon is not strong enough, but William Smith, brother, of the Prophet Joseph Smith, must underscore the above words. William Smith, one of the Twelve, you may understand 'things unlawful to utter,' as did Paul; you may, like Paul, 'speak in parables,' but you have said to me in language that cannot be mistaken that the Book of Mormon provided for the introduction of the doctrine you have been teaching in your 'Elder's [sic] Pocket Companion' written in 1844; you have said further to me – you have said IT HAS BEEN COMMANDED. Many may be deceived by the sophistry of Joseph the younger [Joseph Smith III], but the one man who is picking your words into type will go before the throne of God fully assured that you then had a knowledge of the Celestial Revelation that was not given to the world until August 29, 1852. The world may not heed my words, but when standing before the throne of God in Eternal judgment, William Smith and William Marks shall be my witnesses, and if both of you have lied to me here in time, God help you both then and there in Eternity."

43. See John 5:39.

44. See Romans 15:4.
45. See 2 Timothy 3:17.
46. See Matthew 5:17.
47. Sheen adds these footnotes: "Reader, two treaties [treatises] from the The Elders' Pocket Companion are now before you. In the treaties [sic] named 'Faith,'—etc., he gives the quotation from Section 101, Book of Covenants. Under the head 'Biography' he makes the following historical statement of an affair that occurred before I was born and of which I know of no printed record, while it is possible that there may be. Here is the statement: 'The following *Hymn was sung by Elders, Wm. and D. C. Smith by the request of their aged Father, while on his dying bed, a few hours before his death,' * * * 'Where no chilling winds or poisonous breath Disturb that peaceful shore, Sickness and sorrow, pain and death Be felt or feared no more.'" The brothers sang "Promised Land," written by Baptist minister Samuel Stennett, and made popular during the camp meetings the Smiths often attended during William's youth.

Bibliography

Comprehensive Anthologies and Institutions
Abbreviated in Citations

Community of Christ Library-Archives, Independence, Missouri.
Journal History of the Church of Jesus Christ of Latter-day Saints (chronological scrapbook of typed entries and newspaper clippings, 1830–present), LDS Church History Library.
Journal of Discourses, 26 vols. London and Liverpool: LDS Booksellers Depot, 1853–86.
Perry Special Collections. L. Tom Perry Special Collections, Harold B. Lee Library, Brigham Young University, Provo, Utah.
LDS Church History Library, of the LDS Historical Department, Salt Lake City, Utah.
Selected Collections. Richard E. Turley, ed., *Selected Collections from the Archives of the Church of Jesus Christ of Latter-day Saints*, 2 vols. DVD Provo, Utah: Brigham Young University Press, [December 2002], DVD 18.
Strang Collection. James J. Strang Collection, Beinecke Library, Yale University Press, New Haven, Conn.
U.S. Census. Search under U.S. Census, then by decennial year, and arranged alphabetically thereunder by state, county, and town.

Main Entries

Adams, George J. (Springfield, Ill.). Letter to Peter Hess, July 7, 1843. MS 730. LDS Church History Library.
Adams, George J. (Cincinnati, Ohio). Letter to James J. Strang, March 27, 1846, Strang Collection.
Adams, George J. (Burlington, Iowa Territory). Letter to A. R. Tewkesberry, June 14, 1845. MS 697, LDS Church History Library.
Allen, James B. "Emergence of a Fundamental: The Expanding Role of Joseph Smith's First Vision in Mormon Religious Thought." *Journal of Mormon History* 7 (1980): 43–61.
Allen, James B. *No Toil Nor Labor Fear: The Story of William Clayton*. Provo, Utah: BYU Press, 2002.
Allen, James B., Ronald K. Esplin, and David J. Whittaker. *Men with a Mission: The Quorum of the Twelve Apostles in the British Isles*. Salt Lake City: Deseret Book, 1992.
Allen, James B., and Glen M. Leonard. *The Story of the Latter-day Saints*. Salt Lake City: Deseret Book, 1976.
Amann, Peter. "Prophet in Zion: The Saga of George J. Adams." *New England Quarterly* 37, no. 4 (December 1964): 477–500.
American Civil War Research Database. Enlistment Age Distribution, All Years Union Army. www.civilwardata.com/ca_demo2.html (accessed November 19, 2013).
"Among the Saints." *Nauvoo Neighbor* 3, no. 1 (May 7, 1845): 2.
Anderson, Jotham. *The Recollections of Jotham Anderson, Minister of the Gospel*. Boston: John B. Russell, 1824.
Anderson, Lavina Fielding, ed., *Lucy's Book: A Critical Edition of Lucy Mack Smith's Family Memoir*. Salt Lake City: Signature Books, 2001.

Anderson, Mary Audentia Smith, ed. *Joseph Smith III and the Restoration*. Independence, Mo.: Herald House, 1952.

Anderson, Richard L. *Joseph Smith's New England Heritage: Influences of Grandfather Solomon Mack and Asael Smith*. First ed., Salt Lake City: Deseret Book, 1971.

Anderson, Richard L. *Joseph Smith's New England Heritage, Rev. ed*. Provo, Utah: Deseret Book and BYU Press, 2003.

Anderson, Richard L. "Alvin Smith." In Kyle R. Walker, ed., *United by Faith: The Joseph Sr. and Lucy Mack Smith Family*. American Fork, Utah: BYU Studies and Covenant Communications, 2006, 83–123.

Andreas, A. T. *Illustrated and Historical Atlas of the State of Iowa*. Chicago: Lake Side Press, 1875.

"Annual Conference, The." *Melchisedek & Aaronic Herald* 1, no. 8 (February 1850): 4.

Appleby, William I. Autobiography and Journal, 1847–56, MS 1401, fd. 1, LDS Church History Library.

Applegate, Lloyd R. *A Life of Service: William Augustus Newell*. Tom's River, N.J.: Ocean County Historical Society, 1994.

"Arrest." *Prophet* 1, no. 31 (December 21, 1844): 2.

Arrington, Leonard J. *From Quaker to Latter-day Saint: Bishop Edwin D. Woolley*. Salt Lake City: Deseret Book, 1976.

Atkinson, Grant Davies. "A Sketch of the Life of George Davis Grant." N.p., 1998.

"Aunt Katharine Salisbury's Testimony." *Saints' Herald* 40, no. 18 (May 6, 1893): 275.

Avery, Kevin J. "Movies for Manifest Destiny: The Moving Panorama in Phenomenon in America." Online article, http://www.tfaoi.com/aa/3aa/3aa66.htm, published 1999 (accessed February 20, 2015).

Babbitt, Almon W. (Nauvoo, Ill.). Letter to Brigham Young, January 31, 1848, Brigham Young Office Files 1832–1878, General Correspondence, Incoming, 1840–1877, A–C, 1848, LDS Church History Library.

Backman, Milton V., Jr., ed. *Regional Studies in Latter-day Saint Church History: Ohio*. Provo, Utah: Brigham Young University Department of Church History and Doctrine, 1990.

Backman, Milton, V., Jr., and James B. Allen. "Membership of Certain of Joseph Smith's Family in the Western Presbyterian Church of Palmyra." *BYU Studies* 10, no. 4 (Summer 1970): 482–84.

Bagley, Will. *A Scoundrel's Tale: The Samuel Brannan Papers*. Logan: Utah State University Press, 1999.

Baker, Nathaniel B. "Sixtieth United States Infantry: History of the Regiment." In *Report of the Brig.-Gen. Nathaniel B. Baker, Adjutant General and Act'g Q. M. G. and Act'g as P. M. G., to Hon. William M. Stone, Governor of the State of Iowa*. Des Moines, Iowa: F. W. Palmer, 1867.

Ball, Joseph T., Patriarchal Blessing, July 15, 1845. In H. Michael Marquardt, ed. *Early Patriarchal Blessings of the Church of Jesus Christ of Latter-day Saints*. Salt Lake City: Smith-Pettit Foundation, 2007, 320.

Balliet, Stephen Clay. *The Balliet, Balliett, Balliette, Balyeat, Bolyard, and Allied Families*. Lehigh County, Penn.: Thos. J. Moran's Sons, 1968.

"Baptism Heals: Nephew of Prophet Joseph Smith Relates Experience." *Deseret News*, January 9, 1932, 6.

Bates, Irene M. "Foreword: Lucy Mack Smith—First Mormon Mother." In Lavina Fielding Anderson, *Lucy's Book: A Critical Edition of Lucy Mack Smith's Family Memoir*. Salt Lake City: Signature Books, 2001.

Bates, Irene M. "Uncle John Smith, 1781–1854: Patriarchal Bridge." *Dialogue: A Journal of Mormon Thought* 20 (Fall 1987): 79–89.

Bates, Irene M. "William Smith, 1811–93: Problematic Patriarch." *Dialogue: A Journal of Mormon Thought* 16, no. 2 (Summer 1983): 11–23.

Bates, Irene M., and E. Gary Smith. *Lost Legacy: The Mormon Office of Presiding Patriarch.* Urbana: University of Illinois Press, 1996.
Baugh, Alexander L. "Joseph Smith's Athletic Nature." In *Joseph Smith: The Prophet, The Man,* edited by Susan Eaton Black and Charles D. Tate Jr. Provo, Utah: BYU Religious Studies Center, 1993, 137–50.
Baugh, Alexander L., and Richard Neitzel Holzapfel. "'I Roll the Burthen and Responsibility of Leading This Church Off from My Shoulders on to Yours': The 1844/1845 Declaration of the Quorum of the Twelve Regarding Apostolic Succession." *BYU Studies* 49, no. 3 (2000): 5–19.
Bean, Cheryl Harmon. "LDS Baptisms in Erie County, Pennsylvania 1831–1833." *Nauvoo Journal* 5, no. 2 (Fall 1993): 59–102.
Becker, Anthony J. *The Biography of a Country Town: USA.* Amboy, Ill.: Spencer-Walker Press, 1954.
Becker, Anthony J., and Lillian A. Rapp. *Sublette, Illinois: Our Bit of U.S.A: Sublette Centennial.* Mendota, Ill.: Sublette Centennial Committee, 1954.
Beecher, Maureen Ursenbach, ed. "'All Things Move in Order in the City': The Nauvoo Diary of Zina Diantha Huntington Jacobs." *BYU Studies* 19, no. 3 (Spring 1979): 285–320.
Bennet, James Arlington (Long Island, N.Y.). Letter to Joseph Smith, August 16, 1842. In Hedges, Smith, and Anderson, *Journals, Volume 2,* 135–37.
Bennett, John C. Letters to James J. Strang, March 24, March 28, and April 2, 1846. James J. Strang Collection, Beinecke Library, Yale University, New Haven, Conn.
Bennett, John C. *The History of the Saints; or, an Exposé of Joe Smith and Mormonism.* Boston: Leland & Whiting, 1842.
Bennett, John C. "For the Wasp." *The Wasp* 1 (May 28, 1842): 3.
Bennett, John C. "Ho! For Voree." *Voree Herald* 1, no. 3 (March 1846): 2.
Bennett, Richard E. "'Read This I Pray Thee': Martin Harris and the Three Wise Men of the East." *Journal of Mormon History* 36, no. 1 (Winter 2010): 178–216.
"Bennett." *Wasp* 1, no. 16 (July 30, 1842): 2.
"Bennettiana." *Wasp* 1, no. 15 (July 23, 1842): 2.
Berge, Dale L. "The Jonathan Browning Site: An Example of Archaeology for Restoration in Nauvoo, Illinois." *BYU Studies* 19 (Winter 1979): 201–29.
Bergera, Gary James, ed., *The Autobiography of B. H. Roberts.* Salt Lake City: Signature Books, 1990.
Bernhisel, John M., May 15, 1850. Letter to the Editors of the *Union.* Frontier Guardian 2, no. 11 (June 26, 1850): 3.
Bernhisel, John M. (Washington, D.C.). Letter to Brigham Young, March 21 1850, all in Brigham Young Office Files 1832–1878, Utah Delegate Files, 1849–1872, John M. Bernhisel to Brigham Young, 1849–1866, 1849–1850 March–May, LDS Church History Library.
Bernhisel, John M. (Washington D.C.). Letter to Brigham Young, March 21 1850, Brigham Young office files 1832–1878, Utah Delegate Files, 1849–1872, John M. Bernhisel to Brigham Young, 1849–1866, 1849–1850 March–May, LDS Church History Library.
Bernhisel, John M. May 15, 1850. Letter to the Editors of the *Union.* In *Frontier Guardian* 2, no. 11 (June 26, 1850): 3.
Berrett, LaMar C., and Larry C. Porter, *New York and Pennsylvania, Vol. 2,* in SACRED PLACES: A COMPREHENSIVE GUIDE TO EARLY LDS HISTORICAL SITES. General series editor LaMar C. Berrett. Salt Lake City: Deseret Book, 2000.
"Beware of Strong Delusion, Lest Ye Believe a Lie and Be Damned." *Times and Seasons* 6, no. 18 (December 1, 1845): 1045.
"Bill Smith." *Daily Commercial Register* (Sandusky, Ohio) 4, no. 304 (May 23, 1855): 2.
"Bill Smith, the Mormon Prophet." *Dixon Telegraph* 3, no. 52 (May 4, 1854): 2.
"Biographical Sketch of John Lyman Smith." *Millennial Star* 56, no. 34 (August 20, 1894): 542.
Black, Susan Easton, comp. *Early Members of the Reorganized Church of Jesus Christ of Latter-day Saints.* 5 vols. Provo, Utah: BYU Religious Studies Center, 1993.

Black, Susan Easton, Harvey B. Black, and Brandon Plewe. *Property Transactions in Nauvoo, Hancock County, Illinois, and Surrounding Communities (1839–1859).* 7 vols. Wilmington, Del.: World Vital Records, 2006), 2878,3785.

Blair, Alma R. "The Reorganized Church of Jesus Christ of Latter Day Saints: Moderate Mormons." In *The Restoration Movement: Essays in Mormon History.* Edited by F. Mark McKiernan, Alma R. Blair, and Paul M. Edwards. Independence: Herald Publishing House, 1992.

Blair, Frederick B., comp. *The Memoirs of President W. W. Blair.* Lamoni, Iowa: Herald Publishing House, 1908.

Blair, W. W. (East Paw Paw, Ill.). Letter to Edwin Cadwell, Aaron Hook, and Jotham Barrett, March 7, 1856. P13, fd. 111, Community of Christ Library-Archives.

Blair, W. W. Letter to Joseph Smith III, December 9, 1878. Quoted in Reed M. Holmes, *Dreamers of Zion,* 156.

Bloch, Ruth R. "American Feminine Ideals in Transition: The Rise of the Moral Mother, 1785–1815." *Feminist Studies* 4, no. 2 (June 1978): 100–126.

Blythe, Christine Elyse. "William Smith's Patriarchal Blessings and Contested Authority in the Post-Martyrdom Church." *Journal of Mormon History* 39, no. 3 (Summer 2013): 60–95.

Boatner, Mark M., III. "Pay." In *The Civil War Dictionary,* rev. ed. New York: Vintage Books, 1988.

Bonds and Mortgages, Book 1 and Book K. Hancock County Courthouse, Carthage, Illinois.

Braden, Clark, and E. L. Kelley, February 27, 1884. *Public Discussion of the Issues between the Reorganized Church of Jesus Christ of Latter Day Saints and the Church of Christ (Disciples) Held in Kirtland, Ohio, Beginning Feburary 12, and Closing March 8, 1884 Between E. L. Kelley, of the Reorganized Church of Jesus Christ of Latter Day Saints and Clark Braden, of the Church of Christ.* St. Louis: Clark Braden, 1884.

Brannan, Samuel. "Beware of Strong Delusion, Lest Ye Believe a Lie and Be Damned." *New-York Messenger* 2, no. 20 (November 15, 1845): 157. Also in *Times and Seasons* 6, no. 18 (December 1, 1845): 6–7.

Brannan, Samuel (New York). Letters to Brigham Young, July 22, August 29 and October 9, 1845. Brigham Young Office Files 1832–1878, General Correspondence, Incoming, 1840–1877, General Letters, 1840–1877, Be–Br, 1845, LDS Church History Library.

Brannan, Samuel. Letter to Brethren and Friends. *Prophet* 1, no. 51 (May 10, 1845): 1–2.

Brannan, Samuel (New York), Letter to Brigham Young and Heber C. Kimball, July 22, 1845. Brigham Young Office Files 1832–1878. General Letters, 1840–1877, Be–Br, 1845. LDS Church History Library.

Brannan, Samuel. "Beware of Strong Delusion, Lest Ye Believe a Lie and Be Damned." *New-York Messenger* 2, no. 20 (November 15, 1845): 5. Rpt. under the same title in *Times and Seasons* 6, no. 18 (December 1, 1845): 6–7.

Bratton, Geo[rge] W. (Ottawa, Ill.). Letter to Brigham Young, February 26, 1848, Brigham Young Office Files 1832–1878, General Correspondence, Incoming, 1840–1877, A-C, 1848, LDS Church History Library.

Bratton, Geo[rge] W. (Ottawa, Ill.). Letter to Brigham Young, February 26, 1848, Brigham Young office files 1832–1878, General Correspondence, Incoming, 1840–1877, General Letters, 1840–1877, A-C, 1848, LDS Church History Library.

Brigham Young Office Journal. CR 1234 1, Box 72, fd. 5. LDS Church History Library.

Briggs, E. C. Testimony. In *Abstract of Pleading and Evidence in the Circuit Court of the United States, Western Division at Kansas City—The Reorganized Church of Jesus Christ of Latter day Saints vs. The Church of Christ at Independence.* Lamoni, Iowa: Herald Publishing House and Bindery, 1893, 207. Also *Temple Lot Case.* Lamoni, Iowa: Herald Publishing House and Bindery, 1893, 207. Originally published serially in the *Saints' Herald.*

Briggs, Edmund C. *Early History of the Reorganization: Autobiographical Sketches and Incidents in the Life of the Author.* Independence: Price Publishing Company, 1998.

Briggs, Jason W. "History of the Reorganization of the Church of Jesus Christ of Latter Day Saints, Chapter 1." *The Messenger* (Salt Lake City) 2, no. 1 (November 1875): 1. Chapter II," *Messenger* 2, no. 2 (December 1875): 1–2. Chap[ter]. IV," *Messenger* 2, no. 4 (February 1876): 3.

Briggs, Jason W. (Beloit, Wisc.). Letter to Joseph Smith III, November 20, 1853, MS 4632, LDS Church History Library.

Brooks, Juanita, ed. *On the Mormon Frontier: The Diary of Hosea Stout*, 2 vols. Salt Lake City: University of Utah Press, 1964.

Brough, Chaundelle Hill, comp. "History of George Washington Bratton." July 2004, https://familysearch.org/photos/stories/1703275/history-of-george-washington-bratton (accessed December 30, 2013).

Brown, James (Augusta, Iowa Territory). Letters to Brigham Young, June 13, 1845, and September 24, 1845, both in Brigham Young Office Files 1832–78, General Correspondence, Incoming, 1840–1877, Be–Br, 1845, LDS Church History Library.

Brown, Paul W. "Timber Destruction: The Problem and the Way Out." *America at Work* (St. Louis, Mo.) 6, no. 2 (June 20, 1922): 11.

Bruce N. Westergreen, ed., *From Historian to Dissident: The Book of John Whitmer*. Salt Lake City: Signature Books, 1995.

Bryant, Kevin. "'Attracting No Little Attention': The RLDS Return to Kirtland, 1883 General Conference." *John Whitmer Historical Association Journal* 29 (2009): 59–71.

Bump, Jacob, Leonard Rich, Amos Babcock, and S. B. Stoddard. Letter, October 16, [1846], Community of Christ Library-Archives.

Bushman, Richard L. *Joseph Smith and the Beginnings of Mormonism*. Urbana: University of Illinois Press, 1984.

Bushman, Richard Lyman. *Joseph Smith, Rough Stone Rolling: A Cultural Biography of Mormonism's Founder*. New York: Alfred A. Knopf, 2005.

Call, Anson. Journal. Photocopy of holograph in my possession.

Campbell, Eugene E. *Establishing Zion: The Mormon Church in the American West, 1847–1869*. Salt Lake City: Signature Books, 1988.

"Can't Get the Papers." *Racine Advocate* (Wisconsin Territory) 4, no. 43 (September 16, 1846): 1.

Carter, Jared. Journal, 1832–33. MS 1441, LDS Church History Library.

Census records. Search under U.S. Census, then by decentennial year, then thereunder by state, county, and town.

"Certificate, A." *Melchisedek & Aaronic Herald* (Covington, Ky.) 1, no. 6 (September 1849): 4.

Chambers, William, and Robert Chambers. *Chambers's Miscellany of Instructive & Entertaining Tracts*, 3 vols. rev. ed. London: W. and R. Chambers, 1874.

Christ, Mark. *Civil War Arkansas, 1863: The Battle for a State*. Norman: University of Oklahoma Press, 2010.

"Church Historian Receives Important Document." *Saints' Herald* 112, no. 16 (August 15, 1965): 27.

Church Historian's Office. General Church Minutes, 1839–77. CR 100 318, Box 1, fd. 33. In Turley, ed., *Selected Collections*, 1:18.

Church Historian's Office. History of the Church 1839–circa 1882, CR 100 102, 17, *Selected Collections*, DVD #2. Also in Journal History, April 13, 1846, 1.

Church Historian's Office. Journal, 1844–79. CR 100 1, Box 1, fd. 33, LDS Church History Library.

"General Conference." Reported in *Cleveland Herald*. Rpt. in *Saints' Herald* 30, no. 16 (April 21, 1883): 242–43.

Colburn, Thomas. Letter to Erastus Snow, editor, on May 2, 1855, *St. Louis Luminary* 1, no. 24 (May 5, 1855): 2.

Colburn, Thomas. Letter to Elder Snow, May 31, 1855. *St. Louis Luminary* 1, no. 28 (June 2, 1855): 3.

Collier, Fred C., ed. *The Office Journal of President Brigham Young: Book D, 1858–1863*. Hanna, Utah: Collier's Publishing, 2006.
"Coming to the Point." *New York American*, October 10, 1844, 2.
Compton, Todd. *In Sacred Loneliness: The Plural Wives of Joseph Smith*. Salt Lake City: Signature Books, 1996.
"Conference at Voree." In John Hajicek, ed., *Chronicles of Voree, (1844–1849)*. Burlington, Wisc.: J. J. Hajicek, 1922.
"Conference Minutes." *Times and Seasons* 2, no. 9 (March 1, 1841): 338.
"Conference Minutes." *Times & Seasons* 6, no. 16 (November 1, 1845): 1008, 1014, 1019.
"Conference Minutes of a Meeting Held in Amboy, Illinois, June 10, 1859, P13, fd. 111, Community of Christ Library-Archives.
"Conference of the Church of Jesus Christ of Latter Day Saints, at Voree." *Gospel Herald* 2, no. 30 (October 14, 1847): 2.
Conklin, Wm. "Clearing Land." *Ohio Cultivator* 15, no. 1 (January 1, 1859): 2–4.
Cook, Lyndon W., ed. *David Whitmer Interviews: A Restoration Witness*. Provo, Utah: Grandin Book, 1991.
Cook, Lyndon W., comp. *Nauvoo Deaths and Marriages, 1839–1845*. Provo, Utah: Grandin Book, 1994.
Cook, Lyndon W. *Nauvoo Marriages and Proxy Sealings 1843–1846*. Provo, Utah: Grandin Book, 2004.
Cook, Lyndon W. "'I Have Sinned against Heaven, and Am Unworthy of Your Confidence, But I Cannot Live without a Reconciliation': Thomas B. Marsh Returns to the Church." *BYU Studies* 20, no. 4 (Summer 1980), 389–400.
Corbett, Pearson H. *Hyrum Smith Patriarch*. Salt Lake City: Deseret Book, 1976.
"Correspondence of Friends' Weekly Intelligencer." *Friends' Weekly Intelligencer* (Philadelphia) 3, no. 29 (October 17, 1846): 226.
Cowdery, Oliver (Elkhorn, Wisc.). Letter to Brigham Young, February 27, 1848. Brigham Young Office Files 1832–1878, General Correspondence, Incoming, 1840–1877, Letters from Church Leaders and Others, 1840–1877, Oliver Cowdery, 1843–1848, LDS Church History Library.
Cowdery, Oliver. Letter to Our Beloved Brethren (Kirtland, Ohio), November 12, 1830. In Michael Hubbard MacKay, Gerrit J. Dirkmaat, Grant Underwood, Robert J. Woodford, and William G. Hartley, eds. *Documents, Volume 1: July 1828–June 1831*, THE JOSEPH SMITH PAPERS. General editors, Dean C. Jessee, Ronald K. Esplin, and Richard Lyman Bushman. Salt Lake City: Church Historian's Press, 2013, 211–14.
Cowdery, Oliver. Letter to W. W. Phelps. Letter III. *Latter Day Saints' Messenger and Advocate* 1, no. 3 (December 1834): 42.
Cowdery, Oliver, Letter to W. W. Phelps. Letter IV. *Latter Day Saints' Messenger and Advocate* 1, no. 5 (February 1835): 77–80.
Crawley, Peter. *A Descriptive Bibliography of the Mormon Church, Volume One, 1830–1847*. Provo, Utah: BYU Religious Studies Center, 1997.
Crosby, J. W. "Obituary." *Prophet* 1, no. 47 (April 12, 1845): 3.
Cross, Whitney. *The Burned-Over District: The Social and Intellectual History of Enthusiastic Religion in Western New York, 1800–1850*. Ithaca, N.Y.: Cornell University Press, 1950.
Curtis, V. Alan. "Missionary Activities and Church Organizations in Pennsylvania, 1830–1840." M.A. thesis, Brigham Young University, 1976.
Dahl, Larry E., and Donald Q. Cannon, eds. *Encyclopedia of Joseph Smith's Teachings*. Salt Lake City: Deseret Book, 1997.
Daughters of the American Revolution, New Connecticut Chapter (Painesville, Ohio). "Probate Court Marriage Records, Lake County, Ohio, 1840–1865." Typescript at the Morley Library, Painesville, Ohio.

Davidson, Karen Lynn, David J. Whittaker, Mark Ashurst-McGee, and Richard L. Jensen, eds. *Histories, Volume 1: Joseph Smith Histories, 1832–1844.* In THE JOSEPH SMITH PAPERS. General editors Dean C. Jessee, Ronald K. Esplin, and Richard Lyman Bushman. Salt Lake City: Church Historian's Press, 2012.

Davidson, Karen Lynn, Richard L. Jensen, and David J. Whittaker, eds. *Histories—Volume 2: Assigned Histories, 1831–1847,* Vol. 2 in the Histories series of the THE JOSEPH SMITH PAPERS. General editors Dean C. Jessee, Ronald K. Esplin, and Richard Lyman Bushman. Salt Lake City: Church Historian's Press, October 2012.

Day, Clarence. *The Journey to Jaffa.* N.d., n.p.

"Death." *Melchisedek & Aaronic Herald* 1, no. 8 (February 1850): 4.

Deed to Caroline Louisa and Mary Jane Smith, January 1, 1842. Hancock County Courthouse, copy of original and transcription available at http://josephsmithpapers.org/paperSummary/deed-to-caroline-louisa-and-mary-jane-smith-1-january-1842 (accessed August 19, 2014).

"Died. Enoch Perham Rollins." *Deseret News,* December 19, 1877, 11.

"Died. Smith." *Saints' Herald* 40, no. 49 (December 9, 1893): 787.

Dinger, John S., ed. *The Nauvoo City and High Council Minutes.* Salt Lake City: Signature Books, 2011.

Dinger, John S. "Joseph Smith and the Development of Habeas Corpus in Nauvoo, 1841–44." *Journal of Mormon History* 36, no. 3 (Summer 2010): 135–71.

"Dinner to the Smith Family." *New-York Messenger* 2, no. 6 (August 9, 1845): 4.

Dirkmaat, Gerrit J., Brent M. Rogers, Grant Underwood, Robert J. Woodford, and William G. Hartley, eds. *Documents—Vol. 3: February 1833–March 1834.* Vol. 3 in the Documents series of THE JOSEPH SMITH PAPERS. General editors Ronald K. Esplin and Matthew J. Grow. Salt Lake City: Church Historian's Press, 2014.

"Discourse. By President J. M. GRANT." *Deseret News* 6, no. 4 (April 2, 1856): 4.

Divine Hymns, or Spiritual Songs, for the Use of Religious Assemblies and Private Christians. Wilkesbarre, Penns.: Asher & Charles Miner, 1802.

Divorce proceedings. (1) William Smith vs. Roxey Ann [Grant] Smith, Bill of Divorcement, filed November 20, 1850, Lee County Circuit Court, Illinois, April Term; photocopy in my possession. (2) William Smith and Roxey Ann Smith, Defendant's [Roxey Ann's] answer, filed May 11, 1852, Knox County Circuit Court, April Term 1852. (3) William Smith vs. Roxey Ann Smith, Bill for Divorce, April Term 1853, Lee County Circuit Court, Chancery Book A, 11, 21, Chancery Book B, 246, Lee County Courthouse, Dixon, Illinois. (4) Final Decree, Bill of Divorce, Roxey Ann Smith vs. William Smith, April 26, 1853, Knox County Circuit Court, April Term, Knox County Courthouse, Galesburg, Illinois.

"Dr. Bennett, the Late Mormon General." *Wasp* 1, no. 21 (September 10, 1842): 2.

Edwards, Paul M. "William B. Smith: The Persistent Pretender." *Dialogue: A Journal of Mormon Thought* 18 (Summer 1985): 128–39.

Ehat, Andrew F. "Joseph Smith's Introduction of Temple Ordinances and the Mormon Succession Question." M.A. thesis, Brigham Young University, 1982.

Ehat, Andrew F. "'They Might Have Known He Was Not a Fallen Prophet'—The Nauvoo Journal of Joseph Fielding." *BYU Studies* 19, no. 2 (Winter 1979):133–66.

Ehrhardt, Al (Elkader, Iowa). Letter to LDS Church, August 8, 1973.

Eighth Circuit Court of the United States, Western Division at Kansas City—The Reorganized Church of Jesus Christ of Latter day Saints, Complainant vs. The Church of Christ at Independence, 1892. Complete transcript, microfilm and digitized. MS 1160, LDS Church History Library. Edited transcription in *The Temple Lot Case.* Lamoni, Iowa.: Herald Publishing House and Bindery, 1893.

"Elder Parley P. Pratt." *Times and Seasons* 5, no. 22 (December 1, 1844): 727.

"Elder William Smith." *Times and Seasons* 3, no. 2 (November 15, 1841): 599.

"Elder Wm. B. Smith, of the High Priests Quorum, Present, Reports." *Saints' Herald* 30, no. 17 (April 28, 1883): 269.

"Election, The." *Warsaw Signal* 3, no. 5 (August 6, 1842): 2.

Ellsworth, Sarah. Testimony before James J. Strang, April 23, 1847, John C. Gaylord accuser vs. William Smith accused. Complaint for Adultery, Document 181, Strang Collection.

Enders, Donald L. Interviewed by Kyle R. Walker, June 7, 2013, Layton, Utah.

Enders, Donald L. "The Joseph Smith, Sr. Family: Farmers of the Genesee," *Joseph Smith, the Prophet, the Man*, ed. Susan Easton Black and Charles D. Tate Jr. Provo, Utah.: BYU Religious Studies Center, 1993.

Enders, Donald L. "Treasures and a Trash Heap: An Early Reference to the Joseph Smith Family in Palmyra." *Journal of Mormon History* 40, no. 3 (Summer 2014): 201–22.

"Episodes in Genealogical Research: New Light on William Smith." *Deseret News*, July 27, 1935, 7–8.

Esplin, Ronald K. *The Emergence of Brigham Young and the Twelve to Mormon Leadership*. Provo, Utah: Joseph Fielding Smith Institute for Latter-day Saint History and BYU Studies, 2006.

Esplin, Ronald K. "Joseph, Brigham and the Twelve: A Succession of Continuity." *BYU Studies* 21, no. 3 (Summer 1981): 301–41.

Evans, Max J. "The Stephen Post Collection." *BYU Studies* 14, no. 1 (Autumn 1973): 100–103.

"Extract from Wm. Smith's Fornication Letter." *Daily Cincinnati Commercial* 12, no. 299 (May 22, 1850): 4.

"Extract of Conference Minutes, An." *Melchisedek & Aaronic Herald* 1, no. 6 (September 1849): 4.

"Extracts from Letters." *Saints' Herald* 39, no. 40 (October 1, 1892): 631.

"Extracts from the *Clayton Co. Journal*." In *True Latter Day Saints' Herald* 15, no. 1 (January 1, 1869): 23–25.

"Extracts of Letters from the Elders Abroad." *Evening and the Morning Star* 1, no. 9 (February 1833): 5–6.

Fairbanks, Edward T. *The Town of St. Johnsbury, VT: A Review of One Hundred Twenty-Five Years to the Anniversary Pageant 1912*. St. Johnsbury, Vt.: Cowles Press, 1914.

Faulring, Scott H., ed. *An American Prophet's Record: The Diaries and Journals of Joseph Smith*. Salt Lake City: Signature Books, 1987.

Felt, N[athaniel] H. (St. Louis, Mo.). Letter to Orson Hyde, June 1, 1847. Brigham Young, Office Files, 1832–1878, General Correspondence, Incoming, 1832–1877, Letters from Church Leaders and Others, 1840–1877, LDS Church History Library.

"First Presidency, The." *Zion's Reveille* 1, no. 12 (December 1846): 3.

Flanders, Robert B. "Dream and Nightmare: Nauvoo Revisited." In *The Restoration Movement: Essays in Mormon History*. Edited by F. Mark Mckiernan, Alma R. Blair, and Paul M. Edwards. Lawrence, Kans.: Coronado Press, 1972, 137–62.

Fleming, Stephen J. "Discord in the City of Brotherly Love: The Story of Early Mormonism in Philadelphia." *Mormon Historical Studies* 5, no. 1 (Spring 2004): 3–27.

Fleming, Stephen J. "'Sweeping Everything before It': Early Mormonism in the Pine Barrens of New Jersey." *BYU Studies* 40, no. 1 (2001): 72–104.

"Ford and Moore." *Wasp* 1, no. 17 (August 13, 1842): 3.

"For the *Neighbor*." *Times and Seasons* 5, no. 10 (May 15, 1844): 534.

"Foregoing Communication, The." *Dixon Telegraph* 2, no. 51 (April 30, 1853): 2.

Forscutt, Mark H. "Statement of Obituary." In Frederick B. Blair, comp. *The Memoirs of President W. W. Blair*. Lamoni, Iowa: Herald Publishing House, 1908, 202–3.

"From Nauvoo." *Warsaw Signal* 2, no. 24 (September 3, 1845): 2.

"From the *Nauvoo Neighbor*." In *Prophet* 1, no. 52 (May 24, 1845): 3.

"Funeral of Mrs. Caroline Smith." *Times and Seasons* 6 (June 1, 1845): 918–20.

Galley, Harry D. *Joseph Smith Senior's Children*. Rock Island, Ill.: Harry D. Galley, 2000.
Garrard, Lamar E. "The Asael Smith Family Moves from Vermont to New York, 1806 to 1820." In Larry C. Porter, Milton V. Backman Jr., and Susan Easton Black, eds., *Regional Studies in Latter-day Saint History: New York*. Provo, Utah: BYU Department of Church History and Doctrine, 1992, 14–31.
"General Conference." *Saints' Herald* 30, no. 16 (April 21, 1883): 242–43.
General no. 111, Circuit Court, Lee County, Illinois, vs. William Smith, Criminal Action, term 1849, record B, p. 42, Illinois State Archives, Illinois Regional Archives Depository, Regional History Center, Founders Memorial Library Room 400, Northern Illinois University, DeKalb, IL.
Gilmore, Thaya Eggleston. "Anson Call: Man of Action." *Ensign*, July 2001, 38–43.
Givens, Terryl L. *By the Hand of Mormon: The American Scripture that Launched a New World Religion*. New York: Oxford University Press, 2002.
Givens, Terryl L., and Matthew J. Grow. *Parley P. Pratt: The Apostle Paul of Mormonism*. New York: Oxford University Press, 2011.
Godfrey, Matthew C., Mark Ashurst-McGee, Grant Underwood, Robert J. Woodford, and William G. Hartley, eds. *Documents—Volume 2: July 1831–January 1833*, THE JOSEPH SMITH PAPERS. General editors Dean C. Jessee, Ronald K. Esplin, and Richard Lyman Bushman. Salt Lake City: Church Historian's Press, 2013.
"Good News." *Melchisedek & Aaronic Herald* (Covington, Ky.) 1, no. 7 (October 1849): 4.
Gould, E. W. *Fifty Years on the Mississippi; or, Gould's History of River Navigation*, St. Louis, Miss.: Nixon-Jones Printing Co., 1889.
Graffam, Merle H., ed. *Salt Lake School of the Prophets Minute Book, 1883*. Palm Desert, Calif.: ULC Press, 1981.
"Grand Flare-up in the Mormon Church in St. Louis." *People's Organ*, November 21, 1845.
Grant, Heber J. Letter to S. O. Bennion, February 12, 1924, 666. In Heber J. Grant Letters, MS 1234, Box 21, fd. 2, LDS Church History Library.
Grant, Heber J. Letter to Miss Mariana Shreve, December 3, 1923, 355–57. In Heber J. Grant Letters, MS 1234, Box 21, fd. 2, LDS Church History Library.
Grant, Heber J. (Salt Lake City). Letters to Cousin Thalia [Smith]." August 21, September 5, October 15, November 6, 1923, 266–67. In Heber J. Grant Letters, MS 1234, Box 21, fd. 2, LDS Church History Library.
Grant, Heber J. Letter to "My dear cousin Wallace [Smith]." November 6, 1923, 265. In Heber J. Grant Letters, MS 1234, Box 21, fd. 2, LDS Church History Library.
Grant, Jedediah M. (Philadelphia, Pa.). Letter to William Smith, November 28, 1843. In William Smith, *Defence of Elder William Smith against the Slander of Abraham Burtis, and Others*. Philadelphia: Brown, Bicking & Guilbert, 1844.
Grant, Jedediah M. (Philadelphia, Pa.). Letter to Brigham Young, September 4, 1844. Brigham Young Office Files, 1832–1878, General Correspondence, Incoming, 1840–1877, Letters from Church Leaders and Others, Jedediah M. Grant, 1844–1854, LDS Church History Library.
"Greatest Annual Conference, The." *Melchisedek and Aaronic Herald* 1, no. 9 (April 1850): 2–3.
Greeley, Horace, and Thomas McElrath. "The New Monarch of Mormondom," *New York Weekly Tribune*, 3, no. 152 (August 10, 1844): 2.
Greene, Evan M. Diaries, 1833–1852, MS 1442, LDS Church History Library.
Gregg, Thomas. *History of Hancock County Illinois*. Chicago: Charles C. Chapman & Co., 1880.
Gregg, Thomas. *The Prophet of Palmyra*. Chicago: Charles C. Chapman & Co., 1880.
Gregory, Thomas J. "Sidney Rigdon: Post Nauvoo." *BYU Studies* 21, no. 1 (Winter 1981): 51–67.
Grey-Osterud, Nancy. *Bonds of Community: The Lives of Farm Women in Nineteenth-Century New York*. Ithaca, N.Y.: Cornell University Press, 1991.

Gurley, Zenos Hovey. "Questions Asked of David Whitmer at His Home in Richmond, Ray County, Missouri, 1885." MS 4633, LDS Church History Library.

Hajicek, John J., ed. *Chronicles of Voree, 1844–1849.* Burlington, Wisc.: J.J. Hajicek, 1992.

Hale, Alden (Lowell, Mass.). Letter to James Strang, January 1, 1849, General Correspondence, fd. 361, Strang Collection.

Hales, Brian C. *Joseph Smith's Polygamy, Vols. 1–2: History, and Vol 3. Theology.* Salt Lake City: Greg Kofford Books, 2013.

Hall, Basil. *Travels in North America,* 2 vols. Edinburgh: William Blackwood, 1833.

Hamer, John. "Mapping Mormon Settlement in Caldwell County, Missouri." *Mormon Historical Studies* 9, no. 1 (Spring 2008): 15–38.

Hampshire, Annette P. "Thomas Sharp and Anti-Mormon Sentiment in Illinois 1842–1845." *Journal of the Illinois State Historical Society* 72, no. 2 (1979): 82–100.

Hancock, Mary Salisbury. Autobiography, ca. 1963, 6; original in possession of Mary Dennis; photocopy of holograph in my possession courtesy of Mary Dennis.

Hancock, Mary Salisbury. "The Three Sisters of the Prophet Joseph Smith." *Saints' Herald* 101, no. 2 (January 11, 1954): 35–36.

Hannaman, R. L. Letter to Honorable Hezekiah M. Weed, re: *Roxey Ann Smith vs. William Smith,* Bill of Divorce, filed April 25, 1853, April Term, Knox County Circuit Court, Knox County Courthouse, Knoxville, Illinois; photocopy in my possession. See also **Divorce proceedings.**

Hansen, Debra Gold. *Strained Sisterhood: Gender and Class in the Boston Female Anti-Slavery Society.* Amherst: University of Massachusetts Press, 1993.

Hansen, Klaus J. *Quest for Empire: The Political Kingdom of God and the Council of Fifty in Mormon History.* Lansing: Michigan State University Press, 1970.

Hardy, John, qtd. in "By express." *The New Era and Herald of Zion's Watchmen* (Elkhorn, Wisc.) 1, no. 2 (February 1847): 3.

Hardy, John. *Startling Developments of Crim. Con.! Or Two Mormon Apostles Exposed in Practising the Spiritual Wife System.* Boston: Conway and Company, 1844.

Harper, Steven C. "The Restoration of Mormonism to Erie County, Pennsylvania," *Mormon Historical Studies* 1, no. 1 (Spring 2000): 7–12.

Harris, J. A. "A correspondent from the Albany Atlas." *Cleveland Herald* 11, no. 70 (September 13, 1845): 1.

"Hartford Conference." *Prophet* 1, no. 38 (February 8, 1845): 2–3.

Hartley, William G. "'Almost Too Intolerable a Burthen': The Winter Exodus from Missouri, 1838–39." *Journal of Mormon History* 18, no. 2 (Fall 1992), 16–32.

Hartley, William G. "From Men to Boys: LDS Aaronic Priesthood Offices, 1829–1996." *Journal of Mormon History* 22, no. 1 (Spring 1996): 80–136.

Hartley, William G. *My Best for the Kingdom: History and Autobiography of John Lowe Butler, a Mormon Frontiersman.* Salt Lake City: Aspen Books, 1993.

Harwell, William S. *Manuscript History of Brigham Young.* Salt Lake City: Collier's Publishing, 1997.

Haven, Charlotte (Nauvoo, Ill.) Letter to My dear friends at home, September 8, 1843. In William Mulder and A. Russell Mortensen, eds., *Among the Mormons* (New York: Alfred A. Knopf, 1958), 126–27.

Havergal, William Henry. *A History of the Old Hundredth Psalm Tune: With Specimens.* New York: Mason Brothers, 1854.

Hedges, Andrew H. "'All My Endeavors to Preserve Them': Protecting the Plates in Palmyra." *Journal of Book of Mormon Studies* 8, no 2 (1999): 16–23.

Hedges, Andrew H., Alex D. Smith, and Richard Lloyd Anderson, eds. *Journals, Vol. 2, December 1841–April 1843.* Vol. 2 of the Journal series of THE JOSEPH SMITH PAPERS.

General editors Dean C. Jessee, Ronald K. Esplin, and Richard Lyman Bushman. Salt Lake City: Church Historian's Press, 2011.
"Hell-in Arkansas." http://civilwarhelena.com/history/hell-in-arkansas/ (accessed March 3, 2015).
Herringshaw, Hugh (Nauvoo, Ill.). Letter to William Smith, August 28, 1844, *Prophet* 1, no. 19 (September 21, 1844): 2.
Hicks, Michael. *Mormonism and Music*. Urbana: University of Illinois Press, 1989.
Hill, Marvin S., C. Keith Rooker, and Larry T. Wimmer. "The Kirtland Economy Revisited: A Market of Critique of Sectarian Economics." *BYU Studies* 17, no. 4 (Summer 1977): 391–482.
History of Erie County, Pennsylvania, 2 vols. Chicago: Warner, Beers & Co., 1884.
"History of George A. Smith." George A. Smith Papers, 1834–75. MS 1322, Box 1, fd. 1, LDS Church History Library.
History of Iowa County, Iowa, Containing a History of the County, Its Cities, Towns, &c., The. Des Moines: Union Historical Company, 1881.
"History of Joseph Smith, Senior, Patriarchal Record." Journal History of the Church of Jesus Christ of Latter-day Saints, February 11, 1859, 1–2, LDS Church History Library.
History of Lee County. Chicago: H. H. Hill and Company, 1881.
"History of William Smith." *Millennial Star* 27, no. 1 (January 7, 1865): 7–8.
Hoadly, L. Ives. *Preparation to Profess Religion*. Boston: Congregational Board of Publication, 1858.
Hogan, Edward. "The Curious Case of James Madison Monroe." *Sunstone* no. 172 (August 2013): 30–37.
Holmes, Reed M. *Dreamers of Zion: Joseph Smith and George J. Adams, Conviction, Leadership, and Israel's Renewal*. Portland, Ore: Sussex Academic Press, 2003.
Holzapfel, Richard N., T. Jeffery Cottle, and Ted D. Stoddard, eds. *Church History in Black and White: George Edward Anderson's Photographic Mission to Latter-day Saint Historical Sites*. Provo, Utah: BYU Religious Studies Center, 1995.
Holzapfel, Jeni Broberg, and Richard Neitzel Holzapfel, eds. *A Woman's View: Helen Mar Whitney's Reminiscences of Early Church History*. Provo, Utah: BYU Religious Studies Center, 1997.
Hook, Aaron, and Jotham T. Barrett (Shelburn, Ill.). Letter to the Editors, April 19, 1853. In "Slander Refuted." *Dixon Telegraph* 2, no. 51 (April 20, 1853): 2.
Hook, Rosa A. (Newark, Wisc.). Statement, March 29, 1853. In "Slander Refuted." *Dixon Telegraph* 2, no. 51 (April 30, 1853): 2.
Horne, Dennis B., ed. *An Apostle's Record: The Journals of Abraham H. Cannon*. Clearfield, Utah: Gnolaum Books, 2004.
Horner, John M. "Adventures of a Pioneer." *Improvement Era* 7, no. 7 (May 1904): 510–15.
"House of Representatives." *The Wasp* 1, no. 40 (February 1, 1843): 3.
Howard, Richard P. *The Church through the Years, Vol. 1*. Independence: Herald Publishing House, 1992.
Howard, Richard P., ed. *Memoirs of President Joseph Smith III (1832–1914)*. Independence: Herald Publishing House, 1979.
Howe, E. D. *Mormonism Unvailed*. Painesville, Ohio: By the author, 1834.
Huff, Roy B., and Kyle R. Walker. "Don Carlos Smith." In *United by Faith: The Joseph Sr. and Lucy Mack Smith Family*. Edited by Kyle R. Walker. American Fork, Utah: BYU Studies and Covenant Communications, 2006, 355–98.
Hunter, Kimberly E., and Christina R. Bunting. "Owen County, Bethany Presbyterian Church Records, 1820–1834." Indiana Historical Society Press, 2014, http://www.indianahistory.org/our-services/books-publications/magazines/online-connections/regional/OwenCoBethanyPresbyRecs.pdf (accessed May 2014).
Hutchins, Robert D. "Joseph Smith III: Moderate Mormon." M.A. thesis, Brigham Young University, 1977.
Hyde, Myrtle Stevens. *Orson Hyde: The Olive Branch of Israel*. Salt Lake City: Agreka Books, 2000.

Hyde, Orson. "Bill Smith." *Frontier Guardian* 2, no. 11 (June 26, 1850), 3.
Hyde, Orson. "Cause for Which William Smith Was Excluded from the Church!" *Frontier Guardian* 2, no. 1 (February 6, 1850): 2.
Hyde, Orson. Journal, 1832. MS 1386. LDS Church History Library.
Hyde, Orson (Council Bluffs). In Brigham Young Office Files 1832–1878, General Correspondence, Incoming, 1832–1877, Letters from Church Leaders and Others, 1840–1877. LDS Church History Library.
  Letter to Brigham Young, March 10, 1846.
  Letter to Dear Brethren, March 27, 1846.
  Letter to William Smith, June 22, 1847.
  Letter to Nathaniel Felt, June 29, 1847.
Hyde, Orson (Nauvoo, Ill.) Letter to Samuel Brannan, October 20, 1845. *New-York Messenger* 2, no. 19 (November 8, 1845): 8.
Hyde, Orson (Nauvoo, Ill.). Letter to William Smith, October 28, 1845. *Warsaw Signal* 2, no. 36 (November 26, 1845): 1.
Hyde, Orson. Letter to Joseph Smith, December 15, 1835. Qtd. in Jessee, Ashurst-McGee, and Jensen, *Journals, Volume 1*, 124–28, 128 note 216.
Hyde, Orson. Letter to William Smith, October 28, 1845. *Melchisedek and Aaronic Herald* 1, no. 4 (June 1849): 1–2.
Hyde, Orson (Nauvoo, Ill.). Letter to William Smith, October 28, 1845. In *Messenger and Advocate of the Church of Christ* 2, no. 2 (December 1845): 413–14.
Hyde, Orson. "Mother Smith." *Frontier Guardian* 1, no. 21 (November 14, 1849): 2.
Hyde, Orson. "We Have Just Read a Letter." *Frontier Guardian* 1, no. 1 (February 7, 1849): 2.
Hyde, Orson. "William Smith." *Frontier Guardian*, 2, no. 1 (February 6, 1850): 2.
Hyde, Orson, and John E. Page. Letter to Presidents Joseph Smith, Hyrum Smith, Sidney Rigdon, n.d., n.p. LDS Church History Library.
Hyde, Orson (Nauvoo, Ill.). Letter to William Smith, October 28, 1845. *Warsaw Signal* 2, no. 36 (November 26, 1845): 1.
Important Arrest." *Missouri Republican* 32, no. 101 (April 28, 1854): 2.
"Information Wanted." *Melchisedek and Aaronic Herald* 1, no. 5 (August 1849): 4.
Ingersoll, Peter. Statement, December 9, 1833, Wayne County, New York. In E. D. Howe, *Mormonism Unvailed*. Painesville, Ohio: Author, 1834, 236–37.
Iowa Civil War Union Units 1st through 9th, https://familysearch.org/learn/wiki/en/Iowa_Civil_War_Union_Units_1st_through_9th (accessed March 11, 2015).
Iowa in the Civil War." Transcribed by Sharon D. Franklin, http://iagenweb.org/civilwar/regiment/cavalry/07th/coH.html (accessed March 10, 2015).
"It Becomes Our Painful Duty." *Zion's Reveille* 2, no. 23 (August 26, 1847): 3.
"James S. Quince." Illinois Civil War Detail Report. Illinois Civil War Muster and Descriptive Rolls Database, Illinois State Archives. http://www.ilsos.gov/isaveterans/civilMusterSearch.do?key=205673 (accessed November 5, 2013).
Jarman, Dean L., and Kyle R. Walker. "Samuel Harrison Smith." In *United by Faith: The Joseph Sr. and Lucy Mack Smith Family.* Edited by Kyle R. Walker. American Fork, Utah: BYU Studies and Covenant Communications, 2006, 205–46.
Jensen, Robin Scott Richard E. Turley Jr., and Riley M. Lorimer, eds. *Revelations and Translations, Vol. 2: Published Revelations*, Vol. 2 in the Revelations and Translations series of THE JOSEPH SMITH PAPERS. General editors Dean C. Jessee, Ronald K. Esplin, and Richard Lyman Bushman. Salt Lake City: Church Historian's Press, 2011.
Jensen, Robin Scott, Robert J. Woodford, and Steven C. Harper, eds. *Manuscript Revelation Books, Facsimile Edition.* Vol. 1 in the Revelations and Translations series of THE JOSEPH

Smith Papers. General editors Dean C. Jessee, Ronald K. Esplin, and Richard Lyman Bushman. Salt Lake City: Church Historian's Press, October 2009.

Jenson, Andrew. *Latter-day Saint Biographical Encyclopedia: A Compilation of Biographical Sketches of Prominent Men and Women in the Church of Jesus Christ of Latter-day Saints.* 4 vols. Salt Lake City: Andrew Jenson History Company, 1901–30.

Jenson, Andrew. "William Smith." *Historical Record* 3, no. 5 (March 1886): 44–45.

Jessee, Dean C., ed. *John Taylor Nauvoo Journal.* Provo, Utah: Grandin Book, 1996.

Jessee, Dean C., comp. and ed. *Personal Writings of Joseph Smith*, rev. ed. Salt Lake City: Deseret Book/Provo, Utah: Brigham Young University Press, 2002.

Jessee, Dean C. "The Writings of Brigham Young." *Western Historical Quarterly* 4, no. 3 (July 1973): 273–294.

Jessee, Dean C., Mark Ashurst-McGee, and Richard L. Jensen, eds. *Journals, Vol. 1: 1832–1839.* Vol. 1 of the Journals series of The Joseph Smith Papers. General editors Dean C. Jessee, Ronald K. Esplin, and Richard Lyman Bushman. Salt Lake City: Church Historian's Press, 2008.

Johnson, Benjamin F. *My Life's Review: Autobiography of Benjamin Franklin Johnson.* Provo, Utah: Grandin Book, 1997.

Johnson, Clark V., ed. *Mormon Redress Petitions: Documents of the 1833–1838 Missouri Conflict.* Provo, Utah: BYU Religious Studies Center, 1992.

Johnson, Melvin C. *Polygamy on the Pedernales: Lyman Wight's Mormon Villages in Antebellum Texas, 1845–1858.* Logan: Utah State University Press, 2006.

Jolley, Jerry C. "The Sting of the *Wasp*: Early Nauvoo Newspaper—April 1842 to April 1843." *BYU Studies* 22, no. 4 (Fall 1982): 48–96.

Jones, Gracia N. "Sophronia Smith Stoddard McCleary." In Kyle R. Walker, ed. *United by Faith: The Joseph Sr. and Lucy Mack Smith Family.* American Fork, Utah: BYU Studies and Covenant Communications, 2006, 165–203.

Judd, Mary G. *Jedediah M. Grant: Pioneer, Statesman.* Salt Lake City: Deseret News Press, 1959.

Kay, James (St. Louis, Mo.). Letters to Dear Brother Ward, November 22, 1845, and February 10, 1846. *Millennial Star* 7, no. 9 (May 1, 1846): 135–37.

Kelley, William H. "The Hill Cumorah and the Book of Mormon." *Saints' Herald* 28, no. 11 (June 1, 1881): 161–68.

Kennedy, Inez A. *Recollections of the Pioneers of Lee County.* Dixon, Ill.: Inez A. Kennedy, 1893.

Kennedy, Michael, Joyce Kennedy, and Tim Rutherford-Johnson. *Oxford Dictionary of Music*, 6th ed. Oxford, England: Oxford University Press, 2012.

Kenney, Scott G., ed. *Wilford Woodruff's Journal, 1833–1898.* 9 vols. Midvale, Utah: Signature Books, 1983–85.

Kimball, Heber C. (Nauvoo, Ill.), Letter to William Smith, January 9, 1845, LDS Church History Library.

Kimball, Stanley B. "New Light on Old Egyptiana: Mormon Mummies, 1848–71," *Dialogue: A Journal of Mormon Thought* 16, no. 4 (Winter 1983): 72–90.

Kimball, Stanley B., ed. *On the Potter's Wheel: The Diaries of Heber C. Kimball.* Salt Lake City: Signature Books and Smith Research Associates, 1987.

Kimball, Stanley B. "The Saints and St. Louis, 1831–1857: An Oasis of Tolerance and Security." *BYU Studies* (Summer 1973): 496–501.

"Kirtland." *Voree Herald* 1, no. 9 (September 1846): 1–2.

Knight, Greg, ed. *Thomas Bullock Nauvoo Journal.* Provo, Utah: Grandin Press, 1994.

"Laid to Rest." *Brookfield Gazette* 12, no. 36 (December 26, 1878): 3.

Land and Record Book Z, 584; Land and Record Book B-2, 48; Land and Record Book 38, 37; Quit Claim Deed Record, number 55, all at the Clayton County Courthouse, Elkader, Iowa.

Larson, Andrew Karl. *Erastus Snow: The Life of a Missionary and Pioneer for the Early Mormon Church.* Salt Lake City: University of Utah Press, 1971.

Launius, Roger D. "Anti-Mormonism in Illinois: Thomas C. Sharp's Unfinished History of the Mormon War, 1845." *Journal of Mormon History* 15 (1989): 27–45.

Launius, Roger D. *Joseph Smith III Pragmatic Prophet.* Urbana: University of Illinois Press, 1988.

Legg, Phillip R. *Oliver Cowdery: The Elusive Second Elder of the Restoration.* Independence, Mo.: Herald Publishing, 1989.

Leonard, Glen M. *Nauvoo: A Place of Peace, a People of Promise.* Provo, Utah: BYU Press/Salt Lake City: Deseret Book, 2002.

"Letter from Eld. Wm. Smith," *Times and Seasons* 6 (February 15, 1845): 814.

Lindsay, John S. *The Mormons and the Theatre; or, The History of Theatricals in Utah; with Reminiscences and Comments, Humorous and Critical.* Salt Lake City: Century Printing, 1905.

"List of Agents for this Paper." *Melchisedek & Aaronic Herald* (Covington, Ky.) 1, no. 5 (August 1849): 2.

"List of Letters Remaining in the Cleveland Post Office, August 4th, 1857, Ladies' List." *Cleveland Plain Dealer*, August 4, 1857, 3.

Littlefield, Lyman O. "Still Later from Nauvoo." *New-York Messenger* 2, no. 5 (August 2, 1845): 6.

Livingston, John. *Livingston's Law Register: Containing a Complete List of Lawyers in the United States.* New York: Livingston, 1856.

Lyman, Edward Leo, Susan Ward Payne, and S. George Ellsworth, eds. *No Place to Call Home: The 1807–1857 Life Writings of Caroline Barnes Crosby, Chronicler of Outlying Mormon Communities.* Logan: Utah State University Press, 2005.

Lyman, Edward Leo. *Amasa Mason Lyman, Mormon Apostle and Apostate: A Study in Dedication.* Salt Lake City: University of Utah Press, 2009.

Lyon, T. Edgar. "Nauvoo and the Council of the Twelve." In *The Restoration Movement: Essays in Mormon History*, rev. ed. Edited by F. Mark McKiernan, Alma R. Blair, and Paul M. Edwards. Independence, Mo.: Herald House, 1992, 163–200.

Lytton, Edward Bulwer. *The Lady of Lyons; or, Love and Pride.* In Donald Jay Grout and Hermine Weigel Williams. *A Short History of Opera.* 4th ed. New York: Columbia University Press, 2003, 570.

Mack, Solomon. *A Narraitve [Narrative] of the Life of Solomon Mack.* Windsor, VT: [1811].

MacKay, Michael Hubbard, Gerrit J. Dirkmaat, Grant Underwood, Robert J. Woodford, and William G. Hartley, eds. *Documents—Vol. 1: July 1828–June 1831.* Vol. 1 in the Documents series of THE JOSEPH SMITH PAPERS. General editors Dean C. Jessee, Ronald K. Esplin, and Richard Lyman Bushman. Salt Lake City: Church Historian's Press, 2013.

Madsen, Truman G. *Defender of the Faith: The B. H. Roberts Story.* Salt Lake City: Bookcraft, 1980.

Madsen, Truman G. *Joseph Smith the Prophet.* Salt Lake City: Bookcraft, 1989.

Mahan, Asa. *Autobiography: Intellectual, Moral, and Spirtual.* London: T. Woolmer, 1882.

"Man of Sin, The." *Aaronic Herald* (Covington, Ky.) 1, no. 1 (February 1, 1849): 2.

"Many Are Inquiring." *Wayne Sentinel* 2 (December 15, 1824): 2.

Marks, William. "Epistle." *Zion's Harbinger and Baneemy's Organ* 7, no. 3 (July 1853): 53.

Marquardt, H. Michael, and Wesley P. Walters. *Inventing Mormonism: Tradition and the Historical Record.* Salt Lake City: Smith Research Associates, 1994.

Marquardt, H. Michael, comp. *Early Patriarchal Blessings of the Church of Jesus Christ of Latter-day Saints.* Salt Lake City: Smith-Pettit Foundation, 2007.

Marquardt, H. Michael. "Martin Harris: The Kirtland Years, 1831–1870." *Dialogue: A Journal of Mormon Thought* 35, no. 3 (Fall 2002): 19–25.

Marquardt, H. Michael. *The Rise of Mormonism: 1816–1844.* Longwood, Fla.: Xulon Press, 2005.

Marriage License #12066, Book 1, 219, Clinton County Courthouse, Clinton, Iowa.

"Married." *Wayne Sentinel* 1 (December 3, 1823): 3.

Marsh, Thomas B., and David W. Patten (Far West, Missouri). Letter to Parley P. Pratt, May 10, 1837. LDS Church History Library.
Mayo, Martha, and Connell O'Donovan. "Members and Missionaries of the Lowell, Mass. Branch of the Church of Jesus Christ of Latter-Day Saints, 1835–1860." Unpublished web document. http://people.ucsc.edu/~odonovan/lowell_members.html#hannah_lib (accessed September 12, 2014).
McAdams, Benton. *Rebels at Rock Island: The Story of a Civil War Prison*. DeKalb: Northern Illinois University Press, 2000.
McCormick, Albert E., Jr. *Historical Demography through Genealogies: Explorations into Pre-1900 American Population Issues*. Bloomington, Ind.: iUniverse, 2011.
McPherson, Edward. *The Political History of the United States of America, during the Great Rebellion, from November 6, 1860, to July 4, 1864*. Washington D.C.: Philip & Solomons/D. Appleton & Co., 1864.
McVicker, Maryellen Harshbarger. Email to Kyle Walker, April 9, 2015.
"Meeting." *Nauvoo Neighbor* 3, no. 2 (May 14, 1845): 2.
"Meeting of the Mormons Last Evening." *Prophet* 1, no. 26 (November 16, 1844): 2.
"Memorial to Congress." *Melchisedek & Aaronic Herald* 1, no. 8 (February 1850): 4.
Message from the Council of the Twelve. "Hearken, O Ye Latter-Day Saints, and All Ye Inhabitants of the Earth Who Wish to be Saints, to Whom this Writing Shall Come." *Millennial Star* 27 (October 21, 1865): 658.
Metcalfe, Erin B. Jennings. "Eliza Elsie Sanborn," ca. 2010, unpublished manuscript in my possession.
Metcalfe, Erin Jennings. "Rosanna and Rhoda Hook," ca. 2011. Unpublished manscript in my possession.
Miller, Reuben (Burlington, Iowa Territory). Letter to Bro [Brigham] Young, April 21, 1847, Brigham Young Office Files 1832–1878, General Correspondence, Incoming, 1840–1877, General Letters, 1840–1877, M–P, 1847, LDS Church History Library.
Miller, Sarah, Catherine Fuller (Warren), Matilda Nyman, and Melinda Lewis. Testimonies in Nauvoo High Council. May 1842. MS 24557, LDS Church History Library.
Minute Book 1, 1832–1836 (Kirtland, Ohio), 135, item #7702. LDS Church History Library.
Minute Book 2 (Far West, Missouri), 1837–38. ID# 7235. LDS Church History Library.
Minutes of a Conference held at Nauvoo, April 8, 1846, Leonard J. Arrington Papers, 43–54, Box 12, fd. 2, Merrill-Cazier Library, Utah State University, Logan, Utah.
"Minutes of a Conference held at Walnut Grove, Knox [C]o. Ill. January 30th, 1841." *Times and Seasons* 2, no. 9 (March 1, 1841): 12.
Minutes of a Conference, Held by the Church of Jesus Christ of Latter Day Saints. Cincinnati, Ohio: William Smith, 1846.
"Minutes of a Conference in Philadelphia." *Prophet* 1, no. 17 (September 14, 1844): 1.
Minutes of Address, General Conference, October 8, 1845. Uncatalogued holograph, clerk apparently Curtis E. Bolton, LDS Church History Library.
"Minutes of the Annual Conference of the Church of Jesus Christ of Latter Day Saints, Held at Voree April the 6th, 1847, The." *Zion's Reveille* 2, no. 16 (July 8, 1847): 3–4.
Minutes of the General Conference of the Church of Jesus Christ of Latter Day Saints held at the City of Nauvoo." *Times and Seasons* 2, no. 12 (April 15, 1841): 388.
Minutes of the School of the Prophets, Provo, Utah, 1868–71. MSS 7989. Perry Special Collections.
"Missouri vs Joseph Smith." *Times and Seasons* 4, no. 16 (July 1, 1843): 242.
Moneyhon, Carl. "1861: 'The Die Is Cast.'" In *Rugged and Sublime: The Civil War in Arkansas*. Edited by Mark K. Christ. Fayetteville: University of Arkansas Press, 1994.
Monroe, James M. Journal, 1841–1845. 117, MS 7061, LDS Church History Library.
"More Mormons." *Nauvoo Neighbor* 1, no. 52 (April 24, 1844): 2.
"More Trouble in the Church." *Dixon Telegraph* 3, no. 44 (March 9, 1854): 2.

"Mormon Jubilee, The." *The Wasp* 1, no. 37 (January 14, 1843): 1.
"Mormon Oratory." *True American* (Lexington, Ky.) 1, no. 19 (November 25, 1845): 1.
"Mormon Times in Kirtland." *Cleveland Daily Plain Dealer* 15, no. 114 (May 17, 1859): 3.
"Mormon Times in Kirtland." Notes and commentary by Dale Broadhurst. http://www.sidneyrigdon.com/dbroadhu/OH/miscoh09.htm (accessed February 14, 2012).
"Mormonism Again," *Dixon Telegraph* 2, no. 52 (May 7, 1853): 2.
"Mormonism in New England." *Maine Farmer and Journal of the Useful Arts* 3 (October 9, 1835): 288. In William Shepard and H. Michael Marquardt. *Lost Apostles: Forgotten Members of Mormonism's Original Quorum of Twelve.* Salt Lake City: Signature Books, 2014.
"Mormonism in This County." *Dixon [Illinois] Telegraph* 2, no. 48 (April 9, 1853).
"Mormonism. Lecture by Mr. Stoneman—Reply of a Brother of Joe Smith." *Clayton County Journal* 16, no. 38 (February 6, 1868): 2.
Mormonism—The Young Joseph!" *Weekly Reveille* (St. Louis, Mo). 2, no. 17 (November 3, 1845): 1. Rpt. in "Mormon Oratory," *True American* (Lexington, Ky.) 1, no. 19 (November 25, 1845): 1.
"Mormons and Their Prophet, The." *Congregational Observer* 2 (July 3, 1841): 1. Reproduced in Dan Vogel, ed., *Early Mormon Documents,* 1:477–80; transcribed in the Lyndon Cook Collection, Community of Christ Library-Archives, Independence, Mo.
"Mormons, The." *Warsaw Signal* 2, no. 2 (May 19, 1841): 2.
"Mormons—Oregon, The." *Weekly Reveille* (St. Louis, Mo.) 2, no. 17 (November 3, 1845): 1.
Morris, George. *Autobiography.* Provo, Utah: Brigham Young University Library, 1953.
"Mother Smith, Mother of the Martyred Prophets." *Melchisedek and Aaronic Herald* 1, no. 5 (August 1849): 4.
"Movements of the Mormons." *Warsaw Signal* 2, no. 52 (March 25, 1846): 2.
"Mr. Appleby." *Melchisedek and Aaronic Herald* (Covington, Ky.), 1, no. 4 (June 1849): 3.
Mulder, William, and A. Russell Mortensen, eds. *Among the Mormons.* New York: Alfred A. Knopf, 1958.
Murdock, James. Letter to *Congregational Observer,* June 19, 1841. In "The Mormons and Their Prophet." *Congregational Observer* 2 (July 3, 1841): 1.
Murdock, James. "The Mormons and Their Prophet." June 19, 1841, *Congregational Observer* (Hartford and New Haven, Conn.) 2 (July 3, 1841): 1. Rpt., in James Murdock, "Origin of the Mormons," *Peoria Register and North-Western Gazetteer,* September 3, 1841, n.p., photocopy, M2732.2, LDS Church History Library.
Murdock, Samuel. "The Rev. William B. Smith." *Elkader Weekly Register,* November 23, 1893, 5.
"Nauvoo Charters." *Wasp* 1, no. 40 (February 1, 1843): 2, reprinting article from the *[Springfield] Illinois Register.*
Nauvoo Temple Endowment Register, Land and Records Office, Nauvoo, Illinois.
Neibaur, Alexander. Journal, 1844, LDS Church History Library; also http://josephsmithpapers.org/paperSummary/alexander-neibaur-journal-24-may-1844-extract?p=1.
"New Monarch of Mormondom, The." *New York Weekly Tribune,* August 10, 1844, 2.
"New Order of Things at Nauvoo." *Sangamo Journal* (Springfield, Illinois) 14, no. 40 (June 26, 1845): 1.
"New York Conference." *Times and Seasons* 6, no. 17 (November 15, 1845): 13–14.
Newell, Linda King, and Valeen Tippetts Avery. *Mormon Enigma: Emma Hale Smith,* 2d ed. Urbana: University of Illinois Press, 1994.
Ninety-Fifth Annual Conference of the Church of Jesus Christ of Latter day Saints, April 4, 5 and 6, 1925. Salt Lake City: Church of Jesus Christ of Latter-day Saints, 1925.
Norman, Mary B. Smith (Idaho Falls, Ida.). Letters to Ina Smith Coolbrith, March 27 and April 24, 1908. P13, fd. 955, and Miscellaneous Letters and Papers, P13, f951, Community of Christ Library-Archives.

"Notice." *Times and Seasons* 5, no. 10 (May 15, 1844): 535.
"Notice." *Times and Seasons* 6, no. 21 (January 15, 1846): 1096.
1880, 1890, 1900, etc., as years of federal census. Look under U.S. Census, thereunder by decentennial year, arranged by state, county, and town.
Oaks, Dallin H., and Marvin S. Hill. *Carthage Conspiracy: The Trial of the Accused Assassins of Joseph Smith.* Urbana: University of Illinois Press, 1975.
"Obituary [of Caroline Grant Smith]." *Nauvoo Neighbor* 3, no. 4 (May 28, 1845): 3.
"Obituary [of Jedediah Grant]." *Deseret News,* December 10, 1856, 5.
"Obituary. Mrs. Eliza E. Smith of Elkader." *Elkader Weekly Register* 12, no. 18 (March 14, 1889): 1.
"Obituary [of Caroline Grant Smith]." *Nauvoo Neighbor* 3, no. 4 (May 28, 1845): 3.
"October Conference Minutes." *Times and Seasons* 5, no. 19 (October 15, 1844), 682–85.
Ogden, D. Kelly. "The Kirtland Hebrew School (1835–36)." In Milton V. Backman Jr., ed., *Regional Studies in Latter-day Saint Church History: Ohio.* Provo, Utah: BYU Department of Church History and Doctrine, 1990, 64–71.
Ohio, County Marriages, 1790–1950, microfilm 872467, item 1, image number 371, LDS Family History Library.
Ohio Deaths, 1908–1953, Microfilm 1991300, image number 1849, LDS Family History Library.
"Old Soldier's Testimony, The. Sermon Preached by Bro. William B. Smith, in the Saints' Chapel, Deloit, Iowa, June 8th, 1884. Reported by C. E. Butterworth." *Saints' Herald* 31, no. 40 (October 4, 1884): 643.
"Opinions of the Smith Family," *Voree Herald* 1, no. 6 (June 1846): 1.
Osgood, T. "Messrs. Editors," *Wayne Sentinel* 2 (December 15, 1824): 2.
Osterdock Branch Minutebook, Book 1 (small), entry for June 11, 1893; see also Osterdock Branch Minutebook, Book 2 (large), entry for August 19, 1893. Both in Community of Christ Library-Archives.
Osterud, Nancy Grey. *Bonds of Community: The Lives of Farm Women in Nineteenth-Century New York.* Ithaca, N.Y.: Cornell University Press, 1991.
O'Donovan, Connell, "The Elders' Pocket Companion by Elder William Smith." Web publication, 2009. Available at http://www.connellodonovan.com/pocket_companion.pdf (accessed April 5, 2015).
O'Donovan, Connell. "Joseph T. Ball, 1804–1861: Mormonism's First African American High Priest." Unpublished manuscript, 2011. Copy in my possession courtesy of O'Donovan.
O'Donovan, Connell. "The Mormon Priesthood Ban and Elder Q. Walker Lewis: 'An Example for His More Whiter Brethren to Follow.'" *John Whitmer Historical Association Journal* 26 (2006): 66–71.
O'Donovan, Connell. "The Orphan Child: Priscilla Mogridge Smith Lowry Williams Staines (1823–1899)." *John Whitmer Historical Association Journal* 32, no. 1 (Spring/Summer 2012): 79–113.
O'Donovan, Connell. "William Smith, Isaac Sheen and the Melchisedek & Aaronic Herald," http://www.connellodonovan.com/herald.html (accessed March 6, 2015).
O'Driscoll, Jeffrey S. *Hyrum Smith: Life of Integrity.* Salt Lake City: Deseret Book, 2003.
Paden, Isaac (Knoxville, Ill.) Letter to James M. Adams, April 4, 1846. Strang Collection.
Paden, Isaac (Knoxville, Ill.). Letter to Brigham Young, January 26, 1846, Brigham Young Office Files 1832–78, General Correspondence, Incoming, 1840–77, General Letters, 1840–1877, M–P, 1846, LDS Church History Library.
Page, John E. (Nauvoo, Ill.). Letter to James J. Strang, February 1, 1846, Document 10, Strang Collection.
Page, John E. (Philadelphia). Letter to the President and Council of the Church of Jesus Christ of Latter-day Saints (Nauvoo). September 1, 1841, in Journal History, September 1, 1841, 5.
Page, John E. "Forgetful Prophets." *Gospel Herald* 2, no. 38 (December 9, 1847): 8.

"Patriarch Bill Smith." *Warsaw Signal* 2, no. 18 (July 2, 1845): 2.
"Patriarch Bill Smith, The." *Warsaw Signal* 2, no. 50 (March 11, 1846): 1.
"Patriarch Bill Smith." *Warsaw Signal* 2, no. 51 (March 18, 1846): 2.
"Patriarchs." *Zion's Reveille* 2, no. 1 (January 14, 1847): 3.
Pension File of William B. Smith, Box 48086, 128, National Archives, Washington D.C.:
    Declaration for Invalid Pension, August 8, 1865.
    Invalid pension filed August 26, 1865, Certificate no. 79175.
    Asa Kearr, M. Staples, and C. M. Balderseage, Examining Surgeon's Certificate, June 21, 1882, 123.
    Neely, John R. (Chicago, Ill.). Letter to N. A. Lowry, April 21, 1903, 52, Part 1, Widow's Pension.
    Report of Adjutant General, June 29, 1866
    K. F. Rerdy, Examining Surgeon's Certificate, April 5, 1882, 125.
    Edson D. C. Smith, (Dundee, Minn.) letter to U.S. Pension Office, June 6, 1892.
    William B. Smith, Letters to U.S. Pension Office, July 19, 1875; May 2, 1882; and ca. October 1889.
    Statements of A. B. Hanna, July 27, 1867, September 4, 1873, and March 30, 1882; Examining Surgeon's Certificate, March 18, 1874
    Statement of H. Hamilton, October 17, 1879.
    Statement of J. H. Hill, Clayton County Recorder, April 22, 1899, Part II, 82.
    Statement of L. E. Wagner, October 28, 1887.
    Statement of William H. Ziegler, September 3, 1893
    U.S. Pension Office, Letter to Edson D. C. Smith, March 14, 1916.
People of the State of Illinois vs. William Smith, The.
    Bastardy, Lee County Circuit Clerk, April 7, 1853, Criminal Record, Book B, 348, Dixon, Illinois.
    Bastardy change of venue to La Salle County, in *People of the State of Illinois vs. William Smith*, Bastardy, Lee County Circuit Clerk, September 21, 1853, Criminal Record, Book B, 398, and Chancery Record, Book B, 399, Dixon, Illinois.
    Bond, In Charge of Adultery, Lee County Circuit Clerk, Dixon, Illinois, October 15, 1852.
    Indictment for Rape, Lee County Circuit Clerk, September 21, 1853, Criminal Record, Book B, 400, Dixon, Illinois.
    Indictment for Rape, Bond or Recognizance, Lee County Circuit Clerk, May 15, 1854, Dixon, Illinois, bond posted by Rhoda E. Hook, Aaron Hook, and Elnathan Gibbs.
    Trial, March 23, 1853, Lee County Circuit Court, Dixon, Illinois, Illinois Regional Archives Depository, Northern Illinois University, Regional History Center, DeKalb, Illinois.
    Trial for Bastardy, Criminal Record, April 7, 1853, Book B, 348, September 21, 1853, Book B, 398, and Chancery Record, Book B, 399, Lee County Circuit Clerk, Dixon, Illinois.
Perkins, Keith W., and Donald Q. Cannon. *Ohio and Illinois.* Vol. 3 in SACRED PLACES: A COMPREHENSIVE GUIDE TO EARLY LDS HISTORICAL SITES. General editor, LaMar C. Berrett. Salt Lake City: Deseret Book, 2002.
Petersen, William J. *Steamboating on the Upper Mississippi: The Water Way to Iowa.* Iowa City: State Historical Society of Iowa, 1937.
Peterson, H. Donl. *The Story of the Book of Abraham: Mummies, Manuscripts, and Mormonism.* Salt Lake City: Deseret Book, 1995.
Peterson, J. W. "Another Testimony: Statement of William Smith, concerning Joseph, the Prophet." *Deseret Evening News*, January 20, 1894, 11.
Peterson, John W., Letter to Editor. "Wm. B. Smith's Last Statement." *Zion's Ensign* (Independence, Mo.) 5 (January 1894): 6.

Phelps, William W. (Dayton, Ohio). Letter to Brother Joseph [Smith], June 29, 1840. LDS Church History Library.
Phelps, W. W. (Nauvoo, Ill.). Letter to Prest. Brigham Young, Willard Richards, and Camp of Israel, March 23, 1846. Willard Richards Papers, 1821–1854, MS 1490, Box 4, fd. 1, February 12, 1846–October 26, 1846, LDS Church History Library.
Philadelphia Branch Minutes. Typescript, Community of Christ Library-Archives, Independence.
Porter, Larry C. "Reverend George Lane—Good 'Gifts,' Much 'Grace,' and Marked 'Usefulness.'" *BYU Studies* 9, no. 3 (Spring 1969): 321–40.
Porter, Larry C. *A Study of the Origins of The Church of Jesus Christ of Latter-day Saints in the States of New York and Pennsylvania*. Provo, Utah: Joseph Fielding Smith Institute for Latter-day Saint History and BYU Studies, 2000. Slightly updated from his 1971 dissertation by the same title.
Porter, Larry C. "'Ye Shall Go to the Ohio': Exodus of the New York Saints to Ohio, 1831." In Milton V. Backman Jr. ed. *Regional Studies in Latter-day Saint Church History: Ohio*. Provo, Utah: Brigham Young University Department of Church History and Doctrine, 1990), 1–25.
Post, Stephen. Journals, 1835–1879. MS 1304, LDS Church History Library.
Pratt, Orson (New York City). "Farewell Message of Orson Pratt." November 8, 1845. Letter to *New-York Messenger* 2, no. 20 (November 15, 1845): 1.
Pratt, Orson. *A[n] Interesting Account of Several Remarkable Visions, and of the Late Discovery of Ancient American Records*. Edinburgh: Ballantyne and Hughes, 1840.
Pratt, P. P. "Elder G. J. Adams." In *Prophet* 1, no. 33 (January 4, 1845): 2.
Pratt, Parley P. (St. Johnsbury, Vt.). Letter to Asahel Smith, July 21, 1835. MS 7064, LDS Church History Library.
Pratt, P. P. (New York). Letter to Brigham Young, May 7, 1845. Brigham Young Office Files 1832–1878, Letters from Church Leaders and Others, 1840–1877, Parley P. Pratt, 1845, LDS Church History Library.
Pratt, Parley P. [Jr.], ed. *The Autobiography of Parley Parker Pratt, One of the Twelve Apostles of the Church of Jesus Christ of Latter-day Saints, Embracing His Life, Ministry and Travels, with Extracts, in Prose and Verse, from His Miscellaneous Writings*. 1874; rpt., Salt Lake City: Deseret Book, 1985 printing.
Pratt, Parley P. "Notice." *New-York Messenger* 2, no. 1 (July 5, 1845): 6.
Pratt, Parley P. "Regulations for the Publishing Department of the Latter-day Saints in the East." *Times and Seasons* 6 (January 15, 1845): 778.
Pratt, Parley P. "This Number Closes the First Volume of the 'Prophet.'" *Prophet* 1, no. 52 (May 24, 1845): 2.
Pratt, Parley P. "We Publish the Above." *Prophet* 1, no. 51 (May 10, 1845): 2.
Pratt, Parley P., and Samuel Brannan. "What is 'Mormonism?'" In *Prophet* 1, no. 47 (April 12, 1845): 4.
President Heber C. Kimball's Journal. SEVENTH BOOK OF THE FAITH-PROMOTING SERIES. Salt Lake City: Juvenile Instructor Office, 1882.
"President Wm. Smith." *Melchisedek & Aaronic Herald* 1, no. 8 (February, 1850): 4.
Prince, Gregory A. *Power from On High: The Development of Mormon Priesthood*. Salt Lake City: Signature Books, 1995.
"Proceedings of the General Conference, held at Commerce, Hancock County, Illinois on Saturday the 5th day of October, 1839." *Times and Seasons* 1, no. 2 (December 1839): 30.
"Proclamation of Parley P. Pratt." January 1, 1845, *Millennial Star* 5 (March 1845): 151.
"Proclamation to the Saints, A." *Melchisedek & Aaronic Herald* (Covington, Ky.) 1, no. 5 (August 1849): 1.
Proclamation to the Saints Scattered Abroad, A." *Times and Seasons* 2, no. 6 (January 15, 1841): 274.

"Progress Additional." *Melchisedec and Aaronic Herald* 1, no. 3 (May 1, 1849): 2.

"Prophet Robbed and Deserted—Excommunication of Elder Sheen, A." *Daily Cincinnati Commercial* 12 (May 20, 1850): 1.

"Prophet's Department." *Melchisedek & Aaronic Herald* 1, no. 7 (October 1849), 1.

"Prophet's Sister Testifies She Lifted the B of M Plates, The." *Messenger* (Berkeley, Calif.) 1 (October 1954): 525, typescript copy, LDS Church History Library.

Public Discussions of the Issues between the Reorganized Church of Jesus Christ of Latter Day Saints and the Church of Christ [Disciples] Held in Kirtland, Ohio Beginning February 12, and Closing March 8, 1884 between E. L. Kelley, of the Reorganized Church of Jesus Christ of Latter Day Saints and Clark Braden, of the Church of Christ. St. Louis: Clark Braden, 1884.

"Public Meeting." *Messenger and Advocate* 2, no. 11 (August 1836): 2.

"Public Meeting in Relation to the Late Arrest of General Joseph Smith, A." *Nauvoo Neighbor* 1, no. 12 (July 19, 1843): 3.

Pykles, Benjamin C. "An Introduction to the Kirtland Flats Ashery." *BYU Studies* 41, no. 1 (2002): 158–86.

Quinn, D. Michael. *The Mormon Hierarchy: Origins of Power.* Salt Lake City: Signature Books, 1994.

Quinn, D. Michael. Transcription of minutes. Beinecke Rare Book and Manuscript Library, Yale University, New Haven, Connecticut.

Quinn, D. Michael. "The Council of Fifty and Its Members, 1844–1945." *BYU Studies* 20, no. 2 (Winter 1980): 163–197.

Record of Members Collection, Missouri, Central States Mission, 1904–, 552–53, Reel 4269, CR 375 8, LDS Church History Library.

"Record of the Pilot Grove [Illinois] Branch of the Church of Jesus Christ of L.D.S., The." 1873, Community of Christ Library-Archives.

Records of Early Church Families." *Utah Genealogical Magazine* 26, no. 19 (July 1935): 105.

Reece, B.J.N. *Report of the Adjutant General of the State of Illinois, Volume VI, Containing Reports for the Years 1861–66.* Springfield, Ill.: Journal Company Printers and Binders, 1900.

Reed, John Elmer. *History of Erie County, Pennsylvania.* Topeka, Kans.: Historical Publishing Company, 1925.

Reeves, Thedy Grant. Reminiscence, as told to Joseph Hyrum Grant Jr., November 26, 1904 [sic; should be 1903]. Grant Family Records, ca. 1778–1903. Microfilm #1036844, item #10. LDS Family History Library, Salt Lake City.

"Release of Gen. Joseph Smith, The." *The Wasp* 1, no. 37 (January 14, 1843): 2.

Reports Made to Senate and House of Representatives of the State of Illinois. Springfield, Ill.: William Waters, 1842.

"Resolutions Passed at a Conference of Elders." In Stephen Post, Journal, October 6–7, 1855.

"A Revelation, given March 20, 1850, in Covington, Kentucky, to William Smith." *Melchisedek & Aaronic Herald* 1, no. 9 (April 1850): 1.

"Result of the Election in Illinois, The." *Wasp* 1, no. 18 (August 20, 1842): 2.

"Revelation, Given March 20, 1850, in Covington, Kentucky, A." *Melchisedek & Aaronic Herald* 1, no. 9 (April 1850): 1.

Richards, Samuel W. "The Duty of Marriage." *Contributor* 13, no. 4 (February 1892): 165–68.

Richards, Willard. Diary, 1845. Willard Richards Papers, 1821–54, MS 1490, Box 1. LDS Church History Library.

Richards, Willard. "From Nauvoo." *Warsaw Signal* 2, no. 24 (September 3, 1845): 2.

Richards, Willard, Church Historian's Office. General Church Minutes, 1839–1877, July 6, 1845, Box 1, fd. 35, CR 100 318. LDS Church History Library. In *Selected Collections*, DVDs, 1:18.

Richards, Willard (Platte River). Letter to Reuben Miller, September 17, 1847. Willard Richards Papers, 1821–1854, MS 1490, Box 3, fd. 7.

Richards, Willard (Nauvoo, Ill.). Letter to Elder Wm Smith, Patriarch, August 27, 1845. In Willard Richards Papers, MS 1490, Box 3, fd. 5, LDS Church History Library.
Richards, Willard (Nauvoo, Ill.). Letter to Brigham Young, June 30, 1844. LDS Church History Library.
Richards, Willard. Minutes of Council, May 24, 1845. Church Historian's Office, General Church Minutes, 1839–77, CR 100 318, Box 1, fd. 34.
Richards, Willard. Minutes of Trial of Samuel Brannan, May 24, 1845. Church Historian's Office, General Church Minutes, 1839–77, CR 100 318, Box 1, fd. 34.
[Rigdon, Sidney]. "As We Thought." *Messenger and Advocate* 1, no. 5 (January 1, 1845): 73.
Robbins, Lewis. Autobiographical sketch, circa 1845. MS 18637. LDS Church History Library.
Robison, Elwin C. *The First Mormon Temple: Design, Construction, and Historic Context of the Kirtland Temple*. Provo, Utah: Brigham Young University Press, 1997.
Rogers, Jedediah S., ed. *The Council of Fifty: A Documentary History*. Salt Lake City, Signature Books, 2014.
Romig, Ronald E., ed. *Alexander: Joseph and Emma Smith's Far West Son*. Independence: John Whitmer Books, 2010.
Romig, Ronald E. "Alexander H. Smith: Remembering a Son of Joseph and Emma Smith." *Journal of Mormon History* 37, no. 2 (Spring 2011): 1–58.
Rotundo, E. Anthony *American Manhood: Transformations in Masculinity from the Revolution to the Modern Era*. New York: Basic Books, 1983.
Rudd, Calvin P. "William B. Smith: Brother of the Prophet Joseph Smith." M.A. thesis, Brigham Young University, 1974.
Russell, William D. "A Priestly Role for a Prophetic Church: The RLDS Church and Black Americans," *Dialogue: A Journal of Mormon Thought* 12, no. 2 (Summer 1979), 37–49.
Salisbury, Don Carlos (Tuscumbia, Ala.). Letter to Dear Brother Alvin [Salisbury], August 28, 1862. Perry Special Collections.
Salisbury, D.[on] C.[arlos] (Tuscumbia, Ala.). Letter to Mariah Woolley, August 28, 1862. Photograph of holograph in my possession, courtesy of Mary Dennis.
Salisbury, Don Carlos (Quincy, Ill.) Letter to Mother, Brothers, and Sister, May 8, 1861. Perry Special Collections.
Salisbury, Herbert S. "Reminiscences of Joseph Smith: As Told by His Sister, Catherine [sic] Smith Salisbury, to Her Grandson, Herbert S. Salisbury." *Saints' Herald* 60 (October 8, 1913): 984.
Salisbury, Herbert S. "The Western Adventures of Don Carlos Salisbury," July 18, 1945. Unpublished manuscript, Typescript in my possession.
Salisbury, Jenkins. Letter to Thomas Sharp. *Warsaw Signal* 3, no. 2 (April 8, 1846): 2.
Salisbury, Katharine (Fountain Green, Ill.). Letter to Editors of *Herald*, March 26, 1899, 261.
Salisbury, Katharine (Fountain Green, Ill.). Letter to Dear Friend, February 26, 1889, P19, fd. 46. Typescript copy. Community of Christ Library-Archives.
Salisbury, Katharine (Fountain Green, Ill.). Letter to Dear Sisters of the "Home Column," May 16, 1886. *Saints' Herald* 33, no. 26 (July 3, 1886): 404–5.
Salisbury, Katharine, and Josephine Salisbury. Letter to Elder George Lambert, February 10, 1899, to Bro. George [Lambert]. P21, f92, Community of Christ Library-Archives.
Salisbury, Solomon J. "Old Nauvoo Days Recalled." *Autumn Leaves* 37 (April 1924): 151–58.
Salisbury, W. J[enkins]. (Nauvoo, Ill.) Letter to Mr. [Thomas] Sharp, *Warsaw Signal* 3, no. 2 (April 8, 1846): 2.
Salter, Edwin. *History of Monmouth and Ocean Counties*. Bayonne, N.J.: F. Gardner & Son, 1890.
Saunders, Benjamin. Interviewed by William H. Kelley, ca. September 1884. In "Miscellany." Community of Christ Library-Archives, Independence, Mo.
Saunders, Lorenzo. Interviewed by E. L. Kelley, November 12, 1884. In E. L. Kelley Papers, "Miscellany," Community of Christ Library-Archives, Independence, Mo.

Saunders, Lorenzo. Interviewed by William H. Kelley, September 20, 1884, 4. In "Miscellany," Community of Christ Library-Archives, Independence, Mo.

Saunders, Lorenzo. Interviewed by William H. Kelley, September 17, 1884, verso of p. 13. In E. L. Kelley Papers, Community of Christ Library-Archives.

Scherer, Mark A. *The Journey of a People: The Era of Restoration, 1820 to 1844*. Independence, Mo.: Community of Christ Seminary Press, 2013.

"Sermon by Elder Wm. B. Smith. Delivered at the Saints' Church at Independence, Mo." *Zion's Ensign* (Independence, Mo.) 3, no. 35 (August 27, 1892): 2.

Sessions, Gene A. *Mormon Thunder: A Documentary History of Jedediah Morgan Grant*. Urbana: University of Illinois Press, 1982.

Sharp, Thomas. "Mormon Gull-Traps." *Warsaw Signal* 2, no. 16 (June 18, 1845): 1.

Sharp, Thomas. "Proclamation of Bill Smith." *Warsaw Signal* 2, no. 32 (October 29, 1845): 2. Editorial note, preceding William Smith's "Proclamation" in the same issue.

Sharp, Thomas C. "Trouble in the Holy City." *Warsaw Signal* 2, no. 15 (June 11, 1845): 2.

Sheen, Isaac. "Advice to the Saints" *Melchisedek & Aaronic Herald* (Covington, Ky.) 1, no. 5 (August 1849): 3.

Sheen, Isaac (Covington, Ky.) Letter to Hon. R[ichard] H. Stanton, May 4, 1850. *Frontier Guardian* 2, no. 11 (June 26, 1850): 3.

Sheen, Isaac. "A Prophetic Family Arrangement." *Covington Daily Union*, June 5, 1850, 2.

Sheen, Isaac. "Wm. Smith—The Imposter." *Daily Nonpareil* (Cincinnati, Ohio) 3, no. 185 (May 20, 1850): 2.

Sheen, Isaac. "The Work of the Lord." *Melchisedek & Aaronic Herald* (Covington, Ky.) 1, no. 6 (September 1849): 2.

Sheen, Isaaac, and William Smith. Letter to the House of Representatives, December 31, 1849.

Sheen, John Kirk. "Isaac Sheen First Editor of the 'Herald.'" *Saints' Herald* 57, no. 4 (January 26, 1910): 94–95.

Sheen, John K. *Polygamy, or the Veil Lifted*. York, Neb.: n.p., 1889.

Shepard, Bill. "The Notorious Hodges Brothers: Solving the Mystery of Their Destruction at Nauvoo." *John Whitmer Historical Association Journal* 26 (2006): 260–86.

Shepard, William, and H. Michael Marquardt. "Lyman E. Johnson: Forgotten Apostle." *Journal of Mormon History* 36, no. 1 (Winter 2010), 92–144.

Shepard, William. "Shadows on the Sun Dial: John E. Page and the Strangites," *Dialogue: A Journal of Mormon Thought* 41, no. 1 (Spring 2008): 34–66.

Shepard, William, and H. Michael Marquardt. *Lost Apostles: Forgotten Members of Mormonism's Original Quorum of Twelve*. Salt Lake City: Signature Books, 2014.

Shipps, Jan, and John W. Welch, eds. *The Journals of William E. McLellin, 1831–1836*. Urbana: University of Illinois Press/Provo, Utah: BYU Studies, 1994.

"Shorter by a Head." *Melchisedek & Aaronic Herald* 1, no. 8 (February 1850): 4.

"Singular Committee, A." *Melchisedek & Aaronic Herald* (Covington, Ky.) 1, no. 3 (May 1, 1845): 3.

Skidmore, Rex A. "Joseph Smith: A Leader and Lover of Recreation." *Improvement Era* 43 (December 1940): 716–17, 762–63.

"Slander Refuted." *Dixon Telegraph* 2, no. 51 (April 30, 1853): 2.

Small, William (St. Louis, Mo.) Letter to Benjamin Winchester, November 24, 1845. In *Messenger and Advocate of the Church of Christ* 2, no. 2 (December 1845): 407–8.

Smith, Alexander H. Letter Book, 1897–1901, MS 17756, LDS Church History Library.

Smith, Andrew F. *The Saintly Scoundrel: The Life and Times of John C. Bennett*. Urbana: University of Illinois Press, 1997.

Smith, Andrew F. *The Turkey: An American Story*. Chicago: University of Illinois Press, 2006.

Bibliography 617

Smith, Asael. "Address to His Family." Photographic facsimile reprinted in Richard L. Anderson, *Joseph Smith's New England Heritage*, rev. ed. Salt Lake City: Deseret Book and BYU Press, 2003.

Smith, Caroline Grant (Philadelphia, Pa.). Letter to Jedediah M. Grant, May 5, 1844. Grant Family Papers, 1844–1893. MS 3370. LDS Church History Library.

Smith, Caroline Louisa, and James S. Quince. First Marriage Register, 1839–73, December 8, 1853, Marriage Records of Lee County, Illinois, Book A, 57, Lee County Courthouse (old), Dixon, Illinois.

Smith, Don Carlos, and William Smith (Quincy, Ill.). Letter to Hyrum and Joseph Smith, March 6, 1839. In Joseph Smith Letterbook 2. LDS Church History Library.

Smith, Don C[arlos] (Nine Miles from Terre Haute, Indiana). Letter to Bro. Joseph [Smith], n.d., in Jessee, Ashurst-McGee, and Jensen, *Journals, Vol. 1, 1832–1839*, 280–81.

Smith, E. Gary. "The Patriarchal Crisis of 1845." *Dialogue: A Journal of Mormon Thought* 16, no. 2 (Summer 1983): 24–35.

Smith, Emma, comp. *A Collection of Sacred Hymns for the Church of the Latter Day Saints*. Kirtland, Ohio: F. G. Williams & Co., 1835.

Smith, George A. "Journal and Record Book, 1817–46." LDS Church History Library.

Smith, George A. "History of George A. Smith," 1845. George A. Smith Papers, 1834–1875, MS 1322, Box 1, fd. 1. LDS Church History Library.

Smith, George A. "Memoirs of George A. Smith." In George A. Smith Papers, 1834–1875, MS 1322, Box 1, fd. 1. LDS Church History Library.

Smith, George A. "My Journal." *Instructor* 83 (September 1948): 418.

Smith, George A. "Sketch of the Autobiography of George Albert Smith." *Deseret News* August 11, 1858, 1.

Smith, George D., ed. *An Intimate Chronicle: The Journals of William Clayton*. Salt Lake City: Signature Books, 1995.

Smith, George D. *Nauvoo Polygamy: . . . "but we called it celestial marriage"* Salt Lake City: Signature Books, 2008.

Smith, George D. "Nauvoo Roots of Mormon Polygamy, 1841–46: A Preliminary Demographic Report." *Dialogue: A Journal of Mormon Thought* 34, nos. 1–2 (Spring/Summer 2001): 150–56.

Smith, Hyrum (Commerce [Nauvoo], Ill.). Letter to the Saints Scattered Abroad, December 1839. *Times and Seasons* 1, no. 2 (December 1839): 21.

Smith, Hyrum. Diary, 1832–33, Box 1, fd. 5. Joseph Smith Sr. Family Collection, Perry Special Collections.

Smith, Jesse. Letter to Hyrum Smith, June 17, 1829. Joseph Smith Letterbook, 2:59–61. Joseph Smith Papers, LDS Church History Library.

Smith, John. Journal. LDS Church History Library, Salt Lake City.

Smith, John Henry. *Church, State, and Politics: The Diaries of John Henry Smith*. Edited by Jean Bickmore White. Salt Lake City: Signature Books, 1990.

Smith, Joseph, Jr. "History, 1838–1856," Vol. C-1, created February 24, 1845–July 3, 1845, and November 2, 1838–July 31, 1842, with Addenda September 14, 1840, 20, MS 7513, LDS Church History Library.

Smith, Joseph, Jr. "In Obedience to Our Promise." *Elders' Journal* 1, no. 3 (July 1838): 43.

Smith, Joseph, Jr. Interviewed by David Nye White, Nauvoo, Illinois, August 21, 1843. In David Nye White, "The Prairies, Nauvoo, Joe Smith, the Temple, the Mormons, &c.," *Pittsburgh Weekly Gazette* 58 (September 15, 1843): 3; photocopy at the LDS Church History Library.

Smith, Joseph, Jr. Letter to the Editor, June 22, 1835. *Painesville Telegraph* (Kirtland, Ohio), 1, no. 25 (June 26, 1835).

Smith, Joseph, Jr. (Kirtland Mills, Ohio). Letter to J. G. Fosdick, February 3, 1834, LDS Church History Library. Also available at http://josephsmithpapers.org/paperSummary/letter-to-j-g-fosdick-3-february-1834 (accessed December 12, 2014).

Smith, Joseph, Jr. (Kirtland, Ohio). Letter to William Smith, December 18 or 19, 1835. In Jessee, Ashurst-McGee, and Jensen, *Journals, Vol. 1, 1832–1839*, 132–33.

Smith, Joseph, Jr. Letter to the Twelve, December 15, 1840. *Millennial Star* 1 (March 1841): 266.

Smith, Joseph, Jr., and Kirtland High Council. Letter to Quorum of the Twelve (Kirtland, Ohio), August 4, 1835. In Joseph Smith. "Letter Book" (June 14, 1829–August 4, 1835), 89–90. Holograph.http://josephsmithpapers.org/paperSummary/letterbook-1#!/paperSummary/letterbook-1&p=105 (accessed March 2, 2015).

Smith, Joseph, Jr. "Remarks on Chartered Rights." *The Wasp* 1, no. 34 (December 24, 1842): 2.

Smith, Joseph, Jr., et al. *History of the Church of Jesus Christ of Latter-day Saints*. Edited by B. H. Roberts, 2d ed., rev., 7 vols. Salt Lake City: Deseret Book, 1971.

Smith, Joseph F. (Colchester, Ill.). Letter to Levira A. Smith, June 28, 1860, Joseph F. Smith Papers 1854–1918, MS 1325, LDS Church History Library.

Smith, Joseph F. (Salt Lake City). Letter to William Smith, July 12, 1884. MS 1325, Box 31, fd. 3. LDS Church History Library.

Smith, Joseph Fielding. *Blood Atonement and the Origin of Plural Marriage*. Salt Lake City: Deseret News, 1905.

Smith, Joseph Fielding. *Life of Joseph F. Smith*. Salt Lake City: Deseret Book, 1938.

Smith, Joseph, III (Lamoni, Iowa). Letter to Bro. Heman C. Smith, October 24, 1898, in *Saints' Herald* 46, no. 2 (January 11, 1899): 18.

Smith, Joseph, III (Lamoni, Iowa). Letter to William B. Smith, October 26, 1893. P13, f439, Community of Christ Library-Archives.

Smith, Joseph, III (Lamoni, Iowa). Letter to Bro. Heman C. Smith, October 24, 1898, *Saints' Herald* 46, no. 2 (January 11, 1899): 18.

Smith, Joseph, III (San Bernardino, Calif.). Interviewed by David Seeley, January 1889, Miscellany Collection, P19, fd. 47, Community of Christ Library-Archives.

Smith, Joseph, III, and Heman C. Smith, eds. *The History of the Reorganized Church of Jesus Christ of Latter Day Saints, 1805–1890*. 4 vols. (Independence, Mo: Herald House, 1896); continued by F. Henry Edwards as *The History of the Reorganized Church of Jesus Christ of Latter Day Saints*, Vols. 5–8 (Independence: Herald House 1897–1903; 1952 printing.

Smith, Joseph III, Letters to William B. Smith, Community of Christ Library-Archives:
January 12, 1878. Joseph Smith III Letterbook 1, 275–79
February 20, 1879; July 12, 1879; May 6, 1879; May 15, 1879, Joseph Smith III Letterbooks, Book 2, P6, 163–65.
March 11, 1882.
October 26, 1893, P13, f439,

Smith, Joseph, III. Letter to J[ohn W.] Peterson, November 8, 1893, Community of Christ Library-Archives.

Smith, Joseph, III. "Last Testimony of Sister Emma." *Saints' Herald*, October 1, 1879, 289–90.

Smith, Julia Priscilla (Kirtland, Ohio). Letter to Elias Smith, August 1837. In Elias Smith Correspondence, 1834–39, MS 70621. LDS Church History Library.

Smith, Lucy Mack. *Biographical Sketches of Joseph Smith the Prophet and His Progenitors for Many Generations*. Liverpool: S. W. Richards, 1853.

Smith, Lucy [Mack]. *Biographical Sketches of Joseph Smith the Prophet and His Progenitors for Many Generations*. (Lamoni, Iowa: Reorganized Church of Jesus Christ of Latter Day Saints, 1912.

Smith, Lucy (Nauvoo, Ill.). Letter to Messrs. Babbitt, Heywood, and Hulmer [sic], March 22, 1846. *Voree Herald* 1, no. 8 (August 1846): 3.
Smith, Lucy Mack (Nauvoo, Ill.). Letter to William Smith, January 23, 1845, LDS Church History Library.
Smith, Lucy [Mack]. Letter to Solomon Mack and wife, January 6, 1831, Waterloo, New York, LDS Church History Library.
Smith, Mary Jane. Marriage to Andrew Scott, October 24, 1852, First Marriage Register, 1839–73, Marriage Records of Lee County, Illinois, Book A, 46, Lee County Courthouse (old), Dixon, Illinois.
"Smith—Mrs. Eliza E., wife of W. B. Smith." *Saints' Herald* 36, no. 13 (March 30, 1889), 207.
Smith, Oliver R. *Journal of Jesse Nathaniel Smith*. Provo, Utah: Jesse N. Smith Family Association, 1970.
Smith, Oliver R., ed. *Six Decades in the West: The Journal of Jesse Nathaniel Smith*. Provo, Utah: Jesse N. Smith Family Assn., 1970.
Smith, Robin, and Ron Field. *Uniforms of the Civil War*. London: Lyons Press, 2001.
Smith, Rosanna B. Statement. William B. Smith Pension File. June 21, 1902, 29, Part 1, Widow's Pension, William B. Smith Pension File;
Smith, Samuel H. B. Autobiography, 1860–1863. In Samuel H. B. Smith Diary Collection, MSS SC 870, Perry Special Collections.
Smith, Walter Wayne. "History of the Philadelphia Branch." *Journal of History* (Lamoni, Iowa) 12, no. 1 (January 1919): 117–18. Serialized: 13, no. 4 (October 1920): 509–37.
Smith, William. *See also* items headlined "William Smith" and "Wm. Smith."
Smith, William. "Apology." *Wasp* 1, no. 4 (May 7, 1842): 2.
Smith, William, *Defence of Elder William Smith, Against the Slanders of Abraham Burtis and Others*. Philadelphia: Brown, Bicking & Guilbert, 1844.
Smith, William. Elders' Pocket Companion, ca. fall 1844. Reproduced in John K. Sheen. *Polygamy, or The Veil Lifted*. York, Neb.: n.pub., 1889.
Smith, William B. Epistle, ca. 1850, William Smith Papers, MS 3697, LDS Church History Library.
Smith, William. Interviewed by John W. Peterson and William S. Pender, July 4, 1890, Osterdock, Iowa. Typescript with handwritten corrections by John W. Peterson on May 1, 1921. Miscellaneous Letters and Papers, P13, f1490, Community of Christ Library-Archives, Independence, Mo.
Smith, William. "Introductory." *The Wasp* 1, no. 1 (April 16, 1842): 2.
Smith, William. "Just as Our Paper." *Wasp* 1, no. 2 (April 23, 1842): 2.
Smith, William B. (Elkader, Ia). Letter to William W. Blair, July 24, 1885, *Saints' Herald* 32, no. 32 (August 8, 1885): 514.
Smith, William B. (Elkader, Iowa). Letter to George A. Blakeslee, February 20, 1885, Community of Christ Library-Archives.
Smith, William (Bordentown, N.J.). Letter to Samuel Brannan, November 1, 1844. *Prophet* 1, no. 26 (November 16, 1844): 3.
Smith, William (New York City). Letter to [Samuel] Brannan. *Prophet* 1, no. 30 (December 14, 1844): 3.
Smith, William. Letter to Dear Brother [Brannan], ca. January, 1845, *Prophet* 1, no. 36 (January 25, 1845): 3. Also reprinted as "Letter from Eld. Wm. Smith." *Times and Seasons* 6 (February 15, 1845): 814.
Smith, William (St. Louis, Mo.). Letter to Samuel Brannan, November 14, 1845, LDS Church History Library.
Smith, William (Nauvoo, Ill.). Letter to Dear Brethren, May 10, 1845. *Nauvoo Neighbor* 3, no. 2 (May 14, 1845): 2–3.

Smith, William (Palestine, Ill.). Letter to Sister C_____, July 18, 1851, in *Dixon Telegraph* 2, no. 51 (April 30, 1853): 4.

Smith, William (Voree, Wisc.) "Letter to the Church of Jesus Christ of Latter Day Saints, July 28, 1846." In *Zion's Reveille* 1, no. 12 (December 1846): 3.

Smith, William. Letter to the Editor. *Wasp*, 1, no. 51 (April 19, 1843): 3.

Smith, William. Letter to the Editor of the Prophet. *Prophet* 1, no. 46 (April 5, 1845): 3.

Smith, William (Ottawa, Ill.), Letter to the Editor, September 16, 1847, *Ottawa Free Trader*, rpt., as "A Late Mormon Miracle." *Gospel Herald* 2, no. 40 (December 23, 1847): 2–3.

Smith, William (Warren, Pa.) Letter to the Editor, May 19, 1857, *New-York Daily Tribune*, May 28, 1857, 5.

Smith, Wm B. (Kingston, Mo.), Letter to the Editor, ca. March 1879, *Saints' Herald* 26, no. 8 (April 15, 1879): 125.

Smith, William B. Letter to the Editor. *Expositor* (Oakland, Calif.) 1, no. 5 (May 1885).

Smith, William (City of Joseph [Nauvoo, Ill.]). Letter to Joshua Grant Jr., August 12, 1845. *Nauvoo Neighbor* 3, no. 16 (August 20, 1845): 3.

Smith, William. Letter to Orson Hyde, November 12, 1845 (St. Louis). In *Messenger and Advocate of the Church of Christ* (Pittsburgh) 2, no. 2 (December 1845): 414–16. Also in *Warsaw Signal* 2, no. 36 (November 26, 1845): 2.

Smith, William (St. Louis, Mo.). Letters to Orson Hyde, June 2, 1847, June 22, 1847, Brigham Young Office Files 1832–78, Letters from Church Leaders and Others, 1840–1877, William Smith, 1844–1857, LDS Church History Library.

Smith, William (Osterdock, Ia.). Letters to Edmund Levi Kelley, P19, fds. 48 and 49: September 6, 1891, September 15, 1891, October 15, 1891, October 19, 1891, November 12, 1891, October–November, 1891; March 12, 1892, March 30, 1982, June 1, 1892, July 2, 1892, August 26, 1892, October 3, 1892, Community of Christ Library-Archives.

Smith, William. Letter to Brother [Edmund L. Kelley], ca. 1893. Suplament [sic], Miscellaneous Letters, P19, fd. 49. Community of Christ Library-Archives.

Smith, William (Galien, Mich.). Letter to William H. Kelley, June 5, 1883, October 15, 1891, October 3, 1892, October 7, 1892. Community of Christ Library-Archives.

Smith, William (Hornerstown, N.J.). Letter to Jedediah M. Grant, November 26, 1843. In *Defence of Elder William Smith against the Slander of Abraham Burtis, and Others*. Philadelphia: Brown, Bicking & Guilbert, 1844.

Smith, William (Bordentown, N.J.). Letter to Heber C. Kimball, December 21, 1844. Brigham Young Office Files, 1832–78, Box 42, fd. 13, LDS Church History Library.

Smith, William (Philadelphia). Letter to Respected Br. [George T.] Leach, June 3, 1844. In *Prophet* 1, no. 6 (June 22, 1844): 2.

Smith, William (Nauvoo, Ill.). Letter to Jesse C. Little, August 20, 1845. Typescript by Ireta Andersen, November 16, 1932, Utah State Historical Society.

Smith, William (Bordentown, N.J.). Letter to W. W. Phelps, November 10, 1844. *Prophet* 1, no. 27 (November 23, 1844): 3.

Smith, President Wm. Letter to Brother [David] Powell (Palestine Stake of Zion, Illinois), December 25, 1851, *Messenger* Salt Lake City) 2, no. 2 (December 1875): 1–2.

Smith, William (Brookfield, Mo.). Letter to Richard Randall, February 13, 1879, Richard Randall Papers, 1878–1914, MS 5764, LDS Church History Library.

Smith, William (Cincinnati, Ohio). Letter to Lewis Robbins, January 27, 1846, Brigham Young Collection, 1832–78, General Correspondence, Incoming, 1840–77, LDS Church History Library.

Smith, William (Galena, Ill.) Letter to Brother [David] Roggers [sic], October 8, 1845. Copied by Orson Pratt and sent to Brigham Young, Brigham Young Office Files, Letters from

Church Leaders and Others, 1840–1877, William Smith, 1844–1857, LDS Church History Library.

Smith, William B. Letter to the *Saints' Herald*, ca. March/April 1882. *Saints' Herald* 29, no. 8 (April 15, 1882): 119–20.

Smith, William (Shelburn, Ill.). Letter to Brother [Isaac] Sheen, April 29, 1850, in *Daily Nonpareil* (Cincinnati, Ohio) 3, no. 185 (May 20, 1850), 2; reprinted in *Frontier Guardian* 2, no. 2 (June 26, 1850), 3.

Smith, William (Plymouth, Ill.). Letter to D[on] C[arlos] Smith, December 1, 1840. In "Communications." *Times and Seasons* 2 (December 15, 1840): 252–53.

Smith, William (Armstrong County, Pa.). Letter to Elder D[on] C[arlos] Smith, May 8, 1841. *Times and Seasons* 2, no. 16 (June 15, 1841): 444–45.

Smith, William (St. Louis, Mo.), Letter to Emma Smith, [November] 21, 1845, LDS Church History Library.

Smith, William (Chester County, Pa.). Letter to Joseph Smith, August 5, 1841, LDS Church History Library.

Smith, William (Philadelphia, Pa.). Letter to Joseph Smith, October 28, 1843, LDS Church History Library.

Smith, William (Elkader, Iowa), Letter to Joseph Smith III [also "Dear Nephew"].
  October 16, 1868. Community of Christ Library-Archives.
  (Elkader, Ia.). Letter to Joseph [Smith III], December 12, 1873. *True Latter Day Saints' Herald* 21, no. 1 (January 1, 1874): 19–20.
  January 25, 1879, *Saints' Herald* 26, no. 4 (February 15, 1879): 62.
  May 28, 1879. In *Saints' Herald* 26, no. 13 (July 1, 1879): 206.
  (Hannibal, Mo.), Letter to Joseph Smith III, January 25, 1879. *Saints' Herald* 26, no. 4 (February 15, 1879): 62.
  March 21, 1880. *Saints' Herald* 27, no. 8 (April 15, 1880): 122.
  (Elkader, Iowa). Letter to Joseph [Smith III], Dear Nephew, April 4, 1880. *Saints' Herald* 27, no. 10 (May 15, 1880): 158–59.
  October 24, 1880, *Saints' Herald* 27, no. 23 (December 1, 1880): 369.
  July 23, 1883, *Saints' Herald* 30, no. 32 (August 11, 1883): 507–8.
  October 19, 1883, Miscellaneous Letters and Papers, P13, f2311, Community of Christ Library-Archives.
  March 2, 1884, *Saints' Herald* 31, no. 12 (March 22, 1884): 181.
  Smith, William (Elkader, Iowa), Letter to Dear Nephew [Joseph Smith III], October 16, 1868, *Saints' Herald* 8, no. 1 (January 1, 1869): 22–23.
  (Elkader, Ia.). Letter to Respected Nephew [Joseph Smith III], November 11, 1872. *True Latter Day Saints' Herald* 19, no. 23 (December 1, 1872): 723.
  ca. December 1878, *Saints' Herald* 26, no. 1 (January 1, 1879): 1–2.
  October 19, 1883. Miscellaneous Letters and Papers, P13, f2311, Community of Christ Library-Archives. Also "A Synopsis of the First Chap. of the Gospel of St. William," August 17, 1845, Nauvoo, Illinois, reported by George D. Watt, LDS Church History Library.
  (Elkader, Iowa). Letter to Joseph Smith III, April 18, 1884, *Saints' Herald* 31, no. 19 (May 10, 1884): 290.
  (La Crosse, Ill.). Letter to Joseph Smith III, July 17, 1886, *Saints' Herald* 33, no. 30 (July 31, 1886): 469–70.

Smith, William (et al.) (Shelburn [Palestine Grove], Ill.). Letter to the Honorable Senators & Representatives of the United States in Congress Assembled, January 29, 1850, Brigham Young Office Files 1832–1878, Utah Delegate Files, 1849–1872, John M. Bernhisel to Brigham Young, 1849–1866, 1849–1850 March–May, LDS Church History Library.

Smith, William (Covington, Ky.). "Letter to the Saints Scattered Abroad, Greeting, September 30, 1849." *Melchisedek & Aaronic Herald* 1, no. 6 (September 1849): 1, and continued in 1, no. 7 (October 1849): 1.

Smith, William (Nauvoo, Ill.) Letters to James Jesse Strang:
    March 1, 1846 [date incorrect], *Voree Herald* 1, no. 7 (July, 1846): 31.
    March 11, 1846, *Voree Herald* 1, no. 4 (April 1846): 7.
    March 17, 1846. LDS Church History Library; also James Jesse Strang Papers, 1829–70, WA MSS-186–189, Beinecke Rare Book and Manuscript Library, Yale University, New Haven, Conn.
    April 12, 1846, *Voree Herald* 1, no. 6 (June 1846): 3–4.
    ca. November, 1846. Strang Collection.
    December 2, 7, 19, 1846, Strang Collection.
    December 25, 1846, Strang Collection.
    February 10, 1847, in "Letter from the Patriarch," *Zion's Reveille* 2, no. 7 (February 25, 1847): 3–4.

Smith, William. Letter to Elder Tailor [sic], Editor of the *Neighbor*. ca. May/June 1845, Box 42, fd. 13, Brigham Young Office Files 1832–78, LDS Church History Library.

Smith, William (Shelburn [Palestine Grove], Ill.). Letter to the Hon. John Wentworth, January 25, 1850. Brigham Young Office Files 1832–1878, Utah Delegate Files, 1849–1872, John M. Bernhisel to Brigham Young, 1849–1866, 1849–1850 March–May, LDS Church History Library.

Smith, William (Ellington, Conn.) Letter to Dear Brother Lyman Wight, April 21, 1849. *Melchisedek and Aaronic Herald* 1, no. 4 (June 1849): 1–2.

Smith, William (Bordentown, N.J.), Letters to Brigham Young, August 24, 1844, September 9, 1844, October 16, 1844, December 21, 1844, December 26, 1844, June 25, 1845, August 8, 1854, May 7, 1855, July 13, 1856. Brigham Young Office Files 1832–1878. Letters from Church Leaders and Others, 1840–1877. William Smith, 1844–1857. LDS Church History Library.

Smith, William (Augusta, Iowa Territory). Letter to Pres. B[righam] Young or Lewis Robbins. September 28, 1845. Brigham Young Office Files 1832–1878, Letters from Church Leaders and Others, 1840–1877, William Smith, 1844–1857, LDS Church History Library.

Smith, William (Nauvoo, Ill.). Letter to Brigham Young and Council of the Twelve, June 30, 1845. In George D. Smith, ed., *An Intimate Chronicle: The Journals of William Clayton* Salt Lake City: Signature Books, 1995), 170–71. Also in Dean C. Jessee, ed., *John Taylor Nauvoo Journal*. Provo, Utah: Grandin Book, 1996, 77–78.

Smith, William (Philadelphia). Letter to Brigham Young or Heber C. Kimball, March [no day], 1845, LDS Church History Library.

Smith, Wm., married Eliza E. Sanburne, November 12, 1857." Probate Court Marriage Records, Lake County Ohio, 1840–1865. Typescript, 102, Morley Library, Painesville, Ohio.

Smith, William. "Mormonism." Qtd. in "Clayton Co. Journal." *True Latter Day Saints' Herald* 1, no. 15 (January 1, 1869): 23.

Smith, William. "Notes Written on 'Chambers' Life of Joseph Smith,'" ca. 1875. LDS Church History Library.

Smith, William. "Notice." *Prophet* 1, no. 37 (February 1, 1845): 2.

Smith, William. "Notice." *Nauvoo Neighbor* 3, no. 6 (June 11, 1845): 3.

Smith, William. "Notice to Emigrants." *Nauvoo Neighbor* 3, no. 3 (May 21, 1845): 3.

Smith, William. "Official Notice." *Prophet* 1, no. 17 (September 14, 1844): 2.

Smith, William. "Opinions of the Smith Family." *Voree Herald* 1, no. 6 (June 1846): 1.

Smith, William. "Patriarchal." *Times and Seasons* 6 (May 15, 1845): 904.

Smith, William. Patriarchal Blessing bestowed by Joseph Smith Sr., December 9, 1834. Patriarchal Blessing Book 1, 10–11. LDS Church History Library.
Smith, William B. Pension File. *See* Pension File.
Smith, William. "Proclamation." *Warsaw Signal* 2, no. 32 (October 29, 1845): 1, 4.
Smith, William. *A Revelation Given to William Smith, in 1847, On the Apostacy of the Church and the Pruning of the Vineyard of the Lord.* N.p., 1848, M293. LDS Church History Library.
Smith, William. "Sharp, of the Signal . . ." *Wasp* 1, no. 18 (August 20, 1842): 2.
Smith, William. "Some Well Disposed Persons." *Wasp* 1, no. 20 (September 3, 1842): 2.
Smith, William. "The Saints Will Notice." Unpublished announcement, ca. May 1845, Brigham Young Office Files 1832–78, Box 42, fd. 13, LDS Church History Library.
Smith, William. Sworn statement, October 22, 1883, Clayton County, Iowa, before T. G. Price, Notary Public; published as, "The 'Endowment': Statement of William B. Smith, The Only Surviving Brother of the Seer," *Saints' Advocate* (Plano, Ill.) 2, no. 6 (December 1879): 65.
Smith, William. Testimony, 185–86. In *Eighth Circuit Court of the United States, Western Division at Kansas City—The Reorganized Church of Jesus Christ of Latter day Saints, Complainant vs. The Church of Christ at Independence,* 1892. Complete transcript, microfilm and digitized. MS 1160, LDS Church History Library. Also full transcription in Lyndon W. Cook, William Smith Collection. Item #206, 360–415, Community of Christ Library-Archives, Independence; and *The Temple Lot Case.* Lamoni, Iowa.: Herald Publishing House and Bindery, 1893.
Smith, William. "The Turkey." *The Wasp* 1, no. 2 (April 23, 1842): 2.
Smith, William, vs. Mary Jane [Rollins] Smith, May and June Terms, 1847, Circuit Court Records, Knox County Courthouse, Galesburg, Illinois.
Smith, William. *William Smith on Mormonism.* Lamoni, Iowa: Herald Steam Book and Job Office, 1883.
Smith, William. *William Smith, Patriarch & Prophet of the Most High God. Latter Day Saints Beware of Imposition!* Ottawa, Ill.: William Smith, September 1847.
Smith, William. *Zion's Standard: A Voice from the Smith Family.* Princeton, IL: P. Lynch, March 24, 1848.
Smith, William, and Roxey Ann Grant Marriage License. Marriage Index Book 1, 84, Knox County Courthouse, Galesburg, Illinois.
Smith, William, and Aaron Hook. *William Smith, Patriarch & Prophet of the Most High God. Latter Days Saints, Beware of Imposition!* N.p., ca. 1847, M293,1, LDS Church History Library.
Smith, William, and Isaac Sheen (Covington, Ky.). Letter to the House of Representatives of the United States of America, December 31, 1849, House Miscellaneous Documents, 31st Congress, 1st Session, Document No. 43.
Smith, William, and Isaac Sheen (Covington, Ky.). Letter to President Zachary Taylor, January 1, 1850, National Archives.
Special Conference." *Melchisedek & Aaronic Herald* (Covington, Ky.) 1, no. 4 (June 1849): 4.
Special Report of the Bristol and Clifton Ladies' Anti-Slavery Society. London: John Snow, 1852.
"Speech of Mr. [William] Smith of Hancock County, on the Resolution of Mr. Davis of Bond, to Repeal the Nauvoo Charter, Delivered in the House of Representatives, December 9, 1842." *Wasp* 1, no. 37 (January 14, 1843): 1–2.
Speek, Vickie Cleverley. *God Has Made Us a Kingdom: James Strang and the Midwest Mormons.* Salt Lake City: Signature Books, 2006.
Sperduto, Frant V. "William A. Newell, Class of 1836." *Journal of the Rutgers University Libraries* 29, no. 3 (1966): 74–75.
St. Lawrence Co., New York. Surrogate's Court, Probate Records, 1830–1919. Microfilm 890,065, U.S. and Canada Record Collection, LDS Family History Library, Salt Lake City. See also http://josephsmithpapers.org/back/joseph-smith-pedigree-chart (accessed January 14, 2014).

Staines, Priscilla M. Testimony, Temple Lot Case Testimonies, 528–529, U.S. Eighth Circuit Court, 1892, MS 1160, LDS Church History Library.

Staker, Mark Lyman. *Hearken, O My People: The Historical Setting of Joseph Smith's Ohio Revelations.* Salt Lake City: Greg Kofford Books, 2009.

Stanton, R[ichard] H. (May 14, 1850). Letter to House of Representatives. *Frontier Guardian* 2, no. 11 (June 26, 1850): 3.

"Star in the East, The." *Zion's Reveille* (Voree, Wisc.) 1, no. 12 (December 1846): 1.

Stevens, Frank E. *History of Lee County Illinois.* 2 vols. Chicago: S. J. Clarke Publishing, 1914.

Stevenson, Russell W. *For the Cause of Righteousness: A Global History of Blacks and Mormonism, 1830–2013.* Salt Lake City: Greg Kofford Books, 2014.

Stevenson, Russell W. "A Negro Preacher": The Worlds of Elijah Ables," *Journal of Mormon History* 39, no. 2 (Spring 2013): 216–21.

Strang, James J. Letter to George Adams, May 5, 1846, fd. 60, Strang Collection.

Strang, James J. (Voree, Wisc.). Letter to Dear Brother [Orange L. Wight], September 13, 1848. *Gospel Herald* 3, no. 27 (September 21, 1848): 4–6.

Strang, James J. "Official," *Zion's Reveille* 2, no. 21 (August 12, 1847): 4.

"Synopsis of the First Chap. of the Gospel of St. William, A." August 17, 1845, Nauvoo, Illinois, reported by George D. Watt, LDS Church History Library.

Taylor, John. Editorial. *Times and Seasons* 5, no. 22 (December 1, 1844): 727.

Taylor, John. "Patriarchal." *Times and Seasons* 6 (June 1, 1845): 920–22.

Taylor, John. "We Have Just Received." *Times and Seasons* 5, no. 22 (December 1, 1844): 727.

Temple Lot Case. See *Eighth Circuit Court of the United States, Western Division at Kansas City—The Reorganized Church of Jesus Christ of Latter day Saints, Complainant vs. The Church of Christ at Independence,* 1892. Complete transcript, microfilm and digitized. MS 1160, LDS Church History Library. Also an edited version in, *The Temple Lot Case.* Lamoni, Iowa.: Herald Publishing House and Bindery, 1893.In United States testimony 1892, Court of Appeals (8th Circuit), 501–02, MS 1160, LDS Church History Library.

Terry, Thomas S. Autobiographical sketch, 1857. Val A. Browning Library, Dixie State University, St. George, Utah.

"Texas." *Melchisedek and Aaronic Herald* 1, no. 9 (April 1850): 2.

"The Greatest Annual Conference." *Melchisedek and Aaronic Herald* 1, no. 9 (April 1850): 2–3.

Thomas, E. H. "Life on the Mississippi," 1912–13. Series of articles published in the *Burlington Saturday Evening Post.* Transcription by Georgeann McClure, Iowa History Project, Chapter 37. http://iagenweb.org/history/rivers/burlingtonpost/contents.htm (accessed May 9, 2013).

Thompson, Edward (Keokuk, Iowa). Letter to Hugh Herringshaw, May 26, 1846, MS 22665. LDS Church History Library.

Thurston, Morris A. "The Boggs Shooting and Attempted Extradition." *BYU Studies* 48, no. 1 (2009): 13–28.

"Timely Defense, A." *Saints Herald* 40, no. 19 (May 13, 1893), 294.

Titterton, Robert J. *Julian Scott: Artist of the Civil War and Native America.* Jefferson, N.C.: McFarland & Company, 1997.

U.S. Census.
    1840. Illinois, Stark County.
    1850, Illinois, Hancock County, September 17, 1850, Roll M432_109, 296B, image 60.
        Illinois, Knox County, Township 13 N. 3 E., November 8, 1850, Roll: M432_113, 415A, image 416.
            Illinois, Lee County, Amboy Township, Illinois; Roll M432_116, 117A, images 88–89, 216A.
        Illinois, Knox County, Walnut Grove.

Maine, Penobscot County, Howland, Roll M432_266; 284B, image 145.
1860 U.S. Census, Ohio, Lake County, Willoughby, Roll M653_996, 297, image 133.
Pennsylvania, Erie County, Venango, Roll M653_1108, 1061, image 454.
Wisconsin, Columbia County, Lodi, Film #1032686, Line 48, images 387, 396, and 00389.
1870 U.S. Census, Illinois, Lee County, Amboy, Roll M593_246, 216A.
Iowa, Clayton County, Boardman, 27; Roll M593_383, 152A, image 31.
Clayton County, Mallory, Roll 425, 4A.
Wisconsin, Dane County, Madison, Roll M593_1708, 331B, image 667.
1880 U.S. Census, Iowa, Clayton County, Boardman Township, Roll: 333, 278D, Image 0199.
Missouri, Linn County, Brookfield, Roll 700, film 1254700, 426A.
1900 Iowa, Clayton County, Mallory, Roll 425, 4A.
1910 South Dakota, Sanborn County, Logan, Roll T624_1486, 15B.
1920 Idaho, Kootenai County, Kootenai, Roll T625_291, 27B.
"To the Friends and Voters of Hancock County." *Nauvoo Neighbor* 2, no. 3 (May 15, 1844): 2.
"To the Scattered Saints." *Zion's Standard: A Voice from the Smith Family*. Princeton, IL: P. Lynch, March 24, 1848.
Tourtillott, Duane A. "Book of Remembrance." 1978, Tourtillott Family Papers, Wisconsin State Archives, University of Wisconsin at Green Bay.
Transcript of Testimony. *See* Temple Lot Case.
Tredwell, Daniel M. *Personal Reminiscences of Men and Things on Long Island, Part 1*. Brooklyn, N.Y.: Charles Andrew Ditmas, 1912.
"Trio, A." *Gospel Herald* (Voree, Wisc.) 2, no. 39 (December 16, 1847): 184.
"Trouble in the Church." *Dixon Telegraph* 3, no. 44 (March 9, 1854): 2.
Trouble in the Holy City." *Warsaw Signal* 2, no. 15 (June 11, 1845): 1.
"Trouble in the Mormon Camp." *Warsaw Signal* 2, no. 36 (November 26, 1845): 2.
"Truth Prevailing." *Times and Seasons* 2, no. 10 (March 15, 1841): 350.
Tucker, Pomeroy. *Origin, Rise, and Progress of Mormonism*. New York: D. Appleton and Company, 1867.
Tullidge, Edward W. *The Women of Mormondom*. New York: Tullidge and Crandall, 1877.
Turley, Richard E., ed. *Selected Collections from the Archives of the Church of Jesus Christ of Latter-day Saints*, 2 vols., DVD Provo, Utah: Brigham Young University Press, [December 2002].
Tyler, Daniel. "Incidents of Experience." In *Scraps of Biography: Tenth Book of the Faith-Promoting Series*. Salt Lake City: Juvenile Instructor Office, 1883.
Tyler, Daniel. Reminiscence. In "Recollections of the Prophet Joseph Smith," *Juvenile Instructor* 27, no. 4 (February 15, 1892): 127–28.
U.S. Federal Census. *See* U.S. Census.
Van Dine, Warren L. "Catharine Smith Salisbury." Typescript, 1972. Community of Christ Library-Archives.
Van Wagoner, Richard S. *Sidney Rigdon: A Portrait of Religious Excess*. Salt Lake City: Signature Books, 1994.
Vogel, Dan, ed. *Early Mormon Documents*. 5 vols. Salt Lake City: Signature Books, 1996–2003.
Vogel, Dan. *Joseph Smith: The Making of a Prophet*. Salt Lake City: Signature Books, 2004.
Walker, Kyle R. "'As Fire Shut Up in My Bones': Ebenezer Robinson, Don Carlos Smith, and the 1840 Edition of the Book of Mormon." *Journal of Mormon History* 36, no. 1 (Winter 2010): 1–40.
Walker, Kyle R. *The Joseph Sr. and Lucy Mack Smith Family: A Family Process Analysis of a Nineteenth-Century Household*. Ph.D. diss., Brigham Young University, 2001; published under the same title as part of the BYU Studies/Joseph Fielding Smith Institute for Latter-day Saint History, 2008. All quotations are from the 2008 edition.

Walker, Kyle R., ed. *United by Faith: The Joseph Sr. and Lucy Mack Smith Family.* American Fork, Utah: BYU Studies and Covenant Communications, 2006.

Walker, Kyle R. "Katharine Smith Salisbury." In Kyle R. Walker, ed. *United by Faith: The Joseph Sr. and Lucy Mack Smith Family.* American Fork, Utah: BYU Studies and Covenant Communications, 2006, 308–52.

Walker, Kyle R. "Katharine Smith Salisbury's Recollections of Joseph's Meetings with Moroni." *BYU Studies* 41, no. 3 (2002): 4–17.

Walker, Kyle R. "Looking after the First Family of Mormonism: LDS Church Leaders' Support of the Smiths after the Murders of Joseph and Hyrum." *John Whitmer Historical Association Journal* 32, no. 1 (Spring/Summer 2012): 17–32.

Walker, Kyle R. "William B. Smith." In *United by Faith: The Joseph Sr. and Lucy Mack Smith Family.* Edited by Kyle R. Walker. American Fork, Utah: BYU Studies and Covenant Communications, 2005, 274–91.

Walker, Ronald W. "Qualities That Count: Heber J. Grant as Businessman, Missionary, and Apostle." *BYU Studies.* Special issue, 43, no. 1 (2004).

Wallace, George Benjamin. Journal, 1845, MS 22868. LDS Church History Library.

Ward, Maurine Carr. "Philadelphia Pennsylvania Branch Membership: 1840–1854." *Mormon Historical Studies* 6, no. 1 (Spring 2005): 67–98.

Wasson, Harmon (Binghamton, Ill.). Letter to Emma [Smith] Bidamon, May 14, 1848, Wiford C. Wood Collection, MS f413, LDS Church History Library.

Wasson, Lorenzo D., Emma Hale Smith, and Joseph Smith (Nauvoo, Ill.). Letter to David Hale, February 20, 1841, MS 7395, LDS Church History Library.

Watson, Elden J., ed. *Manuscript History of Brigham Young, 1801–1844.* Salt Lake City: Smith Secretarial Service, 1968.

"We Have Just Received." *Times and Seasons* 5, no. 22 (December 1, 1844): 727.

"We Understand." *Warsaw Signal* 2, no. 5 (June 9, 1841): 2.

Welch, John W., ed., "Jesse Smith's 1814 Protest," *BYU Studies* 33, no. 1 (1993): 131–44.

Whayne, Jeannie M., Thomas A. Deblack, George Sabo III, and Morris S. Arnold. *Arkansas: A Narrative History.* Fayetteville: University of Arkansas Press, 2002.

Whittaker, David J. "East of Nauvoo: Benjamin Winchester and the Early Mormon Church," *Journal of Mormon History* 21, no. 2 (Fall 1995): 30–83.

Wight, Lyman. Journal. Qtd. in Joseph Smith III and Heman C. Smith, eds., *The History of the Reorganized Church of Jesus Christ of Latter Day Saints,* 4 vols. (Independence, Mo.: Herald Publishing House, 1952 printing), 3:34.

Wight, Lyman (Zodiac Mills, Tex.) Letter to Mother [Lucy Mack] Smith, August 21, 1848. *Melchisedeck and Aaronic Herald* 1, no. 3 (May 1, 1849): 4. Postscript to Orange Wight.

Wight, Lyman (Zodiac Mills, Tex.). Letters to Brother William Smith:
August 22, 1848. *Melchisedic and Aaronic Herald* 1, no. 2 (March 1849): 1.
July 26, 1849. *Mechisedek & Aaronic Herald* 1, no. 6 (September 1849): 2–3.
November 4, 1849, *Melchisedek & Aaronic Herald* 1, no. 8 (February 1850): 1.

Wight, Orange L. (Mount Sterling, Ill.). Letter to James J. Strang, August 22, 1848. *Gospel Herald* 3, no. 27 (September 21, 1848): 4.

Wight, Orange. Postscript in letter from Lyman Wight (Zodiac Mills, Tex.). Letter to Mother [Lucy Mack] Smith, August 21, 1848, *Melchisedeck and Aaronic Herald* 1, no. 3 (May 1, 1849): 4.

Wilcox, Pearl. *Regathering of the Scattered Saints in Wisconsin and Illinois.* Independence, Mo.: Pearl G. Wilcox, 1984.

Wilford Woodruff's Journal, 1833–1898. Edited by Scott G. Kenney. Typescript, 9 vols. Midvale, Utah: Signature Books, 1983–84.

Willard, Frances E., and Mary A. Livermore, eds. *A Woman of the Century: Fourteen Hundred-Seventy Biographical Sketches Accompanied by Portraits of Leading American Women in All Walks of Life*. Buffalo, N.Y.: Charles Wells Moulton, 1893.

"William B. Smith, Company G, 126 IL US INF." Illinois Civil War Muster and Descriptive Rolls. Illinois State Archives. http://www.ilsos.gov/isaveterans/civilMusterSearch.do?key=237510 (accessed March 11, 2015).

"William B. Smith Experience and Testimony." *Saints' Herald* 30, no. 16 (June 16, 1883): 388.

"William B. Smith." *Deseret Evening News*, December 19, 1893, 4.

"William B. Smith." *Expositor* (Oakland, Calif.) 4, no. 8 (August 1888): 3, 5.

"William Smith." *Peoria Democratic Press* 4, no. 11 (April 23, 1845): 2.

"William Smith." *Zion's Reveille* 1, no. 12 (December 1846): 3.

"William B. Smith: Experience and Testimony." *Saints' Herald* 30, no. 16 (June 16, 1883): 388.

Williams, Nathan H. "Lucy Smith Millikin." In Kyle R. Walker, ed. *United by Faith: The Joseph Sr. and Lucy Mack Smith Family*. American Fork, Utah: Covenant Communications/Provo, Utah: BYU Studies, 2006, 399–431.

Wilson, Lycurgus A. *Life of David W. Patten: The First Apostolic Martyr*. Salt Lake City: Deseret News, 1904.

Winchester, Benjamin (Philadelphia, Pa.). Letter to Joseph Smith, September 18, 1841. Joseph Smith Collection. LDS Church History Library.

Winchester, Benjamin. "Meeting of the Mormons Last Evening." *Prophet* 1, no. 26 (November 16, 1844): 2.

Winchester, Benjamin. *The Origin of the Spaulding Story, Concerning the Manuscript Found*. Philadelphia: Brown, Bicking & Guilbert, 1840.

Winchester, Benjamin. *Plain Facts, Shewing the Origin of the Spaulding Story, Concerning the Manuscript Found, and Its Being Transformed into the Book of Mormon; with a Short History of Dr. P. Hulbert, the Author of the Said Story*. Bedford, Mass.: C. B. Merry, 1841.

"Wm B. Smith's Last Statement." *Zion's Ensign* 5, no. 3 (January 13, 1894): 6.

"Wm. I. Appleby, if the Truth Is Told by the Frontier Guardian." *Melchisedek and Aaronic Herald* (Covington, Ky.) 1, no. 5 (August 1849): 4.

"Wm. Smith—Fornication—Adultery." *Daily Cincinnati Commercial* 12 (May 22, 1850): 4.

"Wm. Smith's Contradiction of a Utah Rumor." *True Latter Day Saints' Herald* 7, no. 1 (July 1860): 172.

"Wm. B. Smith's Last Statement." [John W. Peterson to Editor], *Zion's Ensign* (Independence, Mo.) 5 (January 13, 1894): 6.

Wisconsin State Census, 1855, Columbia County, Lodi.

Wood, Joseph (Palestine, Ill.). Letter to Jason W. Briggs, September 30, 1851, P13, f80, Community of Christ Library-Archives.

Wood, Joseph (Perry, Ill.). Letter to Bro's. [Ebenezer] Robinson and [Don Carlos] Smith. March 26, 1840. *Times and Seasons* 1, no. 6 (April 1840): 87–88.

Wood, Joseph. *Epistle of the Twelve*. Milwaukee, Wisc.: Sentinel and Gazette Steam Press Print, 1851.

Woodruff, Wilford (Boston, Mass.). Letters to Brigham Young, October 9 and 14, 1844, November 16, 1844, December 3, 1844. Brigham Young Office Files 1832–1878, Letters from Church Leaders and Others, 1840–1877, Wilford Woodruff, 1844, LDS Church History Library.

Woods, Fred E. *Gathering to Nauvoo*. American Fork, Utah: Covenant Communications, 2002.

Woods, Fred E. "The Cemetery Record of William D. Huntington, Nauvoo Sexton." *Mormon Historical Studies* 3, no. 1 (Spring 2002): 131–63.

"Work of the Lord, The." *Melchisedek & Aaronic Herald* 1, no. 6 (September 1849): 2.

Wright, Dennis A. "Caroline Young Harris: The Kirtland Wife of Martin Harris." In *Regional Studies in Latter-day Saint Church History: Ohio and Upper Canada*. Edited by Guy L.

Dorius, Craig K. Manscill, and Craig James Ostler. Provo, Utah: BYU Religious Studies Center, 2006), 111–23.

Wright, Jonathan C. (Nauvoo, Ill.). Letter to William Smith, August 28, 1844. *Prophet* 1, no. 31 (December 21, 1844): 2–3.

Wrigley, Thomas. In Kate B. Carter, ed. *The Mormons in St. Louis*. Salt Lake City: Daughters of Utah Pioneers, 1962.

Young, Brigham. "History of Brigham Young," *Millennial Star* 25 (June 6, 1863): 360–61.

Young, Brigham. Letter to Lucy [Mack] Smith, August 2, 1845, LDS Church History Library; also cited in Dean C. Jessee, "The Writings of Brigham Young," *Western Historical Quarterly* 4, no. 3 (July 1973): 273-294.

Young, Brigham (Nauvoo, Ill.). Letters to Parley P. Pratt, April 10, 1845, May 10, 1845, May 26, 1845. Brigham Young Office Files 1832–1878, General Correspondence, Outgoing, 1843–1876, 1845 January–May, LDS Church History Library.

Young, Brigham (City of Joseph [Nauvoo], Ill.). Letters to Brother Wm Smith Patriarch, June 30, 1845, August 10, 1845. Brigham Young Office Files 1832–1878, General Correspondence, Outgoing, 1843–1876, 1845 June–August, LDS Church History Library.

Young, Brigham (Nauvoo, Ill.). Letter to Beloved Br. William [Smith], September 28, 1844. LDS Church History Library.

Young, Brigham (Nauvoo, Ill.). Letter to William Smith, September 28, 1844. *Prophet* 1, no. 25 (November 9, 1844): 2.

Young, Brigham (Nauvoo, Ill.). Letter to Wilford Woodruff, June 27, 1845. Brigham Young Office Files 1832–1878, General Correspondence, Outgoing, 1843–1876, 1845 June–August, LDS Church History Library.

Young, Brigham, and Willard Richards (Winter Quarters, Neb.). Letter to Orson Spencer, November 25, 1847, Brigham Young Office Files 1832–1878, General Correspondence, Outgoing, 1843–1876, 1847 October–December, LDS Church History Library.

Young, Brigham, for the Council of the Twelve (Winter Quarters). Letter to Lucy Mack Smith, April 4, 1847. Brigham Young Office Files 1832–1878, General Correspondence, Outgoing, 1843–1876, 1847 March–May, LDS Church History Library.

Young, Brigham. Journal, 1845. Brigham Young Office Files 1832–1878, CR 1234 1, Journal, 1844 September 28–1846 February 3, LDS Church History Library.

Young, Brigham. "Notice to the Churches Abroad." *Times and Seasons* 6 (April 15, 1845): 878.

Young, Brigham. Office Journal, 1860. CR 1234 1, Box 72, fd. 5, LDS Church History Library.

Young, Brigham. Patriarchal Blessing bestowed on William Smith, May 24, 1845. Brigham Young Office Files 1832–1878, President's Office Files, 1843–1877, Recommends, Certificates, and Ordination Records, 1843–1871, Blessing of William Smith, 1845 May 24, LDS Church History Library.

Young, E. H. *A History of Round Prairie and Plymouth, 1831–1875*. Chicago: Geo. J. Titus, Book and Job Printer, 1876.

"Youths' Domestic Missionary Society." *Palmyra Herald* 2 (November 6, 1822): 3.

Zimmerman, Dean R., ed. *I Knew the Prophets: An Analysis of the Letter of Benjamin F. Johnson to George F. Gibbs, Reporting Doctrinal Views of Joseph Smith and Brigham Young*. Bountiful, Utah: Horizon Publishers, 1976.

Zion's Standard: A Voice from the Smith Family. Princeton, Ill.: P. Lynch, March 24, 1848.

Index

Note: WBS: William B. Smith
JSS: Joseph Smith Sr.
JSJ: Joseph Smith Jr.

A–B

Ables, Elijah, and WBS, 439–40, 442
Ables, Mary Ann Adams, 439
Adams, George J.
  and church at Augusta, Iowa, 234, 250, 300, 302–03
  and finances, 201–2, 232–34
  and lineal succession, 318, 497
  and JSJ, 313–14
  and Parley P. Pratt, 205, 236, 245
  and WBS "Proclamation," 304
  and plural marriage, 190, 200, 233, 240, 332–34, 338
  and Strang, 319, 329, 338, 353
  as actor, 307–08, 318
  as orator, 187–88
  Church trials, 232–36, 246, 277
  in eastern branches, 190, 198
  personality, 187–88
  recruits WBS, 234, 302, 313
  "thirteenth apostle," 205, 233
  WBS visits, 344–45
Anderson, Lavina Fielding, 19
Anderson, William, 343–44, 437, 365–68, 580–81
Appleby, William I., 317, 365–68, 437
Archer, Evanade, 331, 334–37, 579–80
Arkansas River Valley, 451–52
Atwood, Simeon, 426
Babbitt, Almon Whiting, 211, 372, 468–74
  and debating school, 112–14
  as lawyer, 539
  as trustee, 359, 372, 375–76, 418, 468–74, 482
  JSS patriarchal blessing book, 388–90
Backenstos, Clara Wasson, 340–42
Backenstos, William, 340
Ball, Joseph T., 201, 437–39, 442

Barrett, Jotham T., 415, 418
Beebe, Enoch, 428
Bennet, James Arlington, 162
Bennett, John C., 160–65,
  and James J. Strang, 319–21, 328–37
  and History of the Saints, 185, 310
  and WBS, 317–20, 328–29
  apostasy, 160–65
  spiritual wifery, 181–83, 331–34, 337
Bernhisel, John M., in Washington, 372–73, 387
Bethel Church, 562–63
Bidamon, Emma Hale Smith
  and Caroline Smith, 219
  and RLDS Church, 498
  and WBS, 122–23, 182–83, 219, 227, 258–60, 290–91, 312, 315, 513–14, 555
  on succession, 234, 259–60, 325, 497–98
  parents and siblings, 339–40, 357
  plural marriage, 290–91
  support from Twelve, 290, 315, 469
Bidamon, Lewis C., 357, 498, 513–14, 555–56
Blair, Alma R., 502
Blair, William Wallace, 391–92, 414, 441;
  and RLDS Church, 499–521
Blake, Rosanna ("Rosa") Hook Smith Osborne, 397, 413–16, 421, 580–81
Blakeslee, James, 440, 499
Blythe, Christine Elyse, 269, 272
Bolsinger, Loie May Smith, 524, 536, 558–59, 572
Book of Mormon, coming forth of, 42–44, 54–62
Bordentown, N.J., 193
Boston, Massachusetts, 199, 201, 216, 230
Boynton, John F., as missionary, 89, 91, 94–95, 131–32
Brain, Byron, 429, 433, 444, 535
Brain, Clara, 433
Brain, James, 429, 433, 537, 570
Brain, Mary, 429, 433, 535, 570
Brain, Ward, 429, 433, 535, 570
Brannan, Samuel

and finances, 201–02, 206
and plural marriage, 190, 199–200, 237–40, 245
and WBS's leadership, 236–39, 309–10, 317
Church trial, 235–39, 277
edits newspaper, 188, 197
in eastern branches, 190, 198, 207
personality, 188–89
Bratton, George W., 355, 361, 488–89
Bridges, Vernon R., 454
Briggs, Edmund, 188, 393, 409; and RLDS Church, 498–501, 504
Briggs, Jason
and polygamy, 504
and RLDS Church, 486, 499–501
conversion, 392, 399–400
on WBS, 368, 405, 408, 422, 503–4, 520
Briggs, Silas, 393
Burtis, Abraham, 191–95
Butler, J. J., 487, 490, 502
Bushman, Richard L., on clearing land, 31–32

C–D

Cadwell, Edwin, 348, 414, 502
Cahoon, William, 89
Caldwell, Silas, 383–84
Call, Anson, 99
Capin, Samuel, 368
Carter, Jared, 88–89, 112–13, 115, 302–03, 318, 393, 498
Chambers's Miscellany, 552
Chatburn, T. W., 571
Christ, Mark, 453
Civil War
history, 445, 455
126th Illinois Infantry, 449
soldiers' pay, 442, 447
WBS's motives, 449–450
Clayton County Journal, 532–33
Clayton, William, 157, 203, 229, 236, 241, 253–55, 281–84, 297–98, 302–03, 333, 463
Clinton, Jeter, 428
Colburn, Thomas, 424, 489–90
Coltrin, Zebedee, 89, 93, 129
Cook, Lyndon W., xiii, 137–38
Cooper, James Fenimore, 35
Covington, Mary Ann. *See* West, Mary Ann Covington Sheffield Smith Stratton West.
Council of Fifty, 211, 374, 468, 522
Cowdery, Oliver, 72, 80, 100

Cream Ridge, N.J., 175–76, 191, 365, 367
Cross, Whitney, 53
Curtis, Lucinda Ellen. *See* Lucinda Ellen Curtis Smith Merdock Douglas Flanders.
Curtis, Stephen Z., 365, 383–84
Daniels, Chilion, 425
debating school conflict, 111–24
Dennis, Theodore H., 364
De Valls Bluff, AR, 451–55
Doan, Jacob, 499, 502
Durfee, Jabez and Elizabeth, 166

E–F

Eagle Schoolhouse, 554–56
Edmunds, George, 539
Edwards, Paul M., 520
Elkader, Iowa, WBS in, 1–2, 431, 433–45, 498, 531–36, 548
Elliott, David and Mary, 107–8
Ellsworth, Benjamin, 331, 337, 580
Ellsworth, Sarah, 336
Enders, Donald L., 33, 38
Farwell, Joseph , 414
Far West, MO, 514–17
First Vision, 44–48
Flanders, Lucinda Ellen Curtis Smith Merdock Douglas, 523, 578–79
Ford, Thomas, 161–65
Frontier Guardian, 306, 468, 474, 482
Fullmer, John S., 468–74

G–H

Galena, Illinois, 304, 307–08
Gardner, Joseph, 342–43
Goodale, Joseph, 383–84
Grant, Athalia Howard, 91, 155, 222, 308–09, 347, 565
Grant, Caroline Amanda. *See* Smith, Caroline Amanda Grant.
Grant, George D., 91, 97, 151, 153, 486, 488
Grant, Heber J., and Thalia Grant, 423, 568–69
Grant, Jedediah M., 183–84, 210
and Caroline (sister), 209–10, 217
and WBS, 291–92, 315, 486, 488
as missionary, 191–92, 195–96, 207
conversion, 91, 96
supports Twelve, 202–3
Grant, Joshua (Caroline's brother), 224, 274, 285–86

Index

Grant, Joshua (Caroline's father), 91, 155, 222, 308–09, 565
Grant, Roxey Ann. *See* Smith, Roxey Ann Grant.
Grant, Theda ("Thedy"), 92, 96–97, 99
Greene, Evan, 94–95
Griffiths, Gomer T., 516–17, 555
Gurley, Zenos/Zenas, 393
  and RLDS Church, 486, 498–501, 503–4, 520
  on selection of apostles, 100, 106, 402, 440
Hackleton, Samuel, 167
Haight, Silas, 172
Hale, Emma. *See* Bidamon, Emma Hale Smith.
Hall, Mary Jones Smith, 288–89, 523, 577
Hanna, A. B., 541–42, 548
Hannaman, R. L., 410–12
Hardy, John, 198, 201, 229–30, 275, 332
Harris, Martin, 486
  and WBS's church, 424–29, 534
  and Strang, 425
  mediates between JSJ and WBS, 122–23
  selects apostles, 100
Hedlock, Reuben, 178
Heywood, Joseph L., 359, 468–74
Higbee, Chauncey L., 181–83
Hinkle, George M., 402
Hobart, Otis, and Mary Ann, 383–84
Hodges, Amos, 91, 94, 261–62
Hodges, Curtis, 91, 261, 298
Hodges, Ervine, 261–62, 265, 298, 304, 462, 475
Hook, Aaron, Jr., 413–16, 418, 505
  and WBS, 346, 351–56, 361–68, 382, 393, 396–97
  conversion, 343
Hook, Aaron, Sr., 343, 580
Hook family, money to WBS, 420–21
Hook, John, 342–43, 356
Hook, Mercy, 413, 580
Hook, Rhoda (dau.), 413
Hook, Rhoda Gibson, 343, 349–51, 580
Hook, Rosanna. *See* Blake, Rosanna Hook Smith Osborne.
Hook, William L., 343, 413, 580
Horner, John, 198
Hornerstown, N.J., 184, 217
Hurlbut, Philastus, 111
Hyde, Orson, 174, 180
  and W. W. Phelps, 466
  arranges property for Lucy Mack Smith, 470–74
  as missionary, 88–90
  defends Twelve's support of Smiths, 482
  disaffection in Missouri, 142–43
  edits Frontier Guardian, 468, 474, 482, 485
  on WBS's favored status, 113–14, 274–76, 460–61, 463, 474, 482
  presides in Nauvoo, 322–24, 326, 468
  rebukes Isaac Sheen, 483
  WBS corresponds with, 300, 306, 310, 345, 463–68, 480–81, 485, 488
  WBS threatens, 475

I–J

Ingalls, Ephraim, 407
Ingersoll, Peter, 79–80
Ivins, James, 178
Jackway, Hiram, 37
Jacobs, Zina Diantha Huntington, 221, 297
Jensen, Hyrum, visits WBS, 1–3, 490, 538, 549, 561
Jenson, Andrew, 179
Johnson, Benjamin F.
  and debating school, 112–13
  and JSS blessing book, 388
  on WBS, 115, 155
Johnson, Luke, 322–23
Jones, Mary. *See* Mary Jones Smith Hall.
JSJ. *See* Smith, Joseph, Jr.
JSS. *See* Smith, Joseph, Sr.

K–L

Kelley, Edmund L., 357, 541, 546–47, 549
Kelley, William H., 512, 520, 528
Kettle, Stephen, 353
Kimball, Heber C., 188
  and JSJ's presidential campaign, 523
  and WBS, 204–6, 211–12, 216, 244–46
  purchases lots for Lucy and Emma Smith, 468–69
  support for WBS, 283, 287, 460–61
  vision in temple, 129
Kimball, Stanley B., 418–19
Kirtland Temple, 97–99, 103, 127–31, 424–26, 525, 527
La Ture, Joseph, 572, 559
Lake, John H., 514
Lamoni, IA, 487, 525

Lane, George, 48–49, 51–52
Lane, Selah, 368–69, 393
Launius, Roger D., 543
Law, Wilson, 167
Lewis, Hiel, 340
Lewis, Joseph, 340, 412
Lewis, Levi, 340
Lewis, Melinda, 181
Lewis, Nathaniel, 340
Lewis, Q. Walker, 437, 441
Lewis, Sophia, 340
Lewis, Sarah, 340
Libby, Hannah Maria. *See* Smith, Hannah Maria Smith.
Libby, Nathaniel, 574–75
Libby, Sarah Ann. *See* Sarah Ann Libby Smith Smith.
Libby sisters, as plural wives, 199–200, 240, 410
Lightcap, Joseph, 364
lineal succession, 375, 377, 398, 402, 424. *See also* Joseph Smith III and WBS.
Little Rock, AR, 450, 452
Long, Adam, 364
Lyman, Amasa M., 156, 222

M–N

Mack, Solomon, and Lydia, 23–25
Marks, William, 225, 259–60, 499
Marsh, Thomas B., 84, 137–38, 142
McCleary, Sophronia Smith Stoddard, 22–24, 134–36, 276, 327, 358, 434, 444, 462, 477
   and RLDS Church, 509–10
   at Knoxville, IL., 329–30
   daughter Maria, 358
   shunned, 73
   youthful religion, 52–53
McCleary, William, 134–36
McLellin, William, 112–13, 142
Melchisedek and Aaronic Herald, 360, 368–69, 371, 378, 380–81
Miller, Reuben, 477–78
Miller, Sarah, 181–83
Millikin, Arthur, 273, 358–59
   and Lucy Mack Smith, 418, 471–73, 477
   and WBS, 290, 360, 555
   support from Twelve, 473–74, 482
Millikin, Lucy Smith (JSJ's sister), 266, 358–59, 276, 434
   and Lucy Mack Smith, 471–72
   and RLDS Church, 509–10
   and WBS, 290, 555–56
   nurses B. F. Johnson, 155
   support from Twelve, 462, 471–74, 482
Mogridge, Priscilla. *See* Priscilla Mogridge Smith Lowry Williams Staines.
Monroe, James
   as WBS's scribe, 219, 273
   as Smith daughters' teacher, 226
   on Caroline Smith's funeral, 222
   on WBS's opinions, 221, 247, 253–54, 258–59
   rooms with William, 219
Montrose, IA, 180, 513–14, 524, 573
"Morman" Cemetery, 403, 499–500
mummies, 320, 328, 324, 336, 359–60, 418–19, 431
Murdock, James, 173
Murdock, Samuel
   and Native Americans, 539–40
   as attorney and judge, 539
   employs WBS, 539–40
   on WBS's character, 456, 531, 554, 562
Nauvoo City Charter, 161–64, 167–69
Nauvoo High Council, 181–83, 232, 293, 306
Nauvoo police, 262–66, 269, 279, 304, 462
Nauvoo Temple, 219–20, 320–21, 461
New Egypt, N.J., 191–93
Newell, William Augustus, 191–92, 216–18
Newton, Joseph H., 185–86
Nickerson, Freeman, 238, 406
Nisonger, Henry, 439
Norman, Mary Bailey Smith, 266, 474–75
Nyman, Matilda, 181–82

O–P

O'Donovan, Connell, xiii, 439
126th Illinois Infantry, 449–52, 455
Owen, Thomas, 167
Packard, Philander, 38
Paden, Isaac, 330, 470–71
Page, Ebenezer, 88–89
Page, John E., 174–75, 222, 324, 336, 398–99, 464
Palestine Grove (Rocky Ford/Shelburn), IL, 339, 347–49, 395, 403, 497, 502, 504, 580
Parrish, Warren
   apostasy of, 131–32
   as mediator for WBS, 108–9, 123
Patrick, Shepard G., 421
Patten, David W., 137–38, 257, 394

Phelps, Sally, 321–22
Phelps, William W., 214, 248–49, 251–52, 321–22, 324
Philadelphia, PA, 173–75, 184–86, 193, 198, 206, 210–11, 216, 218, 333
Pickett, Agnes Coolbrith Smith Smith, 134–36, 180, 573
Plano, IL, 487, 510–12
Plymouth, IL, 141, 144–46, 147, 151, 523
Porter, Larry C., 49
Post, Stephen, 424–28
Powell, David, 397
Powers, Samuel, 499
Pratt, Mary Ann, 153
Pratt, Orson, 222–23, 307–08
Pratt, Parley P.
 and Samuel Brannan, 235–36, 239
 dissension among Twelve, 137
 on eastern branches, 203–6, 218, 231, 258, 275, 294, 459–60
 on George J. Adams, 236
 on WBS, 104, 204–5, 236, 238, 244–46, 298, 303–04
 personality, 245–46
 wife's illness, 153
Pugh, J. W., 363

Q–R

Quince, Caroline Louisa Smith (dau. of WBS), 287, 299, 328–29, 417–18, 566
 and WBS, 151–52, 362
 biography, 132, 444, 517, 565
 personality, 183, 210, 226, 266
Quince, James S., 417, 444, 566
Quorum of the Twelve,
 and William's "Proclamation," 305–06
 Last charge meeting, 294
 selection of, 100–101,
Randall, Richard, 514–15
Reynolds, Joseph H., 341
Rice, Henriette. *See* Smith, Henriette Rice.
Richards, Willard, 167, 213, 242, 260, 263–64, 287, 298, 300, 478
Richardson, Stephen and Erepta, 348–49, 439
Rigdon, Sidney, 196, 200, 210, 251, 257–58, 310, 314, 318–19, 467
 and Stephen Post, 428
 leaves Kirtland, 132
Riley, James, 313, 318
RLDS Church, WBS's influence on, 403

Robbins, Lewis, 134–35, 242, 301, 308
Roberts, Ann Sophia Rollins Smith Beckstead
 biography, 523, 579
 marriage to William, 288
 patriarchal blessing from WBS, 579
Roberts, B. H.
 WBS's middle initial, 447–48
 on WBS's appearance, 560
 on WBS's personality, 561
 on WBS's reputation, 1–2, 549
 visits WBS, 1–3, 490–91, 537, 561
Rock Island, Illinois, 308, 445–46
Rogers, Israel, 499, 502
Rollins, Ann Sophia. *See* Roberts, Ann Sophia Rollins Smith Beckstead.
Rollins, Enoch Perham, 285, 566, 579
Rollins, Mary Jane. *See* Taylor, Mary Jane Rollins Smith Williamson.
Rollins, Sophia Philbrook, 285, 566, 579
Russell, William D., 441

S–T

Saints' Herald, 487, 527
Salisbury, Alvin (Katharine's son), 135, 443
Salisbury, Don Carlos (Katharine's son), 442–45
Salisbury, Katharine Smith, 266, 276, 290, 309, 443–44, 462, 524, 555
 and RLDS Church, 554
 and Strangites, 327
 and WBS's visits, 554–55
 in Missouri, 134–36
 in Ohio, 83–84
 in Plymouth, IL, 146, 358
 joins RLDS Church, 509–10
 on persecution, 73–74, 77, 434
 on plural marriage, 523
Salisbury, Solomon, 434
Salisbury, Wilkins Jenkins, 321, 327, 357–58
 and WBS, 146, 290, 298–99, 301, 309, 313–15, 321, 360, 474, 485
 apprehension about safety, 309
 in Zion's Camp, 136
Sanborn, Eliza Elsie. *See* Eliza Elsie Sanborn Brain Smith.
Saunders, Benjamin, 34
Saunders, Lorenzo, 34
School of the Prophets, 93, 97, 126–27
Scott, Andrew, 417, 517, 565
Scott, Caroline ("Carrie"), 417

Scott, Mary Jane Smith (WBS's dau.) 286–87
  and WBS, 151, , 328–29, 362
  biography, 97, 166, 183, 210, 266, 565
  death, 417–18, 517
  illness, 299–300
Searles, Asa, 340
Seixas, Joshua, 126–27
Sexton (spiritualist), 425–26
Sharp, Thomas, 159–61, 163, 250, 270, 286, 289, 292, 304–06, 321, 464
Sheen, Drusilla, 387–88
Sheen, Isaac
  affiliated with WBS, 362–69, 372–73, 378, 380–83
  and RLDS Church, 499, 502
  and Saints' Herald, 499, 504
  as abolitionist, 439
  as printer, 360
  breaks with WBS, 384–90, 402, 410, 440
  opposes Utah's statehood, 483
Sheen, John K., 362, 384–85, 388–89, 583–90
Sheffield, James, 573
Shelby, Jo, 452
Shepard, Bill, 261
Shumway, George R. H., 435
Singley, Margaret L., 134
Small, William, 364
Smith, Agnes Coolbrith. *See* Pickett, Agnes Coolbrith Smith Smith.
Smith, Alexander Hale, 524, 528
Smith, Alva, and Sabrina, 348
Smith, Alvin (JSS's son), 50, 65
Smith, Asael
  in New York, 6
  JSS's mission to, 12–13
  on descendant, 8
  on family unity, 1, 5
Smith, Asahel, Jr., 6, 12–13, 248
Smith, Caroline Amanda Grant (WBS's wife), 180, 223, 286
  death and funeral, 221–24, 229, 236–37, 241, 252, 301, 515, 517, 523, 565
  hospitality, 212
  illness, 132, 153–54, 174, 183–84, 191–92, 207, 215–16
  in Springfield, 166
  letter to WBS, 209–10
  marries WBS, 92, 96–97, 565

treatment for dropsy, 213, 216–18
Smith, Caroline Louisa (WBS's dau.). *See* Quince, Caroline Louisa Smith.
Smith, Clarissa Lyman, 11–12, 16, 299
Smith, Don Carlos
  as missionary, 3–4, 12, 87
  and WBS's hotel, 151, 153, 157
  as newspaper editor, 150
  at JSS's deathbed, 149
  biography, 174–76, 180, 213, 257, 289, 474, 573
  death of, 158
  in Missouri, 134–36, 141
  in Illinois, 144
  in Ohio, 97
  president of high priests, 100–1
  recreation, 34
  testimony of, 68
Smith, Edson Don Carlos
  and LDS Church, 492–93, 571–72
  and RLDS Church, 492–93, 571
  biography, 536, 558, 571
  describes WBS, 541, 549, 553
  marriages, 571–72
  on WBS, 493, 544, 553, 556, 561–62
  temple work for WBS, 493
Smith, Eliza Elsie Sanborn Brain, 429–30, 433
  and LDS Church, 490, 538
  at Elkader, 531
  biography, 517, 524, 529, 569–72
  death, 558–59
  marries WBS, 488, 498, 534, 558, 570
  personality, 537–38, 541, 558
Smith, Emma Hale. *See* Bidamon, Emma Hale Smith.
Smith, George A., 8, 17, 221–22
  and Lucy Mack Smith, 472
  and WBS, 175–76, 263–65, 268, 464–65, 488
  and statehood, 465
  on Book of Mormon, 14
  on JSS as athlete, 37
  on JSS patriarchal blessing book, 388
  unity of Twelve 464
Smith, Hannah Maria Libby Smith, 199–200, 240
  and Provo Relief Society, 575
  biography, 575
  marries George A. Smith, 575
  marries WBS, 288, 523–24, 575

Smith, Henriette Rice
  biography, 577–78
  marries WBS, 288, 523, 577–78
Smith, Hyrum, 476
  and land transactions, 156–57
  and plural marriage, 522
  as mediator, 108–9, 112–19
  as missionary, 87–94
  as Presbyterian, 52
  authority/leadership of, 231, 251, 293, 495
  conversion of, 68–69
  death, 212–14, 231, 267, 301, 459, 461
  letters to grandfather, 8
  marriages, 285–86
  personality, 116–17, 274
  plural marriage, 293
  supports WBS, 254–55, 276–77
Smith, Hyrum Wallace, 422–23, 534
  biography, 389, 398, 422–23, 517, 569
Smith, Jesse (JSS's brother)
  as Calvinist, 4
  compared to WBS, 20, 76
  death of, 19
  greed of, 6–7
  Lucy Mack Smith's dream of, 9–10
  on Book of Mormon, 1, 11–12
  on George A. Smith, 14–15
  on JSJ and Hyrum, 8–9
  on JSS, 9, 20
  personality, 4–7, 11–15, 17–19, 118–19
Smith, Jesse Nathaniel, 465
Smith, John (JSS's brother), 6–7, 11, 14–16, 18–19, 122–23, 248
  and WBS, 268, 299–301, 464–65
  as patriarch, 273–74, 503
Smith, Joseph F., 539
Smith, Joseph, Jr.
  and appointments to family, 101
  and First Vision, 44–48
  and Kirtland Temple, 127–30
  and land transactions, 156–57
  and Springfield trial, 164–68
  as missionary, 3–4, 95
  as presidential candidate, 210
  death of, 212–14, 231, 267, 301, 459, 461, 551
  blesses WBS, 105, 556
  conflict with WBS, 107–24, 177–78
  on marriage customs, 285–86
  ordains John Smith patriarch, 273

plural marriages, 230, 241, 259, 292, 522
  support for WBS, 3, 254–55, 274, 276–77, 460
  Brigham Young dreams of, 477
Smith, Joseph, III
  and lineal succession, 234, 250
  and LDS Church, 504
  and neuralgia, 457–58, 543
  and patriarchal office, 519–20, 528
  and RLDS Church, 498–99, 508
  and Brigham Young, 487
  and WBS's records/journal, 504–05, 512
  appoints WBS high priest, 513, 526
  corresponds with WBS, 503, 507–09, 518, 520–21, 540–41, 548–49
  describes WBS, 56–61, 548–50, 560
  manages WBS, 395, 487, 495, 503, 508–13, 519, 527–29, 550–51
  on mummies, 419
  on plural marriage and WBS, 505, 511, 520–22
  on race, 440–41
  on WBS's Civil War service, 450, 456
  personality, 502, 520, 528–29
  WBS supports, 487, 518, 520, 528
Smith, Joseph, Sr.
  and Kirtland apostasy, 131–32
  and Missouri, 134–36, 140–41
  as mediator (WBS/JSJ), 107, 114–24
  as missionary, 3–4
  as patriarch, 271
  blesses JSJ, 93
  blesses WBS, 105–6, 149
  death of, 149–50
  family devotions, 26–28
  marksmanship, 34–35
  mission to siblings, 7–20
  patriarchal blessing book, 388
  recreation of, 36–37
  religious faith, 4, 22–26
  siblings of, 6
  understands WBS, 564
Smith, Joseph F., 523–24, 539
Smith, Josephina ("Ina") Coolbrith, 474
Smith, Julia Murdock, 226
Smith, Julia Priscilla, 138
Smith, Katharine. *See* Salisbury, Katharine Smith.
Smith, Levira Clark, 165
Smith, Loie May. *See* Loie May Smith Bolsinger.

Smith, Lucy Mack
  and Caroline Smith, 215
  and J. J. Strang, 326, 330, 476–77
  and conflict (JSJ/WBS), 107–8, 122–23
  and WBS, 209, 215, 266–67, 277, 303, 551
  and succession, 268–69, 304
  as grandmother, 215
  in 1850, 358–59
  influence on children, 53
  nurses WBS/Caroline, 139
  on persecution, 75, 80, 212–15
  on JSS as missionary, 18
  property of, 359–60
  religious faith of, 24–27, 41–42, 51–52, 65–66, 83–84
  support from Twelve, 462, 468–74,
Smith, Mary Aikens, 13, 465
Smith, Mary Duty, conversion of, 6, 16–17
Smith, Mary Jane. *See* Scott, Mary Jane Smith Scott.
Smith, Mary Jane Rollins, 347
Smith, Priscilla (JSS's sister), 6, 18
Smith, Rosanna Goyette La Ture Surprise
  biography, 559, 572–73
  marries WBS, 524, 559, 572–73
Smith, Roxey Ann Grant, 92, 517
  and plural marriage, 362, 386–88, 567–68
  biography, 567–68
  cares for WBS children, 308
  divorces WBS, 389–90, 409–13, 567–68
  endowed, 347
  in Illinois, 372–73
  in Kentucky, 373–74, 385
  marries WBS, 347–48, 477, 523, 534, 567
  nurses Caroline Smith, 216, 225, 347
  WBS baptizes, 225, 567
Smith, Samuel, (JSS's brother), 6
Smith, Samuel Harrison
  and WBS, 87–89, 110, 118, 151, 153, 157
  brings WBS and Caroline to Far West, 139
  conversion of, 68–69
  death, 190, 212, 300, 459, 476
  farms with WBS, 97
  in Plymouth, IL, 141, 144, 146
  as Presbyerian, 52
  and succession, 250
Smith, Sarah (JSS's sister), 6, 18
Smith, Sarah Ann Libby Smith
  biography, 199, 240, 574–75
  marries George A. Smith, 574
  marries WBS, 288, 523–24, 574
Smith, Silas, (JSS's brother), 6–7, 11–13
  defends JSS, 12–13, 14, 16, 18
Smith, Sophronia. *See* McCleary, Sophronia Smith Stoddard.
Smith, Stephen (JSS's brother), 6
Smith, Susan, (JSS's sister), 6
Smith, Thalia Grant, 373, 389, 422–23, 534
  as schoolteacher, 568
  and Heber J. Grant, 492, 568–69
  biography, 492, 517, 568–69
  joins LDS Church, 492

Smith, William B.,
Biography, 562–63
  and land sales, 156–57, 177, 227, 260, 320–21
  and mummies, 418–19, 431
  birth order, 22
  childhood/youth, 21–62, 64–67
  church trials, 182–83, 276–77
  converted to Mormonism, 41, 64–72, 71–72, 512, 552–53; on Book of Mormon, 43–44, 550; on Three Witnesses, 71; on Urim and Thummim, 60–62
  death, 562–64
  education, 38
  endowed, 211, 292–93, 522
  family devotions, 63–65
  First Vision, 46–47, 51–52
  health, 174, 218–20, 229, 452–56, 542–45, 548
  in Civil War, 433–57; pension, 453, 541, 543–44, 549
  in Elkader, Iowa, 1–2, 531, 536–37, 549, 553–54, 561
  in Kirtland, 97–134, 329, 525–27; temple, 97–98, 125, 127–30, 329, 525, 527
  in Missouri, 134–40, 515–16
  in Nauvoo, 151–69
  in School of the Prophets, 126–27
  in Zion's Camp, 136, 450
  legal difficulties, 198, 206–7, 415–16, 420–21, 539–40
  marriages (after Caroline), 408, 534, 559–60
  marries Caroline Grant, 96; relationship with, 209–12, 216–18, 224, 408
  member of Council of Fifty, 211, 522
  no middle initial/adopts, 22, 447–48
  old age, 555–57
  personal papers, 388–39, 409–10, 412

Index   **637**

physical appearance, 2, 63, 447, 525, 527, 542, 560–61
poverty, 442, 540–41, 545, 547, 487, 546–47
preaching ability, 38–39, 134, 161, 163, 167–68, 174–75, 220–21, 533, 549–50
"Proclamation," 292, 303–07, 309, 316, 366, 483
singing, 149, 224
speaks in tongues, 93–95
Temple Lot Case testimony, 529

Callings/Employment
as apostle, 100–2, 143–44, 150–58, 460
as Civil War soldier, 498
as editor, 158–61, 356
as elder, 93
as farmer, 488, 538–41; dislikes farming, 31–33, 407, 482, 539–40
as high priest, 99, 513,
as legislator, 161–69, 210–11, 442, 449, 539
as minister, 540
as missionary, 81–82, 87–97, 102–4, 133–34, 155–56, 171–73, 176–77, 211, 361, 507, 513–18, 523–54, 527, 540, 544, 549, 551–52, 562; does not go to England, 144–45, 152–54
as patriarch, 242–43, 248–49, 269–73, 281
as priest, 85–87
as teacher, 81, 85–86
as Sunday School representative, 549
patriarchal blessing of, 76–77
patriarchal blessings by, 438–40
preaches for Baptists, 430–31, 442, 535
shows panorama, 431
tavern/hotel in Plymouth, IL, 141, 144–46, 150–51

Personality/Beliefs
alienates followers, 407–9
and Book of Mormon, 55–59
and ordinances for the dead, 354
and polygamy, 179–82, 186, 190, 198, 229–30, 233, 236–40, 260, 284, 287–91, 294–97, 316, 331, 333–34, 338, 384–87, 396, 408–9, 409–14, 427, 498–99, 521–22, 549, 562; denies plural marriage, 464, 467, 521–22, 523–24
and sealing power, 181, 201, 237–39, 241, 245, 292–94, 459
and Word of Wisdom, 97–98
apprehension about safety, 213–14, 231, 262, 267, 273, 459, 475, 486

aspires to leadership, 231–32, 236, 243–44, 247–48, 250–51, 272, 284, 294, 326–27, 329, 334, 353–403, 405–6, 464–65, 497–98, 503–04, 506–08, 519–21, 527–28, 549, 555
as patriarch, 270–73, 281, 467, 495, 508, 461
compared to Hyrum Smith, 408
compared to Jesse Smith, 20, 76, 106, 564
compared to JSJ, 407–8
entitled to financial support, 201–3, 260–61, 269, 273–75, 460–61, 463–64, 470–74, 479–80, 482, 485–86, 503–4, 518–19, 460–62, 476, 480, 544, 546–47
estranged from family, 358–61
on lineal succession, 204, 243, 248, 250, 259, 264–65, 280–81, 311–12, 325, 327, 330, 464–65, 495–97, 499, 502, 529
on slavery/race, 435–42
on temple work, 516
opposes Utah statehood, 372–73
reminiscences, 527, 550–51
renounces Mormonism/offshoots, 433–34, 506–7, 531, 548
speaking ability, 174–75, 282, 312, 475, 514, 533, 549–50
temperament, 31–32, 37–38, 73, 75–77, 105–24, 147, 171–72, 185, 213–14, 230–32, 247, 254–55, 259, 269, 274, 279, 284, 291, 295–97, 303, 306, 316, 352, 406–75, 478–82, 488–91, 498, 503, 511, 520, 537, 547–48, 552, 556, 560–61, 563–64

Relationships
and George J. Adams, 188, 302–03
and Emma Hale Smith Bidamon, 290–91, 312, 513–14
and Samuel Brannan, 189, 235–38, 246
and Abraham Burtis, 191–95
and Grant family, 96
and Martin Harris, 424–28, 430
and Orson Hyde, 345, 467–68, 478–79, 480–82
and Heber C. Kimball, 214, 246, 283
and LDS Church, 478–79, 482–87, 502, 506
and Parley P. Pratt, 203–6, 231, 244–47
and Sidney Rigdon, 199–200, 364
and RLDS Church, 499–501, 507, 510–13, 529
and B. H. Roberts, 1–3, 490–91, 538, 560–61
and Joshua Seixas, 127

and JSJ, 105, 107–24, 132, 141–42, 176–79, 314, 318, 550–52
and JSS, 105–6
and Joseph Smith III, 503–9, 514, 518–19, 521–22, 528, 540, 548–49, 552
and Lucy Mack Smith, 26, 266–269, 278, 468–74, 477
and James J. Strang, 325–27, 329, 333, 337, 345–48, 353, 470, 474
and John Taylor, 250–53, 279, 287, 295–98, 305
and Twelve, 171, 202, 204, 231, 240–41, 249–53, 257, 458, 462–63, 467, 478–79, 496–97, 473–75, 482, 503–4, 506, 519–21
and Elbridge Tufts, 462
and Lyman Wight, 374–83
and Benjamin Winchester, 195–97, 199–200, 206–7
and Wilford Woodruff, 198, 200–201, 204, 230–31
and Brigham Young, 262–64, 284, 292–94, 301, 362, 422, 459, 475–76, 483–87, 490–91, 495, 503–4, 524, 533
as father/stepfather, 151–52, 183, 210, 301, 418, 517, 534, 537, 556, 563
Smith, William ("Willie") Enoch, 430, 433
biography, 531, 534, 537, 557–58, 570–71
on WBS, 544
Smith, Mary Jane. *See* Scott, Mary Jane Smith.
Snow, Erastus, 177, 198, 290–91, 295, 488
Snow, Lorenzo, 182
Snow, Levi, 103–4
Southwick, Edward, 411, 421
Springfield, IL, 449–50
Speek, Vickie Cleverley, 332–33
Stafford, David, 76
St. Louis, MO, 480–81, 488, 497, 518
Staines, Priscilla Mogridge Smith Lowry Williams
biographical, 287–88, 576–77
marries WBS, 287–88, 523–24, 576
Staker, Mark L., 434–45
Stanton, Richard H., 387
Steele, Frederick, 451–52
Stennett, Samuel, 150
Stevenson, Russell, 439
Stockton, Benjamin, 49–53
Stoddard, Calvin, 110, 118
Stoddard, Sophronia Smith Stoddard. *See* McCleary, Sophronia Smith Stoddard.

Stone, Experience, 348, 499
Stoneman, John T., 531–33, 538
Stout, Hosea, 263, 297
Strang, James J., 318–19, 425–26, 468, 476–77, 528
and plural marriage, 333–34, 337–38
and Smith family, 327–28
and WBS, 335
succession claim, 319, 325
Stratton, Hiram, 298–99, 324, 347, 485
Surprise, Samuel, 559, 572
Syfritt, Jacob, 364, 367, 402
Tadlock, Sevier, and Melinda, 145–46
Taylor, John
and WBS sermon on plural marriage, 295–97
as editor, 162, 203, 230, 246–47, 250, 297–98
on patriarchal authority, 250–53, 257, 272, 279
on Lucy's dream, 267–69
Taylor, Mary Jane Rollins Smith Williamson, 289
biographical, 566–67
divorces WBS, 335, 567
marries WBS, 284–85, 523, 566–67
Taylor, Zachary, 372
Terry, Thomas S., 185–86
Tom's River, N.J., 173, 191
Tourtillott, Thomas, 346–48, 354
Tredwell, Daniel, 368
trustees (Nauvoo), 468–74
Tucker, Pomeroy, 30
Tufts, Elbridge, 261–64, 300
Tyler, Almina, 90–91
Tyler, Andrews, 90–91
Tyler, Daniel, 90–91, 110
Tyler, Elizabeth, 90–91

U–W

Underground Railroad, 435
Underwood, Joseph R., 372
Wallace, George B., 237–38, 309
Wallace, Sarah, 237–40
Ward, Amos, 410
Warren, Catherine Fuller, 181–82
Warsaw Signal, 159–62
Wasp, 158–61, 177
Wasson, Benjamin, 339, 341
Wasson, Elizabeth Hale, 339, 341
Wasson, Harmon, 340, 348, 358
Wasson, Lorenzo, 340, 348

Welch, John A., 17
Wentworth, John, 372–73
West, Mary Ann Covington Sheffield Smith Stratton
- biography, 573–74
- marries WBS, 179–80, 190, 229, 285, 287–89, 390, 410, 522, 573–74
- Temple Lot deposition, 464
- witnesses plural sealing, 577

Whitaker, Benjamin, 145
White River, 451, 453, 455
Whitmer, David, 72, 100, 106, 521
Whitney, Elizabeth Ann, 240
Whitney, Helen Mar Kimball, 261, 286–87, 291, 300, 406
Whitney, Newel K., 240, 282
Wight, Lyman, 464, 515
- and Lucy Mack Smith, 375–76
- and WBS, 374–84, 391, 214, 402, 409, 481
- counselor in First Presidency, 393–94

Wight, Orange, 376–77
William Smith on Mormonism, 512, 550–52, 564
Williams, Susannah, 348
Wilson, Harmon T., 341
Winchester, Benjamin
- and Sidney Rigdon, 199–200
- and WBS, 171, 177, 193–97, 206, 213, 273
- baptized, 94
- converted, 89–91, 193
- patriarchal blessing, 273

Wood, Joseph, 341
- and WBS, 394–97, 402
- as WBS's attorney, 410–13
- as WBS's counselor, 409, 420–21, 505

Woodruff, Wilford, 198–204, 230–333, 239. 243, 247–48, 275, 281
- critiques WBS, 141–44, 438, 459

Y–Z

Young, Brigham, 211
- and George J. Adams, 232–34
- and Samuel Brannan, 235–39
- and Carthage trial, 231
- and Caroline Smith's funeral, 222, 224
- and debating school conflict, 112–13
- and Emma Hale Smith Bidamon, 278
- and Lucy Mack Smith, 282–84, 462–63, 468, 471, 477, 476–77, 492
- history of WBS, 178–79
- officiator at WBS marriages, 284–86
- on patriarchal office, 242–43, 249, 271–72, 279–81, 462, 495–96
- prophecy about WBS, 557
- on succession, 279–82, 292–94, 495–96
- on WBS's misconduct, 141, 201–4, 231, 250–51, 257, 260, 268–71, 304, 316–17, 460–61, 475–77, 483–85, 489, 492, 528
- supports WBS/Smith family, 221, 273–74, 276–78, 282–84, 461–62, 502–3, 566, 574, 577
- WBS writes to, 355, 391

Young, E. H., 146–47
Young, Phinehas, 100
Ziegler, William, 454, 457
Zion's Camp, 136, 515

Also available from
GREG KOFFORD BOOKS

Mormonism in Transition: A History of the Latter-day Saints, 1890–1930, 3rd ed.

Thomas G. Alexander

Paperback, ISBN: 978-1-58958-188-3

More than two decades after its original publication, Thomas G. Alexander's Mormonism in Transition still engages audiences with its insightful study of the pivotal, early years of the Church of Jesus Christ of Latter-day Saints. Serving as a vital read for both students and scholars of American religious and social history, Alexander's book explains and charts the Church's transformation over this 40-year period of both religious and American history.

For those familiar with the LDS Church in modern times, it is impossible to study Mormonism in Transition without pondering the enormous amount of changes the Church has been through since 1890. For those new to the study of Mormonism, this book will give them a clear understanding the challenges the Church went through to go from a persecuted and scorned society to the rapidly growing, respected community it is today.

Praise for Mormonism in Transition:

"A must read for any serious student of this 'peculiar people' and Western history." – STANLEY B. KIMBALL, *Journal of the West*

"Will be required reading for all historians of Mormonism for some time to come." – WILLIAM D. RUSSELL, *Journal of American History*

"This is by far the most important book on this crucial period in LDS history." – JAN SHIPPS, author of *Mormonism: The Story of a New Religious Tradition*

"A work of careful and prodigious scholarship." – LEONARD J. ARRINGTON, author of *Brigham Young: American Moses*

"Clearly fills a tremendous void in the history of Mormonism." – Klaus J. Hansen, author of *Mormonism and the American Experience*

Knowing Brother Joseph Again: Perceptions and Perspectives

Davis Bitton

Paperback, ISBN: 978-1-58958-123-4

In 1996, Davis Bitton, one of Mormon history's preeminent and much-loved scholars, published a collection of essays on Joseph Smith under the title, *Images of the Prophet Joseph Smith*. A decade later, when the book went out of print, Davis began work on an updated version that would also include some of his other work on the Mormon prophet. The project was only partially finished when his health failed. He died on April 13, 2007, at age seventy-seven. With the aid of additional historians, *Knowing Brother Joseph Again: Perceptions and Perspectives* brings to completion Davis's final work—a testament to his own admiration of the Prophet Joseph Smith.

From Davis Bitton's introducton:

This is not a conventional biography of Joseph Smith, but its intended purpose should not be hard to grasp. That purpose is to trace how Joseph Smith has appeared from different points of view. It is the image of Joseph Smith rather than the man himself that I seek to delineate.

Even when we have cut through the rumor and misinformation that surround all public figures and agree on many details, differences of interpretation remain. We live in an age of relativism. What is beautiful for one is not for another, what is good and moral for one is not for another, and what is true for one is not for another. I shudder at the thought that my presentation here will lead to such soft relativism.

Yet the fact remains that different people saw Joseph Smith in different ways. Even his followers emphasized different facets at different times. From their own perspectives, different people saw him differently or focused on a different facet of his personality at different times. Inescapably, what they observed or found out about him was refracted through the lens of their own experience. Some of the different, flickering, not always compatible views are the subject of this book.

Excavating Mormon Pasts: The New Historiography of the Last Half Century

Newell G. Bringhurst and
Lavina Fielding Anderson

Paperback, ISBN: 978-1-58958-115-9

Special Book Award - John Whitmer Historical Association

Mormonism was born less than 200 years ago, but in that short time it has developed into a dynamic world religious movement. With that growth has come the inevitable restructuring and reevaluation of its history and doctrine. Mormon and non-Mormon scholars alike have viewed Joseph Smith's religion as fertile soil for religious, historical and sociological studies. Many early attempts to either defend or defame the Church were at best sloppy and often dishonest. It has taken decades for Mormon scholarship to mature to its present state. The editors of this book have assembled 16 essays addressing the substantial number of published works in the field of Mormon studies from 1950 to the present. The contributors come from various segments of the Mormon tradition and fairly represent the broad intellectual spectrum of that tradition. Each essay focuses on a particular aspect of Mormonism (history, women's issues, polygamy, etc.), and each is careful to evenhandedly evaluate the strengths and weaknesses of the books under discussion. More importantly, each volume is placed in context with other, related works, giving the reader a panoramic view of contemporary research. Students of Mormonism will find this collection of historiographical essays an invaluable addition to their libraries.

On the Road with Joseph Smith: An Author's Diary

Richard L. Bushman

Paperback, ISBN 978-1-58958-102-9

After living with Joseph Smith for seven years and delivering the final proofs of his landmark study, *Joseph Smith: Rough Stone Rolling* to Knopf in July 2005, biographer Richard Lyman Bushman went "on the road" for a year, crisscrossing the country from coast to coast, delivering addresses on Joseph Smith and attending book-signings for the new biography.

Bushman confesses to hope and humility as he awaits reviews. He frets at the polarization that dismissed the book as either too hard on Joseph Smith or too easy. He yields to a very human compulsion to check sales figures on Amazon. com, but partway through the process stepped back with the recognition, "The book seems to be cutting its own path now, just as [I] hoped."

For readers coming to grips with the ongoing puzzle of the Prophet and the troublesome dimensions of their own faith, Richard Bushman, openly but not insistently presents himself as a believer. "I believe enough to take Joseph Smith seriously," he says. He draws comfort both from what he calls his "mantra" ("Today I will be a follower of Jesus Christ") and also from ongoing engagement with the intellectual challenges of explaining Joseph Smith.

Praise for *On the Road With Joseph Smith*:

"The diary is possibly unparalleled—an author of a recent book candidly dissecting his experiences with both Mormon and non-Mormon audiences ... certainly deserves wider distribution—in part because it shows a talented historian laying open his vulnerabilities, and also because it shows how much any historian lays on the line when he writes about Joseph Smith."
-Dennis Lythgoe, *Deseret News*

"By turns humorous and poignant, this behind-the-scenes look at Richard Bushman's public and private ruminations about Joseph Smith reveals a great deal—not only about the inner life of one of our greatest scholars, but about Mormonism at the dawn of the 21st century."
-Jana Riess, co-author of *Mormonism for Dummies*

Mormon Women Have Their Say: Essays from the Claremont Oral History Collection

Edited by Claudia L. Bushman and Caroline Kline

Paperback, ISBN: 978-1-58958-494-5

The Claremont Women's Oral History Project has collected hundreds of interviews with Mormon women of various ages, experiences, and levels of activity. These interviews record the experiences of these women in their homes and family life, their church life, and their work life, in their roles as homemakers, students, missionaries, career women, single women, converts, and disaffected members. Their stories feed into and illuminate the broader narrative of LDS history and belief, filling in a large gap in Mormon history that has often neglected the lived experiences of women. This project preserves and perpetuates their voices and memories, allowing them to say share what has too often been left unspoken. The silent majority speaks in these records.

This volume is the first to explore the riches of the collection in print. A group of young scholars and others have used the interviews to better understand what Mormonism means to these women and what women mean for Mormonism. They explore those interviews through the lenses of history, doctrine, mythology, feminist theory, personal experience, and current events to help us understand what these women have to say about their own faith and lives.

Praise for *Mormon Women Have Their Say*:

"Using a variety of analytical techniques and their own savvy, the authors connect ordinary lives with enduring themes in Latter-day Saint faith and history." --Laurel Thatcher Ulrich, author of *Well-Behaved Women Seldom Make History*

"Essential. . . . In these pages, Mormon women will find *ourselves*." --Joanna Brooks, author of *The Book of Mormon Girl: A Memoir of an American Faith*

"The varieties of women's responses to the major issues in their lives will provide many surprises for the reader, who will be struck by how many different ways there are to be a thoughtful and faithful Latter-day Saint woman." --Armand Mauss, author of *All Abraham's Children: Changing Mormon Conceptions of Race and Lineage*

Mormon Polygamous Families:
Life in the Principle

Jessie L. Embry

Paperback, ISBN: 978-1-58958-098-5
Hardcover, ISBN: 978-1-58958-114-2

Mormons and non-Mormons all have their views about how polygamy was practiced in the Church of Jesus Christ of Latter-day Saints during the late nineteenth and early twentieth centuries. Embry has examined the participants themselves in order to understand how men and women living a nineteenth-century Victorian lifestyle adapted to polygamy. Based on records and oral histories with husbands, wives, and children who lived in Mormon polygamous households, this study explores the diverse experiences of individual families and stereotypes about polygamy. The interviews are in some cases the only sources of primary information on how plural families were organized. In addition, children from monogamous families who grew up during the same period were interviewed to form a comparison group. When carefully examined, most of the stereotypes about polygamous marriages do not hold true. In this work it becomes clear that Mormon polygamous families were not much different from Mormon monogamous families and non-Mormon families of the same era. Embry offers a new perspective on the Mormon practice of polygamy that enables readers to gain better understanding of Mormonism historically.

The Gift and Power: Translating the Book of Mormon

Brant A. Gardner

Hardcover, ISBN: 978-1-58958-131-9

From Brant A. Gardner, the author of the highly praised *Second Witness* commentaries on the Book of Mormon, comes *The Gift and Power: Translating the Book of Mormon*. In this first book-length treatment of the translation process, Gardner closely examines the accounts surrounding Joseph Smith's translation of the Book of Mormon to answer a wide spectrum of questions about the process, including: Did the Prophet use seerstones common to folk magicians of his time? How did he use them? And, what is the relationship to the golden plates and the printed text?

Approaching the topic in three sections, part 1 examines the stories told about Joseph, folk magic, and the translation. Part 2 examines the available evidence to determine how closely the English text replicates the original plate text. And part 3 seeks to explain how seer stones worked, why they no longer work, and how Joseph Smith could have produced a translation with them.

Fire and Sword: A History of the Latter-day Saints in Northern Missouri, 1836-39

Leland Homer Gentry and Todd M. Compton

Hardcover, ISBN: 978-1-58958-103-6

Many Mormon dreams flourished in Missouri. So did many Mormon nightmares.

The Missouri period—especially from the summer of 1838 when Joseph took over vigorous, personal direction of this new Zion until the spring of 1839 when he escaped after five months of imprisonment—represents a moment of intense crisis in Mormon history. Representing the greatest extremes of devotion and violence, commitment and intolerance, physical suffering and terror—mobbings, battles, massacres, and political "knockdowns"—it shadowed the Mormon psyche for a century.

Leland Gentry was the first to step beyond this disturbing period as a one-sided symbol of religious persecution and move toward understanding it with careful documentation and evenhanded analysis. In Fire and Sword, Todd Compton collaborates with Gentry to update this foundational work with four decades of new scholarship, more insightful critical theory, and the wealth of resources that have become electronically available in the last few years.

Compton gives full credit to Leland Gentry's extraordinary achievement, particularly in documenting the existence of Danites and in attempting to tell the Missourians' side of the story; but he also goes far beyond it, gracefully drawing into the dialogue signal interpretations written since Gentry and introducing the raw urgency of personal writings, eyewitness journalists, and bemused politicians seesawing between human compassion and partisan harshness. In the lush Missouri landscape of the Mormon imagination where Adam and Eve had walked out of the garden and where Adam would return to preside over his posterity, the towering religious creativity of Joseph Smith and clash of religious stereotypes created a swift and traumatic frontier drama that changed the Church.

Joseph Smith's Polygamy, 3 Vols.

Brian Hales

Hardcover
Volume 1: History 978-1-58958-189-0
Volume 2: History 978-1-58958-548-5
Volume 3: Theology 978-1-58958-190-6

Perhaps the least understood part of Joseph Smith's life and teachings is his introduction of polygamy to the Saints in Nauvoo. Because of the persecution he knew it would bring, Joseph said little about it publicly and only taught it to his closest and most trusted friends and associates before his martyrdom.

In this three-volume work, Brian C. Hales provides the most comprehensive faithful examination of this much misunderstood period in LDS Church history. Drawing for the first time on every known account, Hales helps us understand the history and teachings surrounding this secretive practice and also addresses and corrects many of the numerous allegations and misrepresentations concerning it. Hales further discusses how polygamy was practiced during this time and why so many of the early Saints were willing to participate in it.

Joseph Smith's Polygamy is an essential resource in understanding this challenging and misunderstood practice of early Mormonism.

Praise for *Joseph Smith's Polygamy*:

"Brian Hales wants to face up to every question, every problem, every fear about plural marriage. His answers may not satisfy everyone, but he gives readers the relevant sources where answers, if they exist, are to be found. There has never been a more thorough examination of the polygamy idea."
—Richard L. Bushman, author of *Joseph Smith: Rough Stone Rolling*

"Hales's massive and well documented three volume examination of the history and theology of Mormon plural marriage, as introduced and practiced during the life of Joseph Smith, will now be the standard against which all other treatments of this important subject will be measured." —Danel W. Bachman, author of "A Study of the Mormon Practice of Plural Marriage before the Death of Joseph Smith"

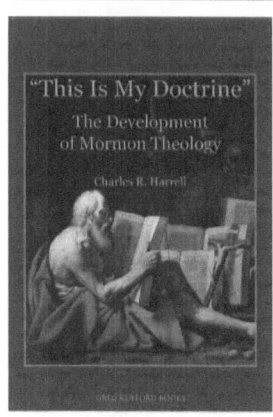

"This is My Doctrine": The Development of Mormon Theology

Charles R. Harrell

Hardcover, ISBN: 978-1-58958-103-6

The principal doctrines defining Mormonism today often bear little resemblance to those it started out with in the early 1830s. This book shows that these doctrines did not originate in a vacuum but were rather prompted and informed by the religious culture from which Mormonism arose. Early Mormons, like their early Christian and even earlier Israelite predecessors, brought with them their own varied culturally conditioned theological presuppositions (a process of convergence) and only later acquired a more distinctive theological outlook (a process of differentiation).

In this first-of-its-kind comprehensive treatment of the development of Mormon theology, Charles Harrell traces the history of Latter-day Saint doctrines from the times of the Old Testament to the present. He describes how Mormonism has carried on the tradition of the biblical authors, early Christians, and later Protestants in reinterpreting scripture to accommodate new theological ideas while attempting to uphold the integrity and authority of the scriptures. In the process, he probes three questions: How did Mormon doctrines develop? What are the scriptural underpinnings of these doctrines? And what do critical scholars make of these same scriptures? In this enlightening study, Harrell systematically peels back the doctrinal accretions of time to provide a fresh new look at Mormon theology.

"*This Is My Doctrine*" will provide those already versed in Mormonism's theological tradition with a new and richer perspective of Mormon theology. Those unacquainted with Mormonism will gain an appreciation for how Mormon theology fits into the larger Jewish and Christian theological traditions.

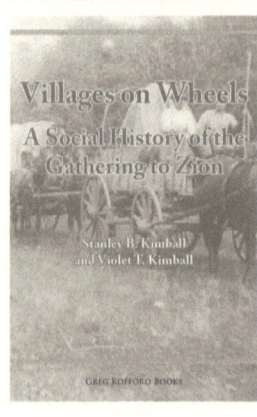

Villages on Wheels: A Social History of the Gathering to Zion

Stanley B. Kimball and Violet T. Kimball

ISBN: 978-1-58958-119-7

The enduring saga of Mormonism is its great trek across the plains, and understanding that trek was the life work of Stanley B. Kimball, master of Mormon trails. This final work, a collaboration he began and which was completed after his death in 2003 by his photographer-writer wife, Violet, explores that movement westward as a social history, with the Mormons moving as "villages on wheels."

Set in the broader context of transcontinental migration to Oregon and California, the Mormon trek spanned twenty-two years, moved approximately 54,700 individuals, many of them in family groups, and left about 7,000 graves at the trailside.

Like a true social history, this fascinating account in fourteen chapters explores both the routines of the trail—cooking, cleaning, laundry, dealing with bodily functions—and the dramatic moments: encountering Indians and stampeding buffalo, giving birth, losing loved ones to death, dealing with rage and injustice, but also offering succor, kindliness, and faith. Religious observances were simultaneously an important part of creating and maintaining group cohesiveness, but working them into the fabric of the grueling day-to-day routine resulted in adaptation, including a "sliding Sabbath." The role played by children and teens receives careful scrutiny; not only did children grow up quickly on the trail, but the gender boundaries guarding their "separate spheres" blurred under the erosion of concentrating on tasks that had to be done regardless of the age or sex of those available to do them. Unexpected attention is given to African Americans who were part of this westering experience, and Violet also gives due credit to the "four-legged heroes" who hauled the wagons westward.

From Above and Below: The Mormon Embrace of Revolution, 1840–1940

Craig Livingston

Paperback, ISBN: 978-1-58958-621-5

Praise for *From Above and Below*:

"In this engaging study, Craig Livingston examines Mormon responses to political revolutions across the globe from the 1840s to the 1930s. Latter-day Saints saw utopian possibilities in revolutions from the European tumults of 1848 to the Mexican Revolution. Highlighting the often radical anti-capitalist and anti-imperialist rhetoric of Mormon leaders, Livingston demonstrates how Latter-day Saints interpreted revolutions through their unique theology and millennialism."
--Matthew J. Grow, author of *Liberty to the Downtrodden: Thomas L. Kane, Romantic Reformer*

"Craig Livingston's landmark book demonstrates how 21st-century Mormonism's arch-conservatism was preceded by its pro-revolutionary worldview that was dominant from the 1830s to the 1930s. Shown by current opinion-polling to be the most politically conservative religious group in the United States, contemporary Mormons are unaware that leaders of the LDS Church once praised radical liberalism and violent revolutionaries. By this pre-1936 Mormon view, 'The people would reduce privilege and exploitation in the crucible of revolution, then reforge society in a spiritual union of peace' before the Coming of Christ and His Millennium. With profound research in Mormon sources and in academic studies about various social revolutions and political upheavals, Livingston provides a nuanced examination of this little-known dimension of LDS thought which tenuously balanced pro-revolutionary enthusiasms with anti-mob sentiments."
--D. Michael Quinn, author of *Elder Statesman: A Biography of J. Reuben Clark*

Women at Church: Magnifying LDS Women's Local Impact

Neylan McBaine

Paperback, ISBN: 978-1-58958-688-8

Women at Church is a practical and faithful guide to improving the way men and women work together at church. Looking at current administrative and cultural practices, the author explains why some women struggle with the gendered divisions of labor. She then examines ample real-life examples that are currently happening in local settings around the country that expand and reimagine gendered practices. Readers will understand how to evaluate possible pain points in current practices and propose solutions that continue to uphold all mandated church policies. Readers will be equipped with the tools they need to have respectful, empathetic and productive conversations about gendered practices in Church administration and culture.

Praise for *Women at Church*:

"Such a timely, faithful, and practical book! I suggest ordering this book in bulk to give to your bishopric, stake presidency, and all your local leadership to start a conversation on changing Church culture for women by letting our doctrine suggest creative local adaptations—Neylan McBaine shows the way!" — Valerie Hudson Cassler, author of *Women in Eternity, Women of Zion*

"A pivotal work replete with wisdom and insight. Neylan McBaine deftly outlines a workable programme for facilitating movement in the direction of the 'privileges and powers' promised the nascent Female Relief Society of Nauvoo." — Fiona Givens, co-author of *The God Who Weeps: How Mormonism Makes Sense of Life*

"In her timely and brilliant findings, Neylan McBaine issues a gracious invitation to rethink our assumptions about women's public Church service. Well researched, authentic, and respectful of the current Church administrative structure, McBaine shares exciting and practical ideas that address diverse needs and involve all members in the meaningful work of the Church." — Camille Fronk Olson, author of *Women of the Old Testament* and *Women of the New Testament*

A House for the Most High: The Story of the Original Nauvoo Temple

Matthew McBride

Hardcover, ISBN: 978-1-58958-016-9

This awe-inspiring book is a tribute to the perseverance of the human spirit. *A House for the Most High* is a groundbreaking work from beginning to end with its faithful and comprehensive documentation of the Nauvoo Temple's conception. The behind-the-scenes stories of those determined Saints involved in the great struggle to raise the sacred edifice bring a new appreciation to all readers. McBride's painstaking research now gives us access to valuable firsthand accounts that are drawn straight from the newspaper articles, private diaries, journals, and letters of the steadfast participants.

The opening of this volume gives the reader an extraordinary window into the early temple-building labors of the besieged Church of Jesus Christ of Latter-day Saints, the development of what would become temple-related doctrines in the decade prior to the Nauvoo era, and the 1839 advent of the Saints in Illinois. The main body of this fascinating history covers the significant years, starting from 1840, when this temple was first considered, to the temple's early destruction by a devastating natural disaster. A well-thought-out conclusion completes the epic by telling of the repurchase of the temple lot by the Church in 1937, the lot's excavation in 1962, and the grand announcement in 1999 that the temple would indeed be rebuilt. Also included are an astonishing appendix containing rare and fascinating eyewitness descriptions of the temple and a bibliography of all major source materials. Mormons and non-Mormons alike will discover, within the pages of this book, a true sense of wonder and gratitude for a determined people whose sole desire was to build a sacred and holy temple for the worship of their God.

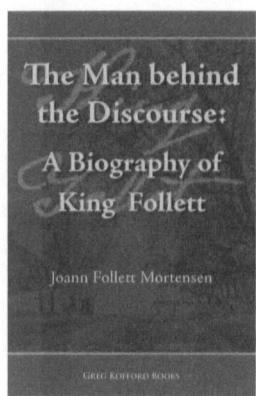

The Man behind the Discourse: A Biography of King Follett

Joann Follett Mortensen

ISBN: 978-1-58958-036-7

Who was King Follett? When he was fatally injured digging a well in Nauvoo in March 1844, why did Joseph Smith use his death to deliver the monumental doctrinal sermon now known as the King Follett Discourse? Much has been written about the sermon, but little about King.

Although King left no personal writings, Joann Follett Mortensen, King's third great-granddaughter, draws on more than thirty years of research in civic and Church records and in the journals and letters of King's peers to piece together King's story from his birth in New Hampshire and moves westward where, in Ohio, he and his wife, Louisa, made the life-shifting decision to accept the new Mormon religion.

From that point, this humble, hospitable, and hardworking family followed the Church into Missouri where their devotion to Joseph Smith was refined and burnished. King was the last Mormon prisoner in Missouri to be released from jail. According to family lore, King was one of the Prophet's bodyguards. He was also a Danite, a Mason, and an officer in the Nauvoo Legion. After his death, Louisa and their children settled in Iowa where some associated with the Cutlerities and the RLDS Church; others moved on to California. One son joined the Mormon Battalion and helped found Mormon communities in Utah, Idaho, and Arizona.

While King would have died virtually unknown had his name not been attached to the discourse, his life story reflects the reality of all those whose faith became the foundation for a new religion. His biography is more than one man's life story. It is the history of the early Restoration itself.

Hearken, O Ye People: The Historical Setting of Joseph Smith's Ohio Revelations

Mark Lyman Staker

Hardcover, ISBN: 978-1-58958-113-5

2010 Best Book Award - John Whitmer Historical Association
2011 Best Book Award - Mormon History Association

More of Mormonism's canonized revelations originated in or near Kirtland than any other place. Yet many of the events connected with those revelations and their 1830s historical context have faded over time. Mark Staker reconstructs the cultural experiences by which Kirtland's Latter-day Saints made sense of the revelations Joseph Smith pronounced. This volume rebuilds that exciting decade using clues from numerous archives, privately held records, museum collections, and even the soil where early members planted corn and homes. From this vast array of sources he shapes a detailed narrative of weather, religious backgrounds, dialect differences, race relations, theological discussions, food preparation, frontier violence, astronomical phenomena, and myriad daily customs of nineteenth-century life. The result is a "from the ground up" experience that today's Latter-day Saints can all but walk into and touch.

Praise for *Hearken O Ye People*:

"I am not aware of a more deeply researched and richly contextualized study of any period of Mormon church history than Mark Staker's study of Mormons in Ohio. We learn about everything from the details of Alexander Campbell's views on priesthood authority to the road conditions and weather on the four Lamanite missionaries' journey from New York to Ohio. All the Ohio revelations and even the First Vision are made to pulse with new meaning. This book sets a new standard of in-depth research in Latter-day Saint history."
        -Richard Bushman, author of *Joseph Smith: Rough Stone Rolling*

"To be well-informed, any student of Latter-day Saint history and doctrine must now be acquainted with the remarkable research of Mark Staker on the important history of the church in the Kirtland, Ohio, area."
        -Neal A. Maxwell Institute, Brigham Young University

The Wasp

Hardcover, ISBN: 978-1-58958-050-3

A newspaper published in Nauvoo from April 16, 1842, through April 26, 1843, *The Wasp* provides a crucial window into firsthand accounts of the happenings and concerns of the Saints in Nauvoo. It was initially edited by William Smith, younger brother of Joseph Smith. William was succeeded by John Taylor as editor and Taylor and Wilford Woodruff as printers and publishers. Some of the main stories covered in the newspaper are the August 1842 elections where local candidates endorsed by the Mormons easily won against their opponents, the fall from grace of John C. Bennett, the attempt by the state of Missouri to extradite Joseph Smith as an accessory in the attempted murder of Lilburn W. Boggs, and the Illinois legislature's effort to repeal the Nauvoo charter.

With a foreword by Peter Crawley putting the newspaper in historical context, this first-ever reproduction of the entire run of the *The Wasp* is essential to anyone interested in the Nauvoo period of Mormonism.

www.ingramcontent.com/pod-product-compliance
Lightning Source LLC
Chambersburg PA
CBHW030320020526
44117CB00030B/231